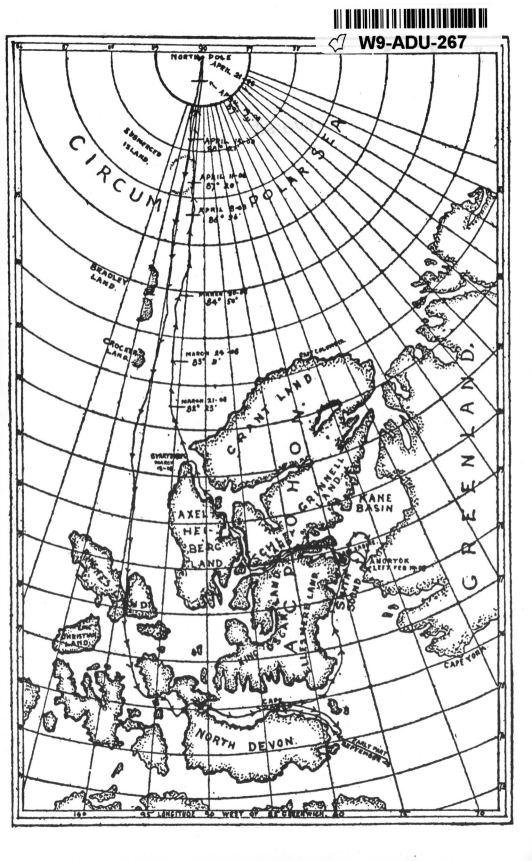

Cook & Peary

Cook & Peary
The Polar Controversy, Resolved

Robert M. Bryce

STACKPOLE
BOOKS

Copyright © 1997 by Robert M. Bryce

Published by
STACKPOLE BOOKS
5067 Ritter Road
Mechanicsburg, PA 17055

Printed in the United States of America

First Edition

10 9 8 7 6 5 4 3 2

Library of Congress Cataloging-in-Publication Data
Bryce, Robert M.
    Cook & Peary : the polar controversy, resolved / Robert M. Bryce. — 1st ed.
        p.   cm.
    Includes bibliographical references and index.
    ISBN 0-8117-0317-7
    1. Cook, Frederick Albert, 1865–1940.   2. Peary, Robert E. (Robert Edwin),
1856–1920.   3. Explorers—United States—Biography.   4. North Pole.   I. Title.
G635.C66H86   1997
919.804'092
[B]—DC20
                                                                    96-38215
                                                                         CIP

To the Pathfinders

To the Librarians who invented indexing and interlibrary loan;
To the Archivists who preserve the past as it was written;
To this twin family of folk who are given so little,
    goes the first credit.
To the forgotten people whose experience has been my guide;
To the protectors of knowledge, whose efforts allow the ascent of the
    ladder toward understanding;
To these, the guardians of the past, present and future—
I inscribe the first page . . .

And to my dear Father, without whom nothing would have been
    possible.

"An Eskimo Legend"

Jealous of men's happiness, Perdlugssuaq, the Great Evil, brought sickness; he struck men on the hunt, on the seas, in the mountains. He was ever feared. He made the Great Dark terrible. But when the night became bright with the love-lorn glamour of the moon, Perdlugssuaq was for the time forgotten; in their hearts men felt a vague, tender, and ineffable stirring—the lure of a passion stronger and stranger even than death. They gazed upon the moon with instinctive, undefined pity. So, as the years passed, and ages melted and remade the snow, the long day was golden with the Beauty that is ever desired, the Ideal never attained; the night was softly silver with the melancholy and eternal hope of the deathless love that eternally desires, eternally pursues, and is eternally denied.

—T. Everett Harré

CONTENTS

EDITOR'S NOTE TO THE READER

"WHATEVER THE TRUTH IS, THE SITUATION IS AS WONDERFUL AS THE POLE," wrote Lincoln Steffens. "And whatever they found there, those explorers, they have left there a story as great as a continent."

The story of Frederick Cook and Robert Peary is grand, and therein lies the importance of this biography of the two men and their epic controversy: only a complete account presenting all the relevant evidence could yield the definitive resolution to the Polar Controversy. In his search for the truth about the discovery of the North Pole and the ascent of Mount McKinley, no less than in his explorations of the human mind, Robert M. Bryce traversed the tremendous hummocks of conflicting information that have thwarted other historians.

Part One is a chronological recounting of events, with all the contradictions inherent in life. The reader is advised to attend to the details, for in them lie clues to the resolution. Why did Roald Amundsen take Cook's side? Why did the *New York Times* take Peary's? What became of Cook's polar records? How many notebooks did he bring back? Was Matt Henson sufficiently literate to take astronomical observations for Peary? Why did Hudson Stuck reject Cook's account of climbing Mount McKinley as soon as he heard the news? Just how many toes did Peary lose to frostbite? The careful reader may discern motives that explain the discrepancies and thus begin to weigh the evidence with a discriminating mind.

Part Two, an analysis of the evidence presented in Part One, assumes an attentive reading of the detail. Just as readers savor the twists and turns of plot in a good mystery and would never think of peeking at the last page, so the reader of *Cook & Peary* should follow the drama of the Polar Controversy as it unfolds to appreciate truly not just its resolution but also the exquisite portraits of heroes, scoundrels and dreamers in the last days of the romantic era.

PROLOGUE

IMAGINE, IF YOU CAN, THE NORTH POLE: A POINT WITH NO DIMENSIONS, NO thickness or breadth; a spot in the mind of man where even the concepts of the mind—time and direction—are no longer valid, where every direction is south and a year is divided into one day and one night; a place whose location can be determined only by other concepts of the mind—numbers and letters manipulated in abstract formulae. It lies more than 400 miles from any solid ground across an ocean more than five miles deep, covered with a jumble of stupendous blocks of ice drifting at the whim of wind and tide and pull of the moon. There is nothing to mark it—no land, no permanent feature. It is indistinguishable by eye from any other point on that vast frozen sea a mile, or a hundred miles, in the only direction from it. To wish to visit it—to try to visit such a place—would seem a mad quest. Yet in the decades before and after the first year of the twentieth century, the mad quest for the North Pole was the ardent dream of many men. It was a time for dreams; a time like all others, and a time never to come again, standing at the end of the past and at the edge of the future in a present unsure whether machines, wealth and comfort had made men unsuited to heroic deeds. The mad dreamers of the North Pole dreamed the dream of accomplishing one last heroic deed—to breathe the frozen winds of the unknown North—to seize the White Grail—to exhale the last great heroic gasp before the spirit of the romantic age departed . . . forever.

Dante, in his frozen hell,
Shivering, endured no bleakness like the void
These men have warmed with their own flaming will,
And peopled with their dreams.

—*from "The Frozen Grail"*

Far away to the left we see a low ridge of unauthenticated land rising abruptly from the Arctic Ocean. We see dog trains, sleds,
packs, and pemmican, pressure ridges, and pen leads. Over the remote north hangs a cloud; it veils the pole. The square object half
concealed amid icy blocks off to the right is, of course, the box of
missing records at Annoatok. Through the fog of Crown Prince
Gustav Sea we dimly descry the figure of Capt. Loose. It is night.
The lamp but half reveals his face as he bends over his heroic task
of revising the data. Then a council chamber appears. Men of
grave mien gathered about a table are examining the celebrated
records. They have long, white hair, which they occasionally tear,
plucking out a handful or two now and then to denote their interest in astronomic records such as never before came within their
learned ken. They are the Faculty of the University of Copenhagen. Behind and above them towers Mount McKinley. Upon its
peak stands the great explorer, proudly wearing his wreath of roses
and brandishing what appears to be a brass tube. There are other
figures, other details in the composition, but these are enough.[1]

TODAY, THIS MIGHT BE MISTAKEN FOR A DESCRIPTION OF THE STAGE SET FOR
some surrealistic play. Yet it is actually only an editorial from the *New York
Times*. But for anyone who read the daily papers during the last four months
of 1909, all of this—every detail—would have been readily comprehensible,
even common knowledge.

For these were some of the important parts of the most sensational news story of the young century and of the greatest geographical controversy of all time, one that lingers to the present day—a dispute so bitter that it divided families and lifelong friends into warring camps over one cold yet burning question: Who discovered the North Pole?

Many of the readers of those newspapers, and certainly most of their writers, could not get enough of the story, and for good reason. "What author would not have given a fortune for such a plot, such a setting, such characters in contrast, such possibilities for dramatic denouement!" one of them exclaimed. "But none of them thought of it, and history gains interest from the strange series of incidents."[2] There was no shortage of those.

When Robert E. Peary reached Annoatok on the west coast of Greenland in August 1908, some said he posted this notice on an abandoned hut he found there:

> This house belongs to Dr. Frederick A. Cook, but Dr. Cook is long ago dead and there is no use to search after him. Therefore I, Commander Robert E. Peary, install my boatswain in this deserted house.[3]

If Peary made such an assessment, he was wrong in every respect. Frederick Cook was then very much alive and somewhere in the high Arctic at that very moment, on a journey that first amazed the world and then was rejected by it. Yet though Dr. Cook has now been dead for over 50 years, the search for him and what he did during that half-year of endless light that makes a polar day has never really ended.

I never intended to write this book. It was simply an inevitable consequence, a part of that search—an attempt to come to some personal resolution of a subject that has fascinated me for more than twenty years.

I became interested in Frederick Cook in a roundabout way. In 1971 I read Chauncey Loomis's biography of the arctic explorer Charles Francis Hall, *Weird and Tragic Shores,* and was strangely disturbed and moved by it. I soon discovered that Captain Hall's mysterious demise was only one of the gruesome and fascinating stories woven around the mad quest for the North Pole. Soon I was frozen in with Elisha Kent Kane at the top of Smith Sound; I watched as Greely's men slowly starved to death, one by one, at Cape Sabine, or I was off on one of the innumerable expeditions seeking the solution to the riddle of the fate of Sir John Franklin.

Before long I discovered the smoldering controversy over who had reached the North Pole first. Like so many others, I had simply accepted as a matter of fact that Admiral Peary had, on April 6, 1909. I had never even heard of Dr. Cook.

When I read about his claim of having discovered the North Pole on April 21, 1908, I was curious as to why his story had been initially accepted and then discredited. I quickly found that there were some who still believed that he had told the truth, and some who believed Peary was the liar.

The only way, I reasoned, that I could resolve the conflicting opinions was to go to the original sources. I wanted to let the explorers speak without an intermediary. I wanted to put myself in the position of a person in 1909, unconfused by later apologists and advocates.

I was soon immersed in a copy of Cook's *My Attainment of the Pole.* The voice of Frederick Albert Cook spoke to me from its pages, and 35 years after that voice had been stilled, it asked me to believe that it spoke the truth.

When I first read that amazing book, I was unprepared to understand the discussion it contained of incidents once familiar to every reader of the newspapers, but the narrative of the polar journey itself I found irresistible. It was certainly an exciting adventure tale—but was there any truth in it?

Still, page by page, it wove its spell: "I felt the glory which the prophet feels in his vision," the voice whispered, "with which the poet thrills in his dream"—and I, too, felt it.

This is the story of the man behind that voice. Not just the story of that bitter contest of priority with his rival, but that of a wholly extraordinary life. It is extraordinary because, by choice and by chance, Frederick Albert Cook was no ordinary man.

Yet, in a sense, it is also the story of Everyman who dreams dreams, who acts upon his dreams, who attempts to make his dreams his reality, and who, once they have taken a tangible form, finds in that reality that dreamers pay a price and must suffer the consequences of their dreaming:

> About the frozen plains my imagination evoked aspects of grandeur. . . . The shifting mirages seemed like the ghosts of dead armies, magnified and transfigured, huge and spectral, moving along the horizon and bearing the wind-tossed ghosts of golden blood-stained banners.
>
> The low beating of the wind assumed the throb of martial music. Bewildered, I realized all that I had suffered, all the pain of fasting, all the anguish of long weariness, and I felt that this was my reward. I had scaled the world, and I stood at the Pole![4]

> After the first thrills of success, a profound feeling of loneliness oppressed me. I sat on my sled and listlessly watched the flag fluttering over the shelter in which my Eskimos slept. Hungry, mentally and physically exhausted, a sense of the utter uselessness of this thing, of the empty reward of my endurance, followed my exhilaration. I had grasped my *ignis fatuus.* It is a misfortune for any man when his *ignis fatuus* fails to elude him.[5]

The voice trapped between those brown covers was persuasive, disturbing and unforgettable.

Many who have listened to that voice have heard something more than the claim to a singular accomplishment. It has struck a deeper chord and disturbed an undercurrent in the human mind where the most basic thoughts arise. It poses the questions of the ages: Is history truth? Is truth itself absolute? It testifies to the power of faith and the tenaciousness of belief, and it strikes at the human heart's basic need for assurance that the affairs of men are orderly; an assurance sought to quell the secret fear that they are, instead, chancy and unpredictable; that in reality, both truth and dreams have no reality, that they are both products of the mind and are sometimes one and the same.

This, and not a point of honor, is why acres of space and oceans of ink were consumed in endless arguments by advocates of both Cook and Peary between 1909 and 1917, when the coming of a Great War proved that the secret fear was ever so well founded. By then, trenches stretched across the ruins of Western civilization and the partisans on both sides of the Polar Controversy were themselves entrenched. Dr. Cook was discredited in the general public's mind, and Peary, now an admiral, was generally accepted as the first man to have reached the Pole. Yet groups of doubters of both claims remained and, among them, partisans avid enough to keep the dispute alive.

About once a decade since then, a major book recounting the fantastic details of the Polar Controversy has appeared. Eventually I read all of these but was still not satisfied. It was obvious that something was still missing; that none of these authors could ultimately put aside his bias for either Peary or Cook, no matter how loudly he professed his neutrality. In reading through some of the references used to bolster their arguments, I discovered that material damaging to one man or the other had been ignored, distorted or at least not given its proper weight.

Goethe said, "It is much easier to recognize error than to find truth, error is superficial and may be corrected; truth lies hidden in the depths." The apologists for both sides were, I felt, steeped in error that needed correction, and it seemed that all they had written had only buried the truth deeper. I resolved to start on a mad quest of my own, into those depths where I was convinced the truth lay hidden in primary documents, and I resolved to correct all errors, to reveal whatever I unearthed and to call it truth.

I say a mad quest. Those who are convinced need no conviction; those who have faith and believe do not need the truth.

This book is the product of that quest: thousands of hours spent, tens of thousands of miles traveled, hundreds of thousands of pages read, and millions of symbols entered into a machine's magnetic memory.

Still, the whole truth lies hidden. I found it could never be deduced from counts of pemmican cans, or averages of miles across the tortured ice of the polar pack, or even by the lengths of shadows cast by the circling arctic sun. Nor did it lie embodied, absolutely, on those pieces of paper, as I had naively believed. I found instead that it lay locked away forever only in the hearts of the men who lived it. It is at those ultimate guardians of truth that the picklock of biography is directed.

As a Paris paper observed days into the dispute:

> Peary and Cook, their characters, their conduct, that is what interests us, and every little item throwing a sidelight upon their natures is valuable.[6]

Some have seen Cook's claims of 1909 as a transparent fraud, carried off by a cheap faker—an unfortunate affair that took away the luster from Peary's richly deserved triumph. Others saw Cook as the ultimate victim and the story of his fall from hero to humbug as the tragic tale of the little man, helpless to resist a rich and powerful establishment bent on his destruction.

In either case it was as plain as black or white.

But life at its dullest is colored by at least shades of gray, and the truth often lies, inaccessible as the North Pole, somewhere in the deepest gray of the shadows that fill the inner recesses of the human mind.

PART ONE

"The Rivals."

To many, explorers seem vain men seeking short cuts to fame, or persons who waste time, energy, and wealth, to win the Impossible, to learn the Unprofitable.

The explorer's master motive . . . his real ardor—is more profound.

It craves, above all, knowledge of itself. . . . The life of man as it is, naked and unshadowed, brutal maybe, life under every stress of fortune—that wins the hungry ear and the deeper charity of these present hours. . . .

Among us who seek on enchanted rivers an answer of those under-thoughts that make life at once a tragic and an ecstatic thing, who dare for nothing but the cause of daring, who follow the long trails . . . the true spirit of the explorer is a primordial restlessness. It is spurred by instinct of pre-natal beginnings and a cloudy hereafter, to search the glamour of unknown peaks and seas and forests for assurance of man's imperfect faith in immortality. It is a creative instinct.

Men with the masks of civilization torn off, and struggling through magic regions ruled over by the Spirit of the North or the South; human beings tamed by the centuries, then cast out to shift for themselves like the first victims of existence—they must offer the best field of all to help this knowledge of ourselves.

—Robert Dunn

CHAPTER 1

The Sunrise of Ambition

THE PRISONER SAT IN HIS CELL, ALONE BUT FOR HIS MEMORIES. STILL, EVEN IN confinement, the eye of his mind was free to survey and summarize the sweep of a spectacular career. And when that inner vision had crystallized itself into words, he took up a pencil to preserve them:

> They have called me the Prince of Liars, but, in truth, I am King of the Luckless.
> Life has taken me to the top of the world, and down into the abyss.
> Kings and felons, savants and savages, have been my associates; I have lived in the rarest luxury of civilization, and in aboriginal simplicity. Once the far horizon was my only confine, which now is a barred cell and the towering walls of the Federal prison in Leavenworth, Kansas.
> Civilized humanity has hailed me as one of history's immortals, only to snatch the laurels from my brow and place there instead the brand of fraud and criminal.
> Wealth has flowed to me in torrents, then trickled away to leave me at last in utter poverty.
> But though Fortune has cast me deep in the shadows; though the world's plaudits have changed to condemning hisses; though I am penniless and ageing, there is no bitterness in me, for I have three things remaining that are above those which have been stripped from me—my friends, my hopes, and my philosophy.[1]

Brave words. Yet Frederick Albert Cook—physician, explorer, lecturer and author, federal prisoner No. 23118—later admitted that this was his blackest hour.

He had always been an introspective man. Now there was limitless opportunity for introspection:

> The purview of life is ever the outcome of memories. Foresight can never be more than hindsight . . . through which to envision the future. If we saw life in one whole sphere, . . . how much more

thorough our culture would become. But we see the unit of human endeavor only in sections—mostly in spectacular sections. History is seldom more than somebody's opinion of the thrill source of life—the stagy artifice of an unstaged world. This is to a large extent unavoidable for the mind does not retain the commonplace in which union of purpose must ever be grounded.[2]

As he paged backward through the mental record of his life to the very limit of his earliest memories, Frederick Cook must have wondered at the chain of chance and circumstance, the opportunities presented or made, then taken or turned aside, that had led him to this place and to this hour.

But life's chances are not all our own. A life is not a story written front to back from birth to death; it is rather a series of related events; a chapter in a continuing story passed one to the next as long as life lasts.

And so, as for countless other Americans before and since, Frederick Cook's chances were ultimately the result of his immigrant parents' decision to leave behind an Old World for the New, to abandon the known for the unknown, and to strike out on a untried path toward a new destiny. It was a course he, too, would follow, but in a different way.

Looking from that barred window beyond the gray walls to the far horizon now denied him, and farther still into the limitless expanse of the starry Kansas sky, he mused: "It is a long step from the doom of Leavenworth to the sunrise of ambition."[3]

There was little to set Theodor Albrecht Koch apart from his neighbors. A plain-looking man of average height and weight, with his high forehead and fringe of dark whiskers framing an otherwise cleanly shaven face, he had the look of an Amish farmer.[4] Born on June 8, 1822, in the town of Schneverdingen, about 20 miles south of Hamburg, he was the first of his family to leave Germany. Why he left is less than clear.

For years he had assisted his father, who held the medical concession in Schneverdingen. After Dr. Koch died, Theodor continued to minister to the sick, despite having no formal medical training. When a licensed doctor complained of this, the townspeople paid to send Theodor to Hamburg to study. But they suffered by his absence and petitioned that he be given his father's concession before he completed his course. Perhaps their request was refused, or perhaps he came to America, like so many other northern Germans of the time, because he had no prospect of inheritance under German law, the estate falling to the eldest son.[5]

Whatever his reasons, he did come, landing at New York in 1855.[6] In the company of several other new arrivals from Germany, he traveled to Newburgh, then westward into Sullivan County. The concentration of Germans already in the area may have caused him to settle in Jeffersonville after a brief stay in Lake Huntington.[7] He must have found the country agreeable, since eventually his three brothers followed, leaving only a sister in Europe.

Among the immigrants already established in the area was Frederick Long, formerly a successful manufacturer of cigars in New York. To escape an epidemic of cholera that struck that city in 1850, he had taken his family west, up the Hudson to Newburgh by raft, then overland by covered wagon. He, his wife and eight-year-old daughter, Magdalena, had come to America from Frankfurt in 1844.[8] Now they intended to go much farther west. But passing through the rolling wooded country above the Delaware River, they paused at a place called Beechwoods, six miles west of Jeffersonville. Here the Longs settled, cleared the top of a hillside and prospered, the family growing to six children.

In Jeffersonville at a community dance Dr. Koch met the fair-haired Magdalena Long. It was an attraction of opposites: he a Lutheran, she a Catholic; he known for having an excitable temperament, she from a family noted for its reserve; he in his thirties, she still in her teens. But if there were objections or obstacles, all were overcome. After a proper period of courtship, they married on March 12, 1858.

For a year, the Kochs lived in Jeffersonville before moving to Beechwoods and finally, in 1860, they settled with their son Theodore in the hamlet of Hortonville at the foot of the Catskills, two miles from Callicoon Depot on the Erie line.

No doubt they lived a hard yet respectable life. Though Dr. Koch enjoyed an extensive practice, cash was scarce; his patients usually paid him with eggs, fruits and vegetables, or an occasional chicken. Of the Koch farm's 15 rocky acres, only two were tillable. But the doctor, fond of horses and hunting, supplemented the larder with game from the surrounding hills.

There, between Callicoon Creek and Joe Brook, in a slab house with two bedrooms and a third room that served as living room and kitchen, the rest of children came—first William, then an infant who lived but a few days, and then Lillian.[9] The Kochs solved their religious differences through choice or circumstance, attending the German Reformed church in Hortonville, where they enrolled their children in Sunday school.

During the Civil War, Dr. Koch found employment as an examining physician for recruits entering the Union Army at Goshen. The payroll clerk listed him on the roster by the English equivalent of his name, Cook. Having been irritated since his arrival in America by the inability of most non-Germans to pronounce his name properly, most calling him "Cox" or "Kotch," Dr. Koch capitulated long before Appomattox, and "Cook" it remained even after he left the Army's service.[10]

The war was over hardly two months when a fourth child arrived on June 10, 1865. They named him Frederick Albert and called him, affectionately, Freddy.

The boy's earliest recollections were of traumatic experiences. At two, while playing with his dog, he had leapt upon the stove. One of its covers gave way and his foot went into the fire, setting his clothes alight. The feel of the fire licking at his leg was frightening enough, but the unexpected bucket of cold water his mother doused him with was even worse, leaving him gasping for breath. He next remembered sitting on a table nursing his burns, helpless as his family fought the rising water of the two creeks lapping at the door. "I watched its advance and cried," he recalled, as he did at the sight of a small herd of deer driven into the nearby woods by hunters. There was the sound of shots, and his tears came at the realization that the beautiful, terrified creatures must die.[11]

Even to one so young, death already had meaning, it was so commonplace. The Longs had fled from New York before its shadow, but few families escaped it completely. Even remote Sullivan County offered no safe refuge, and the Cooks were no exceptions.

They had been fortunate. The cemetery was dotted with tiny graves, but they had lost only one child. And with the addition of August Heinrich in 1868, they now counted five healthy children. But the family's life was irrevocably redirected when Dr. Cook, after a brief illness, died of pneumonia on May 10, 1870, at age 47; Freddy was not quite five:

> Of this tragedy I only remember Father's under-chin whiskers and
> his mud colored suit left hanging on the wall after he was buried. I
> do not remember the funeral, but I do remember tears and a cold
> cry which made me shiver at sometime about the coffin.[12]

Magdalena Cook used the money from her husband's small life insurance policy to build a one-story-and-garret frame house on the high banks above the creek, out of harm's way. Little was left to live on, but with tenacity and frugality the Cooks scratched a living from what they could grow or earn at odd jobs, while Mrs. Cook tried to collect unpaid doctor bills to buy food and clothing. The hard times brought with them hard lessons for young Frederick:

> For a few years we struggled for a bare subsistence. Sour milk and
> potatoes with apples and an occasional rabbit or woodchuck linger
> in my memory of food delicacies. . . . Life here must represent the
> beginning of my schooling for the hardship to follow in wild
> adventures to the brim of the unknown.[13]

The children walked the three quarters of a mile to school on Callicoon Creek. As in many rural places where children provided the farm labor, the session lasted only four months. In his later years Frederick Cook would look back on that one-room schoolhouse next to the graveyard and call it "the most attractive place on Earth." It was through its door that he first entered the world of ideas, a world he embraced and held fast for the rest of his life. Geographical locations especially interested him, and he gathered together every book on the subject that he could obtain.

Not all was happy at school for Freddy Cook, though. Outside of class he seemed always to be in trouble. Rivalries between the town boys and the country boys often led to fistfights. He and his brothers sometimes came home battered and bruised and got an additional whipping to discourage such behavior.

Despite these frequent scrapes, Freddy was known for his "natural reticence." Perhaps he had inherited his mother's reserve along with her large facial features and remarkably fine, clear blue eyes, set below asymmetric eyelids that gave his face an open yet contemplative look. Or maybe the slight lisp with which he spoke made him think better of speaking too much and exposing himself to ridicule.

He had but one particular friend, Peter Weiss—PY, as he was known. PY stuttered. Perhaps their shared speech impediments made it that much easier to talk to each other and to form a common bond. Freddy and PY liked to have adventures and visit forbidden places, like the local swimming hole, where Freddy's career almost ended when he plunged into its depths and nearly drowned. "I shall never forget that struggle," he recalled long after, "and though I nearly gave out, in that short time I learned to swim. It seems to me now I have been swimming and struggling ever since."[14]

But life is never all hardship for a growing boy. The surrounding country was wild enough for any imaginative youngster to find adventure in. Everlasting springs fell from its hillsides, and it was full of secret nooks and caves to explore. Freddy would often venture into the woods, alone or with his brothers, as far as time and nerve allowed, then find his way home, using the position of the sun as a guide.

Without a father, the Cook brothers learned to be independent at an early age. Will Cook remembered that Freddy, especially, depended upon no other if he felt his own efforts would succeed alone. When he decided to build a "bunker," he went out and chopped down the young trees himself, and out of them he fashioned a sled of such quality that it had no equal in the entire neighborhood.[15]

In a countryside so broad and high, with so much to stimulate a boy's imagination, Freddy Cook found himself drawn to the natural world around him and wondered at the things he didn't understand. He learned by observation, and this led to some curious childhood experiments:

> I had noted that if I looked at my dog long enough I would get his attention, and the dog seemingly got the same idea, for he made some experiments of his own. At these times he would look intently for prolonged periods. If in due time my eyes did not respond, a little whimper would come from a seeming distance. When the eye connection was made he would come to my side and proceed to talk. His language was wordless, but I understood. . . .
>
> I next tried the lesson my dog taught me on Mother. . . .
>
> . . . I tried to get her attention from various parts of the room by prolonged gazing without success. Finally I made a boyish discovery that pleased me very much. There was just one place from

which I could always get her attention. That was when I came between her and the stove. . . . It was probably the heat waves that
carried my gaze impulse. . . .

What is the language of the unsaid message of the gaze?[16]

In 1878 Mrs. Cook, seeking better opportunities, rented out the farm for
$25 a year, and the family took the train 48 miles east to Port Jervis. The two
eldest boys were old enough for outside work, and even Fred, now 12, held
part-time jobs while attending Mountain House School.

His first was in a glass factory in Port Jervis. Later Fred took work as a
lamplighter, cleaning, filling and lighting the naphtha lights that lined the
streets of the town. He also helped his two older brothers with the spring log-
rafting on the Delaware, which provided thrills they all looked forward to
with great anticipation.

But even with what the boys brought home and the money she earned by
taking in sewing, Lena Cook was hardly better off than she had been in Hortonville. She sent Theodore to New York City to try to find steady employment. He secured a job in a beer keg factory, and a year later she followed with
the other four children. They found shelter at the foot of South First Street in
the shadow of the Havemeyer Sugar Refinery, along the East River in the
Williamsburg section of Brooklyn. There, August died of scarlet fever, but life
for Fred and the other children continued on its pleasureless course:

> Now I was the baby, about 15 years old. We all worked; sister and I
> went to school but worked on Saturdays and Sundays. Slowly a
> way was made out of poverty to scant but secure subsistence.
>
> I never liked New York. It was slushy and dirty when snow
> came, stuffy, hot and sweaty in summer. There were no nearby
> woods in which to enjoy what a bare footed boy wants, but it did
> serve well to co-ordinate that Indian inclination deep seated in all
> country boys of my age and time.[17]

Fred was now a restless youth seeking an ambition but lacking in guidance:

> This was, I suppose, that nebulous desire which sometimes mani-
> fests itself in early youth and later is asserted in strivings toward
> some splendid, sometimes spectacular aim. . . . I was discontented,
> and from the earliest days of consciousness I felt the burden of two
> things which accompanied me through later life—an innate and
> abnormal desire for exploration, then the manifestation of my
> yearning, and the constant struggle to make ends meet, that sting
> of poverty, which, while it tantalizes one with its horrid grind,
> sometimes drives men by reason of the strength developed in over-
> coming its concomitant obstacles to some extraordinary accom-
> plishment.[18]

Through the good offices of a distant relative, William Ihrig, Will Cook found work selling vegetables in Manhattan's Fulton Market. Mr. Ihrig, impressed by Will's industry, agreed to hire his brother as well. Fred worked in the market on weekends from 2 A.M. until noon. Coming from a household with the plainest kind of fare, he marveled at all the things there were to eat in the world. There he saw for the first time many exotic edibles, including mock-oranges, as grapefruit were then called.

During the week Fred attended P.S. 37, two blocks from his house, where the principal took an interest in him and encouraged his studies. He graduated from grammer school at 16, but as Theodore, and then Will, married and assumed new responsibilities, Fred had to help support his mother. He secured a job as an office boy and rent collector for a real estate agency in Greenpoint, then enrolled in night school.

Fred Cook, age 16.

Fred accumulated enough money to buy a second hand press with which he printed advertising bills for his employer and local merchants, as well as greeting and calling cards. These generated such a demand that he decided to devote his full time to printing. Proud of his work, he designed his own business card. Bordered by a Chinese scene of a boy fishing by a lake, it read: "F.A. Cook, Job Printer, 255 South First Street, Brooklyn."

But Fred Cook always had bigger ambitions. His mother suggested that one of the boys should follow in their father's footsteps and become a doctor. The idea fired Fred's imagination; he decided the advantage would fall to him.[19]

By now he had finished his high school studies and, flushed with a new goal, set out to accomplish it. Fred sold his printing business and used the profits to purchase a milk route in the hope that he could earn enough to pay for a medical education. Milkmen delivered between 2 and 8 A.M. He reasoned this would give him a source of income and leave his days free to finish his college course.

He started out with a small hand-delivered route requiring little capital and a manageable amount of time, buying his milk from Rauch and Hartman, a local milk wholesaler. This milk, a new, richer product from Delaware County, quickly outstripped demand for the standard milk then coming from Orange County. As a result, Fred's business flourished, and his brothers heard opportunity knocking. They gave Fred a loan for expansion, and with it he bought his first wagon and a big brown mare for $150. Theodore, who had become an expert woodworker at the barrel factory, helped modify the wagon to carry glass bottles, which were just beginning to replace the tin cans then in use. Fred moved in with Will on Bedford Avenue and established a milk depot there, renting stable space from their next-door neighbor, Mr. West, a manufacturer of ketchup and pickles.

In 1887 he entered the College of Physicians and Surgeons at Columbia University. As the son of a physician, he received a reduction in his matriculation fee.

In that simpler time, an entrant needed only to be of good moral character and 21 years of age. Two winter lecture series were prerequisites to a course in practical anatomy and the passing of satisfactory written examinations in surgery, chemistry, practice of medicine, materia medica, anatomy, physiology and obstetrics. Practical examinations on a cadaver and for urinalysis competency were also required before a medical degree could be conferred.[20]

Between school and his growing business enterprise, Fred Cook found little time for leisure. He went to work at 1 A.M. and worked through the night, reporting to school by 9, where he remained until 4. Between 5:30 and 1 in the morning, he slept. He worked every day, but on weekends, when there was no school, he tried to catch up on his sleep. Whatever few spare waking moments the young man had, he spent in studying.

It took an hour and a half to travel from Brooklyn to New York on the 23rd Street Ferry. When the college moved from 23rd Street to 59th Street, Fred Cook could not afford the extra hour of commuting time entailed. He transferred to New York University, located more conveniently at 26th Street.

His milk business continued to grow, so Fred returned the favor Will had done him years before by making him his partner. They soon owned six horses and were delivering as far as Rockaway Beach, and their milk wagons now also carried specialties, such as sweet cream and fresh print butter.

As Will took on his share of the responsibilities, Fred had more time for other things. One was more sleep. The grueling schedule he had been keeping had taken its toll; now there was a better attitude for schoolwork, more time for study and a chance for a social life.

When a stupendous blizzard struck New York on March 11–12, 1888, the effects of the unexpected storm were devastating. All transportation, even the elevated railways, ground to a halt, and what electrical and telephone service existed was cut off. At least a hundred people perished, some in attempts to reach their places of employment on foot. Hundreds of horses froze to death along with tens of thousands of the sparrows that plagued the city.

Fred's medical classes were suspended, and the milk business, like all others, closed down. But the storm only posed another opportunity for the Cook brothers to show their ingenuity. Coal was selling at fabulous prices—as much as a dollar a pail at the height of the storm. So Theodore put runners on an 18-foot boat he had built, and hitching their horses to it, Will and Fred made coal deliveries over streets made impassable to ordinary vehicles by the three-foot drifts.

Patches of snow from the "Dakota Blizzard" still remained in shady places as late as June. By then, Fred Cook had met Libby Forbes at a temperance festival at the 2nd Street Methodist Church. Miss Forbes, one of four Forbes sisters from Greenpoint, worked for the French, Shriner and Urner shoe factory as a stenographer, an unusual job for a woman. Soon Fred was seeing Libby regularly. After a courtship of less than a year, Fred proposed. Her family, at first opposed, since Fred was still in school, relented, and the couple married in the spring of 1889.

Fred's final examinations were due in June 1890, just before his wife was expecting their first child, and with Libby no longer employed, money was short. Somehow, though, he managed to keep up with his business obligations during those first months of married life and even found time for private instruction in medical diagnosis.

As summer came round, since Fred was not yet a doctor, Libby's family selected a homeopath for the delivery. There were complications. The baby girl lived but a few hours, and in a week Libby Cook was gone, too, a victim of peritonitis. Fred was shattered. The future had suddenly become a vacuum. Months of loneliness and depression set in.

Word soon arrived that he had passed his examinations and was now a physician. Dr. Frederick A. Cook decided to lose himself in his new work.

He sold his share in Cook Brothers Milk and Cream Company to Will and from the proceeds bought the furnishings and equipment for an office away from Brooklyn and its sad memories.

Though 25 and a widower, Dr. Cook still looked boyish. He decided to do something about it:

> Young doctors of this period considered it important to cultivate a full crop of whiskers to better express the dignity of their calling. . . . I . . . allowed my hairy head to fill out to artistic . . . fashion. Thus beset in facial pride, armed with a diploma from one of the best medical schools of the land, endowed with the usual self-confidence of university graduates, and vested with the sublimity of my profession, I opened an office in New York [at 338 W.] 55th St.[21]

He thought all he had to do was hang out his shingle and the patients would come. But even the addition of his whiskers failed to bring them to his door. He learned quickly that it took hard work and patience for a new doctor

Dr. Frederick A. Cook.

to build up a practice. Suddenly time, which had always been so scarce, became a burden. Dr. Cook sought escape in reading:

> To this time I was an average young man of twenty-five who had risen out of poverty with an unusual hunger for knowledge. I had read very few books of fiction and among books of travel only Dr. Kane's Arctic [Explorations] and Stanley's [In] Darkest Africa.
>
> With time to think and plan there developed a longing to get out over the world into the unknown to blaze the trail for a life of useful adventure.[22]

Kane's *Arctic Explorations*! What other book set so many young men to dreaming of adventures untold? Perhaps the fact that Elisha Kent Kane was a physician himself caused the young doctor sitting in his empty office to look between the covers of that book Dr. Kane had left like a spell upon the nation.

A review of it published in the London *Saturday Review* might almost be taken as a prefigurement of Dr. Cook's own future, and of a book that he would write about his past:

> Looked at merely from a literary point of view, the book is a very remarkable one. . . . The general impression which the book conveys is graphic to the last degree, and its effect is greatly heightened by what Dr. Kane speaks of as defects. It consists almost entirely of extracts from a journal kept at the time, connected by narrative matter more or less compressed from it. An attentive reader can trace the feelings and prospects of the little knot of icebound prisoners, and of their gallant leader with extraordinary clearness, for Dr. Kane is obviously a cultivated man, and by no means unaccustomed to watch the process of his own mind. The hoping against hope, the determination to look at the bright side of things, and the effort to write himself into a cheerful frame of mind, which may be detected in the lines penned by the light of the dim perpetual lamp, in the filthy little den into which the crew was crowded—penned, too, when all but the writer had half forgotten their trouble in sleep—seems to us far better worth having than any amount of artistic composition.[23]

What thoughts stirred in Frederick Cook's mind as he read the incredible adventures of this man, who managed to pack into 37 years of life more than an average lifetime of experiences? Dr. Cook had wished to escape. Perhaps in the pages of *Arctic Explorations* he first glimpsed the route of that escape, and in Dr. Kane's vivid descriptions of the wild people and places of Greenland he heard for the first time the mysterious call of the North.[24]

One morning in the very early spring, as he was reading the New York *Telegram,* he chanced upon a small notice datelined Philadelphia:

> Robert E. Peary, Engineer at the Naval Dockyard, is now engaged in fitting out his expedition to North Greenland. As is well known, it is his intention to try to ascertain the extension of Greenland northwards, by undertaking an excursion on sledges over its snow-covered interior. His companions on the expedition are not yet decided upon.[25]

Dr. Cook had hoped to absorb himself in work and forget his recent tragic losses. But the work did not come, and there was no relief from his thoughts. Now, before his very eyes, had appeared an avenue for complete escape. He immediately wrote to Peary, volunteering to serve as his surgeon without pay, then waited impatiently several weeks before a telegram arrived asking him to come to Philadelphia.[26]

That trip must have been an adventure in itself. Up to then he had never left his native state except for brief excursions into Pike County, Pennsylvania, across the Delaware River from his boyhood home.

As he walked up the steps at 4118 Elm Avenue, opposite Fairmount Park, he didn't know what to expect. Could he hope to be selected with so little experience? His knock at the door was answered by a charming young woman who showed him into the drawing room, where her husband was sitting in full uniform.

The Pearys.

Robert E. Peary, Civil Engineer, U.S. Navy, was an impressive-looking figure as he rose to shake the young doctor's hand. He was 34 years old and six feet tall, his ruddy complexion set off by his sandy, reddish hair and an even redder mustache, large and twisted to pointed ends, which nearly obscured his narrow mouth. When he smiled, fine showed of white teeth set in his squared jaw, marred only by a space between the two front ones. He looked every inch the picture of a proud naval officer. But it was his eyes, most of all, that one noticed. Stern and steely gray-blue, despite the smiling face, they had a veiled appearance that was hard to penetrate, yet they seemed to look right through a man.

Peary invited the doctor to sit down. The tall figure of his wife leaned lovingly on her husband's shoulders as he outlined his plans to his attentive guest:

> With a company of five or six members I shall be landed at Whale Sound, on the west coast of Greenland, in 77° 35' latitude, in the month of June or July. We shall spend the remainder of the summer and autumn in erecting a hut for our wintering, lay in an abundant store of meat, make scientific investigations and excursions to the inland ice, and, if the season is favorable, also establish a provision-depot near the south corner of the Humboldt Glacier. In the course of the winter we shall prepare sledges, "ski," clothes and travelling outfit, and practice running on "ski," and Canadian snow-shoes, for which purpose the head of Whale Sound is well adapted.
>
> When spring begins, four or five of the company will start over the inland ice for the Humboldt Glacier, one or two remaining behind to take care of the house. If good progress is made, we shall continue from the Humboldt Glacier to the head of Peterman-fjord. From here two or three of us will push on, whilst the others return to Whale Sound with the necessary provisions for the home route. Those in advance will continue to Sherard Osborne fjord, go farther on to the head of De Long fjord, and finally push on towards the northernmost point of Greenland. When this is reached, and its geographical position determined, the party will return by the same route to Whale Sound, and the expedition will take the first chance to return to America.[27]

After Lieutenant Peary finished the outline of his expedition, there were many questions for the doctor to ask and to answer. They discussed the techniques of fieldwork. Peary had been in Nicaragua and had made a reconnaissance of Greenland, but he readily admitted that he had yet to master the science of arctic research.

Dr. Cook's first impression was that of "a thoroughly decent fellow, and a strong character." Peary questioned him closely as to his qualifications, but the doctor confessed he had few beyond good health, his medical degree and a strong desire to walk where no others had gone before.[28]

"The life up there under the Pole is terribly hard," Peary said. "Where the expedition is going we will be as much out of touch with the world as we would on another planet. Death will be hovering near us always. Some of us more than likely will never return to civilization. I advise you not to go if there is any fear in your heart."

But Frederick Cook had already had his taste of death. "I am willing to take the chances," he replied. "This is my great opportunity, and I won't be held back by dread of hardships." But as he said the words he shivered a little, inwardly, at the picture Peary painted.[29]

By the end of the afternoon, it was agreed. Dr. Cook would be the surgeon of the North Greenland Expedition. The Pearys asked him to stay for dinner, but he excused himself, saying he had another engagement in New York. As he walked down the steps of the Pearys' Elm Avenue apartment building after saying goodbye, he saw more than the green expanse of Fairmount Park stretching away before his eyes:

> A new school of life now in prospect came over a spreading horizon. The first pages of the art of poleward travel were soon to be set into my book of endeavor. This was quite as exciting as the actual execution of the dream of future adventure.[30]

CHAPTER 2

I *Must* Have Fame

THAT SAME SPRING IN PHILADELPHIA, A YOUNG NORWEGIAN STUDENT WAS also dreaming of adventure. He, too, had just finished *In Darkest Africa,* by Henry Stanley, and was imagining himself penetrating into the interior of that vast continent among its many savage tribes, when his eye was caught by a small notice in the newspaper—a notice similar to that which had attracted Dr. Cook's attention. It struck him in just the same way.

All thoughts of Africa were put completely aside. How wonderful it would be, he thought, to gaze upon those desolate, ice-covered landscapes about which he had so often read. He immediately penned Peary a letter offering his services on the adventure.[1]

Eivind Astrup long remembered his half-comic first meeting with Lieutenant Peary. His English being slight, he armed himself with both English and Norwegian dictionaries along with the required doctors' certificates and testimonials to his character. With these, he entered the corridors of Peary's dockyard office, certain of victory.

A young man of African origin showed him to Peary's workroom, where he was heartily greeted by the explorer. "His whole appearance inspired me with absolute confidence," Astrup recalled. "His tall, lean figure was elastic and sinewy; his features, coarse but determined, were aglow with intrepid resolution."

Nearly at once Astrup's English failed him. Throughout the interview he continually resorted to his dictionaries but confined himself to the simplest of replies, since he hardly ever found the words to express what was in his mind.

As he thumbed their pages, he occasionally caught sight of the lieutenant's black servant coming and going, his face contorted by strange grimaces, as he tried to keep from laughing while watching Astrup fumble with his books. Nevertheless, in a few days, Astrup received word that he had been chosen as one of the five members of Peary's expedition.[2]

By chance, both Cook and Astrup had stumbled across Peary's invitation to adventure. The man who answered Astrup's knock at the door had come into Peary's life by chance as well.

One day Lieutenant Peary was in the establishment of B.H. Steinmetz and Company, on Pennsylvania Avenue in Washington, D.C., picking out a pith helmet suitable for work in the Nicaraguan jungles. He asked the proprietor if he knew of any young Negro man appropriate to serve as his personal valet. Sam Steinmetz said he had just such a "boy" working for him as a clerk, Matt Henson.

Despite his current occupation, Henson had already seen quite a bit more of the world than Peary. As a seaman he had been fairly well around it, quitting the sea only after the death of Captain Childs, who had befriended the runaway black boy on the wharves of Baltimore, made him his cabin boy, and given him all the schooling he possessed. As events would prove, Matthew A. Henson was just the man Lieutenant Peary was looking for, and quite possibly Peary was just the man Henson had been looking for as well.[3]

Henson had been born in rural Maryland one year after slavery had been officially abolished. But the half-century after the Civil War held few possibilities for a black man to make his own way, since what the United States had granted to its former slaves was little more than liberty, and certainly not equality. It was neither uncommon nor considered shameful for a black man to attach himself to a prominent white man and dedicate his own life to his service. Ever since Childs had died, Henson had probably hoped to find another man to serve as he had his beloved captain.[4] That chance had now come, and Matt Henson accepted Peary's offer.

It is tempting, however, to think that something more than chance had caused the meeting between Robert Peary and Frederick Cook. From the false perspective of hindsight, it seems that fate not only had forever preordained the meeting but had also conspired to entangle their lives for all time. And the chance and circumstance of their early lives bear coincidences that only add to this illusion.

Peary had been born at Cresson, at the summit of Pennsylvania's Allegheny Mountains, on May 6, 1856, the only child of Charles and Mary Wiley Peary. Everyone mispronounced Charles Peary's name, but unlike Cook's father, Dr. Koch, he never abandoned the original pronunciation. He always insisted, as would his son, that the vowels be pronounced as a long *e*, as in *weary*.

Like Freddy Cook, Peary lost his father to pneumonia, when "Bertie" was a little short of three; Charles Peary was only 30. Mary Peary, both physically and emotionally frail, responded to this tragedy by returning at once to the comfort and aid of her relatives in Maine, where both sides of the family had resided until her husband had gone to Pennsylvania to seek work as a maker of shooks—the staves used in barrels. Her decision was absolute. She departed, taking the body of her dead husband with her, and settled at Cape Elizabeth, near Portland.

Unlike Lena Cook, Mary Peary had the benefit of an estate of $12,000 that had been left her. This provided amply for her and her son. She tried to raise him as if he were a girl, but as he grew, Bertie proved to be very much a boy—a precocious child with a deep streak of destructive mischief his mother could not understand. Even so, he spoke with a slight lisp and had a shy and

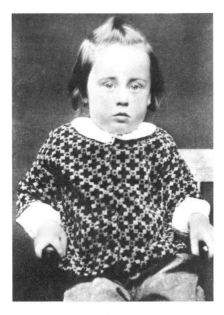

Bertie Peary, age 4.

sensitive nature. These characteristics, combined with his mother's smothering love, made him the object of ridicule and the participant in frequent fistfights to prove himself with the other boys.

Despite periods of resentment of her overprotectiveness, the boy was much devoted to his mother. He suffered agonies with her every illness, fearing her fragile health would soon fail completely and leave him alone in the world.

He attended a number of private schools, depending on where his mother was living at the moment. As he grew up, Bert Peary, fascinated by the natural world around him, spent much of his free time in the Maine woods collecting birds and eggs, earning money as an expert taxidermist.

Some of his collecting trips took him among the many islands of Casco Bay. A heavily wooded one of 17 acres two miles offshore from South Harpswell particularly enchanted him. After clambering over its rocky ledges and wandering through its thick woods of fir, white birch and moosewood maples to the far shore, where there was nothing but the broad sweep of the Atlantic to be seen, he vowed to himself that someday he would own Eagle Island.

Bert entered Portland High School and, although sickly, did well in school. Though still reserved, by the time he graduated he enjoyed a degree of popularity among his fellow students. He even had a sweetheart, to whom he would write long letters expressing his thoughts, dreams and ambitions.

Deciding on a college course, he won the Brown Memorial Scholarship offered by Bowdoin College in Brunswick, Maine. Bert sold his stuffed bird collection to buy his books. When he went off to college, Mary Peary went with him, living together with her son in rooms off campus. Shy with strangers, Bert was aloof at first, but he soon acquired a reputation as an academically brilliant student in the civil engineering course.

During the summer of 1876, he visited the Centennial Exposition at Fairmount Park in Philadelphia. He was especially drawn to the exotic exhibits depicting faraway lands, taking detailed notes on all that he saw there.

On his twenty-first birthday he wrote a letter to his sweetheart, May Kilby, that revealed his restless state of mind:

> It seems almost an impossibility to me how anyone, as some of our
> farmers do, can look forward to living their lives out in the same

place & doing the same things their fathers & grandfathers did before them.

Today as I think of what the world is & that I have my life before me, nothing seems impossible. I wish that as in the story books some fairy might place the mirror of my life before me & tell me to look at whatever scene I wished. Yet if I could do so, I could hardly say but I should close my eyes & refuse to look. How many have wished & wondered about the mysterious future as I do, & yet if the curtain were permitted to be drawn aside, would shrink from doing it for fear of gazing upon rugged rocks & yawning graves in place of the velvety paths they wish for.[5]

Much given to poetry and romantic daydreams, he attended a historical costume party dressed as Sir Lancelot, and once wrote a poem called "Roncesvalles," laden with epic images of knightly deeds traced boldly upon the broad canvas of life. To his diary, which he kept faithfully, he confided,

Tis a glorious life but, ah me! the poetry of the world in this respect is rapidly fading. I am glad that my lot is cast upon the world now rather than later when there will be no new places, when every spot will have felt the pressure of man's foot, & earth & air, & fire & water, the grand old primal elements & all that is in them, will be abject slaves.[6]

When he graduated the next year, Bert Peary stood second in his class of 51. He was elected to Phi Beta Kappa and, on the strength of his athletic ability and enthusiasm, had gained a popular status to match his academic achievements.

After graduation he and his mother moved to Fryeburg, where he practiced surveying in the Franconian Mountains. But without Bowdoin he was at a loss. He often climbed up Stark's Hill just to look out over the countryside and lose himself in dreams.

In December 1878 he went on an extended winter camping trip with one companion, stopping at a hostel near the foot of Mount Katahdin:

I watched Katahdin looming blue, white and cold in the NW from my window as the sun rose and saw the sky above it change gradually from gray to rose gray, then to bright rose,

Robert E. Peary.

then the summit seemed touched with fire which gradually crept down the sides till the whole mountain was a magnificent rose color and every outline was as clear cut as a diamond. Then the sunlight touched the top of the hard wood ridge across the east branch. The light on Katahdin paled and faded till he stood cold and white as usual and the sun had risen. It was as if the grand old mountain on first awakening had been unable to restrain his joy at existing, then remembering that he had his royal dignity to preserve had wrapped himself once more in cold white light.[7]

Ever imagining more heroic times, as summer came on and he contemplated his surroundings, his thoughts wandered to the men who had first visited the country upon which he looked:

> I never thoroughly understood until this Spring and Summer how the early explorers,—Weymouth, Gosnold and the rest—could have given the names Vineland & Acadia to New England. I could see how, to the eyes of Lief, the son of Eric, coming from the frozen shores of Iceland it would seem a tropical country, but to the others it does not seem as if it would. This year, however, the floating clouds, the vivid greens, the soft hazy veils have shown me the secret of the names.[8]

Though he loved its fields and woods and the opportunities they afforded for outdoor pursuits, Maine was too remote to realize his grand romantic ambitions. Perhaps unconsciously, he had transferred his own thoughts to lofty old Katahdin: the joy he felt in existing must be suppressed if a royal dignity were to be achieved; he must leave Fryeburg if he were ever to meet his destiny.

The little place did serve its purpose, however. A careful survey of the town had gained him notice and a trial appointment to the Coast and Geodetic Survey in Washington, D.C.

Although selected for permanent employment, after a year and a half he tired of the work of a draftsman, and though he knew his future must lie elsewhere, his dreams often drifted back again to home. But now they were more often of Laura Harmon, a girl from Fryeburg, although he had become engaged to May before leaving for Washington.

On October 7, 1879, he asked her for his release. In return he received a letter asking for an explanation, and when he had given it, another, reproachful in tone. It closed with the remark that she considered their correspondence at an end, and she requested that if Bert had anything further to say, he should address it to her father. In December she returned all of his letters, and he hers, along with her ring.[9] He informed his mother:

> My engagement with Miss Kilby is a thing of the past. . . . I tell you this that you may know how the matter stands if anyone speaks of

it, yet I rather you would not say anything at all about it and if anyone asks you about it tell them you do not care to talk on the subject. Now it is you and I only, My Mother, and Providence permitting I will make the coming years of your life happy enough to
make up in some degree for the sorrow, pain and anxiety I have
caused you in the past. I am very far from being good but I think I
love you a little though how much I did not know till the past few
months.[10]

His last binding tie to the rural life of provincial Maine severed, Bert
Peary now looked to the far horizon.

He had come upon an article about the proposed Inter-Oceanic Ship
Canal, for which a route was being considered across Nicaragua. The bigness
of the project captured his imagination and filled him with thoughts of
Balboa as he glimpsed the Pacific after climbing the last high hill of Darién. As
he began to read widely on the subject of the proposed canal, he became more
dissatisfied with his routine life. As he told his mother:

I don't want to live and die without accomplishing anything or
without being known beyond a narrow circle of friends. I would
like to acquire a name which would be an open sesame to circles of
culture and refinement anywhere, a name which would make my
mother proud, and which would make me feel that I was the peer
of anyone I might meet.[11]

I don't know whether it is my fortune or misfortune, or whether it
is the sign of an ignoble spirit, but I cannot bear to associate with
people, who, age & advantages being equal, are my superiors. I
must be the peer or superior of those about me to be comfortable,
not that I care to show my superiority, simply to know it myself.[12]

Two years into the life of a government draftsman, he read about a com-
petitive examination being offered to fill an appointment as a civil engineer in
the U.S. Navy with the rank of lieutenant. Now Peary thought he saw a way
toward the name he craved—or at least out of the routine he loathed.

He entered the competition, but, when he took the test he thought he
had done poorly. To it he appended a note that revealed something significant
about himself. "Had I known the direction the examination was to take I
should not have attempted to compete," he wrote, "yet once started it was
against my principles to back out, even though I saw that all the chances of
gaining one of the prizes were against me."[13]

This expressed a trait that would remain throughout his life, along with
others. He had much of his mother's emotional makeup and was subject to
passionate mood swings. Early on, he had observed, "I find every year proof of
my conclusion that I am a creature of pulsations, of ebbs and flows. I know I
am in many things, mentally and physically, and I think I am in everything."[14]

Despite his outward show of confidence, Robert E. Peary had many self-doubts.

In the case of the examination, his doubts were unnecessary. He won the appointment and could soon proudly show off his new dress uniform to his mother. But although now a staff officer, he still had made little progress toward his dream of fame. He was, however, able to fulfill one of his boyhood dreams. With his savings he purchased Eagle Island in Casco Bay.

The appointment gave him an entrée into the social life of the capital. While attending the round of official functions, he worked hard at developing a pleasing personality and good social graces; he even put to use a dancing course he had taken. In 1882, while at Marini's, a popular dancing establishment, he met a charming young woman, Josephine Diebitsch, who assisted her father in an interlibrary exchange at the Smithsonian Institution.

Sent to Key West that same year, Peary promptly contracted yellow fever. He survived the dread disease and also his clashes with the contractor who was building an iron pier there for the Navy. Civil Engineer Peary had been assigned the task of oversight, but after a number of disputes with the man over methods and materials, the untried lieutenant ended up in control of the construction itself. He did his work brilliantly, and by the end of April 1883, the pier was not only complete, but came in $3,000 under budget.

In 1884 his persistent study of the transisthmian canal paid off when Aniceto Garcia Menocal, to whom Peary had been made an assistant when first commissioned, became the project's chief civil engineer. Menocal had been impressed by the young staff officer then, and now asked for Peary as his assistant on a survey of a possible route across Nicaragua. In fulfilling this assignment, Lieutenant Peary showed unusual ability and exceptional initiative under extremely difficult circumstances.

Upon his return from the isthmus, while browsing through a secondhand bookstore in Washington, Peary chanced upon a report dealing with the virtually unknown inland ice cap of Greenland. The report reawakened the intense excitement he had felt as a boy while reading Dr. Kane's wonderful book. He began to read everything on the subject and vowed he would one day see that mysterious interior for himself.[15]

As he studied the subject with his characteristic thoroughness, Peary conceived the idea of attempting a crossing west to east. He began to work out plans in his diary indicating for the first time his consideration of "an imperial highway" across Greenland and perhaps on to the North Pole itself as a possible route to fame.

Though his plans were for the most part practical, there were passages of a different sort as well:

> There is the same wild, fierce poetry and grandeur in the work
> that there is in the Norse Sagas, and it can be prosecuted with the
> same dash and daring that filled the old Vikings, and with the

same dazzling yellow midnight sunlight flashing from every step as shone upon their sails, and tipped their lance heads.[16]

With his ideas sketched out on paper, Peary now considered a voyage to Greenland to see the conditions that actually prevailed there. At first, his mother would not permit her only son to venture his life on such a seemingly senseless aim, but she finally relented in light of Bert's pleading and lent him $500 to mount the attempt.

Peary paid passage on the whaler *Eagle,* which dropped him at Godhavn on Greenland's southwest coast on, June 6, 1886. He then traveled north to Ritenbenk, where he fell in with the town's vice-governor, a young Dane named Christian Maigaard. Together they climbed to the high plateau above Pakitsok Fjord and started off across the ice, dragging their belongings on a pair of nine-foot toboggan-type sleds made of hickory, steel and hide, weighing 23 pounds each. Peary named his sled "Sweetheart" in honor of Jo Diebitsch. Maigaard, lacking a sweetheart, though every bit as romantic as Peary, named his "Princess Thyra," after the youngest of the Danish princesses.

They were delayed by sudden storms and slushy snow lakes. Repeatedly, they had to cross treacherous snow-covered crevasses in the feeder basins of the great glacier over which they traveled. Maigaard had the narrowest escape when he broke through a snow bridge, saving himself only by hanging on to the back of Peary's sledge until he could be withdrawn from the entrance to the blue-black depths below. But when they were finally forced to turn back, dwindling rations, not any lack of nerve, was the cause.[17] Despite having no experience and little suitable equipment, the two men had progressed about 100 miles into the utterly unknown interior.

By the end of July Peary was safe again in Ritenbenk, pen in hand:

> Well my Mother here I am back again in civilization, having accomplished what I came to Greenland for . . . I have shown that one determined man if directed by ordinary intelligence can accomplish anything. . . .
>
> I feel almost as if I had come out of another world. I have worked harder than I ever did before & have had some adventures but I never for a moment doubted that I should succeed & never for a moment feared that any harm would come to me. Were I of a superstitious turn I should have felt a certain awe at times at the way things smoothed themselves out before me, but I only smiled to myself & thought "that is Mother clearing the clouds away."[18]

When he returned, Peary published an account of his trip. Modest though it was, it brought him to scientific notice, resulting in his election to the American Society for the Advancement of Science. This recognition, along with the experience he had gained, fueled his ambition. He determined on another expedition that would succeed in crossing Greenland.

Still, he wanted and needed his mother's approval and tried to convince her that the benefits of his plan far outweighed the risks:

> My last trip has brought my name before the world my next will give me a standing in the world. . . . The trip means to me my Mother, first an enduring name & honor, second, certainty of being retained in the Navy even in case of adverse legislation in regard to the Civil Engineer Corps, third, social advancement, for with the prestige of my Summer's work, & the assistance of friends whom I have made this Winter I will next Winter be one of the foremost in the highest circles in the Capital, & make powerful friends with whom I can shape my future instead of letting it come as it will. . . .
>
> Remember Mother I <u>must</u> have fame & I cannot reconcile myself to years of commonplace drudgery & a name late in life when I see an opportunity to gain it now & sip the delicious draught while yet I have youth & strength & capacity to enjoy it to the utmost. . . . Be indulgent to me again Mother & do not hold me back from that position to which I look with such longing eyes & which will be a source of such unalloyed pleasure to me. . . .[19]

Despite his arguments, his mother was not supportive. But another opportunity to gain what he most desired caused Peary to put aside his dreams of Greenland—at least for the moment.

He would return instead to Nicaragua, this time as second in command to Menocal and accompanied by his new valet, Matt Henson, to make a fresh survey for a route across the isthmus. Before going he wavered about whether he should marry Miss Diebitsch. "That she loves me I know that she can make me happy I think; that she would hamper me less than any woman I have met or am likely to meet I am confident," he confided to his mother. Still, he had reservations. "I shrink from voluntarily chaining myself; & hate to submit my last & fairest dream to the cold light of prosaic daily life."[20] But he did not shrink for very long. Bert Peary proposed in September 1887.

During seven grueling months in the Nicaraguan jungles, Peary laid out the route of the canal and often thought of Jo and his future. But now he had no doubts about his course. On August 11, 1888 immediate Jo and Bert were married. They honeymooned in Seabright, New Jersey; Mary Peary accompanied them.

Only a year into their marriage, Bert nearly lost his wife to a severe inflammation of the kidneys. It was a close thing, and he told his mother how relieved he was that she was now recovering. Despite his misgivings of losing his last and fairest dream, he now realized how much he would lose if he lost Jo. "Whatever Jo's faults or failings may be, & being mortal she has both, she loves me as few men are loved, & as long as she is near me & can touch me she is content."[21]

For the first two years the couple lived a seemingly normal life. But Lieutenant Peary, though assigned routine duties in the dockyards in New York and Philadelphia, had not lost his dream of having his name before the world.

Peary's work in Nicaragua had won him some praise, but most of the credit had gone to Menocal as chief engineer. Peary felt he had gotten far too little; his resentment turned to hatred for his former benefactor. Although Congress appropriated money in 1889 to begin work on the route he had surveyed, it went only for preliminary preparations, not actual construction. And as the legislators watched the French in Panama bog down with what seemed insurmountable difficulties in their attempt to build another Suez Canal across the isthmus, the appropriations dwindled. Peary soon saw that nothing that could fulfill his deepest desire would come out of his struggles in the jungles of Central America.

With his dreams of fame as surveyor and possibly chief engineer of the Inter-Oceanic Ship Canal vanishing in the south, Peary's attentions turned northward again. His path to fame lay there, he had decided, where he alone would receive the recognition as the first man to cross the mysterious interior of Greenland. But while he was still drafting his plans, he received a stunning blow.

Jo remembered the day well and the despondency her husband felt upon hearing the news. He came into their room looking very pale. "Bert, what in heaven's name has happened?" she asked as he sat down heavily on the bed. He only shook his head and seemed unable to speak. Jo was frightened. Then Bert managed to say the words that explained everything. "Jo, Nansen has crossed Greenland."[22]

A Norwegian zoologist, Fridtjof Nansen, had succeeded in crossing the ice cap east to west farther south than Peary's planned route. Not only was Peary bitterly disappointed, he also privately accused Nansen of stealing his plans and deliberately "forestalling" him.

Peary now changed his objective. He would direct his efforts to determining the northern limits of Greenland. He appealed to various scientific societies to sponsor an expedition but received no positive response. The 1884 rescue of the disastrous Lady Franklin Bay Expedition led by Lieutenant Adolphus W. Greely, with its rumors that those few who survived had resorted to cannibalism to do so, was horrifyingly fresh in the minds of potential sponsors. They wanted nothing to do with another arctic expedition.

Meanwhile, time was slipping away. Already, Peary was past 30 and once again tied to a routine job. His inability to realize his ambitions resulted in long spells of depression and self-doubt. But he would not give up his dreams so easily this time.

In 1890 his persistence won him an invitation to lecture before the Brooklyn Institute of Arts and Sciences, where he recounted his 1886 experi-

ences and outlined his plans for determining Greenland's northern extent.
The lecture was such a success that he received an invitation to address both
the Academy of Natural Sciences of Philadelphia and the American Geographical Society of New York.

The members of the academy determined to sponsor his plan, which he
estimated would cost $6,000, in return for transportation on the expedition's
ship of a group of scientists, professors and enthusiasts.

Early in his life Bert Peary had wished for the day when his name would
be known throughout the world. He had been planning for that day ever
since. Now it was finally here, he assured his mother. The North Greenland
Expedition had begun to take tangible form; it would be his chance at the
thing he craved most of all:

> I am starting now on what will be the effort of my life, the
> effort that will make my name known everywhere not only now
> but in the future, & will put me in the position that I <u>must</u> occupy
> or be forever unsatisfied. . . .
>
> Kane cleared $70,000 to $80,000 from his book, & Stanley
> sold his it is said for nearly $200,000 & clears some $50,000 from
> his lectures. Not that I want you to imagine that I am dreaming of
> such results, but there is a long distance between these results &
> $2700 per year, & somewhere in that space I will alight. . . .
>
> . . . Only three know the feelings that I have for Menocal. . . .
> But I must be where his consciousness of my superiority will be a
> constant thorn to him.[23]
>
> The [Maritime Canal] Company are making a strong effort to
> have the Government take the Canal, in which case it is very likely
> to be built by the Army engineers & Mr. Menocal will lose his job.
> If things work well I shall be back then & in the zenith of my fame
> etc. If I could gain it no other way I would give my right hand to
> be in the position that no one could fail to feel my superiority in
> ability & achievement as well as physique over that sneaking little
> black & tan cur.
>
> Fame money & revenge goad me forward till sometimes I can
> hardly sleep with anxiety lest something happen to interfere with
> my plans.
>
> I would turn in my grave if I went into it without having done
> something that would make it impossible for him to ever sneer
> that I owed any of my success to him.
>
> I feel that I am getting warm so I will stop here.[24]

As his plans took shape, the depression of the last few years faded. He
confidently told his mother, "I am working hard, but it is not affecting me as
before, for I am not worried. I see everything clear before me, & success & an
honorable name assured."[25]

He even had arranged that the rights to letters recounting the expedition's progress would go to the New York *Sun* for $1,000, he said. Bert gloated to her about how the *New York Herald* had begged for his story, and how he had refused, remembering his snubbing after approaching its editor in 1886 with a similar proposal:

> I am the independent one now.
>
> Believe me my little Mother, when so many of my prophecies (as that there was actual money in my project, & that I should have revenge for certain slights) are coming true, all will come true, & that in a little time (less than half a cruise if I ever had sea duty) I shall come back stronger & tougher than ever, & with the name of Peary famous throughout the world & through future generations.[26]

The press notices of the coming expedition had served their purpose. Applications poured in from eager young men hoping to find a place in Lieutenant Peary's adventure.

Among them was one from Langdon Gibson. He received Peary's form letter in reply, stating that no expedition member would receive any compensation and that each was expected to pay $300 for his "personal outfit." The letter concluded:

> If, in view of these facts, you still desire to become a member of the Expedition, send me a statement as to your age, height, weight, temperament, place where born, occupation, a physician's certificate as to your health and physical soundness, referenced as to mental and moral qualifications, and, if convenient, a photo of yourself, and I will consider your application.[27]

Gibson replied from Pittsburgh expressing enthusiasm but pleading poverty. He asked that the cost of the outfit be waived, and assured Peary that he wouldn't be sorry if he chose him to go along.[28] Gibson described himself as a lifelong sportsman, skilled in handling boats, who had explored the Grand Canyon of the Colorado. He was also a member of the American Ornithologist Society of Washington, D.C., he said, adept at preparing bird skins.

Gibson's qualifications won him an interview, but it was his splendid physique, above all else, that influenced Peary to choose him as second in command. At six feet and 180 pounds, Gibson was a handsome man of 25, with dark brown hair and gray eyes. Peary waived the cost of the outfit.

The personal interview itself was waived in the case of the final member of the expedition, John M. Verhoeff. Other, weightier considerations took precedence.

Verhoeff, a native of Kentucky, resident in San Francisco, wrote Peary an oddly stilted letter on March 16, 1891:

> Yesterday I read in the Tacoma Weekly News the announce-
> ment of your proposed attempt to reach the pole. Would like to
> accompany you fully realizing that the chances may be nine out of
> ten that I would never return.
>
> Am unmarried, 25 years old, and no one dependent on me for
> support. If you decide not to have me with you, do not take the
> trouble of answering, but treat this communication as confidential
> though you may have received many others similar.
>
> However, if you think favorably you can take the time to read
> the remainder of the letter which treats of my qualifications.[29]

Those qualifications did not look encouraging. Verhoeff was five-foot-
four and weighed only 135 pounds. Other statements hinted at a contentious
nature. Peary didn't bother to "take the trouble of answering."

Receiving no reply, not even the form letter, John Verhoeff penned an
afterthought that he hoped would cause Peary to reconsider him:

> You doubtless received my letter of 14th [sic] inst. signifying
> my desire to accompany you, but I neglected to speak of my ability
> to help defray the expenses.
>
> Would be willing to give $2000 for that purpose. If you are not
> favorable an answer is unnecessary.[30]

He now had Peary's attention. The expedition was sorely in need of additional funds. The lieutenant's estimate of $6,000 had proven far too low, and
he despaired of raising the difference. Hoping to book passage on a whaler, he
had contacted the Dundee Seal and Whalefish Company, but they had refused. The lowest price he could obtain on a chartered vessel was a sealer from
Bowring Brothers at $2,500 a month.

Peary was now "favorable" and accepted Verhoeff's offer with a single
qualification:

> I think everything is satisfactory if one point is clearly understood by
> you, namely that your contribution, generous as it is, cannot entitle
> you to any share in the management or control of the Expedition.
>
> This must in the very nature of the case rest absolutely with
> me. . . .
>
> . . . I think you need anticipate little or no personal risk, but
> you can look forward to any amount of hard work.

For the contributor of $2,000 toward the expedition the cost of the per-
sonal outfit was placed at $50.

The party was now complete. There would be no one to challenge the
leader's absolute authority. As Peary told Verhoeff, "The members of the party
will all be young, like yourself, students & enthusiasts, not one, with the exception of my colored man that I would hesitate to accept as a companion in
every sense of the word."[31]

But just to make sure, he required each to sign a contract recognizing him as sole commander and promising to "loyally aid and support the said Peary by all means in his power, to accomplish each and every object and purpose of the expedition aforesaid." Each man agreed not to write or cause to be written any information about the expedition for one year after the official narrative was offered for sale, and to turn over all material acquired to Peary. These covenants were pledged by each member's "word of honor, as a gentleman" to be faithfully and unqualifiedly observed. In return, the men would get necessary items of equipment, subsistence and transportation and the sum of $50 each on their return to New York.[32]

To ensure that he would be the only source of information about the expedition, Peary was careful to keep even the names of his party from being learned by the press. One of those going, however, was known: Josephine Peary. She became the focus of the reporters' attention. The newspapers vacillated between extolling Mrs. Peary's bravery and loyalty in consenting to accompany her husband and condemning Robert Peary for exposing her to such dangers.

Nine professors, with Dr. Angelo Heilprin in charge, would sail with them, designating themselves as the West Greenland Expedition. But they did not plan to winter. They would have just a taste of adventure and, after dropping off the Peary party, planned to retreat down the coast, gathering ethnological and geological specimens.

With the help of John Verhoeff's money, the expedition engaged the *Kite*, a steam sealer of 280 tons. The newspapers described her as a "dirty and greasy little whaling steamer": her sails discolored from constant exposure, her rigging very strong rather than ornamental, and her decks discolored with the oil of a hundred whales and ten times that many seals.[33]

She was a schooner-rigged barkentine built in 1874 and built to last: her bow a mass of oak from six to eight feet back from the prow; her timbers bolted and keyed together; her propeller, of bell metal, deeply sunken to avoid damage from floating ice.

The captain of the *Kite* seemed as well fitted for ice navigation as the ship. Richard Pike, though nearly 60, was active in mind and body. His rugged yet open and genial face, crowned with a generous crop of white hair, inspired confidence, along with his formidable abilities as an ice pilot. A crusty Newfoundlander, he called the expedition members his "boys," and his advice was heeded without question by every one of them, including Lieutenant Peary.

Richard Pike, captain of the Kite, 1891.

They never tired of hearing his tales gathered on countless whaling and sealing voyages, or how as master of the *Proteus* he had carried the unfortunate Greely to his winter quarters at Fort Conger in 1881. He had also captained the expedition of Lieutenant Garlington, who had been assigned to relieve the Lady Franklin Bay Expedition in 1883, only to be shipwrecked himself. Pike's 600-mile retreat in open whaleboats across seas filled with icebergs and floe ice to Upernavik was already the stuff of legends, and the captain would retell the story endlessly to whoever wished to hear it.

Since his appointment as surgeon, Dr. Cook had tried hard to think of everything he would need for the trip, planning his personal gear thoroughly. It included a few luxuries—among them two cases of ketchup, of which he had grown quite fond after making the acquaintance of his neighbor Mr. West.

His friends had told him that an arctic journey was suicidal, and the insurance underwriters had agreed, refusing him life insurance. Their admonitions had sobered him some from his euphoric state when he had first been accepted by Peary.

Before leaving he wrote a letter to his cousin in Indiana, William Koch, telling of his appointment to the expedition. He had no time for details, he said, but invited him to write to his mother in his absence. The letter ended with what sounded like finality: "I herewith bid you, Good-bye."[34]

On June 6, 1891, the *Kite* lay at the foot of Baltic Street, ready to depart. By late afternoon the throng of well-wishers and curiosity seekers who crowded her decks had been cleared away, and Jo Peary went down to her cabin to find it full of flowers, including a large bouquet from Dr. Cook. Looking at the roses, she felt quite homesick thinking that she would not see another for 18 months.[35]

The sealer soon slid out into the East River and away from the curious crowd that had come to catch a glimpse of the brave white woman bound for the "icy Sahara." Passing beneath the Brooklyn Bridge, Langdon Gibson noticed that the clock on the Produce Exchange Tower read five minutes until 5:00. As she swung out into Long Island Sound, her crew and members of the expedition stood on the deck and watched the bustle of the civilized world slip slowly astern.

Despite his subdued letter to his cousin, Frederick Cook would look back on this moment as one of the most significant of his life:

> We were enroute to the far North. Here began an education, a schooling in self expression, an adventure, not of work and play, the result of which was to merge in the midstream of endeavor, but a life alternately swept from the heights of glory to the depths of despair. Up to now I had sought proficiency in preparedness while invading the domain of books. Hence forth pioneering along the borders of the unknown was to be my chief vocation.[36]

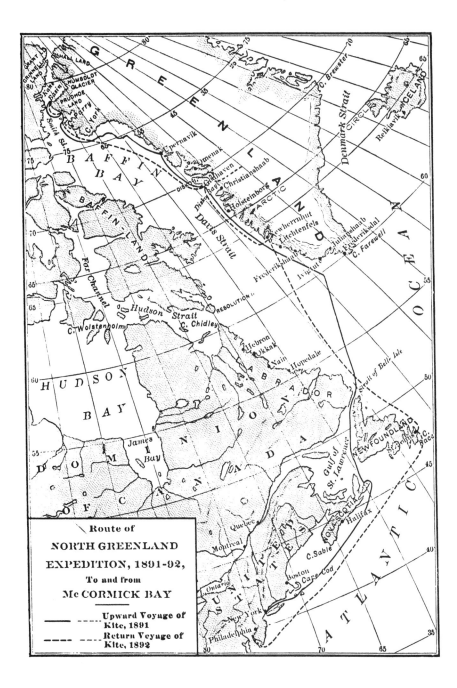

The North Greenland Expedition, 1891–92.

The voyage from Brooklyn was uneventful but by no means pleasant. For many of the expedition this was their first taste of the sea, and it caught in their throats. Despite the beef peptonoids the doctor prescribed to comfort himself and his fellow sufferers, few were able to come on deck when the *Kite* passed the Whitehead Light at the tip of Nova Scotia on June 10, Cook's twenty-sixth birthday.

The *Kite* called at Sydney on Cape Breton Island. While she lay at Victoria Piers, where coal could be had straight from the mines at 90 cents a ton, some boarded the ferry to North Sydney. But they found the town not very lively, a Salvation Army band being the only local entertainment.

While others roamed about Sydney, John Verhoeff had three of his teeth filled, Langdon Gibson went with the dock superintendent to visit a Micmac Indian village, Lieutenant Peary secured three large Newfoundland dogs and Mrs. Peary was treated to a ride in a two-horse tally along the coast. As the vistas of the rock-strewn shore unfolded around every turn, she looked out upon the deep blue of the northern sky mirrored in the deeper blue of the cold ocean and pronounced the scenery "indescribable."

After coaling, the ship sailed for the Gulf of St. Lawrence, triggering another round of seasickness. But this time it did not prevent most of the afflicted from struggling from below to catch sight of the first pieces of pack ice that slowly drifted past.

In the Strait of Belle Isle, the sight of ice was all too common. It grew so thick that further progress was impossible and the *Kite* was secured to a large floe-berg. Through a hole in the ice the expedition members landed a hundred-weight of cod, and in those first hours of waiting, few could resist the novelty of a spirited snowball battle in the middle of June. But as the hours lengthened to days, the expedition members found plenty of time, between taking potshots at the gulls that passed, for gossip and disagreements.

John Verhoeff, whom Cook described as "a cold southerner," embroiled himself in the first of his "rows" with other members of the party, each of which he dutifully recorded in his journal:

> June 16, 1891. Kite still in Strait. Peary, Cook and [Professor Levi] Mengel took a walk several miles over the ice. Probably this night Cook and I had an argument, or rather disagreement, as to whether or not heart is a muscle. Cook claimed it was a muscle.[37]

The excursion mentioned by Verhoeff caused apprehension aboard the *Kite*. When a fog quickly descended, Captain Pike doubted whether "his boys" could regain the ship. A search party was organized. But before it could set out, the adventurers appeared and straggled aboard, exhausted from their struggle over the rough, frozen surface.

As the *Kite* lay motionless, the captain took on ice to replenish the water supply, and the promise of exciting adventure gave way to a monotonous wait.

One member of the expedition had already had enough. Lighting out over the ice, one of the Newfoundland dogs abandoned any prospects of seeing the Arctic in favor of returning to the land of its ancestors, never to be seen again.

On June 22, when the ship was opposite the Cape Norman Light at the northwestern extremity of Newfoundland, a strong wind parted the ice. The *Kite* was released from the pack, and her passengers from their boredom, with a vengeance.

By dawn it was blowing a gale, and the overloaded ship wallowed through the heavy seas much to the discomfort of the once again thoroughly seasick passengers, who had enjoyed little sleep. Adding to his ordeal, Cook's bunk-mate, Eivind Astrup, had the disturbing habit of using the doctor's fine new of leather boots as the receptacles for his distress.

When heavy seas crashing over the deck dislodged the cookhouse and nearly sent it over the railing, few members of the North or West Greenland Expeditions were of much help in righting the matter, nor did they care. As they clung to their bunks in misery below, the cookhouse and its contents were the last things on earth they felt they would ever have use for again.

After three days, the sea finally relented. By then the *Kite* had been blown clear across Davis Strait to Greenland. Those who were able to come on deck were rewarded with a view of the rugged coastline of Cape Desolation, now 20 miles off.

Immense icebergs that dwarfed the little sealer drifted by, sharply etched against the crystalline atmosphere left in the wake of the storm. Comfortably ensconced in an armchair made for her by the ship's carpenter out of an empty flour barrel, Mrs. Peary sat in the surprisingly strong sun and watched them float past.

The morning of June 27, the island of Disco was sighted, and by afternoon the *Kite* was passing up the fjord toward Godhavn. The scenery was very impressive. A blue iceberg, 150 feet in height and pierced with a perfect arch high enough that the *Kite* might have sailed through with her topmasts housed, guarded the harbor entrance.

As the *Kite* dropped anchor in Godhavn's nearly landlocked harbor, a charge fired from her signal gun brought an answering salute from the shore. The captain, the lieutenant and Professor Heilprin went ashore to call on the governor, Mr. Carstens, presenting him with a letter of introduction from the Danish minister at Washington. Soon the whole party followed.

Immediately, they took the part to which they all aspired, rushing up the basalt cliff behind the town. Reaching the summit, they did what they had read all good arctic explorers do upon conquest: they built a cairn. Inside the cairn John Verhoeff placed a record of the names of the conquerors in a tin box with a few American coins. Langdon Gibson's name was placed in honorarium, since just after disembarking, he had sprained his ankle while chasing a butterfly and was thus prevented from joining the others in the climb.[38]

After descending from the heights, the expedition members were further let down by the appearance of the natives. There were no pure-blooded Eskimos left at Godhavn. Those of mixed blood looked simply ragged and impoverished, and certainly not up to the descriptions of the wild savages depicted so vividly in Kane's adventures. Those aboard the ship were eagerly consuming anything offered them by the steward from the now- resurrected cookhouse, when Verhoeff suddenly declared his intention of swimming to shore despite the numerous icebergs dotting the harbor and began to disrobe.

The wretched natives, none of whom had ever voluntarily gone into water of any kind in their entire lives, looked on in mild astonishment as he took the plunge. Alarmed for his safety, Dr. Robert Keely, one of the physicians in the academy's party, jumped into a small boat and began to row after him. Verhoeff, however, reached shore, then resolutely turned around and covered the 200 yards back to the ship without mishap. He received an ovation but almost at once was taken by a chill, and his circulation was restored to normal only after a vigorous rubbing. Dr. Keely, among others, thought Verhoeff's performance sheer bravado and a foolhardy feat, but it was actually the first evidence of trouble to come—evidence that John Verhoeff was a risk taker.[39]

The next day an excursion up the rich green sward of Blaese Dael, a glacial river valley noted for its basaltic columns, allowed a spectacular view from 1,800 feet of Disco Bay and the many icebergs spawned by the Jacobshavn Glacier. But even the beauty of its double waterfall was compromised by its mosquitoes, which Mrs. Peary exclaimed "beat any thing I ever saw even in Jersey."[40]

In the evening the visitors were treated to a sumptuous dinner at the inspector's house and attended a native dance. His sprained ankle notwithstanding, Langdon Gibson waltzed with Mrs. Peary. But it was her only dance; she left, overcome by the aroma of the participants. Those who stayed sampled the native beer made from hops imported from Copenhagen.

Sunday morning the expedition members dressed in their best. Mrs. Peary wore her gray suit but thought her brown hat with the yellow roses made "too much of a variegations" with her already unfashionably sunburnt face.[41] The service at the Lutheran church was not without penance, the expedition members being obliged to crowd into the 20-by-30-foot structure with the redolent natives.[42]

Taking leave of Godhavn, the *Kite* reached Upernavik without incident at 3 A.M., July 1. The time had to be ascertained by the ship's clock, as the *Kite* had now passed into the zone of perpetual summer daylight beyond the 67th parallel. Despite the hour, the governor, Mr. Beyer, came aboard almost at once, delivering the regulations notifying all ships going farther north of the Danes' monopoly on trade with the northern Eskimos.

This, the most northerly of the Danish settlements, had little of the charms of Godhavn's locale, or even its modest improvements. It consisted of two dwellings, several storehouses and 25 dilapidated native huts built into the hillsides. The people occupying them were even more impoverished look-ing and filthy than those of Godhavn. The smell of the rancid meat, seal oil and blubber that clung to their skin clothing was all but overpowering to the uninitiated nose.

But to those members of the expedition who thought about it, there came the realization that soon even Upernavik would seem an oasis. To the north, where the *Kite* was headed, there were only the villages of the wild "Arctic Highlanders."

The visit of a physician being a rarity, Dr. Cook was asked to come ashore. He did what he could for the sick, including removing a piece of bone from one of the Eskimos' arms, the result of a year-old break.

While at Upernavik, the party was entertained by the governor's charm-ing wife, who presented them with beer and bouquets tied with ribbons in the Danish national colors, then plied them with other gifts not to be opened until Christmas. Mrs. Peary, overwhelmed by the Danes' hospitality, thought they "could not be nicer to me if they were my personal friends."[43]

An excursion to the Duck Islands was planned to provided some sport and some necessities as well. But there was little sport, the party bagging 96 of the nesting ducks without any effort at all in the process of collecting 960 eggs and 43 pounds of eiderdown.

Sailing up the coast on July 4, the *Kite* was confronted by a near solid pack that stopped her progress opposite the Devil's Thumb, a prominent rock formation. In celebration of the day and in the absence of anything else to do, the ship's cannon, filled with overripe duck eggs, was fired, and a toast of "Melville Bay Roman Punch," a concoction of snow, rum, lime juice and sugar, was drunk to the Glorious Fourth.

While some hours passed in sawing the lumber for a winter shelter, with little to see on deck, there was once again time for talk below. Inevitably, the conversation turned to Mrs. Peary. One can well imagine the subjects on the minds of young, unmarried men faced with the prospect of having to share close quarters with a married couple. Verhoeff, his cash apparently still in-exhaustible, vowed he would give $500 if Mrs. Peary would return with the ship but confided to his journal, "I did not like the smutty talk."[44]

Spirits rose when the *Kite* suddenly began to move again at 5:30 P.M., July 11. The Pearys went up to the bridge to watch her batter her way through the rotten ice. At 8:45 Lieutenant Peary decided to go down to his cabin to warm up but first stepped to the taffrail to look over the stern. What happened next, Jo Peary would relive in her dreams for months:

> The "Kite" was backing at the moment, and as he leaned over the rail, the rudder struck a particularly solid cake of ice, tearing the wheel from the helmsman's grasp, throwing him completely over onto the deck. As he regained his feet, he called to the officer on

the bridge: "Stop her, Sir, there is a man hurted." Although I had not noticed Mr. Peary step to the rail, and could see him now leaning against it, I knew it was he who was hurt, and I do not know now how I reached him; but I got to him before anyone else, and found him pale as death, standing on his left leg and supporting his right one with both hands above the knee. In a few moments he was carried into the cabin by Dr. Sharp and Mr. Gibson, laid on the table, and his boot and clothing cut from the leg. Drs. Holt, Hughes, Sharp and Keely, of the West Greenland Expedition and Dr. Cook of our party, examined the leg, and pronounced both bones broken above the ankle. The leg was dressed and a box made for it, and the patient made as comfortable as circumstances would permit, on a bed made of rough boards hastily nailed across one end of the little cabin, and covers of blankets. I shall never forget how carefully and tenderly these gentlemen of the medical profession, as well as Mr. Gibson, handled my husband, and how kind and considerate all the members of the Expedition were. From Friday night until Tuesday, I never closed my eyes, nor had any desire to do so. Then Dr. Cook insisted on my lying down, and knowing that I should break down if I did not get some sleep, I did so while Dr. Cook sat with Mr. Peary.[45]

When the ship had gone astern, Peary's right leg had been snapped by the small iron tiller attached to the rudder when it struck the ice. The doctors determined that it was "a good break," however, and that the leg did not need to be set.

A lively debate ensued for the next four days while the *Kite* was again caught in the ice. At one point it seemed she might be "nipped"—her hull crushed by the ice pressure—but the grip of the ice was broken with pickaxes and explosive charges. Professor Heilprin, now fearful of being compelled to spend the winter if the *Kite* went farther north, argued that Peary's party should be put ashore as soon as a landing could be made. Dr. Hughes countered that the academy had allowed the expedition three months to reach Whale Sound and would not abandon the plan prematurely. Heilprin then changed his argument, saying that in light of Peary's accident, the expedition should be abandoned altogether.

Onto this icy scene of boredom and discontent and into the view of the restless explorers, a polar bear chanced to wander. As soon as it came within range, bullets rained down on the unsuspecting animal from 11 rifles trained on it from the deck of the *Kite*. Gibson, who leapt upon the pack as the wounded animal fled, put a bullet in its head at short range as the bear took to the water to make its escape, and a boat was lowered to secure the trophy.

Lieutenant Peary, lying in his cabin, missed all the excitement. He was in great discomfort, but his wife could not do much for him, although she tried her best to make him feel better.

"Can't you tell me where it hurts you most, and what you think might help you?" asked Jo.

"Oh, my dear, pack it in ice until some one can shoot it!" was her husband's reply.[46]

Dr. Cook redressed the leg and made a splint to keep his patient from jerking it against the box, but that night was a bad one for the lieutenant. He was delirious despite a dose of morphine. By July 21, however, Jo's anxiety had eased, and she found time to add to her diary: "This morning Dr. Cook, who is goodness itself to Bert, found that both bones had exuded lymph enough to lightly glue them together & we hope the worst pain is over."[47]

Though immobilized, the ship had drifted north on some unseen current. When a favorable wind sprang up, Captain Pike assured the scientists that the pack would soon separate and allow the *Kite* to proceed. Steam was gotten up, and on July 23 at 6 A.M. Captain Pike's prophesy came true, as the pack parted.

That evening Eivind Astrup watched the play of light on the sky from the low-lying sun. He thought it so heavenly that only a couple of angels were needed to make the vision complete. By ten o'clock that night the expedition's ship had rounded Cape Parry's perpendicular cliffs of red sandstone and basalt, seeking an entrance to Inglefield Gulf, where the expedition planned to winter.

Jo Peary stood on the deck and looked for the first time upon the place that she would call home for the next year, wishing Bert could see it, too:

> The steep red brown cliffs are interrupted frequently by small glaciers reaching down to the water's edge.
>
> The entrance to Wolstenholme Sound was particularly beautiful. Huge bergs guarded the entrance & Saunders Island in the distance & Dalrymple Rock immediately in the foreground stood up like great black giants contrasting with the snow white bergs surrounding them & the red cliffs of the mainland on either side.
>
> Whenever anything particularly striking or pretty appeared I was called by some one on deck & with my hand glass I went upstairs, opened the transom over Bert's head & succeeded in giving him a faint idea of how things looked by tipping the mirror.[48]

Captain Pike kept the *Kite* as close to the southern shore as he dared, looking for a small native village called Ittiblu, supposed to be in Barden Bay. One task of the West Greenland Expedition was to amass Eskimo articles for an exhibit on the peoples of the world to be mounted for the World's Columbian Exposition, planned to celebrate the 400th anniversary of Columbus's arrival in the New World. At Ittiblu they hoped to make a start.

Dr. Cook had been appointed the expedition's ethnologist, and a landing party under his command went ashore from far out in the bay, as the captain feared to go too near the poorly charted coastline.

As the longboat approached the shore, he could see several men running back and forth in front of the village, situated at the foot of steep southwest-facing cliffs. The villagers were all smiles and laughter and did what they could to help land the *Mary Peary* on the extremely rocky beach. They seemed curious about the strangers' mission and followed the boat party everywhere as they inspected the village. Cook was able to learn that the village was not Ittiblu, but Netiulumi, and was given to understand by a map drawn by one of the Eskimos that other natives could be found on the islands in Whale Sound. Peary had hoped he might secure a stone igloo, but the sea was so rough the doctor decided it could not be transported with any safety. So he traded a sawknife, a hatchet and a piece of board for the best skin tent in the village and returned to the *Kite*. "On the whole," he concluded in his report to Peary, "these people were quite intelligent, for not one of us knew a word of their language nor did they of ours, yet we made our selves understood and obtained of their possessions all they could safely spare."[49]

When the lieutenant learned that the entrance to Inglefield Gulf was packed with ice, he directed the captain to enter McCormick Bay.

Because of Peary's incapacity, Professor Heilprin, Dr. Cook and Eivind Astrup rowed ashore with three of the crew to find a suitable location for the expedition's winter quarters. Peary preferred a location on the northwest shore, where he believed the house would be sheltered from the prevailing winds. That side, however, proved bleak and inhospitable, but on the northeast shore they found a good beach running up to a little bluff about 20 feet high, which continued gently but steadily upward toward the rampart of cliffs that marked the edge of the great inland plateau. From the beach to the cliffs a luxuriant growth of yellow poppies and daisies nodded in the bright sunlight. The landing party had difficulty realizing that they stood less than 750 miles from the North Pole and only a short distance from where the Kane expedition had spent two miserable winters frozen in the ice.

A level on the little flower-covered bluff was selected as the site for the camp, and the selection was submitted to the lieutenant for his decision. Since he could only glimpse the spot with the aid of Jo's mirror, Peary deferred to the landing party's judgment.

The *Kite,* unable to anchor because of drift ice in the bay, spent the next four days steaming slowly back and forth while supplies, materials for the expedition's house, six and a half tons of coal and Mrs. Peary's two remaining Labrador dogs, Jack and Frank, were landed in the small boats *Faith* and *Mary Peary.*

Strapped to a board, Peary was brought ashore and placed in a tent where he could supervise the house's construction. In digging the foundation with pickaxes and shovels, the men struck frozen ground at 34 inches. Soon, the walls of the house were standing on the knoll, and by the end of the fourth day, only the roof remained incomplete. Enough progress had been made to allow Peary to give permission for the *Kite* to depart on July 29, but a fog closed in and the ship remained in the bay the following day.

Some of the West Greenland party had climbed up to the ice cap and had reported to Lieutenant Peary that the surface was smooth and unobstructed. In his tent he penned a last letter to his mother:

> I long for the time when I shall be stretching out across it on my way to the northern terminus and to an honorable name & fame. . . .
>
> As to my party I am very well pleased with it & feel much confidence in the members. They are all gentlemen as far as I can discover.
>
> Dr. Cook in particular I feel much confidence in. He is undoubtedly thoroughly posted in his profession, has a very complete supply of medicines, etc., & is patient, careful & unruffled to a degree. This I have had opportunity to test since my aggravating mishap three weeks ago.[50]

Finally, the weather cleared. All but the Pearys came on board to write letters for the ship to carry home. Dr. Keely found the departure a somber affair and recorded the foreboding he felt as the *Kite* made ready to sail:

> It made us all sad and thoughtful, and after exchanging a few souvenirs and well-wishes we bade each other good-by. Three shrill blasts of the whistle and a volley from our guns signalized our departure. Never had I listened to a farewell salute that affected me so sadly, showing the different effect produced by the strangeness of our surroundings and the peculiarity of the circumstances. As their boat rowed off they gave three cheers, but not with the hearty ring that I had heard from the same throats before. The signal-bell in the engine-room rang full speed ahead, and in a few minutes we departed from the most northern white settlement on the globe, leaving our companions to face their chosen duty in that almost merciless Arctic climate.[51]

The *Kite* steamed for the open sea while the rowboat pulled for the bleak shore. But as the distance grew between them, the men at her oars did not share Dr. Keely's feelings. This was the moment that Eivind Astrup and the others had longed for so fervently:

> It was not with any regret that we saw this last connection with the civilized world disappear by degrees on the horizon. We were now alone, and could at our ease start the work we had before us, and to which we had resolved to devote ourselves during the next twelve months.[52]

CHAPTER 3

The Inspiration of All the World

AS THE BOAT ROWED BACK TO THE SHORE, DR. COOK SURVEYED THE SITE OF the house from the sea. It was a beautiful place in the summer sun, he thought, but what would come when the unrelieved blackness of winter descended with its uninterrupted night that had been so miserable for Dr. Kane, Lieutenant Greely and so many others? Only Peary had any experience in the Arctic, and that was minimal. Looking to the interior over which the forbidding ice cap lay, he wondered what experiences awaited on its heights, and about the expedition's probability of success there.[1]

If others were having second thoughts, they were as careful as he not to voice them. Each had come on the expedition as a matter of choice, and all other choices were now fading over the horizon with the *Kite,* anyway. Before the ship was even out of sight, the men, stripped to their undershirts, were back at work on the unfinished roof. The sound of whistling and the ring of hammers were heard where no sounds but those of Nature had ever been heard before.

The roof was still incomplete when the weather changed abruptly. A strong storm swept down from the slopes behind the house, driving the workers from the roof and into the crowded confines of Lieutenant Peary's seven-by-ten-foot tent, where he lay with Jo in attendance. After dinner the men sought refuge under the partial roofing, while the Pearys rode out the storm in the tent, which seemed destined to be swept away by the water running off the hillside in rivulets. All "night" it poured rain.

The next afternoon the skies cleared, allowing the men to resume their labor. By morning, the house was under cover, and none too soon since another storm arose and pelted the house, showing up leaks in the hastily constructed roof. It rained for a week, and since nothing could be done outside, the members of the North Greenland Expedition turned their attention to finishing the living quarters.

The 22-by-12-foot structure was divided into a large and a smaller room. The walls and roof were made of one-inch boards covered with tar paper inside and out. An inner wall of matchboard left a dead air space of about a foot. On the inner wall were hung heavy red woolen blankets for insulation.

The Pearys' room at Redcliffe House, McCormick Bay.

Around the outside would be built a stone wall, four feet from the house and three feet high, designed to keep the cases and barrels of provisions off the ground. Canvas was to be extended from the roof to the wall to form a snow-free passage by which access could be had to the supplies, and also to serve as a place to take exercise and fresh air in bad weather.

The smaller of the two rooms, reserved for the Pearys, was 12 by 7½ feet. Mrs. Peary fitted up the room with a set of curtains across the bed made from two silk flags, one belonging to the National Geographic Society of Washington, D.C., and the other to the Philadelphia Academy of Natural Sciences. A steamer trunk served for a bedtable and held a pitcher and bowl for washing when not in use as a seat. Carpeting was thrown down on the tongue-and-groove board floor, and the expedition's library was put up in rude bookcases along the wall.

The men's quarters, slightly less than twice the size of the Pearys', held their bunks, a table for meals, and a work and storage area. The potbellied coal stove was placed in the partition between the two rooms and set into the floor to its door's level, providing heating to the lowest possible layers of air. Its pipe vented through an opening surrounded by sheet metal just beneath the hut's seven-foot ceiling. Eventually, the men would construct rude chairs to sit on, and Mrs. Peary would sew cretonne curtains for the windows.

On the wall next to her bed, Jo Peary

The living room at Redcliffe House.

lovingly arranged the pictures of her dear ones whom she often thought of longingly. She wondered as she looked at them what they would think if the eyes in the pictures could actually see her now, and what they would say if the lips could speak.[2]

The first Saturday ashore, John Verhoeff told Lieutenant Peary that he did not care to work on Sunday, though he wanted to do as much as the rest. Peary replied that he would not require work on Sunday once the house was finished, but his wife couldn't help making a comment on Verhoeff's request, which the young man duly recorded in his diary:

> Aug 2, 1891. Have little liking for Mrs. P. Said any one who would not make a roof on Sunday would certainly go to Hell. A cut on me.

The outside work, long delayed by the weather, was finally finished August 8, and Lieutenant Peary called for suggestions for a name for the house. "Redcliffe" was selected—after the great sandstone cliffs that rose behind its site. Since it was Matt Henson's twenty-fifth birthday, Peary sent the men hunting while he and Mrs. Peary prepared a special dinner of the celebrant's choosing from the camp stores. Before he left, Matt mixed up a batch of plum duff for dessert, a dish whose recipe he had learned from the cook aboard the *Kite.*

As the hunting party mounted the hill behind the house, its leader, Langdon Gibson, thought about how far from the truth his ideas of Greenland had been. It was warm and starkly beautiful. Still, like Dr. Cook, he noticed a forbidding element as well:

> When reaching the top a most beautiful view lay out before us. . . . Looking from where we stood . . . the icebergs were so numerous it would be impossible to count them. With this view in front of us, the bay at our feet, with our little house and belongings looking like a white dot in the picture, we could see by turning our heads in the other direction the great desolate and unknown ice blink, a huge horizon of smooth ice where no animal exists and where no man has ever trod foot. It is the secret of this ice cap we expect to solve next spring.[3]

Peary was determined that his broken leg would not prevent him from participating in that solution of which he had so long dreamed. Dr. Cook had made him a pair of crutches, though he was still in splints and not expected to be up for at least a week. But with the crutches at hand, nothing Jo said could dissuade her husband from trying them. When the triumphant hunters returned hauling a deer, they were surprised to see their leader standing at the corner of the house snapping their return with his Kodak.

At Matt's birthday dinner, Lieutenant Peary presided at the rude table with the whole group sitting on packing crates. He christened a recipe of spirits of his own design the "Redcliffe cocktail" and used it to inaugurate the first official dinner in the finished Redcliffe House. The chase had given all the men a keen appetite, and they tore into the main course of broiled breast of eider duck with little further ceremony.

Three days later another feast marked the Pearys' third wedding anniversary. This time an incongruous combination of little auk stew and Haute Sauterne was served. If enough such occasions could be discovered, it certainly looked to most of the explorers that whatever else might befall them, at least they were not likely to starve.

As the expedition settled into its new quarters, Dr. Cook had time to reflect on the character of those men with whom he had cast his lot. He later recorded:

> We all had peculiarities which we tried to repress. Those personal idiosyncrasies I had carded as case records like the desk records of a physician's office. Some of these notes were of such a confidential nature that they cannot be printed.
>
> Gibson was in most respects the most dynamic personality. He was over six feet, an evenly developed athlete, grounded in about every angle of sportsmanship. . . . Brother of Charles Dana Gibson, the creator of the Gibson Girl, Langdon also had an eye for art, particularly of the feminine [kind]. . . . Gibson, though outspoken, was ever loyal to the chief and loyal to the best interest of every member of the party.
>
> Verhoeff lived in a grey world. [Though] a graduate of Yale . . . his book learning got him little advantage. He was argumentative on any subject and impractical in his adaptation to camp life, and to Arctic work in general. . . . He also took a violent dislike to Mrs. Peary and to Matt Henson. . . . [But] Verhoeff was good hearted; never said an unkind word about others. . . .
>
> Astrup was a mere boy with good average manly proportions. . . . The largeness of American methods thrilled him. Astrup was poetic in temperament and artistic in expression. . . . He was diplomatic in his comments, loyal to purpose, and faithful to utmost details in service.
>
> Henson was colored with just a little white admixture. He was of average height and somewhat under weight. Serving as camp cook and general servant to Peary and his wife, he had not much time to go astray. He was impulsive and unwise in his remarks. Coming to the men he would carry tales from the inner quarters, and we figured that he would do the same from our camp fires . . . and he suffered from this suspicion.
>
> With these qualities in my files and much more in a subconscious apperception, I could figure out reactions to all issues com-

ing or going. At any rate I thought I could, which in the end amounted to the same thing. A young doctor is ever confident of his capacity, but he soon finds he has much to learn.[4]

Peary, too, had much to learn and had also been sizing up his men and his prospects. If the expedition was to succeed, no time could be lost in readying the equipment for the spring journey. Although unable to actively participate in many of the tasks that must be done, he reasoned that the coming months of delegated responsibility should serve as a testing ground that would determine his choice of the best men to accompany him across the inland ice.

Part of Peary's plan was to make use of the natives in preparing appropriate clothing and to enlist their aid on the trip itself. To this end he drew up orders for an expedition to the nearby islands in Whale Sound. Gibson was to be in charge and was instructed to visit the great nesting grounds known to be on the cliffs of the islands to secure as many birds as possible as food for the coming winter.

In addition, Peary charged Cook with obtaining skins useful in making winter clothing and several pairs of the native skin boots called *kamiks*. As the expedition's ethnologist, he was also to trade for artifacts for the Columbian Exposition's display. But Peary cautioned him "not to run the price of articles too high." His main task, though, was to entice an Eskimo family to settle in the vicinity of the house.[5]

The whaleboat *Faith,* named after the boat used by Dr. Kane, was readied for the trip, and the next afternoon Gibson, Cook, Astrup and Verhoeff cast off.

Rounding Cape Cleveland, the party came upon some floating ice occupied by a herd of walruses. Gibson directed an assault after giving Dr. Cook time to take a few snapshots with his Kodak. At a word all fired in unison, but the huge animals seemed impervious to bullets. With sullen roars the monsters merely rolled off the ice one by one and vanished beneath the water.[6] When they failed to reappear, the *Faith* rowed on toward Hakluyt Island.

Taking watches by twos while the others slept, the boat party approached the island's loomeries. The waves were breaking so high on the shore that it was impossible to land the *Faith,* so they sailed farther, to a point where overhanging cliffs bordered the ocean. Here Gibson shot a few birds, but it was difficult to pick them up from the heavily loaded boat in the crashing surf.[7]

A landing was made a short way up the coast, and after pitching camp, the four men returned to the cliffs, where every cartridge brought down at least one bird from the teeming heights above.

Once back at camp, Cook and Astrup set off down the beach in search of natives. They found none but noticed evidences of recent habitation. Verhoeff took a cross section of the island and then went exploring on his own. Reaching its highest point, he looked out over Smith Sound with icy Grinnell Land rising across its blue expanse flecked with floating icebergs. When he returned, the men roasted fresh eider ducks for dinner, then went to sleep in the lee of an overhanging rock.

The following afternoon they reached Northumberland Island but still found no natives.

As they sailed along its coast the next day, they saw two stone igloos and landed the *Faith*. In his official report to Peary, Dr. Cook described the party's meeting with the "Arctic Highlanders" in matter-of-fact terms:

> When we first saw these igloos from a distance we could see no signs of life, but as we approached nearer and were about to land we saw a man coming down over some hummocks at a short distance.
>
> His general appearance approached nearer that of a wild animal than a human being. He expressed no fear, but came right down and helped us with our boat, and smiled and talked for minutes at a time. We of course knew not a word of what he was saying except *Chimo* [Welcome]. Soon a woman with two children also appeared on the scene. We had lunch and offered them some of it. They seemed pleased at our generosity, ate what we gave them, but apparently did not enjoy any of our foods except the coffee and biscuits. . . .
>
> After this pleasant entertainment I tried to convey to them an idea of what I wanted. I had already examined the stone igloos, but found there absolutely nothing of value to us.
>
> The woman disappeared for a half hour, then returned with a sealskin. She began immediately to make a pair of kamiks, for which I gave a knife.
>
> My original bargain was a hunting knife for two pairs of kamiks, but they did not understand it that way. He said that was all the skin he had, and the appearance of their clothes and those of his wife seemed to bear out his statement.[8]

In his later years, Dr. Cook would again write of this meeting, investing it with far more significance than he had at the time. Looking back through the prism of his subsequent experiences, he had come to realize that this had been for him one of those moments of truth—a point when life's course changes, imperceptibly, yet irrevocably, forever:

> The first meeting of wild and cultured humans must always, as it was to us, be a dramatic event. . . .
>
> . . . The woman was just a little thing, four feet six inches, but in her there was evident a universe of understanding. . . . After a brief preliminary introduction . . . she approached each of us, looked us squarely in the eyes and said questioningly, *ahtingah*. This was repeated so rapidly and so often that we just repeated the word as an answer. This brought extended laughter, but the woman persisted. No other word was offered.
>
> "What does the fool woman mean?" said Gibson.

"She is crazy," said Astrup.

But the peculiar manner of the questioner betrayed the desire to drive in us just one idea. She was more intent and more serious with each effort. We offered food, offered presents, but she would take nothing. . . . Our stupidness now became evident to all. Gibson . . . suddenly . . . got an idea. Rising with a knowing look in his face, he placed his huge hands on her little shoulders, looked into her black eyes and said, *ahtingah?* She promptly said with an expression suddenly cleared of trouble, *"Manee. Manee-ap piblokto ibse,"* and then pointing to her husband she said, *"Ikwa."*

Still puzzled, still too stupid to grasp the import of this wild woman's appeal in the simplicity of one word, we lingered in amazement at her resigned persistence. With motherly intuition she was trying to give us one word with which, as we learned later, we could in time elicit the entire Eskimo language. We were so dense that it took us two days to grasp this woman's teaching wisdom. The word "ahtingah" meant, "What is it—what do you call it—what is your name." When she answered Gibson, she had given her name, Manee, and she supplemented this by, "Yes, it is Manee. You are crazy. There is my husband. His name is Ikwa."

This one word "ahtingah" drilled into us by this savage woman gave us greater aid than all the books of Arctic exploration, for by its use we not only gathered with prompt ease a working knowledge of Eskimo conversation, but an understanding of the essential technique of Arctic life. No explorer can do much in the polar regions without this native insight to deliver life safely through the dangerous periods of famine and frost ever on the horizon of this world in white.[9]

Contact had been established.

Dr. Cook's hindsight was correct. Without the help of these people, pitied or scorned by most civilized eyes, all of his and Peary's future efforts would have ended in futility. They alone possessed the secrets of survival in their harsh land, a knowledge won from centuries of bitter experience and guarded by a society with intricate social relationships and taboos, each designed to conserve human life against a cold and savage environment.

After a night of rain, the next day being Sunday, the men voted on whether they should work or rest. This time even Verhoeff voted to work so that they might return to Redcliffe House and the comfort it already represented to them.

With some means now of making himself understood, Cook tried to coax Ikwa and Manee into the *Faith;* however, the Eskimos seemed reluctant to come along. But after some gentle persuasion, Ikwa got his kayak and dog, and he and his family got into the boat. Ikwa indicated that more "Oiskees" lived just beyond the next cape, so they rounded it and saw a skin tent, or *tupik,* and a man in a kayak approaching them "aglow with smiles." He piloted them to the settlement, where all its inhabitants waited along the shore to see the strangers land.[10]

Cook started to trade with these people and soon had quite an assortment of "ethnological specimens." The doctor also treated one of the children for intestinal parasites, for which the parents seemed to express considerable gratitude. Their mission was now complete, or so they thought. Again Ikwa seemed reluctant to continue. But then he suddenly changed his mind and once again piled his family and all of his belongings in the boat. They set out for Redcliffe.[11]

Ikwa was very greatly astonished at the sight of Redcliffe House and woke up Manee, who to the equal astonishment of the white men had disrobed completely before retiring beneath her deerskin in the bottom of the boat. Upon landing, Ikwa immediately began to erect his tupik.

The men quickly found that with an Eskimo family in residence hunts stood a good chance of success, and soon the party had the skins needed for the clothes they would wear through the winter. Manee set to work preparing the furs, sitting hours on end in the men's quarters chewing the skins to soften them, but resting her jaws on alternate days.

All of the men except John Verhoeff, who would not give up his woolen pants, preferred the skin clothing to their civilized apparel, though they did not wear it on Sundays. In proportion to its weight, the protection from cold it afforded could not be matched. When the seat of his trousers wore out, Dr. Cook patched it with a large piece of bearskin, which, Astrup thought, "with the long, hanging white coarse hair . . . gave him a most quaint appearance."[12]

As if to prove there was a place for a white woman in farthest northern Greenland, Mrs. Peary soon handed

A summer day: Ikwa, his family, Mrs. Peary.

over the cooking tasks to Matt Henson and took to the field to provide the new cook and her seamstress with raw materials.

Strapping on her cartridge belt and .38 Colt, she prepared to join Cook and Ikwa in the hunt. After trotting some distance they came to a stream. The doctor, who was wearing his high rubber boots, carried the guns and ammunition over, then returned for Mrs. Peary.

Once across the stream, they sighted reindeer. Dr. Cook managed to wound one of them, and he and Mrs. Peary pursued it until, seeking relief, the deer plunged into a nearby lake. Having expended the last of their rifle ammunition, the hunters watched helplessly as the wounded animal struggled in the water beyond its ice-encrusted shore. It grew late, but they were loath to abandon their quarry even when Astrup joined them and, thinking the situation impossible, urged them to go back to camp. But Dr. Cook and Mrs. Peary could not be persuaded:

> Nearer and nearer she came to the ice, finally leaning against the edge as if to gather strength, when suddenly the doctor darted over the ice-foot into the icy water, and before the startled animal realized his intention, he had her by her short horns. . . .
>
> The doctor had some trouble in pulling the wounded animal out on the ice, which kept constantly breaking. All this time he was standing knee-deep in the ice-cold water, and before long he had to call to us to relieve him, his feet and legs being so numb that he could stand it no longer. As Astrup had on low shoes, he did not feel like wading out to the doctor who was rubbing and pounding his feet, so I went to his relief. My oil-tan boots kept the water out for some time. Although I could not drag the poor creature out on the ice, still I had no difficulty in holding her, as she made no resistance whatever. After the doctor had somewhat restored his circulation, he came to me and together we pulled the wounded animal out. Then I was asked to kill her with my revolver, but I could not force myself to do it, and Astrup took the weapon and put her out of her misery.

Leaving the deer, the hunters soon reached the river. Ikwa merely removed his kamiks and waded across, but Dr. Cook had to make three trips. First came the rifles; then Mrs. Peary; finally he returned for Eivind Astrup. This last load weighed 183 pounds, and the current was so swift that he did not dare lift his feet from the bottom. When he finally arrived safely on the other side he noticed Ikwa lying on a mossy bank convulsed with laughter at the sight of him carrying Astrup. Once across the river, they quickly reached the house, where Lieutenant Peary had grown anxious waiting for his wife's safe return.[13]

The adventures of the chase were not all confined to land. On August 22, while crossing Whale Sound in the *Faith*, Gibson, Verhoeff, Astrup, Cook and Ikwa suddenly came upon a large number of animals basking on ice floes directly ahead. *"Ah-wick,"* whispered Ikwa. Walruses. The opportunity was irresistible. But their previous encounter with walruses had been atypical, and their inexperience with the animals' usual behavior nearly cost them their lives.

This time the beasts attacked the boat. Nearly a hundred came roaring and snorting from all directions. In the excitement Cook's rifle, held at half

The crew of the Faith: *Cook, Ikwa, Langdon Gibson, Eivind Astrup, John Verhoeff.*

cock, went off, shooting a hole in the side of the boat, fortunately above the waterline, and Gibson, swinging wildly at several walruses that were attempting to hook their tusks over the *Faith's* side and capsize her, buried his mattock in the boat's side rail. They managed to save only one head of the many walruses they slew and the carcass of another.[14]

As the summer slipped toward fall, the rapidly shortening days found the men engaged in a variety of pursuits. Astrup worked as a joiner, making sledges and skis, Peary cut skins to his own patterns, Cook acted as tanner, while Gibson tried his hand at shoemaking. "In these various practical occupations we attained by degrees such skill," Astrup recalled, "that many a time we jokingly expressed a mutual doubt if either one or other of our company had ever done anything else in his former life."[15]

Much was learned by trial and error, however. The first sledge made by Gibson and Astrup proved a flimsy affair and was christened by Cook the "Ah-weak." But as for the staples of life, the doctor was now confident that everything was in readiness for the coming arctic night:

> Situated as we are under the roof of a house as good and comfortable as forethought, practical experience and ingenuity can make it, well ventilated, constantly and thoroughly heated, with no moisture, surrounded by the very best of hygienic conditions, with an ample variety of the proper quantity and quality of food, a sufficient library of interesting and amusing literature and the physical and mental exercise afforded us in the preparation of our sledging outfit, when I consider these advantages I can see no source or time for mental

depression, scurvy or other disease of which other arctic expeditions have complained.[16]

By the end of August, preparations to send a party to establish an advance depot on the inland ice were complete. Peary assigned this task to Gibson, Astrup and Verhoeff. They left on September 3 but, forgetting some of their equipment, returned for it. As they set out again on September 7, snow began to fall. Cook went with them this time to the edge of the ice cap and then returned after each man had packed several 52-pound loads to the top of the 2,500-foot cliffs.

Once on the ice cap, the three men were impeded by drifts that prevented them from making more than a mile and a half a day. When a storm pinned them down in their frozen bags for 36 hours, Astrup became delirious from the cold and Verhoeff's face was frostbitten. Gibson decided to turn back.

Arriving at the house on September 11, they found it deserted, with a note on the door which read: "Have gone to head of McCormick Bay after reindeer. Will be gone three days. Please leave your card. R.E. Peary."[17]

It was a cheerless homecoming for Gibson, feeling that he had failed in his first real chance as leader, made more unpleasant by having to eat cold beans and crackers for dinner. He could manage only rice and mush to celebrate his brother's birthday on September 14, and when Peary still did not return, he sent Verhoeff and Astrup to report to him. Alone, Gibson began to brood:

> It is quite cold in this room, and I am making myself comfortable in my blanket suit which my dear mother made for me. I see the touch of her dear hands wherever I turn my eyes. Each button reinforced, my initial on all my clothing, and even when I sharpen this pencil I found in my chest I do it with the knife given to me by my dear thoughtful mother. I have just been out to stop a dog fight and saw the Mary Peary coming in the distance. So I will put this away.[18]

Lieutenant Peary, disappointed that his men had done so little, asked them to try again. That night Langdon Gibson went for a walk on his snowshoes. The darkening sky was now hung with bright stars and a moon so glaring that the white icebergs looked black against the brilliant horizon. "I don't know why but the whole surroundings inspired me with a strange feeling," he wrote in his diary, "and I soon found myself humming 'Abide with me,'. . . I am thinking of home to-night, and may my prayers be heard to-night."[19]

The depot party, now consisting of only Gibson and Astrup, started out once again for the ice cap on September 22. This time they did not return for a week. Still, they traveled only about 30 miles into the interior, where they were turned back by deep snow.

Though Peary put aside his crutches on October 1, he would still not be able to participate in the preliminary sledge trips for some time—time in which to assess the strengths and weaknesses of his men. But he already felt that some were not up to the great task that lay ahead.

With his constant bickering and his strained relations with Jo, Verhoeff had erased whatever small expectations Peary had had for him. Gibson, too, had been a disappointment. The *Faith*'s rudder had been washed out to sea when left on the beach, and Peary blamed the loss on "Gibson's carelessness and apparent lack of all idea of responsibility."[20] The failure of the depot party to establish an advanced cache on the ice cap along with other incidents about camp had also made Peary believe that Gibson lacked staying power. He was appalled by the man's appetite and, despite his magnificent physique, in Peary's opinion, he had shown badly under adversity. "I have a strong suspicion," he wrote in his diary, "that either from laziness or cowardice the idea of going on this inland ice trip makes Gibson sick to his stomach, but it is too late to change now."[21]

On the other hand, Dr. Cook, who seemed so reserved and unprepossessing at first, had shown initiative, ingenuity and stamina. Nothing had changed Peary's initial favorable opinion of him. Peary now placed Cook in charge of a trip to the head of the bay to build a stone igloo to be used by the spring party.

With the departure of the sun in October, Eskimo families began to arrive at Redcliffe House. The camp now seemed almost a part of the landscape. The autumn snows had covered the house to such an extent that with the native igloos the visitors erected, it looked like nothing more than a series of snow mounds when viewed from a distance. It wasn't long before the explorers had several more expert seamstresses eager for the small rewards that work on the expedition's apparel brought them.

One night two Eskimos appeared at the front door. One said he had come very far to see what a white woman looked like and demanded that she be produced at once. Mrs. Peary put on her wrap and, accompanied by her husband, duly came to the door. The man looked each of the Pearys up and down for some time, then turned to his companion and asked, "Which one is the woman?"

Not all the Eskimos had that reaction upon seeing Mrs. Peary. At first sight, Ikwa immediately took a fancy to her and began to speak. Cook interpreted his words and gestures to mean that it was the custom among Eskimos to temporarily exchange wives with visiting friends. Ikwa asked if Peary would not consider such an exchange and motioned him to sit beside Manee.[22] Peary, through Dr. Cook, finally made Ikwa understand that white men did not have such a custom and that he must decline the offer. Ikwa looked disappointed but did not ask again.

That winter in the main room at Redcliffe House, the whites and natives alike witnessed things strange and new to them. The two groups exchanged stories, and often the Eskimos would sing and dance. Astrup preserved the scene:

> A man or a woman would step on to the floor making the most
> weird grimaces and gestures, the actor reciting more or less impro-

vised songs of very mystic meaning, accompanied by rhythmical
blows upon a gut-skin drum. Round about in a circle the other
Esquimaux would stand, and enjoy themselves in perfect accord
with us all; Matt in the meantime sitting behind on the edge of his
bunk playing hymn-tunes on a concertina out of tune, as a kind of
protest against all this paganism.[23]

The Eskimos were mystified by the ethnological rituals the whites performed on them. Each person's head was measured, as were the other parts of
the body, and the results carefully recorded by Dr. Cook according to detailed
instructions given to the party by the Philadelphia scientists.[24] Then each was
asked to remove all clothing and was photographed front, side and rear by
flash photography. Though the doctor tried to explain what they were doing,
it was all beyond the subjects of the survey. The Eskimos asked if the information was wanted for the purpose of making other people.

This seemed not impossible, since the whites had brought so many marvelous, undreamed-of things with them, like the large Rochester lamp that
stood on the table, which the Eskimos called "baby sun." *Noweeo!* the Eskimo
exclamation at anything wondrous, was often heard in the house.

The flash apparatus was a source of genuine amazement. Peary noted that
the Eskimos, unencumbered by modesty, consented to the prescribed procedures without any question just to experience the novelty of it and eagerly told
newcomers what was in store as soon as they arrived.[25] In all, 75 men, women
and children were thus recorded on film and paper.

All the comings and goings at Redcliffe House made Jo Peary uneasy. She
may have shown pluck in a man's world, but she could not shake off her civilized ideas. "These Eskimos were the queerest, dirtiest-looking individuals
I had ever seen," she wrote in her journal. "Clad entirely in furs, they remind
me more of monkeys than of human beings."[26]

She had little sympathy for their cultural rituals: "He frequently rubs his
face against hers, and they sniffle at each other; this takes the place of kissing.
I should think they could smell each other without doing this, but they are
probably so accustomed to the (to me) terrible odor that they fail to notice
it."[27]

Worst of all, she had forgotten to bring a real broom, and the fact that the
Eskimos were apparently inured to filth terrified her. She was especially uneasy when M'gipsu, her seamstress, worked in the Pearys' room:

> I dislike very much to have the natives in my room, on account
> of their dirty condition, and especially as they are alive with para-
> sites, of which I am in deadly fear, much to the amusement of our
> party. . . . At the end of their day's work, I take my little broom,
> which is an ordinary whisk lashed to a hoe-handle, and sweep the
> room carefully. . . . It answers the purpose admirably but it takes
> me twice as long as it would otherwise have done. After the room

has been thoroughly swept, I sprinkle it with a solution of corrosive sublimate, given to me by the doctor, and in this way manage to keep entirely free from the pests. Both Mr. Peary and myself rub down with alcohol every night before retiring as a further protection against these horrible "koomakshuey," and we are amply repaid for our trouble.[28]

The men were more adaptable or, at any rate, considered some things inevitable. Verhoeff noted matter-of-factly in his diary that he had made his first "capture" and suspected the louse had immigrated to his bed when Astrup had slept in it.[29] He also noted, "Dr. Cook and Mr. Gibson sometimes practice the Husky custom 'Coony' of putting their faces to the women's faces and smelling them."[30]

The Eskimos enjoyed sitting in the warm room, and Gibson thought how curious an evening at Redcliffe would look to an outsider. In the corner sat Kyopahdu, Ikwa's brother, lashing the crosspieces on a sledge, and next to him, half naked, sat M'gipsu, who had taken such a liking to Gibson that she had named one of her children after him. "Poor woman," he thought, "she is utterly unconscious of any impropriety in her actions. Modesty is unknown

Gibson "learning the Eskimos to smoke." Drawing by Astrup.

to these people. And I am truly glad that none of our party by their deport-
ment have ever by word or action given these Inuits reasons to think or act
otherwise."[31] But such sights no longer seemed strange to the North Greenland Expedition. They were now a part of everyday life, and the Eskimos were
almost members of the household.

Ikwa never seemed to tire of laughing at Dr. Cook's big nose, which he assured him would be an absolute danger to his health and safety come winter,
as it would freeze solid. When the Eskimo, in turn, was teased about coming
home with no game, he gave as good as he got. Though Cook had once
bagged an astonishing five reindeer in a single day, his reputation as a crack
shot was not held too highly, and Gibson noticed Ikwa especially loved to
tease him in return:

> He imitates the Dr. creeping up on "Tooktoo" (reindeer) and
> shooting his rifle full of cartridges without success. He also is fond
> of saying "Docty Cook a piuke namee (no good) Bluddy man."
> Ikwa is certainly the life of our camp he always creates roars of
> laughter wherever he is. He is a first class artic comedian. I rather
> suspect that he was not a rich man before we found him. . . . He
> seems however to be much elated by his sudden promotion which
> certainly places him as "King of his tribe" and I can not help think-
> ing that all this sudden fortune thrust upon him may eventually
> prove a curse to him and his family.[32]

For the winter, Peary issued detailed regulations. No one except the off-
duty night watchman could occupy his bunk between 8 A.M. and 7 P.M., nor
could anyone venture more than 500 yards away from the house in the gathering darkness without his permission. Each day was divided into six four-hour
watches in which the man on duty was to perform specific tasks and keep the
fire going. The "fire hole" chopped in the ice near the tide gauge must also be
kept open to draw water from in case of catastrophe. Cook, Gibson, Verhoeff
and Astrup would stand watch. Matt Henson was assigned all the housekeeping and menial tasks, among which were to empty the slop pail and serve tea
to 'the Eskimos.[33]

John Verhoeff thought the regulations unfair, saying Peary should not
have exempted himself and Matt Henson from the night watch.[34] When
Henson was later included in the watch, Langdon Gibson showed a real aversion to sharing the tasks Matt had once done exclusively, especially doing the
dishes.

For those not on duty, many of the hours of the "day" were spent in reading. Dr. Cook preferred scientific works but observed with interest the general
effect any reading had on the party:

> We had a good supply of the high class magazines. . . . These were
> issued monthly . . . a year behind the date. . . . I had for a long time

noted that the diversity of our stream of conversation gradually narrowed as we got farther and farther from the original source of incoming information. From this I had about concluded that the profundity of the brain was overrated and was chiefly a fire which required daily feeding. Since about all the outer source of mental feeding was now absent, and the repercussion of oft repeated stories, jokes and abstracts of wisdom became offensive—about all forms of word exchange were at a discount. The abstract thoughts presented in the magazines gave me the test for source of thought which for some time I had been seeking. . . . In effect it was proven to the satisfaction of all by the repercussion of thoughts out of magazines, that the mind was a mere generating sphere for incoming impressions.[35]

This influx of ideas often resulted in what Gibson called "word jamborees," held by Henson, Astrup and Verhoeff, which often grew so vehement, usually over Matt's theories, that Gibson could not concentrate on writing his journal:

—its all over each man satisfied that the others were wrong, the cook's ideas being most ridiculous. While the other fellows most foolishly dispute him. . . . Some of his arguments while not so refined as those of Sir Isaac Newton are certainly quite as original. He feels deeply injured when you dispute or even smile at his statement.[36]

The thickening darkness caused each person's quirks, especially Verhoeff's, to take on an exaggerated importance. Besides keeping voluminous, detailed records at the tide gauge, he was fond of seeing how little coal he could burn on his watch, much to the shivering distress of other members of the party, who found that water spilled on the floor after his duty ended would freeze instantly.[37] Gibson thought him "undoubtedly a crank."

Gibson also sensed Peary's displeasure with his own performance. This he resented, since Peary had not experienced the terrible conditions on the ice cap that had compelled his return. In his diary, Gibson began to refer to him as "The Invalid" and to Mrs. Peary, who seemed never to stop talking about her husband's merits, as "The Burden." "My whole mind," he wrote, "seems to be focused on one subject just now which is the incongruity of women in the Arctic Regions. Never mind who they are or what they are like."[38]

For her part, Mrs. Peary felt the same way about men in the arctic regions:

I hate the people who surround me more & more every day. Every action speaks of lowness & coarseness. I am afraid I am too much of an aristocrat to ever get used to such people as these. It is very evident to me that B-[ert] does not share this feeling & rather resents it in me. I can see plainly in all that I know of him that he has been brought up to always do & say things for the sake of what others may think or say while I have been accustomed to say what I thought & do as I wished without caring a rap what any one said or thought. The best thing for me to do is to avoid all conversation with the boys; in that way I avoid offending B- by my speech. . . .

The members of the party as they appear to me. Dr. F.A. Cook, an exceedingly coarse man with not an idea of gentlemanly behavior. A former milk man who from his savings studied medicine, although he cannot write a page without misspelling words. How good a physician he is of course I do not know, he was kindness itself to us during Bert's unfortunate accident & a woman could not have been more gentle. This I appreciate highly & shall never forget but his uncouth manners & unrefined talk grate on me constantly. Imagine a physician . . . speaking of "belching up wind from the "stommick" as a sign of fermentation in the intestines" at the table. When he has finished eating he rolls back on his chair & rubs his belly, frequently comes to the table in his dirty undershirt & pants, boasts that he only combs his hair on Sunday which not having been cut since he left N.Y. hangs in stringy masses over ears & neck. The other day while he was marking out something on the table cloth with his fingers a louse walked over his hand. Altogether he is adirty specimen of manhood, but a good worker & a very good-hearted person.

J.M. Verhoeff comes next I suppose; he is an uncanny & very homely dwarf. Nothing gentlemanly about him. Has evidently had no "home training." He has some money & has had a course in a scientific school. He is very eccentrick & thinks himself a model of goodness & smartness. There is no doubt that he is not quite right in the "upper story." He thinks nothing of spitting on the floor & talks of his relatives, one is a policeman, another keeps the poorhouse somewhere &c, &c. He confines himself to 2 meals a day & then just stuffs himself, putting everything on his plate at the same time & mincing it all up. Anything but appetizing for the rest of us. But the boys say he is very good-hearted. He can never attend to more than one thing at a time but this he does thoroughly & can be depended upon.

Next comes Langdon Gibson. There is nothing repulsive about his looks as there is in the 2 former men. He was formerly messenger boy & then clerk in Wall street & it is evident that he has been brought in contact with a better class of people. His appearance I am sorry to say is the only favorable thing about him. He is lazy, shiftless, a flatterer & a thoroughly deceitful fellow, besides being a coward & though he claims to be an ornithologist he knows little more about the birds than the average person who has gone gunning for sport. General education he has none . . . & is continually exposing his ignorance.

Eivind Astrup being a foreigner & not able to always express himself in English seems reticent & quiet when I happen to be in the room so I can't say much of him. He would be a nice bright looking boy if he kept himself clean. The others have taught him to swear & he seems to think it is a big thing to swear as much as possible. The first thing he teaches the natives when they come here is "go to h-" He is still young & I think a gentleman born, so I have hopes of his improvement. These together with the colored boy are the civilized men with whom I am brought in daily contact. Bert thinks I ought to treat them as my equals & see only their good points & feels hurt that I do not do this; he has no idea what it costs me to even treat them with ordinary politeness. I would much rather ignore them.[39]

Dr. Cook knew that the way to avoid such thoughts was to keep the mind occupied, and he sought to do so in any way he could. As the night deepened to unrelieved blackness, he took to sleeping outside in his reindeer bag in temperatures as low as $-50°$:[40]

I got the habit of watching the cold starry heavens from an eye slit in my sleeping bag. It occurred to me that I did not see the stars. That, in effect, all I could see was a white spot in the blue, and that everything else which I unconsciously put into the picture was an illusion, the result of memories of previous schooling. Reasoning with myself a little longer against the unreason of seeing habits, I concluded that I did not see in the white spot a star. Only the beams of light which had been enroute for a million years or more. In the very nature of this blinding light oozing through space, the body of the star itself would forever remain invisible. This strange discovery, proving that all the starry heaven was an illusion, and a delusion, in the course of time revolutionized about all of my thought facilities.[41]

Just before Christmas Jo Peary suffered a bad fall on the ice when no one else was about. She was barely able to crawl to the safety of the house before freezing. Bert gave her a swallow of brandy, and the doctor, after a careful examination, found no serious injury,[42] but she was slow to recover from the fall's effects. Matt Henson then came down with "the grippe," a form of influenza, but on the whole, the party remained in good health.

At the depths of the darkest period Peary noted, "The party are feeling the winter more or less. Matt, Jo and the Doctor especially."[43] But now, as the arctic night slowly began to wane, Mrs. Peary supervised holiday preparations for Christmas Eve, which made the men's moods a little brighter:

In the large room the ceiling was draped with red mosquito-
netting furnished by Mr. Gibson. Dr. Cook and Astrup devised
wire candelabra and wire candle-holders, which were placed in all
the corners and along the walls. Two large silk United States flags
were crossed at one end of the room, and a silk sledge-flag given to
Mr. Peary by a friend in Washington was put up on the opposite
wall. I gave the boys new cretonne for curtains for their bunks. In
my room I replaced the portieres, made of silk flags, with which
the boys had decorated their room, by portieres made of canopy
lace, and decorated the photographs of our dear ones at home,
which we grouped on the wall beside the bed with red, white, and
blue ribbons. This occupied us all the greater part of the day.
About nine o'clock in the evening Mr. Peary made a goodly supply
of milk-punch, which was placed upon the table, together with
cakes, cookies, candies, nuts, and raisins. He gave each of the boys
a book as a Christmas gift.[44] We spent the evening in playing games
and chatting, and at midnight Mr. Peary and I retired to our room
to open some letters, boxes, and parcels given to us by kind friends,
and marked, "To be opened Christmas eve at midnight." I
think our feeling of pleasure at the many and thoughtful remembrances was clouded by the feeling of intense homesickness which
involuntarily came with it. . . . Mr. Peary had carved for me two
beautiful hairpins, and I made a guidon out of a silk handkerchief
and a piece of one of my dresses, to be carried by him on his long
journey over the ice-cap to the northern terminus of Greenland. . . .

I had decided on an early dinner, and then to invite all our
faithful natives to a dinner cooked by us and served at our table
with our dishes. I thought it would be as much fun for us to see
them eat with knife, fork, and spoon as it would be for them to do
it. . . .

At 4:30 P.M. we all sat down to our "Merry Christmas."[45]

The menu was displayed on clever cards drawn by Astrup, each appropriately designed to fit the member of the North Greenland Expedition for
whom it was intended. Dr. Cook's showed a long-haired person with hands on
hips critically examining the pose of a naked Eskimo. The tailpiece was a bottle with a villainous-looking little skull and crossbones.[46]

The evening began with several toasts proposed by Mr. Peary: "To the flag
over us, the brightest that waves, with the hope that our little party may be so
fortunate as to add something to its lustre," he began. "To the loving and perhaps anxious hearts at home, with the hope that some of those mysterious
occult agencies, which we do not as yet understand, may inform them how
comfortable we are."[47] When they had finished, everyone voted it "the jolliest
Christmas dinner ever eaten in the Arctic regions."

Matt then cleared the dishes away and called the Eskimos in.

"It was amusing to see the queer-looking creatures, dressed entirely in the skins of animals, seated at the table and trying to act like civilized people," thought Mrs. Peary. ". . . They chattered and laughed, and seemed to enjoy themselves very much. Both women had their babies in their hoods on their backs, but this did not hinder them in the least. . . .

"At ten o'clock the big lamp was put out and we told them it was time to go to sleep, and that they must go home, which they reluctantly did."[48]

On the last day of the year, several new Eskimos appeared at the door of Redcliffe House and were shown in. Lieutenant Peary took Gibson aside, thinking they might have some fun with the new arrivals:

> Mr. Peary called me into his room and showed me some masks that he had brought from New York. I selected a hideous one and walked outside and put on a suit of Elk skin clothing, fur outside, which makes me appear huge. The fur on the cape stands at least four inches above my head so altogether I looked about 6 feet 5 or 6 inches and broad in proportion. After putting on the mask I knocked at the door, and the usual dialogue took place [in Eskimo] Mr. Peary saying . . . come in.[49]

"I shall never forget the scene that followed," Eivind Astrup wrote of the Eskimo guests' reaction to the apparition coming through the door. "Women and children shrieked in terror; and all, even the most courageous of the men, disappeared through the hut's door with astonishing rapidity. . . .

"Not till far into the forenoon of the following day were the good folk persuaded to come again inside our doors. We explained to them the secret of the masks, and when convinced of their true nature they could not sufficiently express their admiration for such ingenious toys."[50]

Later in the evening, there was another high social occasion. Invitations distributed to each of the members of the North Greenland Expedition announced "An At Home in the South Parlor of Redcliffe, December 31, from 10 P.M. 1891 to 1892." Jo Peary prepared chocolate ice cream and cake with crullers, then dressed in a black silk tea-gown with lace sleeves and a canary silk front, cut square in the neck and filled in with lace. Thus fitted out and wielding a palm fan, she installed herself on her trunk, and with Mr. Peary seated on the bed, tried to have a proper social evening despite the sound of the arctic wind howling outside the house.

John Verhoeff, somewhat caustically, for he had no love for "the woman," as the denizens of the big room called her out of her hearing, described the scene in his diary:

> She appeared in full evening dress and diamonds. We dressed in our best though all except Gibson and I wore kamiks instead of shoes, unless I except the nigger, who looked very spruce and was as much a guest as any one. At midnight Eivind Astrup and I went to the tide gauge to note the reading and on our return we all drank to the New Year. . . .
>
> We had games about 2 P.M. jumping 100 yds, run 100 yds, backward run, 100 yds run on hands and feet. Gibson and I were tied on the jump, he won the backward run, Cook won the forward run and I won the run on hands and feet or "all four." In the forward run Cook took a start of probably three or four yards, but he appeared to be nearly the same distance ahead at the finish. Mr. Peary was referee and time keeper and the nigger was the starter.[51]

Then they retired into their cozy house, which now had, by Verhoeff's measurement, 36 inches of ice on it, for another festive dinner. Verhoeff resolved in the coming year he would put aside his topical novels and start in on the Bible.

After New Year's, the winter settled into a routine, with Verhoeff faithfully attending to his meteorological and tidal measurements, and the others working at the gear that they would stake their lives on, come spring, when they set off across the "Great Ice," as Lieutenant Peary liked to call the ice cap.

Dr. Cook took every available opportunity to study the habits and society of the Eskimo. He amassed a word list, visited their igloos and recorded their legends. As the days passed, he found his first impressions fading and being replaced with a respect for these people who, he began to recognize, had come to terms with their harsh environment through intelligence and cooperation.

As he listened to their stories and gossip, he studied the skills handed down through the ages. He returned their seemingly kind acts with his own. With his medicines he began to take on the aura of an *angekok,* a native shaman, and was allowed to witness many sights others were denied. He was unable, however, to attend an Eskimo birth; even an angekok could not do that.

Gradually, Cook had even taken on the look of an Eskimo; he wore skin clothing exclusively now and never cut his hair. Most of all, he pondered the Eskimo for what he said about all men, for here, it seemed to him, was man in his elemental state. From this perspective, it seemed to him that "modern" man had actually progressed very little, since this "primitive" society often exceeded the latest product of "civilization":

Eskimo. Photograph by Cook.

Human life differs somewhat, but not fundamentally, with the parallels of latitude. . . .

The deeper human sentiments and physical characteristics are very much the same among all kinds and conditions of men. . . .

. . . These northernmost people, almost inhuman in their manner of living, are still, in their relation to each other and to the rest of mankind, very human. They have a deep sense of honor, a wholesome regard for the rights of their fellows, and a sympathetic temperament. Thefts are almost unknown, cheating and lying are extremely uncommon. Quarrels, though frequent, are restrained because of a well-developed habit of suppressing all emotions. Morally, even when measured by our own standard, they are superior to the white invaders of their own country. Physically and mentally they are dwarfed, but sufficiently developed to satisfy their needs. One of the most interesting problems of Eskimo life is involved in the attempt to study in each man the mainspring of his ambition. . . .

What is it that drives a man through storm and snow over ice and into freezing water on into a world of cold misery? The superficial observer will quickly say, "It is the need of food, clothing, and shelter." A more careful search into Eskimo elements, however, proves that those are only accessory to the main ambition of life. The real pivot upon which all his efforts are based is the desire to be rated well among his colleagues, and inseparably linked with this is the love of some feminine heart. Is not this also the inspiration of all the world?[52]

By the end of January, the sky was brightening perceptibly at noon each day. The gloom of the winter left its mark, however, on the party's spirits.

Gibson suffered most from close confinement, though he tried to hide it. Whenever he could, he went outside on his snowshoes during the lightest period of the day just to get away from the others:

> There is an indescribable feeling I have while out doors and by my-
> self. I can jump in the air; crack my heels. I feel happy and per-
> fectly contented there. Perhaps it is that there are no congenial
> spirits here. It is something of an exertion to look pleasant and
> have an ex milkman, at present german doctor, lean on my shoul-
> der and palm me while I smile and joke with him though I have
> several times almost exploded. I might go on and say likewise
> about the rest but I won't. It's unkind and what's the use.[53]

On February 14 Peary, Astrup and Cook packed equipment for a short
excursion, intending to establish a "Sunrise Camp" on the mountaintop to
greet the returning sun. Gibson, who had watch, stayed behind with Matt and
Mrs. Peary. Verhoeff stayed also, so as not to leave a gap in his meteorological
data.

After they had been gone for some time, the temperature suddenly rose,
and the wind rose with it to a gale. Wet snow began to fall. Soon the temperature stood at a balmy 41° and rain was coming down in sheets. The storm
continued without letup, and the snow wall around Redcliffe House began to
melt away. As water poured in on the provisions stored outside and ran in
under the back door, Mrs. Peary felt anxiety about the fate of the party at Sunrise Camp. She had good reason.

At an altitude of 2,000 feet, where it was snowing violently, the men were
snug in their sleeping bags inside an igloo built the previous day by Astrup and
Gibson. But their inexperience with building such shelters proved disastrous.

Dustlike snow began to sift in between the chinks, and finally the violent
wind blew a hole in the wall. Dr. Cook quickly rolled out and plugged the
leak, then retreated to his bag. But instead of the snow-shedding dome of the
Eskimo snow house, they had used their skis as roof beams, and the weight of
accumulating snow on the shelter's flat top caused the whole roof to collapse,
burying the three men beneath the snow blocks. Worse yet, it buried their
clothing, which they had taken off before entering their bags, and the temperature was falling rapidly.

Peary and Cook managed to work their way to the top of the snow heap
that had been their shelter, but Astrup was still trapped. Cook was able to
locate him and kept a breathing hole open.

Finding a shovel, Peary dug out Astrup, but now the doctor said he was
freezing. The lieutenant inched over to him in his sleeping bag and curled up
tightly around the head of Cook's bag to keep out the wind. The doctor, however, reported no relief, so Peary tried a new approach: "I rolled back, got the
shovel, and succeeded in digging a hole, down into the snow. I then got the
Doctor's bag loose, pulled the sleeves out of the frozen crust, adjusted his
hood, and helped him to wriggle to the hole. . . . I then . . . curled myself
round the windward edge of the hole above him."[54]

Finally the storm subsided, but it was some time before the men located their clothing under the wreckage of their snow hut. They dressed rapidly in a temperature of 3°.

Starting back to the house, they got their first glimpse of the rising sun, a sight that had not greeted their eyes in four months. Peary, like the others, was ecstatic:

> Then the yellow sunlight fell upon the highest bluff of Northumberland Island west of us. A minute later Cape Robertson, to the north-west, blazed with a crown of glory,—and then the great yellow orb, for whose coming we had so longed, peered over the icecap south of Whale Sound.
>
> In an instant the snow waves of the Inland Ice about us danced, a sea of sparkling, molten gold. . . . I laughed with the laughing waves of the great white sea, in greeting to the returning sun.[55]

At Redcliffe House, Jo Peary stood at its door and felt the same joy. "Oh! glorious sun, how good it seems to see you again," she thought. "Involuntarily it made me feel nearer home. The same sun was shining on the dear ones at home. I never appreciated the sunlight so much before."[56] The long night was over at last.

CHAPTER 4

A Permanent Drawing Power
for Life

IN THE RETURNING LIGHT DR. COOK EXAMINED THE EXPEDITION MEMBERS. Other than a curious green tinge to the skin, they appeared to have come through the arctic night with few visible effects. Only Matt had been ill with the grippe, and aside from Mrs. Peary's fall and some slight freezes, no one else had suffered any illness or injury.

As Cook had predicted,[1] Lieutenant Peary's leg had healed without complications. Since January Peary had been active, even running footraces. At Sunrise Camp he had put his leg to a practical test, but Gibson was disgusted by the way Mrs. Peary went on and on about how hard of a time her husband had had there. After hearing Peary's description, he thought his own experience in September had been far worse.

Jack and Mrs. Peary.

On February 19, 1892, Astrup and Cook started off to erect a survey marker atop the cliffs at Cape Cleveland. They took along Jack, the Newfoundland dog. Halfway up they found their progress impeded by increasingly icy slopes that also barred retreat. Seeing that the only way out was up, Dr. Cook began to cut steps in the ice with the heel of his snowshoe. As they crept higher, Jack barked anxiously at his inability to follow.

While taking a turn at battering the ice, Astrup lost his grip and heard the snowshoe clatter down the sickening slope and into the gathering darkness below. The two also heard what they thought were Eskimo voices and hollered for help; all the while, Jack continued to howl at his lack of companionship.

Soon, Ikwa and a party of Eskimos arrived at Redcliffe reporting what they had heard to Peary, who hastened with Langdon Gibson to the scene:

> We made good time to the cape, and just before reaching it, heard Jack bark well up the cliff in answer to my shout. Then we left the sledge track, and went directly to the signal flag, following Dr. Cook's track of the day before.
>
> While at the signal staff, a mournful long-drawn-out howl broke through the gloomy, starless night, from the darker gloom of the bluff above us, and filled me with foreboadings. I shouted Dr. Cook's name again and again, without answer, except Jack's dismal wail. . . . Following the tracks as we could through the gloom, we found two or three places where the boys had slipped and slid some distance; and then . . . I saw one of Dr. Cook's snow-shoes lying on the snow where it had fallen from above.[2]

Peary feared the worst—that the two "boys" had been buried by an avalanche. Gibson wanted to climb up immediately, but Peary forbade it. Together they set off at breakneck speed back to Redcliffe to get tools to dig them out.

Flinging open the door to the house, they were astonished to see Dr. Cook and Eivind Astrup sitting at the table calmly enjoying their dinner of reindeer steaks and hot tea. They had finally made the summit and found an easy descent by traveling several miles along the top of the ridge.

The incident made Gibson remember a discussion he had had with the Pearys about prudence. He had said to them, "'In dangerous places it is well to look to each step, a momentary negligence can destroy the chances or the happiness of a life time.' Mr. Peary did not altogether agree with me or rather you could see by his air that he did not. Neither did Mrs. P who has often assured us on different occasions that when her husband ever made up his mind to do a thing you could 'bet yer life' he'd do it."[3]

Gibson took satisfaction in thinking that her words now had a hollow ring. He felt that Peary had failed in not going up immediately rather than going back to the house for tools.

Prudence was not something that anyone thought John Verhoeff possessed, however. His insistence on plunging into holes cut in the ice throughout the winter, and his stubborn clinging to his woolen clothes in the teeth of temperatures as low as −53° had convinced everyone that he had none. After making his noon meteorological observations, Verhoeff decided that he, too, wished to see the sun, and ran the two miles to the cliff at Cape Cleveland. He heard Jack still barking on the ledge and climbed up to help the dog out of his predicament. He was about to start down with the dog when the Pearys and Astrup arrived with the same intention.

Peary ordered Verhoeff not to descend. Though he protested that he was not dressed warmly enough for a long walk, Peary insisted that he should not come down. So Verhoeff continued to climb and, taking a roundabout route, arrived back at the house in about three and a half hours. But Jack remained where he was.

Mindful of the many gruesome deaths on previous expeditions, Peary was determined that nothing should happen to any member of his party. So with the narrow escape of Astrup and Cook during the performance of an assigned duty, he was in no mood to overlook unnecessary risks taken on a whim. When he returned to the house he gave John Verhoeff a severe dressing-down:

> He told me publicly he thought I had done a fool-hardy trick; that
> I had disobeyed orders in going over 500 yards from house, and
> about five minutes more talk which was unnecessary. On finishing,
> his attitude changed and he asked me pleasantly when I returned,
> and after my telling him, he said I had made good time. He prob-
> ably thought his reprimand would have a wholesome effect on me
> without prolonging it, and so changed the subject not wishing me
> to be depressed. Be that as it may, it was not necessary for him to
> reprimand me publicly, especially as what I had done was not ma-
> liciously done. However, I think the 500 yd rule a bug bear.[4]

The following day, Cook and Peary made another attempt to rescue the marooned dog. Cutting steps in the ice with hatchets in the face of violent snow squalls, they finally were able to bring Jack down from his perch.

In the month after his reprimand, the resentment that Verhoeff felt to-ward "the woman" expanded to Mr. Peary and began to fester. One evening Verhoeff confided to Cook that he did not wish to return with the rest of the expedition. He said he felt oppressed and frustrated by the Pearys. The lieu-tenant, he thought, had little faith in him, as evidenced by his public rebuke. He said he could live as the Eskimos did, and hinted that he might make a journey to the highest northern point yet obtained or attempt even the Pole itself.[5]

Toward the end of March an epidemic of the grippe struck. Mrs. Peary came down with it first, then several days later Mr. Peary as well. He ran a high temperature but would not stay in bed. He even threatened to go visiting in Netiulumi. Only Dr. Cook's warning that he was risking pneumonia made him stay put. His patients had barely recovered when the doctor was down with it, followed two days later by Gibson.

After all had recovered, Verhoeff was delighted when the Pearys left with Gibson for a one-week excursion to Herbert Island. It was on this journey that Mrs. Peary had one of her most memorable experiences. On Northumberland Island the party found themselves outside the igloo of an Eskimo named Tahtara when a storm came up. Mrs. Peary had heard about Eskimo habita-tions but had never been in one, and was only persuaded to enter by the rising wind.

After reluctantly crawling through a cramped snow passage, she pulled herself through a tiny hole and into a large room bordered by a sleeping platform of snow covered with skins that "almost crawled away, they were so very much alive," where the family was arrayed.

Mrs. Peary was appalled at the conditions inside the snow shelter, which soon became uncomfortably warm as it filled to capacity with curious Eskimos. All ate from a slab of half-frozen raw meat that looked to her as if many feet had been wiped on it. Resolutely positioning herself between her husband and several native women who had stripped to nothing but their sinishaw necklaces in the now-sweltering interior, she put her teapot to warm on her Florence oil stove. She was careful to see that the lid stayed on at all times to avoid contamination by the filth and insects dripping off the cast-off garments and into the drinking water. "The odor of the place was indescribable," she reported, "well, suffice it to say that was a decidedly unpleasant atmosphere in which I spent the night."[6]

When they returned to Redcliffe, they found that preparations for the spring journey were progressing nicely. The doctor had put to work a number of natives who had recently arrived, the women making kamiks, fur mittens, stockings and trousers, and the men adding to the store of dog food.

Ever since sunset, all preparations had turned toward the journey across the inland ice. Much experimentation had been done with sleds of various types, including one built of corrugated iron. In the end, though, all but four made of ash with no shoeing were discarded. Trials had shown these to be the most durable and suitable to the ice cap's surface. The sleds, built on a framework of skeletal runners according to the design of the legendary arctic sledger Leopold McClintock, ranged from ten to 13 feet and weighed from 13 to 48 pounds. The largest of these sleds could haul up to 1,000 pounds; the 13-pounder, built by Astrup, could carry 400 pounds.

For travel on the ice cap, the men would wear snowshoes or skis, though Astrup alone was skilled at skiing. The others had tried skis but could manage only to outdo each other in grotesque falls.

For traction the expedition had originally planned to use Jack and Frank, but they had proved no match for the natives' animals. Consequently, over the winter Peary had bargained for Eskimo dogs and had obtained a fine team of twenty, including the king dog, Naleyah, and another massive animal they named Lion.

Although they all practiced driving the dogs as much as they could, only Matt Henson had shown any real aptitude. Because of his color, the Eskimos considered Henson a lost relation and responded to his open kindness toward them by teaching him their skills. They were quite sure, however, after watching the *qallunaat,* as they called the whites, that even should they evade the spirits of the dead that inhabited the ice-covered interior, they were too stupid about dogs to ever return alive.

The expedition now had a full set of skin garments adjusted by eye by their Eskimo seamstresses to fit snugly while still allowing for ventilation. Stockings of wool or reindeer skin and underwear of wool were worn as a first layer. Sealskin kamiks covered the legs to the knees; the space between the double soles was filled with soft dried grass to absorb perspiration and insulate the feet. Knee-length trousers were made of various materials depending on the taste of the wearer: Peary's of dogskin, Cook's of reindeer, while Gibson sported bearskin breeches and Astrup wore sealskin. As an outer garment, a *kooletah,* a warm hooded coat made of reindeer-skin, was worn, or a lighter sealskin *netcha* in milder weather. Finally, double mittens—wool and sealskin—protected the hands. Each explorer carried sun goggles with blue-tinted lenses. The whole outfit weighed less than 15 pounds.

As the men prepared to leave on their great adventure, they gave particular attention to their instruments and other equipment: a full array of chronometers, a sextant, compasses, thermometers, barometers, an artificial horizon, a Winchester rifle, ammunition, medicines, sewing materials, knives and personal gear. To determine distance, a wooden odometer wheel six feet in diameter was fitted to the rear of one sledge. Expecting to construct igloos for shelter along the way, they carried reindeer sleeping bags but no tent.

Food and the means to cook it made up most of the load. Prepackaged pemmican made of dried ground meat mixed with melted tallow and raisins was to be the main fare, but there were also biscuits, butter, Knorr's pea meal, condensed milk, powdered beef and chocolate.

All of this lay at the head of the bay but still had to be moved up to an elevation of 1,800 feet to reach the approaches to the ice cap. For this stage of the journey, Peary picked Cook to be in charge.

By now, John Verhoeff must have suspected that he would not be chosen to cross the inland ice. If so, his suspicions were confirmed when Peary took him aside on April 26 to tell him he would stay at Redcliffe:

> In evening while I went outside to bring in ice, being alone, Peary came and said, as I had shown so much interest in my meteorological and tidal observations, he had decided not to send me on the ice for the long trip, but would give me the chance to make my observations undisturbed. Mrs. Peary and I will be alone at the house probably a week or ten days, when the supporting party will return. I spoke plainly with him; Asked him if I would be limited to a certain distance from house, and he said no. Also spoke of the reprimand he gave me on the 20th Feb. He excused himself, said if I felt bad about it, he was sorry, or words to that effect, his lame leg having made him irritable. He said my observations would be one of the principal features of the trip.[7]

It is easy to imagine the bitterness that John Verhoeff felt, though he must have seen it coming. Ever since he had read Dr. Kane's book as a boy, he had dreamed of adventure in the Far North. Now there, he was denied the chance to prove himself. Instead he would be alone with "the woman." What plans began to hatch as a result of his disappointment?

It took three days, beginning April 30, for Cook, Gibson and Astrup, with the help of five Eskimos, to move the equipment in small loads up the steep grades. Gibson had brought a liberal supply of chewing gum with which he hoped to keep from freezing his face by exercising his facial muscles, but the steep climb with a heavy backpack was enough to warm all parts of his body.

When they reached the top of the cliffs, the Eskimos refused to go farther; the interior was the place where the spirits of the dead went, and they loved life. No promise of reward could persuade them to go on, and nothing could convince them that the white men would ever return.

Lieutenant Peary and Matt Henson joined the advance party on May 3. From their position, Peary said, he believed they could reach the ice cap using the sledges. Gibson thought Peary and Henson were slow in coming up and resented that they had borne none of the backbreaking work of getting the outfit to the top of the cliffs.

On the heights they built a snow hut. There the provisions were loaded onto the sledges according to each man's needs. In the process, Henson froze the heel of one foot.

Delays and setbacks plagued the party's advance. Inexperience with the dogs made for many mad tangles and accidents, which Peary found exasperating. Cook managed to foul the traces of his nine-dog team around Peary's skis stuck in the snow, breaking them off two and a half feet from the heels.[8]

The discovery of alcohol leaking from several of the tins made the lieutenant decide to send Gibson back for more fuel and skis. Matt Henson then came forward saying he did not think he could go farther with his frosted foot. Though he would miss Matt's ability with the dogs, Peary confided to his diary that he was not reluctant to send him back with Gibson: "I was glad to have him find this out now rather than later and was not sorry in any case to have him go back. It will be better for Jo."[9]

As the two turned for Redcliffe and moved out of sight across the white landscape, Dr. Cook produced from his medical supplies a package entrusted to him by Mrs. Peary. It was May 6, the lieutenant's thirty-sixth birthday. Inside were a cake, a bottle of Chateau Yquem and a note with birthday wishes for continued good health.

Gibson did not reappear until May 10, thoroughly exhausted from his journey over freshly fallen snow. He was so tired he had to leave part of the load below. It included five canteens of alcohol, canvas dog harnesses hurriedly made by Kyo and Ikwa to replace those of skin that had been eaten by the dogs, and a last letter from Jo.[10] When these had been retrieved, all was in readiness. The four explorers set out up the steep grade toward the inland ice.

It was not long before a gathering storm compelled them to stop. They attempted to construct an igloo, but so little suitable snow could be found that the shelter was big enough for only two men. In this Cook and Astrup took refuge, while Gibson and Peary set out for their previous igloo and quickly disappeared in the drift.

As the storm began to build, the effects of the first week on the trail took hold. Astrup and Cook slept like stones for ten hours as the wind rose in its fury. When they awoke, they found themselves nearly buried by snow drifting through the ill-constructed snow house.

As the storm slackened, Peary and Gibson returned. Crouching behind the igloo for protection from the wind, Peary learned that the two had had all they could handle trying to save their shelter from destruction. It survived the storm but the camp was in a shambles.

Once the wind had subsided somewhat, the explorers could assess the situation. The dogs had broken loose and devoured some of the supplies. Other provisions had blown clear down the slope, but worst of all, two of the dogs were showing the early signs of the dreaded *piblockto,* a disease with all the symptoms of hydrophobia. They howled, snapped at the others without reason and refused all food. The whole expedition was now in jeopardy.

The dogs had to be retrieved, but it was no easy task to gather in the strays. Cook remembered that one of the bigger dogs was particularly troublesome: "The dog at last came into camp and both Peary and Gibson fell over him with blankets. The powerful animal freed himself and bit his captors viciously. Gibson escaped with but a few scratches, but Peary was seriously wounded."[11]

Gibson did not think the injury at all serious, and even though he had voiced private doubts about Peary before, he was shocked by the way Peary now behaved:

> I was much suprised to see how P worried about his hand it did not swell very much, but it seemed to weigh on his mind all day. During which we advanced only five miles. At night he seemed entirely discouraged and loosing all his self respect he went to the medical stores and took such a draught of brandy that in less than an hour the Dr. was compelled to put him in his sleeping bag being much intoxicated. . . . Such scenes are demoralizing to say the least.[12]

Four of the dogs died, but to the men's great relief, the others showed no signs of the disease. More important, Peary's hand healed with no complications, giving confidence in the Eskimos' reassurances that the disease affected only dogs.

It took until May 14 to relay all the supplies onto the ice cap, where there was far better traveling once they had left behind the hollows and slopes that had accumulated drift from above. They also left behind two sledges and some of their supplies to lighten the remaining dogs' loads.

In six days only 11 miles from the head of the bay had been covered, but on the smooth surface over which they now traveled, the pace picked up. In a single day they made 20 miles. The sun glistening on the ice cap's surface grew so intense that they began to travel by night to put the sun at their backs.

By May 17 the monotonous inland ice lay in all directions, unbroken by the sight of any bare land. The only relief from the featureless landscape and the boisterous dog teams was eating. Mealtimes now became the object of eager anticipation. Eivind Astrup was impressed by Cook's "lucky gift of being able to make good and useful things out of strange materials." Over a fire made of the remains of a broken ski the doctor concocted a porridge of hot pea soup and frozen pemmican, which had to be chopped with an axe, that seemed a feast to the famished travelers. "Seldom had any of us eaten a meal with more satisfaction nor with greater delight than that," reported Astrup.[13]

After the men had gone 40 miles in two days, a strong wind began to blow from the southeast. Sensing foul weather, they began cutting snow blocks, and by the time the storm struck, they had finished a comfortable shelter. The cooker was put in service and time passed in pleasant gossip. As fatigue overtook them, they dozed off listening to the gale outside, which successively rose to a thundering roar then sank to a low whisper.[14]

It took two days for the storm to blow out. The men then traveled northeast for two more days. The dogs were a constant source of trouble, with fights and tangled traces. One time, when Gibson dozed off for a few minutes while performing "the costume act," as they called the outside watch designed to minimize these difficulties, the dogs ate half his sleeping bag and bolted down six pounds of cranberry jam.

Another time they ate each other's harnesses and broke loose, devouring all the remaining walrus meat. They even ate the opium pills meant to subdue them with no visible effect whatsoever and had to be trapped the hard way with risk to life and limb. Complicating matters, Cook had suffered a bad fall on May 22 and had to ride on the sledges most of the day.[15]

The party's position was now due east of the Humboldt Glacier, 130 miles inland from their starting point. Peary, christening the spot Camp Separation, announced that two men would return from here. He gave a lecture on the trials that lay ahead, saying they now knew what it was like to travel over the ice cap and that there would be no turning back for those who chose to go on. He insisted that, though others might think the journey ahead hazardous and even foolhardy, he did not consider it either dangerous or difficult. In the end, however, he said, each man would have to decide for himself if he wished to continue. He then asked for volunteers.

Dr. Cook was the first to step forward, but Peary chose Eivind Astrup. That night Astrup expressed his pleasure in his diary: "It went as I always have known it would go. Gibson and Dr. Cook are going home."[16]

The doctor prepared instructions for the use of the medical supplies packed on the sledges:

May 25, 1892. Inland ice E[ast] of Humboldt Glacier.
Sir, Following you will find a few instructions as to the use of your medical stores.

The stores consist of Vaseline, Pancreatin, Antifibrin, Antikomnia, Bismuth & Boric Acid, Ox Gall, Quinine, Cathartics, Opium, Potassium Citrate [and] Iron.

Indigestion. As soon as you find that any of your foods have disagreed with you take as much Bismuth and Boric Acid as you can take on the handle of a teaspoon, follow this in half an hour with one tablet of Ox Gall.

If the fats, the pemmican, etc. continue to give trouble, take regularly, Pancreatin after meal as much as can be taken on the handle of a spoon, one tablet of Ox Gall every night.

Headaches, rheumatic and neuralgic pains. 2 Cathartics, two headache tablets, and one Quinine pill. If necessary to continue the treatment after the first dose and ¼ teaspoon full of Antifibrin morning and night, and what can be taken on the handle of a spoon of Potassium Citrate one hour after dinner.

Snow Blindness.

Rubbing the eye frequently during the day with snow is very soothing. As a wash dissolve 4 opium tablets in ½ cup of water. Use this ad lib.

In case of scurvy symptoms take Potassium Citrate once a day, Quinine 1 pill 3 times per day, and pay particular attention to the digestion and anticular pains, which you can treat as rheumatism, 2 tablets of Iron morning and evening.

Respectfully submitted
F.A. Cook, M.D.[17]

Before they parted, Peary praised Langdon Gibson and Dr. Cook for their performance on the journey, but Gibson was not impressed: "Mr. Peary made some very flattering remarks about the noble work of the surporting party all of which I took little stock in. He is a great hand at this, and especially just before he is going to do something mean. This soon followed."[18]

What followed was the reading of Peary's orders to be observed until he returned. Gibson would command the retreat to Redcliffe, but Cook was to be in charge of the house once they arrived there.

As Astrup looked on, Gibson and Cook were given a sled, two dogs, 28 pounds of pemmican, 50 ounces of crackers, 25 ounces of condensed milk, and eight ounces of alcohol. This amounted to ten days' supplies for a journey back over the same distance that had taken 18 days outbound. Peary asked the two returning men if these supplies were sufficient. Though both agreed that they were, Gibson actually thought they seemed mighty short.

Without ceremony, Eivind Astrup then watched as the two men started back:

There was a moment of hand-shaking, the whips cracked, and we were again on the road—Mr. Gibson and Dr. Cook southward to Redcliffe House, and we two north-eastward to the far off unknown goal, the northernmost cape of Greenland. There was a certain solemnity about this hour of separation, and it will be a long time, I think, before we shall all forget that moment when at midnight we slowly lost sight of each other in the midst of that desert of snow.[19]

For the return, Gibson changed the sledging schedule to an eight-hour run instead of 12 hours, with a ten-minute rest each hour, that Peary had ordered. In this manner, following their own tracks, they arrived in only three days at the camp at which they had been storm-bound. There they recovered from the snow some cranberry jam the dogs had missed and had a special feast. By the time they woke up on the morning of May 28, the wind was blowing sharply and had obliterated their outbound trail. Gibson would have to rely on compass navigation from here to the coast.

He calculated the compass was about 90° out of true to the west. Since this was the first time he had ever attempted navigation by compass, when they camped after going 15 miles, Gibson had a nagging feeling of doubt: "I could not allow the Dr. to think that I was at all worried but it was strange. Such a (far away from home feeling) (out of sight of land feeling) that I did not feel like talking much."[20]

The next few days they nursed their frost-cracked noses against the persistent wind and filled their stomachs with pemmican stews that they wouldn't have touched at home, but that tasted glorious at the end of each monotonous day with nothing to show their progress across the white, frozen plain.

On the last day of May they thought they could see a mirage of land in the distance. By lunchtime on June 1, they had in view real land—a bold headland they recognized. Gibson was overjoyed:

When I first saw it I felt once more like the navigator who I believe I have mentioned before. I felt very much like letting a whoop . . . but instead I am ashamed to confess I affected (perhaps) something of a swagger. I was only compelled to change my course abt 2 points and after going down a gradual slope of 500 feet or more we came to the sledge cache. Here also I forgot to mention was left a 25 # can of sugar. It is needless for me to remark here that our tea was sweet enough from here on.[21]

As they came down off the sterile ice, the spring flowers clinging to the rocks looked especially beautiful. Even several big flies that buzzed in the air seemed exotic. Intending to get up early and go on to the house in the morning, they camped only six miles from Redcliffe. There they sat down and ate all the rest of their food.

At Redcliffe House, John Verhoeff noted, atypically, that while the others were away Mrs. Peary had been "good company," but added:

> To-day in speaking she casually mentioned that I was in charge of the house. I wonder who will be in charge when the supporting party returns? In regard to Mrs. P. she likes very much to speak about people, and I have no doubt that if one of the others were here in my place she would speak as much about me as she now speaks about them. Though I think Cook is her favorite, she likes to gossip about him.[22]

Jo Peary's worries over the fate of her husband took the form of nervousness and sick headaches. Her concern had increased when the lead dog of the supporting party returned to the house, nearly starved to death, 27 days after the party left. But on June 3 she sighted Gibson and Cook approaching from Cape Cleveland. They brought with them a letter from Lieutenant Peary.

> My nightmare is over; the boys have returned, and they bring good news of my husband. I cannot describe how I felt when the doctor, on shaking hands with me, told me he had left Mr. Peary and Astrup both in good health and spirits, and doing good traveling. Both boys look exceedingly well, although their faces, and nose particularly, are much burned and blistered by the sun and wind, and Gibson complains of his eyes. I got them something hot to drink, made them chocolate, and then retired to my room to read my letter.[23]

As Langdon Gibson sat down to transfer his field notes into his diary, he must have reread his last entry, written on April 28, in which he had assigned his soul to God's mercy. It was good to be back at the house; it would be better to be home.

What truce there had been between Jo Peary and John Verhoeff did not survive the return of the others, to whom she declared that the best way to manage Verhoeff was by causing him to think she was displeased when he was pleasing. On June 5 they had a "violent discussion" over liquors, and on June 21 he had an argument with Matt Henson about his putting his lame foot on the table, which nearly came to blows. Mrs. Peary encouraged them to go outside and have at it, but Verhoeff declined, feeling it not right to fight with one "not an equal at home."[24]

Sometimes Verhoeff noted friendlier discussions as well, with Mrs. Peary joining in "generally speaking of her dear hubby of whom she seems to be continually thinking. She tells us nearly every day how far she thinks he progresses. She thinks he is now about to start on his return trip, and will reach the house between Aug. 1 and August 10."[25]

Once in a while there was a laugh to be had from a joke, but when Mrs.

Peary told one containing the word "hell," Verhoeff didn't think a real lady would have said that.

And rarely something unexpected happened. One day Matt Henson was up on the roof stretched out in the sun nursing his still-oozing heel, but he came down in a hurry when Dr. Cook's gun accidentally discharged in the big room, blowing a good-sized hole in the ceiling not far from where he was sleeping.

But usually there was nothing to do but wait. No more messengers would return from the inland ice with glad tidings.

Cook tried to keep as busy as possible, organizing hunts and gathering meat and skins in case they should have to spend another winter. Mrs. Peary, though lonely, took interest in the flowers that quickly came into full bloom, sketching them and writing in her diary.[26]

One expedition member did not imitate their example. It had been hard for John Verhoeff to approve of anything about the Pearys since his reprimand.[27] The doctor noted his sullen mood:

> Verhoeff, the best schooled from a standpoint of book learning, did not do much for himself nor for any one else. He was by nature of an insurgent type and somehow, though a willing worker, he did not fit into any plan of outdoor endeavor. There was evident in him at all times a kind of suppressed bitterness which took the form of a grouch against Peary. This antagonism increased as the time neared to go home. He had already told Gibson and myself in confidence that he would never return in the same ship with Peary. But we did not take this protest seriously for we all had our own impatient spells of complaining.[28]

Cook decided it would be best to try to get Verhoeff's mind off the Pearys. He had long wanted to visit Ittiblu to exhume some Eskimo skeletons for his ethnological collections, so he invited John to come with him. Verhoeff replied that he would enjoy going very much, but the doctor should not expect him to help desecrate a graveyard.

They started off toward the village but were turned back by poor ice conditions. Verhoeff then decided to take a hike by himself. When he returned, he wrote up the journey in the most matter-of-fact terms, apparently with no regard for the dangerous chances he had taken along the way:

> About 8:45 A.M. started for Five Glacier Valley, arriving in about four hours, probably eight or nine miles; made frequent detours on account of lanes of water, but walked through many of them. After getting wet to the waist I crossed from ice to shore west about a mile from the bay. After walking probably five or six miles over stones collecting, after three quarters of an hour's work I succeeded

in getting from shore to ice by floating floes. After two hours'
steady walk I reached our side of the bay and got on a floe, but as it
grounded, I waded to shore. Arrived at the house at 11:50 P.M.[29]

When Verhoeff reached Redcliffe, he found it had turned into an armed
camp in his absence. Matt Henson suspected a murder plot, but who the victim was to be could not be decided. When Mrs. Peary had entered the house
that morning and heard Matt and the doctor talking very earnestly, she sensed
something was wrong and gathered by their tone it was serious. But she
laughed when Cook said he had overheard Kyo and Koolootingwah planning
to kill one of the party, as the Eskimos had never seemed vindictive in the
least. But the doctor insisted on his story, and Matt imagined he knew the
cause. Mrs. Peary had cut off Kyo's coffee and bread and he had blamed Matt.
He was sure he was the one they wanted to do away with. At their insistence,
Mrs. Peary gave each a pistol but thought "the doctor more than anyone else
had reason to fear Kyo, as Kyo makes no secret of his dislike for him."[30]

Despite Mrs. Peary's skepticism, there was indeed some reason to suspect
ill of Kyopahdu. When he came up from Oomanui in November, he had been
an active and willing worker, so trusted that he slept in the corner of the big
room at night. When a widow arrived in December, Kyopahdu went south
with her and did not return until March. It was then that Lieutenant Peary
noted a change in his attitude. He was subject to fits of uncontrollable anger,
and at such times seemed almost insane. In such a state he had twice severely
cut his new wife.[31]

While he was away, the other Eskimos had told some remarkable stories
about him. They said he had once murdered a man and had also killed his first
two wives. He was an angekok of great power, they whispered. Clearly, they
feared and also hated him.

Eskimos believed angekoks had mystical powers and that their spirits
could leave their bodies and travel to the bottom of the sea to communicate
with the spirit world. Consequently, they were not to be trifled with and had
special privileges. Dr. Cook had not been aware of this weeks before, when
Kyo had been one of the party who had helped freight the supplies to the edge
of the inland ice. It was there that the trouble between them began.

Cook expected each of the men to pull his weight, and did not think Kyo
had done his share. So when it came time for him to receive his reward of an
empty tomato box, Cook refused to give him one. Wood was more valuable
than gold in the Eskimos' eyes, and Kyo was very angry. He picked up a gun,
expressing a desire to kill Cook, but the doctor did not take the threat seriously and in the press of his duties soon forgot the incident.[32]

But Kyo had not forgotten.

When the doctor and Matt appeared with their pistols, the Eskimos were
frightened, and when one of the windows was opened for ventilation, they
were convinced there were murderous intentions inside the house. As an

angekok, Kyo shouted, he could not be hurt by bullets, but if others were killed, the Eskimos would kill the whites and destroy their vessel when it returned. Things looked serious, but after a long talk between Dr. Cook and Kyo, peace was declared, and Cook gave him wood for a ring for his kayak in return for a sealskin float.

But such excitement was rare, and for Jo Peary the waiting was interminable. On July 13 she and Dr. Cook set off for the head of the bay. There, in a boggy meadow, Matt had erected a little white tent and laid out the two reindeer-skin sleeping bags that were its only furnishings. He had left Redcliffe the previous day and was not eager to revisit the scene of his possible assassination.

Sitting in the tent, Jo Peary looked out across the bay to the gray granite bluffs beyond, where her husband had climbed to the inland ice. Above all else, she stared intently at the ice cap draping their tops, as she imagined her Bert in its cold, white embrace.

The natives had repeated endlessly that Mr. Peary was *sinnypoh*—dead. Most of them insisted that no one could return from the interior, but one told her that in a dream he had seen one qallunaat struggling homeward. Jo kept up her courage by reading the same paragraph from Bert's last letter over and over again: "I have no doubt I shall be with you about August 1st, but if there should be a little delay, it will be *delay only*, and not danger. I have a hundred days' provisions."[33]

On July 23 a ship maneuvered among the thousands of fragments cast off by the Tyndall Glacier into McCormick Bay. On board, a sharp lookout was kept for the house some of the ship's crew had seen being built a year before. With the red cliffs behind Cape Cleveland now in view, three loud shrieks of the whistle announced her arrival. Captain Pike and the *Kite* had returned to take the expedition home. There came no answer, but a lookout in the crow's nest soon descried a small boat approaching from the shore.

At first he took the skin-clad occupants to be Eskimos, and he feared they had killed the Peary party. Then he recognized John Verhoeff in his woolen suit waving his arms. On the deck, Professor Heilprin waited anxiously for news of the fate of the academy's expedition. He was relieved to hear all was well and surprised by the men's healthy look: "The members of the Peary party who had come out to meet us showed no signs of a struggle with a hard winter. Their bronzed faces spoke more for a perpetual tropical sunlight than for a sunless Arctic night, the memories of which had long since vanished as a factor in their present existence."[34]

The *Kite*'s crew gathered around the three men for a hearty handshake, and Captain Pike invited them to the cabin "to sample a bottle." There Dr. Cook found six letters waiting for him along with a large basket of fruit sent by his mother.

Shortly, a native messenger arrived at Mrs. Peary's camp with news of the ship and a journal from Jo's mother. She read the good news: "All those dear to me have been spared, while there has been a great deal of sickness and death everywhere."35

Since she did not return with the messenger, Professor Heilprin paid a visit to Mrs. Peary at her little tent in the meadow. It seemed strange to her to talk with someone who had been in contact with civilization and to hear fresh news of the world. Professor Heilprin said that Jo's family insisted she return, whatever might be the fate of her husband, and tried to persuade her to come back to the ship with him at once. Unable to do so, the professor started back to join the *Kite* in an attempt to reach the face of Humboldt Glacier.

Next, it was the doctor's turn to journey to Mrs. Peary's camp. Before she left, she penned a note to her husband: "Dr. Cook came up yesterday and urged me to go back with him, and much against my will I yielded."36

Stopped by pack ice and well short of the glacier just opposite Cape Sabine, the *Kite* put about for McCormick Bay to join in the waiting for the explorers' return.

But waiting was no easier for the relief party. They quickly grew restless for a little adventure of their own and thought up an excuse for having it. Led by Professor Heilprin, they struggled up the cliffs with the intention of placing signal posts to guide the returning explorers home. By 9 P.M. they had reached an altitude of 3,300 feet about eight miles into the interior. There they erected two poles 12 feet high, surmounted by a red handkerchief and a crosspiece that read: "To head of McCormick Bay—Kite in port—August 5, 1892."

Here the hardier members of the party separated and moved forward with the intention of placing another beacon a few miles farther ahead.

> Scarcely had the separation been arranged before a shout burst upon the approaching midnight hour which made everybody's heart throb to its fullest. Far off to the northeastward, over precisely the spot that had been selected for the placing of the second staff, [Samuel] Entrikin's clear vision had detected a black speck that was foreign to the Greenland ice. There was no need to conjecture what it meant: "It's a man; it is moving," broke out almost simultaneously from several lips, and it was immediately realized that the explorers of whom we were in quest were returning victoriously homeward. An instant later a second speck joined the first, and then a long black object, easily resolved by my field-glass into a sledge with dogs in harness, completed the strange vision of life upon the Greenland ice. Cheers and hurrahs followed in rapid succession. . . .
>
> . . . Like a veritable giant, clad in a suit of deer and dog skin, and gracefully poised on Canadian snow-shoes, the conqueror from the far north plunged down the mountain slope. Behind him fol-

lowed his faithful companion, young Astrup, barely more than a lad, yet a tower of strength and endurance. . . .

Peary modestly accepted the enthusiastic greeting by the academy's party. Eivind Astrup shook each man's hand, saying in his best English, "It gives me much pleasure." Heilprin thought neither looked the worse for three months' toil in the interior, and both disclaimed having overcome more than ordinary hardships.

The relief party offered them some sandwiches. Peary declined, but Astrup, laying eyes on the first fresh food in many days, devoured them greedily. After a brief recital of the explorers' experiences and an exchange of news, the combined party turned seaward. "Thus terminated a most dramatic incident," marveled Professor Heilprin. "A more direct meeting than this one on the bleak wilderness of Greenland's ice-cap could not have been had, even with all the possibilities of prearrangement."[37]

The next morning aboard the *Kite,* Jo Peary lay sleeping in her cabin.

> I was roused . . . by the plash of oars and loud talking, and before I had fully grasped the idea that the professor's party had returned, some one jumped over the rail and on the deck just over my head, and a familiar footstep made its way hurriedly toward the companionway. I knew it was Mr. Peary, but was unable to move or make a sound. He came rushing down the stairs and rattled at my door, calling to me to open it; but I seemed to be paralyzed, and he forced it open and stood before me, well and hearty, safe at last. . . .
>
> I have been afraid to go to sleep since Mr. Peary's return, for fear I might wake up and find it all a dream; besides, we had so much to tell each other. . . . Mr. Peary recounted to me the events of his journey; how . . . he and Astrup marched on day after day, with their magnificent team of Eskimo dogs, which Astrup learned to handle as well as a native driver.[38]

The *Kite* now steamed down the bay toward Redcliffe House bearing the triumphant explorers, but she had trouble finding a place to land her passengers in the high wind that suddenly sprang up. Finally, the Pearys and Astrup made shore just east of Cape Cleveland, where they were reunited with the rest of the men. The Eskimos could not believe their eyes when they saw Peary and Astrup. They spoke in low, frightened tones and could not be persuaded to come forward and touch them.

But once convinced he was not a ghost, the Eskimos crowded around Astrup. Numerous questions about the fitness of the new coast for habitation spilled from their excited lips. They were not satisfied until he had minutely sketched a rough map of the entire journey and the coast beyond.

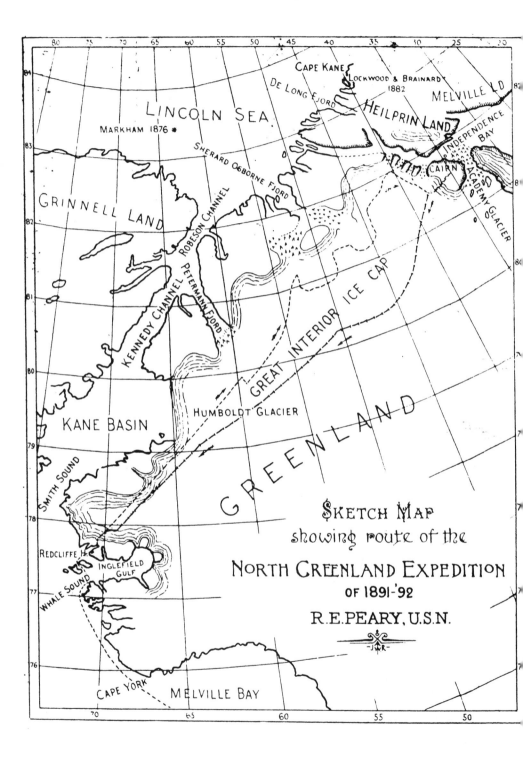

SKETCH MAP
showing route of the

NORTH GREENLAND EXPEDITION
OF 1891-'92

R.E.PEARY, U.S.N.

Eivind Astrup filled his companions in, as well, on what had happened since their parting at Camp Separation. For the next 33 days, he and Peary had shared the long and monotonous journey over the nearly featureless landscape. They had discarded their sleeping bags early in the journey, finding their skin suits, with the drawstrings tightened, adequately warm. Nor had they built any snow huts; the only shelter they erected was a three-sided "kitchen," which served as a windbreak and, in bad weather, as a shelter when a canvas sail was thrown over it.

There were times of danger when the two got caught among great crevasses as they steered too close to the Petermann Glacier's icefall, which Astrup christened "the bottomless pit." But once past the glacier heads, nothing to relieve the flat white landscape of ice came into view.

As they pressed on day after day, Astrup began to be seized by the malady that affects so many northern adventurers—"arctic fever"—a delirium that caused him to hope that his most cherished wishes would actually be fulfilled:

> Are we really to live to penetrate farther northward than any other mortal? . . . Close to the very Pole itself? . . . And with such simple means. . . . There is sufficient strength and enthusiasm. . . . If only the blessed inland ice does not suddenly play us false! . . .
>
> But life is full of bitter disappointments. Scarcely were we on the road that evening when, for the third time, we came in sight of land that barred our course.[39]

They could see mountains to the east and north and decided to turn toward the coast. There, on July 4, they managed to kill several musk oxen, providing the dogs and themselves with much-needed fresh meat.

The next day they struggled up a sharp incline, covered with sharper stones, that terminated in a cliff giving a commanding outlook, which Astrup preserved in his diary:

> We . . . had an excellent view of the extensive fiord which from the east coast cut deep into the country, receiving a gigantic glacier on the eastern side of where we stood, and to the left of us apparently continuing westwards as far as we could follow its high steep

Heavy going near the 82nd degree. Drawing by Astrup.

mountain sides. The bed of the fiord, however, we could not see further than until due north or north-northeast of our place of observation, so nothing sure can be said of its extent westwards or the possibility of its going through to Victoria inlet on the west coast. But one thing is sure: The Greenland inland ice does not extend further north than to the 82nd parallel. Peary gave newly discovered fiord the name Independence fiord (yet uncertain whether he will call it fiord or bay) in memory of the day on which it for the first time was looked down into by human eyes.[40]

They built a cairn on the heights, which Peary called Observation Bluff, and afterward enjoyed the delicacies saved for their "Farthest North": a brandy cocktail, preserved pears and a glass of cream sauterne, served with the usual biscuits and tea, plus broiled musk ox veal and musk ox milk.

After resting for three days, the two began to retrace their steps. On the return they were stopped by occasional storms and slowed by two weeks of fog on the summit plateau. Loose snow, over which the sledge pulled as if it were traveling through sand, also impeded them. But in clear weather they made good time, using a sail on the sled to help the flagging dogs. In the last seven days they fairly flew down the descending slope toward the coast, averaging 32 miles per day.

Astrup told his comrades how, after the unknown had been broached, the trip home had seemed anticlimactic:

> Conversation was impossible, the distance between us being too great; and we had to content ourselves with speculating in how short a time we should develop into true philosophers. All those burning questions which before our departure from civilisation were consuming the minds of mankind we carefully considered— nay, immediately settled. Future plans were conceived, castles in the air were built, periods of life long left behind reviewed, happenings at home recalled, and the time we had spent at school became a vivid and absorbing picture. The whole course of our imagination ran riot. Dead people were pulled out of their graves in order to renew half-forgotten acquaintances, beautiful melodies were mal-treated, whilst all the young ladies for whom one might have felt some attraction from the age of seven and upwards had to dance a fairy dance upon that Arctic snow. But at last the brain struck work, fresh thought refused to flow, originality was paralysed, all material was consumed, and the nightmare of emptiness possessed us.[41]

But now they were back. After 72 days alone with their thoughts, they had returned to the society of their fellows. Perhaps Eivind Astrup felt most proud of his little 13-pounder, the only sledge to make the entire journey.

Dr. Cook examined the returning party and the other expedition members. He found that Astrup had lost considerable weight, down to 159 pounds from 172. Peary, however, at 153 weighed one pound more than at the start of the winter. His own weight had dropped off 22 pounds to 147. Henson was suffering from iritis and a "natural scrofulous tendency." Although only Astrup and Verhoeff had escaped the grippe, "further than this," the doctor reported, "we had nothing to mar our pleasant and joyful occupations."[42]

As a final excursion, the Pearys, with John Verhoeff and Matt Henson, set off for a week's survey of Inglefield Gulf, where the lieutenant was careful to attach to the various capes and glaciers the names of his most important benefactors. Upon his return, Peary ordered that everything be packed and placed upon the *Kite* so that she could leave as soon as possible. But even with the prospect of home and loved ones in the near future, Mrs. Peary felt a twinge of sadness as she heard the order:

> It was with a feeling akin to homesickness that I took the pictures and ornaments from the walls of our little room, pulled down the curtains from the windows and bed, had Matt pack the books and nail them up, sorted the things on the bed, and packed those I wanted to keep. . . .
>
> Could the walls talk they would tell of some very pleasant hours spent there by the members of the North Greenland Expedition of 1891–92.[43]

But the departure was unexpectedly delayed. John Verhoeff had disappeared.

He had last been seen by Langdon Gibson on the shore of McCormick Bay after Peary had given Verhoeff permission to return from Inglefield Gulf ahead of him. Peary had issued Verhoeff three pounds of pemmican, a revolver and 50 cartridges. Verhoeff had also taken his geological hammer and bag.

When Verhoeff met Gibson and two Eskimos, he was tired out, having made a wrong turn that took him far out of his way. At Gibson's camp he lay down without eating and went to sleep. Then he got up, ate a huge meal, and went back to sleep again.

Gibson reported that Verhoeff started off alone early on August 12 to Kookan, an Eskimo village. He wanted to collect mineral specimens, he said, and would be two days in returning. Four hours later, Gibson was surprised to see him coming back. This time he said it would take him four days instead of two, and that he might not be back until even the day after that, so he was not to wait for him. Instead, Verhoeff said, he should send a whaleboat to pick him up near Five Glacier Valley about August 16.

When Gibson arrived with the boat at the appointed time, nothing was seen of John Verhoeff. Gibson stayed a day, then returned to Redcliffe House, thinking he might have missed him. But Verhoeff had not returned. It was now August 18.[44]

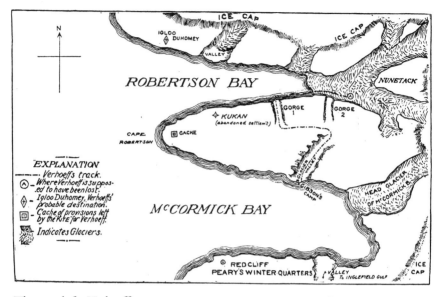

The search for Verhoeff.

A thorough search followed, with a rifle and ammunition promised to the native who found the missing man. While the search parties were in the field, the crew of the *Kite*, in cleaning out Redcliffe House, made a curious discovery. Verhoeff had taken with him or hidden every memorandum book and all his instruments except a few broken ones.

His diary gave no clues as to his intentions. The last entry read:

> Tuesday, August 9, 1892. Temp. at seven A.M. 36½ Mr. Gibson called my attention to a fall of snow; a very few small flakes seen. However, this being the warmest time of the year, the snow seems odd.

Odd, too, was the fact that the missing man had hidden about the house all of his underwear and several good wool suits.[45]

As the search continued, the native women hovered around the piles of goods near the shore that awaited loading on the *Kite*. When Mrs. Peary and the crew supervised the distribution of those things being abandoned, and the poles, lumber, spearheads, pots, knives, saws, scissors and many other wonderful things sent from Philadelphia as gifts for the Eskimos, the natives could hardly believe their good fortune.

It seemed to them especially amazing that the whites would leave their house, the wood of which would supply the needs of the tribe for many years to come. This the Pearys put in the care of Ikwa and Manee, informing them that if they did not return the next year, the house was theirs. Mrs. Peary also gave Frank to Ikwa, since he had formed a strong attachment to the dog.

After five days of searching, freezing weather set in, and Captain Pike feared staying longer in the bay. The only traces of the missing man were some mineral specimens on a flat rock, some bits of label from a corned beef can, and 50 footprints on the approaches to a low glacier.

Before sailing, Lieutenant Peary wrote a precautionary note and left it at Redcliffe House:

August 23/92

John M. Verhoeff
Mineralogist N. Greenland Exped. '91-92

Dear Sir:

Every effort has been made to find you during the past week by the entire party, without success. On the bare possibility that you may still come out all right I have cached at Cairn Point just north of the Cairn [a year's supplies]. . . .

All the Eskimos will look after your comfort to the best of their ability & will take you to Cape York next spring where a whaler will stop for you. You had better plan to get to Cape York not later than June 1st.

Very resp'ly
Robert E. Peary
Comdg NGE 91-92[46]

The *Kite* then reluctantly steamed out of the bay bound for home. Eivind Astrup stood at the rail watching Redcliffe House disappear in the distance. "It was with strange feelings," he recalled, "that at last we lost sight of those winter quarters where we had spent so many happy hours."[47]

On the way to the Danish settlements, Peary fretted over the loss of Verhoeff and how it might reflect on the record of his otherwise flawless expedition. Upon leaving Godthaab, Peary asked Dr. Cook to write a report on the search for Verhoeff to add to others he had already collected from officers of the *Kite*:

Sep 9, 1892

Aboard the S.S. Kite

Sir.

It is exceedingly difficult and quite impossible for me with the present limited information to arrive at a positive conclusion on the peculiar, sad and mysterious disappearance of our companion Mr. J. M. Verhoeff.

Judging from the last and only traces of him after he left Mr. Gibson, the foot prints, their direction, their relative position to the glaciers and the minerals that he deposited on the rock in the glacier bed, it appears to me quite probable that he attempted to cross the glacier at a low level, where it is intersected by numerous deceptive and dangerous crevasses.

Having attempted them in the violent storm which prevailed at that time, he had only to make a misstep or slip to be lost in one of these almost bottomless crevasses.

Whatever is, or may have been his fate, he was instructed for Kookan, was on a perfectly safe and easy way to his destination, but for some reason turned from it, came down over dangerous vertical cliffs only to cross a narrow dangerous glacier, and that after having been previously cautioned and harshly criticized for a previous similar experience.

After a long, systematic and careful search, I feel satisfied that his commander, his companions and the natives did all in their power to discover his whereabouts.

> Respectfully submitted,
> F.A. Cook M.D.
> Surgeon and Ethnologist
> North Greenland Expedition

Lt. R. E. Peary
Commanding[48]

As the *Kite* recrossed Davis Strait, Mrs. Peary thought back to the natives running up and down the shore frantically waving good-bye: "I could not help thinking, have these poor ignorant people, who are absolutely isolated from the rest of humanity, really benefited by their intercourse with us, or have we only opened their eyes to their destitute condition?"[49]

Dr. Cook, reflecting on the same scene, had somewhat different feelings:

> We had from savage intelligence learned a great deal, but wondered if they in turn had acquired much from us. In slowly sailing southward, we discussed the hardships of Arctic life and about all resolved that it was a fool's paradise. All agreed that this was the end of their poleward endeavor. But as a month later we sailed up the Delaware Bay and, still later, enjoyed the fruits of returning explorers in Philadelphia and elsewhere, all changed their minds. This is true of all frigid explorers once they have tasted the other world effects of the ice world, the lure becomes a permanent drawing power for life.[50]

CHAPTER 5

The Conditions of Happiness

As the *Kite* made her way across Davis Strait, Robert Peary could well be satisfied. With utmost economy of means and assisted by untried novices, he had accomplished, nearly to the letter, the program laid before Dr. Cook nearly two years before.

Still, there were two troubling things: the loss of John Verhoeff and what he should report of his discoveries. In the short narrative of his crossing of Greenland that he would append to the book his wife was preparing about her experiences, he wrote of the view from Observation Bluff: "It was almost impossible for us to believe that we were standing upon the northern shore of Greenland as we gazed from the summit of this bronze cliff, with the most brilliant sunshine all about us . . ." [1] And so it was.

Late in June, as he and Astrup had struggled east to get an unobstructed view of the land looming before them, Peary grew increasingly despondent:

> June 30, 1892. Feel less like writing than for last three or four days even. It seems almost sure my dream of years is ended. This cursed land is forcing me more and more to the E. & S. and I have not yet been to the 82nd meridian. But I will do all that man may do. Note land 5 m. distant at first change of course this march. Note appearance of large fjord opening out to N.E. Note ice dunes. [2]

On July 5, as they ascended the bluff, Peary realized the truth but confided it only to his diary:

> Note my understanding as I climbed the last summit and saw that fjord would at last open out before, Balboa's feelings as he climbed last summit to Pacific while my puny discovery is only a Greenland fjord instead of my ambition of years, the N. Cape. [3]

Astrup had noted in his diary the lieutenant's indecision as to whether to call what they had seen a fjord or a bay, and for good reason. If only a fjord, it was no different from the hundreds of others on the Greenland coast, and the land to the north, which Peary had named for Professor Heilprin, continued the uninterrupted body of Greenland for an unknown distance toward the Pole. But if it was a bay, then perhaps it connected with Victoria Inlet on the west coast; if so, Greenland was proven an island. Proof of the insularity of Greenland would be a major geographical accomplishment.

Above all else, Robert Peary had wanted fame. Perhaps he considered the advantages this accomplishment could give as a first step along the road to that goal.

The first word received from the returning expedition on September 11 from St. John's, Newfoundland, was a carefully worded telegram:

> United States Navy claims highest discoveries on Greenland east coast, Independence Bay, 82° north latitude, 34° west longitude, discovered July 4, 1892. Greenland ice cap ends south of Victoria inlet.[4]

On September 23 the *Kite* sailed up Delaware Bay and docked at Philadelphia, where well-wishers thronged the ship to congratulate the leader of the expedition and his assistants. But not all who visited the ship that day were prepared to celebrate. Just before Lieutenant Peary was about to leave the *Kite*, a young woman accosted him and demanded, "Lieut. Peary, what have you done with John M. Verhoeff?" It was the missing man's sister, Mattie.

The lieutenant stood speechless for a minute and then said softly, "I am very sorry that he is not on board."

"Is that all you have to say to me?" she asked, tears welling in her eyes.

"Yes, that is all at present. I will have more to say later."

At the insistence of Miss Verhoeff's uncle, Peary agreed to meet her at the Lafayette Hotel at 3:00. Miss Verhoeff found the result completely unsatisfactory.

"Mr. Peary's treatment of me was far from what it should have been under such sad circumstances," she complained, "and only strengthens my belief that he acted in anything but a kindly manner toward my brother, his companion in a great expedition and his equal, if not superior, in scientific attainment. Mrs. Peary, who should not have been permitted to go with the expedition, needed a body guard, and my brother, who contributed largely to the cost of the outfit, was compelled to perform work that any ordinary member of the crew could have done, instead of preparing his scientific researches, as I firmly believe he is now doing in the far North."

Mattie Verhoeff could not comprehend Peary's surprise at hearing of her brother's scientific education at Yale and his hope to go north to do scientific research. "I have always understood that it was a commander's duty to understand his men," she said, "and I consider Mr. Peary's explanation a very silly one.

"Mr. Peary said that if my brother was alive he was a deserter," she continued indignantly, "and, that as he understood the law neither the Government nor the Academy of Natural Sciences was under any obligations to send out a searching party."

It was only with difficulty that the press assembled from bits and pieces the circumstances of Verhoeff's disappearance:

The crew of the Kite report having seen smoke in McCormick Bay but could not trace it.

Verhoeff's actions from the time the party reached Greenland are described as peculiar and as pointing to an intention to stay and live with the Esquimaux. It is said that he continually wore American trousers and the scantiest kind of clothing, and that almost every day he would go into the water naked where holes had been cut in the ice. He would protest that he was not cold, and did everything in his power to inure himself to the hardships of the climate, and went around with his shoes torn and his bare feet touching the ground.

These facts taken in connection with his mysterious feelers put out during the winter as to the probability of Lieut. Peary letting him stay up north, led some of the Peary party and others of the crew of the Kite who know Verhoeff to the conclusion that he may have taken a notion to stay with the Esquimaus in the hope of making a journey to the furthest north yet discovered, and so win fame.

In speaking of the fate of Verhoeff, Lieut. Peary said he had no right to indulge in surmises, but he gave the impression that he believed Verhoeff was dead.

But little information could be gained from Lieut. Peary, Mrs. Peary, or any of the members of the expedition in regard to the scientific results of their journey. Lieut. Peary and his wife are both under contract to newspapers to give them first the results of the expedition, and the other members of the expedition are pledged to silence.[5]

Peary considered a pledge of silence a necessity. If another expedition was to be mounted, he would have to raise most of the money to finance it through lecturing and writing. He therefore reserved those rights to himself exclusively.

The reception held for the North Greenland Expedition in the library of the Philadelphia Academy of Natural Sciences was a glittering affair. The 1,200 in attendance included both Mary Peary and Mrs. Diebitsch. Lieutenant Peary looked the part of the hero in his full dress uniform as he stood under the academy's large silk flag he had flown from the heights of Navy Cliff, as he now called his observation point. But the center of attention was Jo Peary. She appeared radiant, dressed in a black satin gown with feather and lace trim and carrying a large bunch of red roses. "A most brilliant entertainment," the Philadelphia newspapers declared it, "a fitting close to the most successful of the many exploring expeditions."[6]

But Robert E. Peary was not content to rest on his laurels even one winter. Already he dreamed of a more elaborate expedition to follow up on his discoveries and was planning accordingly: He would first obtain a two-year leave of absence from the Navy; after lecturing from January to May, he would go to Europe to address the geographical societies that had sent him invitations; he would then return to Greenland in the latter part of June and overwinter as before.

He outlined these plans in a letter to his mother, in which he also sought to reassure her:

> The next spring & summer I shall complete the exploration of the northern land which I discovered last summer, returning to Whale Sound in time to come back in September on the ship which will come for me. After my return I shall still have a year of my leave left in which to lecture & write a book. My stay north will be no longer than it was before, & I am not after the North Pole nor planning any work that is not entirely simple, safe & non-sensational. . . .
>
> . . . I believe little Mother that it will be but a short time before you will have a son more famous than Stanley, & with none of the spots that mar his record.[7]

Peary at once petitioned the Secretary of the Navy, B.F. Tracy, to grant him leave. Resistance was stiff. Peary's success had earned him a reputation and, with it, the jealousy of some of the line officers in the Navy who considered him nothing more than a civilian permitted to wear a uniform. Some of them insisted that he was not even "Lieutenant" Peary, as he had been calling himself, but should be addressed as Civil Engineer Peary. His rank, they pointed out, was only an equivalency for protocol, not equal to that of an Annapolis graduate. They saw to it that his leave request was curtly turned down. Civil Engineer Peary was assigned to duty in the Norfolk dockyards.

On October 13, when Dr. Cook reached Brooklyn after the expedition's reception in Philadelphia, he got his own more modest reception at a party in the home of Dr. Robert Smith at 198 First Street. The guests were entertained by George Duryea, the elocutionist, and Miss Emma Jacobs Sand favored them with her rendition of "Ta-ra-ra-boom-de-ay."[8]

Shortly after arriving home, Cook received word that Matt Henson was still suffering with iritis. The doctor sent him enough money to come to New York, where he arranged with an eye specialist, Jackson M. Mills, to examine him. Matt spent the next two months as a guest in Dr. Cook's house, where he was treated without charge by Dr. Mills. In November Cook wrote to Peary on Matt's behalf:

> Matt requests me to write to you in answer to yours of yesterday.
>
> Dr. Mills cauterized his eye yesterday; his eye is much better today, but he had an attack of Malarial fever with severe chills today.
>
> He also thanks you for the money you gave his wife.
>
>   Best regards to Mrs. Peary[9]

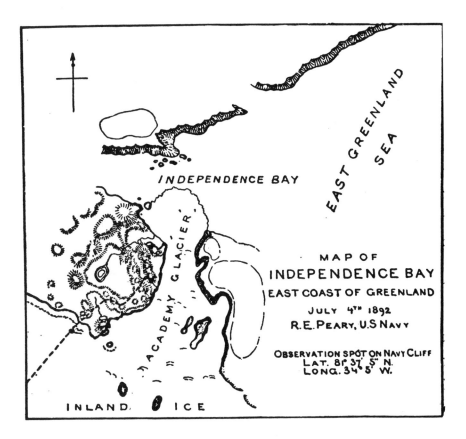

Meanwhile, before the scientific societies that had sponsored him, and as part of the first lecture series of the National Geographic Society in Washington, Peary had described his view from Navy Cliff in detail: To the east lay Independence Bay and, beyond, the East Greenland Sea; below lay Peary Channel dividing Greenland proper from an archipelago stretching farther to the north. His expedition, therefore, had proven the insularity of Greenland.

In Europe, however, there was some doubt of this. Eivind Astrup, in making his own report in the *Norsk Geografisk Tidsskrift,* had noted that no definite conclusion could be drawn from what they had seen from Navy Cliff. In Germany and France critical reports called Peary's conclusions "rash," or worse. "The Norwegians are for the most part truthful observers and, until the contrary is proved, their reports may be accepted with confidence," remarked one such commentary. "The American Polar voyagers, we regret to say, do not always inspire the same confidence, since the exaggerations of [Dr. Isaac] Hayes. Peary himself, according to Nansen, in like manner magnified the distance travelled by him on the inland ice of 1886."[10]

The president of the American Geographical Society, General I.J. Wistar, however, had no doubts. Impressed by Peary's plans and determination, and perhaps by the magnificent mountain in the farthest north the lieutenant had named for him, Wistar intervened with Secretary Tracy, persuading him to cancel Peary's orders and grant him his leave.

With the all-important leave in his pocket, Peary set out to raise the money he would need to sail in the spring of 1893. He contracted with Major James B. Pond, the leading impresario of the lyceum, for a series of lectures beginning in January.

Starting at the Academy of Music in Philadelphia, Peary gave 165 lectures in 103 days. To drum up business, he dressed Matt Henson in his arctic furs and had him drive their Eskimo dog team through the streets of the snow-covered cities where he appeared. His five surviving sledge dogs were as much of a draw as he was. They became so accustomed to the routine that whenever Peary's speech ran long, they would begin to howl, bringing him to a quick conclusion. After the performances, children from the audience were allowed to rush forward and meet the dogs. "Of all the tours I ever had the pleasure of managing," Major Pond wrote, "none met with greater success on a short notice than this one. The profits for those few weeks were about $18,000. Yet Mr. Peary was disappointed, for he was fitting out a second Arctic expedition and needed something like $80,000 for his scheme. . . . Because he could not make $2,000 or $3,000 a day it seemed a loss of time to him."[11]

Time was precious, also, to Jo Peary. She now saw less of her husband than she had in the wilds of Greenland. Suddenly she realized that, as much as Bert loved her, he loved his ambitions more and that she was secondary to her husband's mounting obsession. When he asked her to join him on his tour, Jo gave more than a simple no. "Had I known how matters stood when we were first married," she wrote to her absent husband, "things might be very different now. But I do not feel equal to the separation from you all over again and shall therefore remain at home."[12]

But even Jo's refusal did not keep Bert from enjoying his newfound status. "I have been meeting all sorts of noted men in the last few weeks," he wrote to his mother, "and have invariably been the guest of honor among them."[13]

Peary had received $1,000 for "expenses of the ethnological work in Greenland" from the World's Columbian Exposition's director, Professor F.W. Putnam, of Boston's Peabody Institute. The things Cook had traded for were a very welcome addition to his anthropological exhibit. Peary wanted Dr. Cook to go to Chicago to assist in its preparation. "He would be invaluable," Peary wrote Putnam in January 1893. "Very likely, when I see you, you will be able to suggest some practicable arrangement."[14]

While waiting for instructions, Cook was developing ideas of his own. He wrote to Peary concerning them:

> I have been thinking of your suggestions as to the World's Fair. It has occurred to me that I might take a lecturing tour going through such towns and cities as you did not enter. In this way assist in obtaining funds for your next Expedition.

If you think favorable of this, I will give you a detailed description of my plans.

As to the "World's Fair," if this tour is agreeable to you I would start very soon and make my arrangements at Chicago for a hall or tent such as you suggested. How soon do you think you can give me some definite information as to an exhibit and my connection with it?[15]

In answering, Peary asked for further details, which the doctor supplied:

I have two plans regarding the proposed lecturing tours. In both I wish you to furnish me with the slides and such points as you wish me to clearly bring out in my lectures.

My first plan is to send an advance agent and bill in the usual way lectures in all larger towns or cities along either the NY Central or West Shore RR's, perhaps going into Canada and getting to Chicago in April.

In this arrangement I would allow you say—50% of the net proceeds.

The other plan would be to travel under Major Pond and fill such engagements as you will be unable to attend to.

Your experience no doubt will enable you at once to see which is the better plan or perhaps suggest something else.[16]

Peary had been liberal in his praise of Cook's performance on the North Greenland Expedition. He held up as proof of Dr. Cook's medical skill his own ability to undertake a 1,200-mile journey across the inland ice despite his accident. Cook and Astrup had been singled out as the outstanding members of the expedition, and Peary had every reason to trust his physician and appreciate his services. In his report to the Academy of Natural Sciences he praised Cook as an indefatigable worker and diligent student of Eskimo culture who had compiled a record of the tribe that was unapproachable in ethnological archives.[17] "Personally I owe much to his professional skill, and unruffled patience and coolness in an emergency," he wrote.[18] Above all, Cook had shown the quality Peary valued most—loyalty.

But Peary looked unfavorably on Dr. Cook's proposals. He now suggested another plan: to take a booth and lecture exclusively at the fair. He also offered him the position of surgeon on his next expedition. The doctor, who had personally been over the muddy ground along Lake Michigan chosen for the fair's site, replied:

After thoroughly investigating things at Chicago I have decided it would not pay me to give those lectures as you suggested.

The rental of a suitable place is unreasonably high and there being so many things to see there that I fear it would not prove a successful enterprise. Furthermore, from what they tell me at the fair, things will not be ready by May 1st. Probably not even by June 1st, and that impression seems to have gotten abroad so that even if the fair is opened most persons will delay going until July.

Now, I have decided to go with you on the next trip, and if we start in June, it would hardly do for me to undertake any thing like this.[19]

Peary expressed pleasure at Cook's acceptance, off-handed as it was:

Need I say that I am very glad to hear that you are willing once more to try a hazard of Arctic experiences.

The day after your letter arrived there came one from Astrup long, eager and enthusiastic. He is more than anxious to go again and I am more than glad to say yes to him.

Matt also is eager to try it once more so that I shall have the greater portion of my old party with me.[20]

Herbert L. Bridgman.

A few days later, Peary received a letter from Herbert L. Bridgman, business manager of the Brooklyn *Standard Union,* whom he had met in New York shortly after his return from Greenland. Bridgman was 12 years Peary's senior. He had a perfectly bald dome that drew all the more attention to his small, keen eyes, in which, one associate thought, "always lurked a whimsical smile" not betrayed by his mouth, nearly invisible as it was behind his huge, flowing mustache. He was known in the newspaper business as "a specialist on finding the elusive item in the least likely place." He was also, it turned out, an acquaintance of Dr. Cook's:

Yesterday, a rather curious incident happened. Dr. Cook lunched at the Hamilton with me and the result, without premeditation on my part, was a most interesting talk of two hours covering the past and the future in the North. Thinking the matter over, I felt that I could not in justice to the readers of the Standard Union keep silent and, therefore, I dictated, last evening, my recollection of the conversation making, I suppose, two columns and a half or three altogether. Now, of course, I can't print this without Dr. Cook's permission, nor should I think of doing it without yours. Therefore, if you should receive from me in the course of a few days some proofs, you will understand how they came into being. I will not, either, tax your time to correct them, only assuming that, should there be any special objection to publication, you will inform me as, while we try to make a newspaper, and give the public pretty much all that we know, we do not believe in disregarding honor and propriety to do it.[21]

Bridgman then wrote an apologetic letter to Peary enclosing an actual copy of the *Standard Union* containing his recollections of his conversation with Dr. Cook. He explained that the city editor had been so fascinated by his "copy" that he insisted it be printed.[22]

Cook had recounted his experiences to others besides Bridgman. He had prepared extensive notes for the lectures he proposed to give, and he did not wish them to go to waste. At the suggestion of professional friends, he read a paper before the Kings County Medical Society in Brooklyn:

> It was one of the main objects of the Peary North Greenland Expedition of 1891–92 to thoroughly study these so-called "Arctic Highlanders"; and this pleasant duty was assigned to me. . . .
>
> . . . [In North Greenland,] medicine, as we understand it, is an absolutely unknown art. As you know, neither drugs nor herbs are available, the treatment of the skin by baths and hot applications is never practiced, and the resort which the sick Esquimau has is a sort of faith cure, of a very crude kind. When an Esquimau desires medical aid, an angekok, or priest, is called in, who begins a series of incantations, chants and songs, accompanied by a great deal of expostulation and gymnastics. This is kept up for thirty-six or forty-eight hours, at a stretch, until the medical man is utterly exhausted and stops from sheer inability to longer sustain the strain. During this stage of half frenzy, the attention of the sick man is entirely diverted from himself, and in some cases he forgets all about his pain and trouble. So far as intelligent physiology is concerned the natives have next to none of it, nor are they a sickly race. Colds are absolutely unknown, fevers of the southern latitudes are equally lacking, the only ills to which the Esquimau is ever subjected being those of pneumonic or rheumatic character. From what we could learn, nearly all the fatal cases are one or the other of these classes. The longevity of the Esquimau will compare favorably with that of any other race upon the face of the globe. . . .
>
> . . . During the arctic night, which in the latitude of our headquarters was about 100 days, many of the physiological functions are quite inactive.
>
> Women rarely menstruate during this time. The sexual desire of the men is less, but immediately after the return of the sun there is a reaction; then life begins with renewed vigor.

The sexual desire of the women, like that of animals, seems rather periodical, and when in heat are just as wild as animals in heat. Girls do not menstruate until 18 or 20, but are married at 13.

With all our civilization there were indeed few points that we could suggest to them to make them more comfortable in their cold and icy homes, but they, on the other hand, taught us how to make ourselves comfortable and brave the arctic storms.

We are indebted to them largely for the good health and success of the Peary Expedition of 1891–92.[23]

After he finished, he was besieged with questions. Impressed by his observations and the good humor with which he presented them, his colleagues encouraged Cook to publish his findings in a more extensive form, perhaps even a book. To accomplish this, he would need to obtain the Eskimo photographs from Peary, along with the ethnological data the expedition had gathered. To this end, in the middle of April, Cook visited Lieutenant Peary, who was at the Navy yard in Brooklyn, to ask his permission.

"Not a word can be published by any member of any of my expeditions," Peary insisted. "Their work is my property for my use and may or may not be printed; the issue depending entirely upon my judgment as to its fitness in the scheme of my forthcoming books."

"I was not prepared to receive such a severe reply," wrote Cook. "Up to this time Peary had been democratic and cordial in handling the personal affairs of members of the expedition. I was entirely unprepared for this sudden outburst of selfish autocracy."

Then Peary softened his tone, saying, "I am inclined, Doctor, to extend to you freedom of action, but it is a bad precedent. I cannot do this with others. Every member of my expeditions in the future must be ruled with an iron hand."[24]

Though he had all but made up his mind about what he must do, Cook went home to think over his situation. A few days later he wrote Peary a letter:

> After a second and a more careful consideration of the Arctic question, I have definitely decided not to go on the next expedition.
> I regret that I have left this to such a late day but trust that it will not seriously inconvenience you.
> If however I can be of any service to you in your preparations for the next expedition, particularly while you are in Europe, I shall feel more than pleased to help you.[25]

The same day that Dr. Cook's resignation letter arrived, Peary received another letter from Herbert Bridgman. He had had a second interview with Cook and enclosed proofs ready for publication. But this time he insisted that the paper obtain Peary's formal permission.

Peary sent a telegram forbidding it. "I think," he told Bridgman in his long follow-up letter, "if you will consider the matter for a few moments, you will see at once that the matter in these letters [touches] directly on the narrative that I am now at work upon. Dr. Cook is under agreement not to publish anything in regard to the expedition within a year after the appearance of the official narrative, and this matter is practically nothing but a letter from Dr. Cook. I did not say anything one way or the other about the first letter, because it had already appeared before I had an opportunity to communicate with you about it, and because I supposed that was the only one. I shall be very glad to have Dr. Cook furnish the Union with interesting material, both as a slight return to you for your many kindnesses, and also because I am anxious to have Dr. Cook as widely known in the interest of his practice as possible; but I cannot, in justice to myself, consent to these letters."[26]

Bridgman did not print the Cook material and wrote to Peary immediately:

> While the inability to publish the interview with Dr. Cook is something of a disappointment to me, on account of its value and interest, I assent at once and cheerfully to your decision. . . . Of course, the first interview with Dr. Cook was entirely unpremeditated, and without any idea on the part of either of us that anything was to be printed; but proofs were examined and reviewed by him. The second was in accordance with a definite understanding that it should be published. I am more than ever glad now, that I sent the proofs to you, because while I value, perhaps more highly than anyone, newspaper enterprise, I value good faith more.[27]

Peary accepted Cook's resignation with regrets:

> I need not say that I am very sorry to learn of your decision. Your decision will not seriously inconvenience me beyond the fact that it is a personal disappointment. I have letters from about a score of physicians who are eager to go with me. I expect to be in New York Friday and Saturday of this week, and hope to see you then.[28]

Despite the doctor's resignation and his dealings with Herbert Bridgman, which Peary must certainly have felt were a deliberate breach of contract, he took up the doctor's offer of help. He asked his advice in selecting food items, as well as on some other practical aspects. Cook told the lieutenant that he thought his plan to cover his new headquarters with a double-paned glass roof was a bad idea, but Peary persisted in his belief that it would save fuel by letting light into the house.

Dr. Cook probably had many second thoughts about his decision. The polar world had become his passion. When told of the enthusiastic comments of Eivind Astrup Peary had agreed to take him on the new expedition, Cook confessed in reply that the thought of Astrup's going, not to mention the building heat of the city, "almost makes me disgusted with the civilized world."[29]

As the time approached for his ship to sail, Peary sent Dr. Cook a letter that sounded as if he, too, were having second thoughts. "I am sorry that you are not going with us," he wrote, "but I did not feel that I could urge you against your sober judgment."[30] But there was no chance now that either could reverse his decision; Peary had contracted with another physician to take Cook's place.

Perhaps Peary's renewed regrets had to do with his growing concern over Jo. He needed a good surgeon more than ever—he wanted to take Jo with him again, and she was four months pregnant.

Many of her friends had told her she was acting irresponsibly by going in her condition, but it was only a heart-to-heart talk with the wife of Judge Charles Daly, a prominent member of the American Geographical Society, that caused her to think seriously about the risk she was taking. When she had, she told Bert she could not go. But he seemed so shaken by her announcement that even though she knew Mrs. Daly was right, out of love for Bert she acquiesced. She would go again to Greenland after all.[31]

When the *Falcon,* in command of Captain Harry Bartlett, arrived in Brooklyn bearing the Second Greenland Expedition, Dr. Cook came down to see her off. Though his new surgeon was available, Peary had asked Cook to give each member of the party a physical examination.

Upon arriving at the dock, he found the ship thronged with curiosity seekers, each of whom had paid a quarter to come aboard, as had thousands of others at every stop up the coast. This scheme was part of a last-ditch effort to defray the expenses of Peary's elaborate expedition, which included a wintering party of 14, eight western burros, two St. Bernards, a clutch of carrier pigeons and such exotic equipment as a small oil-driven electrical generator for lighting his new winter headquarters.

Even so, the meteorologist of the expedition, Evelyn Briggs Baldwin, thought the equipment was short on one important commodity. He had heard rumors that Peary intended to stay two years this time but dismissed them upon looking over the supplies. He convinced himself that there was simply not enough food for more than a year.[32]

Dr. Cook had moved back to Brooklyn in November and opened an office at 180 Rutledge Street. With the appearance of the *Standard Union* story, the doctor's notoriety spread, and his practice began to pick up.

Among his patients was the 60-year-old actor Denman Thompson, star of *The Old Homestead,* in the midst of a phenomenal run at the Brooklyn Academy of Music. "I can't sleep," complained Thompson. "When I try I doze off in dreams of Hell, and wake up in the agony of a blazing eternity. I am afraid you can't help me, doctor. Suicide is perhaps my only relief."

As Dr. Cook made an examination he asked, "What did you find in Hell?"

"Fire, fire, nothing but fire," said Thompson.

The doctor admonished him that suicide was only for fools, and after all, he was rich and famous and could have whatever he liked.

"Yes," protested the actor, "but it's monotony and that's Hell's next door."

Finding very little to account for his symptoms, Dr. Cook made his diagnosis: "Den, you have this thing all wrong. . . . Hell is not hot. Hell is a cold, cold place. I've been there. . . .

"I have a cure for all which ails you. Go North. Winter there as the natives do on a half filled stomach. A hungry man in the Arctic finds a new delight and forgets suicide."[33]

Go north! At the time, that was a prescription the doctor wished he could follow himself, but now, as the *Falcon* slipped down the sound on July 2, 1893, bound for Greenland, he no longer had any regrets. He was not aboard, but he would still be going north.

In the spring, at Yale, Cook had given his first public lecture on his arctic experiences. One of the eager young men in the audience was the somewhat retarded son of James Hoppin, a professor of fine arts at the college. After hearing the doctor, he was desperate to get on a ship headed north. The professor wrote for Cook's advice. The doctor saw no harm in the father's giving in to his son's wish. Then Hoppin wrote again, inquiring whether Cook was free to launch a small expedition and include his son in the party, and asked how much it would cost to fit out a yacht for three months.[34]

Cook went to New Haven and met with the Yale professor and within a few hours worked out the details. He thought $10,000 would cover the expenses. The *Zeta,* a 78-foot fishing schooner of 144 tons, was selected and refitted to the needs of the party. The expedition would start within the month for Greenland.[35]

Cook's arrangement with Professor Hoppin was not publicized. It had been announced that he would not go with Peary because of "professional engagements." Perhaps he felt it might look awkward if it became known that he had been planning a cruise of his own to Greenland.

On July 7, Dr. Cook prepared to go by rail to Baddeck, Cape Breton Island, to join Benjamin Hoppin and two other companions chosen for the voyage: Robert D. Perry of Braintree, Massachusetts, a hunting enthusiast who paid $1,000 for the privilege, and E.H. Sutherland of Baddeck, who acted as Hoppin's personal retainer.[36]

Before leaving, Cook wrote a letter to a friend outlining his plans:

> My object is to cruise along the west coast of Greenland to Cape York; there I shall complete my studies among the Arctic Highlanders, take photographs of the landscape, natives and animals, and, if possible, I shall bring back a family of Esquimaux. . . . I expect to prove by this trip that tourists can go there every year under the proper management without danger to life or vessel.[37]

The *Zeta,* sailing under Captain Hebb and a crew of eight, left Halifax July 10 and, after picking up the Hoppin party, coasted along the Newfoundland and Labrador shores before turning east for Greenland. The crossing was uneventful, except for Ben Hoppin's erratic moods.

Though very agreeable in the afternoon, he was a terror in the morning. He would often play with Perry's foxhound, Jack of Diamonds, in the evening and beg to take him to his cabin, treating him royally. But in the morning there would be an uproar and out would fly the dog, followed by a stream of curses.

The original plan was to go as far north as possible, perhaps even visiting Peary's new winter base. When the schooner reached Upernavik on August 16 after visiting Frederickshaab and a four-day stopover in Holsteinborg, however, nothing could persuade the captain to go farther. Robert Perry desperately wanted a polar bear head for his trophy wall. But when Cook and he proposed to cross Melville Bay in a small boat to try for one while the *Zeta* waited safely at Upernavik, Captain Hebb forbade it, and the idea was put aside.

After several days seeing the sights around Upernavik and reacquainting himself with the Danish governor and his wife, Dr. Cook and the *Zeta* turned south for Svartenhuk.

Anchoring off Nugssuaq, Cook and Hoppin started by boat, intending to explore Umanak Fjord, while Perry and Sutherland went hunting. As they landed at Neoktet, which Cook thought looked very romantic, beautifully nestled as it was among the rocks, they were met by crowds of natives who had gathered on the shoreline to see the strangers.

The governor, Rasmus Jensen, insisted on vacating his house in favor of his visitors and prepared to stay the night in a native hut. Before he went, he assured his guests that many interesting mineral specimens and fossils could be found along the coast.

On their way toward the fjord in the morning, their Eskimo oarsmen suddenly asked to land, saying a great storm was raging beyond the next cape. They were put ashore, but their warning was ignored. Neither Dr. Cook nor their Danish guide saw any sign of a storm. But as soon as the boat rounded the cape, it was struck by high seas and nearly driven into an iceberg. When the whites returned, the Eskimos laughed at them, then directed them to a good harbor and a snug stone igloo where they spent the night.[38]

They put in a day gathering fossil specimens and taking in the splendid scenery, then headed back. Although it was 2:30 A.M. when they arrived at Neoktet, the governor nevertheless promptly vacated his house once again. The explorers, who had subsisted on black bread and coffee during the two days' journey up the fjord, now went to the other extreme, having a "ravenous feed" at the governor's expense, then slept until ten in the governor's beds.

When Ben Hoppin and the guide set off for the mountains to go hunting with two Eskimos, Dr. Cook stayed to take photographs. In the evening he attended a dance that lasted until midnight. "The girls did not then want us to leave them," he wrote in his diary. "They asked us to take a walk along those romantic lands. They are really lovable little creatures."

When they left Neoktet the next day, the ever-accommodating Rasmus Jensen lent them his son-in-law, his boat and six oarsmen to row them back to the *Zeta*, which lay 32 miles away. Despite rain and adverse winds, they reached the ship at midnight after a hard pull of ten and a half hours. There had been some anxiety on the ship, since they were one day overdue:

> Eagerly we were questioned about our safety and experiences on this so-called hazardous journey.
>
> Mr. Perry had returned on Sunday having found no game. Both he and Mr. Sutherland have been enjoying life at Nugssuaq. A dance was kept up early night till 12 o'clock with these girls in skin pants.
>
> Everything worth buying has been bought and well paid for. I dare say that these towns have seen more money in the past few days than they will see again in a year.[39]

Among the things purchased were five Eskimo dogs at $2.75 each and a large quantity of dried codfish at 3 cents a pound with which to feed them.

The *Zeta* had hardly been towed out to sea the next morning when a fierce southeast gale blew up and the sails had to be taken in. The sea was very high and the *Zeta*, running before the wind, was driven away from her destination, Godhavn. As the ship rode out the storm, Cook and his party talked over the experiences they had already had on the Greenland coast:

> Our recollections of the last stop are very vivid. Little else is talked about on board the ship.
>
> The dance that the boys had with the girls that wear trousers, they say they will never forget.
>
> The striking arctic scenery that one sees at Umanak Fjord, in which float thousands of bergs, lined with glaciers at its head and to some extent on both sides cannot easily be forgotten.[40]

Ecstacy was soon overcome by uneasy stomachs, caused by the apparently endless gale that had now turned to the southwest. For the next two days no progress could be made against it. Cook guessed they were now perhaps once again off Holsteinborg, but their less-than-bold captain wouldn't approach the coast to ascertain his position. When the weather finally cleared late in the evening of the last day of August, the whole coast from Egedesminde to Holsteinborg came into view.

In the morning someone noticed that the ship's water supply was dangerously low. Dr. Cook suspected a sailor had loosened the stopcock as a ploy to force the captain to make port so that he could get back to the "girls in skin pants." After an unsuccessful attempt to obtain fresh water from a passing iceberg, Captain Hebb decided to proceed to Godthaab.

The *Zeta* now made good time in the fresh wind, sailing 200 miles in 24 hours. As she approached Godthaab, the captain proposed sending in for a pilot. Dr. Cook volunteered to go with the boat, but only a mile from the ship they met a kayaker who offered to guide the *Zeta* in. Negotiating a tortuous passage through the many small islands extending out into the straits, the schooner took ten hours to reach the entrance to the harbor but then was swept swiftly up the fjord on the incoming tide.

Governor A.G. Baumann welcomed them and expressed disappointment that Lieutenant Peary had not visited earlier in the season. He invited the Americans to the hospitality of his house. Its main attraction for the young men was the governor's wife, a cultured young lady, and the first woman in skirts they had seen in two months.

When asked where all the dogs were, Baumann informed his guests that the natives of Godthaab were not allowed to keep dogs, as they tended to eat the domestic goats and also the fish catch as quickly as it was put out to dry. Cook thought Godthaab impressive, boasting as it did the longest road in the whole country—about a quarter of a mile.

The next day the crew repaid the governor for his kindness by inviting him to dinner aboard the *Zeta*. In the evening native boats came from all the fjords around the town loaded with reindeer meat and hides for trade. The only ones who did not get a taste of venison that night were those who were off hunting their own, for here was all one could buy at 10 cents a pound.

Cook and the rest of his party spent the evening planning a trip to Ômat at the end of Godthaab Fjord. They estimated it would take four days to cover the 45 miles and return.

The temperature registered 90° in the sun as their two boats set out on the morning tide. As they advanced up the fjord, Cook found words inadequate to describe it. Huge granite precipices rose from each shore, and icebergs spawned from the main glacier at the head of the fjord floated past. Along the shore were strewn pieces of wood that had drifted across the North Pole from Siberia.[41]

As evening approached, their guide picked out a camping spot on top of a granite ledge covered with thick green moss. Here they erected two tents. The one from Cook's boat he thought quite remarkable:

> Our tent was a model of ingenuity and was the direct result of Mr. Perry's fertile brain. His long experience in hunting and camping after many painful experiences in ordinary tents had led him to experiment with tents of different construction. The present tent is an evolution of these experiments.[42]

The boats were pulled ashore above the high-water mark left by the tides, and after a hearty dinner, the men turned in on the soft moss. The Eskimos carried some eiderdown to sleep on, but the whites were content with their skin bags, for as Dr. Cook noted, "When one has these, comfort is usually assured."[43]

They found breakfast at their doorstep when abundant crowberries and blueberries were discovered on a nearby hillside. Even so, the natives eagerly sampled American food. "They soon repent, however," the doctor observed, "because our delicacies soon cause them to suffer from indigestion just as we would suffer if compelled to live on raw meat."[44]

Here the party split in two. While Perry and his crew crossed the fjord to go hunting with two days' provisions and instructions to return to the ship in three days at most, Cook's boat continued toward Ômat.

At 11 A.M. they landed on a small island, built a roaring fire of Siberian driftwood and prepared lunch. As they ate, they watched the many seabirds streaming up the fjord past the rugged cliffs and caught sight of five whales gliding past, filling the air with their spouted breaths. Talk turned to the possible luck of the departed hunters and the delicacies that could be had if they were successful. The doctor learned that nothing lit up an Eskimo maiden's broad face quite so much as a piece of reindeer tallow, which she chewed as a man chews tobacco, only swallowing every particle of it. Cook speculated that if the Eskimo could be taught to domesticate the animals, as had been done by the Lapps, then both the deer and the natives would prosper.

Above all towered the breathtaking scenery. Perpendicular cliffs stretched away into the distance. The glaciers draping their heights filled every notch and fissure with ice. New-fallen snow covered the summits of the distant peaks, its whiteness accentuated and made dazzling by the deep blue of the mountains beneath the snow line. The scene seemed to change by the minute as the sun was obscured by a cloud or came out fully to play upon each detail and throw it into bold relief. Though he knew he could never do it justice, Dr. Cook tried to capture what he saw on film.

Twelve miles from Ômat, headwinds forced the party ashore. Near their landing spot, the Eskimos indicated there were the remains of Norse dwellings. Not far inland they discovered some ancient ruins overgrown with blue ash and willow. But since the stones were undressed and placed in a semicircle, Dr. Cook suspected they were actually remnants of the houses of the ancient indigenous tribes rather than Europeans. Numerous artifacts found near the ruins, including arrowheads similar to those of the American Indians, reinforced the doctor's conjecture.

When the wind died down, they continued, reaching Ômat at 7:30 in the evening. In Inuit, *Ômat* means "heart," the place being named for the heart-shaped island just offshore. Any visitor to the remote spot was rare, and the Americans, a people the Eskimos had never seen before, received a tumultuous greeting from its residents.

They were met on the shore by the Moravian missionary Otto Heinke and his wife, who invited them to their home, where they were toasted with liebfraumilch and other Rhine wines. Since Dr. Cook and Ben Hoppin spoke some German, they had a good time conversing over many subjects with the

Heinkes. Not wanting him to feel left out, Mrs. Heinke dusted off her much-unused English to keep Mr. Sutherland abreast of the trend of the conversation. Other languages were merely discussed.

Mr. Heinke expressed his awe of the complexity of the Eskimo tongue, saying that in 17 years of effort he had not yet mastered it. They also talked of Nansen, who had visited nearby on his trip across the ice cap. The well-read missionary was quick to point out the many "unpardonable mistakes" about the country the famous explorer's book contained. As the men talked, Mrs. Heinke, with the help of eight native assistants, began preparing a substantial meal, including fresh vegetables from her surprisingly lush garden.

The Danes had said that only the laziest and most worthless Eskimos congregated around the missions, but Dr. Cook noted with pleasure no visible intermixing with European blood among them; these Eskimos had retained more of their own customs than those in the Danish settlements:

> Both the government officials and the missionaries honestly strive to improve the conditions of the poor natives, but they unconsciously degrade them. I believe they would be healthier if left to follow the game and live on native food absolutely. . . .
>
> Their changed habits and customs, the use of tobacco & coffee, the presence of Europeans proving their inferiority, all these things serve to degrade and discourage them so that they are little more than machines now simply eking out an existence.[45]

After a restful night, Cook and his companions bade good-bye to the Heinkes and started back for the ship.

Upon boarding the *Zeta* the morning of September 8, the doctor found that local custom differed below the lands of perpetual daylight: "On the ship things had been rather dull. The governor has, according to Danish rule, forbidden the sailors from coming ashore after sunset. This produced a great deal of dissatisfaction among the crew."[46]

After lunch, since Perry's party had still not arrived, Dr. Cook went ashore intending to trade for bird and deer skins. There he was met by the governor, who asked him to visit the sick, since the local doctor was unaccountably delayed in the outlying villages.

The hospital inmates' situation was most deplorable. Two thirds of the patients had consumption, and a number of natives were suffering from "melancholia and other mental diseases." Some of these had fled to the mountains, where they would eventually starve to death. This and most other afflictions were attributed to the possession of evil spirits.[47]

His duties as a physician discharged, Cook set off for the mission at North Hernhut. There he was treated to a dinner "in the true old German style" by the Moravian missionaries. He commented with racial pride, "It is really remarkable how an intelligent family can be so comfortable in such a desolate country."[48]

Finally, at 10 P.M., the hunters returned, empty-handed once again. Perry had seen thousands of trout and bagged a few ptarmigan, but he had not had so much as a shot at a single deer.

In the morning, while the others explored the fjord, Dr. Cook stumbled onto a bonanza in furs for which he traded at great advantage. By afternoon the *Zeta* had sailed up the fjord, picked up the hikers and put out to sea, guided by native pilots in kayaks, while the women of the village, waving handkerchiefs, stood on the rocks for a last glimpse of the visitors. Not long after the kayaks left them, a fog suddenly lowered, and the schooner was brought up boldly before a group of islands. Captain Hebb blamed the near disaster on the native pilots, but Dr. Cook blamed the timid captain.

The *Zeta* was speeded on her way across Davis Strait by a nor'easter, with great discomfort to the passengers. Below decks Cook tried to catch up on his diary, but the ship pitched so violently that he managed only a few shaky words before giving up. Though the storm blew itself out the next day, all requests to put into a port on the Labrador coast were flatly refused. Dr. Cook was by now thoroughly disgusted with Captain Hebb:

> He is so worried about us being here that I fear he will not stop until he reaches the tropics or some place hoter before he condescends to put us ashore.
>
> Every time we get in sight of land he is uneasy and when ice is reported he nearly faints, so brave and bold is this Capt. of the Zeta.[49]

The weather remained unsettled, and indeed, the only bright spot of the passage came when one of Cook's Eskimo dogs, misnamed Patrick, produced a litter of eight black-and-white pups.

The *Zeta* raised a sail on September 5. She was the *Pembina* of Lunenburg. A Mr. Matner, who had been on the coast for 40 years, was taken aboard from the *Pembina* as a pilot. Now Hebb consented to approach the shore and promptly ran on a bank. Despite much excitement, the pilot told them that there was as much to fear as running on a featherbed, since it was all sand. The *Zeta* floated at high tide but the next day ran aground again, and this time half the ship's ballast had to be thrown overboard to refloat her.

Finally, she made port at Rigolet, where the men had occasion to visit the house of one Tom Soglue. Mrs. Soglue told the doctor that some of their relatives had been taken to Chicago to appear in Professor Putnam's exhibition of peoples of the world, but only one letter had been received from them, expressing a desire to come home, and she was anxious about their welfare. When the doctor said he had visited the fair and met some of her relatives, Mrs. Soglue implored him to try to contact them again upon his return.

In Rigolet they also visited the Hudson Bay Company stores and were treated to that universal celebration in Eskimo country, a native dance. There,

Cook noticed an attractive young girl as she vigorously danced with the first mate.

The voyage of the *Zeta* had been pleasant, yet frustrating for the doctor. Soon he would be back in Brooklyn and at his old routine. Would he ever get back north? Since his resignation from the Peary expedition, he had often thought of going out on his own in some new direction. Perhaps an expedition to the nearly unknown Antarctic would be his adventure. Half an idea of attempting it had been in his mind as he had traded for dogs and furs in Greenland. But he would need money, and lots of it. As he watched the attractive 16-year-old Kahlahkatak dance, perhaps the idea of how he might earn it danced in his mind. He sought out the girl's father, a dog driver for the Hudson Bay Company, and asked permission to take his daughter, along with his 14-year-old son, Mikok, back to the United States.

The results of Peary's lecture tour were not lost on Dr. Cook:

> I studied the quality of Peary's leadership for the lessons it might give in the grounding of my future career. Peary's pose to me was that of false pretense. I had yet to learn that social and political prestige must be attained before an explorer can receive attention for his plans. . . . Judged from this angle, Peary's dramatic pose in the narrative of his experiences on the lecture platform and in his reports fitted the moving picture in demand by news writers. The public was not then, and it is not now, interested in the far reaching depth of scientific exploration.[50]

His break had been complete and final. There would be no more contracts with Peary. He already had his notes prepared on the strange Eskimos of the Far North, and now here would be his great drawing cards—a pair of Eskimos in the flesh.

Whatever he promised or paid, it was persuasive. As Cook sailed from Rigolet, he had the two children with him, having promised to return them the following spring.

During a brief stopover at Battle Harbour, he met a young medical missionary of the Royal National Mission to Deep Sea Fishermen, Wilfred Grenfell, to whom he gave a pair of dogs from which to breed a team for winter traveling.

While anchored at Assizes Harbour on September 27, where the *Zeta* had been driven to shelter by a gale from the northwest, Dr. Cook shifted his dogs, baggage and the children to the *Carrie W. Babson* of Gloucester, Massachusetts. On the way out of the harbor, the *Carrie W. Babson* pulled alongside the *Zeta,* and off Chateau Bay signaled for a race. Excitement ran high as for two hours they surged along, side by side, first one and then the other taking the lead.

When both schooners were forced to seek shelter in Henley Harbour, Dr. Cook had the opportunity to once again go ashore to treat the local sufferers. The Eskimo children were by now suffering, too. Though more than happy to be inside the harbor, as they had been deathly seasick, they were already terribly homesick as well.

When it was safe to proceed, the two ships left the harbor together. But as September drew to a close, they lost sight of each other for a time as they entered the Gulf of St. Lawrence in a rain and snow storm, and parted company for good at Cape North. By the time the *Babson* made Canso, the wind had risen to a gale.

Cook went ashore at Port Mulgrave, Nova Scotia, with Captain Lawson of the *Babson* to telegraph Professor Hoppin that the expedition had safely returned. Then the schooner headed for her home port, and at sunset on October 5, 1893, she slipped into Gloucester harbor and tied up at the wharf of D.B. Smith.

At Gloucester, the *Babson* was visited by a large crowd of curiosity seekers and a few reporters, to whom Cook happily showed off two barrels of bones and artifacts taken from ancient graves. He gave the impression to the reporters that the voyage had been hastily arranged, he himself having decided to go on the spur of the moment. Nevertheless, he assured them, the trip had been a total success. It demonstrated, he said, that a tourist journey to Greenland was safe and reasonable and offered many opportunities for scientific and sporting pursuits.[51]

Once back in Brooklyn, Cook took the children to his brother's house at 675 Bedford Avenue but asked the New York reporters awaiting him there to excuse him. He explained that he had been without sleep for two days and wanted to make up for it. Before he disappeared inside his brother's doorway, however, he was asked about Peary's chances. Cook said he was disappointed he had not been able to persuade Captain Hebb to visit Lieutenant Peary's new headquarters but expressed every confidence in him. "Whatever he starts in to do will very nearly be done," said the doctor. "He is not the sort of man to turn back."[52]

It wasn't long before the New York papers carried amusing accounts of the novelty of the first "full-blooded" Eskimos ever to visit America. The children were amazed at and sometimes terrified of the things they saw there, the trollies most of all, with their sparks and clatter. The city's huge structures especially awed them. After a visit to the Brooklyn Bridge, where they clasped hands nervously as they looked at the water far below, nothing could induce them to climb to the top of the World Dome. "Too high! Too high!" they exclaimed.[53]

Dr. Cook called Mikok "Willie." He did not speak much English but caught on easily to American games, quickly amassing most of the marbles on Bedford Avenue. Cook put his pack of dogs up at his brother's stable behind the milk depot, where they barked and howled without end but seemed friendly enough. Willie took care of the dogs and loved to watch the stablemen grooming the horses, animals the like of which Labrador children had never seen. But he also had a narrow escape there. The defenseless boy was saved by a passerby from nearly being impaled on a wagon hitch by an abusive stable hand. Bicycles, too, fascinated him, but not all new things were to his liking. Like his sister, he detested ice cream.

"Clara," as the girl was called, made a few friends in the neighborhood who asked her to attend Sunday school, but she declined. When asked her age, she was fond of saying, "Sweet Sixteen!" and to the amazement of everybody, she complained about how cold the weather was.

When Dr. Cook took his wolfish pack of dogs out for a walk in Brooklyn with Willie and Clara following behind, he never failed to draw a parade of curious children and bystanders in his wake.[54]

As he had promised Mrs. Soglue, Cook made inquiries to Chicago concerning the World's Fair Eskimos. He learned that they had been abandoned by their promoter, The Esquimaux Arctic Exhibition Company, when the fair had ended. The company had not even provided them the promised means for passage back to Labrador. Some had gone on to California to another exhibit, but ten were still in Chicago looking for a way home. Cook arranged with one of the promoters, Thomas G. Scott, to have the three men, five women and two children sent to New York. When they arrived, he put them up in a tent erected in the backyard of his mother's house on 55th Street. That winter in Manhattan her neighbors were treated to some unusual sights and sounds.

The Eskimos suffered through the warm spells but danced for joy at the sight of the first snowfall. Boys were given to observing them through knotholes in the fence and reported that though they spoke little conversational English, they all could swear the most vile oaths at the slightest provocation.

During the fall, Cook worked on a petition to the American Geographical Society, hoping that they would sponsor his antarctic plans. For the logistics of his expedition he drew largely on his recent experiences with Peary: The vessel would be a steam whaler, the sledge food pemmican, with traction provided by the pack of Eskimo dogs he was raising. The clothes would be of skin, cut to the Eskimo pattern, and there would be reindeer sleeping bags but no tent.

As for the execution, that would be largely theoretical, since almost nothing was known of the antarctic land mass or even what might be the best approach to it. It was his intention, he said, to fill in some of those blanks.

The expedition would leave New York in September 1894, sail to the Falkland Islands to coal and provision, then continue on to Terra Louis Philippe, where it would deposit a cache. Since so little was known of the region, much would depend on discoveries made along the way, he said, but the first opportunity would be taken to penetrate the ice and land a party to overwinter.

If a continent covered by an ice cap like Greenland's was discovered, then an advance station would be placed as far south as possible before the onset of winter. During its darkness all preparations would be made for a sledge journey across the continent in the spring.

"As soon as the sun returns, our actions in the field will again begin," Cook told the society. "The inland party for more southern explorations will then start on their journey across the inland sea [of ice]; the scientific observations will be continued along the coast, and as much of the coast explored on sledges and in boats as the time before our retreat will permit. After the return of the inland party, which will be about the first of March, we will at once begin our retreat."

If the vessel was lost, an attempt would be made to reach the cache on Louis Philippe Land by a combination of sledges and boats, and the explorers would sail for the Falklands.

"I do not believe that anything is to be gained by a large party on polar expeditions," he concluded. ". . . My party will not number more than twelve or fourteen, including the ship's crew. My scientific corps will not be more than four or five, and the other members of the party shall be intelligent, educated volunteers."[55] He estimated at least $50,000, raised by private subscription and his own lectures, would be necessary to carry out his plans.

Like Peary and so many others, Cook was determined to return to the polar wastes. But why? Any man who has felt this determination has had difficulty describing just what his motivation is. Frederick Cook was no exception:

> A resigned dreamyness is the after effect of most Arctic adventure.[56]

> No explorer has ever returned who does not long for the remainder of his days to go back . . . where he must endure by necessary isolation an emptiness of head and belly which can never change—to what purpose?—the lasting thrill of a world unknown which excites every cell of a body to the thrill of living in the face of impending death.[57]

At that moment, far away to the north, another man was contemplating his own motivations and his own dream, which was far more imminent than Dr. Cook's:

> Ugh! These everlasting cold fits of doubt! Before every decisive resolution the dice of death must be thrown. Is there too much to venture, and too little to gain? There is more to be gained, at all events, than there is here. Then is it not my duty?

The thoughts were those of Fridtjof Nansen. The man who had "forestalled" Peary's dream of being the first man to cross Greenland was now frozen in the polar sea, on a special ship he had designed to withstand the pressures of the pack. He had named her *Fram,* the Norwegian word for "forward."

It was his plan to drift across the entire polar basin, perhaps across the North Pole itself, a program nearly every arctic authority considered the most foolhardy ever attempted. He was now locked in the ice for who knew how long, for his dream had taken him totally into the unknown, where there was time to think on the nature of man, and men who would be explorers:

> We are oddly constructed machines. At one moment all resolution, at the next all doubt. . . . To-morrow we throw ourselves heart and soul into these very researches, . . . with a burning thirst, to absorb everything into ourselves, longing to spy out fresh paths, and fretting impatiently at our inability to solve the problem fully and completely. Then down we sink again in disgust at the worthlessness of it all. . . .
>
> It is nothing new to suffer from the fact that our knowledge can be but fragmentary, that we can never fathom what lies behind. But suppose, now, that we could reckon it out, that the inmost secret of it all lay as clear and plain to us as a rule-of-three sum, should we be any the happier? Possibly just the reverse. Is it not in the struggle to attain knowledge that happiness consists? I am very ignorant, consequently the conditions of happiness are mine.[58]

CHAPTER 6

Will You Kindly Come to Our Rescue?

DR. COOK FOUND THE NEWSPAPERS EAGER TO SUPPORT HIS VENTURE. PEARY'S North Greenland Expedition had made good copy and won him friends in the press, and wasn't Cook a friend of Peary's? In any case, Peary's friends knew that the Antarctic did not interest Peary at all, so there could be no "good faith" principles at stake in publicizing the plans of the enthusiastic young doctor this time.

Cyrus C. Adams, whose New York *Sun* had first rights to Peary's narrative, declared, "No one who knows the details of the good, thorough service [Cook] rendered in North Greenland, has any doubt that the right man is at the head of the South Polar project he has now on foot."[1]

Herbert L. Bridgman, who now had no qualms at all, chimed in with a long editorial in the *Standard Union* equating the present with the heroic past:

> Not since Columbus and his caravels put out from Palos four centuries ago, has a voyage fraught with greater or more romantic interest been projected than that which Dr. Cook, our fellow townsman, fully sets forth in another part of this paper. . . .
>
> The work of unlocking the great mystery of the South, the final problem of the surface and structure of the globe, could be entrusted to no more competent hands than Dr. Cook's. Those who know him know that he combines the patience, judgment and zeal of the explorer with thorough medical and scientific knowledge, added to a practical experience of priceless value with the Peary expedition of 1891–2.[2]

With his name before the public, Cook approached Major Pond. Besides Peary, Pond's many clients had included Mark Twain, Henry Ward Beecher, Conan Doyle and Henry M. Stanley. Pond remembered how irresistible Lieutenant Peary's dogs had been, and Dr. Cook had not only dogs but also two real Eskimos. Pond engaged Cook immediately and promoted him in typically flamboyant style:

Important Announcement

It is with pleasure that I am enabled to announce that I have made arrangements for managing the lecture tour of Dr. Cook throughout the United States previous to his sailing for the South Polar regions in September. . . .

Such an undertaking as he proposes is without precedent, and thinking people everywhere will be anxious to see and hear from his own lips the plans of the first great traveler to lay a two years' siege to the almost impenetrable secrets of the Antarctic regions. What a satisfaction it will be when the newspapers are teeming with the accounts of his explorations two or three years hence, to recall the form and character of the man whose achievements will then be the synosure of all eyes.[3]

Cook's lectures showed why Bridgman had been so taken with the doctor's talks. Besides giving the details of his antarctic plans, he devoted part of his lecture to the curiosities of Eskimo society, charming his audience with a humorous and detailed discourse on Eskimo courtship and customs, including their "primitive trial marriages."

Throughout the winter Cook toured New York, New Jersey, Pennsylvania, Connecticut and Massachusetts, at admissions ranging from 25 to 75 cents, illustrating his lecture with a hundred stereopticon views of Greenland. The program also included an introduction to the Eskimo children and dogs on stage:

The serious duties of life began soon enough for both brother and sister. Before Kahlahkatak was 12 years old she could cut garments out of skins and sew them neatly together, with reindeer sinew for thread and with a steel needle procured from a stray whale ship. She could also chew newly tanned skins, to soften them for use. Mikok, for his part, had learned to wield the terrible, longlashed whip with which the Eskimo controls his unruly team of dogs, to throw the harpoon, to build stone traps for hares, foxes and otters, and to balance himself in the frail Eskimo canoe, the kayak. . . .

. . . There was always plenty of food and plenty of clothing. They did not have to eat the old, useless people in the tribe, as did some of the Eskimos further north when the seal catch was not so great as usual. . . .

Thus they lived until Kahlahkatak was 16 and Mikok 14 years old, and then I came along and took them, with many weapons and implements, and a kayak and several Eskimo dogs, to this country. . . .

. . . They are to remain here until next spring, and then they are to go back to their parents.[4]

Although colorfully dramatic, Cook's descriptions were accurate, to the extent of his experience, when applied to the "Arctic Highlanders." But when applied specifically to Willie and Clara, who lived in a log house with their father, a man regularly employed in Rigolet, they were not apt in the least. But Dr. Cook and Major Pond understood that the public did not want to be told these things. They wanted the exotic wild people of the North, not a tamer variety.[5] Even so, the tour was not much of a success, and by March Cook was looking for other opportunities.

He obtained an engagement at Huber's Dime Museum at $300 a week, where he appeared nine times a day on a stage set up to look like an Eskimo encampment. Willie and Clara were soon joined on stage by four of the World's Fair Eskimos he had rescued from Chicago.[6] But after only four weeks his appearances were cut short.

"Altogether, it was a very interesting, and, I may say, instructive show," the museum's proprietor recalled. "Dr. Cook had a knack of holding the attention of his audiences. I wanted him to stay longer, but the Eskimos were discouraged after the death of one of their number, and they asked Dr. Cook to send them home."[7]

Though he no longer exhibited them, the Eskimos were still good for publicity, and Cook made the most of every opportunity to show them off, as well as his dogs, which won three awards at the Westchester Kennel Club show. Already his appearances with the Eskimo children had earned enough attention for him to be named a resident of the American Ethnological Association, and when he lectured before the Brooklyn Gynæcological Society, he took Mikok with him as a living specimen for the doctors to examine.

Before the New York Obstetrical Association, he made public his original observations of the spacing of Eskimo births caused by the four-year lactation period of the mothers. He noted a superabundance of blood in their capillaries that caused them to hemorrhage from the nose at the least excitement and to bleed for hours from a slight cut, and he related how they existed entirely on a meat

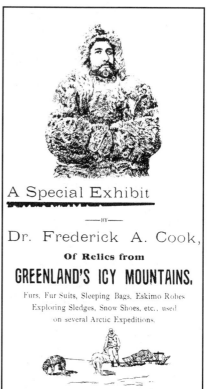

A Special Exhibit

——BY——

Dr. Frederick A. Cook,

Of Relics from

GREENLAND'S ICY MOUNTAINS,

Furs, Fur Suits, Sleeping Bags, Eskimo Robes
Exploring Sledges, Snow Shoes, etc., used
on several Arctic Expeditions.

Ticket to Cook's exhibit of relics.

diet, their only drinks being water and animal blood. Once again, Dr. Cook described the unusual suppressions of bodily secretions and muscular debility during the long arctic winter. "This peculiar condition is due to the prolonged absence of the sun," he asserted, "and I should judge from this that the presence of the sun is essential to animal as it is to vegetable life."[8]

His colleagues were fascinated by the knowledge he had amassed in Greenland and even more taken by the doctor himself, who impressed them as showing "qualities of mind especially suited to the successful pursuit of his favorite study." One marveled that "Dr. Cook is still a very young man but he has the silent and unassuming manner of an older one."[9]

In January 1894 Robert Stein of the U.S. Geological Survey had offered Cook a position as surgeon to his surveying expedition to Ellesmere Land, starting that summer. But he declined, since accepting would have compelled him to give up his antarctic plans, something, Cook said, he had no intention of doing.[10]

He had already ordered stationery with an impressive logo inscribed "Official Bureau of the American Antarctic Expedition. Dr. Frederick A. Cook, Commanding. 15 Hart Street, Brooklyn, N.Y." But while touring with the Eskimos, the doctor could see that he would fall far short of the $50,000 necessary to make this more than ink on paper. He began organizing another venture.

Cook placed advertisements in many popular magazines soliciting sportsmen, tourists, artists, scientists and explorers to join him in seeing the wonders of "Greenland's Icy Mountains." He assured everyone that the dangers associated with the Arctic were exaggerated, and that the voyage would open up a whole new pleasure resort for the summers. He hoped to attract a large group of paying adventurers with a something-for-everyone excursion that would include hunting polar bears in Melville Bay, visiting Peary's new winter quarters in Inglefield Gulf, seeking relics of the legendary expeditions of Kane, Hall and Greely in Smith Sound, and studying the natural history of Greenland along the way.

Word of Ben Hoppin's *Zeta* cruise had spread from Yale to other prestigious schools, and Cook's plans gave rise to much comment in the press. He soon had plenty of takers. Typical was Russell Porter, a student at the Massachusetts Institute of Technology, who had been so fired by one of Peary's lectures that he had applied to his 1893 expedition. Porter had been turned down when his mother had written to Peary asking him not to select her son. Still, his desire to visit the Arctic could not be quelled.

When the doctor appeared at the Mechanics Building in Boston with his Eskimos and arctic paraphernalia, Porter was waiting for him. He thought Cook "a very affable young man, as badly bitten with the [arctic] fever as myself." Porter wanted to go to Greenland but was short of Cook's $500 asking price. "I must have talked the doctor blue in the face about the price, for he finally said, 'Well, Porter, I'll take you on for $300 and make you the artist and surveyor to the party, and in that way you can help work your passage. We plan to leave New York about the first of July.'"[11]

Cook intended to charter the *Newfoundland,* a 600-ton steamer built to haul mail between Halifax and St. John's in winter. When this plan fell through, he decided on the *Algerine,* a 365-ton sealer equipped for ice navigation, but an accident befell her. Instead, the *Miranda* of the Red Cross Line was engaged to carry the excursion's 52 paying passengers. Most were students from Yale, Harvard, the University of Pennsylvania, Chicago University, Bowdoin, Williams and Oberlin, under the charge of professors from the various schools—"a very superior crowd," as one passenger put it. These along with the crew, officers and the 11 Eskimos being returned to Labrador made a total party of 85.

The Cook Arctic Expedition of 1894.

Dr. Frederick A. Cook, Commanding.

S. S. MIRANDA,

The *Miranda* had a reputation as a hard-luck ship. An iron steamer of 1,158 tons, 220 feet long and capable of a speed of 13 knots, she had been built in England in 1884. Immediately after being put into service she ran into the rocks off Port Judith in New York Sound. Subsequently she struck other rocks at Hell Gate, ran down a schooner, collided with an iron steamer and had herself pulled apart towing a raft from Nova Scotia. With such a penchant for disaster, it was small wonder that passengers so lost confidence in her that she was put into the West Indian trade.[12]

If Dr. Cook was aware of this history, he did not indicate it when asked about rumors that the ship was unseaworthy. He simply laughed and replied that the *Miranda* had often traveled through ice much more dangerous than she was likely to encounter on a voyage to Greenland. "She has never had any serious trouble," he said, "and I do not expect that the present trip will prove any exception."[13]

Nevertheless, at the start of her arctic service the *Miranda* resumed her career of mischance. As the anchor was raised and she was put astern to leave Pier No. 6 on the North River, she seemed to drift forward. Thinking the tide was against him, Captain William J. Farrell signaled full speed astern. Instead, the *Miranda* surged forward toward a lighter loaded with iron at the end of the pier. A man on the lighter cried out, "Look out there! What are you trying to do! Make a short cut across town to East River?!" The anchor was thrown over just in time to stop the ship from demolishing the lighter and the pier.[14]

An inspection revealed that the control wires to the signaling device had gotten crossed in a recent overhaul, and so, using speaking tubes to instruct the engine room—a slow process since he stuttered terribly—the captain backed the *Miranda* away from the dock.

Some of the more superstitious sailors who knew the ship's history did not like the incident, especially when several rats rushed down the anchor chains for shore. Rats left unlucky ships, one of the firemen said, and he, too, would desert at the first port of call.

Despite this bad start, the first days of the voyage proved uneventful, the major pastimes being taking potshots at every passing bird or "paying tribute to Neptune." Russell Porter noticed Professor L.L. Dyche of Kansas State University among the chief contributors, even though he had said before the voyage that he had never once been seasick. When Porter expressed surprise at the professor's predicament, Dyche explained his former immunity and maintained his reputation for honesty at the same time: This, he said, was his first ocean voyage.[15]

The big topic of discussion was a rumor that the farther north the *Miranda* progressed, the more reservations Captain Farrell was having about the voyage. The enthusiastic students wanted adventure and nothing to do with a captain who wanted to go home; they thought the captain should be relieved of his duties. But despite the rumor, the *Miranda* steamed steadily northward in fine weather.

Several noted men aboard entertained the students with impromptu talks on their specialties. Professor William H. Brewer of Yale held forth on weather phenomena and icebergs, and G. Frederick Wright of Oberlin, author of *The Ice Age in America,* lectured on glaciology. Professor Dyche spoke on biological topics.

The sea air wrought a wonderful transformation among the stuffy academics and their wards. "Men who appeared starched in linen the first day out are not to be recognized in their yachting caps, jerseys, and wind-proof canvas or leather coats," one passenger wrote home. Cook brought out his stores of arctic supplies, and the students practiced dressing in felt leggings, snow goggles and arctics in anticipation of their adventures in Greenland.[16]

On July 12 the *Miranda* took on a pilot and came into North Sydney to coal. Many in Sydney could not believe that Cook intended to take the *Miranda* to Greenland. They ventured the opinion that it was suicidal to sail an iron ship into the ice-strewn waters "down north" and advised him to abandon such a plan before it came to a disastrous end. Consequently, Dr. Cook and Captain Farrell went ashore to see whether they could rent the wooden steamer *St. Pierre,* then in port, to take the *Miranda*'s place, or hire someone to relieve their ice pilot, Mr. Manuel, to allay the captain's fears should that not be possible. Here, also, the fireman who had commented on the rodent exodus made good his vow to jump ship, and when the *Miranda* left two days later with 800 tons of coal, she was one crew member short despite Captain Farrell's best efforts to shanghai a deserter from a French man-of-war.

Cook had succeeded in neither of his objectives in Sydney, and Captain Farrell, still uneasy about the whole affair, insisted that the *Miranda* put into St. John's to test her compass before going on to Greenland. The ship was pushed around and around at anchor in the harbor by a tug while the ship's compass bearings were compared with another on the deck. This experiment showed that the captain had cause for concern, as the *Miranda*'s compass proved to be at considerable variance. Iron screws used to affix the instrument were the culprits; they were replaced by brass.

Once again Dr. Cook went ashore in search of a second ice pilot, hoping to engage Michael Dunphy, who had served in that capacity on the *Kite.* Dunphy agreed to terms, and his presence gave the passengers added confidence in their safety. But he quickly disabused the novices about any advantages they had ascribed to iron ships in the Arctic, saying, "Why, an iron hull half an inch thick, sir, is like a sheet of paper besides 7 feet of wood and iron, sir."[17]

Michael Dunphy, ice pilot of the Miranda.

Just out of St. John's, the party had need of Mr. Dunphy's services, as the first ice was spotted. Though not much of a piece of ice, the joyful students insisted on rowing out in a boat to photograph it. Ice would soon lose its novelty. The next morning the passengers were aroused by cries of "See the icebergs!" There they were, some 30 of them, ranging in size from a small house to ones that dwarfed the ship.

The captain, against Dr. Cook's urging, took the outer passage, keeping clear of the Newfoundland coast and not entering the Strait of Belle Isle.

Fog settled in. But Captain Farrell, being to the east of the land, kept the *Miranda* at near full speed. As he stutteringly assured Dr. Cook, fog or storms did not worry him but being too near shore did. When Cook protested the dangers of icebergs, the captain insisted he could "smell" icebergs, even in a fog. Still, some huge masses of ice were passing too close to the *Miranda* for Dr. Cook's tastes.

On the morning of July 17, Cook went up on the bridge to talk to the navigating officer. The sea was fairly clear, but there were still patches of dense fog. The *Miranda* was steaming along at a fair clip. No danger seemed imminent, but the doctor had a premonition of disaster. The ship's bell rang for breakfast, and most on the chilly deck went below to get a cup of warming coffee. Russell Porter was one of those sitting at the breakfast table when it happened:

> I heard the signal bell in the engine room to reverse the engines. The thought instantly came into my head that there was an iceberg dead ahead. Without expressing my opinion to my neighbors and

remarking that I had had enough to eat, I left the room and mounted the stairs. I had scarcely reached the deck door when I saw some of the passengers running aft and then the crash came, and what a harsh rasping, exploding noise that was.

Collision with the iceberg.

Cook was standing on the deck talking to two of the passengers when he heard the signal, too, then the terrible thump. At first he took it for an explosion, or thought perhaps the ship had run aground. Then he noticed the large blocks of ice sliding along the forward deck as the order of full speed astern was given. But the ship did not back up; she only pitched violently up and down instead. Then the bow went down hard. There were a few excited cries, followed by a rush by some, including Russell Porter, for the lifeboats:

> I got aft as quickly as possible, fearing every moment that ice would come tumbling down upon us from above. I looked around and there towering up in the thick fog was one of the largest icebergs I have seen as yet, and then turned to my safety. The deck hands were getting the life boats clear, and with them I joined clipping up the cord that bound the canvas coverings, and feeling at any moment I would see the good ship begin to settle down in the sea. But it did not and very soon the captain came back and ordered the crew forward to examine the ship and locate and determine the extent of the damage done. Then I began to feel a little

easier and went up to the bow. There, fully ten feet above the water line the side was stove in, or rather dented in, the hawser pipe broken and the plates around it cracked and separated. Down into the fore hold went the captain and doctor, and came back with the report that everything was dry and sound.[18]

The *Miranda* had burrowed fully six feet straight into the huge berg—125 feet high and 400 long—bashing in the starboard side and tearing away 25 feet of deck railing. Only Dr. Cook's investment in Mr. Dunphy had saved her. He had seen a streak of white ahead and ordered the engines to reverse while he swung the ship to starboard to bring her up square when he saw a collision was unavoidable.

After the assessment of the damage, the *Miranda* turned for Cape Charles Harbour, Labrador, 15 miles to the west. Once in the harbor, the starboard anchor proved useless because of the broken hawse pipe. Emergency repairs could be done where she lay, but because of insurance regulations, Captain Farrell insisted on returning the 400 miles to St. John's for permanent repairs before continuing.

Most of the paying passengers were disgruntled and called a mass meeting in the saloon. Since the original objectives could no longer be achieved, some wished to sail around Labrador and up the St. Lawrence to Quebec and Montreal instead, while others proposed abandoning Greenland for the British Isles. But Russell Porter wanted to see the Arctic and nothing else:

> The doctor laid the matter before the men in a plain and candid way, stating that we must obey the master of the ship and that yet there was a chance of reaching Greenland, although we could not hope to reach the high latitude which we had originally intended. . . . Of all I sympathized with the doctor the most and the captain the least. . . . We members who have paid such a large sum shall get so little from it, but with the doctor it is a great deal harder. Not only has he lost money in this enterprise, but if we do not get to Greenland, it will paralyze all attempts of his to embark on another venture next year and it will ultimately affect his projected expedition to the Antarctic next fall (1895).
>
> Discontent was written on the faces of all the younger members who had come for the hunting.[19]

With the prospect of reaching the polar bears of Melville Bay slipping away with the brief northern summer, five Yale men decided they had had enough of hard-luck ships and voted for a hunting trip to interior Labrador instead. But many of the Harvard men said they had simply "lost their sand" and razzed them as they left the *Miranda*. They were joined by five others and a party of four from the University of Pennsylvania under Professor Hite, whose goal had been the Mealy Mountains of Labrador all along.

The outlook for fulfilling the other goals of the expedition now looked as bleak as the barren hills that rose all around Cape Charles. Devoid of vegetation, they had only the few small houses of fishermen perched on the rocks to relieve their desolation.

While the *Miranda* party awaited a decision on what they would do, some set out to explore the strictly limited charms of the tiny town. Others, sensing nothing to be gained by that, set off across the harbor the six miles to the slightly more ostentatious Battle Harbour. Those who stayed at Cape Charles, among them the "historian" of the trip, Henry Collins Walsh, found amusement to be had even there—at least for the locals:

> So large a steamer had never been there before. We were as popular as a circus in the rural districts of the United States, and the men brought their wives and children over to look at the wonders of the ship and to see the sheep on board—natural curiosities which were much admired and never before seen in that place. One old fellow was very much struck with the ice-water cooler; he thought it the most remarkable piece of mechanism that he had ever seen, and never tired of standing by it and watching people, as they drew a glass of water, with open-mouthed admiration.[20]

The inevitable dance was soon organized, and the Eskimo girls were the belles of the ball, the ladies of Cape Charles being reluctant to dance with strangers. After the dance, the participants were treated to the local refreshments—spruce beer and rum.

In all, 14 paying passengers and all of the Eskimos left the ship at Cape Charles, so many, Dr. Cook thought, that he might exchange the *Miranda* for the *Kite,* which was at St. John's, if extra money could be gotten from the remaining passengers to charter her.[21] Although this was doubtful, they gladly donated a purse to fund the Eskimos' passage home. Clara bid a tearful farewell to Dr. Cook, vowing that she would return to America with her new husband, whom she was bound home to meet.[22]

The *Miranda* steamed south for St. John's on July 22, dodging an unprecedented number of icebergs in the persistent fog, but arrived safely at midnight on July 25.

Surveying the damage done by the iceberg, the townspeople once again called it folly to take an iron ship north, especially since this season had no equal in anyone's memory. Ice was said to be packed clear down to Hamilton, something not seen in more than 17 years.

It would be days before repairs could be completed, so the prospective Greenland tourists had to be content with touring St. John's instead. The major sights were seen in short order, but the inventive amused themselves in out-of-the-way places. When several students showed up at the insane asylum and asked to tour the wards, the doorkeeper replied that visitors were not normally allowed. But when they identified themselves as from the *Miranda,* the attendant deemed the visit completely appropriate. "Walk right in," he said. "Walk right in."

Unfortunately, the *Kite* had been previously engaged, and those who wished to continue the voyage would have to stick with the *Miranda* or watch their "sand" run out. After five days in port, the repaired steamer set off again, this time on a straight course for Frederickshaab on the south Greenland coast. As a precaution, Dr. Cook ordered a double watch for icebergs, but this time the passage was relatively ice-free, and the only things that livened it up were a fight among the stokers and a fire in the pantry.

On the way, Russell Porter got out his arctic gear and planned his dream trip onto the inland ice. He had borrowed the sled Cook had used with Peary and was sitting on the after-hatch pondering gravely his responsibility of caring for this two-year-old "arctic relic" when the doctor approached:

> He broke the ice by asking if I wished to spend the winter in Greenland, that he had heard that I had expressed the desire to do so. I told him I did want to, that I *had* wanted to for many years and were it not for my father and mother I would do it at the first chance.
>
> He told me that Prof. Dyche . . . was thinking of staying in Southern Greenland for the winter to collect specimens and if I really wanted to accompany him, he would help me in every way. Then he said he would give me a complete outfit for wintering there and provisions and coal for the necessary time and secure my return trip next summer, either with him on his excursion vessel (for the doctor intends coming up here twice next year) or on one of the cryolite ships to Phila.; all this and a certain salary if I would do some surveying along the coast and cross the inland ice to the eastern coast. He understands that this would be greatly to his interests, for reasons which I think better not be recorded just now.[23]

The *Miranda* reached Greenland in a fog somewhere near Frederickshaab. But Captain Farrell wouldn't go closer to the coast, even when Dr. Cook urged him to pick up the iceblink of the huge glacier there to check his bearings. Meanwhile, the passengers passed the time laying plans for a trip to the head of Kvanc Fjord and listening to lectures by Professors Brewer and Wright. Late in the afternoon the fog lifted and the coast finally came into view.

The next day the first floe ice was sighted and Captain Farrell quickly stood off. Another period of intense fog set in, but not before Porter made some practice observations of the sun using a sextant and an artificial horizon filled with molasses. If he was to agree to Cook's plan, he would have to master the technique.

When the fog cleared on August 4, the drift ice revealed was unprecedented for a point that far south, and Captain Farrell persuaded the party to give up Frederickshaab and put into Godhavn instead. By now the man had surpassed even Captain Hebb in Cook's estimation. In his diary entry for the day he wrote, "Capt is the most timid man I ever saw. Our progress seems to be effectually stopped by his stupidity. He imagines himself lost with every piece of ice visible."

On the way north, the ship was again beset by fog, but since the sea was glassy calm, a few of the passengers amused themselves by shooting seabirds from one of the ship's boats as it trailed behind the *Miranda.*

Realizing he was off Sukkertoppen, the ever-worried Captain Farrell wanted to obtain reports on ice conditions to the north. Cook tried to reassure him from his experience that he would see no more pack ice until they reached the far northern Danish settlements, but the captain was adamant. Reluctantly, Cook acquiesced to Farrell's desire to put into port.[24]

Still, the cautious captain lay offshore, sounding his whistle and firing up rockets. This finally got the attention of the inhabitants; two kayakers appeared from around the rocky headland. When they reached the ship, Cook conversed with them in words and signs, understanding them to say there was enough water in the harbor to accommodate the *Miranda.* Once there, the ship was secured by hawsers fastened to ring bolts driven into the rocks. The visit to Sukkertoppen gave the passengers a welcome 30 hours ashore, which they spent in trading, exploring, hunting and fishing. Porter went to the inevitable dance at an old warehouse, which he described as "midnight revelry in broad daylight."[25] Trading being brisk, by afternoon the *Miranda* looked like a floating museum of natural history, replete with native implements, birds, skins and 16 kayaks.

Russell Porter joined a small "anthropological" party led by Cook to the Eskimo burying ground to dig up some skulls and other bones. But Porter was less interested in anthropology than in the view from the cemetery. As a talented artist, he was as impressed as Frederick Cook had been the year before: "There I tried to paint in water colors the scenery to the east of us, the grandest, and most beautiful, I have ever seen or ever expect to see. . . . Surely an artist would find subjects which if well handled would make him immortal."[26]

That evening at Governor G.S. Bistrup's house, the usual wholehearted welcome culminated in confections, cigars and songs. The governor assured Captain Farrell that there was no ice along the coast to the north.

The paying passengers finally felt that the expedition was beginning to look worthwhile as the *Miranda* dropped off her pilots and prepared to leave the harbor mouth at 6:30 A.M., August 10.

As she headed out to sea, Dr. Cook was sitting at a table anticipating coffee, biscuits and hot buckwheat cakes when he felt three violent bumps and a sharp side lift that sent everything crashing to the floor. A mad scramble ensued to get to the gangway across the wreckage of cutlery and dish shards that had moments earlier held breakfast but were now merely an obstacle course between the table and the lifeboats. Many fully expected to see another towering mass of ice, but when they reached the deck, nothing appeared to be out of order.

Cook raced to the observation bridge. There he found a sailor with a smile on his face. "Man, what has happened?!" exclaimed the doctor.

"Dun'no—I reckon we been sounding with the keel," the man replied.

Captain Farrell was having difficulty getting even stuttered words to come out of his mouth. At this point Ben Hoppin appeared on the bridge wearing a life ring and carrying the ship's two cats. He abused the captain, saying, "You damn fool! This ship would sink before you could give an order," and then still louder, "Why don't you dumb fool talk!"

When the mate tried to take one of the cats, Hoppin held them even closer as he declared loudly, "Each cat has nine lives; we will need cat lives if we stay with this ship!"[27]

Meanwhile, the carpenter had gone below decks and was soon back with his report. The hold had three inches of water in it and the steam pumps were easily handling it. At first the captain wanted to put out for Godthaab, but Cook insisted that they go back into port to assess the damage. A "violent discussion" ensued on the bridge, the *Miranda* all the while slowly heading seaward.[28]

After going on for some distance, the ship stopped. Captain Farrell ordered distress flags run up to half mast, then the whistle was sounded repeatedly and flares were discharged.[29]

Natives in kayaks soon approached the ship. After paddling around her, they came aboard, pointing over the side and repeating emphatically, "No goot! No goot!" numerous times. The damage was determined to be under the ballast tanks, which had filled with water. The *Miranda* had struck a reef in three fathoms and landed on it twice by the action of the heavy swells. Only the ship's speed had kept her from hanging up on the rocks and ripping her bottom out completely. Captain Farrell now thought better of going on and started slowly back toward Sukkertoppen.

If he hoped to get his charges safely home, Cook decided he must get outside help. He proposed to sail up the coast in a small boat to seek a fishing schooner that might take the party off. Among those chosen to go along was Russell Porter:

> So the open-boat journey was decided on. Dr. Cook unfolded his plans to us in his cabin. In the party were Ladd, Thompson, Rogers, Dunning and myself. He frankly told us what we might expect—hard work at the oars, bad weather, camping on the rocks, etc., but we determined to go, some of us being glad to get the chance.
>
> The governor was kind enough to give us the use of his twenty-one-foot whale-boat and a large tent. To these were added pro-

visions and bags and a crew of six Eskimos, one of whom was a full-fledged "kayaker." We started at five o'clock on the evening of August 10, leaving the crippled ship amid the cheers and good wishes of our comrades.[30]

It was a very rough trip. "How well I remember that evening!" Maynard Ladd recalled. "We six were snugly packed in the stern, our knees locked, and every inch of room occupied. In the bow were the four Huskie sailors, and behind us sat old Jacob Neilson, our half-breed pilot, blind in one eye, but, as we had many opportunities to prove, still skillful in the art of sailing between dangerous shoals and ugly-looking reefs."[31] On that first day they made Kangamuit—some 40 miles in eight hours—and slept in the attic of its church.

Any departure was impossible the next day because of violent winds, so the men passed it profitably in trading. The following day the whole village turned out to see the boat party off, and by evening the 12 tired men were camped in a place they dubbed "Windy Cove."

The succeeding day's journey was a short one. They had hardly started when Cook was advised by Jacob Neilson, who had been watching the sky, to turn about immediately. Having learned to trust Eskimo judgment about weather implicitly, Cook ordered the boat back to shore. Just as they landed, a violent squall struck, followed by two days of sustained winds that trapped them in their tent, which seemed destined to blow off the rocks and into the bay despite the hundreds of pounds of stones they had piled along its edges.

Finally the storm passed, and the Eskimos said it was safe to proceed. The boat crossed the Arctic Circle early on August 16 and by 11 A.M. reached the village of Itirdlek. There they met Jacob Dahl, the resident trader, who said he knew of no schooners on the coast at that time.

The wind had now died out completely, and the mosquitoes came down on the travelers with such vengeance that they put out to sea as quickly as possible, arriving at Holsteinborg at 8. There they heard better news from Governor Muller: Five schooners were off the coast only a few miles away, he said. One, the *Rigel*, had left Holsteinborg only that morning. He assured the *Miranda* party that a kayaker could easily fetch one of the schooners back, but first they must come to his house to eat.

After their adventurous passage up the coast, the travelers didn't have to be asked twice to have a taste of the famous Danish hospitality. Soon they had the pleasure of sitting down to a sumptuous meal of smoked salmon, herring and onions, pickled whale, potted meats, radishes, Knækkebrød, and black bread and butter, served with Carlsberg beer, Danish brandy and grog. After dinner they engaged in the old Danish custom of handshaking. Then came good cigars and pleasant conversation.

As it grew late, Governor Muller directed them to an outbuilding that contained two feather beds. The men drew lots for the privilege of collapsing in one of them. Dr. Cook and A.P. Rogers were favored by the draw, and the other men turned in on the floor.[32]

In the morning, Cook sent Arthur Thompson, Rogers and Porter up the mountain across the harbor to look for a sail. Before they even began the ascent, they caught sight of one west by south, and Rogers went back to tell Dr. Cook. Thompson and Porter pressed on just for the challenge of it, but they had cold water thrown on their fun.

The two were first blanketed by fog. Then, as they climbed higher, rain began to fall and finally snow fell in blinding sheets. Nevertheless, they kept on to the 2,000-foot summit, where Russell Porter fulfilled his dream of standing on the inland ice. Then, soaked to the skin, they started back to the dry village below.

Upon receiving Rogers's report, Cook at once dispatched a native in the direction of Nipisat, where the sail had been sighted. At 4 P.M., the kayaker came alongside the *Rigel,* of Gloucester, Massachusetts. The Eskimo showed Captain George Washington Dixon three letters, one marked to Captain Lawson, of the schooner *Carrie W. Babson,* and the others addressed: "To Captains of American Fishing Schooners." Captain Dixon opened one of these and read:

> Holsteinborg, Greenland, August 16, 1894.
> *To Captains of American Fishing Schooners.*
>
> Gentlemen:—The S.S. *Miranda,* carrying my expedition, with seventy persons on board, has struck a sunken rock coming out of Sukkertoppen; she is now lying at that harbor disabled and in distress. Will you kindly come to our rescue? I am at Holsteinborg with five of the members of my party. Shall remain there until one week from date; then return to Sukkertoppen. If this note reaches you in time to meet me at Holsteinborg kindly do so; if not, come direct to Sukkertoppen, and send a note by kayak at once to Holsteinborg.
>
> > Frederick A. Cook
> > Commanding[33]

That evening there was the commotion at the wharf that the arrival of strangers in Holsteinborg always caused. Their oilskins swinging from side to side, five Gloucester fishermen, clad in sou'westers, led by Captain Dixon and followed by a procession of curious villagers, walked to the governor's house, where the captain closeted with Dr. Cook.

He told the doctor he did not feel justified in abandoning his cruise until he had talked to his crew, since they were working in shares. As far as salvage was concerned, he said he could not get a cent of that as he would be carrying back not the ship but the passengers. Captain Dixon left about midnight saying that if he came up in the offing in the morning fixing her flag, he would take Cook's party to Sukkertoppen and try to make arrangements with Captain Farrell.[34]

The *Rigel* did appear the next morning flying her flag. Dr. Cook and his companions bade farewell to Governor Muller, then rowed out to the schooner standing offshore. The doctor brought with him a fine bundle of eider duck skins obtained from the governor.

All was soon in order, and the *Rigel* departed bearing the boat party, except for the Eskimos, back to the *Miranda*. The Eskimo crew seemed to have a fear of the large ship and decided to go back in the whaleboat.

Though happy to have succeeded in their mission, all in the little party were not content as they stretched out in the hold atop its cargo of fish preserved in salt. As the schooner pounded down the coast in a heavy wind, Porter listened to the complaints of one who felt the voyage had been altogether more than he had bargained for:

> One of the chronic kickers of the expedition, who has book upon the adventure as a big fake, has just remarked that never before did fishing vessel carry such a cargo, first a layer of salt, second a layer of halibut, then another layer of salt and a layer of <u>suckers</u>.[35]

Most of the men were deathly ill on the rough three-day passage down the coast and felt very much relieved to reach the *Miranda* at 8:30 A.M., August 20. The waiting passengers broke into cheers as Captain Farrell put off in one of the ship's boats to meet the schooner, and again when he rowed back with the expedition's boat party and Captain Dixon. Handshaking and congratulations all around greeted Cook and his crew when they came aboard the crippled ship.

Captains Farrell and Dixon then retired to the captain's quarters aboard the *Miranda,* where they agreed that $4,000 would be paid to take the passengers home aboard the *Rigel,* while the *Miranda* would steam, manned by her crew, towing the fishing schooner. Should the *Miranda* be salvaged, Captain Dixon was to receive an award, the amount of recompense to be decided by arbitration.

Meanwhile, word came from the assistant governor at Godhavn that he would not give permission for any of the party to overwinter in Greenland, as Cook had requested by letter from Sukkertoppen. Porter and Dyche reluctantly gave up their dreams of an arctic winter and, like all the other passengers, each packed the one canvas bag in which he was allowed to bring his personal effects aboard the *Rigel* from the stricken ship.[36]

The departure of the *Miranda* from Sukkertoppen on August 22 was a scene that would always stand out in Professor Brewer's memory. While the Danes saluted their guests with fireworks as the whole company sang "America," Brewer noticed tears rolling down Captain Dixon's face as well as those of many others.[37]

At first the weather was fairly calm, but then a heavy sea arose, adding to the discomfort felt by the 39 excursionists in their cramped quarters below deck on the 99-foot schooner. The smell of fish and bilge water was bad enough with the hatchway open, but when it had to be closed because of the waves washing over the deck, the stench, along with the groans of the seasick, made the close confinement seem like a miniature inferno.

The engineers believed that if the weather was reasonably calm, the *Miranda* might survive to sail again, but just in case, the two captains had arranged for the worst. At 12:30 A.M. on August 23 Russell Porter heard three whistles, and coming on deck saw a red light hoisted at the stern of the steamship:

> It had been agreed upon between the two captains that this signal should signify danger and distress, so our skipper mounted the halyards and brought the schooner to port. Suddenly we heard the captain's strong voice across the water. "Heave too under our stern." But we were near enough the sinking vessel and abided our time. We could see lights flitting about the deck of the ship and saw them lower the life boats. A very long and high sea was running and we very much feared for the safe launching of them. Then smoke was seen coming from the stack and I came below thinking they would try to keep her running.[38]

Professor Wright, who had been sleeping in the captain's cabin, was awakened by Captain Dixon's hasty preparations to go on deck as the whistles of distress began to sound, and in a few moments he followed him. Unlike Porter, Wright remained there:

> The suspense of the next three hours was terrible. Now the steamer mounted above us on the huge swells, and now was almost lost in the deep troughs. Fortunately the wind was not strong and the whitecaps were not breaking. Still there were thirty-three souls on the Miranda whose lives were in peril. As day began to dawn, about four o'clock, we saw the first boat approaching us from the steamer. After various attempts she was hauled safely alongside and the members of the steward's department were transferred to the Rigel.[39]

Below decks again, Russell Porter was awakened by the commotion:

> I think I must have been sleeping about three hours when I heard a noise of something scampering on to our decks and ran up to see the first boat load of the unlucky Miranda's crew coming aboard. The other boats were pushing off and at 5.30 o'clock the captain left with the mates and ice pilots. The dories from the schooner put off to the sinking vessel and brought back baggage, provisions, etc. Then the hawser was cast off and we were adrift.[40]

One of the crew, Mr. Clark of the commissary department, told of the last few hours aboard the doomed ship:

> I was sleeping in the ladies cabin when I was awakened by a fluttering sound of inrushing water and air, and very soon after the firemen came up and tried to swing one of the life boats, but smashed it in their cowardly attempt. The engineers went into the boiler room and there examined the damage. The top of the water ballast tank had given way in a weak spot where rust had thinned the plates, and water was rushing in. It was stopped up with blankets, plates and braces and for some time the pumps took care of what came in, but on account of the heavy sea, leaks broke open afresh and it was decided to abandon the ship as the whole tank might give in and fill the hold in a moment. So we left her, and glad I am to be here alive.[41]

And so the *Miranda*, with her rudder lashed to one side and her engines still running, pulled away from the *Rigel* with one pig as her only passenger and with most of the effects of the expedition, including Dr. Cook's arctic "relic," still in her hold. Soon the red light at her stern was lost in the mist, 296 miles west of Sukkertoppen.

Earlier in the voyage Cook had told Porter that the *Miranda's* crew was "ignorant and could see nothing beyond their own vulgar surroundings," and now they proved it.[42] When they came on board the *Rigel,* most were drunk, and many had stolen anything of value from the sinking ship; some of the silverware clattered on the deck as they scrambled over the rail.[43]

The men packed on the *Rigel* were an uncomfortable lot to begin with. Now, the addition of the *Miranda's* crew made the voyage home even more miserable. They got into the schooner's liquor, ate the only hams, drank all of the condensed milk and engaged in the forbidden practice of smoking below decks. This was the final indignity for many of the high-class excursionists on what they now considered a voyage of the damned, though Russell Porter did not agree:

> It was amusing to see some of the more fastidious passengers turn up their noses as they were forced to put up with one inconvenience after another, such as using dirty plates, knives and spoons, salt water for washing, sitting on a bench with a cup of coffee between their knees, a potato in one hand and [a] chunk of hardtack in the other.
>
> But on the whole, I have enjoyed it and if these are the hardships of shipwrecked people I have greatly overestimated the severity of them.[44]

There were now 91 aboard the schooner. To relieve the crowding, the *Rigel* sought the nearest port, Punch Bowl Harbour, and landed the *Miranda's* crew there on August 28, much to the paying passengers' relief. For the ice pilots, Mr. Dunphy and Mr. Manuel, there were three cheers, but for the rest there were "three groans" as they departed.[45]

During a two-day layover in fog-bound Henley Harbour, many of the men were eager for any excuse to have dry land under their feet again. Dr. Cook went ashore with the captains and some of the other officers for a dinner of fresh codfish and herring, while others, looking for amusement, struggled up the oily pier and through the inky blackness until they heard a sound like a herd of runaway cattle in the distance. Using the noise as a guide, they soon found themselves under a house on stilts that contained the revelers.

It was a Labrador dance, but there were only three women in attendance. The rest of the room was filled with smoke and a motley array of sailors, fishermen, and music without variety, so the men quickly returned to the schooner.

The *Rigel* reached North Sydney on September 5. Dr. Cook and Captain Dixon went to the customs house to get permission to land, and the rest of the party followed as soon as arrangements were complete.

While on the *Rigel*, Russell Porter had visions of himself sneaking up Beacon Hill with a three weeks' growth of beard, clad in his skin clothing and carrying all his possessions in his canvas bag. Surely, he thought, as much as he had wanted adventure, he had gotten more than he'd bargained for.

But now, everything was changed. He had been to the barber, had taken a hot bath and was sitting at a table at the Sydney Hotel in a fresh-boiled shirt and civilized suit, having just enjoyed a fine meal of roast lamb and all the trimmings. He was suddenly "another man" but was almost sad that it was all over:

> The party is breaking up and soon Dr. Cook's Arctic Expedition of 1894 will be a thing of the past. I look back over the past two months with a feeling of content and relief that I have seen so much north and come through such hardships and dangers unharmed. . . .
>
> There was a goodly flow of wit, many pointed jokes and several touching remarks which made many of our hearts swell with emotion.[46]

But the adventure was not quite over.

The next morning Dr. Cook returned to North Sydney to see on their way those who had sworn off the sea forever and were going by rail to the United States. The rest boarded the *St. Pierre,* bound for Halifax, where she arrived the next day. Some had a feeling of déjà vu as they boarded the *Portia,* the *Miranda's* sister ship and twin, and left for home. On September 10, off the Cuttyhunk Light, Russell Porter had further reason to feel that he had experienced all this before. He was halfway up the deck stairs when he heard a crashing thud.

At the same moment, Dr. Cook was having lunch when the cutlery slid off onto the floor once more. Parts of a mast crashed through the port windows as another rush for the deck began. When he reached it, it was littered with ropes, spars and sails.

The *Portia* had hit a sailing vessel and cut her in half. The stern was still above water, but the bow had already sunk out of sight. Porter got on deck just in time to see a man struggling with a lifeboat being sucked under by the sinking stern and another man, unable to free himself from the rigging, helplessly disappearing with the wreckage. Of the five crew members, only one—James Murphy of New York, who was picked up clinging to a spar—was saved. He identified the schooner as the *Dora N. French* of Bangor, Maine, carrying a load of coal from New Jersey.

Seeing there was nothing else to be done, the crew of the *Portia* began to cut away the rigging entwined around the bow and anchors. A check below decks found only a little water coming into the forward compartment through a hole six inches wide and two to three feet long, and a few cracks in the plates on the port side. With the foretop mast down and lacking 40 feet of railing, she was declared seaworthy and continued on her journey.[47]

As the voyage mercifully neared its end, like a survived war, it was already taking on an aura of nostalgia for the members of Dr. Cook's Arctic Expedition of 1894 that it certainly did not possess at first acquaintance. Henry Walsh had an idea:

> We were nearing home and a few of us were sitting upon the deck of the *Portia* looking out upon the wrinkled sea. Suddenly it struck me that it would be a pity that so many good fellows already bound together by the ties of common experiences should lose trace of each other when the busy swarming land should be reached. I therefore suggested that we should organize a club as a link to join all the members of Dr. Cook's Arctic expedition and keep them from entirely losing track of each other. The suggestion was accepted, and that afternoon, in the smoking-room of the *Portia* the Arctic Club was formed, which it was agreed should assemble at an annual dinner sometime between Christmas and New Year's day.[48]

Dr. Cook came to suspect that the loss of the *Miranda* was unnecessary. Captain Farrell was later made captain of the *Portia,* and she, too, was lost under suspicious circumstances. There had been a financial panic in 1893 and many ships became unprofitable to operate. The *Miranda* had been insured for $90,000. Perhaps, Cook thought, the loss of the *Miranda* was due not to her own bad luck, or even to a hidden rock in Sukkertoppen harbor, but to something more sinister.[49]

But whatever the ultimate cause had been, for Dr. Cook there was no escaping the realization that the voyage had been a financial as well as a practical disaster, and that all his plans, and his reputation besides, might have gone down with the unlucky *Miranda*.

CHAPTER 7

This Vanishing of the Pole Star

NEWS OF THE *MIRANDA*'S FATE CAUSED A BRIEF SENSATION IN THE PRESS AS RE-
porters scrambled to get the inside story of the disastrous voyage. When they
caught up with Dr. Cook at his house on Hart Street, they found the commander of the expedition undaunted and as enthusiastic as ever.

"A delightful trip, replete with adventures," the doctor called it. "Taken
all in all, I have not heard one member of the party that had a complaint to
make."

When asked of its scientific achievements, he assured them that in only a
little more than two weeks, wonders were accomplished. "All the records of
scientific observation were saved," he said. "No magnetic observations were
made. We were on the wrong side of Greenland for that."

"The tourists and sportsmen enjoyed themselves vastly," he told the reporters. "As to the statement that the Miranda was a condemned vessel, that is
the first I have heard of such a rumor, and it is not true. She was sound, and
was well equipped with everything necessary for such a voyage."

But other interviews disclosed that not every "tourist" agreed with Cook's
assessment. Some expressed bitter feelings or accused him of general mis-
management.[1]

The reporters soon confronted the doctor with more embarrassing revelations: According to Professor Brewer, the crew was drunk when the ship
foundered. Cook replied that he could not understand how Brewer could say
such a thing; he then told the truth without addressing the allegation, saying
that the ship had hit the rock at Sukkertoppen at breakfast, at which time the
crew was most certainly sober. "When a vessel is abandoned, the crew always
help themselves to the liquor," he said of the actual sinking.

Cook declared the accident the fault of the captain, since Farrell had no
charts of his own and had to borrow a set from him, but added that the rock
that did the damage was marked only on Danish charts, which were not available to any but Danish captains.[2]

Despite his pursuit by local reporters, Dr. Cook escaped most personal
blame in the national press. Noting the results of the Peary, Walter Wellman
and Frederick Jackson expeditions in the same year, all of which made little
progress toward their goals in Greenland, Spitzbergen and Franz Josef Land,

respectively, the *Miranda's* loss was put down to unfavorable ice conditions and unforeseeable misfortune. "It does not appear that Dr. Cook, who planned and personally conducted the excursion, was to blame," one national magazine remarked, "except in not having a premonition that the vessel, apparently so well adapted to the purpose, was really the picture of bad luck."[3]

The widespread and sensational coverage that the *Miranda* generated did nothing, however, to help Cook's plans for two more excursions in 1895 to raise money for his prospective expedition to Antarctica.

"My plans for the North are at the present more or less unsettled," he told his chief assistant. "I cannot say definitely that I shall go North. . . . To make the Southern project a certainty, I may be compelled to do so.

"I am more than ever determined to attack the realm of the unknown Antarctic regions. . . .

". . . I have not yet completed all arrangements in the matter of funds. Here is a great opportunity for the one who will come to the front and offer the necessary financial aid,—to write his name across a great and unknown region."[4]

But no one came forward. It was enough to discourage even the most optimistic. Dr. Cook resigned himself to returning to his medical practice, which had been attended by an associate, Dr. Burr, while he was away. He opened a new office in a modest brick building at 687 Bushwick Avenue and bought a white horse, which soon became a familiar sight in the neighborhood as it pulled his buggy on his daily rounds.

In the fall, Cook had a visit from his old comrade Eivind Astrup, who was staying on Clinton Street. He had recently returned on the *Falcon,* which had been sent to relieve Peary. From Astrup, the doctor learned firsthand that even the disastrous voyage of the *Miranda* could not compare with the terrible misadventures that had befallen Peary's Second Greenland Expedition.

The relative ease with which he had accomplished his objectives in 1892, and the acclaim and unquestioning belief his achievements and claims had brought him in America, had turned Peary away from his carefully worked out theories about the superiority of small parties and minimal means for arctic expeditions. He had taken 11 men, his pregnant wife and a nurse, along with all his exotic paraphernalia, with the idea that more would accomplish more.

Things had started well, Astrup said. They had had no trouble establishing a new base in Inglefield Gulf after making a record passage across usually ice-choked Melville Bay. There they had built a glass-roofed house that dwarfed Redcliffe. Finishing on August 11, they named it Anniversary Lodge.

Upon reestablishing contact with the Eskimos, they learned that Redcliffe House had been destroyed, along with the cache left for John Verhoeff, by Kyo and some of the other natives just days after the *Kite* had sailed. Though as reluctant to talk about him as they were of their own dead, the Eskimos indicated that nothing whatever had been heard of Verhoeff since his disappearance. After giving up any idea of a further search for the missing man, the *Falcon* sailed for home on August 20.

On September 12 Dr. Edwin Vincent, Peary's new surgeon, delivered Mrs. Peary of a healthy girl, whom they named Marie Ahnighito. Her skin was so fair that the Eskimos called her "the snow baby," and many came to see the wonder. The joyous birth was about the last bit of joy on the expedition, however.

On October 31 a huge iceberg calved from one of the glaciers in the gulf and set in motion a monstrous wave that stove in the *Faith* and also the new steam launch, *Doris,* while washing most of the expedition's supply of oil into the bay, ending Peary's plans for the generation of electric light.

The burros proved worthless except as dog meat, and the carrier pigeons either had their heads snapped off by the Eskimo dogs or turned stupid as winter approached and froze to death. As Cook had warned, the glass roof allowed heat to escape and had to be boarded over and shoveled continually, since it would not support the weight of the snow. Fuel ran out in March, and the inmates of Anniversary Lodge had to burn walrus blubber and seal oil for warmth. Even so, ice that was inches thick formed on the inner walls.

In the spring the projected return to Navy Cliff also met with disaster. Astrup related how Peary started March 6, 1894, with seven men and five Eskimos, who as before would accompany them only to the edge of the ice cap. He took 12 sledges, whose loads this time included tents and sleeping bags because of the earlier start. They ran into trouble immediately when piblockto struck their dog pack. Astrup then told Cook of his own incapacitation at the place they laid down a cache of alcohol, 26 miles onto the ice cap: "While at the depot, I was so upset by eating some tainted pemmican, that I did not consider it advisable to take part in the adventure, so I remained there a couple of days, and on March 14th returned to the station with Mr. Lee, who had had the misfortune to have one foot seriously frozen, and was unable to put it to the ground."[5]

Since Astrup's gastric distress was severe and Hugh Lee could hardly walk, the two had to be accompanied to Anniversary Lodge by Peary and George Clark. After Peary and Clark rejoined the overland party on March 22, the weather showed signs of worsening. It was the onset of a blizzard. Winds exceeding 45 miles per hour pinned them in their tents for 34 hours at temperatures below −60°. When the storm relented, Peary found that James Davidson and Clark had suffered freezes and decided to send them back with Dr. Vincent, but though suffering terribly, Clark refused to return.

The story of the storm told by Davidson and Vincent was the last word of the expedition Astrup heard until May 1. After a convalescence he started on an extended sledge journey to Melville Bay.

Peary now had with him only the injured Clark; his meteorologist, Evelyn Briggs Baldwin; his first assistant, Samuel Entrikin; and Matt Henson. The original plan of splitting the party at Independence Bay to explore the east coast and the new lands to the north was already impossible for lack of enough men. Now, as the five struggled eastward, the wind-hardened snow ridges pounded the sledges to pieces and more dogs died of exposure and piblockto.

On April 10, 128 miles from his starting point, Peary prepared to turn back. There he buried a cache of supplies, marking it with a 14½-foot bamboo pole.

Ten days later, Frederick W. Stokes, the expedition's artist, met Peary coming down from the ice cap. Stokes thought he seemed dazed and confused, with a wild look in his eyes. His face, red and frostbitten, with its bleached beard and eyebrows, had disappointment and defeat written in every line etched upon it by the blinding storms it had faced. The remainder of the party was soon back at Anniversary Lodge. All were suffering from either severe freezes or snowblindness and were covered with body lice.[6]

After a few days' rest, however, Peary declared his intention to stay another year and try again. But there was not food enough for the whole party to overwinter and he would call for three volunteers when the ship arrived, he said, even though he had implied earlier that there would be no resupply ship for two years.

When Astrup returned to the lodge, he learned the sad fate of the inland ice party: "Many dogs had died during the fearful gales; and Mr. Entrikin, whilst lashing together an improvised sledge, had had both feet frozen, so that he could scarcely use them. The rest of the party were all in an exhausted condition, so that it would have been too risky to persevere."[7] In the weeks it took for the men to recover from their ordeal, they discussed what they should do if a ship did come.

As he convalesced, Peary brooded on his failure to duplicate his earlier journey, and as the days passed, rumors circulated that the lieutenant would not accept anyone as a volunteer who had not stayed with him to the end on the ice cap. The men argued over Peary's confusing signals and were soon thoroughly demoralized, not knowing whether they were in or out of favor. Some were torn between an intense desire to go home and the responsibility they felt to stay until the end of the expedition.[8]

That spring Peary offered the ultimate incentive, a gun, to Panikpa. He wanted the Eskimo to show him the location of what the Eskimos called Iron Mountain, which John Ross, a British explorer, had heard about in 1818. Ross had suspected it was a large meteorite, or perhaps several of them.

Panikpa accepted, and with him as guide, Peary and Hugh Lee set out across Melville Bay. But after going only partway, Panikpa abandoned the journey and returned home. Peary then engaged another Eskimo, Tallakoteah, who said he knew of the *saviksue,* or "great irons."

After many delays on the part of the Eskimo, who apparently had also thought better of revealing the location, Peary finally succeeded in reaching the site. Digging down into the snow, he uncovered one of the iron stones, which the Eskimos called "the Woman" because of its shape and size. He scratched a rude "P" on it in pride of possession but saw no possibility of moving the huge chunk of metal before summer.

As summer drew on, much discontent developed among the party at Anniversary Lodge. Some of the men resented that the Pearys dined in separate quarters. In fact, no men were allowed in the Pearys' apartment at all except Dr. Vincent. Mrs. Cross, the nurse, who did the cooking, carried tales back and forth describing the civilized delicacies the Pearys were enjoying while the men were compelled to eat seal and walrus. The only luxury they had was a taste of champagne on Thanksgiving and Christmas. Some believed that three quarters of the heat was going into the Pearys' room, leaving theirs so cold they could not bathe, even though they suffered terribly from vermin.

There was also much resentment about the presence of Mrs. Peary, some saying that although she had been brave and devoted, they would have been better off without her. As for Lieutenant Peary, they felt he seemed concerned with nothing but red tape and "hogging" all the glory for himself. As one expedition member put it, "it was a perfect Hell."9

Then came the news that many had been hoping for. One sunny evening at the end of July two natives reported the arrival of a vessel. "Enthusiastic hurrahs resounded through the cool evening air," Astrup remembered, "and echoes thundered back from Mount Bartlett's perpendicular rocks, slowly dying away among the distant mountains."10

It was the *Falcon,* but Robert Peary did not join in the cheering. He had decided he could not go home having accomplished so little. By the time the ship had forced a passage into the bay on August 20, Clark and Entrikin had volunteered to stay, but Peary refused them, saying he had enough supplies for only three men, and they would be himself, Matt Henson and Hugh Lee. He had persuaded Lee to stay by promising him a government position on their return.11

When the ship arrived, she carried no spare provisions but instead, by prior arrangement with Peary, brought two huge jack screws to take away the lodge for exhibit in the United States. The men were convinced by this that Peary had never intended to stay two years, and they felt more justified in going home.12

The *Falcon,* with all on board but the chosen three, headed south on August 26. When she reached St. John's, Eivind Astrup mailed a letter home, making clear that "the trouble was with Peary and wife not with the boys."

It was too late for that. After the *Falcon's* arrival in Philadelphia, the press published a letter from Peary to General Wistar criticizing his subordinates and implying that he was carrying on despite their cowardly return. Upon reading this letter, some of the expedition members decided to defend themselves against Peary's insinuations. The papers were filled with damaging statements by the returning party about the management of the expedition, most of their complaints centering on the Pearys' imperious manners and the poor quality and insufficient quantity of food. One disgruntled explorer went so far as to say, "If some of the cheap and ridiculous explorers do not succeed in finding the Pole, they might at least manage to lose themselves."[13]

Astrup wondered whether Peary would repeat the charges when he returned the next year, but concluded it "probably would not pay him."[14]

Throughout the fall of 1894 Astrup visited Dr. Cook's house, discussing with him the progress he was making on the narrative of his two trips to Greenland, which Astrup had begun to write despite Peary's prohibitive contract. It was a good-humored book that skipped over most of the unpleasantries of 1894 but strongly hinted that Peary's 1892 observations from Navy Cliff might not have been accurate.

Eivind Astrup shared Dr. Cook's enthusiasm for the Arctic and admiration for the Eskimos. His book brimmed over with Eskimo lore, and no doubt they spent many hours during its composition comparing notes on their observations of these ingenious people for whom each had developed a deep respect.

Astrup also worked on his careful survey of Melville Bay, made after returning from the ice cap in the spring of 1894. In his conversations with Cook, Astrup expressed his doubts about Peary's claims. He embodied them in a paper submitted to the yearbook of the Christiana Geographical Society.

A French geographer, Charles Rabot, comparing Astrup's paper with Peary's report, which had appeared in the *Geographical Journal,* concluded:

> These two documents and the maps which accompany them present contradictions which singularly weaken the authority of the journey. The map in the *Geographical Journal* establishes the insularity of Greenland. . . . Astrup's map is completely different. . . . Moreover, Astrup's report formally contradicts that of Mr. Peary. "We recognized," writes the former, "the probable extension of Greenland towards the north."

In Rabot's account of Peary's current expedition, he praised Astrup, calling his survey of Melville Bay "the principal geographical result of the expedition." This, and his remarks that the presence of Mrs. Peary "did not contribute to maintain harmony among the explorers" and that the organization and equipment left much to be desired, prompted a heated rebuttal from Professor William Libbey, Jr., of Princeton.

Libbey took exception to all of these remarks, calling them false, and ended by alleging a plot against Peary: "At the last, a conspiracy was formed with the intention of abandoning Lieut. Peary, and this would have succeeded, if he had not persuaded one of the malcontents to remain with him and his coloured man, Matt. Henson."[15]

Peary's friends in the American Geographical Society ridiculed Rabot's taking sides with the young Norwegian. To them it was obvious who should be believed:

> Mr. Peary, a man of proved capacity and honour and experience, was the leader of the expedition and responsible for the result.

There was no responsibility laid upon Mr. Astrup. He was free, if no scruple withheld him, to utter himself in any way that seemed likely to bring a temporary distinction to so young a man. He chose his time well, for his report and map were published when Mr. Peary was again in the frozen North, far beyond the reach of communication for an indefinite period; and this should have given occasion for doubt, if not for suspicion, in a critical mind.[16]

The criticism hurt Eivind Astrup. He departed for Norway on December 2, 1894.[17]

Meanwhile, Mrs. Peary had been soliciting donations, wherever she could gain an introduction, toward hiring a ship to return for her husband in 1895, even though he had told her he planned to go overland the 700 miles to the Danish settlements and take passage to Europe. She wrote to many prominent men, including Gardiner Greene Hubbard of the National Geographic Society of Washington, D.C., trying to interest them in defraying the $12,000 estimated cost of her self-styled Greenland Scientific Expedition of 1895.

Another of her appeals went to Morris K. Jesup. Jesup, a millionaire philanthropist, was a pillar of society. A member of the New York City Mission and Travel Society and vice president of the American Sunday School Union, he had helped found the New York YMCA and was interested in such causes as Anthony Comstock's crusades to suppress vice and obscene literature. But his greatest love was the American Museum of Natural History. He had given it more than $100,000 and was now its president.

Though she came away empty-handed from her interview with Morris K. Jesup, the meeting proved decisive in her husband's career. Jesup, not wanting to look like a soft touch, told her to do the best she could and he would then make up the difference. Her solicitations secured $1,000 each from the American Museum of Natural History, the Brooklyn Institute of Arts and Sciences, the American Geographical Society, Bowdoin College and the Newport Natural History Society.

She then set out on a lecture tour under Major Pond's management to earn the rest. The major found her "in possession of a speaking talent that would have made her a permanent success,"[18] but Jo Peary had no designs on a career upon the platform. She was haunted by the memory of her husband as he staggered, defeated, into Anniversary Lodge in 1894, and her sole desire was to have her Bert home, safe again.

When she fell short of her goal, Morris K. Jesup was true to his word, and in the summer of 1895, all of Jo's efforts and hopes sailed with the *Kite* for Inglefield Gulf to fetch back her husband. But she did not go.

Jo had had a lot of time to think since Bert had told her he would remain in Greenland, but that she must return. She sent a heartrending letter instead:

> When you told me your plan a year ago last April as we sat near
> the shore of Baby Lake, I felt as if you had put a knife into my heart
> & left it there for the purpose of giving it a turn from time to time.

> I have reviewed our married life very carefully, my husband, &
> think I am resigned to the place which you gave me an hour after
> we were married. It was N^O 2 & how it did hurt, has continued to
> hurt & will hurt until the end. A year ago you made it N^O 3 by giving
> "fame" the first place N^O 1 became 2 & N^O 2 became 3. . . .
>
> My Bert, my life, if you have not been successful won't you be
> content to put fame in the background & live for me a little, as you
> once did?[19]

Her apprehensions about his safety were fully justified. When the *Kite*
arrived, the news was even worse than the year before.

In the fall of 1894 Peary had gone seeking the cache he had left in the interior. Much to his dismay, he could find no trace of his 14½-foot marker, and
another storm was rising that would bury it even deeper. As he lay trapped in
his tent with Matt Henson, he felt his chances slipping away like the drifting
snow that scudded against its walls, despondent that he might fail once again.
"Interest in anything refused to be aroused," he wrote; "thoughts of wife and
blue-eyed baby, of mother, pictures of boyhood, happy scenes and memories
before this devil of Arctic Exploration took possession of me, rose and ranged
themselves opposite to the precious hours of my life being wasted, the sacri-
fices of me and mine, all perhaps to end in naught, till it seemed as if with this,
and the unceasing hissing of the wind and snow, I should lose my reason."[20]

After the storm ended, another thorough search was made, but there was
nothing to be seen but the endless white plain stretching in every direction.
Nevertheless, Peary resolved to try again. He devoted all his energies to devising an equipment that would get him to Independence Bay, where he hoped
to live off the land. But he entertained little confidence of real success; he
wanted only to avoid complete failure. Even so, almost nightly, he was awakened by vivid nightmares containing premonitions of his total defeat.[21]

As the time arrived for the journey's start, Peary began a long letter to Jo
that sounded more like a will:

> My Darling,
>   It is the eve of our departure for the great ice, and I sit down to
> write you what I know I shall later hand you myself. . . . The winter
> has been a nightmare to me. . . . The cold, damp, frost-lined room
> has made me think of the tomb. . . .

He then enumerated his improvised equipment and his many problems:

> I have had a great deal of trouble in getting dogs, thanks to the
> loyalty of the Norwegian member of the expedition, who has told
> the natives that he was coming here in a year or two and if they
> kept their dogs for him he would give a gun for every two.

After giving the locations of his journals and other important items, and
what disposition should be made of them, he listed his unpaid debts to the
Eskimos, saying he had promised them a portion of the lodge. He then ended:

Should I not return the rest of the house should go back on the ship. Put on exhibition it will make you independent. All the keys I have put back of the books on the very top shelf.

Good-by my darling.

Bert.[22]

With Henson, Lee and five Eskimos, Peary set out for Independence Bay on April 1, 1895.

It was a tremendous gamble. They took deer and walrus meat in place of their lost pemmican and substituted the less efficient kerosene for alcohol. In so doing, they critically overloaded their sledges beyond their 42 dogs' hauling capacity. This time the Eskimos were persuaded to accompany them onto the ice cap, but they all turned back 128 miles out when Peary failed once again in a search for the lost cache. The three explorers continued, however, and reached Navy Cliff after a grueling journey, at the end of which all but nine of the dogs had died, and they themselves were at the point of starvation.

Lee, in the most critical condition, had to be left in camp while Peary and Henson tried to secure game. After an extensive search, they came upon a herd of musk oxen, shot several of the animals, and fell upon them, devouring chunks of raw meat as they stripped it from the steaming carcasses. Their condition was too frail and their supply of meat too small, however, to risk further exploration. Just getting back across the 500 miles of ice that separated them from Anniversary Lodge would now be challenge enough. It had been a pointless journey. With enough rations on their one remaining sledge for 14 days, the men set out on June 1 to retrace their steps.

Not far along the trail, Hugh Lee, who had been temporarily revived by the fresh meat, collapsed because of constant diarrhea and begged to be left behind. Peary would not hear of it.

At first they shared their meat supply with their dogs, hoping to keep them in harness, but the dogs weakened anyway. Soon, when a dog died, it was no longer fed to its fellows as before; the men now ate the dogs, as no source of food could be spared.

As they descended the downslope of the inland ice into an area of dangerous crevasses, Lee thought the lieutenant showed no caution. He had the impression that Peary was half hoping to fall into one of them and thus avoid facing his own failure should he return.

But return they did, on June 25, 1895, with but one pitiful dog, too weak to pull a sledge, following them into camp. The defeat nearly unhinged Peary's mind; during his convalescence he wondered whether he was going insane and even imagined Matt Henson was planning to poison him.

Lee's impression was accurate; as Peary thought about his two years' record of failure, it was almost too much to bear. When the ship returned for him, how could he own up to it? "I felt that . . . I could not go on board and say that I had failed," he admitted. "It would be preferable to remain where I was. At times I even hoped that the ship would not come so that I might make another attempt next spring."[23]

By the time the *Kite* arrived in August, however, Peary had thought of a way he might salvage something from his two misspent years. He would bring home the great meteorites from Cape York.

He lingered in the North to allow for the maximum thaw. When he arrived at the site where the meteorites had been snow-covered the year before, he found the stones exposed and succeeded in getting "the Woman" and a smaller one, called by the Eskimos "the Dog," aboard. A third, too immense to move, was left where it lay.

The crew of the *Kite* found Peary uncommunicative and morose on the return voyage, and this continued at St. John's, where reporters could get little information out of anyone on exactly what his expedition had accomplished, but rumors circulated of dissension between Peary and his rescuers. They did get L.L. Dyche, who had gone on the relief expedition to collect the natural history specimens denied him on the *Miranda* voyage, to venture a guess about Peary's future. "I don't think that Peary will try another arctic expedition," said Professor Dyche. "His last expedition was a dismal failure."

The explorer found more reporters waiting for him at his mother's house in Portland. There seemed little doubt that he had, indeed, abandoned his dreams. "I shall never see the North Pole unless someone brings it here," Peary declared. "I am done with it. In my judgment, such work requires a far younger man than I. The leader of such a party should be able not only to do as much as any one else, but more than any other man. He should be under thirty, rather than over forty. I am too old to snowshoe twenty-five to thirty miles a day for weeks, and to carry a heavy load during most of the time. For that work one should be a trained man, a thorough athlete, and that I am not. . . . I am done with it. I am not an old man as age is reckoned here, but I am too old for that sort of work."[24]

When Jo Peary wrote to Morris K. Jesup to thank him for his invaluable assistance, she confided to him her husband's despair:

> You know what a blow it is to him to find that after sacrificing everything he finds himself far from the goal of his ambition. He is completely crushed but is trying to bear it as only a strong man can bear the bitterest disappointment of his life. I will not speak of the money he has put into his plans because while we have health & each other I do not give it a thought.[25]

Peary's former expedition companions were not displeased by the first reports of the outcome of the Second Greenland Expedition. They kept a careful watch on Peary and looked to their own reputations. A correspondent kept Evelyn Briggs Baldwin informed:

> Peary, like Br'er Fox, is layin' low. I believe he is still at Portland Me. where he is whining about his old age. . . . From the enclosed clippings you will observe that he must now explain some things in

connection with the expedition which rescued him. My, what a faculty that man has for getting people down on him! . . .

He failed on this last trip over the ice cap because he did not have sufficient provisions and men. He had the men and could have had the provisions. Why did he send the former home and neglect to provide the latter?[26]

Although Peary later had unkind things to say about the men who had not had "the grit" to stay with him in the Arctic, as Astrup had predicted, he did not repeat the charge of desertion.

When he heard of Peary's defeat, Dr. Cook wrote to Samuel Entrikin that although it may have ended Peary's career, the results of his expedition might have hurt other explorers' chances as well. "Peary's failure is sad news," he told Peary's former first assistant, "for it will throw another shadow on Polar work, but it is what you and all [of] us who knew the bad shape of his equipment expected. He has fought hard and against tremendous odds to accomplish something. He deserves sympathy."[27]

Cook hoped that shadow would not fall on him, though there seemed little chance his plans to leave for the Antarctic by November would come to anything now, no matter what the reaction to Peary's failure was. The would-be commander of the American Antarctic Expedition had appeared before the Brooklyn Institute in March, hoping it might sponsor his project. But his experiences with the *Miranda* had caused him to rethink some of his plans. They now called for two wooden vessels of 100 tons each to go to the Gulf of Erebus and Terror. He also tried to promote interest in his project by calling the institute's attention to the strange ball-shaped objects on pedestals discovered by a Norwegian antarctic whaler, which suggested there might be an undiscovered race living in the unknown South. But nothing had come of it beyond formation of a committee to further the project.

Instead, the added publicity only put him at the mercy of cranks and enthusiasts. One man wrote from Brazil that he had invented a flying machine shaped like a bird, and that he was sure the doctor could easily reach the South Pole by sitting in its head to guide it. He also assured him a record-setting pace, claiming a speed of 120 miles per hour for his invention.[28]

In any event, all conventional means of getting there seemed to be fading fast. The *Miranda* voyage had discouraged any potential paying excursionists to Greenland for the summer of 1895. Now, an epidemic of distemper struck his once-thriving pack of Eskimo dogs. Only three survived; these he sent to the old Sullivan County homestead, which had been reoccupied by Theodore Cook and his family. With neither the money nor the motive force for an assault on the Antarctic, Dr. Cook could look forward only to another winter in New York, where the traffic made a soiled and slushy quagmire of the poor facsimile of the polar world that descended occasionally to cover the city's ugliness. For the time being he would have to confine his polar explorations to reading about others' journeys into the realms of his dreams. This he did diligently, spending every spare hour in the libraries of the numerous clubs to which he belonged.

With the turn of the year, Dr. Cook noticed a small story datelined Norway. It was shockingly sad news:

ASTRUP FROZEN TO DEATH

The party that went out in search of Eivind Astrup, the Norwegian who was with Mr. Peary on his second and third expedition, today found him dead in the little Eivedal Valley in the Dovrefjell Mountains.[29]

On December 27 Astrup had started out on skis from Jerkin to Brenna, a town 53 miles distant, to visit friends. He had taken only one day's supply of food, planning to spend the night at a farmhouse midway.

Dr. Cook wondered how such an expert skier, who had survived all the rigors of the ice cap, could have come to such an end on such a simple excursion. He knew that Astrup had been very upset at his treatment by Peary's defenders when he had left for home; could Astrup's death have been something other than an unfortunate accident?

By 1896 the pace of the international competition to reach the North Pole was beginning to quicken. That spring Cook read that Salomon Andrée, a Swedish engineer, was constructing an elaborate shed on Dane Island, off Spitzbergen, with the idea of attempting to reach the Pole in a free-floating, hydrogen-filled balloon. But as summer waned, word came that unfavorable winds had forced him to give up.

About the same time, the biggest news to come out of the North that year again came from Norway. After three years both Fridtjof Nansen and the *Fram* had returned from the embrace of the arctic pack unharmed, but neither had reached the North Pole. Nevertheless, they brought with them one of the most remarkable stories of endurance in the history of exploration.

After several false starts, Nansen and one companion, Hjalmar Johansen, had left the *Fram* in the charge of Captain Otto Sverdrup in mid-March 1895, when the ship had reached about 84° north and it appeared she would drift no nearer the Pole on her own.[30] Nansen planned to travel north for 50 days and then return, whether he reached the Pole or not. He took three sledges drawn by 28 Siberian dogs. Nansen had with him all that he judged necessary for the trip, including two specially designed kayaks.

By April's second week, the ice, which had seemed favorable at first, became more and more impassable; the two men had to struggle all day to make two miles at most. Nansen could see the impossibility of reaching the Pole on his remaining provisions, even though his time limit had not expired. On April 8 he went ahead some distance on snowshoes. Looking out over the pack, he could see nothing but a chaos of iceblocks and hummocks stretching to the horizon. Before turning, Nansen took careful observations of the sun to determine his position and found he had reached latitude 86°13', besting the old "Farthest North" record of Lieutenant J.B. Lockwood of Greely's expedition by more than 160 miles.

He and Johansen started back for the nearest point of land, 450 miles away, because regaining the *Fram,* which might have drifted in any direction, would have been a hopeless task. As the dogs died, they were fed to the others until the men had just one each to help haul their two cumbersome sledges bearing the kayaks, the third sledge having been burned for fuel.

One exhausting day both men fell asleep without winding their watches. By morning both timepieces had stopped. This made it guesswork to calculate their longitude, which requires a knowledge of the exact time.

Week after weary week dropped behind as they struggled on. By July they were beginning to doubt that Karl Weyprecht had charted his discovery, Franz Josef Land, correctly, since they believed it should now be in sight. Yet the horizon disclosed nothing but the monotonous pack. Since they were unsure of their longitude, they greatly feared that they would miss the land entirely and be swept out between Spitzbergen and Greenland when the ice broke up, leaving them at the mercy of the icy ocean in their two frail boats. But before the month was out they sighted the coast, and near the end of August, after a number of harrowing escapes, they scrambled ashore onto the first land they had felt beneath their feet in more than two years.

It was too late to gain Spitzbergen that summer because of the disintegrating ice conditions, so the two explorers built a stone hut and began gathering a supply of meat and blubber to tide them over the long winter night. Throughout it all Nansen faithfully kept his diary, though by now the pages were so black and greasy he had difficulty making out his own words.

In the spring they lashed together their kayaks as a catamaran and, raising its sail, started off for Spitzbergen along the south shore of Franz Josef Land. On June 17, 1896, they were preparing breakfast on that bleak coast when Nansen heard what he thought was the bark of a dog, though he had been obliged to kill his own two faithful animals when he and Johansen had taken to the kayaks. Going to investigate, he soon found tracks and heard several more barks at close range, then a shout—the shout of a human voice! A man in a checkered suit approached, waving his hat. The Norwegian, who in his tattered, oily skin suit looked more the apparition of some wild beast, nevertheless still had a hat to wave back.

The stranger proved to be Frederick Jackson, an English explorer out to reconnoiter the unknown coast. It seemed a rare pleasure to the weary Norwegians once aboard Jackson's ship to reacquaint themselves with what had once been commonplace, as the *Windward* bore them home.

On August 13 Nansen touched Norwegian soil again at Vardø. That same day, the *Fram* drifted free of the ice north of Spitzbergen. Captain Sverdrup had sighted no land at all along the path of her drift over a surprisingly deep sea, at places exceeding 2,100 fathoms. The whole party was reunited on

August 21 at Tromsø, to the wide and joyful national acclaim of the most heroic journey in the quest for the Pole.

At his Brooklyn home, Dr. Cook followed all this with great interest. He noted that despite Nansen's incredible journey, the door was still open for those who coveted the Pole itself. "It does seem to me," the doctor wrote to Evelyn Briggs Baldwin, who had just failed in obtaining the position of meteorologist on Andrée's next attempt at the Pole in his balloon, "that some enterprising American ought to carry the Stars & Stripes beyond Nansen's Farthest North. Certainly the route with which we are the most familiar (through Smith's Sound) is now the only safe path to the Pole. Who will be the victor?"[31]

Surely not Peary. He had confined himself to an attempt to retrieve the last great meteorite that summer and had come back empty-handed.

As 1896 passed, it seemed that Frederick Cook, like Robert Peary, had about given up all thought of returning to the icy regions, though he still gave an occasional lecture about his experiences; he had just recently appeared before the Brooklyn Medical Society to read his paper "Some Physical Effects of Arctic Cold, Darkness and Light."

His house was kept by his mother-in-law, Mrs. Forbes, and the doctor often saw her three remaining daughters coming and going. Soon he was courting Anna Forbes, a schoolteacher, and by the end of the year the couple announced their engagement.

Nevertheless, Dr. Cook continued to follow polar matters closely. He eagerly read the accounts of two Norwegians who had returned from Antarctica. Captain C.A. Larsen, an associate of Nansen's, had landed on Graham Land. Carstens Borchgrevink, sailing with the whaler *Antarctic* under the command of Henrik Bull, had reached Melbourne claiming to have been the first man to set foot on the fabled Antarctic Continent itself, at Cape Adare on January 24, 1895. Borchgrevink had hurried back to Europe to announce the news that he had found lichens there, proving that life existed even in the remotest South.

The untutored Borchgrevink's appearance before the Sixth International Geographical Congress in London caused much discussion among the learned gentlemen gathered there. At the close of the congress a resolution passed calling for a scientific expedition to the unknown continent, which declared "that in view of the additions to knowledge in almost every branch of science which would result from such a scientific exploration the Congress recommends that the scientific societies throughout the world should urge in whatever way seems to them most effective, that this work should be undertaken before the close of the century."[32]

The great scientific minds of Europe had finally caught up with the physician from Brooklyn. The doctor's dreams of seeing that ice-shrouded continent were rekindled, and he dusted off the old plans he had developed in 1893 and began to rethink them in light of his recent studies.

By early 1897, other means having failed, Cook hoped to persuade some wealthy patron to back his attempt. To this end he sought an interview with

George C. Carnegie, a nephew of Andrew Carnegie, the Pittsburgh steel baron and self-styled "Distributor of Wealth," who gave him a cordial reception at their meeting at the Union League Club.

"It is not for the want of men but, as has been the case with all similar enterprises, it is the want of money that stands in the way," he told Carnegie.

After listening to his appeal, Carnegie said, "Doctor, I would like to get interested in your ice business. What color have you to exchange for gold? See me next Monday or write me."

When they next met, Cook "came prepared to give values and scientific research" and "talked utility fast and strong."

"We are not advocating an expedition to the south pole. The knowledge of the surrounding regions is too limited to evolve any theories concerning methods of pushing on to the pole itself. We want a different kind of information regarding the antarctic regions from that sought by explorers in the North. We want a more definite knowledge of the land that is known to exist in vast areas around the south pole. There has never yet been a voyage in those regions, and there is no reason to believe that there are no channels through which a steamer might push far into the great continent that is supposed to surround the pole."

Just as it looked as if he had a compact with the rich man, Carnegie was called away. When he returned a few minutes later, his mood seemed changed. He walked some distance with Cook in silence, then said, "Doctor, there is so much to be done in this world nearer by. Three miles above is all the ice we will ever need. Find a way to fetch it down."[33]

With Carnegie's change of mind, the doctor's last hope seemed to have vanished, but that spring the chance to see the Antarctic came anyway. As he had with the Peary expedition, Cook noticed it in a newspaper. A small article in the New York *Sun* mentioned that the Belgian Antarctic Expedition was about to sail. He telegraphed the leader offering financial assistance and Eskimo dogs, but his application was declined, as all the expedition members had already been chosen.

The doctor returned to his attempts to raise money when fate intervened. After setting out from Antwerp on August 16, the Belgian expedition's ship was forced to put in at Ostend for emergency repairs to her engine. Her Flemish physician took this opportunity to resign for "family reasons," having apparently gotten cold feet long before he saw his first piece of antarctic ice.[34]

One evening a courier appeared at Dr. Cook's door with a telegram; it was from the Belgian leader, one Adrien de Gerlache:

> Dr Cook,
> Brooklyn, N.Y.
> FOUVEZ REJOINDRE MONTEVIDEO MAIS HIVERNEREZ PAS.
>
> Gerlache[35]

Cook had no clue as to what this might mean. At first light, he hurried over to the offices of the New York *Sun* to ask for the help of Cyrus Adams, who was readying the morning edition. Adams translated the message: "Could you join us in Montevideo? We will not winter." Cook immediately answered in the affirmative. In reply came another telegram simply instructing him to meet the Belgians in Rio de Janeiro in September.

The doctor had little to arrange beyond his business and personal affairs. He had already accumulated a good store of polar gear and clothing in anticipation of his own expedition. It was easy to get Dr. Burr to agree once again to take his practice, but it was hard to leave Anna Forbes, especially since she was not well. Dr. Cook suspected something grave, perhaps even pulmonary tuberculosis. He took her to Dr. Alfred L. Loomis, professor of practice at New York University, who reported that Anna's condition was not serious. Relieved, Cook booked passage on the *Helvetia,* which was to sail September 3.

His mother and sister were on the docks that day to see Fred off, but he was nowhere to be seen. When they heard the ship's whistle signal her imminent departure, they begged the captain not to sail, but when Fred did not appear, she pulled away from the dock without him.[36]

He was having second thoughts; Anna had begged him not to go. But in the end, Frederick Cook's desire for adventure exceeded all others; he sailed for South America aboard the SS *Coleridge* on September 20. In his baggage he packed a 10-by-15-foot silk flag, which he hoped to plant nearer the South Pole than any flag before it. "I should have had a longer time to afford better means to prepare for a journey of this kind," he told himself. "To consent by cable to cast my lot in a battle against the supposed unsurmountable icy barriers of the south, with total strangers, men from another continent, speaking a language strange to me, does indeed seem rash. The antarctic has always been the dream of my life, and to be on the way to it was then my ideal of happiness."[37]

It was a stormy passage, but once he had his sea legs, Dr. Cook made the acquaintance of some of his fellow passengers. They soon formed a little group that met in the tearoom regularly to chat. There were two young girls from New England, joining the missionary service in Brazil; four young German men, also headed for Brazil to work in the industrial houses run by other Germans; and the personable young doctor from Brooklyn, bridging the language gap between them, on his way to places that no man had ever visited.

They went ashore at Bahia and had a festive dinner together amid a tropical verdure that seemed exotic to them all. Dr. Cook and his friends spoke enthusiastically of their divergent ambitions, which had, by chance, brought them together. They exacted a promise from the doctor that he would stop and see them on his return journey to America and then bade him a safe voyage and best of luck on the realization of his dream, which seemed far more dangerous than any of their own.

The next day, after weathering one final storm, Cook stood on the deck of the *Coleridge* and gazed at the fabled harbor of Rio de Janeiro with its gigantic, freakish rocks and at the light blue outline of the Organ Mountains looming at the head of the bay, which was bathed in tropical light.

Once ashore, he took accommodations in a magnificent hotel, enjoyed a generous supper, then tried to determine what he should do next. The expedition's ship, the *Belgica,* had left Ostend on August 24 and should arrive shortly, he thought. He scanned the newspapers for word of the ship but could find no "Belgica" among the thousands of Portuguese words printed on the oversized sheets.

Cook called the porter and asked him to telephone the Belgian legation. Upon being handed the receiver, he heard a voice speaking English, much to his relief.

It was Count van den Steen de Jehay, the Belgian minister. After a short exchange of greetings, the count insisted that Cook come to the legation immediately. He would be by in 15 minutes to pick the doctor up, he said. Upon his arrival, the count admonished Cook for his choice of accommodations. "Doctor, they have yellow fever and small pox, unreported, right under this roof; you are young, Doctor, [and] are, I suppose, unafraid of contagious disease, but it is our duty to keep you alive for service on the *Belgica,*" the minister chided. "Are you ready? You will go with your personal baggage to my home in the mountains at Petropolis."[38]

The two boarded the cars of the Principe do Grão Pará cog railway and headed north from Rio to the elevated valley of the Serra de Estrella, where Petropolis lay 2,634 feet above sea level. As the cars climbed higher and through the low clouds, though the vegetation remained lush and exotic, the climate became a cool and preferable alternative to the swelter of the larger city below.

Days went by and still the *Belgica* did not come. The last news of her was that she had left Madeira on September 16. The doctor passed the time studying, preparing his equipment and visiting the coffee plantations and fine summer homes of the foreign legations. The minister's table always attracted a large gathering for dinner with ample interest in things polar. But the Brazilian guests said they would have none of the Antarctic when they were informed that its explorers would be deprived of fine wines, cigars and even a glimpse of the feminine sex.

Finally, on October 22, word came that the *Belgica,* delayed by contrary winds and becalmed on several occasions, had at last arrived at Rio. A start for the city was made at once.

When they caught sight of her in the harbor, at 110 feet long and 26 abeam, she looked diminutive anchored among the ocean liners and warships there. A gray bark with cream and natural wood trim capable of six knots, she had been the *Patria,* a Norwegian steam sealer, until purchased by Gerlache.

Adrien de Gerlache, like Frederick Cook, had long dreamed of the Antarctic and icy conquest and had met equally icy resistance. He had volunteered to accompany the voyage proposed by the Swedish Baron Adolf Nordenskjöld in 1888, but it never materialized. Plans for a voyage of his own had been made in 1894. He presented them to the general secretary of the Royal

Adrien de Gerlache, commandant of the Belgian Antarctic Expedition, 1897–99.

Belgian Geographical Society, Jean du Fief, that September and had been frustrated ever since by a lack of funds. But through persistence and persuasively written articles, sentiment for a national antarctic expedition had slowly taken hold. A rich patron, Baron Ernest Solvay, inventor of the Solvay process of producing soda ash, and the geographical society had together provided 25,000 francs so that Gerlache could visit the Arctic to familiarize himself with polar conditions. But even the 120,000 francs he had collected by 1896 was far less than needed to sail for the Antarctic. Then the Belgian government itself came to his aid, donating 100,000 more, enabling him to purchase his ship. But only a subscription feast organized by Madame Osterrieth in Antwerp in July 1897 and a final contribution from the Interior Ministry assured that the Expédition Antarctique Belge would start that summer. All together, an equivalent of about $60,000 had been raised—a minimal amount for such a large undertaking.

The general plan of the expedition was to reach the Antarctic at the beginning of the austral summer of 1897, then follow the edge of the ice pack, either entering the Weddell Sea or exploring Graham Land and Hughes Bay. A party of four men would debark at Victoria Land, near Cape Adare, and from there attempt to reach the South Magnetic Pole. During the winter, the others would reprovision at Melbourne and return the following year to pick up the explorers. The second year's program would be determined by what was discovered in the first season. In view of this, special equipment and clothing for overwintering were selected for only four persons.[39]

Though supposedly a Belgian enterprise, the original 25 men of the *Belgica* were a polyglot mixture of nationalities; the mate and half the sailors were Norwegian, and most of the scientific staff were foreigners as well.

As the *Belgica* sat in the sweltering harbor at Rio, the ship's officers speculated among themselves about the American who would be their physician. As each boat came alongside, they tried to guess which of its passengers might be Dr. Cook. When he finally did arrive, Captain Lecointe was immediately impressed by his open, sympathetic face. He was also much impressed by his luggage, which consisted of "two sleds, snowshoes, fur coats, a pharmacy especially composed for the polar regions, fifteen coffers and packages and boxes without end"—but no dogs.[40]

The doctor was every bit as curious about his fellow officers. As he came on board in the scorching morning heat, he felt it might be as challenging to be understood as it had been at his first meeting with the Eskimos. He could not speak a word of French. These fears were allayed, though, when Dr. Cook learned that Gerlache could speak some English and the scientific staff all understood German.

The mate of the ship was one Roald Amundsen, whose polar experience, like Gerlache's, was limited to a whaling voyage in the Arctic. Of all the Norwegians aboard, he was the only officer. Amundsen had been sizing up his companions since the *Belgica* had left Antwerp:

> The scientific staff had been chosen with great care, and Gerlache had been able to secure the services of excedingly able men. His second in command, Lieutenant G.[eorges] Lecointe, a Belgian, possessed every qualification for his difficult position. . . . As a navigator and astronomer he was unsurpassable. . . .
>
> Lieutenant Emile Danco, another Belgian, was the physicist of the expedition. . . .
>
> The biologist was the Rumanian, Emile Racovitza. . . . Besides a keen interest in his work, he possessed qualities which made him the most agreeable and interesting of companions.
>
> Henryk Arctowski and A[ntoni] Dobrowolski [his assistant] were both Poles. Their share of the work was the sky and the sea; they carried out oceanographical and meteorological observations.
>
> Arctowski was also the geologist of the expedition—an all-round man. . . . Conscientious as he was, he never let slip an opportunity of adding to the scientific results of the voyage.[41]

Quickly, the doctor gained the confidence of the other officers. Lecointe marveled that although they could communicate only through signs, he felt a bond of friendship fast forming with Dr. Cook. It did not take long for Gerlache to acquaint himself with the American, either, and when he had, he felt very fortunate to have gotten such a man on such short notice:

> For an expedition like ours the choice of companions for the voyage is of the highest importance, especially the choice of the doctor. Not only is it necessary to have an able practitioner, but it is indispensable that he be endowed with the best character. His professional duties absorb but a small part of his time; he must know how to carefully employ his leisure without which his free time would become a danger to the generally good accord.
>
> Guided only by chance, I had a lucky hand. Cook is a charming comrade, helpful, active and ingenious. He will render to the

expedition inestimable services and he will take an important part
in our scientific work. He is 32: the oldest man on the ship.[42]

The doctor, too, was favorably impressed by the scholarly, reserved commandant and the affable captain. But it was the 25-year-old Amundsen who
attracted Cook most. He seemed the most interesting man Cook had ever
met. "He was cold in manner," thought the doctor, "but alluring and friendly
in every act when his profundity could be grasped."[43]

For its physician, the voyage of the *Belgica* would be a further education
in human nature, the finishing school of the study he had begun on the *Kite:*
"I now grasped at its full import that every man differed from others chiefly in
the ground work of the culture behind him. All were far from racial and home
influences, but the national character of each was as permanently set as the
nose."[44]

Dr. Cook was well pleased with his decision to join the expedition. Not
only was his first impression of the ship's company decidedly favorable, but
the *Belgica* herself, despite her diminutive appearance, seemed admirably well
fitted for a voyage of antarctic discovery.

Gerlache, though, wanted Captain Lecointe to have the magnetic instruments tested, and this would require a week. It was the first in a curious pattern of delays by a man who had pleaded and cajoled to be given the means to
reach the Antarctic, but who, now that he had them, seemed in no hurry to
head south.

The delay allowed for rounds of festive appointments, including an audience with the Brazilian president, a banquet at the Restaurant Petropolis and
tours of the city's sights. To the alert doctor, Rio seemed in a stupor of tropical
languor. As he hurried through the narrow streets lined with endless rows of
low houses, the windows and doors seemed full of men, women and children,
all of whom appeared "ill at ease, all doing nothing in various ways."[45]

The idle time resulted in more trouble with the crew; Lecointe had
warned Gerlache even before they had left Belgium that the men would be
unruly. At Ostend two had resigned and one had fallen ill and had to be replaced; several more had been disciplined at Madeira. Now the quarrelsome
Parisian cook, M. Lemonier, involved himself in several fistfights before the
week was out. The naturalist, Emile Racovitza, had decided he could make
better use of his time than loafing about Rio and had already sailed aboard the
fast British steamer *Oravia* for Punta Arenas, where he would rejoin the ship.

The expedition began to break out of its tropical somnambulation as the
time for departure neared. Aboard ship all was bustle and haste as final provisions were loaded. Curious visitors added to the confusion on deck as
photographers snapped the preparations from every angle. Finally, the sightseers boarded tugs to return to Rio, and the *Belgica* steamed out into the open
sea on October 30.

On the way south Dr. Cook, unable to sleep, went out on deck to contemplate the new sights in the southern skies as the familiar constellations

faded over the horizon to the north. "This vanishing of the Pole Star, and the many old friends in the heavens brings to us a vivid impression of the vast distance which we have traversed from our native lands," the doctor thought as he stared at the strange groupings of large stars and empty spaces that seemed extremely dark by contrast. "The new firmament has many charms, but . . . one is more apt to fall into an admiration of Nature than into a profound sleep."[46]

Storms and a fire started by the ship's overheated engines enlivened the passage to Montevideo, where she arrived on November 11 during a massive thunderstorm. It covered the decks in hail and then unleashed torrents of cold rain upon the landing party, which added to the appreciation of the shelter of the Hotel Oriental and its warming cups of fragrant Brazilian coffee. There also awaited some warm and welcome letters from home. Anna Forbes seemed to be improving in health, helping to mollify Dr. Cook's mixed emotions at leaving her.

All in all, Cook found Montevideo more congenial than the torrid, languid life of Rio. Here the look was healthy, and the appearances of thrifty prosperity seemed much in evidence. The change in climate had no effect on the cook's temperament, however, and another fight led to his dismissal and replacement by a Swede.

Chief among the city's attractions were its numerous beautiful ladies. They were a sight that all the men no doubt drank in to the fullest, since soon only the memories of these warm girls of the north would provide comfort in the cold summer to come.

As the *Belgica* steamed down the Rio de la Plata on November 14 for the "Ladyless South," the prospect of receding civilization was on the minds of everyone. They were going farther from home; yes, farther south, but away from warmth and toward an unknown destiny.

The weather, which had been pleasant, now seemed to mirror their increasingly gloomy thoughts. In the afternoon a sudden change seemed imminent. An unusual band of clouds as straight as an iron bar was seen in the west, sweeping rapidly toward the ship. Not knowing what to expect, the captain ordered all sails taken in. A few minutes later Cook noticed that though there was no wind, the sea began to boil:

> The water and the air was lighted with a sort of vague pearly glow. At this time the strange line seemed just over our bowsprit, and extended entirely across the heavens from east to west, but only a little draught of air crossed the bridge. . . .
>
> . . . All at once the bark was struck with terrific force, and stopped as suddenly as if she had struck a stone wall; this was followed by a howling, maddening noise as the wind passed through the ropes and spars such as I have never heard before or since. Everybody grasped a bar or a rope to keep from being swept overboard. . . . From the commencement to the termination, this

strange onslaught occupied but fifteen minutes; but this was as
much as I care to see of a hurricane of this sort, though they are
sufficiently prevalent in this region to receive the special local
name of *pamperos.*[47]

As she passed the unpopulated coastline, which now faded from sight, the
ship's quarters were rearranged, loose gear was stowed away and she was generally snugged down for the notorious weather expected in the "roaring forties."

After two weeks out of sight of land, even the bleak, sandy cliffs of Cape
Virgin at the entrance to the Strait of Magellan were a welcome sight. Once
inside the channel, the *Belgica* anchored each night to avoid the dangers of its
close and unfamiliar confines.

Landing in a canoe at Gregory Bay, the scientific staff happened upon a
group of houses belonging to a Chilean sheep farmer by the name of Menendez. Captain Lecointe and Dr. Cook mounted two intractable horses and
rode eastward toward the main station, where they were greeted by Alexander
Menendez himself. The enterprising rancher proved to have 120,000 acres
and 150,000 sheep. Cook was impressed by the empire he had established on
the barren, inhospitable pampas. Returning to the *Belgica,* the inexperienced
riders got a second taste of their inabilities to handle Chilean horseflesh, resulting in many bruises to their own.

When they reached their canoe, they found it stranded 400 feet from the
nearest water, the tide having gone out. It took an hour of almost superhuman
effort to haul it across the viscous mud, and when they boarded the *Belgica,* all
were covered from head to foot in Patagonian slime.

After another stop at Elizabeth Island, on December 1 they arrived at
Punta Arenas, whose notoriety considerably exceeded its size. Where the
rugged, wild foothills of the Andes met the grassy pampas, a rude city of corrugated iron shacks had been built on a foundation of sheep and gold. The
officers were reunited with Emile Racovitza at the French Hotel, where a large
sack of mail awaited with postmarks of places now so very far away that they
seemed in another world entirely.

While touring the town, Dr. Cook judged it none too refined. The streets
were most notable for their stagnant pools of water and for the tree stumps,
broken carts, tin cans, packing boxes, dead dogs and a host of other refuse that
ornamented and paved their sandy bottoms. Punta Arenas seemed to be
largely composed of saloons, the chief denizens of which were gauchos, gold
diggers, sailors, soldiers, tramps and, serving one and all, the feminine inmates
of Sandy Point.

Cook departed at once to visit the Salesian mission on Dawson Island,
where he wanted to carry out some anthropological measurements of members of the Ona tribe. He was accompanied by Henryk Arctowski, who took
linguistic notes. As he looked about him, the doctor realized that such measurements and notes might not be possible in the near future:

The priests pointed with pride to their work of constructing neat looking houses for native habitation. The so-called houses were mere boxes, well roofed, brightly painted, and so placed as to effectively keep out light and air. Tuberculosis was sufficiently prevalent to thoroughly impregnate the mud floor, and the average life of the Indian here in mission confines was less than three years. Yet the good, but short-sighted Christian workers, believed they were doing noble work. Here, as in all parts of America, if the Indian was encouraged to adhere to his nomadic habits, if he was encouraged to shift his camp frequently and return to shelter tents instead of death boxes, many thousands of worthy lives might have been spared.[48]

Since the *Belgica* was not inscribed on the Belgian Administration of Maritime Affairs register, Gerlache could not employ the usual maritime disciplinary measures to restrain his crew. When one mechanic and four sailors, all Belgians, spent the night on land without permission and returned drunk and disorderly, the commandant had to call upon the Chilean police for help. All were dismissed, and when the expedition left Punta Arenas, the recently acquired Swedish cook, having taken sick, also was left behind.

With her remaining complement of 19 men, the *Belgica* entered the Magdalena Channel and passed up the fjord of the great glacier on Tierra del Fuego. Cook volunteered to accompany Arctowski to examine its geological features.

Arctowski thought the glacier magnificent but the going rough. "We had to hug the extremities of several small hanging glaciers, and climb steep rocks, for along the margin of the basin there is no beach, while the cliffs are mostly precipitous, and to have forced a way among the ice in a canoe would have been an impossibility," he reported. "In the end we were stopped by a river which flows from a lateral valley, and which we made no attempt to cross, the distance still separating us from the great glacier being too considerable and the ground virtually impassable."[49]

Though the season for exploration in Antarctica was already well along, the *Belgica* had lain at Punta Arenas for a fortnight taking on additional supplies. Now Gerlache received a generous offer by the Argentine government of free coal at Ushuaia; she set out on December 14, bound for Famine Reach.

When williwaw winds—sudden squalls that swept down with no warning—buffeted the *Belgica,* she anchored for shelter in Hope Harbour. Dr. Cook and the scientists went ashore to examine the rank undergrowth of its beech forest in a wet snowstorm that soaked them to the skin. "Altogether," wrote the doctor of the miserable experience, "our personal discomforts were such that we were ready to throw science to the dogs."[50]

The next day the ship passed through the Magdalena Straits and among the hundreds of uncharted islands of Whale Boat Sound. Near midnight, finding the anchorage unsafe, she picked her way along in the darkness. After an examination of Londonderry Island, she finally arrived at Ushuaia in the evening of December 21.

Dr. Cook and the other officers had by now all but placed the civilities of their homes behind them and had begun playing the roles to which they aspired:

> At Rio we were done up in good style before we left the ship; dress suits when necessary, the newest thing in neckties, and neatly pressed trousers. At Montevideo our garments were crinkled and showed the effects of the sea. We began, here, to be a little indifferent in personal appearances. At Punta Arenas we did not even try to fix up, but walked about the town as careless of dress as bricklayers; and here at Ushuaia, well—the man who dressed and brushed his hair was an outcast; he was not regarded as an explorer.[51]

At Ushuaia most of the scientists met their first Fuegians, members of the Yahgan tribe living around the mission of the Protestant South American Missionary Society there. Dr. Cook, eager to compare these people at the other end of the earth with the Eskimos, stayed while the ship proceeded to Lapataia.

While the *Belgica* lay coaling for a further week, the men saw the new year come in. Some must have wondered whether it would be their last. Before them were the challenge of the unknown South (though they were tardy in facing it), the worst weather in the world and, as the fates decreed, a small measure of immortality or total oblivion.

Dr. Cook came aboard at Lapataia with John Lawrence, a mission worker he had met at Ushuaia, who wanted to be dropped off at Harberton, farther down the Beagle Channel. On January 1 the *Belgica* steamed east seeking Harberton, the last stop before leaving the South American coast, and the last chance to take on a supply of fresh meat. That evening, while peering through the gathering darkness, the lookout noticed what appeared to be a house on shore, and the bark was turned toward it. Then, mysteriously, the ship's forward progress was arrested. Without a sound she had gone onto a reef of rocks and was stranded as the tide began to fall. At 4 A.M. the *Belgica* began to careen, and by 6 her angle made it impossible to stand on the deck.

The object they had steered toward was indeed a house, that of Lucas Bridges, the son of a missionary-turned-sheep-farmer, who noticed the ship's predicament at first light and rowed out to her:

> Those on board had lowered a boat, attached a kedge-anchor to the stern of it and were paying out the anchor's chain from the sloping deck of the ship. Four men in the boat were rowing furiously, and a number of others on deck were encouraging them even more furiously in French. . . . With every stroke of the oars she bounded forward, and between strokes sprang back exactly the same distance. It did not seem to have occurred to any of them to

load the chain in the boat, pay it out as they rowed away and end up by dropping the anchor. . . .

As I watched the crew's efforts with the kedge-anchor, a man appeared on deck and hailed me in English with a slight American accent. He was a smartly dressed, personable fellow, not much over thirty and full of life; rather below medium height and slimly built. He introduced himself as Dr. Frederick A. Cook, surgeon and anthropologist, member of a party of scientists on a Belgian expedition to the Antarctic. . . .

I suggested to him that, as the vessel had gone ashore at high tide, she might float off with the evening tide if we lightened her as much as possible. I offered to go to Harberton and fetch the eight-ton lighter [my brother] Despard had built. We could bring her alongside the *Belgica* and relieve her of her deck-load of coal before high tide. Dr. Cook spoke to the captain in French. My proposal was agreed to, and the doctor and I set off for Harberton.[52]

While waiting for the lighter, Gerlache could see his carefully laid and dearly bought plans slipping away before his eyes with the falling tide. The ship was now so far over that the whaleboats had to be cut from their davits to prevent their being crushed. Huge timbers intended for possible repairs to the *Belgica* were brought from below decks and placed as props to hold up the ship. Amundsen and Lecointe was then summoned to the commandant's cabin to discuss whether the cargo should be tossed over to try to save the ship. If this was done, the expedition was at an end, and the *Belgica* would have to return in disgrace to Belgium. The three decided that they would await events.

Those events quickly took a turn toward finality when the reinforcing timbers splintered and were swept away in the surf, leaving the *Belgica* to roll on the rocks beneath her. In an instant, all seemed lost. Commandant de Gerlache urgently requested Arctowski to fetch up the flag so that the ship could at least go down flying the national colors.[53]

At this point the *Phantom,* a large salvage brig under the command of a Captain Davis, arrived to assist the *Belgica,* as did the lighter with Bridges, Cook and a crew of 20 Indians. They removed the coal from the *Belgica*'s deck in two loads, landing it on a nearby beach. Then, with the help of a favorable wind and a rising tide, the ship floated free, her colors flying gallantly at the mainmast where Arctowski had obediently hoisted them.

The crisis over, the scientific party disembarked for Harberton. The *Belgica* immediately set out for Porto Toro, a local harbor, to seek shelter and was soon out of sight.

In landing, the scientists let their boat drift away without securing it. Lucas Bridges wondered at their carelessness:

Probably men whose minds are devoted to science should not be expected to be practical . . . but I could not help thinking that, in the desolate regions for which they were bound, the consequence of similar neglect might well be tragic. . . .

I mentioned to them that a party of Ona, real forest warriors with long hair, skin-robes and paint, were encamped less than a mile from Cambaceres. Our visitors were immediately anxious to take photographs of them. On the following morning I escorted them to camp. Knowing that the Ona would be nervous, I went on ahead of the scientists to allay the Indians' fears. . . .

The Ona of both sexes did not like the little magic eye of the camera winking in their direction. I did my best to reassure them; and Dr. Cook was thus able to take some fine photographs, particularly of the women, with their huge loads done up in the orthodox, cigar-shaped fashion and a child or two stowed on top.

With his exposures made, Dr. Cook produced from his capacious pocket a sock containing about two pounds of small, hard sweets of many colours, each with a little seed in its centre. He handed a pinch to each of the numerous natives, then put the remainder, perhaps half a pound, back into his pocket with the remark:

"I think they have all had a taste." . . .

Feeling that this reckless hospitality of the anthropologist might not seem adequate recompense for what they had done at my request, I took a couple of the Ona to the house and gave them a sack of flour. . . .

Before they left our shores to continue their voyage south, I took the scientists to Harberton and introduced them to my father. Dr. Cook was most interested in the Yahgan-English dictionary on which, by then, Father had spent over thirty years of work and thought. Publication was discussed. One of the chief difficulties lay in the printing. Father had used Ellis's phonetic system, but had had to adjust or add to it, to suit the Yahgan pronunciation of various words. Dr. Cook assured him that there was a society in the United States who made a specialty of American aboriginal languages. This society had the necessary facilities to print the work and, Dr. Cook expressed himself quite confident, would be glad to do so. He offered to take charge of the dictionary there and then, but Father feared that the precious volume might be lost in the Polar ice, and would not part with it. He promised to hand it over to Dr. Cook on the return voyage of the *Belgica*.

I was relieved at this refusal, having no great admiration for the seamanship of captain and crew. . . . Their attempts to get out the kedge-anchor had not inspired any greater confidence, nor had the incident of the drifting boat.

For the same good reason, I declined a pressing invitation to join them in their expedition to the Polar regions. The prospect of adventure tempted me sorely, but I was reluctant to place my safety in such unpracticed hands. . . .

So the *Belgica* sailed from Tierra del Fuego with neither the dictionary nor myself aboard.[54]

Captain Lecointe thought the Indians hardly above the level of animals and their language a positive insult to the ears, reminding him exactly of a person in the throes of a bout of seasickness. The doctor felt otherwise.

The magnificently wild Onas, many of them more than six feet tall, clothed in simple robes of guanaco skin, living in such a harsh climate and having no house but a bunch of brush tied together at the top to break the bitter wind, were to Dr. Cook the very essence of savage grandeur. They seemed especially so after his observations of those following foreigners' dictates at the Catholic and Protestant missions.

There was a simmering conflict between the ranchers and the Indians as a result of Ona raids on their sheep herds. As he had before with the Eskimos, Cook pondered their fate in a white man's world:

A European and a Fuegian.

I doubt if missionary efforts will improve the hard lot of this noble band of human strugglers. The efforts thus far made have certainly had the contrary effect, and altogether they do not need a new system of morals as badly as we do ourselves. I do not mean to infer that missionary work, in general, is hurtful to aborigines. There is a legitimate field for such efforts, but it is not among Onas, unless the work is conducted in a new manner by a thoroughly practical man. They need to be placed in a position where they may follow their wild habits without the infectious degeneration of higher life. Individually and collectively they have fewer sins than New-Yorkers. It is true that there are among them no faultless characters, but there are also no great criminals. There are some good and some bad, but the worst and the best are found side by side.

The bitter and the sweet of human life flow in the same stream. They have the same origin and the same termination. The lesson of ages to untutored man has impressed upon him a prescription of moral direction, which is quite as good as, and far more appropriate for him than, the white man's code of ethics.[55]

CHAPTER 8

An Unimaginable Dream

THE *BELGICA* WAS FINALLY ON HER WAY TO THE ANTARCTIC, BUT THE SEASON was now growing late. In this upside-down world below the equator, forsaken by the pole star, the austral summer had begun on December 22, and it was already January 13.

The expedition's goal for the season had not been spelled out; it would take shape as opportunities arose. There were general objectives, however. One was to map the sea bottom along the ship's course.

Sounding as they slowly steamed away from South America, the scientists discovered the seafloor dropped off abruptly to 13,000 feet just off the continental shelf, then started a gradual rise, perhaps toward a vast continent.

At eight in the evening of January 19, an iceberg was sighted—the first tangible piece of the great unknown to the south. A bitter wind from that direction reinforced the chill the sight of this icy mass engendered in the warm blood of the Belgian officers, as the shrill cries of albatross and petrels accompanied the hum of the wind about the *Belgica*'s rigging. The sighting brought on a sudden realization that these seas were totally uncharted and that the leaden atmosphere and the dark depths might conceal any number of unpredictable dangers.

The next afternoon the snowy outline of the South Shetlands could barely be made out, but by evening the ship was approaching the northern end of the island group. As the bark skirted close by Livingston Island, she was in a position no mariner likes, on the lee shore of an unknown coast. The weather became unsettled as she moved slowly south on the evening of January 20.

Morning dawned misty, and while attempting to dodge some small icebergs, the *Belgica* once again ran onto unseen rocks with a thump that made her timbers crack and caused Dr. Cook to come on deck. As the fog suddenly lifted, he could see white crests and black rocks on every side, and as the ship withdrew, he watched some small icebergs being dashed to pieces on them and wondered whether that would be his fate.[1]

The horizon cleared considerably, and the shape of Sail Rock and the dim outline of Deception Island, with its grim heights falling 400 feet straight into the sea, could be seen to port. Soon after passing this impressive landmark, the sailors noted a sea change that they knew foretold nasty weather ahead.

At first the ship tossed gently about, but by morning the sea was occasionally breaking over her deck, which was still covered with coal. Loose coal washed into the scuppers, keeping them from allowing the water to escape. Whoever had deck watch was instructed to clear them as best he could. Hour after hour the sea rose higher as the storm gathered force, and soon great waves rolled over the rails, sweeping anything loose overboard. Dr. Cook, however, could not resist coming up to look at the wild sea.

At three in the afternoon he and Amundsen were on the bridge when they heard an unearthly cry. The doctor went to the quarterdeck and, looking over the stern, saw Carl Wiencke struggling in the water below. The sailor had lost his balance while trying to free the scuppers and had been swept over the side. He was now desperately clinging to the log line, which Cook began to draw slowly in:

> As I brought Wiencke close to the stern, Lecointe, with a bravery impossible to appreciate, volunteered to be lowered into the icy sea to pass a rope around Wiencke. He followed his offer with demands for a rope, which was securely fastened around his waist. With two men at the rope, Lecointe was lowered into the churning waters; but he sank at once with the counter eddies, and nearly lost his own life, without being able to keep near Wiencke. Lecointe was raised, and without delay or undue excitement we managed to tow Wiencke to the side of the ship, where we expected to lower another man. But while we were doing this, Wiencke gave up his grip on the log, and sank. We waited there for an hour, but saw no more of our unfortunate shipmate. Wiencke was a boy with many friends, and his absence was deeply felt in our little party. [2]

Further hope for the man was abandoned. Gerlache ordered the ship to Low Island for shelter.

When the sea eased, the *Belgica* crossed Bransfield Strait toward the unknown continent. Its huge, forbidding ice shelf, 150 feet high and extending as far as the eye could see east or west, was now in view. Soon real land was descried, though its heights were hidden by persistent mists. Captain Lecointe, unable to determine their position on the ship's charts, continued to coast along the ice-mantled highlands somewhat east of south.

The scientists aboard the *Belgica* could hardly wait to get ashore. At ten in the evening, the scientific party rowed one of the whaleboats toward a small island that appeared to be no more than a heap of rocks, its northern exposure bare, but its ravines filled to level with a cap of the ice in whose grip it lay.

Arctowski, Racovitza, Gerlache and Cook all scrambled from the boat onto a small bight, but then the commandant and the doctor were compelled to return to save the boat, which was in danger of being smashed on the rocky ledge in which the landing place ended. The other two men were soon lost to sight in the darkness, but their movements could be traced by the ring of

Arctowski's geological hammer and the cries of alarmed penguins as Racovitza sprang from rock to rock.

The next day the weather began to clear, and another landing was made to determine their position. As always, the doctor volunteered to go along:

> Lecointe and Danco fixed their tripods. Racovitza turned up the stones alongshore, where he found several mysterious crawling things, which he hailed with as much delight as if he had found nuggets of gold; Amundsen remained in the boat, and sought to secure a few sea-leopards that were asleep on the ice near by; while Arctowski and I mounted the inland ice to study its character.
>
> The view which we obtained from the upper slopes of the land-ice was superb. To the east was an island with two bare hills about twenty-five hundred feet high, and from these, expanding in every direction, was a bed of ice and snow. Beyond this, just barely visible, about fifty miles from our position, was the feeble snowy outline of the great mainland, which offered us no hope for a passage eastward.[3]

That first panoramic view of the Antarctic seemed just as remarkable to Henryk Arctowski:

> The silence which brooded over this unknown world was singularly impressive, but occasionally a mountain of ice would collapse with a thundering crash. One could hardly believe one's eyes when these changes in the fairy-like scene occurred, were it not for the dull rumbling growl of the disrupted glaciers. In fact, this realm of eternal ice is so different from anything one had seen that it appeared another world altogether; in sober truth, I do not believe that in any fable the human imagination has described what we have seen there. [4]

The weather was now perfect and the sea as quiet as a millpond. Excitement ran high as the unknown land lay revealed as never before in the suddenly transparent atmosphere.

On the last day of the month, the scientific party prepared for a short expedition inland. They hoped to scale a nunatak on "Two Hummock Island," as they had dubbed the largest one to the east, and get a bird's-eye view of the country for miles around. By taking a round of angles from its heights, they could fix the positions of the newly discovered coasts with some accuracy. Dr. Cook packed his large American flag among his baggage.

The shore party consisted of Cook, Arctowski, Gerlache, Amundsen and Danco. Taking ashore sufficient equipment and supplies for a fortnight, they stowed them on two sledges made to Nansen's pattern and began to laboriously haul them up the incline of the ice cap that extended to the very edge of the sea. At a height of 600 feet they crossed several crevasses with little difficulty and reached a great snowfield that looked down on a glacier cascading toward the bay. Here they camped.

A night of stormy discomfort began as a wind came off the glacier and increased to a force so strong a man could not stand against it. Two men had to hold the tent pole all night to keep their shelter from falling and their effects from being torn and scattered over the ice cliff.

But as the morning light appeared, the wind dropped off. Arctowski and Cook then set out by themselves up the glacier toward the two dark peaks that protruded from its smooth white surface. The trip was a tiring labor.

Despite a thermometer hovering near the freezing point, the heat of the sun was intense, and the men became covered with perspiration as they toiled upward. At 1,600 feet a series of impassable crevasses 30 feet wide stopped them.

After two days' futile effort to establish a higher camp, Amundsen and Cook attempted to get around the crevasses by climbing along the walls of rock bordering that section of the glacier. They roped themselves together with raw silk rope, as climbing would be ticklish business indeed.

During his first field experience, Amundsen appreciated the doctor's already accomplished technique: "It was a long tour and a hard day. We passed huge uncounted crevasses. We were forced to cut our way along a perpendicular ice wall. . . . The Doctor, the experienced Polar explorer, goes ahead, I follow. . . . It is interesting to see the practical and calm manner in which this man works."[5]

Their attempt failed, but on the seventh day ashore, Dr. Cook, once more with Arctowski, tried again. This time they reached the lower of the two peaks. From its heights, a magnificent view of Graham Land stretched out before them.

The doctor unfurled his flag and watched it flutter in the breeze. It was the farthest south the national emblem had ever been carried, and he must have looked at its vivid colors in the brilliant antarctic light with satisfaction.

That evening the shore party heard the whistle of the *Belgica* in the bay below, calling them back. During their absence Lecointe had discovered an opening southwestward and many more islands in that direction.

By February 8 the *Belgica* was steaming into the newly discovered strait in superb weather. Dr. Cook stayed on deck all day exposing more than 100 plates, as panorama after panorama of new lands loomed before his lens.

The *Belgica*'s photographic complement consisted of sophisticated Zeiss glass plate equipment. Although he had very limited experience with cameras, mostly of the simple Kodak type, Cook quickly learned by trial and error: small apertures and longer exposures produced the best results; slow-developing plates were far superior to faster plates for capturing detail.

There was, however, one major difficulty—insufficient fixer. This led him to make some unusual experiments. His hypo supply was running low, and exposed plates would never survive the trip across the equator unless they were

Cook the photographer.

fixed. The doctor remembered mention of prussic acid as a fixing agent for daguerreotypes in an article he had read:

> We had on the *Belgica* twenty gallons of hydrocyanic acid, used to kill animals for specimens. One drop on the tongue and it was all over for the animal. I began to experiment, knowing the grave danger of the poison. In due time I formulated a solution of proper strength, and thereafter we used prussic acid as a fixing bath. Needless to say, nobody remained in the darkroom during the fixing.[6]

These were the brief days of discovery, when Adrien de Gerlache reveled in the fulfillment of his icy dreams. Though slow in making his arrival, he now made the most of his time. When it was over, he could look back at some real achievements:

> During the three weeks which followed, the expedition made a rapid survey of Hughes Bay and the new strait, landing whenever it was more or less practicable. Twenty landings were made altogether between Bransfield Strait and the Pacific. . . . M. Lecointe determined the co-ordinates of the prominent points, and M. Danco determined the magnetic elements whenever it was possible to land the instruments. M. Racovitza discovered and collected . . . representatives of an antarctic fauna hitherto quite unknown. . . .

M. Arctowski did not lose any opportunity of collecting specimens of rocks which should furnish data regarding the geological character of the islands, while Dr. Cook was equally diligent in securing photographs which should prove of real value apart altogether from their artistic excellence.[7]

For Henryk Arctowski's tastes, these surveys were far too short. On some of the landings he was limited to a mere ten minutes ashore, although he saw things there that might occupy a lifetime of study.

Thus the days passed as the *Belgica* slipped among the many unknown islands in the channel. When each officer was called upon for suggestions to name the new lands, two of Dr. Cook's were adopted. He named one Brooklyn Island after his hometown and the other Van Wyck, after the first mayor of

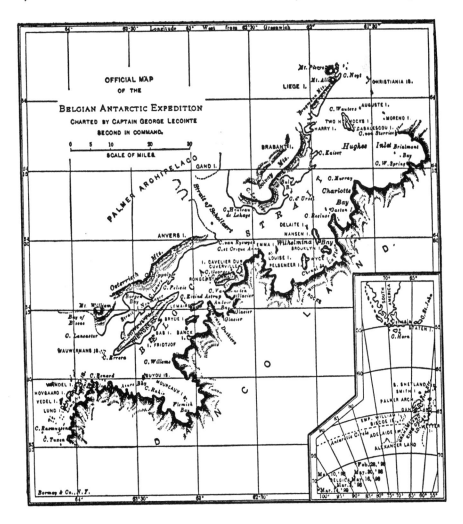

greater New York. The commandant named the strait after his ship; the archipelago that it separated from the mainland he would later name after Nathaniel Palmer, an American sealer who had sighted it in 1820.

On February 11 the *Belgica*, going dead slow in a fog, collided with a small berg, damaging the bowsprit and dislodging her figurehead. The accident was a warning that she was about to leave the relatively safe waters of the strait and enter the ice-strewn Pacific.

Near the northern cape of Graham Land on those Pacific shores, a last landing was made below a spectacular projection of black, craggy peaks, which they named The Needles. Cook and Arctowski reached the snow-free beach beneath them at 10 A.M. and started up the steep, rocky slopes to a little ridge running at right angles to the base of the crags. Once across the inclined plane of snow that led to The Needles' rocky wall, they found that, despite their formidable appearance, the numerous joints and blocks on their faces made climbing them relatively easy. At 300 feet they passed through a belt of mist and stood beneath a perfectly blue sky. The black rocks above the mist had absorbed the intense sunlight and were clear of snow. Looking down, all was lost in the mist bank, which formed a perfectly smooth gray sea below them, on which no ship, not even the *Belgica*, sailed.

The Needles, Antarctica.

As the bark passed out of the strait and coasted southward along the great expanse of Graham Land, Cook found the unknown simply too stimulating and came on deck at all hours, trying to pierce its mysteries:

> The night is of special interest to me. There is something about the air, the water, the ice, and the land, which fixes my attention and makes sleep impossible. There is a glitter in the sea, a sparkle on the ice, and a stillness in the atmosphere, which fascinates the soul but overpowers the mind. There is a solitude and restfulness about the whole scene which can only be felt; it cannot be described. Here, to the east, the face of the mysterious land is clothed by the successive sheets of snows of the sleeping years of countless silent centuries. About us are scores of icebergs, huge table-topped, pyramidal, and castle-like masses, fragments of this same unknown blanket of accumulated snows which clothes every aspect of antarctic land.
>
> Out of the unfathomed blackness of the ocean to the west rise a series of heavy mouse-colored clouds, with their cargoes of vapor, which sail over us in a regular train to deposit their snows on the unscaled heights of the overland sea of ice eastward; under the stream of vapor floating landward there is an occasional puff of icy wind rolling down the stupendous white heights of Grahamland, which suddenly chills the air about us and renders it incapable of suspending its charge of humidity. As a result, there is either an occasional shower of snow or a bank of fog which, for a time, veils the electric splendor of our chilly fairyland.[8]

The bark now entered the outskirts of the antarctic pack—loose and rounded floes, easily pushed aside. Then an onshore wind sprang up and she was in danger of being nipped by the pans and icebergs being squeezed toward the shore. For the first time, the explorers were briefly immobilized by the icy embrace of the Antarctic, with the wild sweep of the high peaks of Graham Land visible to the east for short periods through the persistent high fog.

Approaching the coast whenever the pack allowed, the *Belgica* cautiously picked her way south. Then, without warning, the ship was once more in danger. White crests appeared all around her. She was caught in a hidden circle of rocks, and a current rushing over the reef so taxed the ship's feeble engine she could barely make progress against it. The penguins and gulls seemed to be screaming premonitions of danger as the ship slowly brushed by a stranded iceberg and escaped into the deeper waters beyond.

Leaving the land astern, the *Belgica* crossed the Antarctic Circle and sailed out into the open Pacific on February 15. The men, long sheltered by the numerous islands among which they had passed, now felt the sea's unbroken expanse roll uncomfortably beneath them and experienced violent attacks of seasickness.

The bark now looked the part of an antarctic expedition vessel, her rigging and masts encased in a glassy mail of accumulated frozen spray, her decks so coated with ice that it was difficult to even stand upon them.

By evening only an iceblink indicated the proximity of land to the northeast. Except for a brief sighting of Alexander Island on February 16, the only solid things the men would see to break the monotonous expanse of ice-encrusted sea were the hundreds of icebergs, flat-topped and immeasurable, glistening above the pack.

Coasting southwestward along the pack's edge, the ship was constantly buffeted by the ice. The grating and rasping of the smaller fragments disintegrating on the bow made sleep difficult. What to do next became a topic of debate among the officers. The season was already far advanced. Should they retreat or risk imprisonment in the antarctic pack? The commandant seemed noncommittal.

When the wind rose, the *Belgica* began to take a severe beating, so Gerlache decided to enter the pack to ride out the force of the storm. Once safely within the sheltering ice, there was enough calm for the doctor's thoughts to turn to his surroundings and to what the future might hold:

> The sky here at the edge of the pack generally remains dark at night, there is an incomprehensible metallic glow on the glassy surface of the water, and a sharp phosphoretic glitter from every spire and pan of ice. The night is a long twilight, and when the demons of storm are not hovering about it is a long, dreamy spell of joy. The inspiration of this solitude, the transcendental and indescribable something about this continued twilight from sunset to dawn, and the wine which one drinks with the wintry atmosphere raises the soul into a plane of superhuman existence. The glory of these midnight glimmers will haunt me the rest of my days. . . . The darkness, which is soon to throw the icy splendors into a hopeless, sooty gloom, is gathering its hellish fabric to cover the laughing glory of day. The sunless winter of storm, of unimaginable cold, of heart-destroying depression, is rapidly advancing. We are hoping to continue our voyage of exploration as long as possible, and when the darkness and cold become too great we expect to steal away and winter in more congenial latitudes.[9]

Still the commandant persisted southwestward, battering his ship at times and picking his way through openings as they appeared, in hopes of making discoveries along an unknown coast. But no coast could be seen; only the icebergs of every size and description marked the horizon.

With little else to do, Cook studied the human reactions to these floating mountains of ice. In them he found a lesson in the psychology of his shipmates:

It is curious that the eye generally sees what the mind intends to picture. An illustration of this point is the different forms which we ascribe to these icebergs. The Captain points to a berg, not particularly attractive to anyone, but he insists on describing upon it the face and the form of a beautiful woman, chiseled in walls of alabaster. We look, and try to be interested while Lecointe grows enthusiastic, but we see only dead white cliffs. There are some irregularities, a few delicate blue lines, some suggestive hummocks, and various dark cavities; but these we see in every berg, and with our different mental attitudes we fail to recognize the ascribed topography of a human figure. We dare not, however, admit our ignorance, for which a lack of sympathetic support, especially on a sentimental subject, would be equal to a challenge for a duel on the *Belgica*. The naturalist comes along next, he is always realistic, sometimes poetical, but never sentimental. Upon a small tabular berg there is a shapeless mass of ice-blocks, and these blocks are so piled that one cannot help but notice them. To me the thing seemed like a marble statue of England's Prime Minister, Salisbury, raised upon a huge, rounded block of granite. I heard Arctowski suggest the Egyptian Sphinx, but Racovitza insisted upon the likeness of a polar bear and some one shouted, "It moves!" At once the

picture became real, and the sailors refused to believe that it was
not a living bear. Racovitza's imagination was accepted by all, for
to doubt him was to have humorous abuse and sarcastic caricatures
heaped upon us for weeks.[10]

It now seemed evident that Gerlache had decided to spend the winter in
the pack, though he still said nothing. Although all of the scientific staff were
against the idea, none made an open objection as the *Belgica* continued to
work slowly in the direction that seemed guaranteed to entrap them.

The monotonous journey through the unrelieved whiteness by day was
enlivened by the magnificent sunsets of the lengthening nights. Frederick
Cook stood on the deck and drank deeply of the overwhelming antarctic
wilderness:

> At seven o'clock the long stratus clouds in the south-south-west,
> which were slaty in color, became fringed with a touch of lumi-
> nous gold. This increased gradually until the entire body of the
> clouds was gilded; then the sun, a great yellow ball of dull orange,
> sank under the creamy sheets of waving snows. The great fiery ball
> was only fifty seconds in passing from view, but in this time its face
> changed into at least ten distortions. There is a weird sadness in
> these faces: an expression which is singularly appropriate, because
> we know the good old luminary is quickly leaving us to brighten
> the top of the globe. She seems to feel it, for her face is like that of a
> dying mother sorry to leave her children alone in a world of haz-
> ard. The final parting, however, was more prolonged and more
> glorious than the actual presence. Soon the upper stratus of low
> clouds were showered with a scarlet light, which remained without
> apparent change for thirty minutes. Below and above this were
> narrow belts of bright and glistening silvery blue, while the ice was
> all aglow under a veil of pale magenta. Then followed a long purple
> twilight, which, in itself, is full of delightful charm. It is all an
> unimaginable dream.[11]

But would this dream turn into a nightmare? What were the commandant's intentions? Could the crew survive the rigors of winter with only four
cold-weather suits among them? Whatever the answers, it looked now as if
there was little choice in the matter. But when Gerlache finally asked them
their opinion, Dr. Cook, like the others, had reservations:

> To-night Gerlache is sounding the sentiments of all hands, upon
> their willingness to winter in the ice. . . .
>   . . . If our vessel should be lost, no relief could possibly reach us,
> because it is not definitely known where we may be found. Death
> by freezing and starvation would be our lot if our trusty ship were
> disabled, and such a possibility must always remain in view, in a

battle against the ponderous polar-ice. With this prospect before us we do not take kindly to a voluntary berth among the ever restless floes during the many weeks of sure darkness and unknowable cold.[12]

After hearing the men out, the commandant declared he would go north at once, retracing his course to Graham Land, then on to Deception Island, and from there, as the season for ice navigation ended, return to Ushuaia. Cook and Racovitza would be dropped off for the winter there, and the ship would proceed to Buenos Aires to refit and hire additional crew members for further explorations the following year, perhaps in the Ross Sea. But none of this was to be.

The last day of February, a howling storm forced the *Belgica* back into the pack for shelter, the ship and the ice running before the wind to the west. When the tempest subsided, the pack lay fractured in every direction, with tempting leads open toward the south. Now, the apparently quixotic Gerlache turned his ship in that direction.

But, in fact, this had been his intention all along. For some time the position of the ship had been deliberately misstated by Captain Lecointe. Gerlache had confided his true intentions only to him and the first mate; he hoped to emulate Nansen by locking his ship in the ice and drifting with the pack to a new "Farthest South."

The falling temperatures in the wake of the storm quickly began to cement the damage it had done, and on March 3, 1898, the Belgian Antarctic Expedition found itself frozen in for good, 1,100 miles from the geographic South Pole and 300 miles from the nearest known land. Its members' lives were now dependent on the fate of the ship and destined to drift with her over an unknown sea at the will of the winds.

Dr. Cook tried to be realistic about his situation:

> To be caught in the ice is, after all, the usual luck of polar explorers. It is a life of hardship, of monotony, and isolation, full of certain dangers and uncertain rewards. For success there awaits honorable reward, but for failure there is always ready a storm of condemnation. Our success to the present has been such that we feel proud of our work. We have seized the records to-day and hope to elaborate our observations. Everything which we have done will require careful revising, and this brings to us a new interest and a brighter promise. It serves to divert our attention from the darker side of our future.[13]

Though the doctor may have been resigned to his fate, others retained hope that they might yet break the hold of that sterile place and return to the world of men. The commandant still spoke of Buenos Aires, and there were continued efforts to free the ship. Among themselves the men suspected that these were only for show and criticized the leadership. Even so, a forced gaiety prevailed upon the imprisoned *Belgica*. From the forecastle the sounds of singing and a sailor's accordion drifted aft, where music boxes played cheerful tunes. "In spite of our disheartening prospects, fits of melancholy, and spells of fault finding, there is, in general, hearty laughter and jolly good feeling on board," noted the doctor. ". . . Even the most disheartened among us now begins to see new charms in the curious chance which may make us the first of all human beings to pass through the long antarctic night."[14]

For diversion, Arctowski, Amundsen and Cook decided to try out the pack for traveling—something they might be forced to do should the *Belgica* be crushed. The floes were small and in constant motion, and the risk of jumping between them without falling into the water made the trial an adventure. Arctowski considered the experience "a very agreeable day [that] gave us confidence in ourselves and hope that we should not lack means of amusement."[15]

The men themselves provided amusement to other denizens of the pack. Penguins would often promenade near the ship, eyeing the strange beings from the north with evident curiosity. One sailor practiced the trumpet, and whenever he gave a concert, penguins came from great distances to stand and listen to his efforts. They showed no interest, however, in the sounds made by the ship's clattering mechanical barrel organ, which was often exercised with punched cards containing national melodies and operatic airs.

As the sun began to decline, the *Belgica* was often battered by raging storms. But there were periods of calm when the doctor ascended to the barrel on the mainmast to contemplate their wintering place:

> Only two could rest in the nest at one time, and at best it is a shivery roost, but Arctowski and I resolved to enter it this morning and there spend an hour in study and philosophy. We climbed up over a series of rope ladders which were coated with an inch of hoarfrost in large crystals. The metallic jingle of these crystals made a music full of curious interest, and the gem-like glitter of the masts fired by the silvery beams, as the sun rose over the white splendor of the pack, was a sight which made us hesitate to tread on the bejewelled ropes. Arctowski entered the bottom of the barrel first and quickly kicked and pushed out the frost, sending down a cloud of ice which covered my face and sent streams of sharp crystals down my back. . . .
>
> . . . Our position at the top of the mast is like that of a bird far up under the heavens. The great ugly-looking, but vigorous, giant petrels are dashing past our heads with an air of inquisitiveness. The little dove-like white petrels come to us almost within reach of our arms, and the graceful brown sea-gulls rush over us and around us with a startling buzz. We are inclined to drift into

poetry and philosophy this morning, and everything about en-
courages this mood. . . . There is always a stimulus for an endless
series of interesting observations. It is these tempting studies
which lift the spirits above the even plane of white monotony. It is
this fresh interest in the unknown which makes life tolerable.[16]

Despite the abundant life below and above it, the pack itself seemed to
Dr. Cook to lie, as far as the eye could see, restful and motionless, covered
with the white silence of death. But actually the *Belgica* and her entire surroundings were drifting in concert to the west.

One afternoon the silence was abruptly broken. The ice cracked as pans
overrode each other all around the ship. Thumps and groans from the beams
of the *Belgica* gave voice to her torment as the ice squeezed her sides and the
ship rose a little. But by 8 in the evening the pressure relented, and the bark
settled back to equilibrium, no worse for her ordeal.

As the night lengthened, the aurora australis put in an appearance, draped
like a curtain in the southern sky. To better observe the aurora, Dr. Cook
decided to sleep out on the ice some distance from the ship:

> I had promised myself the pleasure of this experience, but for one
> reason or another I had deferred it. At midnight I took my bag
> and, leaving the warmth and comfort of the cabin, I struggled out
> over the icy walls of the bark's embankment, and upon a floe three
> hundred yards east I spread out the bag. The temperature of the
> cabin was the ordinary temperature of a comfortable room; the
> temperature of the outside air was –4° F. After undressing quickly,
> as one is apt to do in such temperatures, I slid into the fur bag and
> rolled over the ice until I found a depression suitable to my ideas of
> comfort. At first my teeth chattered and every muscle of my body
> quivered, but in a few minutes this passed off and there came a
> reaction similar to that after a cold bath. With this warm glow I
> turned from side to side and peeped past the fringe of accumulat-
> ing frost, around my blow-hole through the bag, at the cold glitter
> of the stars. As I lay there alone, away from the noise of the ship,
> the silence and the solitude were curiously oppressive. There was
> not a breath of air stirring the glassy atmosphere, and not a sound
> from the ice-decked sea or its life to indicate movement or com-
> motion. . . . Every move which I made in my bag was followed by a
> cracking complaint from the snow crust.
>
> At about three o'clock in the morning a little wind came from
> the east. . . . As I rolled over to face the leeward there seemed to be
> a misfit somewhere. . . . My hair, my face, and the under garments
> about my neck were frozen to the hood. With every turn I endured
> an agony of hair pulling . . . but aside from this little discomfort
> I was perfectly at ease, and might have slept if the glory of the

heavens and the charm of the scene about had not been too fascinating to permit restful repose.

The aurora, as the blue twilight announced the dawn, had settled into an arc of steady brilliancy which hung low on the southern sky, while directly under the zenith there quivered a few streamers; overhead was the southern cross, and all around the blue dome there were sparking spots which stood out like huge gems. . . . Finally, as the sun rose from her snowy bed, the whole frigid sea over was colored as if flooded with liquid gold. I turned over and had dropped into another slumber when I felt a peculiar tapping on the encasement of my face. I remained quiet, and presently I heard a loud chatter. It was uttered by a group of penguins who had come to interview their new companion. I hastened to respond to the call, and after pounding my head and pulling out some bunches of hair, I jumped into my furs, bid the surprised penguins good morning, and went aboard. Here I learned that Lecointe, not knowing of my presence on the ice, had taken me for a seal, and was only waiting for better light to try his luck with the rifle.[17]

Time began to be a burden for those less imaginative than the doctor. Monotony began to set in. Ways to add variety to life and direct the mind from negative thoughts were at a premium. One sailor, Henri Somers, who told tales taller than those heard in the South of France, embellished his until even the most credulous crew member refused to believe him. In the end, all stories, real and imaginative, wore thin, and thoughts began to turn to what each man missed most in the world of warmth left behind, so far to the north. The doctor decided to conduct a survey:

I have taken the trouble to make a personal canvass of every man of the *Belgica* to-day to find out the greatest complaints and the greatest longings of each. The result of this inquiry was certainly a lesson in curious human fancies. In the cabin the foremost wants are for home news and feminine society. We are hungry for letters from mothers, sisters, and other men's sisters, and what would we not give for a peep at a pretty woman? Racovitza reminds us daily that he will write a book describing life in the "Ladyless South," and we have all agreed to contribute articles to a forthcoming paper in which we shall advertise our wants. . . . In the forecastle the men are less sentimental and less inclined to poetry. They desire first some substantials for the stomach. Fresh food, such as beefsteaks, vegetables, and fruits are their foremost wants. . . . Our hatred is all heaped upon one class of men. They are the inventors and manufacturers of the various kinds of canned and preserved meats. . . . If these meat packers could be found anywhere within reach they would become food for the giant petrels very quickly. . . .

. . . The things hated most violently are kydbolla and fiskabolla; both are Norwegian concoctions of doubtful stuffs. The kydbolla is said to be a mixture of ground beef and cream, and the fiskabolla is described as a compound of fish and cream. We are, however, ungrateful enough to doubt the usual truthfulness of our Norse friends. The color and consistency of the meats and fish balls are such that no suggestion as to the composition is possible, and thus one idea after another is developed. Some prove by a plausible argument that they are the refuse of the packing-house, defibrinated, bleached, ground, and compressed. Others insist that useless dogs, cats, and what not, have been utilized.[18]

As a respite from frustrated thoughts of the pleasures of home and the shortcomings of the *Belgica*'s larder, Gerlache, Danco and Cook decided to try to reach a huge tabular berg estimated to be eight miles north of the ship.

They set off on skis and found the going fair, even though the ice was deeply crevassed. After making six miles, they noticed that the berg seemed every bit as far away as it first appeared, and since Lieutenant Danco was experiencing severe shortness of breath, they decided to return.

Though they saw no living thing on the ice, as they approached the ship they discovered the ice had a life of its own, nurtured in an inanimate crystal garden of ice flowers. "In form they are flowers, in texture they are gems," observed Dr. Cook. "They bud, if I may so express it, with the first sharp breath of winter, casting their fragile tendrils into a hundred delicate forms wherever a suspicion of humidity can be hardened with sufficient regularity and force. Upon porous young ice, adjacent to open water, is the garden spot for these curious growths. They give the finishing touch of harmony to the rough outline of the frowning cliffs of ice . . . and convert the cold monotony of the pack into a glistening field of beauty."[19]

About the *Belgica* the men busied themselves with their studies or in preparing the ship for the winter night. Danco built a triangular hut in which to make his magnetic observations, Arctowski set up his meteorological instruments on the ice, and Racovitza arranged his specimens of bird and seal parasites for study in the laboratory.

With the naturalist, Cook took an excursion to an open patch of water in which numerous seals and penguins had been reported. Racovitza shot six seals and Cook clubbed all of the penguins to death with his ski pole. "We realized the fact that it was cruel to do this," the doctor apologized, "but the calls of science and the dire needs of our stomachs made the deed absolutely necessary."[20]

On the way to the ship, Dr. Cook noticed that hauling the dead penguins on the sledge over dry snow was extremely laborious, yet if the penguins were simply dragged without support they glided easily. This led him to experiment with shoeing a sled with penguin skin, feather side out. As he suspected, this reduced friction tremendously.

As the sun waned, the sky's ever-varying and spectacular effects were a constant delight to the doctor's curious mind. At night the aurora hung in the sky like some huge, lacy drapery, and by day the sun, distorted by refraction, presented an ever-changing face. Parhelia or paraselenae were everyday occurrences, and when visible, the moon glided, huge and distorted, through the frost mist hovering at the horizon.

The calendar was watched closely to ensure that no birthday of note, no national or religious holiday of Belgium, Norway, Rumania, Poland or the United States would slip by without a feast. On April 9 a special celebration marked King Leopold's birthday:

Announcement by
The Minister of Arts, Feminine Beauty, and Public Works
GRAND CONCOURSE OF BEAUTIFUL WOMEN
Organized in the cold Antarctic, Held under the Auspices of
S.M. Artocho I. —King of the Polar Zone
and
S.A. Roald, Prince of the Kydbolla

> Lecointe, Racovitza and Amundsen, I think, were responsible for the invention. At any rate, anything suggestive of kind, tender, feminine recollections, or of love and poetry, is first championed by one of these gentlemen. It was so in the "beauty contest." For several days they had been electioneering and pointing out the special merits of the women of their choice. The pick had been made from the illustrations of a Paris journal, illustrating women famous for graces of form and manner, and public notoriety. Nearly five hundred pictures were selected, representing all kinds of poses and dress and undress, and anatomical parts of women noted as types of beauty.[21]

The contest soon boiled down to a choice between two beauties: Number 64, Cleo de Merode, and Number 209, the Princess de Chimay, the former Miss Clara Ward of Chicago. Proponents of each tried every inducement to gain the votes of the uncommitted for their choice. Lecointe was the chief advocate of the princess and argued vehemently in her favor. Racovitza was for Cleo and was just as determined to bring her to victory.

Lecointe had early on used his old friendship with his military academy classmate, Danco, and his new friendship with the doctor to secure their votes for his favorite. Lecointe solidified his side by bribing Arctowski with a couple of gigantic cork stoppers needed for his experiments. He had to be constantly on guard to keep Danco from switching his allegiance under Racovitza's intense lobbying, but in the heated arguments that lasted long into the night, Lecointe did not have to worry about Cook's vote. His total lack of proficiency in French made him incorruptible by all counterarguments. Throughout the whole evening of passionate debate, of which he couldn't understand a word, the doctor just kept shouting over and over, "209 Clara, first prize!"

The captain counted heads and loudly declared victory, to even louder cries of protest from the advocates of Number 64. Leaping to the barrel organ, he inserted the roll punched with the notes of *La Brabançonne,* the Belgian national anthem, to celebrate his self-proclaimed triumph. But in his haste he put it on backward, and the musical cacophony, mixed with the shouts in defense of Number 64 accusing him of falsifying the vote, made a frightful din.

Finally, to mollify the combatants, Gerlache uncorked a bottle of champagne and proposed a toast to all the beauties who had provided them with such a merry night.[22]

On Easter Sunday the official winners of the "beauty contest" were revealed. In the end, the vote was announced as having split evenly between the two favored beauties, but the doctor was skeptical of the outcome, if not its implications:

> It is so long since we have seen a girl that I doubt our ability to pass judgment on the charms of beautiful women. . . . The excitement of the contest has been such that a new life and a new stream of ideas are coming over our frosty spirits. To-day we talk of sweethearts, of sisters, of mothers, and of home. For a time we have forgotten the never ceasing sameness of storm-beaten pack-ice and our uncertain future. . . . We can ill afford to go into the spell of the long, unknowable night with the air of despondency which has fogged our mental energy for the past few weeks. . . .
>
> Some one has said we want only our home surroundings, some loving women, fresh food, a few flowers, and our lot will be happy. I believe this, but I also believe it is just these which are all that is required to make Hell agreeable to the average man.[23]

Now all attention turned to securing the *Belgica* against the coming blast of the antarctic winter. The embankments of snow built up around the ship to prevent heat loss by radiation were repaired and improved. The deck was roofed over to permit passage fore and aft without going outdoors, and this too was covered with a blanket of insulating snow. Double storm doors and windows were put in place, and the finishing touches were made to the captain's house in which he would make his observations of the stars to determine the ship's position.

But the largest struggles were against two factors: humidity and isolation. Each man would have to adjust as best he could to whatever the night might bring, but everyone longed for the first cold blast to dry out and dissipate the ice that accumulated on every item on which condensation could collect.

Such relief was soon in coming, as a week of storms swept over the pack in mid-April, dropping the temperature well below the freezing point. The lower temperatures relieved the problems of accumulating humidity but brought on new agonies. Dr. Cook had to make daily treatments of "burns" caused by touching metal objects in the severe cold. Lecointe lost his eyelashes to the metal eyepiece of his sextant, and one sailor who absentmindedly put several nails in his mouth while nailing down the deck lost a good portion of his lip when he tried to remove them.

With the light now insufficient to see its irregularities and numberless cracks, the pack became a no-man's-land, since one careless step might be the last a man would take. With even short excursions now unsafe, the scientists found diversion within the laboratory and the cabin. The commandant and the captain worked on their map of the *Belgica*'s discoveries, the geologist packed and labeled his stones from those newly discovered shores, and the naturalist studied and classified the spoils of the trawls made during the drift among the pack ice.

Some turned their talents toward invention. The commandant was much impressed by the enterprise of Jan Van Mirlo, who toiled to perfect a "veloci-pede sounder." It worked like an ordinary bicycle, but instead of making progress along a road, the pedaling reeled in the sounding wire, an onerous job when done by hand.

The captain noted, dubiously, the doctor's experiments with seal oil lamps to illuminate the coming polar night: "Cook puts to good use the Eskimo system: a tank full of bits of seal grease in which one pricks several wicks. This lamp gives little light, poisons the air with a nauseating odor, and occasions a true, smoky, black rain. Except for these things, it is very good!"[24]

By the last day of April, the period of storms was waning with the wester-ing sun, and the horizon was clearer than it had been in weeks. Daily, there were indications of land, but these always proved to be no more than illumi-nated clouds. Nothing had significantly changed since the *Belgica* had first been held fast by the pack in March except that the once-sterile white expanse was now littered with signs of human activity. Dots of black represented sledges, snowshoes and sundry gear. A small passage on the port side led through the wall of snow to a well-beaten path to the various outbuildings in which the scientific apparatus had been placed.

The first observation in weeks showed that the ship had drifted somewhat to the north. This, combined with the fact that the pan in which the *Belgica* was embedded seemed to be shrinking, gave rise to hope mingled with the fear that the ship might be released sometime during the lightless night but into an uncharted sea infested with icebergs.

The observations also allowed the captain to announce that the winter night of 71 days would begin at noon on May 15. No longer could the dreaded moment be diverted, and Dr. Cook and the others on board found their thoughts turning toward introspection:

The winter and the darkness have slowly but steadily settled over us. By such easy stages has the light departed that we have not, until now, appreciated the awful effect. . . . It is not difficult to read on the face of my companions their thoughts and their moody dispositions. . . . The curtain of blackness which has fallen over the outer world of icy desolation has also descended upon the inner world of our souls. Around the tables, in the laboratory, and in the forecastle, men are sitting about sad and dejected, lost in dreams of melancholy from which, now and then, one arouses with an empty attempt at enthusiasm. . . .

For six weeks we have been so intent in prosecuting the various lines of research and in preparing the bark, as well as our clothing and equipment for the winter, that we have not with sufficient interest, noticed the melancholy decline of the day. It has gone slowly, and the persistent storms have so screened the heavens that it has vanished as if by stealth. Now, however, the gloom of night which has so rapidly followed its lengthening shadow, has suddenly impressed upon our passive minds the awful individual loneliness, and the unfathomable solitude of this impenetrable antarctic wilderness.

Henceforth, for a period which is a blank in human history, the fair-haired goddess of light will repose beneath the polar star over the more hopeful arctic lands. Her pathway is no longer over the familiar hummocks and icebergs and the even spreads of this icy desert under the Southern Cross. Her silvery tresses have swept for the last time this sea of frozen wave; her departing breath has stilled, as by the hand of death, the bosom of this great body of water upon which we have cast our fortunes.[25]

CHAPTER 9

A Year, a Month and a Day

FOR TWO DAYS THE SUN REAPPEARED, REFRACTED ABOVE THE HORIZON BY THE fine ice crystals that hung in the air, but soon the only evidence of the departed day was a brightening at noon. At first this gave every evidence of sunrise, only to fade once again with magnificent color effects. Each day the men gathered to watch the last traces of sunlight and to try to fight off their increasing depression. Their doctor could not find words to express the sensations he felt. "If I could wield a brush, and lay these colors on canvas I feel that one of the ambitions of my life would be accomplished. But I cannot—and what am I to do in black, with an overworked pen, frosty ink, and a mind which is wearied as soon as the cheer of noon-day passes?"[1]

The cheerfulness Cook had noted earlier was fading with the faded sun. Not only were mental facilities depressed and failing, but physical complaints increased with the decreasing light. The close quarters on the tiny bark were beginning to tell as well:

> If we could only get away from each other for a few hours at a time, we might learn to see a new side and take a fresh interest in our comrades; but this is not possible. The truth is, that we are at this moment as tired of each other's company as we are of this cold monotony of the black night and of the unpalatable sameness of our food. . . .
>
> . . . Physically we are steadily losing strength, though our weight remains nearly the same, with a slight increase in some. All seem puffy about the eyes and ankles, and the muscles, which were hard earlier, are now soft, though not reduced in size. We are pale, and the skin is unusually oily. The hair grows rapidly, and the skin about the nails has a tendency to creep over them, seemingly to protect them from the cold. The heart action is failing in force and is decidedly irregular. Indeed, this organ responds to the slightest stimulation in an alarming manner. . . . The sun seems to supply an indescribable something which controls and steadies the heart. In its absence it goes like an engine without a governor.[2]

The most alarming symptoms were those of the physicist. Even before the sun set, Lieutenant Danco had complained of shortness of breath. An examination disclosed that he had a congenital heart condition, and now his heart seemed unable to withstand the strain forced upon even healthy hearts by the lightless days. Dr. Cook worried over him and cautioned him against excessive strain, though he encouraged the others to take daily walks on the ice or go on short ski excursions in periods of greatest light. He and Amundsen made it a practice, usually in the company of the commandant, to time their outings so that they might watch the colors from the sun's hidden disk play on the clouds at noon. By the end of the month, though, even this ceased to be a pleasure, the light in the north degenerating to no more than a feeble yellow haze.

As the night deepened, Adrien de Gerlache, while walking over the polar pack, looked back at his ship and contemplated the unreal world of his realized dreams:

> The immense plain unfolds then to infinity under the soft and sweet moonlight. The Southern Cross extends its arms of sweetly scintillating light to the sky. Here and there, icebergs raise their strange forms with ridges shivering like silver, and project behind them an immense and sad shadow, black on the whiteness of the floe. The immobile *Belgica,* the rigging stiffened by the freezing weather and covered with hoar-frost, disclosing a little life only by the light smoke which rises above the bridge, . . . takes on the aspect of a phantom ship. The sight is of a grandiose and funereal beauty; the dead stars seem to light only a world itself dead.[3]

Each man resolved to occupy himself in a regular regimen to fight off the feeling of lethargy the absence of the sun had brought upon him. Danco continued his magnetic observations despite his failing heart. The commandant vowed to rewrite the ship's log, while Lecointe resolved to work up the hydrographic studies. Racovitza and Arctowski continued working on their collections in the laboratory, while Amundsen and Cook went into a partnership to improve the traveling equipment for a long excursion over the pack in the spring.

By now, the doctor and the first mate had formed a strong bond. Amundsen often made modifications to the doctor's designs that proved valuable but rarely advanced a new idea. Cook's inspirations were limitless, ranging from seal-oil cookers and penguin-skin boots to a 12-pound, three-man tent with one pole, which could be set up by one man, even in a storm, and whose aerodynamic shape could endure all kinds of wind.[4]

In the evening, it became a habit for all the officers to gather in the common room, which they called the Union Club, after the words of the national motto inscribed on the Belgian coat of arms over its doorway: "L'Union Fait la Force." Captain Lecointe listened politely to Dr. Cook's wide-ranging and idealistic ideas. In one discussion the doctor advanced the belief that Europe would unite and that the United States and South America would form a

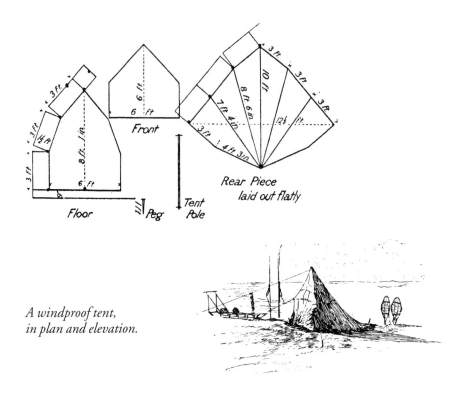

*A windproof tent,
in plan and elevation.*

combine. The world would then settle down to an era of universal peace, he predicted. The captain thought Cook's prophecy naively unrealistic. "One has to find oneself in the Antarctic to believe in the realization of such a semblance of utopia," he remarked; "the extinction of hate and suppression of jealousies, indifference for gold, Universal Peace, what! . . . with or without an international conference at the Hague!"[5]

Gerlache ordered a daily routine to regulate activities without reference to periods of lightness or darkness. But in the sunless environment, Cook and the other men found this schedule difficult to keep:

> There is no dawn,—nothing to mark the usual division of night and morning until nearly noon. During the early part of the night it is next to impossible to go to sleep, and if we drink coffee we do not sleep at all. When we do sink into a slumber, it is so deep that we are not easily awakened. Our appetites are growing smaller and smaller, and the little food which is consumed gives much trouble. Oh, for that heavenly ball of fire! Not for the heat—the human economy can regulate that—but for the light—the hope of life.[6]

Hope of life for Emile Danco was now all but gone. On May 20 Dr. Cook ordered him to stop work, fearing he might develop pneumonia, and forbade him to leave the ship. The physician broke the sad news to Gerlache: the end for Danco was just a matter of time. Gerlache was heartbroken; the lieutenant was his favorite of all the officers.

On June 1 Danco took to his bed and no longer accepted food except for a little condensed milk. He kept up a brave front, talking of the return of the sun and how much he wished to see land again. He would climb to the crow's nest to watch for it when he was better, he declared. Soon, all he could stomach was a little orange juice. The doctor kept vigil over him in a cabin where two candles burned. But Danco continued to slip until Cook had to administer morphine to make him more comfortable.

Because he could not speak French, Dr. Cook implored Captain Lecointe to say some encouraging words to his patient. At first the captain could find none; he felt as if his heart were caught in a vise as he watched Danco slowly open and close his eyes and try to speak. Danco had no relatives—no one whom he could invoke to the lieutenant to encourage the hope of his seeing them again—so he spoke of their days together at the military academy, and their comrades in the regiment. Though ever cheerful, Danco lasted only until June 5.

Dr. Cook tried to console the commandant by saying that even in Belgium the lieutenant would not have lived more than a few years longer. There, he said, he would have died without glory; it was better this way. This appealed to Gerlache's military sentiments and mitigated his grief. "Here," he agreed, "he fell a valiant soldier on the field of honor. . . . He had not only put to the service of the Expedition his intelligence and his life, . . . but he had given to it his entire heart, . . . so well made for absolute devotion."[7]

The body, wrapped in a Belgian flag, lay in state as the crew filed past to pay their last respects in the darkened death chamber. Gerlache consulted with Dr. Cook about freezing the lieutenant's body so that it could be returned to Belgium, but Cook thought this impractical, and depressing for the crew.

A burial in the ice was decided upon instead, after the customary Belgian wake of two days; a porthole was opened to keep the room cold and a single candle was kept going. Lecointe was on watch beside the body of his friend when he heard a quiet knock at the door. It was Max Van Rysselberghe, the second engineer, clutching a bouquet of dried flowers in his hand. He explained that his mother had given them to him just before he had left on the *Belgica.* He had promised her he would never part with them, but under the circumstances, he felt relieved of his obligation and asked that they be accepted for Danco's funeral.[8]

Danco's burial on June 7 was a somber affair set in the dark antarctic wastes. The effect of his passing showed on every man's face as the body, sewn in a bag of sailcloth, was slowly dragged on a sledge by the crew, dressed in their suits of duck.

From the grave site, the Belgian flag could be seen fluttering from the *Belgica*'s main mast, trailing black streamers against the subdued, moonlit sky.

The burial of Lieutenant Emile Danco.

It was so cold—minus 35°—that the hole that had been prepared earlier had frozen over and the crew had difficulty in making another. Each time they succeeded, the water instantly refroze. Instead, a natural crevasse in the ice was located and they prepared for the burial. While maneuvering the sledge to the edge of the crack, one of the sailors broke through the ice and narrowly missed the fate of his comrade. With the sledge in position, despite the intense cold, all of the men uncovered their heads as Gerlache attempted to speak.

At first the commandant was so seized with emotion that he could utter no sound. Finally, he managed a few words of regret, and the signal was given to commit the body to the deep. The metal balls that had been fixed to the feet of the corpse were pushed into the sea. The sailcloth bag jerked off the sledge as if the body of Danco inside had suddenly been reanimated, which caused some of the men to recoil in instinctive horror. Their shudders continued as the bag, containing the lieutenant's body and the engineer's flowers, slowly filled with water and disappeared under the ice, which then immediately closed, as the captain thought, "to better hide its prey."[9]

The depression that had settled over the crew with the dying sun took on epidemic proportions with the death of their comrade. Some had visions of the body floating in a standing position, perhaps right under the *Belgica,* as each man asked himself if the same frigid fate would overtake him in turn.

The first day of celebration after Danco's death happened to be Dr. Cook's birthday. Lecointe made a special effort to get the officers' minds off the saddening event. He decreed that all must appear for dinner in full dress and broke out a bottle of champagne. The captain even wrote out a formal greeting to the doctor in the best English he could muster:

Docteur Cook:
I make fast the occasion from your anniversary in order to you exprime all the sympathy you suggest to me.
In proof from that friendship and because that great day, I take the engagement to mend one couple from your knit stokings.
Dixi,
G. Lecointe.
Ocean glacial antarctique, S. Y. Belgica, 10 juin 1898.[10]

The captain had spent hours preparing his note and was mortified by its reception. Cook could not understand it at all, puzzling over it for ten full minutes, but felt it his duty to respond in kind. His attempt at French was no better, producing nothing intelligible. But as he raised his glass in a sign of appreciation, the others emptied theirs and broke into a chorus of hurrahs.[11] The men shivered through dinner in their inappropriate costumes, many feeling the stiff collars and ungainly neckties something now foreign to them.

On June 22 the *Belgica* experienced the second serious pressure since she had been permanently frozen in place. As the ice squeezed against her hull and the timbers squeaked and groaned, the men were briefly roused to action, but when she settled down again unharmed, they lapsed back into lethargy.

The men's reaction to the dark days to come would be a source of study for the doctor. Gerlache began to suffer from splitting headaches; Amundsen had an irregular heart; Racovitza languished, a feeling Cook had himself. Gerlache watched his doctor watching over his men:

> Cook . . . found numerous occasions among us to prove his unfailing devotion and that he would not lose his head.
>
> This wintering had a curious effect on all: it laid bare our physical blemishes, our "vulnerable spots"; there was not one, afflicted with whatever infirmity, often unsuspected until then, who didn't suffer from it a few days. We were thus providing, in spite of ourselves, constant subjects of observation for the excellent Cook.[12]

Mental depression only compounded the physical symptoms that the doctor noticed had become widespread after Gerlache prohibited the use of penguin as food. Dr. Cook recognized these as the first signs of incipient scurvy but preferred to call the malady "polar anemia," perhaps to allay the instinctive fear all sailors had of the disease. But Amundsen was not afraid to name the curse now upon them:

> Both Dr. Cook and I . . . spent many weary hours, after the day's hard work was done, travelling for miles over the ice in search of seals and penguins, and with great labour had killed and brought to the ship a great number of each. The commander, however, developed an aversion to the flesh of both that amounted almost to a mania. He was not content only to refuse to eat it himself, but he

Hauling a penguin.

forbade any of the ship's company to indulge in it. Consequently, all of us soon got the scurvy. The commander and the captain were both so prostrated that they took to their beds and made their wills.[13]

The sinking of Lecointe's vibrant spirit was especially surprising. One day he came to the doctor resigned to die.

"Doctor, I am going," said the captain. "I will follow Danco. Here are my papers. After I pass away send these to my sweetheart in Antwerp. Death is creeping up to me from my feet. See my ankles? It's all over."

"Men are not dead until the doctor closes the eyes," Cook gently reproached him. "Captain, you are sick, but the end is not yet near. If you come under my orders will you do exactly as told?"

"Yes," said Lecointe. "I am at your mercy. Bring on the guillotine!"

The doctor summoned Amundsen to witness the order and enforce its execution: "Here is a glass of hot water. In the future your usual food and drinks will be stopped. You will eat raw meat, drink hot water and be baked before a hot blazing fire three times daily."[14]

Henryk Arctowski was impressed by the resourceful and imaginative surgeon's efforts:

> In the antarctic regions, thanks doubtless to the detestable climate, the disastrous effects of the polar night are far more marked than in the north. There is a general lowering of the system, and the heart acts feebly. Several of us developed serious symptoms, and without daily care on the part of the doctor, others would not have survived this period of darkness, though it was relatively short. One part of Cook's treatment was very effective and ingenious. Those who were most affected by deficient circulation were made to stand in a half-naked condition close to the red-hot stove, for several hours daily. In this way the action of the solar radiation was in part replaced by rays of artificial heat—in a manner admittedly primitive, but none the less beneficial.[15]

Seeing the good effects his prescription had on the captain, the commandant lifted his ban, and the doctor now prescribed penguin and seal steaks all around. Kydbolla and fiskabolla were gladly put aside, except by the Norwegians. The treatment was now standardized:

> After considerable experiment, I have abandoned drugs as an important aid. Fresh food, artificial heat, a buoyant humor, judicious

clothing, and the least possible humidity are the conditions which suggest a rational treatment. . . . As soon as the pulse becomes irregular and rises to one hundred beats per minute, with a puffiness of the eyes and swollen ankles, the man is stripped and placed close to the fire for one hour each day. I prohibit all food except milk, cranberry sauce, and fresh meat, either penguin or seal steaks fried in oleomargarine. The patient is not allowed to do anything which will seriously tax the heart. His bedding is dried daily, and his clothing is carefully adjusted to the needs of his occupation. Laxatives are generally necessary, and vegetable bitters, with mineral acids, are a decided help. Strychnine is the only remedy which has given me any service in regulating the heart, and this I have used as a routine. But surely one of the most important things was to raise the patient's hopes and instil a spirit of good humor.[16]

Now more than ever, as so many others were failing, Amundsen admired the doctor's resolve and sheer stamina:

It was in this fearful emergency, during these thirteen long months in which almost the certainty of death stared us steadily in the face, that I came to know Dr. Cook intimately. . . . He, of all the ship's company, was the one man of unfaltering courage, unfailing hope, endless cheerfulness, and unwearied kindness. When anyone was sick, he was at his bedside to comfort him; when any was disheartened, he was there to encourage and inspire. And not only was his faith undaunted, but his ingenuity and enterprise were boundless.[17]

The next victim of the polar night was not Lecointe but the ship's mascot, Nansen the cat. Before he died, his symptoms were similar to the reactions Arctowski noticed among the human inmates of the *Belgica:*

Life on board during the polar night was of great interest from a psychological point of view. One finds one's self in conditions of existence altogether abnormal, and crowded against one's fellows in an uncomfortably narrow space. Some became nervous, excitable, and sleepless, with the imagination continually wandering and dreaming. I was one of these. Others, more happily constituted, became chronically tired and indifferent; these slept much. But everybody was content to spend twelve hours a day, or more, in bed.[18]

Though doubtful himself of his prescription's efficacy at the beginning, Dr. Cook gave every evidence of his complete belief in it to encourage the men to have hope. But in the end, he was convinced that the eating of fresh meat and the baking treatments had actually helped many. "If we had not fresh meat to eat and an abundance of fuel to give heat," he recorded, "I am sure we would have an alarming mortality in less than a month. Several lives have certainly been saved by eating penguins, and we shall always owe them a debt of gratitude. And now the sun, though invisible, is rising higher and higher under the horizon, giving us a long dawn from nine until three o'clock."[19]

On July 4 Dr. Cook's flag was run up the masthead in honor of the day, as the wind blew in briskly from the west. The light, now perceptibly brightening, stimulated plans among the few able-bodied for a journey to a great tabular iceberg that had been their companion in the pack since May.

Cook, Amundsen and Arctowski, who had worked up an enthusiasm for the adventure, started off on skis in a temperature of –22°. The trip of only two miles caused considerable difficulty, since all surface irregularities seemed to disappear in the twilight. Arctowski examined the changes the winter had caused in the berg. There seemed to be no evidence of its buildup through accumulated snowfall; rather, it seemed that ice pressure from the prevailing westerly winds had much reduced its bulk. The only life noted on the pack was one emperor penguin, which was added to the larder. The dim and diffuse light hugely distorted size and distance, making the regaining of the ship seem a herculean task.

Even in the dark months, Cook continued experimenting with his cameras. One still, moonlit night he went onto the ice and set up his tripod to expose

The Belgica *in the moonlight. Photograph by Cook.*

a plate for 90 minutes, producing a remarkably detailed photograph of the *Belgica* frozen in the pack, her masts and spars sparkling with their load of frost, their reflected light making the ship appear to be at the center of an illuminated halo.

During the polar night one initially small problem became a growing menace. As the *Belgica* lay coaling at Punta Arenas, some rats with an adventurous spirit had taken passage for the polar regions. With Nansen the cat gone, despite the intense cold below decks, they had prospered by eating the indispensable stores and making nests in the valuable equipment. By midwinter there were so many that they held large mass meetings—"witches' sabbaths," Gerlache called them—on the deck during sleeping hours. The commotion they caused kept the men awake. The stowaways even invaded the sleeping quarters, seeming to single out Cook and Racovitza for particular attention, running over them as they lay asleep in their bunks. The two determined to go on the offensive.

The doctor fashioned long paper cones, which he placed with the pointed ends into the corners of the room. Under a counterattack, the rats would try to escape down the cones. Cook would then spring on the cone and wad up the open end while Racovitza beat the trapped rodent to death with a stick. In this fashion they managed to win back their bunks but made little dent in the overall rat population of the ship.[20]

In the depths of the dark night, a little incident did much to lift the flagging spirits of the expedition's two ailing leaders. On July 13 Gerlache found a small box marked "Open on Christmas Day," which had somehow escaped notice. He showed it to Lecointe, and both men felt something they had not felt in a long time. They savored the intense curiosity aroused by this unexpected little surprise. Carefully opening it, they found inside two smaller packages, one addressed to each of them. Removing the wrapping, each beheld a superb silver pencil case inscribed "Christmas on the Antarctic Sea— Souvenir of L.O." and engraved with the arms of Anvers, which bore the motto *Audaces fortuna juvat*—Good fortune favors the bold. They were from the expedition's patroness, Léonie Osterrieth. The men were thrilled with the little gifts and more thrilled that they had not found them at Christmastime.[21]

By July 21 Captain Lecointe was up and about again and had joyous news. For some time the ship had been drifting north and eastward, and because of this he predicted, based on his celestial observations, that the sun would appear to rise the next day if favored by sufficient refraction. Dr. Cook knew this would do more for the men than any of his efforts had. With his encouragement, the next day before noon, the sun worshipers were out on the ice in hopes of a view of the long-lost home star:

> I am certain that if our preparations for greeting the returning sun were seen by other people, either civilized or savage, we would be thought disciples of heliolatry.

Every man on board has long since chosen a favorite elevation from which to watch the coming sight. Some are in the crow's nest, others on the ropes and spars of the rigging; but these are the men who do little travelling. The adventurous fellows are scattered over the pack upon icebergs and high hummocks. . . . The northern sky at this time was nearly clear and clothed with the usual haze. . . . Precisely at twelve o'clock a fiery cloud separated, disclosing a bit of the upper rim of the sun.

All this time I had been absorbed by the pyrotechnic-like display, but now I turned about to see my companions and the glory of the new sea of ice, under the first light of the new day. Looking toward the sun the fields of snow had a velvety aspect in pink. In the opposite direction the pack was noticeably flushed with a soft lavender light. The whole scene changed in color with every direction taken by the eye, and everywhere the ice seemed veiled by a gauzy atmosphere in which the color appeared to rest. For several minutes my companions did not speak. Indeed, we could not at that time have found words with which to express the buoyant feeling of relief, and the emotion of the new life which was sent coursing through our arteries by the hammer-like beats of our enfeebled hearts. . . .

. . . A few minutes after twelve the light was extinguished, a smoky veil of violet was drawn over the dim outline of the ice, and quickly the stars again twinkled in the gobelin-blue of the sky as they had done, without being outshone, for nearly seventeen hundred hours.[22]

The rising of the sun raised some hopes as well, but much to Cook's disappointment, most of the men's spirits remained low. Amundsen marveled at the doctor's persistence in spite of this discouragement. "Cook's behaviour at this time won the respect and devotion of all," he remembered long after. "It is not too much to say that Cook was the most popular man of the expedition, and he deserved it. From morning to night he was occupied with his many patients, and when the sun returned it happened not infrequently that, after a strenuous day's work, the doctor sacrificed his night's sleep to go hunting seals and penguins, in order to provide the fresh meat that was so greatly needed by all."[23]

Amundsen and Cook continued to make plans for a long excursion as soon as light was sufficient. The original plan of a polar party wintering at Cape Adare while the *Belgica* lay over in Australia had been abandoned with the entrapment of the ship. But now, to keep the men's minds active, Gerlache revived the possibility of an expedition to the magnetic pole while he explored the coast of Victoria Land and perhaps penetrated the Ross Sea with his ship, should they break free in early summer. As preparation for this, a long trip across the ice pack was proposed to harden the men and perfect the equipment.[24]

Amundsen, Cook and Lecointe would make the attempt. They rejected the clothing cut to Nansen's pattern, wondering how he and his companion had made their long journey in such suits, as in even a short ski run the wearer found himself drenched with perspiration. They rated the Eskimo pattern far superior and resolved to experiment with nothing else. The tent Cook had designed was now complete, and they were eager to give it a thorough test.

They decided to make a trial run to an iceberg some miles distant. Gerlache allowed them to select anything they wished from the ship's stores, and the travelers chose things they more craved than needed, including butter, chocolate and fruit. Their sledge, tent and bundles of food, fuel and furs were tossed onto the snow. Then they climbed down to begin the first extended journey across the antarctic pack.

After receiving the cheers of their comrades, the captain ceremoniously draped around Cook's neck the "Cross of the Commander of the Order of the Kydbollers" and pinned the cross of the officer of the same "order" to Amundsen's fur suit:

> These two jewels have been chiseled by Van Rysselberghe: they consist of a brilliant sign, ten centimeters in diameter, made from the bottom of a can, whose front bears the image of a royal penguin with this inscription: "Rapidity! Deprivations!" and on the back: "Scientific Expedition across the ice floe—July 30, 1898."[25]

Once under way, the doctor almost immediately felt the debilitating effects of the long polar night:

> Physically we believed ourselves in fine trim. Every moment of sunlight had been used by us for exercise. We had been on a forced diet of penguin meat, and had undergone the baking treatment to bring our strength to the maximum. We were, however, far from normal, though our ambitions, like the spring flow of rivers, were no longer to be confined to ordinary bounds. Our real difficulty began when we left the large old fields to cross the young ice of leads. Here were huge ridges of pressure-lines all nearly impassable, and the little valley-like spaces between covered by beds of dry snow in very small crystals, over which a sledge runs about as easily as over sand. . . .
>
> At a distance of about a mile from the ship we stopped to take compass bearings of her and the surrounding icebergs for landmarks. The scene here was a picture for the gods. In the north the sun, a great yellow ball of fire, was gliding westward along the horizon, laying beams of gold on the endless sheets of white of the

pack. The moon, nearly full, a bright globe of frosted silver, floated high in the eastern heavens. . . .

Before us, apparently within gunshot, was our destination, the great tabular iceberg, its deceptive nearness urging us on to action, and offering us the hope to be able to camp in the lee of it before night. But in reality it was not less than sixteen miles away. Behind us was the little *Belgica,* the only speck of human life in this rolling sweep of the great south frigid zone. How little and insignificant she seems amid these huge sheets and mountains of ice![26]

Sailing a sledge.

The trio of explorers struggled on across the pack hauling the 270-pound sledge load, with Cook leading and picking the course toward the iceberg without its ever appearing to draw nearer. The going was very slow with much rough ice until they came to the shores of a frozen lake, over which they made splendid progress when they erected a sail on the sledge to gain the wind's assistance. At 3 P.M. they reached the edge of an impassable crevasse, so they picked an old floe and put up the new tent in three minutes.

Once inside, Lecointe complained of a lack of sensation in one foot. Cook examined it and declared the foot frozen due to the narrowness of Lecointe's shoes. He then began to rub it so vigorously that the captain cried out. But his cries only made the doctor smile because they showed the foot still had some feeling in it. There was no need, he told the horrified Lecointe, to amputate it.[27]

The temperature dipped to −31°, but inside the tent it was much more comfortable, since they had lit the cooker to prepare the evening meal. Cook found the apparatus designed by the polar explorer Frederick Jackson severely wanting in efficiency:

> It took us about two hours to thaw out some penguin steak, and two more to make a soup which has the enchanting name of *"bonne femme."* In this we managed to mix a liberal supply of reindeer hair, penguin grease, and other flavoring material. The soup was a failure, —but not quite so much so as the chocolate prepared shortly after. This was made in a can in which the penguin steak had been warmed. It contained, besides chocolate, milk and sugar, much butter, penguin oil, blood, and pieces of fishy meat, some *"bonne femme"* soup, and reindeer fur. Lecointe, who had the honor of having the first cup, received besides the major quantity

of oil, the lighter floating material. He pronounced it "scandalous!" But the other victims who tried it praised its nutritious qualities very highly. After our feed we stowed ourselves away in our bags, falling on each others' stomachs, as our efforts to reach the bottom failed. Finally we went to sleep while the wind roared and the snow dropped on our tent, making a sound like bits of metal; a music which, when comfortably stowed in our bags, proved restful and conducive to sleep.[28]

Altogether, it had been a very tiring day. Still, Roald Amundsen had thoroughly enjoyed himself; he had entered his school of polar technique. "It is a pleasure to make excursions with the company that I had," he wrote in his diary that night. "Lecointe; small, cheerful, witty; never losing hope. Cook, the calm and imperturbable never losing his temper; and in addition, there are the many small things one can learn in the society of such a thoroughly practical Polar explorer like Cook. In his contact with the North Greenland Eskimos, and in his profound study of everything concerning Polar life, he has, without doubt, greater insight in these matters than most men in the field. . . . He has advice on everything. He gives it in a likable and tactful manner; not with fuss and noise."[29]

The next morning they struggled into their frozen furs filled with ice dust, noted that their watches had all frozen during the night, and set off again for the still-distant iceberg. To make better time, they abandoned the sledge, but they soon were stopped by a wide-open channel and decided to build a snow house and wait for the lead to freeze over. The igloo was very comfortable with the sail spread on the floor, and as the silvery rays of the moon filtered through the chinks in its roof, they read and played cards by the light of a candle. Before retiring, Lecointe went outside and thought the opposite view of the candle within the translucent ice walls an even more enchanting effect, reminding him of the cold fire of an opal.[30]

August 2 dawned foggy, and if anything, the lead before them seemed to be widening. Fearing they might lose the position of the ship, they prepared to return to her safe haven. By nightfall they found themselves in an area of small pans and had to pitch the tent on one of these relatively unstable ice cakes and wait for first light. All night long their little pan cracked and groaned as it was forced against the others; the men took turns at watch as a precaution against a complete disintegration of the floe without warning.

In the morning it was still foggy. On board the *Belgica* there had been much worry about the three ice travelers, and a lookout had been fixed to watch for them. One of the sailors, spotting the tent, made a valiant effort to reach it but had to return after breaking through the ice in several places.

Seeing the low-lying fog, Cook told the others simply to go back to sleep and await better conditions. It was nearly noon when they started out on a desperate attempt to reach the ship, just one mile distant. They took only enough food and baggage to establish one more camp, and by using the sledge to bridge small leads, they made good progress. At 2:00 they climbed aboard a vessel that seemed larger and more luxurious than when they had left her.

The weather had actually been exceptionally good while the men had been on the ice. As they had with the decline of the sun, almost unceasing tempests and surprisingly cold weather accompanied its return. On September 8 the lowest temperature of the entire stay in the ice was recorded, −45°, and during October it snowed 25 days of the month.

Despite the trials of the polar night, now that it had ended, the doctor could still not help putting in a few good words for it:

> We have talked only of the discomforts of the night, and of the misery. The long unbroken darkness has not totally blinded us to its few real charms which are strikingly brought out by the awful contrasts of heat and cold, of light and darkness. As lovers of Nature, we found many pleasures for the eye and the intellect in the flashing aurora australis, in the play of intense silvery moonlight over the mountainous seas of ice, and in the fascinating clearness of the starlight over the endless expanse of driven snows. There was a naked fierceness in the scenes, a boisterous wildness in the storms, a sublimity and silence in the still, cold dayless nights, which were too impressive to be entirely overshadowed by the soul-despairing depression. The attractions of the polar night are not to be written in the language of a people who live in a land of sunshine and of flowers. They are found in a roughness, ruggedness, and severity, appreciated only by men who are fated to live in similar regions, on the verge of another world, where animal sentiments take the place of the finer, but less realistic human passions.[31]

The men of the *Belgica* had waited for the night to pass, and now they must wait some more for the summer to thaw the ice. There seemed no end to the waiting or trying to find ways to fill up the time. With his patients better, the doctor's restless mind turned to other problems. He determined to make a boat of sealskin for crossing open leads on excursions, but the idea got no response until he declared the work "scientific." The captain then thought it best that he be given some old boards and sealskin; otherwise, "if one would allow him, he would saw for his famous boat, the table, the library, and the armoires."[32]

Little housekeeping tasks brought with them both frustrations and amusement. Washing clothes was particularly onerous, and various crew members found unique alternatives. Antoni Dobrowlski, the meteorologist's assistant, tried hauling his soiled underwear up the masthead, hoping snow and cold would freshen things up, but he soon learned that weather had no cleansing power. Dr. Cook just rotated through his underwear with a change every eight to ten days, achieving at least an illusion of cleanliness.[33]

Frederick Cook and Roald Amundsen aboard the Belgica.

The doctor presided as the ship's barber and took great delight in wielding the shears. He would cut the hair off only one side or in odd shapes, then pronounce the operation finished and laugh at the passionate and vehement protests from his Belgian customers before evening things out. He himself escaped retaliation by never having his hair cut, allowing it to grow down to his shoulders and binding it up with a ribbon in the front. Arctowski was not far behind in the length of his locks, and Gerlache thought the pair's appearance had taken on the aspect of two apostles. Racovitza's hairstyle was some-what shorter, reminding the commandant of the brushes called "wolf-heads" that were used to clean the cobwebs from ceilings in Belgium.[34]

Laughter was now more often heard in the men's cabins. But as the dark-ness was relieved by the coming of the sun, new torments took its place. The wind seemed to blow constantly from the north and west, and though the sky remained clear, the atmosphere at the surface of the pack was filled by a dense haze of wind-driven frost crystals that hung to the level of the mastheads and stung the skin as if it were being rubbed with emery paper. Though there was now sufficient light, it was not the direct light of the sun, but only this frosted haze that obscured all variety on the pack. By November the light once so longed for seemed oppressive. Insomnia prevailed in a suddenly too-bright world, and men sought relief by hanging black cloths at the windows to simu-late the once-hated darkness.

Most seriously, a crisis of command had developed over the disclosure that when Gerlache had made his will, he had designated that should he and Lecointe die, second mate Jules Mélaerts, a Belgian, would assume command, superseding Amundsen.

Gerlache tried to explain that he had done this because of prior agree-ments he had signed in Belgium, but Amundsen took it as an insult to his honor and officially resigned, although he agreed to continue to execute his duties. "A Belgian Antarctic Expedition no longer exists for me," he wrote to Gerlache. "I see in *Belgica,* an ordinary vessel, beset in the ice. My duty is to help the handful of men gathered on board. For that reason, Captain, I con-tinue my work as if nothing had happened, trying to do my duty as a *human being. . . .*"[35]

With the arrival of summer, all thoughts turned toward an escape from the ice. Since her final imprisonment in May, the pan in which the *Belgica* lodged had changed little. Lecointe estimated that the ship had drifted close to 2,000 miles, but since the drift had been first to the west, then to the east, she had made little real progress from her starting point.

Now measurements showed that the thickness of the pan seemed to be diminishing rapidly. In October lanes of open water had approached within 300 feet of the ship. Gerlache had then ordered the *Belgica* placed in readiness to escape when the first opportunity presented itself.

Amundsen and Cook resolved to make one final attempt on the coveted berg, which had slowly drawn closer to the vessel. Hoping to reach it in a sin-gle day, they took no provisions, tent or sleeping gear.

Just after leaving the ship, they came upon one of the sailors, Adam Tollefsen, who had become mentally unbalanced during the winter, wander-ing on the ice. They thought it best to take him along rather than risk his not being able to return to the ship by himself.

With only what they could carry on their backs, they advanced seven miles with ease in three hours, killed and cached some seals in case of emergency, and then took on the much-broken-up last two miles fronting the object of their desire. Finally gaining the base of the berg, they ascended its icy ramparts. A superb view rewarded them from its top, including 75 huge, white icebergs and the tiny *Belgica* adrift in a vast expanse of blue-tinged ice.

Regaining the ship proved much harder: the pack had been greatly disturbed in their absence. They were without supplies and famished when Amundsen killed a seal. Quickly he cut the seal's throat and drank the warm blood, as did Dr. Cook. Amundsen beckoned to Tollefsen to hurry lest the blood congeal. The sailor was horrified and refused. It took the three until 4 A.M. to reach the *Belgica*.

Once on the bark, Tollefsen fainted and was taken to Lecointe's room and given a glass of alcohol. He then began to accuse Lecointe of trying to poison him, and after being persuaded to eat some buttered bread, he began to rave, saying that he had been taken on the excursion in the hope that it would kill him. Tollefsen soon sank into depression and before long his mind totally snapped. A constant watch was kept lest he harm himself or others.[36]

For Christmas, the officers planned a surprise visit to the crew in the forecastle. Gerlache took cigars and clothes; Racovitza, cigarettes; Cook distributed slides made from his photographs; and Lecointe gave each man a bonus check that he could cash when they reached Australia. The presents made the sailors forget for the moment the seriousness of their predicament.

But New Year's Day is a time for taking stock, and when 1899 arrived, Cook, like all the rest, had to look squarely at the grim prospect that the ship might be entrapped a second winter. The bright days of November and December had done nothing toward breaking the pan, which now seemed as thick as ever, and the weather was again beginning to turn colder:

> If we do not help ourselves, as matters go now there is a great possibility of wintering again in the pack. To do something in this direction, I submitted, yesterday, a plan to the Commandant. It is based on the fact that the sun acts much more powerfully upon water, and upon everything else of a dark color, than upon snow. Keeping this in mind, my suggestion involves the digging of two trenches, one from the bow, the other from the stern to the water, at the edge of the *Belgica* field. These trenches are to be carried through the snow and the superficial fresh water sheet of ice, leaving a narrow current of water from the ship to the lead, which we hope by the aid of the sun will so weaken the ice in this direction that it may break in this line.[37]

Using picks, axes and shovels, the trenches were finished by January 12, but the project failed, since the sun was not strong enough at midnight to keep the water introduced into them during the warmest part of the day from turning to ice. Undaunted, Cook came forward with another plan. Roald Amundsen thought it quite insane:

One day, somebody in the party noticed that the melting ice had formed a small basin of water about a thousand yards from the ship. The rest of us thought nothing of it, as naturally water would form here and there. Somehow, though, to Dr. Cook's restless mind this basin seemed an omen of hope. He declared his firm conviction that the ice would break, and that, when the opening came, it would lead to this basin. Therefore, he proposed what sounded at first like a mad enterprise: that we should cut a channel through the thousand yards of rough ice to the basin and float the *Belgica* through it, so that, if the crack came, the ship could take immediate advantage of it.

I say it seemed a mad undertaking for two reasons: first, the only things we had on board to cut ice with were a few four-foot saws and some explosives; secondly, most of the men were wholly unused to this kind of work and were weak and emaciated. Nevertheless, Dr. Cook's confidence prevailed—at least it would give us something to do besides sitting and contemplating our probable fate. All hands, therefore, turned out, and the enterprise began.[38]

Experiments made with sawing the ice along the route of an old fault suggested by the doctor showed places too thick for the length of the saws. The commandant then proposed a different route, much longer, curving away from the stern. Cook argued stubbornly for his route, but when further experiments showed the longer route to be covered with much thinner ice, he reluctantly agreed, then threw himself into the work.

Sawing the canal through the ice.

At first, great faith was placed in using tonite, supposed to have greater power than dynamite, to blow the ice to pieces. The *Belgica* had more than 2,200 pounds aboard, but in low temperatures the explosive proved very ineffective. The stuff became a joke, some suggesting it might be better used to get up steam. But as the temperature rose, its effectiveness increased.

Still, the canal had to be largely cut by hand with ice saws. The men took ten-minute turns at the handles that pulled the saw chains attached to weights below the waterline. Arctowski, who loved to talk, sometimes would get so carried away by the subject on which he was holding a discourse that he would continue well past the end of his shift. At such times others awaiting their turn took care not to interrupt and would pretend not to notice the time.

No one, from the commandant to the cabin boy, was spared from the work, excepting the cook; since the labor developed enormous appetites, some men consumed seven meals a day. As the first mate attested, it was back-breaking labor that ended in heartbreak as well:

> With the saws, we cut triangular lines in the ice and then applied a stick of tonite to blow the cakes loose. We found that the cakes had a tendency to cling to the edges in spite of the explosive. Dr. Cook then invented an ingenious scheme of cutting off one point of the triangle, which had the effect of freeing the cake at the time of the explosion.
>
> Weary weeks we spent at this labour, but finally the job was done, and we went to bed one night planning to tow the ship to the basin the following morning. Imagine our horror on awakening to discover that the pressure from the surrounding ice pack had driven the banks of our channel together, and we were locked in as fast as ever.[39]

On January 30 the ice had split exactly along the old fault that Dr. Cook had suggested as a route for a passage to the lake of clear water. Now, as the ice drifted westward, it closed the canal, and the *Belgica* found herself in a dangerous position— still frozen in at the apex of the V-shaped pan created by the canal and the open lane along Cook's suggested route. The *Belgica* could not escape in either direction and might well be crushed by the ice pressure instead.

With this possibility before them, the men began work on a large sledge on which a skiff could be manhauled to the edge of the open sea should the ship be lost. From the edge of the pack, they might be able to sail to South America, and

Gerlache ordered rations that would last until April 15, 1900, to be placed in the boat.

When the ice pressure eased on the ship, attention returned to other ideas that might redeem the men's hard labor. One plan involved setting up a winch on the opposite side of the lake of clear water and using the dredge hoists on the ship to pull the pan back to its former position. But after considering the immense weight of the ice, this was judged an impossible feat. Instead, they made a wedge-shaped area of open water behind the ship by cutting blocks of ice and winching them up an inclined plane to ensure that the ship would be free of ice pressure.

In the process, the laborers discovered that the whole stern, including the propeller, was thickly encrusted with ice. To free it, tonite was detonated within nine to 12 feet of the ship. This risky procedure succeeded, and steam was gotten up. Another risk had to be taken in backing the ship into the wedge-shaped harbor, thus exposing her running gear to damage by the ice, but this too was successful, and the *Belgica* lay, safe for the moment, sideways in the little niche they had created for her.

By February 12 the ship sat positioned to sail forward up the canal—if it should ever open again. Escape was imperative. Dr. Cook had already told Gerlache that if the *Belgica* was compelled to stay another winter in the ice, at least four more men would surely die. But just as it seemed hope was gone, suddenly, the next day, the ice went to pieces.

The *Belgica* was maneuvered gingerly astern, and at 3 A.M. on February 15, she was towed forward into the lake. When this had been accomplished, Roald Amundsen, like all the other men, felt an exhilaration mixed with pessimism:

> Now that we were there, we seemed no nearer escape than before. Other weary weeks passed us by. Then the miracle happened— exactly what Cook had predicted. The ice opened and the lane to the sea ran directly through our basin! Joy restored our energy, and with all speed we made our way to the open sea and safety.[40]

They did not get far before they were trapped again, but this time in sight of open water. Here they were held fast for nearly a month, with the ship rising and falling on the ocean's swell. This anxious time lingered in the memory of Roald Amundsen:

> Before we could emerge into open water, we were compelled to pass between two giant icebergs, and for several days we were again held as in a vise between them. All day and all night we were subjected to a terrific grinding pressure, and the noise of ice cakes battering against our sides and splintering off incessantly was at times so loud as to make conversation trying. Here, again, Dr. Cook's ingenuity saved the day. He had carefully preserved the skins of the penguins we had killed, and we now made them into mats and

lowered them over the sides of the vessel, where they took up and largely mitigated the impact of the ice.[41]

Not until March 14, 1899—a year, a month and a day after they had entered the polar pack—did the *Belgica* at last completely free herself of the ice. During that time the meteorologist counted 257 days on which snow fell.

All sail was set for the nearest inhabited place; it lay two weeks away across storm-tossed seas. With only one glimpse of land, the bleak shores of Black Island, they reached Punta Arenas on March 28.

The place had risen in Dr. Cook's estimation since he had last seen it. "The new delights which we saw around this end-of-the-world town were surprising," he thought. "We noticed with considerable interest the worn roads snaking through grassy fields, around groups of trees to the summits of green hills. Behind us were the olive and purple waters of Magellan Strait. The harsh Cape Horn winds, which blew over the forest-covered lands, seemed soft to us; to our frozen perceptions the sweets which these winds brought seemed to combine into one joyous perfume."[42]

The *Belgica* expedition's members lost no time getting ashore. Some sailors rolled with delight on the sandy beach, though for others only a grassy patch would do. The men, so long used to the absence of solid ground, walked with a drunken attitude on the unaccustomed firmness as they strode toward the nearest hotel to reacquaint themselves with civilization.

Gerlache dispatched a telegram to the Royal Geographical Society in Brussels, whose two words, after 14 months of silence, spoke volumes: "Belgica. Adrien."

There were indeed some strange sights ashore—there were women:

> She simply stood and stared at us, and we at her, and then she gathered up a couple of youngsters nearby and rushed away from us into the house, as if we were dangerous characters. Morally hurt by this incident we went along taking some notice of the men who eyed us with considerable interest. Presently we passed a door in which two pretty girls were standing. This sight sent a new sensation through us like that of a Faradic battery. Somehow we all, at the same time, unconsciously brushed aside the year's growth of hair from our faces, and made an effort to arrange our neckties and change the set of our coats, but we were made to realize, more and more, that we looked hideous. The girls gave a sudden giggle, rushed back into the hall, and we had to content ourselves with the rustle of skirts. This rustle of the skirts of these first girls who warmed our frozen hearts would make spicy poetry if we dared to write it.[43]

After cleaning himself up at the hotel, Dr. Cook met Captain Thomas of the Grace Line steamship *Coya*. From Captain Thomas he heard about the Spanish-American War, which had been declared, fought and won since he had departed from Tierra del Fuego. The doctor asked for all the particulars with intense interest and was very grateful for a pile of old newspapers that the captain gave him, filled with all that had happened in the world during his absence.

Cook learned that the Swedish engineer Andrée, with two companions, had gotten away for the Pole in their balloon, *Ornen,* the summer he had left New York. The last message from Andrée came by carrier pigeon 49 hours into the flight. "Good progress toward the North; all goes well on board," the message read. Then there was only silence. The hollow buoy marked "North Pole" that Andrée had planned to drop as he passed over the northern axis of the earth had just turned up. It was empty.

Cook entrusted Captain Thomas with a letter addressed to Miss Anna E. Forbes to deliver when the *Coya* reached New York.[44] The doctor then retired to the hotel's dining room, where he joined the other officers in unabashedly consuming beefsteak after beefsteak as fast as the maître d' could serve them.

Looking through Dr. Cook's newspapers, the Belgians seemed most interested in a French espionage case involving a Captain Dryfus. The scientific staff discussed avidly a report that the liquefaction of air had been achieved, and they all read with amazement of the invention of wireless telegraphy.

The *Belgica* was slated to make a slow return up the coast of South America and then leave for Belgium. Some of the men who were not Belgians decided they could reach home more rapidly on their own, and some of the crew, having dry land under them, decided to stay put and never risk the sea again. Amundsen, still smarting over his demotion, refused to go back with the ship, departing with the deranged Adam Tollefsen by coastal boat for a northern port.

Cook was eager to resume his study of the fascinating Fuegian tribes and obtain the Yahgan dictionary promised to him by Thomas Bridges at Harberton. When the doctor arrived there by cutter from Punta Arenas, Lucas Bridges was very surprised to learn that the seemingly inept scientists had survived their antarctic voyage. Though Thomas Bridges had died soon after the *Belgica* had sailed from Harberton, Lucas felt himself still under obligation for his father's promise to Dr. Cook:

> We remembered how Father had given his assurance that the manuscript would be handed over when the *Belgica* came back from the Antarctic, so we now entrusted that brisk young American surgeon with the priceless dictionary and grammar, together with a great pile of papers relating to the Yahgan language.[45]

The doctor obligingly assented to Bridges's request to examine several sick natives. Bridges introduced him as *Joon,* the natives' word for a magician or wizard. Cook diagnosed one of the Indians as having a stomach tumor, and his daughter, tuberculosis of the hip, both incurable. He left Bridges a phial of opium to make them more comfortable. He also took measurements of a number of healthy Indians and pronounced the Ona a finely developed race.

While crossing the Harberton peninsula to catch his cutter back to Ushuaia, Dr. Cook asked to give some memento to Lucas Bridges in appreciation for his help. Bridges said he would like Cook's fur-lined overcoat, though the doctor protested it was much too small for him.

"I'm not so sure of that. Just let me try it on," said Bridges.

To which Cook replied with a laugh, "You're welcome, but you're twice my size. You'll never get into it."

Bridges managed to squeeze into it, though he looked ridiculous. "My Doctor!" he exclaimed joyfully. "It fits me like a glove!" Which was perfectly true.

Bridges thanked him warmly and the little vessel bore Cook away. But at once, Bridges had regrets:

> When Dr. Cook arrived back at Punta Arenas, he sent me two pairs of snow-shoes that he had used down south. They were a great improvement on my own amateur copies of the Canadian tennis-racket type, being lighter and stronger, and I was very grateful to him for such a present. . . .
>
> . . . A few days after he left Harberton, I sold the fur-lined overcoat for twenty grammes of gold, so I considered that the sack of flour I had given on his account to the Ona Indians a year before had now been paid for. As for Father's dictionary, for an irreplaceable manuscript such as that, two pairs of snow-shoes and a bottle of soothing drugs were a poor exchange.[46]

Returning to Punta Arenas, Cook found that any further anthropological studies would be severely restricted:

> During our absence in the Antarctic, the hostility between the land-grabbing sheepherders and Ona Indians of the islands became intense. Shepherds shot and killed Indians, and the Indians drove sheep by the thousand into the mountains. The sheep men, in desperation, combined interests and sent in two missionaries to act as mediators and to Christianize the savage clans. The net success of this mission was the disappearance of the divine servants. Their hats were found later, but not their bodies.
>
> In the face of this hazard it was considered prudent for me, when I returned to continue my anthropological studies, to work with military representatives and with the still friendly mission Indians of the east and south.[47]

After a month, having done what he could under the circumstances, Dr. Cook started for home, making his way slowly up the eastern coast of the continent. For several weeks he was a guest of *La Prensa* in Buenos Aires at the Principe Hotel. At the newspaper's offices he wrote several articles that he hoped to have published upon his return. His stay in the Argentine capital was pleasant, but when he reached Montevideo he found a letter waiting for him with sad news. Anna Forbes was dead.[48] She had seemed better for a time, but after seeing reports in the press that the *Belgica* was feared lost with all hands, she had taken a turn for the worse and slowly wasted away.

Upon reaching Brazil, Dr. Cook called at Bahia intending to fulfill his promise to the six friends he had seen ashore there, what seemed now a lifetime ago. He located one of the girls and learned to his shock that of all who had gathered in the tearoom of the *Coleridge* with him just two years before, of all those who had bade him come back on his journey home, she alone was still living. All the rest had been claimed by tropical fevers, and he, who had cast his fate to the terrible antarctic solitudes, had been spared.

While in Brazil, he also took sick, and when he set out across the Atlantic, he was violently ill with amebic dysentery.[49] He was still not himself by the time he arrived in New York aboard the steamer *Buffon* on June 23, 1899.

His return aroused enough interest to bring the press once more to his brother's house, where, in spite of his ill health, the doctor, dressed in mourning for his fiancée, summed up the voyage's accomplishments:

> "I think that the scientific results of this expedition were about what they were expected to be. In the first place, the expedition secured a complete series of magnetic observations, extending over an entire year; next, we were the first party to winter in the antarctic regions, and, finally, we have some valuable meteorological records and an interesting zoological collection. . . ."
>
> As an anthropologist, Dr. Cook found much to interest him during a month spent among the Cape Horn Indians. He found three tribes there—the Onas, the Yahgans, and the Alacoolufs. These three tribes are distinct in themselves and are in no way related to any of the other South American tribes. . . . Dr. Cook was surprised to learn that the Yahgans' vocabulary was one of the largest of any of the aboriginal tribes. A missionary named Thomas Bridges had compiled a Yahgan vocabulary of 30,000 words. This compilation is the result of nearly thirty years' work. The language of these Indians is made up almost entirely of nouns and verbs, with suffixes and affixes which give the exact meaning to each word.[50]

After a period of convalescence, Dr. Cook, alone again, returned to his office, whose very familiarity must have seemed strange and unnatural to him. Had it, indeed, been only an unimaginable dream after all?

CHAPTER 10

You Have Chosen the Happier Lot

DR. COOK THOUGHT IT WOULD JUST TAKE TIME TO SETTLE BACK INTO HIS OLD life after he recovered his health. But the youthful dream of being a successful doctor that had sustained the boy from Sullivan County through so many sleep-starved days was no longer enough; it had long since been replaced by other unimaginable dreams. There would now be an urge, persistent and compelling, to return to the white wastes of the world. Medicine was no longer his primary preoccupation or ambition; even to the public he was no longer simply Dr. Cook, but Dr. Cook the explorer. Drawing on his experiences and his dreams, he had begun a new occupation. He submitted the account of the expedition he had written in Buenos Aires to the *New York Herald,* which published it on July 2, 1899.

Writing, from that day forward, would be a steady source of income. He had always written casually, but now he studied writing's formalities, and taking his journal written on the *Belgica* as his sourcebook, he started on several articles. As the only man ever to winter within the polar circle of both hemispheres, he had a unique story to tell. The popular magazines fully recognized this and paid him well for his efforts. The *Century Magazine* thought enough of his work to go to the unusual expense of illustrating his articles with colored plates made from his photographs to better capture the unique antarctic landscape for its readers. The colors applied to them were vivid, almost lurid, in their intensities, just as they were in the memory of Frederick Cook.

He had given one lecture before the Arctic Club shortly after his return, but in November, armed with a set of hand-tinted lantern slides, he set out on a lecture tour of eastern cities. Wherever he appeared, his lectures drew good reviews:

> It was a wonderful story of human endurance and fortitude which Dr. Cook told, and his descriptions, with the pictures, which seemed to bring the very scenes into vision, held his audience spellbound while the lecture lasted.[1]

> Dr. Cook's lecture proved as fascinating in many ways as Nansen's narrative of his adventures in the far north.[2]

He also went to work on the Yahgan dictionary. Cook had decided that it should be transcribed from the private alphabet that Thomas Bridges had used into the ordinary English alphabet. He corresponded with Lucas Bridges for clarification of some points of confusion, making what emendations he thought were necessary, and wrote an introduction to the dictionary.[3]

With the material he had developed for his articles and lectures serving as a nucleus, the doctor soon had in prospect the making of a whole book. For this he was given an unprecedented contract by Doubleday, McClure and Company, calling for a royalty of 20 percent, and as the last year of the nineteenth century began, he bent his energies to finishing his manuscript.

His book appeared in the fall of 1900 under the title *Through the First Antarctic Night.* Its handsome dark blue-green cover was adorned with the image of a king penguin, to whom the men of the expedition owed their lives, standing on the antarctic pack. In the background lay a tiny, distant *Belgica,* a bright orange, life-giving sun rising behind her over the ice. What lay between those covers proved to be a most interesting volume.

Its many illustrations showed not only a high photographic gift but an unexpected sense of design as well. Besides the predictable polar expedition pictures, there were studies of boots and mittens; details of starfish, lichens, penguins' feet and other natural history specimens; and above all others, the breathtaking image of the moonlit *Belgica* beset in the antarctic darkness, its every feature outlined in glittering frost. The book also garnered glittering reviews.

The text's style was youthful and exuberant, yet modest, showing Cook's keen eye for detail and his fine gift for vivid and colorful description, as well as a philosophical and irrepressibly optimistic turn of mind. In the closing pages he wrote:

> In the future exploration of the south polar regions there is the prospect of universal association which has long been the golden dream of science. Indeed, just at present such international alliances are the topics of the hour. . . . Could there be a more fitting seal to this family union than a triple alliance to explore the last great unknown area of the globe? . . . The combined armies of peace could, in this way, march into the white silence, the unbroken, icy slumber of centuries about the south pole, and there collect the needful scientific spoils.[4]

Dr. Cook may have envisioned international cooperation to solve the mysteries of the icy South, but to the north there was no letup in the international competition. Captain Umberto Cagni, of Luigi Amedeo di Savoia, the Duke of the Abruzzi's expedition, had left the *Stella Polare* with the polar dawn and, on April 23, 1900, had captured "Farthest North" for the Italians—86°34'—206 miles from the Pole and 21 miles beyond Nansen's record—at the cost of three men's lives.

With his book finished, Cook again contracted with J.B. Pond to manage a lecture tour, and as before, Pond was unstinting and slightly fanciful in his promotion of the doctor:

> Dr. Frederick A. Cook . . . is personally one of the most charming of men. He is as modest and unassuming as he is accomplished, although he has succeeded in doing some things which no other man before him ever did. . . .
>
> Dr. Cook was the only American [who] ever camped and sledged on the Antarctic continent. While in these far southern latitudes, Dr. Cook, as anthropologist to the expedition, visited and described a cannibal tribe from whom no previous scientist had escaped alive. . . .
>
> . . . Among polar explorers I do not regard any one as more bold, more to be depended upon for accuracy of statement, or whose scientific training better fits him rightly to appreciate the value of each new fact discovered, than Dr. Frederick A. Cook, our fellow-countryman.[5]

Despite all this praise, the lecture tour was not particularly successful. "Here is Dr. Cook," lamented Major Pond, "the first man to set foot on the Antarctic continent. But his unique success does not create the excitement it merits. Times have so changed that it is impossible to bring this, one of the bravest of our young heroes, into public demand. Of late our people have had so much to read about and to talk about that even heroes are common."[6]

With his book in print and his lecture tour at an end, the doctor had but one bit of unfinished antarctic business. In the fall of 1899, Cook had received notice that for his services to the expedition he had been named a chevalier of the Order of Leopold I. Now came word that he had also been appointed to the *Commission de la "Belgica"* established by the Belgian king to arrange the expedition's data for publication. By accepting an invitation to go to Belgium early in 1901, he could make arrangements to have his book published in Europe as well as help with his portion of the data, consisting of a medical report and his observations of the natives of Tierra del Fuego.[7] He accepted and prepared to cross the same ocean that his humble father had crossed just a half-century before. Now, the son would return to receive a knighthood at the hands of a king and bemedalment by the scientific societies of his kingdom.

Cook sailed aboard the *Kaiser Wilhelm die Grosse* on the third day of the first month of the first year of a new century. The nineteenth century was over, and largely due to the voyage of the *Belgica*, he found upon landing that neglect of the continent at the bottom of the world was over as well. Europe was alive with a new taste for exploration in the Far South. The International Polar Commission had designated 1901 as the "Antarctic Year," and the Continent was astir with plans for voyages toward those still-unknown regions. At each of his stops, established explorers and would-be explorers were eager to seek Cook's advice and hear his experiences.

The first were in England, where his book had already been published. There he visited with the alpinists Edward Whymper and Sir Martin Conway. Whymper, who had been in Greenland long ago but was most famous as the first to ascend the Matterhorn, tried to interest the doctor in climbing mountains, but Conway, who had recently been to Spitzbergen, wanted to compare notes on equipment for ice and snow.

Cook also met Sir Clements Markham, president of the Royal Geographical Society. Markham introduced him to a young naval officer whom he had met by chance and subsequently recommended to command the British National Antarctic Expedition. Commander Robert F. Scott was planning to leave for the Antarctic that autumn in the *Discovery*. Though he had privately called the members of the Belgian expedition "a poor lot" after reading Cook's account of their difficulties in adjusting to the antarctic night, he showed much interest in what the doctor had seen and invited him back the next day. Cook, more than happy to volunteer any information that might be helpful, advised Scott on many technical matters of food and equipment learned by cold experience in both frigid zones.[8]

While Cook and Scott were talking, one of the commander's assistants, Ernest Shackleton, dropped in. At Shackleton's request, Dr. Cook went to see him at the Hotel Cecil, where they discussed polar matters late into the night.[9]

Cook next visited France, where he called at the house of Emile Racovitza, now a professor at the University of Paris. The doctor spent several pleasant days there seeing the university and the Louvre, visiting several hospitals and touring the Moulin Rouge. In Paris he also met Jean Charcot, a medical doctor like himself, bent on making his own voyage to the Antarctic.

When Cook inquired about Henryk Arctowski, Racovitza said that he had married soon after his return and was now living in Liége. He also drew the doctor's attention to a sensational story in the papers that said Arctowski had threatened to kill Cook when he reached Belgium.

When he arrived in Liége, Dr. Cook went straight to Henryk Arctowski's house to see what the trouble could be and was relieved to find that the story must have been a fantasy. Instead of being assassinated, he received a cordial reception from his old traveling companion and Madame Arctowski, an opera singer.

From Liége, Cook went on to Uccle, where Captain Lecointe resided. As a result of the voyage, he had been installed as the director of the Royal Belgian Observatory.

The meeting to organize the expedition's documents was to be held in Brussels, but arrangements at the Royal Society were not yet completed. There would be a delay of some days, so Cook decided to fill the time with a tour of Germany.

He took the train for Cologne, stopping in Bonn to tour the Zeiss lens factory. From Cologne he set out to visit Schneverdingen, the place of his father's birth. Arriving by rail in Hamburg, the doctor then continued in a rickety two-horse hack toward his destination 20 miles to the south. There he hoped to inquire whether anyone remembered his family.

In Schneverdingen he found one old man who did. He pointed Cook in the direction of a white house with a straw roof—the only wooden house in the town—as the one that had been built by Theodor Koch's family. But when the doctor knocked at the door, the family occupying it said they had no knowledge of the Kochs.

The weary traveler checked into the town's hotel, a three-story house with a store on the main floor. There he obtained a room for 2½ marks—the equivalent of 50 cents—which also entitled him to three meals and unlimited beer.

In the boarding room he sat with several diners who were drinking black coffee and eating black bread from a common dish. He could hardly make himself understood in Schneverdingen, since the townsfolk all spoke in a dialect of Low German, but little by little he got his questions across. Finally, one of the men got up and brought in someone who had been to America and knew some English. The language barrier bridged, Cook learned that some of his family yet lived in Schneverdingen, and that in fact, the aged sister Theodor had left so long ago still resided there.

Schneverdingen was a factory town; fully half its residents worked at making low leather shoes with wooden soles. Looking out on the town from his hotel window, the doctor may have considered the curious chances of life, especially how a man from a town so provincial could produce a son who had been to such far-flung places. Had not his father decided for America, he must have thought, he might be right at home here taking black bread without butter from the large wooden dish at the center of the plain table, content to trudge to work each day in the shoe factory, for surely no one ever thought of Antarctica in Schneverdingen.

Cook made his way next to Berlin, where he met yet another explorer interested in his polar experiences. Erich von Drygalski, a professor of geography at the university there, like Cook had been inspired by a visit to Greenland to lead an expedition into the Antarctic. His plan was to go south from Kerguelen Island in a special ship, the *Gauss,* which he was having built after the pattern of Nansen's *Fram.* He listened with interest to everything the doctor had to say about his observations while aboard the *Belgica,* especially his descriptions of the south polar pack.

In Berlin, too, the doctor had an audience with the world-renowned pathologist-turned-anthropologist Rudolf Virchow. Together they discussed Cook's encounters with the primitives at both ends of the earth, and Virchow expounded on his theories of race.

As the time for the commission's meeting drew near, the doctor returned to Belgium to join the other 77 representatives charged with organizing the official records. But before the work began, there was to be a round of honors to the expedition's members.

At Antwerp he met Madame Léonie Osterrieth, who was now called "Mother Antarctica" for her critical role in seeing the *Belgica* on her way. At the gala dinner and reception for all the members of the expedition, Cook was greeted by Alphonse Renard, a humorous and influential Jesuit priest and fellow commission member. Renard was a professor at the University of Ghent, where he taught mineralogy, geology and paleontology. He was also a member of the Royal Academy, which had helped persuade Leopold II to subscribe 200,000 francs to publish the results of the voyage.

He was most curious about the doctor's past adventures and asked him about his future plans. Dr. Cook told Renard that he had determined to settle back into the practice of medicine. The priest remonstrated that there were a million doctors, but only one Dr. Cook, the antarctic explorer, so why take such a prosaic course? The doctor replied that it was his "bread and butter." The priest smiled and said, "Isn't that American. We would say it is our bread, but you add butter to it."[10]

In Brussels Dr. Cook gave an address and received a commemorative medal. He had already received by mail in New York the Royal Geographical Society's silver medal, the gold medal of the Royal Belgian Academy of Sciences, Letters and Arts, and another from the Municipality of Brussels for his service to the expedition.[11]

After the ceremonies, the expedition members were received by Prince Albert in lieu of the absent king, who was in France. As did each of the officers of the *Belgica,* the doctor received his white enameled cross identifying him as a chevalier of the Order of Leopold I, and a small poppy-red lapel ribbon that signified the honor.[12]

Roald Amundsen, who because of his resignation did not attend the conference or ceremony, thought Cook's honor especially appropriate. He may well have expressed the sentiments of many of his shipmates when he wrote, "Cook was incontestably the leading spirit in this work, and gained such honour among the members of the expedition that I think it just to mention it. Upright, honourable, capable, and conscientious in the extreme—such is the memory we retain of Frederick A. Cook from those days."[13]

Recrossing the Atlantic on the steamship *Oceanic* in mid-February, Dr. Cook must have thought over the words of the Belgian priest. But in reality, he had no future plans other than the practice of medicine. He was now 35 and had been the span of 151 degrees of latitude; perhaps the time had come to settle down to the work for which he had studied so long and hard.

As he landed in New York, a reporter accosted him and asked him about his trip. Cook characterized the nature of the meeting and the report he had been at work on. "This report is the official record of the expedition," he explained, "the story of which has already been published. There will be eleven volumes in the record. One of them was contributed by me, and contains a vocabulary of 30,000 words of the Yahgan language, which is the tongue of the inhabitants of Tierra del Fuego."

When asked whether he would be serving on any of the other European expeditions then fitting out for the Antarctic, he replied, "No, I am not going with any of them. I have been exploring for many years now, and I think I'll give somebody else a chance."[14]

The doctor reopened his office at 687 Bushwick Avenue, and despite the intervening years, many of his patients drifted back. Still, that office in Brooklyn seemed to him as lonely as the bleak polar wastes. Anna Forbes was dead, and even Mrs. Forbes, who had moved out in a dispute with Dr. Burr during Cook's absence, was gone. But the lure of the poles remained. He returned to the habit of spending his spare time reading everything he could find about his beloved white world. His book was selling so well he had decided to follow it up with another, which he planned to call *Towards the South Pole*. It would recount 36 voyages to the Antarctic, culminating with that of the *Belgica*.[15]

Cook was on friendly terms with the many doctors who lived on Bushwick Avenue, especially Dr. Robert Davidson, his wife and their daughter, Lotta. Often he spent a pleasant evening at the socials held in the Davidsons' parlor. There Lotta introduced him to Mrs. Marie Hunt of Camden, New Jersey, sister of Mrs. Jo Dudley, one of Lotta Davidson's friends and one of Dr. Cook's own patients. She was visiting her sister with her little girl, Ruth. Marie, a 24-year-old brunette of French ancestry, was recently widowed. Something attracted her to the doctor at once, and she would always associate the piece Lotta was playing on the piano—Schumann's "Träumerie"—with the first time their eyes met.[16]

It was not long before Marie Hunt moved from Camden to Brooklyn and Dr. Cook was visiting the Dudley house for no other medical reasons than matters of the heart. For the third time, the doctor resolved to put aside his explorations and settle down. But in the spring of the year he got a call from Herbert L. Bridgman, who asked to meet him on an urgent matter.

Bridgman was now the secretary of the Peary Arctic Club. The club had been officially formed on August 12, 1898, shortly after Peary's departure on yet another expedition, from which he had not yet returned. The club was, in fact, a small group of wealthy and influential men who were backing Peary's latest venture, but their motives were more than simply altruistic.

Peary had saved his dismal record of 1893–95 by bringing back the two meteorites from Cape York. In the eyes of the scientific community this was viewed as a major triumph, eclipsing his failure to achieve any of the stated objectives of his expedition.

By lending "the Woman" and "the Dog" to the American Museum of Natural History, where they were placed on prominent display, Peary had gained a most valuable ally in Morris K. Jesup, to whom Jo Peary had appealed for her husband's relief. After his failed attempt in 1896, Peary succeeded the next year in bringing back the largest of the "Cape York Irons," the huge "Ahnighito," or as the Eskimos called it, "the Tent," reputed to weigh fully 100 tons. Peary had added to the museum's display by inching the iron mass into his tiny ship, the *Hope,* through a remarkable feat of engineering and, in so doing, only added to his reputation with Jesup. Morris K. Jesup became the first president of the Peary Arctic Club.[17]

The club's constitution hinted that Jesup and its other members were as much interested in what else Peary might provide them as they were in his reaching his goal. The document stated that the club was "to receive and collect such objects of scientific interest or otherwise as may be obtainable through Lieutenant Peary's present expedition or other expeditions of like nature." "Or otherwise" often included valuable arctic furs, narwhal and walrus tusks and Eskimo artifacts.[18]

The lieutenant also took care to place his benefactors' names on the newly discovered capes and lands of the Far North. This was no small consideration in itself; as he immodestly told some of them in 1897, "No man could obtain a more royal and imperishable monument than to have his name written forever across the mysterious rocks and ice which form the setting for the spinning axis of the globe."[19]

He even brought back with "the Tent" six Eskimos, whom he turned over to the American Museum. It was ill prepared for their care, housing them in its damp basement. In less than a year all but two, one adult and a boy named Mene, had died of tuberculosis.

But 1897 had been a very good year for Peary. It had begun with a letter dated January 14, in which he outlined his latest scheme that became the basis for forming the Peary Arctic Club. With the delivery of the final "star stone," as the lieutenant was fond of terming the meteorites, Peary's own star began to rise. Among other honors, he was chosen as the first recipient of the American Geographical Society's Cullum Geographical Medal.

In accepting the medal for his arctic achievements, he confessed he felt "a constant intoxication in such work, in the thought 'my eyes are the first that have ever looked upon this scene, mine the touch that has wakened the sleeping princess.'" But what he had done, he said, had been done "for the pure love of doing":

> The midnight sun, the noonday night, equally unapproachable in sublimity; the dazzling brilliance, the universal darkness, the inky sea, the snowy land, the mighty bones of mother earth beneath the feet, the infinite heaven, unbroken, uninterrupted above the head; the crystalline air, biting, it is true, but pure as the celestial ether; the infinite silence, the indescribable desolation, touch and keep in vibrant unison the highest, grandest, noblest, purest chords in human nature.

> My two expeditions of 1891 to 1895, . . . crossed the northern
> portion of the Great Ice Cap from Whale Sound to Independence
> Bay and the northern terminus of main Greenland; reaching an
> unknown portion of the east coast and settling the question of the
> insularity of the Great Arctic Island.[20]

Now, he assured his listeners, he would go on to the very Pole itself. The honors of the present had erased the horrors of the past; he would try again.

In December Peary went to England, where he received the Patron's Medal of the Royal Geographical Society. In London the publisher of the *Daily Mail,* Alfred Charles Harmsworth, made him a present of the *Windward,* the ship that had brought Nansen home. Harmsworth even offered to have new engines installed as part of the gift. In her, Peary planned to "lay siege" to the Pole, as he had put it in his letter. This siege was to last four years.

He was flatly refused leave of absence from his naval duties to accomplish it and assigned to duty instead at Mare Island, California, far away from his powerful patrons. But he used the substantial political influence of one of them, Charles A. Moore, a backer of William McKinley, to prevail upon the president himself to intercede. The orders were rescinded and leave was granted.

With leave, a ship and the substantial monetary support of the Peary Arctic Club, Peary was confident that at last he had the resources to carry out a new plan of attack. He would force his ship as far north up Smith Sound as possible and wait on the northern shores of Greenland or Grant Land for an opportunity to set off across the Arctic Ocean to his destiny. For this effort he would have no large party of potential "deserters." He would take only Matthew Henson and Dr. Thomas S. Dedrick of Washington, New Jersey, as his surgeon.

The gift of the *Windward* was not the windfall Peary had believed her to be, however. A machinists' strike in England prevented her refitting, and she arrived in New York dismally underpowered and inadequate for his plans. Nevertheless, Peary felt he had no time to wait for modifications.

In the fall of 1897 the newspapers had reported that Nansen's captain, Otto Sverdrup, had entered the race for the Pole in the *Fram,* and Peary was hell-bent on beating him into the field to establish his priority to what he called "the American Route to the Pole." Peary, himself, wrote to Captain Sverdrup informing him that the announcement of his expedition's plans had "created a distinctly disagreeable impression over here."[21]

Indeed, Peary's backers publicly scored Sverdrup as a usurper with no sense of fair play. They accused him of breaking "an unwritten law . . . dictated by . . . manly sympathy with heroic endeavour" that honorable explorers kept out of each other's announced field of operations and of "adopting Peary's methods, utilizing Peary's experience and necessarily interfering with his resources of men and dogs in North Greenland, in order to frustrate the labour of ten years and turn to his own advantage, in competition with Peary, all that has been accomplished by Peary's skill and forethought and indomitable courage."

"There is no legal impediment in Capt. Sverdrup's way," one concluded. "He can do these things, if he will, and men will remember him as the one Arctic voyager whom they would gladly forget."[22]

Sverdrup, however, disavowed designs on the Pole, saying he would concentrate on mapping the Greenland Archipelago and the islands to the west, but Peary would have none of it; again he wrote to the Norwegian captain:

> I still can hardly bring myself to believe that you propose to devote your time, energy, and money, in an attempt to anticipate or duplicate work which I proposed nearly a year ago, and the preparations for the execution of which are well under way.
>
> I am sure you will pardon me if I remind you that such action on your part, in entering a field in which I have been at work for several years and assuming objects which I have formally proposed for my own work, will be without precedent in the entire annals of Arctic Exploration.[23]

In his private correspondence, he was not even so polite as this. Writing to Morris K. Jesup, he openly accused Sverdrup of an "unprincipled attempt . . . to appropriate my route, my plans, and my objects."[24] Peary had had enough of "forestalling" Norwegians. With a competitor in the field, nothing could hold him back, not even the outbreak of war with Spain. Despite the hostilities, Peary refused to give up his leave, and leaving Jo, who was expecting a second child in January, he went by rail to Sydney and took passage on the *Hope* from Cape Breton Island on July 7, 1898, leaving the slower *Windward* to come in her own good time.

He was in such a hurry that he even bypassed his customary stops at the Danish settlements. He no longer felt they were necessary. The Danes had no settlements in North Greenland. He had been the first to look upon much that lay there; to him it was, as he would declare it in his diary, "*Mine,* mine by the right of discovery, to be credited to me, and associated with my name, generations after I have ceased to be."[25] It was occupied only by "his" Eskimos, to whom he had given so much, and whom he now thought of as instruments placed there by providence to aid him in reaching the North Pole.

After the ships rendezvoused in Smith Sound on August 13, the *Windward,* under the command of Captain John Bartlett, threaded her way north carrying Peary and the winter party as the *Hope* sailed home after delivering her stores to Etah. The *Windward* made little progress before being frozen in at Cape Hawks on August 18, far south of Peary's planned landing place. A house made of packing boxes was constructed as winter quarters on Cape D'Urville in case the *Windward* should be crushed.

On the wild shores of Ellesmere Land, Peary met his competition face to face:

He came driving along by our track, straight towards us, and I went down to the fjord to meet him. When we met, he asked if I was Captain Sverdrup, which I answered in the affirmative, and we then shook hands and walked together up to the tent, where I introduced [Lieutenant] Bay to him. I asked him to have some coffee with us, but he refused, saying that his tent was not more than two hours' drive from here, and that he was going home to dinner. . . . After staying for a few minutes he said good-bye to Bay, who had been grinding coffee all the time. . . . I took Peary down to the sledge, and watched him disappearing at an even pace, driven by his Eskimo driver. My heart felt quite warm with patriotism.

Peary's visit was the event of the day in our tent. We talked of nothing else, and rejoiced at having shaken hands with the bold explorer, even though his visit had been so short that we hardly had time to pull off our mittens.[26]

The warm feeling was unique to Captain Sverdrup. Though he had no evidence for it, Peary feared greatly that Sverdrup intended to establish a base at Greely's old camp at Fort Conger. The chance meeting with Sverdrup only spurred Peary to action; he decided on a mad tactic to beat him there.

With Henson, Dr. Dedrick and four Eskimos, he set off in the light of the December moon to reach Conger over the ice foot. The little party was endlessly delayed and the moon set; the temperature fell below −50°. In the near-absolute darkness, they groped along the shore. At Cape Cracroft two of the Eskimos buried themselves in a snowdrift with some of the dogs to keep from freezing, but the others continued. In the inky blackness of January 6, 1899, somehow they managed to stumble upon the big building abandoned by Lieutenant Greely 16 years earlier. By then, Peary was in a very bad way.

He had fallen on the ice, and his right arm, hand and fingers were paralyzed and in great pain. Worse than that, he felt nothing in his feet at all. Upon examination, Dr. Dedrick found that Peary's legs had been frosted clear up to the knees, and when the doctor cut away his kamiks and peeled them off, one of Peary's toes on each foot snapped off at the last joint. As he recovered his circulation in the warming hut, he suffered agonies as his nerves reawakened.

There were more agonies to come in the 11 days he was strapped to a sledge in February for the return to the *Windward,* 250 miles away. In an operation aboard ship, Dr. Dedrick etherized the lieutenant and completed the job he had begun crudely at Fort Conger, when he was compelled to remove portions of all but three of Peary's toes. The loss of his toes was just the beginning of four nightmarish years for Robert E. Peary.

In the early spring Victor Baumann, Sverdrup's second in command, visited the *Windward* and found Peary still convalescing. When he expressed his sympathies, Peary simply said, "You must take your chances up here, you know." Baumann offered to take the members of Peary's expedition north in the *Fram* and land them anywhere they wanted. Peary doubted Baumann's generosity and intentions; he believed the Norwegian had come to the ship only to find out what had been accomplished the previous year.

Before leaving, Baumann also made the acquaintance of Dr. Dedrick. He found him well built, of medium height and dressed in Eskimo attire. Though the doctor did not say much, he was very obliging. Captain Bartlett told Baumann how Dedrick "had been the perpetrator of a perfect masterpiece in the hunting line" when, after running out of ammunition while firing on a musk oxen herd, with his hunting knife, he had single-handedly attacked those still standing.[27]

That summer the Peary Arctic Club's relief ship *Diana* arrived under Sam Bartlett and in the command of Herbert L. Bridgman to receive Lieutenant Peary's report and replenish his supplies. Bridgman learned that Peary had been able to do little traveling on his tender stumps; the only things he had accomplished in his first season were to retrieve the record of the British Nares Expedition left on Norman Lockyer Island in 1875 and to gather up the personal papers and other artifacts left by the Greely party in their hasty abandonment of Fort Conger in 1883.

Bridgman was dismayed by what had happened to Peary's feet and tried to persuade him to return on the *Diana* to get proper medical attention. Peary refused to hear of it. He insisted that he would come home only when his leave expired or when he had reached the Pole.

Before the *Diana* departed, Peary wrote an intimate letter to Jo. He had learned from her letters, which Bridgman had delivered, that the baby had come on January 7. Jo had named her Francine. He expressed his pleasure and his passionate love for Jo, and then told her that he had frosted his feet, but tried to make light of his loss:

> This gave the Dr. an opportunity to trim them up a little, & as a result when I come back I shall be able to wear a size shorter shoe. . . .
>
> The Dr. is a faithful, hardworking soul, with some of Verhoeff's characteristics of never admitting that he is cold or hungry or tired, & with the same dogged persistence in doing what he starts on. His great fault is that he is slower (very <u>much</u> slower) than the wrath of God; & he has not enough natural mechanical ability to drive a nail. He is learning however.[28]

That fall, when Jo read of Bert's condition, she determined at once to go north in the spring and fetch him back as soon as she could. She was free to go. Francine had died suddenly on August 7, of infantile cholera, aged exactly seven months. Taking her remaining daughter, Jo sailed north on the *Windward* from Sydney on July 21, 1900, under the command of Captain Sam Bartlett, who took his cousin Bob as mate. But the feeble ship was again unable to penetrate beyond Payer Harbor. Peary was by then back at Fort Conger.

Not long after the *Windward* arrived, Jo made a shocking discovery. An Eskimo woman named Allakasingwah came aboard boasting she was the wife of *Pearyaksoah* (Big Peary), and she had a two-year-old son in her hood to prove it. Jo recognized the woman from a picture in Bert's book, *Northward over the Great Ice,* which had been published just before he left in 1898. The photograph of her lying naked on some rocks was captioned, "The Mother of Seals: An Eskimo Legend."

This discovery, on top of her recent loss, staggered Jo Peary; to think that her husband had fathered a child by "a creature scarcely human" and that it had lived while her own had been taken from her was almost too much to bear. The days that followed brought the details she did not want to know from the Eskimo woman, all innocent of the impact of her words. But when Allakasingwah sickened almost to death, Jo nursed her and arranged that the child not be strangled if she should die, as was the Eskimo custom for orphaned children under three. Some things, however, were already dead to Josephine Peary.

As the summer progressed and Bert failed to put in an appearance, she poured out her heartbreak, outrage, horror and anguish in a 26-page journal-letter, thinking to leave it for him when the *Windward* sailed for home. Her words summed up the bitter harvest brought in by her husband's peculiar route to fame:

> You gave me three years of the most exquisite pleasure that can be had; after that the pleasure was pretty evenly divided with the pain until now it is all pain, except the memory of what has been.[29]

But before the ship could sail, an iceberg grounded across the mouth of the harbor, trapping her. Thus the Pearys wintered, separated now by more than the 250 miles between them.

Peary started south in the spring. On April 30, 1901, he met a party of Eskimos who had mail for him, including Jo's letter. It was the last thing he expected. He thought Jo was in Maine with their new baby. When he asked them when the *Windward* had sailed, they told him that she was still frozen in at Payer Harbor. He hesitated, pausing at the Cape D'Urville box house several days before coming to the ship.

In New York the Peary Arctic Club became apprehensive as 1900 drew to a close without word from either Peary or the *Windward.* This had been the cause of Bridgman's urgent appeal to Dr. Cook. "Peary is lost somewhere in the arctic," said Bridgman. ". . . We can finance a relief expedition to find Peary and bring him back. Will you join us? We need the benefit of your judgment. . . .

"If you go," said he, "the result of your individual work will be yours."

"Very well," replied Dr. Cook, "under these conditions I will go; you may count on me for any emergency and whatever I do will be accessible to you and Peary."[30]

By early June the arrangements for the relief expedition could be announced to the members of the club:

> The Peary Arctic Club has entrusted to its secretary, Herbert L. Bridgman, the command of its expedition of 1901, the fourth of the series since Mr. Peary departed on his attempt to attain the Pole. . . . Dr. Frederick A. Cook . . . has accepted the position of surgeon and will, on the cruise, prosecute his studies of the ethnology of the Arctic highlanders of North Greenland. The club's chartered steamer Erik, formerly the property of the Hudson Bay Company, now belonging to Captain James A. Farquhar, of Halifax, N.S. [will leave] for the North about the middle of next month. . . .
>
> . . . The summer of 1901 is likely to mark the culmination of the work of the Peary Club, though its members, confident as they have been from the outset in Mr. Peary's success, are pledged to stand by him unfalteringly to the end. Three years have elapsed since Mr. Peary left America, and two full seasons' work is to be learned upon the return of the Erik. More interestingly, in a personal and dramatic way, than the geographic work of Mr. Peary, is the fate of his wife and daughter and of the steamer Windward, from which nothing has been heard since her departure from Godhavn, Greenland, Aug. 20, 1900. Expectations and instructions then were that the Windward, with Mrs. Peary and Miss Peary, would return in the autumn, and the hope now is that their detention was due to Mr. Peary's orders, and for reasons which were satisfactory to him. The Erik will take to Mr. Peary for the first time news of the death of his mother in Portland, Me., last November.

Bridgman included an outline of the coming expedition that concluded with the chain of command: "Subject to the discipline of the ship and the conditions of navigation, the authority of the representative of the Peary Arctic Club is paramount, and in event of his disability, and in absence of other directions from Peary, shall devolve upon [the] surgeon, and then upon the captain and officers in order of rank."[31]

On July 8 Dr. Cook left for North Sydney to join the *Erik* and oversee the final preparations. Herbert Bridgman would arrive via the Intercolonial Railroad the day she was scheduled to sail. As had become standard in Peary's voyages, there were to be several rich young paying guests on the *Erik* to help defray the expenses.

One was Clarence Wyckoff, son of an executive of the Remington Typewriter Company. He managed the Booth-Hyomei Company, which manufactured a eucalyptus nasal inhaler, and with his brother, Edward, who owned the trolley lines in Ithaca, New York, was partner in several other diverse business enterprises. Both were members of the Peary Arctic Club. He had brought his friend Louis C. Bement, also of Ithaca. Also on board were the son of the owner of the Brooklyn *Standard Union,* Herbert Berri; his tutor, Limond C. Stone; and Alfred Church of Elgin, Illinois.

Dr. Cook especially took a liking to Wyckoff. Wyckoff enjoyed eating and, not finding the usual ship stores to his palate's requirements, picked up a cartload of extras in Sydney to suit his tastes. The *Erik*'s accommodations were not much more to his liking. The big black sealer had no quarters for passengers at all, and even those for the officers were rather spartan. But with two large barrels clinging to her aft masts 70 feet above her deck to accommodate her ice pilots, an ancient but well-maintained 37-horsepower steam engine and foot-thick square oak planking reinforcing her hull, she was admirably suited for ice navigation, even though she had only recently been salvaged after a severe wreck.

Once aboard, Wyckoff was introduced by Cook to the other members of the expedition, who did not impress him any more favorably than the stores. The first mate, Moses Bartlett, who was volubly drunk, was ordering Captain J.U. Blakeney about like a cabin boy, and Ben Hoppin greeted him with "How are you. Goodbye," then rushed away clad in a heavy overcoat and muffler, even though the weather was quite warm.

The *Erik* left Sydney at 11:50 A.M., July 14, one day late and four men short, including a cook, who, as things fell out, had perhaps gotten a look at what he had to work with and fled. The next day she put in at Port-au-Basque, Newfoundland, remaining three days to search for replacements for the deserters. Ice in the Strait of Belle Isle delayed her further. Wyck-

Clarence Wyckoff, 1901. Photograph by Cook.

off, who was suffering terribly from hives, sat up with his friends and passed the time listening to Cook tell of his experiences in both polar zones. Finally, the *Erik* rounded Cape Ray Light at midnight on July 21, and Labrador quickly faded from sight.

On the stormy passage to Cape Farewell, everyone else was so seasick that Church, Bement and Wyckoff found themselves alone at the supper table. Clarence Wyckoff thought the food none too appetizing:

I happened to be serving soup. We have had rice soup now for about seven days straight, and I for one was rather tired of it. Perhaps the rough weather had something to do with it, but at any rate I was not eating, but rather toying with the rice. I noticed it was peculiar rice for it was corrugated, and then I noticed that there were little black dots at one end of each kernel of rice. My curiosity aroused I examined closer and found that it really was not rice soup at all. The kernels were maggots. I didn't tell the others as I didn't want to spoil their dinner.[32]

By morning the sea had calmed, but a hundred miles south of Godthaab, the *Erik* encountered heavy drift ice, which the captain, who Wyckoff was beginning to think was no better than the new cook at his job, avoided by running to the northwest. On July 26 she crossed the Arctic Circle. First-time crossers had to undergo the traditional "initiation" ceremonies, after which all partook of a bowl of punch, toasting their families, Peary and the success of his expedition. After standing offshore in Disco Bay to wait out a furious sleet storm, the ship anchored on July 28.

At Godhavn Governor Nilsen had no news to offer of either Peary or Sverdrup, though there were rumors among the Eskimos that the *Windward* was lost but that Mrs. Peary was safe at Upernavik. In less than 24 hours the *Erik* was steaming through Wygatt Channel in fine, clear weather and, crossing the great gap of the Umanak Fjord, laid a course for Upernavik.

The ship's meat, which had been hung from the yardarms to preserve it in the arctic air, had a suspicious cheesy odor when taken down. A closer examination showed it to be literally alive with the fat maggots of large flies. The ship's steward tried to convince his patrons that he had seen worse and that the Eskimos even considered ripe meat a true delicacy, but his listeners could not be persuaded. Not that the rest of the ship's fare was all that appealing. Beyond Wyckoff's private stock, provisions appeared skimpy and seemed second-rate at best. Wyckoff, who had taken an interest in the stores after discovering the content of his "rice soup," found the barley no better. Scarcely a kernel was left in the barrel, and what remained was held together by worm webs. He observed the steward hiding things to sell after the voyage and decided most of the stores must have been on the ship the three years she lay wrecked on the rocks while insurance adjusters argued over her fate. By now, Louis Bement had also noticed "a nice assortment of animals in our food," and there was so much grumbling discontent over both the food and the management of the voyage from the crew, almost to the point of mutiny, that the captain appointed Clarence Wyckoff chief steward. He soon was busy overseeing the supplies and planning all the meals.

At Upernavik Inspector Jansen and Governor Knauth knew nothing of Peary or the *Windward*'s whereabouts either, so after the usual social requirements, the *Erik* steamed north for Cape York.

The Erik *with pack ice and iceberg.*

Melville Bay was jammed with ice, but Captain Blakeney put the ship into the "Inner Run" of the whalers—a narrow tidal crack between the fixed floe ice of the shore and the slowly moving drift ice of the bay—while the sportsmen kept an eager watch for bear or seal to replace their putrid meat supplies. But all those seen were well out of range.

When the wind suddenly veered to the east, the cold breath of the ice cap began to freeze what open water there was, and the *Erik* was beset by the pack. Cook took this opportunity to get out on the ice and take some fine photographs of the stranded vessel. Then another sudden shift of the wind freed her, and she continued across the bay. Arriving off Cape York at midnight on August 2, the *Erik* blew several blasts on her whistle to wake the inhabitants of the village.

A whaleboat was lowered and Cook was rowed out to meet several Eskimos approaching in kayaks. Among them were Kokoo, Ootoniah and Sipsu, whom he had not seen in ten years. They recognized the doctor at once and told him that Mitty Peary and Ahnighito were in good health but that food and supplies had run low. They thought Pearyaksoah was either at Etah or somewhere in Inglefield Gulf. They said that he had been at Fort Conger earlier, that his feet had been frozen and that some of the natives had deserted him. Reluctant to give more details, they added only that Pearyaksoah and the angekok Dedrick were piblockto and would not speak to each other.

Piblockto had a wider application than just the name of the dread malady that afflicted sledge dogs. It also referred to brief spells in which individual Eskimos went berserk, tore up their igloos, destroyed their possessions or even ran about wildly outside, naked, in subfreezing temperatures. The Eskimos attributed this condition to "the weight of the world" pressing down on its victim until he could no longer stand the strain. After such a fit, an Eskimo would regain his normal control and go back about his business as if nothing unusual had occurred. But when applied to white men, the word simply meant "insane."

At Cape York Kiota and his family came aboard as guides. The *Erik* passed by ice-choked Inglefield Gulf, paused at Dalrymple Rock to shoot eider ducks and guillemots, and then proceeded toward Etah, intending to check for Peary there. Later, when Kiota came on deck and looked at the coast, he became very excited and loudly questioned the qallunaats' intelligence, before convincing them they were far past Etah and must go back. Not long after the *Erik* turned about, Kiota sighted Annoatok.

Cook, Bridgman and the Eskimo were rowed ashore by Wyckoff and Church. It was a terrible pull against the strong offshore wind, but the whaleboat was finally landed. The Eskimos living in their tupiks at Annoatok were the very picture of arctic prosperity, with an abundance of meat and skins. After the men traded with the natives for anything of value, four more of them were taken into the whaleboat and rowed back to the *Erik*. The new arrivals said Peary was definitely at Etah, and the ship immediately got under way.

There, in the harbor of Foulke Fjord, lay the *Windward* with Jo and Marie Peary aboard:

> August 4, 1901 was a raw chilly day and we had just gone into our comfortable little cabin to get warm after promenading the deck when we were roused by the Eskimo cry of "Omioksoah, Omioksoah" (a ship, a ship). We tumbled on deck & there sure enough we saw the nose of a great black whaler just poking around the corner of the cliff which shut off our view into the sound.
>
> At last, after thirteen months of weary watching & waiting amid the snow clad rocky cliffs & ice bound waters of the Arctic zone, we were to hear from the dear ones at home. How we scrambled for the field glasses, to see if we knew anyone on board. What an excitement, first one, then another familiar figure was recognized. At last the stranger was along side & the oft repeated question "Is every one well in Washington?" was being answered with a "yes."
>
> How happy we felt & how the child danced and clapped her hands for joy. In a moment we were boarded by our friends & once again we shook the hands, heard the voices & looked upon the faces of those who seemed to us to come from another world.[33]

Herbert Bridgman and Dr. Cook were greeted by Jo and Marie as they clambered aboard. The two could hardly wait to get at the sack of mail the men brought with them.

The Windward *and the* Erik *at Etah Harbor.*

Peary was not very specific about the progress of the expedition to date. At the dinner given for the relief expedition that night in the cabin of the *Windward*, it seemed evident to everyone by the silence that little had been accomplished in the direction of the Pole. But only Bridgman and Cook had learned the details.

In 1900 Peary had reached the farthest northern point of the Greenland Archipelago—83°39'N—naming it Cape Morris K. Jesup. From there he had gone out onto the polar pack, but the season was late and the sea was thrown up in immense hummocks along the shore. After struggling a bare 22 miles in a week, he had given up. His 1901 attempt had been even more pathetic; he hadn't reached the shores of the polar sea at all.

It finally came out that there had been a quarrel between Peary and Dedrick, though the details of the disagreement were not forthcoming. To the relief party, it seemed that the harsh arctic environment had indeed unbalanced both men. Most of all, Dr. Cook was struck by the dull and icy mentality that had replaced Peary's former youthful alertness.

Bridgman asked that Peary be given a thorough physical examination, but Cook hesitated until both the lieutenant and Mrs. Peary made the same request. When they did, he and Peary retired to the cabin.

The doctor could see on every part of his patient's body the marks left by unsuitable food, the strain of three years of effort in the harsh climate and the bitter disappointment that had accompanied them:

The Pearys with Cook.

The arm and chest muscles were good but the legs were thin. The feet were crippled by old ulcers, the result of repeated frost bites. Eight of his toes had been removed leaving painful stubs which refused to heal. In the face there was an absence of normal expression, a vacant stare from the eyes, a morbid cherry-brown in the skin of the face. The skin of the body was pale, hard in texture, and hung in baggy folds. Its color was gruesome—not brown like the face—but grey-green with just a little submerged yellow. All outward appearances were those of one affected with some morbid disease.

Repeated examination of the urine gave a little sugar and some albumen, but not enough to warrant a diagnosis of diabetes or Bright's disease. The heart action was irregular and responded too rapidly to mild physical exercise. There was no valvular lesion. The arteries were hard, indicating progressive organic degeneration in the near future. There were varicose veins of serious importance in both legs and a peculiar distension of small veins in other parts of the body. Aside from a well marked and a deep seated anemia, there was nothing to adequately explain the physical disorganization which the general appearance of the body indicated.

Peary's senses were all blunted. The skin lacked that quick response of healthy people. The eyes were dull. There was complaint of a progressive night blindness. Also frequent inflammatory troubles involving not only the eyeball, but the surrounding soft parts. The teeth were in bad shape with caries and pyorrhea. There were premonitory symptoms of scurvy in his gums. The membranes of nose and throat were undergoing some atrophy. The gastric intestinal tract at all times refused to function normally.[34]

To Dr. Cook the symptoms were familiar; they were much like those he had observed in Antarctica, only more extreme. He now made his prescription. As he had with Lecointe, he told Peary that he must eat raw meat, especially liver. When Peary violently refused, the doctor insisted, "Raw meat is between you and your future work. Raw meat is between you and death. Have you learned nothing in ten years? Your present condition is directly due to long use of the embalmed food out of tins. Can't you realize this?"[35]

Cook told Peary that the condition of his feet had finished him as a traveler on ice or snow, because without his big toes he would never be able to wear snowshoes again. He advised him to return home at once to recover his health. In this Jo Peary concurred, but neither she nor the doctor made any impression on Bert's determination. Peary said he would stay until he exhausted his leave or reached the North Pole, but Dr. Dedrick would have to go. The doctor had submitted his resignation before, but Peary had rejected it. Now he had made up his mind that having no medical assistance was preferable to Dr. Dedrick. There would be a meeting to discuss the new arrangements after meat had been gathered for the coming winter.

Peary ordered the ships to sail to the walrus grounds. During the weeks that followed, many exciting incidents of the hunt were recorded in Clarence Wyckoff's diary. Captain Blakeney added to the thrills by ramming the *Erik*, full speed, into the ice floe where Wyckoff and Church were waiting to be picked up, causing them to run for their lives. Later, he nearly sideswiped a whaleboat containing Matt Henson and four of the *Erik*'s paying guests, who were saved only by Wyckoff's shouting instructions to the totally confused captain. After these incidents, Wyckoff inquired of the captain's history. Upon learning that Blakeney had been thrown out of the Canadian government service after wrecking his vessel and had returned to his former occupation as a housepainter before Captain Farquhar engaged him for the *Erik*'s voyage, he wondered how they had not come to grief before. After what he had seen, Clarence Wyckoff thought, Captain Farquhar "could not arrange a summer picnic for me."

But despite the close calls, the walrus hunt was a success. Then the *Windward* sailed for Cape York to trade with the natives, dropping the hunters at Olrick's Bay to shoot reindeer before retrieving Robert Stein and his companion from Cape Josephine. They were returning to the United States after an absence of two years. After hearing about Stein's dismal experiences, Dr. Cook was relieved he had turned down the offer to be his surgeon in 1894. On August 24, the hunts at an end, Lieutenant Peary summoned Herbert Bridgman and Dr. Cook to his cabin to present his plans: Jo and Marie would return with the *Windward*, he said; Dr. Dedrick would also return and be replaced by Dr. Cook.[36]

The Windward *at Olrick's Bay.*

Aboard the *Erik*, Dedrick asked how long it would be before she sailed and was told two hours. Taking a shotgun, he then left the ship in a boat manned by Eskimos, saying he would try for hare. In about an hour, he sent aboard the gun and one hare with a note to Peary, resigning once again:

> You hereby have my forced resignation of the fragment of my position, you having stripped me of my position against your verbal and written assurances.
>
> You will never, by any voluntary act of mine, be deprived of my medical services nor of a helping-hand so long as you remain in the Arctic. If I am not to remain at your headquarters, you can depend on my being at the nearest possible point that I can effect a landing and maintain life.
>
> Enclosed is mem. regarding our financial arrangements.
>
> I shall refrain from making any public comment and private comment on the chain of circumstances leading to the rupture in our relations until we return to the States, when I shall justify my course for the sake of my family and my honor, if I deem it necessary.
>
> Sincerely,
> Thomas S. Dedrick
> (Until now) Assistant and Surgeon
> Peary Arctic Expedition 1898–1901+[37]

Peary, after reading his note, calmly remarked that it was another Verhoeff case. Clarence Wyckoff also received a message from Dedrick asking whether he would give him one of his rifles and one or two hundred cartridges in exchange for a promissory note and mail to his wife the seven letters he had left aboard the *Erik.*

Dr. Thomas S. Dedrick.

Cook said he could not ethically take Dedrick's place until the doctor agreed to give up, physically, the position he had contracted for and return on the *Erik.* After a long conference, Cook and Wyckoff agreed to go ashore and reason with the doctor. Wyckoff suggested that if Dr. Dedrick was insane, as his recent actions seemed to indicate, there would be no shame in making any promise to get him on board and then forcibly detaining him for his own good. In the end, however, the matter of force was left to the negotiators' discretion.

Landing on the sandy beach, they saw the doctor, sitting on a big rock, sharpening a pencil with a long hunting knife. Dedrick shoved the knife in his boot as they approached; Cook quietly warned Wyckoff to watch out. Dr. Cook displayed a friendly attitude and tried to persuade Dedrick to return to the ship. He appealed to him for his family and on the grounds of medical ethics, but none of his efforts made any impression on the man's resolve to remain when the ships sailed. Wyckoff then tried his best:

> His one reply was that a doctor connected with an expedition should not retreat until the expedition did. . . . His honor was more to him than life or anything else and it compelled him to remain as near as possible to Peary's headquarters. The whole thing appeared to me to be simply a quixotic idea - he did not impress me as being in any way insane and I did not feel like giving my word to a sane man that if he came aboard he could return (with the idea of detaining him). Dr. Cook evidently felt the same as he did not mention his going aboard except that he should do so to see Bridgeman. . . . As a last resort Cook remarked, "Well if you won't come we will have to take you." Dr. [Dedrick] jumped up on [a] stone igloo and remarked to [the] Windward's bowswain . . . that he had better not mix with a quarrel that did not concern him

as he was liable to get hurt . . . [but there was] no fight. Dr. [Cook] had been testing him. He would have fought to a finish, crazy or sane.[38]

Two hours later the negotiators were back with news of their failure, reporting that Dedrick had said he would resist any attempt to force his return to the ship. They said, however, that Dedrick had given the impression he valued Herbert Bridgman's opinion, so they suggested that an interview with him might change the doctor's mind. Bridgman then dispatched the two back to shore to bring him on board with a guarantee that he would not be detained against his will. They also took along a proposition from Peary in which he stated that he would accept Dedrick's resignation, transport him to the United States on the *Erik* without forcible detention and, if he went home, would authorize the payment of the bonus he had been promised. But Peary also indicated that although Dedrick, if he stayed, was free to land what personal effects he had on the ship, he would give no assurances beyond that. This time Cook and Wyckoff returned accompanied by the doctor, and Bridgman retired to the quarterdeck with him.

Bridgman used every persuasion, saying that word of his conduct would kill his wife, grieve his relatives and possibly ruin his professional and personal future. If there were differences between him and Peary, he said, they should be settled by arbitration with mutual friends. Bridgman pointed out that the doctor's disobedience of orders put in jeopardy the payment of his salary and bonus. To this threat Dedrick replied that he had several written statements from Peary saying his service had been entirely satisfactory, and that he would put his faith in the decision of the Peary Arctic Club in regard to the payments stipulated in his contract.

In the end, Dr. Dedrick would not be swayed. He told Bridgman he must follow his "mind monitor," that his wife would think the better of him once she learned the circumstances of his decision, and if the Peary Arctic Club would not transport him home at the end of the expedition, he would take a whaler from Cape York in 1903:

> He stated positively, in answer to my inquiries, that he would say or do nothing among the natives to impair Mr. Peary's influence over them, and that he should not attempt to visit Cape Sabine, or Mr. Peary's quarters unless he was sent for. Finally, he declared that further delay of the ship would be useless, and that he should go with the natives to Annoatok tomorrow.
>
> At no time during this interview, which occupied fully an hour, nor in others on the Windward during the preceding week did Dr. Dedrick say in terms what was the matter in difference between him and Mr. Peary, and only while collecting his personal effects on the quarter deck did I gather from his declaration that he had been put under Mr. Peary's negro man Henson, did I have any opportunity to gather what the real trouble was.

The interview closed in the chart room, in [the] presence of Dr. Cook and Mr. Wyckoff, the former urging earnestly upon Dr. Dedrick that another winter in the Arctic might be attended with serious results to him, particularly in regard to his mental condition. Dr. Dedrick laughed at this idea, and declared that he not only knew fully his own condition, but was abundantly able to take care of himself in all respects, with which our efforts and the interview ended.[39]

Before Dedrick left, Bridgman made him hunt up the shotgun to prove it was not on shore. But Wyckoff took one of his new rifles and shoved it in Dedrick's bag, and Dr. Cook made him a gift of 120 cartridges, seven boxes of matches, two bowie knives, a half-pound of Hyler's chocolate and six cakes of Hyomic soap. Wyckoff and Cook also offered him food from their personal stores, since Bridgman pointedly told the outcast he would get nothing from the ship's supplies if he chose to stay. That was Dedrick's choice, and Dr. Cook rowed him ashore.

When Bridgman found out Dedrick had a gun, he was furious. He told Wyckoff he must get it back, since he feared Dedrick might use it on Peary or even Jo and Marie. But Peary seemed unconcerned, fearing only that the rifle would give Dedrick too much influence with the Eskimos. Bridgman protested that Wyckoff had not acted in the best interests of the club, but Peary shrugged it off, saying that giving Dedrick the rifle was no more than "throwing a crust of bread to a starving dog."

At 1:30 A.M. the *Erik* departed to lay supplies at Cape Sabine, Peary's choice for winter quarters. Since the cape was unapproachable because of heavy ice, the supplies, including a box of assorted liquors, a gift from Ben Hoppin, were landed 15 miles to the south, and Peary prepared to go ashore.

In lieu of a medical assistant, Peary requested that Charlie Percy, the *Windward's* steward, stay with him. Bridgman, in spite of everything, expressed confidence that Peary might yet succeed in the coming season:

> Lowering the boat, first went the natives, the gallant fellows who had stood faithfully by their leader in many arduous marches and weary campaigning, obeying him with implicit fidelity; then the ever-faithful "Mat," who handled the natives with a tact and skill which amounted almost to genius, and then Peary himself, after the last good-by and hand-grasp with every one of us, who bade him Godspeed. It was not strange at all, that when little Marie said in broken accents to the loyal steward, "Good-by Charlie, take good care of my father," that some of us found a sudden attraction to the main truck, where our stars and stripes were flying, and that we all of us realized that this was one of the moments which may be historic. Mrs. Peary, on the quarter deck, bade her husband farewell, and then with the same self-possession and confidence which are a part of his nature, Peary himself went over the

side and into the boat, amid our cheers and the volley of our rifles.[40]

It was loyalty that Peary valued above all else, "implicit fidelity" and obedience that he demanded from all who accompanied him, and Thomas Dedrick had failed the test. For that crime and the crimes of his own conscience, the doctor had sentenced himself to another winter in Greenland. As for Peary, fear of failure tied him to the place, despite all the longings for home he had had and those that he knew must come. And so the *Erik* bore away Dr. Cook back to Marie Hunt and home, as Peary rowed away from Jo and back into the icy prison of his frustrated ambition.

It did not take long after the *Erik* returned to Sydney on September 15 for press reports about Dedrick's dispute with Peary to surface. The doctor was characterized as "practically insane." It was said that his state of mind made him "useless to the expedition" and that he had acted in a manner that "imperilled the expedition."

"Instead of caring for the physical needs of his comrades and helping them to stand the terrible strain of the climate, he discouraged them by telling them that they were suffering from scurvy and other diseases," went a typical report. "This, it is said, was the chief reason that Lieut. Peary would not grant to him the authority that might otherwise have been his."

Bridgman denied the report of the *Erik*'s engineer that the doctor had been abandoned without food. When Dr. Cook was asked about this, he replied, "You may be sure that Dr. Dedrick was not turned adrift against his will in the latitude mentioned.

"There were certain difficulties—disagreements you might call them—but I think that Mr. Bridgman is the proper person to explain the whole matter."[41]

Though he did not care to take up the whole matter, what Bridgman explained was that Dedrick was jealous of Matt Henson, and he attributed the doctor's actions to "a slight mental aberration."

Bridgman mailed a letter from Dedrick to his wife explaining why he had not come home. When she received it, Cora Dedrick wrote immediately to the newspaperman, saying the letter from her husband "could not contain much worse news for me. . . . Can I not meet you at your office, and learn the facts of the case: The sooner the more relieved I will be."

Bridgman informed Mrs. Peary that he and Dr. Cook had agreed to meet Mrs. Dedrick at the Hamilton Club to relieve her anxiety but added, "Moreover, since she has invited it, it gives us a chance to place her under obligations, which I think she will regard."[42]

The *Erik* also carried a letter from Peary to Charles A. Moore, the man who had intervened with President McKinley to gain him his leave. It did not even hint at his difficulties, saying, "My grip is still good, I have a year before me, and I have yet to experience the first feeling of discouragement."[43]

It was not true then and it would be even less true in the months to come. During his self-imposed exile at his winter quarters, Peary's Eskimo companions sickened and died, and he was haunted by loneliness, fears of failure and thoughts of his dead mother. The entries in his diary would record just how deep his arctic hell had become:

> Oct. 29 A very hard night. Saune violently delirious all night, talking, screaming, struggling & soiling her couch almost continuously. About the worst night I ever passed. As result of being nauseated all night, I feel a bit weak this morning. . . .
>
> . . . When I look at the pictures in the Heralds, I can hardly realize that there is a world so different from this "Black Hole." Ah Jo and Marie, was I criminally foolish in staying? Shall I really never see you again.

> Nov. 5 Matt & Ahngmaloktok gaining steadily. Pooblah and Saune weaker, but hanging on tenaciously.
>
> I ought to be doing some writing now every day, and I should be made of sterner stuff and not mind my surroundings; but I cannot compose myself to work with the faithful people who have worked and lived and traveled with me for 3 years, passing away about me, clinging to me with their hands, following me with their eyes, mutely begging me to keep them from the dread journey, which would to God I could do.
>
> Took a walk to several places where Jo, Marie & I were in that sunshine, which even now seems so far away. . . .
>
> Nine months from now the ship should be here.

> Nov. 6 A year ago today mother died. How different things will seem when I return. For a week past, the places of my youth have been with me, Bridgeton, Fryeburg, Portland, the Cape. Ah Mother, Mother.

> Nov. 17 . . . Kardahsu delirious again this afternoon.
>
> Is it possible that my compulsory landing at Erik H.[arbor], instead of here, followed by this epidemic among my people has been a means of Providence to keep me from wasting my strength in work to the westward this Fall?
>
> Only these misfortunes, or my own illness, would have kept me from my original plans. If it is so, it will be in line with other occurrences of the past few years. Time will tell.[44]

Nov. 19 . . . Again I built the needed grave, dragged the body to it, and with Ahngmaloktok's wife performed the funeral rites. It destroyed my appetite for the day.

Again all the natives are practically of no use for four days.[45]

Each one of these deaths brings home to me so sadly the thought that mother died while I was absent, when had I been there I might have held her in my arms at the end.

I cannot realize that she is really gone.

Nov. 30   Today is the last day of a most melancholy autumn. How pleasant it would be to put in a year with Jo and Marie visiting the capitals of every country in the world. Dreams, only dreams.[46]

Even little, looked-forward-to pleasures failed to materialize. When he opened his Christmas package that Jo and Marie had left for him, it contained only a picture of Jo and a calendar made by Marie. He had resisted, time and again, opening the envelope before Christmas, even though he thought there would be consoling words from his wife to make the day special. But the package contained no letter.

In his isolation, Peary brooded on Dedrick and documented in his personal memoranda what had led to their dispute. He would have no competitor, and he warned the doctor by Eskimo messenger, "If I have reason to suspect that you are in any way, directly or indirectly attempting to antagonize the interests of the Expedition or if you tamper with any of my caches, I shall feel myself justified in taking efficacious measures of prevention."[47]

In response, Dr. Dedrick made several attempts to offer his medical services, writing that if Peary did not want him at his house, he would stay close by "to relieve any illness existing."[48] But Peary wanted no more of the doctor, even though the natives continued to suffer. In all, six adults and a child died.

That same fall, Dr. Cook had several occasions to correspond with Jo Peary asking her for permission to publish several of the pictures of Bert and Marie he had taken while with the *Erik*. He complimented her on her book for children, *The Snow Baby,* which had just been published by Frederick A. Stokes, and informed her that he had had her elected an honorary member of the Arctic Club, "for which privileges you must pay the penalty of dinning with us once a year." Then he added as a postscript, "I hope to get to Washington in the Spring, and I will then look you up. In the meantime you must come to New York and live among civilized people. Washington is the home of political degenerates."[49]

The doctor did pass through Washington that spring and then went on a lecture tour through the South, appearing in Richmond and New Orleans, among other cities, in March 1902.

As summer came on and Jo Peary was making final plans to sail on the *Windward* to bring Bert back once and for all, she received an announcement in the mail:

> MRS. CHARLES FIDELL
>
> ANNOUNCES THE MARRIAGE OF HER DAUGHTER
>
> MARIE FIDELL HUNT
>
> TO
>
> DR. FREDERICK ALBERT COOK
>
> ON TUESDAY, JUNE THE TENTH
>
> NINETEEN HUNDRED AND TWO
>
> BROOKLYN, NEW YORK [50]

The couple married on Frederick Cook's thirty-seventh birthday. Because it was the second marriage for each of them, they had a simple, private ceremony in the parsonage of the New York Avenue Methodist Episcopal Church.[51] The newlyweds honeymooned briefly in Saratoga and then went to Florida, where Fred had another series of lectures booked.

Upon hearing of his marriage, Dr. Jackson Mills (who had treated Matt Henson's eyes) lamented the world's loss of Dr. Cook as "one of her most enthusiastic, able and earnest explorers," but added, "There is no doubt you have chosen the happier lot."[52]

When they returned to Brooklyn, the Cooks took up residence in a mansion on the corner of Bushwick and Myrtle Avenues that had been built by the late Claus Lipsius, a wealthy brewer. The house, which they had purchased shortly before their wedding, was impressive. Made of stone and three stories high, with a turret on one side, it had no fewer than 84 windows and was filled with elegant, hand-carved trim. Marie's money bought the house; she was very well-to-do from the estate of her first husband, Willis Hunt, a popular Camden homeopath.

Dr. Cook had replaced his familiar white horse and one-lunger with a four-cylinder Franklin and took great pleasure motoring on his rounds, sometimes taking the corners on two wheels. His new office at 670 Bushwick Avenue was fitted out with the latest equipment, including a roentgen-ray machine, an extreme rarity in private practice. He set his office hours for his patients' convenience: daily 1 to 2, evenings and Fridays 6 to 8, and on Sunday 9 to noon.[53]

The doctor's practice prospered as his patients recommended him to their friends. "He was endowed with capacity and judgment of high order," one colleague recalled, "and . . . drew patients to him in great numbers and inspired a confidence that neither time nor absence could destroy."[54]

Ruth, Fred, and Marie Cook, 1902.

The Cooks had hardly settled into their new home that fall, however, when reporters came knocking at its door. The *Windward* had arrived in Sydney with the Peary expedition, and aboard was Dr. Dedrick.[55] Neither man had spoken to the other during the entire trip, but their feud was about to go public.

Herbert Bridgman was the first to speak. He acknowledged that Peary had gathered up extensive papers and other "relics" of the disastrous Greely Expedition but denied rumors that among them were human bones that had been gnawed by human teeth or cut by knives. Greely demanded the papers be returned to him. Instead, Bridgman turned them over to the Peary Arctic Club, along with an initial report on Peary's accomplishments during his four-year expedition.

"Lieut. Peary has done great work," he told reporters, "and has succeeded in going further north than any American has ever done before, he having reached latitude 84.17 which is about 260 [sic] miles south of the pole. His trip on sledges from Cape Sabine to the point reached was about 800 miles each way, and is probably the longest sledge trip ever made. Peary said that he could have gone further north, but the great cost and the distance he could have traversed each day, which was about one mile, made the effort undesirable. The ice was drifting westward, and for that reason, too, it was very hard to make any headway in a northerly direction." However, Bridgman concluded on a doubtful note: "As to whether he will ever make another attempt to reach a point further north in the arctic than he has I am unable to say."[56]

In reality, 1902 had not been much more satisfying to Peary than the previous three and a half years. It had started badly when Dedrick crossed over from Greenland. Peary ordered him to take all of his effects from Sabine and never come back. He wrote up the incident for Jo's benefit:

> The cur on the other side turned up as soon as the ice was safer (Jan 6) anxious to do any kind of work for the expedition. I told him very plainly that I was done with him & as soon as he had his things sent him about his business. Since then he has been writing but I have paid no attention to his letters. He has been no trouble & has not been able to interfere in any way.[57]

As spring approached, Peary despaired of being up to another trial with the chaotic polar ice to the north:

> I seem to have reached the end of the lane. What I gained in Greenland I am losing in Ellesmere Land. Soon they will call me a fake, say I am just hoarding what I can mint from the public's credulity. Yet, would it profit me to confess that all my savings, all my wife's savings, all that I can beg, borrow or steal, have gone into the quite inadequate equipment I have gathered for the next attempt?[58]

But he made the attempt anyway, starting April 6 from Cape Hecla. Fifteen days later, suffering from all his physical impediments, Peary climbed a pinnacle and looked out on the chaos of old ice rubble covered with deep snow; he knew his quest was at an end. In his diary for that day he wrote:

> April 21st—The game is off. My dream of sixteen years is ended. . . . I have made the best fight, I knew. I believe it has been a good one. But I cannot accomplish the impossible.[59]

When the *Windward* arrived, Peary was eager to be gone. The ship stayed less than one day and reached Sydney without incident. Soon he would be home, where he could get proper medical attention and rest. But first he would have to face a battery of questions from reporters who wanted to know about his dispute with Dedrick. They were not long in getting less positive statements than Bridgman's from Peary's former surgeon, who had just arrived by rail from Sydney.

"The report that I was mentally unsound is a malicious lie," Dedrick insisted, "and as to whether the report is true or not I am willing to leave the whole question to a capable and trustworthy commission of experts. . . . This commission can examine all of the evidence, including every word and action, as well as my diary, my resignation and acceptance, and all my correspondence before and since with Lieut. Peary.[60]

"It is very hard to have been maligned as I have been and not talk," the doctor continued, "but I shall, nevertheless, adhere to that determination on my part. Concerning . . . the denial of food to me by Lieut. Peary, even a little coffee without sugar, I shall say nothing at this time.

"The reason I remained in the arctic was purely one of duty to the expedition, and was not for any monetary purpose. When I was a member of the expedition I contracted not to publish articles, and I shall not act otherwise now. There has not been a single day since I left the expedition, over a year ago, that I have regretted the step I saw fit to take, and the knowledge that I acted in an honorable manner has done much to mitigate the unpleasant experiences I had and the vicious attacks made on me."

The reporters asked Dedrick to address the report that he had left the expedition because he was not allowed to have command of it while Peary was away. The doctor called such an idea "palpably absurd."

"Why, if I attempted to answer all the untruthful things I'd be busy with nothing else for a long time to come," Dedrick exclaimed. "Lieut. Peary has not returned as yet, and I do not care to say anything until after he has returned to this country. However, I will make a statement on Wednesday evening at 7 o'clock at the home of Dr. Cook. I cannot state now what subjects I will touch upon, but there will be a statement of some kind."[61]

Wednesday evening, the reporters were on Cook's doorstep, but since Dedrick had not appeared, they turned to Cook for information. He seemed reluctant to say much.

"The Peary Arctic Expedition," Dr. Cook began, "consisted of three men—Lieut. Peary, Dr. Dedrick, and Matt Henson, the colored man, who has been with the Lieutenant for a long time. Of course, as matters were, there could be no such thing as a Lieutenant Commander, although it was Peary's original intention to place Dr. Dedrick in charge of the natives. Later Lieut. Peary found that he could assume charge of the natives himself, and after that, at different times, he transferred that duty to Henson. Out of that grew the various differences between the explorer and Dr. Dedrick, which finally led to the resignation of the latter. . . .

". . . Dedrick thought it would not be right to leave Peary.

"We at length gave up the attempt to persuade him to come home, and concluded that there was something wrong with his judgment. Of course, Dr. Dedrick is sane, and the course he pursued was simply his idea of justice and good faith."

When asked to explain Dedrick's statement about Peary's refusal to give him food, Cook said, "I differ with Dr. Dedrick on that question, and I think that he should have taken the provisions we offered him during the Summer when we were there with the Eric. Dedrick that Winter did go to Lieut. Peary and offered to buy some provisions, and Peary refused to accommodate him. I can easily understand that action by Lieut. Peary, for he had his plans made for the dash for the Pole, and I can see how it was that he did not have an ounce of food to spare.

"You must remember," Cook added, "that these three men had been in the Arctic three long years and passed through three Arctic nights, and an Arctic night is 110 days. I have never known men to live together one Arctic night and not feel like kicking each other. The fact is, this affair is simply the ordinary friction of an Arctic expedition. There are a lot of little details about the whole thing that I have forgotten."[62] And Dedrick never appeared that evening to supply them.

Only after his bonus was denied because Peary claimed he had failed to certify that he had turned over all his diaries, as stipulated in his contract, did Dedrick release a statement to the press. He said he had asked Peary on three occasions for medicine to help sick natives and had been rebuffed, and when he had gone to see him in 1902, offering whatever aid he could, he was ordered to leave immediately. At that time, he said, he felt that his responsibility to stay at Annoatok ended.

Dedrick's statement only hinted at what had happened between Peary and him. Apparently, the doctor had concluded that further insistence on the payment of his bonus was useless, and the details of his differences with Peary were too painful to repeat in public. "The animosity exhibited in the endeavor to brand me and bring me into disrepute . . . and [Peary's] threat to maroon me for a fifth year . . . if I was at the headquarters side of the channel when the ship arrived, make reasons for my resignation unnecessary. A discriminating public can imagine that they exist. They would entail a long and shameful story, and I shall never undergo the mortification of repeating them if I can help it."[63]

Peary refused to reply to the doctor's statement; his attitude indicated that he was not particularly perturbed by the charges. Though Dedrick had said his motives were "as pure as the driven snow, as plain as A, B, C, and as noble as God ever gave a man,"[64] Peary did not think the public was discriminating enough to take them seriously.

In Europe it was not quite so pat. In London Clements Markham of the Royal Geographical Society praised Dedrick for staying north, and J. Scott Keltie, the society's secretary, after receiving a letter from Dedrick alleging some "nameless conduct," asked Peary for his version, so that he might be prepared to meet any criticism. Peary ignored the request.

But when Peary heard that Morris K. Jesup had also received a letter from Dedrick, that was an entirely different matter. Peary seemed deathly afraid of what Dedrick might write to the man noted as a leader in all religious efforts in New York and especially for his support of campaigns against immorality. "I hope you will waste none of your valuable time on him," he wrote to his patron. "Knowing the man, I will ask that any further letters you may receive from him, may be sent to me, for I feel that your time is too valuable for such trifles."[65]

Dr. Cook told Dr. Dedrick that he deplored the rumors circulating about him and wished to stamp out any false impressions. Dedrick was invited to join the Arctic Club. When he accepted, Peary immediately submitted his resignation.

Another four-year expedition arrived home from the Arctic at about the same time as Peary's. When it reached Norway, there were no personal sensations or questionable conduct to explain. There was only a record of solid accomplishment. Otto Sverdrup and the *Fram* had returned.

Sverdrup, as good as his word, had made no attempts on the Pole, but he had made great discoveries. He had charted 1,750 miles of new coasts, enclosing an estimated 100,000 square miles of new land.

Clements Markham praised the results of Sverdrup's expedition, saying they surpassed all that Kane, Hayes, Hall, Greely and Baldwin combined had done. Peary he pointedly left out. Instead, Markham praised "the higher qualities displayed by Peary in the performance of important services to geography."[66]

Once again, praise, foreign medals and comfortable surroundings steeled Peary's resolve. After an operation in October to help ease his difficulty in walking, he moved with a curious shuffling gate, not picking his feet up entirely off the ground, but not limping, either.[67]

By November he was speaking before the American Geographical Society about the merits of his four years in the North, though in reality he had little to show for them. His main emphasis was on his 1900 trip to the north coast of the Greenland Archipelago. Along its shores he had named each cape, bay, fjord and glacier after a member of the Peary Arctic Club, matching the prominence of the feature with the importance of the man—and the size of his monetary contribution. In his speech he again took pains to underline the significance of such an honor. "It may seem to you a matter of little importance," he told his audience, "that these places have been named for these men, but if you reflect a moment, you will see that it is a matter of great importance, for it means that their names will be perpetuated as long as a civilized tongue is spoken."[68]

When he appeared before the National Geographic Society, despite Herbert Bridgman's doubts, Robert E. Peary sounded very much like a man who was not yet cured of his ambitions, and who was certain of the path to his own immortality:

> The man who has the proper party, the proper equipment, and the proper experience, and can start fresh from the northern coast of Grinnell Land with the earliest returning light in February, will hold within his grasp the last great geographical prize that the earth has to offer, a prize that ranks with the prize which Columbus won; and will win for himself and his countrymen a fame that will last as long as human life exists upon the globe. Granted this, shall we let others win the prize from us? . . .
>
> The North Pole is the biggest prize the world has yet to offer; the race for it the greatest race on earth. . . . The winning of the Pole is for all time.[69]

CHAPTER 11

Between the Forbidden Tundra
and the Smiling Snow

DR. MILLS WAS WRONG IN HIS ASSUMPTION THAT FREDERICK COOK HAD made the happier choice, because he wasn't asked to choose. Marie, impressed by her new husband's former exploits, did not discourage future efforts. She even thought that she, like Jo Peary, might want to share in his adventures.

In the fall of 1902 Dr. Cook read reports of the expedition of Alfred Brooks and D.L. Reaburn. They had headed a United States Geological Survey party, which the previous summer had penetrated 450 miles across the almost trackless interior of Alaska and touched the base of a great mountain.

Though well known to Alaskan natives, who called it Denali, "the high one," it had only been described and recognized as a colossal massif in 1896 by a Princeton-student-turned-prospector, William Dickey. After a dispute with a fellow prospector who, although he made his livelihood panning gold, advocated the Democratic rallying cry of "Free Silver," Dickey named the great mountain after the Republican candidate for President, William McKinley, champion of the Gold Standard.[1] Dickey had guessed its elevation at 20,000 feet, which would make Mount McKinley the highest point in North America.

In 1898 George H. Eldridge and Robert Muldrow of the Geological Survey had fixed its position, and the next year Lieutenant Joseph S. Herron of the War Department had discovered a pass across the front range that led to the mountain's southern slopes. Brooks and Reaburn made no attempt to climb the mountain but confirmed that Dickey had not been exaggerating; they estimated its height at 20,300 feet. They also discovered a large glacier draining its slopes, which they named after Willard J. Peters, one of their surveyors.

In the January 1903 issue of the *National Geographic Magazine,* they set forth a detailed plan for ascending the peak and outlined three possible routes to its base. The first two required a single season to accomplish, but the third required spending the winter. It was the first route they described that interested Cook most:

The party should land at Tyonek between the 15th of May and the 1st of June, equipped and provisioned for a three and a half months' journey. . . . For a party of seven men twenty horses would be needed. . . . From Tyonek a boat would be dispatched with a part of the provisions to meet the party at the Skwentna. . . . The pack-train would take a northerly course from Tyonek, crossing the Beluga near the head of tide water, and thence heading directly for the lower canyon on the Skwentna. . . . After reaching the Kuskokwim waters it would turn to the northeast and follow the base of the range, the route being identical with that followed by our party. . . . It might reach the base of the mountain by the first of July. . . . Climatic conditions permitting, a month could then be spent in exploring and ascending the mountain. The quickest way out of the country would probably be to the northward . . . to the Yukon. . . . The cost of such an expedition could be approximated at $15,000 for a party of ten men. . . .

. . . The writers strongly urge that if the expedition is undertaken that it be put under the direction of a man who is not only an experienced mountaineer but who has also had long training in frontier life and exploratory work, for the success of the expedition must depend in a very large measure on its leadership.[2]

In Brooks's plan Cook recognized a feat that could be accomplished in a single season, avoiding the "home-destroying" absence of another polar venture. He must have felt that he met Brooks's requirements—except that he was no mountaineer. But his talks with Whymper and Conway in Europe had interested him in the problems of climbing, and in May 1901 he had attended the organizational meeting of the American Alpine Club in Philadelphia, becoming a founding member. The more he read about it, the more he felt his experience in high latitudes would be applicable to high altitudes. "To men of a polar turn of mind," he wrote, "it is easy to be diverted from solitudes of the Arctic ice fields to the snowy slopes of great altitudes. Polar exploration and high mountain climbing are twin efforts which bring about a somewhat similar train of joys and sorrows."[3] Cook immediately began laying plans for an expedition to Alaska. For a party smaller than ten, the whole expense, he estimated, would be no more than $5,000.

He visited David T. Abercrombie's store in Manhattan and ordered a red Shantung silk version of the tent he and Amundsen had used in the Antarctic, weighing only three pounds. He also put in orders for supplies suitable to the journey outlined by Brooks's article. To pay for them he sought every means available.

In March 1903 he petitioned Peary, now the president of the American Geographical Society, to put his plan before its council in the hope that they would sponsor the project,[4] and arranged a substantial advance for exclusive articles giving an account of his attempt, successful or not, from *Harper's Monthly Magazine*. He also sought companions willing to contribute toward the expenses of the expedition.

The first taker was Ralph Shainwald, a fellow member of the Arctic Club. Shainwald, the son of a wealthy manufacturer of paint, had been on the fruitless Baldwin-Ziegler Expedition. Ralph's father contributed $1,000 to secure a place for him on Cook's venture. For a time, however, it looked as if Dr. Cook might be going back to the Arctic instead—with a second Ziegler expedition.

William Ziegler, president of the Royal Baking Powder Company, hoped to immortalize himself by sponsoring the expedition that first reached the North Pole. His fortune, estimated in excess of $30 million, allowed him to outfit his expedition in a first-class manner. Ziegler's misfortune was in his choice of leaders. Peary's meteorologist, Evelyn Briggs Baldwin, was given the command and failed so utterly and ignominiously that Ziegler dismissed him. The expedition's photographer, Anthony Fiala, recommended Dr. Frederick A. Cook as a replacement, but for some reason the suggestion did not take, and Ziegler appointed the mild-mannered photographer himself to make another attempt the next year.[5]

Cook's second companion was Robert Dunn, a Harvard man who had been to Alaska in the Klondike rush of 1898 and had returned in 1900 to attempt a climb of Wrangell Volcano. In between, he had been a newspaper reporter for Hearst's *American* and the *Commercial Advertiser,* whose reform-minded editor, Lincoln Steffens, recommended him to Cook. Steffens liked Dunn but found him incorrigible, calling him "pride in person."

"He had no respect for anybody or anything," Steffens recalled. "His method of conversation was to draw people out till he discovered what they held most sacred and then to 'spit on the emblem thereof.' He certainly spat upon us, all of us, and all our emblems. . . . He scoffed at those who agreed with him until he had no one to speak to."[6]

No "emblem" was too mighty for Robert Dunn. In 1902 he had been dispatched to Martinique, where just two weeks before, the eruption of Mount Pelée had snuffed out the city of St. Pierre and its 30,000 inhabitants in a matter of seconds. Dunn had climbed to the rim of the smoking crater, and there he spit into it.

Though Steffens had eventually fired the contentious Dunn, he never lost confidence in his reliability as a reporter of facts: "Dunn simply could not lie," Steffens believed. "This born artist had to report things as they were.

"It was this observation about him that prompted me to have him taken along on Dr. Frederick Cook's first attempt to climb Mt. McKinley. I had seen a good deal of arctic explorers, read their books, and heard their gossip, which revealed to me that no book in that field had told it all; they all left out the worst of the wranglings and depressions which were an essential part of the truth about human nature in such tests."[7]

Dunn, who hailed from Newport, suspected that Cook thought he might have some rich relatives who could contribute to the expedition, which was still short of cash. Dunn asked, but the only money he got was from his aunt, Anna Falconnet Hunter, who gave him $1,000 for personal expenses.

"The gentle Doctor came to me in New York with a plan to ascend to the summit of McKinley," Dunn recalled of his first meeting with Cook. "He had been a polar man [but] had never climbed an Alp, nor had I; but McKinley was a simple task, said he, at the rate of 5,000 feet a day. Our arctic outfit assured it—silk tent, oil stoves and pemmican. The uncertainty was in reaching the base."[8]

Dunn visited the doctor's house. He was greeted by Mrs. Cook, whom he later described as "big boned," "plump, with pallor invading her eyes." She called for "Doctor" to come and offered her guest a bad Manhattan.[9] As he waited, Dunn looked at the pictures of Dr. Cook in full arctic regalia that hung on the walls. To him the house seemed "large and sloppy," littered with chairs and stools made of tusks and bones, fashioned into fantastic shapes, and other curiosities from Cook's previous adventures. After hearing the doctor's plans, Dunn had reservations:

> [We were] taking long chances, I thought, on success. Our time for reconnoitering in uncertain weather was too short. McKinley was a very large mountain, quite unexplored, deeply bedded in a great range.[10]
>
> My family feared that Cook was "visionary" and unreliable as a leader. Much I cared. I was conscious of only one danger, the real one of scaling a high alp.[11]

Dunn accepted Cook's invitation of membership in the Arctic Club and agreed to go as "geologist" of the expedition. Even so, he admitted to having little knowledge of the subject and even less equipment—a geologist's pick was all he packed—though he promised to take a winter course at Columbia.

Since the American Geographical Society had failed to take an interest in the project, the remaining funds were made up from Mrs. Cook's ample pocket, and through Herbert L. Bridgman, Cook secured the loan of a compass, an aneroid barometer and a pocket sextant from the Peary Arctic Club.[12]

When all seemed in order, Dr. Cook and the rest of the party, including Marie, boarded the *Northwestern Limited* on May 26, 1903, for the Pacific Northwest. At the Yakima Indian Reservation, 15 packhorses were selected and sent on to Seattle, where the general outfit was purchased.

There they were met by their packer, Fred Printz of Darby, Montana, who had served Brooks in the same capacity the summer before. He was a little man with a big wad of tobacco. Dunn thought him "reserved, self-wrought and young; perhaps a philosopher—you could not tell in a city."[13]

Dunn's first impression of Shainwald had been less favorable:

The Doctor brought with him a college boy he called Hiram, who had enjoyed a summer session of a quarrelsome North Polar expedition, when he made a collection of flowers, which excused him as "our botanist"—though he admitted pistil and stamen were all the same to him. He was small, dark, rotund, and a shameless punster; most self-assertive, and believed himself a young inventor.[14]

He was a Jew. . . . I have the racial, not the religious, repugnance to Jews. I had never relished their race-selfishness, and scouted their tenacity under physical and mental stress.[15]

Dunn didn't think much of the next member of the expedition, either, Walter Miller, a total stranger picked up along the way when a search for suitable pack hands failed:

The Seattle hotel was jammed with applicants—lined and shaggy men, with vast frontier experience, who deserted when our string of fifteen broncos broke loose through the railroad yards; all but one—a pale, thin, slight youth, named Miller, citified, uncouth and low-voiced as they are out on the coast, who having been thrice refused came down to see us off—and sailed with us.[16]

The steamer *Santa Ana,* with the expedition and all its gear, headed up the picturesque coast on Cook's thirty-eighth birthday. Soon they passed Vancouver Island and entered the Inner Passage, coasting between Alaska's wilderness islands, stopping briefly at the few civilized outposts along the

Ralph Shainwald, Fred Printz, Frederick Cook, Robert Dunn, Walter Miller.

coast—tiny Juneau, ancient Sitka, Yakutat. It was the same passage taken by countless others in quest of a golden dream in the Klondike and retraced by those who returned, more often than not, broke and broken by the hardship they found in a vast and heartless land.

At Kayak Island, off Valdez, the last member of the expedition, John Carroll, attracted by Fred Printz's story of a creek he had crossed with Brooks that would yield 12½ cents of color per pan, attached himself to the expedition. In John Carroll, Robert Dunn finally found his kind of man: "Jack was a black-haired, square-foreheaded Apollo of Irish blood, whose partner had died in his arms on the Copper in '98, who began life as a breaker boy at Scranton, Pa., and has been rancher, plumber, and would argue you to sleep upon free will."[17]

As Dunn observed his fellow explorers, he remembered that Steffens had told him before leaving, "You must write exactly what happens, whether you reach the top or not, be the first to tell the whole truth about exploring. The rows, the bickering—,"[18] and decided to take up that assignment:

> The passion of the long trail, I knew, brings out the best in you and the worst, and all in scarlet; and while the law of compensation wisely provides that in the after memories which make up life, only what is pleasant survives, it did not seem to me quite fair to nature or the blessed weaknesses that make us human, in recording things, to forget too much. The tragic moment in the heat of the trail's struggle, the thing as it was to you as you were—to note that with all the passion of heroism, the beastliness or triumph of the moment—would not such a record among real men in the end all turn out fair?[19]

And so Robert Dunn resolved to keep a diary that left nothing out—from his point of view—and would spare no one, not even himself.

The steamer arrived off Tyonek after midnight on June 23, well after the starting date suggested by Brooks. From the deck of the ship, Dr. Cook could see in the twilight a snowy crest far to the north:

> This peak like a star on a cloudy night would blink and disappear with marvelous quickness. It did not seem to us as being very far away, nor did it give the impression of great altitude, but there was a mystery about the thing which kept one's attention pointed. This in reality was Mt. McKinley, one hundred and fifty miles away, the ultimate destination of the impatient adventurers on board the *Santa Ana,* the new Eldorado of the big game hunter, the gold seeker, and the mountaineer. . . .
> We were all the wildest kind of dreamers.[20]

At dawn the packhorses were slung over the side and, though nominally guided by Swedish sailors in boats, were largely left to their own devices to swim the half-mile and tumble ashore wet and exhausted on the beaches of Cook Inlet. It took a long time to find and corral the horses scattered up and down the beach, and one, Bosco,[21] which had nearly kicked its stall to bits on the voyage north, busted down the fence and evaded all attempts at capture rather than risk further immortalization in Robert Dunn's diary.

It was hard work dodging the hooves of kicking horses, nursing "chawed" fingers and readjusting constantly slipping cinches. But in two days of horse-breaking at the government corral, Printz, who deemed the horses "not jest the animals I would have chosen," tried to make a pack train out of cayuse chaos.

Dunn, like John Verhoeff before him, was uncomfortable with the presence of a woman in what he considered a man's world, and when the doctor suggested Mrs. Cook might accompany them part of the way overland, he was violently opposed. He offered the $1,000 his aunt had given him to keep Marie Cook off the trail, which the doctor accepted. He could have saved his money. Tyonek was an impoverished settlement of 20 Indian families, six white men and a single woman, and when Marie Cook found her ideal of roughing it up against the real thing, she decided on a retreat to the more attractive confines of Valdez to await the return of the expedition.

Afterward, Dunn wondered whether the doctor's suggestion about Mrs. Cook's going on the trail had been a bluff to part him from his money. It was just the first of many things about the expedition's leader that Dunn would wonder about. He had already been sizing up Cook and found him stolid and hard to read:

> I think he would face death and disaster without a word, but through the insensitiveness of age and too much experience, rather than by true courage. I cannot believe he has imagination; of a leader's qualities he has shown not one. He seems our sympathetic servant. I suspect no iron hand behind his innocence.[22]

> The Doctor seems green at this Alaskan game. He doesn't even smoke, and that makes me uncomfortable.[23]

Leaving Bosco to the mosquitoes, on June 25 the pack train set out, with each of the 14 horses bearing 150 pounds of supplies, and arrived the next day at the Beluga River, appropriately filled with white whales. Here Cook split the supplies in two, he and Miller taking half in a boat that had been brought up from Tyonek by Miller and Shainwald. After ferrying the men across the river in the boat, he placed Dunn in charge of taking the pack train overland along the trail pioneered by Brooks. They were to meet in eight days at the Skwentna ford and decide the best course from there.

That evening, after drifting down the Beluga, Cook and Miller found themselves in an embarrassing situation. As they were approaching the mouth of the Susitna, the tide suddenly went out, leaving them for the night on a

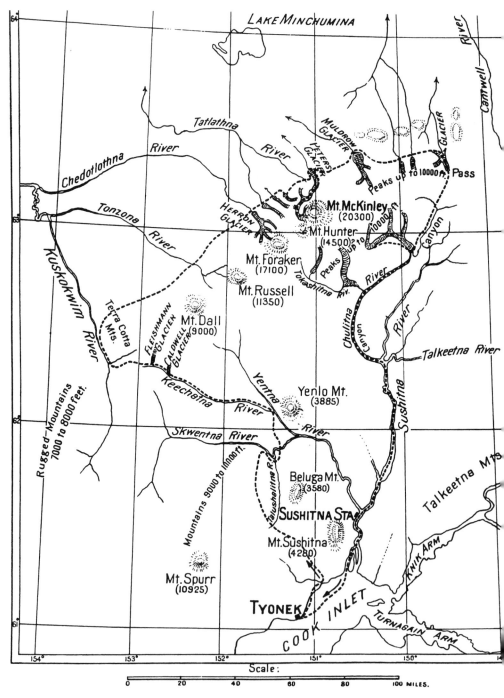

Dunn's map of the route of Cook's 1903 expedition.

mud bar. The strong tide of Cook Inlet raised the fear that the boat might be swamped when it came back in, making for a sleepless night. Much to their relief, it came in very gently, and they made for the river's mouth. But even with the aid of Stephen, a Siwash Indian they enlisted to help, it took four days of strenuous poling and hauling to cover the 20 miles to the trading post at Susitna Station, a small Indian settlement. The uniformly bad weather did nothing to discourage the hordes of mosquitoes and gnats that followed the boat in black clouds, making the trip even more of a torment.

At the station they exchanged boats and picked up another native helper, Evan, who assured them it would take at least 20 more days to reach the designated meeting point. But by July 8 they were camped on a small island in the middle of the Skwentna River awaiting Dunn.

That very day at noon the pack train appeared at the riverbank. Dunn was in no mood for an exchange of pleasantries. The tone of the doctor's "Hello, Dunn" brought Stanley's "Dr. Livingstone, I presume?" to the mind of the exhausted leader of the pack train, and the sight of Cook in his mosquito-proof hat irritated him. "If a man can't stand the 'skeets as God made him," fumed Dunn, "he's no right up here."[24]

Dunn's story of life on the trail made the boat journey sound like a vacation jaunt: "Oh, our beautiful oaths! Hot, hungry, dizzy, insane with mosquitoes, we struggled waist-deep in yellow muck, unsnarling slimy cinches, packing, repacking the shivering, exhausted brutes. . . . It was endless. It was torture."[25]

Jack had also shown a bad temper, and Shainwald had been, in Jack's opinion, "a fifth wheel." Hiram had shot one of the horses in the head by accident with his .22, on which occasion Printz had remarked, "Alaska ain't no place fer little boys with girls' guns." Fred Printz had shown a long-suffering disposition. When his foot was stomped by a cayuse and turned blue at the ankle, he consoled himself by thinking that though he was missing the "Fourth o' July" dance in Darby, he couldn't have done much dancing anyway, with his foot all wrapped up in electrical tape.

Dunn begged Cook to exchange Shainwald for Miller, but the doctor said that things had gotten along well as they were and there would be no changes. The horses, showing the wear and tear as much as the men's tempers, had their packs lightened, with the excess to be taken the 20 miles to the Kichatna River by boat while the pack train continued overland.

Dunn, still trying to get a handle on the doctor, wondered whether the 'skeets would have chewed off his long hair by the next time he saw him:

> He's just told me awesomely he'd been afraid Miller would have yielded up his spirit to mosquitoes on the river, and propounded a weird theory that their poison in the doses we get injures and depresses the blood. I like him, but then,—I haven't hit the trail with him yet. He's just given me a pair of bedroom slippers. "To wear

about camp," he says. I thanked him. . . . He says "How?" instead
of "What?" when you ask a question.[26]

The boat had to be taken into the Yentna River to reach the Kichatna.
Cook, Miller and their two Indian helpers paused along its course long
enough to climb a spur of Mount Yenlo. Their path lay over broad marshy
meadows in which they often sank to their waists in icy water. Then they
picked up a bear trail that led to the base of the mountain, ascended through a
dense forest on its lower slopes and pitched camp on an old glacial shelf above
the five-foot grass that clothed its upper reaches.

In the morning, they had a magnificent view of the easterly slope of the
Alaska Range and the vast fertile lowlands that ran up to it. Over all, 75 miles
to the northeast, towered the huge beehive-shaped summit of McKinley,
loaded down with all the snow that could balance upon its sheer slopes. Food
having run short, lunch came at the expense of several ground rats before they
started back for the boat.

Arriving at the meeting place late on July 13, they found the pack train
encamped on the south bank. Now the boat would be sent back in care of the
Indians, and the whole expedition would proceed overland with the horses.

From Dunn's report, the second leg of the pack journey sounded as if it
had been even worse than the first. Horses went down in the yellow mud slews
with disheartening regularity. They constantly entangled their packs in the
thick underbrush of alders, which lacerated their legs and through which a
trail had to be hacked with axes.

The mosquitoes were horrible, as were the green worms that had stripped
the trees bare; they clung by the hundreds to drying horse blankets and
formed a scum on the packs. Then there were the yellow-bellied horseflies that
blackened the sunny sides of the birch trees. Printz would run them through
with a straw, saying as they flew away, "Thet's how I like to serve you gentlemen." The flies ate half the hair off the pack animals and were so thick on the
horses that they could be pulled off in handfuls. When they were, the sores
they left oozed blood.

The strain of the journey had continued to tell on the men as well. More
and more, Ralph Shainwald and his numerous foibles and idiosyncrasies had
become the target of the frustrations of the other men. They yelled at him for
his "stunts" and called him ugly names, they "lost" his cherished mosquito-
proof hat in the fire, which they fueled with his bulky botanical gear as well,
and they used his college flag, which he hoped to fly from the top of McKinley,
to wipe the dishes. "I pity him," Dunn wrote in his diary. "Nine men out of
ten fresh from the city wouldn't do half as well—couldn't stand this. . . .

". . . But he is long-suffering and doesn't kick. Yet I prefer volatile men like
Jack to the easy-going sort. I'd rather see a man break loose and rip things up,
than swallow everything in muteness."[27]

But Dunn's preference was now talking about going back with the Indians down the Kichatna, so to make sure his judgment of men was not misguided, Dunn talked Jack out of it.

Dunn tried to get Cook to assign duties to keep down the "kicking" over Ralph's alleged failure to do his fair share. He also fretted that the doctor might be just as bad. "An expedition of this sort will not run itself, unless the leader sets an example by getting up first, starting breakfast, and leading tirelessly in every job," he complained. "It's the only way to escape giving orders, which the Doctor won't do either. He just fusses with his instruments—junk, I call them—and like most tenderfeet is an incessant boot changer."[28]

So the discontented expedition hit the trail all together for the first time: "Jack and Printz chopped trail ahead, the Doctor led the train with L.C., the lead horse, groaning under the junk boxes, then four horses, then Ralph lazily moving his fat little legs and shouting just in time to drive them off the trail; then four more beasts, then Miller, tall and silent in brown khaki, then five, and yours truly, the peevish rear guard."[29]

The going was better now, but the horses' legs were swollen double from contact with the alders, and the horseflies had left many of them dazed and septic. The pack train had to cross and recross the river as they took to traveling in its bed. Shainwald insisted on riding the horses across, prompting a fistfight with Dunn, who was sick of Hiram's self-assertive ways.

Dunn muttered that the horses would play out long before they got near Mount McKinley, but Printz, though he too thought they should be rested, at first would say nothing. "He was the greatest diplomat I've ever known," wrote Dunn, "to offend, even to disagree with anyone to his face—except Hiram—he found impossible." And besides, Printz said, he was "sorta contracted" to the doctor.

When Dunn decided he would speak up, Cook seemed indifferent:

> His pack train is going to the devil, and he doesn't pay the least attention. He just packs and unpacks his instruments. I wonder if he can use a theodolite after all?[30]

> Our chief's down there by the river, praying over his junk, smiling at screws and nickel cases, lifting, stroking his old Abney level. I no longer ask him to show quality; I wish he'd show something. He's too silent; hopeful without being cheerful; slow-witted.[31]

> It was funny to see the Doctor bucked off the big buckskin fording a creek yesterday. Away he went after his mosquito hat, and didn't get it. Then he tied a red handkerchief over his ears, so he looked like a Bashibazuk. It must have been a fearful loss, that mosquito hat. . . . Now he is telling about killing pelicans [*sic*] in the Antarctic. . . .

. . . Move tomorrow? No one knows. The Doctor said we'd try it, and see how it goes. . . . The Doctor won't tell if we're going two hours or twenty. He can't make up his mind. He can't seem to grasp the situation.[32]

Progress was slow, anyway, because it rained almost incessantly, so Cook finally decided to do as Printz recommended through Dunn: rest the horses a full day and then take them on for three hours a day until they recovered. Still they played out. Dunn was disgusted and ran ahead to the doctor saying something about "having sense knocked into him some time."

"Dunn, it doesn't do any good to talk like that," Cook said quietly.

"I'm sorry if I put my feelings too strongly sometimes," Dunn apologized, but the doctor only answered, "Dunn, you talk too much and too loud all the time."[33]

When they reached the Tatina River, they had to ford its twisting path 40 times in two days. But as they entered the higher lands, the horses gradually recovered.

Looking for Simpson Pass, last seen by Herron's expedition, Miller and Dunn went ahead to scout but reported only a blind canyon. When they came into camp, Jack was complaining of pains in his chest, the same complaint he had voiced off and on for about a week. Dr. Cook had first diagnosed it as neuralgia, and it wasn't improving Jack's quick temper one bit. But now the doctor said he thought it might be pleurisy.

By July 27 Herron's elusive pass still had not been found. A trip up a promising valley by Dr. Cook and Fred Printz had turned up nothing, so Dunn decided to do a little exploring on his own:

I left camp, saying nothing. In half a mile, Fleischmann Glacier pushed its flat blueness out upon huge slate moraines. Waded the stream near the pot-hole, and mounted the boulder-strewn esker. It appeared to wall a niche in the blind range. I rose, still keeping west; the walls seemed to slip apart; my heart was burning; a steeper, darker valley opened—and, quite against all physiographic law, turned narrowly downward, bent to the west among sharper, darker mountains truncated by cloud. The pass! The Kuskokwim valley, illimitable, untrodden unto the tundras of Bering Sea! . . . How chary life was of such triumphs as this; what wonder men went to the devil, seeking in civilization to counterfeit such intoxication.[34]

The next day Cook led the pack train up and over the pass Dunn had rediscovered, crossing a huge ice bridge to a grassy meadow that marked the divide. The splendid spruce forests of the Kuskokwim then came into view. As they descended the steep pass, it became more and more evident that John

Carroll could not go on. Dr. Cook was for sending him back; the others balked at his recrossing the pass alone. But after several days, they came to regard Jack's complaints with less seriousness and agreed he should return.

He was given the weakest horse, an ax, a skillet, a milk can, a cup and grub for ten days. The others wanted to have him sign an agreement that he had returned of his own free will and relieve them of any responsibility, but the doctor forbade it. "Must be an Arctic wrinkle," Robert Dunn noted. On August 1, as Jack retreated up the pass on the moth-eaten gray, Robert Dunn and the others started on the last 150 miles to the base of McKinley:

> The wilderness unfolded, vast and dumb, there in the west; low, translucent mountains hovered far beyond the horizon, across some aqueous gap. Over all the great Kuskokwim was sprent, a long-drawn lacework of crackly glass bits, dazzling in the eight o'-clock sun. Ghostly shadows filled the low ridges and flat hollows of this no-man's waste, burned and naked, dull carmine with fire-weed. Never was wilderness so vast and serene, so without inspiration, without even melancholy; so powerful, so subtle, so unplanetary.[35]

A week later they rose over a dome-shaped mountain and saw the broad gravel bed of the Tonzona River far below. The doctor continued to mystify Dunn. He had already characterized him as "dull and gentle," "so kind and colorless" and "lacking a ruling mind." Now, as the pack train descended, Dunn had come to think of him as something of a joke. "He's a fearful combination of stubbornness and indecision," he decided. "Long ago he said he expected and wanted criticism, but no one now dares advise or suggest anything; but may laugh in his blue shirt sleeve instead, at some of his moves."[36]

On this side of the divide they came upon large numbers of caribou. They had hoped to live off the land, though except for a bear, they had been unable to shoot anything other than the one horse. Fred Printz, the acknowledged hunter, shot just as poorly as the rest and had taken to blaming Cook's ancient Winchester .44—which he referred to as his "Antarctic blunderbuss"—remarking, "Like some of them horses, it was a good gun once." But now, as they plugged away at the caribou, Dr. Cook vindicated his gun by bringing one down, though the others said it was their shots that had killed it. With fresh steaks in prospect, they settled into camp, where Dunn found a good use for his unexercised "geologist" skills: "I have been digging out a sleeping-hole to fit my hips, with the geological hammer. Fred is changing his socks. He's always doing that; has at least three pairs in commission—sleeps on one, which takes more courage than I have."[37]

At breakfast on August 12, several tremors shook the camp, and there was a verbal earthquake as well when Dunn's constant carping finally struck a spark. When he remarked sarcastically that one of the doctor's "moves" was the "cleverest" yet, Cook told him that he had quite overstepped his bounds. Dunn backed off: "The crowd stared, as if a dynamite fuse were discovered fizzling out under our noses. I forbore. The idea of taking my remark seriously."[38]

In the days to come, there were more arguments and more miles to cover. On they went, up the hills and down again, ever northeastward toward McKinley.

Caribou were now constantly in sight, and dinner often just wandered into camp. Printz wolfed down plate after plate, which caused Cook to ask whether he was off his feed. Printz's reply that "a hawg eats fast, y'know; and don't take no small bites" drew a smile from the doctor wide enough for a rare glimpse of his gold tooth.

On a summit Printz would say, "Gawd, I can see Seattle. Let's go to the dance tonight." The doctor said it was good practice for McKinley, which finally was in view over the endless ridges, its bulk striking Dunn with awe— and something else again—at such close range:

> Falling mists defined a blur in mid air; a white feathery dome; tiny specks of rock and ridge lines developed, threw out the long, curved summit in breathless and suppressed proportion—sheer on its broad face, buttressed by tremendous white haunches, to right and left, which quaked and quivered through the mist, mounting 20,300 feet to the very zenith. . . . We descended suddenly to . . . the stream where Brooks had camped, at the very base of Mt. McKinley; altitude, 2,600 feet, fourteen miles as the blow-fly flies from the summit; camped with forty-six days' incessant travel— ten days faster than the government—behind us. . . .
>
>   . . . I began to think, and think, and think. . . . This was a strange place, a strange hour, an unnatural quest. How did it all come about? Why am I here? What for? Who are these companions? . . . A hundred answers . . . came . . . romances, confessions, wills and testaments, undreamed tales of death, triumph and transfiguration—between the forbidden tundra and the smiling snow.[39]

The camp was on the headwaters of the Tatlanthna River. They had hoped to arrive at this point on August 1, but it was already the 16th; the early Alaskan winter snows would soon begin to cover the highlands and freeze the grass on which the horses depended for forage.

For five days, continuous rain and drizzle made prospects for starting bleak, but they could wait no longer. Nursing a fire, they huddled in a Fuegian windbreak as the doctor outlined his plans.

One man would have to stay below and read the barometer, he said. Cook asked for a volunteer. None spoke up. They hadn't come this far to miss the main chance. So he decided that all would go on, and whoever showed worst on the first day's climb would return. Miller and Dunn were sent to the last willow thicket to bake zwieback—bread double-baked to remove all the moisture—to use on the mountain, a task they found difficult in the driving rain. The packs were arranged in 40-pound loads: an eiderdown robe that could serve as an overcoat or part of a sleeping bag, the silk tent, rope of horsehair, and provisions—fuel and food for ten days. Inexplicably, there were only three ice axes, so the fourth man would have to use the tent pole.

Dr. Cook studied the mountain for a possible route:

> To the northeast there was a long ridge with a gradual slope, but this ridge was impossible as a route to the summit because of several lesser peaks, which absolutely barred the way. To the southwest there was a more promising ridge, also interrupted by a spur, but which we hoped to get around. The western face of the great peak between these ridges, above twelve thousand feet, was an almost uninterrupted cliff of pink granite, so steep that snow would not rest upon it. Hence the only way to the summit from the west was along the southwesterly ridge.[40]

They crossed the river and ascended a narrow valley to 4,200 feet and established a base camp. It continued to rain all night, and they were forced to move to higher ground when the stream they camped next to overflowed its banks and into the tent.

The next morning, despite the bad weather, they started with five horses over the moraine of a glacier flowing from one of the valley's amphitheaters and then went onto the glacier itself. Cook named it Shainwald Glacier after his long-suffering companion. The doctor led, sounding with his ice ax. It was slow work finding a safe route between the crevasses. Some had to be jumped, which the horses would do only if they were beaten into making a terrified leap. Some horses broke through and had to be hauled out again as snow bridges collapsed. At 7,300 feet the horses were halted while the doctor and Shainwald went another thousand feet up.

Dunn, Fred Printz and Walter Miller waited in the silk tent, where a smell like mildewed cotton filled the air. Since little could be seen ahead, Cook and Shainwald returned and waited for the weather to clear. They had a dinner of zwieback and caribou ribs in the crowded tent. "The zwieback was voted a success," recorded Dunn. "The Doctor is going to use it at the North Pole. Now and then as the clouds parted overhead to let down a chill silverish light, conceal the wavering edge of this snowy cistern, reveal shreds of sky too cold and lustrous to be blue—Fred would say, 'Yes, sir, a hundred and sixty acres more of heaven cleared off. She looks like the break-up of a hard winter.'"[41]

When morning came, Dunn found the view all too clear: "Never were such steep walls, such hanging glaciers jeering at the laws of gravity, such overbrilliance of sunlight and azure sky. . . . Southwest, we looked out over sharp-angled black slate and irony tuff, clean-cut and glistening as if created yesterday."[42]

Miller said he would be the one to take the horses back at the end of the day and read the barometer. Though Dunn thought this unfair, since Miller seemed to have "shown" as well as anyone, in fact he had volunteered.

Leaving the horses at camp, the five began their assault up the talus that spilled from the east wall of the moraine of the glacier, stopping every 200 steps to catch their breath. Once on the snow slope, Cook, carrying the tent pole, fell and rolled nearly to the bottom. When he recovered his balance and climbed to the top of the first ridge, he did not like what little he could see. "No possible slope from here either," he said, "and even if we can get up the ridge to its peak, we're not sure of getting further." The doctor said they should return, and since no one objected, they started back down the talus as it began to drizzle again.[43]

Gingerly they urged the horses back over the same crevasses they had crossed earlier in the day and were soon packed in the tent at the bottom of the glacier from where they had started. It was silent in the tent except for the thunder of an occasional avalanche, at which Fred would habitually remark, "Another lumber wagon." Nothing was said of the first defeat.

The next day, in a blinding snowstorm, reconnaissances by Dunn and Printz failed to turn up any more promising route. Then Cook and Shainwald came in. Hiram had seen signs of a route, he said, and he enthused over how easy it would be to climb the mountain from that angle. Dunn was suspicious of just how much they could have seen under the existing conditions and even more of whether the doctor was up to the task at all:

> That sort of insincerity makes me boil. As if it would do any good for God Almighty, in such a story book, Arctic-traveler fashion, to lie in order to keep up our spirits. Pretty examples of courage men must be to rig up a fool's paradise around them to give them courage. . . .
>
> . . . I felt that the Doctor was not trying his best to climb the mountain; that recognizing it was beyond us, he was making half-hearted tries to escape our judging him a quitter. . . . Every member of the party, except myself, had always spoken as if he thought that to reach the summit of Mt. McKinley would be little harder than scaling—Pike's Peak for instance. . . . Nothing, apparently, could shake these opinions up to now. . . . If the others' confidence were only a prop to determination, I hold that a pretty false, even cowardly, frame of mind in which to approach a great task; and if such self-deception is customary, as it seems to be, in polar ventures, it is easy to understand their constant failure. . . .
>
> . . . I was angry with myself for having consented to come with these people, whose experience on snow mountains was nil— though, God knows, mine is small enough. . . .
>
> The Doctor determines on a certain move; he has the feat accomplished before starting. He will not hear of difficulties, and

when his unreasonable dream of success turns out a nightmare, he
is all meekness and dependence, and asks your advice in a hopeless,
demoralized way. . . . I criticize him with no conceit that I could do
better: I couldn't, with our equipment and personnel, do as well—
I can't keep my temper nor take anything in life, even reaching the
summit of McKinley with such placid, stubborn seriousness.[44]

The only remaining prospect seemed to be in the direction of the outflow
of Peters Glacier, which required skirting along the front range. As the pack
train began to toil to the north toward the foot of the glacier, Dunn went with
the doctor "in the deadening silence usual in his companionship" to have a
look at it from a nearby peak:

At last I broke silence. It took some effort to make him discuss
our rebuffs and chances on McKinley. He expressed the same blind
confidence we should reach the summit, now tinged with a melancholy ill concealed by a smiling naivete, which made confidence
ring even less sincere. The momentary rasp in his throat, the precise phrasing, grated on my outworn nerves. At last, in a moment
of real depression, he said: "Yes, I'm afraid it may be as Professor __
said, that it would take two seasons to climb this mountain."I was
for once all tact and sympathy, but it was like drawing teeth.[45]

Of course, failure would be more terrible for him than for me. In
my selfishness, I had never thought of that, till this real flash of
doubt bared the poor man's heart.[46]

From the top of the peak, Cook picked out a camp for the next day on the
north side of the glacier. Reaching the great expanse of ice was hard enough,
but crossing it, he and Dunn found themselves sliding on clear ice one moment, then ankle deep in soft muck the next. They hit for some sparse spruces
along a roaring stream that flowed out of the huge mass of ice. There they rejoined the pack train and made their second base camp.

After crossing the river the next day, the men came upon the remains of a
recent campfire. They thought it might be a Siwash camp until they found
some Kodak film wrappers and a pair of overalls. These were the traces of
Judge James Wickersham of Fairbanks, who had made the first attempt on the
mountain just two months before. Not knowing this, they took it to be the
stopping place of surveyors, who Fred Printz said were "as thick as gamblers in
these parts."[47]

Straight toward McKinley they headed, between the glacier's moraine and
the white granite peaks. Climbing the lateral moraine, they looked upon
Peters Glacier—a mile-wide sheet of ice stretching to the vanishing point—
with countless hanging glaciers draped from the mountains' walls beyond.
Across the glacier they hoped to gain the south arête and find a feasible route
to the top, but time was running out. On August 25 they started up.

For three days they explored the river of ice, looking for a route. Robert Dunn said words would mock and crawl to detail that trek, but as usual, he found them in wretched excess:

> Hanging glaciers, split by irony pinnacles, overhung like titanic crocodiles, vomiting brown chaos into jagged black cavern-mouths, under smooth pillars of pearly marble. An azure wrist of ice—a snow bridge—buttressed a huge detrital cone on the white plain, and beyond a city of brown pyramids huddled at the mysterious bend, where one huge feeder scuffed up under the "pink cliffs" in the cirrus gloom of three linear miles overhead, just tipped by the weak, slow-moving sun.[48]

On August 27 Dunn, who had outdistanced the others, was confronted by an awesome sight:

> Suddenly a wall of ice peeked out from behind the buttress—ridged, pinnacled ice, growing into an enormous serac, the whole breadth of the glacier, massing into a white Niagara, hinting of the world's end, the unknown range, and the hid deserts of the moon. It towered, widened. I was planning to scale it and return before eating; but, aching with hunger, I saw the human trio behind crawling along an ice ridge, and waited.[49]

Shainwald had been dispatched to bring up the horses, and after lunch the remaining four roped together in twos. "We started up the ice-fall," Dunn recalled, "struggling among its wrecked white skyscrapers that jutted out in cubes and blocks beyond gravity angles; crawled along little snow ridges, shinned miniature Matterhorns, where the sudden deeps were chill and ugly. A blizzard began. We tried lead after lead to the top of the chaos, but steepness and the driving snow herded us back."[50]

At 4:00 the doctor decided to continue up the serac with Fred and see whether there was a way to the top, instructing Miller and Dunn to return to camp and bring up the rest of the equipment with Ralph when he brought the horses in from the spruce camp. Dunn argued against Shainwald's being taken on the climb but was rebuffed by the doctor. Sullenly, he started back to camp with Miller, as Printz and Cook disappeared behind a veil of falling snow.

At camp there was no sign of Shainwald. Entering their tent, Dunn soon dozed off as Miller went on and on about his amorous adventures in Room 10 of the Bohemia Hotel. By morning Ralph still had not come, and Miller's stomach was giving him trouble. He insisted on starting for the serac, however, but soon collapsed. After the contents of his backpack were cached in a rubber coat, Miller started back for camp while Dunn continued on alone.

Dunn met Cook and Printz heading down to camp to see what was keeping the others. Hearing of Miller's predicament and Shainwald's absence, Printz went back for another load while Cook and Dunn mounted the serac:

We roped up the serac by a crafty combination of snow pinnacles, toward a tiny speck on the vast polar plain—the tent—which it seemed I'd never, never reach; where six inches of snow had fallen in the night as an avalanche hurtled past. The Doctor's anticipations were working smoothly. He was jubilant. Sure! He'd found a way to the summit of McKinley. "Unless we have very bad luck," he said, "we shall be there within five days.". . .

We were to climb this big spur, though the rocks above still looked to me very steep. . . .

Cook and Dunn on the icefall.

The Doctor has just said over the pea soup, "We shall spend a night on top of McKinley. I don't think that has ever been done on so high a mountain in such a latitude—why, I don't understand." So, another litter of chickens is hatched out and counted.[51]

When the sun struck the red silk the next morning, Dunn and Cook continued upward, resting frequently between winding around hidden crevasses and probing snow bridges with their ice axes. After reaching the foot of the ridge they planned to climb, they cached their loads and returned to the tent to await the others. When they did not appear, the two started down the serac and back for base camp.

There they found Printz and Shainwald asleep in the tent. Ralph, not able to find the horses, had gotten himself lost trying to find camp and had spent the night on the glacier. Miller was now below looking for the lost cayuses. He soon appeared with the horses, and after a good night's sleep the other four started back for the silk tent left at 7,500 feet, reaching it by evening.

They broke out the mountain food—pemmican—which Dunn thought looked like mushroom spawn and tasted like plum cake. Here they sorted out what they would take to the summit, discarding most things but food and warm clothing.

On August 29 they started to ascend the slope stretching upward for 3,000 feet, taking 50 paces between resting places stomped out of the hard-crusted snow. Dunn thought how freakishly peculiar they looked in the dark-tinted sun goggles each now had in place.

Before long the incline increased to such an extent that steps needed to be

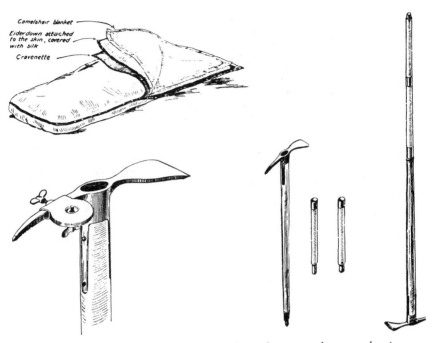

Camelshair blanket
Eiderdown attached
to the skin, covered
with silk
Cravenette

A sleeping bag, an ice axe with a camera tripod attachment, and a tent pole – ice axe.

cut. Each had to be hewn out of the ice after removing the 14 inches of snow covering it. The chosen route stretched upward beneath a huge overhanging wall of ice that ended in two rock balconies, dubbed "Fred's rocks" since Printz had first spotted them. Among the four, there were only the three ice axes; Dunn had the tent pole, which, he was now painfully aware, was no substitute.

The men took turns cutting steps, and when it became Dunn's turn he gladly exchanged the pole for an axe, but he also got a chorus of criticism from those behind for cutting the steps too far apart. At least he had the pleasure of being the first to catch sight of a new peak in the range—a giant peak.

They rested for lunch, but one taste of the cheese they had laboriously lugged up convinced them it was too salty to eat. Once they had decided on a zigzag course up between the overhanging cornices, they did not rope up, fearing that a slip by one might take them all. Just that possibility now filled Robert Dunn's mind:

> As the steps changed from a stairway to a stepladder, the other
> three betrayed no excitement, no uneasiness. Neither did I at first,
> but I felt both. . . . As hour succeeded hour, I lived each minute
> only to make the false step, cursing inwardly, but only at what then
> would be said by our civilized friends, their pitiful comments on

this party, that with no alpine experience just butted blind into the highest mountain on the continent. . . .

Climbing Mt. McKinley with a tent pole. Sometimes I boiled in those dizzy, anxious places that I had put myself in such a position with such men. My blind neglect of the Doctor's silence on alpining now reproaches in another way. It is not bringing out his lack of staying power, as I thought, but his foolhardiness. . . .

One requisite of the explorer—besides aversion to soap and water—is insensitiveness. I understand why their stories are so dry. They can't see, they can't feel; they couldn't do these stunts if they did. . . . So I can't help admiring Hiram and the Doctor and their callousness, which is not bravery, not self-control. Their brains do not burn, horrifying the present with the supreme moments of life. It's better so. Where would we be if there was another fool like me along?[52]

By 5 P.M. they reached a massive snow cornice, climbed it and pitched camp. There were not three square feet on the level, so they dug into the wall to get a flat space, spiked down the tent and crawled inside. The aneroid read 9,500 feet.

Dunn wondered out loud what would happen if the overhang should give way under them during the night. The others changed the subject. Soon they were all laughing:

This is a great joke; there is something devilish about just being here. Everyone is in a bully humor, more tolerant of his fellow than ever before on the trip. Aren't we the only ones in all this dastardly white world? How would it pay for the only four creatures in the universe to be the least at odds? We depend on one another. And yet, perhaps our devotion is—only the warm tea.[53]

The Doctor has been a real companion the last two days. Probably he realizes this is the final effort, and is making a grand play to come up to scratch. At any rate, to-night I'm convinced he's really trying for all he's worth to get up McKinley; that this is the actual, hell of a bluff I promised myself to make on the mountain. Even if we fail, the worst suffering will be over—the days following the first repulse—and then, Oh! how I shall feel for him, perhaps an undeserved pity, but it will turn all the tables of my regard. . . . And all my righteous disgust of the past and revulsion of race toward Hiram have vanished. To-day we exchanged the brotherhood that civilized people do *not* fool themselves into believing is always the heroism of explorers in a tight place. I know it's hollow and meaningless; take away the danger, and all will be as before.[54]

It was a wakeful night for Robert Dunn as he struggled to justify the terror he felt as the hours slowly crept by:

> I can feel the deathlike silence. No one is asleep, yet no one
> dares move lest he tell his neighbor he's awake. A cold blue from
> the nether world forms with the awful twilight a sort of ring about
> the tent which magnifies the texture of the silk, and rises and falls
> as I lift my head from the pillow of trousers and pack. It is a sort of
> corrupted rainbow, or what the halo of a fallen angel might be like,
> I think—the colors burned and wearied out. . . . I am not cold, but
> I shiver, and shiver; . . . I doze.[55]

The next day they resumed the slow climb upward. As they did, the huge
massif of Mount Foraker appeared, 17,400 feet high, looming below McKinley's southern haunches. All Robert Dunn's icy fears were just one misstep
away:

> Whew! Those next four hours! I had the tent pole, of course—
> no one would touch it on that stretch. . . . A hundred times I con-
> cluded . . . I was not meant to climb mountains; a hundred times
> more I called myself a fool, seeing the awkward rears of Hiram and
> the Doctor; . . . I turned just for the delicious suffering of seeing
> the hateful Below spring upward . . . with Foraker leaping like a
> rocket into the sky, the far pond-spattered tundra sweeping sky-
> ward in waves. . . .
>
> Doctor was in the lead. It was my turn to cut, but he did not
> seem inclined to take the tent pole and give me the ax. . . . I offered
> and offered the pole, but couldn't tell if he withheld the ax because
> he thought I'd rather stay behind, or didn't want to give it up. I was
> content enough behind, but I felt he thought he was sort of sacri-
> ficing himself to me. "It's all ice here. Look out," he would say
> calmly between most deliberate steps; and stopping to hack a little
> deeper. "Are they too far apart?"—just the things I should say
> ahead there, but I was not saying them; words of big consolation; I
> admired him mightily. . . . "It's getting a little leveler," said the
> Doctor. It was. And then I would ply him with questions about
> that, laughingly fishing for more assurances. "Rocks ahead, the
> edge of a ridge, something, see them," he said. So there were.
> "Thank you, thank you," I said, as if that were all the Doctor's
> doing. "God! I admire the way you take this slope," I'd exclaim.
> And, by heaven, with all these mean pages behind, I still do.[56]

They continued to climb for another hour before they reached the spur
top, and there, looming before them and apparently blocking their path, was a
sheer pink cliff:

The Doctor dropped his pack and ran, mumbling an order to camp at the first flat spot, dashing through the deep snow toward our coveted ridge, now so black and puny. I saw it was hopeless. . . .

. . . Here where the black ridge leading to the top of the pink cliffs should have flattened, all was absolutely sheer, and a hanging glacier, bearded and dripping with bergschrunds, filled the angle between. . . .

. . . Looks like another brood of chickens hatched out dead.[57]

As they pitched the tent after leveling off a spot for it, the barometer read 10,800 feet, then adjusted to 11,300. Cook, from his position above them, looked out on the awesome view of the glacial ice 7,000 feet below.

Inside the tent the men were settling in for the night when Cook came in:

"Never, never," he said solemnly, "have I seen anything so beautiful." That from him! The Spirit of the North, like Moses, has struck water from the rock. But it's so. I've seen it. No cloudfloor hides the forbidden tundra, no mist softens the skeleton angles of these polar alps; only a wan red haze confuses the deeps of the universe, warning that they, and we and life at last is of another world.[58]

They slept late. Then Printz and Cook went back up to look at the prospects. While they were gone, Dunn apologized to Ralph Shainwald for all he'd done and said on the trip out. They talked earnestly about their pasts. Dunn was trying to make his peace, for as much as he had been terrified by the ascent, he feared even more the going back.

Finally, the other two returned and the doctor announced that they were checkmated by the sheer cliff ahead. Shainwald did not want to go back and argued a dozen routes, but the doctor insisted. So camp was packed up, those things of no use kicked off the ridge, and they started downward.

The descent was everything that Dunn had feared:

How I got over Fred's rocks don't ask. I've heard of persons sweating blood, and something red kept dripping from my forehead in that most ghastly descent. I remember I talked incessantly to the Doctor of the various sorts of courage; how easy it had been for me to stand on the crater-edge of Mt. Pelee just after St. Pierre had been destroyed, because life or death there *was not in my own hands,* as here; which suggested new problems about cowardice and responsibility I've not solved yet. Half way down, the Doctor insisted on taking the tent pole, for which I put him forever on Olympus between Leonidas and Brutus. We strung along Peters, each stopping dazedly in his tracks now and then to gaze back and upward, and slept at the Doctor's and my lone camp of the 26th.[59]

Rebuffed by the mountain, they now were faced with getting out of the country before winter took hold; already the grass was frozen at Miller's camp and the horses were gone. It took two days to find just seven; the others were given up for lost.

Though rations were short, Cook decided not to return the way they had come. He proposed keeping along the face of the range, crossing it north of McKinley, abandoning the horses, and then rafting down the Chulitna and Susitna rivers to Tyonek. This would take them into totally unexplored country.

With no guarantee of game or even that a pass existed over the range in that direction, Dunn felt Cook was taking such a chance "because finally defeated on McKinley we must propitiate Science by some sure-enough exploration."[60] Nevertheless, all agreed to set off on the course suggested by the doctor, who led the way with his wooden compass day after day:

> He "works out our position" each night with a pencil and a straw. We've lugged pounds of instruments which haven't been used at all, and now we're lugging them home. "There's a good chance to use your theodolite," said Miller to-day, pointing at an angle of Muldrow [Glacier]. Doc only smiled, as often before at that remark. Sometimes as we plug along I feel, from what I've seen here and elsewhere, not much will be done in Northern exploration till it gets in the hands of some one Napoleonic, brutal perhaps, but with a compelling ego and an imagination; away from the bourgeois and cranks.[61]

The brotherhood of danger felt on the slopes of the mountain had once again dissolved, as the weary grind of the trail with all its petty and real irritants—the lost horses, the bad food, the footsoreness—overwhelmed all good intentions. All was again as before.

At least now they had a ready supply of fresh meat, bagging caribou and moose almost at will as they passed the outflow of the Muldrow Glacier.

On September 8 Cook asked Dunn and Printz to join him on a climb to the summit of a mountain they called Blackhead. From its 5,300-foot heights, Dr. Cook had a good view of the summit upon which they had hoped to stand:

> An almost constant stream of clouds swept over and around the mountain from the east. . . . Now and again we could see the summit, and from here it resembled very much the crown of a molar tooth. Four tubercles were distinctly visible; the saddles seen from the west formed two, and to the east were two rather higher and more distinct. These tubercles of this giant tooth are separated by large glaciers, whose frozen current pours down very steep slopes. If it were not so very difficult to get at this side of the mountain, we reasoned that here the upper slopes might offer a promising route.[62]

The horses wandered off each night with regularity, so Cook ordered a watch to keep them in camp, saying he would take the first turn. Late that night Dunn was awakened by voices. Soon Shainwald was rummaging in the tent for the binoculars. The horses were gone! And on the doctor's watch! Dunn was livid, but Printz, even though disgusted, kept his feelings to himself, for as Dunn had recorded, "He's always hiding what he really thinks about the trail and the outfit while preaching the abstract laws of existence."

But even Fred spoke up after the doctor started up a glacier with Shainwald. Before leaving, Cook had told Miller that when Dunn and Printz found the horses they should bring them up to the pass. Printz doubted loudly that there was a pass here, or anywhere, on this side of the mountain and thought it was just the doctor's excuse not to chase after the horses he was responsible for losing. They decided to wait for Cook to return, but when he didn't, they followed.

It began to snow. There were more dangerous crevasses and more horses to be roped out when the snow bridges gave way under them. But there was also a pass, and from the head of it they looked out on the easterly foothills of the Alaska Range with its black, ragged peaks, dotted by spots of fresh snow.

In two hours they descended 3,000 feet down a steep talus slope and rested on the other side of the range. The horses had suffered terribly on the nearly vertical slope, leaving a trail of blood dripping from the cuts made by the sharp stones. But the animals, once out of that purgatory of a pass, had reached horse heaven and luxuriated in the grass, which on the south side of the pass had not yet been visited by frost and was still green and soft.

From their camp that night Cook watched the moonlit mountains over which they had passed as he listened to the cry of wolves and the rumble of avalanches in the distance. He had won his gamble and could, for the moment, revel in the vast Alaskan wilds in contentment.

Cook had predicted that once across the range they would reach the coast in two days by crossing the foothills of the Chulitna's valley and aiming for a big glacier rumored to push near to the river's banks. The route necessitated fording the icy river 40 or 50 times a day as it wound back and forth across their path. The crossings of the Chulitna's tributary, which Cook named Bridgman River, became more and more dangerous, as the men had difficulty standing in the swift glacial stream. Dunn had trouble just walking on dry land after one of the horses slipped on a boulder in midstream and came down with its full weight on his foot. Soon the river was too deep to wade at all, and he, like the rest, had to take to riding crouched on the back of the terrified animals as they plunged into the icy stream:

> Again and again we just escaped; the beast stood upright circling
> down-stream, treading water, ready to topple over, till the current
> eased, or a hoof struck a boulder safely. We began to value life; each
> kneeling on a haunch like a circus-rider, wigging an ear, banging a

neck, blinding an eye with your hand, as the shivering, overloaded beast snorted in the icy mudwater . . . and your eyes play about on the racing shore line, and the whirlpool sneaks toward you.[63]

Both Cook and Shainwald had near brushes with death in the river, and Miller and Printz ran double jeopardy because they couldn't swim. Clearly, the fording was becoming too risky, but Dunn could get nothing out of the doctor about when or if he might take to rafts:

> To-morrow'll be worse than to-day. I've just told the [Doctor] so. He simply went on eating, not even winked. Of course he never told us in so many words that he intends driving the pack train to the glacier, but has often given that impression. He gives nothing but impressions; you have to be a mind-reader to draw him out.[64]

By September 14 Cook had decided they had reached the place where the horses could no longer follow. Supplies were running critically low. The sugar was wet and syrupy and the beans were sprouting in their bag. The bread was too hard to bite, even after soaking, and was filled with chunks of green mildew, which made it look like currant cake. The tea was gone. Dunn dumped the meat out in the sand in the rain—at a safe distance from camp—as each chunk had to be deeply shaved before it could be eaten.[65]

They felled 84 cottonwoods along the river, intending to build a raft. Dunn thought the doctor so nifty at skidding the logs to the bank that he said, "You must have worked in a lumber yard once." The doctor only replied seriously, "I don't know that I have."[66]

They named the raft *Mary Ann.* Once launched, the cottonwood did not seem to have enough buoyancy for the safety of the whole party, so Printz and Miller took her for a try while the others packed the horses for another swim.

Though all got across, it was a near thing. The water was so swift and dangerous that all now agreed the horses must be abandoned. Fortunately, they had come to a place with dry spruce, and after two days in camp, they had strained backs, raw shoulders and two new rafts to show for their labor. As they ate the last of the beans and some slimy pea soup, Fred Printz fretted over the lack of salt and speculated on how ugly the squaws might be at Susitna Station, where he planned to satisfy his craving for as big of a chunk of Climax Plug as he could get into his mouth.

When it came time to shoot the horses, they were nowhere in sight. No attempt was made to find them; they were left to their chances, slim as they might be, with the coming Alaskan winter.

The spruce rafts christened *Mary Ann II* and *Ethel May,* after Miller's friend in Seattle, "the less said about the better" were pushed off from shore, and the men set off downstream.

Rafting down an unknown glacial river proved an exciting and backbreaking business. The rafts careened from shore to shore, brushed off canyon walls, grounded in the shallows and had to be hauled off inch by laborious inch, then shot ahead again only to be jammed between the boulders that could not be fended off with a drift pole. They thundered down tunnel-like chutes, never knowing whether the ripples and eddies ahead were the prelude to an unseen waterfall.

To Robert Dunn, it was as real a physical challenge as climbing Mount McKinley:

> You must be very handy with a pole. You must have a hair-fine eye for moving angles, strength of an eddy, strike of a cross-chop, depth of foam ruffling over a stump. You must be surer of the length of your pole than a polo-player of his mallet's reach. You must know, just as a frog foretells rain, how many times between this drift-pile and that eddy your raft must swing, that the dead water may catch its hind end right; how long momentum will hold you, to twist the fore end to catch the riffle six yards beyond, so you just shave the bowlder in mid-channel, swinging straight from a broadside. . . . It's a pretty game.[67]

On September 18 they stopped to repair the *Mary Ann II,* which had scraped through her underlashings. The next day they came upon ice embedded with gravel at the river edge—the finger of some gigantic glacier. Taking two days' worth of pemmican, Cook, Shainwald and Dunn struck out for its pothole. The doctor pronounced the immense mass of ice "the most wonderful accumulation of glacial debris" that he had ever seen. Ascending steep slopes, they could see the course of the glacier winding from the great peak. On the southeastern side they spotted a lesser glacier. Dr. Cook named the two after his wife and daughter, the larger, Fidele; the smaller, Ruth.

The slopes of McKinley from the east looked more promising. "Three spurs offer resting-places for glacier ice, over which a route to the summit may, perhaps, be found," thought the doctor.[68]

Regaining the rafts, they again pushed off and continued toward Susitna Station. The worst of the rapids were past them, but they were not always able to avoid the dangerous sweepers that hung out over the banks. One time a raft had to be freed by cutting away the tree it had lodged in, and another time Cook was brushed off into the river and Shainwald had to pull him out of the water on the fly.

After many misadventures and yet another canyon, a tent hove into view along with two strangers walking along the shore. "Which way did you come? By the Talachulitna?" they called out. "Them Indians at the Station'll go crazy when they see you," they said. "You're a hard lookin' lot with them red handkerchiefs tyin' up yer hair." The sourdoughs had been digging flour gold since August; they gave the explorers salt and tobacco in exchange for their rotten meat. "See me spit on the rocks," giggled Fred. "I chew it tags an' all. It'll take a hell of a lot till I catch up."[69]

It was still 100 miles to the station and 30 beyond that to Tyonek, but on September 23, after more exciting emergencies, they finally made clear sailing and were floating effortlessly toward civilization. "Beautiful! beautiful! beautiful!" exclaimed Fred Printz. "See the view change without you movin'."

Two days later they raised smoke around the bend and heard the bark of Siwash dogs and savage shouts. Coming ashore, they met a man who volunteered the latest news—up-to-date through August 10.

"But yer know the Pope's dead o' course," he drawled, "and them cardinals held a sort o' political convention, where Cardinal Gibbons he acted as a sort o' boss, and they chose another. And Roosevelt, he's agreed to complain to the Czar o' Rooshia about them massacred Jews, and someone's killed that Queen Dragon of Servia, and jumped her claim to the throne, an' Rooshia's goin' to fight the Japs. . . . There ain't much happened this summer!"[70]

The prospectors at the station didn't ask whether they had gotten to the top of McKinley. Didn't care. But they looked with interest over the rock specimens hauled from the mountain for traces of color; they ran fingers over the maps and asked questions about things they knew meant golden ease if they could only be interpreted properly from the clues.

The Indians said a man fitting John Carroll's description had been at the station in mid-August. It must have been him, since he had taken their boat. Robert Dunn was annoyed at that. The five men procured an old dory as a substitute and drifted off toward Tyonek.

As for McKinley, it would have to wait for another season. But the doctor hadn't given up:

> It is not likely that the highest peak in North America will be abandoned as impossible of ascent until the great mountain has been thoroughly explored for a route from every side. I hope to be able to make an attempt from the east. . . . Any attempt to reach the summit is sure to prove a more prodigious task than Alpine enthusiasts are likely to realize. . . . It is an effort which, for insurmountable difficulties and hard disappointments, is comparable with the task of expeditions to reach the north pole.[71]

As their boat put Susitna Station far behind them and floated toward a steamer for Seattle and home, Robert Dunn may have thought about his conversation with Cook on the way back from Fidele Glacier.

The doctor and Ralph had been comparing notes on arctic explorers they had met, when Dunn interrupted. "Don't you think," Dunn had asked, "that the leader who rouses personal devotion and enthusiasm in his men, though he be sometimes unfair and his temper quick, would reach the Pole before the easy-going, forbearing, colorless sort?"

"Dunn, your sort of leader would have to be an angel, too," said the doctor.

"Well, then, only an angel will reach the Pole—and climb McKinley," thought Dunn.[72]

CHAPTER 12

And Therefore to the Top of the World

AT THE ARCTIC CLUB'S ANNUAL DINNER IN DECEMBER 1903, DR. COOK presented a modest account of his expedition, illustrated with the excellent photographs he and Miller had taken. Though altogether a pleasant evening, at its end some members asked him to take care of some unpleasant business: to prevail upon Robert Peary to reconsider his resignation from the club.

But Cook had already written to Peary, who refused as long as Dr. Dedrick remained a member. "As you are well aware, he is a cur of the first water, and I never will knowingly retain my connection with, or membership in any of the organizations to which he is admitted," he responded, adding, "I congratulate you on the work which you did on Mt. McKinley, and am sincerely sorry that you did not attain the tip top. I hope you may tackle it again and win out."[1]

Soon there was more unpleasantness at the club involving Dr. Cook. Robert Dunn had taken Lincoln Steffens's advice to tell all, and the first of a series of articles based on his diary had appeared in *Outing*'s January 1904 number. Its contents so outraged the members of the Arctic Club that they called for Dunn's expulsion, and a motion was offered to that effect.

Steffens, by letter, urged Dunn to fight the club's expulsion order when he returned from Japan, where he was covering the outbreak of the Russo-Japanese War. Meanwhile, Steffens wrote an indignant letter to Rudolph Kersting, the club's secretary, protesting that Dunn was being punished for telling the unvarnished truth about the failings of human nature during such a trial, rather than simply reporting its dull scientific results.

When Dunn returned, he appeared at the hearing on the motion to expel him just so that he could "spit on their emblem." Though Dr. Cook was not pleased with Dunn's exposé, he nonetheless defended him before the club and tried to minimize the scandal. But Dunn voted against a motion to reconsider his own expulsion, and when it passed nevertheless, Dunn resigned anyway.[2] After the session, Steffens resigned as well.

Unlike Dunn's, the doctor's account of his expedition, which concluded in February, was totally without controversy. The writing of it gave him material for an additional lecture, entitled "Climbing Mt. McKinley: Incidents of the first exploring and mountaineering expedition to America's greatest peak."

He now had three lectures to choose from, which he billed collectively as "The White World of the Two Frigid Zones: The Story of Poleward Exploration, Picturesque, Educational, Entertaining."

Also in February he received word that the Eighth International Geographic Congress would be held in the United States. It was being organized by the National Geographic Society, which had grown from a handful of geographical savants in 1888 to a truly national organization. The upsurge in membership was due to the efforts of Gilbert H. Grosvenor, editor of its official journal, the *National Geographic Magazine.*

Grosvenor, a former schoolteacher, was the son-in-law of the inventor of the telephone, Alexander Graham Bell, who had been a founding member of the society and its second president. Grosvenor had sought to expand the society's membership by changing its magazine's format from a strictly dry and scientific journal to one of wide popular appeal. Bell had made Grosvenor the assistant editor for that purpose in 1899 at the princely salary of $100 a month and defended him through a number of internal conflicts that resulted in the ouster of the unsalaried long-time editor, John Hyde. By 1903 Grosvenor had become, at 27, not only the editor of the magazine but director of the society, and he would rule it with an iron hand.

In the words of an associate, he was "an absolute monarch" whose opinions, judgment and word in anything to do with the magazine were final. He laid out three simple principles regarding articles to be included in it: each must be absolutely accurate, of permanent value and devoid of all partisanship and controversy.[3] His plan was starting to show results; membership was increasing.

Naturally, Dr. Cook had been a member for some time, and when he learned that the society would be sponsoring the meeting, he was one of the first to register to attend. He would go, along with Dillon Wallace, as a representative of the Arctic Club.

The congress's attendees were a veritable who's who of geography, and Dr. Cook recognized many old acquaintances among the delegates, including Henryk Arctowski, Alfred Brooks, and Professors Heilprin and Brewer. On September 7, 1904, the congress was opened by its president, Robert E. Peary.

Peary, after two years back in civilization, was an entirely different man from the one who had sailed so silently home on the *Windward* in 1902. Gone were the nightmares of failure and the discouragement he had felt that last horrible winter at Payer Harbor.

For the first two consecutive years since 1891 he had not been beyond the Arctic Circle. But he returned each summer to Eagle Island, where he had built a modest Cape Cod house on its sea-facing bluff to escape the oppressive summer heat of Washington, D.C., where he was assigned to the Navy Yard, near the centers of power.

With the approval of Morris K. Jesup, Bridgman had tried to introduce a measure giving the Thanks of Congress to Peary for his explorations.[4] Though it went nowhere, Perry had, by normal longevity of service, been promoted to commander, and despite the little he had to show for his four-year "siege of the Pole," he had been decorated by the Paris and Scottish Geographical Societies. He also had received the Daly Medal of the American Geographical Society.

Having recovered his health and his confidence, he would make one last effort to reach the North Pole. In the years since his return he had reasoned that all he really lacked was a suitable ship. But this one last effort would be expensive—$100,000, he estimated, for the ship alone.[5] That spring he had written:

> My ship . . . must be of a strength to resist and a shape to lift to the pressure of the ice, and with power to smash and wedge and squeeze her way through the ice-floes. A massive, powerful steamer, not a sailing ship with auxiliary engines. . . .
>
> . . . I expect soon to place the contract for the hull of my new ship, and the supervision of this and the raising of the balance of the funds will occupy me fully for the next ten months. There will come the repeated trials of the ship and engines. . . .
>
> . . . I hope to reach the northern shore of Grant Land in early September [1905], winter there with my ship, and very early in February begin the sledge journey which, God willing, shall attain the pole.[6]

Now, as he stepped forward to introduce the congress's distinguished guests, Peary knew he would have his ship; the Peary Arctic Club would see to that.[7] It had just incorporated and would sponsor another expedition. Its members, too, had forgotten all the failures and discouragements of the past—if they had ever known of them.

At that moment, Peary's stock was never higher. Obtaining leave was now an easy proposition, since his friends in high places included the man who now sat in the White House itself. When his new ice ship was finished, Peary would ask the president of the United States for the honor of naming her after him, to put his personal seal on the new venture. Theodore Roosevelt would not refuse.[8] The advocate of "the strenuous life" thought Peary a model for American manhood—determined, never-say-die and ready to take on any physical challenge—in short, a man like himself.

But even with all of this, perhaps most satisfying of all to Peary was that Jo had borne him a son, Robert E. Peary, Jr., on August 29, 1903.

The Roosevelt.

Peary now came forward to speak, and although he did not ignore the flurry of activity in the direction of the Antarctic, he was not long in getting around to the area nearest his heart:

> It has been somewhat the fashion during the past few years, in the interest and enthusiasm excited for antarctic work, to decry further arctic work as not likely to be of value, and to assume that in the antarctic region alone is there a field for really valuable scientific investigation. I do not at all agree with this view. There are no 3,000,000 square miles of the earth's surface that do not contain scientific information of value much greater than the cost of securing it.
>
> Further than this, I believe in doing the thing that has been begun and that is worth doing before shifting to a new object.
>
> There is no higher, purer field of international rivalry than the struggle for the north pole. Uninfluenced by prospects of gain, by dreams of colonization, by land lust, or politics, the centuries' long struggle of the best and bravest sons of England, Germany, Norway, Sweden, Holland, France, Russia, Italy, and the United States, whose able delegates are here to-day, has made this field of effort classic, almost sacred.
>
> The conquest of the pole is a man's work as well as a geographical and scientific desideratum, and its attainment would move the man and the geographer in every one of you.
>
> The south pole, from a practical geographic point of view, is no less a prize (but I do not consider it a greater) than the north pole, but the north pole has a place in history, in literature, in sentiment, if you will, which the south pole will never hold. . . .
>
> I will note here but two other geographical feats of primary magnitude yet to be accomplished by the explorer.
>
> The culminating peak of Asia remains yet to be won.
>
> The culminating point of North America remains yet untrodden by human foot.[9]

The sessions in Washington heard the reading of a variety of papers. In the spring, Peary had asked Cook to prepare one on his antarctic experiences.[10] He had done that and also had written two others. The first paper, in which he told of his efforts to carry out the last feat Peary had spoken of, was entitled "Results of a Journey around Mount M'Kinley." The second was an account of the voyage of the *Belgica,* and the third, a comparative view of the Arctic and the Antarctic.[11]

Among other papers presented, one particularly caught the doctor's attention. It was titled "Some Indications of Land in the Vicinity of the North Pole," by Dr. Rollin A. Harris of the U.S. Coast and Geodetic Survey. In it Dr. Harris argued the evidence in favor of an undiscovered body of land in the polar basin northwest of Greenland.

In support of this theory, he advanced several arguments: the prevailing currents seemed to indicate their deflection by an unknown land mass lying in this approximate area; the traditions of Eskimos living on the northern fringes of the Arctic Ocean included one that a land mass did indeed exist to the north; the disruption of the tides north of Alaska indicated a moderating effect explainable by intervening land.

Cook had already read with interest the narrative of Otto Sverdrup's expedition of 1898–1902 that had appeared in the *London Times,* which Herbert Bridgman had gotten for him especially, at his request.[12] Sverdrup had discovered a number of islands lying west of Ellesmere Land. Now Harris said that he believed these islands might extend to the northwest, perhaps even to the very Pole itself. If so, this would greatly simplify efforts to attain that coveted point by significantly shortening the distance to be traveled over floating pack ice.

When Sverdrup's book, *New Land,* appeared, Cook carefully noted the Norwegian's movements and studied his maps. He was especially interested in his reports of abundant game along the route he traveled, which culminated in a point on an island the captain had named for his chief benefactor, Axel Heiberg. Sverdrup called the cape Svartevoeg because of black cliffs that rose precipitously from its shore, 520 miles from the geographical pole.

Dr. Cook was not through with the urge to go exploring. He began working on plans for a motorized boat that might enable him to navigate the treacherous rivers of Alaska for a second try at McKinley. But reading was the only exploring the doctor would do that year or the next.

Late in 1904 Dr. Cook delivered his lecture on Mount McKinley before the members of the Canadian Camp, an outing organization. After the lecture he met a physics professor from Columbia, Herschel Parker. Parker had taken up mountain climbing as a way of building up his strength and had made several ascents, including Assiniboine in the Canadian Rockies.

Parker waxed enthusiastic about Cook's description of the Alaska Range and offered $2,000 toward another attempt on Mount McKinley if he would be included in the expedition. The two went to Parker's house on Fort Greene Place in Brooklyn to discuss his latest plans to reach the summit.[13]

Cook told Parker he believed that there was a pass at the head of the Yentna River that would lead him to the southwest face of the mountain. Alfred Brooks had agreed that there was a good chance of this, though he still thought the best way to reach the mountain was from the northwest. But this time, the doctor explained, he planned on taking his power launch to move supplies up the river and save the strain of heavy loads on his pack train.

Though a lack of funds kept Cook from high adventure in Alaska in 1905, the year still held out great promise of a different kind of adventure. Marie was expecting a child that spring.

On May 30, while the doctor was at the Brooklyn wharves seeing Dillon Wallace off on his expedition to Labrador, Marie felt the baby coming. She wished and wished that Fred would come home, but by the time he put in his appearance, he had missed the whole blessed event. Marie was very upset, but the baby was fine, a healthy girl. They named her Helen and asked Lotta Davidson to be her godmother.[14]

Among the many congratulations and gifts was a bankbook containing a short note:

> Dear Miss Helen:—
>
> By the enclosed book you will see that you are the Mistress of 2000 Cents. You may like to know that this Great Fortune has been laid at your feet because of your Excellent Taste in being born on Herbert's Birthday and taking Helen's Name. Both wanted to show how much they approve of you—though it will be some time before you can joyfully "blow it in"; during which we hope You and It will Grow and Prosper. That you may be as Beautiful as your Mother and as Good as your Father is the ardent wish of
>
> > Your Sincere Friends
> > The Bridgmans
>
> (Please [do] not read this with either your Father or your Mother standing by.)[15]

The year 1905 saw the pace of exploration quickening in the Arctic. Roald Amundsen was negotiating the northwest passage in a tiny ship, the *Gjøa,* and planned to stop at the magnetic pole along the way. Walter Wellman, a Chicago newspaperman-turned-explorer, who had failed in his sledge attempts on the Pole from Spitzbergen in 1894 and 1899, had reentered the race and was readying a 185-foot-long dirigible, christened *America,* to fly to the Pole.

Also in the race was Peary. He had sailed in his new ship from Sydney on July 26 for a more tried-and-true approach over the "American Route"— through Smith Sound to Cape Sheridan. He had chosen Bob Bartlett as her master, and if he could place the *Roosevelt* at the top of Grant Land, Peary believed he should surely win. As always, Matt Henson accompanied him. Matt was relieved to be heading north again after various menial jobs and an unsuccessful stint as a railway porter.

As Peary was making his preparations to leave, he had received a letter from Callicoon Depot, New York, offering the services of "T.A. Cook, Builder of Special Sledges for Arctic and Ant-Arctic Explorers."[16] It was not the first time Peary had been offered this assistance. In 1903 he had received a similar offer:

> Seeing you are again gowing north we would verey mutch to build your sledges for you of your own Disine or of mine. . . . We make this our specalety we have the good white hickorey growing here the best to be found & have maid sledge building a study for years. . . . To get the best results the lumbr must be picked out in the thrie

and onley chuse cutts ground thru again each part of a sledge must be chusen from a cut perlicular to the strain putt it in the sledge then again the best results for toughness and spring to it the timber must be cut at the right season to get these results I have disind a sledge that with this timber with a lignumvitie shoie adops itself frum soft snow to rough sea ice with least amount of frictine on the runer this sledge ways abut sixty lbs and will cary a load of frum five to eight hunder lbs. . . . This sledge is entirely Flexible with a wide spase of give to it so as not to Break on rough Jerneyes. . . . This sledge is <u>interchangible</u> in every part. . . . If you are in new york in the near future I would be pleased to call on you and talk these sledges over.[17]

Now Theodore Cook, whose spelling and grammar had not improved in the interim, tried to interest Peary in several new models. Peary asked for the prices of Cook's special hickory and other hardwoods and also for a photo of his eight-foot sledge but ultimately wrote back that he did not think the sledge was suited to arctic conditions and turned down Cook's offer to ship him an example of his workmanship. He also said that he had found a source of cheaper wood but invited Dr. Cook's brother to visit the *Roosevelt* should he happen to be in New York.[18]

The Cook brothers were rumored to be working on something other than conventional sledges at Callicoon Depot, as well. Stories appeared in the New York papers that winter about a motorized vehicle being tested by Dr. Cook in Sullivan County that he hoped to use in an assault on the South Pole.

Actually, the doctor was planning a return to Alaska for another try at McKinley. Cook had not been able to forget the big mountain and found its call nearly as alluring as that of the Poles. "The mountain climber and the arctic explorer in their exploits run to kindred attainments," he wrote. ". . . Both suffer a similar train of hardships, . . . followed by a similar movement of mental awakening, of spiritual aspirations, and of profound and peculiar philosophy. Thus the stream of a new hope, of dreams and raptures is started, and this stream seeks a groove down the path of life for ever after. It follows that he who ventures into the polar arena or the cloud battlefield of high mountains will long to return again and again to the scene of his suffering and inspiration."[19]

On his new attempt he wanted Russell Porter, his old compatriot from the *Miranda,* to go with him.[20] Cook had heard of Porter's work as topographer on the latest Ziegler fiasco.[21] The leaders of both of Ziegler's expeditions, Evelyn Briggs Baldwin and Anthony Fiala, were members of the Arctic Club and often visited Cook's house. Although each had failed miserably in his attempt to capture the North Pole for Ziegler, they had nothing but praise for the work of Russell Porter. Porter had still not shaken off the call of adventure himself and agreed to listen to the doctor's proposal:

He took me to his home in Brooklyn and unfolded a plan for conquering the highest mountain on the North American continent,
Mount McKinley. It was a wonderful prize, he said, almost to be
had for the asking. He had tried to ascend it a year or two before
but failed and thought he now knew how to turn the trick. His
plans were almost completed and he needed a surveyor, for he was
going into virgin country.[22]

While in Washington in 1904, Cook had discussed with Alfred Brooks
the best line of attack. Brooks was flattered that the doctor had followed his
advice of 1903 in approaching the mountain along the trail he had pioneered.
He had publicly praised Cook for choosing to strike out into unknown territory for his return, calling his discovery of the new pass across the range at
6,100 feet a more important result than the scaling of the 20,300-foot mountain would have been.

By March 1906 Cook was in contact with Brooks again, trying to have
Porter put on the Geological Survey's payroll for his trip to Alaska. But Brooks
said no government funds remained to pay for a survey, and besides, he knew
nothing of the man's ability to do the work properly.[23]

Nevertheless, plans were firming up for the expedition by April. Cook
had again secured an advance from *Harper's* and had taken up Parker's offer of
assistance. But the biggest contributor was Henry Disston, heir to his father's
Philadelphia saw-manufacturing fortune, who agreed to put up $10,000 if
Cook would arrange a big-game hunt for him in the foothills of the big
mountain in the fall. Also to go was a friend of Professor Parker's, Belmore
Browne, a small, wiry artist and outdoor enthusiast, whom Parker had met by
chance in the smoking car of a westbound Canadian Pacific train. Walter
Miller agreed to go again as photographer, and as for a horse packer, despite all
his doubts about the doctor's horse sense on the last trip, Fred Printz would
also go again. Other than an additional packer, whatever other manpower
they needed would be hired in Alaska. This time, Marie would stay home with
the children. She had been cured of "arctic fever" at her very first exposure.

The expedition started overland to Seattle on May 1, 1906. As in 1903,
the horses would be picked up at the Yakima Indian reservation, but this time
Printz was to bring along another man of his choosing to help him do the
packing. Printz chose Edward N. Barrill—or Brill, he wasn't particular about
what he was called—a blacksmith from Hamilton, Montana.

Porter was amused by his first meeting with "Big Ed":

We moved on to N. Yakima. Here Prof. Parker was told to look
for a man, Brill by name, who belonged to our party. He—Brill,
was described as a very big man, wild eyed, heavy black mustache,
carried a rifle, in fact, a man to be careful about. When Prof. Parker
and I alighted at the station, the professor walked off among the
people on the platform sizing them up. I watched him step before

a giant, approaching him from the rear. He seemed to hesitate some time, letting his eye run up and down the big figure, weighing the chances as to what might happen if he was the wrong man. These moments were very funny to me while the professor played the Sherlock Holmes. Then he braced up to the man, I saw them shake hands and laugh and knew he was Brill. Later the Doctor appeared and we came on over the Cascades to Seattle, leaving Brill and Printz to bring the ponies.[24]

On May 16 the party took the *Santa Ana* north from Puget Sound, as before. On the way, much had to be done to get the outfit in shape, especially adjustments to the motor launch that Dr. Cook had had built along the lines of a Peterborough canoe, with a mere 20-inch draft. He christened the launch *Bolshoy*, after the Russian name for Mount McKinley, which simply meant "big."

Russell Porter was impressed with both the launch and his companions:

All is well so far. The entire party and outfit are on board. The men seem congenial. Everybody is happy. Just now six of us are in the riverboat....

This boat has been built for our own purposes, is flat, open, roomy and forty feet long; has a twenty-five horsepower Lozier gas engine. The doctor hopes with this boat to get us and much of our equipment close under Mt. McKinley perhaps 30 miles from the summit. This means much.[25]

Fred Printz, Frederick Cook, Belmore Browne, Edward Barrill. Photograph by Parker.

At Seldovia, a little village at the mouth of Kachemak Bay, they transferred to the tug *Neptune* for the last leg of the journey, 150 miles up Cook
Inlet, the tug pulling the *Bolshoy* behind her. She anchored off Tyonek on the
morning of May 29.

The horses were once again dropped overboard and swam for the beach.
This time they got an unexpected welcoming committee in the form of a pack
of Siwash dogs that attacked and scattered them as they struggled ashore. The
dogs chased six of the horses so far inland that they were given up for lost.

As before, the packers were to go overland to the headwaters of the Yentna
and there meet the boat party. While the horses were being broken to their
packs, Cook planned to take the *Bolshoy* on a trial run up the Susitna River
with part of the outfit, dropping off Browne and Porter to do some surveying.

Except for a tendency for the engine to suck sand into the water jackets,
the trip went off without a hitch, and the *Bolshoy* arrived at Susitna Station
early that evening. Its inhabitants couldn't credit the boat's journey. They said
the river was at its worst. Next morning the launch headed back for the rest of
the outfit and to start off the pack train.[26]

From their landing place at Alexander, Browne and Porter set out across
the ten miles separating them from the great granitic boss of Mount Susitna,
having agreed to meet the launch again in two days.

The doctor, Miller and Stephen, the same Indian employed three years
earlier, sped back down the river hoping to reach the inlet before the tide went
out and left them stranded as it had in 1903. They at first made swift progress,
but the tide suddenly turned and they were aground. The boat floated at midnight, though, and they put on power. A blow was coming out of Turnagain
Arm and was raising whitecaps several feet high. With ten miles of mudflats
ahead and a gale behind, Cook urged Stephen to guide them into Fire Island,
but Stephen argued for Tyonek. Then the carburetor began to balk and the
boat pitched so wildly that they dared only crawl about in the dark, unwilling
to light the lantern because the smell of gasoline filled the air. By 2 A.M. there
was enough light to see they were clear of the shallows, and they set a course
for Tyonek. At daybreak they dropped anchor there and sounded their
foghorn for a boat to take them ashore. Professor Parker had the cook hastily
prepare some hot food, which was ready when they landed, and nothing had
ever tasted better to the hungry, exhausted men.[27]

At Tyonek they were still looking for the horses. The search continued
until June 2 without success. The abbreviated pack train headed north the
next day with Printz, Barrill and Samuel P. Beecher, a local man Cook had employed to help. This time the horses carried only enough supplies for 30 days
and a folding canvas boat for river crossings; the rest was loaded in the *Bolshoy,*
bound for Susitna Station and the now long-overdue relief of Browne and
Porter.

On board were the doctor, Professor Parker, and two other hired hands,
Russell Ball and William Armstrong, to help unload supplies and return to
Tyonek once the water grew too shallow for the boat's draft.

When she arrived at the station after picking up the famished mountain climbers, the natives clustered around the launch and speculated on whether the boat, which had set a record in coming from Tyonek, could buck the current of the river above the station, as Cook proposed to do. At first their skepticism was gratified when the engine balked and the explorers had to retreat.

The propeller tunnel was cleared of snags, and on the next try the *Bolshoy* steadily climbed upstream. To the cheers of the onlookers, she disappeared toward the Yentna.

The boat had little trouble as long as the water was deep enough, but in the shallows she scraped bottom and damaged her rudder, which Belmore Browne fixed by diving under the boat.

When she reached the limit of navigation, camp was made not far from Mount Yenlo. It would be days before the pack train came up. To fill the time, an exploring party would go in search of the pass Cook expected would lead to the Kuskokwim Valley. The plan called for Professor Parker and Ball to remain at camp while the other five would go in a canvas boat, tracking it up the river. But the frail craft was not up to the abuse, so Armstrong and Miller were left with the boat while Cook, Porter and Browne continued on foot, taking three days' supplies and Porter's topographical instruments in their rucksacks.

The going had all the rough Alaskan obstacles: roaring icy streams that rose suddenly in the afternoon as their feeder glaciers melted in the sun, thickets of dense alder and undergrowths of devil's club on which an axe had to be used, and plenty of tormenting mosquitoes. But their reward came with their first majestic view of McKinley and the Alaska Range. Belmore Browne, being an artist, was captivated by the amount of light that lingered at all hours, enhancing the mountains' grandeur.[28]

They had many narrow escapes in crossing the swift river and food grew short, as predicted progress far exceeded reality. But Porter found the doctor undaunted:

> As the stream meandered from wall to wall, there was almost continuous wading in the ice water. . . .
>
> . . . Whatever faults Dr. Cook may be accused of, the trip up that glacial stream brought out his sterling qualities as a companion in such pioneer work. Always in good spirits and ready for more than his share of the drudgery, resourceful, and considerate of the others.[29]

Eventually the river led into a canyon. The three climbed its walls to avoid the swift and treacherous water below, hoping to get a glimpse of their surroundings. Forced to climb higher and higher, around every bend they expected to see the valley of the Kuskokwim spread out before them. But there was always another obstruction to block the view.

Even though it was the height of summer, they had to cross a number of snowslides that blocked their path. Browne recorded how treacherous such travel could be: "The Dr. got in a serious position yesterday on an almost per-

pendicular snow bank, that dropped 1,000 feet below. He got on it and could
not turn back and finally succeeded in reaching the far side of it with the aid of
a hatchet."[30]

Finally they crested a ridge and could see the rounded sheep hills of the
Kuskokwim, and beyond, a mass of unknown mountains. From this vantage
point the pass looked possible for men to the Tonzona River, but they decided
to descend the 2,500-foot-deep canyon to see whether the route was really
passable for packhorses.

After a very difficult descent of the precipitous canyon walls, they reached
the river, only to find it dangerous and apparently unfordable. Here they
stopped to rest and have a good meal before retreating to base camp. They
needed to; the only way out was back up the canyon walls, and Porter was acting strangely and seemed about to collapse. The other two men joked with
him to try to make him feel better, even though there was not much to be
happy about.

The home trail had all the outward trials and then some. They had been
on short rations since their big feed in the canyon and were now almost out of
food. Their last four meals had consisted of a cup of tea and a third of a slice of
bacon. It seemed they could talk of nothing else but thick caribou steaks and
other delicacies they had no hope of getting.[31]

When the three reached camp, it was a welcome sight indeed. Absent
eight days with just three days' rations, they wasted no time in trying to make
up the deficit.

The pack train still had not come up, so the *Bolshoy* was moved downstream to a more protected anchorage, and for the next four days all the men
engaged in the brutal work of chopping trail through the alder thickets.

When the horses arrived, there were only 11 left. Disaster had struck just
one day out of Tyonek. After they had been turned out to graze, six had fallen
into a burning seam of coal. By the time they could be extracted, only three of
the unfortunate animals could be saved. The others were scorched so badly
that they had to be destroyed.

On June 25 the remaining horses were sent up the prepared trail, while
Armstrong and Ball headed downriver with the folding boat. As it had in
1903, the pack train was forced to ford the swift glacial rivers that wound,
snakelike, back and forth along its route. Many were too deep to be waded;
the raging glacial torrents had to be crossed on horseback, with each man
crouched behind the packsaddles. Professor Parker immediately showed a
great aversion to such crossings. Even though he took the precaution of wearing a bulky inflatable vest under his coat, his tendency to panic worsened at
each crossing. He had the narrowest of escapes when his horse turned halfway
across a swift chute and lost its footing. Luckily the current swept Parker past
a point and Barrill helped him ashore, but the horse disappeared from view in
the rapids. Fred Printz seemed most upset that all the tobacco was on the professor's horse and was relieved when it was found, miraculously unharmed,
farther downriver.

After an earlier close call, Herschel Parker had confided to William Armstrong his fears about crossing the frigid rivers. "Armstrong," he said, "the world at large thinks a man foolish who climbs mountains, but if he were to drown trying to ford a river to reach the mountain, what would they say of him?"

Armstrong was one of those who thought that way. "I, for one, think the man who will climb the mountain above snow line is a fool," he replied, "and I classify him with the man who tries to swim the whirlpool rapids and the man who jumps from the Brooklyn Bridge."[32]

After several days during which acquaintance with all the miseries of the trail were renewed, the expedition reached the mouth of the canyon. There Cook, Printz, Barrill and Browne mounted horses to see whether the pack train could be taken through safely.

Even though the horses were stripped of their packs, in each of the first six crossings there were moments of doubt as to whether all four animals would stand on the opposite shore. Then the canyon split. Cook and Printz took the right fork while Browne and Barrill explored the other. The doctor and Printz quickly found that their fork offered no possibilities of safe passage and followed the others into the left fork.

After six more desperate fords, Browne and Barrill managed to climb on foot to a point where they could see the sheep pastures of the valley beyond. Here Browne killed a bear, but they left the meat when they discovered the animal was covered with festering scabs from a recent fight. When they returned to the river, it had risen greatly from the afternoon melt. It looked impassable, but hunger drove both horses and men to risk a crossing.

Somehow the horses managed to make the opposite bank at each ford, despite the raging torrent that would have swept a man away like a leaf in a tempest, until they attempted the main channel:

> The roar of the water made talking impossible and great blocks of green ice jammed the stream and threatened the horses. . . . At the first ford where the two streams joined Brill's horse lost its footing and he and his mount were swept past me in a smother of spray. At times I could see nothing but the angry water, as they were pulled under by the whirlpools. Then my horse was seized by the current and down we went with the choking freezing flood, full of small pieces of ice, sweeping us past the rugged cliffs. At last we crawled ashore and lay shivering on the rocks until the circulation returned. There is something terrifying about savage glacier water; it was 8 o'clock p.m., as well, and a chilly wind was moaning down the canyon. The cold seemed to sap the life from us. . . .[33]

After resting on the rocks, they summoned up their courage again, managing three more fords before sunset. Browne's horse collapsed after the next ford, though, and Barrill's refused absolutely to cross. He spent the night on the far bank. Browne continued alone, on foot, into camp. There he found

Dr. Cook, who had had an almost identical experience to his own, having nearly drowned in the icy river. The only difference was that Printz, who had abandoned his horse, had returned on foot along the canyon walls. In the morning, the river was well down and Printz had no trouble bringing Barrill and the horses in.

Stymied in their attempt to cross the range through the canyon, the explorers returned to base camp and set out across the east fork of the Yentna on July 3, toward the southern foothills 65 miles away, a route dotted with low-country slews filled with treacherous quicksands. As they slogged through two days of heavy rain, the boggy country took its toll on the horses, and black clouds of mosquitoes dogged the exhausted animals' every step.

Professor Parker, by now thoroughly sick of the soggy going, pronounced the climbing of Mount McKinley a marine enterprise. Parker was so worn out by the hard travel that he could no longer mount his horse without the assistance of two men. A day of rest was called while some of the men climbed Mount Kliskon, which, at 3,900 feet, was more of a hill in a land of giants. It did afford a good view of the surrounding country, however, allowing them to pick out a miner's trail that led 18 miles over the mountains to a mining settlement called Sunflower.

There they met J.A. MacDonald, the camp's promoter, who lent them a Siwash guide who styled himself Susitna Pete. Pete was supposed to know every foot of the country around the big mountain but proved more a source of amusement than information. More icy fords brought them to the head of the Tokositna River, where the lower reaches of two glaciers led back into a tangle of wild mountains.

After climbing a high ridge to the west of the river on July 19, Belmore Browne and a few of the other tired men got an unobstructed view of the great mountain's southern and western flanks:

> We reached the top to find McKinley and all its tremendous foot-hills directly in front of us and at the first look we all said "un-climbable." The Professor came up for a short time and also saw how impossible it was. To climb Mt. McKinley from the S. side, we would have to scale 18,000 feet of as difficult rock cliff as the world can produce.[34]

Professor Parker descended again with most of the others, but Cook and Browne pitched the tent for an all-night vigil hoping to study McKinley's upper slopes when they would have less cloud cover. "During the night I was constantly awakened by the booming of great rock and snow slides," Browne wrote in his diary. "At intervals during the night we got up and looked at the mountain hoping that all the clouds would withdraw, but only an occasional glimpse could we get. . . .

". . . The Dr. has I think given up all hope for making the top this year and I sympathize with him in his great disappointment."[35]

After two more days of rain they decided to go on to the next ridge by crossing a wide glacier covered with crushed granite, which Cook named for Clarence Wyckoff. On the other side they met the pack train and camped beneath a giant boulder. From the ridge top they could see to the north the glacier that Dr. Cook had named for his daughter in 1903.

In the morning, the approaches to the glacier below were seen to be barred by a wide river flowing out of its ice wall. The men skirted its face without finding a break until they reached the base of a range of magnificent knife-blade peaks, which they named the Tokosha Mountains. Here, Cook turned back because he thought the going too dangerous for Professor Parker.

The professor, Dr. Cook and Belmore Browne set out for the ridge above, with Printz and Barrill carrying supplies to the top before returning to the horses. The three pitched the silk tent.

During the night there was a fierce rainstorm. The little tent rattled like a sail but did not blow down. From the ridge they had hoped to get another point of view to survey prospective routes to the summit. But from this angle, too, the mountain looked absolutely unclimbable. In any case, they could see that the terrain was too rugged to make any real progress toward the mountain before Henry Disston was expected at Tyonek for the promised hunt. The expedition now retreated toward the coast.

For Belmore Browne this was a relief:

> We no longer had to exert all our energy of mind and body toward the overwhelming mania of speed, regardless of cost. We drifted, rather, as a band of gypsies would, as free and irresponsible as children. Laughter and rough jokes rippled back and forth along the pack-train, and we learned to play wild, shrill marching tunes on the turned edge of a red willow leaf.[36]

The march back didn't seem so carefree to Professor Parker. He had reached his limit as they faced crossing the numerous streams that flowed out of the Kahiltna Glacier. "The 'Professor' got scared at the first ford," wrote Belmore Browne in his diary, "and I had to lead his horse far below and take him across the different rivers, he riding and myself swimming."[37]

When they reached the site of Youngstown, an abandoned gold rush camp, on July 30, Belmore Browne and Russell Porter learned that the expedition would have to split up. Cook wanted the horses driven down the river to the Kichatna, where he would join Disston. The doctor conceded that there was no possibility of making an ascent from this side, so Parker decided to return to New York at once.[38]

Porter set off to map some of the peaks near McKinley, leaving Barrill and a miner named John Dokkin to care for the animals and to prepare for the hunt. Cook took Browne and Miller to retrieve the *Bolshoy*, after arranging to meet the rest of the party downriver. When they reached the river, they found the boat on a mudflat. They slept on the rocks without blankets, then worked to free the *Bolshoy* in the morning. Browne would drop the anchor in shallow water and sit on it while Miller and Cook worked at the hoist, making one foot every 20 minutes.[39] Finally she came free, and after gathering up Parker, Beecher, and Printz, they reached Susitna Station on August 1.

Here they found some men who had suffered a terrible experience. Their boat had been smashed in an attempt to run the rapids of the Kahiltna's canyon. They had been forced to stand on a partially submerged boulder for four days. When finally taken off by a rescue party with a tracking line, their feet and legs were black and swollen from the long immersion in the glacier water.

J.A. MacDonald witnessed Dr. Cook's response to the emergency. "Although tired and worn and in a bad physical condition himself," the miner recalled, "he gave his unlimited attention to a party of prospectors . . . brought into camp in an almost dying condition just before his arrival. He spent hours working over these men, and did not give himself a thought until they were properly cared for."[40]

The trip had been hard on the launch; the rudder was gone, taken away by a snag, and other damage had been done by trees overhanging the river. When they reached Turnagain Arm, the boat, which now was being steered by sweeps secured to the stern deck, ran into heavy winds blowing off the shallows of Cook Inlet, which built up a gigantic sea.

A decision had to be made to retreat upriver or try for Tyonek before the full fury of the coming storm unleashed itself. Cook decided to keep on, saying that they would seek protection in the Beluga River if the worst happened. The sea rose so high that Printz and Browne, who were at the sweeps, had to be attached to ring bolts on the deck to keep from being swept overboard.

As the storm worsened, they tried to make the Beluga River as planned but found its entrance guarded by a line of impassible breakers. Just then, the engine sputtered and stopped, and it seemed doubtful that the 30-pound anchor would keep the launch from being dashed on the lee shore. As the *Bolshoy* drifted toward destruction, Cook and the others below deck worked feverishly to clear glacial silt from the engine. When only 100 yards from the surf, the engine revived and the *Bolshoy* pulled slowly away from the breakers.

The sea pounded the *Bolshoy* so violently that Parker kept crying out, "What have we struck?" Cook then directed that they try to enter a creek near Tyonek. In attempting this, the launch was caught by a huge comber and almost swamped; then she retreated. But suddenly the waves began to subside as the tide undercut the wind's action in the opposite direction, enabling the boat to make Tyonek.

Browne and Printz made a landing in the boat's canoe, and a crew of Aleut boatmen came from shore and removed the rest of the thoroughly wet and miserable complement from the *Bolshoy.* Generous glasses of hot whiskey at first brought them around and then induced sleep.

The next day Professor Parker accompanied Dr. Cook to Seldovia to meet Henry Disston, but he was not there. They found instead a message saying that he would not arrive for another two weeks. Cook gave the professor a telegram to be sent from Seward telling the sportsman he would be waiting for him at Tyonek. From Seldovia the professor boarded the SS *Bertha* and departed on the first leg of his trip to New York. Cook then made arrangements with a local man named Bill Hughes to rent a 12-horse pack train at $30 a day to replace the horses he had lost, intending to use them for the hunt in the direction of Kichatna Pass.[41]

On August 25 Disston wired that he would not be coming at all. The hunt was now called off, and Cook made assignments to his men to best use the remaining time before winter set in. He directed Printz and Miller to take some of the horses and go up the Kichatna in search of game. He would drop them at Youngstown, he said, to speed them on their way.

Returning to Seldovia, Dr. Cook sent off a message to Herbert L. Bridgman:

> My Dear Bridgman,
>
> I have heard nothing from you, though I wrote you two months ago. There has been little to report. We have worked hard, and to the present time have explored about 1,000 square miles. We are now arranging our final efforts, and I hope to wire you from Seward about our work early in October. If the telegram is of sufficient importance, give it to the Associated Press. Yours cordially.
>
> F.A. Cook.[42]

At the same time, he wired Herschel Parker, saying that he had decided to explore the southern foothills of the mountain using the *Bolshoy,* with an eye toward picking out a route for another attempt the following year. Belmore Browne asked to go with him, but the doctor assured him that he would be doing only a reconnaissance and would make no attempt to climb the mountain, just as he had assured Professor Parker before he had left for New York. He sent Browne to the Matanuska River to gather some specimens for the Brooklyn Institute.

The *Bolshoy* had to be carried overland from Tyonek Creek and refloated after being trapped for a week when the steamer *Caswell* beached across the creek mouth in a storm. In the process, the *Bolshoy*'s circulating pump was damaged, and a new one had to be installed at the machine shop of the Kasilof salmon cannery. Finally, Cook took the *Bolshoy,* repaired and loaded, up the Susitna on August 27 with Printz and Miller aboard. He was eager to proceed before the coming winter so diminished the river's water level that it would impede his return.

At Youngstown the next day, the doctor exchanged Printz and Miller for Barrill and Dokkin and continued upriver. The launch ascended the first 60 miles without mishap. As they entered the Chulitna, however, they were de-layed trying to find deep water in a series of slews. After lining the boat over ten miles of narrows, they reentered deep water. Passing through canyons with 300-foot-high walls, they reached the Tokositna River and camped below the glacier Dr. Cook had explored briefly in 1903. Here, Barrill built a dock to secure the boat, and a camp was established on the riverbank.

As the weeks passed, the parties sent into the field slowly drifted in. Browne and Beecher came down to Seldovia. Miller and Printz returned on foot to Susitna Station after their horses gave out on the trail.

Cook and Barrill arrived at the station with the *Bolshoy* flying a big flag on September 22. The next day Porter joined the others at the station after finish-ing his topographical survey south of the mountain. As he walked up to Porter, Barrill said, "Go back and congratulate the Doctor. He got to the top."

Porter listened as "they described a hair-raising dash to the very summit. Following the Tokositna Glacier they had climbed the northeast spur, digging into the very face of vertical ice walls when night overtook them. The account was all very thrilling."[43]

The entire party went in the launch to Kenai, where, after a wait of a few days, they all boarded the steamer *Tyonek,* bound for the village of the same name.

Late on the night of October 2, a telegraph messenger knocked on the door of 604 Carlton Avenue in Brooklyn. Herbert L. Bridgman paid the $12.50 collect charges and opened the telegram. It was dated September 27:

> Tyonek Alaska.
> H.L. Bridgman, Brooklyn, NY.:
>   We have reached the summit of Mount McKinley by a new route in the north, and have mapped 3,000 miles of country. Re-turn to Seattle by next steamer. Fred. A. Cook[44]

Bridgman telephoned Herschel Parker and other members of the Explor-ers Club, who, despite the late hour, met at the club's rooms in an all-night session. Parker was distraught, maintaining that Cook's message couldn't be correct, as it seemed to claim that he had ascended the mountain in the region he had explored in 1903 and had given up as hopeless.

Bridgman tried to confirm the cable but failed. "All human knowledge concerning both branches of the Cook family may be represented by 0," he reported. "I have—however—no reason to doubt the authenticity of the dispatch—which to satisfy others—I am asking the telegraph company to investigate."[45]

At Seldovia, Browne and Beecher had heard rumors that Cook had climbed Mount McKinley but had discounted them, since it seemed, after their summer of experiences on the trail, he would have had no time to even reach the mountain since they had last seen him, much less climb it. But now the doctor arrived with the rest of the expedition members and confirmed it. By a lucky chance they had hit upon a workable route, he said, and had reached the summit on September 16. Browne and Beecher listened intently as he outlined the ascent.

After setting up their base camp, they had started with heavy packs to explore the approaches to the mountain afforded by Ruth Glacier. John Dokkin had turned back partway up the glacier, but in three days he and Barrill had made such good progress that they decided to press on to the top of the 12,000-foot ridge that loomed before them to examine possible routes they might try another year. Once on top of the ridge, they were encouraged to go on by a break in the weather. They continued climbing for two more days and, after a number of harrowing escapes and a miserable, sleepless night spent in a hole dug into the nearly vertical slope at 14,200 feet, realized they had a chance of reaching the summit. The weather held, and despite headaches, nosebleeds, snowblindness and other evil effects of the high altitude and intense cold, Cook related, they managed to struggle to within 2,000 feet of the top on the seventh day of the climb. Now came the final effort to reach the top:

> Very early on the morning of the eighth day we made the dash for the top. In our climb we encountered two peaks. We chose the southwestern. We reached the top at 10 o'clock. We intended to stay there two hours, but actually stayed only twenty minutes, so great was our suffering.
>
> About 200 or 300 feet below the peak we left a record of our visit—made out of a pile of stones and an American flag. With this we left the names of our party, the line of march, the date, and the temperature.[46]

Cook made preparations to leave Alaska, but contrary to his words to Herbert Bridgman, many steamers left Seldovia before he returned to Seattle.

The delay was caused by a complaint brought by Bill Hughes, who said he had a contract that the doctor had not honored and was owed $600 for the use of his pack train for 20 days at $30 a day for a hunting trip to the Kichatna Pass. Cook said he owed nothing, as it was only a "provisional agreement," and besides, the trip was never made. But Hughes disagreed and filed suit.

A trial date was set for late October at Seward. To fill the time, Cook began to write an account of his conquest of the mountain for *Harper's Monthly Magazine*. Porter stayed on to work on some illustrations for the article. Barrill also stayed with the doctor in Seldovia, as a witness in the dispute with Hughes.

The other members of the party had left Alaska, proud to have been a part of the history-making expedition. In Tacoma a reporter caught up with Belmore Browne and asked for his comments on the feat. "Too much cannot be said in praise of Dr. Cook for his courage and tenacity," said Browne. "The trip will place the name of an American with the foremost mountain climbers of the world."[47]

But in New York another expedition member was not so happy with the news of the doctor's success. "He may have ascended one of the peaks of the range, but I do not believe that he made the ascent of Mount McKinley, which is the highest peak in North America," asserted Herschel Parker. "And even if he did so, he was without scientific instruments. . . . At best, he could not have had more than an aneroid barometer, which would be valueless in the determination of Mount McKinley's height. So that any news that he has ascended Mount McKinley is totally without interest to the scientific world."[48]

In an interview later in the month, Parker gave more details of the reasons for his disbelief. Parker assumed that Cook had gone hunting with Disston and could not understand how he could have gotten back from Kichatna Pass before October 4. Furthermore, he had a promise from the doctor, he said, that he would make no further attempts to climb the mountain that season.

"This fact being a pledge, as it were, from Dr. Cook, alone makes it impossible, to my mind, that the information from him is correct," said Professor Parker, with no concealment of considerable feeling about the whole matter. Nevertheless, Parker still expressed the highest esteem for Cook and did not absolutely deny the famous Alaskan telegram but said he would not be convinced that it was true until he had talked the matter over face to face. "He will have to tell me how he did it before I can believe that it was done," the professor insisted.[49]

But another former Alaskan companion seemed to confirm Cook's exploit as true. "It was at Seldovia, Alaska, early this month," said Robert Dunn, "that I met Dr. Cook. I had just returned from a cruise among the Bering Sea volcanoes, and in the course of a conversation Dr. Cook told me that by unexpected luck, after he had practically given up hope of climbing Mount McKinley, he had, accompanied by a single packer, succeeded in reaching the summit of the peak from the northeast side. . . .

"That Dr. Cook had reached the summit of the great peak was no more a surprise to me than to many others in Alaska who understood that the attempt had been given up for the year, but a sudden change in the weather that had baffled Cook all Summer would make an ascent quite easy according to the nature of the route described to me.

"I do not understand why the authenticity of Dr. Cook's dispatch from Tyonek would ever have been questioned," concluded Dunn.[50]

On October 25 Cook was ordered to pay Bill Hughes $600 and court costs of $15.18. Cook was free to go, but only after borrowing a substantial sum of money. The judgment had left him flat broke. The doctor lost his hat there, too. He gave it to a miner who wanted to put it on display at the Alaska-Yukon Pacific Fair; as he reckoned, since it had been to the top of McKinley, it was "the highest hat in history."

When Cook and Porter arrived in Seattle on November 7, he checked into the Butler Hotel. The doctor was talking with a representative from the *Seattle Daily Times* there when, suddenly, a door burst open. In rushed Ruth from the adjoining room. She looked at him in the most confident way, and he regarded her for some time in astonishment before asking, "Where's your mother?" Marie came in from the next room, where she had been covertly watching the scene with amusement. The reporter slipped out quietly and left the doctor to the family reunion "that was all the happier because of the surprise it contained for the leading man." After Fred's departure, Marie and Lotta Davidson had decided on an extended western tour. They had swung as far south as the Grand Canyon and had visited San Francisco just after the disastrous earthquake. Then they had come north to await his return.[51]

The Mazamas, a mountaineering club headquartered in Portland, asked the doctor and other expedition members to describe their Alaskan experiences. When he told his story publicly for the first time two days later before 500 cheering admirers at the Alaska Club, Dr. Cook was joined by Russell Porter and Belmore Browne. "When it came Dr. Cook's turn to speak," reported the *Seattle Post-Intelligencer,* "he was given a reception which American audiences seldom give to anyone save a national hero."[52]

Like the narrative he was writing for *Harper's,* his account proved to be filled with thrilling details. He had had no intention of making a climb, he told his audience, but only of surveying a future route, so they carried no cumbersome equipment. "We did no relay work or double-tripping," he said. "Rapid marches, light packs, and but the prime necessities of camp life characterized our methods of action. We aimed to carry on our backs about fifty pounds each, and this pack was to contain all our needs for ten days, independent of each other and independent of our base camp or a supporting party."

An ordinary horsehair rope, the silk tent, pemmican and an alcohol stove, two thermometers, three aneroid barometers, a watch, a prismatic compass and a 5-by-7 camera and six film packs, together with a rubber floor cloth, tent pegs, aluminum kitchen gear and a pocketknife made up the outfit. They each wore lightweight underwear and a flannel shirt with wool trousers and socks, shoepacs and a felt hat, with sections of their sleeping bags held in reserve for colder weather, and did all the climbing dressed in this manner.

Cook outfitted for climbing.

They had started up Ruth Glacier on September 8 at an altitude of 1,000 feet, along an old caribou trail. The doctor described how on the evening of the second day he and Barrill crossed a bend in the glacier and its first northerly tributary and pitched camp on a beautiful moss-carpeted point about 15 miles from Mount McKinley. Dokkin had already retreated, fearing the crevasses that had to be crossed, and had been given instructions to read the barometer.

The next morning they made an early start, climbing the big boulders of the lateral moraine with the rope securely fastened between them, and before dark pitched the tent at what Dr. Cook calculated to be an altitude of 8,000 feet. Beyond the camp towered a ridge 4,000 feet higher, which he hoped to reach before turning back.

As he settled into his bag that night, the doctor explained, he had every reason to be pleased. In three days they had pushed 35 miles into the foothills of an unexplored country and were now in a better position to attack the mountain than at any previous time during their siege of three months. Sleep was difficult, however, because of the thunder of distant avalanches and the creaking of the glacier below them. "That third night we felt as if we were at the gates of Hades," he said. "We were about ready to quit and seek a more congenial calling. But dawn brought its usual inspiration."

With the lifeline secured, they started to ascend:

> We chose the lateral moraine of the cerac of the first glacial tribu-tary as a route into an amphitheater. Here we found ourselves ris-ing into the breath of avalanches too numerous and too close for our sense of safety, but there were no other lines of ascent, so we pushed on into the gathering basin and into the clouds. . . . With an eye on some rock, we picked our way through mist, over dan-gerous ceracs, to the frowning cliffs that made the circular rim of the amphitheater. Here at noon we dropped in the snow, ate some pemmican, and rested long enough to permit the clouds to part and give us a peep at the cliffs above. . . . There was no place to camp in the regions above unless we reached the top of the ridge. . . . Rising from ridge to ridge and from cornice to cornice, we finally burst through the gloomy mist on to a bright snow-field, upon which fell the parting glow of the sun settling into the great green expanse beyond the Yukon. We were on the divide, the wall between the Yukon and Susitna. . . .

Here they built a snow house, Cook told his audience. Thin rubber sheets were spread on its floor; then they crawled into their bags once again and ate their fill. The doctor noted that he had heard mountain climbers often suf-fered from indigestion but said he did not experience any difficulty with his menu of pemmican, tea and biscuits and slept comfortably for twelve hours.

By morning's light, to the east, among the seemingly impossible cliffs, he spotted several promising lines of attack over narrow overhanging glaciers and steep ice-sheeted ridges. But all of them, and those to the west also, were crossed by avalanche tracks:

> Our only chance . . . was along the cornice of the northeastern arête upon which we were camped. For some distance there was a smooth line of crusted snow, with a sheer drop of about 4000 feet to either side. At about 13,000 feet this line was barred by a huge rock, with vertical sides of about 1000 feet. Beyond this rock there were other cliffs of ice and granite, and beyond this was a steep arête, over which we could go from the west to the northern face on to a glacier and into a valley between the two peaks which we now saw made the summit. . . .
>
> . . . With half a notion to climb to the summit, but with a more determined resolution to pick a route for a future ascent, we adjusted our rucksacks and life-line and started along this cornice. . . . We found a way on a narrow cornice around the big rock. . . . Without stopping for lunch, we continued difficult step-cutting all day. Our rise in altitude was very little, but we got beyond this barrier, out of the area of windy cliffs and frigid crags, out on a steep snow-sheeted arête. . . .

By his calculations, they had reached 14,200 feet by 7:30; it was −11° and growing dark. Caught on the ridge, they had no choice but to hang on, Cook said, so they dug a seat into the 60-degree slope, wrapped themselves in a bundle with all their belongings and, lashing it to their axes securely driven into the ice, waited for dawn. "The thought of going to the top of the mountain was dispelled by the misery of that awful night," the doctor reported. But after a night spent in mild arguments, "we dragged ourselves out of the icy ditch of terrors [and] we were able to see that we had passed the barriers to the ascent.

The slopes above were easy, safe, and connected, but the bigness of the mountain was more and more apparent as we rose above the clouds."

The sleepless night and high altitude rapidly took their toll. "Soon after noon we swung from the arête easterly to the glacier. Here, owing to fatigue, we were utterly unable to proceed," he said. "The snow was such that we were able to build a snow house, and in it we packed ourselves for a long rest" at 16,300 feet. "The snow and the rocks glittered with a weird brightness seeming to come out of the earth—darkness above, light from below."

Drawing by Porter from To the Top of the Continent: *Cook and Barrill in the icy ditch of terrors.*

Starting out on the morning of the sixth day on the mountain, they dragged themselves another 2,000 feet to the soft snow of a gathering basin within easy reach of the top and pitched the tent. From here Cook said he could see "several miniature ranges running up to the two main peaks about two miles apart . . . with one main peak to the southeast where the highest point lay." They settled in for a night of rest before making a try for the top.

It was a restless night that Cook described. The temperature settled at −16°, though it seemed colder to the doctor than −60° at sea level. Breathing and heartbeat were labored, and it was impossible to dispel a sense of chilliness even with hot tea. After hours of waiting for light, Cook related, with numb fingers they packed their sleeping bags and a light emergency ration in a rucksack and then, with grim determination and a flag, started for the summit. The sun had risen out of the great green lowlands beyond Mount Hayes and was moving toward the iceblink caused by the extensive glacial sheets north of the St. Elias group. His route lay over a feathery snowfield between rows of granite pinnacles, the doctor said.

He then graphically recounted the struggle to make the unwilling muscles of his stonelike legs pull his body to the goal of his mind. Every hundred steps they halted, leaning on their ice axes to rest:

> I shall never forget, however, the notable moments when the rope became taut with a nervous pull, and we crept impatiently over the heaven-scraped granite toward the top.
>
> We stood up under a black sky so low that we felt as if we could nearly touch it. We had reached the top. What a task! Without the aid of a guide we had at last reached our goal. Almost unconsciously our hands were locked, with a look of satisfaction at each other; not a word nor a yell was uttered. We had not the breath to spare. It was September 16, 1906, ten o'clock in the morning, the temperature −16°; the altitude 20,391 feet. Then followed a long gaze over the cold wide world spread out at our feet. To the south the eye ran over the steaming volcanoes, Redoubt and Iliamna, down Cook Inlet to the point of Kenai Peninsula and the Pacific, two hundred and fifty miles away. Narrow, winding, pearly ribbons marked the courses of the Kuskokwim, Yukon, Tanana, and Susitna rivers. Out of the Pacific rose a line of clouds drifting over the Chugach Mountains, to deposit their snows in the glaciers of the Alaskan Range. A similar train of clouds came out of the Bering Sea and swept the western side of the range. These clouds blotted out most of the mountains near the main range. This lower world of lesser mountains did not impress us so much as the little skyworld about us. Here, under our feet, was the top of the continent, the north pole of our ambitions, probably the coldest spot on earth, and we were the most miserable of men at a time when we

should have been elated. Nevertheless, I shall always remember, with a mental focus sharpened by time, the warm friendship of my companion, Edward Barrille, the curious low dark sky, the dazzling brightness of the sky-scraped granite blocks, the neutral gray-blue of space, the frosty dark blue of the shadows, and, above all, the final pictures which I took of Barrille with the flag lashed to his axe as an arctic air froze the impression into a relief which no words can tell.[53]

Dr. Cook concluded by telling how it took just four days to reach his base camp. He gave no details of the descent, although in his diary of the climb he had written of his emotions when he reached the spot where they had dug in for the night, and how they had relieved their suffering from snowblindness from the glare off the ridges of ice by rubbing their eyes with snow. Despite the subzero temperatures, their faces were burned and cracked and felt hot. They reached the *Bolshoy* on September 20 and started for Cook Inlet.

The local press noted the pride with which the three told of their accomplishment: "Mr. Belmore Browne, the naturalist of the party, and Mr. Porter, the topographer, spoke. There was a note of enthusiasm, an apparent love of their work, in every word they said, that is seldom seen after anticipation is turned into reality."[54]

In Tacoma the doctor was entertained at the home of George Browne, Belmore's father. Belmore seemed eager to present Cook to all his acquaintances and to share in the limelight of his great Alaskan feat.

When Dr. Cook arrived back in New York on November 27, he went to see Herschel Parker to tell him how and why he had made the climb despite his assurances that he would not make another attempt. After the meeting, Parker evidently had a change of heart. He no longer said that the doctor had not made the ascent, but he continued to maintain it had been simply a feat of endurance, not of much use to science. "To any one familiar

Barrill and the flag on the summit of Mount McKinley. Photograph by Cook, as printed in Harper's Monthly Magazine.

with the conditions and topography on this side of Mt. McKinley such a trip must certainly seem a most brilliant achievement of mountaineering and exploration," said the professor. "Unfortunately, however, no accurate information can be gained with regard to the altitude of the mountain, except from the results of Mr. Porter's triangulations."[55]

Cook was invited to lecture before the Explorers Club, and on December 7, 1906, the club members elected him to succeed General Greely as their president. But the honor was tempered with sadness the next day, when Dr. Cook's mother died.

In the coming days, the doctor would be in great demand. He was a guest of honor of the American Alpine Club, delivered an illustrated lecture on the climb before the Association of American Geographers, and spoke on his conquest before the annual dinner of the Arctic Club. When Cook was unable to attend a banquet for the Duke of Abruzzi, Professor Parker presided over a showing of lantern slides that included the doctor's pictures taken during his climb of McKinley.

But though Parker had been won over, there were still people who doubted the doctor's claims. Principal among these were Alaskans who considered the feat simply impossible or at least too difficult to have been done so easily, especially by someone from "Outside," as they termed anywhere but Alaska.

Before Dr. Cook even began his 1906 attempt, Hudson Stuck, an Alaskan archdeacon of the Episcopal Church, had confessed to Alfred Brooks that he would rather climb Mount McKinley than find the richest gold mine in Alaska and predicted that the doctor would fail again.

Archdeacon Stuck bet Brooks a total of $5 that Cook would not reach various altitudes on the mountain, much less the summit. But after Cook's announcement of his success, Stuck refused to pay and stated his reasons with less than Christian charity.

"Cook is a prig," the clergyman wrote to Brooks. "Moreover I find it hard to contain within myself my vehement suspicion that he is an ass. And a prig and a vehemently suspected ass will never climb Mount McKinley. God forbid!"[56]

Still, Brooks insisted he had won. "I have gone over the matter in detail with Doctor Cook and am convinced he reached the summit of the mountain," Brooks chided the archdeacon. "I have heard him lecture on the subject, seen his photographs and there is no doubt in my mind."[57] Nevertheless, Brooks never got his money.

On December 15, 1906, a dazzling gathering of 400 guests assembled at the New Willard Hotel. There was a good showing of Washington's elite—senators, congressmen and ambassadors with their wives in their best finery. The occasion was the annual banquet of the National Geographic Society, and the guest of honor was Robert E. Peary. He was back from his latest expedition, and though he had failed once again to reach the North Pole, he had eclipsed the record for the "Farthest North" held by Captain Cagni since 1900. In the attempt, however, his new ship had been battered practically to pieces and had still not reached New York.[58]

Perhaps even more important, from the northern tip of Axel Heiberg Land he had seen a new land far to the west and named it Crocker Land, after the backer who had saved his expedition by paying off the $50,000 balance owed on the *Roosevelt*'s construction costs. Surely this was the farthest northern land yet discovered, perhaps even the edge of Dr. Harris's "Arctic Continent."

The society had decided that such feats deserved a special award. Peary would be given the first Hubbard Medal, a three-inch gold disk bearing a map of the globe struck by Tiffany and Company especially for the occasion. Marking the spot of Peary's record, 87°6'N, was a glittering Montana star sapphire.

After an invocation by the chaplain of the Senate, Dr. Edward Everett Hale, the guests took their places at the 12 long tables. A moment of silence was observed in memory of the first president of the society and the medal's namesake, Gardiner Greene Hubbard; then the current president, Willis L. Moore, proudly told of the society's growth from its tiny beginning in 1888 to 18,000 members, among whom could be counted the best men of the best nations of the world, the lawmakers, the highest representatives of the church and the men who had made the greatest discoveries in science. Nor did he believe the society had yet reached its zenith. "We are not modest in our ambitions," he declared. "We wish to know all about the earth, and the waters under the earth and the heavens above the earth."[59]

The Italian ambassador then rose in praise of the guest of honor, who had bettered his countryman's record. "In the fields of science," the ambassador said, "there is no place for low feelings; in the competition for the conquest of the globe, there is no sentiment of envy. All work for humanity. I am therefore happy to tribute, on behalf of the Italians, to you, Commander Peary, to your courageous and faithful followers, to your intrepid companion, Mrs. Diebitsch Peary, the most sincere expression of our deep, warm, and heartfelt admiration."

Peary, if not humble, could afford to be magnanimous in acknowledging the ambassador's congratulations. "The fact that such names as Abruzzi, Cagni, Nansen, Greely, and Peary are indelibly inscribed upon the white disk close to the Pole," he declared, "shows conclusively, if anything were needed to show it, that these efforts to solve the northern mystery represent the biggest, cleanest, most manly example of friendly international rivalry that exists.

"It is a magnificent galaxy of flags that has been planted around the Pole, and when eventually some one of them shall reach the Pole itself, it will add to its own luster without in any way detracting from the luster of the others or leaving any sense of injury or humiliation in its wake."

President Moore then announced the election of several new honorary members to the society: George Dewey, hero of the late war with Spain; Roald Amundsen, who had succeeded in negotiating the Northwest Passage and locating the North Magnetic Pole,[60] and Morris K. Jesup, president of the Peary Arctic Club. Jesup sent regrets that he could not attend to see Peary receive the medal, saying, "He is worthy and entitled to all the honor that his country can bestow."

After more toasts and speeches, Alexander Graham Bell arose to introduce a special guest seated at the head table. "I have been asked to say a few words," the inventor began, "about a man who must be known by name, at least, to all of us, Dr. Frederick A. Cook, President of the Explorers' Club, New York. We have had with us, and are glad to welcome, Commander Peary, of the Arctic regions, but in Dr. Cook we have one of the few Americans, if not the only American, who has explored both extremes of the world, the Arctic and the Antarctic regions. And now he has been to the top of the American continent, and therefore to the top of the world, and tonight I hope Dr. Frederick Cook will tell us something about Mount McKinley."

Cook approached the podium to the applause of the banquet guests and began to speak:

> I would prefer to tell you tonight of the splendid achievement of Commander Peary and of the noble character of the man who has succeeded in pushing human endeavor to the utmost limit of endurance, all with the unselfish motive of carrying the honor and the flag of his country to the farthest north, but your chairman has put me to the task of getting to the top of our continent.
>
> In the conquest of Mount McKinley success was mostly due to our use of the working equipment of polar explorers, and among polar explorers Commander Peary has worked hardest to reduce the outfit to its utmost simplicity. Thus indirectly to Commander Peary should fall a part of the honor of scaling the arctic slopes of our greatest mountain.

The overly modest doctor was only just approaching the summit of his vivid description of the climb when the door to the hall burst open and President Roosevelt was announced. Not wishing to delay the proceedings, Cook left his hearers hanging on the cold, windswept apex of North America, concluding, "It would, however, take me several hours to tell you what we saw. This I will reserve for a future occasion."

Dr. Cook then stepped down and made room for President Roosevelt's presentation of the Hubbard Medal to the commander.[61] The President did not take long in sounding one of his cherished themes:

> Civilized people usually live under conditions of life so easy that there is a certain tendency to atrophy of the hardier virtues. And it is a relief to pay signal honor to a man who by his achievements makes it evident that in some of the race, at least, there has been no loss of hardier virtues. . . .
>
> . . . There is need that we should not forget that in the last analysis the safe basis of a successful national character must rest upon the great fighting virtues, and those great fighting virtues can be shown quite as well in peace as in war. . . .
>
> . . . You (turning to Commander Peary) . . . who for months in and months out, year in and year out, had to face perils and overcome the greatest risks and difficulties, with resting on your shoulders the undivided responsibility which meant life or death to you and your followers—you had to show in addition what the modern commander with his great responsibility does not have to show—you had to show all the moral qualities in war, together with other qualities. You did a great deed. . . .

In accepting the medal, Commander Peary said:

> The true explorer does his work not for any hope of rewards or honor, but because the thing he has set himself to do is a part of his very being, and must be accomplished for the sake of accomplishment, and he counts lightly hardships, risks, obstacles, if only they do not bar him from his goal.
>
> To me the final and complete solution of the polar mystery which has engaged the best thought and interest of the best men of the most vigorous and enlightened nations of the world for more than three centuries, and to-day quickens the pulse of every man or woman whose veins hold red blood, is the thing which should be done for the honor and credit of this country, the thing which it is intended that I should do, and the thing that I must do. . . .
>
> As regards the belief expressed by some, that the attainment of the North Pole possesses no value or interest, let me say that should an American first of all men place the Stars and Stripes at that coveted spot, there is not an American citizen at home or abroad, and there are millions of us, but what would feel a little better and a little prouder of being an American; and just that

added increment of pride and patriotism to millions would of it-self be ten times the value of all the cost of attaining the Pole. . . .

Tonight the Stars and Stripes stand nearest to the mystery, pointing and beckoning. God willing, I hope that your adminis-tration may yet see those Stars and Stripes planted at the Pole itself.

It was a grand night for Peary. He was back in his element, and he had made it clear that he had not finished with the Pole. The only thing he may have regretted was the poor choice of words Dr. Bell had used in introducing Dr. Cook. Frederick Cook had not reached the "top of the world." No, that was the thing that was intended *he* should do; that was to be *his* destiny.

CHAPTER 13

The Wind-Loved Place

EARLY IN 1907 THE NEW YORK PAPERS CARRIED REPORTS THAT DR. COOK HAD revived his plans to lead an expedition to Antarctica. There were more rumors of mysterious motor vehicles for an assault on the Pole, and Captain Robert Scott, who was planning another voyage to the Antarctic himself, was concerned enough to write Herbert Bridgman asking just what the doctor's intentions were. But in truth, Cook's funds to mount any such venture were exhausted. Despite the attention it had gotten him, the McKinley expedition had left the doctor "miserably hard up."[1]

Henry Disston's failure to appear and pay for the expected hunt had saddled Cook with obligations he could not meet. The money put up by Professor Parker and advanced from *Harper's* had been expended on the *Bolshoy,* the horses, the outfit, and the disastrous judgment against him in Seward. The doctor had to borrow $1,000 from Marie just to cover the return expenses of the expedition members. He was able to pay Ed Barrill only half what he had promised him. For the others, like faithful Fred Printz, there was only a promise.

John R. Bradley.

Russell Porter sympathized with the doctor's circumstances but still wanted his salary and payment for work on a topographical map Cook planned to sell to the Geological Survey. Porter was due $770.[2] Dr. Cook was counting on proceeds from the map and a tentative arrangement with Doubleday, Page to publish a book on his latest adventure, but nothing was yet in hand. When a new opportunity presented itself that might alleviate his financial embarrassment, he seized upon it.

At the Arctic Club in 1905, David T. Abercrombie had introduced Cook to John R. Bradley. Bradley was a brusque and undiplomatic man. He could afford to be. He had started out as a faro dealer in New Orleans, where he once broke every professional gambler at Bud Renaud's gaming house. Already the owner of the Bacchus Club in El Paso, in 1898 John, along with his brother Ed, whose specialty was racehorses, had opened the Beach Club in Palm Beach. Notorious for allowing women at the gaming tables, it had quickly become one of the country's premier gambling establishments and had made the Bradley brothers millionaires. The profits from the Beach Club allowed Bradley to do pretty much what he pleased, and he pleased to indulge his hobby of shooting big game all over the world.

Dr. Cook had been trying to persuade him for two years to go hunting in the Arctic, but Bradley had gone to northern Mongolia instead. When he returned in December 1906, however, he contacted the doctor. He was considering his suggestion to go north.

"In the spring of 1907 I had fully made up my mind to go that year, and invited Dr. Cook to go as my guest," Bradley remembered. "That is the way the idea originated. He was to photograph Eskimos and I was to shoot walrus and polar bear."[3]

If they were to leave that summer there was much to be done. Bradley contacted Bowring Brothers, seeking to rent a sealer, but their terms were not to his liking. Not only did he think the price high, he did not wish to be under the command of a captain reluctant to risk losing the company's vessel chasing polar bears among the dangerous ice floes of Melville Bay. With no time to build a ship, Bradley and the doctor went up to New London to look over what might be for sale. Finding nothing suitable, they next visited Gloucester, where they spotted a likely vessel, a fishing schooner of 111 tons named *George W. Lufkin.*

The doctor thought she would do, but just to make sure, Bradley wanted a second opinion. On May 25 Dr. Cook took Bob Bartlett, master of Peary's ship, *Roosevelt,* to see the *Lufkin,* and he pronounced her "as safe a ship as ever left for the Arctic."[4] Bradley paid $7,000 to Benjamin Smith of the Pew Gorton Company for her and put the schooner in dry dock at the Moran Shipbuilding Company to be overhauled.

Next, Bradley engaged Moses Bartlett. Captain Bartlett was an imposing man at six feet tall and 184 pounds. At 49 he had been north three times with Peary, who had described him as "weather beaten, grizzled, keen of eye." He had a fabulous reputation as an ice pilot, and like many of the Bartletts from Brigus, Newfoundland, including his second cousin, Bob, he had an equal reputation as a hard drinker. But he had promised Bradley that he would stay off the bottle for the duration of the voyage.

The first mate was Mike A. Wise and the second, John Bartlett, one of the captain's nephews. These and five sailors made up the crew. Bradley also hired an engineer, whom he called Jack because of his unpronounceable Hungarian name, to look after the engine he was having installed in the yacht. Bradley's personal servant and Dr. Cook rounded out the ship's complement, but Bradley still needed a good cook.

When he happened to notice an advertisement in the *New York Herald* that one Rudolph Franke was offering himself as a traveling companion for a hunting trip to the Far North, Bradley responded. Franke was astonished just to receive a reply to his ad and even more astonished when the address given him turned out to be an apartment in an elegant section of West 67th Street.

He had hardly had time to look at the numerous trophy heads staring down at him in the entrance hall when

Moses Bartlett, captain of the Bradley.

Bradley entered, shook his hand and asked him to sit down. He was planning a trip to the Arctic, he said, and wanted a dependable man to prepare his food.

Franke told him he had experience in that line with the Lloyd Company and the Hamburg American Line and could provide favorable references. Bradley offered him the position then and there. "I accepted," recalled Franke, "with the understanding that I would stay for a year or a year longer, for an expedition in the Far North is dependent on ice, wind and weather, and other unpredictable circumstances which make it impossible to give extremes in length of time. Bradley paid me, as is customary, a considerable sum in advance and gave me a letter of recommendation and a ticket for Gloucester, Massachusetts with instructions to look up his traveling companion, Dr. Cook."[5]

Franke crossed the river that night and celebrated his good fortune with friends in Hoboken's Little Germany, drinking until morning. As a boy he had read the tales of explorers in faraway places and had been stricken with wanderlust ever since getting his first whiff of the sea at Hamburg. His wanderings had taken him to America and now, by an incredible chance, his ad, which had been no more than a lark, would be his passport into the wilds of the Arctic on a millionaire's yacht.

But with the dawn he began to think of the dangers he might have to face. Still, he resigned himself to stand by the agreement he had made without much serious thought:

> I had willingly given my word. I had to be a man and fulfill my
> duty to the last second. I felt the urge of the new. Yes, a longing for
> the unknown, and as I stretched out in bed I had these misgivings

but regained my perspective. Yes, a joyful urge to get started possessed me.

Late next afternoon, I reached Gloucester and took myself and Mr. Bradley's letter to meet Dr. Cook, who already had been busy for several weeks with preparations for the hunting trip. . . . At Dr. Cook's I met Captain Moses Bartlett . . . and soon we found ourselves in serious discussion about regulations governing food and equipment. . . .

Now, there was plenty of work, and when I look back to those days I still wonder at Dr. Cook's confidence and ability to organize. Dr. Cook gave all the orders for the equipment and oversaw the execution to the smallest detail.[6]

Cabins were built for Bradley, Cook and the officers. The schooner was braced fore and aft, her bow and stern sheathed with steel plates, her sides with oak. The rigging and sails were replaced, and to give her maneuverability, she was fitted with a 55-horsepower Lozier gasoline engine.

Dr. Cook had been given carte blanche to equip her as he saw fit and had purchased four months' supply of food, plus another year's allowance in case of shipwreck. This was packed away in uniform-sized boxes weighing 50 pounds apiece. Five thousand gallons of gasoline were taken into the yacht's tanks, and all the other equipment was put aboard and stored away.

As Dr. Cook saw to all the preparations for Bradley's big-game hunt, he was making preparations of his own to hunt for something even bigger. About four weeks before sailing, Bradley and the doctor were having lunch at the Holland House when Cook asked, "Why not try for the Pole?"

"Not I," replied Bradley. "Would you like to try for it?"

"There's nothing that I would rather do; it's the ambition of my life," said the doctor. He thought it would cost only about $8,000 or $10,000 more to furnish an equipment for this purpose. After some figuring, Bradley exclaimed, "We'll fit this expedition for the Pole, and say nothing to any one about it."

"We did not want the newspapers to get at it," Bradley explained later. "Peary was waiting to go, and we did not want him to beat us into Etah and get all the dogs; moreover, I wanted to shoot on the way up and did not want to be in a hurry. . . .

"We figured this way: In case we got up to Etah and found the natives were not well, or the dogs scarce, or any other conditions unfavorable, we would call it a hunting trip and return quietly home again."[7]

Bradley wrote out a check for $10,000. The two men drank a glass of sparkling burgundy to seal the compact, and after saying good-bye, Dr. Cook took the 3rd Avenue El for the Brooklyn Bridge, where he changed trains for Bushwick. The whole way home he was lost in thought about the coming adventure.

His office was full of patients when he arrived. After the last had been seen, he quickly ate dinner and went off on his rounds. When Fred got back to the house, it was silent. The children were in bed. There was time to tell Marie about his pact with Mr. Bradley, but he hesitated. Marie had already spoken against the hunting trip; she argued that he should wait a year to recover from the strain of the McKinley climb. When he disagreed, Marie had kept asking plaintively, "Well, suppose you don't come back?" But he knew his chance had now come and would not come again. He said nothing about the North Pole.[8]

Dr. Cook did his best to secure his financial position. He attempted to collect old bills and visited a friend at the Mutual Insurance Company, Charles Wake, seeking life insurance. He was turned down. Wake also declined Cook's invitation to accompany him on his polar quest. Next Cook engaged an associate, Dr. Cordes, to take over his practice. He had left for Gloucester on his birthday and thereafter spent five days a week there, returning to Brooklyn on the weekends.

The doctor had something to occupy every minute. He even designed a special flag to fly from the mast of the yacht he had decided to name after his benefactor. On it he drew a stylized globe with arrows pointing to the poles.[9]

How do you like this idea for a flag

While at home he worked feverishly at his McKinley manuscript, for which he had finally received a contract. It was a rush job, which left much for Marie and his editor to do before it could go to press.

Hurriedly, he gathered his personal gear and supplies, including one of his brothers' finished sledges and enough parts and raw materials cut by Theodore to construct ten others. Now, at last, he could try out all his ideas about equipment and ice travel and apply the theories he had formed in his many hours of reading and study.

All haste was necessary to get away on July 1, the appointed sailing date. But the engine on the yacht and the 75-horsepower motor of the 30-foot launch, constructed in the style of a whaleboat, were still not thoroughly trustworthy. Even so, it was decided to sail. They would test the engines along the way and put in for repairs if necessary.

At 7 P.M. on July 3, the *John R. Bradley* slipped out of Gloucester harbor on an easy swell and into the calm and beautiful night. It was Rudolph Franke's twenty-ninth birthday, which he thought a good omen that counterbalanced the number of the ship's complement—13. In just 40 days the boat had been transformed from a dirty schooner into a gleaming white arctic yacht trimmed in gold at a cost of $30,000, double what had been estimated.[10]

As she sailed north, her namesake was not aboard; he would join her later at Sydney. But she carried four passengers who would leave the ship there and await the *Bradley's* return—Marie, Ruth, Helen and Marie's maid.

The weather was fine on the first day of the run to Sydney. The ladies enjoyed being on deck in the bracing sea air to watch the colors run up in honor of Independence Day. The next day the engine showed some independence of its own, balking for the first time, and since Jack could not remedy the problem, Captain Bartlett determined to lay over at Sydney to put things right before setting out for Greenland. As the *Bradley* sailed with the power of the wind on her sails like some great white arctic bird, Dr. Cook listed in his diary, among the articles he might write as a result of the cruise, "The Sport of Getting to the North Pole."

He would need whatever money he could earn from his writings; he had left most of his McKinley debts—to Porter, Printz and the others—unpaid. But he had squared himself with Ed Barrill before leaving. He sent him $200, thanking him for his loyalty and faithfulness but cautioning him not to tell Printz he had been paid. He suggested that Barrill get Printz to "push" Disston for the money instead.[11]

At Sydney Cook sought an electrician and a gasoline-engine expert to look after the Lozier. There, John Bradley, who had come up by rail, got his first look at his finished yacht. Over dinner at the Sydney Hotel he learned of the needed delay, then left for Battle Harbour by mail steamer at midnight to go hunting until the *Bradley* reached Labrador.

It took two days to overhaul the engine. Fred used the time to take Marie to Baddeck, where she planned to summer with the children. While in Baddeck, Cook was invited by Gilbert Grosvenor to Beinn Bhreagh, Alexander Graham Bell's summer home, where Grosvenor edited the *National Geographic Magazine* from a tent set up on the hillside of the palatial estate above the beautiful Bras d'Or. There he discussed his theories about routes to the Pole with Grosvenor and then returned to the yacht, which sailed from Sydney at 9:30 A.M., July 11.[12]

By July 12 Newfoundland was in sight. The weather was stormy, so Captain Bartlett ran the *Bradley* into Bonnie Bay, a slash in its rugged coast. Here Dr. Cook and Rudolph Franke left letters for home. The next day they rendezvoused with Mr. Bradley at Battle Harbour, and the yacht headed out across Davis Strait for Greenland on July 15.

Out on the open ocean, the ship encountered headwinds that piled the sea in great waves. Fortunately she sailed well, because the engine gave constant trouble. Even Dr. Cook stood watch as engineer for several nights during the crossing, tinkering with the Lozier and pondering the balky motor's problems, but otherwise it was an uneventful passage. Ice along the shore prevented calling at Holsteinborg, so Captain Bartlett turned the *Bradley's* prow toward Godhavn. The sea was alternately smooth as a mirror, then heavy and rolling as she sailed up the coast, crossing the Arctic Circle and into perpetual summer daylight on July 26.

It all seemed routine now to the doctor: the obligatory stop at Godhavn, the greetings from Governor Baumann and his beautiful wife, the natives' visits to trade, the invitation for the crew to the inevitable Eskimo dance. But to Rudolph Franke it all seemed wonderful indeed. He had thrilled to his first encounters with icebergs and the wild and beautiful coast of Greenland. He attended the dance and noted that endurance counted far more than rhythm.[13]

But the *Bradley* did not stay long; the ambitions of the two men who had organized the expedition pulled them ever northward—when the equipment cooperated. The next day the chain broke on the pump. Then on July 28, after anchoring in Disco's harbor at 6 P.M. and setting out for the shore in grand style in the motor launch, it too broke down. The millionaire and his guest had to paddle ashore "feeling cheap" to meet Governor Fenker, who offered the usual hospitality nonetheless. The ship then sprang a leak at the screw plate, but the damage was easily repaired at low tide, and after the water tanks were filled, John Bradley was impatient to start north again.

While crossing Disco Bay, the engine froze up once more, but by August 2 it was working perfectly as the yacht approached the Duck Islands in fine, clear weather for some sport. Just offshore, however, a sudden fog lowered like a curtain, and the disappointed hunter ordered sail set for North Greenland.

The fog seemed a strictly local phenomenon; an hour later all on deck shed their coats and hats beneath as a sun that seemed as bright as Palm Beach's shone down incongruously on the hundreds of bergs floating past as the *Bradley* entered Melville Bay.

Captain Bartlett ordered an approach to the shore, held closely by much rotten ice. As the yacht picked her way through the pans and leads, Bradley became eager for action. He offered $5 in gold to the first man to spot a bear, but saved his money when he himself spotted one, though it proved to be on an inaccessible floe. Then another with a cub was sighted, but the yacht, in a precarious position just then, could not be stopped.

On August 5 the ship was caught in the ice. Huge pans crunched together, forming hummocks where the superimposed sheets pressed against the yacht's sides with tremendous force. The crew had a day's hard exercise with picks and axes, keeping her from being nipped.

The next day a sudden gale raised a sea the likes of which Dr. Cook had never seen so near a large ice field. The ice split and heaved in undulating hills as clouds of gray vapor hurtled down from the land like smoke from an erupting volcano. But the storm went as quickly as it had come, and all the next day the yacht, making for Cape York, continued to pick her way through leads against the shore until she found open water at last.

As the *Bradley* approached the cape in a stiff southerly breeze, thousands of little auks streamed past, along with a little drift ice. A landing party discovered that most of the natives were away hunting, so the yacht set out for North Star Bay in a mounting snowstorm that soon covered her decks to a depth of five inches and pasted the ropes and sails with ice.

Many on board were terribly seasick. Rudolph Franke went below to find Jack lying, white as a sheet, in front of the engine. The kitchen looked just the same, but for a different reason. A barrel of flour had been tossed on the floor, and a tin of petroleum had been upset, too, making it so slippery that Franke had to sit on the sideboard while he thought about what to do. He wanted to fix lunch for the exhausted crew, but lighting the stove would be dangerous, so he decided on canned meat and zwieback.

While rummaging in the storeroom, Franke spotted a chest labeled "Creme in Bottles." That puzzled him, as cream was always carried aboard ship in tin cans. He took the chest down and opened it.

> And what did the chest reveal? Twelve carefully packed bottles containing whiskey of the best brand; so the Pole was not yet lost! The label on the chest was a sly trick, a ruse perpetrated by Moses Bartlett. Bartlett went after whiskey like a bear goes after honey. Even though he had sworn not to drink, since Bradley had forbidden it, Bradley did not completely trust the old sea-dog. The find seemed like a gift from heaven; a good drink for the cold and long-suffering, hard working crew. Of the men at watch and at work on deck, half frozen and discouraged, many came down and refreshed themselves with a "soul-warmer."[14]

As the *Bradley* passed Conical Rock at 7:30 A.M., most of her crew were interested in nothing but "hugging the fires," and though the stove was still out, the whiskey served nicely. When the storm finally abated, Dr. Cook and Mr. Bradley were amazed at how good-natured the captain and crew had been through the whole ordeal. They were the only ones not in on the secret of the salutary effect of "Creme in Bottles."

By noon the next day, the storm had given way to a dull gray-blue light, and the yacht was groping among icebergs and hidden rocks off Cape Atholl. It took three hours to work into Wolstenholm Sound, but by 5 P.M. she was approaching North Star Bay. Cook and Bradley were now in the high arctic paradise of their respective dreams.

The doctor watched the icebergs blinking in every color of the spectrum and the bits of drift ice vying with each other in rival blues and greens, as the cries of thousands of seabirds filled the air. His patron grew restless to do battle with walrus and polar bear as he neared the promised game haunts and couldn't wait to land.

Once again, the engine on the yacht was out of commission; she had to be towed into the bay by her dories and the motor launch. Here Dr. Cook greeted many of his old Eskimo acquaintances and met a stranger as well, a Dane with Eskimo blood named Knud Rasmussen, whom the Eskimos called Kudnu.

Rasmussen had first met the Arctic Highlanders in 1903 when he had accompanied L. Mylius-Erichsen's Danish Literary Expedition, which had come north to trade with the natives and to gather their folklore. As with so many others, this first arctic experience had lured him back again, and he was now encamped at North Star with several other Danes. Cook invited him aboard the yacht for dinner, but Bradley said he could not tolerate the smell of the man in his private cabin and asked that he be served at the captain's table. The way in which Bradley loudly gave orders and Cook quietly obeyed led Rasmussen to mistake Dr. Cook for Bradley's personal secretary.

John Bradley was not long in organizing a walrus hunt using the launch. Several Eskimos in their kayaks preceded it as they stalked a large herd lying on ice pans in the bay. But as the natives quietly approached, the animals, one by one, rolled off into the water. Repeated attempts at stealth failed.

Now desperate to get a walrus before they all disappeared into the sea, Bradley ordered a frontal assault. The engine was opened up on the launch, and she drove ahead at full speed past the startled natives and among the sleeping animals. Apparently, the sound of a gasoline motor was new to them, as they surprisingly remained in place until it was too late. The boat's charge bagged four fat bulls.

Hauling them ashore, the Eskimos cut up the animals and invited the visitors to their tupiks for a feast. Franke was repulsed by the look of the raw, oily flesh and upon tasting it rushed out, feeling ill. This mortified his hosts, but Kudnu tactfully explained that Franke was just unused to eating such a delicacy. Outside, the curious Eskimo children gathered around the young stranger as Franke offered them candies. He noticed among them a boy who looked remarkably white. Upon inquiry, he was told the boy was Robert Peary's son, Anaukaq, whom Peary called Sammy.

That evening, Franke decided he would try to do something with the quivering piles of walrus meat collected on the deck. He seasoned it with pepper, salt and onions and offered it to the crew, who thanked him with a small mutiny that saw his walrus dish unceremoniously thrown overboard. To avoid receiving the same treatment, he had to appease their wrath with more "Creme in Bottles."

The next day the launch went south once more after walrus but soon had to turn about as its engine failed again. Sail was set on the yacht for a rescue, but then the wind died, and the frustrated hunters had to be ignominiously hauled back to shore by Captain Bartlett with the help of three Danes in a dory.

The engineer now began working in earnest on the yacht's ever-problematic motor, and in lifting it out, he found that a loose universal joint had bent the propeller. For repairs to be made, the ship would have to be beached. After sounding the soft bottom near the east shore, Captain Bartlett grounded her.

The maneuver was successful, the falling tide leaving the *Bradley* lying on the beach. Dr. Cook thought her a doleful sight when out of her element and looked upon the stranded yacht with a feeling of melancholy, as if having witnessed the death of a friend. Since she lay at such an angle that she could not be boarded, Cook and Bradley took to the launch, where they set their evening table.[15]

The engineer soon reported that the propeller had scraped away about two inches of wood from the *Bradley's* bottom where it had rubbed against it and advised cutting away more—enough to clear the blades—rather than attempting to repair the severely bent propeller without proper tools.

While waiting for things to be righted on the yacht, John Bradley set up his powerful harpoon gun on the shore for target practice, bending the harpoons against the rocks with every discharge. The others contented themselves with trading with the natives and the Danes. Knud Rasmussen offered a fine musk ox skin and head for a supply of brown sugar, salt, alcohol and baking powder. The repairs completed, with all hands pulling at the anchor chains, the *Bradley* was hauled off on the 4:00 tide and, after a last run at walrus, sailed for the northern settlements on August 14.

At Ittiblu they found a lone woman and two small children. She was so overjoyed at having someone new to talk to that she talked incessantly of all the tribal news from many months past. To escape her constant chattering, and in hope of finding guides to organize a reindeer hunt, the captain sailed into Bowdoin Bay. There Dr. Cook was reunited with Manee and her two children.

Cook and Bradley counted four tupiks at the village of Karnah but no men, though a considerable number of women, children and dogs gave them a welcome. Here the natives had such an abundance of blue fox skins, walrus ivory and narwhal tusks and traded at such a disadvantage that Cook ordered the storeroom locked to prevent all the excess supplies from being bartered away.

The season seemed ten days early, with much ice in Inglefield Gulf and snow already settling on the highlands. They intended to go to Olrick's Bay for deer. Then a stiff wind blowing out of the gulf half changed their minds for the walrus grounds farther north. But when they arrived at Kookan in half a gale, they finally found native guides, and when the weather cleared, Bradley and the doctor took two with them to hunt reindeer. After struggling up the heaps of immense boulders strewn along a steam valley that fell from the plateau, they camped on its summit. All they got for their trouble was a single blue fox.

On August 20 the *Bradley* dropped off the Eskimos and in a gathering snowstorm headed for the most northern of the natives' permanent settlements, Etah, under reefed sail. She passed Cape Alexander, entered into Smith Sound, and by the time the yacht made Foulke Fjord, half a gale was blowing again. Wind was a familiar feature at Etah. There, between the fjord's 1,200-foot cliffs of pink sandstone, which funneled the wind off the glacier, four tupiks were seen on the pebbly beach, just inside the first projecting point on the north shore. The Eskimos there said most of the men were at Annoatok, twenty-five miles farther north. A reconnaissance from a high bluff showed no

Sealskin tents, Etah.

significant ice in that direction, so it seemed like a good chance to use the motorboat. The tanks were filled and she set off the next morning for the most northerly inhabited spot on earth.

For once, the launch ran beautifully. As John Bradley, Mike Wise and Dr. Cook approached their destination, suddenly their guide, Tungan, cried out, "Look! there is Annoatok!" Scattered about on the bleak shore were 12 sealskin tents, which served as summer shelters for an equal number of vigorous families. Nearer the beach, seven stone igloos were under construction for the winter. In their immediate vicinity turf and moss grew; everywhere else within a few hundred feet of the sea the land rose abruptly in steep slopes of barren rock. But it looked like a land of plenty to Dr. Cook:[16]

> The wealth in food and furs of this place fixed my determination on this spot as a base for the polar dash. We were standing at a point within seven hundred miles of the pole. The strongest force of men, the best teams of dogs, and an unlimited supply of food, combined with the equipment on board the yacht, formed an ideal plant from which to work out the campaign. The seeming hopelessness of the task had a kind of weird fascination for me. Many years of schooling in both polar zones and in mountaineering would serve a useful purpose.

Annoatok seemed just as prosperous now as it had in 1901; Cook told Bradley of his determination to stay. Bradley warned that he would not be coming back, but Cook wished no relief. He assured Bradley he could go overland to Upernavik and from there get a ship to Copenhagen. He had $500 in gold that Marie had given him at the last moment, and he would pay for his passage with that, he said. In response to the doctor's plan Bradley simply responded, "OK, you're over 21."

Dr. Cook rejoiced at his great good fortune. "Only good health, endurable weather and workable ice were necessary," he wrote later. "The expenditure of a million dollars could not have placed an expedition at a better advantage. The opportunity was too good to be lost. We therefore returned to Etah to prepare for the quest."[17]

On the voyage north Rudolph Franke had heard rumors that Dr. Cook meant to try for the Pole. After the hunters had departed for Annoatok in the launch, he began to hear other rumors as well:

> Late one afternoon, Captain Bartlett entered my room and I noticed in spite of his calmness a secretive look that something was bothering him which he evidently did not wish to disclose. But, I knew the old fox, and after he had emptied the glass of whiskey many times, he came nearer and reported to me that Dr. Cook would like me to accompany him on the planned expedition, but I surmised that Bartlett's confidence was due more to his fondness for whiskey than for me, and consequently I did not pay much attention. In the evening I went ashore to be with the Eskimos before leaving, for I was not only fond of them, but had gotten to really like some of them. As I approached a group, they invited me to go with them to Annoatok, a tiny settlement farther north, which I, however, refused point blank. They laughed and I went on my way.[18]

When the launch returned from Annoatok, Franke thought to himself how easy his experience in the Far North had been and that he would soon be headed home. But this satisfaction was soon replaced by other emotions: "The next morning Dr. Cook sent for me in the presence of Bradley. Captain Bartlett had not lied and the Eskimos had known more than I, for Cook asked whether I would stay with him and accompany him. I hesitated a while, but there was little time for consideration. As I knew Cook as a man of character with the ability to organize, I shook his right hand and accepted."[19]

Late in the evening, Dr. Cook sat down to write letters to send back to New York. Some were official, like that to the Explorers Club's secretary announcing his intentions:

Etah, Aug 26, '07

> My Dear Walsh:
>   I find that I have here a good opportunity to try for the North Pole and therefore I will stay here for the year. I hope to get to the Explorers Club in Sept of 1908 with the record of the Pole.

My plan is to cross Ellesmere land and reach the polar sea by Nansen Strait.

I hope you can induce some of the men of the Explorers Club to come up and meet us at Cape York. If such a project is feasible talk to Mr. Bradley about it.

Long life to the Explorers Club. Here is for the Pole with its flag.

Yours Cordially
Frederick A. Cook[20]

But there were other, more personal ones, too:

Annoatok, Aug. 27, 1907
Greenland
700 miles from the
North Pole

My Dear Ruth,

This is bad news for you. I am going to stay and go to the North Pole and will not come back for one year. I am awfully sorry to be away from Mama and you and Helen. Tears are in my eyes as I write this and how I long to take you in my arms and kiss you and love you and also Helen and Mama—but I am so far away. I can only love you and hope that the time will be short. Be a good girl love Mama and Helen and think of me often.

Your Loving Papa[21]

The yacht left Etah trimmed and ballasted, with supplies on deck ready to throw off at short notice. "None of us slept," Dr. Cook recalled, "and by the time all was ready . . . we were off Annoatok with a strong easterly wind and a good deal of ice in the bay. The dories were loaded and the launch towed them in. This unloading required five hours and it proved an exciting time. Things were thrown ashore anywhere a landing could be effected."[22]

John Bradley was anxious to get out of Smith Sound before the season grew too late and compelled him to stay the winter, too. Storm signs appeared on the horizon. There was no time for long good-byes. Bradley grabbed Cook's hand and then put his hands on the doctor's shoulders and shouted above the rising wind, "Get there and get back!" As Cook and Franke left the ship, the Eskimos simply shouted, since they had no word for good-bye.[23]

As he rowed the dory slowly ashore, Rudolph Franke was again having second thoughts about his hasty decision: "I had given several letters and quickly parted. As the bright sails of the schooner disappeared over the horizon, my heart became heavy, for now we were two white men, all alone for months, maybe years, cut off from the world and civilization and probably slated to die in a region of eternal ice."[24]

The wind was strong with a lot of spray, and Franke, who had insisted he was "proof against cold," had gone ashore wearing only cotton underwear and a Gloucester jacket, much to his shivering regret now. But then he had a thought that warmed him: "My apprenticeship as a Polar explorer was to begin. A sort of wild inspiration—the call of adventure—possessed me and no more was I freezing."25

As the yacht's topmast settled under the storm-tossed sea, the men's attention turned toward devising a shelter. They picked out a spot at the foot of the cliff, behind the pebbly beach, that looked like it would be sheltered from the wind. This was important. *Annoatok* meant "the wind-loved place."

A house was begun by piling the uniform packing boxes to form walls enclosing a space 13 by 16 feet. The boxes were anchored by strips of wood and a few longer boards. For the roof, box lids served as shingles. A covering of thick turf provided insulation that would still allow for circulation of air. A table was built around the post that supported the roof. The two men slept in the rude shelter that first night, but until the house was finished eight days later, the supplies were piled nearby, covered with the *Bradley's* old sails, which had been brought along for that purpose.

By September 1 a small stove was in place, but there was no fuel for it immediately. The last load to be landed was coal, which in the gathering storm had been left in the dories on the shore where the rising surf had swamped them. Ice then drifted over them. When unloaded three days later, they were found to be heavily damaged by the ice. After the five tons of coal were ashore, it would require more hard work to repair the dories for the walrus hunt.

Now, the first of Dr. Cook's careful plans went awry. In its first test, the little stove had to be constantly watched to keep up a draft; what was saved by the economy of its size would be lost through inconvenience. The hard coal they had brought would help make up for the work of tending it, however. The filth associated with the soft coal usually used on polar expeditions would be eliminated, as would the constant cleanings of the stovepipe.

Once settled, Cook and Franke began to explore their surroundings. Occasionally, across Smith Sound, they caught sight of Bache Peninsula and the inland ice of Ellesmere Land, over which they hoped to travel when the sun returned. Despite his hasty choice, Dr. Cook thought Annoatok a practical place from which to launch his try for the Pole:

> It is rather far south as a winter camp for a polar dash — 78° but the very great advantage of starting with fresh stores, dogs and expert sledge men, and travelling through a game country for the first 400 miles are not to be overlooked. Furthermore, it obviates the need of a large party. It eliminates the risk to the ship and makes a yearly communication with the main base a certainty. Counting all the advantages on both sides of a far north station and a lower station—it seems to me Annoatok is an ideal starting

point. If my judgment is right the success or non-success of our campaign will tell.[26]

These first gray days ashore, the two white men began to settle into a routine. Dr. Cook made every effort to gain the confidence of the Eskimos and direct their efforts toward the multitude of preparations necessary for his polar journey. They were delighted with *Tatsekuuk*'s liberality of inviting them to his warm house each afternoon to have a cup of tea.

Cook occupied himself with planning the equipment while Franke, eager to get into the field, went hunting for hare around Inglefield Cape and into Rensselaer Harbor, where Kane had wintered. But Dr. Cook knew it was more efficient to let the natives hunt and then barter with them for food, using his own abundant supplies of tobacco, cartridges and biscuits for trade, than to do it themselves:

> There was a complex activity suddenly stimulated along the Greenland coast which did not require general supervision. The Eskimos knew what was required without a word from us, and knew better than we did where to find the things worth while. An outline of the polar campaign was sent from village to village, with a few general instructions. . . .
>
> Each Eskimo village has as a rule certain game advantages.
>
> In some places foxes and hares were abundant. Their skins were in great demand for coats and stockings, and the Eskimos must not only gather the greatest number possible, but must prepare the skins and make them into properly fitting garments.
>
> In other places reindeer were abundant. This skin was very much in demand for sleeping bags, while the sinew was required for thread. In still other places seal was the luck of the chase and its skin was one of our most important needs. Of it boots were ordered and an immense amount of line and lashings was prepared.
>
> Thus in one way or another every man, woman and most of the children of this tribe of 250 people were kept busy in the service of the expedition. The work was well done and with much better knowledge of the fitness of things than could be done by any possible gathering of white men.[27]

The natives were also preparing for winter and had their underground houses to get in order. But reluctant to enter them until they had to, they clung to their tupiks as long as they could, even as the first snows began to cover the ground. It would not be long, though, before the tupiks would be taken down, and Dr. Cook was made to think of the coming night and its attendant trials. "The snow has come to stay," the doctor wrote in his diary. "The dark veil of the long night is slowly falling over us, and these grey days, humidity and stillness serve to increase the saddening effect of the gloom of the long night."²⁸

Working on the equipment presented many challenges to the explorers' ingenuity. The hard hickory was difficult to bend for sled runners, but this impediment was overcome when Franke suggested using several lengths of stovepipe as a steam bed. When the men found themselves short of three-foot lengths of wood, Koolootingwah, a particularly clever Eskimo, straightened barrel staves by heating their convex sides over the stove and then patiently standing on them until they were cool and flat.

Hunters soon returned from Humboldt Glacier, telling of the failed deer hunt—bad news that could threaten the expedition's plans. But they brought even more disturbing news in the form of a piece of wood. It was painted white, and Dr. Cook thought at first some accident might have befallen the *Bradley*. Closer inspection showed it was probably part of a deck rail made of hard pine. Since the *Bradley*'s rail was of oak, it could not be from hers.

The doctor asked the natives to bring back more of the wood, saying, "We must soon solve this problem." Koolootingwah then volunteered that another native had told him of seeing the smoke of a steamer crossing the sound, but that it did not come back. Captain Bernier, with the Canadian vessel *Arctic,* was known to have wintered at Pond Inlet; perhaps she had met disaster.²⁹

On September 13 there was a remarkable sunset, so beautiful that even the natives came out of their tupiks to admire it. The dogs were not without aesthetic appreciation either, getting up a howl that struck Dr. Cook as "music out of harmony with the scene." The evening was made doubly memorable with a program of dogfights as entertainment. Most ended in the capitulation of the weaker animal without much real damage being done, but two determined canine gladiators kept at it until they had literally chewed the ears off each other.

Soon the inevitable storms that accompany the going of the sun set in. "Even the Eskimos to-day abandoned their tupiks for the winter igloos," Dr. Cook noted. Now the Eskimos began visiting the house even more often to get away from their underground shelters. "We have adopted the plan that every one who absorbs the heat of our house and the tea which we freely serve must work," he wrote. "We therefore set [them] at working whips, parts of harnesses and sledges and so on. In a little while we will have a factory here for polar equipment."³⁰

Dr. Cook took novel approaches in his dealings with the Eskimos. He lent Angodlu a gun in return for nothing more than a percentage of what the hunter might get in skins. Sometimes he was a bit too generous. He had set a price of three biscuits for an eider duck, and as he watched his biscuit supply dwindle rapidly, he made a note to himself: "This is expensive meat, we must try to get the price lowered."³¹

The doctor made other agreements as well:

> We have given Koolootingwah wood for a sledge with the understanding that it is loaned and when we leave, if he has proven worthy, the sled is to go to him. This is a system of arrangement which we will adopt with all our sleds, guns, knives and tools.
>
> Neucapingwah took the .22 and went out after hare. This is also a part of the routine of our daily life—nearly every day some of the young men borrow the .22 and try for hare—if they succeed we give them a little tobacco. If not, there is no reward except a cup of tea, a biscuit and a warm reception.[32]

Koolootingwah was the native Dr. Cook believed stood out above all others, and he went to great lengths to ensure his loyalty. He told the Eskimo he was to be the chief helper and would get a fair supply of tea, coffee, sugar, tobacco and biscuits in return, but that he must not tell the others. Though Koolootingwah agreed, the doctor thought it "rather doubtful that this attempt at secrecy will succeed, because the natives keep no secrets. If this news spreads all the natives will demand a similar favor."[33]

In the middle of September the two white men indulged in the rarest of arctic luxuries—a bath—but the amount of humidity that accumulated as frost on the walls from heating so much water was decidedly unpleasant.

The box house felt so warm and cozy that Cook and Franke shivered at the thought of going out to take their daily exercise, but they knew they must keep in shape. These outings were made more tolerable when Eginguah brought the doctor a pair of bearskin britches. The doctor recorded his delight: "It is a day of rejoicing . . . they are a prize."[34]

As much as the whites did not want to leave their hut, the Eskimos wanted to enter it. So many wild-looking men in fur suits crowded the tiny house at any time that it reminded Franke of a robbers' den. The Eskimos were especially fascinated with the darkroom Dr. Cook set up inside by chinking all the cracks in the box house with absorbent cotton flour paste. They never tired of seeing the red light and watching the pictures appear on the paper; "Noweeo!" they exclaimed. Then they whispered to each other of the power of the great angekok from the south.

Franke had by now picked up enough of the simplified language the natives used when talking with whites to understand some of what they said. "The Eskimos had great admiration for Dr. Cook," Franke was certain. "Although they had a word, 'angekok,' for doctor in their language, they spoke of him as Doctorsoah, the big medicine man, for in his earlier journeys he had in a self-sacrificing way helped them with medicines and had gone throughout the settlements."[35]

Franke marveled, too, at how Cook managed to overcome every eventuality and gained the confidence of these strange men of the North:

> I felt honest admiration and wonderment at his ability and understanding of people. He knew how to put the right man in the right

Rudolph Franke in the box house.
Photograph by Cook.

place. No failure, no work was too much for him, and everywhere he knew how to help with advice and assistance, helping with his own hands. In bed at night, he busied himself with the work of the next day, thinking of all the changes and circumstances that might arise for the expedition. In spite of all the work, Cook was everywhere. He examined, led or encouraged us, and all that with a calmness, foresight, and understanding and generosity which filled me with astonishment and respect.[36]

Rudolph often found Dr. Cook sitting by the shore, watching with fascination as the ice foot was slowly built up by the incoming and outgoing tides. The entire length of Smith Sound had been so ice-free that Cook had speculated on how far he might travel up and down the coast if he only had a motor launch like the *Bradley's*. For future reference, he even sketched a double-pulley device that could be used to raise such a boat beyond the danger of ice and tide. But by September 17 the sound was choked with ice, and the Eskimos said that in a month it would be suitable for sledging.

Cook gave special attention to the sledges upon which all his hopes would eventually ride. He carefully standardized their runners' widths at 30 inches so that each could follow in the others' tracks. A large tent would be hauled on a special sledge on which it could be quickly erected. He hoped this might be practical as a shelter on the trail and intended to try it out in the field over the winter.

The completed sledges were lined up outside the box house awaiting a good test. The men now had to be careful to bring everything else inside, since the snow was starting to build up around the house and anything left out was unlikely to be seen again before summer.

One major job that still needed doing was the manufacture of pemmican for the trip north, as the *Bradley* had left an inadequate supply. The two men experimented with drying walrus meat, and soon their efforts were pronounced a "howling success." "[This is] the only article which we greatly need," Cook declared. "This invention is likely to have an important bearing in the future success of our venture and therefore we are giving it a good deal of our attention."[37]

The meat was taken from the caches along the shore and allowed to thaw in the box house. Then, after cutting it into six-inch strips, they hung it on hooks for three days, collecting any moisture and oil that dripped off in a large pan. When the meat was thoroughly dry, they mixed it with fat in equal quantities, packed it in tin cases and wired them up. Drying walrus meat soon filled the rafters and also filled the house with its distinctive aroma. They would make 1,500 pounds of the concoction, and when the last of the meat came down, Franke thought the house looked strangely large, it had become so much of a fixture.

The fading sun still gave enough light to work outside for 12 hours of the day. There was not much room in the box house anyway, which was usually filled with crying children; women working at chewing and sewing skins, dog harnesses and other articles of equipment; and men hoping for tobacco or a hot drink. With all the comings and goings, the door seemed more often open than closed, so a snow vestibule was constructed, and a protective wall of snow was erected around the entire house.

Dr. Cook now wished for the deep snows to come, since the dogs were getting to be a bother. They climbed on the roof and attempted to scratch their way through the sod to the fragrant walrus meat hanging just below their reach. They constantly raided the shed that the men had built behind the house and made off with supplies until Cook devised a door out of the back of a chair covered with coal sacks. One of the dogs suspected of having piblockto was destroyed, lest an outbreak of the mysterious ailment stifle all their plans.

No details were too small to attend to. The doctor noticed the difficulty in keeping socks dry. "To overcome this I am devising a more porus bottom," he recorded in his diary. "Taking a woolen stocking we have cut strips of hare about ¾ in. wide and sewn them in, leaving a space of about ½ inch. The sole is made of blue fox tails. The next experiment will consist of cutting slits along the dorsum of the foot and above the ankle to the side of the leg and setting in strips of camel hair blanket."[38]

None of these exotic ideas seemed to cure the problem, so Cook took to wearing four pairs of woolen socks around the frigid floor of the house, while Franke preferred the native hareskin stockings with the hair worn inside, even though these required more frequent drying.

Though the floor at −10° necessitated warm footgear, the rest of the house was warmer by degrees: two feet higher on the bunk it was +36, at head height, 65, and under the roof, 82.

Outside the comfortable house, the pack ice seemed to alternately leave and blow back into Smith Sound, until it formed more permanently just as the sun had almost waned for good. As the light faded, Dr. Cook felt as depressed by the thought of its departure as he always had before. He noticed a similar reaction among the Eskimos as well. The children did not seem to mind and continued digging in the snow for their own amusement, but the adults seemed saddened by the sun's decline. Along the shore he found women standing near the ice foot in silence, with tears rolling down their cheeks. The only sound that could be heard was what the Eskimos called "the weeping under the ice"—the creaking and groaning of the congealing waters.

When snow finally covered the box house at Annoatok, the men inside suddenly felt very uncomfortable. With the addition of the insulating white blanket, the little stove was now too much for the space. To remedy the lack of circulation, they dug a hole lower than the door's level and drilled tiny holes in the roof's sod covering for ventilation. This arrangement had its drawbacks, however. When the temperature suddenly rose, the roof's covering of snow melted, then froze to the floor after dripping through the vent holes.

October 10 was a red-letter day. Eskimos had been out all fall stalking reindeer but had always returned empty-handed; now the *tooktoo* hunters arrived with four deer. "We adopted a new rule to-day to feed the workers," the doctor wrote of the celebration that followed. "The tooktoo hunters were invited with their families to dinner and we served them with just the things which we also [had]. The menu was rather elaborate: tooktoo steaks, potatoes, french peas, biscuits, rice with strawberry syrup, a raisin cake and peaches. It was a great treat to the simple good-hearted creatures and we enjoyed their companionship."[39]

As he had suspected, having done this for the hunters, Dr. Cook had to give dinners to everyone. He and Franke quickly wearied "of this equal treatment for all—whether useful or otherwise to us" and henceforth gave dinners only as rewards after worthy deeds.[40]

In ten days the sun would set. Cook was anxious to field test some of the new sleds, the "house sled" especially, before it disappeared. With this purpose he set off with the natives on October 15 for a 14-day hunting trip to the Humboldt Glacier. The first two days they camped on the ice pack in the house sled, which could be set up in ten minutes, but since it was cumbersome to haul and cold to live in, they quickly abandoned it for a snow house. Lack of success made them return early, and just in time, since they were greeted by a terrible blow on the day they arrived back at the box house.

It had been stormy before, but the storm of October 23 seemed almost like a hurricane. It piled snow over everything, including the dogs, which were completely buried. There was no damage, however, since the men had taken to throwing their waste water over the snow wall. Though this destroyed "the artistic effect," it had so thoroughly cemented the protective wall that no storm could now have any effect on the house.

A lamp had been burning constantly for the past two weeks as the light coming in the small south-facing window faded, and the sun officially set on October 25, though light would be visible at noon for some time to come. As winter began, Dr. Cook had a right to be pleased. "At midnight or thereabouts we celebrate our second month here," he wrote of the event, "—and a pleasant two months it has been training and preparing for the long march. We are looking for days to celebrate but we can find few. Our birthdays do not occur till June and August, months when we should be well on the trail homeward."[41]

With the darkness, the same symptoms observed on the *Belgica* began all over again. Dr. Cook prescribed a routine to combat the lethargy of the night:

> It seems to be difficult also to prolong any one line of mental occupation for more than a few hours without undue fatigue. So I have arranged quite systematically to rise at six, Breakfast at 6:30, sit down to my desk for literary work at 7:30 and remain there until the brain refuses to work which is usually at about 10. Then we have coffee and I go out for exercise. Returning at noon we have dinner and at about 2 pm we begin serious manual labor—working sledges and equipment and keeping the men at work. At about four I sit down to read—at 5 the natives are served daily with tea and biscuits and at six we have supper.[42]

There was certainly no lack of company. The Eskimos at least provided diversion as the monotony of winter came on; they amazed Cook at every turn. One learned the function of every part of a new Winchester rifle in less than five minutes, a task that had taken Franke two hours of study.

The hunters continued to bring in meat and blue-fox skins, and the house was always crowded with others working on the expedition's equipment or just wishing to take in the latest marvel. Only once did they willingly leave.

Rudolph had decided to try out his recipe for sourdough bread but found he had no cream of tartar. When he substituted sauerkraut juice, the smell of the baking bread sent the Eskimos scurrying to their foul-smelling igloos and set Dr. Cook to pondering the cultural education of the olfactory lobes.

The weather had turned dull and gloomy, but still the winter landscape held endless fascination for the ever-observant doctor. Surprised at how ice-free the sound remained, even in November, he began to worry that he might be prevented from crossing over in the spring to Ellesmere Land to begin his trek to the Pole.

He looked with satisfaction, however, upon the three sledges he and Franke had built with the Eskimos' help in the last week. They had now completed seven, made of the second-growth hickory chosen only from those trees growing on the hillsides of his brother's farm. Dr. Cook had studied the Eskimo sleds for their weak points and found the floor most likely to break. As always, he recorded his observations in his diary: "It is important to note that most hard wood becomes stronger in low temperatures while soft wood usually becomes more brittle. As a general rule it pays to use hard wood. In the end this will be a savings in weight."[43]

He also constructed hickory snowshoes. These he made narrower and shorter than the normal racket shoe, and with a turned-up end, because he noticed as the winter progressed that deep drifts of snow were a rarity, the strong prevailing winds having scoured them off.

To test the equipment, the doctor planned a journey to gather the supplies still needed. In the light of the November moon, the month the Eskimos call *Tutsarfik,* Dr. Cook bade good-bye to Rudolph and started southward. So loaded down with trade goods was the sled train as it left Annoatok that it reminded Franke of the arctic equivalent of a merchant caravan.

It would be a severe and brutal test. On this trip Cook would learn to travel like an Eskimo, to eat like an Eskimo, indeed, what it was to *be* an Eskimo, and he shuddered at his own feeble inferiority:

> We have crawled like foxes among the rocks and crevasses at a mad pace until we are all so bumped and bruised by slipping and falling in the thickening darkness that we must rest and mend up. This kind of travel is new to me. I never would have ventured on the glacier in bright light without being roped but here we go pell mell over seracs or miles of glacial ice with only the instinct of the natives and the dogs to guide us, but some how we get along very well—I wish that I could picture this kind of life. It is the most desperate kind of a trip that I have been forced to make. The eye of the caucasian is not sufficiently keen to venture out on the level. I cannot see the irregularities of the snow sufficient to place a footing, yet these people go along at a pace which takes one on the run to keep up. . . .
>
> It is hard to conceive how a sledge or human beings can stand this kind of abuse.[44]

But the pace soon slowed. He spent days in an igloo listening to the monotonous chanting designed to drive away the low ice haze that kept them from traveling, and when they moved on, they had to stop, out of Eskimo custom, at every igloo for a visit.

They made one of these social calls at the igloo of an Eskimo named Kessir, who without much conversation offered them slabs of raw, frozen walrus meat hacked off with an axe. Dr. Cook marveled at how easily large quantities sat on the stomach. Kessir was a good host and also set out his great delicacies of putrid auks and their dried eggs for his guests. The doctor especially liked the eggs and ate them with relish.

By the time they reached Etah, all things Eskimo were beginning to have an alluring appeal:

> Mrs. Anninah is a remarkably pretty woman of 20—she is married 7 years has no family but has developed a cult of domestic weakness peculiar to herself with a skin about white and a figure as near perfect as it is possible for an eskimo woman to be. She sits daily in

her position sewing. It is a picture worth reproducing. As she sits she seems perfectly nude. The little strip of fur which modesty dictates is lost to view; holding between her toes a strip of fur she sews all day.[45]

On December 4 they arrived at Oomanui, where Cook again met Kudnu. When his trading was completed, the doctor left with the Dane letters for Marie and John R. Bradley, as well as one for Herbert L. Bridgman:

> Oomanui Wolstenholm Sd.,
> Dec. 6, 1907
>
> My Dear Bridgman:
> I have this opportunity to send a letter to Upernavik by Rasmussen during this moon, and I must hasten to report our progress to the present. I have a hundred dogs and as many more as I desire, with 15 of the best men of the tribe, assembled here for the attack over the new route—across Ellesmereland, out by way of Nansen Sound and back by Kennedy Channel, thus using to good advantage, the drift and the musk-oxen so abundant in Ellesmereland.
> All of my equipment is ready and we hope to start for the goal, late in January, with men and dogs well fed and under normal conditions unlike the half-fed and utterly demoralized condition of the people and their dogs when wintered in the Far North. Like my predecessors, I feel confident of success, as our equipment means perfection.
> When we return we will push southward at once to Cape York and Upernavik.
> With kindest regards to Mrs. Bridgman and all my friends, I am,
> > Yours faithfully,
> > Frederick A. Cook.[46]

The weather was better for most of the homeward journey but became thick again as they left Etah for Annoatok, where they arrived December 11:

> At home at last after a tremendous effort from Etah. The wind blew a half a gale and the snow drove into our fur garments through every crevice. As we came out of the last pressure angle I fixed myself on the sledge and turned from the wind in such a manner as to suffer least from the blow. How long I sat in this position I do not know. I dozed from time to time. At last Koolootingwah said "Tokor." I turned to face the wind and saw a light; a few moments later more lights—a welcome sight. It was Annoa-

tok, wind swept, snow decked, dark and gloomy, but still our
home. With a big fire and an abundance of food no place ever
aroused greater delight.[47]

Home at last! Now he could satisfy his craving for a pan of Rudolph's biscuits! Soon, however, the joy of being home gave way to more worries over
whether everything would be ready in time. In less than two months, he reckoned, he would be on his way to the Pole. Despite his optimistic report to
Herbert Bridgman, there was so much still to be done—some of the sledges
were not yet finished, and much of the equipment needed modification. But
though his ambition for the future remained high, his willingness to be up
and doing for the moment was gone, snuffed out by the blackness.

In the wake of Dr. Cook's visit, more and more Eskimos, excited as children at their first circus, arrived to see the wonders of the white men's house.
One item proved particularly popular with the visitors—coal oil. Cook told
them it was a hair invigorator, and its use had helped keep the box house tolerably free of lice. Franke thought there was one drawback to this method of
pest control, however. The smell of kerosene combined with the distinctive
native aroma was almost too much for him.

Dr. Cook also noted with amusement that the women had taken to asking for soap, but when they washed with it in a basin, they began by doing
their feet and, working upwards, finished with their faces.

Late in December one of the Eskimos brought in a harpoon shaft—more
evidence that a ship might have wrecked on the coast in the fall. Dr. Cook
asked Koolootingwah to cross Smith Sound as soon as the ice permitted to
look for evidence of white men; Franke wondered, if they were found, what
effect this would have on their plans.

"Even today I can see myself with Dr. Cook in our arctic dwelling on
Christmas Eve as I asked him the question about the possible ship wreck and
if our expedition to the North Pole might be in vain," Franke remembered of
that anxious time. "Cook dropped his head in his hands, but then the physician came to the fore—the real friend of man—'To save human lives is our
first duty,' he said. This quiet resignation will be unforgettable as long as I
live."[48]

On this December 24 there were two things to celebrate: the coming of
Christmas and the midnight of winter, just passed. The sun was now on its
way back; soon it would flood the white landscape with its blinding light, and
they must be ready when it returned. But first there would be a feast!

Franke prepared roast arctic hare, potatoes, green peas, French rice,
onions, peaches, cake and tea, but all else was missing:

> This Christmas Eve in the uttermost settlement of the arctic
> there were no bells, no choirs—only the icy storm outside, howl-
> ing and whistling, delivering gruesome melodies and filling us
> with terror—no gifts to exchange, but Dr. Cook and I clasped

hands and with tears in our eyes promised to stay together and endure to the last. After a short refreshing walk outside we went to bed, but for a long time we lay awake thinking of our loved ones at home and wondering what the future would bring.[49]

From Christmas to New Year's Day a holiday was declared. Franke had saved some delicacies, and since he noticed that "the greatest thing for the children of the Far North is eating, eating, eating," they would be given two meals daily.

On Christmas itself, the white men were invited to festivities in the igloo of an Eskimo they called "Bismarck." A huge meal of cooked walrus meat was served, which everyone alike dipped out of a large kettle with a long knife. Franke was still not fond of walrus, though he now thought it better than beans and bacon, at least. After dinner, pipes were lit, and Cook and Franke handed around raisins and chewing tobacco for dessert.

Inside the small stone igloo 18 men and one woman danced to the monotonous beat of a skin drum while others, trying to crawl through the low doorway, were kept out by kicks as they attempted to enter. The smoke grew so thick from the tallow candles and tobacco that the swaying, chanting forms of the dancers were almost lost to view, and the atmosphere grew so heated that everyone had to strip to the waist as if they were in the tropics.

After the Eskimos chanted their songs and swayed and bowed interminably, Franke was asked to sing. He tried a song called "Outside There Blew a Cold Wind," which seemed appropriate but was lost on his audience. Then he tried another, from the "Wild Hunter," which seemed more appreciated. Getting up his courage, he moved on to a medley from Wagner's *Ring,* for which he received hearty applause.

Toward evening, longing for a breath of fresh air, Rudolph Franke left the igloo at which the feast had been in session and started back for the little house of boxes. In the east he saw the harbinger of arctic dawn, hanging wraithlike above the horizon. The long night was beginning to wane:

> I saw the red glow of the northern lights . . . after the long, long, terrible polar night the first weak indication of the gradual reappearance of the day-star which gives new life and confidence. Leaning against the cliff, I marveled at the cold starry night until a heavy gust of wind came down from the Humboldt Glacier and aroused me from my thoughts and dreams. It was an impressive and unforgettable Christmas in the Arctic.[50]

CHAPTER 14

I Have Been to the Pole!

BY THE TURN OF THE YEAR, EVEN FEASTING HAD LOST ITS CHARM, AT LEAST for the white men, and the unrelieved presence of the polar night left little room for cheer. Even the Eskimos seemed restless and could spend only a short time in their igloos before planning some errand just to get away, so Cook dispatched a party under the leadership of Koolootingwah to look for traces of the suspected shipwreck.

The brilliant light of the moon was enough for the Eskimos' keen eyes to pick out a route to the other side of Smith Sound, which they reached in one long, unpleasant day of travel. A howling storm blew out of the Humboldt Glacier as they crossed the sound, and on the far shore they encountered a large polar bear, which raided the sleds and made off, with Ootah in pursuit. The bear escaped but not before biting Ootah in the seat of the pants for his trouble. The storm had one benefit, however; it crusted and packed the surface of the snow, which made travel easier.

Upon their return, Koolootingwah reported no signs of white men. Their worries about the need for a possible rescue put to rest, Cook and Franke were eager to be off on the adventure that would begin with the polar dawn. But Dr. Cook was not without doubts as to their chances.

Surprisingly, there was still much open water in Smith Sound. The doctor was afraid this would prevent a crossing by the heavily loaded sledges when the sun reappeared. Even so, he continued to refine his plans. He toyed with the idea of returning by way of Prince Patrick Island or Herschel Island and then on to Alaska, thinking that if he came back via Crocker Land the total distance would not be much greater than the additional journey to Upernavik from Annoatok.[1]

Yet, even with so much left to do, the arctic night once again all but stifled the two men's enthusiasm. Cook was wakeful and could not sleep; Franke, who had no difficulty sleeping, still felt exhausted. They had to force themselves to do even necessary tasks.

By January 14, 1908, they were ready to make an attempt to establish an advance depot for the coming campaign. Franke was assigned this important duty. He started at 4 P.M. for Ellesmere Land in the company of three Eskimos driving 45 dogs, pulling five sledges carrying light loads of 250 pounds each. His orders were to cache the supplies at the head of Flagler Bay.

For the next few days, Cook brooded on the bitter fate he had chosen for himself. "Alone in a big cold world," he wrote in his diary. "If a man were to select a place to frustrate evildoers artificially he could find no more appropriate place than to place an individual isolated in this land of torment with its cold wind to be feared [more] than the fire of hell and its darkness more degenerating than the influence of the devil. . . . Every rule of life is broken to give full swing to the insidiousness of this life-sapping darkness."[2]

To improve his mental outlook, he returned to his baking treatments. He felt like a new man after sitting in front of the fire. But soon there would be no fire and no shelter—only the merciless arctic wastes, stretching endlessly and unbroken, between him and his goal. "How cozy the house is," he thought.[3] "Alone with my plans to conquer the pole—How the ideas come and go with the doom of night. . . ."[4]

After four days he was happy to have the companionship of some Eskimos who arrived with gossip from North Star Bay, and the next day Franke returned. The doctor was eager for every detail and encouraged by Rudolph's report. The news that the ice of Smith Sound had been good for traveling, and what open water remained at its center was easily gotten around, was especially welcome.

Even in temperatures below –70°, Franke's Jaeger underwear had frozen like a sheet of iron when he perspired while struggling with the sledges, of which only one had broken, at the very beginning while descending from the ice foot onto the pack.

The moon was so bright that it enabled them to see Greenland all the way across Kane Basin, and Franke described as overwhelming the sight of the massive expanse of ice glittering as far as the eye could see. After a long day's march of more than 28 miles, they had reached the rafted ice against Cape Sabine. Once ashore, they were too tired to build an igloo, so they took refuge in Peary's dilapidated house, which offered some shelter.

While in the shack at Sabine, Franke said, the Eskimos drew a distinction between the structure and its builder:

> Koolootingwah said, "Peary *iglu pijuk,* Peary no good." I had to laugh at the Eskimo's remark for his comment sounded as if Peary's house was good but Peary, himself, was no good. I told him he must not talk like that about one whose hospitality he had accepted, because as soon as Peary came North again he would be the first to board Peary's ship. But there I got into a hornet's nest— Koolootingwah took me to one side and told me how Peary had sent away the angekok Dedrick, who had come from Etah, and who was friendly to the Eskimos, without food and drink into the cold, although they wanted medicine because they had been infected by Peary's white companions. . . . He showed me the spot where Dedrick stood when he was mercilessly turned away by

Peary. When I expressed doubt [about Peary's treatment of
Dedrick] the good Koolootingwah said, "Dead Eskimos. Peary no
good." It is true that Peary in inhuman brutality refused the help
of his former expedition doctor and let the Eskimos die under the
worst suffering. The bodies of the unfortunate victims were not
even covered, as is the custom in the Arctic, with stones and rocks,
but left for the foxes and ravens, and I could find the human bones
scattered around Cape Sabine.[5]

The snow had been too soft and deep to continue past Cape Veile, so
there they stowed their supplies under some rocks and returned to Annoatok.
        Perhaps most important, Franke, who had never had such a field experi-
ence, had held up surprisingly well. Cook noted that his companion did have
one physical disadvantage for a polar explorer, however. Since he was balding,
he could not draw any long hair over his face as the Eskimos did in extreme
conditions. In the bitter cold, he and the other men had run beside the sledges
to keep up body heat. Still, Franke suffered minor frostbite to the cheek, nose
and one of his big toes.
        The "day" was growing brighter, though the sun would still not be visible
for almost a month. The polar night was fading rapidly; the Dipper was now
barely visible at noon. Yet the men felt ever more lethargic and had to force
themselves to exercise and sit before the fire to build up their strength. On
their walks outside they took great pleasure in the fact that they could now see
their own footprints, and Dr. Cook noted the difference in the psychological
effect of the same amount of fading light as opposed to that of the returning
sun: "[Then] we thought of our isolation from the world of life and our long
deprivation of the comfort of friends and loved ones. . . . Now we think of the
light and heat and renewed life of the coming day of months and of our success in the field of action and an early return to home and everything that is
dear to us."[6]
        Final details occupied them fully. Adjustments had to be made to dog
harnesses, sledges and clothes, and all the women were still sewing birdskin
shirts.
        The doctor had noticed in his photography experiments that amber fil-
ters seemed to cut down on the actinic rays of the sun better than any other
color. He now constructed amber-lensed goggles as an experiment against
snowblindness.
        The folding boat also needed to be prepared. Cook had asked the manu-
facturer not to impregnate it with the ordinary waterproofing compound, as
he had discovered in Alaska that this made the canvas very fragile in low temperatures. Instead, he mixed his own, omitting the turpentine and adding one
third the volume of ozguk seal fat instead.
        But even if everything had been ready, it would have been impossible to
even think about starting, since hunters had taken all the dogs and gone to the
walrus grounds at Nerke.

The two white men knew the little luxuries they now enjoyed would soon be only a memory, and any notable day was never allowed to slip by uncelebrated. January 27 was the Kaiser's birthday, and since both had kind feelings for the fatherland, they toasted Wilhelm II with roast hare, erbswurst and sauerkraut.

The coming dawn triggered equinoctial storms that piled the snow to such heights outside the box house that the wind could no longer be heard and the door could not be opened. Franke had to cut a hole in the side of the house so that they could crawl out and clear it away.

Koolootingwah returned from Nerke on February 5 telling of great storms that had swept many of the snow houses into the sea. Two sledges were lost, along with several valuable fur coats, which would have to be replaced before the expedition could move. This occupied the Eskimos during another huge gale that swept in from the southeast. Franke busied himself constructing a special box for the little alcohol field stove. Indeed, during the forced confinement there was no idle time for anyone. "In about two weeks the rear guard, the last train of sledges, will leave here," the doctor reckoned. "I should very much like to be in the advance guard but there are so many little things to be attended to that all my time for at least 10 days will be spent in these final arrangements."[7]

As suddenly as the fierce storms had arisen, there came a complete calm almost as startling in its abruptness. During this lull, Okiu and his young wife appeared, just back from a journey to Cape York, with much news and a strange tale to tell. "Peary's ship has been crushed and Peary has been nailed to a cross by white men because he has caused suffering and starvation among the natives at Cape Sheridan," said Okiu. "His spirit is soon to hover over the Eskimo land in a balloon and from it Peary is to shout at his Eskimos."[8]

But Peary's ship had not been crushed; it was not even at Cape Sheridan. The *Roosevelt* was still in New York. The contractors had failed to meet their deadline of July 1 for installing new boilers. Peary was reported to have been beside himself at the delay, and by August he had abandoned any hope of going north in 1907.

At least Walter Wellman and his airship were out of the race. Peary, who had no faith in mechanical methods of travel to the Pole, was not surprised to hear the fate of the journalist-turned-aviator's latest expedition.

The *America* had been towed out to sea by the steamer *Smeerenburg Sund* and then cast adrift on September 2, 1907. But after struggling against southwest winds for three and a quarter hours and making only 15 miles, Wellman landed his airship safely on a Spitzbergen glacier. She was taken back to Europe for repairs and another try the next summer or at least that of 1909.

Then came another severe blow to Peary's plans. Morris K. Jesup died on January 22, 1908, and despite his other millionaire backers, Peary said he was severely strapped for funds and still needed $100,000 to get away in 1908. He was reduced to appealing for the donation of pennies from American schoolchildren to make good the deficit run up in trying to accomplish his great patriotic undertaking.[9]

Peary's anger over the delay of his expedition and his anxiety over his benefactor's death were nothing compared with his feelings when he had learned in October 1907 that Cook had not returned with John Bradley but was instead encamped at Annoatok.

The first official word of Cook's intentions to try for the Pole came from Herbert L. Bridgman, who, like Henry Walsh, had gotten a letter from Cook upon the return of the *Bradley.* Bridgman immediately phoned Bob Bartlett.

"Did you know that Bradley was back with the schooner and that Dr. Cook has been left north to go to the Pole?" asked Bridgman.

"What?" exclaimed the captain.

"Exactly that," said the newspaperman.

"But how on earth can he make it without equipment or ship?" asked the captain anxiously.

"He can't," said Bridgman with finality, and hung up.

"I was stunned," Bartlett recalled, "but felt Dr. Cook's daring could only be rewarded by complete failure."[10]

The two men's assumptions were upset when Bridgman obtained an interview with John Bradley. The gambler was quite willing to talk and told Bridgman he had left Cook with everything he could possibly need and expressed confidence he would succeed.

"But how is he going to get home?" Bridgman asked.

"The natives have gone across that ice for thousands, perhaps millions, of years," said Bradley. "I do not see why Dr. Cook cannot."

"Well," Bridgman muttered, "he might. He certainly has the nerve."[11]

This was indeed an unexpected turn of events, even for the up-and-coming newspaper in New York, the *Times,* which editorialized:

> The news that Dr. Frederick A. Cook, scaler of icy mountains, and an expert in both arctic and antarctic exploration, is already safely housed at Etah, in Greenland, 650 miles from the North Pole, and amply provisioned for eighteen months, comes as a sort of surprise. . . .
>
> We have more faith in him than we have in the vociferous explorers who would fly to the pole and back again in an incredibly short time. The sledge, the boat, and the legs are still the arctic explorer's only trustworthy means of locomotion.
>
> That Cook has got the start of Peary does not count for so much. Peary will be in the race. But it is to men of this sort, who prepare to encounter the obstacles of the arctic in the reasonable way, that we must look for any further knowledge of the geography of the far North. Dr. Cook knows his business, and he has started in the right way.[12]

Although Peary refused to believe that Cook had even the smallest chance of success, he soon had suspicions of Cook's motives. They were aroused one day in the fall of 1907, when a fellow explorer, Vilhjalmur Stefansson, called on him.

Stefansson had been a member of the Mikkelsen and Leffingwell Expedition, which had set off the previous spring to search for the continent Dr. Harris had postulated as lying north of Alaska. Their ship, *The Duchess of Bedford,* had been crushed off Banks Land, and they had experienced very rough going trying to penetrate north of Flaxman Island by sledge. One day they took eight hours to move 200 yards, and their total northing was only about 100 miles. Stefansson had returned by way of Herschel Island and Fort Yukon.

When he arrived in New York he went to see Peary, who was staying at the Grand Union Hotel. Stefansson told Peary of the rumors current in Alaska that Cook had gotten only halfway up Mount McKinley and gave him the names and addresses of some of the doubters. Stefansson suggested that if Cook had been bold enough to lie about McKinley, he may have gone north with a dishonest intention—to fraudulently claim the Pole.

Peary's first reaction was to dismiss this. He told Stefansson he knew Cook well and that he didn't think he would do anything dishonorable. Furthermore, Peary was sure that "his" loyal Eskimos would never assist someone in competition with him for the Pole. Anyway, Peary said, Cook would convict himself should he fail to bring back the record he himself had left at Cape Thomas Hubbard in 1906 when he had sighted Crocker Land, and that surely Cook lacked the ability as an ice traveler to get even that far along his proposed route.

Stefansson was not so sure as Peary. He thought the Eskimos had no sense of competition and would remember Cook only as Peary's assistant in 1891. They would be able to get him as far as Cape Hubbard, he suggested, and leave him there, free to invent the rest of his journey to the Pole.

Since Peary remained unconvinced, Stefansson took his concerns to Herbert Bridgman. Bridgman was much more interested.[13]

If Peary was truly unconcerned in 1907, that feeling did not last long. He was soon writing letters to various scientific organizations stipulating, "If Dr. Cook returns and claims to have reached the Pole, he should be compelled to prove it,"[14] and by May 1908, Peary would write a letter to the *New York Times* in which he cried foul, just as he had earlier with Sverdrup and Nansen:

> I beg to note that Dr. Cook . . . has about him my Eskimos and dogs, assembled at Etah with the expectation of meeting me there last Summer; that he is appropriating for his own use the services of the Eskimo, whom I have trained in the methods of protracted serious sledge work, and is utilizing their intimate knowledge of the routes and game resources of the land to the north, which they have gained under my lead and guidance. . . .

. . . In order that there may be no misunderstanding as to my position in the matter, I wish to say that I regard Dr. Cook's action in going north "sub rosa" . . . for the admitted purpose of forestalling me, as one of which no man possessing a sense of honor would be guilty.[15]

Stuck in the United States, Peary could do little about Cook but write letters. Later, he even wrote one to Teddy Roosevelt casting doubt on the character of Cook's backer, and Cook by association, calling him a "card sharp" who ran a "gambling hell" where even women were allowed to gamble.[16]

With Cook absent, the Explorers Club was without a president. Its members decided to offer Peary the position. At first he would not accept, but his wife counseled him that he should. "I must say I hate the idea of your being associated with such men as Cook & Walsh," she told him. "They are all fakes. But in view of present conditions it might do you considerable harm to antagonize these people. Harm in the way—that they would assist Cook in every way just to annoy you. . . .

". . . Even if the sentiment of the club is against Cook now, if he returns during your absence they would be inclined to do more for him if you are not their president than if you are."[17]

In the end, Peary accepted the offer on the same condition that he had urged upon the scientific societies in his letters—that proof be demanded if Cook claimed the Pole.

He was now president of the Explorers Club, but the only positions Peary really wanted had already slipped through his grasp. He had long expressed interest in being the chief of the Bureau of Yards and Docks. The top job in the Civil Engineer Corps, it was the only one allowed to hold the rank of rear admiral, which was his real interest in it. It had come vacant while he was away in 1906, and Jo Peary had pleaded with the Navy Department to keep the position open, hoping that if Bert were appointed he would never return to the Arctic. But by November 1906, when Peary finally reappeared, the position had been filled.[18]

On December 29 of that year, Peary had received an offer that interested him even more. Alexander Graham Bell was willing to nominate him to the vacant post of secretary of the Smithsonian Institution. It was a position that Peary was willing to work for, especially when Bell intimated that his acceptance "need not affect [his] relations with the Peary Arctic Club."[19]

Peary wrote several draft letters outlining how it would benefit the Smithsonian's regents to make the appointment, but he was willing to postpone his plans to reach the Pole only temporarily:

It will be taken for granted that I have given up arctic work.
Should circumstances so shape themselves that later Mr. B would give out the statement that the R[egent]'s had granted me a

year's leave to complete my northern work, the news would go to every corner of the civilized world.

During the progress of the Expedition, the name of the I[nstitution] would be constantly associated with its movements, and on its return with materials and collections for the I[nstitution] its name would be made a household word, and the objects and needs of the Museum brought to wide popular notice.

Peary wanted the job so much that he promised that if his administration did not meet approval at the end of two years, "you shall have my resignation without the least hesitation."[20] But the appointment never materialized, and he had returned to preparing for his departure in July 1907 to establish his winter base at Cape Sheridan.

But in that month it was Cook, not Peary, who had departed for the Far North, and now he was planning to leave Annoatok for the very Pole itself. "We are gradually securing our dogs in good condition," the doctor wrote with relief. ". . . Ikwa tells us that all the natives below are bound this way and most have decided to give us from one to five dogs. This seems to harmonize with . . . the natural helpfulness of the people. We have given them liberally all winter and have counted on a reward when the campaign opens, but the manner in which nearly everybody hesitated to part with their dogs made us feel anxious. I had planned a trip to the Gulf to secure the dogs but the incoming natives seem to bring us about all we want."[21]

Things were now almost in readiness. Still, there were little nagging worries as the day for departure approached. "About once a month Rudolph gets a notion that we have lost a day," Cook noted, "and so we watch with eager interest the phases of the moon to keep tabs on our date for if we should gain or lose a day it would be a serious business in determining our positions."[22]

They tried various experiments to secure the supplies against the dogs. Light tin cases, each holding 80 pounds of pemmican, worked best. "It seems grand to get our things securely packed and perfectly stacked for transportation," he thought. "In a few days we will be on the march to the pole. What will be our luck?

"We had planned to send a party to-day to Ellesmere Ld. but there is a gale blowing out of the Sd. which makes this start impossible, and since this start cannot be made to-day we must wait a few days and all start together. . . ."[23]

When the weather cleared, the advance party left Annoatok under the leadership of Koolootingwah to cross to Ellesmere Land and hunt for the musk oxen reported to be there by Captain Sverdrup. The rest of the expedition would catch up with them at the slaughter grounds and then push on to the polar sea.

Before the last remaining details were worked out and the records of the expedition were placed in a trunk for safekeeping, Dr. Cook sat down to write some letters. He expected that Knud Rasmussen might visit in the spring and wanted him to have the hospitality of his hut; he also wanted the Dane to do him a favor.

February 20, 1908

My dear Rasmussen:

> I expect to leave in a day or two for the far north and if you come this way you will be welcome to use my house and its provisions during your stay here.
>
> We find the natives will in a small way help themselves to things lying about, so do not allow them to rummage about among our things and if you go away even for a short time lock the doors. Tungwingwah will tell you where everything can be found so make yourself comfortable.
>
> We expect to get back about the middle of May or the first of June and will start at once for Upernavik. There is a chance of our being carried too far east and in that case we will go to Shannon Island[24] and down the east coast of Greenland. There is also a strong possibility of our finding much land to the westward of Crocker Land and in that case we may follow the land and go to Alaska—but both of these possibilities are rather remote and I really expect to be in Upernavik before July first.

Yours Very Cordially,
Frederick A. Cook.

P.S. If you could leave me a few boxes of 44-45 Winchester cartridges here it would help me very much.

F.A.C.[25]

He then wrote a second letter and put it in an envelope marked "To Whom It May Concern." In it the doctor asked that if they should not return, their library, the trunks on the bunk and the narwhal tusks outside be transported home.

As February drew near a close, 11 sledges, loaded to capacity, their teams totaling 103 dogs, stood ready to start for the Pole. Franke looked for the last time at the box house and already felt nostalgia for the memories it contained and the comfort it represented. But after consuming one last steaming kettle of walrus meat, the drivers cracked their whips, and as the dogs strained to start the heavy sledges, the men bent into the sharp, cold wind from the northwest and toward their uncertain fate.

Franke worried about how the overloaded sledges would perform on the pack ice, but they proved dependable and practical. Open water diverted their track to the north, and there the dogs, picking up a fresh bear trail, bounded forward despite their heavy loads. At 4 in the afternoon it grew too dark to travel, so the men stopped and built three igloos. Despite the hard day's traveling, the Eskimos immediately unloaded several sledges and dashed off in pursuit of the bear but returned unsuccessful after a couple of hours.

In the morning they continued northward and then made directly for Pim Island. The day was made memorable by the first glimpse of the sun above the horizon, after an absence of more than four months. As always, it was a sight that buoyed men's spirits and heightened their ambitions after the long darkness, and Rudolph Franke was no exception. "In an awesome silence we watched the wonderful spectacle with new courage and zest for life after the long, terrible, melancholy night," he recalled. "Although bitterly cold, we still had a feeling of warmth and, since a good German likes a drink on joyful occasions, to keep this feeling of warmth, I fetched a sack from my sled. I had a four-liter can covered with reindeer skins and also covered with the sack. I filled it mornings with hot coffee or tea. With this warm drink we celebrated with joy the reappearance of the sun."[26]

After this break, it proved a long afternoon's work to make Cape Sabine, where they arrived late in the evening. Some of the dogs' paws were tender from the sharp ice, so Cook decided to camp there for a day to allow them to heal. When the tired explorers got into their sleeping bags, they discovered them to be crawling with lice. The Eskimos remedied this by using the insects as a convenient snack, much to Franke's amazement.

Once on the trail again, the going was very slow, since the wind had scoured the snow off, leaving bare ground. The temperature fell to $-45°$. Nevertheless, they reached the cache at Cape Veile and loaded its contents onto the already groaning sledges. Then they ran into an area of deep, loose snow, which made gaining a few more miles terrible work, and the men were glad to settle into their vermin-free bags in a warm igloo that night near Cape Rutherford.

It took another day of hardship pulling the sledges through deep snow to reach Flagler Bay. There it was so cold that two axes were broken in attempts to chop frozen walrus skin to feed the dogs, and the petroleum was so congealed that it had to be preheated with the alcohol stove before it would light. That evening dogs were heard howling on the opposite cape.

As they were fixing coffee the next morning, Kudla arrived from Kooloo-tingwah's advance party, reporting the same problems—unfavorable snow conditions—either loose and deep or none at all. Worse yet, they had killed just one musk ox and a dozen hares.

Their report greatly disturbed Dr. Cook. His whole plan was predicated on slaughtering the polar oxen that Sverdrup had reported in abundance right up to land's end. If he had to draw upon his sledge supplies, he would not have enough food on the sleds by the time he reached the polar sea to sustain him to the Pole and back.

Franke noticed his companion's concern but reasoned that together they would do the best they could by sharing all the hardships, just as they had pledged each other to do. He was not in the least prepared for what was about to happen:

> Soon [Dr. Cook] called me into his snow house and told me point blank that he could not take me with him and that I must immediately return to Annoatok with Kudla and Esjehu to guard our station with its supplies. He would send me further news and regulations with the Eskimos whom he would send back when they reached the Polar Sea. I stood as if I had been struck by lightening! In light of these revelations, I gave Cook arguments against them and begged him to at least let me accompany him overland to the Polar Sea and then return with the Eskimos to Annoatok. But that didn't help at all. Did Cook want to get rid of me? Did I somehow fail in my duty? Was I not supposed to go any further because I was not an American? Similar thoughts swirled in my head, but I had to obey orders, partly because of the appearances white men must keep up before the Eskimo. There was no time for arguments. I was crushed. . . .
>
> A brief hand clasp and we parted—Cook to the West and I to the East.[27]

Franke reached Cape Sabine the following day, but he hardly noticed where he was. He had been so depressed that he neglected to take normal precautions and had frozen his nose and the end of one of his big toes. While Franke sat dejected, the Eskimos dismantled part of Peary's wooden house and loaded the precious stuff onto the sledges. It was a terrible night for Franke, spent in mental and physical pain.

In the morning, when the Eskimos said they would have to lance his toe, it made no difference to him. They made an incision with a hot knife, which froze instantly to the flesh and had to be raised up with needles and cut off. Then they removed the nail and wrapped the toe in a filthy provision sack, but it gave him no more trouble and healed perfectly.

They arrived back at Annoatok about March 5, though Franke was not quite sure of the date, since he had left the daily log to Dr. Cook, a fact he now very much regretted. He decided to keep one himself from now on.

The Eskimos were joyous to be reunited with their friends, but Franke now felt desperately alone. A sense of his own freakishness came over him, and he had trouble expressing his feelings to the Eskimos. He could not shake off his sense of isolation, and although he at first felt hatred for Cook, this soon passed, as he realized that it was the doctor's presence he missed most.

Cook had taken with him all the scientific and nautical instruments except a mercury thermometer, an aneroid barometer and a heavy ship's compass. To help him keep track of the days, Franke rigged up a sundial with two poles arranged with the aid of the compass and set his battered alarm clock to this. He began to record each day's events and weather to give his life purpose, but all in all, his daily routine was monotonous and uneventful. To pass the time he made several sledge trips, including one to Petowik to hunt walrus, remaining there for ten days.

On May 5 men were sighted on the ice of Smith Sound. All of the Eskimos who had gone with Dr. Cook had returned except two young men named Etukishuk and Ahwelah. They brought with them a letter from the doctor to Franke:

> March 17th 1908, Polar Sea
> North of Cape Hubbard.
>
> Dear Rudolph:
>
> Thus far it has gone very well, but the weather has been awful cold. We got no musk-ox until we had crossed Ellesmereland, but since we have secured 102 musk-ox, 5 bears and about 150 hare.
>
> The Eskimo will probably return slowly, for they like this land very well, I do not expect the Eskimo to reach you until about the middle of May. If we are lucky we will take a short cut back and will get to Annoatok by the end of May. . . .
>
> . . . To the present we have seen nothing of Crocker Land, and I am taking a strait course for the pole. The boys are doing well and I have plenty of dogs. I hope to succeed. At any rate I will make a desperate attempt.
>
> While I expect to get back to you by the end of May, still I wish you to be ready to go to Acponie, the Island off North Star, where the whalers' steamers come, by the 5th of June, and if I am not back go home with the whalers, I think however we will be back.
>
> Gather all the blue fox skins you can. These must be our money on the return trip. If you can get a few bear skins take them, also Narwhal and Walrus tusks, but do not give too much for them.
>
> The dogs that come back that belong to us turn over to Panikpa to feed and work.
>
> If Kudnu (the Dane) is still there urge him to wait for our return either to Annoatok or at North Star, for I am anxious to go to Upernavik at once on our return, and he can be of much use to us.
>
> There is likely to be much open water between you and Etah so you had better send the trunk, the Narwhal tusks and all things for the return to Etah at least, if not further, as soon as you can.
>
> I have regretted many times, that you are not with us, but at the moment it seemed best to send you back and on the whole you are of more assistance to me at the house to guard and care for our things, than there in the field in this awful cold and wind. I trust you are of the same opinion.
>
> So good-by and now for the pole.
>
> Yours cordially
> Frederick A. Cook.[28]

Franke faithfully carried out Cook's instructions as best he could. Even by the middle of the month travel by boat was impossible, so Franke took the luggage and started overland for Oomanui with Eskimo guides. But they had to abandon it at Arwagluarwi Point after Franke injured his leg in an unsuccessful attempt to cross the glacier; he returned to Etah to fetch the boat. As June began they again set out, but bad weather forced a six-day stay at Cape Alexander. It was not until the first week in July that they reached their destination, and that was too late to catch the Dundee whalers, who had already sailed. Dejectedly, Franke started back, resigned to another winter in the Arctic.

"Floating ice, heavy rain, my lame leg and the impaired boat made our return trip more difficult," Franke remembered, "but we managed to live through it. . . . On the return trip my leg pained me dreadfully and I did not feel at all well. As we entered the harbor of Etah the Eskimos cried "*Oomiaksoah, Oomiaksoah!*" ("Ship, Ship!")[29] It was the *Roosevelt.*

On August 2 Peary had gotten his first information on the movements of his rival from a letter Franke had left at Oomanui on July 13 explaining his predicament, and now here was the man himself. But Peary was now aboard the *Erik,* which was away hunting walrus and organizing the expedition. Franke was a terrible sight when he reached the *Roosevelt.* He came aboard begging for food but was sent away by Charlie Percy.

The next morning, at the suggestion of the ship's surgeon, Captain Bob Bartlett brought Franke back. The captain severely reprimanded Percy, then ordered the steward to prepare Franke something to eat.

When Peary returned with the *Erik* on August 11, he was told what Franke had revealed of Cook's winter at Annoatok and his departure for the Pole. Peary asked his surgeon, Dr. John Goodsell, to examine Franke. With his wild hair and fur clothing, Franke reminded Goodsell of an ancient Teuton ready to do battle with the Roman invaders. The surgeon found him to be in poor condition, however, exhausted and suffering from scurvy.

At the examination's conclusion, Peary called Franke in for an interview. Peary told him that he would be allowed to go home on the *Erik* on condition that he turn over all the supplies under his care to him. Franke hesitated to do this, torn between loyalty to Dr. Cook and an intense desire to avoid another arctic winter. When Franke repeated Cook's desires expressed in the letter addressed "To Whom It May Concern," Peary ignored them, insisting on his previous condition for Franke's passage back to America. Peary convinced Franke that Cook's furs were needed to clothe his own companions and assured him that he had never sent any skins or ivory back from any of his expeditions.

Commander Peary promised to settle the whole matter in the best way with Cook; nevertheless, Franke took a day to think it over before settling for the terms Peary had laid down. What else could he do? he reasoned. He was in no condition to stay, and there seemed little chance any other ship would call. Still, he felt he was abandoning his post, despite Cook's instruction to return if he did not appear by June 5.

He wrote a long letter giving his reasons for acceptance of Peary's terms, ending with:

> Now you see, Mr. Peary, that I justify my steps in every line and I beg you to take care all the property of Dr. C. After advise of your Surgeon I should take care of myself and it would be foolish to stand a second winter. Please lend me your helping hand furthermore, I will be very thankfull. In another paper you will find a statement of the provisions and supplies and in leaving them I give you full power to use them. Excuse my bad english I am foreigner. I remain, Sir,
>
> Respectfully yours,
> Rudolph Franke.[30]

Franke attached an inventory of all the considerable supplies left at Annoatok, though he noted that in his absence the Eskimos had helped themselves to the milk and sugar.[31] In addition to the supplies, Franke handed over the letter Cook had sent from the polar sea and those he had left at Annoatok. He did not want to give the letters up, but he had no power, in his exhausted condition, to resist the demand. When he felt better, he asked that he be given back the letter sent from the polar sea and received it after Peary had a copy made.

Peary dispatched a motorboat to fetch the trunk full of blue fox skins and narwhal tusks left on Arwagluarwi Point and personally took the keys to Cook's house at Annoatok from Koolootingwah, to whom Franke had entrusted them.

With Peary's demand settled, Franke received some clothes from the crew members and threw away his lice-infested furs. Then he borrowed $20 from one of the passengers, a young man named Harry Whitney, who along with three others had paid to accompany the expedition to do some hunting.

Before the *Erik* sailed, Franke heard rumors that the ship would carry a rich cargo back to the United States and saw bundles being stored in the hold. What could these be but Dr. Cook's furs, he thought, since Peary had had little time to gather any number of pelts? As Rudolph Franke packed his few remaining effects, his journal and that of their winter together written by Dr. Cook, along with a number of photos they had taken, he wondered whether he had done the right thing.

On August 17 Franke signed a receipt for $50 in gold for passage and expenses to New York City. Peary then made ready to get under way for Cape Sheridan.

The commander had taken care to question every Eskimo who had been with Cook. He seemed so obsessed with where Cook had been and what his intentions were that Ross Marvin, Peary's private secretary, could not help mentioning it in his letters to a friend. "Dr. Cook seems to be the whole topic of conversation here but whatever I will tell you I wish you would consider it as confidential," he wrote. "He sent all but two of his natives back from Cape

Hubbard, where the Com had been last summer *[sic],* & said he was going on to Crocker Land but not the pole. . . ."[32]

"Perhaps you may think I ought to tell you more about the Dr. Cook affair but as things seem to be so mixed up here I hesitate about saying much of anything about it, and as far as actual news goes there is not much to be said. Dr. Cook is not back and no one knows where he is."[33]

Even though Peary had written to the *Times* that Cook's encroachment on "his" Eskimos would cause him difficulty in obtaining dogs, he had no trouble securing 246. He did not wait for the Eskimos to give them up voluntarily, as Cook had, but assigned Matt Henson to procure them. "Acting under orders, I obeyed, but it was not a pleasant task," Matt recalled. "I have known men who needed dogs less to pay a great deal more for one pup than was paid Nipsangwah for his pack of seven. The dogs are a valuable asset to this people and these two men were dependent on their little teams to a greater extent than on the plates and cups of tin which they received in exchange for them."[34]

The *Roosevelt's* burly Newfoundland boatswain, John Murphy, volunteered to stay and guard Cook's supplies. The cabin boy, Billy Pritchard, was assigned to keep Murphy company and to keep the log. Though the boatswain was perfectly illiterate, Peary nonetheless wrote out lengthy instructions for him to follow:

> The following are instructions for your guidance while in charge of the station here for the relief of Dr. Cook. . . .
>
> . . . No active measures can be taken toward searching for Dr. Cook until at least February or March and it is probable that he will return himself some time during the winter as soon as Kane Basin closes so that he can come across from Ellesmere Land where he undoubtedly now is.
>
> Should he not return, it will be better for you to send the Eskimos in search of him while you remain in charge of supplies and the station, than to go yourself. . . .
>
> Should Dr. Cook return or be brought back in bad condition you will take every possible care of him and endeavor to bring him around as speedily as possible.
>
> Should he return in good condition you will still remain absolutely in charge of the station and will not permit Dr. Cook to interfere with you or with your control of the natives.
>
> Dr. Cook authorized his assistant Frank to go home on the whalers if he himself did not return this spring. This would have meant the abandonment of all his supplies and equipment to the Eskimos.
>
> Franke has now turned over all these supplies and equipment to me so that Dr. Cook has no longer any claim upon them.

> You will however take all possible care of his equipment and
> supplies and on his return allow him to use them. Any of the sup-
> plies landed from the Roosevelt which Dr. Cook needs you will
> give him and take his receipt for.

But the bulk of the orders were not about Cook at all. They were detailed instructions concerning trading with the Eskimos for every kind of skin and for unbroken narwhal tusks and how they should be preserved. Peary then closed with a lengthy postscript giving more instructions on gathering walrus and seals, specifying what should be traded for each.

"Mr. Whitney having expressed a desire to remain here for the winter will make things in many ways pleasanter and easier for you," he told Murphy. "It will be advisable for you to use Dr. Cook's supplies and particularly the broken packages first, in order to avoid loss as these goods are already over a year old and some of them doubtless improperly packed."[35]

Despite his orders establishing a "station here for the relief of Dr. Cook," Peary had already written his true intentions to Jo in a letter that the *Erik* would bear back to her. The "relief station" was a precaution he was taking only for himself:

> I have Sammy on board to prevent Cook from taking him back.
> The Cook circumstances have given me a good deal of extra
> work & trouble, but have worked out satisfactorily.
> I have landed supplies here, & leave two men ostensibly in be-
> half of Cook. As a matter of fact I have established here the sub-
> base which last time I established at Victoria Head, as a precaution
> in event of loss of the R-[oosevelt] whether going up this fall or
> coming down next summer.

Peary enclosed various letters to Jo concerning the "Cook affair."[36]

On August 18 Franke, still brooding over his dealings with Peary, watched the *Roosevelt* steam slowly north and vanish from sight among the ice of Smith Sound. Peary had forbidden him to take anything aboard the *Erik* besides his personal effects; he was not even allowed a pair of dogs he wanted to donate to the Catholic relief mission ship *St. Bernard*. The *Roosevelt* was hardly out of sight when he began to hear grumblings among the crew of the *Erik* about Peary's unfair treatment of them, though while the commander had been present they had seemed totally subservient.

The day after the *Roosevelt* sailed, the *Arctic*, under the command of Captain Joseph Bernier, anchored in Etah's harbor. Captain Bernier had hoped to try for the North Pole himself in 1908, but the Canadian government had ordered him to visit the islands discovered by Sverdrup and claim Canadian sovereignty over them instead. One of Bernier's assignments was to deliver 15 boxes of relief supplies sent by Marie Cook. Bernier also had 11 letters for Dr.

Cook, which Franke took on the doctor's behalf. He gave them to Harry Whitney for safekeeping, since he did not trust Peary's men to deliver them. When Bernier tried to obtain a team of dogs to aid his explorations, Boatswain Murphy, following Commander Peary's orders, would not allow him to have a single animal, and after caching Cook's supplies slightly south of Etah, the *Arctic* left Foulke Fjord bound for Jones Sound.

The meeting with Captain Bernier made Franke all the more depressed and resentful of Peary. Certainly, he thought, Peary must have known the *Arctic* was coming to Etah but had kept silent in order to extort from him Cook's provisions and furs for his personal gain. He felt he now realized the extent of Peary's unscrupulous nature and began to fear for Dr. Cook's safety in case of his return, as Peary seemed capable of anything. But he had asked Panikpa to keep a watchful eye on things at Annoatok; in this, at least, Franke took comfort as the *Erik* left Etah on August 21. He did not know that at that moment Panikpa was bound for Cape Sheridan aboard the *Roosevelt*, along with many of the Eskimos who had accompanied Dr. Cook across Ellesmere Land, for further questioning.

With the departure of the *Arctic* and the *Erik*, Harry Whitney turned to preparations for the coming arctic winter. From Franke's description, he thought he would have a comfortable headquarters at Annoatok, more central to the hunting grounds than Etah. So on August 27 he set out for Cook's house.

Whitney found the box house filthy, dripping with moisture and virtually uninhabitable. The only way to set things right, he believed, was to dismantle the whole thing and move it to a better location 200 yards to the south.

In rebuilding the house he reduced its size to 10 by 12 feet and lowered the roof to conserve heat. Billy Pritchard and the Eskimos helped him seal up the cracks with strips of the leftover boards as far as they went. Then they put a layer of canvas over the rest. Snow soon piled up against the house, making it nearly weatherproof. Boatswain Murphy decided to shuttle back and forth to Etah to best fulfill Peary's instructions, but Pritchard remained, most of the time, at Annoatok. Confident now that things were in order, Harry Whitney settled in for the long winter night.

The box house's former tenant was on his way home, but he was far from happy. Though the weather was beautiful, the events of the last few weeks hung gloomily over Rudolph Franke as the *Erik* steamed south. When she touched at Godhavn, he did not even go to the dance. He was glad of one thing, though—that he was not part of the crew, as he observed, like Clarence Wyckoff in 1901, that their treatment was miserable; it seemed that Captain Sam Bartlett and the steward were managing things to line their own pockets.[37]

Even the prospects of a tranquil voyage vanished when, on the evening of September 22, while crossing Davis Strait in a "black fog," the *Erik* collided with an iceberg that stove in her bow. After some frantic activity, it was determined that the severely damaged ship could still make port. Franke went below to discover that his trunk was also a casualty of the accident. Many of the photographic plates were destroyed, but he was able to save Dr. Cook's diary.

The next day the *Erik* limped into Brigus, where Franke was hospitably received by Moses Bartlett. Here he discovered that it was not September 23 after all, but September 30. Despite all his efforts, he had lost seven days during the nightless arctic summer.

Rudolph Franke next went to St. John's and then to Sydney, where he caught the train for New York. There he was met by Captain B.S. Osbon, secretary of the Arctic Club, to whom he related his adventures in Greenland.

Bradley Osbon was a first-class "character" who described himself as a "sailor of fortune." Born in Rye, New York, in 1828, he had gained fame as a reporter for the *New York Herald* with Admiral Farragut at the Battle of New Orleans during the Civil War. Osbon had been made a petty officer of Farragut's ship to get around Navy regulations, which forbade civilians aboard. During some of his later exploits, he received other "promotions." He was named a captain in the Argentine and Chinese navies and an admiral in the Mexican Navy; the last title was often used derisively by his enemies. And he had made many by his outspoken views.

One of them was Robert Peary, whom Osbon found insufferable. Osbon knew him personally, knew all the inside gossip about him and considered him unbearably arrogant. When the captain heard about Peary's arrangement with Franke, he published a notice in the Arctic Club's bulletin that there would soon be a "sensation" revealed concerning Dr. Cook and Commander Peary.

Under Osbon's influence, Franke wrote a letter to Mrs. Peary, sending her versions in both German and English, asking her to set things right with Cook. Otherwise, he said, he would have to report the affair publicly. Jo Peary simply ignored the letter, though it worried her because other things had recently appeared in the daily press that cast an unfavorable light on her absent husband.

The day before Peary had left Etah for Cape Sheridan, a dispatch appeared carrying news of the fate of Mylius-Erichsen, who had led a Danish expedition into eastern Greenland in June 1906. Erichsen's plan had been to explore the unknown section of Greenland's eastern coast and link up with Peary's discoveries of 1892–95 from the south. He would then proceed up the Greenland Archipelago to Peary's Cape Morris K. Jesup, filling in the only other part of the coastline that had not been explored. He had not been heard from again.

In March 1908 a relief party under Lauge Koch found the body of one of the Erichsen party, a Greenlander named Jørgen Brönlund, in a cave. From Brönlund's neck hung a bottle containing a survey sheet; a diary lay nearby that starkly told his tragic tale. "I perished in 79° N. latitude, under the hardships of the return journey over the inland ice in November (1907)," the last entry read. "I reached this place under a waning moon, and cannot go on because of my frozen feet and the darkness. The bodies of the others (Erichsen and Hagen) are in the middle of the fiord (south of Amdrup Land). Hagen died on November 15, Mylius-Erichsen some ten days later."[38]

Erichsen had undertaken his journey on the assumption that Peary's observations at Navy Cliff had been accurate, but where he expected the coast to extend westward along the shores of the "East Greenland Sea," described by Peary in 1892, it continued north. The journey was so much farther than he supposed that his provisions ran low, but he decided to push on, hoping to find game. When he reached the vicinity of Navy Cliff he was amazed to find that there was no East Greenland Sea at all; solid land extended to the east through 22 degrees of longitude, or about 190 miles. The point from which Peary had made his observations looked down on a narrow fjord only a few miles wide. Greenland itself extended north as far as could be seen. There was no Greenland Archipelago.

Jo Peary was not alone in thinking about the implications of Koch's report for her husband's future. Geographers wondered how an explorer of Peary's reputation could have been so wrong in his observations. A few, like B.S. Osbon, saw it as more ammunition with which to disparage Peary.

Peary and Cook may have been far away somewhere in the Arctic and out of all contact with civilization, but neither had been forgotten. The supporters of each man were planning for the future. The friends of Dr. Cook worried over his failure to reappear in the summer of 1908, and the friends of Commander Peary worried over what would happen when he did.

The Arctic Club appealed to John R. Bradley for help in mounting a relief expedition, but he declined, saying Cook's avowed intention was to return by blubber boat to Copenhagen and that he needed no help. In fact, he said, he expected him to turn up shortly. In any case, the *John R. Bradley* had been sold and was not available.

To help raise money, the club sponsored a benefit performance at the Lyric Theatre on January 26, 1909. Even though Julia Marlowe, the premier Shakespearean actress, headlined the bill of noted actors and singers, few were willing to pay the stiff $3 admission.[39] The club also gave a euchre party at the Waldorf-Astoria, which Mrs. Cook reluctantly attended after being given assurances it would not be improper.

Marie Cook had waited the whole summer of 1907 on a farm on Cape Breton Island for the *Bradley*'s return. When the yacht arrived without Fred, she had returned with Mr. Bradley on the express to New York City.

Soon after reaching home she was disheartened to read the criticisms of her husband after his letters had been published. "I'm so sorry that the papers see fit to misjudge Doctor in reference to his intentions, and his work," she intimated to a confidant. "His friends criticize his lack of confidence as well as the papers. How I should love to feel his staying was accidental & not prearranged."[40]

Marie had grown concerned as the winter passed without word from Fred. Then, on July 11, 1908, she received his December letter from North Star Bay. Fred wrote that he would reach the Pole or die in the attempt; she was confident, however, it would be the former. She had moved his picture low on the wall and had the children kiss it each night so that they would remember their father when he returned.[41] The only other word she had was a wire from St. John's, Newfoundland, reassuring her that Dr. Cook was in a land of plenty and undoubtedly safe. The message was from Robert E. Peary via the *Erik*.[42]

Jo Peary was concerned about her own husband, but for other reasons. Osbon had made good on his threats, causing Herbert Bridgman to rescind his own counsel of silence. He went against Peary's expressed wishes by allowing Jo to publish Franke's letter in which he turned over Cook's supplies to Peary to use as he saw fit.

When, on March 23, 1909, she sat down to write her customary yearly letters to be delivered by the Dundee whalers, all these events weighed heavily on Jo's mind:

> Surely you will come this Fall. You <u>must</u>. I could not face another winter without you. I <u>never</u> have wanted you as I have this last year. The children have been fairly well & things have gone well but <u>I need you</u> . . . .
>
> Cook & his friends may give you trouble. That dog Franck told Osbon of the Arctic Club that you stole all of Cook's furs & ivory valued at $5,000. & sent them as presents to Roosevelt your wife & others & drove Franck out of the country at the point of your rifle. Osbon published this & a lot of similar rot & I simply had to allow [the *New York Times*] to publish some of the correspondence between you & Franck. The matter is to be taken up again when you return according to Osbon. Adm. Schley is pres. of the Arctic Club & is soliciting money for a relief ship for Cook to be commanded by Dillon Wallace.[43]

She would have some good news for Bert, however, when he did return. After years of haggling, she had finally come to an agreement to sell the Cape York meteorites to the American Museum of Natural History. The "star stones" brought $40,000. Jo put the first $10,000 into AT&T gold bonds to mature in 1936. At the same time, she invested another $10,000 in U.S. Steel stock.[44]

But the Erichsen revelations and Osbon's allegations and threats were not her biggest worry. Jo Peary had another problem in the person of Mene. He alone had remained in America when the only other surviving Eskimo of the six Peary had brought down from Greenland in 1897 sailed home with the explorer in 1898. He was now 19 and at the center of an acute embarrassment to her.

Sensational stories about the orphan had appeared in one of the New York newspapers as early as 1907. But now, more specific details emerged. Shortly after his father, Quisik, had died, Mene had been present at a funeral at which he believed his father had been laid to rest in the garden of the American Museum of Natural History. This, it was now revealed, had been an elaborate ruse. In fact, the bodies of his father and the other dead Eskimos had been sent to the museum's macerating and bone-bleaching facilities in upstate New York, where the flesh had been removed and some of the organs, including the brains, had been put into specimen jars for study. Quisik's skeleton had been mounted and put on display in the museum itself.

Peary had always tried to separate himself from all adverse publicity, and as the Eskimos he had brought south began to sicken, he had tried to shift blame, saying he had brought them to New York only at the museum's request. When they began to die, he had washed his hands of them completely. But as interest in Mene's story grew, Peary's role was being reexamined, and that could do nothing to help the commander's carefully cultivated public image.

Commander Peary had refused Mene's request to take him home when he sailed in 1908, perhaps because Mene had threatened to tell his countrymen of his own treatment in America and so turn them against helping Peary on his next expedition.

In May 1909 the *San Francisco Examiner* ran a melodramatic drawing of Mene shrinking in horror at the discovery of the case filled with his own father's bones, captioned, "Why Arctic Explorer Peary's Neglected Eskimo Boy Wants to Shoot Him," accompanied by an article filled with additional lurid details.[45] Jo Peary was angry but also afraid.

Mene had gotten an agreement from Mrs. Cook that he would be given passage on the *Jeanie* when the Arctic Club sent the ship north to relieve her husband, but the $1,000 the club had raised was not nearly enough. Then the Peary Arctic Club hired the *Jeanie* instead, and Herbert Bridgman refused to honor Mrs. Cook's agreement. But now, since it appeared that the story would not die so long as Mene could give interviews to the press, Bridgman decided it would be good to give him his wish and offered the Eskimo passage—under certain conditions.

In an interview with Marie Cook, Bridgman placed the *Jeanie* at her disposal to bring back her husband, if he could be found. Marie insisted on reimbursing the club for any expenses it might incur on Doctor's behalf beyond the $1,000 the Arctic Club had raised.

Though the Peary Arctic Club had no shortage of money, Herbert L. Bridgman made every effort to spare its millionaire members unnecessary expense. He took the Arctic Club's $1,000, then collected another $5,000 from Harry Whitney's mother, who was anxious for her son's safety, and bragged to Sam Bartlett that he had avoided any agreement to make the payment contingent on Whitney's actual return. "We get the $5,000 before we leave, and are to do our best," Bridgman wrote.[46]

He also made a secret offer of exclusive press coverage of the voyage to the *New York Herald* for another $1,000. Several conditions were also attached to the agreement he drew up with the *Herald*, however: no news could be sent about the Peary expedition, and "upon junction with Peary, [the *Herald*'s] representative will confer with him, and use concerning the work of Peary and of the 'Roosevelt' only such material as Peary approves."[47]

Bridgman believed that with Peary as censor there would be something to be gained besides the money. "I am rather inclined to think," he wrote to Mrs. Peary, "that the 'Herald' man on the spot, with what I should be able to give him beforehand, would get 'the rights' of this whole Cook-Mene, etc., business, in a way which would be advantageous."[48]

At first the *Herald* was undecided as to whether it should accept the deal, but at the last moment, Bridgman was able to tell Jo Peary that it had: "At the fifty-ninth minute of the eleventh hour the 'Herald' has made good its application, and according to the terms of the agreement, of which I enclose copy. I hope everything will work out all right, and that we shall have an ally."[49]

But Bridgman was most proud of the agreement Mene's guardians had signed as a condition of his being taken back to Greenland. They agreed to allow Peary to choose the debarkation point of Mene, to let Peary decide what he could take from the ship's stores, and to forever waive claims of every kind against the owners of the *Jeanie;* Bridgman had given nothing binding in return. "Mene Wallace still has no contract nor anything else signed by me," he gloated to Jo. "They all signed the memorandum of which I sent you a copy."[50] He also assured her that anything that Mene might land would be thoroughly searched for firearms.

In the letter Jo sent to her husband by way of the *Jeanie,* she expressed her wish as she pulled this latest thorn from her side: "I hope you take Mene over your knee & lick him until he begs for mercy. On no condition allow him to return to the country."[51] She was unsure whether Bridgman was doing the right thing, however, in sending a reporter on the ship, which only added to the sense of foreboding that had come over her. "Oh if I were only sure I would get a wire from you this Fall," she wrote to Bert. "The suspense this time seems worse than ever & I feel all the time as if something awful were coming to me. Dearest Sweetheart you must come to me soon."[52]

By his maneuvers, Bridgman believed that the Peary interests had been made to look magnanimous toward both Cook and Mene while ridding themselves of two problems at once, as he had no intention for the *Jeanie* to look for Cook at all—just as Peary had given secret instructions to John Murphy that he was to make no serious efforts in that direction.

And so it was that spring had come to Annoatok without any relief parties having been sent across Smith Sound to search for the missing doctor, when on April 15, at 10:00 P.M., two Eskimos burst into the box house and excitedly told Harry Whitney that they had sighted some black specks far out on Smith Sound. Though Whitney could not make them out at all, the keen-eyed Eskimos stated emphatically that they were three men approaching over the ice.

"Who they were we could not imagine," Whitney remembered thinking as he scanned the sound, "for none of our people had crossed during the winter, and it was remarkable that these men were without dogs."

Whitney instructed three Eskimos to fetch their sleds. After going several miles, one pulled ahead and neared the strangers. To his surprise, one walked like a white man, though he had to look carefully even as he got close to otherwise distinguish him from his two Eskimo companions. Harry Whitney soon caught up.

"Great was my astonishment," he recalled, "when the white man introduced himself as Dr. Frederick A. Cook, who we had come to believe had long since perished in the North. . . . He was as greatly astonished to meet a white man here as I was to meet him.

"The three men were sights to behold. Human beings could not be more unkempt. They were half starved and very thin, terribly dirty, and Dr. Cook, like the Eskimos, had long hair reaching to his shoulders. For many months they had been without dogs and had hauled a sledge a long distance from the southward. Open water had prevented their taking a direct course across Smith Sound from Cape Sabine, and they had been forced to make a long detour to the northward to accomplish the passage. In the very rough ice they abandoned the sledge, and made their course direct for Annoatok, which at this time could be seen plainly in the distance. . . .

"After a short delay we turned back to camp. . . . In camp the hungry men enjoyed a good hot meal, then slept for several hours, after which Sipsu and Etukishuk . . . went back on the ice and late in the day brought in the abandoned sledge."[53]

"Mr. Whitney offered me unreservedly the hospitality of my own camp," the doctor remembered of his homecoming. "He instructed Pritchard to prepare meal after meal of every possible dish that our empty stomachs had craved for a year. The Eskimo boys were invited to share it." Whitney declared Cook was the dirtiest man he had ever seen as he helped scrub his angular anatomy between courses.[54]

Boatswain Murphy returned to the box house from Etah to find Cook there but left for Etah again after a dispute with the doctor. Whitney was glad to see him go. He told Cook of many months of bickering with Murphy, of Murphy's bullying methods and of a final quarrel over Cook's stores and the Peary provisions at Etah in which the boatswain flared up with savage fury and seized an axe. Pritchard had grabbed a gun, as had Whitney, and by threatening to shoot they succeeded in bringing about more amicable relations.[55]

By this account, Whitney quickly gained Cook's confidence as someone sympathetic, and so he imparted his secret to him. "I have been to the Pole," the doctor said in a low voice. Pritchard was nearby and overheard. Later, when he discovered that the cabin boy had written the news home in a letter, Cook made him take it out. He enjoined both Whitney and Pritchard to keep the news from Murphy and Peary, though he authorized them to say he had beaten Peary's "Farthest North" of 1906.

The doctor thought how odd it sounded to say for the first time in English, to someone who could understand all that it really meant, the words he had repeated to himself over and over again—"I have been to the Pole!"

The Eskimos' companions were less concerned about where their comrades had been. What they wanted to know was how they had managed to survive a winter without dogs. That, in their estimation, assured the two young hunters' place in legend forever.

Once rested, Cook began to take an interest in the arrangements Peary had made to dispose of his supplies. When he read Murphy's orders, he became indignant and wanted to know why the house was no longer where he had built it. He copied Peary's orders, word for word, and wrote additional notes about "Peary's Grab": how Peary had taken his supplies on the pretense of establishing a relief station; how they had been traded away for skins and used to feed the dogs; how he had taken the Eskimos north who had been instructed to mount a relief expedition should he fail to return. Dr. Cook was angry; he made careful notes on what the Eskimos told him about Peary's doings at Etah the previous summer:

> The Roosevelt went northward with 2 young girls for P. cabin, Annodou and Evllie both 13 years old crying bitterly were taken from their mothers and families forced on the ship and taken north for the lust of him who seeks the pole. . . . Illegitimate children are scattered among the tribe who are not wanted by the Eskimos and at least two should bear the name of Peary and an equal number bear the earmarks of his colored servant. Seeking to avoid a more liberal distribution of Peary offspring has thus taken two young girls of 13.
>
> Franke—driven from the Eric & not even given a cup of coffee . . . having missed the Whalers and the Eric his last chance to escape death under pressure forced Franke to turn over the things which did not belong to him.[56]

He also carefully noted the names of Peary's Eskimo wife and children, as well as Matt Henson's.

Despite his weak condition, Dr. Cook insisted on starting off for the Danish settlements as soon as he could; he must beat Peary back to civilization. The next three days he spent getting ready to head south.

As Cook packed his things, Whitney suggested that he should leave his instruments with him for safekeeping and asked, as a special favor, that he leave his North Pole flag as well. Whitney said he had arranged with his friends to send a ship, which would surely come. Why risk them on the hazardous trip he planned? The doctor assented to the kind offer and left several boxes in Whitney's care for transport home. Cook also gave Whitney, at his request, his one surviving polar sledge. It had been shortened by half and badly cut up, some of the wooden strips having been slivered for firewood; its steel runners had been made into knives. Its appearance confirmed Cook's story in Whitney's mind, and he thought it a perfect souvenir of their meeting.

Before he left, Dr. Cook toyed with the idea of leaving a letter for Peary, and began to write:

Annoatok April 21 1909.

To Com R.E. Peary
    To say I am surprised at your disregard of arctic

He crossed this out and began again:

Your unwarranted [illegible: possibly "treatment"] of my inter-est has set abomie to our living friendship. Under the guise of a relief station for which you had no authority you have sought to rob me of my belongings to satisfy your crazy thirst for barter. You have ordered your agent to assume possession to dispossess the Eskimo caretakers and to use my property at the same time giving orders which would make all relief work impossible. The relief station is therefore a humbug and the unseen succoring hand is that of a hypocrite. For all of this you must answer in the due course of time. For the present I desire to give notice that you will be compelled to pay for damages of the misdeed.

Everything stolen must be paid for the blue fox skins & nar-whal tusks which you took must be replaced. Franke's return pas-sage & his expenses I will pay in cash taken. You stipulate the price.[57]

He took the note with him. But he did leave instructions for the distribu-tion of the supplies that he still considered his own:

Annoatok, April 21, 1909

To Harry Whitney:
    All of my belongings here and at Etah are to be given to the Eskimos, and to see that this is properly done, you are hereby appointed director and guardian of my house, with the station and all of its equipment and supplies.

Mr. Murphy as Peary's agent, may remain as tenant of the house until you leave with the understanding that the rental is to be re-garded as full pay for Franke's return passage on the Eric and all ex-penses incurred thereby.

The house and most of the supplies and equipment at Annoa-tok is to be given to Etukishuk and Ahwelah. The things at Etah are to go mostly to Koolootingwah. 30 bags of coal are to be deliv-ered to you by Mr. Murphy and equally divided among the 3 Eski-mos above mentioned.

You are at liberty to use any of my property either for your own use or for other urgent purposes. When you leave everything must go to these Eskimos unless your companions are in need.

In subsequent notes I may change these orders. Also a change in your environment may call for a different arrangement. In this case or in any case, you are in full power hold possession and act according to your own judgment.

Yours very sincerely,
"Frederick A. Cook.[58]

As he left Annoatok, Cook bade farewell to Ahwelah. The doctor called to him and, with Etukishuk and Harry Whitney, started for Peary's old camp at Etah, where they opened the cache left by the *Arctic*. Its chief attractions were clean underwear, tins of butter and a letter from Marie.

From Etah the three continued south with a sledge load of trade goods as far as Cape Alexander. There the doctor met Koolootingwah and asked him to accompany him, but the Eskimo was hesitant. *"Peari annutu"* (Peary will be angry) was his reply, but the doctor insisted. He also induced Pewahto to accompany him.[59] It was nearly 800 miles along the coast to Upernavik, but the doctor was confident after his recent experiences that he would make it, just as he had told John R. Bradley, and set off with his three Eskimo companions.

The four crossed the Crystal Palace Glacier and entered Sonntag Bay, where they were overtaken by a raging gale. Descending to the coast, they reached Nerke, where they met Eskimos engaged in the spring hunt. At Nerke there was much eating and gossip about the trip to the "Big Nail," as the Eskimos called the North Pole.[60]

Continuing down the coast, they passed Northumberland Island, where Cook had met Ikwa so many years before and had been given the key to the Eskimo language, and then the little party passed beyond Inglefield Gulf to Ittiblu. There they ascended the glacier and struggled through the deep snow with only the wind-piled sastrugi to give direction to their course. After arriving back at the shore in Booth Sound, they rested, then crossed Wolstenholm Sound and reached Oomanui.

There the Eskimos wanted to rest again, but Cook was eager to be off, and after exchanging his traveling companions for Myah, Angodlu and Iokoti, he was back on the trail again. In the first week of May he reached the farthest outpost of Danish Greenland—Tassuasak.

At Tassuasak he was shown Danish regulations by Charles Dahl, the official in charge, saying he must send back or destroy all of his dogs for fear of infections they might bring to the south. Neither man understood the other's language, but they sat up all night talking nonetheless. The doctor found he could not start a sentence without grunting, as was the Eskimo habit.

The sledges then turned back for the north, bearing gifts for the Eskimos and tobacco for Harry Whitney, which the doctor had purchased from the Danes. Here, too, the doctor paused to write a long letter to his wife:

My Dear Mary,

    I am 700 miles closer to home in the first Danish settlement . . . back within reach of the civilized world in spite of Peary's bunglesome hindrance. . . .

    During our long and lonesome winter of 1908–9 at C. Sparbo we finally made ourselves very comfortable in an underground den, but I suffered from a mental torment all the time. I imagined and often dreamed that you had left me for another, that you had secured a separation like Dr. Charcot's wife and married someone better suited to your disposition. So certain was I of this that the pleasure of return to Annoatok was suffocated by an overbearing sadness. Your letter however, though lacking love sentiments dispelled this idea. . . . The test has been severe, but it will serve us as a renewed bond of love for all times. . . .

    Poor Ruth, she is in my eye constantly, thin—with glasses—tall and ungainly—at her age—how I long to take her in my arms—and Helen sweet little child with whom I am barely acquainted. What an heavenly re-union there will be upon my return. Kiss and squeeze the children for me and have them return the same for you.

Ever Your Lover,
Fred.[61]

After a week in Tassuasak, Dr. Cook started for Upernavik in an oomiak, a native boat made of skins, and reached the settlement at 5 A.M. on May 21, 1909.

He went to the home of Governor Hans Peter Kraul but paced up and down in the street outside, not wishing to disturb him so early. Someone noticed the hard-looking traveler before the door, however, and the governor soon came to the window to inquire what was the trouble. The doctor suddenly grew conscious of his own wild appearance. His face was bronzed and haggard and his hair long and straggling. He wore an old sealskin coat, worn bearskin trousers, stockings of hareskin, and seal boots. He felt reassured in a bath and clean underclothing secured a week before, but he was not surprised when the governor asked, "Have you any lice on you?"

Over breakfast Cook told the governor of his adventures. "We talked together for more than half an hour," Kraul recalled, "before Dr. Cook, after having shown me his route on the map, in reply to my inquiry, 'then you have been at the North Pole?' quietly said 'Yes, I have.'"[62]

Although polite and pleasant, Kraul was skeptical. But during the month he remained with him, Cook worked at finishing his narrative begun the previous winter. His notes and papers lay scattered about, and as the governor read them his doubts faded.

At Upernavik Dr. Cook left a letter for Captain Bernier, thanking him for his delivery of the supplies to Etah and outlining, for the first time, his polar journey:

Upernavik, May 23, 1909
Dear Captain Bernier:

I hasten to write you the first letter after being sealed behind icy barriers for two years. . . . . It was the supplies which you so thoughtfully left in charge of Mr. Whitney which enabled me to come to Upernavik. . . . My large store of supplies and my station was . . . used for barter with the natives to satisfy Peary's commercial greed. The splendid assistance which you

Cook at Upernavik, May 1909.

have given . . . is a happy contrast to the bunglesome hindrance and injustice of one of my own countrymen. . . .

We have pushed into the boreal center and picked the polar prize, but the effort was dangerous beyond all conception. . . .

The pole was reached on April 22, 1908. The return was forced slightly westward of the northward route, but above the eighty-fifth we drifted eastward and south. Below the eighty-fourth we drifted strongly westward with fog, open water, and an active pack of small ice. We were hopelessly carried to the west, unable to reach our line of caches along Nansen Sound. We were pushed into Prince Gustav Sea, without food or fuel. Still unable to press eastward, we went with the ice south. Food and fuel were now exhausted, but polar bears came along as life-savers, and with them we went into Wellington Channel, hoping to be able to reach the whalers in Lancaster Sound. But we were soon stopped by failing food supply and jammed small ice. With no game this short route to an early ship was no longer possible, and to satisfy the pangs of hunger we sought Jones Sound. Here, after a long run of hard adventures by boat and sledge, a cruel necessity forced us into winter camp in September at Cape Sparbo, without fuel, food, ammunition, or winter clothing. With no dogs, no shelter, and no guns our outlook was nearly hopeless, but fortune came our way.

Bows and arrows, harpoons, lances, and other implements were made. The musk ox and the bear were taken with the line, the lance, and the knife. Small game was secured with the bow and arrow and the slingshot. Foxes were trapped in stone traps. The walrus and the seal were attacked and secured in our little folding canvas boat. An underground den was built, and the winter of 1908–09 was passed with a taste of savage life, for we had not a morsel of civilized food, not even salt. A new equipment was devised, and as the sun of 1909 rose over the hills of North Devon, we started for Annoatok February 18, dragging dried musk-ox meat as food and moulded tallow as fuel for 30 days on our sled. Deep snow, bad ice, open water, and continued storm made the return slow and arduous. We reached Annoatok after a run of hard luck on April 5.[63]

No news of the world had reached Upernavik for about a year, but there were some old newspapers that the doctor read with much interest, as he had been gone for nearly two. This situation was remedied by the arrival of Captain William Adams's Dundee whaler *Morning*.

The captain told Cook of Ernest Shackleton's journey to within 94 miles of the South Pole; about "The Merry Widow," the sensational musical that was the toast of Europe; that Taft was now president; and that Holland had an heir at last, the newborn Princess Juliana. In exchange, the doctor outlined his trip to the northern axis of the earth and received the captain's hearty congratulations. Captain Adams gave Cook a bag of potatoes, which seemed to the doctor's mind the greatest of delicacies and a royal reward.

On July 20 the supply ship *Godthaab* arrived from South Greenland. Aboard were Inspector Jens Daugaard-Jensen and a group of scientists under Professors Thompsen and Steensby. Dr. Cook took the opportunity of booking passage on the *Godthaab* to Umanak. On the ship he discussed the details of his journey with her captain, Henning Schouby.

At Umanak the ship took on coal and then proceeded to Egedesminde, where the doctor checked into the King's Guest House, the only hotel in Greenland. Knud Rasmussen, who had heard of Cook's having reached the Pole after passing south, thought he could be of help and sent a letter to Cook at Egedesminde:

> My heartiest congratulations on your happy north pole journey. Your victory is the greatest in the history of arctic exploration. It will bear its reward in itself, but great victories always bring envy to light, and you will, on your return, have to reckon on a big fight with ever-ready doubters. I therefore mean to be of great help to you, if I, when during the Summer I am visiting the polar Eskimos at Cape York, get a thorough interview with your companions, if I happen to meet them.
>
> In order to help me in getting the interview as complete as possible, I ask you to give me a short resume of your journey before you leave Greenland, and I ask you to send this to Umanak by the Hans Egede on the 3d.[64]

Rasmussen did not meet Cook's companions, who were farther north, but he had the opportunity to talk with 35 Eskimos who had. But upon returning to Umanak, he found no reply to his letter aboard the *Hans Egede*.

The *Godthaab* went north again, and when she returned bearing Knud Rasmussen, he said the Eskimos he had met confirmed that Cook had indeed reached the North Pole. "Cook jumped and danced like an 'Angekok' when he had looked at his sun glass and saw that they were only one day's journey from the 'great nail,'" they told him.[65]

At Egedesminde a modest dinner was given Dr. Cook, at which he was introduced by Inspector Daugaard-Jensen. The inspector reported that, independently, Knud Rasmussen, Captain Schouby and Professor Steensby had spoken to different parties of Eskimos of the Cape York tribe, who all said that they had heard news that Cook had reached the "Big Nail."[66]

Cook at Egedesminde, July 1909.

The doctor then talked informally about his journey for 45 minutes. Rasmussen next rose to say that not only had the Eskimos given the same story, but they had given even more details. Rasmussen also predicted trouble ahead.

Peary would permit no rivalry, he said. He told of Peary's domination of the blue fox market and how he had forbidden the Eskimos to trade in ivory with anyone but himself. Further, he alleged that presents sent the Eskimos for their assistance to Mylius-Erichsen's 1903 expedition had been taken away by Peary so that they would be compelled to trade with him alone.

Captain Schouby then spoke, telling how he had become convinced of Cook's success. "I am of a very skeptical nature," he said, ". . . but when I had once got the man on board in Upernavik, we soon became very good friends. One day we sat in the cabin; he brought forward his observations and showed them to me. 'Look here,' he said, 'these two sheets contain the observations I made on the day I discovered that I had only fourteen seconds left to reach the North Pole, believe me, I was glad.'"

When he looked over the doctor's calculations and observations, they "astonished" him, Schouby said, and he judged that they were accurate, adding, "He told me that he had definitely told the two Eskimos, and Panikpa (the father of one of his companions), to tell nothing whatever about the journey" to Peary.[67]

Then it was Professor Steensby's turn to speak. He related that the natives had told him their tribesmen with Dr. Cook had reached a place where the sun appeared to stay at the same height and never varied. Among the 30 guests at the dinner in the King's Guest House that night, there seemed to be no doubts he had.

The next day, August 9, 1909, the doctor sailed from Greenland. Inspector Daugaard-Jensen had intervened to secure him a berth on the *Hans Egede,* even though all were already occupied. It would take three weeks to reach Denmark.

Everyone noticed Cook seemed very anxious to be off, but once at sea he relaxed and chatted with anyone on board who spoke either English or German. He told of the awful privations he had suffered at Cape Sparbo and how he and his companions had reverted to Stone Age methods to survive. During the voyage, Cook was often questioned by Professor de Quervain, the leader of a Swiss anthropological expedition, and became very friendly with C.M. Norman-Hansen, a Danish eye doctor and poet. "Now we are laughing," Cook said to de Quervain in recounting the terrible experiences of that winter, "but for two years we have not laughed."[68]

Professor Steensby, too, took an intense liking to the American doctor and thought he knew why Cook had succeeded where so many others had failed:

> During the homeward journey . . . together with Dr. Cook, I had many conversations with him about ethnographical themes and particularly his "dear" and "admired" polar Eskimos, and I conceived the greatest admiration for his intelligence and fine grasp of the moral as well as the material culture of the tribes.
>
> It was in one way lucky for Cook that he did not return from the Pole as early in last spring [1908] as he had anticipated, but that he was obliged to winter at Cape Sparbo, because when the description of this wintering, where he had no European weapon to use, is published, one will see what an excellent polar Eskimo Cook had become, and one will not be surprised that this man was able to reach the Pole.[69]

On August 29 Dr. Cook gave his first formal lecture about his polar attainment aboard the *Hans Egede*. The enthusiasm of several Danish correspondents present was evident, and Daugaard-Jensen advised the explorer to publish an account at his earliest opportunity. "These reporters are friendly to you," said the inspector, "but in their excitement are liable to give four different stories and it will take the rest of your life to correct these, it is therefore important for you to get your own outline of the work of the expedition published first."[70]

On his advice the doctor retired to his cabin and reworked the 2,000-word synopsis of his journey he had written while at Upernavik. The captain suggested he telegraph it from the nearest port with a wireless. That port was Lerwick, capital of the Shetland Islands and the farthest northern city in Scotland.

Cook aboard the Hans Egede, *August 1909.*

CHAPTER 15

I Show You My Hands

ON THE MORNING OF SEPTEMBER 1, 1909, THE *HANS EGEDE* STEAMED slowly up Brassay Sound and into the fine harbor of Lerwick on the island called Mainland. A skiff was soon lowered and two men rowed away toward the docks and curing stations of the herring trade, for which the town was the center. The men aboard could scarcely be distinguished from any rough sailors, and if they were noticed at all on their errand, it is unlikely that even one of the town's 4,500 residents suspected the sensational news the little boat bore.

Upon landing, the ship's mate and Dr. Cook made their way past the ancient stone houses that dipped their gable ends into the sea and up narrow Commercial Street to a hillside lane that led to Hillhead, where the telegraph station lay. After the operator assured him that his messages would be secure, Cook handed them in, along with others from the *Hans Egede*.

The first was addressed to Belgium:

> Lecointe, Observatory, Brussels:
> Reached north pole April 21, 1908. Discovered land far north.
> Return to Copenhagen by steamer Hans Egede.
> Frederick Cook.[1]

The second went to Marie in Brooklyn:

> Successful and Well. Wire address to Copenhagen.
> Fred.[2]

The operator read the messages and looked up, unable to hide his surprise. Then the doctor gave him the 2,000-word statement. But the operator said he would not be responsible for it, suggesting that it be given to the American consul for safekeeping. Cook set out for the American consulate but, unable to locate it, went to the Danish consul instead, who agreed to hold the statement until receiving a reply.

Returning to the telegraph station, Cook wrote out a third telegram, to be sent to the *New York Herald*:

> Reached North Pole April 21, 1908. Discovered land far north.
> Have left sealed exclusive cable of 2,000 words for you with

Danish Consul at Lerwick. Expect $3,000 for it. I go steamer Hans Egede to Copenhagen.

Frederick A. Cook[3]

A fourth message was left for Harry Whitney's mother, assuring her that her son was well. Then the two men returned to the boat, and only two hours after she anchored, the *Hans Egede* disappeared down the sound and resumed her voyage to Denmark.

That afternoon in Copenhagen, Maurice Francis Egan, the genial Irish-American minister to Denmark, was handed two telegrams by Director Ryberg of the Greenland Administration Bureau. The first, from the captain of the *Hans Egede,* addressed from Lerwick, read:

> Hans Egede passed. All well. American traveler, Dr. Cook, on board. Has been at the Pole. Expects to be in Copenhagen on Saturday.
>
> Thorsen[4]

The second was from Daugaard-Jensen:

> We have on board the American traveler, Dr. Cook, who reached the north pole April 21, 1908. Dr. Cook arrived at Upernavik in May of 1909 from Cape York. The Eskimos of Cape York confirm to Knud Rasmussen Dr. Cook's story of his journey.[5]

The greatest enthusiasm ensued upon the reading of these messages, and as word filtered out into the city, visitors thronged the legation. Minister Egan

James Gordon Bennett.

could not remember such excitement before in the Danish capital. "The town was stirred as if Holger Dansker had risen from beneath the vaults of Kronborg Castle—the castle of Elsinore—and walked in the streets," he recalled. "Nobody questioned the truth of the story, for Knud Rasmussen's name is a talisman, and the officers in Greenland do not take travelers' tales seriously unless the travelers have serious claims. The whole city of Copenhagen was in an ecstacy of expectation."[6]

Cook's telegram was forwarded from New York to the office in Paris where the owner of the *Herald* ran the paper.

Born with a gold spoon in his mouth, James Gordon Bennett had inherited the *Herald* at 31 on the death of his father and namesake. The younger Bennett was educated abroad and, like John R. Bradley, had something of a reputation as a sportsman. He had introduced polo to Newport and he loved the race, whether horse or yacht and, later, automobile or aeroplane.

Also like Bradley, Bennett did pretty much as he pleased. He had unlimited income and could buy anything or his way out of any difficulty. One associate described him as "a creature of unrestrained desires. If impulse called he obeyed, and no rule existed but to be broken. . . . The consequences might entail little more than signing a check."[7]

Though losing ground to its aggressive rivals, the *Herald* was still the most powerful paper in New York, a three-cent daily in a city full of one-cent competitors. Bennett ran it *in absentia* from Beaulieu, his villa halfway between Nice and Monte Carlo. He rarely visited New York, but he took care that no one in the *Herald* organization attained any real power that could possibly challenge his own.

Bennett must have thought it somehow fitting that he should publish the exclusive account of the first man to reach the North Pole, since the *Herald* had a long association with explorers. In 1869 he had sent Henry M. Stanley to Africa to find Livingstone, and Bennett had also fitted out the *Jeannette* expedition in 1879, which, though it came to utter disaster, did much to reawaken the quest for the Pole.

To Bennett, Cook's asking price was a ridiculous bargain, considering the news it offered. He lost no time in wiring Lerwick:

Cable Dr. Cooks 2000 words immediately. Herald will pay three thousand dollars & cable tolls. Send via commercial cables.
James Gordon Bennett
New York Herald[8]

As soon as it came off the wires, the story was set up and appeared in the Paris edition of the *Herald* on the morning of September 2. New York had to wait a few hours before its morning edition exhibited it under a triple-banner headline:

In its first words the doctor announced to his readers:

After a prolonged fight against famine and frost we have at last succeeded in reaching the North Pole.
A new highway, with an interesting strip of animated nature, has been explored.

Big game haunts were located which will delight the sportsman and extend the Eskimo horizon.

Land has been discovered upon which rest the earth's northernmost rocks.

A triangle of 30,000 square miles has been cut out of the terrestrial unknown.[9]

There followed an outline of a harrowing trip that culminated in that previously inaccessible spot at the apex of the earth. The doctor then related his feelings as he stood at the top of the world and looked upon what so many others had seen only in their ambitious dreams:

After all the observations had been taken with a careful study of the local conditions, a sense of intense loneliness came with the further scrutiny of the horizon.

What a cheerless spot to have aroused the ambition of man for so many ages!

An endless field of purple snows. No life. No land. No spot to relieve the monotony of frost. We were the only pulsating creatures in a dead world of ice.[10]

It was not just a press sensation; it was the scoop of all scoops. Delighted, James Gordon Bennett sent off a telegram to await the arrival of Dr. Cook in Copenhagen, saying he had never spent $3,000 more gladly.

Every news organization sent a representative to catch any crumb that might fall off the *New York Herald*'s table. But the *Herald* itself had no more to offer. Dr. Cook was on the high seas, out of range of all questions, unable to provide the details and clarifications that every reporter craved. There was nothing to do but wait.

To mark time and to fill columns, interviews were sought with anyone who had ever been near a pole or seen a piece of arctic ice and everyone who knew the doctor or who had once met him. First on the list were other polar explorers.

Admiral George Nares, the crusty veteran of the British Polar Expedition of 1875 and the captain of the *Challenger,* was openly antagonistic to the doctor's claims. "The rate at which Dr. Cook says he traveled is the weakest point in the story," he declared. "He went north at marvelous speed, beating his own time coming back. He tells us that his speed was due to the fact that he found the ice fields beyond the eighty-sixth parallel more extensive, that the crevasses were fewer, and that little or no crushed ice was thrown up as barriers. For two days he traveled over ice which resembled a glacier surface, in others words, smooth ice. I cannot understand that." Nares also made comments objecting to the doctor's conduct, saying Cook had taken "Peary's Eskimos" and that Peary had been "keeping these Eskimos there for years to help in his advance to the pole. He has been feeding them and teaching them

European ideas."[11] Apparently, Peary's letter-writing campaign of 1908 had taken effect.

If Britain's old arctic contingent was skeptical, her young antarctic heroes were willing to give the benefit of the doubt. In London Captain Scott volunteered, "When I saw Dr. Cook in 1901 he gave me valuable information, which proved of considerable service to me on the *Discovery* expedition. He impressed me with being well fitted for polar exploration"; then he added, "It must be imagined that Cook had extraordinary good luck in getting northward at [twelve miles a day]."

Ernest Shackleton, the hero of the hour, chimed in, "The news, if true, is a remarkable achievement. I am not in a position, from the particulars at hand, to make any extended comments, but the difficulties in the way were enormous."

Other polar veterans showed less reserve. General Adolphus W. Greely called the journey "the most extraordinary feat in polar exploration." Even this wasn't enough for the Duke of Abruzzi, who rated it "the greatest achievement of the twentieth century." Roald Amundsen, Cook's old friend from the *Belgica,* called it simply "the most brilliant sledge trip in the history of polar exploration."[12]

But Admiral George W. Melville, a veteran of the ill-fated *Jeannette* expedition, called it a fake. He qualified this by saying he did not believe that Dr. Cook was a fake but that the whole report was a press canard.

Next, old associates were turned up. Dr. Dedrick praised Cook's plan of taking only Eskimos and living off the land. Dillon Wallace assured the press that the doctor was "a man of extreme reliability, fairly scientific," who had "always manifest truthfulness in every report," and John R. Bradley was convinced that "there lives no man that surpasses Cook in nerve, judgment, and persistence."

Dr. Keely could not credit the claim, however, remembering the conditions prevailing in the Far North in 1891. He concluded that Cook must be suffering from a delusion. But Rudolph Franke, who witnessed all the careful preparations, defended his companion's veracity: "I lived with him for months, helped him in preparing his outfit and constantly saw how he acted in his relations with men of all classes. When he says a thing he means it, he never makes any statement which he cannot prove; he never gives a promise which he does not keep."[13]

Even Jo Peary was willing to comment about Dr. Cook's achievement. "I have been expecting to hear this report ever since I knew Dr. Cook started for the Pole," she scoffed. "It has been a standing joke at the Explorers' Club and in our set in New York. It is a great surprise to me that Dr. Cook has been able alone and with but two Esquimau boys to accomplish in so short a time what so many others of much greater experience and better equipment have failed in doing. I am sorry Dr. Cook has wrested the honor of discovering the Pole from my husband, but I congratulate him."[14]

Anthony Fiala, hearing the dissenting voices, expressed his confidence that "no man would be foolish enough to make such a claim unless he had proofs to back it." This was to be a trend: a call for proofs. Just as Peary had ordered—if Cook returned claiming the Pole he should be compelled to show proofs—the first to call for them was Herbert Bridgman.

"Dr. Cook will, of course, recognize the moral and honorable obligation and insist that his claims to the highest geographical distinction be irrefutably established," Bridgman told some reporters. "The word of the Eskimos who went with him will be of use in getting at the proof. . . . The Eskimos cannot write, but Mr. Peary has told me that they can draw a map of the north pole and the regions surrounding that is remarkable for its accuracy. With this skill, the Eskimos ought to be in position to help Dr. Cook establish beyond doubt his claim. . . . If Dr. Cook has reasonable proofs the credit for having discovered the north pole must go to him."[15]

With the subject of proofs broached, reporters asked scientific experts what evidence could be provided that would be irrefutable. They got a variety of answers, but Professor W.D. McMillan of Chicago University gave one that seemed to be the opinion of many. "I know of no scientific test which a sufficiently informed but unscrupulous explorer could not meet except a verification of his description of the country traversed by a second expedition," he said. "The credibility of Cook's report must rest upon his character as a man, together with the internal and external consistency of the report itself."[16]

If there was skepticism in the New York press and calls for proof among Peary's friends, there was no doubt in Brooklyn. The person who received Cook's message on Bushwick Avenue was not Marie—she didn't live there anymore. When the Knickerbocker Trust Company, in which she had deposited most of her money, failed in the Panic of 1907, she no longer could make payments on her mortgage and had to sell the house. First she moved to an apartment in South Brooklyn. Later she went to live with friends in South Harpswell, Maine, not far from Peary's home on Eagle Island.

Dr. Robert Davidson, Lotta's father, who lived across the street from the Cooks' former residence, was first to read the message of success from his old friend. He called to his wife, "Doc has got there!"

Dr. Davidson told the reporters at his door that Mrs. Cook had never lost her courage and was sure Doctor would not be lost. Just before she left for Maine, the doctor continued, she said she expected to receive word at any moment that he had accomplished his ambition. "I knew he would succeed," his friend declared. "He always did. He was very quiet, unassuming, precise and methodical. . . . He is a wonderful man. He has never truly been known."[17] Dr. Davidson sent the telegram off right away to South Harpswell, special delivery.

When it arrived, Marie Cook was not there either. She was out trolley riding between the villages; a desperate competition among the reporters ensued, all in vain, to find her and obtain the first interview. They easily located another member of the Cook family, however.

At 749 Bedford Avenue they found William Cook, his sleeves rolled up, waiting on some customers.

"Did you think he would find the north pole?" asked a reporter.

"Who, Fred? You bet I did," replied the dairyman, chomping on a cigar. "I didn't know he was going after it until he sent back word from that place up in Greenland—Etah, I think, they call it. I thought he was just on a fishing trip up in Labrador. He always did have a notion that he would get up to the north pole some day, and when they told me that he had started I said to myself: 'Fred will find it if any one does.'

"I am feeling pretty good over it to think that my own brother has done what so many others have failed in doing. . . . This is a fine thing for Brooklyn, isn't it?"[18]

Finally, Mrs. Cook broke her silence and gave out a nondescript statement through the *New York Herald* thanking her friends for their interest and expressing her pride that the Pole had been discovered by an American; she steadfastly refused all requests for interviews from any other paper.

As the content of Cook's cable was absorbed in Europe, the Paris press was reported to be jubilant, Berlin's convinced, but not London's. Lord Northcliffe's *London Times* editorialized:

> The evidence is as yet very incomplete, but it has the appearance of *bonae fides,* and the previous record of the explorer as a serious man is *prima facie* evidence that he is not likely to mislead the world about his achievements. When he telegraphs to his wife that he has been successful, and to the Director of the Belgian Observatory that he reached the north pole on April 21, 1908, and when a high Danish official telegraphs in the same sense to his Government from the steamer at Lerwick which had Dr. Cook on board, we are bound to accept the statements as serious.
>
> If by any chance further investigations were to show that Dr. Cook had been mistaken in his latitude and had not quite reached the mysterious spot after which Peary, Nansen, and Wellman had striven in vain, there would be a reaction in opinion that not even the most hardened explorer would like to face.[19]

The British skepticism bothered James Gordon Bennett. He sent wires to Copenhagen asking for a dispatch refuting the criticisms and for a photostatic copy of Cook's log entry for April 21, 1908.[20] But Bennett, like everyone else, could only wait for a reply. Hard stories were so scarce that by September 4 news of the polar conquest had degenerated to mere trivialities.

Descriptions of a Doctor Cook hat and a Cook cocktail were given space to fill the void. Soon there appeared a 5-cent cigar bearing the explorer's likeness and New York street vendors hawking blue-eyed Eskimo dolls. But the biggest boon of all went to the manufacturers of confections.

It began with an interview with John Bradley. Exasperated by endless and often ridiculous questioning, the gambler put his tongue in his cheek when asked how Cook had persuaded the Eskimos to venture onto the dangerous sea ice. "An Eskimo will travel 30 miles for a gumdrop, for his is the sweetest tooth in the world," Bradley replied, adding that his yacht had gone north with two barrels of them among her stores. Instantly, there appeared bags of "Cook Gumdrops" in the windows of all the candy stores, along with the slogan "A little gumdrop now and then is relished by the Eskimen."[21]

The first contact with the *Hans Egede* came on September 3 off the Skaw, when the Danish torpedo boat *Sobjornen* roared up and stopped opposite the vessel. Through a megaphone, Captain G.C. Amdrup asked for confirmation that Cook had reached the Pole. When given, the *Sobjornen*'s crew broke out in cheers and threw their caps into the air. The captain shouted an outline of the reception to come, and the doctor's measurements were shouted back so that he could be properly attired for the festivities.

When the *Sobjornen* returned to Copenhagen with this critical information, it also brought word that the *Hans Egede* was approaching Skagen and would arrive in the harbor sometime the next morning. This was the news awaited by the throngs of reporters who had begun arriving in the Danish capital after the receipt of the first cable.

Among them was a young man named Philip Gibbs, representing the London *Daily Chronicle.* He had reached Copenhagen the evening before

Philip Gibbs boarding the Hans Egede.

and, by sheer chance, fell in with Knud Rasmussen's wife and a young friend of the Danish explorer, Peter Freuchen. As a result of their good graces, he found himself that night aboard a motor launch plowing through a very rough sea to intercept the *Hans Egede.* He sighted her in the early light of dawn, far up the Cattegat. Gibbs's luck had put him in a unique position among English-speaking reporters.

Scampering aboard, the thoroughly drenched and seasick reporter frantically tried to identify Dr. Cook. One of the passengers pointed out a man on the deck as "The North Star," as the Danes were now calling him.[22]

"There I saw a sturdy, handsome Anglo-Saxon-looking man, in furs, surrounded by a group of hairy and furry men, Europeans and Eskimos, and some Arctic dogs. There was no journalistic rival of mine aboard, except the young Danes with us. . . .

". . . I studied the appearance of Dr. Cook. He was not bearded, but had a well-shaven chin. He had a powerful face, with a rather heavy nose and wonderfully blue eyes. There was something queer about his eyes, I thought. They avoided a direct gaze. He seemed excited, laughed a good deal, talked volubly, and was restless with his hands, strong seaman's hands. But I liked the look of him. He seemed to me typical of Anglo-Saxon explorers, hard, simple, true."[23]

Gibbs's first impression didn't last long. Though he later admitted that he knew nearly nothing about polar matters, upon questioning the doctor in the saloon with three enterprising Danish correspondents who had simultaneously arrived on a pilot tug, the reporter understood the explorer to say that he had no diary of the trip with him and no observations—in fact, no papers of any kind. He had left them with a friend in Greenland to be returned to New York.

When he pressed the doctor for what evidence of the achievement he did possess, Gibbs noticed a certain defensiveness about his reply: "He spoke with a sudden violence of anger which startled me. Then he said something which made suspicion leap into my brain.

"'You believed Nansen,' he said, 'and Amundsen, and Sverdrup. They had only their story to tell. Why don't you believe me?' . . .

"From that moment I had grave doubts of him. . . .

"By intuition, rather than evidence, by some quick instinct of facial expression, by some sensibility to mental and moral dishonesty, I was convinced, absolutely, at the end of an hour, that this man had not been to the North Pole, but was attempting to bluff the world."[24]

While Gibbs was having his intuition of deceit, the rest of Copenhagen was innocently awaiting the arrival of the polar hero. The harbor was crowded with Danes from the common man to the crown prince, who, like Minister Egan, was dressed in formal attire and top hat for the occasion. He was talking with the commander of the king's yacht, Commodore Hovgaard. The harbor was brilliantly blue and filled with small craft, many displaying the Stars and Stripes, which waved limply in a slight breeze, the only remainder of the previous stormy night. Whistles and sirens sounded at 10 A.M. as the *Hans Egede*, flying all her flags, came into sight, and several bands struck up "See the Conquering Hero Comes."

The prince, Minister Egan and members of the Royal Geographical Society, along with other dignitaries, boarded a launch and soon were alongside the ship. There they saw a man with an unkempt mustache and long hair, shod in leather moccasins and wearing a shabby black coat and a disreputable-looking cap, standing at the top of the ladder.

Where Minister Egan saw "a modest-looking man, with a kindly face, under a cap that Robinson Crusoe might have worn,"[25] Philip Gibbs noticed something else again: "I never saw guilt and fear more clearly written on any human face. He could hardly pull himself together when the Crown Prince of Denmark boarded his ship and offered the homage of Denmark to his glorious achievement.

"But that was the only time in which I saw Cook lose his nerve."[26]

As Egan identified himself, Dr. Cook said, "You are the first American I have shaken hands with for over two years." Cook quickly qualified the statement, the minister later recalled: "Afterward, he explained, with that careful regard for exact truth which is his characteristic, that he had in the meantime shaken hands with Mr. Whitney, but that *he* looked so much like an Esquimau that, for the moment, Doctor Cook had forgotten his nationality."[27]

After brief greetings aboard the *Hans Egede*, the welcoming committee took the doctor into the launch. As it approached the landing place with the crown prince standing next to the explorer, a tremendous shout arose from the shore and from the throats of all aboard the hundreds of small craft and ships in the harbor.

Upon stepping ashore, Cook stood for a moment acknowledging the cheers by bowing slightly and doffing his cap, looking a little dazed at the reception. A bouquet of flowers was pressed into the explorer's hands. The crown prince set off immediately for another engagement, but the rest of the party had to literally fight their way to the waiting carriages as the crowd closed in. The police seemed powerless in the crush of happy, excited people.

William Stead, the dean of British correspondents and William Randolph Hearst's man on the spot, seized the doctor to keep him from falling:

Cook's arrival in Copenhagen. The man with the beard is William Stead. At the extreme right is the crown prince of Denmark, doffing his top hat to Cook.

> I was immediately behind him when the crowd burst, and seeing that he was ill prepared for a scrimmage, I flung my arms round him under his armpit, and pressing backward with all my weight I somewhat eased the pressure from behind. . . . Dr. Cook had to give up his flowers, one of his cuffs was torn off and carried away as a trophy; once or twice it seemed as if we should be carried off our feet. . . .
>
> My face was close against Dr. Cook's left ear, and as we pushed backward and forward and swayed to the right and the left making

a slow advance toward the carriage that seemed as inaccessible as the North Pole, I began a series of "Talks with Cook.". . . . I was close to him in all conscience. . . . There is something in the touch of a man, especially when you are at close grips with him.[28]

The carriages were, indeed, impossible to reach as the crowd swept them against the low, wire fence surrounding the gardens of the Meteorological Department, where the official greeting party now sought refuge. For a moment it looked as if they might be crushed against its high iron gates, but someone opened them, relieving the pressure. Once safe inside the building, Cook panted, "I used to be a football player, but this is the worst I ever saw!"[29] and expressed regret to Minister Egan as to the condition of his top hat, which itself had barely survived the ordeal.

The crowd surrounded the building and called for the doctor to speak. After some urging, he reluctantly appeared on the balcony to increased cheering. "My friends," he said, "I have had too hard a time getting here to make a speech. I can only say that I consider it an honor to be able to put my foot first on Danish soil."[30] After bowing and waving his hat in acknowledgment of their cheers, he retired inside again.

From there, Commodore Hovgaard smuggled the man of the hour out a back door and into his carriage, which proceeded toward the Hotel Phoenix, where the doctor was to be the guest of the Geographical Society. After a slow

progress through streets clogged by the cheering, curious crowds that lined the whole route, the Phoenix, decorated with masses of flowers and flags, finally came into view. The Danish minister of commerce, Johan Hansen, greeted him at its door, toasted him with champagne and called for three cheers for his long life, before inviting him to a banquet in his honor at the municipal building.

The weather-beaten explorer was then put into the hands of Copenhagen's finest barbers and tailors. A dentist was called in, several chipped teeth were attended to, and when the time came to accompany Minister Egan to the legation, Cook reappeared, perfectly groomed and faultlessly attired. It was a metamorphosis hard to credit, for anyone in a position to make the comparison.

Cook transformed.

The legation overflowed with reporters and those just wishing to get a glimpse of the doctor, so there was little respite to be obtained even there. Cook answered questions freely and was full of praise for the faithfulness and loyalty of his Eskimo companions, whom he said he had made arctic million-aires with the contents of his house at Annoatok.

In the afternoon, Minister Egan presented Dr. Cook to King Frederick at Bernstoff Castle. The monarch talked with him for an hour and invited him to dinner the next evening. Princess Marie and the Princess George of Greece then asked him to tea. But still more was to come before the weary traveler would be granted rest.

At the Phoenix, William Stead had arranged for Cook to meet the press of the world, who were clamoring for an interview. Stead led him in and seated him at a large table. The doctor bowed his face in his hands, as if trying to get a grip on himself after being shuttled about the Danish capital nearly nonstop for the nine hours he had been ashore.

The reporter from the London *Daily News,* who witnessed the ordeal over which Stead presided as moderator, felt almost guilty seeing that the doctor was so very tired:

> There was something pathetic in the fact that he was called on to prove his claim as the greatest explorer the world had ever known. . . .
>
> We seemed to be making history, and behind the greatness of it there was something grotesque.
>
> Here was a man whose greatness will live as long as the world lasts arraigned like a prisoner in the dock, charged with discover-ing the North Pole. For an hour he was submitted to a searching cross-examination and sat there answering questions. . . .
>
> He smiled indulgently now and again as if he pitied our in-credulity, but never once did he decline to answer questions, and they were put to him baldly and directly. It was a trial of veracity. Dr. Cook, with his back to the wall, was fighting to convince a world of unbelievers. The picture will ever remain with me out of to-day's record of a little, sturdy man with dreamy gray blue eyes that seemed to vision the desolate days. . . .
>
> A very ordinary catalogue of a man's features, but that is the most remarkable thing about him. He is just a man of the type you see every day. If there is anything persistent in his individuality it is those haunting eyes, the eyes of a man who has looked for an empty horizon. He turned this way and that, replying like a wit-ness giving evidence before a royal commission. . . .
>
> I felt, I think all felt, that the verdict of the Copenhagen jury was quite unanimous as to the discovery of the Pole.[31]

This feeling developed as the doctor answered all questions in a calm, simple and direct manner without hesitation. During the interview he gave clarifications of several troubling passages contained in his initial report. He stated that the lowest temperature measured −83° Fahrenheit, not centigrade, as the Paris edition of the *Herald* had printed it, and that his assertion of eliminating 30,000 square miles from the unknown was based on his ability to see 15 miles to either side of his lines of march. It did not imply, he said, that he had discovered a landmass of this dimension, and certainly not that he had actually covered all this ground personally. He denied that he had lost track of time. He affirmed that he spoke Eskimo fluently. He explained why he had sent Franke back, and he stated the bases on which his claim would be tested.

"I realize, gentlemen," said the doctor, "that, despite the fact I have absolutely nothing to gain from misrepresentation of actual facts, but on the other hand have everything to lose, the nature of my accomplishment of April 21, 1908, when I planted the American flag on a spot at latitude 90 degrees north, calls for proof to the scientific world.

"I understand that in a case of this sort my reputation and my past count for naught, but I believe that in a carefully prepared diary which I kept and in the painstakingly accurate astronomic observations I made will be found the proof demanded by the world. Corroborating this will be the evidence of the two brave and uncomplaining companions of my trip, the Esquimaux Etukishuk and Ahwelah. . . .

". . . I am satisfied that no scientific man acquainted with the Esquimau and his traits of personality will place so low a value on my intelligence as to presume that I would pin my hopes of proof in such an issue as this to a lie concocted by me and placed in the mouths of these men. . . .

"An Esquimau is a better judge of Arctic conditions and Arctic travel than a white man, and there is no real reason why as witnesses the word of Etukishuk and Ahwelah will not be quite as acceptable to the scientific world as would that of any white man."[32]

Again and again, he was asked to describe the conditions surrounding the North Pole and the nature of the observations he had made there.

"Concerning the ice around the pole, so far as I could see, it was slightly more active there than at one or two degrees south. It drifted somewhat more to the south and east. Its general character is not very different from that at other places. . . .

"I do not claim to have put my finger on the exact spot; I do not claim to have put my foot on it, but personally I think we have been at the spot. When the observations have been figured out again it is possible that there will be found slight errors and differences, but I am certain that a gunshot fired from where we were would have passed over the pole.

"I do not assert that I am perfectly familiar with making astronomical observations, especially in the polar regions. I think that all explorers will be satisfied with my data."[33]

When asked if he thought that these observations could be faked, he replied, "Why should I sit down and invent observations? I did not do this thing for anything but sport and because I take a real interest in the problem.

It would not do me any good to invent these things. The only witnesses I had were two Eskimos, certainly, but in all polar expeditions observations have been made by one man. . . ."[34]

The questions were endless and often trivial. What were his future ambitions? Was it true that he had remarked to the king that he would like to see the South Pole? "Oh, I would like to see it all right," he answered, "but my desire is not sufficiently keen to prompt me to make the trip. Right now the greatest desire of my life is to see my wife and children. It is my purpose to get to New York just as soon as possible."[35]

After a grueling hour, Stead intervened, or the 60 reporters would have kept on through the night. At the end of the press conference, the correspondents swarmed around the explorer, many of them shaking his hand or patting his shoulder. One not present to be convinced was Philip Gibbs. He spent the afternoon typing an account of his interview with Cook aboard the *Hans Egede,* which was soon on its way to the *Daily Chronicle.*

That evening at the dinner in the magnificent municipal building, Dr. Cook was acclaimed by numerous speakers, and when glasses were raised to "Our honored guest," there were nine rousing cheers.

In response, the doctor rose to speak. "I thank you very much for the warm and eloquent words," he began, "but I am unable to express myself properly. It was a rather hard day for me, but I never enjoyed a day better. . . . The most important factor in my expedition was the Eskimo and dog world, and I cannot be too thankful to the Danes for their care of the Eskimo, and now they also have instituted a mission at Cape York. Had I not met with the right Eskimos and the right dogs and the right provisions I could not have reached the pole. I owe much to the Danish nation for my success."[36]

The doctor excused himself early; it *had* been a tiring day. But before retiring, he took time to send off a wire to the White House announcing that he had reached the North Pole.

President Taft, from his summer home in Beverly, Massachusetts, congratulated him on his report, saying it "stirs the pride of all Americans that this feat which has so long baffled the world has been accomplished by the intelligent energy and wonderful endurance of a fellow countryman."[37]

Dr. Cook spent the next day being greeted by Danish explorers and men of science. The Rector Magnificus of the University of Copenhagen, Professor Torp, and the royal astronomer had asked permission of Minister Egan to talk with Cook in private at the chancery. In a short time they emerged convinced of the truth of the doctor's story and of his ability to take celestial observations. "As there were certain questions of an astronomical nature with which I myself was not sufficiently acquainted," the rector explained, "I called in Prof. Strømgren, who put an exhaustive series of mathematical, technical, natural, and scientific questions to Dr. Cook, based particularly on those of his contentions on which some doubt had been cast. Dr. Cook answered them all to our full satisfaction. He showed no nervousness or excitement at any time. I dare say, therefore, that there is no justification for anybody to throw the slightest doubt on his claim to have reached the north pole and the means whereby he did it."[38]

Professor Torp then told the minister that the university had decided to bestow an honorary degree and petitioned the king, as president of the university, for permission to do so, saying, "All must admire the courage and ability he has manifested in the accomplishment of this great task."[39]

A quiet lunch was planned at the American legation. But even there the doctor could not escape the press of questions. He was asked once more for his feelings upon his arrival at the Pole. "Let me confess," he admitted, "I was disappointed. Man is a child dreaming of prodigies. I had reached the pole, and now, at a moment when I should have been thrilled with pride and joy, I was overcome with a sudden fear of the dangers and sufferings of the return."[40]

After leaving Copenhagen, the doctor announced, he would visit Paris and then go to Brussels to meet with members of the International Polar Commission there. Georges Lecointe, who welcomed this chance to see his old friend again, took the opportunity to express his anger at the widespread skepticism that had initially greeted Cook's claim. "I am indignant at the idea that Dr. Cook's statement of his discovery is accepted as untrue by some people," fumed the Astronomer Royal. "I know Dr. Cook personally, and I vouch for his sincerity. He is truth itself."[41]

Others came to the doctor's defense. Otto Sverdrup said, "It is a shame that jealousy should strangle justice." Nansen expressed confidence in Cook's trustworthiness, and Lieutenant Herron defended the explorer's claim to have climbed Mount McKinley, the initial doubts about that feat having been recalled in the American press.

Through it all Mrs. Cook kept silent, leading to rumors of coolness between her and her husband. Lotta Davidson denied this, however, saying no one could have been more loyal and uncomplaining, despite the desperate financial strain the doctor's absence had caused.

After Cook left the *Phoenix* to have his portrait made at the photographer's, as every member of the royal family had asked for one, word arrived that the *Selskabets Guldmedalje*—the gold medal of the Royal Geographical Society—would be presented to the explorer.

That evening Cook was the guest of honor at the royal palace, Charlottenlund, where the entire royal family, down to the smallest child, was present. At dinner the doctor sat at the right hand of the king—an honor no one could remember ever having been given to a private individual. After the dinner, which was a quiet affair, the three princesses, Ingeborg, Thyra, and Dagmar, and all the children gathered around Dr. Cook to hear a recounting of his adventures. He took delight in telling the youngest children about the polar bears and other animals of the Far North, answering their every eager question.

The splendid evening was marred by only one unpleasant report. It had been widely rumored that King Frederick would bestow upon his dinner guest the Doonebog—the Gold Medal of Merit with Crown—given only to those who rendered mankind the most distinguished service, but for some reason he had changed his mind, and the evening passed without the honor being conferred.[42]

Despite a pouring rain, a large crowd gathered outside the doctor's hotel to cheer him that night. In his rooms at the Phoenix he was visited by Otto Sverdrup, whom he had never met before, and by Roald Amundsen, who greeted him enthusiastically, kissing him on both cheeks.

As the crowd in the street clamored for the doctor's appearance at the window, the three explorers talked of expeditions past and future. Amundsen was planning to take the *Fram* to the Bering Sea for another try at the Pole and asked Cook about the conditions he had encountered.

The doctor demurred, saying he could only duplicate the feat of Nansen and Sverdrup. Instead, why not try something new? Why not try for the South Pole?

Amundsen seemed to sit in meditation on his friend's words, then said, "The Fram is not a good sea boat for the heavy South seas. But this is the thing to do. Let me think it over." After a further silence the Norwegian objected: "Scott has a fleet of ships, ample funds to fit an army of men with an equipment which will make my expedition look like a peanut wagon."

"For that very reason you should give him a race," said the doctor. "Scott's overload will hang him. You know that the South Pole will never be reached except by dogs or wings."[43]

On September 6 Cook had the pleasure of being left pretty much alone, though yet another dinner was planned for that evening. Except for a reception for the diplomatic corps and lunch with the Egans, he spent most of the day trying to catch up on the immense stack of wires and letters of congratulation that had piled up in his suite. Minister Egan had suggested a private secretary and recommended Walter Lonsdale, who was visiting the city. Lonsdale was soon employed, helping Cook with the seemingly impossible task of answering them all.

Even while they were at work, the doctor could not be totally free of the inquiring press. One reporter who came to his rooms noticed he seemed to care for none of the congratulatory messages but kept looking for one from his wife. He interrupted the explorer in this process long enough to ask if he was getting tired of so much adulation. "No man could honestly say that he was tired of such attentions after so short an experience," Cook replied, "but I do feel that I am getting more attention than my share. Now, what shall I do about this?" he said, picking up an invitation from Prince Adolphe Frederic of Mecklenburg-Schwerin to address the Berlin Colonial Society. "I should like to do that, of course, but I want to get to America."

"I suspect there are a few people there who would like to see you," the reporter suggested.

"I know of three," said Dr. Cook, smiling. Then the telephone rang. It was a message from Mrs. Rasmussen asking when she could come to see her husband's friend.[44]

Finally, the cable he sought emerged from the massive stack. It said simply, "Thank God all well. Marie."[45]

Among the other hundreds of letters and cables were fabulous offers for lecture and literary rights to the explorer's story. Curtis Brown and Massie, literary and dramatic agents in London, estimated literary rights would bring a minimum of $40,000 but said that the lecture rights were "impossible to estimate."[46] Their guess of what the doctor's story was worth wasn't even close.

Benjamin Hampton, owner of *Hampton's Magazine*, had already guaranteed the doctor $100,000 just for magazine and newspaper rights. When the doctor didn't reply to the offer, Hampton's agent pleaded for just 15 minutes to present a proposal, saying he was authorized to pay "whatever price you ask."[47] William Stead weighed in with an offer from William Randolph Hearst to double any offer the doctor received.[48] And the lecture rights? The impresario of the platform, Frederic Thompson, offered $250,000 for the first 250 lectures.

Faced with such prospects, Cook had no shortage of advice from friends old and new. Ralph Shainwald, his old climbing partner, put aside business in France to come to Copenhagen. Shainwald cautioned Cook about selling the newspaper rights too cheaply, certainly not for less than $100,000.[49] E.G. Wyckoff, Clarence's brother, who was also in Europe and had come to Copenhagen, volunteered to go on a tour of the continent to secure the best price. Minister Egan was against *Hampton's* and thought it unseemly to sell the rights to Hearst, suggesting his own publisher, the *Century Magazine*, instead, but Stead naturally disagreed. Cook, however, seemed resolved out of loyalty to give the rights to James Gordon Bennett.

The Hotel Phoenix was besieged by visitors, including Harper & Brothers' vice president, Clarence W. McIlvaine, who hoped to get a piece of the explorer's story or perhaps even the rights to his book. The other Copenhagen hotels resented the monopoly the Phoenix was holding, so Minister Egan took the doctor to lunch at the Bristol, but they could hardly eat for all the autograph seekers at their table.

At the dinner given that evening for the foreign correspondents by the dominant Copenhagen newspaper, *Politiken*, Dr. Cook sat in the gilded ballroom of the Tivoli Casino, wreathed in roses, with an ice sculpture of "The North Pole" slowly melting in front of his place, listening to the flattering speeches and toasts being given in his honor. A whisper started around the room that Peary had returned, claiming to have reached the North Pole. Though the whispers reached him, the doctor showed no reaction at all.

"Dr. Cook did not lose a fraction of his poise," observed one dinner guest, "yet the intelligence, as a silent undertow, carried away the enthusiasm of the diners. Only the personality of Dr. Cook kept the banquet from disintegration. The speeches were fewer than had been expected, and were noticeably listless. But with the fortitude which drove him footsore and weary through the long polar night, Dr. Cook himself spoke at greater length than usual, with more humor and keener interest."[50]

Once again he praised Sverdrup, John R. Bradley and his faithful Eskimos, as well as the Danish nation. After Cook resumed his seat, a man tiptoed in and handed the doctor a piece of paper. On the paper was written, "Peary says, 'Stars and Stripes nailed to the Pole.'"

Philip Gibbs witnessed the dramatic moment as the startling news was announced: "I stood close to Dr. Cook when that message was handed to him, and I am bound to pay a tribute to his cool nerve. He read the message on the bit of flimsy, handed it back, and said: 'If Peary says he reached the Pole, I believe him!'"[51]

Instantly, the reporters pressed around the doctor hoping to get his reaction. But he simply replied that he was glad to hear the news. "I am proud that a fellow American has reached the pole," he said. "As Rear Admiral Schley said at Santiago, 'There is glory enough for us all.'"[52] Some insisted that the message must be someone's idea of a joke, but the doctor disagreed; then he went to the window to acknowledge the cheering crowd standing below in the pouring rain. Leaning out of the little window, he said, "You kindhearted people, I thank you."[53]

Many in the United States greeted the news of Peary's return at this dramatic moment with disbelief as well. Dr. Roswell O. Stebbins, chairman of the Arctic Club's committee that was planning a welcome for Dr. Cook, was one of them. "That is truly extraordinary if it is really true," Stebbins exclaimed. "That the pole should be twice discovered in that short space after all these years of failure on failure is most remarkable. It is what I had been hoping earnestly for ever since Dr. Cook sent in his report—that Peary would succeed. Then the matter could be settled, once for all, they could corroborate each other; Cook's story could be verified by Peary's. . . .

"With the knowledge that there is enmity between the two men over that difficulty regarding the blue fox skins, and the anger Peary's friends feel that Dr. Cook should have profited from Peary's hints as to the best course, and should have taken over the dogs and Eskimos Peary planned to use, I foresee trouble," said the dentist nervously. "Had they filed quite independent reports it would have been different, but Peary must have heard of Cook from Harry Whitney, who was at Etah, so that when he sent his story he knew of Cook's."[54]

The news was no joke; it had been confirmed by the receipt of a one-word telegram forwarded to Herbert Bridgman from Indian Harbour, Labrador. The message read: "Sun"—the prearranged code word for "Pole Reached. *Roosevelt* Safe."

Bridgman had been in South Amherst, Massachusetts, when the word came, and when the New York reporters intercepted him at Grand Central Station on his return to the city, his statement sounded like the opening salvo in the fight Dr. Stebbins had predicted.

"Coming at this time, the news from Commander Peary is very gratifying," the newspaperman said. "It is unfortunate that a controversy over the real discovery of the pole should have arisen, but that is Commander Peary's own fight, and I do not think that I should comment upon the announcement by Dr. Cook that he reached the pole in April of last year. Commander Peary is quite capable of attending to that controversy and of settling all doubt about the matter."[55]

"Cook's word must be taken the same as any other man's," Bridgman continued. "I have not the slightest doubt that Dr. Cook believes implicitly that he has reached the North Pole, and that he made his observations with the utmost care, but I do believe that he has made mistakes in the reading of his instruments that will rob him of the glory. I think that when the records are submitted to scientists there will be flaws.

"I think, when Mr. Peary gives to the world his account of the stories told by the two Eskimo boys who accompanied Dr. Cook their narrations will do much to prove or disprove Dr. Cook's claim. They are a simple minded people but they have a strange and wonderful intelligence regarding geography."[56]

The president of the Peary Arctic Club, Thomas Hubbard, was more circumspect in his remarks when informed of Peary's message. "Of course as soon as I am sure that Peary sent the cablegram I am sure that the report is true," said the general.

"As for Dr. Cook, I know little about him. I don't care to say anything in criticism of his statements, for they may easily have become confused in some respects before they came out in print. Any insinuation by any one at all that Peary is not telling the truth is beneath consideration. Commander Peary is no faker; what he says is right."[57]

That was just about the way the whole world felt. Peary's word was indisputable. If he said he had done it, then it was done. Little skepticism could be found anywhere on the pages of the world's press, with the possible exception of Copenhagen's.

Denmark had not finished with its honors to the man who claimed priority over Peary by nearly a year. So many wanted to attend the presentation of the Royal Geographical Society's gold medal on September 7, an honor previously granted to only nine men, including Nansen, Scott, Sverdrup and Sven Hedin, that they could not be accommodated in the society's small chamber. So the Palais Concert Hall was engaged.

Once again, the royal family attended. Along with 1,200 other persons, they waited expectantly for the doctor to enter the hall. Some had paid the equivalent of $200 to gain a seat, and one of the 500 tickets for the dinner to follow at the Phoenix was impossible to obtain at any price.

*Lecture at the Palais Concert Hall,
September 7, 1909.*

Dr. Cook was introduced by the crown prince, who had asked for the honor of presenting the society's medal to him. When he did, Cook accepted the box containing it with a stiff little bow; a full five minutes of unrestrained and enthusiastic applause followed before he could speak.

His lecture, delivered before an immense map of the Arctic, nine meters square and surmounted by the Stars and Stripes, began with a lengthy description of his preparations for his great northern journey. When his long pointer had at last traced his route to that magic spot marked on the map by the American flag, his audience was surprised that he had so little to say about the Pole itself—a mere 268 words, ending with, "I have been within a circle a kilometer in diameter where the pole is situated. I am satisfied that that is quite sufficient for practical purposes. I will say no more until my book is published."[58]

To William Stead, his presentation seemed curiously unemotional. "There was no gesticulation," he observed. "He went straight on with his lecture as if he were a university professor methodically giving an expository lecture to his class. His great anxiety was to confine himself to what he had already said, and to say no more."[59] When Minister Egan noticed this same thing and mentioned it to Cook, the doctor replied, "I must keep something back."[60]

The lecture was a distinct disappointment for the scientists, who had asked for as much specific information about the North Pole as possible. Their feeling could be summed up by the description of the lecture filed by the New York *Sun's* correspondent: "It must be said at once that never since the news of his success reached the civilized world, never since he landed in Copenhagen, has the American explorer made so poor, so weak a showing."[61]

For Philip Gibbs, Cook's performance only confirmed his suspicions. At first he had been politely skeptical about the authenticity of Cook's statements, then he reported that the doctor had no documents with him to prove his claim and had presented none to the Danish scientists who had interviewed him. Now he openly denounced Cook as a fraud, characterizing the lecture as "a fairy tale" filled with "awkward pauses" and delivered with a flushed face and a "forehead beaded with perspiration," though others, like Stead, reported that he had told his story coolly and without hesitation.[62]

In the coming days, Gibbs would make other charges, including that Knud Rasmussen's wife had received a letter from her husband in which the Danish explorer had renounced his belief in Cook's claim. Mrs. Rasmussen issued a denial of Gibbs's allegations but then could not be found for confirmation. The *Daily Chronicle* asked Gibbs to explain, then refused to send him to America to continue his coverage of the story.

The lone dissenting voice in an almost universal chorus of praise in Copenhagen, Gibbs became, at once, a marked man. *Politiken* published a caricature of him, branding it "The Liar Gibbs." The Danish poet-doctor Norman-Hansen challenged him to a duel, and when Stead caught sight of him on the street one day, he called out, "Young man, you have not only ruined yourself, which does not matter very much, but you have also ruined the *Daily Chronicle,* for which I have had a great esteem."[63]

September 8 was to be a quiet day for Cook and the press, since the explorer planned to spend it secluded at Count Holstein-Ledreborg's Roskilde Castle, a few miles outside the city. But all was changed when the contents of Peary's latest communications from Labrador were published:

> Cook's story should not be taken too seriously. The Eskimos who accompanied him say that he went no distance north. He did not get out of sight of land. Other men of the tribe corroborate their statements. Kindly give this to all home and foreign news associations for the same wide distribution as Cook's story.

To his wife he wired:

> Good morning. Delayed by gale. Don't let Cook story worry you. Have him nailed. Bert.[64]

If the world had been amazed by Peary's coincident arrival on the scene of Dr. Cook's triumph, it now became apprehensive about the consequences of one explorer calling another a liar. *Le Temps* in Paris had already cautioned: "As a matter of fact, it is agreed that the north pole is covered with moving ice, and one might say that it is a problem resting in the domain of metaphysics. When some one says he has been there let us believe him, because if criticism on this metaphysical question ever commences it will never end."

The rest of the world's press, though they might not have agreed with Paris on this point, surely agreed that the whole thing was taking on an aspect "exceeding the wildest romance."[65]

Although Cook remained outwardly unruffled by Peary's charges, he was less restrained in private. He dispatched a wire to John Bradley via the Explorers Club in New York City:

> Call the Peary bluff try to secure a ship to go from St. John's after eskimos at my expense.
>
> Cook[66]

Peary's charges did nothing to dissuade the Danes, however. "Dr. Cook's apparent confidence is the greatest factor working in his support in Copenhagen," reported one correspondent who witnessed the explorer's utter assurance in his own claim. "Those who have had the opportunity to talk with him are only of one mind, that he is an absolutely sincere, simple man, or deserves a pedestal in history as one of the greatest of actors."[67]

That is exactly what Philip Gibbs believed the doctor to be, and he felt that his act was symptomatic of something much more sinister in his personality:

> That personality is so strange and so powerful that I believe if Cook claimed to have come from Mars there would be many people who would say, "We believe him because he tells us so. Such a simple, honest man would not deceive us."[68]

> I must now say that this man Frederick Cook is the most remarkable, most amazing man I have ever met. He calls me his enemy, but I have no personal animosity against him, and I will say honestly that I am filled with a sense of profound admiration for him. If he is an impostor he is also a very brave man—a man with such iron nerve, such miraculous self-control, and such magnificent courage in playing his game, that he will count for ever among the greatest impostors of the world. That and not the discovery of the north pole shall be his claim to immortality.[69]

Gibbs demanded that Cook give him proof of his claim or he would "destroy" him, but the Danish press only mocked Gibbs's arrogance and his continuing criticisms as desperate attempts to save himself from his initial misjudgment; his demands had no effect.

On September 9 the honorary degree that Rector Torp had mentioned to Minister Egan was conferred on the explorer with all the dignity that the university could muster. At 1:00 the crown prince, in morning dress and accompanied by the princess, and the prince of Greece and Princess George entered and took their seats on the dais in the Great Hall, which was packed to capacity. Outside, a crowd of thousands waited in the street. Dr. Cook sat on the floor beneath the tribunal.

The officials filed into the hall in procession to the strains of Beethoven's *Eroica* Symphony. After ascending the tribunal, Rector Torp gave a brief address outlining the development of polar exploration and saying that the degree should be conferred upon Dr. Cook not only for his achievements in the field but also because he had "given us something that makes us look up to the doer as a man of thought and action, a true homo sapiens."[70] The rector then spoke directly to Cook saying, "Whether your scientific research will rank very highly or not, the faculty gives you this degree in recognition of your great achievements in exploration and the qualities you have shown therein."[71]

There was a large round of applause, but the doctor did not understand that the degree would now be conferred, and although he acknowledged the cheers, he failed to ascend the dais. Rector Torp, realizing this, descended to the floor, handed him the red moiré case containing the diploma inscribed *Summos in Philosophia Honores* — *Fredericum Albertum Cook*, and motioned for him to ascend the throne.[72]

While the minute and a half of applause lasted, the doctor looked pleased and a trifle shy. But when the clapping stopped, he paused and, after looking sternly around the hall, said with a sharp staccato manner in his clear voice, "I accept this degree with due appreciation of the honor done me. By it you have stamped my journey to the Pole. All my records of observations and papers of every kind are to be examined forthwith by a proper tribunal. When that has been done they will be sent here for you to see and examine first. I ask you only to wait until then. I do not want you to examine mere fragments, but want you to examine it all.

"Since unfortunate rumors have been circulated, I will, at my own expense, send a ship for the Eskimos who were with me. They will be taken to New York and examined there by Rasmussen, whom I regard as the greatest authority on Eskimo and the Eskimo language.

"I can say no more, I can do no more, I show you my hands."[73]

After the ceremony, Cook asked Gould Brokaw, a millionaire friend of Minister Egan's, whether he would take his yacht *Fedora* to Greenland to fulfill the promise he had made before the university, but Brokaw did not want to risk his craft on such a perilous trip, though he offered to take the doctor back to the United States on her. Cook then asked Otto Sverdrup to captain the voyage but was advised by the Danish Greenland Administration that it would be impossible to return to Etah before spring. Then he retired for the night to Count Holstein's castle with the Egans.

That evening, Roald Amundsen made up his mind. On a piece of Dr. Cook's personal stationery, he wrote out a letter to Daugaard-Jensen

"I show you my hands," at the Great Hall, September 9, 1909.

asking permission to pick the 50 best dogs Greenland had to offer and to acquire 14 suits of sealskin. He would turn south and give Scott a run for the Pole.[74]

In light of Peary's charges, Minister Egan advised Dr. Cook to make a statement, but the doctor said he wished no controversy with Peary. Still, he did not seem to be able to decide what he should do. Finally, he was persuaded to draw up a response:

> I did not deem it well at first to reply to the attacks of Commander Peary. I thought it better to maintain the reserve becoming a gentleman. Besides, if Peary has reached the pole I am glad of his success. It does not prove that I have not succeeded, and before him. . . .
>
> I am asked for proofs of my veracity. Well, I will give proofs, for I solemnly bind myself to submit all the documents and instruments to the geographical societies of America and Denmark or to any assembly of scientists any one likes to name. I think that declaration will suffice to prove my good faith.
>
> One must not be astonished that I refused to furnish proofs to various personages. I want to present the results of my work as a whole and not to private individuals, but to constituted bodies. I think those who have doubted my word will not doubt that of the geographical societies which I shall take for judges.
>
> I shall say no more. I hate this quarrel into which it is being sought to drag me. I am satisfied that I have done what I have done and know that in a little while no doubt will be possible.[75]

Cook's indecisiveness puzzled William Stead. He could not understand the way the man vacillated over little matters and failed to do things obviously in his best interest. It seemed so out of character for one who had accomplished such a great deed. But after reviewing the extraordinary circumstances, he felt it could be explained:

> He does not strike us as a man, but rather as a child,—a naive, inexperienced child, who sorely needed some one to look after him, and take care of him, and tell him what he ought to do in his own interest. It was really almost pathetic to see his efforts to readjust himself to the busy, bustling, new environment of modern civilization. . . .
>
> . . . A rather annoying thing about this infantile side of his character was his inability to make up his mind and stick to it about almost anything. Perhaps this was due to his consciousness of being in strange surroundings and feeling that he ought not to be governed by his own judgment. . . .
>
> If he had been as indecisive and as changeable in the Arctic regions he would never have got anywhere, and certainly could never have got home. Yet there was never any trace of impatience or of fear. He was always as cool as a cucumber, calm, composed and collected.[76]

Some of the advice that seemed to confuse Cook had come from Minister Egan. "I must accuse myself of an error of judgment in suggesting to Dr. Cook that he should leave Copenhagen at the first opportunity," the minister confessed. "He was desirous of going to Belgium, in which country, he said, lived one of his closest scientific friends, the astronomer royal, I believe. It seemed to me that his delay was making a matter for serious scientific consideration seem frivolous, and the subject of sentimental and sensational discussion."[77]

More came from Georges Lecointe, who told his friend he would get a great welcome in Belgium but urged him to return immediately to the United States "for your sake." When Cook received a telegram from his brother Will urging the same thing, it confirmed his resolve to cancel all other European engagements.[78]

Dr. Cook left Copenhagen on the yacht *Melchior* on September 10. The man who ten days before had been generally unknown, who possessed only the clothes on his back and a mere grip full of papers when he landed at Copenhagen, prepared to depart with five large trunks and most of the highest honors of the Danish nation. A committee of university and geographical society officials, still stating their unshaken belief, saw him off. These included Sverdrup and Amundsen, who would accompany him as far as Norway.

Women showered the doctor with flowers as he stepped from his automobile. The *Oscar II* of the Danish-American Steamship Company was reported to be booked to capacity. In a private reception in the *Melchior*'s saloon, Admiral de Richelieu assured him, "Green-eyed envy and jealousy are doing their envenomed work, but we in Denmark believe in you absolutely."

"I want to thank you for the great honor that is mine in going home on a Danish steamer," the doctor replied. "Since I cannot reach home on an American steamer or an expedition vessel, it is fitting that I should go home on a steamer of the land which has given me such happy days. You have made my return so happy that the tortures of the past are forgotten. You have been my friends; you have fought my battles. With a full heart I say farewell to the people of Denmark."

To a call from reporters for a statement to be issued to the world, the doctor replied, "Don't you think that would be rather presumptuous? All I want is to get home to my wife and children and to finish my work."[79]

A large crowd stood on the wharf and cheered as the doctor doffed his

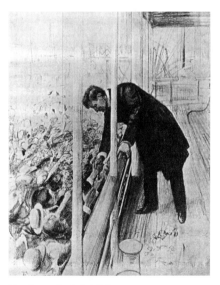

Cook on the Melchior.

hat from the topmost rail, and then the *Melchior* pulled away and glided out among the other ships, spangled with flags and sounding their whistles.

Minister Egan was there to see him off as he had seen him in. "On Friday, when he left, he was loaded with honors and followed by the acclamations of the people . . . and the cheers that greeted him were as much a tribute to his personal character as to his epoch-making exploit," Egan recalled. "Kindly, simple, firm, and sincere, he had, in a short time, made the sons of the Vikings love him."[80]

When the minister arrived back at the legation, he found a box containing an exquisite new top hat, which had been sent with Dr. Cook's compliments.

The weather was absolutely brilliant for Cook's arrival at Christiansand at 11:00 the next morning. He was saluted by seven guns from the fort at the order of King Haakon, and an official entourage visited the *Melchior* as throngs of sightseers in small craft darted around the ship. The explorer then transferred to the *Oscar II* to sail home to America.

In welcoming Dr. Cook, the captain paid tribute to him in a brief address:

> It is our proud task to take Dr. Cook home and deliver him to the American nation, which is waiting with open arms to receive the most famous explorer of modern times. . . . What the citizens of the United States will do with him we can well guess. Such an opportunity to shower honors on a man does not occur frequently. For centuries, men of all nations have been seeking the top of the earth. Many have lost their lives in the quest. Dr. Cook has done better. He has reached his goal and deserves and will receive all the glory due to the achievement. He did not devote his indomitable courage, his wonderful strength and his powerful will to the task for the sake of fame, but in order to solve a problem which had hitherto baffled all men in all time. In reaching his goal he has attained a place of honor in the annals of exploration and his name will be inscribed in letters of gold on the roll of famous Americans.
>
> Bravo, doctor! Your fellow passengers on the *Oscar II* speaking in behalf of many millions of all nations are proud of you.[81]

The "Cook Days" were over. Dr. Cook was gone. But his brief stay in Copenhagen had left many puzzles in its wake. In Laussane E.G. Wyckoff learned that Cook had already disposed of the book rights to Harper & Brothers, just when his efforts on the doctor's behalf seemed assured of securing a guarantee of at least half a million dollars. He wrote to the doctor, imploring him not to sell the magazine rights too quickly. But it was too late. Cook had let James Gordon Bennett have his story for a mere $25,000.

The Danish writer Georg Brandes, who had lunched with the explorer, could not understand such actions or his ineffectual rebuttals of the charges made against him. "I consider Dr. Cook a good, honest, sincere, but *maladroit* man," said Brandes. "Could anybody have bungled more completely his affairs when he was here than he did if he wanted us to believe in his veracity? . . . But all this does not change the fact that he has, like Aladdin, found the treasure, and that Peary detests him like Noureddin. . . . But we must not overlook the fact that [Dr. Cook's] feat was a brilliant one, and that he himself is the perfectly simple hero. These are not small things as the world goes today."[82]

In England two reporters also pondered the stirring events of the last eight days. One was William Stead, to whom the doctor had said of his arctic hardships, "The process is so complete that it seems to wipe out the traces of memory. I only seem able to remember clearly the most recent things. You, for instance, think of the North Pole that seems to me now so far away behind a veil that [what] I remember clearly is the cruel hardship of the final escape from the Arctic. It was then we suffered most,—it is most recent and is most vividly impressed on my memory."

Stead thought back over these words and the puzzling man who had said them:

> Who knows but that this fierce fire of physical exertion which burns out the cells of the brain and makes a man new from day to day may be responsible for some of the things which have mystified us about Dr. Cook? . . .
>
> . . . I do not venture to have an opinion on the scientific value of the credence he may have or may not have. But I do possess an elementary enough sense of justice, and I protest against treating a hitherto reputable American citizen as an infamous fakir before we have heard his evidence, seen his papers, checked his calculations, and examined his proofs.
>
> It may be that he will fail to prove his case. If so, we shall bow to the authority of the tribunal to which he has appealed. But if he were declared by the competent authority to have not made good his claim, while I should bow to the decision, I should reserve my own judgment as to Dr. Cook. Mistaken he may be. A fakir, a liar, a deliberate scoundrel who set forth to make a fool of the whole human race, that he is not. He is both too honest and too limited to have conceived so colossal a fraud.[83]

The other was Philip Gibbs. Though he had staked his reputation and career on that moment of intuition aboard the *Hans Egede*, he, too, was not quite sure what to think:

> It was marvellous on the day when the doctor's degree—the highest honor of the University—was conferred upon him, and before all the learned men there he ascended the pulpit of the University chapel and in a solemn oration stretched out his arms and said: "I show you my hands—they are clean!"
>
> At that moment I was tempted to believe that Cook believed he had been to the North Pole. Sometimes, remembering the manner of the man, I am tempted to think so still. . . .[84]

CHAPTER 16

We Believe in You

THE DAYS SINCE SEPTEMBER 2 HAD BEEN UNBEARABLE FOR JO PEARY. DR. COOK was in Copenhagen receiving honor after honor, but where was Bert? She ardently hoped for a message from him and kept a lookout for any boat bound for Eagle Island that might be bringing word. Even so, she missed seeing the approach of the long-awaited messenger.

At 1 P.M. on September 6 Marie had answered the knock of a stranger at the door. He asked for Mrs. Peary. Her mother was in her room with a sick headache, she said. The man identified himself as a reporter from the New York *Sun.* He wanted to know her reaction now that Commander Peary had announced he had reached the Pole. Marie shouted for her mother to come.

As Jo Peary arrived at the door, another man was seen coming up from the beach where he had landed his boat; it was Steve Toothacher of West Harpswell with a telegram. "I have good news for you, marm," said Steve. "It's from Captain Peary."

Jo Peary read the telegram:

> Have made good at last. I have the D.O.P. Am well. Will wire again from Chateau.
>
> Bert[1]

She interpreted D.O.P. as "darned old pole" but conceded that the "D" might stand for something stronger. Jo told Marie to run the flag up. Since her dad had planted it at the Pole, she said, it should be flying at Eagle Island, too.

Now that it was official, Jo Peary could hardly contain herself. "I knew it! I knew it!" she cried. "I have been thinking all day that we should hear good news to-day. Oh, I am so glad, so glad! . . .

". . . You don't know what it means to me. Twenty-three years he has been working for this, and during all this time I have just existed, that's all. Hardly a year of real happiness during all that time have I had because of the worry and anxiety and fear. But it is all over now. No one knows how much my husband has suffered or sacrificed to reach the pole. Many times he has risked his life. The best years of his life have been spent in that frozen country, far removed from every comfort and from everything. It has been his life's work. He has studied and labored for success, and now that it has come no one can appreciate how happy it makes me."

376

Then came the inevitable question about Bert's rival. "I don't want to talk about Dr. Cook's discovery. There has been too much said about that, and I don't want to comment on it. Whatever I might say would be misunderstood, anyway, and people are so unkind about such things. If he reached the pole ahead of Mr. Peary it makes no difference."[2]

"Just glory, that's all!" enthused Marie. "I knew he would succeed all the time because I have had dreams that he would. We don't want to talk about the other man who claims to have reached the pole. We know, mama and I, that papa got there any way, and that's enough, isn't it?"[3]

Crawling up on his mother's lap with a Sunday supplement, six-year-old Robert E. Peary, Jr., wasn't so easily impressed. "Don't talk about the pole any more," he said, "I'm tired of it. Read this funny story, mamma."[4]

Soon, boats were arriving from all over, loaded down with the press. Jo Peary welcomed them with an apparent slap at Mrs. Cook, whose somewhat backhanded congratulatory telegram was among those brought over from the mainland. "No, I am not going to run away and hide from the newspaper men. I have nothing to conceal and am willing to tell you everything I know. We shall begin life again when Mr. Peary gets home. I shall not hear of his going north again."[5] When she had done with the reporters, she started packing.

It took several days after Peary's assertion that Cook had not been to the Pole for an account of his own journey to be published. The *New York Times,* which had purchased in advance the exclusive rights for $4,000, expected it immediately, but it was "delayed." Peary's original announcement had been accompanied by only a bare itinerary. Peary had started for the Pole from Cape Columbia on February 22, 1909, and reached it on April 6, it said. He had left the Pole April 7 and returned to Cape Columbia on April 23. Both his charges and his itinerary raised the eyebrows of many in the exploring community.

"I am rather surprised to see Commander Peary quoting the Eskimos to the effect that Dr. Cook never reached the pole," said Dillon Wallace. "Their whole idea of life is to say what pleases. . . . They are all in awe of Peary and would not like to offend him. They would, for the sake of being agreeable, willingly declare that white snow was black."[6] Dr. Dedrick, however, was not at all surprised, and far more blunt.

"To those who know Mr. Peary best it is not surprising that Mr. Peary might really think in his egotism that his own statement that the Eskimos said Dr. Cook did not get a hundred miles from land must be taken by everybody as a conclusion of the whole matter," said Peary's old foe. "What other man but Peary but would have brought these two important Eskimo witnesses immediately to this country to substantiate the assertions he makes against a rival?

"Mr. Peary's statement that the Eskimos gave him these facts must be judged in the light of the conditions under which the statements were made. . . . To please Mr. Peary, in which art of pleasing the Eskimo is most adept, the

Eskimos, in expectancy of gifts, could easily say or have their remarks twisted to the semblance of saying that Dr. Cook did not get very far toward the pole. Here was a man on the spot with a ship. Dr. Cook was but a memory to the Eskimos.

"Mr. Peary's record breaking trip from the pole must have necessitated his making as high as forty or forty-five miles many days. A further proof of Dr. Cook's claim is not needed when Peary says he returned from the pole in sixteen days. The only wonder is that with all this speed and the incessant haste with which the Roosevelt was rushed back to the telegraph station Mr. Peary had to be nudged up from the New York end of the wire before this could be got out of him."[7]

Many noticed the same thing. The main objection to Dr. Cook's account had suddenly vanished; his sledges' "incredible speed" looked like the progress of a log cart compared with Peary's. Even Herbert Bridgman found this impossible to deny.

"I must admit that the figures in Peary's statement showing the increasing rapidity with which he travelled as he neared the pole itself confirm Dr. Cook's statements that he travelled faster the further north he went," said the secretary of the Peary Arctic Club, "and it would seem also that Peary's figures banish all skepticism as to Dr. Cook's claims in the matter of fast travel.

"I am convinced, however, that when Peary gets back he will be able to prove the error of the belief entertained by Dr. Cook, that he, Cook, reached the actual pole."[8] Bridgman then boarded a train for Sydney in the company of Gilbert Grosvenor and George Kennan, an explorer and lecturer.

As further details emerged about Peary's polar journey, they resulted in more bad press for him. When it became known that his chief assistant, Ross Marvin, had drowned while returning across the arctic pack ice and that Marvin's mother had only learned of it on the evening of September 8, B.S. Osbon took the opportunity to heap scorn on the man who had accused Dr. Cook of unethical conduct. "What does Commander Peary do as soon as he comes into communication with civilization but keep all the wires going to advertise himself to the uttermost parts of the earth regardless of the feelings of everybody else," scoffed Osbon. "He telegraphs to every man in town and then to everybody out of town he can think of. There must have been sheaves of those dispatches about Peary by Peary. . . .

"Could he not have realized that this anxious, aged woman was waiting for news of her son?"[9]

But many had another reaction when they got one of those telegrams announcing Peary's success; their endorsements of Cook began to cool. The National Geographic Society, whose president, Willis Moore, had declared his belief in Cook, now became cautious. Though the society had dispatched an eminent member to Europe to invite Cook to its annual dinner, at which it planned to have President Taft present him and Ernest Shackleton with gold medals, it now decided it would wait for proofs to be presented. The Explorers

Club, which had invited Cook to a banquet for all explorers in connection with the Hudson-Fulton celebrations, now wished it hadn't, since its own president was now calling Cook a liar, and the invitation had caused Herbert Bridgman to resign as chairman of the dinner committee. The Arctic Club alone stuck to its offer and continued to plan a welcoming dinner for the Brooklyn explorer. But now its representatives were careful to say that the dinner was not to be considered an endorsement of his claims.

If Peary's wireless messages had instilled caution in geographical circles as to Cook's honesty, the commander did nothing for his own image when he sent a telegram to the *New York Herald,* which promptly published it:

> Battle Harbor Sept 10
>
> Do not imagine Herald likely be imposed upon by Cook story, but for your information Cook has simply handed the public [a] gold brick. He's not been at the pole April 21, 1908, or any other time. The above statement is made advisedly and at the proper time will be backed by proof.
>
> Peary.[10]

When the *Herald* wired for the particulars of Peary's proof against Cook, he disavowed that he intended his telegram to be published but stood by it nonetheless. Peary then added:

> As regards the details of my evidence in refutation of Cook's story I am sure the Herald and others will acknowledge the force of the situation when I say these details will await a corrected detailed account, with sketch map of Cook's journey, over his signature.
>
> At this distance I have only fragmentary and contradictory information concerning Cook's version of his story, full of self-evident errors of hurried transmission and typesetting.[11]

"If Mr. Peary is in possession of direct evidence, as he claims," the *Herald's* editor caustically replied, "he should produce it at once instead of waiting for the appearance of Dr. Cook's story, with the intention of trying to pick flaws in it.

"If the information he possesses is too fragmentary and contradictory to permit of his controverting Dr. Cook's story, it would have been, to say the least, more dignified to wait until he obtained the correct story before launching his charges."[12]

When the narrative of Peary's expedition was finally printed in three parts in the *New York Times* on September 9, 10 and 11, it bore a remarkable similarity to Cook's report—not only in his incredible speeds, but in his descriptions of the ice and weather conditions and the very Pole itself. Most amazing was that Peary, too, had taken with him no one capable of verifying that he had reached the Pole. He had sent back Captain Bartlett, the last witness who could independently fix his position by a navigational sight, when 133 miles from his goal. Like Cook, he had with him only Eskimos—and Matt Henson. Suddenly, it was one man's word against another.

In Paris *Le Temps* was quick to point out, "Peary now proceeds alone, and whatever suspicion was raised against Dr. Cook is equally applicable to him. Peary's recital up to the present time offers nothing more worthy of credence than Cook's."[13]

"One fact alone is certain," quipped *Le Soleil* as it observed the growing confusion; "it is that Dr. Cook arrived before Commander Peary at the telegraph office. . . . It is difficult to understand why so much noise has been made over the news. Without doubt such a feat is proof of great endurance, but the good it will do to humanity appears almost nil."[14]

Nevertheless, everyone in the exploring establishment understood what was at stake. Captain Frank A. Houghton realized there would be a fight to the finish. "One thing is certain," declared the first master of the *Roosevelt,* "that now one must stand and the other fall, and the one who falls will fall hard. If Commander Peary does not substantiate his charges against Dr. Cook he will be in a bad position. If Dr. Cook is what Commander Peary says he is, he will hardly be able to live in this country."[15]

As she prepared to board the train for Sydney with her children, Jo Peary was not unhappy to escape this storm of charges and countercharges. She was accompanied by the poetess Elsa Barker, an intimate friend of Herbert Bridgman's and the representative of *Hampton's Magazine,* and Henry E. Rood, representing Harper & Brothers, each hoping to secure the rights to the commander's story.

Marie Peary bristled when reporters called her "the Snow Baby" and also resented that her father had instructed her mother to bring the "kids" along. "No kid, no indeed," she fumed; after all, she would be 16 on Sunday. Robert E. Peary, Jr., carrying a big silk flag and his teddy bear, Polaris, marveled to his mother, "Won't it be strange for dad to be home?"[16]

After rushing to Sydney, they spent day after day waiting for the *Roosevelt* to come the 450 miles from Battle Harbour. She was reported coaling; then, being cleaned and painted. Jo Peary just couldn't believe this, remarking impatiently, "The idea of their staying up there to fix up and one here just dying to see them."[17]

The press corps shared Jo's sentiments and decided to do something about it. If Peary wouldn't come to them, they would find a way to reach Peary. They sought any boat that could make the trip. One enterprising journalist even tried to charter the French cruiser *Isly,* which the French captain most indignantly refused.

The first to get away was a group of journalists from the Associated Press aboard the tug *Douglas H. Thomas* on September 12, followed by the Canadian government cable ship *Tyrian* the next day with 17 more reporters, five photographers and a stenographer. The *Thomas* arrived at Battle Harbour in a gale at noon, September 13, after a rough voyage. On board was Henry Rood, bearing a letter to the commander from Jo:

> Sweetheart, Sweetheart after all your privations & sacrifices now when you should be showered with honors & have everything your own way, this miserable creature causes a disturbance which can't help but annoy you & take from you pleasure of your success. I am nearly crazy & have been since Sept 1st when the news first came. If you can only keep still & not discuss this creature until you have had an opportunity to see what he & others have said it would be far better. Oh, to know what is best.[18]

At Battle Harbour, Commander Peary was still keeping Gordon Spraklin, the telegraph operator, busy as never before. Among the wireless messages was one to New York City:

> Personal and Confidential can you meet at Bangor Maine about first next week desire your advice regarding most destructive way of presenting and disseminating my evidence of falsity of Cooks story.[19]

The recipient was General Thomas H. Hubbard. The general was a commanding figure. As one associate recalled: "There was in his appearance a sense of power, of dignity and integrity which inspired universal confidence in his character; . . . tall, erect, with a well-knit figure and splendid bearing, he was always a striking personage in any company."[20]

General Hubbard, who had contributed $20,000 toward Peary's expeditions, had assumed the presidency of the Peary Arctic Club on the death of Morris K. Jesup. His title stemmed from a brevet commission during the Civil War while a member of the 30th Maine Volunteers. He had been a highly respected lawyer representing banking and railroad interests before retiring in 1908 to devote his time to the financial management of similar enterprises, including Western Union. Hubbard also owned the *New York Globe and Commercial Advertiser.* He was a wealthy and influential man, indeed.

His interest in Peary no doubt stemmed from their membership in the Bowdoin College alumni association; they had first met at its 1903 annual meeting. Hubbard always had a soft spot for his alma mater. He had been a trustee of the college since 1889 and in 1903 had donated Hubbard

General Thomas H. Hubbard.

Hall to house the college's library. In its vestibule was carved the inscription "Dedicated to Truth and to Books as the Depositories and Teachers of Truth." The following year the general gave Bowdoin another gift, the Hubbard Grandstand, which also had a motto carved in stone: "Fair Play and May the Best Man Win." He took up this theme in its dedication speech. "Sometimes, let us hope, the best man will be the Bowdoin man," he had said. "But . . . from whatever field they come, may the best man win. No true athlete should wish to win without [fair play]. . . . Victory unfairly won is not success. The worst defeat is to score an unearned record."[21]

Hubbard may have had these words in mind as he wrote to Peary when he first heard of his questioning of Cook's claim. He wanted fair play and left the issue in Peary's hands:

> About the Cook matter—you know the man and know what he probably has in the way of proofs, and you know what you have, and, for these reasons, are the one competent judge as to the treatment the matter should receive. I hesitate to make any suggestions and so merely submit impressions that any outsider may have. . . . His story, of course, must be determined according to the facts. . . . I take for granted that when you come here you will be thoroughly prepared with facts, put in proper form.[22]

Upon receiving Peary's telegram, however, the general seemed to lose his hesitancy about making suggestions and advanced one explaining why Peary's narrative was so like Cook's: Cook had copied it from Peary. "Peary returned to comparative civilization on April 23 and the news of his success was at once disseminated among the Eskimos assembled near the Roosevelt," the general speculated. "Dr. Cook then had from the end of April to the end of August to hear the story and model his after the original. I do not say that he did this, but he could have done so, and this thought no doubt at once struck Commander Peary when he learned that Dr. Cook claimed to have outstripped him in the race for the pole."[23]

There were many who thought Hubbard's idea ridiculous, among them Captain Houghton, who sniffed at the general's remarks: "Those who are familiar with conditions in the arctic will at once see the absurdity of such a theory. As a matter of fact, the Eskimos seemed to have spread the story of Dr. Cook's discovery along the Greenland coasts."[24]

The sort of arguments and points being raised by Bridgman and Hubbard disgusted Cook's friends and reminded them of things they had heard in the past. Now they voiced suspicions of a plot. Dillon Wallace recalled whispers that had been floating in the explorers' clubs for months:

> I have reason to believe a conspiracy has been on foot to discredit Dr. Cook should his polar dash prove successful and that this conspiracy had its birth two years ago, when those who are responsible

for it first heard that he was in the North prepared to attack the pole. The plan of which I speak included, first, the persistent spreading of a rumor that Dr. Cook had not in fact scaled Mount McKinley and that his claim to have done so was willfully false. This was followed by an insidious effort to impress upon the public that he was an imposter. . . .

These slanders first came to my ears in the fall of 1908 *[sic]*, and I took occasion then to denounce their originators. . . .

I was never able to actually trace them to their source, for the man that fathered them was too cunning. . . .

These men were afraid of Cook because they knew well his courage, good judgment, determination, temperamental balance, experience and general ability as an explorer. They gave him full credit—as all the world did—as an authority of high standing upon Arctic and Antarctic exploration until they learned that he was a dangerous rival of Mr. Peary for polar honors. Then they forgot past friendships and, like a thief in the dark, tried to knife him in the back. Can one imagine anything more contemptible than the course they have pursued?[25]

Peary's supporters were equally outraged by charges made by the doctor's advocates. One that especially incensed them was the story of Dr. Norman-Hansen, the Danish doctor who had met Cook after his return to the Danish settlements in Greenland. Dr. Hansen gave a sensational account of Cook's reception at Annoatok:

Peary had given the boatswain a written order, which commenced with the following words:—"This house belongs to Dr. Frederick A. Cook, but Dr. Cook is long ago dead and there is no use to search after him. Therefore I, Commander Robert E. Peary, install my boatswain in this deserted house."

This paper the boatswain, who could neither read nor write, exhibited to Dr. Cook and the latter took a copy of this wonderful document. . . . Dr. Cook gave me a lively account of how . . . Mr. Whitney, during the whole Winter, was treated like a dog by the giant boatswain, and how he had witnessed the sailor calmly bartering Dr. Cook's provisions for fox and bear skins for himself. Dr. Cook also had to put a good face on the unpleasant situation. He had to beg to get into his own house and had to make a compromise with the boatswain with strong fists.[26]

Stories like Hansen's, as well as Peary's own statements, were losing Peary much sympathy, especially in light of the gentlemanly stance of Dr. Cook toward his rival. Peary's supporters chafed at his delay in returning and wondered what could be keeping him in Labrador so long.

The reporters at Battle Harbour found the *Roosevelt*'s crew sworn to secrecy about the expedition, but Peary himself agreed to talk. In the loft of John T. Croucher's whitewashed fish shed, Peary met the correspondents. As he sat on a tool chest and leaned against a roll of netting in the dim light from two small windows, the explorer, dressed in his rough blue woolen shirt, jeans and rubber hip boots, looked powerful and impressive.

The correspondents eagerly asked their questions, but they noticed a certain reticence in Peary's replies. "The answers came slowly and deliberately," one noted, "the explorer weighing his words so that by no slip should he be trapped into any statement that conflicted with the lines he had originally planned."[27]

The commander reiterated that he had proof that Cook had not been to the Pole but continued to withhold its nature. When asked about the conditions at the Pole, he was not very forthcoming, especially to questions whose answers were intended to be compared with Cook's reports. He declined to say whether there was any ocean current there. He refused to state the temperature he observed. He said he had no means to measure the ice thickness. When asked whether he had seen any of Dr. Cook's "purple snows," he replied, "That is a range of information that I do not care to impart now." He shrugged his shoulders when he was asked about the possibility that an unknown continent lay to the west. He did say that there were no animals at the Pole, and no land. When asked why he did not take another trained navigator to verify his position, he replied: "Because after a lifetime of effort I dearly wanted the honor for myself." He firmly denied that he had written any such notice as Norman-Hansen had described, declaring Cook dead at Annoatok.

Although there was not much to be had about the previously inaccessible Pole, the commander was more than willing to expound upon the ease of his success in reaching it. He said it was due partly to favorable head and tail winds, but mostly to the improvements he had made to his sledges, combined with his physical prowess:

> They were improvements similar to those which a yacht builder would develop in a yacht, after he had been building racing craft for ten years. The strain on the dogs was reduced, the sledges were stronger, less liable to breakage, and went over the ice with 20 to 30 per cent less resistance.
>
> You must understand that there is no riding in sledges when you go hunting the pole. . . .
>
> . . . The training consists of good habits, with sound, healthy body as a basis to work on. One must be sound of wind and limb, to use the horseman's phrase, and he must not be a quitter. That's the kind of training that finds the pole.

When the reporters insisted on asking about the other claimant, Peary became excited and irritable. "Is it possible that Cook went and you missed him?" one asked.

"No—hold on; I take that back." The commander leapt to his feet. "Cook says he was there the year before. There are hundreds of routes he could have taken and I not seen him."

"Is it possible, then, that Cook was there first?"

"Don't say Cook. Eliminate names from the discussion."

When Peary was asked for the names of the Eskimos with Cook at Etah, he again leapt to his feet. "My statement covers all I have to say on Cook," he said.

The news conference ended abruptly when a reporter asked how he had felt upon reaching the Pole. Commander Peary rose from his seat. He drew himself up to his full height. His voice was steady and solemn as he turned and faced the questioner.

"Can't you imagine," he said, "how a man feels after spending twenty-three years of the best years of his life, who had given parts of his body, the body God gave him, in accomplishing his ambition, when he attains it?"[28]

The explorer suddenly looked weary and, after promising to meet the reporters again later in the day, disappeared through the hatchway and down the ladder.

After waiting at Sydney for over a week with no indication that the *Roosevelt* was planning to leave Battle Harbour, Herbert Bridgman, pleading urgent business matters, prepared to return to New York. At the railroad station, he was asked about press reports that he was leaving to attend a strategy meeting of the Peary Arctic Club to launch a formal challenge of Cook's claim. The plan was said to include a publicity campaign via the newspapers, a searching inquiry into the details of Cook's climb of Mount McKinley and an expedition to interview Eskimo witnesses.

Bridgman didn't deny it, saying, "There is nothing to be given out on that subject until the scheme has been passed upon by the club."[29] With that he boarded the train. General Hubbard at the same time left Bar Harbor.

Bridgman's first action upon arrival from Sydney was to resign as president of the Brooklyn Institute of Arts and Sciences and to threaten the institute's director, Franklin Hooper. If the institute persisted in its plans to honor Cook, who sat on its executive board, Bridgman warned, it could expect no more dealings with the Peary Arctic Club.[30]

As Peary held court in the fish loft in Battle Harbour, his rival drew ever nearer to his native shores. It had been a pleasant voyage for Dr. Cook. He was relieved to be away from the friendly crush of Copenhagen and out of range of the press's constant questions.

He had time to relax and slept ten hours a day, but when he was up he was not idle. He held talks to entertain the passengers in the saloon, using a map drawn by the ship's engineer to illuminate his journey. In these he revealed the chief reason for his success where all others had failed. "I returned to the primitive life," he said, "in fact became a savage, sacrificed all comforts to the race for the pole."[31] The doctor stood patiently for photographs with almost every one of the ship's passengers. His skin suit was put on display, but he declined all requests to put it on.

By September 15 the *Oscar II* was off Cape Race and again within wireless range. Starting that day, the installments of Cook's polar narrative began to appear in the *Herald,* one every other day.

When the ship was opposite Boston and it looked as if she might make New York on September 20, her wireless operator received several desperate messages from the Arctic Club imploring the captain to slow down so that the plans for Cook's reception would not be upset. Even though this would cost the steamship company $500 to feed the 1,100 passengers an extra day, Captain Hempel decided to lay to off Sandy Hook until dawn.

The press had been clamoring for a reply to Peary's charges ever since it reestablished communications with the liner. By wireless to Boston, Cook issued his statement:

> Why should Peary be allowed to make himself a self-appointed dictator of my affairs? In justice to himself, in justice to the world and to guard the honor of national prestige, he should be compelled to prove his own case; he should publish at once a preliminary narrative, to be compared with mine, and let fair-minded people ponder over the matter, while the final records by which our case may eventually be proved are being prepared.
>
> I know Peary, the explorer. As such he is a hero in arctic annals, and deserves the credit of a long and hard record. To Peary, the explorer, I am still willing to tip my hat, but Peary's unfounded accusations have disclosed another side to his character which will never be forgotten.[32]

The *Oscar II* arrived off Fire Island at 3 P.M. on September 20. When the plan to lay over till morning was announced, some of the passengers were disappointed at the delay, but all took it good-naturedly.

Dr. Cook was home at last, and it was an exciting time to be in New York. A joint celebration for the 300th anniversary of the discovery of the Hudson River by Henry Hudson and the 100th anniversary of the invention of the first practical steamboat by Robert Fulton was about to get under way. A great military parade was slated for Fifth Avenue, and a naval review to be led by reproductions of the *Clermont* and the *Half Moon* had attracted a large international armada to the harbor. Spectacular illuminations with millions of electric lights were planned along the city's streets, and a magnificent court of honor had been erected. Wilbur Wright and Glenn Curtiss were set to dazzle the crowds with daring demonstrations of their rival flying machines. It was even rumored that Wright would risk a flight around the Statue of Liberty from Governors Island. With all this plus a chance to greet the two polar heroes, New York's plate was full indeed, and millions of visitors were set to descend on the city to take part in the festivities.

But Cook cared for none of this. He told others on the ship he simply wanted to see his family and that he was apprehensive about the reception planned for him. "I feel anxious to get ashore," he confided to them. "It seems about ten years since I left, instead of only two and a half, but I dread the ordeal of landing tomorrow. I would much prefer landing quickly and quietly without a repetition of the scenes at Copenhagen. I hope that I shall be left in peace with my family by to-morrow night at least."[33]

He wired to Marie to come out to the ship, but John R. Bradley cabled back that she was not feeling well and would rather wait until dawn. During the night, several tugs bearing the advance guard of the New York press, determined to board the liner, were turned away. The only person allowed aboard was Anthony Fiala, representing Hearst's *American,* who climbed the rope ladder and held a brief conversation with Dr. Cook in the cabin before departing. The doctor asked Fiala about Marie, his children and the arrangements to meet him. When asked in return about Peary's attitude, the doctor laughed, put his hands behind his head in a characteristic thinking attitude and then fell silent.

At half past midnight, the ship proceeded to quarantine, where she arrived at 4 A.M. There she was dressed in flags to greet the reception committee led by Captain B.S. Osbon aboard the *Grand Republic,* which had been chartered by the Arctic Club. The club had offered 2,500 tickets to board the boat but had sold a bare 424. What the purchasers lacked in numbers, however, they would make up for in enthusiasm.

At sunrise Dr. Cook could be seen pacing the deck and peering into the low mist for the first sight of the *John K. Gilkinson,* which was scheduled to bring Marie and the children out to greet him. At that moment the tug was approaching the Danish liner accompanied by scores of smaller craft, including the *New York Herald*'s dispatch boat, *Owlet,* flying flags spelling out, "Welcome Dr. Cook."

When at last he caught sight of the tug, the doctor waved his derby excitedly at the woman on its deck in the light brown cloth suit and black-feathered hat, who fluttered her handkerchief back and called, "Fred, here I am." Turning to Captain Hempel, he said, "I guess I'll go aboard the tugboat right away."

"All right, sir. You are not timid about descending the rope ladder, are you?" the captain asked. Dr. Cook smiled slightly and went over the side as the ship's band struck up "Hail to the Chief." When he was halfway down the companionway, the swell sent the tug crashing into the side of the liner and Cook had to scamper up the ladder to avoid her. Then, in a second attempt, he nimbly let himself down again and leapt the intervening distance to the *Gilkinson.* Dashing up to the hurricane deck, he held out his arms to Marie and without a word enfolded her in them. They embraced for some moments, her husband patting her back. All Marie could manage to say was, "Oh, Fred."

"Where are the children?" he asked.

"Hurrah for my Papa and the Pole!" cried Helen as she came forward with Ruth, holding a parasol made out of an American flag. Their father picked the two girls up and kissed them. Helen he put on his shoulder. As cheers rang out over the water from the passengers on the Danish liner, the explorer was reunited with his brother William and sister Lillian, whom he kissed unreservedly, and her husband, Joe Murphy. Finally, John R. Bradley stepped forward. The two men took each other by both hands and talked quietly for a few moments before the whole party retired to the cabin. The passengers on the *Oscar II* broke out into a chorus of "For He's a Jolly Good Fellow" as she prepared to leave quarantine.

For half an hour the *Gilkinson* lay dead in the water, surrounded by the boats bearing the press, while the doctor visited with his family. Then he emerged from below and went up to the tug's pilothouse, and she puffed away toward the Statue of Liberty.

Off Bedloe's Island she met the *Grand Republic*. The side-wheeler, sirens wailing, was decked out in flags of all nations, her white hull standing out boldly in the gathering morning light. A young woman dressed in a smart mauve outfit leaned over the rail shouting, "Uncle Fred, Uncle Fred!" and he blew a kiss to his niece Lillian. All 423 other passengers of the *Grand Republic* were also gathered along the starboard rail, giving her a distinct list.

As the tug's party was transferred aboard at 9:00 and "The Star-Spangled Banner" rang out across the water, Dr. Cook involuntarily drew back at the sight of the throng that rushed to greet him as he came over the deck rail, as a massive battery of cameras clicked and whirred. He was powerless to resist the excited crowd and was soon hoisted on their shoulders and carried around the deck. Everyone screamed his name and shouted various greetings all at once, so that Cook's protests that there was no reason to make such a fuss could not be heard.

It had been planned that he would pass through an honor guard from the 47th Regiment. After that the doctor was supposed to be met with a wreath of white tea roses, to be placed ceremoniously around his neck by Miss Ida A. Lehmann of Brooklyn, daughter of the secretary of the Dr. Cook Celebration Committee of 100, who had written a greeting speech:

> You hero of the North, come to us, your friends, associates and business acquaintances of your neighborhood, Bushwick. Your record with us was one of honor, character and conscience and your word the synonym of truth. We believed you from the far North and are here to proclaim you a "gentleman of Bushwick."[34]

As it was, the honor guard in their white and blue uniforms were too busy trying to help Captain Osbon keep the guest of honor from being crushed to death to perform their designated function, and Miss Lehmann barely managed to lasso the doctor with the wreath, which itself was soon crushed to lifelessness as he was buffeted around on the deck.

"Git back! Give 'im air!" bellowed Captain Osbon to no avail. The press of people was too great, so it was announced that Dr. Cook would go up to the top deck where there was more room. This set off a dangerous stampede in which, miraculously, no one was trampled. The explorer was there greeted by Bird Coler, the Brooklyn Borough president, who apologized that the mayor of New York had declined to greet him.

Captain Osbon, feeling upstaged, loudly asserted that as the representative of the Arctic Club's president, Admiral Schley, he had something to say and demanded to be heard. When he finally had the attention of the crowd, he stepped forward and said, "How do you do, Doctor Cook?" At such an anticlimax, everyone roared with laughter.[35]

Standing under the Arctic Club's flag, with its white bear on a green field snapping in the wind, Cook read a speech barely audible over the shrieking of ships' whistles in the harbor:

> To a returning explorer there can be no greater pleasure than the appreciation of his own people. Your numbers and cheers make a demonstration that makes me very happy and should fire the pride of all the world. I would have preferred to return first to American shores, but this pleasure was denied me. Instead I came to Denmark and the result has come to you by wire.
>
> I was a stranger in a strange land, but the Danes with one voice rose up with enthusiasm and they have guaranteed to all other nations our conquest of the Pole.

At these words three cheers for the Danes ended any idea of finishing his prepared text, and the rest of the speech appeared only in the newspapers:

> You have come forward in numbers with a voice of appreciation still more forcible. I can only say that I accept this honor with a due appreciation of its importance. I heartily thank you.[36]

After shaking hands with everyone on deck, Dr. Cook retired below with his family.

The reception was set for noon, but it was only 9:30. So the *Grand Republic* spent the time cruising up the North River as far as Spuyten Duyvil to the toot of whistles from every craft in the waterway, while the Squadron A band played "Auld Lang Syne" and "Home, Sweet Home." Since it seemed that most aboard the *Grand Republic* were overcome with joy, Cook's great reserve was all the more evident by comparison. "Dr. Cook neither at this moment nor at any other time during the uproar, . . . gave evidence of being a man of emotion," observed one reporter. "If he is he conceals it absolutely. While bands smashed out stirring marches and the crowd cheered, or later as all the East River let loose with steam whistles . . . Dr. Cook talked on with his wife or with Bird S. Coler, or what not, as if he were waiting for a crosstown horse car."[37]

*The reception committee, New York, September 21, 1909: Captain B.S. Osbon,
Ruth Cook, Fred Cook, Marie Cook.*

The *Grand Republic* docked briefly at 130th Street to let off several hundred who had had enough. She then passed back down the river under the
towers of the Brooklyn, Manhattan and Williamsburg Bridges, the last still
under construction and festooned with workers, who had the best view of all,
hanging from the cables. After one more turn in the river, she docked at
Williamsburg's South Fifth Street wharves below the sugar refineries to a
tremendous cheer from the thousands waiting on shore.

In the shadow of those refineries Fred Cook had felt the bitter sting of
grinding poverty; from those wharves he had swum as a boy, and from beneath those bridges the *Kite* had taken him to Greenland and had set the
young doctor from Brooklyn on the first step along a road that had now led
back again to his old neighborhood and to world acclaim.

As the sidewheeler tied up, even the deck band was drowned out by the
great blast of whistles from every ship in the harbor, including scores of foreign warships assembled for the great naval parade. These, combined with the
deep wail from all the whistles of the sugar refineries along the waterfront,
from whose windows protruded hundreds of heads and whose fire escapes
were dangerously overloaded with humanity, made a shattering din. As he descended the gangway, Cook turned to his wife and was heard to say, "Is this
possible? And this—this is home."[38]

The New York police were out in force, forming a cordon 100 strong around the Cook party. Even so, it took ten minutes to push a path through the crowd on the dock, estimated between 5,000 and 10,000, though it was only 50 feet to their objective. That was an automobile belonging to John W. Webber, founder of the Bushwick Club, the first in a long line assembled for the occasion. Once the Cooks were safely in the car, the parade was set in motion. A huge flatbed truck carrying a brass band led the five-mile procession to the Bushwick Club, as more than 200 auto horns sounded an accompaniment.

Along the route stood 100,000 people, many waving handkerchiefs. In front of the Catholic schools, as hundreds of children pointed their tiny flags and shouted, "Cook! Cook!" the polar hero stood up in the tonneau and bowed deeply. It seemed everyone in the whole borough was in the streets, and in truth no one could have done much else, as the crowds blocked trolley traffic and interrupted all normal business.

Cook acknowledged their plaudits by raising his hat, smiling and bowing. The police accompanying the motorcade did little to discourage the scores of boys who milled around the doctor's car as it made its way through Brooklyn's familiar sights. The houses all along Bedford Avenue were decorated with flags and bunting. The doctor looked long at the milk depot there, with the huge wooden bottle, painted white, on its roof, bearing the inscription "Cook Bros.," where he had worked so many hard hours to put himself through school. All of the milk wagons were lined up along the curb, and a huge sign read, "It takes a milkman to discover the North Pole!"

The triumphal arch in Brooklyn.

As the procession turned the corner, directly opposite his old home on Bushwick Avenue the doctor caught sight of the triumphal arch erected by his neighborhood association over the intersection of Myrtle and Willoughby. Cook looked up almost in disbelief as he drew near the huge canvas and wood-frame structure as high as the El viaduct next to it. Surmounted with laurel wreaths and garlands, it bore a giant golden globe with a flag flying from its top. It dripped with painted icicles and electric lights and was decorated with arctic scenes, shields, more flags, and a portrait of himself, crowned with the words "We Believe in You." Four snow white pigeons were released as the doctor's car passed under the archway.

On Hart Street there was a great surge around the car in front of the Bushwick Club, which was nearly hidden in the folds of the flags that encircled it. The police kept back the crowd, though, and the doctor, looking limp but still bowing, entered the club. He appeared briefly on the building's balcony, but despite cries for a speech he could not be heard and once again simply bowed. As he stood there he remarked to his 93-year-old great-uncle, John Maerach, who said he had come to witness "Fred's triumph" even at a risk to his health, "This is home. These shouts mean everything in the world to me."[39]

After Cook had had an hour's rest and a light lunch, the doors were opened for a public reception in the billiard room. The club officials announced that the doctor could not shake hands with so many wanting to see him, but he occasionally took the hand of a particular friend. He was offered a chair but insisted on standing to greet those who filed past. Most of the 5,000 who did so were orderly, but one man who insistently screamed, "He is not Dr. Cook! He is simply posing as the intrepid discover of the Pole!" had to be dragged away by police, as did several amorous women, one of whom managed to land a kiss square on the doctor's mouth before being restrained.

After three hours the doors of the club were closed, to the disappointment of thousands of people still waiting to get in. Between 4:30 and 6:30 the doctor conferred with John R. Bradley and rested. Bradley wanted Cook to go after Peary, even sue him for slander, and advised him to retain a lawyer. Bradley allowed the press three minutes with the doctor, during which they learned little more than that the Pole was a cold and icy place. The greeting committee and their guest of honor then retired to dinner in the banquet room on the fourth floor, which was festooned with flags and bunting.

There, Mrs. Cook sat with her husband next to the club's president, Louis Berger, at the apex of the U-shaped table. During the meal, a great chorus of voices was heard outside singing Beethoven's "The Lord's Day." The voices were those of the United Singers of Brooklyn, 500 strong, who had come with the Bushwick Club Band to serenade Dr. Cook. At the conclusion of the piece, the doctor went out on the balcony again. He looked out over the huge crowd that stretched a block in each direction along Bushwick Avenue and blocked Hart Street, as the singers launched into "I Greet You." His appearance also set off a chorus of automobile horns and the banging of tin pans.

"For a while he stood there," one reporter recorded, "bowing and smiling that smile that seems to have become more a matter of habit than a sign of pleasure, and then he opened his mouth to speak. The hubbub kept going with even more vigor than before. Then he smiled a real smile as he realized that it was a hopeless task to try to talk to that crowd."[40]

When the mighty chorus had finished "Sweethearts at Home," the officers of the club, by raising their arms, obtained a lull and the doctor declared, "For the honor, the cordiality and kindliness of the welcome, I thank you!"[41] and then returned to dinner. At its conclusion, the explorer addressed his hosts.

"You have shown me that it is good to go to the Pole," he began. "In returning it was a delight to receive the cheers of other nations. But there is no human ecstacy so great as that which comes from the hearts of one's own people.

"If I talked for an hour I could not adequately express a suitable appreciation of this momentous welcome. To feel this cordiality for one moment is to dispel all the discomforts of the Arctic quest."[42]

The doctor then went downstairs to receive the United Singers. Handshaking was forbidden, and all attempts to do so were met by shouts of "Just salute Dr. Cook and pass on!" from the club members. Even this did not intimidate some, who refused to be satisfied with a bow and stood stock-still until Cook drew his hand from behind his back and turned it to over to the mercies of the zealous admirer. As the people filed past, the explorer showed signs of weariness, passing his hands over his face and rubbing his eyes before returning again to the task of smiling.

At 9:30 it was announced that Dr. Cook would be given a rest. The club's officers then whisked him out the side door to an automobile surrounded by motorcycle policemen, which sped away toward the Waldorf-Astoria, where rooms had been reserved by Marie. Once there, the Cook party was quickly ushered in the 33rd Street entrance, and the doctor retired for the night, refusing all callers.

In summing up the dramatic day, the press expressed surprise that despite the huge crowds, only a few women and children had been slightly trampled, and even more amazing, that with more than 200 automobiles on the street at once, there had not been a single accident. Most of all, though, reporters marveled at the center of all this attention:

> His rugged nature, concealed beneath an aspect of constant smiles, seems as nearly unemotional as it is possible to conceive.
>
> Not even when the melodramatic features of the welcome that was prepared for him gripped the nerves of spectators and brought unbidden tears to manly eyes did Dr. Cook appear to be touched. The crowds roared and stamped, whistles blew and horns honked, and several times the doctor was almost swept off his feet, but he showed no sign of great joy or pride. Behind his dancing blue eyes of shallow depth there lies either wonderful power of self-control or an innate insensibility to the ordinary emotions.[43]

That same day at Sydney, the *Roosevelt* finally arrived—but not before another strange delay in Commander Peary's already much-delayed return from the Far North.

All reports had said that she would make port the day before. A holiday had been declared and the whole town had turned out to greet the explorer. A private yacht, the *Sheelah,* had put out to sea with Mrs. Peary and the children. But as the hours dragged by and the *Roosevelt* did not appear, the *Sheelah* returned with Mrs. Peary in tears.

The *Roosevelt* was next reported at St. Paul's Island, 70 miles out of Sydney, cabling messages in the wake of the startling confession of her cabin boy, William Pritchard, who had announced that he had known since April of Cook's North Pole claim.

Peary's backers had pointed with suspicion to the apparent fact that Cook had not told anyone of his great discovery before his arrival in Danish Greenland. Whitney hadn't said anything about it when he was aboard the *Roosevelt,* and Pritchard and Murphy had sworn at Battle Harbour that Cook had never mentioned it, either, though Bo'sun Murphy now admitted that Cook had claimed to have been beyond Peary's "Farthest North" of 1906.

With Pritchard's unexpected revelation, the *World's* correspondent reported: "Speculation is rife over the possibility of a rebellion among certain members of the *Roosevelt* crew who were sworn to silence concerning Dr. Cook." He noted that some of the men were "bearing themselves as men who had been badgered for weeks over that single issue of fact" and also that "there is no doubt of the fact that Peary exercises an almost savage dominance over the members of his expedition. He is a man of tremendous physical energies and said to have a volcanic temper."[44]

On September 21 the *Sheelah* went out again and this time, meeting the *Roosevelt* coming toward the harbor, came alongside and lay to. When his family came on board, Peary received a kiss from Marie and a smart salute from young Robert. He then went to his cabin with Jo and in 20 minutes emerged in so exuberant a mood that he caught Marie about the waist and waltzed her around the deck. The commander ordered Captain Bartlett to run up the "North Pole Flag," a huge American banner with a diagonal white stripe across it bearing the words "NORTH POLE" in foot-high letters. The *Roosevelt* then proceeded to the harbor, where she received a rousing welcome.[45]

Despite Peary's ban on interviews, Matt Henson couldn't resist giving his version of things when surrounded by eager reporters. "[Dr. Cook] ordered [his Eskimos] to say that they had been at the North Pole," Henson declared, then added, "After I had questioned them over and over again they confessed that they had not gone beyond the land ice."[46]

"You people needn't worry about Dr. Cook," Matt sang out confidently. "He's never been to the pole. Commander Peary and I are the only ones that have ever been there except our Eskimo servants. . . .

"It's a joke to talk about Dr. Cook's experience. He never had any experience with sea ice in his life. What the old man said about him in that book just meant that Dr. Cook was a good strong sort of a fellow to work around on land ice. . . .

"The old man has taught me to take observations almost as well as he can. I took a lot of them on our trip to the pole. . . . The commander took me to the pole because I knew latitude and longitude so well and all about sea ice. . . ."

Of Harry Whitney, Henson remarked, "He was only on board our ship about a week. . . . On the 23d [of August] we got to North Star Bay. . . . The *Jeanie* was there waiting for us, and lay alongside until the next day. The Eskimos came out in their kayaks from shore and said a whaling ship had left some letters for us down at Cape York. Then Mr. Whitney said he guessed he'd go on the *Jeanie.* I guess he knew what he was doing all right. He wanted to get away before there was any trouble.

"The next day we got the box of letters at Cape York. That was the 25th. That's when we found out that Dr. Cook said he had been at the North Pole. The captain of the whaler had written a letter to the Commander telling how he met Dr. Cook and Dr. Cook said he had been to the North Pole."[47] At that point a man pushed through the crowd of reporters and took Henson aside. The interview was over.

But even Peary could not contain himself when he heard of the great welcome given Cook earlier in the day, vowing it would not be long before he would "annihilate" Cook's claims to the deed for which he was being honored in New York:

"What I have to say," said Peary with an inflection that was almost a snarl, "will not be very long delayed, you may rest assured on that score. But at the moment I cannot tell to a day when I will be ready to speak.". . .

Meanwhile, Peary declared with that wolfish grimness that translates the tremendous vigor of the man, he will keep his sleeves rolled up, avoid public demonstrations, attend no banquets. He stated this succinctly thus:

"Acting on the advice of Gen. Hubbard and Herbert L. Bridgman, President and Secretary of the Peary Arctic Club, I wish to thank all my friends for kind wishes and invitations, but prefer not to accept any invitations for public receptions or orations until the present controversy is settled by the competent authorities."[48]

When asked whether he had any comment on Pritchard's story, Peary said, "Not the slightest" with a finality "that made some of the interviewers jump," and when asked at what time he had first heard of Cook's claim he began to answer:

"I heard while in Etah that"—His jaws snapped together like a bear trap, and he flung himself back in the chair so that it creaked and rocked. Winking his eyelids and working his jaws for a moment, he said more softly than he had yet spoken:

"I do not wish to say any more yet. Let us waive that."[49]

Peary also answered the question that was on the mind of every Cape Bretoner: why had he taken a Negro instead of the stalwart Newfoundlander, Bob Bartlett, with him to the Pole?

Peary replied that Henson was the most skilled man he had with the sledge but then gave the real reason, which was exactly the one he had given to Dr. Dedrick years before: "I did not feel called upon to share the honors that might occur with any other man. When twenty-three years have been sacrificed to obtain an object one cannot be expected to share the accruing honors with one who had not put in one hundredth part of the work that I have."[50]

In this context, the real difference between Bartlett and Henson was made clear; as he had already assured General Hubbard: "I am the only white man to have ever reached the Pole."[51]

The citizens of Sydney gave the returning explorer as warm a reception as they possibly could. It was marred only by several injuries resulting from the collapse of the veranda of the Sydney Hotel while Peary was speaking to a throng of admirers gathered on it that exceeded its carrying capacity.

The Pearys were pleased at the enthusiasm, but the commander declined to attend the planned dinner, saying he wanted to spend the evening with his family. That night he dispatched Henry Rood with a number of papers to see General Thomas H. Hubbard.

During his first day ashore, Cook managed for the most part to avoid newspapermen, but that could not last for long. He had already issued a short statement concerning the growing controversy between him and Peary to try to stave them off:

> I have not come home to enter into arguments with one man or fifty men, but I am to present a clear record of a piece of work for which I have a right to display a certain amount of pride. When scientists study the detailed observations and the narrative in its consecutive order, I am certain that in due course of events all will be compelled to admit the truth of my statement.
>
> I am perfectly willing to abide by the final verdict on this record by competent judges. That must be the last word in the discussion, and that alone can satisfy me and the public.[52]

But of course that could not be the last word or satisfy the press. The newsmen seemed insatiable for news on the subject, and when they got their chance at a formal interview on September 22, they were well prepared. Some had the help of Peary backers, including skeptical scientists, in framing questions designed to test the doctor's knowledge and attack what they considered flaws in his first report, sent from Lerwick.

Cook appeared at the press conference in the Waldorf-Astoria's second-floor parlor at 4 P.M. He was accompanied by his secretary, Walter Lonsdale, and Ruth, who stayed only a few minutes before climbing down from her father's lap. Sitting comfortably in a chair, legs crossed, his hands thrust into his pockets, the doctor asked, "Well, gentlemen, what can I do for you?"

For the next hour and a half he took each of the 32 correspondents' questions in turn. The reporters noticed his relaxed and conversational tone of voice and his direct gaze. "His replies were, as a rule, given slowly," one observed, "the explorer evidently carefully weighing each word before giving it utterance. Yet there seemed to be no reluctance on his part to meet the questions fairly and fully."[53]

When asked whether he considered Commander Peary his friend, he replied: "I don't know. I always treated him as a friend and until I know more about the situation I shall continue to do the same."[54]

Many questions centered on his ability to take astronomical observations. When asked about his compass course to the Pole, he said, "Well, that changes every day," and referred the questioner to his published map. When asked whether his determination of the Pole's location was based on observations of Polaris taken 12 hours apart, he asked, "How are you going to take an observation by the polar star when you have a continuous sun? There is no night; you cannot have any stars; there is no darkness."

Asked just what observations he did take, he said, "We made regular astronomical observations, such as would be made by the compass and other instruments. We merely made the nautical observations that a captain would have made aboard a ship," but he declined to describe any single observation in detail.

"The astronomers say that in the latitude you mention the midnight sun would have been visible on April 1 and that if you really saw it for the first time on April 7 you must have been 550 miles from the pole instead of 234. . . . What is your explanation of the apparent discrepancy?" asked one skeptic.

"[Up to that time] the northern horizon at midnight had been so obscure that we could not tell whether the sun was below the horizon or above it," Cook calmly replied.[55]

The doctor maintained that he would not be able to produce his full record before two months, since it would take that long "to embody all the loose memoranda into one consecutive record of the trip from the scientific standpoint."[56]

He was asked about the report that the condition of his sled and equipment cast doubt on the possibility that he could have attained the Pole with it. "I do not see what they could expect," he replied. "We came back to Etah with half a sledge. Our sleeping bags had been fed to the dogs. We were ourselves dragging what was left of the sledge and the instruments and records. We had come back to land from the pole with two sledges."[57]

Never did the doctor contradict himself or falter. Only once did he look uncomfortable with a question. When one reporter insisted that because of the curvature of the earth he could not have seen 15 miles to either side of his route, as he had said in Copenhagen, unless he was at an elevation of 150 feet, he replied, "Well, if there is any land up there it is always at a considerable altitude—at least 1,000 feet—and certainly we would have seen any such elevation within a horizon of fifteen miles. We saw none."[58] He then changed the subject.

He lost his patience only once. When the reporters persisted in asking about his relationship with Peary, he straightened himself in his chair and said, "Now, gentlemen, I think you have gone far enough on the Peary matter. I shall refuse to answer any more questions involving Commander Peary. So far as I am concerned, the Peary incident is closed."[59]

Many times he held his interrogators in thrall, especially when he talked of his experiences during the winter at Cape Sparbo and his return to Annoatok. "The circle of listeners was hanging breathless on every word," one awed correspondent reported, "and Dr. Cook was leaning forward, a far-away look in his eyes, and speaking in low tones as though the memory of those days and nights haunted him."[60]

But the most dramatic moment came when someone asked to see the records of his trip. The doctor paused for a moment, then jumped up and excused himself. He returned in a few minutes with a small, well-thumbed notebook, its 173 pages filled with a clutter of minute writing, all in pencil. He showed it freely but would not let it be handled. He turned the leaves over and pointed out the interlineations and corrections but would not allow a word of it to be copied.[61]

The polar notebook shown to reporters at the Waldorf-Astoria.

This book was the first real, tangible thing anyone had seen in support of Cook's statements, and it bore every indication of being what he said it was. He explained that he had three such books, containing 100,000 words describing his dash to the Pole and slow journey back.

Just as in Copenhagen, his manner and openness, rather than his answers, seemed to sway the press, and the little book went a long way toward convincing some who had been doubters of Cook's sincerity. At the end of the interview every reporter asked for the doctor's autograph.

As he prepared to take his leave, Cook told the reporters that he was starving himself so that he could do justice to the dinner planned by the Arctic Club for the next evening, as he had practically forgotten how to eat while in the Arctic. Other than meeting with a few agents and preparing his speech, he said, he would take most of the next day off.

On the evening of September 23 a grand assembly gathered at the Waldorf-Astoria. For the preliminary reception in the Astor Gallery, a plaster bust of the explorer in arctic garb had been installed. Dr. Cook, a half hour late, entered arm in arm with Admiral Schley and shook hands with more than 600 admirers.

The hotel's vast banquet hall was draped in rosettes made of intertwined flags of the United States and Denmark, and over the head table hung the giant burgee of the Bradley Arctic Expedition, the one that Dr. Cook had sketched for Marie in his letter from Gloucester. All 1,185 guests, who had paid from $5 to $30 to attend the Arctic Club's banquet, were dressed in their best formal attire.

The Arctic Club of America's banquet at the Waldorf-Astoria, September 23, 1909.

In the box of honor sat Mrs. Cook, wearing a corsage of roses and a gown of white silk with an overbodice of silver lace and gold lamé, decorated with tiny pearls, gold pellets and mother-of-pearl disks in a stunning Art Nouveau pattern. She was accompanied by Mrs. Schley, wife of the club's president.

Dr. Cook entered the hall to excited applause, and after the strains of "For He's a Jolly Good Fellow" had died away, the crowd settled down to dinner.

During the meal there were numberless toasts to the explorer's health, including one from Count Harald Moltke of Denmark, who said, "I raise my glass to the American conqueror, from whose deeds are derived such benefits that he shall ever be considered a pioneer in the realm of high example." When Bird Coler said Dr. Cook had "invaded the dominions of the north and dragged its king from his icy throne," some wondered whether this was more than a figure of speech.

At 10:00 the doctor was introduced by Admiral Schley. Then, to a great cheer, Cook stood up to speak:

> This is one of the highest honors I ever hope to receive. You represent most of the frigid explorers of Europe and nearly all of the Arctic explorers in America. Your welcome is the explorer's guarantee to the world—coming as it does from fellow workers, from men who know and have gone through the same experience—it is an appreciation and a victory, the highest which could fall to the lot of any returning traveller.
>
> The key to frigid endeavor is subsistence. . . .
>
> . . . With due respect to the complimentary eloquence of the chairman and others, candor compels me to say that the effort of getting to the pole is not one of physical endurance, nor is it fair to call it bravery, but a clear understanding of the needs of the stomach and a knowledge of the limits of the brute force of the motive power, be that man or beast.

Cook next paid homage to his backer, and to shouts of "Three cheers for Bradley!" the man who had financed the great adventure was compelled to stand on a chair and acknowledge the acclaim.

Then the doctor made reference to the controversy raging in the press:

> One of the most remarkable charges brought out is that I did not seek a geographic license to start for the pole. . . .
>
> . . . Now, gentlemen, I appeal to you as explorers and men. Am I bound to appeal to anybody, to any man, to any body of men, for a license to look for the pole?

This rhetorical question brought a resounding chorus of "No!" from the audience:

> Another criticism is the charge of our insufficient equipment. . . . An army of white men, who at best are novices, is a distinct hindrance, while a cumbersome luxury of equipment is fatal to progress. We chose to live a life as simple as that of Adam, and we forced the strands of human endurance to scientific limits. . . .
>
> Now, as to the excitement of the press to force things of their own picking from important records into print—to this I have taken the stand that I have already given tangible account of our journey. It is as complete as the preliminary reports of any previous explorer. . . .

> . . . I cannot sit down without acknowledging to you, and to the living arctic explorers, my debt of gratitude for their valuable assistance. The report of the polar success has come with a sudden force, but in the present enthusiasm we must not forget the fathers of the art of polar travel. There is glory enough for all. There is enough to go to the graves of the dead and to the heads of the living.[62]

After his address, the guest of honor adjourned to the Grand Ballroom, where he shook hands with more than 2,000 supporters. He received the hearty congratulations of many old associates, including Langdon and Charles Dana Gibson, Dr. Dedrick, Captain Houghton, Franklin Hooper and Clarence Wyckoff. The session concluded just after midnight.

"My hand is a little sore but otherwise I never felt better in my life," he told the Arctic Club officials. "It has been a great night and I hardly know how to express my appreciation for the cordial reception which has been given me by my fellow explorers. It is needless to say that the memory of this occasion will ever be cherished."[63]

It seemed by the evening's end that Dr. Cook's oratory had certainly conquered his audience, and it seemed likely that it would soon conquer more, with the announcement of a national lecture tour beginning at Carnegie Hall under the management of William Gray.

The next two days the doctor kept out of the limelight; few got to see him. One who did was Rudolph Franke, who urged Cook to sue Peary over the theft of his furs, but the doctor said he preferred to let the whole matter "blow over." He passed some time enjoying a drive through Central Park, shopping for evening dress and visiting with Dr. Dedrick. But most was spent preparing his lecture and attending to his correspondence.

More than a thousand envelopes and telegrams were piled high in his rooms. Some were from scientists and dignitaries, entrepreneurs and hucksters, but most came from ordinary citizens. They contained congratulations, requests for pictures and autographs, commemorative poems, and at least two lucky pennies of the brand-new Lincoln design.

The thousand would grow to many thousand more, among them letters from the famous and the common alike, from Buffalo Bill to Edwin Andrew:

> My dear Doctor Cook
> I would like to know if you saw Santa-Claus and I would like you to come to 22 Park Ave Danbury Conn and take Edwin Andrew to the North Pole.
> So long.
>> Yours truly
>> Edwin Andrew but you do not know me.[64]

Cook also found time to visit the offices of the *New York Herald,* whose employees gave him an enthusiastic greeting. Ever since Pritchard's admission of what had transpired in Annoatok, at the *Herald,* as everywhere else, re-porters' interest had turned to Harry Whitney. Suddenly, he seemed to hold the key to the great Polar Controversy.

The first word from Whitney came to Cook on September 26 in a telegram sent the day before from Labrador:

> Started for home Roosevelt. Nothing arrived for me. Peary would allow nothing belonging to you on board. Said to leave everything in cache at Etah. Met Capt. Sam, North Star. Did not go back. After going schooner bound at St. Johns. Take steamer home. Hope you well. See you soon. Explain all. Good shooting.
>
> Harry Whitney[65]

When reporters gathered to get his reaction, they noticed the usually calm doctor was considerably agitated. Yet when he spoke about his records that had been left behind, he seemed as confident as ever. "I don't believe they are lost," he said, "or that there will be any trouble in getting them. The only dif-ficulty now is that it is the worst time of the year to send for them. You see, the long arctic night is beginning there . . . but there is no danger of losing them, as I have said—at least I don't think so."

"Suppose you were not able to produce them along with the proofs which are to go to the University of Denmark, do you consider that the scientists might throw out your proofs?" asked one correspondent.

"That is for them alone to say," Cook replied. "The originals that I gave him were blurred, and I took a copy of these and brought it back with me. The duplicates I gave him were not proofs that were all right—that had not been blurred. The originals of these proofs I brought with me. I have them now."

"Your trip toward the pole might be of no avail, then, if you fail to get your instruments?" his questioner persisted.

"Again I must say that that would be for the scientists to determine," Cook maintained.[66]

The day after he got word that his belongings would not be returned to him as expected, Dr. Cook sat down to write a letter to Professor Torp that did not quite agree with his statements as reported in the press:

> New York, September 27, 1909
>
> [Dear Professor Torp:]
>
> When in Copenhagen I told you that I had with me only the worked up observations as published, otherwise I would then have left the papers for immediate examination. I have since received nothing from my cache at Etah. Mr. Whitney, with whom the in-struments and part of the original data were left was unfortunately compelled to return for a part of the way on Mr. Peary's ship. In doing so, he was deliberately forced by Mr. Peary to leave behind everything belonging to me. Thus part of the records and instru-

ments which are now necessary to prove my case are buried among the rocks at Etah. I did bring with me original diaries, the elucidations of which has given the subject matter for the published narrative. Most of the astronomical field notes, however, were contained in a separate book which was left with the instruments. Without the instruments and the entire series of original field notes it seems unwise and impossible to submit for final examination the present report.[67]

He then put the letter aside without sending it and returned to the preparation of his first lecture to be given before an American audience.

While Cook's graphic description of his journey to the North Pole was appearing on alternate days in the *New York Herald,* the paper assigned Roscoe C. Mitchell, one of its reporters, to be Cook's personal agent and to protect its own interests in the doctor. Reporters from other newspapers now began to complain about the interference of such "handlers" whenever Cook appeared to answer their questions. Some also speculated on just how much help the doctor was getting from them in framing his experiences for publication.

Nevertheless, many found the serial account of Dr. Cook's polar adventures irresistible and would eagerly read each article to its conclusion on October 7. Only one installment had appeared before some were predicting the narrative would become "a classic."

The *Washington Post* suggested that there was something additional to be learned in reading between the story's lines:

> Incidentally, the manner of the telling of the story throws a strong light upon the character of the writer. There is little of the mathematical scientist in the teller of this story. . . .
>
> His report is to the people, and he knows the manner in which they want it. A round, well garnished tale, with lights and shadows and a constant appreciation of the dramatic, is to be the result. The man is one of the people, full of red blood, a lover of glory, something of a sensationalist and armed with a large sized ladle and a good story. He promises to work overtime.[68]

It was in this manner of a "report to the people" that Dr. Cook approached his lecture at Carnegie Hall on the evening of September 27, 1909. A big crowd assembled outside the hall even though the parquet seats were going for $5 apiece. Hawkers were selling white placards emblazoned "YOU ARE A LIAR," but none seemed in evidence in the galleries.

Admiral Schley was supposed to introduce the speaker but was unaccountably delayed, so Anthony Fiala stepped forward in his place. "Those who have lived in snow houses may throw hot water," Fiala concluded his remarks to laughter, "but none who knows the doctor would do so." With that, Dr. Cook entered through a small stage door and went straight to the front of the platform and bowed. He received three cheers and a two-minute ovation from the house of 2,500 and a scattering of empty seats, and when he began his speech by announcing that he had reached the North Pole, his next words were once more drowned out by cheers. Then he began again:

> I feel that I have reached the highest pivot of happiness to be able to stand before an American audience and to tell you that on April 21, 1908, I reached the North Pole. The problem with which we had to deal had claimed the energies of the minds of adventurous men for ages. In our campaign was nothing very wonderful.
>
> We used no aeroplanes, no submarines, no motorcycles. We reduced the distance to the simplicity of primitive man. . . . Civilized man does not often descend to the scientific limits of the savage. He will live otherwise as long as he can. We had no other way.[69]

As he had in his *Herald* story, he told of his conception of the voyage of the *Bradley*, of the preparations made during the long night at Annoatok and of his parting with Rudolph Franke. Then, as he would in the coming days in the pages of the *Herald*, he conveyed to his listeners how he set out across Ellesmere Land with the remaining Eskimos on his quest for the top of the world. As he told it, the journey was packed with dramatic detail.

The temperature had fallen to −83° as he crossed over the divide and passed into Bay Fjord, where the long-sought musk oxen were at last secured; now his sledge supplies could be reserved for the polar attempt and caches laid for the return. With well-fed dogs, rapid progress was made up the smooth ice of Eureka and Nansen Sounds to the frowning cliffs of Svartevoeg, the northernmost point of Axel Heiberg Land. From its heights Cook looked out for the first time in his life on the jumbled ice of the polar sea.

There he made a cache and pared down the sledge gear and supplies to the barest essentials, selecting Etukishuk and Ahwelah to accompany him, and the 26 best dogs to pull the two sledges. Each was loaded with 600 pounds of food and gear designed to last three men 80 days. Koolootingwah and Inugito were chosen to help the polar party on its way while the other six Eskimos prepared to return to Greenland.

The five started out over the ice foot toward the northwest on March 18. Once clear of the blocks thrown up on the shore, they found the ice fairly smooth, and camp was pitched on a large floeberg 26 miles out.

The next two days' travel was equally encouraging. The floes were separated by zones of troublesome crushed ice thrown up in pressure lines, but progress remained good, and the ice axe was needed only when a way around them could not be found.

The support party had already stayed for a day longer than planned, and when they departed it was with empty sledges and hungry dogs. They selflessly left all the food to Cook and their two countrymen for the long journey still before them.

By dead reckoning Cook calculated their position as latitude 82°23'N, longitude 95°14'W. Heiberg Land was now only a dull blue haze on the horizon. The Pole lay 460 miles beyond.

The next day Cook estimated they advanced 29 miles in 14 hours. That night utter fatigue and a fierce gale lulled them to sleep in their snug snow house.

In the morning the sky had cleared, and indications of open water to the north could clearly be seen on the horizon. After several hours of travel, they mounted some great ice hummocks and saw before them a tremendous cut several miles wide. Peary had called this "the Big Lead," and it seemed to bar all further progress:

> A thin sheet of yellow ice had already spread over the mysterious deep and a profusion of fantastic frost crystals were arranged in bunches resembling flowers. Through this young ice dark vapors rose like steam through a screen of porous fabrics and fell in feathers of dust along the sparkling shores. Etukishuk went east and I west to examine the lead for a safe crossing. . . .

Ahwelah began a snow house while they were gone.

Though no way across was found, Dr. Cook said he thought the crossing could be made in the morning when the temperature reached its lowest, and they retired for the night:

> The groaning ice and the eagerness to reach the opposite shores kept us awake for a long time. . . .
>
> [In the morning] though the ice was hardly safe it did not seem wise to wait longer, for the western skies were darkening with a wind that might destroy the new ice and compel a halt for a long time.[70]
>
> On snow shoes and with spread legs I led the way. The sleds with light loads followed. . . . In two crossings all our supplies were safely landed on the north shores and from there the lead had a much more picturesque effect. . . .
>
> . . . With the big lead and its many possibilities for troublesome delay behind, a course was set to reach the eighty-fifth parallel on the ninety-seventh meridian. What little movement was noted on the ice had been easterly, and to allow for this drift we aimed to keep a line slightly west of the pole.

A set of observations obtained March 24 showed their position as 83°31'N. The clouds still visible above Grant Land were not the only indications of land. To the west were suggestions of what Cook believed might be Crocker Land, but persistent mist screened the horizon, so he couldn't be sure of it:

The dogs sniffed the air as if scenting game, but after a diligent search one seal blow hole was found and an old bear track, but no algae or other small life was detected in the water of the crevices. At the big lead a few algae were gathered, but here the sea was sterile. . . .

Near midnight, signs of a big blow appeared in the west; a strong igloo was erected:

> We expected a hurricane and had not long to wait to taste of its bitters. . . . In a few moments the dogs and sleds were buried under banks of snow and great drifts encircling the igloo. . . .
>
> Early in the morning, after a rush of but a few hours, the storm ceased as suddenly as it came and left a stillness which was appalling. The dogs soon began to howl desperately. . . . We rushed out. . . .
>
> The storm driven snows had buried and bound them in unyielding frost . . . so much so that few could rise and stretch. . . .
>
> It was too early to start, so we disrobed again, slipped into the bags and sought a quiet slumber.
>
> A few hours later we were rudely awakened by loud explosive noises. Looking about nothing unusual was detected about the igloo and a peep through the eye port gave no cause for the disturbance. It was concluded that the ice was cracking from the sudden change of temperature in quite the usual harmless manner and we turned over to prolong the bag comforts.
>
> Then there came a series of thundering noises, with which the ice quivered. Ahwelah arose and said that the house was breaking. I turned to rise and sank into a newly formed crevasse, which up to that moment was bridged by snow—a man in a bag is a helpless creature—and with water below and tumbling blocks of snow from above pressing one deeper and deeper the case was far from humorous at a temperature of forty-eight below.
>
> Still the boys laughed heartily. Their hands, however, were quickly occupied. Ahwelah grabbed my bag and rolled me over on snow of doubtful security. They then slipped into furs with electric quickness and tossed the things out on safe ice. . . .
>
> A few moments more of sleep and we might all have found a resting place in the chilling deep. That experience kept us ever watchful for the dangers of the spreading ice in all calms after storms. . . .[71]

Now the initial enthusiasm began to wane. "With senses blunted by overwork and benumbed with cold," the doctor said, "we sought the comfort of the bags." More and more, thoughts centered on food and warmth:

The mind, freed of the agitation of frost, wandered to home and better times under these peculiar circumstances; there comes a pleasing sense with the touch of one's own warm skin, while the companionship of the arms and legs, freed of their cumbersome furs, makes a new discovery in the art of getting next to one's self.[72]

But even the most elementary of pleasures was often interrupted without warning.

> I was awakened by falling snow blocks.
>
> Forcing my head out of the ice encased hood, I saw that the dome had been swept away and that we were being buried under a dangerous weight of snow. In some way I had tossed about sufficiently during sleep to keep on top of the accumulating drift, but my companions were out of sight and did not respond to a loud call.
>
> After a little search a blow hole was located, and in response to a louder call came Eskimo shouts. Violent efforts were made to free the bags, but the snow settled on them tighter with each tussle. I was surprised a few moments later as I was digging their breathing place open to feel them burrowing through the snow. They entered the bag without undressing and half emerged with shirt and pants on, but with bare feet. . . .
>
> . . .[After retrieving the rest of our clothes] the dogs were freed of snow entanglements and fed, and a shelter was made in which to melt snow and make tea. A double ration was eaten and then the sleds began to move again. . . .

It was a torturous day, and only a few more miles were covered before camping again at midnight. But with dawn came the pleasure of Cook's first major discovery.

The morning of March 30 was beautifully clear; the mist had vanished and land was seen to the west. "The land as we saw it gave the impression of being two islands, but our observations were insufficient to warrant such an assertion," reported the doctor:

> They may be islands, they may be part of a larger land extending far to the west. What was seen of the most southerly coast extends from 83 deg. 20 min. to 83 deg. 51 min., close to the 102d meridian.
>
> This land has an irregular mountainous sky line, is perhaps eighteen hundred feet high, and resembles in its upper reaches the high lands of Heiberg Island. The lower shore line was at no time visible.

From 84 deg. 23 min. extending to 85 deg. 11 min. close to the 102d meridian, the coast is quite straight. Its upper surface is flat and mostly ice capped, rising in steep cliffs to about twelve hundred feet. The lower surface was so indistinctly seen that we were unable to detect glacial streams or ice walls. Both lands were hopelessly buried under accumulated snows.

Cook named the new discovery Bradley Land. But its sighting was to be the last break in routine for a long time to come, though progress improved

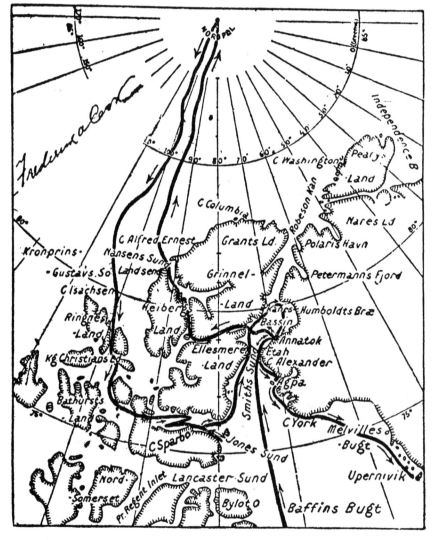

Map, drawn and signed by Frederick A. Cook.

steadily as the fields became larger and thicker and the pressure lines less troubling. Nevertheless, a sense of terrible isolation continued to worsen. "We were alone—all alone in a lifeless world," he said. "Now, as we pushed beyond the habitat of all creatures—ever onward—into the sterile wastes, the sun sets. Beyond was night and hopelessness. With eager eyes we searched the dusky plains of frost, but there was no speck of life to grace the purple run of death."[73] Still they struggled on:

> In spite of what seemed like long marches, we had only advanced 106 miles in nine days. Much of our hard work was lost in circuitous twists around troublesome pressure lines and high, irregular fields of very old ice. The drift ice was throwing us to the east with sufficient force to give us some anxiety, but with eyes closed to danger and hardships the double days of fatigue and glitter quickly followed one another....
>
> ... In dreams heaven was hot, the other place was cold. All nature was false; we seemed to be nearing the chilled flame of a new Hades. In our hard life there was nothing genuinely warm. The congenial appearances were all deception, but death offered only cold comfort. There was no advantage in suicide....

As the midnight sun appeared, they started to travel at night, when the sun was lowest, but the long marches of the past were no longer possible. Even so, by April 11 they had passed the 87th degree of latitude and had the momentary exhilaration of a new "Farthest North." But now, Cook said, he had to decide whether the time had not actually come for turning back, short of the ultimate goal, still 160 miles away.

An inventory of remaining supplies persuaded him to risk it, and he was encouraged by the next few days on the trail, as a new kind of ice was encountered:

> From the eighty-seventh to the eighty-eighth parallel we passed for two days over old ice without pressure lines or hummocks. There was no discernible line of demarcation for the fields, and it was quite impossible to determine if we were on land or sea ice. The barometer indicated no elevation, but the ice had the hard waving surface of glacial ice, with only superficial crevasses. The water obtained from this was not salty, but all of the upper surface of the ice of the polar sea makes similar water. The nautical observations did not seem to indicate a drift, but nevertheless the combined tabulations do not warrant the positive assertion of either land or sea for this area.
>
> This ice gave a cheering prospect; a plain of purple and blue ran in easy undulations to the limits of vision without the usual barriers of uplifted blocks. Over it a direct air line course was possible.

But utter monotony and bone-weariness at last dampened all enthusiasm. "To eat, to sleep, to press one foot ahead of the other, was our steady vocation," Cook told his listeners:

> Words and pictures cannot adequately describe the maddening influence of this sameness of polar glitter, combined with bitter winds, extreme cold and an overworked body. To me there was always the inspiration of anticipation of the outcome of ultimate success, but for my young savage companions it was a torment almost beyond endurance. Their weariness was made evident by a lax use of the whip and an indifferent urging of the dogs. They were, however, brave and faithful to the bitter end, seldom allowing selfish ambitions or uncontrollable passions seriously to interfere with the main effort of the expedition.
>
> But on the morning of April 13 a strain of agitating torment reached the breaking point. . . . Large tears fell from Ahwelah's eyes and piled a little frost of sadness in the blue of his own shadow for several minutes; not a word was uttered, but I knew that each felt that the time had come to free the fetters of human passions. Slowly Ahwelah said: —"Unne Sinig pa—oo ah tonie i o doria." "It is well to die—beyond is impossible.". . . [74]

Not a sound could be heard from the audience as it hung, spellbound, on this desperate and crucial turning point in the story. Cook explained how he urged his two faithful companions to go on by telling them how far they had come and how close the Pole was. Hearing this, they found new courage, and the trek continued.

Only 100 miles now separated them from the goal, but the wind's satanic cut dulled their progress and sapped the men's energy. Too tired to build a snow house, they now turned to the silk tent for shelter. Some things, however, never changed. "It seemed that something must happen," explained Cook, "some line must cross our horizon to mark the important area into which we were pressing," and all three kept a close lookout:

> As we neared the pole the imagination quickened, and a restless, almost hysteric excitement came over us. The boys fancied they saw [bear] and seals, and I had a new land under observation frequently, but with a change in the direction of light or an altered trend in our temperament the horizon cleared and we became eager only to push further into the mystery.
>
> From the eighty-eighth to the eighty-ninth [parallel] the ice was in very large fields and the surface was less irregular, but in other respects it was about the same as below the eighty-seventh. We noticed here also an extension of the range of vision. We seemed to see longer distances and the ice along the horizon had a less angular outline.

The color of the sky and the ice also changed to deeper purple blues. We had no way of checking these impressions by other observations; the eagerness to find something unusual may have fired the imagination, but since the earth is flattened at the pole perhaps a widened horizon should be detected.

On April 19 the three pitched camp on an old floe. Cook described how he stayed up to take observations at noon, as the Eskimos drifted off to sleep. When his calculations placed him just 29 miles short of his ambition, he was so overjoyed, he said, that his excitement awakened Etukishuk. When he told him they would reach the "Big Nail" in two average marches, Etukishuk woke Ahwelah with a kick and the two went out with field glasses to look for it.

Further sleep was impossible, so they hitched up the dogs and set off, but their enthusiasm soon flagged and they camped again, sleeping until after midnight on April 21. This would be the long-looked-forward-to day:

> We were all lifted to the paradise of winners as we stepped over the snows of a destiny for which we had risked life and willingly suffered the torture of an icy hell.
>
> The ice under us seemed almost sacred. When the pedometer registered fourteen and a half miles we camped and calmly went to sleep, feeling that we were turning on the earth's axis.
>
> The observations, however, gave 89 deg. 59 min. 45 sec. We therefore had the pole, or the exact spot where it should be, within sight.
>
> We advanced the fifteen seconds, made supplementary observations, pitched the tent, built a snow igloo and prepared to make ourselves comfortable for a stay long enough for two rounds of observations.
>
> Our position was thus doubly assured and a necessary day of rest was gained. Etukishuk and Ahwelah enjoyed the day in quiet repose. But I slept very little; my goal was reached, the ambition of my life had been fulfilled; how could I sleep away such overwhelming moments of elation? . . .
>
> The sun indicated local noon, but time was a negative problem, for here all meridians meet. With a step it was possible to go from one part of the globe to the opposite side from the hour of midnight to that of midday. Here there is but one day and one night in each year. The latitude was 90 deg., the temperature –38.7, the atmospheric pressure 29.83. North, east and west had vanished. It was south in every direction, but the compass pointing to the magnetic pole was as useful as ever.[75]

The doctor paused, and from the silent audience someone was heard to say in quiet awe, "First at the Pole!" But the doctor did not linger there long. "During the first hour of April 23 backs were turned to the pole and to the sun," he continued. "Our exploring ambition had been thoroughly satisfied. There were few glances backward."

Soon, Cook said, he realized that the winning of the Pole was not the ultimate test; that would be returning to tell about it. The first days passed quickly with fair progress, but with the goal obtained, the terrible strain of the outward journey now crushed down upon them fully.

The explorer explained how he now aimed to the west to counter the observed easterly drift of the ice, hoping to make land somewhere near his starting point. But they drifted east nonetheless, so he steered more westerly still:

> With weary nerves and compass in hand, my lonely march ahead of the sleds was continued. Progress was satisfactory. . . . These hard fought times were days long to be remembered, but only the marks of the pencil now remain to tell the story of a suppressed existence. . . .
>
> The dogs, though still possessing the savage ferocity of the wolf, had taken us into their community. . . . To remind us of their presence frost covered noses were frequently pushed under the bag, and occasionally a cold snout touched our warm skin with a rude awakening. We loved the creatures, however, and admired their superb brute strength. Their adaptability was a frequent topic of conversation. . . . They offered their fur as shelter and bones as head rests to their two footed companions. . . .

The ice became heavier below the 88th parallel, but speed was essential. Some of the dogs had already been fed to their fellows, and the men had hardly enough food left for themselves to get back, even if they experienced no serious delays. But as the days wore on, they were trapped in the tent several times by gales, as precious hours slipped away.

The last observation had placed them on the 84th parallel, but that had been 20 days before. Persistent mist had prevented any further checks. When the sky cleared at last, Cook discovered they had unaccountably drifted to the west. They were far down in the Crown Prince Gustav Sea, "with much open water and impossible small ice as a barrier between us and Heiberg Island," where their caches of food had been placed:

> With the return to Annoatok rendered impossible by the unfortunate westerly drift our only alternative was to go south with the ice. We hoped in this course to find game for food and fuel. The Scottish whalers enter Lancaster Sound and touch at Port Leopold. The distance to this point was shorter than that to Greenland, and by this route I hoped that I could return to Europe during the same year, 1908.

Cook then lined his route through Hassel Sound between the Ringnes Islands, where lifesaving bears were secured, before drifting with the ice into

Norwegian Bay and Wellington Channel. He said they landed on Devon
Island, crossed it and reached Jones
Sound but secured nothing but small
game. Here they released their dogs,
abandoned one sledge and took to
the folding canvas boat:

> Early in September we were
> beset on the shores of Baffin Bay
> with neither food, fuel nor
> ammunition. New implements

*Hauling the sledge to Annoatok,
February 1909.*

> were shaped, and we returned westward to Cape Sparbo to seek a
> place to pitch a winter camp. An underground den was built of
> stones, bones and turf, and with our primitive weapons we fought
> the walrus, the bear, the musk ox and other animals. Thus food,
> fuel and skins were secured and death by famine was averted.
>
> The winter and the night of 1908–1909 were spent preparing
> food and equipment for the return.
>
> On February 18, 1909, we started with a remodelled sled and
> reached our camp at Annoatok in the middle of April. Here I met
> Mr. Harry Whitney and told him of our conquest of the pole.
>
> Because a ship was to come after Mr. Whitney to take him
> direct to home shores, most of my instruments were intrusted to
> his care. Anxious to gain a few months in the return home, I pro-
> ceeded by sled over land and sea southward to Upernavik and from
> there onward to Copenhagen by Danish steamers.[76]

After the explorer finished his lecture and the applause had died away,
members of the audience came up to congratulate him and shake his hand.
But he explained he had to be off, as he was expected as a guest at the Harlem
Casino and at dinner in the Bronx.

Not everyone was so impressed by the doctor's performance. The *Sun*'s reporter remarked, ironically, how far the doctor had come in so short a time—
not from the North Pole to land in just 53 days, but from Huber's Dime
Museum to Carnegie Hall in just 16 years. But he predicted a short run for
the doctor in his appearances on the platform:

> Notwithstanding Dr. Cook's prowess as a pole discoverer it was
> plain that he will never win great fame for his platform delivery
> owing to an unfortunate trick he has of slurring his words together
> and a nervous habit of punctuating his sentences with a dry cough.

Throughout the lecture, lantern slides made from his photographs were
thrown upon a large screen. They were beautifully tinted with delicate hues of

blue, yellow, purple and red. But the *Sun*'s reporter was no more impressed by the doctor's photographic abilities than by his stage delivery:

> Dr. Cook's most interesting picture, the one of his igloo at the pole itself, has been "touched up" so much and in so unintelligent a manner that its value as a record is seriously interfered with. As you face the picture the strong shadows on the roof of the igloo are to your left, showing that the sun must have been at the photographer's right, whereas the sledge and the jutting cakes of snow and ice in the foreground, on the opposite side of the picture cast their shadows in the opposite direction.[77]

Despite all the warm receptions the doctor had received, the question mark put over Cook's story by Peary and his supporters still needed to be dispelled. Suddenly, shadows and other such details, which would ordinarily not have been noticed, were deemed important; everything the doctor did, or had done, was now a subject for the closest scrutiny.

CHAPTER 17

Into the Hall of Bribery

WHEN HE ARRIVED AT BATTLE HARBOUR, HARRY WHITNEY WAS SURPRISED TO find himself the storm center of a polar feud of which he had not the slightest idea, since Peary had never even mentioned to him that he had reached the Pole himself.

As soon as the *Roosevelt* had put in at Etah, Whitney had told Peary of Cook's arrival in April and, complying with the doctor's request, stated that Cook had said he had gone beyond Peary's "Farthest North" of 1906. Peary made no comment but immediately went to his cabin.

The next day Cook's Eskimo companions came to Whitney and asked him what Peary's men were trying to get them to say. Peary's men had shown them papers and maps, they said, but they did not understand these papers.

Previously, they had told Whitney that they had been to the *tigi shu*—the "Big Nail." Whitney stated to the reporters who met him in Newfoundland that he had heard nothing of Cook's Eskimos' retracting their statements or saying they never went out of sight of land, until he reached St. John's. To the best of his knowledge, he said, Cook's two companions never varied their story, though Whitney admitted that Peary's men could have gotten such a retraction without his knowledge.[1]

Since the *Jeanie* was overdue, Whitney explained, he had arranged to go south on the *Roosevelt*. Although Peary forbade him to bring along anything belonging to his rival, he repacked Cook's belongings in his own luggage and had it sent aboard. But before sailing, Peary asked him to give his word of honor that he had nothing of Cook's with him. Whitney then admitted that he had the instruments and flag Cook had used, along with some other effects, and that he planned to take back as a souvenir the little sled Cook had used. But Peary would not allow a single thing of the doctor's on the ship, so Whitney packed Cook's belongings in a gun case and, with the help of Bob Bartlett, buried it under a pile of rocks on the beach at Etah.

These sensational revelations reinforced the popular impression that Peary was a man who had lost all sense of propriety in a fit of jealous rage, his mind having become "unbalanced by egomania and chagrin," as one paper put it. These feelings found expression on editorial pages of many others throughout the country:

Every day or so something new comes to the surface which shows that Dr. Cook well knew the manner of man he was dealing with. . . . The refusal of Peary to let any of Cook's property be brought back on the Roosevelt is another act confirmatory of Cook's good judgment in trusting nothing to Peary's generosity or honorable dealing with a rival.[2]

Why, the public will ask, should Peary not have brought home his rival's notes and instruments? If Cook was "faking" the notes should prove that fact. The inference from the refusal to bring them will be that Peary was afraid to do so. . . .

The evidence on which Peary decided that his rival's claim was fraudulent . . . will now need to be overwhelmingly conclusive to offset in any degree the impression that has been forming of Peary's actions.

Whatever the outcome of the controversy, there is no doubt that as a tactician Dr. Cook has displayed qualities far superior to those of his rival.[3]

The further this most deplorable controversy is carried the worse is Commander Peary made to appear. It is quite clear now that his mood after returning to Etah from the pole and hearing that Dr. Cook had reached the goal ahead of him was—and still is—blind fury, breaking the bounds of good judgment and good taste, indeed, of ordinary discretion.[4]

Straw polls showed Cook ahead of Peary by as much as 35 to 1 for the title of discoverer of the North Pole, and a Yonkers paper offered $5 in gold for the best defense of the doctor's claim. Now, as the Whitney revelations sank in, they brought a new wave of support for Cook from a country already greatly impressed by his gentlemanly restraint in contrast to Peary's surprising outbursts. This led to incredible shows of popular affection wherever the doctor appeared.

On September 29, 10,000 cheering admirers greeted Dr. Cook at the Philadelphia railroad station. A hundred mounted police cleared the way for the automobile that took him to the Bellevue Stratford, where he was met by the mayor and a delegation of scientists. The doctor consented to two press conferences and, with the patience and directness that never failed to impress his hearers, answered many of the same questions he had been asked again and again since his return to America.

At Philadelphia's Academy of Music that night, a capacity audience of 3,000 wildly received the explorer's appearance before its curtain. "From the words of introduction which brought him upon the stage to the last echo of the ovation which broke out at the end of the lecture, Cook held his audience in thrall," one witness reported, "convincing as much by his manner and voice as by the words that he spoke, and gaining for himself the unmistakable stamp of popular approval." Still, some felt that the lecture lacked dramatic effect and that his controversy with Peary had made it desirable that Cook enlarge more on "certain vital points."

His pictures were judged excellent and called forth spontaneous outbursts of applause when flashed on the screen. The cheering began when, after his introduction, he said simply, "I have come here to tell you how, on April 21, 1908, I reached the North Pole." For several minutes he was unable to proceed. Clapping and shouting, the audience "showed beyond the shadow of a doubt that they believed him."[5]

Dr. Cook and the aviator Glenn Curtiss were the special guests at the Hudson-Fulton Banquet on Staten Island on September 30. Governor Charles Evans Hughes paid tribute to their daring in their respective fields, and when Dr. Cook took leave after a brief speech, there was a storm of cheers and cries of "Oh, you Cook!"

While Cook was receiving the acclaim of thousands, Peary had arrived in Maine, where he was given a hearty welcome all down the state. After stopping at Bangor to confer with General Hubbard, Peary moved on to Portland. In his welcoming speech, Governor Bert Fernald assured him that "great deeds are imperishable. A great life as a good example never dies," and President William Dewitt Hyde of Bowdoin proclaimed his journey to the North Pole "a triumph of mind over matter, of will over force."[6]

After this reception, Peary retired to Eagle Island and his self-imposed exile, interrupted by additional conferences at Hubbard's home in Bar Harbor. On a train bound there from Portland, the commander gave a rambling interview in which he issued various criticisms against his rival, which the press dubbed his "fourteen points."

Among them were the Eskimos' story that Cook had not gone out of sight of land, Cook's failure to bring back Peary's record from Cape Thomas Hubbard, his negative opinions of Cook's abilities as a sledger, and various criticisms of Cook's provisions, equipment and his decision to leave his records with Whitney. This last point, he theorized, was a scheme to either lose or destroy them, since he could not conceive how any man could have separated himself from such priceless possessions.

Although obviously contemptuous of Cook's claim, Peary also expressed his contempt for doubters of his own word. "My position is unassailable, because I have the backing of my own conscience," he said. "I do not care who doubts the proof I offer, who turns against me or what question arises, I have the conviction that I did go to the North Pole."[7]

Outside of New York, the press was filled with outrage at Peary's ravings:

> Commander Peary's bombastic bulletins have destroyed confidence in his reputed triumph. The language attributed to him in

various despatches is not that of a trained scientist, nor is it the calm utterance of a disciplined officer of the American Navy.

Only by promptly repudiating those ridiculous messages can Commander Peary hope to regain the confidence that once was reposed in him and which now seems to have been transferred to Dr. Cook, whose statements have been dignified and convincing.[8]

His "fourteen points" interview was too much even for Peary's backers. Henry Rood sent him a telegram that was only a little less than blunt:

You are evidently being misquoted respectfully suggest no further interview until full statement appears wire me here also pleasantville where to meet you day you reach NY.   Rood.[9]

By the end of September, General Hubbard was doing all of the talking publicly. "You may quote Commander Peary as saying that if Cook's belongings had been received on board the Roosevelt Commander Peary would have been blamed if Cook had made any claim that they were not all right,"[10] the general said as Peary stood by, smiling.

Peary reached New York at 7:30 A.M. on October 1, unnoticed by all but some reporters and a few friends who greeted him at Pennsylvania Station. Peary excused himself immediately and went across the street to have breakfast.

Herbert Bridgman thought it would be advantageous, now that he knew the *Bradley* would not participate, for Peary to appear on the bridge of the *Roosevelt* as part of the Hudson-Fulton Celebration's naval parade up the Hudson River. There he would be out of any reporter's reach and yet could display himself to the people and counter some of the publicity Cook's unchallenged lecture tour was garnering him. But even this carefully controlled event went awry when the steering gear on the ship broke two miles below West Point, leaving the *Roosevelt* dead in the water. When it could not be fixed immediately, Peary took a tug to Fishkill, boarded a train for the city and from there took the night express for Portland.

Peary's rival was bound for New England as well. By the time he reached Boston, where he was to lecture that evening in Symphony Hall, Cook, who had seemed shaken when first confronted concerning the telegram from Harry Whitney, once more sounded confident. "I can say that those records are not absolutely important," the doctor declared, when asked again about the papers he had left with the Connecticut sportsman. Would he ever again attempt the Pole? someone asked. "Never again," he said with a smile.[11]

When Cook wired Whitney to meet him at Boston, Whitney wired back that he could not come. By October 4 Whitney was beginning to feel persecuted by the press. As he told the *World*'s reporter, "If only something else will turn up that will make them forget me, I will be happy. I have been dragged into this thing by the neck. If any one will show me a quick way out of it I will take it—provided that way does not lead north again. Hunting Arctic game is great sport, but I've had my fill of it."

Back in Brooklyn the next day, the doctor learned of a proposal to put Peary's records before a board of scientists to be chosen by Ira Remsen, president of the National Academy of Sciences. The panel would be made up of members of the academy, the American Geographical Society, the American Museum of Natural History and the National Geographic Society. Only the National Geographic Society failed to give a tentative assent to the arrangement, but when Peary expressed a willingness to submit his records to such a panel, it reluctantly agreed.

Cook, however, when asked to do the same by the American Geographical Society's representative, repeated that his records would go first to Copenhagen. "The Danish people expressed confidence in me when I landed there, and they gave me their medal of honor. I assured them that they would have my proofs, and they shall have them," he insisted.

"I would like to see the discussion at an end—that is certain, but the way is open before me. I have only one course to pursue. You must remember that other explorers have had their own time to present their proofs. Why should not the same courtesy be given to me? . . .

". . . Anyhow, it makes no difference. I have made up my mind and shall stick to what I have decided to do."[12] Cook then set off for the Brooklyn Academy of Music, where he was received by 2,000 homefolks, who at the sight of him cheered for a full two minutes before he could speak.

Peary had returned to Eagle Island. He said he had important business to attend to there and welcomed the opportunity to catch up on a number of pressing matters. But he still found time to write daily letters to Bridgman and Hubbard about strategies they might consider for discrediting Cook.

He studied Cook's narrative in the *Herald* and sent critiques of various points. He worried endlessly over how best to present his evidence against Cook and suggested that Frank W. Perkins, acting head of the Coast and Geodetic Survey, Willis Moore of the National Geographic Society and friendly representatives of the press, including Henry Rood of *Harper's* and William Reick of the *New York Times,* look over his statement before its release.[13]

Two American Museum of Natural History officials had questioned Matt Henson about Peary's mysterious proof that Cook's story was a fake, and Peary was furious. He cautioned Herbert Bridgman that what they got from Henson must not be allowed to become known: "If Henson's version of the Eskimo narative is kept absolutely quiet until our statement is out there is no harm, but every additional person who becomes familiar with the substance of that statement, increases the chance of either the Herald's or Cook's friends getting hold of it, and their making it public."[14]

Hubbard met privately with officials of the organizations from which men might be selected to rule on Peary's polar records and concluded that the panel should not sit for at least two weeks and that Peary should be consulted as to which scientific bodies' members should be selected.[15]

All this would take time, and General Hubbard was concerned that his ban on Peary's appearances would be a financial hardship for the commander.

But when he offered to lend him some money, Peary demurred. "At present I am not in need of funds," he wrote Hubbard. "Mrs. Peary has lived very simply & quietly during my absence, & saved a little for this very time.

"We are also living inexpensively here now, I would not change places with our friend Cook for twice what he is reported to be gathering in."[16]

Peary did not mention meteorites or AT&T Gold Bonds, but he admitted that even his "inexpensive" lifestyle afforded him the hiring of a photographer, an assistant and two clerical aides, who were helping him "get some of [his] material in shape." Also helping him with his important business at Eagle Island was another houseguest, a young astronomy professor named Hudson Bridge Hastings, whose services he had obtained through the good offices of the president of Bowdoin College. Peary had engaged Hastings to check up the astronomical points in Cook's published statements, but he kept reminders to himself of other, similar matters he wanted to ask the bright young man about:

> —Hastings—
> Read over, modify, & check Cook's time matter. Tables of refraction. Check up midnight sun. Check up methods of keeping course. How near can noon be approximated by sun culmination at time of Marvin & Bartlett Observations. Series of questions.[17]

Although Peary was out of the reach of the press, Cook was always readily available. He was asked if he intended to fulfill his lecture dates in view of the imminent issuance of Peary's indictment against him. "Most assuredly," Cook said emphatically. "I don't see that I am obliged to cancel my lecture engagements until my proofs are passed upon."[18]

His next stop was Washington. On the way he called on Colonel George Harvey, managing director of Harper & Brothers, at his home in Deal Beach, New Jersey. The doctor said it was just a social call, but there were rumors of a contract, in the range of $250,000, for the explorer's forthcoming book.

The colonel told his visitor that he wanted a few magazine articles to counter the Peary propaganda and prepare the way for the book, but unknown to Cook, Harper & Brothers, through Henry Rood, was simultaneously seeking information about the nature of Peary's proofs against him with an eye toward breaching the contract signed in Copenhagen with Clarence McIlvaine.[19]

In Washington Cook was greeted by 8,000 at Union Station. As he was driven to the New Willard Hotel, he acknowledged the cheers of the crowd gathered along Pennsylvania Avenue by standing on the seat of his car and doffing his derby. In the afternoon he was given an informal reception at the National Press Club, and he lectured that evening at the National Theatre, which was filled to capacity.

Peary had many friends in the capital, and one of them, who was in attendance, assured him that Cook's performance had been a disaster. "I doubt if it is physically possible for any man to have successfully achieved the task he claims and to fail so utterly to look and act the part," he reported. ". . . The whole address was in the last degree impersonal; as if indeed the speaker was repeating an old, old story of some one else's accomplishment; and one could almost feel the audience chilling under the narration, which might have concerned a visit to Arlington or Great Falls as readily as a visit to the pole."[20]

The next morning Dr. Cook was honored at an official reception at the District Building. He then took the train to Baltimore.

At that hour, Commander Peary was at the Portland train station awaiting the arrival of General Hubbard from Bar Harbor. When his train came in, the two men walked up and down the platform talking together under the glaring arc lights; occasionally they stopped while Peary emphasized a point. General Hubbard was seen to accept a large white envelope from Peary on which he made a few notes. The general then boarded a train for New York.

Arriving there, he immediately went into conference in his office at 60 Wall Street with the members of the Peary Arctic Club. When the meeting was over, Hubbard announced the club's unanimous decision to issue Peary's report to the newspapers the following week. Reporters pressed the general to reveal its contents, but Hubbard vowed his position was neutral in the matter. "It is not my place to take a part in the controversy other than I have brought back the statement of Commander Peary," the general said. "I am not concerned in anything that Dr. Cook claims, and will not express any opinion. When Commander Peary's statement is issued the people will be able to decide. I do not feel called upon to try to influence public opinion in any way. I think Commander Peary's statement will stand for itself."[21]

By the time he reached Pittsburgh, Dr. Cook had caught cold. At the Duquesne Gardens that night, he received a glowing introduction by the astronomer John A. Brashear, but when he started to speak, he was so hoarse he could hardly be heard. At his first inaudible utterance, there was a mad rush to the front of the auditorium, and it took police 15 minutes to clear the aisles before the lecture could go on.

His appearance in St. Louis caused an even wilder scene. For mile after mile, people stood along the tracks to wave as his train passed the outlying villages and towns. Most of them saw Dr. Cook standing on the platform of the last car under its awning, bowing and lifting his hat. As the train backed into Union Station, the doctor caught sight of a vast crowd, estimated at 15,000, and involuntarily recoiled, saying, "We're in for it here." The crush was tremendous. Nevertheless, he turned aside all suggestions that he seek a side exit, and after asking that some officials look after Mrs. Cook, he plunged into the sea of humanity.

He not only survived the ordeal, but seemed none the worse for it at his lecture that evening. Indeed, his cold seemed better, and although still hoarse, he could be heard plainly. It was rumored that the doctor had been paid $10,000 to come to St. Louis. It is safe to say, if the fervor with which the huge crowd sang the "Star-Spangled Banner" when he appeared was any indication, that none thought the price too high.

In the evening the doctor entrained for Kansas City, leaving Mrs. Cook to recuperate from her experience at Union Station at their St. Louis hotel. At the cavernous Convention Hall, despite its notoriously bad acoustics, the doctor seemed to be over his cold and was clearly audible to the 15,000 who had come to hear him.

As always, reporters were waiting when he reached the Congress Hotel. "How did you get your longitude when you were so near the pole, and how did you overcome the difficulties of determining it so exactly?" one asked.

"That is a question of no importance. Our observations are not exact. Any person who has a chronometer and a sextant and an artificial horizon, and who understands them perfectly, can determine the approximate longitude. Of course it becomes more difficult as one nears the pole, but the difficulty is not hard for one to overcome."

"What about the marked charts that Peary is reported as saying your Eskimos made of your journey? Do you consider them of any importance?"

"Not of the slightest importance. The Eskimos were told to tell no one of our discovery."[22]

The next day Cook, who had returned to St. Louis, rode at the head of the Centennial Week parade in the landau of Adolphus Busch, drawn by four horses and surrounded by mounted police, along a parade route lined by an estimated half-million cheering people. That evening he set out for Cincinnati and another enthusiastic welcome.

There he was greeted by a large and friendly crowd, but the pace was apparently taking its toll, as an astonished group of businessmen at the Chamber of Commerce were to find out:

> The explorer bowed and stepped in front of the rostrum. He held in his fingers a piece of paper about the size of a postage stamp.
>
> "Ladies and gentlemen," he began, and then looked at his paper. "The reception comes from cold-blooded business men," and looked at his paper again. "It pleases me greatly. Thank you."
>
> Then he bowed his way out. When he had gone [Chamber of Commerce] President Roth looked about him and tried to smile, but he couldn't when he saw the faces in front of him.
>
> Some one said, "Well, what do you know about that?" and the meeting adjourned.[23]

In Milwaukee there were more crowds and more questions.

"Did you expect to come back when you started?"

"Oh, yes; otherwise I should not have gone," was the reply.

"Mr. Bradley stated that he looked upon your return as a 100 to 1 shot."

"If I had looked on it that way I should not have gone," repeated Dr. Cook. "No man has any right to take such chances as that."[24]

Then it was off for his remaining stops in Ann Arbor, Detroit, Chicago, Cleveland and Buffalo.

On October 13 the long-awaited proof that the man being celebrated across the country had, in fact, made no such journey as he claimed was issued to all newspapers in a copyrighted story by the Peary Arctic Club. It consisted of a statement signed by Peary expedition members Donald MacMillan, George Borup, Bob Bartlett, Matt Henson and Robert E. Peary.

The statement's preface, written by Herbert L. Bridgman, explained that in order to prevent any accusations of undue influence, no direct questioning of the Eskimos had been done by Peary himself, that Cook's two Eskimos had been questioned separately, yet had told the same story, and that Etukishuk's father, Panikpa, had confirmed that the same story had been told to him by his son.

According to the statement, the Eskimos said that they had proceeded to the tip of Axel Heiberg Land, as Cook had said he had done, that they had camped there for some days and then, with two other Eskimos, had started north over the pack. These two had returned after one day on the ice. Cook and the remaining two Eskimos had camped on the ice for one more day and then turned west, then south, eventually reaching Cape Northwest on the coast of Heiberg Island. The two Eskimos traced their route on a map provided by Peary:

> From [Cape Northwest] they went west across the ice, which was level and covered with snow, offering good going, to a low island, which they had seen from the shore of Heiberg Land at Cape Northwest. On this island they camped for one sleep.
>
> The size and position of this island, as drawn by the first boy, was criticized by the second boy as being too large and too far to the west, the second boy calling the attention of the first to the fact that the position of the island was more nearly in line with the point where they had left Heiberg Land (Cape Northwest) and the channel between Amund Ringnes Land and Ellef Ringnes Land.
>
> This criticism and correction was accepted by the first boy, who started to change the position of the island but was stopped, as Commander Peary had given instructions that no changes or erasures were to be made in the route as drawn by the Eskimos on the chart.[25]

From this point, the statement said, the three had traveled southward along the eastern coast of Amund Ringnes Island. In almost all particulars from this point on, the Eskimos' story, according to the statement, was similar to Cook's account, except that the Eskimos said they did not cross Devon Island to reach Jones Sound and that two small islands were discovered southeast of Ellesmere Land on their trek toward Annoatok in the spring of 1909.

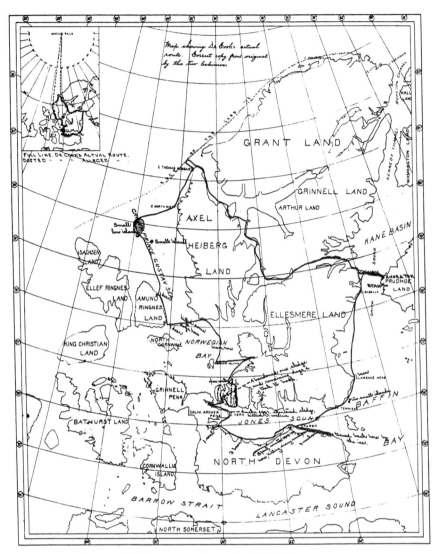

Peary's map showing Cook's route as drawn by the Eskimos.

Reporters confronted Cook with Peary's statement in Cleveland. The correspondents noticed a confident smile flicker momentarily across his face as he read the article. "It is the same old story," said the doctor when he had finished. "I have replied to the points raised a dozen times. I fully expected to see something of the kind. The document looks formidable over so many signatures and will probably appear so to the public. There is, however, nothing in it, as it is based upon the distorted and evasive replies of persons who were told not to give any details."[26]

The proof the Peary Arctic Club presented fell as flat as Dr. Dedrick had predicted it would after Peary's telegram of September 8. Dedrick, after reading the statement, said that of the signatories, only Matt Henson had sufficient knowledge of the Eskimo language to have understood so complex a story. The doctor also pointed out that Sverdrup, who had been over the whole area, could not have missed an island 25 miles long and 17 wide such as the Eskimos described lying so close to Heiberg Land. He also remarked on the story's statement that the Eskimos could not remember how many dogs they had with them. This he pronounced an impossibility, since dogs meant so much to their own survival.

Professor Dyche called the Peary Arctic Club's statement "absolutely incredible." "How unlikely it is," said Dyche, "that [Cook] with more than twenty years Arctic experience, fired with an ambition of a lifetime, would give up just at a time and place when one of the greatest trophies the world has to bestow upon a brave and daring explorer was standing within his reach, beckoning him to come on."[27]

The statement credited to Cook's Eskimos was so anticlimactic that it added to the public's resentment of Peary's behavior. The press outside of New York City gave voice to these feelings. Typical was the reaction of the Rochester *Post-Express:*

> At last Peary has discharged the bomb that was to blow Dr. Cook to pieces and destroy his claim to be the discoverer of the pole. After weeks of preparation, after many dark threats, after denunciation that has been mortifying to all true Americans, after long consultations with his lawyers and other advisors, after studying Dr. Cook's narratives, Peary brings forward his alleged "proofs" that Cook never went beyond land. And what do they consist of? Absolutely nothing except what Peary says the Eskimos said, that is all. And this officer of our navy, who once paid tribute to Dr. Cook's character as a man and a scientist, expects the American people to accept those "proofs" and denounce one of their own scientists a faker, liar and fraud.[28]

Even Commander Peary's friends doubted that the statement would end the matter. "There might be circumstances under which the evidence of these young men would be of greater value," admitted Cyrus Adams of the New York *Sun.* "It is not very likely that . . . their evidence will count for very much in the final settlement of the controversy."[29]

But even before the Eskimo statement had been released, General Hubbard had said that if this document was not enough to destroy Cook's claim, there would be more evidence forthcoming. He now hinted at what form this would take.

A committee of the Explorers Club was considering Cook's Mount McKinley climb, he said. When asked about rumors that he had submitted certain affidavits to the committee, Hubbard said he would have something in a few days.

The editor of General Hubbard's *New York Globe* confidently predicted: "It looks as if we are approaching the exposure of the biggest piece of humbuggery the century has known—an exposure so complete that even the credulous will be convinced."[30] The *Globe* was in a good position to know. In its pressroom the linotype was already being set for the story Hubbard believed would bring on that conviction.

During the days of the doctor's triumphant swing through the Midwest, the New York papers were full of rumors from farther west still. As early as September 5, stories had appeared in the *Sun* recalling the doubts expressed by Herschel Parker of Cook's McKinley ascent, and one, purporting to be an interview with Fred Printz, stated flatly that the doctor and his climbing partner, Ed Barrill, had perpetrated a fraud:

> He evidently sized us up, and taking Barrim *[sic]* ascended an adjoining mountain, a mere foothill in comparison. This mountain was about 10,000 feet high, and photographs were taken of adjoining peaks for the purpose of deceiving the public, but no views were taken in the direction of Mount McKinley. . . .
>
> Barrim told me afterward that Cook offered to give him hush money.

The article quoted Printz as saying that he and Barrill had not contradicted Cook, even when approached by Walter Miller to expose the doctor, hoping that by keeping quiet they would eventually get the money the doctor owed them.[31]

Professor Parker was more circumspect now than in 1906 but still equivocal. "I do not know whether Dr. Cook climbed Mt. McKinley or not," he said.

"A man of science quite naturally asks why he did not make photographs of the other summit of Mt. McKinley, only a short distance away, and of views about him, since he stated that he saw from the top of the mountain the Cook Inlet Mountains 200 miles away, the smoking Iliamna, and Redoubt. These photographs of the approaches to Mt. McKinley summit in themselves would have settled the question. . . .

"I am a friend of Dr. Cook, but in matters of this kind scientific proof is needed. If Dr. Cook has climbed Mt. McKinley then he has made a bad case of it, as the lawyers say."[32]

Parker expressed this opinion on the very day Peary first accused Cook of fraud, September 8; a number of letters written that same day expressing doubts of Cook's Alaskan claims soon began arriving at the office of Herbert L. Bridgman.

The parties supposedly having evidence against the climb were pointed out by J.E. Shore, a U.S. Commissioner in Leavenworth, Washington. He also reported Cook's debts to his packers and his many unpaid bills to others in Alaska as well. Shore advised Bridgman to see Cook's creditors before the doctor could "'fix' his Alaskan 'fences.'"[33]

General Hubbard engaged an old friend and business partner in Washington State, a lawyer by the name of James Ashton, to round up Printz and Barrill and to act on Shore's suggestions. When reporters got wind of it, the general denied he knew anything about Ashton's intentions, and Ashton said that though he had been employed by a New York law firm on behalf of one of the rival polar claimants, he did not know which one. Walter Miller and William Armstrong, who had been with Cook in Alaska, aided Ashton in his endeavors to interview the men pointed out by Shore.

Late in September, one of the letters repeating Alaskan rumors about Cook's McKinley climb was printed in the *New York Times*. It came from a Cornell geologist, Ralph Tarr, who had been on Peary's 1896 expedition. Tarr was aghast that Bridgman would allow any part of his letter to be published, and others in the exploring community were shocked at what even the heavily edited version contained. Caspar Whitney, *Collier's* editor for its *Outdoor America* feature, called Tarr's letter "ridiculous . . . hearsay and second-hand gossip," and decried the trend the controversy was taking in the press:

> No language can be strong enough to condemn these efforts to prejudice the public mind and to blacken the character of Dr. Cook. It may develop that Dr. Cook is a liar, as Commander Peary declares, but he has solemnly affirmed that he did climb to the top of Mount McKinley, that he did reach the North Pole, and his statements are entitled to respect and he to a hearing, before being judged or defamed. Meanwhile, such facts as he has presented are more convincing than the "circumstances" and gossip and fancies which have been brought forward by his detractors to confirm their flimsy "evidence."[34]

By October the rumors about what Barrill was going to do were almost as numerous and varied as the spellings of his name in the newspapers. Whatever his intentions might be, the *Times* pointed out that he was uncharacteristically closed-mouthed about them:

> Barrille is a French-Canadian, and the difficulties the people in these parts had with his name led to various contractions of it, so that it was cut from Barrille to Burrill, and finally to Brill, the name by which he was known to the other members of Dr. Cook's expedition. . . .
>
> Also he has the loquacity of his people, which has resulted in more or less skepticism around here as to the exact value of the

tales he tells. But of late he has developed a reticence not at all in accord with the reputation for talkativeness he had hitherto enjoyed. And his taciturnity goes with a shrewd business sense that seems likely to do him a very good turn before he is through with the present incidents.[35]

The paper reported that Barrill possessed a little red diary that would "forever disprove" Cook's claims at McKinley. A man who had read it, said the *Times,* vouched for its genuineness: "This man says that the book bears on its face the evidence of its authenticity. It shows its age and the usage it has had, and in the manner and matter of its contents gives every reason for belief in its truth."[36]

Ed Barrill. Drawing by Russell Porter, 1906.

However, the *Herald* quoted another man, C.G. Bridgeford, Barrill's partner in the real estate business, who said just the opposite. "Barrille has shown me his diary a score of times," Bridgeford testified, "and I can say positively that his records correspond with Dr. Cook's story to the smallest detail. There is no doubt in my mind that Dr. Cook succeeded in reaching the summit of Mount McKinley. I have heard Barrille tell the story many times and it has always been the same."[37]

Some rumors said that the packer had signed affidavits against Cook, and others that Barrill would testify in the doctor's behalf. The *Herald* even reported that Barrill had defeated a plot to discredit Cook and had fled Seattle to avoid temptations of "every persuasion."

In fact, the doctor had been warned from Tacoma that Barrill could prove troublesome and that Belmore Browne, too, seemed to be positioning himself for self-promotion at the doctor's expense.[38] Cook had already sent a telegram to Barrill asking him to come to New York at once, but he received no reply.[39] Before leaving for the West, in his suite at the Waldorf, Dr. Cook penned a note to his former climbing partner:

> I am very anxious to see you to talk over the past and the future.
> I enclose $200 cash—and if possible would like you to meet me in
> St. Louis on Oct. 6. I will pay all expenses and pay you liberally for
> the time lost. It is important that I should see you. Kindly give no
> press interviews whatsoever.[40]

He also finally acted on John Bradley's advice; he phoned for an appointment with a lawyer.[41]

Though Barrill failed to appear in St. Louis, when Cook returned from the Midwest, he expressed no fear of what his packer might say. In fact, he freely admitted he had sent money to Barrill to have him come to New York, and he hoped Printz would come as well. "I want to have them where everybody can question them and end this talk about my ascent of Mount McKinley," he said.

"It is true that after the expedition was over there was money owing to several persons. I was not responsible for the bills, but the society that had care of the expedition must have overlooked these payments. When my attention was called to the bills I promptly paid them. As in everything else, I invite the closest inquiry in this matter."[42] This invitation was accepted, and how mistaken Cook and the *Herald* were about what Barrill would say was not long in being known.

True, the two packers had been urged to sign affidavits against the doctor, but rather than "steadfastly refusing to yield to their persuasions," as the *Herald* reported, they had already struck a deal. A series of telegrams from James Ashton to General Hubbard outlined how negotiations were progressing:

> Sept. 21, 1909:   Armstrong assisting me. Necessary to assemble men here account their unpaid wages and expenses when members expedition. Understand amounts due run two thousand dollars or more. They unwilling to make affidavits unless paid. Shall I proceed.
>
> Sept. 25, 1909:   Encountering difficulties will report soon as possible.
>
> Sept. 27, 1909:   May be Wednesday or Thursday next. Pushing hard as possible without endangering situation.
>
> Sept. 30, [1909]:   Difficulties account parties increasing claims Make sure protect drafts which will run over amount stated Many interferences causing continuance Wild demands and indecision of parties
>
> October 1, 1909:   Barrille and Printz here with me. Could get nothing definite or competent until today. Stenographers working hard having Barrille's diary transcribed. Have drawn for five thousand covering everything. Impossible do better. Statements show great fake.

On this day, Ashton drew on the Fidelity Trust Company a customer's draft for $5,000 made out to himself and charged it to the account of Thomas H. Hubbard.

Ashton next asked for instructions as to how the affidavits and Barrill's original diary should be transported to New York. He suggested they be carried east by Walter Miller or sent by mail. But Hubbard insisted Ashton carry them to New York personally. He boarded the Burlington Northern *Lake Shore Century* on October 8.[43]

When Peary was informed by Hubbard of the nature and impending arrival of the affidavits, he wrote to the general, impatient to have them published. He hoped they could be ready by Monday, a traditionally slow news day, so that they would get maximum attention.[44] But at the *New York Times,* William Reick, who had also been apprised of the affidavits' content, had a different idea. It was all in the timing, he said.

Dr. Cook had been offered the Freedom of the City of New York, an honor previously extended to only three men—the Marquis de Lafayette, the Prince of Prussia and Charles Dickens—and never to any American citizen. Reick hoped that perfect timing of the release of Barrill's affidavit might cause the withdrawal of such an unprecedented honor. "When the people have a perfectly open mind it is then time to give them serious facts," Reick assured General Hubbard, "and I think by about next week the proper moment will have arrived."[45]

William C. Reick, one of the men Peary had suggested to review the Eskimos' statement before it was published, was described by Peary to General Hubbard as "one of the best newspaper men in New York and my personal friend." Until 1903 Reick had been city editor of the *Herald,* the most powerful position at the paper short of the ultimate power, its owner, James Gordon Bennett. To Bennett's ever-suspicious mind, however, Reick had become too powerful, so Bennett reorganized the paper and kicked Reick upstairs, naming him president of the New York Herald Company. When Reick subsequently resigned in 1907, Bennett couldn't understand why he had left.

Albert Crockett, a *Herald* employee who knew Reick well, suspected the reason, and a chance meeting in Germany with the *Times's* owner, Adolph S. Ochs, who was taking the cure at Carlsbad, only confirmed his suspicions about why Reick had quit. "After my talk with Mr. Ochs," remembered Crockett, "I was convinced that one reason was that Reick aimed at revenge . . . and knowing Reick as I did, I am within reason in saying that the chance to get even weighed quite as heavily with him as any thought of personal gain."[46]

On October 12 the *New York Herald* reported from Missoula, Montana, that a bribe had been offered:

> Edward Barrille, the guide who accompanied Dr. Frederick A. Cook to the top of Mount McKinley, Alaska, in 1906, has been

approached, it is asserted here, with an offer of $5,000 to make an affidavit to the effect that the Brooklyn explorer never completed the ascent.[47]

Fred Printz, however, when contacted at his home in Darby, Montana, seemed to be keeping his options open. Despite the previous statement attributed to him in the *Sun,* he was now quoted as saying, "As far as I am personally concerned, I do not know that Dr. Cook climbed Mount McKinley, but I am certainly willing to accept his word. I made two trips with him and I learned during those times that he was honest and truthful. Barrille is the only man who can say positively that Dr. Cook scaled the peak, and if he signs such an affidavit you can stake your life that he is telling the truth." He then added, "I cannot understand why any statement from us is desired, but every inducement has been offered to us to swear to something which is far from the truth."[48]

The day after the publication of Peary's version of the Eskimo testimony against Dr. Cook, the other shoe fell. The affidavit signed by Barrill appeared in the *New York Globe and Commercial Advertiser,* and it agreed in every particular with the statement attributed to Fred Printz in the *Sun* more than a month before.

When the affidavit proper, with a sketch map of where Barrill said he and Cook had actually gone, was followed on October 15 by a literal transcript of the packer's diary, C.G. Bridgeford's recollection of its contents proved the more accurate. It supported the doctor's description of the climb to the last detail.

Countering this, Barrill said in his affidavit that the entries covering the dates September 9 through 18, 1906—the days Cook claimed he was climbing Mount McKinley—were fictitious and were dictated to him by Cook. The *Herald* scoffed at this idea:

Barrill's diary entry for September 16, 1906.

Frequently the literary guide has taken "his pen in hand" to record that the weather was "ruff," referring doubtless to pressure ridges. He also sees "glasiers" or, again, "glasers." Also possibly in view of the verdict of an interested world he has recorded on more than one occasion, "Think it will be cold to-night. It is getting cold now." Also he further announced that in a moment when Dr.

Cook was "jubilat" they had "a grait time" shaking hands on top. He says that portions referring to the top were dictated by Dr. Cook, although he does not assert that the spelling is that of the Brooklyn explorer. The guide declares that in the diary the pages from September 9-12, *[sic]*, 1906 were dictated by Dr. Cook, who seems, if that be true, to have an adroit method of mimicking the Barrill rhetoric.[49]

Dr. Cook was in Atlantic City the day the Barrill affidavit went to press. That evening reporters handed him a copy of the *Globe* and he read the allegations for the first time.

He skimmed the story twice, showing greater surprise as he went on. After he had finished, he said, "I never even knew that Barrill kept a diary. I never saw it, consequently I could not have asked him to alter anything whatever. The only thing I ever saw him do was to make sketches. Any statement of his that I suggested the changing of dates and altitude is a lie."

"As usual," one of the newsmen noted, "he never once lost his self-control. There was no sign of anger in his expression, and he talked straight into the eyes of his questioners."

"I do not feel that it would be proper for me to make any answer to these charges until I have had a chance to see Barrill," said the doctor, "or until I know something definite of the manner in which the affidavit was secured. I cannot but think that some undue influence must have been brought to bear on him."[50]

The whole thing was so unexpected, Cook said, adding with a smile, "Why, I have not even had a chance to read my own book relating to the ascent of Mount Mckinley. It was published while I was away, and I did not even read the proofs, although I believe Mrs. Cook did go over them."

After Cook had a chance to collect his thoughts, he said in an interview with the Associated Press, "I have always had the most complete confidence in Barrill, and cannot comprehend why he should have sworn to such a story. The fact that Gen. Hubbard is proprietor of the Globe throws a light on the affair which was not previously apparent. I shall see Barrill, I hope, when I reach New York, but I do not know when or where.

"It appears to me that there was money behind his statement. He was perhaps annoyed that he had not been paid his wages, but that was not my fault, and I remedied that matter as soon as I got back from the pole."[51]

Reporters, acting on Cook's suggestion, interviewed General Hubbard about the allegations made by the doctor's supporters as to the statement having been bought. He called such reports "all bosh."

"How about $5,000 being offered to Barrill for an affidavit attacking Dr. Cook? . . ."

"No money was given to him for his signature," the general answered.

"Since the question of the ascent of Mount McKinley was raised recently," continued Hubbard, "I have sought to ascertain the exact facts. For that purpose I commissioned a correspondent in Tacoma to ascertain the truth. He made a thorough investigation and this affidavit and others were obtained. Before the publication I told Barrill that he would surely become a storm centre and that some persons would probably call him a liar, and told him to make sure that everything he said was absolutely true. He told me that the affidavit was correct in every particular."[52]

The *Globe* editorialized on its own revelations:

> Smashed is Dr. Cook by the sworn narrative of Edward N. Barrill. . . .
>
> The similarities between the Mount McKinley hoax and the north pole hoax are readily discernible. In one case as in the other there was a dissipation of the party and a reduction of the number of witnesses. In both there was a careful preparation of a fabricated record. . . . Measurably successful in fooling the world concerning one mental journey, one can understand why the other was projected, and why an objective was selected whose pretended attainment would fructify into a fortune from lecture receipts.
>
> The Mount McKinley revelation means the exit of Cook, the intrepid explorer, and the entry of Cook as one who has chosen a queer road to immortality.[53]

But even the editor of the *New York Times* could not avoid an obvious flaw in the testimony of Ed Barrill:

> It will be at once objected, of course, that if Barrille falsified his diary, "doctored" it at the command of Dr. Cook, as he said he did, then his testimony now cannot be accepted. He may have been persuaded by somebody else, it will be urged, to "doctor" his present story. Allowing all due weight to that objection, the fact remains that this witness to whom Dr. Cook appealed for support in his Mount McKinley story testifies against him, just as the Eskimos to whose testimony he appeals testify against him.[54]

Nevertheless, the affidavit of Edward N. Barrill had a chilling effect on much of the pro-Cook press. After its publication, the coverage of Cook by the *Herald* declined precipitously, so much so that Peary inquired of Bridgman whether James Gordon Bennett had given up on the doctor or, conversely, whether Bennett had left for Denmark to "fix things up" in Copenhagen.[55]

The doctor's support in the public's mind appeared to be as solid as ever, however. When George Kennan wrote an article "proving" by calculation that Cook could not have carried sufficient food for a journey of 88 days on two sledges, he got scores of replies pointing out his fallacies of both arithmetic and logic. He also got a storm of vituperation from the doctor's supporters, who, though they said they admired Cook as a model of gentlemanly behavior toward Peary, were not about to spare Peary themselves. Kennan refused to repeat the worst but gave examples of the abusive tone of his correspondents, who described Peary as "jealous, disappointed, and vindictive"; a man of "narrow vision and a craven heart"; "unworthy of confidence and utterly devoid of the instincts of a gentleman"; "a man whose home-coming brings as much shame as fame to the people of the United States"; an explorer who "went to the Pole like a lady"; a "tom-cat on the back fence"; and "a blackguard and a poltroon."[56]

Mass-produced postcard showing support for Dr. Cook.

Despite Barrill's sensational charges, the aldermen of New York City seemed unmoved. They had determined to go ahead with the ceremony granting their native son the Freedom of the City of New York, which had been scheduled for 2:30 on October 15. Not even General Hubbard's letter to Mayor McClellan asking him to delay the ceremony had had any effect.

When the explorer appeared, 15 minutes late, in formal dress and top hat, he entered City Hall with Brooklyn Borough President Bird Coler and went to the office of the chairman, Patrick F. McGowan. Dr. Cook had received a protest from the Explorers Club saying that he should accept no such honor until its committee had settled the controversy now swirling about his Alaskan claims; he asked McGowan for a postponement.

Along with two-thirds of the aldermen, Dr. Cook's two brothers, his sister, Captain Osbon and Henry Biederbeck, a survivor of the Greely ordeal, had come to witness the ceremony. Two members of Peary's expedition were also there, Donald MacMillan and George Borup, both of whom declined to be interviewed. MacMillan sent a note in to the doctor asking to talk with him, but he did not acknowledge it.

Two minutes of cheers greeted Cook when he entered the Aldermanic Chamber. The first order of business was the presentation of a gold medal, which had not been ready in time for the gala dinner of September 23. On its two-and-one-half-inch diameter was engraved an explorer standing with a flag at the apex of the earth and the date April 21, 1908. As Dr. Stebbins, representing the Arctic Club, handed it to Cook, it fell to the floor and rolled away but was quickly retrieved and put in his hands. Then Alderman McGowan spoke.

"I deem it only fair to Dr. Cook to say that he wanted this action of the Board of Aldermen postponed. . . . The Chair has . . . absolute confidence in Dr. Cook . . . and for that reason a postponement has been refused, although Dr. Cook, with his characteristic manliness, requested that we wait until all proofs are in."[57]

Dr. Cook was then given the mahogany box containing a 15-by-23-inch engrossed sheet of vellum representing the honor being bestowed. On the illuminated scroll were represented his igloo at the Pole and a team of dogs pulling a sledge, with the schooner *John R. Bradley* riding at anchor in the distance. At its top rested the Seal of the City of New York upon two draped American flags. The first initial of Cook's name held the figure of Columbia seated on a throne, holding aloft a laurel wreath about to be placed on the explorer, clad in furs and holding a flag. The inscription on the scroll began, "Whereas the mystery of the ages has been solved. . ." It was signed by the mayor.[58]

As the alderman handed the scroll to Cook, the flash powder in one of the camera trays set afire a huge cloth bag intended to catch the smoke of the flashlight. It blazed up, scorching the picture of George Washington that hung on the east wall. After the commotion this caused quieted down, Cook made a brief speech:

> In trying to thank you for the great honor conferred upon me to-day, I feel how poorly mere words can express my high appreciation. I cannot wish for a greater distinction than the freedom of this great city, the city with which I have grown up and of which I am so proud.
>
> I have attempted many things and perhaps gained a little, but never have I anticipated such an honor as to-day. This is the proudest moment of my life, and to feel that you have confidence in me amidst the unfounded statements and against the false affidavits published during the last few days, creates a feeling of pride in me—worthy pride in the knowledge that my countrymen believe my word. I will substantiate every claim I have made with every proof within the power of man, and believe me, ladies and gentlemen, when I say that this tribute paid me to-day will never be misplaced.[59]

After the ceremony Dr. Cook retired to the Waldorf-Astoria to confer with his lawyer. When he emerged in the evening, reporters were waiting as always. Asked whether he had kept a diary in Alaska, he replied that he had, but that it had been in storage for over two years and he wasn't even sure where it was.

"Do you not think that the production of your own diary of the ascent would go a long way toward refuting these charges that have arisen?"

"No, I do not think so; the book does that, for it contains the complete record. The book is practically a reproduction of the diary, and the record is worked out better than in the diary and contains more than does the diary."

"Doctor, don't you really think that the diary, being the original record of the trip, is better proof than the printed book?"

"No, I don't see that it is."[60]

Cook said he knew nothing about Barrill's being in the city or having testified before the Explorers Club. He then cut the questions short, as he said he must hurry to meet an engagement to act as the honorary starter for the all-day auto race at the Brighton Beach Speedway.

Doubleday, Page could not have agreed with the doctor more about the authority of his book. They immediately ordered a new printing of *To the Top of the Continent.*

When asked, General Hubbard confirmed that Barrill was in New York. Barrill had come to see him, he said, and had assured him that every word in the affidavit was true, but the general disclaimed knowing where he was staying. Frederick Dellenbaugh of the Explorers Club said he knew but could not disclose the address without breaking a confidence.

Barrill had also met with two members of the Explorers Club at the Century Club on October 13. One was Marshall Saville, curator of archaeology at the American Museum, acting president of the Explorers Club and chairman of the committee investigating Cook's Mount McKinley climb. Barrill had told them substantially the same story as would appear in his affidavit the next day. Ed Barrill then left for Missouri without appearing before the full committee to answer questions. According to the two interviewers, General Hubbard had told Barrill that he saw no reason why he needed to be in the city for the next few days; he never returned.

Dr. Cook was next feted by 200 Danes at a dinner in his honor at the Danish-American Society on Pierrepont Street in Brooklyn on October 16. He rose from his seat beneath a huge arrangement of white chrysanthemums labeled "The North Pole. Discovered by Dr. Cook" and bearing the sentiments of his hosts, "We Believe in You," to make a special announcement.

"Now, ladies and gentlemen, there is just one word more I want to say to you. Within the last two or three days things have happened which I could never have believed possible. I have tried to be calm, but I now see that in future my campaign must be changed. My next move will be to cancel all my lecture engagements as far as possible, and I will devote my time to preparing my data to be placed before the University of Copenhagen."[61]

Some thought the doctor looked downcast as he spoke, but his statement delighted the assembled guests. At the end of the evening he was led around the hall, crowned with laurel leaves and followed by the floral pole. He confided to his host that he had come to the decision "suddenly, within the last few hours." The lectures being canceled were estimated to have been worth $104,000 to the doctor.

Next, he disclosed that he had asked Anthony Fiala, Professor Parker and Belmore Browne to go with him to Mount McKinley and recover the records he had left on its summit. Parker and Browne, who were being interviewed by reporters when Cook's request arrived, refused it instantly, saying they would never again risk their lives with such an incompetent leader as Cook. They said that they had decided to return to Alaska themselves, however, and try for the summit by a route from the north and that they considered Mount McKinley a "free peak," in other words, one that had not yet been scaled.

Browne delivered his refusal to Dr. Cook himself. Fiala also declined, saying he had no experience as a mountain climber. Cook then asked Professor L.L. Dyche. He accepted at once and began organizing an expedition to retrieve the records, to leave in the spring of 1910.

When Cook next met the press, his lawyer accompanied him. The doctor's formerly ever-present smile was gone, and he appeared serious. He said that under legal advisement, he would have nothing further to say about Mount McKinley. He then excused himself to prepare for his second western tour, with stops in Toledo, Columbus, Canton, Ann Arbor, Duluth and Minneapolis. Before leaving, however, he said he intended to reply to a summons received from the Explorers Club committee.

Barrill's sudden departure had left the committee with just two relevant witnesses, Belmore Browne and Herschel Parker, who had testified October 15. In light of Barrill's affidavit, they were now far more outspoken than they had been in the past. Under questioning, however, they were unable to state positively that Cook had actually said there would be no further attempts to climb the mountain after Parker left, and they seemed confused about just what equipment had been available to him for another attempt. They emphasized suspicious aspects of Cook's photographs and tried to explain the reasons for their belief that his pictures had not been taken anywhere near "the top of the continent's" highest point.

Cook appeared at the club's room in the twenty-second-floor suite of the Parker-Clark Electric Company at 11 A.M. on October 17, accompanied by his lawyer, H. Wellington Wack, a dignified-looking gentleman with a pince-nez, who always carried a little green bag. Wack suspected that Peary was behind the whole McKinley investigation. He had heard talk that Peary had attempted in vain to obtain the scientific record of Cook's climb from his publishers in 1908, and after all, wasn't he the president of the Explorers Club?

Nevertheless, several old friends and sympathizers of Cook's were among the members of the committee, including Anthony Fiala; Henry C. Walsh, the "historian" of the *Miranda;* and Caspar Whitney, the editor who had pleaded for patience with the doctor's claims until he could produce his proofs. The other members of the committee were Chairman Saville; Walter C. Clark, Parker's business partner; Charles H. Townsend, director of the New York Aquarium; and Frederick S. Dellenbaugh, the secretary of the American Geographical Society and confidant concerning the whereabouts of Edward N. Barrill.

The doctor shook hands with each man and even with Professor Parker, who was also present. The professor belatedly took the opportunity to tell the doctor that he could not accept his invitation to go with an expedition to locate his records.

Wack produced from his green bag a letter that he had planned to send when it looked as if Dr. Cook's prior commitments would preclude his personal appearance and began to read it aloud. It said that his client needed more time to gather his material on the McKinley climb, since the controversy over it was entirely unexpected. The lawyer also asked that any questions for his client be prepared in advance, in writing, so that he could answer them as soon as he returned from his western trip.

Cook and Wack were asked to wait outside while the committee considered these requests. Some of the committee members argued for an immediate statement, that day, and a written reply later. Others saw the lawyer's request as only fair, considering the extraordinary circumstances. Although there were differences about how to proceed, the members seemed concerned to act both fairly and with all due dispatch.

After considerable debate, the committee decided that Dr. Cook should give whatever statement he desired immediately and put whatever else he wanted to say in writing at his leisure. The two men were then summoned from the hall. Addressing Wack, Caspar Whitney said, "I think I express the sense of the Committee when I say we want him to understand that we are not meeting here in an antagonistic spirit. He is a fellow member and he must feel that he is in a position to defend it. . . . If Dr. Cook could say two or three words that would give us any comfort we would be very glad to hear them."

In reply, Cook spoke up. "Now gentlemen I appreciate your good offices, but I have come back here and have been suddenly thrust into a controversy and I have not had time to breathe, have not had time to eat, and it doesn't seem to me that you should expect me to go into any details just at this moment. I have now definitely decided to cancel my lecture contracts at once, just as soon as I can. . . . I want to be reasonable and fair, and I shall try and prepare as much of the data as possible. . . . If there is really anything about the book gentlemen that you would want to have cleared up, I should like to have that put in writing as a request. . . . It would help me a great deal and save a great deal of time in meeting the problem."

At the end of the meeting, Wack expressed his thanks to the committee for its evident fairness and pleaded with its members to keep all of its proceedings in confidence.[62]

As Cook was about to leave, he expressed uncertainty about just what the committee wanted him to produce in support of his claim. Chairman Saville specified his original diary as the best data that he could provide. He also asked that Cook provide any original unpublished photographs in his possession in addition to the negatives of the pictures that had been reproduced in *To the Top of the Continent*. The doctor promised to comply and also agreed to appear before the committee in about one month or as soon as he had finished with his lecture obligations. He then retired to the Waldorf-Astoria and slept for the balance of the afternoon preparatory to his taking the midnight train for Toledo. Before retiring, he directed that the free lecture he had arranged in Hamilton, Montana, Barrill's hometown, also be canceled so that he could turn his attention to his proofs as soon as possible.

It was at this point, when it seemed that his honesty was being denied by all of the witnesses to his claims in Alaska and at the Pole and questioned by people who had once trusted him, that a testament to the doctor's veracity arrived in the form of a letter from Knud Rasmussen. Not only was this totally unexpected, but it appeared in the unlikeliest of places—the pages of the *New York Times.*

In his letter, Rasmussen detailed the story he had heard in interviews with 35 members of the Eskimo tribe to which Cook's companions belonged. Unlike the Peary version, Rasmussen said the story the Eskimos told him supported Cook in every detail. They, too, had traced the route of their tribesmen on a map, which indicated a long journey over the polar pack from the tip of Axel Heiberg Land that did not regain land until it was summer. The Eskimos said that Cook's companions had told them that they were prevented from returning to Heiberg Land by "deep crevices in the ice" and confirmed their southerly journey to Jones Sound. They also supported Cook's account of securing musk oxen there without ammunition and of the torturous journey to Annoatok. Of the spot Cook identified as the Pole, the Dane wrote:

> The Eskimos have told their friends that they were very much surprised when Cook told them the goal was reached, because the spot was not the least different from all the other ice they had passed over. They had often asked Cook to return, but that was only because they had a feeling that they were very, very far from shore and that they would never get back alive again. It is, therefore, apparent that the expedition was not forced back by the hindrance of ice, but because the leader said the goal had been reached.

Rasmussen said his faith in Dr. Cook was unshaken by Peary's charges, which he had read in newspapers that had been delivered to him in Greenland through the date of September 10. "Personally, I want to express my unreserved admiration for Dr. Cook," Rasmussen said in closing. "A man who with his bare hands has passed a Winter at Cape Sparbo, a man who on his feet has taken a walk to Annoatok through deep snow, through twisting ice and utter darkness, that man certainly deserves to have been the first at the pole. His name is Frederick Cook. No one in the world can name him as a swindler."[63]

The *New York Times* had no choice but to print Rasmussen's letter, since he had specifically requested it to do so, though the paper ran several analyses of it that sought to minimize it. Nevertheless, the editor could not but marvel at its contents:

> His letter, written at Julianshaab, Greenland, Sept. 25, reads as if it had been composed with full knowledge of what the Eskimos told Peary, and of the map which accompanied Commander Peary's statement, although the statement and the map were not published

until Oct. 13. The letter reads as though it had been prepared in refutation of the Eskimos testimony and of their map.[64]

Despite Rasmussen's amazing letter, the doubt Barrill's affidavit had placed in many people's minds remained. Still, most maintained that only when Cook's proofs were submitted to a scientific tribunal could the merit of his claims be fairly decided upon.

Peary was dismayed that the testimony of the Eskimos and the sworn affidavit of Edward Barrill had not been the knockout punches to his rival's claims he expected them to be. He could not understand how matters that were so clear to him were still so lost on the general public. "The events of the past six weeks have been a National Disgrace," he raved to Herbert Bridgman.

"An unprincipled adventurer disgracing the name American, has deliberately insulted the Royal family of a friendly nation and placed an ineradicable slight and slur upon their entire people; then, backed and aided and abutted by a gambler, and a yellow paper, has caused this country to make a hysterical fool of itself; and finally has deliberately and intentionally stolen thousands of dollars, by as fraudent a trick as was ever practiced by green goods man or confidence sharp."[65]

Peary had not only failed to dispatch his rival, he now also was beginning to worry about a faithful associate—Matt Henson. Henson had written to Peary asking permission to accept an offer of a series of lectures under the promoter William Brady. "I would also like to have the negatives and the ice pictures specially which you have of mine and would like you to loan me one of the slide maps which you have from last trip," Matt added.

Even though Peary's reply was negative, Henson decided he would accept the proposition anyway. As Henson had said in his postscript to Peary: "I have been with you a good many years on these trips and have never derived any material benefits. I am not getting any younger and it has come to an issue where I have to look out for myself."[66]

Years later, William Brady recalled the genesis of Henson's lecture tour: "I tried to land Cook when he reached Copenhagen on his way back. But he knew all about lecture-tours and had already got himself booked for a tour before he ever started for the Pole. . . . I also tried to land Peary when he turned up with his story and started the public wondering about Cook. But Peary didn't even give me the courtesy of an answer. For third best—and a pretty good third too—I got Mat Henson. . . . He was an intelligent, good looking, soft-spoken, dead-panned, modest fellow who, I was sure, would easily ingratiate himself with audiences. A set-up—but it didn't work.

"I broke him in for his lecture tour at Middletown, Conn. . . . Receipts that afternoon were $13.80. For the evening performance they climbed to $23."[67]

When he came on stage, Henson looked very nervous. He hesitated frequently over his prepared text and often had to be prompted from the wings.

Finally he abandoned his script entirely and just answered questions. Henson showed 70 views of the Far North, one of which he said was "the only photograph of the pole in existence." He had kept some of his pictures from the trip, including those made on the polar journey, and decided to use them when Peary did not accede to his request for pictures.

When Peary had heard from Professor H.C. Bumpus of the American Museum that Henson was planning to show these, he had been extremely anxious to get hold of them. "I should prefer that at present all the photographs and slides of his now in your possession should be sent on to me for examination," he told Bumpus. "It was the distinct understanding of every member of my party who took a camera North, that all of their negatives should be turned over to me. This should have been done with these photographs of Henson's. . . .

"It would be only another perversion of truth and equity, of which there have been so many instances in the present extraordinary state of affairs, to have the photographs taken by a surbordinate member of my party as a result of my permission and forbearance in use * * * before my own."[68]

Peary then fired off several telegrams to Bridgman in not so gentle a tone:

> If Henson, as newspapers say, has pictures of NP. or the sledge journey he has lied to me, and these pictures must on no account be shown by him I doubt the papers. P.[69]

Peary's objections gave Brady the free publicity every promoter dreams of, and he was now confident Henson's lectures would be a success. "Obviously, we needed some big stunt to get Henson out of Peary's shadow and in the limelight on his own," Brady recalled. "Henson himself supplied that with the big argument he got into with Peary about who had exclusive rights to Henson's pictures of the expedition which we used as stereopticon slides—including the crucial shot of Peary, himself, and the three Eskimos at the Pole."[70]

When Henson appeared at the Hippodrome on October 17, Peary sent Herbert Bridgman to get a close look at his "North Pole" picture and to be on the scene to control any damage. The crowd of 500 seemed lost in a house that sat 3,000. Bridgman introduced Henson but didn't think much of his pictures or his talk, though Henson said a few unsettling things. He stated that "[Cook's] Eskimos told us that he had claimed to have been to the pole when we took them aboard our ship at Etah." But he added, "They laughed at it and so did we." Henson also volunteered that before leaving the United States in 1908 he had heard that Cook was planning to fake a trip to the Pole and that he had not climbed Mount McKinley.[71]

After this appearance, Brady decided to cancel the two lectures he had scheduled at Carnegie Hall, since overhead was high and sales very light, and move west. He took Henson to Pittsburgh: "But the farther we went, the heavier the losses were. . . .

Matthew A. Henson.

"As it was, I had to compromise his contract, pay him off and let him drop into undeserved oblivion."[72]

When it was rumored that Henson would challenge Cook to a debate, Peary wrote to Bridgman. "It strikes me that anything of the kind would be unwise for three reasons," Peary told him. "It is likely to make a fool of Henson by giving him pronounced megalomania; it will put him in a position to be tangled up and made to say anything by emissaries of the Herald, and it will introduce into this matter the race issue."[73]

On his tour Henson had already made a number of revealing statements about Peary's journey to the North Pole, among them that Peary had been little more than baggage, having ridden on a sledge much of the way. Furthermore, Henson stated that since he himself had been in the lead, he was actually the first man to reach the Pole. Peary assured General Hubbard that Henson's statements were "all lies" and later complained that "Henson, after my looking after him for years, after giving him a position in the advance party with me on all of the expeditions, and after permitting him to go with me to the Pole this time, . . . has now, for the sake of a few dollars, deliberately and intentionally broken faith with me."[74]

In less than a year, Henson's failure as a lecturer had effectively relegated him to obscurity, but Peary was not one to forget such "disloyalty," even from a man who had been faithful for over two decades. When it came time to distribute the small bonus checks the Peary Arctic Club had voted to all the members of the 1908 expedition, he wanted it made clear to Henson that it was no bribe. "[If] he has any idea whatever that his check was anything especial, . . . I hope you will disabuse him of that idea completely and permanently," he instructed Bridgman. "I would not have him get the idea that I am endeavoring to do anything for him or that I am trying to get solid, or any allied idea for a thousand dollars.

"He has deliberately and premeditatedly deceived me and broken his explicit and thoroughly understood word and promise to me and I am done with him absolutely."[75]

Dr. Cook's own lecture tour was just about to end, too. But upon his arrival at his last scheduled stop in Minneapolis, he found a telegram awaiting him, inquiring if he would still be coming to Montana:

People are anxiously expecting you and ready to give you a cordial welcome despite newspaper reports. Montana congratulates you on being the first to reach the North Pole, please advise early so arrangements can be made.

F.H. Drinkenberg, Mayor of Hamilton.[76]

Even his confidential agent, Roscoe Mitchell, who had been in Hamilton several days, sent a telegram strongly urging him to come, saying there were a thousand people in Hamilton willing to swear Barrill had told them he had climbed McKinley. Once again, the doctor changed his plans and decided he would go to Hamilton after all. As Cook's train sped west toward Montana, Herbert L. Bridgman stood before an audience in Amherst, Massachusetts, and in reference to him said, "It becomes us not to strike a man when he is down, but always speak respectfully of the dead."[77]

Mitchell and Cook's Montana lawyer, General E.D. Weed, had announced in the local newspapers that the doctor would come to Montana to confront his accusers on their home ground. Nevertheless, Mayor Drinkenberg seemed to be right in his estimate of Montana's feelings. At Butte an enthusiastic crowd of 4,000 greeted the explorer's train and he was compelled to shake hands with most of them. Before leaving, he was given a handsome copper plate commemorative of his visit. When the *North Coast Limited* finally pulled into Missoula, it was 11:06 P.M. Even so, a small crowd of enthusiasts was there as well, and the doctor had barely checked into the Savoy Hotel when he was hustled off to the grill room, where his health was toasted voluminously.

The next day Cook addressed the students of Montana State University and then went by automobile the 50 miles into the Bitter Root country to Hamilton. Its streets were crowded with people who wanted to shake his hand; considerable time passed before he was allowed to retire to the Ravalli Hotel, well pleased with his reception.

That evening Dr. Cook was introduced to an audience of 1,200 at the Hamilton Opera House by the town's mayor; he then stepped forward to deliver his now familiar lecture on his polar attainment. During the lecture, the audience's polite attention gave him the confidence to add a special postscript written just for the occasion:

> I have come to your Commonwealth, not to seek revenge, not to enter into a controversy with men in whom I only had every confidence, but to ask for a fair deal. There is no malice in my heart. . . .
>
> My veracity has been attacked by men residing in this community. They have fallen into evil hands, and the temptation was too great. They have sold their birthright for silver, and there probably was more than thirty pieces. . . .
>
> At the time of my arrival in New York . . . there began a warfare to rob me of the glory of an achievement which was, and is rightly, mine. . . .

> When this warfare failed, the enemy began this flank move-
> ment on the climb of Mount McKinley; men with money to burn
> in the flame of infamy entered the arena. Men of this community
> whom I had previously believed honest fell as victims. Their state-
> ments were absolutely untrue. . . .
>
> Your fairness and your faith is a pledge of human nature worth
> more than millions thrown into the hall of bribery. . . .
>
> My records are on the summit of the Alaskan peak, and, accom-
> panied by unbiased, fair-minded men, I pledge you my word that I
> will again reach the top of the mountain and bring back this un-
> questionable proof of the success of my former expedition.[78]

But the doctor had made a grave mistake. His statement was taken as an
opportunity for Colonel Charles M. Crutchfield, Barrill's and Printz's lawyer,
working under the instructions of James Ashton, to rise and call for the two
packers to stand and reply to the doctor's imputations.

When Barrill started to come forward, Cook scolded that he had the
opera house for the night, and if Barrill wished to speak he could hire it tomorrow. This statement caused an uproar, and Dr. Cook retired behind the
scenes as some uncomplimentary remarks were hurled after him. Montana
senator Joseph A. Dixon, who had engineered the confrontation, went back-
stage but was unable to persuade Cook to return. But since there was no back
door, the only way out was through the hooting crowd in the theater.

In the doctor's absence, J.M. Durston, managing editor of the *Anaconda
Standard,* introduced a motion of doubt by all the people of Montana in
everything that Cook claimed. This resolution caused a near riot between the
partisans on the two sides, as there were many Cook supporters in the crowd,
and another lawyer, Roland J. White of San Francisco, stepped forward to defend the doctor.

Deepening the legal debate, a local member of the bar, Mr. McCulloch,
objected to the resolution saying, "If you want to say that Dr. Cook acted in
bad faith in refusing to cross-examine these guides, well and good. If your
resolution, or the impact of it, is that because he has not cross-examined these
men that you do not believe he reached the north pole, I absolutely refuse to
be bound by any such action."

After a half hour of constant demands for the doctor to face Barrill, Cook
resigned himself to this as the only way that he could escape from the theater.
Once he was back on the stage, the crowd quieted to hear the long-awaited
confrontation.

Barrill and Printz were asked to identify themselves and both stood up.
Barrill, for the most part, reiterated the charges made in his affidavit. When
asked by Roland White for whom had he made his affidavit, he said, "the
American people," but for whom, specifically, he wouldn't volunteer. Cries
came for Dr. Cook to question Barrill personally.

The doctor used this opportunity to make one more effort to quell the hostility and put an end to the proceedings. "First let me say there has been a mistake in the statement of my coming here," he began. "When we cancelled all engagements west of Minneapolis, I also cancelled our intention of coming here. I never stated that I was coming here to challenge these men. We cannot be responsible for newspaper reports. Again I must say to you, as I told the Mayor, I came here at his invitation to tell the story of our polar campaign. Now, I see nothing to be gained by a discussion of the problem to-night. We climbed Mount McKinley."

"How far did you go?" someone called out.

"I have left the record at the top of Mount McKinley," the doctor answered. "I have already said we will organize an expedition to go to the top of Mount McKinley to get these records. We will invite some one opposed to me to join the expedition to see fair play. When I say this to you, ladies and gentlemen, there is nothing further to be said on the problem, and I cannot see that any resolution that you may pass to-night can possibly change that one way or the other."

But the audience would not be pacified. They called for Barrill to speak. Barrill asked Cook exactly where he put the records on the top of Mount McKinley. The doctor began, "You deliberately and falsely—"

Barrill cut him off with "You're another."

"Your statement is untrue," retorted the doctor.

Now came shouts for Cook to make his own affidavit. He called for pen and paper and calmly wrote out a statement that he and Barrill had climbed the mountain and stood at its summit on September 16, 1906. When he had finished, he said, "I have stated, and I have written it out, made an affidavit, that we have been to the top of Mount McKinley. After I have said that, the evening is at an end, and I do not care to stay any longer."

There were more catcalls, and Senator Dixon rebuked the doctor, saying that he would stay till morning if it were his reputation at stake. The evening was decidedly not at an end.

Barrill repeated the key part of his affidavit, that they had climbed only a small point of rock and that Cook proclaimed he would publish it as if they had scaled the great mountain. Barrill estimated this point as having a height of 8,000 feet. He added that only two months after his return he had told several men, including his family doctor, that Cook's story was false.

Barrill said he had gotten five or six letters from Cook since their return from Alaska. The last one, which he had recently received, contained two $100 bills, he said. He also attested that before Cook had left on his polar trip, he had written from Labrador, "For God's sake, keep still, and when I come home I will bring you a chunk of the pole."

He had gone to New York, said Barrill, but did not see the doctor. When asked if he had seen representatives of the Peary Arctic Club instead, Barrill professed that he would not have known it if he had.

Cook denied having written such a letter from Labrador and countered that Barrill had written to him trying to get money for Printz; that was the money he had sent when he had asked his packer to come to New York at his expense, he said.

From the audience, Printz protested when the doctor said the packer had been paid in full—$500 since his return. Barrill insisted that he had the letter he referred to that promised him "a chunk of the pole," but Cook again denied writing it. Barrill added that he had received the $200 to visit Cook in New York but that he had not gone.

Cook then turned to Printz and said, "I want to ask Mr. Printz if he made an affidavit concerning the facts in this matter—you made it in Missoula."

"They prepared an affidavit and asked me to sign it," Printz replied.

"Did you make an affidavit and ask $1,000 for it?" asked Cook.

"He said he would give $1,000 for it—he would have given $1,000 for it quick enough if I had taken it," responded the packer.

Cook then recounted an Associated Press report that Printz had asked for a bribe of $1,000. He said that Printz had also asked Roscoe Mitchell, his representative, for a bribe and that Printz had written a letter asking for $350 to come to New York to deny the story Barrill had told. Printz denied all this. But when Cook insisted that Printz had written him such a letter, Printz asked why he should make such a request when he could get $1,000 and stay home.[79]

From that point on there was more heat but scarcely more light. Then a resolution affirming the county's faith in the two Montana packers was put to a vote. It passed, and the meeting broke up.

"After the meeting," a local correspondent observed, "Dr. Cook, who did not allow himself to become ruffled or excited in the least during the affair, but bore himself as a calm and perfect gentleman throughout, went to the Ravalli Hotel and chatted until a late hour with a big crowd that gathered there to hear him talk about his experiences in the North. . . .

"When seen by a reporter after the meeting Dr. Cook said he did not care to discuss the result of the meeting at present. He evidenced no special concern about it and did not appear in the least downhearted or grieved over what had happened."[80]

Press accounts of the lively evening in the opera house were an embarrassment to Mayor Drinkenberg, who said that the citizens of Hamilton were not nearly so unruly as the reports seemed to indicate and that the affair was all Cook's fault, anyway.

When details of the Montana meeting reached New York, the subject of the letter promising Barrill "a chunk of the pole" was pursued with General Hubbard. When asked whether such a letter was in his possession, the general replied: "I will not say that I have any such letter as Barrill speaks of. I don't want to talk about the matter now. I will say that I have more ammunition in this Mount McKinley affair, but as to letters—not a word."[81] In fact, the general did not have such a letter, but he wanted it very much and had Barrill searching for it.[82]

The reports of the melee in Montana pleased General Hubbard immensely. "I should say that Barrill got considerably the better of Dr. Cook," he told the press. "It appears that the people of Hamilton gave a vote of confidence to Barrill at that meeting. That shows the sort of impression Cook made as to his truthfulness."[83] The general directed Ashton to get the stenographic record made by the *Anaconda Standard,* every word of it, for future reference.

At Helena the next day, the doctor received a much different reception than he had gotten in Hamilton. Montana governor Edwin L. Norris introduced him at the Harnois Theater with words that emphasized a desire for justice and fair play. The Helena Civic Club presented him with its own resolution, expressing "not only our confidence in him and the results of his work, but even more, our admiration for the manner in which he has conducted himself under exceedingly trying circumstances."[84]

Despite departing on this positive note, when he returned from the West, friends noticed the strain the trip and the confrontation with Barrill had placed on the doctor. His lawyer agreed that it had been a mistake to go to Hamilton and advised him that he should waste no more time before getting his records together for the University of Copenhagen. H. Wellington Wack suggested that he go to the country without notifying anyone so that he could get a few days of total peace before beginning. After a consideration of various options, they settled on the Hotel Gramatan in Bronxville.

The last day of October the newspapers reported that the National Geographic Society was asking Peary to come to Washington to present additional data. The society's president, Willis Moore, was careful to point out that the society was in no way dissatisfied with the material Peary had already forwarded to them but that several things had been left out "by inadvertence." But there was more than inadvertence behind the inadequacy of what Peary had forwarded and more than met the eye about the society's offer to take up Peary's proofs and relieve the other scientific bodies of this responsibility.

The original plan had been to let the National Academy of Sciences settle the validity of the rival claims. But when Bridgman and Hubbard attempted to influence the composition of the committee, President Remsen wavered, fearing the academy was becoming involved in an increasingly partisan and bitter dispute.[85]

Having failed to stack the committee, the Peary Arctic Club was more than happy to have the National Geographic Society step into the breach. Gilbert Grosvenor was a tried and true friend of Peary's, and his power over the society's affairs was now nearly absolute.

In March 1907 Grosvenor had written to Peary, informing him that he was the recipient of $1,000 to be put toward his North Pole Expedition—the very first subscription ever made from the society's own funds. He had apologized it couldn't have been more and expressed his every confidence that Peary would succeed this time.[86]

Grosvenor publicly professed the society's neutrality, but as early as October 5, 1909, he had sought to reassure Peary that although the society's magazine had printed Cook's report from Lerwick, he did so only because he felt he had no choice:

> I have held our Oct number for 3 weeks hoping your statement would be out and that it would be unnecessary to mention anything except your work and the achievements of your splendid associates. But we could not wait longer and as we all believed that we could help you most by treating both you & Cook alike until the facts were published, the resolution already sent you by Prof Moore, was passed by the Board. . . . We feel for you and Mrs. Peary in such a trying experience, but the end is very near; greater honors and reward than you would otherwise have experienced I am confident, will be showered upon you presently, from every quarter of the globe.[87]

Before anyone had examined Peary's evidence, on October 12 Grosvenor sent him a telegram to make arrangements for his first lecture on his polar conquest:

> National Geographic Society has been anxiously waiting your appointment of date for your address. Will give you a tremendous welcome.[88]

The baldness of this indiscretion took even Peary by surprise, but the next day he was happy to accept by wire nonetheless:

> Pardon inadvertence. Was under impression everything off under existing circumstances. Delighted come to Washington. Will fix date after conferring General Hubbard. Illustrations under way now. Regards.[89]

Though Peary had steadfastly repeated Hubbard's edict that he would accept no offers for lectures until the matter between the two claimants was settled, in light of Grosvenor's telegram he told General Hubbard he could see no harm in making an exception—under certain additional circumstances: "If the Geographic Society desires a lecture in the near future and are prepared to emphasize, by the presence of the officers of that Society on the platform, by suitable introduction, and by the distinguished and official character of the audience which they will gather for the lecture, their belief in the status of my work, such lecture might have its value."[90]

With this commitment in hand, once the National Academy of Sciences had bowed out, the society immediately appointed a three-member subcommittee to consider the merits of Peary's polar claim on October 15.

Even so, Peary was very cautious about what he would offer the society as proof of his discovery of the Pole. The commander was adamant that Cook could not possibly have original celestial observations, and he insisted that until Cook filed his data with some reputable scientific body he would allow no one to see his own original records.[91] He instructed his lawyer, Charles Nichols, to inform President Moore and Gilbert Grosvenor that they were not to publish the fact that he would not allow his observations out of his hands until Cook turned his over. He also told Nichols to tell the society that not only would he not be sending his original records, but that he could not appear, either, saying, "I will ask you also to emphasize the fact of the impossibility just at present of my coming to Washington in person, on account of the work here demanding my constant supervision."[92]

What he sent the society with his transmittal letter was a condensed summary of his dash to the Pole, a report on the expedition, three certificates by Marvin and Bartlett showing that they had reached certain latitudes, and one by himself indicating his arrival at the North Pole, along with a profile of soundings made on the trip.

But President Moore's request for "more information" and another by one of the subcommittee members, asking him to send the instruments he had used on the trip, made Peary see that he now had no choice but to appear in person with his original data. But he wanted no emphasis laid on the instruments because of the furor over his having ordered Cook's instruments buried at Etah. He also wanted his visit to the society to be as unpublicized as possible. He asked his lawyer to make the arrangements with one of the subcommittee members:

> Write Mr. Gannett in regard to the matter of making no pronounced point of the instruments, for reasons indicated in my last letter to you.
>
> Mr. Gannett speaks of the Committee meeting me at [Hubbard] Memorial Hall. You might also suggest for Mr. Gannett's consideration whether a meeting at my hotel might not be less conspicuous and less likely to attract the attention of newspaper men.
>
> Of course I am entirely at the service of the Committee, but it seems to me that if I go quietly to a hotel without registering and instruct the office to keep my presence quiet, and then the members of the Committee drop in quietly and come directly to my room, it might be generally advantageous.[93]

Commander Peary arrived in Washington on November 1 and telephoned from Pennsylvania Station. He visited the society's rooms on 16th Street briefly, and then, with Rear Admiral Colby M. Chester, went to the admiral's residence, where the other members of the subcommittee, Henry Gannett and Otto H. Tittman, awaited him. Willis Moore and Gilbert Grosvenor were also present as observers.

The meeting was brief. Immediately after it adjourned, Moore announced that Commander Peary had been invited to speak before the society, leaving little doubt as to what the subcommittee had decided. Peary left the city on the midnight train for New York.

When the National Geographic Society's board of managers met two days later, it confirmed the expected verdict by issuing the formal report of its subcommittee to the press:

> The sub-committee to which was referred the task of examining the records of Commander Peary in evidence of his having reached the north pole beg to report that they have completed their task.
>
> Commander Peary has submitted to this sub-committee his original journal and records of observations, together with all of his instruments and apparatus and certain of the most important of the scientific results of his expedition. These have been carefully examined by your sub-committee, and they are unanimously of the opinion that Commander Peary reached the north pole April 6, 1909.
>
> They also feel warranted in stating that the organization, planning, and management of the expedition, its complete success, and the scientific results reflect the greatest credit on the ability of Commander Robert E. Peary and render him worthy of the highest honors that the National Geographic Society can bestow upon him.[94]

In the evening, President Moore elaborated on the report. The proofs submitted by Peary and examined by the subcommittee were absolutely conclusive, Moore said. Even though there were friends of Dr. Cook on the committee, he maintained, the data were examined on their merits, "and every member of the committee was convinced that no loophole for error had been made. Not only did the committee see the several notebooks on which the Commander had jotted his observations and memoranda, but the instruments with which he made his observations were closely scrutinized by the scientists."[95]

The notebooks, Moore said, made a complete and consecutive scientific account of the trip to the Pole. He emphasized that Commander Peary's presence in Washington was only for the purpose of allowing him to explain abbreviated statements in his notes, for filling in the narrative and for clearing up details not sufficiently clear from the notes. Moore also announced that the same subcommittee had been asked to look into the claims of "other explorers" to settle the question of whether anyone had reached the Pole before April 1909. The subcommittee had been authorized to examine the "proofs" of such explorers "no matter where they are to be found," he added.

To this end, Willis Moore wired the University of Copenhagen requesting that members of the National Geographic Society be present at the examination of Cook's data. Next, a society delegation went to the Department of

State and closeted with Assistant Secretary Huntington Wilson. There were rumors that the delegation's mission was to have the department put diplomatic pressure on Denmark to release Cook's data upon receipt. Whatever the intentions, it was all very hush-hush. When reporters appeared on the scene, several members of the delegation denied who they were.

The secretary expressed willingness to give the society's members letters of introduction, as he would to any private citizen, but since the National Geographic Society was in no sense a government agency, the department, he said, could not intervene on its behalf with a foreign government.

In Maine Peary issued a statement saying that he was "deeply gratified" by the society's decision to vote him a special gold medal. His gratification took on tangible form almost immediately, with the announcement that he had settled a substantial deal for the publication of the personal narrative of his expedition and had signed a contract at the reported rate of $1.20 a word for the first rights to his serialized story; the total gain to Peary was rumored to be $200,000.

Just after the announcement of the findings of the society's subcommittee, James Ashton, who was about to leave Washington to tie up some loose ends in the Hamilton affair, received a request from Henry Gannett for an audience. Ashton kept General Hubbard fully informed:

> New Willard
> Washington
>
> Novr
> 4/09
>
> My Dear General
> . . . Prof Henry Gannett has been very anxious & I have met him at his request, Admiral Chester & the other gentleman & several times with Prof Gannett as he has been keen on my explaining all details to him.
>
> I enclose copies of 2 telegrams sent Barrill by me in response to his of 25 Oct (copy of which you have)
>
> The detailed report of the Hamilton Proceedings (in the Times) show these 2 telegrams had the desired effect.
>
> The Reporters & particularly the Herald Reps. have bothered me considerably here but have accomplished nothing to comfort things strangely enough your statements are all corroborated by mine.
>
> In a reasonably short time I think Barrill should state that he will go to McKinley for nothing but his expenses with any official Expd^n to demonstrate the truth, the Expd^n to pay his services only after he has so demonstrated. I suggested this to Gannett & he agrees. In view of Conditions I consider the Labrador letter is now in best shape possible. The affidavits to follow in due time.
>
> This research Committee of the National Geographical Society is a far-reaching affair if properly handled.

Get them to Parent the Expedition in the Spring. Have them send 1 or more Reps to Copenhagen at the proper time. Gannett & I have discussed these features & I feel sure they will help wonderfully.

I believe Admiral Chester can Mathematically & astronomically convince the Danes.[96]

On November 6 Admiral Chester stunned an audience of scientists gathered at the University Club in Washington by denouncing Dr. Frederick A. Cook as a deliberate faker. His astronomical analysis illustrating that Cook could not possibly have reached the Pole was surprising enough, but not half so surprising as his statements made after it, indicating his reasons for disbelieving the doctor had climbed Mount McKinley. Chester was quoted as saying that at the 1906 lecture before the National Geographic Society, Cook himself admitted to him and several other persons that the photographs taken apparently at the top of Mount McKinley and at the niche in the side of the mountain wall in which Cook claimed to have slept were not pictures of these places. Admiral Chester said that Dr. Cook admitted that he had left his camera behind him before he reached these points in his journey to the summit of the mountain.

"Dr. Cook made this admission just after he had completed his lecture and had received the congratulations of many scientists," said Chester. "At the time his explanations seemed plausible, but recently Dr. Cook has declared that he made the pictures in the positions which they seemed to represent. These statements on his part helped to bring about my disbelief of Cook. At first I was inclined to believe that he reached the pole, as I believed that he had reached the top of Mount McKinley."[97]

At 1:50 P.M. the next day, Dr. Cook paid his bill at the Waldorf-Astoria and started for Bronxville. Through his lawyer, Cook issued a statement refuting Admiral Chester's astronomical analysis. It also said that he would send his records via the *United States* of the Scandinavian-American Line on November 25 and that they could be expected to arrive in Copenhagen on December 7. Of Chester himself, the doctor's statement said, "This is the unbiased gentleman who displayed such anxiety to pass upon my record, and who now desires to go to Copenhagen as an unprejudiced witness. Do the American people wonder that I have kept my promise to the scientists of Denmark?"[98]

Cook's attorney steadfastly refused to disclose the doctor's whereabouts, saying simply that he had retired to the country to rest and finish his records. The lawyer also intimated that another reason for the move was that he had knowledge of a conspiracy to "crush" the doctor and that spies had been planted at the Waldorf to intercept his messages.

In light of the University of Copenhagen's negative and somewhat indignant response to its request and the embarrassingly biased statements of Admiral Chester, the National Geographic Society announced that it would not be sending a delegation overseas after all and that an entirely new subcommittee would be appointed to rule on the claims of "other explorers" to priority at the Pole.

With the unanimous verdict of the National Geographic Society confirming his claim, Peary no longer felt it necessary to refrain from all honors. He would lecture, but not extensively and only before a few scientific societies, he said.

At the National Geographic Society on November 12, the newly certified discoverer of the North Pole revealed the key to his success to the many prominent guests who came to hear his first public speech about his greatest exploit.

"The fundamental keynote of my success was experience," he told his audience. "Nothing else did it and nothing else could. If the Pole could have been won by a streak of luck or a grouping of fortuitous circumstances or a mere fluke, it would have been won long ago. . . . In the campaign I made I not only utilized but needed every item of the specialized equipment and every iron nerve of the party's veteran personnel. . . . Could a man reach a pole unfatigued, . . . he might experience some peculiar sensations. But a man worn out with fatigue as I was could not analyze his sensations. I did have one overpowering feeling, however, and that was that I had made good to myself, to my friends, and to the flag I had carried there."[99]

At the dinner tendered him by the Peary Arctic Club, the commander showed its members the first pictures of his expedition, including one of a huge ice hummock flying the American flag near the spot he had calculated to be the top of the world. The explorer heard, with pleasure, Admiral Chester's comparison of his polar expedition to the campaigns of Alexander and Napoleon, and then Peary followed up the analogy by once again laying emphasis on experience as the one factor that allowed him, alone, to conquer the North Pole.

On Thanksgiving Day Walter Lonsdale boarded the *United States* with a bundle containing Dr. Cook's completed polar records and sailed for Denmark. The press had learned that the day before Lonsdale embarked, the doctor had drawn a $15,000 foreign letter of credit on the Carnegie Trust Company, indicating that he, too, was going abroad, and though the press had quickly located him at the Gramatan, by the end of the month Cook seemed to have done so, his whereabouts being once again unknown.

In his absence, H. Wellington Wack appeared as his spokesman. He said Cook would be going to Naples on the *Caronia* for a rest and there await the University of Copenhagen's decision. The lawyer intimated that the doctor was in a highly nervous state and was suffering badly from indigestion caused by an inability to readjust to a civilized diet. Wack then repeated the accusation of a plot against his client.

The *New York Times* reported, as news, an interview with the lawyer that seemed intended to make light of these contentions. According to the *Times,* Wack dramatically described the plan to steal Cook's records using the intervention of a lady who was to drug Lonsdale with a champagne Mickey Finn.

The lawyer was confident, the *Times* said, that the diabolical scheme would be thwarted. The "record" carried aboard the *United States* was simply a dummy package, Wack said; the real records had already been forwarded aboard another ship.

The story went on that Wack had asserted there were three private detectives watching Cook constantly during his recent stay at the Gramatan, but that he had hired detectives to watch "The Opposition's" detectives, and in the process the plot had been exposed. When the reporter asked who would be interested in such a dark deed, Wack was reported to have said, "Who? . . . You ask me who? I'm not mentioning any names, but I could if I wanted to. Who do you think would be interested in stealing Dr. Cook's records?"

The reporter admitted he couldn't guess and asked, "What would be the object in stealing the records?"

Wack looked disgusted. "The object?" he cried. "Why, that is perfectly plain. Suppose Dr. Cook announced that the data that would prove he had discovered the north pole—the original data—had been stolen on its way to Copenhagen. What would the people say? They would say that Dr. Cook was faking, wouldn't they? They would say he had fixed up a story because he didn't really have the data. They would be apt to call his integrity in question. Dr. Cook saw all that. We all saw it. We talked it over and decided on this scheme of ours to circumvent the plot."[100]

With this story, the *New York Times* had ceased to treat Cook and his associates seriously. A lead article the next day began this way:

> Is Dr. Frederick A. Cook, the explorer, sequestered in a quiet nook, recovering from his fright over that plot to steal his arctic observations?
> Did Dr. Cook, in disguise, leave yesterday on the Cunarder Caronia for southern France, there to compose his nerves?
> Has Dr. Cook started on a dash to the south pole, or to the north pole, or to Mars, or has he dashed anywhere?
> It is all a mystery. . . . [101]

And the 50 reporters waiting at the gangplank of the *Caronia* had failed to solve it. They saw no one resembling the doctor bound for Naples. He was then reported aboard a ship headed for Havana, but the "Dr. Cook" aboard turned out to be only an unfortunate man who happened to resemble the missing explorer.

A canvass of Cook's friends only added to the confusion. One reported that the doctor's associates had been so fearful of porch climbers that the windows of his rooms at the Gramatan had been nailed down and that he had refused to use the phone because it "leaked." One was quoted as reporting Cook on the verge of a complete nervous collapse and that he had exclaimed, "If this keeps up a few months longer I shall be in the insane asylum!"

Charles Wake, the insurance man, was the only one who claimed to know the whereabouts of the disappeared doctor but said he would not reveal the place. John R. Bradley, becoming concerned that the venture with which his name was so intimately associated was taking on the aspect of a comic opera plot, phoned Wake and demanded that he tell exactly where Dr. Cook was. Wake refused. Bradley, not used to being refused, was indignant:

> I can't understand this confounded business. Why there has been so much secrecy about Dr. Cook is too much for me. What's the use in trying to hide him? What has he done that he should be secreted? If he has gone abroad without letting me know, I want to say that I don't thank him for it. The least he could have done was to inform me of his plans. I'm sure I have given every evidence that I was one of his warmest friends. . . .
>
> . . . Plot nothing! Who the deuce would want to steal [his proofs]? They're not good to eat. The trouble is, some of the doctor's advisers kept telling him detectives were on his trail, and that if he didn't take care they would break into his rooms at the Gramatan and get away with his data. I told him it was all rot. If those stories hadn't been [put] into his ears he would probably not have to be sneaked away like this. I suppose the poor man was scared half out of his wits.[102]

In an official statement issued from his office at 40 Broadway, H. Wellington Wack continued to maintain that his client had gone with the *Caronia* for rest and to finish his book about his polar expedition but emphasized that he was not in seriously ill health. The statement closed with what seemed to be a calm refutation of the *Times*'s erratic revelations of the last few days: "The fantastic stories attributed to those who represent the explorer have no foundation. Evidence of an attempt to steal his original observations had cautioned him to employ reasonable safeguards in transmitting them to Denmark."[103]

Peary, as much confused as anyone by the stories in the *Times,* was growing increasingly concerned about just what the doctor and his advisers were really up to. He anxiously asked William Reick for information. Was Cook really physically or mentally affected by the trend of events? Was he really going abroad? Had the records really started for Copenhagen with Lonsdale?[104]

He imagined all sorts of plots himself that were going to be carried out on the doctor's behalf to see him through: Bennett had gone to Copenhagen to smooth the way with the Danish press or influence the university; the expedition to Mount McKinley that the Mazama Club of Portland was planning was nothing but a cover to bring back fraudulent "records" from the "top" of McKinley or to plant some there; Bennett had already carried a set of manufactured polar records personally to Denmark, where they would be "sprung" before the Peary Arctic Club could assert its own pressure on the Danes.[105]

Bridgman had previously tried to calm Peary's fears, but as the *United States'* sailing time had neared, even he had felt nervous at the prospects but had finally decided matters were in good hands. "This moving into the dark is ticklish business," he said, "and I am inclined to think that Mr. Reick and the 'Times' can lead the procession effectively; at any rate that it would be an error of judgment to try to forestall or anticipate them."[106]

There were certainly plenty of offers to help: offers to write damaging articles against Cook for the Danish press came from several Danes, including Peter Freuchen, and also from Henryk Arctowski;[107] offers from persons who claimed influence with the Danish royal family; offers by visiting Danish academicians to wire back home all the doubts being raised in the United States about Mount McKinley, which had received little attention in Europe.

Yet despite the Eskimos' story, the Barrill affidavit and the tens of thousands of words printed in "proof" of Cook's imposture, even General Hubbard had expressed his doubts to Peary that all of this had been enough:

> My impression is that when Dr. Cook's record is submitted in Denmark, it will be found pretty good, but not an original. I should suppose that he would be employing his time now in getting up the best record he can make—and that may be a very convincing one—and that he will send no original data, but will make some excuse for sending only a copy. As you and others have told me, any skillful man can make up a set of proofs, which, if accepted as original and genuine, would be conclusive.[108]

The week the doctor dropped out of sight, another polar explorer arrived in New York. Roald Amundsen had gone there to promote his projected voyage in the *Fram* across the Arctic Basin. Reporters found him totally ignorant of the controversy surrounding the claims of his old friend.

"I was amazed when I reached this country and learned that doubt has been cast on the statements made by Dr. Cook," Amundsen said. "The Scandinavian press generally has been strangely silent with reference to the controversy that has been in progress here between the supporters of Dr. Cook and Commander Peary. It was all news to me. . . .

". . . I have no desire to be dragged into this controversy. Dr. Cook says he has reached the pole, now let us wait until the scientists in Copenhagen have passed upon his proofs. This seems to me to be the proper way."

When asked whether polar observations could be faked, Amundsen gave his opinion: "That could be done, of course, but nobody would be foolish enough to postpone this work until after he returned from the arctic regions, knowing that the moment he struck civilization he would be called upon to furnish just that sort of proof."[109]

CHAPTER 18

Tell It to the Danes!

J~~UST WHERE WAS~~ FREDERICK COOK? THAT WAS THE JOURNALISTIC QUESTION of the hour, and it received many answers. He was reported to be taking a cure at sanitoriums in Maine and New York or to have sailed for Europe, several destinations in Germany being the most popular suppositions.

H. Wellington Wack was adamant that all the speculation about his client's "disappearance" was nonsense. The doctor had simply gone to Italy for a rest, the lawyer repeated. That, indeed, had been the plan, but Dr. Cook had not followed it.

In New York City Charles Wake, whom Cook had entrusted with his original notebooks, waited in his office for the doctor to appear. Wake had himself only recently returned to the city after five days in Bronxville, having gone there at the urgent request of Dr. and Mrs. Cook.

Letters they had received telling of plots to steal the polar records or even murder Dr. Cook had left them distraught. Wake had found the doctor so unhinged that he could not sleep day or night. His condition so alarmed Wake that he had even acceded to the Cooks' request to leave the door between their adjoining rooms open at night. The doctor wanted to go immediately to Copenhagen and finish his records there, but Wake advised against this.

At first, Wake was inclined to make light of the whole "plot" business, but soon it became obvious to him that Cook's every move was being shadowed by as many as six detectives. The doctor seemed practically a nervous wreck, and as the days wore on, Wake observed, "He became even more uncommunicative than usual and would not express his thoughts."[1]

Wake had left the Gramatan with the polar records, which he locked up in his office upon his arrival in New York. The plan called for Lonsdale and Cook to come there on November 24. But they did not appear at the appointed time. Then Lonsdale called asking to meet Wake at a different location, where he related what had happened.

On his way from Bronxville, the doctor told Lonsdale he believed he had at last shaken off the detectives and had a chance to get away unnoticed. "Now, I'll be able to get some sleep," Cook said. "I will take the first train for Philadelphia, and will write Wake under the name of Fred Harper telling him my plans."[2] After a number of evasive maneuvers, with Lonsdale's help, he shaved off his mustache, cut his hair short and, donning a slouch hat, started for Jersey City.

As he listened to the story of Cook's secret departure, Wake became incensed. But when Marie Cook came begging him to help her, as she had no idea of Doctor's plans and was fearful of what would happen next, Wake pledged he would, even though his faith in her husband had been shaken. The next day Walter Lonsdale boarded the *United States* carrying with him copies of Dr. Cook's proofs that he was the discoverer of the North Pole.

In fact, Cook had not gone to Philadelphia. In Jersey City he had changed trains for upstate New York. A few days later, Marie Cook got a letter posted from Toronto:

> If the hounds are still pursuing you put my original records in a safe deposit box and leave the key with Wake; if they are not following you, bring the records with you. My life is of more importance than the polar matter, which can wait if necessary.[3]

On December 4 Marie Cook quietly sailed for Europe with the original records. She instructed H. Wellington Wack before leaving to discontinue all expenses on her husband's account and to forward to her certain papers pertaining to the Mount McKinley matter.[4]

The *United States* arrived at Copenhagen after an uneventful voyage on December 8. Walter Lonsdale went directly to the Landmandsbanken, where Cook's proofs were locked in the safety vault. He then went to the university, where he explained that he did not have the original notebooks but that they were en route. The representative of the university asked that the material he had be turned over immediately. The following day, the records were given to Professor Elis Strømgren and Rector Carl Salomonsen, and a Konsistorium was called to examine them.

Weeks had passed without any word whatever from Dr. Cook. But if he was in eclipse, Peary's star was on the rise. His lecture before the National Geographic Society had drawn the dignified and important audience Peary required, and the society found its membership increasing at a phenomenal and gratifying pace.

Peary had given his next public lecture December 1 before several thousand guests of the Geographical Society of Pennsylvania in Philadelphia's Academy of Music, where he was unequivocally introduced as the discoverer of the North Pole. Not everyone, however, was ready to stamp such a declaration in gold.

The National Geographic Society had voted him a special medal but had not yet had it struck. The subcommittee appointed to examine the question of whether anyone had reached the Pole before April 6, 1909, had not delivered its report, and it had not been decided whether the medal should be inscribed to "The Discoverer of the North Pole" or something else.

Meanwhile, the critics continued to hammer away at Peary's absent rival's claims. Dr. John Stockwell of Cleveland University now came forward to "prove" once again through highly technical and assumptive arguments that the doctor's observations could not have been made anywhere nearer to the North Pole than 581 miles.

The press hinted at attempts to influence the Danish government through diplomatic channels and of bribes being offered Danish newspapers to print anti-Cook articles and to give the Mount McKinley doubts a prominence they had not yet received. In Denmark, however, astronomers' allegations and even the sworn statements of his Alaskan-expedition associates were taken as just an extension of the baseless campaign being waged with unlimited funds by Cook's jealous enemies. Belief in the man Copenhagen had welcomed in September seemed scarcely lessened there by the events of the intervening months. But on the very day Cook's proofs were handed over to the rector of the university, the first serious doubt was introduced into the minds of the faithful Danes. New allegations that directly involved Denmark appeared in the *New York Times.*

On December 3 William Reick had sent a cryptic telegram to Commander Peary:

> I have what I consider most important development yet where can I reach you.[5]

He then met Peary, swore him to secrecy, and instructed him that in all future correspondence on this development, Cook would be referred to as "Black." On December 6 Reick urgently asked Peary for a sample of "Black's" handwriting.

The next day, two men signed a long statement at Westchester, New York, swearing that Cook had employed them to manufacture a set of faked observations to fool the Danish scientists. The affair, as reported in the *Times,* had an innocent enough beginning.[6]

Just before leaving for the West in October, John Bradley had introduced Cook to an insurance man named George Dunkle, who had helped raise money for the Arctic Club's relief expedition in the winter of 1908–09. Dunkle said he wanted to talk to the doctor about insuring his original records, but actually he had another business proposition in mind.

Dunkle knew an indigent Norwegian sea captain named August Wedel Loose. During the press debate over Cook's proofs, the captain had suggested to Dunkle that it was probable the doctor did not really have any reliable navigational records and was trying to buy time. The two thought perhaps they could be "of service" to the explorer. In nearly three full pages of newsprint, by far the largest amount of space it had devoted to a single story on a single day in the entire momentous year that was now drawing to a close, the *Times* spared its readers not a single detail.

After some preliminary conversation about insuring Cook's "proofs," Dunkle related in his affidavit, he came to his real reason for the visit:

It was a rather delicate matter to approach. I had sense enough to know that if I came right out and let the doctor know I had suspicions of his observations he would probably turn upon me and order me out. I didn't propose to do it that way. The doctor seemed to be tired out, and I remarked that I must be going. Just before I started for the door I said: "Well, doctor, I hope all this public criticism doesn't bother you." He smiled and said, "Oh, I guess not." He remarked that he had not had time to do much else than attend to his lecture engagements and banquets up to this time, but that he would soon have to get down to real work and that then he would send his proofs to Copenhagen. Then I thought I saw my chance.

Dunkle suggested that the doctor might need some help in getting his records off in a timely manner and mentioned that he knew a navigator of wide experience who might be of help in putting them in shape. Dunkle said the doctor seemed interested in this but said only, "Well, Mr. Dunkle, I may have occasion to call on you on that insurance matter. I am glad you called. I wish you would leave your card."

Once he was sure the doctor had returned from his western trip, on November 3 Dunkle sent up his card to Cook's suite on the tenth floor of the Waldorf-Astoria. Dr. Cook sent down his own card asking that he come up. Dunkle thought the doctor looked very nervous when he greeted him with a hearty handshake and, according to Dunkle, said, "I tried to reach you over the telephone this noon. I want to get in touch with your friend you spoke about. . . .

". . . All I want him for is to go over some of the observations with me. They are all right, but there are some things that I want to see about. . . .

". . . I don't know that there is anything he can do, but from what you say I guess he can help with a few points. It's nothing vital, you know, but some details that I want."

Dunkle said he assured Cook that Loose was "the very man he wanted," then departed.

The next day Dunkle brought Captain Loose to see the doctor, introduced the two, and then retired from the scene. Once alone, Loose said, he was not long in reassuring the doctor:

> "Now, Dr. Cook, maybe you have been to the north pole and maybe you haven't. Perhaps you think you have and maybe you are wrong about it. You don't need to have any worry about it, though, for I can supply you with sets of proofs that I will guarantee will pass at Copenhagen."
>
> "Is that so?" he asked.
>
> "I know what I am talking about and I am not going to fool you," I replied. "But there is one thing about it, doctor, I would like you to answer some questions."

"I am willing to answer any questions you put to me," he said. "I will try to answer them. I believe I have been to the north pole. I am sure of it. What is it you want to know?"

"It is to satisfy my mind about the observations you have in your possession, and what I shall be expected to furnish, that I am going to ask you these things," I said.

"All right, go ahead," said the doctor.

"I want to know how you found the north pole," I said to him.

"Why, I used my compass to go to the pole," he replied.

"Did you have your compass corrected?" I asked him.

"No, but I assumed it was correct," he told me.

"Then if you didn't have it corrected, so you could know if there was any error, you would never have been able to tell when you reached the pole, if you relied on the compass alone," I said.

"Well, I had a chart on Nansen's and Sverdrup's expeditions when they reached approximately the same distance toward the pole from opposite routes," said the doctor. "I thought from their observations that there was a path crossing the pole, and following the 95th meridian west, in which path there was no compass error, other than that the needle would point due south, instead of due north, and I presumed that if I followed that path I would cross the pole. If the reckoning of Nansen and Sverdrup was correct, then it was only a matter of latitude, and I could rely upon my dead reckoning for that."

To this I said: "Dr. Cook, you are making a great mistake. You are an independent explorer, and you should not rely upon any presumption based upon what other explorers have done. You mustn't go by the figures of Nansen or Sverdrup. You must have your own figures."

In response to other questions, Loose said, the doctor stated he had not taken his chronometer time from the *Bradley*, he had made no time sights at Annoatok and, in fact, did not know even the latitude and longitude of the place. At this point, Loose remarked wryly, he could see that he had "a lot of work cut out" for himself. Loose then specifically inquired about some of the troubling aspects regarding his observations as they appeared in the *Herald*'s series:

> I asked him what was his reason for putting down his observations at the north pole clear down to the second when every navigator knows that seconds are not usually considered. He replied that he had been very careful to get the exact observations—that by putting them down in seconds he believed they would be more convincing. . . .
>
> . . . [After finishing with my questions] I felt ashamed of him. Here he was saying that he had taken observations and that they

were accurate, and yet he didn't have any way of knowing that they were, because he could not check up his time. I wondered if any other explorer was ever in that fix before. . . .

I had gone at the doctor so hard that I was afraid that he'd get mad. I didn't want to let on what I felt—that he had not been to the pole. I hated to be that harsh with him, so I kept my thoughts to myself.

We went on talking and I told the doctor that I had better fit him up with a complete log all the way to the pole, with every sort of observation in it. If he didn't want it for any other purpose, I said, it would be of use in checking up his own observations, although I felt that they were sadly lacking, if he had them at all. I wanted to ask if he would show the observations to me, but I did not want to embarrass him.

Loose then left Cook, he said, with the understanding that he would get the tables and charts he would need and work out backward the positions of latitude and longitude mentioned in the *Herald*'s series. Loose's affidavit exhibited a paper on which the doctor had written, "Svartevaag—start March 17–18. Strong wind.—haze. March 30—obs. Latt. & Long. Daily observations to April 23." which the captain said were his instructions for the job.

On November 5 George Dunkle once again sent up his card and was summoned to Dr. Cook's rooms. He felt the time had come for him to talk business:

We did not go into details. . . . I told Dr. Cook that if Capt. Loose succeeded in making observations that were of use to the doctor in getting his records accepted at Copenhagen it would certainly be worth a considerable price. I told him that I would figure the matter out and would charge him a fair price for the services rendered, but that, everything considered, it would be a good round price. He asked me what I thought I ought to receive, and I told him it all depended on what Capt. Loose did for the doctor.

"Well," the doctor replied, "I can't say right now exactly what Capt. Loose is going to do. I have asked him for a complete set of observations going up to the north pole. If I get them and they are of any use to me I am willing that you should receive a good, round sum. What I mean is, that if the University of Copenhagen scientists accept my proofs, as I suppose they will, and Capt. Loose has been of assistance to me in getting them accepted, it will be worth considerable to me and I am willing to pay for it."

That was pretty straight talk, and I asked the doctor if he had any doubt that his proofs would be accepted—that is, those proofs he already had in his possession. He replied: "There are some things that I want to put in my observations to make them complete. I have overlooked certain things and it is in these matters that Capt. Loose may be of avail."

They agreed to meet again in Bronxville the next morning. Cook said he was far from well, needed quiet surroundings and was going to the Gramatan there.

Loose arrived in Bronxville on November 6 calling himself Andrew H. Lewis, but the hotel clerk said that Cook had not arrived. Loose thought Cook was playing games and made a scene, later regretting that he might have drawn attention to himself. But when Cook did arrive, he was not in the least upset, as he had been at their last meeting, and seemed glad to be away from the city.

Once again closeted with Cook, Loose said, he pressed him about his observation of 89°59'45", and when he expressed his amazement at its precision, the doctor replied that he had taken a great deal of care in making it.

Loose suggested that his observations should take into account the theory that there was a depression of five or six miles at the Pole and proposed ways to account for any possible depression without committing himself one way or the other.

Loose said the doctor admitted that he could not describe the method for taking an azimuth "without looking it up," and when asked what he understood by the true bearing of a heavenly body, he made the same reply. This led the captain to be more straightforward.

"It seems strange to me that you could be certain that you discovered the north pole if you didn't know how to take the observations that would take you there," the captain ventured, but the doctor replied that he had been guided by the Nansen and Sverdrup charts, the same as he had said before.

Loose could not get some points over to the doctor at all, he said. He kept insisting, for instance, that Loose put the temperatures down for all the times the observations were made, even though Loose held that the temperatures were unimportant:

> "They won't prove anything," I told him. "I'd like to know who is going to bother about temperatures if the observations are not there." Well, that didn't seem to make any impression on the doctor, and he kept insisting that the temperatures go in. He informed me that, although I might not think it, he did actually have his observations, with the exception of the longitudes, which he wanted me to furnish, and the latitude observations which I had already supplied. He thought that these did not matter much if they were not in, and I answered that if he put his proofs in without them he would find out that it did make considerable of a difference.
>
> "You'll find that the Danish scientists are going to be very particular about this thing," I said to him, "and I would advise you not to throw away anything that I have given you."

"Oh, no; I shall not throw anything away," he replied, "I want all the data you can furnish me."

When he returned to New York, Captain Loose conferenced with George Dunkle on how things were progressing.

"Dunkle, do you know what this means?"

"What means?" he asked.

"Our working out this stuff for Dr. Cook," said Loose.

"What about it?" asked Dunkle.

"Why, it means that if the Copenhagen scientists pass his proofs we will be the real discoverers of the pole." Loose told him he hadn't had the slightest idea how far Cook had been from knowing how to put in his proofs.

"It's a shame to think what might have happened to him," the captain remarked.

Dunkle said he had visited Bronxville several times during the week and received six $20 bills from Cook on the veranda of the hotel. Dunkle did not like the look of the doctor. He seemed extremely nervous, his face was pale and he appeared to be on the verge of a breakdown.

When Dunkle suggested that Loose had already shown that he could be of considerable service to the doctor, Dunkle said Cook agreed.

"The Captain," he said, "seems to understand what he is doing, and the observations he has already submitted are accurate and will be of great value in checking up."

I said: "Dr. Cook, you know that Capt. Loose can fix up a set of observations which will help you prove to the Copenhagen scientists that you reached the north pole, don't you?" He replied: "Yes, I believe he can." I told him: "There is no question about it. Now, a service like that is worth a good deal of money," I went on, and Dr. Cook agreed that it was, and that he was ready and willing to pay.

"We are going to charge a pretty stiff price for a few days' work," I said. He asked, "How much?"

I told him it would cost $2,500 before the records left here and a bonus of $1,500 more if they were accepted by the Danes.

He gasped some at that and finally said: "All right, but it seems a big price."

I assured him that we thought we had the market cornered, but didn't want to squeeze him, nevertheless the data were worth the price and to this he afterward agreed.

Cook had lent Loose some books of his own and given him $50 to buy some nautical almanacs and charts, plus $20 more. The captain purchased them from John Bliss and Company on Front Street. The books the doctor requested were delivered, but the captain didn't have the heart to tell Cook that he had lost many of the other books that he was working from, including Cook's copy of Sverdrup's *New Land,* when he had taken a fall while trying to catch an electric trolley and knocked himself out. "He had trouble enough already, and I didn't want to add to it for fear he might lose his nerve entirely," Loose said. "He had seemed to be so nervous when I saw him the last time that I really felt sorry for him."

Dunkle again visited the Gramatan on November 15, at which time, the insurance man alleged, Cook asked that Loose come and stay at the hotel for several days. The doctor said there were many things coming up that he needed assistance with and that he was constantly being shadowed by detectives. Dunkle said the doctor declared: "You don't know what tricks the opposition is up to. They would steal my records if they could."

According to Dunkle, Cook could not be persuaded to leave the Gramatan, but the doctor offered to pay Loose's hotel bill if they agreed to stay and volunteered to go down and register them himself. Dunkle said he was aghast at this lack of secrecy and suggested that he register Captain Loose instead. "Oh, I guess you're right," the doctor was said to have assented. Dunkle registered Loose under his alias of Lewis, but Dunkle used his own name. They obtained adjoining rooms on the same floor as Cook's.

Before leaving in the morning, Dunkle was given $70, making the total they had received from Cook $260. The doctor insisted that Loose stay until he finished his calculations, as he was anxious to see them off to Copenhagen as soon as possible. Loose said he told the doctor it would not take long to finish the job, but the doctor now asked for two sets of observations at the Pole, taken at six-hour intervals over 48 hours. Loose asserted that the doctor explained that the two different sets were needed to compare the results with and without a depression at the Pole, as "he had not made up his mind" whether there was one. He also insisted that Loose leave in the seconds when figuring out the altitude of the sun backward from his reported sight at noon on April 21, 1908.

Loose's affidavit stated that he stayed up late into the night working on the new requests, finally retiring after taking a time sight by the stars from his hotel window when he remembered that Dunkle had borrowed his watch.

Loose also claimed to have worked out a complete set of chronometer sights to establish Cook's local time at Annoatok. At one point he asked if the doctor had a record of the weather on January 15, 1908. Cook went to his room and soon returned saying the weather was clear. Loose said he used this information to establish his sight on several stars, which would have been visible on that date, to correct his local time:

> I had another sight on Capella, west, on Jan. 15, showing an apparent altitude of 46 degrees 32 minutes 30 seconds at 4:51 A.M., apparent time. I asked the doctor if he could imagine that he got up early enough for such a sight, and he asked:

"Was that necessary?"

I replied, "It certainly was."

"Well," replied the doctor, "as that is an important detail of my journey, I doubtless did get up at that very hour or some time before it. You are safe in putting the observation that way."

According to Loose's affidavit, he provided the doctor with assumed corrections for each of his three chronometers and the compass variation at both Annoatok and Svartevoeg. Loose had now given the doctor everything he thought he needed, he said, for documentation of a trip to the Pole, but there was still the matter of the return:

> When I submitted the latitude sights to Dr. Cook at the Gramatan they covered only the trip to the pole and at the pole. I remarked to the doctor that it would be a good scheme—a very wise scheme—if he would send over to Copenhagen the latitude sights on his way down from the pole. Dr. Cook looked stumped for a minute and then I said to him:
>
> "Well, that'll be all right, doctor. You can say that you got to the pole and that everybody knows you got back and that you left the return observations in a cache somewhere."
>
> "Yes, that's right," replied the doctor. "I did leave them in a cache at Etah, where my instruments are. I'm going to get them next Spring if I can."
>
> I laughed and said, "Yes, if you can."

Dunkle said he came up from New York on November 19 to ask how things were going:

> "You are confident your record will be all right?" I asked.
>
> "Quite satisfied," he replied. "There are many points that Capt. Loose has cleared up for me, and I am glad I had him to work on them."
>
> "He has furnished you with some observations that he tells me you didn't have, and which were necessary in order to have your records passed at Copenhagen," I suggested.
>
> "Well, I guess that's true," assented the doctor. "I thought I had everything I needed, but I find I overlooked some vital things."

Dunkle attested he saw Loose hand over a number of items to the doctor, including a course protractor, a divider, some charts, sets of observations, including compass variations, and the two volumes of *New Land* that belonged to Cook. Before they parted, both men strongly urged Cook to submit the records the captain had worked out and not to send his own. Dunkle then said that the doctor agreed to pay $740 the following Monday to make his payments an even $1,000, and to deliver an additional $1,500 before the records left for Europe.

According to Loose, the two men shook hands, and Cook expressed his hope that Copenhagen would look favorably on his proofs. Loose left the Hotel Gramatan satisfied, he said, that he had done all in his power to provide the doctor with everything he could need to make good his claim. After all, it meant a bonus of $1,500 if the data passed and an extra $500 for himself. That, he said, the doctor had promised him in the event of a favorable result.

The deed was now done. Loose added just one other thing to the affidavit he made for the *Times:*

> During my stay at the Hotel Gramatan Dr. Cook had in his possession in his rooms there all the calculations I made for him. Some of these he returned after having kept them a day or longer, or a sufficient time to have copied them. He did not return the latitude sights from Svartevoeg to the pole, nor the chart of his supposed route to the pole, which I worked out for him from an improved map of my own, similar to the Admiralty charts. He also kept all the books on observations and polar information which I had bought for him at his request.

At no time, said Captain Loose, was he allowed to see any of Cook's original records, but that several times the doctor read data to him from a ten-inch-square notebook. Loose said that he noticed the latitude positions the doctor gave him for certain dates were different from those printed in the doctor's narrative in the *Herald* but that most were identical.

George Dunkle waited for Cook's arrival the following Monday, but he did not appear. Dunkle then set out for Bronxville. There, he said, he was told by Walter Lonsdale that the doctor was too busy to see him. When Dunkle met Cook briefly on the train platform, he was afraid to say anything since he was with Charles Wake. Dunkle boarded the train and returned to New York. It was the last time he saw Cook. When he called at the Gramatan the next week, Cook was no longer there and his whereabouts were unknown.

To many who read the Dunkle and Loose affidavits, the whole idea that Cook would enter so casually into so dangerous and risky an arrangement with total strangers seemed preposterous, the alternative monstrous and the conclusion obvious:

> Dr. Cook is either the greatest and at the same time the stupidest charlatan who ever attempted to impose upon a skeptical world, or he is the victim of the most malignant and devilishly ingenious persecution that hatred and envy could devise.[7]

> Last week it was still the thing to maintain that the astute doctor could have made up a perfect set of polar observations, 800 miles from the pole, while wintering in an arctic igloo; this week the same doctor is suddenly transformed into such a pitiful ignoramus that Dunkle and Loose become his indispensable $4,000 aids in

the forging of the precious records. Doubtless the Danes have perspective enough to see the uproarious absurdity of the contrast.[8]

Then, too, there were others who thought they saw a pattern to the Dunkle and Loose allegations. Here were men who, like Barrill before them, admitted that they had engaged in a deliberate plan to deceive, swearing now to
be telling the truth. Others were skeptical because the affidavits had appeared
in the *New York Times,* which had increasingly favored Peary, and because the
paper announced it had sent copies of Dunkle's and Loose's affidavits to
Copenhagen a day *before* it had made them public. The affidavits' timing
seemed suspiciously close to the final decision on the doctor's claims and had
been disclosed only after Cook's proofs—which were now alleged to have
been largely created by Loose—had been locked up in a Copenhagen bank
vault. This made many believe that the whole thing had been designed to
place doubt in the minds of the scientists about to sit in judgment of Cook's
claims.

Nevertheless, the sensational allegations of Dunkle and Loose seemed to
be supported by a number of circumstantial details. Loose had indeed purchased navigational books at the place indicated, and a check of the Gramatan's registry certified that a George Dunkle and a Mr. Lewis had been
registered at the times stated. Furthermore, Dunkle and Loose had carefully
kept the doctor's cards he had sent down to them at the Waldorf and his "instructions" to Loose.

Then, much to Cook's supporters' horror, Walter Lonsdale confirmed
that Cook and Loose had actually had dealings involving polar observations,
although the doctor's secretary denied any intent to deceive. "Loose set to
work at home, checking observations made by Cook, always with the distinct
understanding that no corrections or alterations were to be made," said Lonsdale. "Loose was understood to be an expert navigator, well versed in taking
observations. Dr. Cook consented to his doing the checking purely to satisfy
his own curiosity.

"Loose, however, could not settle down to work at home, so he was . . .
brought to the hotel in Bronxville with Dunkle to look after him. . . . He was
naturally placed in possession of observations made by Dr. Cook in the arctic
and north pole regions.

"Loose, however, did not inspire confidence and was told by Dr. Cook
that he did not want his services or figures, and he was discharged."[9]

Cook's friends worried that if he did not surface soon his disappearance
would be taken as an admission of guilt. But Walter Lonsdale thought he
knew why the doctor had remained silent even in the face of these serious allegations. "When one recalls the state of mind and health of Dr. Cook during
the last few days of his stay at Bronxville, N.Y., it is quite easy to conclude that
he is not in a fit state to come forward and meet the case," he said.[10]

In the days following the Dunkle-Loose affidavits, the newspapers
printed dark hints that the mounting evidence against the honesty of the once-

trusted doctor was putting a tremendous amount of pressure on the Danes to look very carefully at his polar proofs.

On the eve of Denmark's taking up the study of his rival's records, Commander Peary was the guest of honor at the National Geographic Society's annual banquet. Lionized by speaker after speaker and in toast after toast as the discoverer of the North Pole, he then stepped forward to receive the society's special gold medal. As he stood before the distinguished audience gathered at the New Willard Hotel, holding the presentation box, he acknowledged the gales of applause. The box, however, was empty. The society, still hedging its bets, had presented no medal—which was still to be "suitably inscribed." It was waiting for Copenhagen and studying the calculations of August Wedel Loose, which it had obtained from the *New York Times*.

Bob Bartlett actually got a silver medal, presented by the British ambassador, Viscount James Bryce. And it was Bartlett who perhaps unconsciously summed up what that evening really signified. "I tell you," he said, "it is worth any price to stand in a company like that, with an organization like the National Geographic Society behind you, and men like Bryce, Moore, Grosvenor and others in front of you, and hear words of praise."[11]

The Dunkle-Loose affidavits had caused the Danes' belief in Cook to falter by the time the expert commission appointed by the Konsistorium sat to consider his proofs, yet most still believed that the doctor would make good his claim. Snow began to fall just after the commission began its deliberations in a small and ancient brick building at the university on December 16. Some saw it as a good omen for the consideration of polar records. Everyone said that the longer the scientists sat, the better for the doctor. It took just one day to come to a decision.

Robert A. Bartlett, captain of the Roosevelt.

On December 21, 1909, the University of Copenhagen released its findings. The report said that on December 16 Cook's proofs were delivered to the commission. They consisted of two documents. One was a typewritten report, 61 folio pages in length, describing his polar journey, which the commission found was materially, though not exactly, a repetition of the serial narrative that had appeared in the *New York Herald*. The other, according to Walter Lonsdale, was a complete and exact copy of the entries written in one of Cook's notebooks between March 18 and June 13, 1908, the time Cook said he was on his way to the Pole and back again. These entries covered 16 folio pages. The typewritten information did not contain "any original material of astronomical observation whatsoever, but only results."

None of the doctor's original notebooks were submitted for examination. Though Lonsdale had assured the scientists on his arrival in Denmark that they had been sent to Europe by another channel, they had not yet arrived.

In just one day, the report continued, the "Commission singly had acquainted themselves with the material received and so had convinced themselves that it was entirely valueless for the determination of the question, whether Dr. Cook had reached the Northpole." Therefore, the chairman called a full meeting of the commission on Friday, December 17, to write its report.[12]

When Walter Lonsdale appeared at this meeting to answer questions, he brought with him a letter from Dr. Cook postmarked Marseilles, December 14, 1909:

> My dear Lonsdale—After many wakeful nights, I have come to the conclusion that it is unfair to the Danes to ask them to accept our incomplete record—as a final proof of the conquest. Though it leaves me in an unfortunate position, I prefer to submit the digest which you have as a preliminary report asking the university to forgo the final examination until the things are brought from Greenland. . . . The report can, if the authorities so choose, be published but nothing else. Read the enclosed letter to Professor Thorp over carefully and make a copy of it before you send it.[13]

The letter referred to was the one Cook had written on September 27, saying it was "unwise and impossible to submit for final examination the present report" given the fact that his instruments and some of his data had been left in Greenland because Peary would not allow them aboard the *Roosevelt.*

The commission's report continued:

> There is in the documents submitted to us a not permissible lack of such guiding information which could show the probability that the mentioned astronomical observations had actually been undertaken; neither has the more practical side of the question—the sleigh trip—been described by such details which could help to control the report. The Commission is therefore of the opinion that there can not in the material which has been submitted to us for examination, be found any proof whatsoever of Dr. Cook having reached the Northpole.

The long-anticipated official decision of the University of Copenhagen on the data submitted by Frederick Albert Cook to prove he had reached the North Pole on April 21, 1908, consisted of just 50 words:

> In accordance with this declaration of the expert Commission, the Konsistorium wishes to state, that the material which has been submitted to the University for investigation, does not contain observations or information which could be considered to prove that Dr. Cook had reached the Northpole on his last polar trip.

The verdict was unlooked for so soon, and its conclusions, though rumored beforehand, were totally unexpected by many. The *New York Times* headlined that Cook had no observations of his own and had used Loose's, even though the report explicitly stated that there were no observations whatsoever, but only results. But this lack of observations shocked Cook's supporters almost as much as if he had used false data.

The *Times* devoted columns to the outraged comments of members of the Konsistorium, who, it reported, called the doctor a liar and a swindler and declared that they had been hoaxed. Knud Rasmussen, who had been asked to sit in on the deliberations and who so recently had defended the doctor's claims, was quoted as saying: "When I saw the observations I realized that it was a scandal. . . . No schoolboy could make such calculations. It is a most childish attempt at cheating."[14]

Although the *New York Herald* tried to put the best face on the situation by saying that the Danes had ruled the doctor's claim "not proved" but not discredited, either, their decision was seen in most geographical circles as absolute and the doctor's claim as irrevocably crushed and exposed as an audacious and brazen fraud.

One scientific bystander in Copenhagen called the decision "a geographical judicial murder," but some on the committee saw the verdict as their scientific duty, though they found the outcome embarrassing and distasteful. "It is the saddest day of my life," said Professor Olufson. "As an explorer there seems to be no doubt Cook is absolutely unreliable. . . . We took Cook's word as a bond. . . . We must be careful not to repeat the error." Others were just glad that it was over. Professor C.F. Pechüle stated with finality, "The university is now done with Cook— we leave the rest to America."[15]

There, he was being vilified in the press. Some editorials called him Ananias, Munchausen, a "thimble-rigger," "a contemptible cheat" and a "monster of duplicity."

Some editors, however, were more charitable. They refused to believe that any man could have been so foolish as to intentionally try to hoax the world without possessing a shred of evidence and expressed the belief that the doctor had realized that he was mistaken and knew the observations he had would not stand the test. Others concluded that the doctor must be suffering from mental delusions brought on by the hardships he had experienced in the North.

In the face of this storm of criticism mixed with pity, the doctor alone remained utterly silent. For days, friends, former friends, and enemies gave their reactions to the events of the preceding four months.

They ranged from disbelief to glee over the doctor's dismal showing after his repeated confident assurances that his proofs would be found completely convincing. Cook's family, naturally, would not admit that he was any of the things he was being called in the newspapers. His brother William said, "Fred never lied to me. I don't care what the Danish fellows have done. I won't believe he did not discover the north pole until he comes here and admits it himself."

Cook's business associates sought to save face. John R. Bradley tried to take it good-naturedly. "All I know is what was in the evening papers," he said. "If I had been fooled, why, I am not the only one, and every man has got to be fooled once in his life. All I can say is that I am a good sport and know how to take my medicine." But for a man like John R. Bradley, that medicine must have been a bitter pill to swallow. He immediately made plans for a long shooting trip in the West.

James Gordon Bennett said there was not the slightest possibility that he would prosecute Cook for selling him a false story.[16]

Captain Osbon was stubbornly undismayed. "I stick with my friends until they die!" he declared. But many of the doctor's other old friends were devastated by the decision.

Georges Lecointe was particularly sorry. "I have however not to conceal to you how painful I feel what has arrived to Dr. Cook; firstly for the family; secondly, as Dr. Cook is one of my old companions," lamented the captain. "Perhaps he will furnish some complementary proofs of his declarations; I do wish sincerely but I dare not believe strongly in it."[17]

"The important question now is whether he is a swindler, or merely ignorant," remarked a completely mystified Roald Amundsen. "I prefer to believe that Dr. Cook himself was confident that he had arrived at the north pole. This must have been a fixed idea with him. If he is swindling he must have changed his character in the past ten years."[18]

Other explorers and recent acquaintances reacted with varying degrees of denial of their former endorsements. Shackleton declared that he was unwilling to criticize Cook. Nansen, however, said he had never believed in him and pronounced him "practically a dead man," adding that he "ought to vanish from the consideration of the world." Minister Egan, under fire for his cordiality to the returning explorer, announced he had never espoused Cook's cause in any way.[19]

But most of the doctor's former advocates simply had a feeling of helpless resignation in light of the findings of what had always been seen as the tribunal of choice and the court of last resort:

> Whatever the future may bring forth is hidden, but now the popular decision must be that Dr. Cook is a faker of colossal assurance. If he did reach the pole, it is pitiable that he should be so discredited. If he did not, it is pitiable that a man's thirst for fame should drag him to such depths. If the first is true, he, largely by his own fault, is a terribly wronged man. The only other alternative is that he has shamefully wronged his Nation and the nation that trusted him.[20]

In his own nation, as the news from Copenhagen was absorbed, the common man had various ways of expressing his disillusion. Merchants all over the country found themselves stuck with a glut of unsalable "Cook" toys just before the Christmas shopping season and discounted them heavily; in Brooklyn plans were abandoned for erecting a shaft with commemorative tablets on the little triangular plot in front of Cook's old house on Bushwick Avenue. In Minneapolis the Reverend G.L. Morrill donated his autographed picture of Cook, of which he had been so proud when the doctor had given it to him on his triumphal western tour in October, to an auction to raise money for the Christmas fund; it fetched 2 cents. "Tell it to the Danes!" became a popular exclamation in response to any questionable statement, and in New York Senator Chauncey Depew, after chiding a female acquaintance for her staunch defense of Dr. Cook, found in her reply what he thought was the key to the doctor's long run of confidence: "Well," she said, "Cook is a liar and a gentleman, and Peary is neither."[21]

After the dailies had had their say, the more sober news journals looked back on the incident and tried to sum up what it all had meant:

> The collapse of Cook's case before the University of Copenhagen completely puts an end to his claim to the discovery of the North Pole, and with equal completeness establishes his standing as one of the monumental impostors of history. . . .
>
> . . . As for Peary himself, he has been defrauded of something which can never be restored to him. . . . False as it has been proved, the claim of the cheap swindler has dimmed the lustre of the true discoverer's achievement. He will receive the full acknowledgment that his work merits, in the form of recognition from scientific and other bodies and a sure place in history; but the joy of the acclaim that should have greeted him at the triumphant close of his twenty-three years' quest can never be his.[22]

Peary, nonetheless, was relieved and delighted. He wired William Reick:

>   Congratulations to The New York Times for its steady, insis-
>   tent, victorious stand for the truth.[23]

But Peary's joy was brief at best. To many minds, not even the verdict of
the Copenhagen scientists had ended the matter. Reputations had been staked
on the doctor's veracity, and he still had a few friends willing to speak for him
in his absence.

One of these was Arctic Club president Admiral Schley. He suggested
that although Cook may have been discredited by an impartial scientific
board, Peary had been judged by his friends at the National Geographic Society. Admiral Schley proposed that Peary turn over his records to the same
commission that had examined the doctor's.

Peary declined all public comment on the admiral's proposal, but in his
private correspondence with General Hubbard he immediately wrote:

>   I fear that the Schley suggestion in regard to sending my
>   records to Copenhagen is a vicious one. . . .
>   Of course, my records will be accessible to any reputable organ-
>   ization, but I object to being bulldozed by sore, disgruntled, or vi-
>   cious partisans of Cook, into any line of action that they may sug-
>   gest, and it would seem entirely inappropriate that the record of an
>   American explorer should be sent to a foreign organization, even
>   should they ask for it. . . .
>   I submit for your consideration the desirability of having Mr.
>   Reick, through the machinery of the New York Times and its affil-
>   iation with the London Times, immediately instruct some able
>   representative in Copenhagen to obtain a statement from the
>   Copenhagen University that they have no desire to examine any
>   further Polar records or observations, and have this statement sent
>   out by the Associated Press. . . .
>   Should it seem inadvisable or impracticable to get immediately
>   an official statement to this effect from Copenhagen, an unofficial
>   statement might be sent out to the effect that there is no reason to
>   believe that Copenhagen has any desire to examine Peary's proofs,
>   which unofficial statement might pave the way for an official one
>   later on.[24]

The very next day, the *New York Times* printed a story headlined DANES
DON'T WISH TO SEE PEARY'S RECORD. The "unofficial" statement came from
Minister Egan, who was in the United States on a leave of absence. The Schley
proposal was dropped.

Also dropped was the National Geographic Society's investigation to see
whether anyone had reached the Pole before April 6, 1909. Its panel voted to
accept the conclusions of the Konsistorium in Denmark without any review
of the evidence they had once so eagerly sought. Ironically, the committee

lauded the "conscientious and fearless position" taken by the Danes and held it up to the board of managers of the National Geographic Society as "an example worthy of emulation."[25]

One by one, the clubs and societies that Cook had helped to found deleted him from their membership lists. Still, Walter Lonsdale reserved judgment:

> Dr. Cook has been excluded by both the Explorers and Arctic Clubs of America; friend after friend has forsaken him; he is looked upon as a Munchausen or worse and, for the time being, is a doomed man. All of which he has brought upon himself by his stubborn silence since the verdict of Copenhagen University. Had he come forth immediately, he would certainly not have achieved his present unenviable position. At least he would have received the benefit of the doubt until his remaining papers, with original field notes and observations which he says are at Etah, were brought down this summer. The existence of these papers is now very much doubted. But it will be wise to defer passing final judgment in the case, until this has been investigated, and the papers— should there be any—are examined.[26]

Although the immediate victory had been won, by the reaction of Schley and others Peary could see that not all were convinced. He had already thought of another approach, however.

"After the appearance of the Dunkle and Loose affidavits, I suggested to Mr. Reick that there was just one thing more for the Times to do to clean up this whole matter," he told General Hubbard, "and that was to get a confession from Cook himself.

"I may be wrong, but I cannot rid myself of the idea that, if the right kind of a man was near Cook and could work on him continuously, such a result might be accomplished.

"If it could be done, it would be absolutely final and conclusive and would remove the last chance of anyone longer believing in the impostor, and it is, perhaps, the only way in which the matter could be concluded in the minds of some people.

"As a matter of practical business newspaper enterprise, I believe that a story with the headlines 'Cook's Own Confession' might be a big thing."[27]

But Hubbard had a different idea. Yes, they must make the exposure of the imposture utterly convincing, but to do it they must find the evidence on the slopes of Mount McKinley.

Several expeditions were planning to go to the mountain to try to prove or disprove the statements of Cook or Barrill. Herschel Parker and Belmore Browne were making plans to attack the peak from the north, and Herbert Bridgman had already pledged $3,000 to outfit an Explorers Club expedition to check the doctor's route from the south. General Hubbard wanted Parker and Browne to lead this expedition and offered to foot the bill, under certain conditions.

He wrote: "I want . . . an expedition . . . that will go to Mt. McKinley next spring and summer- not primar[il]y for the purpose of getting to the top of the mountain, but to follow Dr. Cook's alleged September route; to re-photograph the points his book says he photographed, and to determine, beyond any question, how far he did go and where he took his photographs. The party ought to include the guides and the photographer who were with Dr. Cook, so that they can identify the places with which they are familiar, and that the guide who was last with him can show the spot where he says his photograph was taken."[28]

At first Parker and Browne stuck to their own plans, but when they found themselves short of funds, Parker expressed a change of heart. Using the excuse that a friend had determined that their proposed route was unclimbable, he wrote to George Little, the librarian of Bowdoin College, who had already put Hubbard's proposition before the professor:

> Since seeing you I have completely changed my plans and have decided to cooperate with Gen. Hubbard in regard to the Mt. Mckinley affair. . . .
>
> [Browne] has already written Printz and Barrill whom we expect to have with us. . . .
>
> . . . We hope to obtain several sets of these photos taken by different members of the party.[29]

In the end, neither packer would be taken on the expedition, because, according to Browne, "We realized that Barrill's testimony could not be believed by many people as he had confessed to having made misrepresentations concerning his Mount McKinley climb. We, therefore, determined to depend on our own investigation and on Dr. Cook's photographs alone in our search for evidence."[30]

Although Parker and Browne were planning a return to McKinley to prove Cook's fraud at the Pole, in Alaska itself no further proof was necessary. As word of Cook's debacle in Denmark spread to the most remote areas of the Territory, there was simply a sigh of relief. To an Alaskan's way of thinking, because the doctor was a proven fraud in his polar claims, McKinley was still unclimbed. The dreams of those who had hoped to be the first to stand atop its icy ramparts were reborn with the death of the doctor's polar pretensions.

Among the hundreds and hundreds of congratulatory letters sent to Robert E. Peary in the wake of Copenhagen's decision was a letter from one who cherished just such a dream—Archdeacon Hudson Stuck, the man who had refused to pay his bet with Alfred Brooks in 1906:

> I am so greatly rejoiced at the news that the imposture is already detected and exposed, that I cannot forebear venturing to write you with my warmest congratulations.

> One is sometimes tempted to regret that we in America have no such illustrious means of rewarding distinguished merit as they have in England. Over there they would make you Lord Peary of the Pole, and the heralds would set the North Star in an azure field for you, that your posterity to the remotest generations might proudly bear the symbol of your great achievement.
>
> But in the world's chivalry of geographic exploration your place is secure for all time.[31]

Alaskans had always doubted that Cook could have climbed McKinley so easily, if at all. One reason was their very familiarity with the great mountain. Many had panned for color, months at a stretch, around its foothills, and most were convinced it was absolutely unclimbable, at least by a "Cheechaco." That was what galled them most, that a city-bred explorer from "Outside" had come to Alaska and claimed to have done the thing that the "Pioneers" thought an impossibility. When Barrill's affidavit had been published in the *Fairbanks Times,* there were few in Alaska who had disbelieved it.

In Bill McPhee's saloon in Fairbanks that October, Tom Lloyd had done some big bragging. For 2 cents, he said, he would show what a real Alaska Pioneer could do. He would climb McKinley and plant a flag on the summit that could be seen in Fairbanks and, incidentally, prove that Cook never saw the top of the mountain. Tom said he wanted to "give the Cheechacos 'the laugh' by proving that what the Easterner brags about and writes about in the magazines and which to the Easterner is impossible, the sourdough Alaskan performs as a part of 'the day's work.'"[32]

This boast gave Bill McPhee a laugh all right—at Tom Lloyd. At 53 and portly, he wasn't much better than the average Easterner, McPhee declared. But when Tom insisted he could do it, McPhee put up $500 to bankroll an attempt. Two other merchants matched McPhee's stake, and to sweeten the pot, McPhee made a forfeit bet of $5,000 that one of Lloyd's men, if not Tom himself, would reach the summit before the Fourth of July 1910.

Lloyd selected three tough sourdough miners he had working his claims and two surveyors to handle measurements and photography. The six started by dogsled for the mountain the day Copenhagen's decision reached the front page of the New York newspapers, December 22, 1909.

With Cook disposed of, Peary was asked what he would do now that he was the undisputed discoverer of the North Pole. Rumors had it that he would be called back to duty, but Peary had other plans. He might visit Europe, the commander replied, but for the next six months he would be devoting himself to the preparation of the narrative of what he called his "final polar journey." Despite this declaration, Peary's publishers were finding that the commander was more than willing to leave the telling of what he termed "the last great earth story" to others.

At that moment the staff of *Hampton's Magazine* was busily readying the first installment of "Peary's Own Story," scheduled to appear later that month. On the staff of the magazine was Elsa Barker, the poetess who had accompanied Jo Peary to Sydney. Mrs. Barker had written a poem dedicated to "Peary and his band" entitled *The Frozen Grail,* which had appeared in the *New York Times* just before they steamed north in 1908. Its closing lines ran:

> And shall he fail? They never fail who light
> Their lamp of faith at the unwavering flame
> Burnt for the altar service of the Race
> Since the beginning. He shall find the strange—
> The white immaculate Virgin of the North,
> Whose steady gaze no mortal ever dared,
> Whose icy hand no human ever grasped.
> In the dread silence and the solitude
> She waits and listens throughout the centuries
> For one indomitable, destined soul,
> Born to endure the glory of her eyes,
> And lift his warm lips to the frozen Grail.

It had been reported that Peary was so taken with the poem that he had clipped it from the paper and carried it with him to the Pole itself.

Ever since their meeting with Peary in Sydney, Elsa Barker and a young, well-groomed writer, T. Everett Harry, had beseeched him to grant *Hampton's* the exclusive rights to his story. Barker had paved the way by writing to him immediately after his return, describing how she would handle the telling of his conquest:

> It must be a great classic, for it will live forever. It is through this story, principally, that your name will go down the ages. . . . It will be quoted from forever, and it will be translated into every tongue. . . . It will be read as history—as we read the younger Pliny on the destruction of Herculaneum and Pompei, and as we read Caesar. . . .
>
> There is no labor too great, and no inconvenience too great, to have this book made perfect.[33]

From Sydney, Mrs. Barker had dispatched another letter via the *Tyrian* to Battle Harbour; this time she used other inducements:

> I am down here for a magazine to offer you a pile of money for . . . your North Pole story. . . .
> . . . I am crazy with joy that you have won. I knew you would.
> I came down from Portland with Mrs. Peary & the children, and Mr. Bridgman met us at North Sydney. He looks about thirty - he is so happy.

You can have ten thousand dollars, <u>advance</u>, or more, immediately, if you can give the story to me. . . .

It would be a good <u>omen</u> to arrange magazine rights through one so enthusiastic about the Polar work as I am.[34]

Ben Hampton was absolutely desperate for Peary's story. His offer of "whatever price you ask" had been ignored by Dr. Cook in Copenhagen, but Hampton had been working the other side of the Atlantic as well, sending T. Everett Harry to visit William Cook the day his brother had announced his discovery. Day after day the young man came to Bedford Avenue, hoping to ingratiate himself with the dairyman and induce him to accompany him to Europe.

At first William was reluctant. "No, no, I wouldn't embarrass Fred," the modest man protested. But Harry persisted. "Think how glad he'd be to see your face among those thousands of strangers. You needn't intrude upon your brother," cajoled Harry. "All I ask is that you introduce me to him and help me in any way you can so I can engage his attention and land his story." Seductively, he played on William Cook's sympathies and his pride, painting a picture of the man looking on while his brother was showered with medals and honors by a foreign king, and offered him first-class passage and $500 for this pleasure. In the end it was all too much to resist, and the day Dr. Cook landed in Copenhagen, William Cook agreed to Harry's offer.

Trouble was, it was Saturday, and the banks would be closed for the Labor Day holiday and would not open until Tuesday—the same morning the first available ship was scheduled to sail. Hampton decided to get the cash and meet Harry on the dock at Hoboken.

On Tuesday morning, as the bells on the *Kronprinz Wilhelm* sounded all nonpassengers ashore, Harry grew frantic. Ben Hampton was nowhere in sight. In a panic he phoned the office and demanded to speak to Reginald Kauffman, the managing editor. "Ben's on his way," assured Kauffman, "but have you seen the *Times*? It publishes a message from Peary that he reached the Pole." When Harry told William Cook the news about Peary, it reminded the milkman that he had a telegram in his pocket. "This came first thing this morning—in the rush I forgot to open it," he said sheepishly. "Guess it's an answer from Fred to the cablegram you sent telling him we are coming."

Harry tore open the envelope. It read: "No use your coming. I will arrive in N.Y. Sep. 21 on Oscar II."

Just then up rushed Ben Hampton, breathless, disheveled and clutching a fat wad of bills, which he pressed into Harry's hand just as the last bell rang out for departure. Harry hurriedly showed Hampton the cable and told him the news from the *Times*. Ben Hampton ran his hands wildly through his hair as he often did in a high state of excitement. "You better take Brother William back home," he said, "and come back to the office for a conference."

By the time Harry got there, Ben Hampton had developed a whole new strategy. "There's going to be a hell of a fight," he said. "Cook has the public with him. But Peary's got the organization." Hampton decided to switch his bets to Peary and sent Harry off to Sydney.

Cook or Peary, Hampton had the idea that this polar business held the key to getting a jump on his competitors. He was certain that it would push *Hampton's* circulation of 350,000 over the half-million mark and establish him as the king of the 15-cent magazines. As Ben Hampton waited and watched his chances for any part of the polar story slipping away to others, he anxiously telegraphed Harry: "You must win or I am up against it now."[35]

Harry and Barker had settled in at Portland, where they lay siege to Peary on Eagle Island, bombarding him with every inducement. Harry emphasized Ben Hampton's advertising skills and how he would use them "and other ways" to influence "sore newspapers and pro-Cook papers," as *Hampton's* offers for Peary's story gradually increased from the original $20,000, and Peary held out to consider his options.

But as week after week slipped away, no amount of persuasion had availed. On October 23, 1909, T. Everett Harry took a more direct approach. He sat in his room at the Lafayette Hotel and typed a five-page diatribe about the injustices of the press against the object of Ben Hampton's literary desires and its unwarranted praise of Dr. Cook:

> When I read this stuff, in intelligent reputable journals I boil up within me. Is this our journalism? Is this what our editorial brains amount to? Are these men mad? Or are they deliberate and damnable liars? Can it be that because they feel this fulsome and dirty fakir Cook had, through the yellow press, got the mob running after him like a pack of wagging-tailed dogs they are willing to pander their brains, their souls, their little abilities, the truth— everything that is honorable? Or are they so obtuse and purblind that they believe this rot they write, that they credit this abomination from Brooklyn? . . . I'd hate to think that our papers . . . are rotten, and that they are attracted to Cook as vultures are to congenial carrion! And yet, after your lucid statement, after the testimony of Barrill, after Cook's own manifest inability to defend himself, they remain in their slough of lies and misrepresentations and wallow, like hogs grow fat on foulness.

Harry was just warming to his task. He went on to praise Peary, "who fought for a heroic Ideal" and in the hour of victory was forced to suffer "vile misrepresentation." But what could you expect, said Harry, when all history bore witness to "the Glorification of the Lie!"

> The mob acclaims the fool! It offers incense to the charlatan! It builds temples to superstition! It supports the quack, fawns to the trickster and deifies or canonized the fakir! . . . And when, on Calvary, the Symbol of Truth was nailed up, who jeered, and danced, and howled and mocked—the scribes and pharisees!

The scribes—we have them today, in our Bennets, our Hearsts, our Pulitzers. . . .

. . . Commander, do pardon this outburst; but I shouldn't sleep if I did not get it off my mind. . . . Just now I can fully sympathize with the feeling of a Spanish Inquisitor when he eyed his heretics. I should feel a fierce and holy joy in putting the tumbscrews on James Gordon Bennett, the correspondents to his "Readers' Column" and in dipping Cook in boiling oil!

It was not until his two-page postscript that Harry came to the point:

Oh, Commander, I hope and pray you will let Hampton have your story! I know the earnestness, the eagerness, the power of the man. I know his enthusiasm, his sincerity. . . . If need be [he can] put his hands on the editorial necks of these whelps and choke them into right doing. . . . It's simply a means of causing men in positions to form public opinion, to tell the truth to that public and do justice in writing of a man whose boots they're unworthy to touch.[36]

Perhaps this flattery worked, but more likely it was Ben Hampton's $40,000 offer that convinced Peary that Elsa Barker should ghost the discoverer's first detailed account of how he reached the North Pole. The contracts were signed within the week.

To whet enthusiasm for the series, Barker published an article in her own name in the December issue of *Hampton's*. Peary's true greatness was not appreciated, she maintained, but now that the Cook claim lay in ruins, it could no longer be denied:

We of the twentieth century are too near this man in point of time to see him in his true historical perspective; but the labor of Columbus in giving to the world another hemisphere was easy and brief compared with the labor of Peary. . . .

. . . At last, at the age of fifty-three *[sic]*, he reached the goal, the goal of daring dreamers for three hundred years.

The fame of Peary is secure. The newspaper incidents attending his return to America, in September, 1909, will have their little paragraph in the school histories of future centuries, paralleling the troubles of Columbus five hundred years before. Peary has not given the world another hemisphere; but he has proved that the spirit of man is indomitable in its struggle with physical environment. In the history of the human race, that has not happened heretofore.[37]

The turn of the New Year promised to see Robert Peary make up for all the time he had refrained from accepting any honors for his achievement.

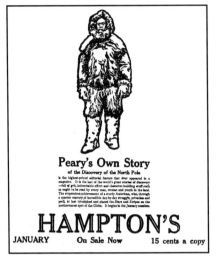

Peary's Own Story
of the Discovery of the North Pole
is the highest-priced editorial feature that ever appeared in a
magazine. It is the last of the world's great stories of discovery
—full of grit, indomitable effort and character-building stuff such
as ought to be read by every man, woman and youth in the land.
The stupendous achievement of a sturdy American, who, through
a quarter century of incredible day-by-day struggle, privation and
peril, at last triumphed and placed the Stars and Stripes on the
northernmost spot of the Globe. It begins in the January number.

HAMPTON'S

JANUARY   On Sale Now   15 cents a copy

With Ben Hampton's money in the bank, he began negotiations for a series of lectures. He refused all offers of less than $1,000, pointing out that Cook had been paid much more for telling his completely fabricated tale. The newspapers speculated that he might easily gain $100,000 in the first year alone.

He got a tenth of that in one night. On February 3, 1910, at the Metropolitan Opera House, a national testimonial given in his honor awarded him a purse of $10,000 donated by 31 prominent New Yorkers. In his acceptance of the purse, the commander said he would donate the money toward the American Antarctic Expedition he had announced the previous day, which was to be organized in conjunction with the National Geographic Society.

By then, he had also signed a contract with Frederick A. Stokes and Company to produce his North Pole narrative in book form at a price rumored to be more than $150,000. He immediately asked for "a first class literary man," who could assist in the preparation of the material for the book. "What I want is someone who has the big, masculine literary instinct," he told Stokes, "as well as literary practice and training, to take hold of and revise material already written, cut out such portions as do not seem desirable, transpose portions and, if necessary, strengthen, under my direction."[38]

Stokes recommended A.E. Thomas, a former reporter for the New York *Sun,* "a man of unusual energy, good judgment and capacity for work."[39] Peary approved the choice, as long as Thomas's contribution was kept entirely confidential, and asked Stokes to set him to work revising the first three *Hampton's* articles for starters. But Stokes objected that he needed at least an outline of the proposed contents of the whole book before he could really begin.

Beyond the *Hampton's* material, Thomas had to rely on personal interviews with Donald MacMillan and Captain Bartlett, although they seemed reluctant, Thomas thought, to say anything that Peary might not like. For many details he was forced to draw upon the voluminous diaries of Dr. Goodsell, which were furnished by Peary. Peary himself, it seemed, was too preoccupied with trying to get a retirement bill through Congress to be of much help.

A number of bills had been introduced into both houses of Congress to, variously, award Peary a gold medal, vote him the Thanks of Congress for discovering the North Pole, and retire him with the rank of rear admiral at the highest pay grade—$5,625 per annum—retroactive to April 6, 1909. A Senate bill passed without question on February 9, but despite an intense pro-Peary propaganda campaign, in the House the Peary bills were in trouble.

Peary's actions during the months since his return from the Arctic had made him many bitter enemies. Even though his supporters used the collapse of Cook's claim to justify Peary's attitude during the controversy, many simply saw him, as one newspaper put it, as a "coarse-grained and ill-tempered boor," and Cook's Copenhagen fiasco had made some congressmen leery of any polar claim. Furthermore, the secretary of the Navy, George Meyer, objected to the wording of the bill that had passed the Senate. The secretary said the bill's reference to Peary as "Commander" was incorrect and should be changed to "Civil Engineer," his proper title as a staff officer. Meyer also pointed out that, as a staff officer, Peary could not be made a rear admiral, as only the chief of the Bureau of Yards and Docks could hold that title in the Engineer Corps. "It seems to me," concluded Secretary Meyer, "inappropriate to confer upon him a title for which his previous education, training, and services have not fitted him."[40] He did not object to the retirement of Civil Engineer Peary with the *rank* of rear admiral in his own corps, however.

Even when Peary confidentially let it be known that he would forgo his pension and settle for retirement as rear admiral, the House bills failed to clear the House Rules Subcommittee on Naval Affairs. Some members insisted on a hearing, since granting such honors to Peary without a hearing, one of the committee members said derisively, would be as advisable as making Matt Henson a captain in the U.S. Navy.[41]

At first a hearing seemed a mere formality, but it soon became evident that at least one member of the committee, Representative Robert Bruce Macon of Arkansas, seemed intent on making it a test of Peary's polar claim. Peary blamed this on the jealousy of the line officers; to jump him two ranks and then retire him with the highest pay grade in that rank was more than many of them could swallow. Peary now saw he had a real fight on his hands.

The first witnesses called on March 4, 1910, before Subcommittee no. 8 of the Committee on Naval Affairs were two of the three men who, on behalf of the National Geographic Society, had examined Peary's records: Henry Gannett, now president of the society, and Otto Tittman, superintendent of the Coast and Geodetic Survey. The third, Admiral Chester, was out of the country and could not appear.

Under questioning, Tittman said that in his official capacity at the Geodetic Survey he had been provided with no proof related to Peary's North Pole expedition other than a line of soundings and tidal observations, and even for these, he had never seen the original records. When asked to detail what other evidence he had examined while a member of the society's subcommittee that decided Peary had found the Pole, Tittman deferred to Henry Gannett and excused himself to appear before the House Appropriations Committee. Thus it fell to Gannett, assisted by Gilbert Grosvenor, who had accompanied him to the hearing, to explain the nature of the examination of Peary's records by the National Geographic Society in November 1909.

Gannett testified that none of the subcommittee had seen any original records of soundings made on the trip to the Pole. Peary, Gannett said, had brought his diary of the journey, "which had all the earmarks of being the original," and read the entries in it from three or four days before Captain Bartlett left him, at approximately 88° north latitude, until Peary reached land again at Cape Columbia. But the society's president was not sure whether anyone had read the whole record. Gannett explained that they had also examined Peary's observations, which were not in his diary but on separate sheets of paper. Gannett said there were no longitude observations among these, only ones for latitude.

Further answers disclosed that none of the other members of the expedition, and explicitly Matt Henson, had been called to give corroborating testimony before the society's subcommittee, and that Peary's instruments had not been inspected or tested, but were merely looked at after nightfall as they lay in a trunk at Pennsylvania Station.

Gannett, after some prodding, admitted that anyone with enough knowledge of navigational mathematics could concoct convincing observations without actually having reached the Pole. He agreed that a set of observations without a narrative and without a knowledge of the character of the man who was making the claim would not be sufficient proof of such a journey. By implication, the society's subcommittee had had no testimony but Peary's unsupported word that he had made the journey recorded in his journal or that he had made the observations at the places indicated on his loose slips of paper.

When he was asked about the value of Peary's testimony and whether he believed Peary had reached the Pole before he saw Peary's proofs, Gannett explained, "Everyone who knows Peary by reputation knows he would not lie; I know him by reputation. . . . I certainly did."[42]

The subcommittee decided after hearing Gannett's testimony that the examination of Peary's records was not as methodical and exhaustive as had been implied by the society's official report; they wanted to see the original records for themselves. Gannett, however, informed the congressmen that Commander Peary did not wish to have his original observations or his polar journal made public, but he declined to speak for the commander as to his reasons. The congressmen voted to call for them nonetheless.

On March 7 the hearings reconvened with the expectation of examining the commander's records. What they got instead was a brief statement from Representative De Alva Alexander of New York, a close friend of Thomas Hubbard's, acting as Peary's personal representative. He explained why they would not be granted this opportunity: "Commander Peary and his friends say that contracts signed months ago with his publishers render it impossible to make his records and scientific data public now. It would not only subject Peary to heavy damages . . . but it would be breaking faith with his publishers."[43]

The "Peary Bill" was then tabled and the proceedings adjourned.

Atlanta was scheduled as Peary's first stop on a series of lectures under the management of the Civic Forum. It proved a very inauspicious start. Governor Joseph M. Brown refused to introduce Peary at the lecture. Governor

Brown, who turned out to be something of an armchair explorer, said he believed Peary was a faker and expressed his belief that Dr. Cook was the true discoverer of the North Pole. "What proof does Peary bring save his own word?" asked Brown. "Cook brings the same and as good. If Cook has handed us a gold brick, Peary has handed us a paste diamond.

"It is up to Peary to explain how Cook's story can be false and his identical story can be true. The American people will not accept his smile as proof that he is not as great a faker as he charges Cook to be. . . . Peary's selfishness has disgusted the country."[44]

Perhaps as a result of the governor's denunciation, the audience in Atlanta was very sparse. But even in Pittsburgh there was suspicion of Peary's claim. Stung by the demise of Cook's claims after his enthusiastic introduction of the doctor at his lecture in 1909, Dr. John A. Brashear demanded proof before Peary spoke there. Peary's manager offered to cancel the Pittsburgh engagement and any other to prevent the commander from receiving a further affront. But he added ruefully, "Within the past week, the state of public sentiment has become worse than indifferent, owing to the non-submission to the Congressional Committee of the proofs that Committee demanded."[45]

Peary fulfilled his engagement in Pittsburgh, but one account of the lecture reported only 65 paying customers in the audience. The balance of the lectures in the South had to be canceled for want of ticket sales.

Though Peary's spokesman had indicated before Congress that the commitment to his publishers was the primary consideration in not producing his original records, at *Hampton's,* Elsa Barker was experiencing difficulty in getting them as well. Peary was not providing copy that she could rework into a convincing narrative, despite extensive interviews designed to obtain a framework on which to hang it. Mrs. Barker could see that she had taken on "a gigantic labor" in agreeing to do the Peary series and pleaded for his assistance:

> As you may imagine, I have many anxieties and responsibilities in regard to this enterprise of the Magazine, and I have tried to keep an eye on everything—even the advertising department—in accordance with my promise to you last November.
>
> As to the articles themselves, of course, I must go right along with them to the very last word, as you cannot have a sudden break in the continuity of the general style, each writer's style being as distinctive from any other as his own hand writing. A break would show badly in the Magazine, and still more badly in the book itself. I have had so little time during the last seven months to think about myself that I had forgotten that while I may have a man's ability for work and a man's will, I have only a woman's nerves. . . .
>
> Of course I cannot break down before the end of this work, any more than you could have broken down on the road to the Pole. I merely tell you the situation, in order that you might help me all you can.[46]

As the first anniversary of his discovery approached, Elsa Barker wrote to the commander hoping to get enough information about Peary's proofs to convince anyone that he had, indeed, found the Pole. Though she had received a copy of his diary covering his time there, it did not contain the information she needed. "I hope you will have sent me before this reaches you more of the data which I need for April 6th and 7th," she wrote. "That is the climax of the story, and the possibility is very great. If we do not have an article which will make everybody sit up and take notice, it is our own fault.

"I hope you will have found time to dictate two or three thousand words relative to those days. Your eyes being so tired from the observations, there are no entries in the journal. The whole world is intensely interested in what you did during those two days, even to minute details. You know humanity is simply a many-headed child, and children all love stories. Even my associates on the Magazine are as curious about this as are the little boys in the street. The instinct is universal."[47]

As an illustration of her associates' curiosity, she attached a memorandum from *Hampton's* editorial staff indicating the trend of the comments the *Hampton's* series was generating:

> The tone of many letters that come to us is that of impatience. Writers say that Peary has not substantiated his claim to discovery; has not presented any scientific data. Readers are impatient for him to clear up the apparent mystery about the location of the North Pole. Of course this is very good from a circulation standpoint, but we must take special pains to make good in this respect in the July and August articles. . . . I am expecting, and I know the public is expecting, to get a very clear understanding of just how Peary knew he was at the Pole,—expecting the most interesting and instructive popular science article that it is possible to write. . . .
>
> Along lines of general criticism of lack of scientific data in reports published thus far, it has been questioned that he got any nearer the pole than Cook did, because his descriptions of the conditions are so similar to those described by Cook. It has been said of his lectures that they lack detail in the events of the last few days of the dash to the Pole, and that he describes too quickly the return journey. I am convinced that careful attention to detail and putting into popular form the Commander's scientific observations are the chief essentials of the July and August articles.[48]

Frederick A. Stokes was equally frustrated and had his secretary write to the commander: "Mr. Thomas is becoming disturbed about the possibility of completing his work or even doing a satisfactory amount of it before the time of your departure for Europe. He has been able to do nothing for a week for lack of copy."[49]

Most of the complaints to *Hampton's* came from the heartland, where

Dr. Cook still had a strong following and where many believed Peary to be an unworthy hero, even if he had succeeded. In Kansas the *Emporia Gazette* editorialized:

> There are legions of people in this country who will believe that Congressman Macon is doing the right thing.
>
> He says there is no more proof that Peary discovered the Pole than there was that Cook discovered it, and he is right. When Peary first returned from the Arctic he declined to make public his alleged proofs, because he wanted to use them in his magazine narrative, and his magazine narrative presents nothing that can be considered proof. Dozens of geographers and other experts have criticized it, and have pointed out that it presents all sorts of inconsistencies. Peary has been asked a hundred times how it was he went to the pole an inch at a time, and returned wearing seven league boots, and he never has explained.
>
> His attitude has been so insolent from the first that the people are tired of him. He has profited by the humiliation of Cook. Because Cook has proved a faker, it has been taken for granted that Peary must be genuine.
>
> The latter has disgusted the people by the mercenary spirit he has shown. While writing about his devotion to science, his chief concern seems to be nailing the money.[50]

Peary's friends had seen to it that his recall to active duty was postponed. Instead, he would make his tour of Europe. As he prepared to depart, news came that Mount McKinley had been climbed. The conqueror, however, was neither Herschel Parker nor Belmore Browne.

Tom Lloyd had returned to Fairbanks on April 11 with the news that he and three of his party had reached the summit and there had attempted to plant their flag tied to the 14-foot spruce pole they had carried with them for that purpose. But there was nothing but ice and snow on the true summit, Lloyd said, so they climbed the lower North Peak for good measure and there erected the flag on a rocky outcrop.

The April 12 *Fairbanks Times* had trumpeted the news:

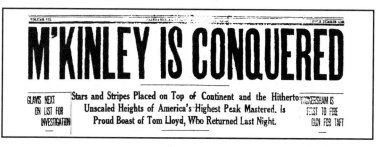

> Lloyd asserts that he has positive proof that Dr. Cook never climbed the mountain and that he will be able to demonstrate this to all. He says that he has photographs taken at the various heights and that the scenery on the upper reaches of the mountain is appalling in its grandeur. . . .
>
> The ascent was made, to a considerable extent, over the trail traveled by Dr. Cook. While Lloyd is reticent as to details, he claims that the party was able to determine beyond peradventure that the doctor never reached beyond a certain point.
>
> Tom is unstinting in his praise of the men who stayed with him on the trip. . . . He is becomingly modest in regard to his share in the conquering of the 20,464-foot mountain that, so far as is known, was never climbed by human being before.

Tom Lloyd had a right to be modest, as it turned out.

On April 26 Peary and his family sailed for Europe aboard the *Kronprinzessin Cecille.* Accompanying them, and sharing in most of the honors, would be Captain Bob Bartlett. Peary would first go to London to address a dazzling audience, including King Edward, at the Royal Albert Hall.

Early in the morning of May 4, Halley's Comet, that ancient harbinger of doom and disaster, hung brightly in the predawn sky as Peary polished his speech. That evening, Robert E. Peary looked nervous as he came on the stage to receive the applause of the 10,000 gathered to greet him. One, however, was absent: the king was indisposed.

As Peary proceeded through his 90-minute lecture, and as lantern slide after lantern slide was thrown upon the screen to illustrate his triumphant march to the earth's northern axis, the overheated projector shattered the glass images before the eyes of the audience. Nevertheless, when he had finished, Peary stepped forward to acknowledge the thunderous applause and seemed almost overcome with emotion as he was presented the special gold medal of the Royal Geographical Society from the hands of the society's president, Leonard Darwin.

Although he had been introduced as the conqueror of the North Pole, on the edge of the medal was inscribed simply: "Robert Edwin Peary, 1910. Presented by the Royal Geographical Society, for Arctic Exploration 1886–1909."

As he held the medal up before the vast audience, the golden disk slipped from its box, fell to the floor with a hollow clang and disappeared between the floorboards of the platform. Awkward attempts to retrieve it were accompanied by laughter.

Peary's Royal Geographical Society medal, 1910.

The next day, after Peary's second lecture in Queen's Hall, it was announced that Edward VII had died of pneumonia, and Peary's European itinerary had to be rescheduled around the king's funeral. What, if anything, the superstitious Peary thought of this sequence of events is not known.

From London the Peary family went on to Berlin, Rome, Vienna and Budapest, as Peary collected his gold medals and Bartlett several silver ones, along with the praises of scientific dignitaries and royal personages. Returning to Great Britain, at Edinburgh he received an honorary degree and was presented by the Scottish Geographical Society with a replica of a sixteenth-century three-masted ship in full sail, such as Hudson or Davis might have used. Two feet high, mounted on wheels and made of more than 100 ounces of silver and gold, it was a most magnificent trophy.

His tour of England and Scotland prevented Peary from seeing off Captain Robert Falcon Scott on June 1, when he sailed for the Antarctic on his ship *Terra Nova* with hopes of duplicating Peary's success at the other pole. But before leaving England, Peary was presented to the new king, George V, at Marlborough House.

At Antwerp there was another gold medal waiting, the same as had been given to Dr. Cook in silver in 1900. But on his return to Berlin for a lecture engagement, Peary received something he did not desire. At the Hotel Adlon he was served legal papers in connection with a suit filed by Rudolph Franke, seeking the recovery of the property he alleged Peary had extorted from him at Etah in 1908. Peary refused to accept them at first, but he was reminded by the bearer that he had been legally served before witnesses and could not ignore the service.

On June 11 the Peary party boarded the *Mauritania* to return to the United States; despite the ill omens at Albert Hall, all in all, the tour had been a total triumph.

While the discoverer of the North Pole was being covered with glory, the man who had first claimed that title continued, even in his absence, to accumulate allegations of deceit. In January a statement had appeared by Governor Muller, who said that Cook had cheated him of $500 in his short stay in Holsteinborg while seeking assistance for the stricken *Miranda* in 1894, and in May a story with the headline COOK TRIED TO STEAL PARSON'S LIFE WORK alleged that the doctor had tried to claim credit for the Yahgan dictionary he had obtained from Lucas Bridges at the conclusion of the *Belgica's* voyage. Between the two were the negative reports on Cook's Mount McKinley claims given by members of the Lloyd party.

When Peary arrived again in New York, Mount McKinley was back in the news. After the *New York Times* had carried an exclusive story about the conquest of the great peak on June 5, criticisms began to appear and shortcomings started to be pointed out. Tom Lloyd's two surveyors had quit before the climb began, so there were no independent scientific witnesses. The sourdoughs had lost their barometer, so they couldn't measure the exact height of the mountain. None of the pictures that Lloyd produced showed any evidence of having been taken at a very great height, and it was rumored that Tom had admitted in private that he himself had never gotten near the top, though he said some of the others had.

Still, the other three men refused to contradict Lloyd. The members of Lloyd's party signed an affidavit at Fairbanks on June 11, 1910, saying that on April 3, all four had unfurled the flag on the northern summit of Mount McKinley. Even so, considering Lloyd's lack of proof and the contradictions that had surfaced, the whole thing was put down as just more of Tom Lloyd's big bragging. Many suspected Lloyd had just spun a yarn designed to avoid the huge forfeit bet made by Bill McPhee. By the time the ice-dust settled, as one local writer put it, "You couldn't get the price of a meal ticket from any newspaper or magazine on earth for carrying a grand piano to the summit of McKinley and then telling the story of the feat."[51]

Even so, Herbert Bridgman thought he might get some anti-Cook publicity out of the affair. Lloyd and his party were offered honorary memberships in the Explorers Club and the Peary Arctic Club, and Tom Lloyd was given an all-expenses-paid trip to New York to speak to the clubs' members.[52]

The Explorers Club's own expedition under Parker and Browne was unaware of the doubts of Lloyd's claims. At the time his story appeared they were on their way up Ruth Glacier to trace Cook's route and, if possible, duplicate his summit picture. They followed the doctor's example in every respect, even using a boat that was a copy of the *Bolshoy.*

In the *Explorer* they had proceeded rapidly up the rivers to the very place Cook had disembarked four years before. There they found the log cabin built by John Dokkin when he stayed to prospect that winter. On the way they passed another expedition, which, without the inventive doctor's example to follow, was having a hard time poling an unwieldy boat up the Chulitna.

This was the expedition of the Mazama Club. Claude E. Rusk, its leader, was a lawyer and one of the men who had volunteered in October 1909 to accompany Dr. Cook to retrace his climb, and the Mazama Club was the same mountaineering club that had so heartily welcomed Cook in Seattle on his return in 1906. Rusk was cosponsored by the *New York Herald* and the *Oregonian* and therefore seemed disposed to be biased toward Cook's claim. Peary even suspected that the expedition's real intention was to plant false records on the summit to aid the doctor.

With the head start provided by the *Explorer,* Parker, Browne and three other expedition members reached Ruth Glacier well ahead of Rusk and after much hard traveling came to a place they recognized from Cook's photographs, which Browne now described in his diary:

> June 22   Camp 11
>   Glacier Point! The historical camping place of Dr. Cook. We are at the fork of the Ruth Glacier or the point where Ruth Glacier comes out of the great cliff lined gorge below 5 mammoth peaks.

Glacier No. 2 joins it from the east and . . . beyond which rises
the mountain where Dr. Cook faked his Mount McKinley pictures. I have the the *[sic]* mountain photos of "The Top of the
Continent" with me and from them we can tell almost to a dot
where Cook went. It seems a pitiful thing as one stands surrounded by the overwhelming grandeur of these noble crags—he
must have had some pretty unhappy moments![53]

They did not reach Glacier Point with nearly the speed that Cook and
Barrill claimed, because they backhauled loads up the glacier to ensure
enough supplies for an extended siege.

They wanted good weather to duplicate the doctor's photographs for
General Hubbard, so instead of pushing on to the base of McKinley, they
waited in camp until June 28 for it to clear. Once on the tributary glacier, they
looked long and hard at the surrounding mountains for the 8,000-foot peak
that Barrill had said was the one in Cook's photograph, but none looked
likely. Farther on they climbed a saddle, and looking back toward the main
glacier, they recognized the location of one of Cook's photographs that he said
had been taken from McKinley's flank. Actually, the main slopes were still 19
miles away.

Continuing from the saddle up a snow cornice, Browne suddenly heard
Professor Parker, who was in the lead, yell, "We've got it!":

2.35 P.M. June 28th Tuesday—Eureka!!! Am sitting on the peak (?)
(it is a little rock on a saddle) that Dr. Cook faked as Mt. McKinley, it is pretty well smothered in snow but is easily recognizable.

We are waiting for good photographing conditions before getting our pictures. . . .

Looking away in any direction one can see nothing but a sea of
great grim silent snow smothered rock ribbed peaks. . . . Such a
scene of desolate savage beauty has never blessed my eyes before.
. . . This is a land for a man to love! We keep wondering how Cook
must have felt standing here alone with Barrill (we have located by
several photos of his the very rocks he stood on). In civilization his
deed seems criminal but here its a sacreledge as well.

The peaks about us are remarkable for their broken character—
I have never before seen rock so rotten seemed cracked and disintegrated by the forces of nature. Peaks stand about us that look as if a
breath of wind would send them crashing and rumbling to the
glaciers far below. . . .

The snow is about 10 ft. deep where Barrill stood and the cornice has changed being in places over 10 ft. deeper. This prevents
us from showing the middle peak of the first 3 Ruth Glacier peaks
in its proper position to correspond with Cook's photo. But these
differences are of slight moment as the features of rocks that show
are all the proof required. . . .

> Prof. Parker's hypsometer . . . places Cook's peak approximately
> 5,100 ft. above the sea [and a mere 250 feet above the glacier]. . . .
> This indeed is a low altitude for the "Top of Our Continent"![54]

After retracing their steps to the main glacier and ascending to where it bent sharply to the left, Parker and Browne spent the next three weeks trying to line out a route toward the top but were unable to find any way to get over the great seracs that fell down the eastern and southwestern ridges of the mountain. They concluded that the mountain was a lot easier to conquer with pen and ink than with ropes and ice creepers.

Before they abandoned their attempt, they climbed a mountain they named Explorers' Peak and looked out over the amazing array of rugged, unnamed crags before selecting one that seemed outstanding for one final task: "On the east stood a magnificent mountain that rose in the shape of a rock-ribbed, ice-encrusted throne, above a broad base whose lower snow-fields had been carved into buttresses by the glacier winds. This peak we named Mount Hubbard after General Thomas H. Hubbard, president of the Peary Arctic Club, whose lifelong interest in exploration has been of such great benefit to mankind."[55]

The Fake Peak.

The Mazama party was not nearly so well equipped as Hubbard's. Though it also reached the bend in the glacier, it had less time and no more luck reaching the summit by the doctor's alleged route from the south. Every man with Rusk came away convinced that no approach from this side of the mountain could ever carry off a victory over the mighty uplift in anything like the time Cook had claimed. As Rusk and his climbing partners looked out over the magnificent maze of peaks at the head of the great gorge of Ruth Glacier, he was utterly in awe and believed that he now knew the truth:

> Are there, any other place on Earth, such mountains as those
> stupendous piles that culminate the Alaska Range? . . .

What glorious mountains they are! Unique and stupendous; immutable and lone![56]

To the northwest of our camp the monstrous form of Mt. Mc-Kinley rose to a dizzy height, the summit twelve miles away in an air line. But between us and the massif of the mountain a succession of precipitous ridges barred the way. The whole southern and eastern faces of McKinley are torn by stupendous precipices where even the snow can find no spot to cling. These great walls rise from the very base of the mountain to the summit itself. From the more gradual northeast slope, however, a long, high ridge leads down. To reach the crest of this ridge is the problem of the ascent. The lower part is broken by precipices and the slopes are frightfully steep. It seems to be separated from the range by deep-cut passes and it is doubtful if one could find a route from the roof of this range to the top. . . .

. . . As we gazed upon the forbidding crags of the great mountain, and realized that it would require perhaps weeks or months in which to explore a route to the summit, we realized how utterly impossible and absurd was the story of this man, who, carrying a pack, claims to have started from the mouth of the Tokositna on the eighth of September, and to have stood on the highest point of McKinley on the sixteenth of the same month. The man does not live who can perform such a feat![57]

The Mazama party also independently confirmed that some of the pictures in *To the Top of the Continent* were misrepresentations, and that none of these were taken beyond the seventh peak along the glacier—the point where Barrill said the doctor had turned back. Foggy weather prevented them from investigating the peak that Browne believed was the one represented as "the top of our continent," but they identified from afar the peak they thought most likely to be the one in Cook's summit photograph. They named it "Mazama Peak," but it was not the same one Parker and Browne had photographed and named "Fake Peak."

As they retreated down the glacier, Parker and Browne returned once more to the Fake Peak to take more photographs. Some melting had taken place, exposing more of the rocks, but much of it still remained smothered in snow.

When the expeditions returned, the two leaders made their reports. Parker and Browne had failed to climb Mount McKinley, but that didn't matter to General Hubbard. He had gotten everything he wanted.

"This morning," he told Peary, "I had a talk with Professor Parker and Belmore Brown. They followed Cook's route and have photographed the summit which he gave in his book as the top of Mt. McKinley, 5300 feet above sea level and sixteen miles from the top of the mountain. Their

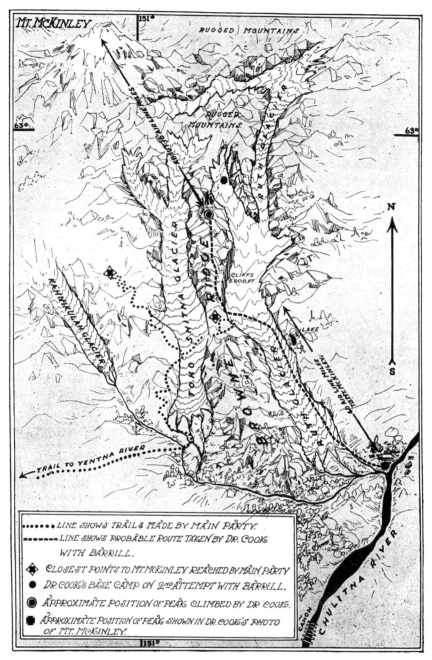

Belmore Browne's map showing Cook's route in 1906.

photographs are exact reproductions of the prominent features shown by Cook's picture. . . . Nothing could more clearly prove Cook's deliberate intent to impose on the public. . . . The reading public should be informed in a way that will be impressive and that will reach everybody who reads the newspapers. I think this can be arranged without much trouble."[58]

In an interview given before his expedition set out to prove his former friend's fraud, Herschel Parker had astounded the reporter when he had little but praise for Dr. Cook anyway. "Cook was a delightful companion," said he. "He is one of the best outdoor men I ever knew. He is brave as any man can be, he is strong and enduring, and no man can go further on any trip than Dr. Cook can—if the starting conditions are equal. The trouble with Cook was that he lacked totally executive ability and scientific knowledge. He could not plan, he could not direct an expedition, and he could not take reliable observations. But give him the single stunt of climbing a mountain or fording a river, and he will go as far as any man. There are few men of my acquaintance that could follow him over a tramp of a day or a month."

"Then why did he fake that Mt. McKinley climb?" asked the reporter.

"He needed the money," was Professor Parker's explanation. "He had tired of being a practicing physician, and determined to make his living as an explorer. He liked the life. But up in Alaska he found himself bankrupt, and harassed by claims some of which, at least, were unjust. He could not have gotten out of the country if he had not raised money somehow."

Now, after Parker's return, even having declared that his expedition had forever destroyed the doctor's claims, he still called Cook's 1906 attempt "a glorious failure." As for Tom Lloyd, Parker was less forgiving. After reading his account, he called his claim to the summit "manifestly a fabrication" and maintained "that Dr. Cook did not have anything on the Lloyd party when it came to fiction."[59]

Perhaps the professor, having been over the same ground, owed his continued respect for Dr. Cook to the recognition of the daring of this man who, with just a 40-pound pack and a single companion, had penetrated such an awesome and unknown wilderness and gotten as far as he had and back in just two weeks, even though Parker was now sure the doctor had failed in his ultimate goal.

In the end, Claude Rusk, too, having seen the overwhelming obstacles barring Cook's route, reluctantly came to the same conclusion:

> Now I can say without fear of ever having to retract, that he did not climb Mt. McKinley.
>
> Originally, I was a believer in Dr. Cook, and it was only when the proof of his deception became too strong to resist that I lost faith in him. I entered upon the Mt. McKinley project absolutely without prejudice against him, and would have been only too glad to have found his claims just. In many respects Cook is a remarkable man, with numerous admirable qualities. The pity of it all is

that he should have spoiled a great career by his failure to resist a unique temptation.[60]

That is all for Dr. Cook. He had many admirers who would have rejoiced to see his claims vindicated, and I, too, would have been glad to add my mite in clearing his name. But it could not be. As he sowed so has he reaped. If he is mentally unbalanced, he is entitled to the pity of mankind. If he is not, there is no corner of the earth where he can hide from his past.[61]

CHAPTER 19

I Suppose I Am

PEARY'S EUROPEAN TOUR HAD BEEN GRATIFYING, BUT HIS ELATION MUST HAVE quickly faded as he thought of all the unfinished business awaiting him at home. The Congress had suspended consideration of his promotion bill, and he knew he could not now avoid a personal appearance before the subcommittee, one of whose members was openly hostile to him.

There had been all sorts of wrangling. Attempts to bypass the subcommittee, accept the findings of the National Geographic Society as official or amend the bill had all failed. When the subcommittee proposed that Admirals Melville and Schley and General Greely form a three-man board to examine Peary's proofs, the *New York Times* asked sarcastically why Dr. Cook and "The Admiral of the Mexican Navy," B.S. Osbon, shouldn't sit in as well. After some behind-the-scenes persuasion by a lobbyist hired for Peary by General Hubbard, the idea was quashed. Peary even asked former President Roosevelt to appear before the subcommittee on his behalf. TR diplomatically declined.[1]

It was now Peary who was crying conspiracy to General Hubbard:

> You can accept it as a fact that there is an organized, vicious, and unscrupulous campaign to discredit me, if possible.
>
> The reason for this is, as I have already indicated to you, that if I can be discredited, such a result will (at least in their own mind) rehabilitate a great many individuals, organizations and newspapers.
>
> The three parties of this campaign, in the order of their importance (and I believe, activity) are "the line," the New York Herald, and Cook and his friends. . . .
>
> . . . The Herald was the patron and backer of Cook, and while it has been quiescent in this matter since last November, Bennett would jump in again, with all his unscrupulous ability, if he felt he had the slightest chance to discredit me, because if such result could be accomplished, it would not only justify him for the lying campaign which the Herald waged against me last fall, but would also be a body blow to the man, whom Bennett probably hates more than any other one, William C. Reick, of the Times. . . [2]

The *Times* kept up a running editorial campaign against Peary's opponents, saying that the subcommittee's "behavior would be detestable in a community of molluscs" and lamenting as a national disgrace its failure to vote
American honors for a hero who had been honored all over Europe. When
Representative Macon had said he personally believed Peary had turned south
a day or two after leaving Captain Bartlett and if he did not get Peary's proofs
would "expose the whole business on the floor of Congress," the *Times*
taunted, "Turn yourself loose, Mr. Macon, and let us see you perform."[3]

Besides his difficulties in Congress, Peary's literary contracts were an endless source of irritation. Though *Hampton's* had said that Peary's proof, when
published, would "prove his claim beyond all cavil," the articles had been unconvincing. Many inconsistencies had been pointed out in the press, and
Stokes had warned Peary that he should "scrutinize every statement that may
give the slightest opportunity to the enemy" in his manuscript to avoid future
criticism.[4] Peary agreed that his book must not perpetuate any of the errors
that had escaped notice in *Hampton's*. But he was unwilling to assume this task
himself, suggesting instead "someone who could put themselves in the place
of a critic anxious to prove Peary a liar out of his own mouth."[5]

Nevertheless, when the book was published in September 1910, it was
found to be full of errors. The most grievous one, it seemed to the horrified
Stokes, was on the large colored map that accompanied it. Even now, when
Peary's adversary seemed to be condemned to complete obloquy, the specter
of Dr. Cook had insinuated itself into the commander's own book. There, just
above Crocker Land, in the otherwise blank Arctic Ocean, lay Bradley Land!

"It is cruel that this insidious and unpardonable mistake should have occurred," fumed Peary's infuriated publisher. "It is especially deplorable because a mistake of this kind is more annoying to Commander Peary than any
other that could have been made. He has telegraphed us expressing his annoy-

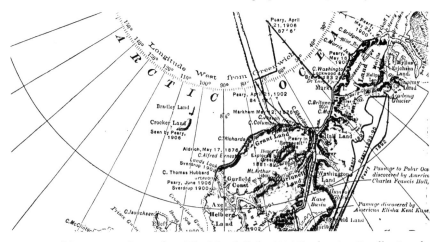

Portion of the suppressed map from The North Pole *(1910), showing Bradley Land.*

ance, and has in so doing given us the very first expression of disapproval of anything that we have done in our valued relations with him."[6] Stokes recalled all stock on hand and had them destroyed, but some copies had already been sent out—some of them to sharp-eyed reviewers.

The North Pole was not a financial success. Stokes's salesmen in all parts of the country reported resistance from store owners. From the South one wrote, "The feeling that he has not proved his case seems to be universal," and in the West, Peary's failure to send his proofs to Copenhagen was mentioned. But in the East, merchants were more pragmatic. One noted that sales of *Hampton's* had dropped 50 percent when it ran Peary's story and considered the book a bad risk; another said he still had copies of Peary's 1907 book, *Nearest the Pole,* that he couldn't sell.[7]

Just before Peary had sailed for Europe in the spring, word had come of the collapse of his antarctic scheme. Peary had first proposed the expedition in 1905 and had been planning it ever since he returned to the *Roosevelt* in April 1909. At Cape Sheridan he had filled page after page with elaborate plans needing hundreds of thousands of dollars to finance. Since he so strongly objected to "usurpers" in the Arctic, he justified his own proposal to enter the Antarctic by saying he would stay far away from Scott's announced route; instead, he would establish a base via the Weddell Sea.

He had sent feelers to England to gauge British reaction. On January 5, 1910, he had received a letter from Captain Scott welcoming an American expedition but informing him that Dr. William S. Bruce had designs on the same route Peary proposed. Even so, Peary continued to make his plans.

Peary had originally thought he might lead the expedition personally. But in light of all the controversy the North Pole dispute had evoked, Herbert Bridgman and Thomas Hubbard thought his participation in "anything short of perfect success . . . would detract from the great achievement already reached" and advised "it would be better to let the National Geographic Society take the lead and facilitate them as much as we are able."[8]

Arrangements along these lines were made, with the *Roosevelt* set to sail in August. The society circulated a letter predicting that the expedition would be "a project which promised unusually rich scientific results, with the well-defined possibility of bringing to our country an honor such as it now holds in the north."[9] But for every pledge of money, the society got a letter abusing Peary, some of them "very violent." In the end, the American Antarctic Expedition had to be abandoned for lack of funds.[10] For this, Peary's friends blamed Dr. Cook and the cloud he had cast over honest exploration.

As for Cook, he had not been heard from for ten months. In that time sightings of the missing explorer in New York, Bermuda, the south of France, Venezuela, Callao, Pernambuco, London, Paris, Rome, Berlin, Toronto, Edinburgh, Jerusalem, Jericho and Halifax had been reported. All these proved false. But even in his absence, the doctor held a certain fascination for the press. How someone who had achieved such notoriety could go anywhere without being recognized by somebody would have seemed impossible. "The queer part of it is that there is no particular need for him to remain in concealment," argued the *New York Times*. "Using the audacity with which he is well supplied, and utilizing the credulity which he is so skillful in inspiring, he could still make something of a fight against the Copenhagen decision—could still make a colorable plea for a suspension of judgment. But the man remains what he has always been—inexplicable—obviously mad, but most methodical. That in all these months he has nowhere been recognized is the culminating mystery of the strange career. It is to be hoped that he will be found at last, if only that the psychologists may investigate him."[11]

One columnist believed he had the answer to why no reported sightings had been confirmed—Cook was in northern Greenland:

> Dr. Cook knew a thing or two. He knew, for instance, that any announcement of his purpose of going to the arctic regions to recover his proofs would result in a counter movement on the part of his enemies to beat him to them, and to destroy them. He had seen enough to convince him that his enemies would stop at nothing whatever in order to rob him of the credit of his great achievement. . . . He stole a march on his enemies, and if he lives to get back to his own country he will come back with the goods, and all the world will acknowledge that he was indeed the man who discovered the north pole.
>
> It is hard to understand how those who believe that Peary reached the north pole can consistently refuse to believe that Cook reached it also, whether his papers show it or not. Cook got back first and told his story first. Peary, coming later, substantiated Cook's story in every important detail. If Peary reached the north pole and Cook did not, then Cook is the best guesser the world has ever produced.[12]

Actually, the Arctic was no longer on the doctor's itinerary. But it was on other people's minds. In January 1910 John R. Bradley had said he planned to consult with Otto Sverdrup on the possibility of a joint search for Bradley Land. And later in the same month, Rudolph Franke announced his own expedition to Crocker Land and Bradley Land. These came to nothing. Then, Joseph Bernier announced that he would be going to Bradley Land to claim it for Canada. This was taken more seriously, because Captain Bernier was a veteran arctic explorer and because he said he would stop first at Etah to pick up Etukishuk as a guide.

But there was another ship going north as well, the *Beothic,* a new iron sealer of 471 tons. She had been chartered by none other than Harry Whitney and Paul Rainey, another millionaire hunter, at a cost of $70,000 for the summer. Her captain was to be Bob Bartlett.

Immediately, rumors flew. Although her advertised mission was just a hunting trip, the presence of Bartlett and Whitney, the two men who had buried Cook's belongings at Etah—and the fact that Whitney had said repeatedly he never wished to return to the Arctic—stirred speculation as to what the game would be.

The *Beothic* sailed from Sydney on June 19, 1910. On August 30, her rivets leaking from collisions with the ice, she returned to Battle Harbour. Paul Rainey characterized as "a joke" Danish reports that at Upernavik in July the *Hans Egede* had hailed a yacht, whose crew members said they had John R. Bradley aboard, and that he and Whitney were bound for Etah to get Cook's records. Though he absolutely denied the *Beothic* had anything to do with these reports, Bartlett confirmed that his ship had visited Etah, the first vessel to do so since the *Roosevelt* had left the previous summer. He stated positively, however, that none of Cook's records were now there.

The sportsmen had also chosen for a "hunting ground" Cape Sparbo and took along Etukishuk as a guide. As the *Beothic* had approached the coast, Bartlett had seen two herds of musk oxen grazing on the rolling country around the cape, which was dotted with wildflowers, ground willow, grasses, moss and nesting birds. Near the shore, the Eskimo pointed out Cook's winter igloo, a hubblestone house whose roof of whalebones and sod had collapsed. Inside, Bartlett, Rainey and Whitney found it comfortably lined with musk ox and polar bear skins in magnificent condition.[13] Rainey took moving pictures of a musk ox hunt; Bartlett captured musk oxen and a polar bear for the Bronx Zoo, and after dropping off Etukishuk at Etah, they sailed home.

When the ship reached Bristol, Rhode Island, Paul Rainey reported he had brought no records of any kind back from Etah. At Glen Cove, Long Island, Rainey disembarked the animals and himself, after settling what the newspapers described as "a serious disagreement" with Whitney over how the spoils would be divided. Whitney then sailed with Captain Bartlett for Newfoundland to return the *Beothic* to her owners.[14]

En route to New York from Bartlett's home, the two chanced to meet Peary's lawyer, Charles Nichols, at North Station in Boston. Nichols wrote to Peary: "Captain said that he was very anxious to see you and that he had started once or twice to write you, but he could not write what he wanted to say and he thought some of coming to Eagle Island to see you, but was afraid the newspaper reporters would get hold of it and make game of it. Whitney wished to be remembered to you and sent his regards many times."[15]

Only Rainey was publicly forthcoming with any details about the *Beothic*'s visit to Etah:

> From the outset our expedition attracted a great deal of attention, the press and the public assuming that we were going after Dr. Cook's records. . . . But although it was not my original intention to visit the cache at Etah where Cook's records were said to be

concealed or his igloo at Cape Sparbo, I did, as a matter of fact, visit both places and secured interesting photographs of each. . . .

. . . The afternoon of the 25th [of July] I went ashore with [Harold] Hemment [the photographer] and several Eskimos and visited this much-discussed cache. I refrained from touching or opening it, on account of not wishing to be mixed up in the Peary-Cook controversy. The cache is a stone igloo. . . . The top has fallen in. The contents, whatever they may be, being covered with canvas, it was impossible for me to see anything. It seems peculiar, however, that an explorer returning from the pole and reaching a point where he could have obtained plenty of help from the Eskimos, should have left valuable records in a place so unprotected.[16]

Despite his stated unwillingness to mix himself in the controversy, Rainey volunteered that Etukishuk had asserted while on the *Beothic* that Cook had never been out of sight of land on their polar trip and that he had never seen Bradley Land.

The discoverer of that supposedly mythical place continued to remain just as elusive. After nearly a year of rumors and false sightings, the question of where Dr. Cook had been since the fall of 1909 was still a topic of speculation almost as mysterious as where he had been in the spring of 1908.

The last reliable word anyone had from Cook was on December 24, 1909, in a letter postmarked Cadiz, to Walter Lonsdale in Copenhagen. In it, Cook said he could be reached by writing to Mrs. Elmer H. Dudley, Mrs. Cook's sister, at 340 East 18th Street in New York, but he said nothing of the Danes' decision three days before.

On January 3, 1910, Lonsdale received a registered package from Gibraltar. The writing on the wrapper was Mrs. Cook's, and her fingerprint was in the wax seal that closed it. It contained one of Cook's original diaries. This Lonsdale presented to the Copenhagen scientists, but after examining it, they said its contents did not alter their decision. It was identical, in part, to the typed transcript sent previously, and there were no indications of Loose's observations in it.[17]

After mailing the notebook, Marie and Fred had decided on a trip to South America to try to escape their anxieties. The Cooks boarded the steamer *Cadiz* at Barcelona; not a soul on board spoke English, and the doctor was able to get some rest. When he had regained some physical and mental balance he began to worry again. He regretted he had not gone to Italy or kept in touch with Copenhagen: "For the first time, fears that my departure from New York might be construed as an admission made me uneasy. I hazarded all sorts of guesses regarding this—but never dreamed of what had been printed and what the public was saying about me."[18]

Upon landing at Montevideo, the Cooks went to Buenos Aires, and after a pleasant sojourn of a month in the Phoenix Hotel there, where the doctor began dictating notes for the book he planned to write, they returned to Montevideo.

On board the German steamship *Osiris,* which sailed from that city bound for Chile, were a druggist from New York, Frederick L. Upjohn, and his traveling companion, 17-year-old Daniel C. Riker. They asked to be thrown together with any Americans on the voyage and fell in with a Mr. and Mrs. Craig, whom they at first took to be modest, middle-class Americans. But the two soon noticed some peculiarities about the Craigs. They seemed reluctant to say anything about their pasts, even as to where they were from or when they had left the United States.

To pass the time, the boy spent several days with Mr. Craig, beating him regularly at double solitaire and checkers for hours on end. He noticed that Mrs. Craig, who usually called Mr. Craig "Fred," seemed to catch herself one time when she called her husband "Doctor." When Riker mentioned this to Mr. Upjohn, he suddenly realized who the Craigs were. At dinner that evening Riker and Upjohn dropped a remark about the North Pole to see their reaction. "I thought he was going to faint," Daniel Riker recalled. "He began talking about something else and would not take his eyes off the table, while his wife got as red as a beet, and also tried to change the subject."[19]

When Daniel tried to get a photograph of the dinner group, the Craigs protested they were not properly dressed, and when he insisted, Mr. Craig tried to get behind the others and pull his hat down over his face. Young Riker was sure that if this was not Dr. Cook, he was most certainly an escaped crook. At the first port, Valdivia, Upjohn went ashore and wired the *New York Times* that he had found the missing explorer.

At Corral, Chile, the Craigs sequestered themselves in the Hotel Oddo, which was soon besieged by reporters. When Max van Rysselberghe, the engineer of the *Belgica*, who had returned to Chile to live, presented his card, Mr. Craig refused to receive it. But they secretly met later, and Mr. Craig confirmed his true identity to his old shipmate. He told him he was working on a book that would reestablish his claim to the North Pole.

At the Cooks' every stop in Chile—Santiago, Valparaiso, Los Andes—they thought they saw reporters and imagined the crowds of people were staring at them at every turn. The doctor was seized with the old panic of being pursued and realized he might forever be a freakish object of curiosity wherever he went:

> For the first time the really world-wide interest in this mad quest began to dawn upon me, and for the first time, with a sense of almost paralysing terror, I faced the immeasurable extent of my world-wide ignominy. It filtered slowly into my mind, this thought—that throughout the world, in the huts of Andean mountaineers as well as the meeting halls of scientists, in the isles of the far southern Pacific as well as the great cities of America, in

the desolate homes of Russia, of deep Africa, wherever men lived along the trail of railroads and the tributaries of rivers, in the most remote of places where news slowly spread—there, everywhere, men had heard of the man who announced the discovery of the North Pole, who had dined with princes, and who, branded an impostor and liar, was a self-elected fugitive among men.[20]

His fear of pursuit was not shaken off until his arrival at Mendoza, Argentina, where the Cooks stayed a week with a relative of van Rysselberghe's wife. They then quietly returned to Buenos Aires. The doctor had vanished again.

One paper offered William Cook $1,000 for his brother's address. Another offered $5,000 to the doctor himself for any statement he cared to make. But for many more months there would be no further word of his whereabouts.

He had gone back to Montevideo and there received newspaper clippings bringing him up-to-date on the decision at Copenhagen, the Dunkle-Loose exposé and the drubbing he had taken in the American press. He also received word that his two daughters, who were in the Hamilton Institute for Girls, a private boarding school in New York, were being annoyed by reporters and curiosity seekers.

When Marie Cook read the papers, she had terrible fears, imagining her children were being ridiculed and abused. She insisted on returning to New York at once. Together they decided she should quietly get Helen and Ruth and meet again in London.

As she left Montevideo in April, Fred stood on the dock watching Marie sobbing as the boat pulled away. The doctor later recalled his thoughts as he stood on the pier: "She was going home. Going home! . . . What a flood of longings, like the remembrance of singing birds in winter time, of a sudden came to my heart with that thought! Going home!"[21]

Dr. Cook tried to lose himself in the jungles of Paraguay but soon decided he must be in a position to communicate with Marie. He returned to Montevideo and booked passage for Italy but changed ships at the Canary Islands for Liverpool instead. At the Canarys he took the opportunity to post a letter to Marie:

> Dearest Thought.
>
>   I wonder if you are so ill at ease without me as I am without you. Things are dull here. The passengers are either soldiers or missionaries from Africa. Interesting in a way but awfully coarse. Before bedtime every night a large proportion are so drunk that that *[sic]* the hilarity becomes scandalous. This thing worries me for I wonder if you had the same kind of cattle on your boat. . . .
>
>   I should not have permitted you to go unaccompanied. No one *[sic]* upon whom so much depends should be better protected. I do

not think that I can ever let you go alone again. This is a result—of hours and days of worry—and also of a selfish love—for all love is selfish—it hates to have others tread on its pleasures. We must always be to-gether.

You are all to me—how much am I to you?

Fred.[22]

The well-traveled physician arrived in England near the end of April and took up residence in London in early May. He engaged rooms at the Hotel St. Erman in Westminster and found, to his surprise, that no one recognized him. But his stay there gave him no pleasure. "My life was aimless and futile," he wrote of this idle time. "Day by day I sat thinking—thinking until it seemed my brain must exhaust itself repeating the rigmarole of unhappy, unsatisfactory thoughts. The verdict of the world regarding me became, each day, more unendurable, and although my case seemed hopeless, the old questions recurred insistently. What can I do? Can I explain? Will people believe me?"[23] For the first time in his life, Cook took up smoking cigarettes.

Marie and the two girls were reunited with him in London in June, and together they set out across Europe on a tour of France, Holland, Switzerland, Italy, the Austrian Tyrol and Germany. In September the doctor was recognized by an old acquaintance in Munich. He acknowledged knowing the man but insisted on being called "Mr. Coleman." However, he now really wanted things to be as they had been—to be "Dr. Cook" again.

"Mr. Coleman" returned to England while Marie placed the girls in the exclusive private school at the Cours de l'Étoile in Neuilly, just outside Paris. Back in London, the doctor checked into the Hotel Capitol, near the Strand, where he had an unexpected visitor.

"I lived at the same hotel for five weeks with him," recalled H. Wellington Wack. "He seemed quite prosperous but terribly worked up at being thought a fakir. We talked often about his future plans. He seemed anxious to get back to this country, but didn't know what business he would enter when he did come back."

Wack suggested to the doctor that he was now a man without a country, to which he replied: "I want to unpack my heart to the American people; I want to forget about the north pole. I want them to take me back with respect."[24]

He now knew he could not last forever in self-elected oblivion. "I wanted the people of my country to believe in my honesty; I wanted to be able to go home, to take my children home. I think it is chiefly because of them that I have resolved to state my case, whatever the result may be, and to face my countrymen."[25] He would reveal his continued existence to the world on a trial basis, he decided, to prepare it for his full return. He reestablished contact with Walter Lonsdale and through him made a secret arrangement to meet a reporter connected with the New York *World* at a certain address to give an exclusive interview.

When the reporter arrived, he found the address belonged to a dingy room in London's West End. After waiting for a time, he felt that the promised meeting was just another false alarm and was about to leave when he heard a rattle at the door. It opened cautiously, halfway. The bearded face thrust through the opening broke into a smile. It belonged to a well-dressed man who held out his hand and said, "I am Dr. Frederick A. Cook and I am immensely glad to see you. You are the first person to whom I have admitted my identity or to whom I have spoken in my own name, except my wife and children, since I left New York, Nov. 25, last year. I have heard myself discussed in various places and under different circumstances, but my incognito was only once penetrated—by newspaper men in Santiago, Chili—and then I got away before the suspicion could be made good or verified."[26]

He did not seem at all like the reportedly broken man who had fled New York, the correspondent thought. Instead, he stood looking robust in a dark suit and derby hat, carrying gray gloves and a walking stick. His beard was a Vandyke, grizzled on the sides, his hair brushed forward to shorten his forehead. But there was no mistaking the eyes—"The blue-gray, rather near together, observant eyes, bearing then, in the dim little room in West End, London, the same smilingly ironic gleam that is so prominent in that famous photograph that shows him with his neck garlanded receiving the freedom of New York and the homage of its crowds."

Looking around at the grimy little room, he beckoned the correspondent to go with him to his apartment. On the way, the reporter saw a little of what life had become for Dr. Cook. They took a cab, and all the while the doctor glanced around furtively at the people in the street. He had the cabby take some evasive turns before doubling back to the hotel near London's theater district.

Incredibly, the reporter thought, the man whom every reporter had been searching for in the farthest-flung corners of the world claimed to have been living in London for some time, registered at a prominent hotel under his own name. Once inside, Cook refused to take the lift, saying it put him too close to strangers, with no possibility of escape.

The reporter found the apartment comfortably furnished, large and airy, with suitcases packed and piled in the hall. Now the doctor, chain-smoking cigarettes, began to talk more freely:

> A year's absence from one's country under these circumstances is a long, long time. But it was necessary. I was like a deer that had been driven into a cold stream. I simply had to get away from perturbing conditions—the conditions that surrounded me.
>
> As a matter of fact I expected to carry out a plan I had agreed upon with my counsel. This was that I should go to Italy for a few weeks on the Caronia—just for a few weeks rest.

After that had all been arranged, and even the tickets bought, a motley lot of friendly advisors pestered me with other plans. And this, added to the great weariness, mental fatigue and the disgust that had come over me—the disgust at the conspiracy that was despoiling me of the result of my life work—these things caused me suddenly to leave New York. I left for anywhere—anywhere that I could be absolutely alone. . . .

. . . I left New York for Toronto, Canada, Nov. 25. I told nobody of my intention. I shaved off my mustache and put on a soft hat instead of the derby I usually wore. I adopted no other disguises. Nobody apparently recognized me in Toronto. From there I went to Halifax where I sailed for Liverpool. I sailed on the steamship Virginian. At Liverpool I took a train for London and went straight to a prominent Westminster hotel. I registered there as F. A. Cook. . . .

When I say I told nobody of my departure from America, I have omitted my wife. She knew. Within a few days of my departure from New York my wife sailed for Naples. From there she made her way to Gibraltar, and it was there, in the shadow of the big rock, that we met just before Christmas, 1909.

The reporter thought he detected a twinkle in the doctor's blue eyes as he described how he had escaped notice during most of the next year. He especially noted it when Cook remarked that he had been present at Peary's London lecture in the Albert Hall and had not been recognized and that he had sat in the grandstand in Edgeware Road to watch the funeral possession of King Edward without being noticed. When the reporter said that surely he must have seen the king of Denmark in the cortege, the doctor shook his head, saying, "There were so many kings there and they passed so quickly that you had hardly time to recognize them."

About his future plans, Cook was reticent. He implied that he would soon publish a dignified book recounting his recent adventures. "In due time," he said, "I shall have an important message for the American people and all who are interested in the truth of my Polar work. But I cannot now indicate its import.

"I did not run away from my task, but from the intolerable conditions that were created to ruin it and to goad and harass me. What I so dearly earned may have been filched from me, but only temporarily. It will come to me just as I shall come back." At this point the doctor stood up. "Every world achievement has aroused envy and engendered intrigue," he continued. "My work is not dead nor, as some would wish, am I.

"I shall be leaving London presently, but only to perfect my plan to fight for my own at the proper time and place."

The reporter noticed that the look of ironic humor that had played on the doctor's face as he had spoken of evading all of his pursuers had vanished. His voice now grew very emphatic:

> Those who believe that my journey over the ice from Cape Sparbo to Annoatok during the Arctic night while I was starving bereft me of tenacity or patience don't appreciate the fact admitted by all competent to speak, that to travel from Sparbo to Annoatok, in the Arctic night with no dogs and no food, dragging my own sledge, is a more difficult performance than going to the Pole. Having endured the hardships of that journey and survived I have learned to endure all that my enemies have invented and I will survive.
>
> My friends, however, must trust me a few weeks longer. I will not betray their confidence.
>
> The North Pole was discovered exactly when I said it was— April 23, 1908.
>
> I see in Peary's story—among other things which I will deal with at the proper time—he says he returned to his ship only four days after Bartlett's return from the point fifteen miles south of the 88th degree latitude—that is about 135 miles from the pole.
>
> Can it be believed that Peary, with his negro associate, Henson, could have travelled north 135 miles over an unbroken trail and south 135 miles, making 270 miles in four days, less the time spent in observations? Why he could not have done it without an aeroplane.
>
> That is a very striking point; for Peary you know, has only one toe on each foot—the little toe. He hobbles on the march. Bartlett, on the other hand, is much younger and has ten toes. He was, moreover, the fastest of Peary's crew. He made the trails in advance of Peary. On Bartlett's return journey he must have travelled much faster than Peary could have travelled either north or south. If Bartlett was sent back fifteen miles from the 88th degree and Peary reached his ship only four days behind him, what conclusion can you arrive at?

Dr. Cook made a motion of dismissal. "However, I am not concerned with any part of Peary's performance at present. I intend to devote myself to my own claim without challenging his story, however improbable. When I am again attacked I shall be prepared to carry my campaign into the enemy's midst."

The reporter asked when he would return to New York, thinking how different this homecoming would be from his last. "It won't be long, I hope," said Dr. Cook. "You see, while I feel very well most of the time I have not yet got over those three terrible months of 1909. Moreover, I expect corroborative evidence and will await that."

When asked about his observations, Cook sat silent before volunteering, "But I have a full answer to everything, and I will deliver it in my own time."

A few weeks after the interview with Cook in London was printed in the New York *World,* Peary received a letter from J.S. Keltie, secretary of the Royal Geographical Society, asking him to send his original observations or certified photographs of them. Keltie told him that his data had been recalculated by the society's expert computer and that the results were very favorable, but "it would be better to have the originals rather than copies, so that no-one could have any grounds for insinuations. This I write to you confidentially and on my own account, so that you will consider it as private."

Keltie added that he had recently talked with a very gentlemanly man whom he took to be a journalist, named H. Wellington Wack. He reported that the man had talked an hour in Cook's defense but had added nothing really new in his favor. Wack assured him, Keltie said, that Cook was not in the Albert Hall during Peary's lecture and, in fact, was not even in London at the time.[27]

Now that Dr. Cook had revealed himself, the *New York Times* positioned one of its London correspondents to try to find out what his next move would be. The reporter, Ernest Marshall, who had been the *Times's* man in Copenhagen, wrote to William Reick that he was not having much luck.

He had waited outside the address on Hanover Street Reick had provided and had kept watch on Lonsdale, but Cook's secretary had caught on to him. Lonsdale told Marshall it was no use, as he was communicating with Cook in a way that defied detection. He did volunteer, however, that he was more convinced than ever of the truth of Cook's polar claim and thought the world would agree when his "proofs," which Lonsdale said he was working on with the aid of scientific authorities, were produced in about a month. Lonsdale called the interview with the *World* a "mistake" that both he and Cook "deeply regretted." They had resolved to say nothing else until the "proofs" were ready, he added.[28]

Marshall could not locate the doctor because Cook was no longer in London. He was in Canada.

In the company of William Cook, T. Everett Harry, Ben Hampton's representative who had secured the Peary story, had been dispatched to London to make Dr. Cook an offer.

Peary's series had been a spectacular financial disaster for *Hampton's.* Not only had the stories not put the magazine at the top of the 15-cent business, as Ben Hampton had confidently expected, but the enormous amount he had spent on advertising the series, $50,000 on the first article alone, added to what he was paying Peary, had nearly bankrupted it. Ben Hampton hoped to save his publication with another costly gamble—a series of articles by Cook telling why he faked a claim to the North Pole.

Harry put this proposition to the doctor baldly, but the doctor calmly stated that he could not write such a series because, in fact, he had reached the Pole. Harry cabled Hampton that Cook was favorably inclined to give *Hamp-*

ton's a story of his recent travels but was adamant about holding to his claim and would give no confession of fakery.[29]

Hampton would not take no for an answer, however. He instructed Harry to bring the doctor incognito to Quebec. When they arrived on October 29, Harry found another message telling him to come to Troy, New York, where they met his managing editor, Ray Long, who Hampton hoped would be more persuasive. According to Harry, Long laid out a scenario for Dr. Cook.

"One can imagine your starting out on the long trip to the Pole. Storms, blizzards. Food runs short; suffering from hunger, cold; lost in the blizzards. While you think you're going straight ahead, you're traveling in a circle. Later you realize in a sort of delirium that you simply imagine you got to the Pole."

To Long's recitation, Cook listened in silence, his face inscrutable.

"What you suggest is interesting, Mr. Long," he said, "but not true. I got to the Pole."[30]

Long argued and suggested, but Cook was willing to admit, as he had at Copenhagen, only that although it was impossible to locate the North Pole precisely, he had gotten to the approximate area, and therefore was its discoverer. Harry then said to Long that perhaps that admission would be enough to satisfy Ben Hampton.

After some discussion, Cook agreed to go secretly to the Palatine Hotel in Newburgh, New York, and write a series of articles, then go back to London. His official return to America would be timed to coincide with the release of the first of the series in the January 1911 issue of *Hampton's Magazine.*

Hampton's offices were soon buzzing with rumors about a prospective series with Dr. Cook. Lilian Kiel, a stenographer at the magazine who had taken the dictation of Elsa Barker's ghosted account of "Peary's Own Story," said that one day she heard Ben Hampton and Ray Long talking, apparently about the upcoming Cook series.

"We can't do it; we're under contract with Bob," Long said. Hampton replied, "Never mind, we'll fix it up with Bob."

In any case, "Bob" already knew something about what was afoot. On October 20 Hampton had written to Peary: "There are certain matters in connection with Dr. Cook that I do not want to trust to a letter, but which I think would interest you a good deal. I do not know that it will work out to be of any importance or advantage to you, but at the same time you will be entertained by knowing some of the things that have recently come to my attention."[31]

Lilian Kiel soon learned that the rumor that she would transcribe Cook's story was untrue, because Cook insisted that his own niece do the typing. Still, there were plenty of other rumors and many hasty trips by Harry to the Palatine Hotel. Some said that alienists had been called in but that Cook had refused to be examined by them. Just what the series' theme was to be was a matter of speculation, though it was expected to be sensational.

When he had finished his articles for *Hampton's,* Cook sailed for Europe via Canada, leaving behind a story that, though filled with psychological insights, had not provided the admission of fraud that Ben Hampton hoped would sell more magazines. Cook had, however, signed an agreement that provided that *Hampton's Magazine* would make "no editorial guarantees whatsoever." So the editorial staff cut through the signed galley sheets of the first article and inserted paragraphs that were more to their liking:

> No one should discredit me until he knows what I have endured during the two and a half years of Arctic experience—until he hungers with me, freezes with me, shudders with me in the specter-ridden Arctic night, and grows mad with me in the glaring, burning, long and crazing Arctic day. Not until then can he understand my mental condition. . . .
>
> Did I get to the North Pole? Perhaps I made a mistake in thinking that I did; perhaps I did not make a mistake. After mature thought, I confess that I do not know absolutely whether I reached the Pole or not. This may come as an amazing statement; but I am willing to startle the world, if, by so doing, I can get an opportunity to present my case. By my case I mean not my case as the geographical discoverer, but my case as a man. Much as the attainment of the North Pole once meant to me, the sympathy and confidence of my fellow-men means more.[32]

The other three articles were left pretty much as written, but all negative references to Robert E. Peary were edited out.

Lilian Kiel thought she was out of the "North Pole specialty" until called one day into T. Everett Harry's office and asked to take a memo.

"Statement for the Press," said Harry, and he began to dictate:

> I have come back to America branded as few men ever have been branded in history—as an impostor unparalleled in the world, and one who has held his country up for scorn. I have come to state my case rather than plead my cause. I have come to explain how I came to believe that I reached the North Pole. . . . I shall tell everything possible about myself, and when the time comes, face the public and answer the charges made against me. . . .
>
> That my efforts, misguided and deluded perhaps, have resulted in ignominy for myself and added anything but glory to the proud record of American achievement, is a thing that I can hardly bear.

Here Harry paused and Miss Kiel blurted out, "There you see, Dr. Cook is a Faker, after all!"

Her remark prompted Harry to confound her by saying he was not and that he had indeed discovered the North Pole! At this remarkable assertion, Lilian Kiel could not contain her puzzlement and asked how, then, he could give such a statement to the press. She just could not understand it. Harry, taken aback, told her, "Stenographers are not supposed to 'understand' anything," and continued:

My whole aim in coming back is to prove, if possible, that I did not premeditate a lie for money. . . . I shall bare my soul to friend and foe . . . to have them say, "Cook may have unconsciously lied, and may have deceived himself, but he did not deliberately try to deceive others." . . . Only by reading the full frank confession of my life, my life's work and my life's tragedy, can anyone understand me, understand my motives, and my present convictions. . . .

. . . For the position of suspicion and disgrace in which I find myself I blame no one excepting myself. I want it to be understood now that I do not intend to enter into any controversy with Commander Peary, and that my feeling is that Commander Peary deserves the honor of a notable achievement, which was the result of sacrificing life-work. I have never questioned Commander Peary's claim to the discovery of the North Pole. I do not now. I did not consciously try to filch an honor which belonged alone to Commander Peary. . . . If I unconsciously effected a depreciation of Mr. Peary's claim, I am sincerely sorry. . . . I was the victim of a goading, mad, insatiate ambition. It filled my brain and devoured me. . . . But I can say, unflinchingly, and with all the force of which I am capable, that I did not deliberately lie, that I did not purposely try to steal an honor to which I had no claim. . . .

Miss Kiel just couldn't get over Dr. Cook's pleading for clemency. T. Everett Harry was pleased, he said, that she had that reaction—it was just the one he hoped the statement would evoke. He then told Miss Kiel to sign it "Frederick A. Cook," leaving off the "Dr." and also his own initials, as they were not necessary.[33]

Early in December, extracts of the first Cook article were given to the press by *Hampton's,* and editorials began to appear based on the snippets given out. Peary claimed to be uninterested in the whole matter when his lawyer inquired about what Ben Hampton was up to:

It is true, I understand, that Hampton is going to publish some material by Cook.

Whatever the matter may be called, you have doubtless by this time observed that it is having a most satisfactory effect apparently in every section.

I have yet to see a favorable editorial.

I think our contract with Hampton is concluded, and I do not think that his publication of the story will hurt us at all.

I know nothing about the inside of the matter further than that Hampton told me in New York, about ten days ago, that he had the manuscript of Cook's "confession" given him by brother William, and that he was considering the purchase of it (price $3000.)

He asked me what I thought about it (i.e. the main proposition of his publishing the story, he did not show me the manuscript) and I told him I had no comment. . . .

Between you and I, I could see no objection to his publishing it.

After reading a considerable number of editorials on Cook's "confession," I am inclined to think that he has more thoroughly alienated those who were still inclined to stand by him, and has more completely damned himself, than he would have done by a full, free and frank confession that he did the thing with the deliberate attempt to deceive.[34]

But Herbert L. Bridgman was not so sure. He accused Hampton of playing "a treacherous and piratical game." "From what I hear in newspaper articles, I think Mr. Hampton will find that he would better have invested his energy and capital in other wares," Bridgman predicted. "All the same, the return of Cook stirs up more or less senseless and worrisome talk, subtracting so much from what is Peary's rightful due."[35]

The January issue of *Hampton's* appeared on December 17 bearing a picture of Walter Wellman's cat, Kiddo, who had been rescued with his master off the New Jersey coast when Wellman's latest venture, a transatlantic dirigible flight—like his third attempt at reaching the North Pole in 1909—had ended in the sea. The picture was crossed by the bold announcement DR. COOK'S CONFESSION.

At that moment, faithful to the plan, Cook was bound for Hoboken after an absence of more than a year. At first he had not been recognized with his long, unkempt hair and grizzled beard—his name was not even on the original passenger list. But he had now returned to his former appearance and identity.

Although initially unsure of how he would be received, Cook found most of his fellow passengers cordial, especially the women. He took time to pay attention to their children, regaling them with stories of the people and animals of the Far North. When one little girl asked, "Are you the Dr. Cook who went to the North Pole?" the doctor replied, "I suppose I am."

A horde of reporters awaited the ship as it tied up at the German Lloyd Line's pier. The representative of the *World,* which had taken to referring to

Cook since his fall as the "Gumdrop Explorer," was anything but open-minded about the second coming of the ex-hero of the North Pole:

> Doc Cook, champion faker of the world, came gayly and openly back to America last night on the North German Lloyd steamship—O, nerve of steel!—the North German Lloyd steamship GEORGE WASHINGTON! . . .
>
> . . . He wore the same grin, the same sly twinkle in his eyes that he had when he fooled the public of New York and stood bowing to its cheers, his neck garlanded with a huge horseshoe of roses. Needless to say there were no garlands for the Doc last night, no shrieking whistles of acclaim; no frock-coated Aldermen; no big, cheering crowds. The only thing that might be regarded as a decoration peculiarly applicable to the Doc's vicinity were the Yuletide drapings of the George Washington's main saloon, for these were of evergreen goods.[36]

The reporters encountered the doctor smilingly ensconced in a comfortable chair in the saloon, his hands thrust into his pockets. When he withdrew them, they noticed the large gold ring glittering on his left hand. It complemented the handsome jeweled stickpin in his neat cravat, which contrasted with his fine, dark gray suit and derby hat.

As they pressed in to ask their questions, Cook was greeted by T. Everett Harry and asked to be excused for a half hour. The passengers of the steamship, who had assembled in the saloon to hear the doctor answer the newsmen's questions, soon began to make news themselves while waiting for him to return:

> The whole Cook controversy was on again, just as hot as it was a year ago. In twenty minutes the scene in the ship's drawing room was so promising of at least half a dozen fist fights that the oldest and most blasé ship news reporter hugged himself with delight at the prospect.
>
> Men called each other liars to their faces, shook their fingers under each other's noses, and broke friendships which seven days on the ocean in hourly contact had served to cement. Women stood on chairs and joined vociferously in the arguments shouted by the men on both sides of the question of whether or not Dr. Cook had reached the pole, and whether or not he had been ostracized on his "return from Elba."[37]

At one point, when it looked as if two contestants in a shouting match might actually come to blows, a young man stepped to the ship's piano and began to pound out the chorus of "T'row 'm Down, McCluskey," and the wave of laughter that resulted disarmed what a moment before had looked to be a serious situation.

When Cook reappeared, he handed out a typed "interview," which, for the most part, referred the reporters to his forthcoming articles in *Hampton's* for answers to their questions. Nevertheless, the press insisted on asking them anyway.

Most he turned aside, but when one asked, "Well, did you climb to the top of Mount McKinley or is there room for doubt on that score as on the north pole discovery?" the doctor replied, "No room for doubt this time. I got to the top of that mountain all right." When asked if he thought Peary had reached the Pole, the doctor said, "He says he did; you had better ask him. . . . I still believe I reached the pole though I am not sure I did." To another question he replied, "I am through with exploration. I have had enough. I am here to settle down as an American citizen." Then would the doctor be challenging Peary to a debate? "Certainly not. Impossible!" he exclaimed. "Why impossible?" the reporter persisted. "Why, it is not my way," Cook replied.

"I do not know what my plans for the future will be," he said. "I have no plans whatever for going on the lecture platform. I have not returned to America with the intention of making money out of my Arctic experiences. Money did not prompt the writing of my story, as I have seen suggested in certain newspapers. As I have said, I have come back solely for the purpose of rehabilitating myself and my family by setting matters right with my countrymen."[38]

Dr. Cook then set off, intending to go to the Waldorf-Astoria, where he had reserved the same suite of rooms on the tenth floor he had occupied 13 months before, but his brother, Will, who met him on the dock, persuaded him to stop first at his house on Bedford Avenue. It was good to be home in spite of everything. The Waldorf could wait. He spent the night at William's house.

The articles that were supposed to set matters right had instead stirred up a storm of negative comment in the press. They emphasized the privations and the conditions that made accurate observations in the high Arctic difficult, if not impossible, and with the insertions made by *Hampton's,* they seemed to waffle between uncertainty about reaching the Pole and a renunciation of his claim. With such inconsistencies as the insertions created, the press hooted about Cook's insincerity and his apparently low opinion of the public's credulity:

> The fact is that Dr. Cook's abnormality is not temporal; it is constitutional and therefore habitual, and it shows up just as clearly in his pseudo-confession as it did in the previous products of his vivid imagination.[39]

> That he should attempt to capitalize his shame into more dollars by once more playing upon the susceptibilities of the public tops any summit of impudence yet attained by impostors in history.[40]

At any rate it is clear that we have not heard the last from Dr. Cook. Now let Rider Haggard and H.G. Wells look to their laurels.[41]

In his series, Cook acknowledged uncertainty about his celestial observations at the Pole but said that another, more simple observation had convinced him he had actually been there—that of his shadow. It seemed to stay a consistent length at all times of the day. This condition was only possible at the Pole, he said, where the sun would appear to the eye to be at a constant height as it circled the horizon every 24 hours.

Not all the reviews of "Dr. Cook's Confession" were totally negative. A magazine that made its living analyzing the merits of writers thought it had finally grasped Cook's true talent:

> At last, as he casts aside all pretense to scientific reliability, Dr. Frederick A. Cook may be taken seriously. His reputation as an explorer is, of course, gone forever. But his reputation as a descriptive writer has suffered no eclipse. . . .
>
> [His conviction that he reached the Pole] rested, he tells us, upon the behavior of his shadow. . . .
>
> . . . Of course an honest man would have said all this long ago, and of course no scientist on earth would have paid any attention to such proof . . . [which] has hardly enough precision in it to satisfy the mind of a child. . . .
>
> His record as a descriptive writer remains. . . .
>
> . . . This is vivid and real. It is not imaginative literature. It is obviously descriptive of actual and unusual experiences. As such the record is worth preserving, irrespective of the writer's reputation for veracity, which, as the newspaper comment seems to indicate, is irremediably lost.[42]

If Peary felt satisfaction that the doctor's credibility seemed shattered by his "confession," little did he know his own reputation for honesty was about to be put to the test. Not even President Taft's specific call for recognition of the great achievements of Robert E. Peary in his annual message to Congress could stave off a hearing.

On January 7 and 10, 1911, Captain Peary appeared before Subcommittee no. 8 of the Committee on Naval Affairs, Chairman Thomas S. Butler of Pennsylvania presiding. Peary had been promoted by normal seniority on October 20, 1910. Now he was asked to give evidence justifying the bill that would retire him with the rank of rear admiral and the Thanks of Congress for his discovery of the North Pole.

Peary, as he always had, emphasized before the subcommittee that his success was the result of his long arctic experience and superior equipment. But upon questioning, it seemed he had made little use of either on his last expedition. He admitted that his "clipper-built" sledges had shattered with startling regularity, that his thermometers developed bubbles so that he had to estimate temperatures, that he had no chart of known compass variations, that none of his soundings above 85°34' north latitude found bottom, and that his sounding apparatus had broken and had been discarded five miles south of the Pole on the return journey.

At the Pole itself, he testified, he had made no chart of his movements. He repeatedly stated that he had taken no observations for longitude and no checks for the variation of the compass during the entire trip, even though he had always taken these observations on his past attempts to reach the Pole.

Although the publication of *The North Pole* had cleared away his stated objection to presenting the subcommittee with his original observations and journal, he still refused to leave them overnight for a thorough examination. The congressmen had to examine them on the spot. Even then, they noticed a number of peculiar features.

The celestial observations were not in sequence in the journal but were taken on loose slips of paper. Representative Ernest W. Roberts noticed that the crucial memorandum given to Peary by Bob Bartlett certifying that he had left his commander 133 miles from the Pole seemed to be written in three different kinds of pencil. Peary did not explain why this was so, though he did not disagree with Roberts's assessment.

When the journal of the polar trip was examined, subcommittee members noticed that its cover was inscribed: "No. 1 Roosevelt to ——— & return, Feb. 22 to Apr. [28 crossed out] 27, R.E. Peary, U.S.N."; the date of the return had been recorded, but the point achieved had simply been left blank. The pages for April 7 and 8, 1909, the days Peary said he had been at the Pole, were blank, and April 6, the day of the discovery, had the key event written on a loose slip of paper and inserted, though there was a regular entry for the day itself. The sharp-eyed Roberts also thought the book unusual, considering the brutal conditions under which it must have been written, since it was free from any sign of the oily food consumed by polar explorers. "It shows no finger marks or rough usage; a very cleanly kept book," he noted.[43]

Peary also stated that he had told no one, with the exception of Captain Bartlett, that he had reached the Pole until he wired the news himself.

Despite all this, most of the subcommittee was favorably disposed to take Peary's word. As Representative Butler put it, "We have your word for it, and we have these observations to show that you were at the North Pole. That is the plain way of putting it—your word and your proofs. To me, as a member of this committee, I accept your word; but your proofs, I know nothing at all about."

Still, there were some not willing to accept Peary's bare word. Questioned about his speed, he estimated that he had traveled more than 50 miles on his best day. One skeptical subcommittee member contrasted this with Peary's recent performance in a physical test required for promotion by the Navy. In that test, Peary had taken 15 hours and 39 minutes to walk 55 miles on the paved roads of Washington, D.C., spread over three consecutive days, separated by two nights of sleep. Even so, Peary insisted that he made his arctic miles on foot and did not ride the sledges. Sympathetic subcommittee members tried to justify such speed by comparing it with records made by mail carriers and dogsled racers in Alaska, which antagonistic members pointed out had no relevance to a journey over the jumbled, treacherous and ever-moving polar pack ice.

Further questioning brought out that Peary had not only not taken any longitude sights, though he insisted that he stayed on the 70th meridian all the way to the Pole, but that all of the sights taken for position until he parted from Captain Bartlett were single sun shots made by his subordinates, which precluded any independent checking of any of his positions.

But the really tough questioning lay ahead. Representative Robert B. Macon of Arkansas was about to take up the *New York Times*'s challenge; he was about to "turn himself loose":

> Mr. Chairman, the committee having under consideration a bill for the purpose of promoting Capt. Peary to rear admiral for the discovery of the North Pole . . . and remembering that this country and every other country has been infested with bogus heroes as well as real ones, I consider that we ought to go into this matter upon the merits of the case and not becloud it by comparing his marches in a polar region with a dog race in Alaska. . . .
>
> . . . It is too serious a matter, and hence in my examination of the gentleman I propose to deal with the meritorious facts in connection with his case as I see them.

Mr. Macon then took up his questioning of the captain:

> You said, I believe, that you took no longitude observations at all?
>
> Capt. Peary. I took no observations for longitude at any time on the trip.
>
> Mr. Macon. Then, you do not hold to the teachings of other scientists, which is to the effect that unless you take the longitude observations you can not know exactly the direction in which you are traveling?
>
> Capt. Peary. I do not care to go into a discussion of general principles. I am willing to give the facts in regard to the work.
>
> Mr. Macon. Then, you took no observation, longitude or otherwise, for a distance of 133 miles after you left Bartlett at 87° 47'?
>
> Capt. Peary. No, sir.

Mr. Macon. And without that you managed to make a straight course to the pole without anything except conjecture or estimate to guide you. Is that it?

Capt. Peary. I leave the observations to answer that question. I am satisfied that I made that distance, was in fairly close limits, as I have done on other journeys on previous expeditions.

Mr. Macon. How did you come to the conclusion that you were 4 or 5 miles from the pole toward Bering Sea when you had not taken any longitude observations?

Capt. Peary. I did not know that until I had taken my observations.

Mr. Macon. But you took no longitude observations?

Capt. Peary. I took no observations for longitude.

Mr. Macon. What character of observations led you to conclude that you were west of the pole 4 or 5 miles?

Capt. Peary. The observations taken by me at those two places of which I speak. After I had taken the series of observations which I had noted, I felt I knew approximately my position, as indicated in the book.

Whenever Macon asked such uncomfortable questions, one of the congressmen sympathetic to Peary attempted to interrupt his train of thought and more than once derailed it. As a result, some lines of questioning were never completed. At one point an argument erupted over several questions Arthur L. Bates of Pennsylvania believed were "foolish" and quasiscientific. But the representative from Arkansas was determined to have his say. Macon turned next to Peary's speed:

Capt. Peary. We made the distance from the camp where Bartlett left me to Camp Jesup in 5 marches.

Mr. Macon. That was 133 miles; it would be 26⅗ miles per day. Can you call to mind the travels of any explorer that disclose such a record as that— 5 days' marching with an average of 26⅗ miles, over an unknown sea of ice?

Here Peary offered an excerpt from a speech by Representative Moore of Pennsylvania, with accompanying data furnished by Gilbert Grosvenor, editor of the *National Geographic Magazine,* which compared Peary's marches along the smooth ice foot and across the ice cap of Greenland with his polar performance to show that better times had been made. The excerpt concluded with this statement: "In the history of polar explorations no one has had so much and such long-continued training in ice work as Peary; his speed is the result of long years of practice, resulting in great physical endurance and skill in the use of the sledge."

This did not satisfy Macon, who insisted on knowing whether any other explorer had ever achieved such a record under "like conditions and circumstances." Once again Macon was interrupted, but he eventually returned to the subject:

> Mr. Macon. Getting back to the distance, I would ask if you joined with your friends in protesting against the report made by Cook of having traveled a little over 24 miles a day with light sleds and a small party up in the Arctic belt, and some of them went as far as to say it was impossible to make 24 miles a day up there?
>
> Capt. Peary. I do not recall stating that it was impracticable to make 24 miles a day up there.
>
> Mr. Macon. Captain, did you read the report that Dr. Cook made of his discovery of the pole before you denounced him as a faker and his report as a gold brick?
>
> Capt. Peary. That is answered on the face of the circumstances, by a comparison of dates.
>
> Mr. Macon. Did you not corroborate him in many things about the route, the travel to the pole, even to the descriptions surrounding the pole, the description of conditions surrounding the pole?
>
> Mr. [William F.] Englebright. I would like to supplement that by adding this to it: When Dr. Cook published his story did he not have the newspaper accounts of yours first?
>
> Mr. [Albert S.] Dawson. I would like to inquire whether the committee is going into the Cook question at all?
>
> Mr. Bates. Now, Mr. Chairman, men who are scientists and explorers do not, I am sure, desire to make criticisms in public hearings, and it is not pertinent to this inquiry in any manner or shape whatever.
>
> Mr. Macon. I believe you said, Captain, that the Eskimos that you selected to go with you to the pole would walk through hell with you if you said so. I believe that language is in your book, and that they, and Henson, the colored man you took with you for witnesses, were as pliant to your will as the fingers of your right hand. You made that statement, did you not?
>
> Capt. Peary. If that is in my book, I will stand by it.
>
> Mr. Macon. Do you really think those men would walk through hell for you, or was that just a figure of speech?
>
> Mr. Bates. What do you think about it, Brother Macon?
>
> Mr. Macon. I don't know; I am trying to find out.
>
> Mr. Bates. What has that to do with whether Peary reached the pole?

    Mr. Macon. It has something to do with it when you take into account all of the circumstances in connection with this question.

    Capt. Peary. I think those men would go with me out on the ice just as far as I went, even if they felt pretty well satisfied in their own minds that their ever coming back to land was a doubtful question. That is my opinion.

    Mr. Butler. Of course that statement presupposes that there is a hell.

    Mr. Macon. And it presupposes that they would say whatever the captain told them to say and abide by it.

    Mr Butler. Are you through?

    Mr. Macon. I am.

    Mr. Butler. Mr. Englebright?

    Mr. Bates. I think that last remark better be struck out.

    Mr. Macon. I do not think the committee has anything to do with it.

    Capt. Peary. I will ask, Mr. Chairman, that that be struck out of the record, if permissible.

    Mr. Butler. We will take that up in executive session.

Macon was finished, but Peary's ordeal was not over. Representative Roberts turned to the examination of his records by the National Geographic Society, of which Peary had a curious lack of recall, considering that the society's endorsement of them had established his claim as discoverer of the North Pole.

He could not recall the time of his arrival in Washington; he could not recollect his movements once he had arrived; he could not remember whether he had visited the National Geographic Society's rooms on 16th Street; he could not say specifically who was at the meeting at which his records were examined or what the panel examined in them; and he could not give details as to the procedures or thoroughness of the examination.

Representative Macon was taken aback, however, when Peary introduced a letter signed by Leonard Darwin, the president of the Royal Geographical Society of London, which seemed to say that Peary had not relied upon the National Geographic Society alone to verify his proofs. It said in part: "Copies of the observations taken by you at the pole . . . have been thoroughly examined by us. In the opinion of my council there is nothing in this or any other new matter which has come to their notice that in any way affects the position indicated [when you were presented] with a special gold medal . . . for your explorations, during which you were the first to reach a pole of the earth."

The hearings concluded with the calling of Hugh C. Mitchell, an expert calculator at the Coast and Geodetic Survey who, with the assistance of Charles R. Duvall, had recomputed Peary's calculations and concluded that he had indeed been at the Pole. Mitchell displayed a chart illustrating their findings.

Because of Peary's unwillingness in his testimony to state absolutely that polar records could be manufactured, Mitchell was asked about Otto Tittman's opinion that such records could be faked and how such fakes might be exposed:

> Mr. Butler. Suppose these figures submitted to you by Capt. Peary had been made here in Washington or in New York or Boston, how could you have detected it—how could you have made the detection?
>
> Mr. Mitchell. Well, that is rather a difficult question to answer. I believe it is altogether a matter of experience that any dishonesty in observations or computations will show up in the reduction of those observations or computations. I can not say that at a particular point a certain figure would show that something was wrong; I can not say that. It is purely a matter of experience in the past.

Mitchell failed to tell the subcommittee that his examination of Peary's data was not a part of his government duties; he had been hired by Peary to do so.[44]

On January 21, 1911, the subcommittee reported out the Bates Bill, as the Peary legislation was officially known, to the full committee and recommended its passage—four votes to three.

Despite the close call, Peary expressed his confidence to General Hubbard that his position would be unassailable once the bill reached the House floor. He felt he had the votes but was concerned that the "Thanks of Congress" might be stricken from the final wording.[45] Just in case, Hubbard continued to pay Lucien Alexander, the Philadelphia lawyer he had hired to be Peary's lobbyist, to shepherd the bill through the House as it came out of the Naval Committee onto the floor.

Representative Roberts attached a lengthy and curious "minority report" to that of the full committee, in which he characterized the National Geographic Society's examination of the Peary records as "anything but minute, careful and rigorous." He noted that Peary's remembrance of this examination was "delightfully vague and uncertain." Nevertheless, Roberts had been convinced by Mitchell's "independent" recomputation of Peary's figures, though he was skeptical that it would, at this late date, put an end to the questions surrounding the captain's claims:

> Assuming the astronomical observations upon which this chart is based to have been made by Capt. Peary as he states they were made—and there is nothing in evidence to the contrary—I am forced to the conclusion that Capt. Peary was within a very short distance of the pole; sufficiently near to warrant the claim that he reached the pole.[46]

Mitchell's testimony had carried the day; the Peary bill was, despite the "minority report," reported out of the full Naval Affairs Committee unanimously—but only because R.B. Macon was out of the city attending to the christening of the battleship USS *Arkansas.*

Once back in the House, Representative Macon led the effort to defeat the bill, though he knew he had little chance of success. Macon summed up his prospects in the ensuing debate on the House floor. "Mr. Chairman," he began, "I realize that my efforts to defeat the passage of the bill to promote and retire Capt. Peary are herculean in their proportions when I consider that I have the combined influence of the administration, a paid lobby of the Peary Arctic Club, and the National Geographic Society to contend with, but having right upon my side, as I see it, I am going to do everything in my power to defeat it. . . ."

The congressman then espoused an almost biblical suspicion of scientific theories and caused laughter in the galleries by describing those who "accept any kind of a so-called scientific statement or discovery without question, because [otherwise] . . . yellow journals . . . will call them ignorant blatherskites."

> Because I would not accept the unsupported and unreasonable tale of Mr. Peary and allow great honors to be heaped upon him without corroboration, some of the newspapers of the country, like the New York Times and the New York Post, that are edited by pea-eyed, pin-headed, and putrid-tongued infinitesimals, have been trying to persuade the public to believe that I am almost alone in the position I have taken; but, sirs, if they could but read the vast number of petitions, letters, and newspaper clippings that I have received from practically every quarter of nearly every State in the Union, . . . and if Mr. Peary could see what they say about him I am sure he would not pursue his inane quest further. . . . They catalogue a list of misdeeds about this wonderful self-alleged discoverer that would cause anyone to seek a hole in which to hide from the public gaze whose skin was not too thick to be pierced by a spear. . . .

After skewering his enemies, Macon asked for reason to prevail:

> . . . Some of the committee were in earnest in their desire for the real facts in the case . . . but the best information, or so-called proofs, that they could get from the alleged discoverer, when summed up, were a lot of guesses, speculations, assumptions, estimates, and evasions, and from these four of the subcommittee of seven solemnly reported that the proofs were sufficient to establish the self-serving declaration of the gentleman to the effect that he had discovered the pole. . . .
>
> And yet we are asked to accept the bold statements of the gentleman as God-given facts concerning everything that he claimed

to have done on his journey, when they are contradicted by a combination of every reasonable physical and scientific impossibility.

The congressman's subsequent analysis considered each of these impossibilities down to the smallest detail:

> He claimed that his chief food was pemmican, and that it consisted of about 30 per cent grease; that he held it with his hand when he ate it, and hence grease and smear must have been left on his hand, and yet he prepared his diary with that hand and never made a single smear upon a single page of the entire book while he was doing it. Such a thing may have been possible, but I do not believe it.

When he had finished with Peary, Macon blasted Hugh Mitchell, saying his own examination of Mitchell's report "from start to finish indicates rank presumption and wild guesswork concerning everything he did in connection with the computation of the observations submitted by Peary."

Representative Macon then summed up his feelings about the whole matter: "I have given more time and thought to this alleged discovery than I have to any other public question that I remember to have undertaken to investigate in my whole life, and the more I have investigated and studied the story, the more thoroughly convinced have I become that it is a fake pure and simple."[47]

During the House debate Peary received support from an unexpected quarter in the form of a letter to the chairman of the House Committee on Naval Affairs:

> Dear Sir:
>
> From various sources I am informed that my prior claim stands as a bar to Mr. Peary's demand for national honor. My object in writing you is to clear the way for Mr. Peary.
>
> My claim of the attainment of the Pole is a personal one. I was not in the government pay; nor has the government or any private society advanced my cause in any way.
>
> I ask for nothing. Within my own bosom there is the self-satisfying throb of success. In spite of unlimited funds to discredit me in a persistent campaign of infamy waged against me, that throb remains; it always will remain, and it is the only reward I expect.
>
> Give Mr. Peary the honors—the retirement with increased pay. His long effort in a thankless task is worthy of such recognition. My reward will come with the reward that our children's children will give.
>
> Very sincerely yours,
> Frederick A. Cook[48]

Peary was not amused. "The matter shows," he wrote General Hubbard, ". . . that while Cook . . . is giving the impression of working a magnanimous and self-effacing game, he is really endeavoring to be vicious.

"Not that it amounts to anything, one way or the other, only it is interesting in showing what a consummate cur he is."[49]

As the bill was being deliberated on the floor of the House, Hubbard got word that Macon had obtained from a man in Nebraska a "mare's nest" of information that he planned to "spring" just before the bill came up for a vote. When Bridgman heard of it, he worried: "I'd like to know what this Omaha man has, for it may be that the record will be dangerous." Hubbard had already heard something was afoot and had sent out inquiries as to just who this Captain Thomas F. Hall was and whether he could be taken seriously.[50]

Before Hubbard could receive anything on Captain Hall, word of success arrived. The Peary bill passed the House of Representatives March 3, by a vote of 154 to 34. However, the final wording of the bill had been amended to read: "That the Thanks of Congress be, and the same are hereby, tendered to Robert E. Peary, United States Navy, for his Arctic Explorations resulting in reaching the North Pole." All references to "discovery" or "discoverer" were deleted.

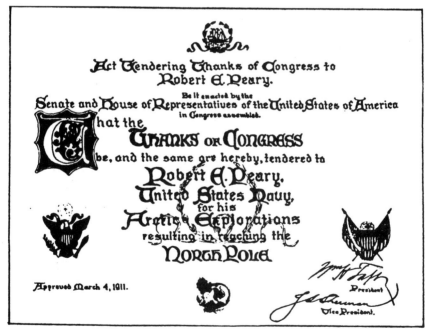

Even so, R.B. Macon was not satisfied. Before the roll call he denounced Peary, according to the newspapers, as a "willful and deliberate liar, dirty little pilferer of words, and contemptible little ass." So bitter were his remarks that they were not even printed in the *Congressional Record.*

On March 4, as the Bates Bill reached President Taft's desk for signature, a telegram arrived from Omaha accusing Peary of a long list of scurrilous crimes. It seemed that one recent supporter had had a radical change of heart:

> Peary is covered with the scabs of unmentionable indecency, and for him your hand is about to put the seal of clean approval upon the dirtiest campaign of bribery, conspiracy and black-dishonor that the world has ever known.
>
> If you can close your eyes to this, sign the Peary bill.
>
> Frederick A. Cook.[51]

Whether Taft's eyes were open or closed, his hand signed the bill. Relieved, Peary telegraphed Hubbard:

> Thank God the fight is over! President signed Bill this forenoon.[52]

Frederick A. Cook's reappearance, even though it had started off so well—from Peary's point of view—with his "confession," still rankled Peary and worried Bridgman, who thought Cook might yet cause trouble.

Cook's first official statement since his return was designed to meet a new "Eskimo story" being circulated by Knud Rasmussen. This time, rather than corroborating Cook's account, as he had in October 1909, Rasmussen quoted Cook's Eskimo companions as saying that Cook had been nowhere near the Pole and had failed even to give the rewards he had promised them for accompanying him.

Cook blasted the Danish explorer's qualifications, credibility and motives. "Why," he indignantly wrote, "did Rasmussen first launch out into this polar controversy and defend me, later to discredit me and then to champion Peary? . . .

". . . The only rational explanation of Rasmussen's irrational course is to credit him with an ambition to get into the limelight. . . . But need an explorer stoop to the depths of a literary muck-raker to get public attention?"[53]

It would be an ironic question considering what was to follow.

Cook's attack on the Dane represented the opening shot in a public campaign to reestablish his claim to the North Pole, the initial steps for which had been taken almost immediately upon his return to America.

On January 17, 1911, Cook had written to the University of Copenhagen accepting the *Herald's* interpretation of its findings:

> As indicated in my letter to Rektor Torp in November of 1909, my field data is incomplete, and therefore I preferred to rest my case upon a report and reduced observations.
>
> Your verdict upon this was "not proven." I accept that and thank you for the courtesy displayed during trying times of public agitation.
>
> Kindly send to the Waldorf Astoria, N.Y. my note book and other material.[54]

On January 26 he addressed a meeting of the German Pioneer Literature Club in the back of Rudolph Klein's wine shop on West 124th Street. Cook discussed the Copenhagen decision and the difficulties of establishing exact positions near the Pole but reasserted his claim to have been within a reasonable distance of the spot nonetheless.

Soon, despite his disclaimer of any plans for the future, Cook was reported to be in Chicago, the motion-picture capital of the country, to establish something called The North Pole Moving Picture Company.

Peary could see trouble coming and wrote his assessment to General Hubbard:

> Neither ridicule, nor harsh names, nor anything else, will have any effect upon him, as long as the newspapers are eager to publish his rot.
>
> He started from the other side, last December, whining.
>
> He "wanted to spend Christmas at home with his family"; he "had made a mistake in saying that he had been at the North Pole; he did not believe that he had now." He "never had any doubts but what Peary had been there, and that Peary would receive all the honors due him for that."
>
> He comes over leaving his family behind him.
>
> He finds that he is let alone, except for some unpleasant criticisms in the papers, which do not trouble him a particle. He grows more confident each day, and insists now that he did reach the Pole. He does not believe that I did. He attacks everyone who does not agree with him, and he will go still farther before he is done, if he is left undisturbed.[55]

It did not take long for Peary's prediction to come true.

On February 12 Cook appeared on the stage of Oscar Hammerstein's Manhattan Opera House as an "added" feature to a six-part vaudeville card directly after the Panklebs, an act billed as "Comedy Clay Modelers." Herbert Bridgman hired a stenographer to get a running account of the whole thing.

Cook said he was appearing gratis in exchange for the opportunity to place his story before the public. This statement was viewed with some skepticism by the audience, which greeted it, as they had his appearance on the stage of the crowded house, with a mixture of hisses and catcalls mingled with some cheers. The doctor then displayed the fruits of his recent Chicago venture, showing a set of "historically accurate" motion pictures dramatizing episodes of his polar experiences, entitled "The Truth about the North Pole."

The opening scene showed the "Arctic Trust," a "nefarious body in active operation," thrown into consternation when it learns that Dr. Cook has started for the Pole. Meanwhile, at the box house in Annoatok, Dr. Cook, played by himself, leaves "Franke" in charge of his belongings and sets out on his journey north. In the next tableau, Franke, ill and despairing, starts on a desperate trip south. In due course, the "Roosevelt" arrives and stirs new hope in the febrile Franke. With true melodramatic instinct, "Peary," depicted as a "very, very bad man," according to the stenographer, ruthlessly extorts Cook's property from a starving Franke as the price of his return to America, then seizes Cook's stores and places his henchmen in charge. During the unfolding of the events at Annoatok, Dr. Cook is shown in a split tableau struggling northward until the great goal is reached and his sextant shows the position as 90° north.

Upon his return, travel-weary and worn out, he is denied entrance to his own house by the brutal bo'sun "Murphy." Dr. Cook then entrusts to "Whitney" his instruments as he departs. When Peary reappears, he is furious at the news that Cook has returned, and "the sole owner of the North Pole" orders Whitney to remove all of Cook's belongings from his effects in spite of his pleas for fair play.

When the Arctic Trust learns of Cook's success, one of their agents is shown on the way to Tacoma for the purpose of bribing Ed Barrill into swearing Cook never climbed Mount McKinley. In the final scene, Cook's welcome at Copenhagen was shown on half the screen as the backers of Peary, depicted as "a ghoulish lot of old dried up scientists, who hesitate at nothing," are thrown into confusion and anger on the other, followed by a depiction of the impotent rage of the author of the "Gold Brick" dispatch.

During the showing of the film, one loud protestor had to be forcibly removed from the theater. But though the stenographer was impressed by an occasional "really remarkable scene," most of the audience seemed "seized with an uncontrollable desire to snicker and laugh outright at Dr. Cook in the Arctic regions."

In his talk that followed, Cook denounced Peary and his backers in no uncertain terms. Bridgman's stenographer took down his lecture word for word:

> Now, Ladies and Gentlemen, I have tried to maintain patience. I have tried to show the attitude of fairness and manliness. My faith in human nature was such that I counted on meeting gentlemen in a public question, but I find I am dealing with dogs. . . . Today I will throw off the mantle of diplomacy and seek with a knife the brutes who have assailed me. . . .
>
> . . . For three months mud-charged guns from every point of the compass were directed at me, all the world blushed with shame. The "Arctic Trust" in the meantime bribed men to sell their honor and mind. . . . Cook must be downed at all cost! . . . What chance for fair play have I, all alone, a mere man, against such a combination? It is all a shame-faced underhanded battle, and to meet it we have made the moving picture, and I am here to see that the picture is started around the world on its eye-opening mission.

At first, the audience listened patiently, but as he went on, they became restless, and their intermittent clapping and hissing seemed unrelated to the words heard from the stage. At one point an urchin in the highest balcony shrieked, "Git der Hook!" and sent the entire audience into convulsions of laughter, but the doctor only smiled and went on to the finish:

> I have reached the pole. What is my reward? . . . I have simply sought to be credited with the fulfillment of a personal ambition. This the Arctic Trust refused. It is little enough to seek—an empty ambition perhaps, for I only ask that my footprints be left in the polar snows. . . . Will you deny me that? . . .
>
> . . . I challenge each and all to answer. If this is not the underhanded effort of a lot of thieves, let them explain.[56]

Bridgman forwarded the stenographic report to General Hubbard, who passed it on to Peary with his comments: "It is rather laughable, although venomous. The way in which he was treated by the audience shows that the address did not have much effect, except to cause laughter. Very likely Cook is inviting legal proceedings — a libel suit, or something of the sort—in order to pose more effectively as a persecuted man. I think he should be let alone."[57]

That they had done, and none of Cook's efforts had stopped the Peary promotion bill and his retirement papers from reaching President Taft's desk.

A formal reception was planned at the Brooklyn Institute of Arts and Sciences to celebrate the second anniversary of Peary's arrival at the North Pole. After badgering the president's secretary until he secured Taft's signature on his promotion and retirement papers, Peary asked Herbert Bridgman to take precautions so that the celebration would look enthusiastic.

"If . . . the sale of tickets should not be sufficient to fill the house completely," he instructed him, "then those in charge of the lecture should see to it that the house is thoroughly 'papered.'"

"As you, of course, have learned from your press dispatches, our matter is now un fait accompli, or, as the Washington Times puts it, 'tis finished.'"

"I have my parchment commission, carrying out the act of Congress, and I have my orders of detachment from all duty.

"Again, my lasting obligations to you for your unswerving loyalty and invaluable assistance."[58]

The day before Peary's reception, Dr. Hooper, director of the institute, received a letter posted from a New York hotel:

> My aim in writing this letter is, not to challenge Peary's Polar claims, not to fortify mine. History will deal with the merits of both. Nor do I protest against the honoring of Peary, except in its bearing upon a call for cleanliness in public life.
>
> You are about to honor Peary. You invite our wives and daughters to come and do honor to a man under a cloud of indecency. We have a right to expect that the Brooklyn Institute in its efforts to uplift man by the high aim of Arts and Science gives us clean words from clean lips.

Investigation will show that the charges specifically outlined below are true, and if so cleanliness is impossible from Peary, and therefore by the right of every father and mother of the city whose honor and intelligence you represent there is here a call for a halt. Either prove Peary innocent or refuse to put on him the clean mantle of the grandest Institute of our city of homes.

Peary has used the most sacred of our institutions the public schools to gather subscriptions to pay for this pretended effort of getting to the Pole. Part of this money thus taken from the hands of our innocent school children was used to promote an immorality that would put the White Slave Trade to shame. Can you put the veil of innocence on this?

Later the ship Roosevelt was used as a harem. This ship was flying the American Flag, was engaged in a mission for which the government was responsible, was equipped at public expense. Its leader drawing an unearned pay as a naval officer. I charge that this ship was used as a den to satisfy a craving which leads to moral rottenness. Will you put a white blanket over this?

Here Americans are put to the shame of seeing the Stars and Stripes floating over an Arctic Hell. And, under the cover of wild people, beyond the reach of medical help the flames of unmentionable diseases—diseases now sapping the life blood of the world's last clean aborigines. Will you have our wives and daughters shake this man's unclean hands?

Stepping from the same ship of sin Peary took from my companion and myself, with the hand of a buccaneer and the heart of a hypocrite things worth thirty-five thousand dollars. This was done, not to insure expedition needs but to satisfy a hunger for commercial gain. While thus engaged in a crime for which he would be hung in a mining camp, he did the most dastardly thing ever attempted by a public official.

He abandoned two helpless little children.

Through the veins of these little souls, weak hearts pump Peary blood. With eyes closed to the most noble human passions—these helpless little ones were left to shiver and freeze in the cheerless North, where white blood unfitted them to the frigid tortures. These Peary children are to-day in the death-dealing Arctic environment, crying for bread and milk and a father. The meanest thief would not stoop so low. But the man whom you seek to honor did it. . . .

Peary seeking funds for legitimate exploration has passed the hat along the line of easy money for twenty years. Much of this money was in my judgment used to promote a lucrative fur and ivory trade, while the real effort of getting to the Pole was delayed seemingly for commercial gain.

Thus engaged in a propaganda of hypocrisy he stooped to immorality and dishonor, and ultimately when the game of fleecing
the public was threatened he tried to kill a brother explorer. The
stain of at least two other lives is on this man. This Peary record
covers a page in History against which the spirits of murdered men
cry for redress.

I insist that in this Polar march, this man Peary has left behind a
trail of blood-and-sin - which in the interest of public decency
should be investigated. Thorough investigation will show that in
his play with the Pole and in his assault of rivals, Peary has stooped
to every crime from rape to murder.

We have traced to the door of Peary, an arrow pointing to the
dirtiest campaign of bribery and conspiracy and black dishonor
that the world has ever known. Can you put the seal of clean approval of the City of Churches, on this?

Respectfully submitted,
Frederick A. Cook.[59]

After reading this, Peary seemed genuinely concerned about what Cook
might do. "If I were in Cook's place and frame of mind," he told Bridgman, "I
should follow up his move of today by going to the academy affair tomorrow
night, and attempting to create a scene there, whether during the course of the
lecture or the reception which follows."[60]

Peary asked Bridgman to station at the entrance to the institute a plain-
clothes detective who would throw Cook out should he dare to put in an appearance. But he decided not to dignify such charges and to follow Bridgman's
oft-repeated advice: "Silence is a mighty hard argument to answer."

Cook did not show up that night; the only disturbance came after the
ceremonies had ended, when the crowd leaving the institute was given hand-
bills advertising a lecture to be given by Dr. Cook, entitled "The North Pole
and After."

This time Bridgman didn't bother to send a stenographer to take down
his words:

What I will say tonight is a call and a challenge to Mr. Roosevelt and Mr. Peary, who, as a team have pulled together on a wagon
freighted with pro-Peary lies and the loot of other men's credit. . . .

. . . For twenty years, Peary has gone North at public expense,
not so much to explore new lands, as to enjoy beyond the reach of
the law, the privilege of a plurality of wives. The same privilege
which is denied the Mormons of Utah. Peary gets that privilege,
with the endorsement of Mr. Roosevelt, the consent of the government, and the backing of the Navy. . . .

. . . Peary has proven himself a Buccaneer in the arctic, an assas-
sin in the field of geographic honor. His murderous assault has left
the stain of the blood of envy on the flag of Freedom. History will

deal with Peary, the Explorer; but I call upon Mr. Roosevelt and manly men to quarantine Peary, the man, to the island of immoral contagion. His bearing on the Polar problem is a leprous blot on the fabric of clean human endeavor.[61]

"Cook is certainly a reckless slanderer, but it seems to me best to let him go his own way," Hubbard had cautioned Peary. "Answering him, or calling him to account for slander, would help him. Kicking against nothing, as he is doing at present, must tire him out."[62]

His letter had had no effect on the festivities, his speeches drew little attention, but Frederick Cook was not about to fade away. He was instead constructing the apparatus he hoped would reinstate his claim to the North Pole, and he would do more yet.

Cook hired T. Everett Harré, as Harry now styled himself, to rework his manuscript about his polar journey and represent it to various publishers. Harré was glad to be off the staff of *Hampton's Magazine,* whose dual polar publishing disasters now seemed certain to doom it to receivership.

Harré had a difficult task. It was rumored that Peary's own narrative was selling very slowly, even though he was now considered the "true" discoverer. Doubleday, Page was stuck with the reprints of Cook's two previous books, which it had rushed to press to take advantage of his short-lived hero status, and now took a cold view of yet a third. He didn't even bother to solicit Harper & Brothers. As the allegations had mounted against the doctor in the fall of 1909, Cook had voluntarily released them from his contract.

When Harré exhausted all prospects, Cook established the Polar Publishing Company to publish his polar narrative, sell off the remainders of his

other books and manage the series of lectures he planned to give once the new book was released. To this end he set up offices in the Marbridge Building on 34th Street, the same building that contained the offices of *Hampton's Magazine.* He made Harré the company's manager. By April Cook felt confident enough to send word for his wife and children to return from Europe.

The newspapers, which knew nothing of the tampering of *Hampton's* with Cook's series that was then still running, simply could not fathom how he could be claiming the Pole once again. Nevertheless, the Polar Publishing Company's letterhead boldly proclaimed Dr. Cook's book, *My Attainment of the Pole,* as "the sensation of the decade—eagerly awaited for two years." When it appeared on August 1, it proved less than that to most reviewers.

The *New York Times,* naturally enough, dismissed it as a total fantasy. Its caustic review was written by Cook's former companion, Henry Collins Walsh.

Less biased reviewers found the book overwritten and filled with inexplicable mistakes. More than that, they took exception to its contents, which went beyond the narrative of Cook's alleged journey to the Pole, questioning its motives and even its authorship:

> It is vague, loose, verbose, full of patent inaccuracies and almost incredible flashes of ignorance; the language is bombastic and sometimes grotesque; and the object of the book is less to show how the North Pole was reached than to assure us in a crescendo of assertion that Frederick A. Cook was certainly the first and probably the only man to reach it. . . .
>
> We acknowledge that the volume, as a speech for the defense, makes out a superficially plausible case; but . . . whether the author is trying to delude the public or has succeeded in deluding himself . . . delusion is the prevalent atmosphere of the whole affair. . . .
>
> The attack on Peary strikes an impartial reader as the real object of the book, though the avowed purpose is to prove that Dr. Cook reached the Pole. The attack fails on account of its very intensity. . . .
>
> . . . Cook has now revealed to us . . . his animosity against Peary. We know that it is universally recognized that, whatever may be his faults of taste, Peary is a man of high character and honorable conduct; and the malignant and unjustifiable attack made upon him recoils upon his assailant. . . .
>
> . . . Our deliberate conclusion is that Dr. Cook's mental equilibrium was disturbed at the time of this journey, and that he was not in a fit state to know where he was. It is impossible, except on the hypothesis of a rapid breaking-down of his faculties, to reconcile his clear scientific description of the Antarctic voyage of 1898 with the wordy rubbish to which he has put his name for the Arctic journey of 1908. The hyper-sensitiveness to color suggests some special disturbance of the optical centres. The vagueness as to dates and times convinces us that there can have been no systematic diary. The voluntary separation from instruments and notes on the author's return was not the action of a sane explorer; and the failure to take any steps to recover them is inexplicable if they existed. The efforts of this book, published long after the events, to make out a plausible case, have failed, and so egregiously as to inspire a doubt whether they are actually the work of the man who figures as the explorer and author.[63]

Nevertheless, despite its generally negative reception, Cook set off on a tour of the West to promote the new book. His lectures were sympathetically received and were a considerable success but failed to move many books at a pricy $3 a copy.

Ironically, one of the first orders came from Herbert L. Bridgman, who bought two copies and passed one of them on to Hubbard, who gave it to Peary. Peary was not impressed. "It will hurt Cook worse than anybody else," he thought, "unless he is already so badly damaged that he is immune."[64]

With Peary's own book in print for more than a year, other members of his expedition petitioned to write their versions of the North Pole journey. George Borup was first, weighing in with a manuscript dripping with college slang. Even its gee-whiz style was brought under the watchful eye of Peary's lawyer, who deleted the few provocative paragraphs he detected. But now Dr. Goodsell wanted to publish his sober diary, and that was something else again.

"In the case of George Borup," wrote Charles Nichols, "I read all his manuscript and thus made suggestions which he carried out; the object being that there would [be] no conflict in statements and no new sensational developments for the newspapers. But in the case of Dr. Goodsell, I do not see how this can be done, for he wants the consent on his original agreement to show his publishers. While I do not question his loyalty, yet from what I have heard, he might unintentionally blunder, so if given free and unlimited authority, he may overstep the bounds of propriety and good judgment when interviewed by reporters. Capt. Bartlett, Borup and Macmillan are all right, and I would match either against the sharpest reporter or interrogator.

"If you think best, you could insert . . . the following clause 'provided also that all manuscript shall be read before publication by Herbert L. Bridgman, Secretary of the Peary Arctic Club,' for you know the calibre of the Doctor."[65]

Even Matt Henson wanted to have a book published. Despite his vow that he was "done with him absolutely," Peary agreed to Henson's proposition. Frederick A. Stokes, whom Peary asked to do the job, baldly declared his firm had no interest in a book by the only other civilized witness to the greatest feat of exploration of the age—after all, he asked, who would buy it? But Peary insisted. He even offered to insure Stokes against loss for a small printing. Stokes refused this offer but accepted $500 to be applied to advertising the book.

In return for writing its introduction, Peary and Stokes would have the right to review Henson's manuscript. When they did, Stokes wanted several statements cut out about Peary's high-handed methods with the Eskimos, including his technique of obtaining draft animals, and Peary asked that Henson's statement about Cook's being "not even good for a day's work" be softened or deleted. Strangely, when the book was printed, all these remained in the text.[66]

During the summer, Dr. Cook, who had now been joined by Marie and the children, embarked on a chautauqua tour through eight midwestern states. At the same time, Evelyn Briggs Baldwin, who had old scores to settle with Peary, denounced the Dunkle-Loose affidavits as forgeries and announced his belief in Cook.

By September Cook had renounced his *Hampton's* articles as fabrications. "They were to be a series of heart-to-heart talks, embodying the psychological phases of the polar controversy and my own actions," he explained.

". . . Imagine my amazed indignation when, on reaching the shores of my native country, I found that the magazine which was running my articles, in which I hoped to explain myself, had blazoned the sensation-provoking lie over its cover, 'Dr. Cook's Confession'! I had made no confession. I had made the admission that I was uncertain as to having reached the exact mathematical pole. . . .

"I felt impotent, crushed, in my very effort to explain myself I was being irretrievably hurt. But misrepresentations do not make history. The American people cannot always be hoodwinked."[67]

Next, Cook announced that he would lecture on the Continent, where he hoped to reestablish his claims and spend some time with his wife and children, who would be returning to Paris.

As he and his family prepared to board the steamer *Lapland,* he was asked whether Copenhagen was on his itinerary. The doctor just smiled and said he was going to present scientific data to back his claims, then hurried up the gangplank. But a return to Denmark was, indeed, the very first item on his European agenda.

Dr. Cook's reappearance in the Danish capital got a decidedly mixed reception. He was met at the train station by what was described as a "howling jeering mob" that followed the Cooks' carriage and its strong police escort to the Phoenix Hotel.

A lecture, arranged for October 24, was to be given across the street from the Phoenix in the Palais Concert Hall, where he had made his first address and received the geographical society's gold medal just two years before. The hall was crowded far in advance of the scheduled time. At 8:15 Dr. Cook stepped before the curtain and was greeted by a mixture of applause, hissing and whistling from an audience of 1,500.

The explorer was introduced by Count C.E. Holstein-Ledreborg, whose father had entertained Cook at his castle in September 1909, and who was still a firm believer in him. Suddenly, C.M. Norman-Hansen, the eye doctor who had met Cook in Greenland and had been his former champion, leapt to the platform screaming, "I want to speak! I want to strike Doctor Cook down—and a swindler he is!"

This outburst threw the audience into an uproar. They hissed Norman-Hansen mightily and called for him to be taken away. "We paid to hear Cook, not this regular cartoon!" they shouted. But Norman-Hansen seemed hysterical; he jumped up and down on the stage and tore his hair. Count Holstein urgently requested that those who did not want to hear the lecture should leave the hall and retrieve their money. Three persons availed themselves of his suggestion. The count then tried to calm the audience by saying, "Let us listen quietly to Dr. Norman-Hansen. This meeting is to be reported in all the papers of the world. Let us therefore behave like gentlemen." But Norman-Hansen continued his tirade, displaying a copy of *My Attainment of the Pole* and yelling, "This book is a swindle and a lie!"

The Danish newspapers had reported that Norman-Hansen had six questions he wanted to ask the doctor, but when invited to do so he denied he had any such intention. "Dr. Cook smiled ironically," one newspaperman recorded. "Norman-Hansen [had] called Cook on the telephone and said that he would come to the meeting and strike Cook dead in six questions. He also declared that he would create a scandal and stop the meeting."

Norman-Hansen was trying his best, but the audience continued to ridicule him when he demanded that Cook step down from the platform. He seemed to have gone mad as he leapt onto some of the people sitting on chairs at the side of the stage. He rolled a manuscript he was carrying into a ball and threw it into the audience.

The spectators demanded that the madman be removed, but he shrieked all the louder, "I have come here to hiss at him, the nervy swindler! All his pictures are fake or stolen pictures!" Then suddenly he departed by the side door with three or four gentlemen in his wake, stopping to yell from the corridor three times, "Down with Cook!"

The stage now abandoned to him, Dr. Cook stepped forward to deliver his lecture. For the most part, the audience listened quietly while the doctor talked of his journey to the Pole. But when some of his pictures were shown, purportedly taken at the Pole itself, there were some "differences of opinion" expressed from the audience.

Cook then went on to analyze the Peary attacks one by one. This part of his speech won much sympathy:

> After the lecture Cook had won a crushing victory over his opponents. Applause shook the hall, but Cook did not come before the curtain again.—While the audience waited he was led through a rear door to the Hotel. . . .
>
> A resume of the meeting between Dr. Cook and Norman-Hansen gives the following result: Dr. Cook behaved like a gentleman. Dr. Norman-Hansen absolutely did not.[68]

New Yorkers were treated to a very different version of this incident. According to the reporter for the *New York Times*, Norman-Hansen had asked the audience to leave, and all but a few middle-class patrons had left with him en masse. After the lecture, said the *Times*, Cook was pelted with rotten eggs as he entered his carriage to return to his hotel.

Herbert Bridgman had every reason to believe the *Times* when he received correspondence from the explorer Thorvald Mikkelsen, who had attended the lecture and supported the newspaper's version of things. "Cook," Mikkelsen wrote, "took it very quietly and insolently. . . .

"I believe that he has felt the opinion so strongly against him, . . . but on the other hand I am sure too that he will try to give the impression where he comes, that we believe in him in this country, and that we honor and admire him, which naturally nobody does."[69]

Cook's performance in Copenhagen shocked Fridtjof Nansen, whom some of the papers confused with Norman-Hansen. He called it "Horrible!" and urged the press to ignore Cook. But even the *New York Times* could not restrain its grudging admiration for his cheek—or whatever it was that drove the man:

> It certainly took something very much like moral courage for Dr. Cook to appear again on a public platform in Copenhagen. . . .
>
> . . . The mystery of Dr. Cook is not his alternating bravado and cowardice—that phenomenon is common enough—but his inability to see the utter worthlessness of what he offers in vindication of his veracity. That inability is apparently real and it constitutes a sort of madness. Showers of bad eggs and decayed vegetables will not cure it.[70]

Before he left Copenhagen, Dr. Cook offered all of his lecture receipts to the Cape York mission, to be used to help the Eskimos. The offer was refused.

From the Danish capital he set out for Berlin to meet Otto Baschin, custodian of the Geographical Institute there, then went on to Brussels and finally Paris to see his family before returning to the United States on November 5.

Back in New York, Cook denied that he had been egged by the Danes, though he admitted to "slight hostile demonstrations" by the populace. When he read the article detailing his experiences in Denmark in the *Times*, he filed a $100,000 libel suit against the paper for its account, as well as for previous allegations it had printed, including that he had used Captain Loose's figures in the material sent to Copenhagen and that he had tried to steal credit for Thomas Bridges's Yahgan dictionary.

General Hubbard kept Peary abreast of how the doctor had interpreted his reception at the scene of his former triumph: "Cook represented that he was rather pleased with his reception in Copenhagen. He had, as we know, considerable success in the West, and evidently, when he went abroad, he thought he could there repeat the role of an injured explorer and make headway by abusing you. He seems to have been convinced of the contrary."[71]

As 1911 drew to a close, it seemed to Admiral Peary's friends that he now had everything that he deserved—the Pole, the medals, the retirement, the promotion, substantial financial reward and undying fame—and that Frederick A. Cook had nothing.

And yet, with everything, Peary was not happy. His lawyer kept asking him to forward materials that he could pass on to his German lawyers as evidence in the Franke suit. "I should have taken up the letter to you in connection with the Franke case before this," Peary wrote in trying to explain his neglect, "but if you knew how sick I am of everything connected with the whole business, not particularly this detail of the Franke suit, but the whole proposition of the last two years, you would understand."[72]

CHAPTER 20

Veritas

ALTHOUGH THE ACCOUNTS OF COOK'S RECEPTION IN EUROPE VARIED WIDELY, there was little doubt that he had indeed met with considerable success in the West in 1911 and was now enjoying it again in 1912. His venue was the tent lyceum that had been developed to bring culture to the great heartland of America.

The Chautauqua Managers Association had originally given him a trial of just three lectures in Illinois and Missouri to prove himself. Some of its members had objected even to that, saying, "Dr. Cook, of North Pole fame, as scientist, traveller, explorer, is a legitimate chautauqua attraction, but Dr. Cook, personal enemy of Peary, exploiter of hate, making a personal justification, is just as much out of place on the chautauqua platform as any man would be discussing another man's morals in the presence of ladies."[1]

But as Cook's lectures filled the tents and the cash boxes, opposition melted away. His manager, Gilbert W. Baker, set his terms: $90 plus half the gate receipts, or a flat rate of $200. The chautauqua circuit forbade personal attacks, so his more vehement charges against Peary were toned down or stricken. Instead, as Cook spoke to his audiences of men in straw hats and women in white cotton dresses, enjoying their picnic baskets under the striped tents on those broiling midwestern afternoons, he dwelt largely on the frigid polar journey itself, the privations of the winter at Cape Sparbo and his own campaign for vindication.

When he spoke, he held the closest attention of every man, woman and child. Many small boys well up in the front and at the sides were in a perfect position to escape into the pleasant grounds, but none went. Instead, their eyes remained fixed on the speaker, their ears turned to his modest yet commanding voice.

Eastern newspapers characterized Cook's new lecture venture as "capitalizing deceit," but the midwestern press was more open to conviction. There, the doctor found thousands willing to listen to his story and, upon hearing it, be completely won over:

> Dr. Cook told in simple, straightforward manner, before a large
> audience, the story of his achievement; as he explained details of

photographs taken by him on the way to the Pole, as they were thrown upon a screen the audience soared with him to the arctic heights—to other world dreams. The hearts of his hearers beat to the passions of frigid wilds.[2]

There are, perhaps, many people who have concluded that Dr. Cook did not discover the 'top of the world'—some who will even go so far as to claim he did not come close; and it will be of interest to these folks as well as to many believers to hear him tell his story. Even if one does not believe that he discovered the Pole, one must admit that he is a great explorer and traveler, and has had a wide and thrilling experience, from which he may easily draw an interesting tale.[3]

Anyone who imagines that he is discredited—that he has been universally branded as a faker and the greatest liar of the century—should have seen an audience of five thousand at the Grundy County Chautauqua here to-day scramble to hear him lecture, rise up and call him great, and finally shoulder and shove one another in an effort to shake his hand and assure him that they were convinced that he had the 'Big Nail' in his pistol pocket.[4]

This is what Dr. Cook wants. He says the verdict in the North Pole controversy rests with the people, and that if the people believe he has told the truth he is satisfied.[5]

Among his listeners at Celina, Ohio, was the Reverend E.C. Stellhorn, pastor of the Zion Lutheran Church of Saint Marys, Ohio. When he got home, he wrote to his friend William Koch:

Why weren't you at the Celina Chautauqua last evening? . . . We felt sure that you would not miss so good a chance to hear that celebrated cousin of yours, Dr. Fred'k Cook on "Who found the North Pole?". . . He talked for more than two hours to one of the largest gatherings ever at the chautauqua. The large open air auditorium was literally jammed with eager listeners and the attention was such that one might have heard a peanut drop on the sawdust underfoot. The hearty and long-continued applause following the lecture evidenced that the immense throng was pleased. Do I think that Cook got to the North Pole? I certainly do. To see and hear the man is to believe his claims. . . . You missed something when you let this opportunity slip by.[6]

That's the way many who heard the doctor felt, and many left with another feeling as well. As one editorial writer put it: "He sent his audience home thinking of the smallness of human nature when a great prize is at stake."[7]

But the men whom Dr. Cook was charging with that smallness were little concerned with his ability to draw large crowds in the Midwest. After all, did it make any difference whether the entire population of Yankton, South Dakota, or Red Oak, Iowa, believed absolutely in the doctor's story? They began to take notice only when Cook spoke in a place they considered important, symbolically or otherwise, like Copenhagen—or Portland, Maine.

When he proposed to speak there in February 1912, at the very high school that had graduated Robert E. Peary, there was a violent protest. The school board canceled his lecture.

The story made the eastern newspapers, something Peary wanted to put a stop to. "Wouldn't it be practicable also to arrange such an order [not to handle any Cook material] with all of the NY papers except the Herald?" he asked Bridgman. "I know that the *Times* a year or more before I went North the last time had such an order in regard to Cook because they were then aware that he was a common fakir."[8] An agreement was eventually made with the Associated Press to ban all coverage of Cook.

But for the most part, the doctor's lectures did not draw any national attention beyond occasional sarcasm. Peary and his friends were convinced that this was Cook's last gasp and that he would soon wear himself out "kicking against nothing" but silence. There was time for other matters now in the admiral's retirement, though most still centered on the consequences of his polar quest.

Honors and business opportunities were still coming in. Peary had endorsements for cigarettes, ammunition, Pianolas, rifles, pencils, razors, watches, toothbrushes, whiskey, toothpaste, socks and cameras already committed to or under consideration. He was promoting the "Peary coat," a heavy fur greatcoat he had designed, for which he was negotiating a $5,000 advance and a 10 percent royalty on every coat sold. He still gave an occasional lecture, never for less than $1,000, unless it was good for publicity. His writings were not selling well, however.

Jo's books, *My Arctic Journal* and *The Snow Baby,* consistently outearned his own narratives. *Northward over the "Great Ice"* had stopped selling completely, and in Germany his royalties from *Nearest the Pole* had amounted to all of $2.30 in the last year. Sales of *The North Pole* there were almost as bad, and his German publisher said this was because the book contained no proof that Peary had reached the North Pole. He therefore declared his payment of 25,000 marks for the rights to Peary's book null and void and filed suit to recover it.

Another book about his North Pole expedition had been a failure as well. Just as Frederick A. Stokes had predicted, Matt Henson's *A Negro Explorer at the North Pole* had aroused little interest, though some reviewers noted it was unexpectedly well written.

In his odd moments, Peary toyed with the design of a medal that he wanted to have presented by the Peary Arctic Club. Perhaps he remembered the suggestion of the Reverend Stuck about "Lord Peary of the Pole" because, as he worked on the design, it resembled what a badge for just such a title might look like. But his first sketch of it had actually been made on a page in his diary on his journey toward the Pole. There it lay—"The Order of the North Pole," above the entry for April 5, 1909, the eve of the great discovery itself—among page after page of personal memoranda.

Onto those pages the ideas had flowed: "North Pole" suits, tents, cookers; "Peary" snowshoes, sleds and fawn skin coats, all made official by the stamped-on emblem of the "North Pole Flag." Then, souvenirs would need to be distributed to the best political advantage: his sextant and artificial horizon to the Navy Museum; a piece of sounding wire to the Prince of Monaco; a sledge to the National Museum and one to TR; polar equipment for a "permanent tableau in honor of MKJ"; pens and flag fringe for the D.A.R.; and, naturally, a gold-mounted watch with suitable inscription for Herbert L. Bridgman.

There would need to be pictures:

> Have Borup take a 5" x 7" 3 1/2 to 4 ft. focus portrait of me in deer or sheep coat (face unshaven) with bear roll, & keep on till satisfactory one obtained.
> Have Foster color a special print of this to bring out the gray eyes, the red sun burned skin, the bleached eye brows & beard.
> frosted eyebrows, eyelashes, beard.

Then, there was the money to be made: "have Harpers' take entire matter . . . (100-[thousand])"; "Look up Thompson Hippodrome proposition.

Robert E. Peary, 1909. Photograph by Borup.

Modify perhaps, . . . 15.- (an original amount) Make society affair, auction boxes & seats," and to this he appended a roster of the knighthoods and ranks achieved by former polar explorers as rewards for their exploits and as precedents for future honorees.

Finally, there was the matter of an appropriate monument:

Mark I.[sland] monument for Mausoleum?

Faced with marble or granite, statue with flag on top; lighted room at base for 2 sarcophagi? Bronze figures Eskimo, Dog, Bear, M.O., Walrus, etc, etc, or bronze tablet of flag on N. Pole & suitable inscription. Bust.[9]

Now, as he filled in its details from the sketch in his polar diary, he devised the medal he would award himself: a five-pointed star set in a gold frame, a sliver from the Cape York "Star Stones" forming each arm, and on each would be inscribed one of his five great achievements. On the reverse was to be inscribed Peary's chosen motto: *Inveniam viam aut faciam*, "Find a way or make one."

Peary called it "the Iron Cross of Polar Exploration," and at its center would be set a perfect three-and-a-quarter-carat blue-white diamond, emblematic of the North Pole as

Peary's sketch for "The Polar Star."

"that splendid frozen jewel" of discovery he had so often spoken about. An order was placed with the firm of Berry and Whitmore Company by the Peary Arctic Club for $1,200 to make it.[10]

As for Archdeacon Stuck himself, though Parker and Browne planned to try again in 1912, and though another group of sourdoughs had been sent out by the *Fairbanks Times* hoping to keep the Cheechacos from carrying off the oft-disputed prize, he still nurtured the hope that he would be the first to stand on Denali's icy summit. But that spring Peary's thoughts were no longer on Mount McKinley; they were a pole apart from his usual train of thought, as he wondered who would win another prize in the race to the South Pole.

Amundsen, who had announced his intention to head south, instead of north, only after arriving in Madeira, had established himself on the Ross Ice Shelf, and so had Captain Scott. There was no question in Peary's mind whom he wanted to win.

"I sincerely hope we shall hear soon that Scott got there, and got there first," he told General Hubbard. "That route was his, and he deserves to win the prize.

"Whatever may be said, Amundsen's action in secretly entering Scott's field of work was not honorable.

"This is the third instance of this kind by Norwegians within the past 25 years."[11]

When a telegram arrived stating that Amundsen was at Hobart, Tasmania, with the *Fram,* but that Scott had beaten him to the Pole, Peary was overjoyed. But the next day William Reick wired Peary that his hopes had been dashed. The first wire was mistaken. Amundsen had reached the Pole on December 14, 1911. There was no word from Scott.

Peary was disheartened that the usurping Norwegians had apparently won out, and called Amundsen's announcement that he would now try for the

North Pole "a play to the galleries."[12] Peary still hoped Scott might have beaten the Norwegian without his knowing it and would soon emerge with the news. But if Scott didn't, he believed "Amundsen will have deliberately stolen the prize from Scott, and while I imagine it will be necessary to recognize his accomplishment, still there will be a pronounced reservation in the minds of many."[13]

Bridgman was anxious, however, that Peary befriend Amundsen instead of criticizing him. He feared that Cook would now claim part of the credit for the discovery of the South Pole, saying he had shown Amundsen the way, since it was evident that Amundsen's equipment and technique owed more to Cook than to Peary. He also thought that anything Peary might say good of Amundsen would be to his advantage in his continuing battle with Cook by making it "absolutely and overwhelmingly impossible for [Amundsen] to be used in any relation in antagonism" but he also thought any statement by the Norwegian favoring Peary's claim over Cook's might only "resurrect the dead by indirect advertising."[14]

Peary pronounced Bridgman's advice "first rate," adding that Admundsen should be "fully posted as to the light in which Cook is now regarded here."[15]

"A Lost Opportunity," 1912.

Amundsen already was "fully posted," yet when his book, *The South Pole,* was published later in 1912, he had many kind things to say of his old shipmate as he knew him in 1898. He wrote of Cook's then-honorable character, and for the first time he told, in detail, the story of Cook's role in saving the *Belgica.* "Little did his comrades suspect," Amundsen mused upon Cook's fate, "that a few years later he would be regarded as one of the greatest humbugs the world has ever seen. This is a psychological enigma well worth studying. . . ."[16]

The news of his friend's success in the enterprise he had advised him to undertake took longer to reach Cook than it did Peary. At that moment, he was on his way back to Europe aboard the *Mauritania* for a second lecture tour there.

Peary planned to go to Europe as well, to attend the Tenth International Congress of Geography in April, but he made private inquiries first to be sure Cook would not also be there. Before going to Rome, however, he would attend a grand dinner at the American Museum in New York City, where he would be presented the Polar Star to commemorate the third anniversary of his discovery of the North Pole.

When he learned of the plans for the dinner, General Thomas Hubbard expressed some reservations; he was growing tired of the whole Pole business. "I recognize the magnitude of the event . . . and the merits of the Admiral," he wearily explained to Herbert Bridgman, "but one can have too much of a good thing."[17] Hubbard didn't come, and neither did the Polar Star, which, due to technical difficulties, had not been completed.

With his retirement, Peary may have gotten the "polar bacillus" out of his system, but he had passed on to others the "arctic fever" it caused. Donald MacMillan and George Borup were two of its victims.

Hardly back from Peary's 1909 expedition, MacMillan had broached the idea of a follow-up expedition of his own to Crocker Land. To sell the idea, MacMillan played up how such an expedition would help end the Polar Controversy, then raging, by "a disproof of the existence of Bradley Land. An examination of the commander's cairn at Thomas Hubbard and Dr. Cook's cache at the same place to disprove statements of Dr. Cook. An examination of box at Etah, if still there. The bringing back of the sledge of Dr. Cook and the two boys if necessary."[18] Though all this seemed no longer necessary, and perhaps even undesirable, he and George Borup had made detailed plans and had obtained Peary's blessing to look for the land he had sighted from the heights of Axel Heiberg Land in 1906. With the backing of the Peary Arctic Club and the American Museum, where Borup now worked, they announced in February that their expedition would sail for Etah in the summer of 1912.

Peary was still fussing over the design of the Polar Star when he received word that George Borup and a companion had drowned on April 27, while canoeing in Long Island Sound. After four full paragraphs about his self-awarded medal, Peary expressed his shock at the sad news to General Hubbard: "What a terrible thing Borup's death is. I can scarcely bring myself to realize it. It will be a most serious blow to the Museum's Expedition. They will be able to find no one who can fill his place."[19]

Peary's assessment of Borup's loss was accurate. The Crocker Land Expedition was put off for one year. Also postponed was the European geographical congress because of imminent hostilities between Italy and Turkey. The admiral would not have to worry about running into Frederick Cook in Europe after all.

There, during March, April and May, beginning in Berlin, Cook was touring the big cities of Germany, Austria, Hungary and Switzerland—wherever German was spoken. Although the doctor's claims had raised much doubt in the German press, there was also an undercurrent of admiration for a fellow German who dared to risk the censure of the scientific establishment.

Cook took with him a German-American newspaperman, Harry Distler, whom he had met in Buffalo. Distler would harangue Cook's audiences in German before the explorer came out, setting the tone for his attack on his rival. Cook's speeches were a mixture of German and English, as his mastery of German was inadequate for formal speech making and his accent too thick for many to understand. By the end of May he had spoken at Munich,

Salzburg, Strassburg, Heidelberg and Frankfurt, always closing with a 15-minute attack on Peary in English.

After seeing his family in Paris, he went on to Belgium and a cordial greeting from Mme. Osterrieth, who had not forgotten the *Belgica*'s debt to the American doctor. Nor had Georges Lecointe, who made Dr. Cook and his wife his guests. Then Cook returned to Germany, lecturing at the universities of Bonn and Berlin.

Cook's appearances in Germany, despite widespread initial skepticism, had gained him many supporters who were won over by the doctor's forthrightness. In the German capital he found some reevaluation of attitudes toward his claim taking place since the release of *Meine Eroberung des Nordpols,* the German translation of *My Attainment of the Pole.* It received a favorable reception and good reviews:

> The book shows the clever researcher on the difficult way to the Pole and on his return over the limitless wastes of ice water with its inhuman difficulties. Everything is told in such a self-effacing and sympathetic way that we can rejoice in its simple heroism.[20]

> The contents of the book have held us chained from beginning to end. The descriptions are simple and modest and so natural. It can be no lie what this man lets us experience, and even if it is a lie, it has earned a place in every library.[21]

The doctor, apparently still well-heeled, took first-class lodgings with Distler throughout the trip and again visited with his family before sailing from Bremen aboard the *Prinz Friederick Wilhelm* in June for the summer round of chautauquas.[22]

When summer came, word from Alaska that Parker and Browne had returned to Fairbanks came with it. Following roughly the same route as that claimed by Lloyd and the sourdoughs in 1910, they had climbed to a point they estimated to be 464 feet below the actual summit on a horseshoe-shaped ridge that formed the top of Mount McKinley. There, on June 29, they were driven back by a fierce storm to their last camp at 16,615 feet. A subsequent attempt two days later was met with the same result, and because of their inability to digest the fatty pemmican they carried as mountain food, they were inadequately nourished for another attempt. The climb was then abandoned.

Ironically, the men owed their lives to the indigestible pemmican. On July 6 a great earthquake associated with the concurrent cataclysmic eruptions of the Katmai Volcano shook the area around Mount McKinley and shattered the icy Northeast Ridge over which they had descended. A cloud of ice-dust racing at 60 miles an hour overtook the men's camp ten miles away and covered it to a depth of several inches. If the climbers had remained for another attempt on the summit, undoubtedly they would never have been heard from again.

Though Parker and Browne had come within a hair's breadth of the top, the summit had not been reached, and they contended that no one else had reached it, either. In the narrative of their attempt, they gave additional evidence that the sourdoughs' story was pure fantasy. With binoculars, they studied the ridge of the North Peak from every angle, looking for their famous flagpole, but saw nothing. In fact, they declared that the North Peak was, if anything, a far harder spot to reach than the true summit, two miles distant and about 800 feet higher on the South Peak.

The rival *Fairbanks Times* expedition had done far less, defeated by a deep crevasse at 9,000 feet on the saw-toothed top of the North Ridge. So McKinley remained unconquered, and the way remained open for Hudson Stuck to fulfill his ambition. Stuck had found an ideal partner for the enterprise in a hardy pioneer named Harry Karstens and was readying to leave on his own attempt the following spring.

But the near conquest of the great mountain was eclipsed by the real conquest of the South Pole. With all the attention being given Amundsen and his impending tour of the United States, Peary was careful to look to his own reputation, lest it be overshadowed by that of the latest polar hero.

When Amundsen was honored on January 11, 1913, with its special gold medal, the National Geographic Society made sure Peary was at center stage along with him. He acted as toastmaster at the gala gathering of 700 at the New Willard.

During the evening, many references were made to the remarkable growth of the society's membership since Peary's endorsement by its subcommittee. It now stood at 170,000. Its annual income had reached $370,000, and a surplus in the reserve fund of more than $175,000 enabled it to contribute to worthy enterprises. The society would soon vote Amundsen $20,000 for his proposed drift expedition to the North Pole.

Peary himself handed Amundsen the medal for the discovery of the South Pole, and in accepting it, Amundsen said, as Dr. Cook had done on a similar occasion a little more than six years before, that Peary deserved some of the credit for the great feat he had accomplished; it was the news of Peary's own conquest that had sent him there, Amundsen declared.[23]

Cook was also looking for new opportunities to present his story to as many people as he could. The chautauqua circuit was confined to the summer months and the lyceum courses to churches, armories and social halls during the balance of the year. But the lyceums were all but dead in the big cities of the East, where they had been replaced by that potpourri of entertainment of sometimes questionable taste known as vaudeville. There Cook thought he might find a new audience that he would never reach from the more or less legitimate lyceum platform. After another European trip in December 1912 to spend Christmas with Marie and the girls, he signed a contract for the 1913 winter season.

Before setting out on his first vaudeville tour, Cook sat down to write to the librarian of the Albany Society of Civil Engineers, Clark Brown. Brown had written to Cook first in 1910 and continued to write. He, like many others, had followed the Polar Controversy closely and had noticed many inconsistencies in Peary's story. Brown was soon put in contact with Captain Osbon, Captain Hall of Omaha and other Cook stalwarts and began to supply them with the results of his studies. He was particularly fascinated by magnetic variation, which he thought held the key to the Cook and Peary claims, and had written to many polar experts asking them in which direction the magnetic compass would point near the geographic pole.

When Jean Charcot got one of Brown's letters, he wrote to Herbert Bridgman. Bridgman wanted to know what this man was up to and requested a meeting with Brown after a lecture Bridgman was giving on Peary in Albany.

At the interview, Bridgman tried to find out. "Are you not asking some pretty hard questions? What are you trying to do," he asked Brown, "figure out some new system of gravitation or what? What are you trying to get at? You wrote me that you were preparing something for publication."

"I believe that only one white man has been to the North Pole," said Brown, to which Bridgman replied, "Everybody agrees to that."

But Brown said he knew one who didn't. "Cook says two. . . . I have not made up my mind yet what he really believes, but he says two."

A letter from Dr. Cook soon settled what he really believed:

> In the beginning I was inclined to grant that Bridgman's underling had reached the Pole, but . . . it is now positively provable, from a scientific standpoint, that Peary never tried to reach the Pole. . . .
>
> His whole claim, therefore, as you have said yourself, is a humbug and an imposition upon the American people. Every man in Congress, who voted for the Peary pension, is a party to that humbug and this must be brought out in the next Congress, when I shall demand a hearing before the Naval Committee.[24]

But Cook would not give voice to this opinion on the vaudeville circuit.

It was against many of his friends' advice that he had decided to present his story from the vaudeville stage, especially the stage of Alexander Pantages.

"Pan," as he was called, had started out as an illiterate floor sweep in the Klondike who had the good sense to separate the gold dust from the ordinary dust that he gathered up from the floors of the gold-rush saloons. With the earnings from this novel mining activity, he had gone to Seattle and opened a combination bootblack parlor and fruit stand, and later, a dime museum. By 1913 he was still illiterate, but he was also rich, with a chain of thirty "middle-time" theaters stretching from Edmonton to San Francisco, and he didn't much care what kind of acts he put on their stages so long as they made the cash register ring.

He booked the normal entertainment pastiches, but he also hired a lot of what were known in the business as freak acts—persons who had gained some notoriety or infamy. Pantages was known for his stable of "convict talent," including forgers who sang, swindlers who did skits and former gang members who simply talked about their lives of crime. Pan told the doctor he wasn't particular about what he said, just so he said it twice a day in exactly 28 minutes. About half the doctor's "act" consisted of hurling charges at Peary that the papers called "a little short of horrible."

The orchestra began playing "America" and the doctor would appear before the curtain and announce in "a plaintive wail," according to one antagonistic witness, "Ladies and Gentlemen: to me this is not amusement. Vindicating my claim is my most painful duty." Then he would launch into a brief account of his polar journey, illustrating it with stereopticon slides. When the flag was shown fluttering above the North Pole, the theater orchestra would strike up "The Star-Spangled Banner." The lights were then brought up; the last half of his talk could not be illus-

trated, because, as one reviewer put it, "no one has invented absolutely fireproof pictures."[25]

A vitriolic attack on Peary followed, concentrated on his seizure of the doctor's supplies, his "moral contagion" and his shameless leaving of his own children, so ill fitted to the polar climate, to freeze in the Far North. Finally there was an account of his own "battle for recognition" against a "black-hand campaign of bribery" to discredit his polar claims. "The doubts are all due to the machinations of just ONE man, aided by his band of arch conspirators," he declared. "That one man is R.E. Peary."

The doctor then invited his audience on another journey—this time to Washington, D.C., "the home of the steam-roller," with its three "monkey wrenches," Gannett, Tittman and Chester, "who never saw a piece of glacial ice and couldn't tell the difference between the North Pole and a barber's pole." He closed by blasting Peary's approval by the National Geographic Society and Congress.

While Cook was on the Pantages circuit in Tacoma, Raymond P. Tarr, whose brother had offered in 1909 to help Bridgman discredit Cook's McKinley claim, wrote to Bridgman as well, saying he should not underestimate Cook's ability to make a comeback:

> The man Cook is here this week, giving his lecture in vaudeville and I am putting it mildly when I say that he is making a hit and gaining almost universal sympathy. He has been feted and dined in

Portland, Seattle, Vancouver and here. After his first lecture I went to his quarters at the back of the stage in the local theatre and said, "Dr. Cook, I wish to say that I don't think you are doing your cause any good by pursuing that sort of policy." With his nauseating smile he replied that he had been doing this sort of thing for the past two years, and occasionally people come to him speaking as I do, "but I am continually increasing my favor, nevertheless." He also stated that he has many things up his sleeve to spring and among others he promises a congressional investigation that will at last satisfy his countless followers. "I shall get congressional recognition and have Peary thrown out of the navy."

Judging from all that I can observe I feel that he is not making idle boasts. . . .[26]

Tarr may have exaggerated the doctor's reception in Tacoma, since the real point of his letter was to make money. He tried to interest Bridgman in financing a $15,000 investigation, with $100 a day for himself, into rumors that Cook had kept double books in outfitting the *John R. Bradley* at Gloucester and had pocketed half the money his benefactor had provided to finance his polar trip. Bridgman declined the offer.

Despite the low esteem in which the admiral held vaudeville, any news of Cook's success rankled Peary. Bridgman asked Melville Stone of the Associated Press to look into the reliability of the reports from Washington State. When he had, Stone assured Peary that the men who accepted Cook's story were all nonentities and that his favorable reception was greatly exaggerated. He advised Bridgman that Peary could only hurt himself by taking any notice of "this charlatan, who has taken his proper level by appearing with dancers and negro minstrels on the vaudeville stage."[27]

In Pantages's vaudeville houses Cook shared that stage with the likes of Rice, Ball and Baldwin, three comic acrobats who specialized in slapstick routines, and Ned Wayburn's English Pony Ballet, but he was satisfied that his appearances really did further his cause.

"Now, of course, I am working to clear my name of the shadow placed upon it by Lieut. Peary and his bought press," he told one interviewer. "For two and one [half] years now I have told the real facts to the world. But it is a big task for one man to fight the official clique at Washington; men who have contributed money to Peary's polar work for 20 years do not wish to see me have justice. I am striving to force a government investigation of the charges against me. To that end I have gone before the public on the vaudeville stage at the sacrifice, perhaps, of some dignity, but I am more than compensated by the large number of people whom my words reach. In three weeks of vaudeville speaking in San Francisco I put my story before 35,000 people, and many of them wrote letters to Washington. . . .

". . . I bore slander in silence as long as a man could bear it, hoping the thing could be settled in a gentlemanly manner.

"Now I am telling facts cold and hard as the Arctic glaciers."[28]

The newsman noted that despite the determined words, the doctor looked pale and worn out. "His manner has in it a patient listlessness that you observe in men who are bent under loads that tried their souls," he observed. Though his story was compelling, the reporter decided, "there is not a thing in his talk that tends in any way to clear up the mystery. It might be true and it might not be. Lie or truth, his story is, however, of absorbing interest.

"[He is] either the discoverer of the North Pole or the biggest liar that ever talked," the correspondent concluded.[29]

Another reporter offered that in the meantime, the doctor was raking in the money. "True," replied Dr. Cook, "but I am spending in my defense $150,000 a year and am making only about $120,000." He assured the man that every story put out to discredit him was manufactured by a bribed press and that none of the honors the Danes had awarded him had ever been withdrawn.[30]

On February 9, 1913, the doctor was starting a week's run in Los Angeles, sandwiched between a "girl act" and a motion picture, before moving on to Honolulu, when he read a dispatch that Captain Scott had perished in the Antarctic. At first he tended to discount the story, but it was soon confirmed.

Scott had reached the South Pole on January 18, 1912, but on the return journey, man-hauling the sledges, his party had frozen to death in their tent just ten miles shy of a ton of food cached on the ice for their relief. With his tragic diary were found pictures proving that Amundsen had beaten him to the Pole. They showed Scott and his discouraged comrades standing in front of Amundsen's black tent, left there a month earlier, still flying the Norwegian

Scott's men at Amundsen's South Pole camp, January 18, 1912.

colors and the burgee of the *Fram*. There would be no argument about who stood first at the South Pole, though a different kind of bitter controversy would cast a shadow over Amundsen's triumph.

Dr. Cook must have felt strong emotions as he looked at those pictures. The tent was of his design—exactly like the one he had made on the *Belgica* with Amundsen's advice so many years before.

Peary was shocked at the news of Scott's death. It had been Mrs. Scott who had designed the special gold medal the Royal Geographical Society had given him in London in 1910. He sent her his condolences and contributed $100 to the captain's memorial fund.

It so happened that Amundsen was due to speak in New York when the news of the Scott disaster overtook him. Bridgman wired to Peary that it might be advantageous if the admiral wrote a brief eulogy to be delivered after the lecture.[31]

There would be no dinner for the pole anniversary in 1913. Peary would be going to Rome to attend the Tenth International Congress of Geography. He was looking forward to the trip. Things appeared to be brightening on all fronts. A favorable decision against his German publisher was all but assured, the Franke case was in limbo, and it seemed as if nothing could spoil his enjoyment of being in the limelight again and picking up a few more honors.

Best of all, Cook seemed to be fading as a serious threat. Letters written by the doctor's boosters to the Navy Department had not been received favorably, and one Cook had written personally to President Wilson had not even been acknowledged. But General Hubbard alerted Bridgman that Cook's and his advisors' voices were no longer the only ones to be heard; the Polar Controversy seemed to have taken on a life of its own:

> A Philadelphia gentleman, named Balch, has, I am told, lately published a book for the purpose of proving that because Peary was at the Pole, Cook must have been also—and first. Mr. Balch is, I believe, a Harvard graduate and a man of some literary distinction. A man named Brown, at Albany, says he has a book resulting from 3 years of labor, now ready for the press, proving to his own satisfaction that Peary did not reach the Pole. These things are, in a way, trivial, but the record which was to have been given at Rome should dispose of them.[32]

The "record" Hubbard spoke of, a paper entitled "To the Students of Polar Exploration," was presented at the international congress and printed in its acts. Its introduction by Hubbard stated that Peary's calculations had not been previously published to protect them from "improper use" but said "they have been repeatedly submitted and offered to impartial and reliable bodies qualified to determine their value." Hubbard assured his students of polar exploration:

Always Peary has reported, as a real explorer should report, exactly what he has accomplished. Always he has given the true record, whether it was what he had hoped it might be, or fell short of his hope. . . .

. . . The uninformed must be brought to know, as the well informed already know, that the attainment of the Pole, or of any point of latitude, is susceptible of mathematical proof and does not depend on mere assertion.[33]

This "mathematical proof" took the form of the 1911 "recomputation" of Peary's observations, for which Peary had paid $280 to Mitchell and Duvall, whom Hubbard called, nevertheless, "independent of any other person," and a reproduction of facsimiles of Peary's latitude sights and the certificates of Marvin and Captain Bartlett given on the northward march in 1909.

It also included a narrative section written by Hugh Mitchell, attempting to show that observations of the sun at a very low altitude with an artificial horizon were possible with good accuracy. He used sights of the setting sun taken from the third-floor window of an office building in Washington, D.C., made when the sun's apparent altitude was lower than two degrees above the horizon. Since these were accurate to two minutes, he argued that those made by Peary in the Arctic in 1909, when the sun was at an altitude of nearly seven degrees, must have been at least that good.

Whatever the "Students of Polar Exploration" who read it thought of Hubbard's paper, there was little doubt of what Peary's geographic peers thought of the conqueror of the North Pole. Peary was ecstatic about his reception in Rome. He was seated in the position of honor wherever he went, and he was elected general secretary of the International Polar Commission.

In the Italian capital Peary had an audience with King Victor Emmanuel; in Cairo he had lunch with Kitchener. In Geneva, St. Gallen, Rouen, Marseilles and Paris he was awarded four more gold medals and a gold plaque. In the French capital, President Poincaré himself decorated him with the Grand Cross of the Legion of Honor, "the highest grade that can be conferred except upon a sovereign or ruler," Peary gloated to General Hubbard. It was a most satisfying tour.[34]

When he arrived home, he found his young compatriots were involved in new enterprises in his old domain. The Crocker Land Expedition had finally gotten away on July 2, and Bob Bartlett had agreed to captain an expedition in search of new land north of Alaska led by Vilhjalmur Stefansson. Captain Bartlett was eager to go north, but he was not at all sure of his ship, the *Karluk,* the expedition members "who like to have the trip but not the work," or the leader himself, whom he thought "the best natured man I ever met" but incapable of tough leadership. As he told Peary, "It is a Fiala job all right, only I will see that there is no come back with me. It's the New Land or bust. . . . I would love to land on Crocker Land. Hope to God she stays afloat long

enough to get near it. . . . I hope with all my heart that things will come out better than I anticipate."[35]

Another of Peary's old associates was back on the tent circuit for the summer, and his momentum was beginning to build. A new edition of Cook's book had just been issued by Mitchell Kennerley in New York through the influence of T. Everett Harré; Kennerley simultaneously published Harré's "Eskimo romance," *The Eternal Maiden.* Sixty thousand copies had been printed of *My Attainment of the Pole,* and Cook was selling the new edition at cost—$1—wherever he appeared. It contained several appendixes of new material supporting his polar claims, including an article by Peary's former meteorologist, Evelyn Briggs Baldwin, filled with state-ments culled from Peary's narratives that appeared to support his rival's claim. It also had a contribution by the Philadelphia lawyer-geographer Edwin Swift Balch, whom General Hubbard had mentioned. Like his book, *The North Pole and Bradley Land,* Balch's essay argued the truth of Cook's claim by comparing his reports with those of other explorers, including Peary.

Most of the new material, however, was focused on forcing a hearing before Congress or a group of impartial polar explorers and ended with an invitation to readers to "kindly write your congressman calling for an investigation." What was more, Cook had started a postcard and petition campaign, and mail was beginning to pile up in Congress, especially in the offices of the senators and representatives of Michigan and Washington.

Once again Peary began to fret over Cook's staying power and how he might be stopped once and for all:

> He is [a] natural liar, he has a manner that is convincing with many, he is persistent, & the average individual memory is short.
>
> He convinces many with whom he is brought in personal contact.
>
> The applause he receives at his cheap shows, keeps him encouraged & the longer he is left alone the more impudent he becomes.
>
> His not having to act on the defensive, leaves him free to devote all his attention & energy to the offensive.
>
> There must be some quiet ways of putting him on the grill without advertising him.[36]

The counterstrategy settled upon was a 35-page packet of materials signed *Veritas*—"Truth"—containing a résumé of Cook's Eskimos' statements, Barrill's affidavit, Dunkle and Loose's testimony, the Copenhagen decision and editorial comment tending to undermine the doctor's veracity, designed to make anyone thinking of openly supporting him think twice. It also called the charges of Peary's immorality among the Eskimos "a deliberate, intentional and malicious lie."

Newspapers and prominent people at many of the doctor's scheduled lecture stops began to receive this material, anonymously, in advance of his lecture dates, but these were often hard to obtain with enough advance notice to make an effective mailing.

Peary, who valued the support of the powerful so highly and who had received the benefit of that support so often, seemed convinced that if Cook could be discredited utterly in all official circles, he would be discredited entirely with everyone, for all time, and at this he kept hammering away. He had recently discovered Cook's name among the recipients of the Order of Leopold, and he wanted something done about it.[37] In August an agent was sent to Belgium to "take up the matter of the purification of the Order of Leopold" but had no luck. The agent reported that it seemed to be the Belgians' policy "to let sleeping dogs lie."

Another tool for chipping away at Cook's credibility presented itself that summer, when Hudson Stuck emerged from the Alaskan wilderness and announced that his party had finally conquered North America's highest peak, reaching the summit on June 7, 1913. Stuck took the same route Parker and Browne had tried in 1912. But the Northeast Ridge no longer looked the way they had described it. It was now a broken chaos of ice blocks loosened by the earthquake from which Browne and Parker had so narrowly escaped. Above the broken ridge, however, their route could easily be followed by the landmarks they had described. But of Cook's route the archdeacon said:

> It is quite impossible to follow his course from the description given in his book. . . . Doctor Cook talks about "the heaven-scraped granite of the top" and "the dazzling whiteness of the frosted granite blocks," and prints a photograph of the top showing granite slabs. There is no rock of any kind on the South (the higher) Peak above nineteen thousand feet. The last one thousand five hundred feet of the mountain is all permanent snow and ice; nor is the conformation of the summit in the least like the photograph printed as the "top of Mt. McKinley." . . .
>
> But it is not worth while to pursue the subject further. The present writer feels confident that any man who climbs to the top of Denali, and then reads Doctor Cook's account of his ascent, will not need Edward Barrille's affidavit to convince him that Cook's narrative is untrue. Indignation is, however, swallowed up in pity

when one thinks upon the really excellent pioneering and exploring work done by this man, and realizes that the immediate success of the imposition about the ascent of Denali doubtless led to the more audacious imposition about the discovery of the North Pole—and that to his discredit and downfall.[38]

Besides the archdeacon's newfound Christian charity toward the downfallen doctor, the Peary forces had other reasons for regret. Stuck had failed to obtain a clear picture of the summit—all the films had been spoiled in his attempts to expose them in the bitter conditions that prevailed there.

If he denied Cook's climb, Stuck established part of the claims of the Alaskan sourdoughs. He said that while opposite the North Peak, he and his companions had caught sight of their flagpole perched, snow-encrusted, above the outcrop of rocks nearest its actual summit. Stuck denied, however, the possibility of their having also climbed the South Peak in 1910, as Tom Lloyd had originally claimed.

The *Fairbanks Times,* whose own expedition had been sent out hoping to beat the Cheechacos to the summit the year before, was relieved and thankful that the deed was now all-Alaskan. "To Archdeacon Stuck and . . . the Taylor-Anderson party . . . the people of the Tanana and of all Alaska owe a real debt," it said. "After all the attacks upon the summits of McKinley by expert mountain climbers from the Outside, it has remained for true Alaskans to clinch the hazard and to win. They have shown the world that we have here the stuff of which Pearys, Scotts and Amundsens are made."[39]

That fall Dr. Cook, the man pointedly left off the *Fairbanks Times's* list of polar heroes, was appearing in Chicago and St. Louis on the stages of J.M. McVicker's vaudeville houses and in the East in the establishments of F.F. Proctor in the company of E.B. Baldwin, who was now actively supporting Cook's claims. Baldwin had never forgiven Peary for his treatment in 1894. As early as 1911 he had denounced Peary and had submitted evidence against him during the congressional fight over his retirement bill. After it passed, he had set to work writing a book that he hoped would vindicate Cook and relegate Peary to the status of an also-ran in the race for polar honors.

The initial trickle of letters supporting Cook from the Midwest and Northwest was becoming a torrent. Every ticket holder where Cook spoke was handed a petition to Congress written, according to one witness, in the style of a "get-rich-quick mining brochure," and rumors were circulating that Miles Poindexter, a senator from Washington, was interested in taking up Cook's congressional fight. Still, it took a sensational incident to put Cook over.

Fred High, the editor of *The Platform,* an independent magazine covering the chautauqua-lyceum field, had arranged it. High, in his early days, had been on the stage himself as a comic impersonator and elocutionist, and he knew how to work an audience. Ever since he had taken up Cook's cause in 1911, he had been devoting a page or two in each issue to promoting Cook and his claims, satirizing the National Geographic Society[40] and demeaning Peary, though he steadfastly maintained his neutrality in the polar dispute. He billed Cook as "The Man against the System," compared his character to Lincoln's and his fate to that of Jesus Christ, and hawked "Cook's Book," which was offered as a premium to chautauqua managers, from *The Platform's* pages. He had also masterminded Cook's postcard and petition campaign.

What High wanted most was a confrontation with Peary. He attempted continually to learn Peary's lecture schedule far enough in advance to book the doctor into the same town on the next day. He finally succeeded in Benton Harbor, Michigan, where Peary was scheduled to speak in the Bell Opera House. He selected one of his articles accusing Peary of various immoral acts and, using the telephone book for an address list, blanketed Benton Harbor and nearby St. Joseph with 2,000 copies.

In response, Peary secured an attorney and asked that the Cookites be placed under bond to keep the peace. The announcement that Peary would appear at the lecture under police protection "to guard the speaker from possible harm from the audience, local or otherwise" did not sit well with the good citizens of the "Twin Cities."

The evening of November 17 the house was packed, and among those seated in the balcony were Cook's claque. With them was one law officer determined to keep order, though the Cook partisans had promised there would be no demonstration.

When Peary appeared, he received a thunderous ovation. No serious incidents interrupted Peary's talk, but at one point a small man quietly appeared on stage and slipped a list of questions onto the speaker's podium. The admiral refused to look at the questions or even to glance in the direction of the balcony. When he had finished, Peary bade his auditors good night and left the stage. The audience remained, thinking the lecture would be followed by an answer to High's charges. But Peary had been ushered out the back door under police escort and did not return.

The doctor arrived the next day declaring, "Tonight I will face the issue once and for all and I will either make Admiral Peary answer my charges or he will be in a position where he will have to give up his uniform in the United States Navy." That night on the Bell's stage he accused

The Cook-Peary Controversy Breaks Out Anew

Dr. Frederick A. Cook

Will Lecture at

The First M. E. Church Jackson, Mich. Saturday, Nov. 29 8:30 P. M.

Under Auspices of the Wallace Class. E. F. Jordan, President

Peary of "every serious crime, almost, within the laws of the United States"; he brought no police guard, but he brought down the house, receiving an ovation "never before equalled in the lecture course history of Benton Harbor. . . . From the parquet to balcony [the audience] cheered him wildly, enthusiastically applauded his 'I reached the north pole first,' and fairly made the rafters ring when the doctor raked Peary fore and aft with destructive verbal canister."[41]

Dr. Cook's frank and open manner made its usual good impression as he repeated that he was sure that truth would prevail in the end. As proof of the truth of his own statements about Peary, he said, "This is not the first time I have voiced these sentiments in public. For four years I have spoken on the same lines and to 3,000,000 of people. If the charges are not true, I would have been jailed long ago, but nothing of that character has so far befallen me."[42]

Fred High howled in the next day's paper as he explained to local readers the cause of the dramatic confrontation in their city:

> For almost three years [*The Platform*] has fought Cook's battles . . .
> and dug under the naval rhinoceros hide of the man who has been
> pensioned as a rear admiral but who had to have six police to pro-
> tect him, who mistook Benton Harbor for a frontier settlement or
> a mining camp instead of a city of culture, a soldier afraid to leave
> without police protection. . . . This battle has only begun and we
> expect to keep it up until Cook is vindicated or put in jail.[43]

Peary asked his Michigan lawyer, Victor M. Gore, to investigate what had happened in Benton Harbor and to run down everything he could on High, Gilbert W. Baker and a man named Ernest Rost, who apparently was Cook's agent. He could not have been pleased with Gore's report:

> I find this town has gone wild over Cook. The doctors gave him
> a banquet that afternoon; prominent citizens dined him before his
> lecture; . . . his appearance and lecture were received with tumul-
> tuous applause. He was introduced by a prominent physician as
> the first man to reach the top of the earth. The whole meeting was
> an ovation for Cook. I will send you papers . . . [44]

To counteract the bad publicity, Peary had Gore publish a letter in the Benton Harbor papers containing "original documents" refuting Cook's allegations that he had cheated Franke, stolen Cook's stores or attempted to starve Cook on his return to Annoatok. Cook had even signed a receipt for the stores he had provided to him for his relief, he said. As to the charges of personal misconduct, he made no comment.

Cook replied that the letter was almost totally false, that he had never signed a receipt for supplies received, and he implied that Peary had bought British recognition by agreeing to withdraw from a race to the South Pole against Captain Scott. For the honor of the Navy, Cook declared, Peary should either "give up his uniform or commit Hari-Kari."[45]

The incident at Benton Harbor convinced Peary that decisive action must be taken to neutralize Cook and his enthusiastic followers. But first, the movement in Congress had to be squelched.

Gilbert Grosvenor was dispatched to convince Senator Poindexter that, ultimately, any publicity he would get out of taking up Cook's cause would be of an undesirable nature. Peary was sure that Poindexter was pro-Cook because he had been opposed in the last election by James Ashton, of Barrill affidavit fame. He was also sure that Cook was working "tooth and nail" to get his hearing and that a measure of revenge was in it, since Cook was now saying that it was a great mistake to have passed the Peary retirement bill.[46]

On December 16 Victor Gore sent his invoice to Peary and advised him that the sensation at Benton Harbor had been short-lived:

> During the last two weeks the excitement occasioned by the visit of Dr. Cook has wholly abated. No permanent impressions seem to remain. It was remarkable the extent to which his advance agent, by personal interviews and a free distribution of Dr. Cook's Book had persuaded a number of good people into the belief that Cook had actually discovered the North Pole. . . .
>
> I am sending you under separate cover the final chapter with reference to Cook's visit to this city. It is the turning over to his agent, Baker, by the doctors of the city of the medal inscribed "To the discoverer of the North Pole—Frederick A. Cook, April 21, 1908."[47]

The papers the lawyer sent contained an account of Cook's reception of the medal:

> The applause that followed drowned Cook's reply. The explorer bowed low and for the moment seemed to be surprised.
>
> "I thank you from the depths of my heart," he said. "This gift touches me deeply."[48]

On the same day, Peary received word that the first part of his plan had worked perfectly; he wired General Hubbard:

> Grosvenor had a near 2 hours seance with Poindexter today and has Poindexter's promise that he will do nothing for at least 4 weeks. That ought to be enough time for some skyrocketing. details later.[49]

The details of what would be included in the "skyrocketing" were rapidly taking shape. Cook's movements would have to be closely watched to prevent a repeat of what happened at Benton Harbor. But all that could be learned of Cook's plans was that he had two more engagements in the West before a week's run in a New York vaudeville house in mid-December. After that it was believed he would be going to Europe for six months.

Hubbard and Peary decided to hire the William J. Burns Detective Agency to track Cook's every move and compile a schedule of his upcoming lectures and theatrical engagements when he returned from Europe. Frederick Cook became Special Investigation #2140 in Chicago, where he had his office at Steinway Hall, and #5039 in New York City. Special agents bearing numbered codes would keep tabs on his movements, hecklers would be hired to confront him at his lectures and informants would be planted within the Cook organization itself.[50]

In New York on December 6, Ralph Shainwald and his wife dined with Evelyn Briggs Baldwin. Baldwin's book, which he thought might settle the polar dispute in Cook's favor, was now nearing completion. He had lent his manuscript to the doctor to read while on the road. But during dinner the Shainwalds were surprised at Baldwin's negative stance toward the doctor. He spoke of controversial aspects of the Mount McKinley matter as if they were new to him and said he had discovered among Cook's material the original of one of the pictures that had appeared in *My Attainment of the Pole* that caused him to doubt Cook's veracity.

After dinner Baldwin took the Shainwalds to Cook's suite at the Prince George Hotel on Fifth Avenue to show them the picture. They were amazed that Baldwin seemed to have the run of the place. After rummaging through Cook's unlocked trunks, Baldwin remembered that the photograph was no longer there. Shainwald was disturbed by this, but he was even more disturbed by Baldwin's next admission—that he had it at another location:

> I wondered how Baldwin would come to remove this picture under the circumstances as it certainly was Dr. Cook's property. . . .
>
> . . . I ask him whether he had spoken to anybody else about the picture. He said, "Yes, the enemy knows about it too."
>
> After a time I suddenly said to Baldwin "When did you see Bridgman last?" "About three weeks ago," he replied.
>
> A little later Baldwin admitted that he had seen Bridgman several times. . . . I simply said to Baldwin "Be very careful about Bridgman." His reply was "You don't need to worry about me, Bridgman is the biggest faker I know."

Dr. Cook had given Baldwin access to his rooms and material to aid him in preparing an appeal to Congress. He had returned half of Baldwin's manuscript by mail from Cleveland. The doctor liked it but had made suggestions in the form of a large number of interlineations proposing changes Baldwin should make so that the manuscript could be used as the basis of his appeal. Cook had also given permission for Baldwin to use his two stenographers to speed the work.

When the doctor returned to New York, he was told by the Shainwalds of their suspicions about Baldwin:

> We had a full talk. . . . Cook was loath to believe anything wrong
> about Baldwin, we suggested however, that on returning to his
> rooms he investigate to see whether any of his material was
> missing.
>
> At about midnight we were called to the phone and Dr. Cook
> laboring under great emotion informed us that not only was the
> film missing of the ice island but in addition a film taken of Peary's
> eskimo son and one or two other films. But even more astonishing
> was the fact that a great many pages dealing with the northern
> journey had been clipped from Dr. Cook's note books.[51]

On December 19, from the stage of the Patterson, New Jersey, vaudeville house, Cook announced a new development in the conspiracy against him, which he now called "The American Dreyfus Affair." His trusted associate, Evelyn Briggs Baldwin, had vanished, he said, and simultaneously, someone had taken from his private trunks "valuable original data." Could no one be trusted? he asked.[52]

When Baldwin read of Cook's announcement in the papers, he was indignant. He had just gotten back from Philadelphia, where he had met with Edwin Swift Balch, and went to see Cook at the Prince George Hotel.

When Baldwin arrived, Cook said, "You have been to see Bridgman." Baldwin denied that he had. But Dr. Cook insisted he had it on good authority. Baldwin replied, "Whoever made such a statement was a ——— ——— liar," and added that he had no use for a coward who would bring up to a man an anonymous falsehood without disclosing the source.

Baldwin then demanded back the second half of his manuscript. Cook said he wanted to take it with him on his upcoming European tour, but Baldwin refused, saying he did not wish to have it out of his hands any longer. "He then produced it, but in a suspicious manner," remembered Baldwin.

"Dr. Cook realized that I was through with him, and had become convinced as to certain conclusions I had been resisting through all the years of his conflict with public opinion. He wanted time to make erasures. Some whole pages of the manuscript he tore out. I found they were pages where he had written in substitutions for what I wrote. His erasures, done so badly that the matter can even now be partly read, were of pencil notes he had made which altered the meaning of certain passages and made a rather impartial study a defensive propagandist volume."[53]

When he emerged from the confrontation, Baldwin admitted to reporters that he did have some of Cook's original papers but said that they had been given to him. "I am engaged in making an independent investigation of the doctor's case from original sources," he explained. "I am going into the whole matter scientifically and deliberately. The outcome of this investigation will depend upon what I find, for I do not wear Cook's collar or anybody else's.

"I have gone to him and told him he must turn over to me every scrap of original field notes, every original observation and the original negatives of his photographs. I have told him I must have them by to-morrow and he has promised to give them to me. If those notes and other things establish that Cook reached the pole I am going to say so and work in his behalf for a Congressional investigation; if they do not I am going to say so. I am going to give him a chance."

After this interview, it was the doctor's turn. Cook said that Baldwin had explained everything satisfactorily and that there had simply been a misunderstanding.

"Mr. Baldwin has been engaged for two years in writing a book which attacks Peary's claims from scientific deductions, and when the manuscript disappeared coincident with his departure I was worried. I have always regarded Mr. Baldwin as my friend and still so regard him. Recently he insisted on making changes in his book which I regarded as unnecessary, but he was so positive about it I yielded.

"When he left without explanation after this incident and certain important papers disappeared simultaneously I could not understand it. I have never charged Mr. Baldwin with taking the papers. I hope to recover them all."[54]

Cook boarded the *Lusitania* on Christmas Eve 1913 to return to London. But his tour was extremely short. He lectured first at the Metropolitan Music Hall in Paddington, then at the Pavilion. His run at that famous London vaudeville theater lasted exactly one night. The vast house seemed as empty as the Arctic. Those who were there all seemed afflicted with severe coughs; one woman shouted, "Liar!" The balance of his engagement was canceled.[55]

After that, Peary's informants could find no trace of Cook on the Continent, and it was rumored that because of the London fiasco he had sailed quietly for the United States. He arrived from Southampton on the *Oceanic,* January 13, 1914.

On January 25 Cook resurfaced in Takoma Park, Maryland, a suburb of Washington, denying he had received a cold reception in London. "I came home before I had planned because I received an urgent message to return," he explained. "Therefore I delivered a few speeches, saw my family and then took a boat. I will go back to Europe later."[56]

The message was from Baker, High and Rost. It said:

> Baldwin a complete traitor. Papers attack you bitterly and refuse to take any refutation except from you. Situation serious. Return soon as possible.[57]

The first result of Peary's new campaign had apparently been the defection of E.B. Baldwin. On December 28 an article had appeared in the *New York Times* in which Baldwin denounced Cook. Soon afterward, Baldwin, who in recent years had been in a fix for money for all his exploratory schemes and who was in the process of petitioning Congress to finance a polar drift expedition, reportedly paid off many old debts and appeared clad in an expensive new wardrobe.

Peary now proposed to Hubbard that Baldwin go on the lecture circuit, armed with a set of slides and some documents dealing with Cook. He suggested his lecture might be entitled "The real story of the North Pole, with some inside facts about Cook the faker." But given Baldwin's own dubious reputation as an explorer, the idea got an unsympathetic reception from Hubbard and was quickly dropped.[58]

Having failed to get Peary's backing, Baldwin appealed to Fred High to put him on the platform. High, who always professed that he was willing to listen to any evidence, pro or con, concerning Cook's claims, rebuked him as a "Judas" and taunted him to produce evidence that proved Cook a faker. Baldwin apparently provided none.

Meanwhile, General Hubbard's investigations were starting to bear fruit. Burns's agents discovered that Cook planned to lecture at the Panama-Pacific Exposition in San Francisco in 1915. Hubbard contacted an associate justice of the California Supreme Court, who intervened with the fair's board of managers to have his concession vacated. One informant reported that Cook's press agent's position turned over rapidly because of the doctor's bad habit of not paying what he promised. Peary suggested that perhaps a confederate could be installed in that position who would be "in constant confidential touch with him" without exciting suspicion.[59]

Wherever information could be obtained as to the doctor's engagements, *Veritas* was sent ahead of him, and paid interrogators were planted in the audience to ask embarrassing questions. But despite all of Peary's schemes and Hubbard's elaborate countermeasures, at the Bellevue Presbyterian Church in Pittsburgh on April 3 and 4, 1914 everything seemed to go wrong for them when Fred High went the Benton Harbor encounter one better.

Not only did he get the same house for the day after a Peary lecture, but when Peary came forward to deliver it, Dr. Frederick A. Cook was sitting right there in the front row looking back at him. Some noted that Peary seemed ill at ease, and if Peary ever glanced at him, it would be the last time the two men would ever see each other.

At his lecture the following night, Cook not only denounced Peary as usual, but he also dramatically pointed out one of Peary's agents seated in the crowd as the "miserable sneaking coward" responsible for distributing *Veritas* in advance of his lecture.

After it was over, Dr. Cook explained to reporters what he was trying to accomplish. "Very early in the controversy I realized that if I could get Peary into court the injustice of the entire propaganda of insinuation could be passed upon by a jury of fairminded men," he said, "and that such an examination would be almost as good as a national investigation. Peary's advisers have been too shrewd to give me a cause of action—but I had hoped that I could force him into court to defend his uniform. To the present I have tried every means except by the use of an axe or gun to get Peary before a fair tribunal."[60]

Cook had repeated again and again at his lectures that the Danes had accepted his claims after a careful examination of them, and despite some newspapers' interpretation of the University of Copenhagen's decision, they had never rescinded the honors they had bestowed on him. The doctor was rather indefinite about the sequence of events in Copenhagen when he talked, mixing his unquestioned initial acceptance in September 1909 with the verdict of the university the following December, and Peary saw this as deceptive. He wanted an official statement of the Danish government's attitude toward Cook's claim. To this end General Hubbard petitioned the Danish Minister in Washington.

In reply, Minister Constantin Brun sent Hubbard a copy of the university's annual report for 1909 with a translation of its decision, saying he thought that would be sufficient as to Denmark's official position. He intimated that the status of Cook's honorary degree was just then under consideration, but no decision had been made because of the ill health of some of the committee members. He also told the general that although Cook had indeed received the Geographical Society's gold medal "as a recognition of his valuable work in the service of the geographic science," Cook's name had not been inscribed on the official list of recipients pending the receipt of satisfactory proofs that he had reached the North Pole, which he had promised to send to the university. Since the doctor had not yet done so, the Dane implied that the medal alone was not emblematic of official recognition. Minister Brun enjoined Hubbard, however, not to reveal these facts publicly without his permission.[61]

Except for that night in Pittsburgh, Peary's plan seemed to be going well, but Cook was not idle. Ernest C. Rost, the man Peary had asked his lawyer to investigate, had moved with his wife, Etta, to a flat at the Winton on Harvard Avenue in Washington, D.C., but for security and for the prestige of its address, they were having their mail sent to the New Ebbit Hotel. This placed Rost in position to lobby for a congressional hearing of the doctor's case.

At first glance it would not seem that Ernest Rost had a lot to recommend him for the job. He was an artist and photographer. But this had given him an eye for detail. He noticed things that others overlooked, both in pictures and on the printed page, and he was capable of clear exposition of what he saw. His wife acted as his private stenographer and editor, and what they wrote together had no chance of "leaking" to the Peary camp. They would make a formidable team that would have a lasting influence on the Polar Controversy.

On April 30, 1914, Cook's mail campaign resulted in Senator Poindexter's introduction of a resolution to establish the priority of Dr. Cook's claim to the North Pole and to appropriate $300 to strike a special gold medal to be given to him with the Thanks of Congress.

By the end of May, each member of Congress had received a complimentary copy of *My Attainment of the Pole* along with a letter from Cook himself, in which he said he wanted to place it "in the hands of the men who guard our National Honor" so that he might obtain the only reward he really wanted: "the appreciation of my fellow countrymen," which had been made "impossible by the campaign of abuse which has been waged against me."

The doctor also said he wished to appear before the committee that would consider Senator Poindexter's joint resolution:

> Before this committee I hope to have an opportunity of appearing and presenting my polar proof, including all of my original data and observations, together with the expert opinion of many of my colleagues and the corroborative evidence given by Peary himself, as worked out by several scientists. In the committee room, I hope and expect to get a square deal. . . .
>
> With the present Congressional half-recognition of one Polar claimant and absolute indifference to the other, the Glory of the American flag first at the North Pole, goes down to history with the sting of unnecessary bitterness.
>
> Will you lend your influence to an adjustment of this problem?
>
> Respectfully yours,
> F. A. Cook.[62]

Three days later, in Boston, Cook had a lawyer try to attach the property of Robert E. Peary there against 56 depositions seeking $35,000 in damages for various charges made by Peary against his client since 1909.[63] Meanwhile, pro-Cook mail continued to inundate the Capitol. Obviously, Cook was spoiling for a fight, and Peary told General Hubbard he was afraid he was going to get his way:

> The game is to mail until this material assumes such proportions as to seem irresistible, then dump it on the Committee & give it to the press.
>
> Just as Cook got his bill into Congress in spite of almost universal judgment to the contrary, so he is going to get his hearing before the Committee, with all the prestige of Congressional attention, & its enormous advertising value, sure as hell.[64]

The Cook forces were working on other fronts as well. The Justice Department received a personal appeal from Rudolph Franke for redress of his treatment at the hands of Peary at Etah in 1908. Franke now said the stolen property was worth $40,000 to $50,000 and asked official Washington to deal with these "two criminals, Peary and Bridgman."[65] The Justice Department, saying it had no jurisdiction, referred the matter to the Department of the Navy.

On June 23 Congressman Charles B. Smith of New York introduced joint resolution 282, requesting the secretary of the Navy to make an official statement preparatory to the Congress's declaring a definite priority concerning the discovery of the North Pole.

In response to Congressman Smith's resolution, Secretary of the Navy Josephus Daniels replied: "The department has never conducted any investigation or made any findings in regard to the discovery of the North Pole, and is . . . unable to submit a report of finding in reference to the matter under consideration."[66]

Though many thought Poindexter's resolution was as big a joke as Dr. Cook, it too was prompting some interesting responses. Edward S. Brooke, who had been the Crocker Land Expedition's motion-picture cameraman, sent Senator Poindexter a letter saying that while he was in Greenland, Dr. Cook's two Eskimos told him that "they went far from land for a long time," thus contradicting their story as related by the members of the Peary expedition.[67] Another letter came from the Danish explorer Ejnar Mikkelsen, who said that he had heard through a mutual friend of the doctor's how Peary's claim had gained approval. "Good God!" he exclaimed. "That committee of the National Geographical Society have certainly taken matters easy. It seems really incredible."[68]

Mikkelsen, who had confirmed the nonexistence of Peary's 1892–95 reported discoveries while looking for Mylius-Erichsen, added that Peary had not answered his inquiries about glaciology. He surmised "that he does not like that I brought back the information that the Peary Channel did not exist."

Cook's onslaught by mail and maneuvering in Congress infuriated some senators, such as Elihu Root, who vowed to fight to the bitter end against any actual attempt to rehabilitate the discredited doctor. But for many, Cook's efforts simply aroused their curiosity. Knowing a curious congressman could be a dangerous thing, Peary thought it best to "educate" those aberrant enough to take Cook seriously. To this end Hubbard rehired Lucien Alexander as Peary's personal lobbyist. Alexander moved in immediately on the center of all the trouble, Senator Miles Poindexter.

In his speech introducing his Cook resolution on the Senate floor, Poindexter had maintained that Archdeacon Hudson Stuck's account of his climb to the summit of Mount McKinley upheld the doctor's on "every material point." Alexander wrote to the senator, tactfully pointing out that Stuck himself had denied that Cook had climbed McKinley.

Poindexter replied that he was well aware of the archdeacon's attitude. But he told Alexander that Stuck and Peary were "interested judges" since Cook stood between them and their priority at the mountain and at the Pole, respectively. Even though each denied the doctor's claims, he argued, the narratives of their own journeys confirmed Cook's statements when he said he had been first at each. Poindexter said Cook's reports were so like Stuck's "it would have been impossible for Cook to know these facts without ascending the mountain."[69] Nevertheless, Poindexter's resolution was referred to the obscure Library Committee, where its opponents hoped it would die a quiet death.

Meanwhile, Alexander had sent a letter to the chairman of that committee on June 5, in which he quoted the archdeacon's repudiation of Cook's claims from Stuck's recently published book, *The Ascent of Denali*. In this letter he also tried to portray the doctor, by quoting some of T. Everett Harré's advertising copy for Cook's lectures, as nothing more than a snake-oil salesman out to part suckers from their pocket change. "Dr. Cook is the most widely advertised man in the world," Harré's copy ran. "Every country on the Globe either supports or condemns him for what he has or has not done, Hence: <u>He is an International Drawing Card—A Hero To His Friends and A 'Curiosity' to His Enemies</u>. In either case they are now flocking to see and hear this man, paying as much as ONE DOLLAR for the privilege, during his present lecture tour. . . . You have the ability to make the 'Killing' of your life with this feature production."[70] Alexander now sent copies of this letter to all the members of the Senate.

Alexander also flooded the Senate with a four-page tabloid entitled "The North Pole Aftermath in the United States Senate. Editorial Comments upon Senator Poindexter's Joint Resolution and the Baldwin Exposé." It contained reprints of editorials going back to 1909 but concentrated on unfavorable reviews of the senator's attempts to resuscitate the "gumdrop explorer," implying that such attempts would result only in unfavorable publicity for anyone else foolish enough to lend credence to the doctor's disallowed claims.

By July 1 Peary's lobbyist could confidently report to General Hubbard that the tract had had its effect; the joint resolution was all but dead. Even so, how had things gotten this far? How could this man have come back from utter ignominy to insinuate himself into the very halls of Congress? How could anyone who knew the facts give Cook a second thought? These were questions that Peary must have asked himself over and over. But the biggest question of all was where Cook's money was coming from. Peary knew firsthand that the kind of campaign he was waging in Congress was enormously expensive. This led Peary to redouble his efforts, since the only way to stop Cook now, he believed, was to cut off his source of revenue. To this end he drew up his master plan.

Peary proposed nothing less than a massive mailing campaign of his own. "Educational" material would be sent to newspapers and prominent persons wherever Cook went. Every chautauqua association in the country needed to be "educated" with a modified version of the *Veritas* packet. Then the same tactics could be brought to bear on the vaudeville houses. He believed an intensive campaign could cut Cook's financial base in half by the end of the season.[71]

Lucien Alexander was reluctant to approve Peary's tactics when he reviewed them with General Hubbard, fearing they might actually result in the unwanted investigation by Congress. He agreed with Gilbert Grosvenor, who had told him privately that he thought Peary was making a mistake in sending *Veritas* out anonymously. Alexander discouraged its continued use, suggesting instead that "The North Pole Aftermath," with a few of the editorials marked to attract the reader's eye, be used, along with more hired interrogators to disrupt Cook's lectures.

"The beauty of the editorials' blanket sheet is that we say nothing," counseled the lobbyist. "The editors of the newspapers do all the talking . . . [in] language much stronger . . . than any paper or brief written in Peary's interests at his behest, could with good grace employ."[72]

Finally, Alexander suggested sending Mitchell and Duvall's recomputation of Peary's observations to persons in official positions, "who would not understand it but would be impressed by it." To counter Representative Smith's resolution, Alexander even wrote personal letters to President Wilson and the secretary of the Navy, advising them of Cook's tactics and enclosing a marked copy of "The North Pole Aftermath."[73]

For the time being, the matter seemed under control. The Poindexter resolution was safely bottled up in the Library Committee, and Smith's had not been reported out. But pro-Cook petitions continued to pour in from Washington, Michigan, Iowa, Ohio and Illinois, which might yet become irresistible.

Meanwhile, Peary's informants were continually gathering intelligence to carry out his master plan, and General Hubbard continued to pay out $25 a day plus expenses to the Burns agency, whose detectives regularly filed encrypted messages on their subject.[74]

One operative, "No. 11," got close to Cook for a considerable time and provided much information. Perhaps this was L.S. McMahan, the mysterious character the Cook men called Mac, who seemed to turn up wherever Cook did, giving friendly advice and asking about where the doctor would be appearing next. He offered $100,000 to finance another try for the Pole by Dr. Cook, bragged about bribing public officials, then pledged $5,000 as "a retainer" for Miles Poindexter to help him carry on Cook's fight in Congress.

By constant surveillance, Peary got a rather complete picture of Cook's movements and advance notice of his lectures. For each place the doctor was to talk, Hubbard's agents supplied the names of prominent civic leaders, pastors, newspaper publishers, and theater or chautauqua managers. Each received a packet of anti-Cook material, either *Veritas* or "Aftermath," as seemed appropriate.[75]

In the summer of 1914 General Hubbard got a letter from Peary's old and faithful associate Hugh J. Lee. Lee related to the general his impression of Cook's book: "He appears to have written it after all the ammunition had been fired at him and all the statements are so nicely explained." Lee also mentioned that Bob Bartlett, contrary to what he had told Peary, seemed "to be of the opinion that Peary was mistaken about Crocker Land being land and he thinks the MacMillan expedition will prove beyond any possibilities of doubt in the minds of everyone that Cook is a faker. He thinks there is no land."[76] Lee did not know it then, but Donald MacMillan had already confirmed Bartlett's opinions beyond any possibilities of doubt—in regard to Crocker Land, at least.

MacMillan had set out from Etah intending to follow essentially the same route Cook had in 1908 to the tip of Axel Heiberg Land and then, taking a course west of true north, strike out across the polar pack up the 95th meridian for Crocker Land.

MacMillan may have sincerely believed the doctor's polar journey to be a fabulous concoction, but he had enough respect for Cook's description of his route across Ellesmere Land to take an entirely different one from Flagler Fjord to Eureka Sound, having noted the difficulties detailed in Cook's book, a copy of which he had along for amusement.

The route he chose across the Beitstad Glacier was so treacherous in its own way that some of his Eskimos deserted. While crossing the glacier, his dogs, which had to be fed exclusively on pemmican that inexplicably contained salt, were coughing up an oily yellow liquid and passing a brown one. Once down from the heights and back on Cook's route, seven musk oxen were procured, and the dogs responded to the change in diet by making 90 miles in three days.

By the time he was ready to set out across the polar sea, MacMillan had sent back all but three men and was in a situation similar to that described by Dr. Cook in 1908.[77]

He had with him one white companion, Ensign Fitzhugh Green, and two Eskimos, Pewahto and Etukishuk, whom MacMillan had come to regard as his "main Eskimo." His dogs, however, were in far worse shape than the healthy animals Cook claimed to have picked from a large pack. The tainted pemmican had taken its toll; all were weak, and some had already dropped dead in the traces.[78]

MacMillan had spent considerable time after reaching the tip of Axel Heiberg Land looking along the shore for the cairn Peary had said no explorer could have missed. Peary had briefly claimed that Cook could not have reached the cape because he had not brought back the contents of this cairn. But after a careful search without success, MacMillan had to give up. With his dogs fading fast, he decided he could wait no longer if he was to have any chance of reaching Crocker Land before the season became too far advanced.

He departed Cape Thomas Hubbard on April 16.[79] The first day the ice was rather rough near the shoreline but became smoother farther out, and they progressed ten miles before camping. The following day the going was still good for the first three miles, until they were stopped by an open lead in which they tried to take a sounding. But the pick ax they used for a weight was carried away under the ice by a strong current and lost.

On April 18 they made 12 miles more, even though confronted by much open water. The Eskimos did not like the looks of the ice conditions and asked MacMillan to turn back the way *Tatsekuuk* had, but Macmillan refused.

They were now 25 miles from shore, and Etukishuk indicated they had already passed, several miles back, the spot where the doctor had abandoned his quest for the Pole.

The next two days the men traveled across relatively smooth ice with few pressure ridges and made good 53 miles. These mileages were achieved even though the Eskimos rode the sledges on every level stretch. The white men walked most of the way, however, hoping to save the badly failing dogs.

On April 21 they covered 18 miles in eight hours. They were now nearly 100 miles from land, yet nothing was in sight on the horizon, even though the mist that usually hung low on the ice had disappeared when all the leads had frozen over.

The next morning, however, MacMillan was inside their igloo when he heard Green's excited shout that Crocker Land was in sight. "We all rushed out and up to the top of a berg," MacMillan wrote in his diary. "Sure enough! There it was as plain as day—hills, valleys, and ice cap—a tremendous land extending through 150 degrees of the horizon. We had even picked out the point to head for when Pewahto remarked that he thought it was mist . . . resembling land. As we watched it more narrowly its appearance slowly changed from time to time so we were forced to the conclusion that it was a mirage of the sea ice. This phenomenon has fooled many and many a good man and deceived Peary, I believe, in 1906 when he stood on the heights of Cape Thomas Hubbard. Two or three days more will tell. Clear weather and good going is our prayer."[80]

After pushing on another 18 miles in six hours the next day, they camped. Pewahto wanted to go back, since he feared being so far from land, but MacMillan insisted he continue. The weather remained fine, and an additional 24 miles were covered the following day. They had thought they had seen land in the morning of the previous day, but it had faded away in the afternoon when the sun worked south and west. Now, as they calculated their position, they estimated they had reached the place where Crocker Land should be, but there was only ice. MacMillan sadly recorded in his journal: "In other words we have done what we came to do—prove or disprove the existence of Crocker Land. So my dream of 5 years is over."[81]

Here the ice changed abruptly to "a chaotic mass of leads and pressure ridges extending in all directions as if acted upon by a strong tide or a current."[82] They struggled on one more day but made only a few miles before MacMillan gave up and ordered the men back to land.

The return was even easier than the going, and in four days they had Cape Thomas Hubbard in view. From out on the sea ice, MacMillan caught sight of what appeared to be a cairn high on a point above the foreshore, and although they were tired, he insisted on visiting the cairn and retrieving the record it contained. After a struggle over the pressure ridges near the shore and up three snow-crusted hills, he reached the snow-covered cairn and at its base found a cocoa tin. It contained a piece of Peary's silk flag and a surprisingly short message. This must have been the spot from which Peary had seen Crocker Land, but of the sighting of what he said were the most northerly rocks on earth, there was no mention. The record simply read: "Peary, July 28, 1906."

MacMillan looked out to sea and thought he could see land as well. He believed that if he had been there in Peary's place, he would have declared the discovery himself. But later, along the low foreshore to the southwest, Fitzhugh Green discovered another of Peary's cairns. The message it contained stated that on the day Peary subsequently claimed to have seen Crocker Land he had "a clear view of the northern horizon," yet there was again no mention of land, the "discovery" of which Peary later said had been the second most important result of his 1905 expedition.

But of all this the world had received no news in August 1914, and, if it had, the report would have been buried on an inside page, lost in the descriptions of the war that had broken out in Europe between the Triple Alliance and the Central Powers.

The rumors of war that had swept the continent since the assassination of Archduke Franz Ferdinand of Austria-Hungary at Sarajevo in June had already made up Marie Cook's mind. She had left for home with the girls and heard news of the war's beginning by wireless while still at sea. Most in America, however, were not that worried. The European war was expected to be a short one, and anyway, it was very far away.

By the end of August the chautauqua season was drawing to a close. Peary's agents reported Cook had canceled a two-week engagement to attend to urgent business in Washington. They also found out he had secured engagements in eastern vaudeville houses that would carry him through the winter, something he had not been able to do in 1913. Among these were Keeney's in New Jersey, Keith's in Pennsylvania, Shubert's in upstate New York and Willie Hammerstein's in New York City itself.

Also among the reports Peary had received was that Cook had a statement from a "girl" saying that Cook's name had been forged to his *Hampton's* series. "He appears to have a mania for affidavits," Peary raved, ironically, about the value of sworn statements as evidence. "He seems to think this is the cure for every charge against him. He must have a trunk full in all."[83]

Peary was preparing suggestions and reviewing questions to be used by the "anti-Cook interrogators" at the doctor's speeches and theater engagements. He outlined general points to avoid and ones he thought would hit the mark; he advised staying away from technical matters by asking questions concentrating "on his record and put to him in carefully considered form so as to reduce as far as possible his opportunities for evading the main point, a procedure in which he is very expert."[84] But the trouble with this plan was that it exposed in the questioner a knowledge of complex details that the general public did not possess or understand. It was easy, therefore, when Dr. Cook was faced by such questioners, as he had been at Pittsburgh, to point them out to his audience as minions of General Hubbard, whom Cook now described as "Peary's Press Agent." Often, this was enough to silence the questioner, who did not want to draw attention to his employer.

Cook's constant travel for the chautauqua—sometimes 70 tent meetings in a season—was grueling, not to mention the two-a-day performances in the vaudes, but it was a life not without its compensations. He traveled up and down the country, to just about every state, and often met famous people at the tent lyceums and in the theater districts. He made the acquaintance of many, including Clarence Darrow, Thomas Edison, Henry Ford, John Burroughs, Elbert Hubbard and Fritzi Scheff. One day, in Chicago, he even met Rigo, the gypsy violinist who had run away with Clara Ward, the Princess de Chimay, whom Cook had helped make "the most beautiful woman in the world" aboard the *Belgica* in the wilderness of Antarctica. He must have heard hundreds of interesting tales from the many odd and clever people who performed on the boards, and on the lyceum circuit he was often invited for dinner or entertainment at the cultured homes of the towns he visited.

It may be taken as something of a microcosm of Dr. Cook's life at this time that within the space of less than two weeks in September 1914, he appeared before a vaudeville audience in Newark, wedged between an act featuring the comic antics of seven trained bulldogs and "Morey's spectacular mechanical reproduction of the Titanic disaster,"[85] a dignified audience at a lyceum course in Nashville, and finally, a very distinguished assembly at the Masonic temple in Washington, D.C.

Free tickets for his Washington appearance had been distributed by Cook's lobbyist, Ernest Rost, and more than 100 members of Congress heard the man who was asking them to recognize him as the discoverer of the North Pole. Even as he spoke, supportive cards and letters were pouring into their offices, and by the end of the year it looked as though some sort of investigation would be inevitable.

The push for a hearing to establish Cook's priority at the Pole had become so strong that news of it reached even to the most remote inhabited spot on earth. "To us who know the facts and who know Etukishuk and Ahwelah so well," wrote Donald MacMillan from his winter quarters at Etah, "it seems almost incredible that there are still people who believe in Cook. . . . [Etukishuk] pointed out where they camped, what they did, and where they stopped on the Polar Sea which I judged to be about fifteen miles from land. . . .

"I have Dr. Cook's book with me and many a laugh these two boys have had over it as we have read certain parts of it to them. If it will do any good to bring Etukishuk back with me to the States I could easily do it. . . ."[86]

Peary cautioned his former assistant against such a course of action. He wrote that to bring an Eskimo from the North would probably result in the man's death or, worse yet, turn him into another Mene.[87]

CHAPTER 21

A Perversion of History

PEARY DIDN'T NEED ANY MORE PROBLEMS IN THE FORM OF UNPREDICTABLE Eskimo witnesses. He had plenty to deal with already. True, Poindexter's resolution was dead, and he'd been so humiliated that he confided to Ernest Rost that he wished he'd never even heard of the North Pole. But Rost had found a new sponsor to keep Cook's cause alive in the person of Representative Charles B. Smith of New York, who introduced yet another resolution on January 21, 1915.

Joint resolution 408 called for the establishment of "the priority of discovery of the North Pole and the region contiguous thereto." It was referred to the Education Committee of the House. On the same day, Representative F.O. Smith of Maryland entered a resolution calling on the postmaster general to explain why the National Geographic Society enjoyed special franking privileges worth $300,000 per year, since it was "not national (in the sense that it is not a bureau of nor connected with the National Government in any capacity whatsoever), is not geographic, is not scientific, and is not a society, but is simply and solely a private publishing house."[1]

Lucien Alexander had left the city, confident nothing would come of any of this, but still he did not want to be caught off guard. For some months he had been accumulating a mass of material on the polar dispute, arranged in a card file for easy access in his Philadelphia office. Part of it consisted of contradictory quotations attributed to Dr. Cook on a variety of subjects, filed as "Cook vs. Cook."

Alexander had cause to use his file when Representative Smith unexpectedly secured a hearing on the evening of January 28 under the pretext that several foreign explorers who were in the country only a short time wished to give testimony in regard to the congressman's resolution on polar priority. The chairman, Dudley M. Hughes of Georgia, could not get a quorum for an official meeting but agreed to meet informally to accommodate these witnesses. The members who did appear were told that the explorers had not yet arrived but that there were others present who should be heard; they were all old friends of Cook's.

The witnesses were evidently gotten together in some haste. The first, Edwin Swift Balch, declared he had no prepared remarks. Balch was now the author of two books defending Cook's claims, the latest being *Mount McKin-ley and Mountain Climbers' Proofs*. By comparing later climbers' accounts with Cook's, it attempted to show that Cook must have made the climb himself, since their descriptions matched his. Before the committee, Balch simply gave an extemporaneous explanation of how Cook's priority at the North Pole and on Mount McKinley could be established by the comparative approach he had used in his books.

Then came Clark Brown, the Albany civil engineer who had had the confrontation with Herbert Bridgman. Brown had lately been supplying Rost with all kinds of material that the lobbyist hoped to work into the *Congressional Record*. Brown, too, argued that Cook's claims could be substantiated circumstantially.

Congressman Horace M. Towner of Iowa was curious about the engineer's interest in polar matters, especially since Brown was candid enough to say that he had never been north of Plattsburgh, New York.

"[The Polar Controversy] was a subject for a long time that most everybody was reading and talking about," responded Brown, "and I soon reached the opinion that the matter was not receiving that careful and thoughtful consideration that it deserved. . . . There are [a] few of us, who, as we go through life, can see an opportunity to do something really worth while, and I thought that there was an opportunity, perhaps, for me to develop something which would be worth while, and perhaps cause my name to be remembered after my death."[2]

Like Balch, Brown seemed desultory and unfocused. At one point he inexplicably introduced the text of a newspaper clipping in which Dr. Brashear of Pittsburgh denounced Dr. Cook.

Next, at Congressman Smith's suggestion, Ernest Rost produced letters from 32 men "with arctic experience" who he said were ready to endorse Cook's claim. Among them were staunch supporters of the doctor like Professor Dyche, Dillon Wallace, Admiral Schley, Ralph Shainwald, Rudolph Franke and John R. Bradley. But surprisingly, the list also included such unlikely names as Hugh J. Lee and Harry Whitney. It soon developed that only one of the 32, Middleton Smith, the aging last survivor of the Point Barrow Expedition of 1882, was in the hearing room.

One other witness, however, was worthy of attention. She was Lilian Kiel. Unlike the others, she had a carefully prepared statement recounting how Dr. Cook's "confession" had been created and issued over his signature.

At last, the committee members sat up and took notice, asking her questions that betrayed a genuine interest. If not Dr. Cook, then who authored the "confession"? one asked. Miss Kiel identified its author as T. Everett Harré, even displaying a photograph of the former subeditor of *Hampton's Magazine* while saying sarcastically, "This is a picture of the noble gentleman. You can see the intelligence in his face."

When the congressmen remained skeptical that Cook had known nothing of the changes interpolated into his story, she not only repeated that he did not know anything about them, but added that Cook had been so heart-broken over the incident that he had only recently even looked at the articles to see what had been done to them. "Between ourselves," Miss Kiel told the congressmen, "he did not read a portion of it until last October, when I forced him to read the insertions. He knew that they had lied and misrepresented his story, or they could never have printed 'Dr. Cook's confession' on the cover. He did not know what they had done, but he did know that they had faked his story."

Furthermore, she stated that this was not the first instance of the magazine's having taken liberties with an explorer's story. As the stenographer who had taken down the magazine's Peary series, she said, she knew the inside story of how those articles had been created as well. Kiel asserted that Peary "did not write his own story. . . . Mr. Peary had no story, he had no data, he had nothing to present to *Hampton's Magazine*. . . . Mr. Peary merely answered questions. From those notes Mrs. Elsa Barker made up the story."

When she had concluded her testimony, the chairman thanked Miss Kiel for entertaining them with her "interesting" recollections, to which she replied, "I did not come here, gentlemen, to entertain you. I merely came to show you one of the many wicked methods which were employed to denounce Dr. Frederick A. Cook, who, in my opinion, is the discoverer of the North Pole. However, I am not a scientist. To me it is immaterial whether Robert E. Peary is the discoverer of the North Pole, or whether Dr. Cook is the discoverer. As I have repeated several times, I am here simply in the interest of justice." The committee adjourned at 10:25 P.M., giving every indication that it would meet again to consider Cook's case. But that would not happen.

When Lucien Alexander heard about the late-night goings-on in the Education Committee, he returned to Washington and went straight to Capitol Hill, where he got an appointment with Representative Simeon D. Fess, a committee member who had not attended the informal hearing. Peary had pointed out Fess to Alexander as a likely foil to Representative Smith should Cook's bill ever get out of committee. Alexander closeted with him from 8:00 to 11:15 on the evening of February 1, and the next morning Fess went to the Education Committee. Alexander wrote General Hubbard as to the results:

> The committee on convening decided to make the session an executive one. Several expressed the opinion that Cook in fairness should be heard as was Peary. Fess took hold and poured fact after fact into the committee as to Cook's faking methods and all were silenced and a resolution adopted killing the Smith resolution. Fess did not disclose where he got his information and neither you, Peary or the P.A. Club were in any way involved in the matter.[3]

When another similar resolution was brought before the Education Committee, it was again defeated, but only on a tie vote—6 to 6. Consequently, Alexander stayed in Washington to see if he could engineer something that would keep Cook from springing any more surprises. He button-holed members of the committee and made sure the January 28 hearing minutes were suppressed. He decided against introducing any pro-Peary resolutions because, if they should fail, it would provide more ammunition for the "Cook crowd." Likewise, speeches from the floor that would allow Cook's proponents to respond directly were ruled out. Instead, Alexander decided it would be best to have an "extension of remarks" speech put in the *Congressional Record* to counter four such speeches on the doctor's behalf already introduced by representatives of Illinois, Kentucky and North Dakota and mailed out under their franking privileges to their constituents. To this end he courted several congressmen who were eager to help, but in the end they all seemed too small in stature for his purposes. The man he really wanted for the job was Simeon D. Fess.

When he met with Representative Fess again and asked him to take up Peary's fight in Congress, Fess was reluctant to become publicly involved in the controversy but willing to do everything in his power to help if the matter ever reached the floor.

Lucien Alexander used every argument to change his mind. After all, he told Fess, he was from the Midwest, Cook's stronghold; he was a former president of Antioch College and the president of a chautauqua. If it was he who struck the blow against Cook, Alexander declared, it would go a long way toward demolishing the faker forever. Still, Fess remained hesitant, having been warned by colleagues to avoid the messy dispute. But when Alexander told Fess that as a member of the American Historical Association, it was his duty to prevent "a perversion of history," Fess finally agreed to ask for permission to publish an extension of remarks provided another congressman would do likewise and share the burden.

Alexander immediately suggested Congressman A.C. Hinds of Pennsylvania, whom he considered a lightweight but loyal. Over dinner, he made a deal with Hinds that his remarks would be short and unobtrusive, placing all the weight on Fess. The next thing Alexander did was to write Fess's speech. Using material from his card file as his sourcebook, he kept two stenographers busy into the early morning hours.

Alexander continued to polish his draft all the next day until he laid it before Fess at 1 A.M. on March 3. The congressman went over it three times. He changed practically nothing and seemed delighted with it. Alexander was rather surprised, he told General Hubbard, that Fess "was willing to stand for all my 'copy,' which at places 'called a spade, a spade'—a thing we, from the Peary standpoint could not wisely do."

When Alexander showed his draft to Peary that evening, he thought it "just the thing." There was one small problem, however. Alexander had written every word of the speech but had discreetly left the title to the congressman. It was already at the printer's when Alexander found, to his horror, that

Fess had dubbed it "Dr. Cook, Still in Front of the Stage." Alexander told the representative that this was just the sort of advertisement Cook desired, and the chagrined Fess had to retrieve the speech before it went to press.

After it was printed under the title "The North Pole Aftermath," Alexander boasted to General Hubbard of his triumph: "The Fess speech, in accordance with your wishes is not written from the standpoint of Cook vs. Cook, but rather as <u>Dr. F. A. Cook, liar, vs. U. S. History.</u> You see, Fess as a member of Congress & of its 'education' Committee can say things & bang Cook effectively – of course in a dignified manner – in a way that would not score if done by you, Peary or a direct representative."[4]

Alexander felt he finally had in the Fess speech what he wanted—a written-to-order antidote for the massive mailings of material that others had introduced into the *Congressional Record* on Cook's behalf, saying it "will probably be more convincing to the popular mind than anything we will ever have again."[5] Alexander judged the men working for Cook as "shrewd but unprincipled" and feared other "honest but misguided" men like Poindexter might yet come to Cook's defense if left unchecked.

Evidence of just how right Alexander's assessment was appeared the same day as Fess's speech, when Thaddeus H. Caraway of Arkansas also put into the extension of remarks for March 4 a verbatim transcript of the suppressed minutes of the ex parte committee meeting of January 28. A Cook sympathizer had tipped Ernest Rost that one of the committee members still had a copy of them. Late at night two stenographers were gotten into his office and a transcript was secured. When the minutes appeared in Congressman Caraway's speech under the title "The Attack on Dr. Frederick A. Cook," they created more grist for Dr. Cook's congressional mail mill.[6]

Seeing that he was in a serious battle, Alexander now gave in to the suggestions he had previously rejected. Immediately, 20,000 copies of a pamphlet containing "The North Pole Aftermath" were printed and distributed. By April more than 100,000 had been printed, and Alexander had developed his own master plan for their distribution, which he sent to General Hubbard for approval after discussing it with Peary and Gilbert Grosvenor.

Peary would distribute the copies of the Fess speech already printed at $40 per 1,000 for postage. A further printing of 42,000 was earmarked for members of the American Medical Association. Copies would be sent to all school districts in the Midwest, where Cook was strongest, to put an end to pro-Cook essay contests being promoted in some of the schools there as class activities. Personal correspondence with midwestern school principals was suggested to stop this pollution of innocent minds. Alexander was aghast at the thought that "otherwise they will probably be pro Cookites all their lives, as well as their parents, brothers and sisters." Individual correspondence with those 32 men "with arctic experience," whom Rost had mentioned, was also suggested to find out who were really unrepentant Cook supporters. The Fess

speech would also be used to counteract a letter Fred High had sent to ency-
clopedia and textbook publishers, seeking to have mention of Cook's claim
inserted in their new editions.

Alexander also wanted every YMCA, Elks, Rotary and other civic club to
receive copies. Also, he revived the idea of a counterlecturer who would blast
Cook from the platform.

And still he was not finished. Alexander also wanted to "educate" the
vaudes with the Fess speech and to tail Cook's agents to keep abreast of their
movements. He suggested an anti-Cook editorial be printed in the New York
Sun that could be sent to all Associated Press papers for their permanent files,
as well as having similar stock articles written for journals to be printed over
impressive authors' names.

In all, he thought 400,000 copies of "Aftermath" would take care of it, at
a cost of $1.50 per 1,000, now that the plates had been made.[7] To distribute
them widely, Gilbert Grosvenor volunteered the National Geographic Society's membership list if Fess would use his franking privilege.[8]

Alexander was also very much interested in the whereabouts of Rudolph
Franke. On the strength of an affidavit by Peary, Franke's case had finally been
dropped by the German courts. In it he swore he had not coerced Franke in
any way to obtain his property, including requiring its surrender as a condition to allow Franke to returned to America.[9] But since Peary had vowed to
fight the suit to the bitter end, fearing that to do otherwise would be used as
an admission of guilt in future Cook propaganda, his legal expenses had been
steep.[10]

Franke's arctic experience, like so many others', had changed the course of
his life, and he dreamed of returning there some day. While in Germany, he
had unsuccessfully applied for Count Ferdinand von Zeppelin's proposed expedition to the North Pole in one of his huge airships. Franke had given a few
sparsely attended lectures, billing himself as "Dr. Cook's Commissary General," and had published an account of his experiences in the Far North under
the same imprint as the German edition of *My Attainment of the Pole.* His
book had not caused as much of a stir, and with the demise of his legal case,
Franke had returned to America. He was now reported to be planning to em-
bark on another journey to Greenland, and Alexander went to New York to
see what he could find out.

Evidently, Franke had come to America to stay, perhaps to avoid the war,
as he had brought his wife and taken up residence on 39th Street. When
Alexander visited the narrow, run-down, five-story tenement above a barber-
shop in an Italian-American neighborhood, he learned that Franke was no
longer there. He did, however, find an acquaintance, a Mrs. Hunting, who
could supply some details.

She said he had been sent "to the North Pole" by a rich gentleman from
Philadelphia, whose name she couldn't remember, and that he had taken
along his best friend, Arthur Haark. Alexander asked if the wealthy gentle-

man's name might possibly be Disston, but the woman said no, she didn't think so. Alexander next suggested Bradley, then Whitney. "Bradley was his name, I feel sure," she replied. The woman added that Franke had told her that he would not be back until at least the fall of 1915. Mrs. Hunting felt sorry that when he did return he would find out that his wife had died of cancer on New Year's Day.[11]

Just what Franke was really up to worried Lucien Alexander. He was deathly afraid that he would bring back one or both of the Eskimos who had gone with Dr. Cook, that they would be coached into vouching for the truth of the shadow story to prove Cook reached the Pole and that they would destroy the "somewhat contradictory" Eskimo evidence Rasmussen had sent down from Greenland.

A Pearyite's worst nightmares unfolded in Lucien Alexander's mind as he imagined, as only a man who had thoroughly familiarized himself with all the byzantine loose ends of the Polar Controversy could do, what Cook's next moves would be: he would return to McKinley and climb it by the Parker-Browne-Stuck route and "find" his record, then say that the picture he had taken in 1906 was an innocent substitution, since

> his own picture of the real top(?) had not come out right (film had spoiled) and he simply had to have a picture for his book so he made one of another rock by photographic process instead of having one painted to use as an illustration; that when he was attacked he had to keep quiet about it <u>until</u> his tube was found. It is really all most simple. <u>Some</u> people would not believe him or his Eskimo—but he has <u>already</u> got the Admiral Schleys and the Senator Poindexters and the Edwin Swift Balches—and his new fakes would get him more than half the world. . . .
>
> If Franke brings back one or both of the Eskimo, Cook <u>and</u> his Eskimo would be the biggest vaudeville drawing card Keith ever put on the circuit—just fancy Cook and Etukishuk showing audiences in a darkened theater with a lamp for the sun and Etukishuk casting real shadows on the stage "just how" they took the shadow dial at the Pole as mentioned [on] pp 307-9 of Cook's book! And think of Etukishuk in broken English telling the audiences in a six word speech "It was all just that way" and then waving the American flag over Cook. All Cook needs is a Hammerstein back of him to boom him . . . it will create a sensation. . . . Whitney is already on record as saying the Eskimo went to him & said they did not understand Peary & his men when they came to them and asked them about Cook's journey.[12]

Notices soon appeared in the press that Cook would be undertaking another business venture and making another journey, but this time it would be no shadow show with Eskimos on the stage of Keith's, and he would go nowhere near Mount McKinley. Instead, he told the Chicago press, he would attempt the last great physical conquest left to man—the ascent of Mount Everest.

"I will be detained in Chicago until some time in June," he said, "making preparations for my next adventure. . . .

"For this trip we will have everything of an up-to-date nature. . . . I am taking special pains in the purchase of a moving picture outfit as it is my intention to show the world the discoveries of the trip. I plan one film on the 'Round the World' tour in its entirety and another featuring the conquest of Mt. Everest."13

Cook said he planned to sail on the British steamer *Mongolia.* There was talk about taking some Boy Scouts along and even a rumor that one member would be Kathryn Fife, an Osage Indian crack shot from Oklahoma. But when the party was settled on, it consisted of just three—to "lessen the chances of discord"—Dr. Cook, Dr. Frank P. Thompson of Chicago, and Edward S. Brooke, late of the Crocker Land Expedition, as cameraman. The presence of Brooke bothered Bridgman, who began to worry that he might have been planted on the expedition by the Cook forces to gather damaging information against Peary in Greenland.

Lucien Alexander took credit for Cook's apparently hastily planned expedition. "From the extent of the announcements as to Cook's trip to the Himalyays," he told General Hubbard, ". . . I think we may assume Cook really expects to go, and I can readily understand his desire to get out of this country now that he finds people posted thru the Fess speech wherever he goes."

Alexander had information that John W. Ruskin, a world traveler and lecturer, planned to stand in for the doctor during his absence to keep the Polar Controversy alive. Peary's lobbyist estimated that Cook had canceled 70 chautauquas to make the trip, but he would not get away that easily if Peary had his way. It was the admiral's idea to have the words Alexander had put into Fess's mouth accompany Cook around the world.

Alexander liked Peary's idea and wrote to prominent people, including Secretary of State William J. Bryan, to get the addresses of missionaries and consular and commercial agents all along Cook's planned route. He also thought Gilbert Grosvenor would be able to supply a list of correspondents in each country on his itinerary. "If this plan is carried out," Alexander concluded, "it ought to do a lot to head off his being feted in Asia as the simon pure discoverer of the North Pole and from building upon that upon his return."14 Three thousand to five thousand of the admiral's copies were slated for Asia, and a copy was sent to all-first class passengers aboard the SS *Mongolia.*

Alexander had been writing his thoughts directly to Peary because General Hubbard had been ill for a considerable time. It was not considered serious, even though Hubbard was only able to pencil yes or no next to the points of Alexander's "master plan." Then on May 19 the general suddenly died of erysipelas. The "master plan" was now in limbo, since it was largely the general's money that was to fund it, and Alexander didn't know how, or even whether, to approach his heirs and executors about such a confidential matter.[15]

Lucien Alexander had given himself and Simeon D. Fess too much credit for Cook's departure, however. Actually, he had been planning the trip for quite some time. With the demise of his latest efforts in the Education Committee, perhaps Cook had seen the writing on the wall. How long could he keep up interest in his recitation of the story of a grievously wronged man? And how long could he maintain the grueling round of chautauqua-lyceum-vaudeville appearances that had resulted in nothing concrete in Congress? He was now nearing 50. Perhaps it was time to move on to something else.

That something else was embodied in the incorporation of the Orient Film Company, which was capitalized at $210,000 in the state of Maine. Originally, Cook planned the venture with Harold M. Weir, who would be the photographer and vice president of the company. Stock was issued to raise money for the enterprise and circulars were sent outlining the company's prospects to potential shareholders:

> The Cook-Weir expedition will leave San Francisco during the month of May 1915 and proceed to Calcutta, India via Honolulu, Yokohama, Hong Kong and Singapore. From Calcutta the party will then proceed to Katmandu the capitol of Nepal, where headquarters will be established. From Katmandu Dr. Cook will lead an expedition to ascend Mt. Everest (the highest mountain in the world) . . . which has never been attempted. . . .
>
> . . . The story of the ascent of Mt. Everest, the exploration of the Himalayas and the country traversed by this expedition will prove of greatest interest and value to the world, and the arrangements will be made to place this material before the public in such a manner that the value of the motion pictures secured by the expedition will be greatly enhanced.
>
> All motion picture companies who have produced such types of feature films have made and are making profits upon their initial investment which probably have not bee[n] surpassed by any other legitimate staple business.
>
> The Orient Film Company offers to the purchasers of its preferred stock an opportunity to participate in the earnings of a company which will unquestionably yield substantial profits.[16]

Dr. Cook had gone back to studying all the details he could find about his objective, just as he had in the old days. A little of the fire he had formerly felt when facing a formidable challenge seemed to have been rekindled:

> Of the great and interesting tasks, the battles wherein man goes to war with nature at its worst, Mt. Everest is the last challenge to the explorer. For four hundred years men with veins bursting for

physical action who did not care to sacrifice themselves on the alter
of war, turned to the farthest north or the farthest south. But now
the slogan must be- highest up- nearest Heaven.[17]

Just at that moment, countless men, whether they cared to or not, were
being sacrificed "on the alter of war" and finding the depths of the European
trenches the shortest route to the reality of the doctor's lofty metaphoric goal.
The war that had been expected to end in a matter of weeks in August 1914
had bogged down in a stalemate on two fronts and had become a true world
war through entangling alliances and dreams of conquest or opportunity by
many not compelled to take sides. Even so, the little party from the isolation-
ist United States that boarded a train in Chicago on June 8, 1915, had little
idea of the depths of the war hysteria that now gripped the rest of the world.

The Orient Film Company had been able to raise only $9,600 from stock
sales, Weir had backed out and the trip was in severe doubt until Dr. Thompson threw in most of his cash on hand to get the expedition ready to go.[18]

Frank Thompson, a small, wiry man with an open expression and very
prominent ears, was an eye doctor. He had no mountain-climbing experience,
but he had unbounded confidence in Dr. Cook. It was not shared by his insurance company, however, which canceled his life insurance policy upon
hearing of his rarefied ambitions. But actually, for Thompson, the expedition
to Everest was not the main attraction.

He had first met Cook shortly after the doctor's return from his 1903 expedition to Mount McKinley. Thompson had written to inquire about a big-
game hunt in Alaska, asking Cook to stop by when he was in Chicago. The
chief lure for Thompson now was the chance to hunt tigers, rhinoceros and
elephants in India.

After briefly looking over the Panama-Pacific Exposition in San Francisco, the three adventurers embarked on the *Mongolia* of the Pacific Mail
Steamship Company on June 12, with through tickets to Hong Kong.
Though every first-class passenger had duly received Fess's speech, it seemed
to have made no impression. In fact, Dr. Cook's willingness to give entertaining talks about his experiences added to the passengers' enjoyment and gained
him many friends before they reached Hawaii on the seventh day out. The
Mongolia spent a day and a night at Honolulu, before sailing for Japan.

Cook found the port of Yokohama 11 days, and a world apart, from the
soft breezes of Hawaii. The piers were crowded with tradesmen selling every
conceivable ware, and hundreds of rickshaws lined up to take the passengers
wherever they wanted to go for 30 sen. There were free accommodations at
the Grand Hotel, and the free rail passes the passengers received allowed Cook
to see some of the country. He and Thompson visited Kōbe and Kyoto, and
he took Brooke to Nagasaki to film the huge industrial complexes there.

The prosperity of the Japanese impressed Cook. There was much talk of a
"Japanese menace" in Hawaii, and the industry so obviously displayed by

everything he now saw set the doctor to thinking about Japan's future. "Pretending . . . a superior civilization, Japan will seek to conquer and build an empire over the ruins of subjective peoples," Cook predicted.

"To do this, however, she must quickly enlarge. . . . Just how Japan can [do] this and save herself from international reproach, is the big question now at hand for solution. . . .

". . . The common American assertion that the Jap fleet is aimed for the American shores, is to my mind entirely without foundation. Only a strong alliance with some strong European power, would make such a daring project thinkable. . . . No, to Americans there is no Japanese menace. The Jap is too wise a soldier to assume such a risk."[19]

On July 6 the *Mongolia* departed Yokohama bound for Manila, four days away. There Cook, Thompson and Brooke transferred to the Spanish freighter *Alicante* hoping to save several weeks of travel time to Calcutta—time they would need for their attempt on Everest. She was not the *Mongolia* however; her accommodations were spartan, and she was slow. They spent a miserable, sweltering six days on her, relieved only by the ample supply of good Spanish wine she carried, before they arrived at the Straits Settlements on the Malay Peninsula.

At Singapore the British officials were cordial but nervous. They had just put down a mutiny among the Bengali troops during which it was rumored many had been killed, and they feared more trouble. Here the Cook party gladly left the *Alicante* and took passage on a Japanese freighter, the *Hakata Maru,* which was crowded to overflowing with Indians leaving Singapore in the wake of the disturbance.

When she reached Penang two days later, they were detained aboard ship, searched and their cameras seized before they were allowed to land. Cook had the notion that his party was suspected by the British of espionage.

When Dr. Thompson went to the chief of police to find out what was going on, the policeman voiced the opinion that Thompson had a German accent. This offended the doctor, who was of Danish descent; he went to the American consul to complain. The consul explained to Thompson the cause of the nervousness on the officials' part. Several days before, the German raider *Emden* had fired on the port; the consul told Thompson that he should report any further incidents to him.

Cook's party took a room at Raffles Hotel, but everywhere they went, Cook, Thompson and Brooke were shadowed. They didn't think much of Malaya—the people seemed languid and aimless, suffering from a sort of war malaise—and considering the reception they had received, they were only too glad to be off again.

On July 22 they caught sight of the mountains of lower Siam and Burma. But their greeting in Rangoon was, if possible, even less cordial than it had been in Penang. Their passports were declared improperly stamped, they were arrested, taken to police headquarters and questioned for several hours. Then they were told they could not proceed to Calcutta, or even leave Burma, and were returned to the ship, where they were put under guard by six soldiers.

After two days, word of their plight reached the American consul, whose protests at their treatment cleared the way. Entering the Bay of Bengal, some relief was found in the monsoon winds, which moderated the heat and dissipated the smell of rotting fruit, putrid fish and their thousand unwashed fellow passengers. When Cook's party arrived at Calcutta, Thompson resolved to forestall any more trouble by going directly to the American consul general, James A. Smith. Thompson pleaded with Smith to try to get approval as quickly as possible for them to enter Nepal, setting a deadline of five weeks as the latest they could hope to begin the long journey toward Everest. Cook and his fellow travelers then settled into the Great Eastern Hotel to wait.

Dr. Thompson wrote to his wife, Olivia, about their tribulations to this point but tried to reassure her that everything was fine anyway. She was apparently something of a worrier, and he wanted her to know that local officials had told him that tigers were far less fierce than their reputations and that of the 69 kinds of poisonous snakes in the district, few were ever seen. He even took the trouble of going to the zoological gardens and measuring their fangs, which he maintained were not long enough to penetrate ordinary shoe leather. He reassured his wife that their victims invariably were the barefooted natives.

But most of all he wanted her to know there was nothing at all to worry about in regard to their attempt on the greatest mountain in the world:

> Since I have become intimately acquainted with Dr. Cook I realize
> he knows much more than I ever supposed & he absolutely knows
> all about mountain work. If you could only see how nice & easy he
> goes about getting things ready for the higher altitudes where
> weight has to be reduced to a minimum and hear him talk about
> how to avoid avalanches & where to climb to make the most dis-
> tance with the best expenditure of energy & in fact all the details of
> making the climb you would have the same regard for him &
> his abilities that I have; from what I hear from others about the
> Himalayas he is the only man in the world I would care to make
> the attempt with. We have talked over the plans for climbing the
> mountain everyday since leaving the U.S. & the more I talk to him
> about it the more I am convinced there is absolutely no danger.[20]

As the five weeks passed without word from the consul general, they despaired of ever getting out of Calcutta, much less into Tibet, so Thompson applied for permission to go to the Sunderbans, in the eastern part of the Ganges delta, to hunt tigers. But then word arrived summoning Cook to the consulate, where Smith explained everything that he had been able to discover:

> We were told unofficially of the secret charges on file at the police
> department against us. British spies, it seemed, had followed us

from Chicago, but their work was incomplete. They reported that we had left San Francisco with a group of seditionists, en route for India, to start a revolution,—that we had a great sum of money to finance such a project,—that I had been seen with the German Consul, Roderick [whom Cook had met in Europe and visited out of courtesy], at Honolulu,—that we had booked passage to Hong Kong,—and then, to avoid meeting examination there, we had trans-shipped at Manila,—and that 40,000 Mauser rifles had been secretly delivered into the mouth of the Ganges, by someone [on the day Thompson had picked out for his tiger hunt there]. A letter had been intercepted wherein Mr. Brooke mentioned our eagerness to make a dash for the frontier. . . . We were restrained, under official orders. At the end of about thirty days it was definitely learned that the . . . suspicions had no real foundations. However . . . we would not be allowed to go to the Himalayas.[21]

Hoping to salvage something out of his long journey, Cook petitioned that they be allowed to go to Sikkim to climb Kanchenjunga, which some suspected might be higher than Everest, and Thompson tried again to gain permission for a tiger hunt, but both were to no avail.

The long detention in Calcutta had severely depleted their funds. Less than $3,000 remained, and they had no original footage to show for it. So they determined to go to Borneo, the only neutral territory where they felt they could get some unique motion pictures.

They took a boat to Colombo, Ceylon, where they arrived September 9, then boarded another Spanish freighter back to Singapore, expecting to catch a Dutch ship bound for Borneo, 350 miles away. But once they reached Singapore, the British authorities would not allow them to leave their ship, so they were compelled to sail for Manila, a detour of more than 2,500 miles.

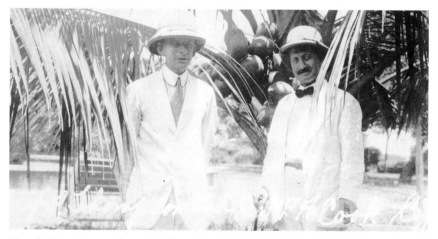

Frank Thompson and Frederick Cook in Ceylon, 1915.

In Manila they met Tom Hardigan, owner of the Manila Hotel and a Chicago native, who knew Dr. Thompson. He arranged passage to Zamboanga on the island of Mindanao, whose subgovernor was another acquaintance of Thompson's from Oak Park. He wrote a letter of introduction for them to Governor Rohrer in Jolo, who, after reading it, invited Dr. Cook and his party to stay at his home.

The governor lent them the government launch, a 28-foot motorboat, which Cook thought capable of reaching Borneo from the east. Their object was to film the Dyaks—its famous "wild men"—reputed to be headhunters and savages of the first order; it would be a chance for Dr. Cook to have at the equator a taste of the primitive life he had already experienced at both ends of the earth. Before leaving Jolo, they secured the services of an interpreter named Bill Schuch and two Moro guides. Schuch claimed he knew a few things about Borneo, besides the lingo, and also how to keep hold of his head—literally. The Dutch were supposed to have banished the practice of head-hunting in their domains, but who knew what went on far up the rivers where the "wild men" lived?

Their first stop was Siasi, where Brooke captured on film the sponge and pearl fishers who dove beneath its harbor's crystalline waters. There they laid in a supply of fish and rice and started off through the chain of islands to the southwest on October 10, bound for Tawi Tawi.

Near the port of Bongao, at the island's tip, they ran aground in high seas. After getting free, they went on despite waves that rose so high they washed into the tiny craft. But there was no danger since the launch had been provided with a number of air tanks and was practically unsinkable.

A few days later, the adventurers landed at Sandakan, notorious for its gambling and opium dens. Here they took on a Moro pilot to guide them to Sipitang. He said he was very qualified, since he knew the waters well from his days as a pirate. That evening, as a beautiful half-moon rose over a mirrorlike sea, they left the coast of British North Borneo, embarked on a southeasterly course.

They finally sighted the mountains of Dutch Borneo rising in the west on October 19. Soon they entered the Sebuku River, which they ascended about 15 miles. On the Sebuku they saw one Dyak house, but its residents were far too civilized for an entertaining film, so they started back for the coast.

The coastal inhabitants were even less photogenic, being a half-breed mix of Chinese, Malays and Indians living in houses built on stilts in the shallows. Dr. Thompson joked he had seen better-looking "wild men" on the streets of Chicago. The true aborigines, however, had not been met as yet. They lived only on the interior rivers, and the coastal villagers indicated that the best way to reach some of them was up the Belayan River far to the south. Three of the locals were then added to the little boat as interpreter, pilot and cook.

The journey was long and tiring. The thermometer stood at more than 100 degrees, and the impossible half-breed dialect was too much for even Bill

Schuch to understand. The cooks made weird dishes of fish and monkey meat, which to the white men's tastes were not much of a relief from their staple diet of rice and wormy pancakes.

At noon on October 23, after ascending the river 30 miles, they reached Belayan with its Dutch trading posts, neat buildings and long, wide, straight streets. Set apart among huge coconut palms was a cluster of huts surrounding the palace of the sultan of Belayan.

On the dock to greet them was the controleur, Mr. L. Ludolph. The official was very helpful with information about the best way to reach the interior. He said they could take their motorboat only one day farther upriver. From there they would need to travel as the natives did, in dugouts, to reach the aboriginal settlements. Even then, Ludolph said, travel in the evenings would be difficult because the rivers fell a great deal during the day, only to be refilled by nightly rainstorms. He secured for them a 50-foot dugout canoe and crew of nine at a wage of one rupee each.

The next morning Cook and his party cast off in the rain with the dugout in tow. The doctor was excited to think that he would soon meet men who lived much as their ancestors had 1,000 years before, and this time, unlike the Onas or the Eskimos, there would be great numbers of them. Some estimated a population in excess of 2,000,000 lived on the island five times the size of New York State.

Soon all vestiges of civilization vanished, and the dense tropical jungle crowded down to the riverbank. The low, swampy region through which they first passed was infested with crocodiles and biting insects, but as the boat climbed higher, this gave way to a more pleasant landscape. Beautiful mountains rose before them, and the banks of the river were carpeted with a profusion of plants.

The journey went just about as Mr. Ludolph had said, and on the third day out they began to see little plots of rice and bananas tended by aboriginal women, who seemed shy but not unfriendly. By evening they saw, far in the distance, a huge house perched above the riverbank on stilts. It was the outskirts of the village of Punyan. Since it was growing dark, they determined to camp on an island just offshore and go into the big Dyak town in the morning. Before they could set up camp, however, the evening storm broke over them, wetting all of their belongings. The river became a raging torrent that seemed to bury the lowlands.

The water had hardly subsided when a group of Dyaks suddenly appeared from the jungle and greeted the strangers with smiles. Dr. Cook was impressed with how tame the "wild men" looked. "The 'Wild Man of Borneo' is one of the best specimens of the human family that I have ever seen," he noted, "—physically, mentally and ethically far above the aborigines of most other parts of the world. . . .

"He is well developed, has a soft, light skin, with a golden hue, often nearly white, with black hair, brown eyes, and a very intelligent physiognomy.

He presents a picture of refinement, rather than that of a savage. The men are about five feet three inches high, and the women a little less than five feet. The women, though adorned with little clothing weigh their ear lobes down with heavy jewels, and by way of decoration, the entire leg is tattooed from the ankle up. The designs have considerable artistic merit."[22]

The Dyaks helped the strangers collect their belongings and carried them across the river toward the long house that seemed to simply materialize out of the inky blackness of the jungle night. Climbing up slippery ladders, they reached the floor of the house, 14 feet above the ground. The house of split wood and reeds was about 300 feet long and 50 wide, half of which was a great room partitioned into apartments, one for each family. The rest of the house was open and reminded Cook of nothing less than an enclosed street. There 200 Dyaks, talking in low tones, gathered to meet the strangers.[23]

The native men motioned that they should come near the fire, where they took off their wet clothes and hung them up to dry. The Dyaks, men, women and children, watched this procedure carefully as they chewed betel nuts. Then the white men indulged their own curious habits by smoking a number of Philippine cigarettes, while, through Bill Schuch, they carried on a halting conversation with their hosts.

The "chief" was, surprisingly, interested in the course of the war, but they could give him little recent information. Some of the women wanted to know whether white skin was not a sign of sickness and what was considered beautiful in the strangers' own country. In exchange, Dr. Cook repeatedly tried to draw them out about the ancient custom of head-hunting, but they seemed reluctant to talk about it. The day had been tiring, and it was not long before all were asleep.

Early in the morning, just before dawn, the cocks began to crow and the dogs and pigs came to life under the big house. The women arose, put down the ladders and, carrying baskets of bamboo tubes in which they transported water, went to the river. There, some bathed in a fenced pool constructed to ward off crocodiles. When they returned, they blew up the embers from the night before and put on a large pot of rice for breakfast. Some of the rice they wrapped in leaves for lunch. When it was ready, the men got up and ate, and after they had gone out to hunt or to fashion tools, boats or paddles, the women and children had breakfast. The women spent the day in gossip while they pounded rice and prepared fruits and nuts for supper. As evening fell, the usual violent storm blew in, and it seemed to Dr. Cook to be very civilized, considering the experience of the previous night, to be under the roof of the wild men.

After the ladders had been pulled up, the men recounted myths and animal tales by the light of resin torches, while the sound of a nose flute hovered over the flickering shadows thrown upon the reed walls. This soon died away, but the noise of the pigs and dogs fighting for their sleeping places under the house kept Cook awake. When they finally settled down, their voices were replaced by the shrieks of countless insects, tree frogs and, occasionally, something bigger. With no physical fatigue, he found it difficult to sleep in such strange surroundings. In the dim light of the torches he could see the hollow eyes of a row of human skulls staring back at him from a high shelf and thought, "It takes a long time to school the nerves to this kind of novelty."[24]

After two days with the Dyaks, having captured on film some of their life and ritual, the white men started back downriver to Belayan and from there to the sea and up the coast. They visited Koenpeng on November 1, but an attempt to land in Lahad Datu in British North Borneo was refused, so they set out again for Jolo, arriving there without incident on November 6.

At Jolo they found that not all the headhunters were confined to Borneo. While in Governor Rohrer's office, they witnessed the delivery of a sack by two Moros. It contained a head that had recently belonged to a notorious local brigand, who they hoped was not their former pilot. While at Jolo they were introduced to the sultan of Sulu's executioner, who, since his job had been legislated out of existence, had little to do but look grim. The sultan himself was nothing more than a figurehead, but he retained the trappings of power, a palace and a mosque. Nothing could induce the sultan to grant their wish to film his harem, which he maintained despite a legal proscription against polygamy.

Money and film almost exhausted, Dr. Cook and his party determined to head for home. Because of the growing menace of German U-boats, they were advised not to go back by way of the Suez Canal as they had originally planned. Instead, they decided to retrace their steps and go home by way of San Francisco. So, for the third time they set out for Manila. There they boarded the *Persia Maru* for Japan.

From Nagasaki, they went by rail to Yokohama. Since Everest had been denied them, Dr. Cook had suggested climbing Fujiyama, 62 miles southwest of the city.

Few attempted to climb the sacred mountain in fall or winter. Nevertheless, on November 24 Cook procured Japanese guides and they started up the perfect volcanic cone on horseback. When the footing became too insecure for the animals, the climbers shouldered their packs and continued on foot, spending the night in a shack at 9,000 feet. The weather seemed very much to Dr. Cook like the Arctic all over again after so many months in the tropics, but a pleasant fire soon warmed the men and the rice they cooked over it. The view in the morning was enchanting:

> Under our feet was a sea of clouds; beyond, an endless expanse of floating mist churned up into huge wavy lines, like that of a typhooned sea. Here and there a low peak piercing the clouds, made an isle; in other places, a break permitted the eye to descend to the far-off lowlands. The scene changed every second, and the glow of the rising sun poured a liquid color that offered a glory never seen on low lands. . . .
>
> We started for the top. Under the crest however, we were

stopped by soft, avalanching snow. The Japs would not go farther. Our position, however, was such that we could get a view of the top, and also of the great mountainous expanse below, which was all that we were after.

The descent was quickly made. Before midnight of the second day we were back to our little hotel at Gotemba.[25]

When the men reached Yokohama on November 30 expecting to rejoin their ship, they learned that the *Persia Maru* had run into a concrete pier while coming into the harbor and was so heavily damaged she could not proceed. They were told it might be weeks before the ship could leave Japan, so they checked into the Grand Hotel to reassess their situation.

While there, Cook gave an interview to a reporter from an English-language Tokyo newspaper. He attributed his expedition's failure to "spyitis." "I can't understand what the trouble was," the doctor told him. "It was perfectly evident that we three, ignorant even of the language of the people we were going among, were not able to start a revolution. All they had to do was to search our trunks to make sure that we weren't carrying anything that would be handy in raising an insurrection."[26]

Cook thought they might go overland on the Trans-Siberian Railway to Europe and there take passage to the United States. After inquiring at the Russian consulate as to the feasibility of their plan, they had their passports amended for Russia and sought advice about traveling through the war zone. The Russians suggested sending their baggage by ship, as its safety could not be guaranteed. Brooke agreed to stay with the precious film and return on the ship once she had been made seaworthy again. Bidding him good-bye, Cook and Thompson caught a train for the west coast and from there embarked for Fusan by steamer.

From the window of the train they boarded there, Corea, under the yoke of Japan, seemed a modern, prosperous-looking place indeed. But once they crossed the Yalu River at Antung and entered Manchuria, time seemed to have slipped back several centuries. Snow had begun to fall by the time they reached Ch'ang ch'un, where they met a train bound for the main line of the Chinese Eastern Railroad. Having had no intention of going to Siberia, in changing trains they discovered Manchuria was quite cold enough for them. The two doctors were chilled to the bone in their light summer suits and envied the natives hustling about in their fur coats and hats.

By the time they reached Harbin, the temperature had fallen to −10°, and the most common vehicles on the streets were heavy sledges pulled by bow-collared horses. At Harbin they began to observe the first hints of the war raging far to the west. The city's huge saloon, built in the heyday of Russian influence in Manchuria, was totally out of vodka, and its large station was thronged with people dressed in furs and quilted rags; every fifth man seemed to be a soldier. Here they boarded the train for Khailar on the Russian frontier.

Khailar was just seven days away from Petrograd, but even so, real signs of the war were surprisingly few. As Cook watched Siberia's vastness roll by outside his coach window, he thought its sterility much exaggerated. Indeed, he thought one day it might become one of the greatest producing countries in the world.

Near Lake Baykal the train was sidetracked next to a line of heated boxcars that contained German prisoners of war. The doctor held a brief conversation with them in German from the window. They had no overcoats and said they got only one meal a day, but more than food or clothing, they wanted one thing: *"Wann wird der Krieg zu Ende?"* they asked again and again—"When will the war be over?"

As Cook and Thompson got off the train in Petrograd, only eight hours overdue, they came face-to-face with the war's reality. The front was now less than 200 miles off. The hospitals were full of wounded, and refugees from Riga clogged the streets. Soldiers and military equipment were everywhere.

It took two days to make arrangements to get out of the country via Finland, and once their train crossed the border into Sweden, the passengers seemed to breathe a collective sigh of relief; they had arrived in neutral territory. But the doctor realized more and more that there really were no neutrals in this war that was threatening to swallow up civilization itself. "All of the world's resources," he thought, "were mobilized, not for any common good, as each of the belligerents would have you believe, but to risk by a gamble with death-dealing weapons the fate of future empires - empires to be built in the future, as in the past, at the expense of weaker nations - and this, in the day of our Lord, 1916, we call 'christianity' and 'higher civilization.' There is more justice in the wilds of Borneo!"[27]

While in Sweden, Dr. Thompson received word that his wife and son were in Copenhagen. They had come over on Henry Ford's "Peace Ship," an ocean liner he had hired at the suggestion of a group of pacifists who would go to Europe in an effort to persuade delegates from the neutral nations to call a conference that would negotiate an end to the war. Ford had agreed to do so without much thought as to any expected results beyond the publicity it might gain for himself. When called upon to defend it, however, he soon convinced himself that he had embarked on a great cause.

But what seemed like a noble goal to the American industrialist was held up for ridicule in both America and Europe. As the "Peace Ship" sailed across the Atlantic, the violent internal wranglings that arose among the individual peace activists became the butt of so many jokes that by the time of its arrival, the mission had been practically laughed to scorn in the American press.

When Cook and Thompson arrived in Copenhagen just after Christmas, they visited Henry Ford's ship. It must have been with some emotion that Dr. Cook stepped upon her deck, because she was none other than the *Oscar II,* the ship that had borne him triumphantly to America a little more than six years before.

Cook's visit to the "Peace Ship" only added to the laughs being had at the pacifists' expense. Sixty reporters asked Dr. Cook questions, many of which Dr. Thompson thought most insolent, for nearly two hours. The contempt in which the "gumdrop explorer" and "greatest faker of the age" was held by the New York papers was used to heap more abuse upon Ford's enterprise.

When a rumor circulated that Cook was seeking a passport to enter Germany, the *New York Times* scoffed: "Just as he found the pole where no pole was, so he could doubtless find victory for the Germans, backed up with affidavits and gumdrops."[28] "Probably enough," the *Times* added, "he intends to look for peace and to write a book about finding it."[29]

Like the rest of Europe, Denmark was absorbed in the war news, so Cook's third appearance in the Danish capital did not cause a widespread stir. The doctor paid a call on Minister Egan, but Egan was too preoccupied with diplomatically handling the Ford pacifists to give any attention to Cook. Some, however, including Count Holstein, welcomed him and affirmed their belief in him.

Cook found it even more difficult to get out of Europe than it had been to get in. Fear of German submarines had diminished the number of passenger liners crossing the Atlantic and caused those that still did to go as far north as possible. Dr. Thompson had just about resigned himself to booking the only immediate passage for the party—the bridal suite on a new Norwegian liner at $2,000—when Dr. Cook was offered the position of ship's doctor on the *Kristianiafjord.* Cook volunteered Thompson's services as well, and together they sailed for America on January 12, 1916. Cook, Thompson and his family got the bridal suite for free.

On the high seas, in between caring for the illnesses among the passengers, Dr. Cook was absorbed in thoughts about the war that had turned the carefree Europe he had known in his exile into a no-man's land:

> Since, I have wondered who is responsible for the World War that has stabbed the heart of all mankind!
>
> I am inclined to place the blame upon. . . . he who has served for us the national histories of all ages. He has dramatized crimes . . . deaf to the cry of countless millions of souls sacrificed on the altar of injustice —blind to the river of human blood that has poured down through the valley of ages, – he has made plausible fiction of the leprous disease of conquest.[30]

As Dr. Cook approached home shores, his own war for congressional recognition of his polar claim was continuing as well. Ernest Rost had not been idle in the doctor's absence. A new spokesman had been found in the person of a representative from North Dakota, Henry Helgesen. Rost had installed himself in Helgesen's congressional office and was hard at work supplying him with ammunition for a new assault.

On January 13, 1916, Helgesen had made a speech on the House floor entitled "Government Maps of the Arctic Regions Corrected," in which he reiterated his original attack, made a year previously, on the accuracy of Peary's discoveries in the Far North. In that speech he had shown that such features as "Peary Channel," "Independence Bay" and the "East Greenland Sea," as well as "Crocker Land," did not exist and asked the Hydrographic Department to strike them from the official government charts. This had now been done, he said, proving the inaccuracies of Peary's so-called discoveries.

The speech was followed by an extensive "extension of remarks" printed in the *Congressional Record* on February 12, which contained a verbatim copy of the testimony given before the Naval Affairs subcommittee by Gannett, Tittman and Peary himself in 1910 and 1911. This testimony had received little attention in the press at the time; only the favorable report of the full committee had been widely quoted. Along with the full text of the hearings, Helgesen published an astute analysis pointing out the many contradictions, prevarications and suspicious features it contained. Now that they were readily available in full, Peary's answers could be used by anyone wishing to foster doubts about his claim to the Pole.

Helgesen's speeches marked the beginning of a new stage in Cook's battle with the Peary forces. Up until now, Cook's agents had been content to leave Peary's claims alone, but since the Fess speech, which had done much to destroy confidence in Cook's credibility, the plan had shifted to one that would put Peary in the same position of distrust. If Peary's reputation for veracity could be torn down, they figured, then his claim to the North Pole might fall, too, leaving a void to be filled by a congressional examination of the doctor's prior claim.

Though they came from a new quarter, Lucien Alexander recognized the true source of Helgesen's remarks:

> There is no question but that Mr. Helgesen's deliverance is but a continuation of the Cook plot to build up a mass of material having a semblance of being official, and which is to be used in Cook's efforts to discredit Peary and aid himself in establishing his own claim. . . .
>
> There is no doubt in my mind that he will succeed sooner or later, and perhaps much sooner than we anticipate. . . .
>
> . . . There can be no doubt but that the Associated Press ban on Cook news would fall if an extensive Congressional hearing got under way. . . .
>
> Had the advice I gave last fall been followed I do not think that [the] Helgesen attack . . . would ever have been delivered. . . . It now stands on the face of it as a rather serious indictment of Peary's credibility,—and to those of us who know him, it is absurd that such a thing should happen.[31]

Alexander's original plan had been cut short by the sudden death of General Hubbard. The general's executors had pledged to honor the items he had agreed to, but beyond that, nothing had been done. Herbert Bridgman was reluctant to spend the balance of funds in the Peary Arctic Club's treasury unless an emergency arose in Congress. And since it seemed to Bridgman that the wide distribution of the Fess speech had effectively put an end to Cook's chances for an official hearing, he had asked Alexander to cease operations as of November 9, 1915.

But Alexander had continued corresponding with Admiral Peary and now angled to be reemployed to counter Helgesen's latest attacks. "Cook is the man who ought to be kept on the defensive—yet that is the position into which they are very shrewdly getting Peary," he warned Bridgman.[32]

The two Helgesen speeches, though not flawless, were excellently researched. They relied on original documents, displayed official replies to letters of inquiry and, for the most part, drew logical if not always supportable conclusions. But their main conclusion—that Robert E. Peary could not possibly have reached the North Pole—seemed unavoidable. The speeches were widely distributed under Helgesen's franking privilege, and they had a decisive effect on interested parties who read them.

Letters commenting on the speeches poured into the congressman's office from polar explorers, engineers, college professors and other persons of some standing. "I have read your analysis of civil engineer Peary's North Polar narrative," wrote General Greely. "It will be difficult for anyone reading your analysis, based on official documents, to come to any other conclusion than that drawn by you."[33]

"You have so thoroughly established your points," one correspondent assured him, "that only the knowledge that your exposition can not be shaken prevents, or will prevent, Peary from attempting an answer. What you have done in the polar inquiry seems to me a classic piece of work."[34]

"Kindly permit the expression of my admiration of your courage and thoroughness in the reduction of Mr. Peary to oblivion," wrote another.[35]

Although it was the congressman who received the compliments, in truth Henry Helgesen had not written a word of the material that was the stimulus for the letters of praise. Like Fess, Helgesen had simply signed his name. The speeches had been prepared by Ernest C. Rost and his wife, Etta, in their Washington flat, and the Rosts had done their work well and tirelessly.

Because Ernest Rost believed that carbon copies would not get any attention, Etta was endlessly at the typewriter making "originals" of pro-Cook material to send to as many as 96 congressmen and senators for each mailing. Rost worked diligently, digging for discrepancies in Peary's story, comparing his narratives for contradictions and writing letters of inquiry for Helgesen to sign to obtain evidence. He also found time to have a booklet published declaring Belmore Browne's picture of Fake Peak itself a fake, retouched to make the details of the skyline conform to the contours shown in Cook's summit photograph.

To obtain interviews, Rost represented himself as Helgesen's private secretary and even invaded the enemy's camp, obtaining negative evidence from Dr. Goodsell, who had fallen out with Peary over his failure to grant his former surgeon permission to publish his own book about the 1909 expedition.[36] Rost's work was so intense that he sometimes was incapacitated by severe headaches brought on by long hours of concentration.

Etta Rost, justly proud of the work they had done, wrote to a friend:

> Yes, I did all of the typing of this "last Helgesen stunt" and of the other Helgesen (?) stunt; . . . and if anyone thinks that is all I had to do with those two speeches, they are greatly mistaken. Of course, the fact is not for general publication, but since Mr. Helgesen frankly told Doctor I suppose there is no harm in my telling you, that every word of this last analysis (Cong. Record, Feb. 12,) was written by the Rosts. . . . Ernest and I together read the proof for the speech of January 13th, but when we were about half through with the one of February 12th, Ernest had one of his bad headaches, and Miles [Poindexter] came to the rescue, and helped finish it. Any apparent mistakes in the "Hearing" are ones that occur in the original which we didn't dare correct, for fear some one would jump on us for not printing it exactly "as is."

While Etta was satisfied with their work, she didn't know how much longer she and Ernest would be employed at it. Dr. Cook was in arrears in paying them, though he was as agreeable as ever to let them continue their efforts:

> Yes, Doctor has gone to Chicago, (and other places) and will not return to Washington until February 28th. He seems to expect great results from the Chicago business affair, and I certainly hope he will not be disappointed, for MUCH depends on his actions in the near future. I enclose herewith a copy of a Resolution which Ernest succeeded (after much diplomatic coaxing) to get introduced. Now, if Doctor wants a Hearing and investigation it is UP TO HIM! He was told rather plainly when he was here just what must be done to bring that about, and—as usual—agreed to do it.
>
> No, I am not worrying about the financial end of things—but I am still waiting to be shown! But one thing is certain—we can't wait forever! Of course, it is too bad if he is really "broke.". . . It certainly was something more than "hopes" that he lived on while he was away. Yes, I know I am an ugly, uncharitable beast, who just won't understand; but never mind, I too, am still HOPING!!!![37]

The resolution Rost had written was introduced by Charles B. Smith on February 16. It called for an investigation to see whether any American had reached the North Pole and was referred to the Education Committee, but on March 23 the committee voted unanimously not to call Dr. Cook.

Despite their strained relations with "Doctor," the Rosts were not finished with Peary yet. They had done a vast amount of research, and they were not about to let it go to waste.

On August 3 Helgesen introduced a bill to repeal Peary's retirement and pension. In the accompanying speech, he presented the Rosts' detailed comparative analysis of Peary's *Hampton's* articles with his book *The North Pole* and made further comparisons with Henson's *A Negro Explorer at the North Pole* and Borup's *A Tenderfoot with Peary.* Peary's *Nearest the Pole,* his congressional testimony and the books published by other polar explorers, including Sverdrup, Nansen and the Duke of Abruzzi, were also combed for compromising evidence. This analysis disclosed numerous discrepancies, contradictions, mistakes, improbabilities and absurdities, all of which had the cumulative effect of undermining the veracity of Peary's account of his polar journey of 1909.

But the most devastating attack was saved for last. It took the form of an analysis of Peary's entire career, taking as its motto: "Wherever Mr. Peary went, some one was there before." It cited allegedly false or exaggerated claims on his so-called reconnaissance of Greenland in 1886. It pointed out that Peary's observations in 1892 and 1895 from Navy Cliff were erroneous—and that he had not, in reality, crossed Greenland at all, but only reached the head of a deep fjord, and that since the salient features he described hadn't any existence, his claims of having proven the insularity of Greenland at that time were false. The speech then turned to the Cape York meteorites, saying they had been described in Sir John Ross's book about his expedition of 1818, and though Peary had removed them, they were not his discovery. It also showed that Peary had tried, in 1907, to claim the discovery of "Jesup Land," when it was actually the same island Sverdrup had named Axel Heiberg Land in 1900. Though Peary made no contemporaneous mention of this discovery at the time, in *Nearest the Pole* he claimed to have seen "Jesup Land" in 1898.

The printed remarks attempted to show that Peary was a highly inaccurate cartographer, who filled his maps with fantasies while at the same time eliminated features that did, in fact, exist. Readers were also reminded again that Crocker Land did not exist and once more were given the body of evidence that cast severe doubt upon Peary's North Pole discovery. The only claims Helgesen left standing were the "Farthest North" of 1906 and the discovery of the most northerly cape of Greenland, which, the speech said, in light of Peary's demonstrated inaccuracies, needed to be verified.

In conclusion, the congressman summed up his thesis:

> Peary's claims to exploration and discovery have been given to the world through the mediums of his magazine articles, his books, and (in the case of the North Pole) through his testimony before the Naval Committee of the House. His magazine articles contradict his books, his books contradict each other, and his testimony before the House Committee on Naval Affairs is at variance with both books and magazines. In view of the facts which I have presented, and since Robert E. Peary's claims to discoveries in the Arctic regions have been proven to rest on fiction and not on geo-

graphical facts, . . . our taxpayers need no longer be compelled to raise $6,000 annually of retired pay to reward Civil Engineer Peary for services which he never performed.[38]

Even before this lengthy speech, Cook's supporters had managed to insert in the *Congressional Record* more than 100 pages of pro-Cook material, and the seriousness of Helgesen's latest attack was not lost on Lucien Alexander; he cautioned Peary against inaction:

> [Cook] has dumped too much impressive looking material into the Congressional Record to make it safe not to be prepared. . . . He has made a great deal of headway the last year—he and his force are everlastingly "at it." . . . It will not do for us longer to close our eyes to the situation. The matter for your own sake should now be your first consideration over everything else upon which you are spending or may spend energy. The matter is too vital a one for you longer to neglect.
>
> Cook has created a very dangerous situation—one that will be several fold harder to combat than if my advice had been followed to finish him after we had him "on the run" and he went to Asia.[39]

Besides the Helgesen mess, Alexander had other grave worries. Mene Wallace had returned to America and he had an announcement to make. "I've got a big story about Peary and Cook," the Eskimo told the press. "After I get a lawyer for a manager, you know, the same way as you would open up any show, I'll tell you the price."

When asked if he had solved the Polar Controversy, he replied, "No, I don't know who discovered the North Pole, I don't know that it was ever discovered by anybody. What I know is what the Eskimos who accompanied Cook and Peary tell me. They may not be scientists but they made their observations just the same. For instance, you remember that Peary had four Eskimos with him on the last 180-mile *[sic]* dash to the place where he said, 'Here we are—we go no further.' I've been living with Ootah, Eginguah, Seegloo and Ooqueah, who were with Peary. They know just how many days passed during the journey. Wouldn't it be interesting to compare their record with Admiral Peary's proofs of his discovery? I've also talked with Etukishuk and Ahwelah, the men who accompanied Dr. Cook on his expedition in 1908.

"All this information is locked up in here," Mene said, pointing at his head. "Tomorrow, after I see a lawyer, I will be ready to receive offers."[40]

To Lucien Alexander's mind, Mene's testimony might be the most dangerous of all:

> Of course I understand Mene is crooked but that makes him all the more dangerous for off hand the world will believe he speaks the truth, and even if we could prove him a liar we would at the same time be proving that at least one Eskimo will be like C-,

and if one will, why not others? The thing cuts both ways. Mene will be very difficult to refute. The Eskimo set of stories which I presume he will dole out to Cook's great joy, is precisely the sort of thing I have feared. . . .

I felt there was little doubt about there being such a contest after Helgesen's material . . . but this Mene Wallace warning makes it my duty to speak out plainly without a moment's delay. . . .

An answer of some sort should have been made to Helgesen's diatribes. . . . When you have such a bunch of rascals to deal with as this Cook outfit, with so much at stake, it does not do to assume the world will realize the true inwardness of their world-wide machinations, for the <u>world</u> <u>won't</u>. You ought either to go into this thing thoroly from the ground up—or drop it altogether and do nothing except appear as a witness if summoned. The latter course you cannot afford to take but I believe it a lot better than going into this matter of Cook's fight unless fully prepared on every point. . . .[41]

Alexander's letter must have struck a chord. Peary rehired him at his old salary of $500 a month plus expenses. But an unexpected sequence of events was about to dissipate all of the fears his lobbyist entertained.

The high hopes for the product of the Orient Film Company were not being realized. Cook's silent film was advertised as containing "Weird and Fascinating Scenes of Wild People. — In the Lands of Paganism, Superstition, Tropical Splendor. — Thru Unknown Jungles Among Nature's Giants and Smallest Creatures. — In Wonderful Motion Pictures Full of Remarkable Scenes and Human Interest. — Entertainingly described by Dr. John W. Ruskin, Naturalist and Traveler."[42]

But Cook himself had returned to the lecture and vaudeville circuit, and Ruskin had not been on the road long before he sensed financial failure:

The big punch is the entire last reel of Borneo. . . .

[But] I am absolutely sure the first four reels would not be acceptable . . . without you personally with them, and even then, I doubt whether they would satisfy. . . .

. . . [Though] I talked to several thousand people outside of the theatre, our gross was $365.00 on the six days, one half to the theatre. . . .

I made the fatal mistake of putting the pictures at 25 cents. The price should have been from 25 cents to $1.00. At a price of 25 cents in the legitimate theatres the movie fans will not come, and it is too cheap to attract the people who are used to paying more. . . .

So far as the South is concerned, . . . it would be necessary to do at least $1500.00 per week gross to make it go. This is unlikely.[43]

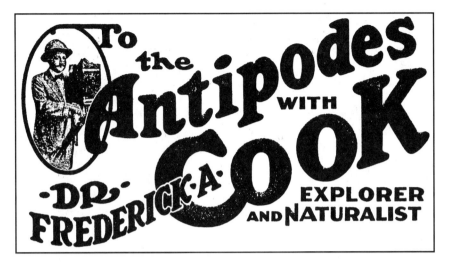

As hopes for the film faded rapidly, Dr. Cook found his own drawing power diminishing as well. His circulars now asked: "Is there any interest in the Polar question? It is a live issue, that is the answer."[44] But in truth, it was not.

The doctor's absence of nearly a year hadn't helped, but it was really the European war that had turned people's attention from the polar question. President Wilson was running for reelection on the slogan "He Kept Us out of War," but it seemed only a matter of time now before America would enter it on the Allies' side. Somehow, the seven-year-old question of who was the first to stand on a mythical point at the top of the world seemed of minor importance in the face of the pressing realities of the present.

Even though another joint resolution calling for an independent commission to hear Dr. Cook's claim had been introduced in June, and Helgesen had authored yet another bill to revoke Peary's retirement, Peary seemed to be less and less concerned. His interest now lay with the Aero Club of America, and his appointment as chairman of the National Aerial Coast Patrol Commission was absorbing most of his time; his new theme was "Preparedness through Air Power."

Apparently, Dr. Cook felt his chances were gone—that the attention of the people and the Congress could never be focused sufficiently again to bring about a hearing of his claims. The Orient Film Company was a bust, and further money spent to lobby Congress would only compound his shaky financial situation. As Etta Rost had said, "<u>MUCH</u>" depended on the doctor's actions, and his action now was to terminate the services of Ernest C. Rost.

Rost sued Cook for $3,818.64, the unpaid balance of what he said the doctor owed him for wages and expenses. Cook's lawyers argued that Rost's work had been unsatisfactory, and since there was no contract, the doctor would not pay.[45] But whether they ever got their money or not, the Rosts would make sure the doctor paid one way or another.

On September 4, 1916, Henry Helgesen announced that he would place in the *Congressional Record* yet another extension of remarks on the North Pole question. But this time the subject would not be Peary's credibility. It would be Cook's.

He began by denying that he had ever really been a Cook partisan but had defended Cook only out of a sense of justice. "If Cook's opponents are sure—as they claim to be—that he is a fraud," he asked, "why not give him a hearing, let the American public know officially the fraudulent nature of his claims, and close the matter with finality? . . . Apparently Cook's detractors have not feared that he could prove his claims so much as they have feared that an investigation would bring to light charges against Peary even worse than those already proven; hence their reluctance to mete out justice to Cook.

"I have therefore set myself at the task of analyzing all of Cook's official evidence. . . ."[46]

Helgesen's remarks on Cook's record began with what amounted to a personal note by the Rosts questioning their former employer's sincerity:

> In 1915, when matters looked as though a hearing might be granted him, he decided on an eight months' tour around the world, though I happen to know that those persons who had his interests at heart remonstrated with him against such a course. The present year, on the more or less plausible excuse of a Chautauqua lecture tour, he went to the West, at a time when, with a little extra effort on his part, his friends hoped to secure for him the hearing which he has so long professed to desire. These actions may possibly be reasonably explained, nevertheless they lend color to the theory that Cook does not desire a bona fide hearing and investigation.[47]

The speech itself related how Helgesen had written on August 3 asking Cook whether he was still willing to let his claim be judged by the information contained within his book, *My Attainment of the Pole,* as he had said in its preface. Cook replied in the affirmative, and Rost now took him up on it. In 28 pages of fine print, Rost closely analyzed Cook's book and pointed out numerous minor errors, discrepancies of dates, internal inconsistencies and contradictions.

He compared John R. Bradley's statements and those in Franke's book with Cook's and found many more. Most telling were his analyses of other explorers' narratives showing how Cook might have used them as a basis to embroider a fanciful story of his journey to the Pole and back.

Rost pointed out discrepancies in lunar phases, which had apparently been erroneously taken from an almanac for 1908 rather than 1907. He called attention to suspicious revisions of Cook's astronomical observations between the first edition of *My Attainment of the Pole* and subsequent ones that could not be explained away as typographical errors. These revisions gave the same required results while neatly correcting a fatal internal mathematical error that would have brought into question the observer's competence with navigational instruments.

Rost scrutinized Cook's photographs and disparaged the shadow data that Cook said convinced him he had reached the Pole. He derided the lack of any observations for magnetic variation and the inadequacy of certain features of Cook's claimed ones for longitude and latitude. He theorized a rationale for all of Cook's "discoveries" along the way to the Pole—Bradley Land, the Glacial Island far out at sea, his description of conditions at the Pole itself— and he questioned Cook's veracity throughout, up to and including his accounts of the events at Annoatok upon his return, using Whitney's book as a comparison.

Considering that Cook had had plenty of time, three serial accounts and three editions of his book to correct any unintentional errors, Rost had Helgesen sum up the evidence he gave:

> After a careful, analytical reading of Cook's book, remembering that the material contained in this book has been revised by Cook six times . . . is it possible for anyone who gives this matter any thought or study at all to believe that Dr. Cook ever attained or remotely approached the North Pole?[48]

By the time Rost won his lawsuit, Cook had already lost through the words his unpaid lobbyist had put over Helgesen's signature. Etta Rost was right, and her revenge was complete. Still, despite Helgesen's surprising attack on Dr. Cook, Lucien Alexander was worried about the damage that he had already done to Peary:

> Our inaction for so long a period has enabled them to so shift matters as to force us into a defensive position. . . . I sometimes feel overwhelmed at the mass of material of a type so apt to impress the superficial, and some of it the thinking man too, and even the scientist, which they have gotten into Helgesen's extensions. Since I have grappled with his "remarks" in detail I have been more than surprised at the mass of them—and most of them things that sooner or later must be met.[49]

Alexander had arranged for another Fess speech, which he advised Peary to distribute in a manner similar to the first one. But Lucien Alexander also wanted to go over Peary's personal papers, to see "what facts you have in rebuttal of the charges made."

Though Hugh C. Mitchell had for some time been preparing just such a reply,[50] Peary wrote back saying he was dispensing with his lobbyist's services. Alexander was shocked that the admiral had taken the advice he had said Peary couldn't afford to take—to drop the matter altogether. He called such an action "a monumental blunder" and pleaded with Peary to reconsider:

The situation at present is no longer one requiring us to fight Cook's claim; the ground has been completely shifted and has become almost entirely a case involving your attainment of the Pole. While that is not a pressing matter at the moment the numerous Helgesen contentions should not be left as they stand for on their face I am sorry to say they are formidable (and I say this not only as your counsel but sincerely as your friend as well), and unanswered they are bound to impress future historians. And now while we have the matter in hand is of course the time to prepare the answers, and if your diaries and records have errors we ought to explain how that happened and determine in the light of the facts the degree of publicity that is desirable and not leave the matter for some possibly unfriendly historians of the future.[51]

But Peary could not be persuaded. He had already made up his mind and had written to Congressman Fess declining his further offers of help. "The material inserted in the Congressional Record by Mr. Helgesen and circulated under his Congressional frank I at first attempted to read," he told the congressman, "but owing to his garbling of quotations and misrepresentations, I threw it down in disgust.

"To attempt to read through, much less to discuss, a mass of material prepared thus, would be a waste of time."[52]

Despite Peary's disclaimers, he *had* read Helgesen's remarks—and he had read them very closely. He even made comments on the margins of his copy of them. About their contents he was livid. He wanted General Greely removed from the National Geographic Society's board of governors and Edwin Swift Balch expelled from the American Geographical Society. He was sure it was they, and especially Greely, who were supplying Helgesen with his material.

His seething anger was taken out in fantasy memoranda directed at his enemies or simply written for himself. In one he advocated that a "distinctly lighter & smaller" man contrive to assault Dr. Cook in public in an attempt to show that the doctor was a physical coward and so discredit him in the western states. In another he told Helgesen that he was a "dupe," a "liar" and an "ignoramus" who had "prostituted his office" to the interests of a vaudeville scheme, and challenged him to bring formal charges to the secretary of the Navy against him.[53]

But Peary saved his bitterest attack for General Adolphus W. Greely:

> G- the martinet, G- the unfit, G- the coward weakling, G- the cannibal who kept his own contemptible life by subsisting upon the flesh of better men than he, G- the murderer whose inefficiency slowly starved his men to death, while he returned to pass as a great arctic explorer, critic & authority. Greely, whose Arctic experience & record are a horror & a disgrace.[54]

Peary sent none of these ravings, however, and he met none of Helgesen's charges publicly. Alexander's services were dispensed with for good on March 15, 1917.

With Rost gone, Mene Wallace received a letter from Congressman Helgesen's office advising him: "There is nothing in the circumstances in the case to warrant you in predicating your future conduct on any interest that Mr. Helgesen might have in your particular version of the Peary-Cook controversy, and I want to assure you that so far as this office is concerned you are perfectly free to make any disposition of any information you have as you deem best for your own interests. . . ."[55] No one else was interested in his "big story," either, which remained in Mene's head, never to be told.

On April 10, 1917, Henry Helgesen suddenly died. By the end of 1918 Mene, too, was dead, victim of the influenza epidemic that swept the world in the wake of the Great War.[56]

As for Dr. Cook, by then he was living in Wyoming, where he had gone in search of a new life.

CHAPTER 22

The Meanest Men in the World

DR. COOK HAD FIRST GONE TO WYOMING AT THE BEHEST OF DR. THOMP-son, who, with a group of other Chicago men, had invested a good deal of money in an oil speculation in Lincoln County headed by a man named Abner Davis.

During their trip around the world, Thompson had plenty of opportunities to learn of Cook's varied experiences, and he had developed an unbounded admiration for his friend's abilities. Thompson was convinced Cook had acquired a knowledge of geology through study and practical observation, so when he became suspicious about his oil investment's actual worth, he asked Dr. Cook to make an on-site inspection.

The doctor arrived in Kemmerer in December 1916 and met Davis. He was shown the venture's holdings, including a dome—a structure of deformed sedimentary rocks that often indicates the presence of oil—in whose vicinity there was even some surface seepage. After looking over the extensive property, Cook thought that although there might be oil on the land, it seemed unlikely there would be enough production to make a profitable, ongoing proposition.

When he reported this to Dr. Thompson and the others, they withdrew from Davis's company. Abner Davis made a huge profit anyway, not from bringing in an oil well but by selling off his undeveloped holdings to other speculators. Nevertheless, Thompson was happy to be out of the oil game.

His visit to the Wyoming oil fields had just the opposite effect on Cook, however. Davis might not have found oil, but others had. The doctor was by no means alone in seeing a golden future in Wyoming. With America's entrance into the war looming as a real possibility, the price of oil was going up, and Casper was at the center of the new prosperity. The city's population had rapidly risen from 2,000 to 15,000 as the oil fever took hold, and it seemed to Cook as good a place as any to begin again.

He returned to Lincoln County early in 1917 and there met Frank G. Curtis, a former New York attorney, now president of New York Oil Company. Cook told Curtis that he hoped to catch on with some oil concern. Curtis, it turned out, was a staunch believer that the doctor was a wronged man in regard to his claim to the North Pole and was only too happy to give him a trial. He took Cook 45 miles north of Casper to show him the largest oil field in the Rockies at Salt Creek, adjacent to the federal oil reserves at Teapot Dome. They also visited the promising Grass Creek field, opened up just the year before. After a few weeks, Curtis hired Cook to prospect for oil and recommend likely places where claims could be filed on public land or leased from private owners.

When the United States entered the war in April 1917, the oil companies smelled boom times ahead and redoubled their efforts to obtain leases on any likely tract. Dr. Cook looked over the anticline formations to the southwest, then recommended some land near Hidden Dome, 19 miles from Worland. Gas was struck in September.

He also went to investigate the domes close to the hot springs near Thermopolis, where that summer a wildcat well had struck oil at a depth of 1,000 feet. Thermopolis lay north of the Bridger Mountains at an elevation of 4,397 feet. Its semiarid climate encouraged little vegetation to cover the concentric hogback ridges rising 2,000 feet higher. Twenty-three miles northwest of the town, Dr. Cook recognized the sharp rocks of a number of domes interrupted by low ridges and gravel-covered terraces running in a belt 25 miles wide along the south margin of the Big Horn Basin.

One of these, the Cottonwood Anticline, had an especially steep southern slope. Government geologists who had surveyed the ground in 1913 considered the area barren of oil, as two wells drilled near the crest of its sandstone outcropping had failed to hit anything, not even water. Nevertheless, Cook advised New York Oil to acquire property there.

By the end of the year, he had recommended land that was put into a corporation at an appraised value of $500,000. Fifty-one percent of the stock issued was divided among Frank Curtis, Herman Curtis, who had abandoned his prune business in California to join his brother, and Dr. Cook. The rest of the stock was sold to raise capital for development. The company was chartered as the Cook Oil Company, a subsidiary of New York Oil, with capital of $1,000,000, and Cook took up residence in Thermopolis.

With the recent strikes of heavy, dark oil near the domes, competition among speculators intensified. Since there was a limit on how much acreage could be held by any one person, royalties were given just for the use of a person's name to acquire property, and nearly everyone in the countryside "owned" some. Disputes over boundary lines near Worland resulted in several incidents in which Harry Sinclair's Standard Oil crews dismantled New York Oil rigs on ground both claimed they had rights to. Unfortunately for its competitors, the sheriff of Worland held royalties to acreage controlled by New York Oil under his name and had the Standard men arrested. But when New York Oil sued Standard Oil for claim jumping, the result of the trial was simply to divide the disputed ground equally between the two.

Despite its promising prospects, New York Oil had only a few "show wells," useful for attracting investors with new capital. Its real business was in holding land and taking royalties when others developed it on lease.

Although he now termed himself a "petroleum technologist," Cook still gave an occasional lecture on his past adventures. He had been turned down for the Ambulance Corps because of his age, but he still tried to do something for the war effort by writing brochures for the Rocky Mountain Sheep Association promoting wool production.[1]

He also continued to read voluminously. In the fall of 1917 he read an astonishing report carried by the Associated Press indicating that more than just British agents had followed him around the world. The revelations came in the testimony of a Hindu named Sukupar Chatterji.

Gustav H. Jacobsen, a wealthy real estate dealer, was on trial in Chicago with three codefendants charged with conspiracy. One of the defendants, George Paul Boehm, Chatterji alleged, had revealed a plot to him while he was in Manila. Boehm was to kill Cook and his party, and their identities were to be assumed by Boehm's agents, who in the guise of the explorers would go through the countryside fomenting revolt against Great Britain.[2]

Chatterji had been kept in solitary confinement in Manila for six months before he confessed to the alleged conspiracy and was then sent to the United States to testify. Also implicated in the plot was the German military attaché to its United States embassy at the time, Captain Franz von Papen, who had been expelled in 1916 for questionable activities that seemed intended to compromise America's neutral status in the war.

But to Dr. Cook the report must have seemed merely a souvenir of his former life. He was absorbed in the petroleum business full-time now, and it looked as though the only claims he would be making in the future were in the land office in Thermopolis and as though his exploring days—for anything but oil—were over. The Polar Controversy seemed dead, given up even by its two principals. But at that moment there quietly appeared a new factor that would fuel the dispute for decades to come.

The "mare's nest" from an Omaha man that General Hubbard had noted in 1911, and that Bridgman had feared would fall into the hands of Congressman Macon, had developed into a full-fledged book, which in more than 500 pages of closely argued analysis came to the conclusion that Peary could not have reached the North Pole in 1909 and, in fact, had perpetrated a deliberate hoax in claiming to have done so.

The author, Captain Thomas F. Hall, was the well-to-do and well-respected owner of the Hall Distributor Company of Omaha, which manufactured feed-grain machinery. Descended from Massachusetts Pilgrim stock, he had gone to sea as a young man and experienced there the thrill of an adventurous life, which he continued to live vicariously through his study of polar expeditions. When Cook's report came from Lerwick, he had at first been skeptical, but as he read Cook's serial narrative, he had become enthusiastic over the doctor's accomplishment, then fascinated by the kaleidoscopic events of the great Polar Controversy that ensued.

In the introduction to his book, Hall avowed strict neutrality on the question of whether Cook or Peary was first at the Pole. But he believed, he said, that by careful, logical analysis the true conqueror would emerge, once all the layers of accusations and counteraccusations were stripped from the known facts, as presented in the statements of the explorers themselves and their witnesses. The book gave evidence that his quest to "unfold the truth," as he put it, had driven him to the point of obsession. Part of the driving force seemed to be a visceral dislike for Robert E. Peary.

Not only did Hall's book, *Has the North Pole Been Discovered?* attack Peary's North Pole claim, but it also systematically assailed the one other claim that even the Rosts' speeches for Congressman Helgesen had left intact—the "Farthest North" of 1906. By exhaustive analysis, Captain Hall attempted to show that this claim prefigured in all the same suspicious features Peary's polar claim, and he declared it, too, a hoax.

Every aspect of Peary's polar narrative—his photographs, his reports of his speed over the polar pack, his navigational techniques and observations, and the results that had been recomputed by Mitchell and Duvall—was minutely examined. Discrepancies within Peary's book and conflicts with the writings of Borup and Henson and Peary's own congressional testimony were pointed out and belabored in multiple comparisons. Meticulously drawn diagrams and charts, demonstrating graphically the incongruities of Peary's claims, complemented a text that demolished them verbally. Hall also ridiculed the manner in which the National Geographic Society had examined Peary's records and how others had blandly accepted its findings without further investigation.

He then compared the several versions of Cook's journey as told by Cook's Eskimos and decided they conflicted to such an extent that they were worthless as competent testimony. In a similar fashion, he dismembered the various lines of "evidence" that had been advanced to prove Cook had not reached the Pole, pointing out the ludicrous aspects of the critics' arguments.

Mount McKinley he studiously avoided, calling it irrelevant to the polar question; Dunkle and Loose were pronounced likewise, since Cook had used none of their calculations to try to prove his case. He was willing, however, like Cook, to accept the generous view of the Copenhagen decision as one of "not proven."

Hall demonstrated to his own satisfaction how all the "evidence" presented against Cook did not stand up under logical inquiry or meet the test of scientific scrutiny, and so could be safely disregarded as "proof" that Cook had not reached the Pole. Therefore, the captain reasoned, there was nothing left to disprove Cook's claim except what could be gleaned from an analysis of Cook's narrative itself. In so doing, Captain Hall was able to excuse *My Attainment of the Pole* for what inconsistencies it contained under his own rules of logic, and declared he found nothing in it inconsistent with the possibility that Cook might actually have reached the vicinity of the North Pole in 1908.

As for the only other such attempt at analysis that Cook's story had ever received, that of Congressman Helgesen in 1916, Hall dismissed it as being an "apparently puerile, picayunish, pettifogging attempt at juggling with clerical errors" made to "create prejudice against Cook for personal reasons." In the end, Hall declared Cook's narrative "unimpeachable," placing much emphasis, as Balch had, on the priority of Cook's descriptions of conditions on the way to the Pole and in its vicinity as a basis of belief in the doctor's truthfulness and accuracy.

Although Captain Hall believed that his logical arguments were "unassailable," he also knew that his book would not change the minds of those who did not wish to be convinced:

> Thousands of persons, through the influence of an organized press bureau campaign *believe* that Peary reached the North Pole in 1909. The *belief* must be well nigh universal that he reached 87° 6' in 1906.
>
> Many persons *believe* what they *want* to believe. Shakespeare wrote:
>
> "When my love swears that she is made of truth,
> I do believe her, though I know she lies."
>
> The fact that Mr. Helgesen and others whose writing I have reviewed will resort to such methods as I have herein exposed not only indicates, but is *strong evidence* that each of them *believes* (or fears) that Cook reached the Pole, *which they regret.*[3]

The crux of the trouble with Peary's narrative conflicts and subsequent actions, Hall said, was that they proved that many of Peary's statements of fact were invented fantasies. "But it was not the falsehood itself that was significant," he maintained. "It would not have been significant even if he had falsified every sentence in his story. But the significance rested in the FACT that the falsehood proved INVENTION, and proving invention, SOLVED THE PROBLEM.

"When anyone can catch Cook at business of that character it will be Cook's undoing."[4]

Hall contended that Cook's narrative was free of such error and that unless something in it could be found that was invention or some explorer eventually produced evidence that contradicted Cook's descriptions of physical phenomena encountered on his journey to the Pole and back, history would certainly award him the honor of being the discoverer of the North Pole.

Though a highly respectable effort, Hall's book betrayed the author's personal animus for Peary and his hope of Cook's eventual vindication, which compromised the captain's pleas of neutrality. Still, for Peary's claims, the appearance of *Has the North Pole Been Discovered?* would be a truly devastating blow, and yet, this remarkable book had little immediate impact. Hall had it published at his own expense by R.G. Badger in Boston and then sent it to more than 1,000 libraries around the country, where it lay, for the most part, unnoticed, itself waiting to be discovered.

Meanwhile, Dr. Cook had found employment as a field geologist with some of his leaseholders, notably Empire State Oil Company. In September 1918 New York Oil brought in the first well on the supposedly "barren" Cottonwood Anticline, or Hamilton Dome, as it was now being called; more important, it was the lightest oil yet found near Thermopolis.

But in the bitter Wyoming winters, oil prospecting and drilling all but stopped, and with it so did income for "petroleum technologists." That fall, just after the Great War had finally ended, news of new oil strikes in Texas lured Cook to Fort Worth.

Although oil fever was running high in the Lone Star State, the distinctive geological formations of Wyoming were absent, and finding oil there was much more of a speculation. The divining rod was not yet out of favor, and the location of oil was as much a black art as a science.

As he looked around Fort Worth that winter, Dr. Cook caught the infectious optimism feeding the fantastic boom in oil. The huge demands of the war had driven the price from 64 cents a barrel in 1916 to nearly $2. In response to new strikes in Eastland County, the city was in a boom of its own—in real estate—with prosperity written on its upwardly expanding skyline. Soon, Fort Worth would be billing itself as "the Chicago of the Southwest." Even so, choice office space was at a premium. Most of that had been taken over by high-powered speculators looking for high visibility to sell shares they said would make investors rich and, at the same time, to convince the credulous of their prosperity.

It was so difficult to find a room that one recent visitor cautioned against even going to the city because "they hang you on a hook down there." The best hotel, the Westbrook, which was booked so solid it had a ten-day limit, was doing land-office business, literally, with an oil lease concession operating out of the lobby. There, Dr. Cook was presented with a study in contrasts as "ermine capes and tobacco juice; hip boots and Paris hats" intermingled, and where prospectors in corduroys swapped stories and made deals with men in garish silk shirts and boots tooled with intricate scrollwork.

If the Westbrook was impossible, a room could be obtained at $3 a night, without bath, for those willing to sleep with three others, or a cot could be arranged in the hall for $2. Everything else was as outrageously expensive: pecans were 5 cents for two; apples, 10 cents each; a $50 suit imported from Dallas picked up 50 percent in value in the 22-mile transit; women's clothes brought whatever the market would bear. The streets were thronged with everything from decrepit bicycles to shining new foreign cars with names no Texan would dare even try to pronounce.

The rule seemed to be this: the closer to the oil fields, the higher the price—of everything. In Wichita Falls a spot in a "tent hotel" where the "oil maggots," as the oil seekers were known, slept was going for $2 and up. In Burkburnett, a "mushroom city" on the site of the big oil strike of July 1918, Dr. Cook found himself on the literal wellspring of all this newfound wealth. An old white farmhouse sat among a forest of spindly wooden derricks clus-

tering on the horizon. The town itself looked like something out of a Hollywood western with imposing false fronts and streets of mud so deep and sticky
with oil they could be crossed only on boards.

The cotton crop hung unpicked on the bushes, even at offers of a fabulous wage of $3.50 per 100 pounds. After all, in the oil fields unskilled
laborers made $7 a day, a driller made $16 and a tool dresser the equivalent of
a colonel in the U.S. Army—nearly $20.[5]

But in Texas, just as it had been in Alaska, most of this apparent prosperity was illusion. Only 1 percent of the hundreds of oil companies that had
been formed had made a profit out of their speculations.

Nevertheless, Cook was so impressed by what he saw in Texas that he decided to stay. At first the doctor worked as a geologist for interests controlled
by Marriner Eccles, a sugar beet king, and Tex Rickard, a fight promoter.
Then, with W.E. Clark and a friend of Dr. Thompson's, Joe Taylor, he leased
some likely acreage in Oklahoma and Texas, and in February 1919 established
the Texas Eagle Oil Company as a common-law trust, with capital stock of
$300,000 and modest offices in Fort Worth at 603½ Main Street.

Soon, the papers ran full-page ads touting the difference between Texas
Eagle and other oil promotions:

> GET INTO A SOUND COMPANY
> DR. COOK THE EXPLORER, AND A GROUP
> OF WELL KNOWN SUBSTANTIAL
> MEN ARE BEHIND THIS ORGANIZATION.
> . . . With the claws of an eagle we have gripped the oil fields of
> Mid-Texas. ONLY 10,000 SHARES OPEN TO PUBLIC subscription.
> Capital $300,000. Fully paid, non-assessable, par value $10 per
> share.
> THIS COMPANY IS AS SOUND AS A BANK. Insured profits, verified
> accounts, open books, No secrets.
> Deposit your money with us with the same confidence that you
> have in your bank.

In New York Bob Bartlett clipped one of these ads and sent it to Admiral
Peary, remarking sarcastically on its margin, "Here's your chance to get rich
quick."[6]

Peary had once told Helen Bridgman that the discovery of the North Pole
would make him one of the "World Men," of which he reckoned there had
been only a handful in all of human history, among whom he included
Caesar, Columbus and Napoleon. Though he was an honored man, its conquest had not made him that, nor even what he had imagined it would as he
had sat penning his grandiose notes in his polar diary ten years before. If most
of the apparent wealth of Texas was illusion, illusory, too, was the everlasting
glory Peary had hoped to win by capturing "that Frozen Jewel of the North."

As the United States negotiated with Denmark to acquire the Danish West Indies, Peary had suggested Greenland be included in the purchase. "Greenland represents ice, coal, and power in inexhaustible quantities," he had argued. "And stranger things have happened than that Greenland, in our hands, might furnish an important North Atlantic naval and aeronautical base. . . .

". . . With the rapid shrinking of distance in this age of speed and invention, Greenland may be of crucial importance to us in the future."[7] But when the United States signed a treaty purchasing Denmark's Caribbean colony in 1917, it renounced all interests in Greenland based on Peary's explorations there. With that renunciation, any secret dreams Peary may have had that he might be seen one day, as Henry Stanley was in Belgium, as the father of a colonial empire had also vanished.

Yes, he had the fame he said he must have and the money that went with it, but he was running out of that most important commodity of all—time. His running battle with Cook had been a nagging drain on both his time and his money, and the many doubts it had raised about his own claim and character had compromised his fame. Even after the verdict at Copenhagen had brought him forth from his exile on Eagle Island to accept the plaudits of the world, Peary continued to spend most of each summer there, incommunicado, isolated by the three miles of sea between him and South Harpswell, without so much as a telephone to intrude. He spent the days walking its wooded paths and having improvements made to it that nature had not thought of, including a pool that filled at high tide and allowed the cold Atlantic's water to warm in the bright summer sun.

The house itself remained to the casual eye as it had been—a modest one-and-a-half-story Cape Cod—but now it incorporated many imaginative and unique features. Most notable were two turrets built into the cliff below the house. Peary called these his "bomb proofs," and in them he stored the mementos of a lifetime.

One he dubbed his "Cave of Memories" and filled it with his boyhood collection of mounted hawks along with the skins, tusks, skulls, horns and all the other arctic trophies of his manhood.

The other was his personal office and retreat, circular and substantial, with windows that looked out on the bay from its large desk. In it was installed his library and 50 wooden packing cases containing his papers—tens of thousands of sheets representing every phase of his life, including his polar records—nailed up, inaccessible as the Pole itself. The North Pole had become a subject, despite all his former desire to reach it, that Peary now was glad was rarely mentioned as a stirring issue. Winters he spent in Washington, D.C., close to the seat of power, and it was there that he turned his energies to one that was.

Briefly, in 1916, he had considered running for the Senate on the Republican ticket, but consistent with his youthful inclinations, he saw little chance for victory and decided against it. As the war grew more desperate in Europe and unrestricted submarine warfare was unleashed by the Germans, Peary had advocated airpower for coastal defense. His advocacy had resulted in his election as president of the Aero Club of America.

Upon the admiral's return in late 1917 from an extensive speaking tour on the club's behalf, he complained of unusual fatigue, abdominal numbness and nausea. His personal physician, Commander Howard F. Strine, discovered that Peary was suffering from pernicious anemia, an incurable blood disorder.

He was given injections of iron and arsenic and ordered to bed for eight weeks to prevent further blood destruction through exercise. As an experiment, he was fed red bone marrow in the hope that it would have some effect on his declining red cell count, which was now half the normal 5,000,000 cells. But even with the "incurable" pronouncement, Peary was outwardly confident. "I have not at any time felt any apprehension in regard to my condition," he told an acquaintance, "because I could not believe that a perfectly sound, smooth running machine could be put out of commission permanently, because the steam pressure had run a bit low."[8]

After his confinement, Peary felt considerably better. He resolved to conquer pernicious anemia just as he had conquered everything else he had ever set his mind to. Even though he knew it was a losing game, this time he had no choice but to enter the contest.

For most promoters and investors, oil was also a losing game. But every man who chose to play also hoped he would beat the long odds. And like every other of the hundreds of independent oil promotions in Fort Worth, Texas Eagle aimed to spread its wings. It was "building on a strong, sure foundation—building for the future," one of its brochures declared. "It intends to be in the oil business ten, twenty years from today. It has faith in the oil future of Texas and it plans to grow and develop with the state."[9]

But $300,000 was slight capital for a company with such big aspirations, and with $100,000 needed to sink one well, the money that had come in quickly dissipated. To provide more capital, in August 1919 a subsidiary company, the Texas Eagle Producing and Refining Company, was created with additional stock amounting to $2,500,000.

This second Texas Eagle had an impressive list of names on its board, including bank presidents, prominent manufacturers and even a former U.S. senator. Cook was president of the company, and William Gould Brokaw, whose yacht Cook had tried to borrow in Copenhagen, was listed as vice president.

A handsome booklet sent to prospective investors proclaimed that the new company had been organized to profit from refining crude oil. Texas Eagle, the brochure went on, was preparing to engage in the erection of refineries, the laying of pipe and the distribution and marketing of its products throughout the United States under the trade name TEPARCO.

The circular said profits of 100 percent were not uncommon for well-located and efficient refineries, and that Texas Eagle would transform an open field in Fort Worth into one with a capacity of 10,000 barrels a day and profits of $9,000,000 a year. In the center of the booklet was a picture of the prospective refinery with a train of 30 tankers each labeled "Texas Eagle," ready for loading, and it asked whether the investor was not also ready to get on that train before it began to roll toward "a big future, rich in promise of reward to those who become associated with it."

These were small claims in the fantastic world of promises of wealth beyond measure that was Fort Worth in 1919. Although many companies formed with the honest intent of bringing in an oil well, unfortunately the oil boom had also attracted many who had no such intention. They saw that vast amounts of money could be made instead by cashing in on people's gullibility. The methods used to raise capital by such promoters were limited only by their imagination, but they quickly fell into several familiar patterns as the boom progressed.

Oil promoters sometimes gave free tours of producing oil fields in which they had no actual share, after which potential shareholders were harangued with promises of easy money and unlimited ease to persuade them to buy stock. Some used late-night telephone calls telling of spectacular opportunities that just couldn't wait, or a string of highly enticing letters to persuade investors to part with their cash. These played on greed and fear, and if no response was received, appeals to shame and envy were tried.

One ever-present problem for promoters was how to get their advertising to people most likely to invest in their promotions. "Sucker lists" of those who had previously invested in oil were, sometimes clandestinely, bought and sold at high prices on the theory that former investors were more likely to be interested in further oil speculations or were just plain susceptible to high-pressure sales techniques.

Once some likely investors had been found, an ever-popular ploy was to declare a dividend early in the promotion, even if the "dividend" was derived from stock sales rather than earned income. These dividends, sometimes as much as 100 percent, almost invariably served to entice those who received them to invest even more money and also to attract new investors who hoped to reap such huge and sure profits for themselves.

Some scams involved the payment of "royalties" so infinitesimal that stockholders could never hope to recover their original investments; others involved the sale of worthless stock, usually on attractive terms, paid for on a time basis at very reasonable rates. After a few payments had been gathered in, the promoters would melt away with no further solicitations.

Chief among the assets of any promoter who wished to be successful was the acquisition of the services of "pens," as the writers of hot copy for the letters sent to the names on the sucker lists were called. A good pen could almost name his price, often getting a percentage of the profits from all stock sold under the influence of his persuasive prose. Some promoters went one step further, setting up a figurehead who would lend prestige to the company's promotion, around which a pen could build his crusade for cash.

Perhaps the most notorious example was "General" Robert A. Lee, who before he became the symbol of the General Lee Oil Company was a janitor at the courthouse in Denton, Texas. In addition to his name, he bore a bewhiskered resemblance to his almost-namesake of Civil War fame. On the strength of this he was given the persona of his famous nonrelative as a southern gentleman. One of the promotional pieces gotten out by his managers was a booklet entitled *The Honor of the Lees,* which touted their sacred honor, fidelity and innate ability, and which was mailed by the thousands. Outrageous as this may seem, the company took in nearly $2,000,000 as a result.

Mail flowed in and out of Fort Worth at the boom's height, literally by the ton. The appropriately named J.H. Stamps, a railway mail clerk on the Amarillo–Fort Worth line of the Fort Worth & Denver Railroad, recalled that on just his run alone there were often 20 sacks of mail addressed to one oil firm or another, and 32 mail trains a day passed through the city.[10] Post Office receipts jumped from half a million dollars a year in preboom days to nearly a million by 1919.

In addition to the money flowing in torrents directly to promoters, brokerage houses controlled by them made hefty commissions selling their own stock, while numerous "tip sheets"—newspapers purporting to be guides to oil investments—boosted the holdings of the oil promotions that owned them or paid them for the space. Some tip sheets took a negative approach, earning money from payments made to them for not attacking questionable promotions in their pages.

As long as pretense and subterfuge could be maintained, a company's stock could be sold, even though totally valueless. When continued deceptions finally lost their appeal, dishonest promoters would simply fold up the company, establish a new one with a new name and new personnel, and start over again.

Since surrounding states, like Arkansas, had passed "blue-sky" laws that prohibited excessive promotional promises, a considerable number of dishonest oil promotion schemes had gravitated to Fort Worth. With these flam-

Tip sheet.

boyant promoters in competition with legitimate companies for the vast amounts of capital needed to drill for oil, even those who had no intention to defraud were often driven to adopt marginal practices to keep from going under.

Many oil companies, like Texas Eagle, were organized as "trust estates," a perfectly legal arrangement not requiring a state charter. Many of these, however, were little more than a license to steal, the trustees often being given almost absolute power over all the money the company received. The amount of capitalization could be increased at will, and no controls were placed on the use of incoming funds, including the payment of dividends. The trustees fixed their own salaries and charged expenses to the company, with the stockholders having no say in anything whatever until the liquidation of the trust. In most cases, all the trustees were obligated to do was divide the value of the trust estate with the stockholders at the end of the life of the trust—if there was anything left to divide. Worse yet, the courts in Texas had ruled that although they had no control over its operations, the stockholders could be considered partners who were liable for the trust's indebtedness in case of failure.

Though many of these trusts had little intention of developing their potential oil lands, because of the huge influx of mail-order money, even these companies gave the illusion of immense success. In Fort Worth, that mecca of liquid wealth, prosperity reigned, and an incurable optimism overtook every newcomer who did not know the precarious structure of oil promotions and the tremendous risk involved in the business of finding oil.

Being new at the oil investment game, Dr. Cook made the mistake of buying at the top of the market. His choice of properties showed that whatever field experience he had gained in Wyoming did not apply in Texas. His expensive acquisitions failed to provide enough production income to offset the cost of field operations. In fact, the doctor himself had been the easy victim of unscrupulous fellow promoters who unloaded their worthless properties at premium prices.

Although Cook had given an occasional lecture on his polar attainment in Fort Worth as late as 1919, if he had finally put the Polar Controversy out of his mind in his struggle for success in his oil ventures there, he was forced to recall it by the news that now came from Washington, D.C.: Robert E. Peary was dead.

In the spring of 1919 Peary had made his last public appearance at the National Geographic Society's rooms on 16th Street to present Vilhjalmur Stefansson with the Hubbard Gold Medal, which had been instituted to reward his own "Farthest North" in 1906. Stefansson, a Canadian of Icelandic parentage, was the new rising star among polar explorers. This came as the result of his unexpected emergence from the Arctic in 1916 when all had given him up for dead.

Captain Bartlett had been right in doubting the quality of his ship. She had been crushed in the ice 60 miles northeast of Wrangel Island with the loss of 11 men. But long before she sank, Stefansson and two others had left the *Karluk* and struck out toward Banks Island on March 28, 1914, and did not return. It took them 96 days to reach the island, where they spent the winter at Cape Kellett. Living Eskimo fashion, catching their food with spears, they spent the next year exploring the Canadian Archipelago.

Stefansson's story of survival was a great one, but it was another tale for which he was most famous. In 1912 he had returned from Alaska bringing news of a tribe of "blond Eskimos," which he speculated might be the remains of a Nordic race that had mingled among the aborigines in ancient times. The *Seattle Daily Times* printed a big story rating Stefansson's discovery of a "lost tribe of whites, descendants of Leif Eriksson . . . ranking next in importance from an ethnological standpoint to the discovery of the lost tribes of Israel."[11] But Stefansson's announcement had also received considerable derision from the scientific world.

Roald Amundsen, who had sailed through the same area in his epic negotiation of the Northwest Passage, called it "the most palpable nonsense that ever came from the North."[12] His public denunciation of the "blond Eskimos" was the first indication of the enmity the Norwegian felt for the younger explorer.

Stefansson's most recent expedition, aimed at exploring the ethnology and geography of the same region, originally was to have been sponsored by the American Museum and the National Geographic Society. The now-prosperous society had offered the explorer $22,500 but, like the museum, withdrew from the expedition in favor of the Canadian government at its request. In 1919 Stefansson had returned with more sensational news. This time he said he had proof positive that Dr. Cook had not gone to the North Pole.

The evidence consisted of the discovery of an island that he called "Second Land," later named Meighen Island, very close to where Cook had given his bearings in the Crown Prince Gustav Sea on his return from the Pole. Stefansson said this proved Cook could not have taken the route he claimed, since if he had actually been at the position he gave, he would have been on the island itself, or surely would have seen it.

At the ceremonies honoring Stefansson, everyone who saw Peary noticed the inroads disease had made upon the once-robust explorer. For some time the admiral had been on a program of transfusions to boost his rapidly declining blood count, but by the end of the year, Peary was not helped even by transfusions and was often hospitalized. In one of his last letters he had confided to a friend, "I had confidently expected to be entirely myself before now but am disappointed."[13]

The last of 35 transfusions was given to Peary on February 13, 1920. It had little effect. He was allowed to go to his home at 1831 Wyoming Avenue, where, surrounded by his family, he slipped into a coma and died quietly at 1:28 A.M. on Friday, February 20. Condolences poured in from all over the world. Obituaries, especially that of the *New York Times,* were effusive.

As his North Pole flag flew above the gravesite and as Navy seaplanes circled overhead, Rear Admiral Robert Edwin Peary was laid to rest with the full military honors befitting a national hero.

Besides the grieving family, the funeral at Arlington National Cemetery on February 23 was attended by a cross section of the political and geographical establishment. Vice President Thomas R. Marshall, Chief Justice Edwin D. White and various cabinet members were there, along with Gilbert Grosvenor, Willis Moore and Alexander Graham Bell of the National Geographic Society. Dr. Bryant, whose association with Peary extended back to the 1891 West Greenland Expedition, was joined by the president of the Explorers Club, Vilhjalmur Stefansson; Dr. Isaiah Bowman, director of the American Geographical Society; Dr. Henry F. Osborn of the American Museum; and Henry Wise Wood of the Aero Club. Other faces among the crowd were those of Captain Bartlett, Herbert Bridgman, Donald MacMillan, Admiral Chester and Simeon Fess.

One who was not present was Matt Henson. When he heard of his old commander's death, he went into the washroom of the Customs House in New York, where he was employed as a messenger boy, and turned on the water so that others would not hear him crying.

Herbert L. Bridgman, in a memorial service at the Explorers Club, summed up his estimate of his beloved friend:

> Grave, calm, and perfectly self-contained, yet as far as possible from chilling reserve or bored indifference, with a sense of real humor, which, among intimates, could take and make a joke with the best—yet always with a fine and inborn sense of the courtesies and conventions, of the rights of others, and the value of time.
>
> Peary rarely in my hearing talked much about himself, his use of the first person singular was sparing to the last degree. . . . Even when the great prize had been won, and the victory of twenty years achieved, his manner, tempered by repeated repulse and disappointment, did not outwardly change, and no man ever heard from him a boasting or vainglorious word.[14]

Kenneth Sills, the president of Bowdoin College, held up Peary's life as an example:

The discovery of the Pole . . . was one of the most idealistic performances of the century. It meant that man could conquer; that he is
a superior being—that will dominates material difficulties. . . .

. . . A poor boy with nothing but his talent and his character to
rely on, [Peary] became a world figure. . . .

. . . His career is a great and wholesome inspiration to all the
young men of the land; for what has been done can be done. His
years of sacrifice for an ideal are a rebuke to those . . . who count
success only in the terms of huge profits.[15]

If Peary's arch-rival was mentioned at all in the press in connection with
his death, it was only to make further accusations. Dr. Keely, who had witnessed the inception of the inextricable entanglement of the two men's lives
on the North Greenland Expedition, expressed the opinion that the battle
with Cook had hastened the end of Peary's life.[16]

Frederick Cook's thoughts on the passing of Robert Peary are unrecorded.
At that moment he too was fighting for his life, but only for his financial life.

Texas Eagle's original capital quickly vanished in promotion costs and
down dry holes. To raise yet more capital, a new venture, the Texas Eagle Oil
and Refining Company, was organized out of the remaining assets of the first
two companies in February 1920, as a stock company under the very liberal
laws of the state of Delaware, and recapitalized at $5,000,000. Cook's part-

Stock certificate, 1920.

ners, with the exception of J.W. Taylor, took the opportunity to get out, but the doctor contributed his trust certificate and personal lease holdings in exchange for one quarter of the new company's stock.

There followed a massive mail-order appeal in which Dr. Cook used his name recognition to drum up investors. His ads said he believed his new company had a 99 percent chance to make good and that no inside clique owned promotional stock, and he held up the hardships he had endured in the Arctic as badges of his honesty and fortitude. His unbounded faith in the future was this time founded on new holdings acquired near proven fields in Desdemona, an area known for wells with high initial yields but also for early exhaustions.

The campaign produced $800,000. Even Dr. Thompson caught the enthusiasm and began investing in oil once again. But promotional expenses devoured a third of the company's new income, and the soil of Texas swallowed up the rest. By the time the price of oil peaked at $3.07 a barrel and began to decline, it was too late for the Texas Eagle to take flight.

By summer the board of directors had met and decided to refinance or find a buyer for the company. Its lawyers had been sent to London to try to arrange for stock to be issued on the London Exchange through the financial firm of LeRoy Ferry and Company, at a cost of $8,500. The lawyers said they had a favorable report on Ferry, but to make sure, Dr. Cook ordered one of his own from Bradstreet's. Its report cautioned him to "exercise care in any contemplated dealings pending a more extended experience of trading."

The London Stock Exchange Committee refused to list the issue, so Ferry proposed the formation of an English company capitalized at a million pounds sterling to take over Texas Eagle. Expenses to Texas Eagle would be $100,000, to be repaid out of the public issue returns.

Cook denounced the proposal, calling it a high-handed effort to get more money under false pretenses by LeRoy Ferry and his own lawyers, whom Cook accused of working both sides of the street, and it was rejected by the board. Attempts were then made to sell off the remaining 117,000 capital stock shares through a Chicago investment house, but this and all other attempts to come to a financial arrangement to save the company went nowhere.[17]

That winter it seemed evident that even his new venture was doomed. Announcements were sent out saying that "owing to the unusual rainy season and weather conditions together with freight congestion," the site of the Texas Eagle refinery would remain an open field. Stockholders, who once were given to expect $9,000,000 a year in profits, were now told that the company would be concentrating on the acquisition of new wells and the marketing of the crude oil obtained, but they were also assured that the company remained financially sound, with no indebtedness.

On February 1, 1921, the first and only annual report of the Texas Eagle Oil and Refining Company appeared. It painted a bleak picture of the future,

saying the economic downturn had done its worst and that small companies
had to look to mergers to increase their assets and resources. Therefore, it was
announced, Texas Eagle had acquired Mitchel Production Company, which,
if nothing else, had equipment worth $300,000 that could be liquidated for
ready cash. Economic factors, the report went on, had now made refineries
unprofitable, but the company still hoped to build one to refine its own oil
when production reached 2,000 barrels a day.

The bounds of credulity, as far as Texas Eagle was concerned, had been
reached. The war was over, demand had slackened and the price of oil had
fallen drastically. The wells that were coming in all over Texas could find no
customers for their black gold. But Texas Eagle had done even worse—it had
drilled nothing but dry holes on land that had cost more than $175,000. The
money coming in from stock sales was too slight to drill another well; everything was invested and nothing returned.

Cook had little encouraging to tell Dr. Thompson, who had bought some
stock in his friend's enterprise and now offered him a loan to keep his company afloat:

> Things here are not looking good—hopes of improvement are
> increasing but these hopes are based mainly on the general recov-
> ery of the business and it is my judgment that there will be very lit-
> tle change until December. . . .
>
> . . . There is a general merging & consolidation going on—and
> it may be best for us to do likewise— It seems to be the only way to
> protect my interest and that of the stockholders—you are pro-
> tected as matters stand now but I am not.
>
> No stock can be sold so long as the scalpers and brokers offer
> Texas Eagle Stock at the present prices.
>
> So you see I have before me a hard road to travel but some way
> the problem must be worked out.[18]

But there would be no improvement even in December, and for Texas
Eagle, December would be very short. In Breckenridge on September 6, the
Eagle's creditors attacked it, and a receivership was granted. As his last act as
president, Cook sent out a letter urging his stockholders to merge with the
Revere Oil Company. Some of them filed litigation to prevent the merger, but
it was eventually approved, and the Texas Eagle Oil and Refining Company
went out of existence on December 5, 1921.

As the new year came in, Cook was virtually out of the oil business but
still in the news. In January a strange story appeared on the wires of the Associated Press that briefly revived discussion of the doctor's polar claim. A Harvard graduate named Kenneth M. Clark said he had met a vagrant Eskimo
while in northern Quebec who had in his possession a notebook containing
Frederick Cook's name. In it were notes and data said to indicate positions as
far north as 89°. When asked about this report, Cook expressed confidence

that it represented part of his lost records. He predicted that more such discoveries would be made and eventually he would be recognized as the true discoverer of the North Pole. But recalling the Arctic, he said, made him quite content to remain in the sunny Southwest.[19]

On the thirteenth anniversary of the recognized discovery of the North Pole, the National Geographic Society unveiled a new marker for Peary's grave at Arlington for which it had paid $2,954. It was not the mausoleum of Peary's dreams but a white granite globe with the Pole marked by a shining bronze star. On its base was inscribed: "Robert Edwin Peary. Discoverer of North Pole. April 6, 1909."

At the dedication, Gilbert Grosvenor addressed a distinguished gathering that included President Harding:

> [Peary] was ever an ardent supporter of The Society's ambition to enlist the interest of every man and woman in scientific work . . . by making geographic knowledge intelligible and attractive to all persons. No member was more enthusiastic than he, nor pushed harder to increase its numbers, nor took greater happiness in helping it grow to more than 700,000 members. . . .
>
> . . . I voice the feeling of every member of this organization when I say to Mrs. Peary that our hearts are filled with inexpressible tenderness and gratitude that the precious privilege of placing this monument at his resting-place has been granted by her to the National Geographic Society, which loved him so well, and which with all the world rejoices that he "made good at last," and that an American has become the equal of Hudson, Magellan, and Columbus.[20]

In Texas Frederick A. Cook's dreams that the success of his oil enterprise would become *his* everlasting memorial had come to worse than nothing. It might be imagined that those dreams would now have to be abandoned. But though he had been a three-time loser with Texas Eagle, Cook, too, hoped to "make good at last."

Where others saw risks, the irrepressibly optimistic doctor saw opportunities. Inspired by his own company's demise and merger into Revere Oil, on March 1, 1922, he had launched a new venture, conveying 121 acres in LaSalle County as the company's basis under the law. "In the endeavor to iron out the various Texas Eagle problems, I am still quite busy with Revere Company," he wrote to Dr. Thompson, who was about to leave for a hunting trip in Africa, "but in the meantime I have organized the Petroleum Producers Association, which is arranged for the express purpose of taking over and salvaging other companies. We expect to begin closing contracts for these companies within the next ten days."[21]

PPA, as it was called for short, was, like the original Texas Eagle, a common-law trust with Frederick A. Cook as the sole trustee. In April the first trust certificates were issued through a brokerage house in which Cook had an interest. Cook explained the basis of his new approach: "There were properties here in Texas being neglected . . . which were valuable if under a new head . . . and I felt that stockholders in the combined organization could be put in a position to make some money upon what otherwise would have been almost a lost hope. . . .

". . . By the first of April we were beginning to make our arrangements . . . and along about the middle of May we bought the Petrolia property . . . which cost thirty thousand dollars. . . . It is the one field that produces helium gas in commercial quantities [and] therefore has a splendid future."[22]

An aggressive mail-order campaign was launched to raise capital and persuade holders of stock in other companies to merge with PPA by exchanging their old stock at a rate of par plus 25 percent. Nearly a quarter of a million such letters were sent out, but the results were not more than enough to cover the costs of the promotion. Perhaps feeling it was image that was lacking, PPA then moved to the most exclusive address in Fort Worth, the elegant 24-story Farmers and Mechanics Bank Building.

This helped, but PPA's fortunes changed quickly when Dr. Cook hired a new "pen" in the person of Seymour Ernest Jacobson Cox. S.E.J., as he liked to style himself, was known as "Alphabet" Cox, for obvious reasons, but he also was known as "Lucky" Cox, as he always seemed to avoid running afoul of the law in a long career of questionable activities.

He had been born in Michigan in 1885 and started work at 12 as a bill-boy. He had also been a factory hand before finding his true calling as a salesman. After the Illinois blue-sky law had put an end to his line of dubious health-related promotions, he had left Chicago for the South. His "luck" had not been infallible, however. He had served a sentence for forgery in Illinois at the tender age of 15. He'd also been fined for fraudulent use of the mails in 1914 but had escaped what seemed would be a sure conviction in Houston in 1921, not long before coming on board with PPA.

The personable and irrepressible Cox had created and folded company after company in his charmed career. He lived the high life with his attractive wife, Nelda, even if his promises of fantastic wealth always seemed to elude his stockholders. His highly visible and flamboyant lifestyle included racing his $150,000 Curtiss monoplane, "The Texas Wildcat," for the James Gordon Bennett trophy in Paris, and the aura of aviation only added to his mystique of success and persuaded many to trust him with their money.[23]

The value of a good pen was inestimable, and Cox's gift for alluring claims and his ability to manipulate language to appeal to a potential investor's greed or feelings of inadequacy approached art. With Cox as pen the fortunes of PPA began to turn around.

Cox's talents were well compensated. He occupied a four-room suite in the Texas Hotel and drew a salary of $2,000 a week. Yet the money spent on Cox's abilities showed an immediate return. Mail poured into PPA's offices by the sackful. One of PPA's employees later recalled a typical day in the mail room: "Dr. Cook had a long table on which the contents of mail sacks were dumped and sorted. Bushel baskets were provided into which valuable contents of letters were placed. Checks, currency and money orders were placed in different containers. Many times these containers would be filled from one mail delivery. After the receipts were checked and counted, they were bundled, placed in a suitcase and carried to the banks."[24]

With Cox's genius at work, PPA took in half a million dollars in two months. By September 15, 1922, PPA was ready to declare a 2 percent dividend, which its promotional literature said would be paid monthly. By the first of October the company's advertising letters boasted an interest in more than 100 operating wells.

One of the most profitable aspects of the company's business had nothing to do with returns from its oil wells, however. It came from the printing and mailing of other oil companies' promotional literature, much of it of a questionable nature. In its on-site print shop scores of typists, stenographers and Address-O-Graph operators prepared more than 20,000 circulars for mailing daily, at a profit of 6 cents apiece.

But most of the company's cash flow derived from solicitations to exchange the stock of defunct companies with former interests in thousands of dormant acres of unproven oil potential—or no potential at all.

Most of these mergers were accomplished by a technique known as "special trusteeship." Often the trustee was O.L. Ray, a one-time officer of the defunct Dupont Oil Company, who was driving a bakery wagon when he came to Cook looking for a position with PPA. Ray, in the role of special trustee, solicited the stockholders of the target company by mail.

"After investigating every possible opportunity to better our position," one letter ran, "I have made an agreement very much to your advantage. . . . I have arranged for you to enter the Petroleum Producers' Association. . . . When you convert your stock into Association shares . . . your original investment will be well placed and thereafter you will be in a position for the double profit always possible in oil. . . ."[25]

Using this method and others, by the end of December 1922 PPA would merge 313 oil companies and capitalize them at $380,861,000. The exchange of old stock for PPA shares would net it nearly $90,000,000. Unfortunately, Dr. Cook's high-profile, spare-no-expense business methods swallowed up most of the money as it came in, leaving little for field operations.

More money derived from the selling of stock for oil speculations set up by means of a PPA loan, in exchange for a percentage of any profits that might develop. Two of these ventures were Amalgamated Petroleum, a company headed by S.E.J. Cox, and the Smackover Petroleum Syndicate under O.L. Ray.

Smackover was the latest sensational oil find near the town of El Dorado, Arkansas. It literally came in with a bang. A blown well of enormous gas pressure ignited in a towering finger of flame, which pointed to the likelihood of a great store of oil beneath the Arkansas fields.

In one of his promotional letters for the Petroleum Producers Association, Dr. Cook used the metaphor of the burning well to warn investors away from crooked promoters:

> I stood on a hill about a half a mile away watching this shaft of light and heat as its wicked tongues of flame leaped and roared. . . . I was standing there with the black of the night behind me and the clear white light of this burning well in front of me, wondering if possibly all this roaring fire wasn't in reality sent as a kind of warning to the fake promoters—the meanest men in the world—the most contemptible human rodents that ever breathed God's pure air.
>
> I don't believe that the man who would wilfully defraud the public and take from the investors who are willing to help develop nature's resources the money which they have so carefully saved, without giving them a fair return, deserves much better an end than might be typified by this flaming gas well. . . .
>
> I wonder after all if his Satanic Majesty isn't retaining just a little supply of the old fashioned hell-fire torment for the reception of a few phony promoters.[26]

The combination of Cook's conspicuous visibility and his former reputation in some quarters as someone not above phony claims himself, along with the presence of S.E.J. Cox, who had so recently slipped through the fingers of postal inspectors in Houston, made PPA a prime target for scrutiny.

In August 1922 Post Office inspectors had begun a limited investigation in Fort Worth into the practices of oil promoters. In September more postal inspectors arrived and were soon joined by Federal Trade Commission investigators. Together they leased a suite of offices that took up most of a floor downtown and settled in for a lengthy stay.

The chief postal inspector, John Swenson, became a familiar face at the offices of PPA, where he obtained Cook's permission to examine the files of the company. His inspectors took much interest in their contents. During the weeks they studied them, Swenson had long conversations with Cook and other officers of the company and traveled throughout Texas and Arkansas to look over PPA's field operations.

When a government auditor asked to see the books, the secretary-treasurer, Fred K. Smith, assured Cook there was nothing out of order but cautioned him about surrendering them voluntarily. But Cook granted the request anyway, repeating to Smith what he had often said to Inspector Swenson: he had nothing to hide.

PPA certainly looked successful to the general business community. It had become one of the largest employers in Fort Worth among the independent oil companies, and the tip sheets touted its potential:

It is automatically conceded, Dr. Cook has built the Petroleum Producers Association into one of the dominating independent operating concerns in the Mid-Continent field, owning more than 100 actual producing oil wells—several additional ones under process of drilling, and his success can be attributed to the fact of confining his expenditures and operations to exclusively proven acreage.

They are almost certain their next dividend is going to be of such an enormous cash expenditure, as to shock many, if not all, of the other independent operators.[27]

There were others, however, who not only doubted PPA's prosperity; they doubted its president's honesty as well. In New York on January 10, 1923, Herbert S. Houston addressed a meeting of the Associated Advertising Clubs of the World. Houston, once a member of the Peary Arctic Club, was now chairman of the National Vigilance Committee, a consumer watchdog organization formed by the advertising lobby, and it had been watching events in Texas closely. He singled out a "gigantic stock reloading scheme" there for special mention. "This scheme led to the discovery of our old friend Dr. Cook," Houston told his audience. "He did not discover the North Pole, but we certainly discovered him, and it would appear that he is in a fair way toward securing as much publicity for his present exploits as for some of his earlier forays into the realms of fancy and imagination."[28]

The National Vigilance Committee sent consumers information circulars on the practices of suspect oil promoters for a small charge. When one of PPA's stockholders wrote to Cook about the things the committee said about his company, he responded personally:

You advise that you have paid good money for certain reports that were not favorable . . . alleging that we are a fly-by-night concern. . . .

. . . The concern that wrote you a letter to that effect is a bunch of black mailers. . . .

. . . It is true that the advertising clubs are kicking me and saying some very unkind things about my plans of operation, . . . but there is a cause for this unfair publicity, and the reason is because I positively refused to give the newspapers any advertising. . . .

The newspapers were instrumental in urging the Government to make an examination of the records of the Petroleum Producers Association, which has already been done, without criticism. . . .

. . . I have been vigorously assailed because I was the Cook who discovered the North Pole. Newspaper writers alleging that I did not discover the Pole, upon which they have no facts to offer, nor have they ever been able to repudiate the statement and the report that I have given in such a way as to convince any man with average intelligence, but that I accomplished the things I said I did, which fact cannot be disputed with any degree of accuracy. . . .

. . . It is unreasonable to believe a man having spent the greater part of his life in the furtherance of Civilization and the betterment of mankind, would engage in any kind of an unfair scheme or inaugurate any kind of methods that were of an illegitimate nature, and I therefore believe, the hardships that I have endured during my life, are of such a character as to convince you . . . beyond a question of doubt, that I have lived a life that is entirely worthy of respect and the approval of any intelligent man or woman in this United States. . . .

If you do, or if you do not, cooperate with me in the way of making an investment in the securities of this Association, you have my good will, and if there is a time in your life when I can serve you, irrelative and irrespective of the sacrifice that I might be required to make, I want you to feel perfectly free in commanding me, either day or night, because when the time comes in my life that I get so narrow minded in the recognition of humanity, then that is the time when I want to pass into the world beyond.[29]

But the National Vigilance Committee was not the first to impugn Cook's methods. Along with the other merger operations, Revere Oil and Pilgrim Oil, PPA had also relentlessly come under attack in a tipsheet called the *Independent Oil and Financial Reporter* for alleged fraudulent practices, and in November 1922 the *Fort Worth Press* had joined in, running a letter cryptically signed "Uncle Panther":

Dear Doc Cook:
I have read with much interest your fulsome "sucker list" letters telling of the great number of producing wells which the Petroleum Producers Association has acquired. . . .
. . . As I recall, you state in some of your literature that the Petroleum Producers Association owns or has interest in "upwards of 100 producing wells."
From Austin I learn that the total oil production you have reported to the state comptroller, in accordance with requirements of a state law, is 362 and a fraction barrels.
I await with greater interest than ever, doctor dear, your explanation.[30]

In truth, despite its air of prosperity and S.E.J. Cox's high-flown rhetoric, PPA was in deep trouble. Wells drilled in promising territory had not struck marketable quantities of oil. Just to keep the operation going, Cook had sold his interest in Cook Oil Company to the president of Empire State Oil, Walter Look, for $40,000.

The *Independent Oil and Financial Reporter* stopped its unfavorable comment after changing hands; it was rumored that a group of oil promoters, including Cook, had banded together and bought out the offending tipsheet to silence it. The *Fort Worth Press,* however, continued the attack.

The day after Houston's speech in New York, the *Press* published a big exposé of the merger companies in general and PPA in particular. Though this was its first open attack, it was not its last; it found many opportunities to mention the activities of "doctor dear" in 1923. The first incident of the new year had nothing to do with oil, however.

On January 30 at 10:45 P.M., a policeman, accompanied by private detective J.H. Griffin, entered room 818 of the Texas Hotel. There, the two reported, they found Dr. Cook and a lady who had apparently fainted upon the uninvited callers' arrival. They alleged that Cook was in possession of a pint of gin. Both he and the woman were described as "undressed" at the time of the unexpected intrusion.

Cook was arrested and taken to the city jail, where he spent the night. In the morning, before U.S. Commissioner George Parker, he pleaded "not guilty" to the possession charge and was released on $500 bond. Speaking through his lawyers, PPA's president denied that he had been in possession of any liquor or that the woman was even in the room with him. He insisted he was being "jobbed" by his wife, who had immediately filed suit for divorce.

In her filing petition, Marie Cook, who was said to be living in a separate apartment at the time, charged cruelty and inhuman treatment and asked for custody of Helen. She alleged that her husband had been infatuated with several women of late, and to satisfy her suspicions, she had hired Griffin, who had trailed him to the hotel. Marie Cook further stated that she had seen the woman with her own eyes and asked an injunction from Judge R.E.L. Roy to restrain her husband from withdrawing bank funds connected with three operations in which she said he had a controlling interest—PPA, Smackover Petroleum Syndicate and Vitek Oil—and also to prevent him from molesting her.

The next day, Cook was ordered to appear before Judge James Wilson on February 19 on the possession charge. Vice charges against him were dropped for lack of evidence. The divorce, however, would proceed.[31]

Soon, there were rumors that Marie Cook had entered into secret negotiations with her husband's lawyers and that he had agreed, among other considerations, to pay her $15,000. Even though Cook's lawyers now acknowledged that a woman had been in the room with Cook, they stated it was she who had rented the room and that she had enticed him into the predicament.[32]

The *Press* gleefully published on February 8 that Cook had "got it in the neck" in New York City when stockholders of the Allied Oil Corporation had razzed two of his "handy men," W.P. Welty and Fred K. Smith, out of town. The *Press* maintained that the whole affair was another fraudulent attempt on PPA's part to acquire the valuable property of another company.[33]

Welty, the "fake trustee," as the *Press* described him, had called a special meeting of Allied stockholders, but they would have none of his proposals, and he and Smith were asked to leave.

On February 9, the *Press* continued its tattoo, headlining DR. COOK, FRAUD ARTIST, QUITS PAYING DIVIDENDS. The article declared that PPA's highly advertised 2 percent monthly dividends had been suspended and again blasted Cook's company as a fraud scheme.

As a result, Cook filed suit against the *Press's* editor, Leon M. Siler, for $1,000,000. The suit, which accused the *Press* of "malicious and criminal purpose," took exception to the paper's various descriptions of Cook as a "promotor of gush and hot air, falsehoods and misrepresentations, trickery and fraud" and as a "faker, flim-flammer and fraud artist." Instead, his suit asserted that he was "a good, true and respectable citizen," held in "high esteem and repute."[34]

But it was not Dr. Cook who first got into court. He had other enemies besides the *Press.* On February 16 one F.H. McLaughlin filed suit in Judge Roy's court as a PPA stockholder, asking for an injunction to restrain Cook from dissipating the assets of his company. McLaughlin's suit asserted that "Cook and his associates have been carrying on a system of financial pyramiding" and had defrauded their investors by "holding out alluring promises and hopes of vast returns" and "from time to time paying out to pretended stockholders pretended dividends."

McLaughlin further alleged that PPA had made no profits or profitable investments and that its dividends were paid from money received from stockholders. McLaughlin estimated the assets of Cook's company at about $17,500, total, and said his suit sought to preserve these. It charged that the continued operation of PPA was "constantly creating debts, liabilities and obligations in vast sums of money, for which the stockholders will become liable" and asked that a receivership be declared.

Finally, the suit alleged that dividends had been suspended because they would amount to $120,000—more than the entire assets of Cook's company—and that the dividend was never intended to be paid but was merely a promotional promise to attract more money.[35] For himself, McLaughlin asked $1,000 actual damages and $11,000 exemplary damages from Cook and Fred K. Smith, alleging a conspiracy to harm and defraud him.

Cook's lawyers maintained McLaughlin was merely a PPA stockholder being used by a disgruntled promoter named F.W. Strang to get even with Cook. Cook's lawyers asked for an injunction restraining Strang from doing any more litigating against him in other people's names. At the hearing on Cook's request for the injunction, it was insisted that PPA was solvent and that Strang had already filed $2,000,000 worth of suits against the companies that he said controlled the *Independent Oil and Financial Reporter,* including one for $150,000 against Cook's.

Herbert C. Wade, representing Cook, said Strang had filed the receivership suit simply to embarrass Cook and that Strang had alleged Cook was part owner of the paper that had libeled him. Strang, Cook's lawyer contended, was on a vendetta against these men and was said to have declared, "I might go to jail or to hell, but I will take as many as I can with me."

At the hearing, Fred K. Smith, who identified himself as "auditor" of PPA, gave some insights into its financial structure. He testified that PPA had no outstanding debts and that it owned 80 to 90 wells that were currently producing oil but that the production of these wells was not sufficient to cover the operating expenses of the company. Smith estimated PPA's cash on hand to be $15,000. When asked if PPA was making money, Smith said he "thought so."

Smith denied PPA had any interest in the tipsheet in question but said Cook had paid $1,000, chargeable to his personal account, to the paper's business manager. Surprisingly, Smith asserted that PPA had never merged any companies but "simply merged the stockholders." "There have been no mergers of companies in Dr. Cook's organization," he said. Finally, he stated that there was no aftermarket for PPA certificates, as they were non-negotiable.[36]

After Smith stepped down, Dr. Cook testified before Judge Roy that he had never had any interest in the *Independent Oil and Financial Reporter*. He said he owed Strang nothing and had refused to settle out of court for $750, as Strang's lawyers had proposed, because he "regarded it in the light of being a blackmail."

He also denied he had attended a conference at which a plan to buy the *Reporter* had been discussed, but he admitted he had lent its publisher, Chester Bunker, $1,000. Though he had not given it to help buy out the *Reporter* specifically, Cook said, he had not put any restrictions on Bunker's using it as he saw fit, but again denied he knew anything about oil promoters trying to get hold of the paper.

As far as Strang's estimate of PPA's net assets, Dr. Cook said that PPA had no fixed capital but that approximately $2,000,000 in outstanding stock had been issued. He estimated PPA's total assets at $100,000, this being in land owned in fee, leases, oil wells and equipment.

Neither McLaughlin nor his lawyers appeared to defend their petition, so Judge Roy dismissed their request for a receivership.[37]

Some of his friend's mounting troubles filtered back to Dr. Thompson in Chicago. He wrote to Cook of his concern, who in reply tried to minimize matters:

> Most of the difficulty, which you have been hearing about, has been adjusted and cleared up. On the whole, it is a great deal of the "Tempest of the Tea-pot" and we seem to be scheduled to have newspaper criticism, favorable and unfavorable for the rest of our days.
>
> An Organization as large as ours is at present, with immense interests extending all over the United States; and any line of business would be sure to create a lot of enmity, and in this position, we can not escape a certain amount of trouble. But we are going

right along, minding our own business, and from a legal standpoint, all of our cases have been disposed of.

It is with me a big problem to determine upon the line of development, during the next few months: whether to increase or de-
crease our activities. . . .

It is also a very vital question: whether to handle and develop
the Syndicates, as we have in the past. . . . All of these are doing
very well, under the present excitement.

We are expecting a big boom in the Corsicana Field within the
next thirty days, and if this develops, we will have something very
valuable in the way of proven acreage. . . .

. . . As to the Stock you mention, . . . the Postal Authorities have
been examining the Books of Revere for the past three months,
and during the time of the Federal activities, it did not seem wise
to have the Stock re-issued. They have about completed their action now, and we ought to be able to get the Stock very soon.[38]

But the settlement of the McLaughlin case had by no means disposed of
Cook's legal woes, nor had the federal activities quite run their course. A
grand jury had been empaneled on March 12, and on April 3, 1923, a commissioner's warrant for Cook's arrest for using the mails to defraud was issued.
Dr. Cook, who was in Little Rock when he heard about the warrant, returned
to Fort Worth and immediately surrendered to federal marshals. He was
arraigned before U.S. Commissioner Parker, waived examination and was
released on $25,000 bail in connection with his PPA activities and $15,000
for those related to Revere Oil Company. The next day, F.W. Strang again petitioned that PPA be placed under a receiver.

On April 20 the grand jury handed down 18 separate indictments against
Cook and 91 other officers and employees of 14 oil companies, including 20
employees of the Petroleum Producers Association. The indictment against
PPA consisted of 12 counts, which alleged that Cook and his associates, in
founding PPA, had "devised the said scheme and artifice to defraud" and that
"the defendants schemed and planned that they would make and cause to be
made to the persons to be defrauded false and fraudulent pretenses, representations and promises, orally and by letters, circulars and advertisements, and
through agents, as to the business, operations, profits, earnings, dividends and
prospects of said Petroleum Producers Association." Each of the counts gave a
specific example of an alleged fraudulent action by the persons named in the
indictment, concluding that they "at all the times mentioned herein were
known by the defendants, and each of them, to be false and untrue . . . with
the purpose and intent of inducing the said persons to be defrauded to pay to
them, the said defendants, large sums of money for shares or units of the said
Petroleum Producers Association" and having "devised the said scheme and
artifice to defraud . . . did unlawfully, wilfully, feloniously and knowingly, . . .

place and cause to be placed in the Post Office of the United States. . . . certain postpaid postal card and writing to be sent and delivered by the said Post Office Establishment of the United States. . . . "[39]

Henry Zweifel, the district attorney, said the government estimated that the fraudulent activity of the indicted promoters was vast, with 100,000,000 to 200,000,000 shares of bogus stock having been sold to as many as 2,000,000 victims. Now that the government had uncovered them, Zweifel confidently pronounced, fraudulent oil promotions would be ruthlessly pursued until they were stamped out.

Incoming mail to the companies under indictment was cut off. Each piece received was stamped "FRAUDULENT" by postal authorities and returned unopened to the sender. In PPA's case, a day's mail amounted to as much as $25,000 in investment capital. With no incoming money, insolvency was all but assured for the companies under indictment, regardless of the outcome of their officers' trials.

Cook's lawyers, Herbert Wade and Joseph Greathouse, went into conference with visiting Federal Judge Benjamin Bledsoe, who gave them until May 14 to file petitions in the case. On that day, they filed to quash the indictment. The motion said the indictment was vague, and in any case, since the others indicted were only agents and employees, Dr. Cook wanted a separate trial. Some of the individuals indicted, the petition stated, were not even connected with PPA on the dates cited in the indictment. Further, the petition alleged that John S. Pratt and David Cahill, special prosecutors working for Assistant Attorney General John H.W. Crim, were improperly in the grand jury room at various times, and that two of the jurors were not drawn from the jury box but were "bystanders and interlopers." The petition further alleged that when it was found that the grand jury was two jurors short, two had been brought in without an order being entered for the action.[40]

Cook's motion to quash was thrown out on the grounds that he had not acted expeditiously in challenging the competency of the grand jury, and preparations were begun for the coming trial. As chief defense attorney, Cook chose Dallas lawyer Joseph Weldon Bailey.

Bailey, who had been the junior senator from Texas for two terms between 1900 and 1913, was a piece of local color and regional history. He had been a political phenomenon. First elected to the House of Representatives, he rose to the position of House minority leader in his third term on the strength of his oratorical skills. But after being elected senator, he had become disillusioned with the tilt of the national Democratic Party toward the philosophy of its Progressive wing; he resigned at the end of his second term.

He still looked the part of the stereotyped southern senator, even at this late date favoring a frock coat and broad-brimmed hat. His voice was mellifluous and his speeches eloquent. He knew every oratorical trick in the book and was well schooled in political trench warfare. Described as being possessed of a "nauseating vanity," he was said to have more personal enemies than any man in Texas. Whatever the trial's outcome, the choice of Bailey ensured it would not be dull.[41]

Though PPA had been hit hard by the indictments, its case did not go to trial first. That dubious honor went to the General Lee Oil Company, against which the Justice Department felt it had the strongest case. Lawyers for its promoters, Charles Sherwin and Harry Schwarz, tried to have the indictments thrown out, maintaining they had been granted immunity by federal agents and that the courts had no authority over a trust estate. But both of these contentions were ruled against, and the case proceeded to trial late in May before Judge Bledsoe.

The government brought 78 witnesses forward to prove the claims of the company's promoters mendacious. Upon conviction, they received ten-year sentences, were released on $30,000 bond and promptly fled to Mexico. "General" Lee got two years in Leavenworth.

Though it was hoped the result of the General Lee case represented local sentiment, the government could not be sure that the favorable reaction to the stiff sentences was really an approval of its campaign of oil prosecutions in general, since the Ku Klux Klan was very strong in Fort Worth and both of the convicted promoters were Jews. So special prosecutor John S. Pratt had already suggested to Assistant Attorney General Crim several ways of strengthening the chances of further convictions. One was indictment in other states chosen after a careful canvass of the records of the judges presiding in those jurisdictions, so that if a change of venue was necessary, it would maximize the chances of a result favorable to the prosecution. If the trials went forward in Fort Worth, however, additional judges would be necessary, and judges from these chosen jurisdictions would be given preference.[42]

On July 10 Cook was again indicted in Cleveland in connection with the activities of the Revere Oil Company and Pilgrim Oil, two of the companies that had used his facilities to print and send out promotional literature. Placing the threat of indictment over the defendants in every state where PPA stock had been sold was a strategy special prosecutor David Cahill thought would yield several benefits. "The morale of the defense is now somewhat broken as they realize the power of the government to prosecute them all over the Union and the purpose to use that power," he told Crim. ". . . I firmly believe from what I hear that one result of other indictments in other districts will be to drive some of the defendants into the arms of the government here and to materially strengthen the government's cases."[43]

By the end of July Zweifel advised setting over all of the oil fraud cases for 30 days, scheduling the PPA trial for September 3 with Judge James C. Wilson presiding. Wilson was a worry to the prosecutors because he was known to be lenient in such cases, but Zweifel advised Crim "inasmuch as Judge Wilson has been so nice and agreeable about our entire campaign of Special Judges, etc., I feel like that we should not do anything to interfere with his plan [to try the case himself] at this time."[44] Zweifel didn't think it really mattered who tried the case, since he thought only Cook and one or two others would not plead guilty.

While legal countermeasures against the indictments continued throughout the summer, some of the indicted officers of PPA, including O.L. Ray, called at Zweifel's office to sound him out on the consequences of a guilty plea. Ray asked what sentence, for instance, Cook would get if he pleaded guilty. Zweifel suggested to Ray that he would recommend a fine and two years in the penitentiary but stipulated that approval of this plea bargain by the trial judge would be necessary.

Zweifel took this development as a hopeful sign that a lengthy and expensive trial would not be necessary in the case of PPA and informed Crim that "Viscoid tendered," the code words for Dr. Cook, might be ready to strike a bargain:

> Be advised Viscoid tendered and associates seeking settlement and advise me your view on settling basis of year and day with stiff fines for tendered and principal associates with fines for minor ones.[45]

Ray then took Cook with him to see Zweifel, but the doctor was apparently not interested in pleading guilty. Throughout the two-hour interview, he insisted he had done no wrong and talked about his hopes for PPA. The doctor asked Zweifel whether there was any way to fix things up without having to go to the penitentiary; Zweifel replied that the only way to escape this punishment was to fight the case. But Cook insisted he was perfectly willing to incorporate his company and conduct it on any line that seemed right and fair. At this point, Ray told the doctor there was no use in further talk. For himself, he said, he was ready to plead guilty and take his punishment. Dr. Cook, however, left the interview without indicating what his course would be.[46]

On September 17 Cook's defense team met with the federal prosecutor to discuss ways to avoid the expense of a long trial. After the conference, Senator Bailey advised Cook to turn down all plea bargains, as Zweifel had implied that the best the doctor could do would be a two-year sentence and a fine of $5,000 if Cook pleaded guilty. Bailey was confident that with Judge Wilson presiding, he could do better than that even if he was convicted. But things did not work out as he predicted.

Zweifel had scheduled so many trials that Wilson's docket was filled to overflowing. "Special judges" had been lined up to assist—judges known to be tough on offenders in similar cases.

Because of the government's need for more time to prepare its complex case against PPA, and a desire to get past the heat of summer in Fort Worth, the court date had already been pushed back to October 1. But it soon became obvious that the overcrowded docket would not allow the case to come up even then. By October Judge Wilson had been bumped from the case in favor of Judge Grubbs from Alabama. Then the trial was postponed again to October 15; when an appeals court judge was taken ill, Judge Grubbs was called to sit in his stead.

Cook's lawyers were left guessing as to whom they might draw next, most bets being on Judge Bledsoe. But unexpectedly, Judge Wilson invited John M. Killits from the federal bench in Toledo to hear the case. Bailey set out immediately to see what he could learn about Judge Killits.

Through contacts with several of Killits's enemies in Ohio, Bailey discovered that Killits could not be more different from kindly Judge Wilson. He had been on the federal bench since 1910, had tried fraud cases in Ohio, New York and California, and was known to be very tough. He was also very stubborn and had once been cited for contempt of a Supreme Court order, but this had been dropped when he subsequently complied. He was also said to control his court very tightly and to be so uncompromising that his actions in several instances had caused a decision to be overturned on appeal.

With such strong personalities as Bailey and Killits involved, a collision seemed inevitable, and with the steady stream of pretrial publicity that Zweifel had been feeding to the local press, the public and the reporters looked forward keenly to a spectacular show trial that the government hoped would put an end to fraudulent oil promotions in Texas.

CHAPTER 23

At the Head of the Fraudists

SPECTATORS BEGAN ARRIVING AT THE COURTHOUSE EARLY TO GET THE CHOIC-
est seats for the opening session of the trial on October 15, 1923. Standees
lined the back of the courtroom by the time the bailiff announced that all
should rise and shouted, "The Federal Court for the Northern District of
Texas is now in session—God save the United States and this honorable
court!"

The selection of the jury and alternates took up all of the morning and
the first part of the afternoon sessions. Seven of the 21 defendants, it was
learned, had put in a plea of guilty and would be sentenced at the end of the
trial, but the trial's key figures, including Dr. Cook, had pleaded not guilty.

The doctor sat behind his attorneys, shuffling through a large stack of
papers before him on the table:

> Graying hair, falling long over his neck and temples; parted on
> the left side and combed back on the right.
>
> Stolid expression on a somewhat seamy face, with a distant look
> in "cold gray Norse eyes" wearing shell-rimmed glasses part of the
> time; reddish mustache; a face old and heavy.
>
> Black sack coat, black necktie loosely adjusted; white shirt.
>
> Unpressed black trousers.
>
> Betraying no nervousness; his demeanor indicating rather a
> mild curiosity in the proceedings; only a frown now and then to
> show personal concern.
>
> That's Dr. Frederick A. Cook as he sits in federal court sur-
> rounded by fellow defendants and attorneys, in his trial for use of
> the mails to defraud.[1]

When the jurors had finally been seated, John S. Pratt, special assistant to
the prosecutor, outlined the government's contentions. At the outset he acknowledged that the case was very complex. He confidently asserted, however, that the proof would show beyond all doubt that the Petroleum
Producers Association was founded by Frederick A. Cook as a scheme to defraud and that Cook was not an oil man but a confidence man.

In a rambling opening statement, Pratt outlined for the jury the way the Petroleum Producers Association allegedly operated. It would obtain the stockholders list of some defunct or insolvent company and send letters urging them to exchange their stock for PPA securities by paying a 25 percent fee over the par value of the stock they held. For example, if a stockholder had 100 shares with a par value of $1 each, he could receive 125 shares of PPA stock by the payment of $25 and an exchange of his certificates. To induce this exchange, the prospective stockholders were flooded with literature touting the advantages of merger with PPA, including a 2 percent dividend paid monthly on all outstanding stock, an interest in 100 producing oil wells and many other assets, all of which, Pratt said, were nonexistent or valueless.

Though PPA literature said that such a merger would resuscitate stockholders' investments by providing more efficient management and development of their assets, Pratt alleged that this was "bunk," since only a dozen of the more than 300 companies merged by PPA had any real assets whatsoever beyond their stockholder lists and valueless stock certificates.

Further, Pratt asserted, the prosecution would show that PPA made attempts to merge many companies without any authorization and that some of the companies targeted had protested or brought legal action to prevent solicitation of their stockholders by PPA's "special trustees."

Stock in PPA was also sold directly. Pratt alleged fraudulent promises of future profits, as well as misleading statements about current oil revenues, had been made to induce previous investors to buy more shares at $1 each. Pratt also asserted that a supposedly independent brokerage under one H.O. Stephens had simply been a front, controlled by Dr. Cook and intended to boost the stock of PPA and other companies in which Cook had an interest.

Yet another scheme, said Pratt, was to advertise that all remaining PPA stock was about to be sold to a syndicate for $2 a share but that the present stockholders could purchase it up to a certain date at the old price of $1 a share. This, he alleged, had been merely a deceit to panic stockholders into buying more worthless shares.

All these schemes and others, Pratt claimed, were parts of a plan to induce potential investors to send good money after bad, and although he admitted that PPA itself did have some assets, he maintained they could not possibly support the fantastic future profits forecast in its avalanche of promotional literature.

When Pratt started to read from some of the circulars issued by PPA, defense attorney Joseph Weldon Bailey arose to object. The point of the opening statement was not to present evidence but to tell what the proof would show, he said. He was overruled. The judge allowed Pratt to continue.

This exchange, though mild, was the first of many that would grow more and more bitter as the trial progressed. Like Killits, Pratt was from Ohio, brought in specially to try the case; he was also a friend of Judge Killits's, and there was some speculation in the press that Bailey would appeal to sectional sympathies to win favor for his clients from the southern jurymen.

For all of these fraudulent actions, Pratt continued, the defendants were responsible. From a table piled high with a mountain of envelopes, Pratt produced the deed of trust, which he introduced as Government Exhibit no. 1. It gave Dr. Cook virtually absolute control over the Petroleum Producers Association. Although it had been signed by two other men who had not been indicted, one supposedly the head of the directors' board, Pratt excused this by saying they never were asked for advice nor had they ever attended a PPA meeting, and their names were used without authorization. The unauthorized use of signatures was a common practice in PPA operations, he asserted.

Senator Joseph Weldon Bailey.

At the conclusion of the prosecution's opening remarks, Judge Killits ended the afternoon session by announcing that the trial would be lengthy and any defendants desiring to absent themselves from the courtroom during the proceedings would be allowed to do so upon application to the court.

The next morning Senator Bailey stated the case for the defense. It was quite simple, he said: the officers of PPA had every honest intention; they had simply failed to find oil.

"The defense will show," began Bailey in his rich voice, "that Dr. Cook formed the Petroleum Producers Association to take over a few rundown companies, rebuild them, and put them on an operating basis. Cook is not guilty of any fraudulent scheme of promotion as the Government charges....

"Cook would have made a success of this enterprise had not the Government come along and interfered when it did."[2]

Herbert C. Wade then made a brief general statement for the men he represented. Cook had agreed to shoulder the expenses of most of the defendants, and his own lawyers represented them as well. Wade was followed by the lawyers for S.E.J. Cox and Ambrose M. Delcambre.

A stir was caused by the appearance in court of Marie Cook. This was thought remarkable, considering the scandalous allegations she had brought against her former husband only a few months before. Nevertheless, she sat next to the doctor and now seemed to be on the most friendly of terms with him. With rare exceptions, this was the position she would occupy every day of the trial.

The prosecution then called as its first witness C.W. Whitmer, a real estate operator from Freemont, Iowa. Whitmer had purchased 200 shares of the Burk-Hoyt Oil Company and had received what the prosecution said was a typical run of letters urging him to come into PPA. The first was a "teaser"— a postcard to arouse curiosity:

> An important letter which brings a message and documents from a long silent friend – one you have probably misunderstood – should reach you in a few days. Watch for it – I must be certain of its delivery – hence this card. If it does not get to you within a week, pen me a note.
>
> F.A. Cook[3]

The "long silent friend," it turned out, was the failed Burk-Hoyt Oil Company, and in the weeks that followed, Whitmer was deluged with literature urging him to merge his stock with PPA. The letters read to the jury were filled with extravagant promises and descriptions couched in colorful language.

Whitmer was told that PPA offered him "stepping stones to greater results for small companies—sustained effort and assured returns to investors—conservation—economy—vigorous drilling activities—profits to stockholders." He was also apprised of "the men who manage the affairs":

> This association was founded by its president, Dr. Frederick A. Cook, petroleum technologist, who for the past ten years has devoted his time to the oil industry. The sec'y-treas. is F.K. Smith, an aggressive expert in finance and organization. The directing board is headed by E.A. Reilly, who drilled the famous Trapshooter wells of Kansas. His associates on the board are: T.B. Ridgell, former District Attorney of Breckenridge, closely allied with the wonderful oil development of Texas; and T.O. Turner, one of the best known field managers of the Southwest.[4]

After reading about their 2 percent monthly dividends, Whitmer exchanged his shares for the required fee. In subsequent mailings Whitmer was told that the price of stock had been raised to $2 a share; the company was about to develop what it believed was the main oil pool in Texas, and it was drilling a well expected to produce 20,000 to 30,000 barrels per day. PPA expected its stock to surge. "Fifty dollars a share will be cheap for it when our first well is completed," one letter read, and the $2 stock offering was about to be withdrawn "for reasons that must be perfectly obvious to you."[5]

These letters were followed by others pushing the can't-miss potential of a syndicate being developed to exploit the new finds and urging Whitmer to buy personal leases in the new concern when it was floated. The letter was signed "Yours for quick profit and a sure one. Frederick A. Cook."[6]

Although the PPA literature built up its officers' credentials and the company's potentials, it was just as careful to warn Whitmer of "the meanest man in the world"—the fraudulent promoter:

He robs the investing public not only of their cash, not only of the money which they might use themselves to build up a competence for their old age, but he robs them of that vastly more important thing – he robs them of civilization's greatest asset, he robs them of a belief in human nature and their fellow man. . . .

. . . But just remember this: Any time any investment is offered to you; and any time any great new opportunity is presented, it is the brains and integrity of the men backing the proposition and not the proposition itself in which you are investing.

Look before you leap.

Think before you write the check and then think five times before you send it.

And this applies just as much to any investment that I might offer you. . . . I am going to do my best to protect those who become associated with me against the loss of money if you will simply be guided by my experience and take advantage of the knowledge that I have gained through years of dealing with oil men and promoters.

With the assistance of a good clearheaded investigator I am preparing a series of articles on How to Avoid The Pitfalls of Fraudulent Financing. . . .

. . . Yours for better business and higher business ideals.

Frederick A. Cook[7]

Another letter signed by Cook assured stockholders that he himself had invested $50,000 in the company, that he controlled no stock and that there was no inside group getting special treatment.[8]

Though he had been promised monthly dividends and had gotten one, Whitmer next learned that for efficiency's sake, PPA would henceforth pay dividends quarterly. This was to save the expense of sending so many small checks, the letter said. But PPA's solicitations continued to come.

"Eastern Brokers," he was informed, were requesting a block of stock at double par, but in fairness to the current stockholders PPA would allow Whitmer to double his holdings for only $1 a share—an offer limited to 30 days. When no order was forthcoming, Whitmer received another letter urging prompt action:

From the Bowels of Mother Earth and direct from the reservoir of Nature's Eternal Gift, the Petroleum Producers' Association and their shareholders are today receiving credits from more than 100 actually producing wells, and with many more under process of drilling in the most profitable oil fields in the entire world.

We say it with cash dividend checks—not promises or flowers. . . .

. . . Should this letter find you short of funds, then take advantage of the partial payment plan where we have provided a way for men and women to grasp an opportunity that is of a meritorious nature by paying 25 per cent cash with their subscription and the balance in 30 and 60 and 90 days. . . .

Even if it becomes necessary for you to borrow the money, the conditions entirely justify the sacrifice and you owe it to yourself and loved ones in providing for those who are dear and near. . . .

Sincerely Yours,
F. A. Cook,
President.

P.S. . . . Fear no embarrassments by inviting your neighbors and friends. I am with you with clean hands to the end of the world.[9]

At this point, Senator Bailey objected that neither Cook nor any man on trial had written this letter. Prosecutor Pratt retorted that Cook was nevertheless responsible for literature sent from his office and that the letter was written by H.O. Stephens, one of the defendants, with the knowledge and approval of Dr. Cook.

Bailey again objected, saying that the prosecutor was testifying while not on the stand. He was overruled by Judge Killits; the senator registered his exception to the ruling.

Pratt continued to read letter after letter into the record, each of which seemed more fantastic than the last:

The blast of the whistle has already been sounded announcing the landing of the Petroleum Producers Association safe into the clutches of riches, by the penetration into the greatest oil field on earth which is Smackover, Arkansas, adding immeasurably to the enormous volume of holdings we already own. . . .

Startling it is, but ever so true. I have witnessed the belching forth from Mother Earth a week ago, a well estimated making more than 25,000 barrels of oil, worth millions . . . erupting from the earth unto a volcano. You will be overjoyed, as I am, when you realize the enormous credit the shareholders of this Petroleum Producers Association are receiving from this gigantic gusher. . . .

. . . It is your privileged right to own an opportunity to make money. If you have made some, it is your right to make some more. If you have not, here is your opportunity to start on the road to prosperity.[10]

Bailey once again objected, saying that Cook had never written such a letter, but the judge ruled that if it had been sent out from his office, it did not have to be his physical effort. When Bailey persisted that a citizen was entitled to protection against the introduction of testimony that was not competent, Judge Killits admonished him that there was no need to make such a suggestion to the court, adding, "But it might appeal to a jury for a little while, until the jury is instructed. . . ." This statement drew a heated objection from both Wade and Bailey.[11]

Whitmer testified that he continued to receive mail from PPA describing itself as "the most substantial organization for fabulous dividends of any organization that has ever offered to the public their securities" and that those securities "will forever stand the acid test." In one letter, Cook assured him that he was "sweating blood for you and the other shareholders" and was "instrumental in the saving of your losses that could have been saved in no other way than by the exertion on the part of myself of unusual efforts, foreseeing the possibility of serving humanity in a clean and legitimate way." Cook further assured him that PPA was "an Association with immeasurable possibilities, stupendous and gigantic returns."[12]

In addition to the endless flood of PPA literature, Whitmer explained, he also began to receive mail promoting the Smackover Petroleum Syndicate. If anything, this literature, signed by its president, O.L. Ray, was even more aggressive than PPA's. In one circular, Ray promised, in his folksy way, the greatest strike of all time:

> RAY PAYS
> 100% CASH DIVIDEND TO HIS PARTNERS. . . .
>
> Old partners, I want to tell you right here and now that I don't take off my hat to any operator in the Smackover field. . . .
>
> I got to looking over these here papers and watching what the other fellow was doing to see if all my partners were getting a square deal. . . .
>
> . . . Then I see when they was declaring a flock of 100 PER CENT CASH DIVIDENDS. THEN AN IDEA STRUCK ME. THEN I SAID TO MYSELF, RAY, OLD HORSE, maybe some of your partners kind of feel themselves slipping and don't think they're in on one of the best bets in the Smackover field. . . .
>
> . . . I put over a deal that allows me to pay a 100 per cent cash dividend to all my partners that were in with me on this deal on January 12, 1923, and I'm going to lay the cash to them on February 12th next. . . .
>
> . . . I'VE GOT THE WORLD BY THE TAIL AND A DOWN HILL PULL AT SMACKOVER I EXPECT TO WHACK MORE THAN A TWO MILLION DOLLAR JACK POT WITH MY PARTNERS.[13]

Again the defense objected: the letters of O.L. Ray were immaterial to the indictment. Once again it was overruled. When Sylvester Rush, who had been examining Whitmer for the prosecution, was finished reading one of the PPA letters, he asked Whitmer, "Did you make a fortune?" Whitmer replied, "I haven't seen it yet"—to snickers from the spectators. The total proceeds on his investment were $3.10 in dividends. Most important, he said that he had been persuaded to exchange his stock by the statements made in the PPA literature he received—especially the promise of 2 percent monthly dividends.[14]

During cross-examination, Senator Bailey tried to establish what would be the two thrusts of the defense's rebuttal: that the witness had made no complaint against PPA until he was solicited to turn in the letters by U.S. postal inspectors and that since he had previously invested in an oil company that had made no returns, he surely should have been aware of the risk involved in another similar investment.

Whitmer's testimony required more than ten hours to take, and reporters quickly figured that if all the government witnesses who had been subpoenaed took as long, the trial would last 215 days at nine hours a day. This was not desired by either side, so they agreed to avoid repetitions by reading into the record only unique parts of future exhibits.

Most of the subsequent witnesses would not require nearly so much time. The prosecution had already established the trend of its case. Witness after witness would be put on the stand simply to identify the letters the prosecution characterized as "lurid" and "spectacular" as actually having been received through the U.S. mails, sent by a company that had fulfilled none of its promises.

Two other things had to be established, however: that the claims in the letters were fraudulent and the promises were therefore unfulfillable, and that the defendants had known this and had consciously intended to defraud by the use of those promises. Under the law, this was what was termed "guilty knowledge."

After Whitmer was dismissed, a series of witnesses were called to lay the groundwork for such proof by linking Dr. Cook to the letters of Amalgamated Petroleum and the Smackover Petroleum Syndicate as well as those of PPA and, in so doing, give evidence of repeated use of the same fraudulent means to sell worthless stock.

A multigraph operator testified that the proofs of PPA letters were routinely left on Cook's desk for final approval by either him or his private secretary. An advertising jobber testified that copy for Ray's Smackover Petroleum Syndicate, though prepared by others, was given final approval by Cook.

The volume of letters was testified to by Virginia Brown, one of the many "girls" employed to get out mail for PPA. She said as many as 300,000 pieces of promotional literature had left its offices in a single week, though she admitted this was extremely exceptional, estimating an average week at about 50,000.

At one of the numerous objections of Senator Bailey and Henry Kahn, who was representing S.E.J. Cox, Judge Killits cited a similar case to assert what the jury had to consider.

"[The jury was] obliged to look to human motives, to get inside the man's mind and see the movements there, because in that kind of a case, as here, guilty knowledge was an important and an indispensable ingredient the State had to prove. . . . The State must go further and prove that he knew it was counterfeit; that he had reason to know it was counterfeit, and among other things allowed to be established in that case, not as conclusive, but as one of the incidents of the case to make up what the proof of guilty knowledge which the State had to establish beyond a reasonable doubt. . . ."[15]

Such legal arguments and the repetitious testimony caused interest to wane considerably by the fifth day of the trial. Only a handful of spectators heard the testimony open with Thomas Laity, a farmer from Ada, Kansas, who had requested the return of his money when he read in a Dallas paper that Dr. Cook had been arrested in a hotel room with a woman who was not his wife. Judge Killits ruled the charges against Cook that had angered Laity were inadmissible but said the witness could state that he had demanded his money back "for certain reasons." In reply to Laity's demand, Cook wrote asking him not to be influenced by "scandal sheets," including the *Fort Worth Press:*

> This is not the first time that the Press have ever endeavored to persecute me, but each and every time I have come through with my colors flying, for I am dealing absolutely on the square with each and every shareholder. . . . My skirts are clean; my character is pure; my conscience is undisturbed. . . . I might add that as far as my adversaries are concerned, they may continue their campaign to the bitter end, but the results they are endeavoring to obtain will never be acquired.
>
> Poverty or ill health or adverse criticism might hinder a man's progress, but they cannot kill his ambition or his soul or the determination of his will, or the wonderful brilliance of his mind, if he is made of the stuff from which the world's leaders are moulded. . . .
>
> The affairs of this Association, I feel, are growing in leaps and bounds to such a magnitude that it is almost uncomprehendable by the most optimistical investor, therefore, it might be, if you will stop and consider, this, that my enemies are jealous of. . . .
>
> I am not appealing for sympathy. I care absolutely nothing for sympathy, but it injures my great feeling of pride to know that even one of my many kind friends will quietly turn round and accept the charges of the Press as being correct, and condemn me before the bar of justice has spoken.[16]

Laity, however, continued to ask for his money. He did not get it, nor did he get a penny in dividends, he said.

Under cross-examination, Laity admitted he had invested in 15 other oil companies without success and knew oil investment was risky but repeated that he had been induced to exchange his stock by the "good promises" made in PPA literature.

When an attempt was made to dissociate Cox from all transactions after December 1, 1922, the date he had moved out of PPA's offices, it was denied by Judge Killits, who held that "any one who sets a train of circumstances in motion having an unlawful purpose in view, he cannot escape . . . by merely withdrawing from the association."[17]

Judge Killits then struck at one of the contentions of the defense by saying, "It will be no weakening of the Government's case to show that anybody went in with eyes wide open.

"The test of this situation is whether the scheme itself was a fraudulent scheme, no matter how extravagantly conceived, and whether to assist in the execution of the scheme, there was a prostitution of the mail service of the United States. That's all there is to it."[18]

However, Killits was quick to qualify his remarks by saying to the jury, "You must take from what you have heard, no impression whatever as to what the court considers the merits of this case at any time during the progress of this case.

"If some impression comes to you that the Court is passing on the facts in this case, you will not let that have any weight with you, because you will be ultimately charged to disregard that altogether."[19]

Senator Bailey, in reply, stated the defense's main theory. "We stand on the proposition that our plan was an honest one," he said, "and we spent the money received under it in an honest effort to make an oil company, and if that is our case we are not guilty, and if that is not our case we are." To which the court conceded, "There is a very clearly defined line of demarkation here. If you are honest, no matter how unfortunate your scheme might have been, how bad your judgment, if you are honest then of course you are not guilty."[20]

On October 19 Judge Killits wrote to Judge George Hahn, one of his friends in Ohio, the first of a series of letters giving his impressions of the trial as it progressed:

> The trial is well under way. The sixth witness, out of 283!! whom the gov't has summoned, is now on the stand. . . . Chief for the defense is Senator (ex) Joe Bailey. He's some politician and, perhaps, he can't help bringing into the trial the tactics of a politician. It is hard to keep back the thought that many of his observations to the court are specially for jury impression. . . . I suggested that to him Wednesday. He got it very quickly and became very sore, but since has been as mild as a sucking dove. . . . If I weren't so confounded lazy I would keep a diary. . . . You see the job a Northern judge [has] to keep sectional lines in the dark.[21]

During the sixth day of the trial, the prosecution attempted to link Cook directly to the composition of the letters sent out over his name. Postal Inspector John S. Swenson testified that Cook had told him during their many conversations that he had approved the letters.

Next, the prosecution started to introduce evidence that the companies being merged were without assets and so demonstrate that PPA's only interest in them was to obtain "sucker lists." Charles E. Taylor, former mayor of Little Rock, testified that this was true in the case of the Arkansas Chief Gas and Oil Company, a firm that had no assets whatsoever beyond its list of 1,000 stockholders, which he sold to R.L. Maxwell, one of the defendants, for $250.

More hints about the trend of the defense's case were given when Senator Bailey indicated that the success of the Standard Oil Company and other large concerns would be held up as examples of enormous sums that had been made by small investors in oil stocks in the past, thus proving that Cook's promises of big returns on small investments were possible.

The second week of the trial opened with arguments about whether PPA stock had been unfairly exchanged equally with worthless stock of companies that had no assets, as well as being sold at $1 par. Senator Bailey objected that this was immaterial to the indictment, but he was overruled by Judge Killits, who said such action would constitute discrimination and therefore fraud and that any evidence of a scheme to defraud, even though not specifically mentioned in the indictment, would be allowable.

In the afternoon, F.T. Connor of the Allied Oil Corporation testified about the failed "unauthorized takeover attempt" the *Press* had reported, which had been stopped only by a court injunction.

Senator Bailey, in his cross-examination, attempted to prove that Allied was in fact dormant and therefore that it was perfectly proper for PPA to solicit its stockholders. He also offered that the solicitor's calling himself a "special trustee" implied no official capacity. To an objection, Judge Killits ruled that the status of Allied did not seem material. The jury, he said further, must decide the intent of the solicitation on the basis of what a "man of average understanding" would infer from a letter purporting to be from a "special trustee for stockholders," that is, whether the "special trustee" had some official capacity. The judge then took a swipe at Bailey's contention of the previous week about Standard Oil by saying, "I will say right now, you are not going to load this record up with a lot of extraneous proof as to the value of oil property that does not figure directly in this case." This drew a vigorous objection from the senator, which ended in the judge's asking Bailey to take his seat.[22]

The next day another row developed between Bailey and Killits over the senator's contention that despite its previous agreement, the government was reading the same circulars over and over to imprint them on the jurors' minds. Bailey then turned toward the jury and remarked that the only institution that had made any money out of the mass of literature sent out by PPA was the government, in what it got from the postage stamps used to mail it.

At this Judge Killits exploded, calling the remark "pure buncombe." Bailey excepted to the court's characterization of his remark. "I treat the Court respectfully—intend to," the senator exclaimed; "I think I am entitled to be treated respectfully by the Court, and to characterize what I said as 'buncombe' is not respectful treatment."

"I don't withdraw it," said the judge.

"Of course you don't, Federal judges never do," retorted Bailey.

Killits then requested that the senator face the court when addressing it. Bailey angrily excepted again. "Just a moment, until I get through with this situation," interrupted Killits as District Attorney Zweifel attempted to continue his examination of the witness. "I have been somewhat considerably embarrassed because Senator Bailey suggested his hearing was somewhat deficient, and unfortunately I am in the same situation. I can hear a man plainly when he looks at me when talking to the Court and not to the jury."[23] Bailey excepted to the judge's remarks.

On the ninth day of the trial, Martin Jachens, a disabled veteran, testified that he had actually made money on oil stocks—in a company operated by S.E.J. Cox—though he had lost money with PPA. Cox's secretary, R.D. Mooney, then testified that he had written a number of letters for Cox pertaining to the merger of some of Cox's companies with PPA and that Cook had changed some items in the letters to make them more to his liking before sending them out.

Further links between Cox and Cook were testified to by another witness, a former PPA employee named Herman Danielson. He said that Cox had gotten 15 percent royalties on all stock sold on the strength of his letters written while at PPA. When Cox's letters had gone out, he said, PPA's receipts had jumped from $1,500 a day to more than $5,000. Soon after this, Cox had left PPA and established the offices of Amalgamated Petroleum in the Neil P. Anderson building. Mooney had said in his testimony that he believed some disagreement with Cook over the authenticity of this increase in receipts had caused Cox to quit PPA.

The evidence concerning Cox continued the next day when T.E. Nolan, one of the original trustees of the Amalgamated Petroleum Company, took the stand. Nolan testified that Amalgamated was the brainchild of Frederick A. Cook and that Cox was its guiding hand.

Senator Bailey objected that the testimony about Amalgamated's dealings was immaterial, as they had not been mentioned in the indictment; besides, he said, after December 1, 1922, Amalgamated had been separated from PPA. When the prosecution contended that the evidence it was introducing would not be held against Cook, Judge Killits allowed its admission.

During cross-examination, defense counsel W.P. McLean tried to get Nolan to admit that he had had differences with Cox. Nolan denied this. McLean also asked if he knew Cox had invested $20,000 of his own money in Amalgamated and that he drew no salary. Nolan denied knowing about Cox's investment but confirmed that he drew no salary, adding that his expenses were all paid out of company money, at any rate.

Ten days into the trial Henry Zweifel received permission to hire a man to guard the case files, after he reported to the Justice Department that an attempt had been made in the night to steal them.[24]

The next day the prosecution produced 14 more witnesses who identified reams of letters and repeated testimony about unfulfilled promises and unauthorized merger attempts. Repeated, too, were the contentions of the court that Senator Bailey was facing away when addressing it and "looking at the clouds" outside the window. Bailey objected strenuously; then the judge said that if it was inadvertent, it should be corrected.

The prosecution next attempted to prove that the assets of PPA were so inconsequential that they did not, by any stretch of the imagination, justify the claims made in the company's promotions. Witnesses testified that nine of the wells in which the company had interests in the highly promoted Petrolia field altogether pumped only 6.1 barrels of oil per day that could be credited to PPA. Eight more produced a total of only 2.1 barrels per day to their credit. Another yielded 0.6 barrels. The entire oil income from these wells was estimated by W.R. Mitchell, a buyer of crude oil, at $2,100 for the entire period from June 1, 1922, to February 8, 1923—virtually the whole life span of the Petroleum Producers Association.

But even these amazing figures failed to overshadow the star witness of the day, one Mary A. Phillips, who limped to the stand in her faded blue suit. Mrs. Phillips identified herself as a 66-year-old widow living solely on the pension of her husband, a deceased Civil War veteran. She related in a thin and quavering voice that she had repeatedly written to Dr. Cook regarding PPA's endless solicitations, explaining that she was in poor health. Cook, she said, had written her back urging her "to look at the bright side of things; that most always black clouds had a silver lining." She said she had made payments as small as 50 or 60 cents at a time.

Mrs. Phillips testified that she had literally sold the carpets off her floor to buy more PPA stock. "I repeated so many pitiful stories," she said plaintively, "and they were all the truth that I thought I could not tell him anything more to satisfy him—that he would take pity on me and would not send to me for more money."[25] When the prosecution asked exactly what carpets she had sold, it was quite enough for Bailey, who objected to her whole testimony. Judge Killits sustained the objection to the identification of the carpets but allowed her other testimony to stand.

In cross-examining her, Senator Bailey developed that Phillips had personally been brought down from Coshocton, Ohio, by the local postal inspector to testify because her health was so poor. She maintained, however, that she had not informed anyone of what she would testify to, not even on the way to the trial. Upon leaving the witness stand, Mary Phillips stopped at the defense table and, shaking her finger in Dr. Cook's face, berated him by shouting, "They ought to put him at the head of the fraudists! That is where he belongs!"[26]

The next day the newspapers carried stories that Cook had authorized his attorneys to turn over $100 in cash to Mrs. Phillips to compensate her for her losses.

The first direct mention of Cook's polar claims surfaced the thirteenth day of the trial in a letter read into evidence in which were the words, "I am the Cook who discovered the North Pole." Most of the day's 13 witnesses were meant to hammer home the same message to the jury: the companies merged had no properties, so PPA's statements that they would turn these defunct companies into prosperous ones by developing their assets more efficiently were obviously fraudulent.

One witness, H.E. Robinson, a defendant who had pleaded guilty, testified that in September 1922 PPA and two other "merger" companies had contributed toward buying out the *Independent Oil and Financial Reporter*. Robinson further stated that he had to persuade Cook to go in on the deal, since the doctor said he thought that it might cause trouble later, but that he finally went along with it at the recommendation of Fred K. Smith.

On October 28, during the cross-examination of Robinson, two incidents brought to a head the growing enmity between Senator Bailey and Judge Killits. The first concerned one of Bailey's private papers that had gotten mixed up in the papers of District Attorney Zweifel. When Senator Bailey aired the incident in front of the jury, Judge Killits said it was trivial, insinuating that Bailey's comment was part of a movement calculated to "create the impression that there was an atmosphere of unfairness, of chicanery . . . toward one or more of these defendants."[27]

Again, Senator Bailey took vigorous exception to the court's remarks. But the bursting point came when Bailey tried to get Robinson to admit that he had cut a deal with the government. "Didn't the United States either through Mr. Zweifel or through some other agent or representative, agree that if you would plead guilty they would let you off with a fine?" he asked.[28]

Judge Killits instructed Robinson that he need not answer, since no officer of the government could make any such agreement, but not before Robinson had denied it. Then there was this exchange:

> Mr. Bailey: It may not, if Your Honor please, be binding on the Court, but they made it; they made it.
> The Court: Go on. He has answered the question; go on. Wait a moment. You say they have made it?
> Mr. Bailey: Yes, not binding the Court, but the district attorney has said to people — Now, probably I ought not to say this in the presence of the jury.
> The Court: You ought not to say what you said.
> Mr. Bailey: I will step there and tell the Court what I know.
> The Court: No, no, no, no, no. We won't talk about it at all.
> Mr. Bailey: Have the record show that the Court objected to the question as I state it, that I stepped to the bench and offered to state to the Court privately why I had done that —
> The Court: Just a moment.
> Mr. Bailey: But the Court declined to hear it.

The Court: This Court will not permit Senator Bailey to testify to anything unless he takes the witness stand. . . .

. . . The Court is not interested in Mr. Bailey's information, and don't need it.

Mr. Bailey: I know.

The Court: Just a moment, Senator; you have a bad habit of interrupting. The Court refused to hear Senator Bailey's statement because this is not the time for any statement of that kind to be made at all, to any person, much less to be made openly as a positive fact, in the presence of this jury. . . .

Mr. Bailey: I will ask Mr. Wade to conclude the examination of this witness.

The Court: The Court will direct Senator Bailey to conclude the examination. It is his witness.

Mr. Bailey: Senator Bailey does not feel that he can do justice to this examination under these circumstances, and declines to proceed.

The Court: Do you ask the Court's permission to withdraw from the case?

Mr. Bailey: If the Court keeps this up, I will have to do it.

The Court: If Senator Bailey keeps this up the Court will have to speak more sharply to him.

Mr. Bailey: All right, let it stand either way. I am not in the habit of continually having a Court lecture me. Never before has a Court refused to let me state to him the basis upon which I had made a statement in the presence of the Court, and to which the Court objected. Now, under those conditions I don't feel like I am willing to continue this examination.

The Court: Senator, I have been looking for just this scene for some time. It does not surprise the Court at all; I have expected it; I have expected that your methods would bring you to just this point. This is not the first time that in the presence of this jury you have asserted a fact which you should have testified to under oath. . . .

Now, what you might have had to say to the Court . . . would not have mended the situation in any way . . . the situation that you made deliberately — I withdraw the word "deliberately" — that you made yourself; it would not have mended it any; it would have made it worse. . . . If it were a fact, you could use it to the discredit of certain witnesses; that is, you could use it argumentatively, I mean. . . . You know why — you know why you put the question to this witness. . . .

Now, I am not saying that that was a plan on your part, but that was the effect of what you offered to do, and that is the reason why the Court would not hear you. . . .

Now, if you feel . . . you are disqualified from cross-examining the witness . . . the Court will waive the situation and let Mr. Wade do it, because we want the defense to have the best chance possible, and want the defendants to be properly tried by the Court and by the jury, without any reference to what their counsel may do.[29]

Killits then relented, allowing Wade to examine Robinson on the matter of any "deal." But under repeated and strenuous questioning, he was unable to shake the witness from his testimony that there had been none and, specifically, that Zweifel had not said if he pleaded guilty he would be let off with only a fine. Robinson also maintained that he had not told the district attorney what his testimony would be.

As Wade cross-examined the next witness, he was interrupted by Judge Killits, who took umbrage at his line of questioning. At this, the defense vigorously objected. This outburst on top of all that had gone before was too much for Judge Killits, who dismissed the jury and called the defense team to the bench.

Killits said he had the "belief" that the defense was baiting the court, making insinuations against it and addressing the court in a disrespectful and indiscreet tone. He again complained that Bailey did not face the court when addressing it. The judge conceded that calling Bailey's remark about postage stamps "pure buncombe" might have been improper but said there was provocation for it.

"There are many things that have happened," he told Cook's lawyers, ". . . that don't get into the cold record. . . .

". . . I never presided in a case where there was that sort of atmosphere towards the court that exists here; this submissive air of martyrdom, this assumption of flagellation; this insidious suggestion that the Judge on the Bench is a partisan, not so much in words as in the very way in which you sit on your chairs, and the way in which you act."[30]

The judge admonished the defense, lest they violate their oaths as officers of the court, to conduct the trial so as to give the jury confidence in the bench. He simply wanted to receive the respect due the bench, he said, and he would forget everything that had happened to this point. Killits conceded that "probably we would not find any single instance, or perhaps not a combination of several instances [in the trial record] which would seem to justify what the Court has said just now . . . but much of it has been in the line of attitude and inflection and conduct; not in words spoken."[31]

The judge called for a fresh start and asked for the jury to be brought back, but Senator Bailey interrupted, saying he had "a very unpleasant duty" to perform. Bailey then called for a mistrial on the grounds that the court had accused the defense of misconduct.

After some discussion Judge Killits ruled on the motion: "Now, gentlemen, I am not surprised that this matter came up at this time. I have been looking for it because it has been moving this way. I say again that I am not concluding that it was deliberately pushed to this point as a purpose—as a studied plan of campaign; I am not prepared to say—utterly disclaim saying any one of you have been unprofessional in your handling of the case.

"This motion is denied. You may have your exception."[32]

Defense attorney McLean then made a rambling and disjointed speech that sounded like a peace overture, saying the judge had been influenced by what he had heard on the street and that the attorneys just wanted to get on with the trial.

And so the trial continued, but the truce, if anyone thought one had been made, did not last long; by the end of the day W.P. McLean had accused Judge Killits of intimidating the jury. The judge gave McLean until the next day to apologize for such a "grave accusation." "You will give until tomorrow fifty years and I won't do it," McLean retorted, "because I think your remarks are prejudicial. . . . I will never apologize to you as long as I live!"[33]

Before counsel, Killits had been careful not to say he thought the defense unprofessional or their actions deliberate, but he was more candid when writing to his friend Judge Hahn:

> The motion which was denied Tuesday to break the case was on the ground that the court had lost confidence in counsel for defense. As to one of counsel the assertion was true, emphatically so. I have never seen a viler pettifogging shyster in my life. Arrogant, insolent, unfair, hypercritical and hypocritical – a combination of Uriah Heep, Pecksniff and Spenlow and Jorkins.[34] Except that two of the other counsel were, until checked, constantly drunk in court, and another is a shallow pated nervous firebrand, the eight average up well in all respects. . . .
>
> . . . When I sent the jury out last week, to clean up, I told him . . . that it was the thought of some observers that he was pursuing a course with a view of baiting me into some sort of indiscretion that the case might break. Then an amusing thing happened. Counsel McLean, who had been jovially and verbosely drunk for several days, interrupted to say something and said that more than a hundred citizens, in the banks, in his office, on the street corners, and about the court, had said to him that that was Baily's purpose but that I should be kind to the Senator because he was as God made him. My! how Baily liked that. . . . Will be here certainly until after Dec. 1.[35]

When Judge Killits ended that stormy session by telling McLean to come to court in a condition to address the bench in the right way, McLean said he would not come at all. Nevertheless, the next morning he apologized profusely to the judge, who accepted and instructed the jury to disregard the incident in their judgment of the defendants.

When testimony resumed, the defense continued trying to show that the prosecution's witnesses should have known from firsthand experience that oil investment was very risky business. One such investor, L.B. Wade, stated that "Dr. Cook's letter read so good I just couldn't help merging" and caused a ripple of laughter in the courtroom when he baldly admitted he "just took the gambler's chance."

Testimony concerning the personal visits of PPA agents disclosed that at least one represented the company as being backed by the world's largest oil producer, Royal Dutch Shell, and that not all stockholders were as complacent about PPA's dealings with them as the defense had attempted to show. One said he had sent copies of its circulars to the United States commissioner, declaring them "a bunch of swindlers that ought to be behind bars."

The collisions between the judge and the defense became even more frequent, with Bailey declaring at one point that he had never seen anything like the court's conduct in his 39 years of practice before the bar. And Judge Killits took extreme offense at what he perceived to be the senator's questioning of his right to examine witnesses, saying that the court had a right to see that the facts were developed and asking who dared to challenge the court's right to do so.

The government then tried to build a chain of evidence linking the brokerage house of O.H. Stephens to PPA. A stenographer testified that Stephens's brokerage occupied just one small office on the floor above PPA's offices; an advertising man testified that Cook had initialed Stephens's promotional brochures; and an equipment contractor testified that the office fixtures had all been lent to Stephens by Cook. The prosecution attempted to show by exhibits that Stephens heavily recommended the stocks in which Cook had an interest and that his brokerage was merely a front for another of Cook's elaborate fraudulent schemes to sell worthless stock.

The prosecution next called another defendant who had pleaded guilty: O.L. Ray, author of the colorful Smackover promotional literature already read into the record. Ray described how he had persuaded various officials of oil companies to sell Cook lists of their stockholders and testified that, in most cases, no properties or assets of any kind were included in the purchase price. Ray asserted that Cook knew they had no assets, though he could not say whether he had informed Dr. Cook of each and every company's condition. Later, he said that he informed Cook if there were assets left in a company. When Herbert Wade objected that his testimony was therefore conflicting and should be stricken, he was overruled by Judge Killits.

Ray maintained that as a man of little education, he was incapable of writing the merger letters to which his name was signed. When officials of other companies objected to PPA's merger attempts, Ray asserted, he went to Cook and advised him he had better drop the attempt. Asked what the doctor said upon receiving this kind of advice, Ray replied, "I would just go to him in a general way and sometimes ask him to send a letter and retract it; sometimes he did and sometimes he would tell me they would quiet down – soften up – that did not amount to nothing; let them rave."

"He said, 'Let them rave; they wanted a few hundred dollars; they would be quiet after a while.'"[36]

Ray stated that he had authorized his name to be used on just one letter, but he later found that it had been multigraphed onto 58 mailings of letters advocating the merger of companies, and when he asked what he would get for the use of his name, Cook replied "nothing," as he was paying all of the expenses. According to Ray, Cook did say, however, that he had a reason for using Ray's name so extensively; he wanted to get it before the public, since he planned on using Ray to promote a new oil syndicate he was going to launch. In all of these mergers, Ray said, he had no authority to say he was appointed or acting as trustee from anyone in the target companies, but only from PPA.

Under cross-examination, Ray said he had not investigated a single one of the companies to ascertain the condition of the properties. He also admitted that the Smackover Petroleum Syndicate was formed not by Cook but by himself, and that he himself had made the arrangements to sell stock through Cook and split the proceeds 50-50 with him. Cook's half would go to pay for advertising and for preparing and mailing Smackover literature. This arrangement resulted in the sale of $104,000 worth of the stock.

To write the material, he said, Cook hired a man named Lambert, but Ray admitted that the information about the Smackover syndicate contained in the circulars came from himself directly to Lambert. Ray further admitted that Cook's only connection with his promotion was the addressing and mailing of the circulars from PPA's office.

At this point the defense requested that all of Ray's testimony about the Smackover syndicate be disallowed, since the indictment referred only to the formation of PPA to perpetuate fraud in two ways: through the merger plan and by the direct sale of its own worthless stock. Bailey contended that the arrangement between Cook and Ray was a personal transaction not within the scope of the indictment and, therefore, inadmissible.

Killits, however, cited admissibility under the rule of "similar transactions"—which could be used to show a pattern of fraudulent intent—and Ray continued to testify. He said that he and Dr. Cook had jointly decided that to be a success, Smackover would have to pay a 100 percent dividend, as many of its competitors had done to attract investors. The money for this dividend came from an advance on a note, $4,800 from Dr. Cook himself; there were no revenues from oil at the time to justify such a dividend. Ray said that not only had letters promoting the syndicate been sent from Cook's offices but that he had supplied the names for solicitations from his "sucker lists."

Bailey again objected, saying all mailings made after Ray had formed his company should be stricken from the record as having nothing to do with the indictment and that Cook could not be held responsible for the contents of another company's advertisements, even if he had performed the service of sending them out. His objection was again denied.

Under re-cross-examination, Bailey addressed Ray's contention that he had not enough education to understand the letters sent out over his name, a statement that if true would protect him from "guilty knowledge." Ray, he maintained, was posing as an uneducated man but had been "smart enough to get out of this case."[37]

Bailey got Ray to admit that wells had been drilled for the Smackover Petroleum Syndicate with the intention of finding oil. Ray also admitted that on several occasions Dr. Cook had written to objecting oil companies saying he had been badly informed as to their condition and was dropping any further attempt to merge them into PPA. Ray, like Robinson before him, denied he had made a deal for leniency in exchange for testimony against the other defendants.

Under Bailey's questioning, Ray stated that it was never his intention to swindle anyone. When Bailey pointed out that he had pleaded guilty to having had such intentions, and that even if he had made misrepresentations, if they were not made with the intention of swindling, he could not be guilty, Ray seemed confused and restated that swindling was never his intention.

Postal Inspector J.S. Swenson was recalled and occupied the stand for most of the following day, testifying to his investigation of PPA and its field operations. Swenson said he had asked Cook to turn over a list of all leases, royalties, properties and production, but that when he received the list it had no production totals on it. What Swenson found in the field, he said, was a pattern of exaggeration. In one case a well continually advertised as yielding 25,000 barrels of oil a day was producing only 500.

Swenson admitted that Cook had said he was welcome to any information he wanted and that if he found anything wrong he would be glad to correct it. Bailey then asked him if he had pointed out anything that was in error in PPA's advertising letters. Swenson said not specifically, but stated that he had told Cook that the whole merger plan was wrong. When Bailey asked Swenson if he knew that H.O. Stephens had written his own brokerage letters, Swenson volunteered that Stephens had told him that was not true; that he had submitted all his copy to Cook for approval.

Bailey then questioned the way in which the fraud order against PPA had been issued, alleging that it had been rushed through on May 7, 1923, without giving Cook's lawyers time to respond. Swenson confirmed that the hearing and issuance of the fraud order had taken just one day but insisted there was nothing irregular about it. There had been a ten-day notice given, he said. A wire from Bailey asking to keep the hearing open had been received, said Swenson, but only after the order had been issued when no one appeared to represent PPA at the hearing.

Swenson's testimony was interrupted to call R.C. Lomax, auditor of the State Comptroller's Office, to testify to the actual oil production of PPA as filed quarterly at Austin. He reported that the four quarterly reports, signed by either Cook or his production superintendent, showed a paltry total of 5,709 barrels with a value of $7,022.

In rebuttal, Bailey tried to demonstrate that though the oil runs were small, they were showing a steady increase, that the figures did not include revenues from Arkansas or Oklahoma, where PPA had additional holdings, and that they included no royalty incomes whatsoever.

On November 7 S.E.J. Cox returned to court after an absence of nearly two weeks. It was said he had been attending to field operations and had brought in a well.[38] Many of the other defendants had also taken advantage of the judge's ruling that they need not be present during the trial to look for work or attend to other business.

George A. DeMontrand, another defendant who had pleaded guilty, in emotional testimony, outlined his role as a PPA scout. He said he had been paid $11,000 for the lists he had obtained of 40 to 50 companies that Dr. Cook wanted to merge. DeMontrand said Cook told him not to tell Swenson what he had been paid for the lists. When he told Cook he thought the deal was crooked, DeMontrand testified, "He told me that he had worked for Humanity's sake, but now he was working for F.A. Cook, was the very words he told me. He told me from now on out he was working for F.A. Cook, that is the very words he told me."[39]

Among the other witnesses in the trial's third week was Milton Lory, a journalist who testified that a *Pictorial Oil News* item praising Dr. Cook as the savior of the small investor had been written in PPA's offices as a collaboration between himself and S.E.J. Cox.

Damaging figures were offered in the testimony of an expert accountant, H.B. Matheny, who had examined PPA's books. He testified that the books began in March 1922 but were somewhat incomplete before July 13 of that year. He said the books were turned over to him by Fred K. Smith under the instructions of Dr. Cook. These included the regular books and books of accounts, including cash books, general ledger, record of cash receipts and disbursements, bank statements and canceled checks, bank passbooks and a separate book including a record of oil production. Cook also turned over a large number of canceled personal checks for examination, since he was in the habit of giving his personal checks for expenses early in the history of the company. Matheny also said he had access to all of the company's files.

The accountant stated that the entries in the books were complex and it was necessary to reclassify many entries to make sense of them. His examination had taken nine weeks. The books showed that Cook had directly advanced $53,643.17 of his personal funds to PPA and had been repaid all but $10,651.45. Other personal checks brought the unpaid advances to more than $21,000.

Tables developed by Matheny from PPA's books showed that the company had operated at an enormous loss amounting to $306,719.69 up to March 1923. By comparison, the total income from oil production and royalties was a mere $14,468, and PPA's bank balance on January 31, 1923, stood at only $5,660.77.

Most of the income was derived from the sale of stock in the amount of $2,030,000, which, since it was outstanding, Matheny said should be added to the company's deficit. When asked the book value of this stock that had been sold at $1 or $2 par, Matheny answered 9.3 cents per share.

The accountant testified that the company had never actually paid the monthly dividends that had attracted so many investors. PPA had paid two dividends, he said, one in cash and one partially in stock six weeks apart, and although PPA letters declared it would thereafter pay 6 percent quarterly dividends, none of those had ever been paid, either. In fact, he asserted, such a quarterly dividend, if paid, would have required an outlay of $120,000—far more than the company had in cash at the time.

The photostatic reproductions of the tables prepared by Matheny that were handed to the jury showed that most of the money collected from stock sales had been spent to operate PPA's office. $50,492.80 had gone for postage and envelopes alone—80 percent as much as the entire expense over the same period for all field operations, $63,916.62—while expenses associated with the acquisition of stockholder lists exceeded $85,000.

The books disclosed evidence that supported some of the prosecution's allegations, among them the $1,000 paid to the fund to buy the *Independent Oil and Financial Reporter.* The contention that Cox had dissociated himself from PPA when he moved to his own office was contradicted by subsequent payments to him well beyond that date. Examination of the books also showed absolutely no properties acquired by any mergers, with the exception of the Rose City Petroleum Company.

Using the tables, the prosecution elicited testimony from Matheny that the first dividend PPA had paid, in the amount of $10,054.21, could not possibly have been paid out of oil runs, as there had been no oil income up to the date it was paid. At the time of the second dividend of more than $19,000, PPA had oil revenues amounting to just slightly over $1,000 to its credit. Prosecutor Pratt pointed out that paying dividends from stock sales, which he contended had been the source of the dividends, was illegal, and that PPA knew it was, since it had stated this fact in some of its own promotional literature.

Matheny's tables also disclosed the infinitesimal nature of some of the interests in the "more than 100 actually producing wells" held by PPA. In one case it owned a 0.000162 percent interest, which entitled it to one barrel in 6,000 produced.[40]

Matheny stepped down so that Paul Vitek, another controversial oil promoter, could be called to identify his books and testify to his arrangement to have Cook act as his agent in selling stock in the Vitek Oil and Refining Company.

Matheny then resumed the stand to testify that his examination of the Smackover Petroleum Syndicate's books, and those of the Vitek Oil and

Refining Company, showed that Cook had received enormous sums of money from his interest in sales of the stock of these companies—$260,699.96 from the sale of Vitek stock alone.

Under cross-examination, Matheny confirmed that Cook had not objected to an examination of PPA's books, all the while asserting he was an honest businessman. He also conceded that the treasurer, Fred K. Smith, was cooperative in explaining his accounting system. Only the oil production record had not been handed over immediately upon request, he said.

Matheny was asked whether the audit he had made of PPA's books showed them to be regularly kept or if there were changes or erasures in them. "There were a good many accounts which were not included in the PPA books," Matheny explained. "The accounts which were in those books were of such a nature that it was necessary to make many reclassifications and adjustments of items, particularly in connection with the accounts receivable to which had been charged hundreds of items."[41] When pressed if there were any irregularities, such as mathematical errors, he said, "No attempt as far as I could see to cover up anything. Whatever irregularity, if you call it such was one of omission rather than one of attempt to cover up something."[42] "They do not show [debts outstanding] in any instance excepting a few small items that had to do with the purchase of furniture or office equipment which have not been paid for," he added.[43]

Defense counsel Wade wanted to know how the witness could say that PPA took in only $440,000 but managed to lose $1,600,000. Matheny explained that the outstanding stock was a liability and that they had sold more than $2,000,000 worth, so it was simply a matter of subtraction. Wade maintained this was absurd, since a company could not lose money it never had, but Matheny defended his figures. Wade also developed that there was nothing on the PPA books of any consequence regarding the activities of either O.L. Ray or Paul Vitek. At the end of the accountant's testimony, the prosecution rested its case, having called 160 witnesses.

As had the prosecution's, the essence of the defense's case could be discerned in the testimony of its first witness, J.Q. Corbett, an oil driller, who testified about the efforts the defendants had made to find oil. For the most part he, and those who followed, asserted that the attempts had been real, and that all drilling locations were in areas where they had every expectation of success. But in the end, all these wells, even those that had struck oil, failed to yield significantly for either Amalgamated Petroleum or PPA.

At 3 P.M. on Friday, November 9, Dr. Frederick A. Cook was called to the stand. The doctor began his testimony with great deliberation, seeming to weigh each word before he said it. Cook went briefly into the history of his experience in oil, starting in Wyoming in 1916. He recounted how he had come to Texas and decided to stay, and told a little about his various Texas Eagle ventures. He then described why he had decided upon the merger scheme to build up his Petroleum Producers Association.

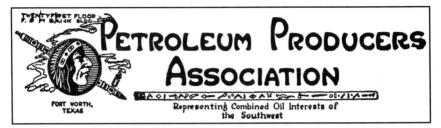

"The fact that the Texas Eagle was combining with the Revere Oil Company, approved by the receiver and the order of the court convinced me that was a reasonable method under which many other companies of that type could be handled," he began. ". . . Now that was the theory that I had in mind when I began to develop the idea regarding the Petroleum Producers Association. . . .

". . . We learned as we progressed . . . that it took a long time to get in the stock, to transfer the properties. It was practically impossible in the beginning to say just what the properties were, or what the values were or what the outstanding indebtedness was. . . . So we gradually developed our elastic system in the first stages of the limited merger plan. . . . We used the word 'merger' in a rather limited way. . . . In other words, the idea of a complete merger was seldom undertaken and could never be finished for a long time. . . . In that spirit we gradually got to the point where we outlined the plan of special trusteeship that has been brought up so often."[44]

The doctor then explained the rationale behind the "special trustee" method of merging companies: "Sometimes that trustee was appointed by an officer of the company; . . . more often he was asked to act by myself, on the theory that since we would succeed to the stock of the inactive company we acquired, our interest would be exactly the same as that of the stockholder. . . . In those cases we sent out, first a letter, which letter was so arranged as to be suitable to nearly all cases. We of course made some mistakes."[45]

Though the doctor admitted that O.L. Ray had done "about as he told" in his testimony, he said that Ray had been enthusiastic about his role and had asked to be a special trustee for as many companies as possible. Cook denied that he had advised Ray to pay a 100 percent dividend on the Smackover Petroleum Syndicate stock but said it was true that PPA had an interest in more than 100 wells, though he admitted they did not produce much oil.

Cook maintained that all merger activity had ceased after the postal inspector had called it wrong. "About the first of December of last year we had decided for various reasons to discontinue taking over companies," he said. "Scouts were being called in. . . . Smackover at that time was beginning to be the rising star of the East for oil. . . . Ray suggested that he organize a syndicate and he desired to be the sole trustee. He asked if I would advance him some money for that purpose. He asked if I would sell his stock, to which I replied in the affirmative."[46] Beyond that, however, Dr. Cook denied having anything whatever to do with O.L. Ray's business.

The doctor flatly contradicted Ray's testimony that he had attempted to take over any going concern against the wishes of the officers, and in the instances in which this had happened accidentally, the pursuit of the company had been dropped when he realized his mistake, he said. He also stated that far from selling stock to people who could not afford it, PPA had sent out a half-million circulars in which he advised potential investors not to invest money they had saved to buy a home, which read in part: "A home for the family is far more important in the quest of happiness than the best and most profitable investment in the world. Neither wealth, power nor fame are worth the risk of the loss of your home. Do not take a chance. Buy that home first."[47]

After two and a half hours, Cook was asked to step down and S.E.J. Cox's secretary, R.D. Mooney, was called to refute the testimony of Thomas E. Nolan that Amalgamated Petroleum Company was Cook's brainchild. Mooney disclosed that after Inspector Swenson had begun his investigation, Nolan and Cox had gotten into a fistfight, and after being knocked down, Nolan had angrily declared, "That lick will send you to the penitentiary." Mooney testified that Cox had instructed the officers of Amalgamated Petroleum not to accept money from anyone who spoke of sacrificing the necessities of life to buy stock, and to use only truthful statements in advertising literature sent out by the company. He defended Cox as honestly looking for oil and testified that Cox was the largest stockholder in the company with $17,000 worth, and that he drew no salary.

When the trial resumed the next day, Dr. Cook was recalled. Cook denied any financial interest in the Amalgamated Petroleum Company or any connection with the letters sent out to promote it, once it had been established independent of PPA; all he had gotten out of the deal was a piece of property that was put into PPA, he said. As for letters written for PPA, Cook admitted he had given Cox information to help him write them but insisted he gave only information he had been able to verify. When asked if he had ever made a statement in any letter that he knew to be untrue, Cook replied, "I certainly did not."[48]

Cook said that Welty and Smith had acted on their own behalf when they solicited Allied Oil Corporation, that he owed no money to PPA but rather the company still owed him money, and that Paul Vitek had been the source of all the claims made for the oil wells at Vitek's Smackover operation. He had simply repeated Vitek's statements in good faith, all the while trying to get an accounting from him of the oil being produced there, but to no avail.

When at one point Dr. Cook tried to make an explanation after answering a question asked by the defense, John Pratt interrupted to say he had answered the question. To this, Mr. Linden of the defense team excepted, saying counsel could not tell his witness when to stop. Judge Killits supported Pratt, saying Cook should just answer yes or no. Herbert Wade then excepted to the court's remark, which in turn caused an exception by Sylvester Rush to Wade's exception, accusing him of misconduct in attempting to interfere with the court. Then another exception by Joseph Greathouse, followed by a speech on the government's methods in the trial, gave a further opportunity for Judge Killits to dilate upon what he perceived as his ill treatment by the defense team.

Did Greathouse know, asked the judge, that the continued exceptions to the court's statements were very annoying? Greathouse said he could answer the question, but if he did, the judge might send him to jail. When Killits called for a courteous answer, Greathouse said that if the judge insisted, he would "answer it sometime, your Honor, outside of the court room."

"You may be now approaching the jail in that sort of attitude," the judge replied hotly.[49]

Greathouse again excepted to the court's remarks and to Rush's tactics, and Rush chimed in with his own exception. As the lawyers approached chaos, Judge Killits moved to check the flaring tempers of both sides.

"I think counsel for the defense is very much out of order," he said. "... We do not propose to stand insolence and impudence and stage-plays from either side, and we may be pardoned on the assumption that we possess our own share of weaknesses of human nature to become irritated when exceptions seem multiplied. . . .

"All along through this case the court has realized that some of the counsel in it are more familiar with other courts than with this one, and having their training in courts presided over by a different judiciary; they may have gotten the wrong impression of what are the privileges.

"There has been an atmosphere throughout the entire trial of the case as though the law here were being administered in an unusual way; as though rights were being infringed upon. That is all very very annoying. . . .

". . . I have never been in a trial in my nineteen years on the bench, . . . when so many exceptions were taken to the exercise by the court of it[s] plain rights. Why we were not permitted to interrogate the witness on any question. . . .

"All you need to do is to say in the presence of the court you except to what the court has said without amplifying it by any exhibitions of temper, wounded pride or anything else."[50]

When Bailey began to raise further objections, Judge Killits refused to hear them and adjourned until 2 P.M. but first allowed the defense to introduce documents showing that attempts to correct errors in PPA circular letters had been made, and a directive to "adjusters" was put in evidence to show that effective December 1, 1922, PPA had stopped merging companies. These documents also stated that the company's sources of income included not only oil runs but also leases and other assets, supporting the contention of the defense that dividend payments were not from oil runs alone.

At the beginning of the afternoon session, Judge Killits was evidently still rankled by the scene that had ended the morning session. His first words were to the court reporter: "Mr. Reporter, the first thing you do, the Court directs you to enter an exception in behalf of every defendant on trial to what the court said—everything that the Court said at the close of the forenoon session, while this witness was on the stand."[51]

Senator Bailey said he did not wish to except to everything but only to the court's imputation that the words in the record were delivered in an offensive tone or manner. He also said he wanted to reserve an exception to the statement that "because one of the attorneys for the defendants had been trained in the emasculated judiciary system of Texas, he did not know enough about the Federal practice to properly conduct his client's case."

Judge Killits said he had "made no such remark as justifies any such exception as that," but Bailey insisted that the record would bear him out.[52]

During cross-examination, Dr. Cook had frequent lapses of memory. In one instance, he had trouble remembering many details about a transaction in which he had acquired a piece of property from the Doublehead Oil Company. Pratt tried to show that PPA had never obtained ratification from that company's stockholders before selling off some of its assets. After much wrangling, Zweifel requested that Cook bring in his files for the Doublehead Oil Company to settle the matter.

Bailey objected that the prosecution could ask for nothing from the witness, whereupon Judge Killits intervened and asked for the records. The defense demurred that it would be impossible to find all the transactions in Doublehead stock because of the way the filing system was arranged, but it was directed to make an effort to bring them to court, and the judge adjourned the trial for the day.

The next morning Cook was late for court; his lawyers said that he was still trying to gather his records. Zweifel then abruptly asked that the request for the records be withdrawn and testimony resumed.

When Cook regained the stand, the prosecutors dwelt on their contention that the Petroleum Producers Association lacked valuable assets. When they denigrated the original 121 acres conveyed by Dr. Cook to establish the company, saying they had no oil potential and suggesting their only value was as farmland for raising onions, Cook disagreed.

On the contrary, Dr. Cook asserted, he had so much faith in PPA's future that he had put much of his own money into it. In fact, he said, the company still owed him money. Prosecutor Pratt wanted to know how this could be, since the deed of trust that formed PPA stipulated that Cook was entitled to one eighth of all moneys it received from any source. Cook replied that he had never taken his salary or any royalty. "[In] my own judgment," he said, "I did not think I ought to take it until the time the company was in good shape, in a well organized shape, and paying it." Pratt jumped on this remark, asking if all of PPA's literature had not claimed that the company was already in such shape. Cook simply said that he was certain that it soon would be.[53]

The doctor defended the statements in some of the letters read in evidence that investments in PPA were as safe as in a bank by saying "investing in a bank is not safe," since several had failed just that year, and insisted it was comparable. He refused to admit PPA had no income from oil, not even enough to cover office expenses. "I don't know anything of that kind," he said.[54]

Pratt relentlessly pursued the source of PPA's dividends. When asked of his knowledge of the oil income his company had, Cook referred Pratt to his bookkeeper. But Pratt pressed on, trying to make Cook admit that there was little income from oil. "It was insignificant, wasn't it?" he asked. "It was small," the doctor responded. "It was not nearly enough to pay any dividends, was it?" Pratt persisted. "It was small," Cook repeated. "It was not enough at any time to pay your office rent, was it?" insisted the prosecutor. To which the doctor said, "Well, I don't think that is – I don't know."[55]

Cook maintained that he had other sources of income from which dividends could be paid, citing the sale of several properties in Oklahoma. He described a deal in which he said he had sold two pieces of land for $29,000. On close questioning, however, Pratt extracted the admission that only $500 had been collected from this transaction—in January 1923—long after any dividends had been paid out, but Cook maintained he would have been paid the money had the indictments not been handed down.

"But our dividends were based not upon any one thing," repeated the doctor, "they were based upon what we felt would result from the development of our production, our oil fields, our wells, and from the sale of properties."

"The fact is, isn't it, that the reason for paying the dividends was to stimulate the sales of your stock," declared Pratt.

"That is not a fact," retorted Cook.[56]

During his testimony, Cook displayed little knowledge of the inner workings of his own company, at one point not being able to recall the names of the men on its board of directors. He seemed especially mystified as to its holdings and financial status, at one point saying, "I looked at the books so infrequently." He also seemed willing to accept Matheny's evaluations of his company's records absolutely. This apparent lack of knowledge prompted Pratt to ask caustically just what his function was at PPA.

"Well, I came there about 6:00 o'clock in the morning," said the doctor, describing his daily routine, "before the help came in I reviewed to some extent the affairs of the day previous. . . .

"Then, when the help came along, I would talk to various heads of the departments; I would also talk to the men out in the field, or . . . go out in the field, and look over . . . possibly the contracts or agreements we had to make during the day, and then late at night I would stay there until ten and eleven o'clock at night; I would watch the general work being done at night."[57]

As his testimony continued hour after hour, Cook often mumbled his answers and had to be asked to speak up. He protested that Ray's and DeMontrand's testimony about his statements concerning unauthorized takeovers of going concerns was untrue. He also denied that he had used sucker lists or that he had ever heard the term until he had come to court, even though some of the PPA letters already read used it to warn investors against crooked promoters. When Pratt argued that merger was never his intention and never had, in fact, been carried out, Cook disagreed. But Pratt pointed out that the certificates were often never exchanged for the old stock and suggested that the sole purpose of obtaining the lists was to solicit 25 percent additional in exchange for PPA's worthless stock. He charged that since the "assets" of these companies did not exist or, at least, were never acquired, the whole merger plan to develop assets was fraudulent. To none of this would Dr. Cook admit.

Pratt next questioned him about his dealings with O.L. Ray and H.O. Stephens. Cook insisted that the "OK" he had placed on the letters of Ray's company were simply permissions to run the letters on the Address-O-Graph and did not reflect his approval of their contents. In the case of Stephens's letters, he did not repudiate them but denied they were anyone's responsibility but Stephens's, and now that he had heard them read, he said, the claims they contained made him "doubt as to the man's sanity."[58]

In response to questions by Pratt, he denied the testimony of Herman Danielson that Cox had gotten 15 percent of the profits from stock sales made as a result of his promotional letters. Further, he denied the contention that the $1,000 he gave Chester Bunker was paid to get favorable publicity or to buy off the offending tipsheet. He also denied approving, over the objections of Paul Vitek, the sending out of a photograph purporting to show a gusher that he knew was a fake.

Although he admitted that one of his meager wells had been advertised as a big producer, he said that he had corrected this as soon as Postal Inspector Swenson had brought it to his attention. In any case, he contended, it was oil industry tradition always to describe a well by the rate at which it came in, even if this level of production fell off later.

He maintained that he had none but honorable intentions. "In substance, I told Mr. Swenson that I believed we were an honest business," he said, "and we were within the law, and that if he found any errors, or had any suggestions to make, that we were ready to change. Then I also told him our office was open to him, and that he might have anything he wanted from our office."[59]

Why, he declared, he had put $65,000 of his own money into PPA. No, he said, the advisement that the stock would soon sell for $2 was not an inducement to buy more stock at $1. Finally, Dr. Cook replied to the suggestion that he had offered to sell his interest in PPA at any time after the indictment was handed down by saying, "Oh, no." With this he was excused after 15 hours on the stand.

During his testimony, Dr. Cook had disclaimed knowledge of most of the letters that had gone out over his facsimile signature. However, Judge Killits now said that Cook, as sole trustee of PPA, was responsible for all circulars sent out of his office whether or not he had knowledge of their specific contents.[60]

Bailey agreed to this only if the intentional scheme to defraud asserted in the indictment could be proven by the government. Killits conceded this point.

At this admission, the senator then declared that the only question in the case that mattered was whether or not Cook contrived a scheme to defraud, and everything else was immaterial. To speed up the process he proposed skipping several scheduled witnesses and immediately calling PPA's field manager to testify that it was actually actively engaged in the business of finding oil.

T.O. Turner testified concerning his experience during the 50 years of his working life, the last 26 in the oil business. He had met Cook in Wyoming in 1916 and had gone to work for him at PPA in June 1922.

When asked whether it was true that he was the vice president of the board of directors, he discounted this, saying the board never met, Dr. Cook preferring to conduct business in discussions with each department separately. Turner said he had told Inspector Swenson that if there was anything wrong with PPA's operations, he owed it to him to tell him about it. Turner said that Swenson had replied: "Well, Turner, I think you are all right. If they were all like you, we would not have any trouble."[61]

Turner testified that he believed that the Vitek well was capable of 25,000 barrels, since when he visited it in January 1923, he was told it was flowing 1,500 barrels "pinched down," a method used to control high-pressure wells. PPA, he said, had drilled nine wells while he was in their employ, and the expectations of finding oil at these locations had seemed good, based on the surrounding wells and topography. He said that PPA had 9,400 acres in leases, 120 tracts in which they had a royalty interest, of which 32 were actually producing, and that PPA had an interest in 174 finished wells, of which all but 18 were producing.

Turner also said that he had advised Cook against giving a dividend, because he wanted the money spent on more field operations to find oil. But Cook, Turner testified, wanted to declare the dividend, even though the company had not earned anything from oil.

Under cross-examination, Turner stated that some of the claims attributed to him were not correct, but he wished to explain what he did say. An argument over this ensued before he was finally allowed to relate how he had made speculative statements, informally, similar to those that appeared in PPA's circulars, but had made no absolute statements to that effect.

When the defense tried to introduce evidence that the Stephens Brokerage Company was an independent concern, the court disallowed it on the grounds that the date of the material to be introduced had been issued a month after the indictment. That was the very point, Senator Bailey said; it proved Stephens's was an independent concern still in existence despite the demise of PPA. Even so, he was denied.

The PPA treasurer, Frederick K. Smith, next took the stand and testified about his relationship with Dr. Cook. Smith threw some light on how the declaration of trust had been written. Cook had asked for examples of such documents, Smith said, and when he brought him several, Cook copied the parts from each that suited him. Smith denied he had represented PPA when he went with W.P. Welty to New York to work on the possible merger of Allied Oil. It was an entirely private venture, Smith said.

After lengthy discussion over whether Smith could be cross-examined on the financial assets of PPA, it was ruled that he could, but not before Pratt admitted that PPA's claim of an interest in 100 oil wells was indeed true. Pratt maintained, however, that deception had been practiced because the circulars implied that dividends were coming out of revenues from those wells, when the proof showed, he said, that those wells' revenues couldn't even pay PPA's rent.

Surprisingly, Senator Bailey agreed with Pratt, saying he believed the people who received the literature were meant to think just that. Judge Killits termed his statement "a pretty damaging admission," which caused Bailey to interrupt: "I am not afraid to make it; I don't shrink from it, and I think the men who made it believed it, without any doubt. I don't shrink from it, and I have no objection to Mr. Pratt asking any questions about those wells, or even about their production. The only thing I don't believe he has a right to go into, is to go into the question of expenditure, whether these people spent the money wisely or not."[62]

Killits responded: "There is in the circulars already read within the last ten minutes to the Court, a concrete, positive assurance, unmistakable in its terms, that dividends are not being paid on speculative profits, or assumed profits, or on assumed enhancements of values, but that they are actually being paid from current oil runs. . . . Now, the evidence, now tends to show that that statement is not true."[63]

With this Bailey differed, saying that no direct statement of the source of the money paid in dividends had been made. His argument was that since part of the profits distributed to the stockholders was gained by buying and selling interests in wells, leases, royalties and other properties, the list of assets was constantly changing, and if these assets were honestly thought of as having increased in value, though no actual hard profits were in hand, dividends could be paid legitimately on that expectation and belief. The men clearly expected to pay what they promised, or simply hoped that they would.

"If these oil wells – I mean, if these dry holes had been oil wells," insisted the senator, "this company would have been rich, and we would never have heard of this lawsuit; there is the difference between hope and expectation and fact. There never was a man drilled an oil well in this state that did not hope to find oil at the bottom of it, and he did not expect to have to go as deep as his neighbors went. It is the excitement of gambling."[64]

Several employees of PPA rebutted the testimony of O.L. Ray and the alleged PPA takeover attempt of Allied Oil under the leadership of W.P. Welty. But most of the rest of the testimony for the day was taken from witnesses who continued to testify as to the promising aspects of PPA property at Kosse and Corsicana, on which most of the optimistic statements were based that had been used to circularize prospective stockholders. The defense then introduced a number of exhibits showing evidence of many contracts to drill wells and assignments of leases to demonstrate that PPA was making an honest attempt to strike oil.

As the trial approached a conclusion, Judge Killits dropped his friend another line:

> The case is free from error, so Judge Rush of Omaha says. Rush is Government's old time expert on Sec. 215 – an encyclopedia of all adjudications. . . .
>
> I am also sending <u>rough</u> abstract of the remarkable deed of trust. I made this hurriedly during the interruptions of the trial as a guide for preparation of charge. I might say that this itself is a badge of fraud, but of course will not go that far. It is of great influence in the trial and will be used to determine the limits of Cook's high responsibility to share purchasers. It is in evidence from his own witness – that Cook prepared the instrument by getting a number of others together and combining those provisions which he specially desired.
>
> Note especially parts. 6 6½ 7 8 10 11 & 12. Did you ever see anything like it? . . .
>
> Warned everybody this morning that profuse talking is hereafter barred, all possible subjects having been exhausted. Baily shows signs of choking. He wants to orate in taking an exception. . . . I wish I had him where local conditions put him and myself on equal terms.[65]

On the last day of testimony, when Bailey called District Attorney Henry Zweifel to the stand, a murmur ran throughout the courtroom. When Bailey attempted to question him about any deals he had cut with defendants who pleaded guilty, the court intervened, saying that the district attorney was privileged under the law to refuse to divulge anything that he had done by way of the execution of his office. But Zweifel said he had no objections to telling everything he had done in connection with the case, and Bailey was allowed to proceed.

Zweifel testified concerning his pretrial meetings with individual defendants and all of the defendants' attorneys, denying that he had cut any deals to obtain testimony. Judge Killits then took the opportunity to admonish Senator Bailey for his "unsworn testimony" about the deals Zweifel had supposedly cut with defendants now that Zweifel had sworn under oath that he had made no such deals. The court was right in rebuking "any person, no matter how exalted he is, or how much he magnifies his own lofty position," who tried to place an unsworn assertion of fact before a jury, he maintained. "No man in Texas is big enough to do that," declared the judge.

Killits refused to hear Bailey until he was through, although the senator was seething as the judge went on to call "Senator Bailey's personal feelings and pride" "immaterialities." When he finally spoke, Bailey was vehement. "I except to the speech which the Court has just made in the presence of the jury," the senator said with emotion, "upon the ground that it is bitterly vindictive, and presented and intended to discredit me before the jury, and before this community.

"We are through with our evidence."[66]

Judge Killits then instructed the jury to disregard the "utterly unsought controversies we have had with Senator Bailey in this case" as having nothing to do with the merits of the case whatever; he then made a long speech saying they must divorce any feelings of perceived unprofessionality on the part of counsel or unfairness on the part of the judge from their minds. Upon completion of the judge's remarks, Senator Bailey took his exception.[67]

Several witnesses were put on the stand to rebut the defense's witnesses. Inspector Swenson, when recalled, said he had never told Turner he was "all right," and Paul Vitek returned to say that he had told Cook not to use a picture of a well gushing oil, since he knew it to be fake, but that Cook used it anyway.

The last witness was M.E. Smith, a broker called to identify a document dated June 27, 1923. At once the defense objected, saying that the testimony concerned a matter long after the indictment had been handed down and therefore was immaterial, but Judge Killits allowed the questioning to proceed.

Smith said that on June 24, 1923, Cook offered to sell through him his entire interest in the Petroleum Producers Association for $50,000. In evidence of this, the government introduced its 890th and last exhibit—a list of all the properties, including leases, royalties, lands held in fee and a refinery site in Little Rock, which Smith said Cook had furnished him in support of the proposed transaction. The last page of the document was missing, and the witness could not recall what it contained. He testified that Cook had said that the refinery site alone was worth the price he was asking.

Efforts by the prosecution to question Smith on PPA's oil production were denied by the court and the evidence was concluded.

Judge Killits announced there would be no session in the afternoon; that would be reserved for a meeting with counsel to discuss the law in the case and to arrange for the order of the closing arguments and charge to the jury, which he set to begin Monday. Before adjourning, the judge informed counsel for A.M. Delcambre that he would instruct the jury to acquit his client because of a mistake in the indictment by the prosecutors.

As it had been early in the trial, the courtroom was crowded long before final arguments were to begin at 8:15 A.M. on November 19. Dr. Cook came into the courtroom carrying a leather portfolio and took his seat with his attorneys. Marie Cook sat with him, as did Mrs. Cox with her husband.

The first to speak was Special Prosecutor Pratt, who addressed the jury for three and a half hours. In his remarks he called Cook a crook and a liar, and Cox a "peach." "It makes no difference whether Cook hoped for success," Pratt said. "If he got money by false representations, it is a crime and it makes no difference what he did with the money. Practically all of the companies Cook merged did not have a nickel's worth of assets and Cook was buying only sucker lists. The attempt to take over going concerns without their consent was outrageous. The deal to take in the Allied Oil Company is the worst example of this, and brands the defendants, Cook, Welty and Smith as being without conscience. It was the crookedest deal I ever heard of."

Pratt reread a number of PPA letters and then exclaimed sarcastically that Cook wanted the jury to believe that his OK of such stuff was an idle, perfunctory act. Further, he declared scornfully, "the literature conveyed the impression to the reader that Cook owned 100 wells that constantly poured into his coffers a stream of gold. But the income from these wells was not enough to pay his office rent." Throughout it all, Dr. Cook sat impassively and showed no reaction whatever to Pratt's words. In fact, the session for once was free from all outbursts and disputations other than those being formally presented.

In their closing statements, the defense team struck the theme that Cook and Cox were on trial only because they had drilled dry holes, and that if they had found oil, there would have been no prosecution.

On the last day of arguments, November 20, Senator Bailey addressed the jury for three hours. "It is the same old story," he said dramatically, "crown the victor, crucify the loser. If Cook used the money he obtained to build up an honest oil company he is not guilty; if he didn't he is guilty." Bailey justified Cook's merger scheme from history, saying that only the large companies survived in the oil game. He pointed out that Cook had cooperated fully with government agents, had willingly provided the evidence they had used against him and had offered to correct any irregularities they found—hardly the actions of a perpetrator of fraud, he said. He differed with the prosecution's argument that none of the companies Cook had merged had any property, and he bitterly characterized the defendants who had testified for the prosecution as "informers" who had sold out their fellows for a light sentence, while it was they who actually had gotten the most out of PPA's operations.

Senator Bailey boldly declared that Cook had not formed PPA as a scheme to defraud and that he had made no false statements willfully. He asserted that the officers of PPA would never have paid even one 2 percent dividend "even if they were rascals" had it not been their intention to continue paying them.

He attributed many of PPA's allegedly false statements to information taken from others in good faith, including Paul Vitek. The senator also hinted at a deal with Vitek for his testimony, since the evidence clearly showed that Vitek was guilty of many of the same "crimes" that the officials of PPA were accused of, yet he had not been indicted. He admitted that in some cases, like Allied Oil, mistakes had been made but said they were innocent mistakes.

In reference to the possible prejudice of the judge, Bailey remarked that it was up to the jury to decide the case as they thought, not as the judge thought.[68]

By the time Henry Zweifel finished the last speech for the prosecution, there had been 17½ hours of argument. Now only one thing remained—the charge—before the case was ready to go to the jury.

The judge cautioned the jurymen that in the discussion of the case he was about to make they might get the impression the court was stating proven facts or had an impression of the merits of the case. He assured them that if that notion was conveyed, it was unintentional, and that it should not weigh in their judgment of the case in the slightest degree. Judge Killits then began to read from a thick document he held in his hands; he would not finish for more than three hours. As he read, he also cautioned them, over and over, that they must judge the case on its merits and not on the conduct of the defense attorneys or the judge, however that might have been perceived.

The offense being tried, Judge Killits stated, was the use of the mails to defraud and nothing else—not that a fraud had been committed, but only that the mails had been abused to aid in a fraud. Even if the enterprise was intended to benefit the investors eventually, the judge said, the use of the mails to convey fraudulent statements to get the money to fund that enterprise was illegal.

Contrary to several of his statements during the trial, Killits now seemed to say that it was unnecessary for the government to prove that PPA was organized as a fraudulent scheme, only that it "was working fraudulently at the time the mails were used" at any of the times laid in the indictment.

"The evidence of the character of the scheme is such in the record as to justify a finding from you beyond a reasonable doubt . . . that the Government's charge in this behalf is true," he told the jury. "Whether you should so find or not, is for you only to say. . . . One false statement of the character described in the indictment, deliberately made, to influence him to whom it was addressed, to come into the Association with his money, and seen to have substance and character to produce that result, if made through the mails, is sufficient to support a verdict of conviction."[69]

The big question, said Judge Killits, was the intent of the defendants, which was a condition of the mind, but he maintained that "when we see a man doing one thing, and we see what it naturally accomplishes, we naturally assume he did it on purpose, with intent; when we see him doing the same thing over and over again, and producing the same results, we are more certain not only that he intended to have done what his acts bring about, but that his doing these things proves that he had a general plan to work in that way."[70]

Each of the individuals' capacities and their reactions to the circumstances they faced in the matters explored in the evidence must be weighed in determining their intent, the judge said, and each must be looked at individually unless proven to be part of a conspiracy. After defining the legalistic meaning of "conspiracy," he dwelt on the original declaration of trust that had set up PPA and given Dr. Cook its sole control.

"Here . . . Cook has prepared the documentary groundwork of his scheme," he said, "he is the sole judge of what may or may not be done, and the only brake on him is that of exercising good faith, with the burden wholly upon the other parties to prove that he acted in bad faith at any time. You will not understand that the Court is advising you that the scheme, as outlined in the Declaration, is intrinsically dishonest. One could exercise all its extraordinary powers given to him as trustee without violating any law of morals or legislation. Cook . . . is entitled to the presumption that he intended to operate in good faith. . . . Organization through a Declaration of Trust is not unusual, as we have said. We do not, however, wish to be understood as saying that the Declaration is in the customary terms.

"But . . . he was in control . . . of an instrument capable . . . of working . . . a large reward for dishonest action, with little chance of loss or risk.

"In nothing we have said," Judge Killits continued, ". . . are you invited to lose sight of a possibility . . . that . . . Cook . . . may not have been, at all times, when action was taken, counted on by the prosecution as fraudulent . . . self deceived. Self deception is a perfect defense to any charge of fraudulent conduct, and conviction cannot be had so long as a reasonable doubt of its absence exists." But he added, "You will note, however, that when the charge is that fraud was committed by and through deliberate misrepresentation of material existing facts, there is no room for reasonable doubt on the subject of self deception. When it is clearly proven that a conscious lie has been uttered, there is an end to any valid claim of self deception."[71]

Killits then addressed the main contention of the defense: that the promoters of PPA had worked honestly to find oil for their stockholders and had simply failed. "The nature of the business of oil investments is, of course, a circumstance which has a place in this case," he said.

"Sincere optimism is allowable even if it should seem to us foolish. . . . But the law does, in fact, include everything intended to defraud by suggestion, promises and predictions as to the future, as well as to intentional misrepresentations of the present. So . . . [if] the literature purposely indulged in alluring suggestions and predictions, for the future, without sufficient basis of present fact, or reasonable warrant, intending thereby to derive profit by inducing reliance among ignorant or credulous people . . . you have a situation covered by the statute."[72]

"The more highly speculative and chancy is the business in hand," concluded the judge, "the most care should be exercised in making statements of fact."[73]

At the end of the charge, Senator Bailey excepted to many of the points made by the judge. Among these were his dwelling on the declaration of trust, which Bailey asserted was "calculated to make the jury feel that that declaration was an extraordinary one, and out of the usual run of such documents," and the judge's statement that it was not necessary for the government to prove that the Petroleum Producers Association was devised from the start as a scheme and artifice to defraud, as the indictment explicitly stated. He also objected to any reference to the law regarding conspiracy, as no question of conspiracy was alleged in the indictment.

It was 6:00 before a final word was given to the jury by Judge Killits. He cautioned them not to be too hasty, yet not to feel that they had to plow through every piece of evidence again to come to a decision, and then dismissed them to consider their verdict on the 168 counts brought against the 14 defendants. With that, the trial was adjourned until 9 A.M.

As the jurymen filed out to begin their deliberations, Cook returned to his hotel. "I was resigned by this time to expect a verdict of guilty," he remembered of that moment, "so the strain of the overnight wait for the jury's report was not extreme. I slept, though fitfully, that night, for the last time a free man. Half waking, I reviewed my career in vivid dreams. I saw the flag and the snow hut at the Pole, the flaunting mirages under the spiralling sun, the tall cliffs of Cape Sparbo, the muskox lunging against the sealskin noose, the walrus sprawled on the drifting pans."[74]

Despite the judge's admonition, or perhaps because of his charge, the jury did not take long to decide—just 20 hours. When the court was called to order at 4:30 P.M., Mr. Gray, the foreman, announced that the jury had reached its verdict and handed it to the court clerk, G.B. Buckley, to be read. Monotonously, he recited the defendants' names and the verdicts. On all counts, each was adjudged guilty as charged of violation of the Federal Criminal Code, section 215: use of the U.S. mails to defraud, with two exceptions. "Lucky" Cox was found guilty on only eight of the 12 counts against him, and A.H. Delcambre, as the judge had recommended, was acquitted.

As the verdict was read, Cook sat "like a graven statue just under the Judge's bench. A face already gray became grayer, lines in his face, already deep, became deeper." With his chin on his breast, his eyes never seemed to leave a figure on the carpet.

Cox, whose facial muscles twitched nervously throughout the reading, when it was over, hurried to the water cooler, quaffed a glass of water, then sat down again.

The first to be sentenced was Dr. Cook. Judge Killits called him forward. Cook stood expressionless as the judge spoke:

> Cook, what have you got to say?
>
> This is one of the times when your peculiar and persuasive hypnotic personality, fails you, isn't it? You have at last got to the point where you can't bunco anybody. You have come to a mountain and reached a latitude which are beyond you.
>
> History gave us Ananias, then we had Machiavelli; the twentieth century produced Frederick A. Cook. Poor old Ananias, he is forgotten, and Machiavelli was a piker. But we still have Frederick A. Cook.
>
> Cook, this deal of yours, and this conception of yours, and this execution of yours, was so damnably crooked that I know the men who defended you, defended you with their handkerchiefs to their noses. It smelled to high heaven.
>
> I wish I could do with you as I might, the way I feel about you; I wish I were not circumscribed by some conventions that I think

are mistakes. . . . I don't think you ought to run at large at all; you are too dangerous.

Undoubtedly you have those ill-gotten gains laid away somewhere. Counsel told me this morning that you couldn't make appeal bond and I said any man not under the spell of your hypnotic personality would know you could make any kind of bond. Right now you are holding money of people of poor means all over the United States.

I don't see how any living man who has any appreciation of the standards of decency or honesty can suggest that you ought to hold a penny of it. Every penny of it was robbed from orphans and widows, and credulous old people; people in the depths of poverty; people anxious to get money enough to ensure a decent burial.

Haven't you any honor at all? Haven't you the honor to place it in the hands of a trustee to be sent back to those you stole from, those you robbed—widows, orphans. Oh, God, Cook, haven't you any sense of decency at all? Or is your vanity so impervious that you don't respond to what must be calls of decency to you? Aren't you haunted at night? Can you sleep?

I'm conscious of the fact that you are under indictment in my district and the same record produced here can be poured into the ears of honest farmers of Ohio just as it was poured into the ears of honest farmers of this district of Texas. If it wasn't for that the sentence would be a good deal stiffer. I know what my colleagues on the bench in Ohio would do to you. I couldn't try your case there, tho. One contact with you is enough. Thank God, you can be indicted in every district in the United States.

What's the use of talking to you? Your effrontery, vanity, and nerve are so monumental, so cold-steel, so impervious, so adamantine to what I have to say that the only satisfaction I get in saying that is that I know I am voicing the feelings of the decent people of Texas without any question; those of them that have brains enough not to fall for what some of these foolish people call your personality. I don't know where it is. They call it "personality," whether it is poker face or false face.

The prosecuting officers have suggested to me that I be not quite so stiff on you. I am not going to do you justice, Cook. I am not going to give you what you ought to have. I suspect you will get the balance of what you ought to have somewhere else. Those people you swindled in the northern Ohio district ought to have a chance to look at you. You ought to be carried around from district to district to be exhibited. I can not express the abhorrence I have for such a crook as you are.[75]

Judge Killits then pronounced sentence: 14 years, nine months in prison and a $12,000 fine—$1,000 for each count—the maximum allowable. In addition, he assessed Cook the costs of the trial, estimated at $12,869.11, and set appeal bond at $75,000. Senator Bailey objected at once to the severity of the sentence and gave notice that he would appeal.

In sentencing all the men who had pleaded guilty, Judge Killits followed the recommendations of District Attorney Zweifel, saying that such a practice was entirely proper. All got off with a $500 fine except O.H. Stephens; his sentence amounted to a $1,000 fine and 90 days in jail.

But for those who had maintained their innocence, there was little mercy. Fred K. Smith got seven years, $12,000 in fines and had his bond set at $35,000. W.P. Welty received a sentence of two and a half years, a $7,000 fine and a bond of $7,000. W.L. Braddish got the same, despite his pleas for clemency.

Then PPA's sales manager, Leslie A. McKercher, came forward. Before sentencing he was asked, like the others, if he had anything to say. McKercher said that whatever he had done, he had done it because of the faith he had in Dr. Cook as a man.

"Do you still have faith in him?" asked Killits.

"Yes, Sir," declared McKercher.

"Poppycock," retorted the judge. "Anyone who has read that disreputable declaration of trust 'heads I win, tails you lose' can not make me believe they still have faith in the man who wrote it." McKercher got six years, a $1,000 fine and a bond set at $15,000.

Next it was Cox's turn. He had nothing to say before his sentencing. Judge Killits did, however. "Well, Cox," said Killits, "this is a case of the pitcher going to the well once too often. I don't want to say anything to add to your discomfiture. You know how I feel about this nasty, despicable scheme. You're no martyr." For Cox there were eight years and $8,000 in fines. His bond was set at $35,000. After pronouncing Cox's sentence, Judge Killits immediately said he would deny any motion for a new trial, even though none had been made.

The judge then turned his attention to the defense team. "I note from a transcript that you, Senator Bailey, are of the opinion that Federal Judges do not change their minds."

"I've never seen one that did," Bailey responded.

"Under the bombardment of insolence to which the court has been subjected I am glad it was given me to be patient enough not to send someone to jail during the progress of this trial," Killits declared.

Bailey then called to the attention of the court that one of the jurors was illiterate. Killits said that made no difference in a federal court.

The remaining seven defendants were called to the bar and District Attorney Zweifel urged that the judge be lenient in their cases. "Con men," said the judge, "are among the most despicable. Everything is fish that comes to their nets—widows, orphans, life insurance money, carpets off the floors, as you have heard in this case." He informed them that their citizenship was revoked but that he would recommend it be restored if they appealed to the president. He also advised them not to participate in any attempted appeal of the case but to go to the penitentiary for three months and then make their appeal for clemency, and if their record was good, he would advise in favor of it. The men were given sentences of one year and a day and a fine of $1,000. Bond was set for each at $4,000.

Judge Killits then admonished the jury for convicting Cox on only eight of the 12 counts but said it made no difference since he was imposing the maximum sentence as if it had found him guilty on all counts.

When court had been adjourned, the defendants who were given time were taken the four blocks to the Tarrant County jail in a police patrol wagon, where they were locked up in the fifth tier of cells. Soon after their arrival, T.O. Turner, who had been greatly affected by his sentence, had to be taken to the hospital ward of the jail. Jailor Fitch locked the rest into cells by twos and allowed no visitors.

In the morning they were served a breakfast of bacon, light bread and coffee, but their only visitors were several newspapermen, who reported that Cook appeared broken, with an "immobile look on his face, the same as when Killits flayed him."[76]

The new prisoners were allowed to place an order for groceries, which included a large supply of cigarettes. During the day they were let out into the corridor, where they amused themselves playing dominoes and cards or spent the time discussing what had gone wrong at the trial. The *Press's* reporter believed that the disastrous result of their venture into the oil game had not yet really hit home. "They all seem," he thought, "to be men who have had a vision of wealth, or, better, a dream; and are having a hard time realizing that their bubble has burst. It is a far cry from the fantasies of high powered oil promotion to the cold reality of a jail, and Cook and his associates hardly seem to have felt yet the chill shadow of the bars. They said they had expected an acquittal—and then the verdict, like a thunderbolt."[77] Once in a while one would get up, go into his cell and sit leaning over with his head in his hands.

To the correspondent's surprise, the other convicted men still seemed to look to Dr. Cook for leadership and appeared to be on a most friendly basis with him. The prisoners expressed several desires to the reporter. Most of all they seemed concerned about how the public perceived them now that they had been convicted. Several put in orders for out-of-town newspapers. They also asked that someone send up a checkerboard.

As Cook approached, the newsman studied his subject's changed appearance since the sentence had been pronounced. "Cook's face," he reported, "seems more heavily lined than before and his eyes reveal an inner strain and suffering that he will not permit to pass his lips. As he walks along the runway of the tier of cells, there is an aimlessness to his gait, an unsteadiness of sudden age, and a droop to his shoulders. He smiles at times, however, and converses with affability."[78]

"I had only altruistic aims in my ventures," said the doctor, still maintaining his complete innocence. "I wouldn't deliberately swindle even a swindler.

"I only had one dream. Call me visionary if you will, but within me was an abiding desire to find an oil field that would remain a monument to my name and memory, and all the money I received was spent to that end."[79] But he now acknowledged that it was too late to save that dream that had been embodied in the Petroleum Producers Association. "I am broke," he declared. "Every penny I made went into the company. Much of it went into dry holes. The books show where the money went. That should have been developed. The Government knew it.

"It is not true that I have a large amount of wealth hidden away. Nor is it true that I collected $366,000 from Paul Vitek for handling his stock."[80] When asked to comment, Cook had no reply to Killits's denunciation of him.

The doctor's several experiences with extreme isolation had taught him that inactivity had a disastrous effect on both the mind and the body. He declared he was forming a "Cook Brigade" of two squads to do regular exercise together. Cox, because he had lost an eye as a youth, was the only nonveteran of the Great War besides Dr. Cook. He was designated the "bugler," blowing reveille on a comb. Ever the wordsmith, Cox composed a song, "Marching on Leavenworth," to the tune of "Marching through Georgia," to get them into the yard. There they did drills and calisthenics to keep in shape.

One who was not in the "brigade" was O.H. Stephens. Though he professed no fear of being with the others, he was confined in a distant cell by federal order.

The out-of-town papers arrived; their editors seemed to feel justice had been done. "By succeeding so admirably in this conspicuous case," said one, "the effect will be increased a thousandfold. It will hurt legitimate prospecting, of course, but there is too much oil any way, so the country can well afford to pay that price for the victory won at Fort Worth."[81]

In the news magazines, the doctor's latest fall from grace was a cause for yet another caustic review of his entire career:

> Dr. Cook is perhaps the century's greatest faker, and in a country which worships at the shrine of advertising and accepts any oil speculator who succeeds he ought to receive some recognition. If Barnum is a national hero, why not Frederick A. Cook? Dr. Cook might appropriately be made the hero of a great national saga. He too was a poor boy who advertised his way to fame. He began sell-

ing fruit in Fulton Market; he peddled milk—and in course of time he was decorated by the King of Denmark *[sic],* given an honorary degree by the ancient University of Copenhagen, granted the Freedom of the City of New York, and entertained at a monster dinner at which Admiral Schley presided and many men now living who would prefer to remain nameless joined to do him honor. He made a small fortune in advertising an ascent of Mt. McKinley and a trip to the North Pole, neither of which he had ever taken, and after he had been thoroughly exposed, he returned to fame as author of a series of articles explaining that he was not really sure whether he ever did get to the Pole or not. . . .

. . . Dr. Cook, instead of laughing at the world, tried to make more money out of whimpering. There may be more joy in heaven over one penitent sinner, but this earth hates the breed. Dr. Cook might be forgiven his oil swindle—lesser men than he have "got by"; he can never be forgiven his apologies for fooling us.[82]

Herbert Bridgman, who had said somewhat prematurely once before to "speak respectfully of the dead," now was sure the doctor fit the category. To him and Robert E. Peary's other old friends, the conviction in Fort Worth was not mere justice for a felony. To them, it seemed to have been more than that. They were certain that it had finished any chance of any more polar "comebacks" by Cook for all time. To them, it seemed a fitting climax to the doctor's strange career.

CHAPTER 24

The New Era

THE DAY THEY WERE LOCKED IN THE COUNTY JAIL, THE CONVICTED OIL MEN read in the papers that Harry Houdini, who was appearing in Fort Worth, had escaped from a straitjacket while suspended by his feet from the *Telegram* building. Senator Bailey assured his clients that their escape would be easier than that. The judge's behavior ensured the conviction would be overturned, he said.

Whatever else they may have read in the papers about what strangers and old enemies thought of them, Dr. Cook and his associates could have no doubt that their friends had not forgotten them. They sent food, cigars, and cigarettes, as well as flowers, which Cook arranged in the various cells. They also sent the checkerboard.

Soon all were engaged in a round-robin checkers tournament in which a special prize was offered for the elimination of Dr. Cook. This came early, as the doctor freely admitted his skill at checkers was "somewhat rusty."

Friday was visitors' day. Among the first was Marie Cook, who told her ex-husband that Senator Bailey had also assured her that the verdict would never stand. Raising the money to make the appeal would be difficult, however, and there seemed no possibility of making the bond.

Cook's lawyers were not long in beginning their challenge to his conviction, nevertheless. Senator Bailey, still smarting from Killits's numerous rebukes, wanted badly to get even. He publicly called the trial "a farce and travesty on Justice," and fueled by money given by other nervous oil promoters, he began work. But the wheels of justice grind slowly, and day after day the former officers of the Petroleum Producers Association whiled away their time behind bars.

For the doctor there was little to relieve the days of empty idleness. One morning he received an unexpected package from T. Everett Harré. It contained his latest book, a novel, uncomfortably titled "One Hour and Forever." Marie came regularly on visitors' day, but she now needed transportation. While she was delivering breakfast to the jail one day in early December, federal marshals had seized her Packard Twin-Six. Her chauffeur came in to tell her they were going to take possession, and when she went out it was gone. Later that month the car was sold for $741 in back taxes.[1]

Cook's daughters wrote to him. Ruth was now at Cornell, but 18-year-old Helen was still at home with Marie. He was always pleased to hear from them and tried to be optimistic.

"I know that the greatest hardship falls on you and Ruth and Mother," he wrote to Helen, "but if we all do the best we can there will be brighter days for us all."[2]

To Ruth, he held out hope that the appeal would exonerate him but told her "before we can file our writ of error . . . the record of the trial must be copied—this . . . is expected to cost $6000 which we must pay."[3]

Still, it was hard to be truly optimistic. The record was the second longest in Texas judicial history, surpassed only by the 20,000 pages generated by the Texas-Oklahoma border dispute. And Judge Killits was insisting that the whole record must be printed, all 12,000 pages, not just those sections containing the assignments of error, which amounted to only 112.

The dull routine of the day was not improved when, on December 13, all of the other PPA prisoners except for Cox, Welty and McKercher left for Leavenworth to begin serving their sentences. A bad checkers player can only stand so much of the game, so the ever-adaptable doctor looked for something different to occupy his time.

One of the new arrivals at the jail was John Western, an Australian who was being held by immigration authorities until he could be deported. It so happened he was an expert in fancy needlework; Cook asked if he would teach him to embroider. Soon the doctor was hard at work on his first piece. It gave creative satisfaction, and he found that he had a real flair for it. When Marie visited, he would ask her for thread of the shades his vivid imagination dictated, to be sewn into his latest design.[4]

Christmas brought a little cheer in the form of a complete dinner for 80 served by Sheriff Carl Smith, including 137 pounds of turkey with all the trimmings. In the banquet room stood a Christmas tree covered with colored lights, supplied by the First Methodist Church and the Union Gospel Mission.

Still, a man so used to action, so accustomed to active observation of an active world, could not eliminate the negative thoughts that his fate had thrust upon his often-idle mind:

> To me all was dark. It was my blackest hour. There was not the hope of another sunrise, but also there was no end to the execution. While thus in the damnation of utter despair, a friend said, "Doctor don't you hate the world?"
>
> There was bitterness, depression and disgust in the very air about, but did I hate the world? . . . Did I hate any body or anything, or the source of my trouble? No. I was seeking a remedy, but could not co-ordinate thoughts.
>
> At this time another friend spoke. One who had millions to burn. Said he, "Doctor, what a wonderful experience you have had

and are having. What a life! I have spent my money to find life, to get thrills. . . . You get everything going and coming without money cost. Lucky victim!". . .

But, my friend of millions was right. The excess baggage of wealth delays the pathfinder. But, again I wondered. How can trouble give values, how can damnation give thrills and how can the shadow of death give color to life? It took time. It took a long time for me to see through this confusing haze, through the seeming unreality of life when near death. But as I escaped the doom of the end, I found, as I think all men will find when the doors of eternity are open, that man's most enduring vintage is brewed and aged under a rain of tears. . . . How can those know life who have never suffered? Those who have lived on the even road of peace and plenty are ever near-sighted. Hunger billboards the destiny of most men. I have been in heaven and I have been in hell, in so far as human consciousness can ever give feeling to such places. I have been to the top and to the bottom of the globe and fairly well around it, but I feel that my mental life has only just begun.[5]

In the outside world, the pace of the oil prosecutions had slowed considerably; the harsh verdict against PPA had produced the desired effects. Fort Worth postal authorities reported their receipts had fallen more than a third since it had been handed down. What further convictions were obtained resulted in light sentences of, at most, a year and a day; the phony oil promoters continued to operate, but their tactics no longer included the methods that had brought down PPA.

In January S.E.J. Cox was taken away to Houston to stand trial in connection with his dealings with Bluebird Oil. As a result he got five years and a $15,000 fine. But the sentence was to run concurrently with his previous PPA conviction, and he went to Leavenworth to start serving both. Cox was the last of the PPA men to go, leaving Cook alone with his embroidery, his thoughts and his reading.

Several stories came to the doctor that seemed to bear out his lawyers' contention that if PPA had brought in a gusher, there would have been no prosecution. One account had it that a group of crooked promoters who were under threat of grand jury action sent drilling equipment to a property they owned just to give the appearance of serious activity. When the truck broke down short of the chosen site, they sank the well then and there—and struck oil. They were not indicted.[6]

A second concerned a notorious promoter named Pat Marr, who guaranteed "Ten Gigantic High-Grade Smackover Gusher Wells" and "100% dividends" to his investors. He had been summoned to Washington to explain to postal authorities why a fraud order should not be issued against him. On the way, he received word that one of his wells had come in and that he had an offer of a buyout for $1,500,000. Marr declared a 100 percent dividend, and the fraud order was not issued.[7]

For some time, Judge Killits had been complaining that Cook had too many privileges at the Tarrant County jail, especially his easy access to the press. He cited the delay in producing the record from the stenographic notes of the trial as a stall tactic on Cook's part and insisted he be sent to Leavenworth at once. But in a letter to the attorney general's office, Henry Zweifel cautioned against this, saying Judge Wilson affirmed that it was local practice that until a man's case record had been presented and approved, he could not make bond and so could remain in jail rather than beginning his sentence. Zweifel said Wilson "did not believe we should adopt any different practice . . . just because it was Dr. Frederick A. Cook" and that Wilson should be placated, since he thought Killits's sentence unjustified and was having regrets that he had not heard Cook's trial himself.

Zweifel enclosed a letter from the court stenographer, which indicated that the transcription of the record was proceeding as rapidly as possible. Marie Cook, the stenographer said, had not requested the record until December 23 because she had to solicit the funds. She then had paid for the work one volume at a time but now assured him that she had enough to cover the balance. The transcript had so far progressed to 5,000 pages.[8]

Zweifel himself shared Judge Wilson's view of Cook's sentence and had said so privately on many occasions. This made John Pratt suspicious of Zweifel's loyalty. Pratt wrote to Assistant Attorney General Earl J. Davis that Judge Killits was corresponding with the convicted PPA men at Leavenworth, trying to convince them of Cook's perfidy in making them dependent on his defense team and then having them "ruthlessly sacrificed without having any chance to make a defense" since Cook feared their testimony would incriminate him.

Pratt proposed going personally to Kansas to obtain statements from the incarcerated men. His idea was to introduce these into the appeal proceedings "in order to illuminate the real atmosphere of the trial and further explain the various incidents which counsel for Cook claim constitute prejudicial misbehavior on the part of the court."[9] This course of action was approved by the Justice Department on March 19, 1924.

On May 7 Judge Killits denied Cook's writ of error and refused to accept his affidavit *in forma pauperis* in which he requested relief of the cost of printing the trial record since he was without funds. In refusing Cook's petition, the judge said, "We decline to be added to the long line of individuals . . . who have been duped by Cook's stupendous misrepresentations. To believe his affidavit or anything he may say on the subject to the effect that he is too poor to make his proceedings in error in the way required by the statute for the convenience of a burdened court and government is to discredit his intelligence and foresight. We find him lacking in neither characteristics."[10]

Killits did reduce Cook's bond to $45,000 but conditioned this as a supersedeas bond, refusing to change its status to a mere bail bond, because he saw Cook's application as an impoverished litigant as not made in good faith. The judge thought it was incredible that Cook could have possibly dissipated the huge fortune taken in by PPA in so short a time. He estimated Cook had at least $250,000 concealed beyond the reach of his creditors or the government, and the only way any of it could be gotten back was to keep the bond high.

Killits also objected to the bill of exceptions filed by Cook's lawyers. Of the 23 assignments of error, three were irrelevant, he said, because they concerned matters before and after the trial, and 17 had to do with the perceived treatment of the defense team at the hands of the court. Because of Killits's opinion of his own treatment, he considered these beneath contempt. Of the remaining three, the judge believed they came nowhere close to showing that the verdict might reasonably have been favorable to Cook had these things not occurred.[11] On this basis, the judge refused to sign the document, and after a heated discussion that included "a sharp exchange of remarks," Herbert Wade asked to be excused from the court, a request the judge was more than happy to grant.[12]

The night of June 9 Dr. Cook had trouble sleeping and got up. He was reading a story in the *Saturday Evening Post* when he heard noises and voices coming from the reception room between the two wings of the jail. Suddenly a grate in the wall opened. The same voices said they were about to "bust out" and asked if he would like to go, too. The doctor said he did not care to go that way. "If I can't get out without breaking jail, my good friend Judge John M. Killits will see that I'm taken care of," he told them. The next day, in recounting the incident to reporters, he said, "When I leave jail I'll walk out in broad daylight, thru the front door with my head up." He just smiled when told the two jailbreakers had already been captured.[13]

Cook soon learned from the newspapers that Killits had asked President Coolidge to remit the fines and shorten the jail terms of all the PPA defendants except Cox and himself. Killits's intransigence caused Cook's lawyers to petition the court of appeals in Atlanta. On July 7 all three appeared in Georgia to argue for his release on bail as a pauper.

During the hearing, Senator Bailey stated to the court that Judge Killits had only filed his memorandum opinion instead of entering the character of the order of his decision on Cook's pauper petition, as required, and so the court should recognize it. Then Henry Zweifel, to John Pratt's utter amazement, seemed to confirm Bailey's assertion. Since the court had no records before it, based on what it had heard, it agreed that Cook could proceed with his writ of error without printing the record of the trial, but it refused to reduce his bond to an appearance bond.

The request for Cook's release was denied on August 1, so Wade filed for a writ of habeas corpus on the doctor's behalf, saying he was being held in jail unjustly and illegally. But this also was denied. Wade then appealed to Judge Wilson.

At the hearing, with Cook present, Senator Bailey argued that the original bond of $75,000 was the highest ever in the state for any crime, including murder, and so was clearly unjust. In reply, Judge Wilson said he was inclined to grant Cook bail, but because of the ruling of the circuit court he felt he had no jurisdiction to do so. He noted, however, that while the court had upheld Cook's claim to be a pauper, it left the bail of $45,000 intact, requiring a man legally recognized as without financial means to raise an enormous sum to gain his liberty. The effect, said Judge Wilson, was that bail, which he believed was designed to get men out of jail, was being used to keep Cook in, but the court had so ruled. The doctor could not hide his disappointment at the judge's decision.[14]

Immediately upon hearing of the ruling in Atlanta, Judge Killits had requested a search of the circuit court files, and insisted that he had filed his order. It was, indeed, among the records. Pratt was furious with Zweifel and demanded an explanation. Although Zweifel was able to explain to the attorney general's satisfaction that he had merely been misunderstood, Killits and Pratt were in an unforgiving mood; the judge took up correspondence with the circuit court to try to get it to reverse its ruling.

Judge Wilson, who went on record at the habeas corpus hearing as sympathetic to most of the arguments of Cook's lawyers, wrote a confidential letter to Attorney General Harlan F. Stone about the PPA trial and its aftermath.

"The people generally were shocked at Judge Kittit's conduct at the end of that case [and] regarded his conduct as brutal and inhuman," he told Stone. ". . . You would be able to understand this all better if you would read the stenographic report of Judge Killits remarks at the time he sentenced Dr Cook. For my part, I exceedingly regret that I made the mistake of requesting the assignment of Judge Killits to the trial of this particular case."

Wilson was concerned that as a result of Pratt's and Killits's pressing the matter of the circuit court's ruling, the court would conclude, "and it can do so from the record, for that matter, that it was not possible for any man to get a trial, a fair trial, at the hands of Judge Killits, and particularly that it was not possible for Dr Cook to do so. . . .

". . . I say to you frankly that I sometimes think Judge Killits is not quite right. I think that Dr Cook should have been convicted, I believe the sentence imposed was extreme, but I nevertheless am anxious to see this case affirmed since the matter of the penalty can be taken care of. There is absolutely no question in the mind of anyone about the guilt of Dr Cook."[15]

Henry Zweifel also advised the Justice Department to back off, saying, "To require this record to be printed means a denial of an appeal in this case.

"Rich in mountains of testimony as to Cooks' guilt, the Government can well afford to be liberal with Cook. It is dangerous not to be. Cook is claiming that he did not receive a fair trial, and therefore our every act should be more than fair."[16] In the end, the government decided to waive the printing of the record and instead purchased for $750 the carbon copy of the stenographic transcript to plan its case.

None of his lawyers' legal maneuvers having had any effect, the doctor marked his first anniversary behind bars on November 21. There was nothing left to do now but wait for the appeal itself to be heard.

On February 2, 1925, arguments were made on Cook's behalf in New Orleans for a new hearing of his case. His lawyers focused on the way the grand jury that indicted Cook had been seated, and on the remarks of Judge Killits at the trial, which they contended had prejudiced the jury and prevented Cook from receiving a fair trial. But Herbert Wade was severely admonished that his attempts to state that Killits had been reversed several times before because of his attitude were improper and immaterial.

Henry Zweifel summed up the government's argument as to why a new trial was unnecessary:

> The evidence which was produced before the jury was almost beyond comprehension in its proof of deliberate, willful falsehood and misrepresentation. It establishes beyond any question and without any possibility of a doubt that Cook and his associates were not oil men, nor were they in good faith seeking the production of oil, but from the evidence they could be and were justly and properly characterized as confidence men and "bunco steerers." . . . The fraud was clear and emphatic, the proof of the mailing of the several letters in furtherance of the scheme was undisputed and justice was done by the jury when they returned into court with their verdict of guilty.[17]

The next day the court denied the appeal, saying Cook's objection to the competency of the grand jury could not prevail because it had not been prompt. As for the other points of the plaintiff's brief, the court found that since "it is not questioned, and it is not fairly open to question, that evidence adduced warranted the verdict rendered," the record did not show reversible error was committed in admitting or excluding evidence or giving or refusing instructions to the jury, or that the right of Cook's counsel to submit evidence to the jury was improperly abridged in any way.

The court was of the opinion that although not all of Judge Killits's actions or statements to Cook's counsel were "approved or commended as proper and justifiable in the exercise of the large discretion vested in the court in the conduct of the trial," these actions were not grounds for reversal because "the incidents complained of were not influential in bringing about Cook's conviction, and did not affect his substantial rights."[18]

In a last-ditch attempt, Wade put in a motion for a rehearing with the circuit court of appeals, contending that District Judge Bledsoe had given them until May 14, 1923, to file their motion to quash and that they had done so within that agreement,[19] but on March 11 the request was denied. After considering their chances in the Supreme Court, Cook's lawyers dropped all further actions on March 27, 1925, and their client prepared to join the others in Leavenworth.

On the eve of his departure, Cook told the press, "I'll be back some time. Texas has been the scene of my bitterest trouble, but I plan to make it my home when I am free again." Before the doctor started for Leavenworth, Judge Wilson recommended that the 16 months Cook had spent in the Tarrant County jail be credited toward his sentence.[20]

Cook's friends said he would never serve his full term; an investigation would be made and he would be exonerated. Memories of these words were all the hope Cook had left as he was led out of his cell to be handcuffed to Texas Marshal Sam L. Gross for delivery to the federal penitentiary. So, on April 6, 1925, the sixteenth anniversary of the discovery of the North Pole by Robert E. Peary, the other claimant, clutching a small suitcase and several bundles containing materials for embroidery work, set off on the overnight train to Kansas.[21]

The trip to Leavenworth faintly reminded the doctor of his lecture tours. Passengers pointed him out to one another with evident excitement, though it was now the handcuffs and not a recognition of who he was that caused them to do so, and when the train arrived at the station in Kansas City, there was a crowd of reporters and photographers waiting. No interviews were allowed. Cook was taken into a police wagon for the final ride to the penitentiary.

Marshal Gross had been as kindly and pleasant as the early spring day, but the anticipation of what was to come had made the trip an ordeal for the prisoner. His first sight of the prison made him think of the tomb:

> Before me were the ponderous walls of stone and steel with glass port holes – windows that offered no outlook. Behind was the world of life. . . . Now as the huge stairway to the big penal institution was to engage my feet, the doom of damnation spread mental crepe everywhere.
>
> As I stepped and stepped up and up into the unknown of a dark future world, the nothingness of time before creation was near. The emptiness of life after the body cools was not far off. The immense outer door opened and closed with a sickening metallic ring. The rattle of keys, and the icy slabs of marble in the dark interior, completed the feeling of one who enters the mausoleum in which he expects to be planted for the final rest. As I now walked under the huge rotunda and eyed beyond the long, lone, lane of mystery, incomplete and in ill repair as is everything everywhere in prison, where the hope of future departs, then came the thought, – so this is Leavenworth, brimmed with the tears of men lost – a weedy wilderness – a weeping willow jungle, where everything

> grows – where nothing withers but [the] essential goodness of the human heart. It was cold. Leavenworth is always cold. It is the coldest spot on earth.[22]

As Cook contemplated his fate, Marshal Gross led him inside to transfer his commitment papers. After this had been done, the doctor was strip-searched for contraband and then ushered into the waiting room outside the warden's office.

Warden W.I. Biddle soon appeared and, in a friendly manner, invited Dr. Cook inside. There was a meeting of the parole board in progress, which he suspended long enough to introduce the doctor to those present. The warden assured the prisoner that everything would be done to make his stay as easy as possible. He then said to the guard, "Put Doctor Cook through in the usual way."

The next stop was the receiving department. The block-long walk to the small brick building seemed a mile, and beyond that loomed one mysterious building after another; surrounding all stood the high, austere wall that excluded any view of the far horizon. The doctor was issued a set of prison clothes—not the stripes he expected, but a woolen suit of gray-blue—given a physical examination and fingerprinted. He was then led to the photographer, "where names are exchanged for a number." "For a few hours we thus went through a troublesome set of introductory formalities," he remembered, "but I heard and saw very little – my receptive sense was blunted by deep seated grief, and despondency. I felt like a caged animal with a desire to shout the call of the wilds. Though everybody was kind, nothing suited me. Everywhere there was the cold feel and smell of impending death."[23]

Passing through the yard, Cook was greeted by a man he had known in Texas, who took his hand warmly, but the man was reprimanded harshly by a guard for doing so. At 10:30 the doctor was locked into a receiving cell. The snap of the locks grated on his nerves, making a sound that symbolized, to Cook's mind, doom and the end of liberty.

Soon a guard approached and tried to engage in small talk, but the doctor didn't feel much like talking. The guard offered the newcomer some friendly advice: "A prisoner

Cook behind bars, 1925.

gets what he gives, not more. Remember that, and act accordingly." This little kindness endeared the guard to him out of proportion to the act. Their conversation was interrupted by the sound of a bugle. Gongs rang and keys rattled in an irritating manner. It was dinner call.

In the huge main hall no conversation was allowed. The lines of hungry men shuffled silently to the narrow tables and waited for the wagons to come down the aisles and the food to be passed along the lines of inmates. But the doctor did not feel like eating and returned to his cell unfed but not hungry.

Dr. Cook could find no ray of bright hope in his dark cell. He trusted no one except the guard who had tried to befriend him. All others at their very sight aroused feelings of persecution. Just as he was thinking that another week in that icy little cell would turn him into a paranoiac, his friend returned "with a glowing smile which could not be mistaken for anything but good news."

The guard rolled two cigarettes, lit them and handed one through the bars. "Doctor you are in luck," he said after taking a puff. "You have the best job—and the best place for a [berth] to sleep in the institution. Your loneliness is at an end. Tomorrow you leave my picture gallery—to work in the hospital and to loaf in Parole H. Big Tim Murphy is there and he will curse you out often enough to give life a new meaning. The Warden will do the rest for he needs your medical capacity. We are short of Doctors and there is a small-pox epidemic. Good news isn't it?"

"Yep," said Cook as he thought, "If he had added leprosy and the Black Plague – it would still have been good news for me."[24]

Warden Biddle was happy to get Dr. Cook. Though there were already 49 doctors among the 3,185 prisoners, most of them had been imprisoned for violation of the Harrison Drug Act and could not be trusted in the hospital.[25]

"Parole H" proved to be a large cellar dormitory with double steel gates; below it was "the Hole"—solitary confinement. Parole H was occupied by 80 men he did not know; of all the PPA men sent to Leavenworth, only one remained when Cook arrived—S.E.J. Cox. The others had already been paroled, except for T.O. Turner; he had died there.

Some of his cellmates came forward and shook hands with the newcomer, but all the doctor could feel was "an unresponsive creepiness" at their touch. He was glad to be out of the dismal receiving block, and there was a faint feeling that perhaps he might soon be in a position to do some good, but he regretted the loss of his kindly friend, the guard.

In the hospital he was introduced to Dr. Huey, the physician in charge, and Dr. Mereness, who assigned him to the operating room. It was the first room in the prison that seemed to him to have a purpose other than to rob a man of his normal life.

Despite the guard's mention of an epidemic, there was little to do, but there was plenty of time—time to look from the high windows of the hospital at the new surroundings below. The sheer size of the place and the antlike lines of men coming and going worried him. How could such a den of suffering humanity endure without riot, murder and the violence of personal combat? he wondered. He simply could not place himself in the vision before him. "I was a convict myself, but like other newcomers, I was to myself—not the commonplace villain for whom prisons are built. No, I was not yet ready to merge into this picture of degradation and damnation."[26]

Adjustment came slowly for the doctor. For a long time he imagined himself the only sane man among those in the huge damp cellar. As he looked upon his cellmates, he noticed the frozen, emotionless cast of their faces that seemed to indicate a blunting of the senses and a premature dulling of the mind brought on by the mere tiresomeness of existence.

There was one dynamic, if not rational, personality among these men, however, the doctor thought. He was the man the guard had mentioned, Big Tim Murphy. Once a prime figure in gangland Chicago, he was as strong as a bull and could bellow just as loudly.

"Tim expressed himself in dramatic eloquence, using chiefly swear words in poetic alignment. . . . An impressionist with a limited mental range, Big Tim was nevertheless the emperor of his domain," Cook soon learned.

"Hurling at me volley after volley of violent curse words, Tim promptly kicked me out of an attitude of silence and cold indifference into an atmosphere of insurgency. The spirit of this warfare was directed first against myself, and out of this I gained a valuable lesson – for as I learned later a man must know himself before he can understand others, must know himself before he can wield a power over others, and eventually must know himself, or die unknown."[27]

The doctor found that behind the violent exterior of men like Big Tim lay some likable traits, if one could be patient enough to wait for them to emerge and sympathetic enough to appreciate them when they did. Cook was coming to realize that he had been cast in with another class of men as worthy of study as the primitives who had so fascinated him before: "[Big Tim] taught me that I was in a world unknown – in a walled city of human degradation which required the search light of science, and when this mental attitude arrived some discoveries were made.

"Days, weeks and months now passed in dull routine, but my ever expanding interest took on new forms – even dullness and monotony offered subjects for study."[28]

But living in the group dormitory, Dr. Cook had periods of recurrent anger and nervous depression that left him in no mood to write or to study, even if he had been given the opportunity. Still, he realized that he needed something to avoid the monotony imprinted on his fellow prisoners' faces, something to give a mental stimulus and constant occupation. In the dark cellar of Parole H, Dr. Cook resumed his handiwork. The hours passed more quickly as his fingers embroidered the dictates of his mind upon a piece of cloth. Even after his transfer to "Banker's Row," where 12 to 15 former professionals lived in relative comfort above the deputy's office, he continued his embroidery, making table runners with floral designs, and as his fingers were occupied by the needle, he thought about his future course. At length, he decided that the guard's words would be his motto, and he vowed to give whatever he could.

Work occupied the day, but it often seemed to Cook more like a madhouse than a hospital. About a third of the prisoners in Leavenworth were "hop-heads"—drug addicts. Looked down upon by the staff and the other prisoners alike, they received little care. When they arrived, most were thrown in the "bullpen" on the hospital's top floor and given "twilight sleep"—scopolamine—to calm them. Their insane shrieks and beating against the walls were regular sounds in the wards below when the sedative's effects dissipated.

At first Cook felt the same revulsion for these desperate men, since they were unable even to explain the habit that had reduced them to an almost subhuman state. But when he delved into their psychology, he began to realize that in the sum of their individual weaknesses there might be something larger to fear: "I was led to believe that modern civilization is going under the cloud of a plague, more destructive in its economic strain than that of all the wars of history."[29]

"The opium blight, if not checked, will, eventually, sap the life blood of half of all mankind," he predicted. "It can be stopped by the stroke of the pen, under an international agreement."[30]

Dr. Cook proposed a treatment plan involving some of the techniques he had used on his depressed shipmates aboard the *Belgica* so many years before. He prescribed epinephrine and strychnine as heart stimulants, to ease their withdrawal from opiates and its consequent nausea. Water, sunlight, exercise and fresh meat were provided to bring the body's natural balance back into line. Tonics such as cod liver oil were prescribed for convalescents instead of sedatives. Although he admitted this was a crude system of treatment and the problem needed far more study, at least the screaming madness of the narcotic ward was eliminated, and the doctor's reassuring presence seemed to have a calming effect on his patients.

Despite this success in relieving the physical symptoms of addiction, Cook realized this was no cure; the answer to stopping addiction and preventing its return lay wholly within the psychology of the addict. "This man is a by-product of social disorganization," he thought. ". . . If something is not done to correct this disaster the gulf of modern civilization will be filled in and obliterated by the drug-shot dead.

"But what can be done? . . . Condemnation, abuse, isolation, punishment never has and never will salvage human derelicts. There is no drug cure for the habit and there probably never will be. . . . It is not difficult to take the patient from the habit and place him back in society as a fairly normal individual, but the great unsolved problem is to devise means to keep him there and away from drugs."[31]

By his success with the hop-heads, Dr. Cook rapidly gained the confidence of the prison doctors. After six months they made him night warden of the hospital, a position of trust that left him in charge 16 hours a day, from 4 P.M. to 8 A.M. He requested and received permission to transfer from Banker's Row to the hospital so that he could be on call. Here he had a small, well-lighted room to himself, a good bed, running water and a chair.[32]

Prison rules forbade inmates to write for publication, and they were limited to three letters a week. Each was censored before being sent out and could pertain only to business or family matters. So the doctor had no opportunity to answer the many letters he received each day. Mostly he wrote to Dr. Thompson, and he let it be known that he did not wish any visitors, as they tended to disturb his scrupulously observed routines. In those long, silent hours of night duty, Cook jotted down his observations of prison life and began to draft his memoirs.

Just before Christmas, he learned what had become of his Texas dreams. After the receivers were finished with the Petroleum Producers Association, there was a cash balance of $71.10 left in its account, plus $4,000 in miscellaneous assets. The rest had been sold for $18,841.74, of which the court-appointed receivers took $7,230 as their fee. He also learned that he had been indicted for the third time, in connection with his association with Paul Vitek and his Smackover operations. This did not worry him a great deal, since the indictment against him in Texas for his part in the Revere and Pilgrim Oil companies had been dismissed by kindly Judge Wilson, and he had every reason to believe the same would come of this indictment.[33]

On January 20, 1926, Dr. Cook made an exception to his self-imposed isolation when he was informed that a man by the name of Amundsen had requested a visit.

With the South Pole, the Northwest Passage and the fixing of the North Magnetic Pole to his credit, Roald Amundsen was considered, the world over, the greatest living explorer—except in England. The English had never forgiven him for beating Scott to the Pole. They considered Amundsen's secret change of plans in 1910 a cowardly deceit, unworthy of any sportsman. Many held to the idea that Scott's discouragement at having been beaten to the object of his ambition, rather than his own inefficiency and refusal to use dogs rather than men to haul his sledges, was the telling factor in his failure to return. This, and the suicide of Hjalmar Johansen, Nansen's traveling companion, with whom Amundsen had clashed in a bitter disagreement over his authority on his South Polar expedition, had caused him much personal pain. His later activities had been bold, but all had fallen short of their object—the North Pole. A drift journey to the Pole in the *Maud* had been a failure, and an attempt to fly there in 1924 had come down short at 87°44' north latitude.

The Norwegian now was touring the country to raise money for his latest venture, a crossing of the polar basin by airship with his rich American backer, Lincoln Ellsworth. In the Midwest, Amundsen had met Thomas Hall.

He and the old captain had talked for an hour and a half of their common beliefs about the claims of Cook and Peary. Amundsen mentioned that he wanted to visit Dr. Cook but did not know if it would please him. The captain encouraged him to do so and also to veer a little out of his course and go over Bradley Land on his coming flight.

Amundsen told Hall that at his landing spot in 1924 he had seen two geese and one auk fly away in the direction of Bradley Land and considered this "certain evidence of its existence."

Hall reminded Amundsen that if he sighted Bradley Land, it would make Cook the discoverer of the North Pole and thwart his own ambitions but that he was sure Amundsen was "big enough to overlook that point." As the captain told Edwin Swift Balch: "He agreed with me, and I think he wants to be the one to see it and to announce it. If he goes out of the way to do so, it will show his greatness."[34]

Captain Hall and Amundsen agreed on other things besides the likely existence of Bradley Land. Neither had any use for Vilhjalmur Stefansson. Hall had said of him, "He will probably go as far from truth to uphold Peary as I have shown he was willing to go to besmirch Cook."[35] In a supplement to his book that he had printed in 1920, Hall had blasted MacMillan's and Stefansson's veracity. Amundsen told Hall that Stefansson had admitted to him that all the business about the "blond Eskimos" was a publicity stunt. "That was for the reporters," he had said.[36] Neither Hall nor Amundsen believed in Stefansson's reliability as an explorer or as a man. At the end of their meeting, Captain Hall had high hopes that the truth would be "unfolded" at last.

By the time he reached Kansas City, Amundsen had thrown off all doubts about seeing his old companion from the *Belgica*. "I owed my life indeed to his resourcefulness in extracting us from the dangers of that expedition," Amundsen recalled. "I felt I could do no less than to make the short journey to the prison and call upon my former benefactor in his present misfortune. I could not have done less without convicting myself of base ingratitude and contemptible cowardice. . . . Even had I known that he had been guilty of baser crimes than those with which he was charged, I would still have felt my duty and my inclination to be the same. Whatever Cook may have done, the Cook who did them was not the Dr. Cook I knew as a young man, the soul of honour and kindliness, lion-hearted in courage. Some physical misfortune must have overtaken him to change his personality, for which he was not responsible."[37]

When he entered the warden's office, Dr. Cook was immediately struck by the contrast between Amundsen and himself. The Norwegian's face was ruddy from his long summers in the brilliance of a never-setting sun, while his own was pallid with the shadow of his confinement. The two old friends clasped hands, and this grip was not broken as they sat on a bench and talked quietly while guards and curious officials looked on.

Inevitably, their talk turned to Amundsen's plans and recent defeats. Amundsen told Cook he thought he had gone far enough north on his abortive flight to the Pole in 1925 to verify all of the descriptions of the pack, and he talked of his airship, *Norge,* and the perils of the coming flight.

Though he appeared to be the picture of health and freedom, the doctor could feel a sense of pessimism and bitterness that seemed to have overtaken his friend, and Amundsen soon gave voice to it. "Now what is the situation?" he said. "We have much in common, so little time to talk. You are in prison, but all men are barred some where. You have suffered more than you ever will here. Our lot has been a hard one. From the depths of poverty to the heights of glory. From brief spells of hard earned success to the scourge of condemnation. I have wondered for years how you stood it all. I have had the same, with perhaps not so much of the knife in it, but with quite as much of the pain of envy. . . .

". . . Men have stabbed you out of the darkness. They have stabbed me in broad daylight."[38]

At the end of the 45-minute reunion, Amundsen rose to go, saying he would come again if he survived his upcoming polar flight. But before he left he expressed his faith in his old friend. "I want you to know," Amundsen said, "even if all the world goes against you, that I believe in you as a man."[39]

Though no reporters were allowed to interview the prisoner, a guard volunteered that Amundsen's visit had had a distinctly positive effect on Cook. "Finding such a champion as Amundsen is to Dr. Cook almost like getting a reprieve from prison," said the guard. "Dr. Cook looks like a new man despite his 60 yrs."[40] Cook wasted no time in sending a letter to the Kansas City *Journal-Post* declaring that future visits to the Pole, such as Amundsen's imminent flight, would certainly vindicate his claim to the attainment of the North Pole.

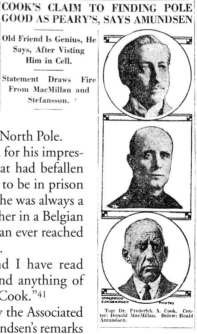

COOK'S CLAIM TO FINDING POLE GOOD AS PEARY'S, SAYS AMUNDSEN

Old Friend Is Genius, He Says, After Visiting Him in Cell.

Statement Draws Fire From MacMillan and Stefansson.

Top: Dr. Frederick A. Cook. Center: Donald MacMillan. Below: Roald Amundsen.

In Fort Worth Amundsen was asked for his impressions of his visit with Cook and of what had befallen him. "I don't know whether he deserves to be in prison or not," he told some reporters. "To me he was always a genius. When we were young men together in a Belgian Antarctic expedition I said that if any man ever reached the North Pole it would be Dr. Cook. . . .

"I have read Dr. Cook's story and I have read Peary's. In Peary's story I have not found anything of consequence not covered already by Dr. Cook."[41]

When this interview was reported by the Associated Press, there was general amazement. Amundsen's remarks were widely interpreted as meaning that Cook had as valid a claim to the North Pole as Peary. As the furor his words generated began to break over him, Amundsen protested that he had been misquoted, but it was too late.

Adolph S. Ochs, the owner of the *New York Times,* was "indignant that he should mention [Peary's] name in connection with the infamous Dr. Cook."[42]

Gilbert Grosvenor was outraged. He considered Amundsen's remarks a slur on Peary's great accomplishment. Amundsen was informed that an invitation to lecture before the National Geographic Society on his proposed aerial voyage had been withdrawn. Amundsen called Grosvenor's action "silly" and protested again that he had been misquoted, but when the criticism did not abate, the Norwegian cut short his American tour and prepared to return to Europe.

"Maybe they will grow up someday," Amundsen said to a reporter who accompanied him to his New York hotel room. There he found a small package waiting for him. When he opened it and saw its contents, his voice broke with emotion as he held up a beautifully embroidered linen table runner 15 inches wide and four feet long. "Well, and whom do you think this is from?" he asked. "The man I once thought was going to discover both the North and South Poles. Now, poor fellow, he is in Leavenworth Prison. And he did every stitch of it with his own hands. It is pathetic. Yes, it is from Dr. Cook. I am more touched by this gift than by almost anything that has happened to me in a long time."[43]

Captain Hall was disappointed in Amundsen's attempted retraction of his remarks about Dr. Cook and his failure to hold the ground he had staked out at their interview. He concluded that he may have overestimated the man. "Will any leader of an expedition after his strenuous effort to reach the goal of his ambition, further strain himself to prove that the honor and the glory really belongs to Cook?" he asked a friend.

"It does look as if not any of them would. All explorers are by nature ambitious for glory. It is at least temporarily to their personal interest that the present status of both Cook and Peary in the public mind be undisturbed, i.e. that they both be considered eliminated as claimants." But still, Captain Hall looked forward eagerly to the *Norge's* flight that coming spring:

> All this to me, even at my advanced age, causes interesting thoughts. There looms in my vision a possibility at least of Cooks early redemption. . . .
>
> Explorers as a class are perhaps unusually amenable to the mutations in human affairs. But it seems that the life of this Man-meteor in his unequal and unfair contest with the vicissitudes of fate, had not been wholly unlike that of the Pearl Diver described by Browning,
>
> "A pauper, when he prepares to plunge,"
>
> "A prince when he rises with the pearl."[44]

General Greely, now the grand old man of the Arctic, had taken the opportunity of Amundsen's remarks to once again voice his own doubts that either Cook or Peary had reached the Pole, though he said that Cook, unlike Peary, may have lacked the navigational experience to know exactly where he had been and was simply under the illusion that he had.

In light of the interviews with Captain Amundsen and General Greely, newspapers that had treated Dr. Cook as a joke for years began to reconsider their words:

> At any rate, the captain and the general, between them, have shown Cook to the public in a new light.
>
> The former has focused attention on a fact hitherto little stressed—that the "doc" had a highly honorable record to his credit before the Mount McKinley and north polar episodes. The latter, while refusing to accept his claim to attainment of the earth's hub, assumes that he was honestly mistaken.[45]

Immediately, Donald MacMillan came forward to restate the evidence against Cook, but it was left to Vilhjalmur Stefansson to cast doubt on Amundsen's and Greely's motives by suggesting "that they had a notion that the North Pole would some time be visited by either themselves or their friends, and desired to prepare the public mind for the idea that both the Cook and Peary stories were doubtful, so that they themselves might be considered the first undisputed visitors."[46]

But there was much more than two interviews to worry the keepers of Peary's memory. Already, in 1924, an article in the *Manchester Geographical Journal* by an English cleric named J. Gordon Hayes had systematically attacked Peary's credibility. But he was far away, and his article got little notice in America. The most threatening figure to Stefansson was William Shea, an investigative journalist whose articles for *The Independent* had resurrected and elaborated all the old doubts about Peary first expressed in Congress in 1911.

He also had unearthed an article by Matt Henson that had appeared in 1910 in the *Boston American,* which contradicted Peary's account in many crucial respects. Shea emphasized Peary's physical shortcomings and Henson's assertion that Peary had ridden most of the way on the sleds. Stefansson feared that Shea's views would make their way into a series of books on the twentieth century called *Our Times* by his editor, Mark Sullivan, and would then achieve permanent form.

Stefansson had gauged Shea right. He had established contact with Captain Hall and with Dr. Cook at Leavenworth, and he was drawing on their expertise to dismember Peary's claims. Soon, a review of *Has the North Pole Been Discovered?* by Henshaw Ward, an English teacher and writer, also appeared in *The Independent.* The captain's book, which had lain dormant in those many libraries he had given it to eight years before, suddenly became an active voice in the renewed chorus of doubt.

Stefansson dismissed these critics, as well as Amundsen and Greely, by saying: "None of the writers of pro-Cook and anti-Peary articles and book reviews has ever traveled afoot or by dog sledge over the drifting ice fields of the Arctic Ocean. This likewise applies to those who have criticized Peary in the newspapers within recent weeks. . . . In other words, no one has yet questioned Peary's accomplishment who has had experience in the same field."[47]

But legs and dog sledges were no longer the preferred means of making polar discoveries. On May 9, 1926, Commander Richard E. Byrd reported he and his pilot, Floyd Bennett, had reached the North Pole from Kings Bay, Spitzbergen, in their airplane, *Josephine Ford,* and had seen nothing but ice the entire distance.

Two days later Amundsen got away from the same base in his dirigible, *Norge,* and crossed the polar basin via the Pole, landing at Teller, Alaska, on May 13. He had seen no land either. At last there was indisputable independent confirmation of Cook's first report—there was nothing at the Pole but moving ice.

The nearly simultaneous announcements of Byrd and Amundsen refocused attention on the Polar Controversy but brought no conclusion to it. Amundsen had not made any detour to search for Bradley Land.

Stefansson had already begun a dialogue with the offending article writers and by use of his prestige and considerable charm tried to dissuade them from their views, or at least from airing them. In the coming months, Stefansson would write to the Reverend Hayes that "so far as the published evidence goes you have the best of the Peary argument" but intimated he knew of unpublished evidence that prevented him from agreeing with Hayes that Peary did not reach the Pole.[48] He even took up correspondence with Captain Hall himself, now in his mid-80s.

Hall assured Stefansson that he was not a Cook partisan but had had no change of heart about Peary. "I tried to make clear . . . my object in writing the book," he told Stefansson. "It was, in substance, to unfold the truth. . . .

"The truth about Peary is, that he did not go to 87°06' in 1906, nor to the North Pole in 1909.

"The truth about Cook is, that no one but himself knows whether he reached the Pole or not.

"There is a superabundance of evidence in Peary's book and in the books of his comrades to convict him of deception.

"I am unable to find anything in Cook's book that is evidence against his claim."[49]

"Peary is eliminated," Hall concluded. "If Bradley Land is proven nonexistent, Cook is eliminated. If it exists, Cook is the discoverer. It seems to be studiously shunned, as if its existence was feared."[50]

Stefansson learned through the publisher William Morrow, who had been Stokes's secretary when Peary's book was being written, that it had been ghosted, but Morrow recommended he see the writer himself for details and gave him A.E. Thomas's address.

To this end Stefansson arranged a luncheon with the one-time newspaper-man, now a famous playwright, who remembered Peary as "an earnest, honest, single-track personality to whom most things meant nothing and a few everything." Thomas confirmed that most of his data for *The North Pole* had come from Bartlett, Borup, MacMillan and Goodsell, and that none had come from Henson, whom he understood "he was not supposed to consult with." But Thomas believed Peary had read all of his proofs, although he said he was surprised at how few changes he had made in them. Stefansson sent a memo on this meeting to Isaiah Bowman, the director of the American Geographical Society.[51]

Next, Stefansson and Bowman together interviewed Matt Henson, who held to his story that Peary had been little more than baggage after Bartlett had left, riding on the fifth sled. Henson also stated that Bartlett was slow on the trail and, at the point he turned back, was in no shape to continue, as both of his legs were badly swollen.[52]

Bowman was for letting the Peary family decide whether Henson's allegations and Thomas's authorship should be made public. But Stefansson decided to say nothing and wait to see what developed. What developed was that when the critics had started to appear, the family had given approval to Commander Fitzhugh Green, MacMillan's companion on the Crocker Land Expedition, to write the first biography of Peary, a project that Herbert Bridgman had toyed with. But at the time of his death in 1924, Bridgman had not gotten beyond accumulating a number of remembrances of Peary by his associates.

In the preface to Green's book, which now appeared under the imprint of G.P. Putnam, Jo Peary wrote: "It is my hope that this work will create a clearer and better understanding of a character that is too little known or appreciated."[53]

Green's biography, whose proofs and galleys were all checked by the Peary family, was a maudlin affair that one reviewer called "a hodgepodge of sentimental slush." Its readers learned of Peary's origins and birth:

> It is as though that group of good people were laid like an egg of Destiny in the womb of a clean nature for the single purpose of bringing forth a finer specimen of the race than the commonplace mechanics of gestation could achieve.[54]

And of his death:

> He died a poor man. . . . He had sunk all his earlier earnings into his expeditions. The tragedy of the controversy robbed him of what he might have won through lectures and writing. . . . No, there lay no taint of greed in Peary's polar search.[55]

As for what lay between, rather than fulfilling Jo Peary's hope, Fitzhugh Green felt compelled to explain why "many in Peary's command used to return hating him in a way that murder couldn't gratify." In so doing, he had left much space for reading between his lines by refuting, among other things, charges that Peary was "inhuman," cold, greedy, venial, unsympathetic, ungenerous and that he had a mania for fame.

In what may have been a veiled reference to Dr. Cook, Green admitted that Peary was incapable "of being automatically able to inspire his men by that hypnotic charm some men have, the weaker more often than the strong character . . . [with] a blurred and fuzzy humaneness, so reassuring to the doubtful or suspicious."[56]

When the book was released, Gilbert Grosvenor disliked the context in which the National Geographic Society was mentioned and indignantly objected. Green, in turn, promised to change the offending passage in the second printing.[57]

Stefansson may have dismissed Peary's critics publicly, but in private he was very anxious about the growing insecurity of Peary's claim. Adding to his worries, now came reports that Ross Marvin's death on the 1908 expedition had been no accident; one of Peary's Eskimos had confessed to having killed him, causing some to recall that Dr. Cook had written in *My Attainment of the Pole,* "Marvin's death . . . does not seem natural."

In prison, Dr. Cook was naturally interested in the renewed discussion of the Polar Controversy, but he had some more immediate concerns. Besides his duties as night warden of the hospital, he was allowed to lecture to groups of inmates on his experiences as an explorer. He also had been made superintendent of the prison school, taking as his motto: "An openminded adventurousness must be the first cause in adult education." He taught vocational subjects along with reading and writing. But now the routines he had established for himself and his position as trusty seemed to be in jeopardy.

"The entire institution has been under official suspicion," it seemed to him. ". . . Secret Service men, spies, inspectors and under cover investigators come and go as a regular phase of life in the walled city of trouble. . . .

"Upon my state of mind this turmoil had a sad effect. The local officials had been good to me. The prisoners were respectful and friendly. To me the outside investigators were blood hounds trailing game for their own vicious purposes."[58]

But the reasons for the investigations were well founded, and if they were not understood by the doctor living in his private room off the hospital ward, they were well known to every inmate behind the bars of the locked cell blocks, even to newcomers to Leavenworth like Joseph Weil.

Weil was in for a stretch as an accessory to bank robbery. But although he freely admitted he was a "master swindler," he denied being anything so coarse as a bank robber. Weil had used his unusually persuasive personality and a little bribe money to obtain the privileged position of Dr. Cook's secretary.

Joe Weil was much taken with the doctor and took time to study his past. "He was a tall, kindfaced, mild-mannered man," Weil recalled, "who was friendly to everybody and who exercised the utmost tolerance towards the prisoners. . . .

". . . My own research convinced me Dr. Cook actually did discover the Pole. My association with him convinced me there was nothing about him that was faked. I became his friend, just as everybody else in Leavenworth was his friend."[59]

Although Joe Weil believed Cook was clean, he knew some prison doctors weren't. One took money, sometimes as much as $10,000, to ensure that a negative Wassermann test appeared on the parole report of any man about to be released, since no man with syphilis could be considered for parole. This same doctor rented out the parole room to convicts who could pay. "A man with money could have almost anything he desired brought to him in the parole room," reported Weil. "Actually, for the wealthy convicts—and there were many, such as bootleggers, racketeers, and gangsters—Leavenworth was more like a gentleman's club."[60]

Among the things brought in were cases of morphine-laced cigarettes, which one guard was smuggling using a Christian Science worker as the unwitting delivery man.

The extensive investigation cleaned out the corrupt officials and guards. Blood testing was moved to the University of Kansas and duplicate records were kept, ending any chance of Wassermann test blackmail. By the time it was over, practically the whole prison hierarchy had been replaced, all the way up to the warden, who was now Thomas B. White, and someone new, Dr. Bennet, had been placed in charge of the hospital.

On March 19, 1927, Warden White received a judicial order from Judge James C. Wilson in Fort Worth. Wilson's recommendation that Cook be given credit for time in jail in Texas had been ignored, and the judge thought Cook's sentence was far too long for a man nearly 60—a life sentence, in effect. Taking advantage of a law passed in 1925, Judge Wilson had granted probation to Cook for time served and ordered him released. Warden White wired Washington and received the reply: "Continue to hold Frederick A. Cook pending further instructions from department."

When Judge Killits heard of Wilson's action, he said that if Cook was released, he would have him arrested and brought to trial in Ohio for mail fraud; a bench warrant for that purpose was issued in Cleveland. Before Wilson's order could be executed, however, the government appealed on the basis that the law did not apply, since it had been instituted after Cook's conviction. Judge Wilson agreed to hold his order in abeyance until a ruling could be made.

In June Judge Wilson's order was vacated by the appeals court. In turn, Cook appealed to the United States Supreme Court for a writ of certiorari, which was granted. His case was docketed for a hearing in the fall.

That summer G.P. Putnam and Peary's son went north on the *Effie M. Morrissey*, a schooner captained by Bob Bartlett, to investigate the reported murder of Ross Marvin. Accompanying them was William H. Hobbs, a professor of geology at the University of Michigan and a vehement supporter of Peary; Cook had called him "a coward faker and embryo militarist" on a visit to Ann Arbor in 1916. They were joined by Knud Rasmussen, who had come from Copenhagen especially to assist them. When the *Morrissey* returned, Putnam said he had obtained the true story behind Marvin's death.

He reported that Marvin, in a fit of rage, had threatened to leave behind on the ice one of the two Eskimos who were with him. The other Eskimo, Kudlooktoo, who had been practically a household member of all of Peary's expeditions since he had been selected as the "Snow Baby's" playmate in 1893, then shot Marvin with his own rifle to save his companion.

Putnam's explanation was enough to squelch the story but it did not satisfy critics like William Shea or Captain Hall. Dr. Cook, too, held his own opinion. "The later reports of Marvin's murder are unconvincing to me," he wrote Shea. "I am sure if some one will carefully go over the letters Marvin sent home that a different motive can be found for the death. I am equally sure that Peary, Henson and Bartlett knew of Marvin's death and that there was a conspiracy to suppress the facts that later came from Denmark. The incentive for this tragedy has not yet been told."[61]

Even Donald MacMillan refused to believe Putnam's explanation, since he remembered Marvin as the most kindly and even-tempered of men. Besides, MacMillan declared, Marvin and his alleged murderer were the best of friends, though the two Eskimos hated each other. MacMillan preferred to adhere to the theory that Marvin's death had been simply an accident after all.

Meanwhile, Cook waited patiently, hoping for release on Judge Wilson's order. On November 22, with Assistant Attorney General Mabel Walker Willebrandt handling the government's case, arguments were heard before the Supreme Court. She maintained that the Texas courts had lost all jurisdiction over the petitioner after his sentence had begun and cited several legal precedents for continuing to hold Cook.

The court's decision, written by Chief Justice William Howard Taft, who as president had sent his congratulations to Cook at Copenhagen, ruled that the Probation Act of 1925 did not empower the trial court to place on probation a defendant who had begun serving a sentence prior to its passage.[62]

This outcome was a bitter disappointment to Cook, but at least, despite the housecleaning at Leavenworth, none of his privileges had been taken away. In fact, he was assigned even more responsibilities.

When S.E.J. Cox arrived at the penitentiary, he had, naturally enough, been made the editor of the prison newspaper, *The Leavenworth New Era*. When "Lucky" Cox was released on parole on July 20, 1926, he had vowed, "Hereafter I will think faster and act slower." Succeeding him as editor was Colonel Charles R. Forbes, a man who had, as one observer commented, "every needful quality of the universal good fellow and high-class confidence man." Forbes was no common criminal, however. The former director of the Veterans Bureau was doing time for bilking the government out of millions by illegally selling the bureau's supplies and for grotesquely fraudulent practices in the construction of its hospitals.

After Forbes took over, an article in the prison's paper caused a stir in the national dailies. It was signed by the colonel, but the contents came directly from Dr. Cook: a lengthy argument for the validity of Cook's claims in the wake of the polar flights of the previous year.[63] It seemed that Cook had discovered another advocate, but Forbes's article was nothing compared with what the doctor himself would do once Forbes had been released.

Cook was then asked to edit the paper, and he began by renaming it simply *The New Era*. The doctor had been a contributor to the paper before, writing a humorous column called "Give Kansas Back to the Indians," but now that he was its editor, he saw the serious possibilities the paper offered. He had plenty of material from his late-night jottings, and he could set his personal stamp upon it. But he had hardly begun when he was incapacitated by a hernia requiring surgery.

Even this redounded to the doctor's benefit. When news of his operation was broadcast, he received a deluge of Christmas cards and notes from well-wishers. Cook had already petitioned once for executive clemency in 1926. Now, citing his health status, the doctor appealed again to President Coolidge. He continued to maintain that his sentence was excessive and his actions in relation to PPA's business transactions showed no intent to defraud. As his petition declared:

> So thorough was his belief in the Petroleum Producers Association that he sold [his] Wyoming interests and placed all the money with the company. All other funds and all his property were also placed in the company. He worked night and day for the success of the company and he continued to do so and continued to invest additional funds to the day of the trial. Could a man do this if he did not believe in the project?[64]

By the end of February 1928, Herbert Wade had persuaded Judge Killits to sign an order vacating the indictment pending against his client in Ohio, but Wade despaired of ever convincing Killits that Cook was penniless. The judge remained adamant in insisting that Cook pay the fines levied against him as a condition of parole.

Killits was still as certain that Cook had vast wealth stored away as when he discouraged a request by C.J. Stillson of the Prison Problem League, who had contacted the judge at the behest of Dr. Thompson, to discuss the convicted man's plea for clemency. "Cook was justly convicted," he told Stillson. ". . . I owe a public duty to oppose Executive clemency to him . . . at this time;

and unless he pays the judgment against him, . . . I will continue to always oppose his release.

"I know a great many well-meaning people still believe in Doctor Cook, and that it is hopeless to argue with such. If they are not convinced by the revelations concerning him, argument would be a waste of time. I know also, that his plausibility has persuaded many people that he is penniless; and that he cannot take any step towards repairing the expense he has caused his government as the result of his crime. But I have seen nothing to suggest that he is, except his word which, in view of his monstrous prevarications in the past, carries no weight."[65]

When Dr. Cook had made a full recovery, he was ready to begin his work as editor in earnest. At last he had the vehicle with which to reestablish communication with the outside world.

Through exchange programs, *The New Era* was sent to publishers and libraries across the country, from which Cook received other periodicals in return. Everyone who had written to the doctor, and whom he could not answer because of the restrictions on his correspondence, was now placed on its mailing list and received a free issue every month, mailed at the government's expense. These copies generated more requests, and the subscription list grew ever longer. Cook began to write most of the paper himself, and though polar subjects appeared occasionally, the articles he wrote showed a surprising variety, scope and depth of thought.

Almost anything was seed for the doctor's fertile mind, and the exchanges of *The New Era* for other publications brought a rich harvest of new ideas to the doctor in return, which he clipped and filed for future reference. Cook was especially taken with Einstein's general theory of relativity, John Watson's psychological philosophy of behaviorism and the writings of H.G. Wells on man's place in nature. These he adapted and transformed as subject matter for the paper.

Readers were treated to essays with metaphysical titles: "The Prospect of Heads," "Seeing the Unseen," "A Concept of Pre-creation." They were also asked provocative questions: "Is There a White Race?" "What Dies after Death?" "Do We Think in Words?" Unusual ideas appeared in features styled "Frontiers of a New Horizon" and "Other Worlds to Conquer." These contained experiences from the editor's career and an introduction to some of the ideas that Dr. Cook claimed "priority" to, such as "Power Theory," "Cellular Therapy" and "Feeling Perception."

Sometimes the articles were just offbeat. The doctor wrote of a method of bringing cold air down from the upper atmosphere to moderate the climate, a very individual explanation of baldness, and of a eugenicist future where pygmies and giants would be bred to perform specialized tasks in a world increasingly controlled by machines.

Often his pieces had a tinge of leftover nineteenth-century sentimentality or were merely banal, but sometimes they were inspired and visionary. A frequent subject was the interaction of men with each other or Man with Nature, and in each he theorized on the role of the tyranny of experience and the imposition of self as the interpreter of perception:

> The mental eye recreates all in symbolic form to fit its preconceived pictures of experience.
>
> Lacking experience, it is hard work for the mind to deal with unfamiliar abstractions, that do not fit into the scheme of life conditioned by previous experiment.
>
> We see only through the eyes of experience. . . . Things become real in feeling channels of thought—nowhere else. . . . To every man the world and all it implies begins and ends in mental visions.[66]

He applied this theory to many aspects of life: It was perception that created truth; everything beheld was interpreted in the light of experience, and this interpretation provided a reality that did not exist absolutely. The mind—the accumulated interpretation of perception through experience—then, was merely a "by-product of the brain":

> We begin somewhere, end no where, the intervening space is all that life offers. . . .
>
> . . . Today is the meeting place of yesterday and tomorrow, both have forever gone when today extends into the future. Time has no real existence. It is but a word-figure to express motion of the earth around the sun with relation to sunshine and earth shadow. Time is thus a symbol for degrees of space, distance, and like gravity it becomes lost in the usual grip of electric magnetic power.
>
> What we do today then is all that matters to the individual. . . . Does it give best color? . . . Your answer must always be no, for else implies human perfection, a condition never attained.[67]
>
> In his inter-relations, man feels what he believes others to feel, not more. From this mortgage on self there is no escape.[68]

He had, through his idea of "feeling perception," reduced the five senses to "extensions of the brain" that provided the material for interpretation into "reality," and he had reduced the universe via Einstein into "circles of power" that lay at the basis of all creation. In an essay entitled "A New Alignment Which Seems to Explain Nature—God—Life and Death," he wrote: "What follows is a new alignment of observation, thought and deductions outlining a theory so far reaching that it must be regarded as revolutionary to all of our ancient beliefs." Indeed, there were no limits except those that were self-imposed, he said; there was no longer an excuse for ignorance, he believed, and "with the knowledge of all ages thus before us, even speculation takes on the form of scientific analysis."[69] Anything, he reasoned, might be comprehended now that the line between reality and dreams had been erased.

In another essay, he instructed his readers how to get into the mood to think about the unknowable:

> Let us sit by a window a few hours before sunrise. Our purpose is to figure out the conditions before creation, with no local distractions, mind and body can be at ease. For three hours pre-creation is our problem to the exclusion of all other desires. We look with all attention into the dark blue of a cold star-lit night. Now, what was there before the stars appeared?[70]

Nevertheless, it was the feeling sense of sentient Nature, and not the reasoning power of Man, that was all important, the doctor concluded; "man may feel the unseen, but he will never see the unfelt."

The intellect and all its conceptions—time, space, society, morality, reality, immortality—lay in shambles in that little room off the Leavenworth hospital ward, mere illusions built of incoming perceptions from a universe that gave them no notice outside of the by-product of the brain.

With such a universe as he perceived, there was little room for puny Man and his pretensions to set himself above Nature:

> To speak of subduing nature is a false pretense. . . . It represents the inbred, inexcusable conceit of men.[71]

> We may seek the big bodies of the domain of stars, or the minute sphere of atoms—the infinity above and the infinity below—and still there is a beyond. . . .
> The claim of human superiority does not stand the test of time. The universe was far along in an orderly dominion before the coming of man. It will continue in the splendor of its spheroid rule after man and his self-made morality and immortality fades into the ever changing picture of other living powers. Man does not lead, and perhaps he does not even follow. He is carried along in the river of eternal life, to make and break the connections of nature's must-be, in the interchangeable power of eternity.[72]

In light of this, Dr. Cook advocated strict control of animal resources so as not to exploit a species and drive it to extinction. He warned against the plundering of the natural world and used the mechanization of whaling as an example. "If these methods are pursued for a few more years," he believed, "the antarctic seas, the last resort of the greatest animals of our day, will be depleted and in a few more generations only the skeletons will remain to tell the sad story of the last great world encircling animal. . . . Future generations will suffer from their depredations but there is a higher duty, that of protecting animated nature—what right have we to use the destructive war machinery of man against innocent inoffensive animals who by the same laws of creation have as much right to live as we have?"[73]

Still, the doctor often returned to the conventional world in his essays and had much to say about it. On social issues, he advocated racial and ethnic tolerance. "He who condemns a man because he hails from other lands or is clouded in shadows of a darker skin is weak in judgment, [and] mentally and ethically stupid," he declared.[74] He advocated the equality of women and men and asserted, "Our method of rendering woman less troublesome by reducing her station in life has few precedents in animated nature." To deny her any place but the one men assigned, he saw as the breeding ground of the war between the sexes. "If she stands straight and noble with the strength of a daring heart, if she spurns the arts of twining weakness, we pass her by. Inconsistency is man's privilege, is not this the battle line?" he asked.[75]

Based on his observations of the Eskimos, he felt trial marriages could serve a legitimate purpose but thought, considering the present social inequality of the sexes, they would be used to take advantage of women. He was against the rod, saying violence against children would beget violence, since the example of adults set their patterns of behavior, both mentally and physically, for the rest of their lives.

In the medical line, readers of *The New Era* were apprised of the use of "Fish as Brain Food," "The Dangers of Mineral Oil" and "The Delusion of Cough Syrup." Its editor advocated overlooked sources for human nutrition, such as earthworms, and argued that a study of primitives' diets might offer clues to a cure for cancer.

His visions of the future included a society on wheels, and he predicted that one day "great transcontinental roads for motor vehicles crossed and crisscrossed by thousands of good roads in every other direction will in turn revolutionize the social and economic habits of all the people of North America."[76] As for the society of nations, he was still as idealistic as he had been in Antarctica and held out the hope that "our age will perhaps place among its important archives a record of the fading picture of autocracy."

The prison newspaper had become a crucible for his speculations and thoughts, which he hoped would be "suggestive raw material to give resourcefulness to other thinkers, those who are seeking to envision the mirages of worlds beyond." After all, he said, "Men in prison think because they have nothing else to do"; it was Dr. Cook's belief that "we need men who think in terms of a 1000 years," and that it was, in the end, only ideas that counted for anything as a product of existence.[77]

Eventually, *The New Era* became a small magazine. Inside its front cover little poetic essays began to appear on commonplace things: clouds, potatoes, sand, stars. Its convict editor elicited scores of letters of praise from ministers, social workers and respectable men and women from all walks of life. *The New Era* soon was receiving national attention and its editor new respect. The *Literary Digest* noted:

> He has shown great versatility and a wide range of interest in his contributions. In his editorials he has struck a consistent note of hope, urging his fellow prisoners to spend their time learning trades and preparing to lead better lives upon release.[78]

Not all of this appealed to the inmates themselves, however, some of whom criticized the publication's contents as "highbrow," but this was exactly Cook's intention. He saw for *The New Era* the role of a "pathfinder" to a higher mental and moral life:

> We have endeavored to blaze a trail through your mental domains by keeping, ever in view, the elements that make for a better perception and a higher intelligence. We believe that the best way to eliminate vice is to give a pleasing relief to virtue and we, further, believe that the best school to greater wisdom is in setting a groundwork to a more stable system for self-seeking knowledge.
>
> Our subject matter may, at times, have appeared to be an array of generalities, but there was always the plan to offer an introduction to a better system of mental hygiene—not by any set rule of psychology—nor by preaching goodness or condemning badness, but by appealing to feeling instincts which are deepseated in every one. As the pathfinders, we have tried a new trail by way of the old home sentiments nearest to the heart of every man.[79]

But there was a dark side to Cook's prison writings, too—things that never appeared in the pages of *The New Era*. One was a manuscript he called "Man, the Poor Fish," a cryptic and apparently sarcastic and bitter allegory of his own persecution and incarceration.

In May 1928 Cook read that Roald Amundsen was feared lost in the Arctic. Amundsen had become embroiled in another bitter controversy, this time over who should have credit for the *Norge*'s triumphant voyage across the polar basin. His Italian pilot, Umberto Nobile, was claiming full credit, with the backing of the National Geographic Society.

To prove that Amundsen was superfluous to the enterprise, Nobile had attempted to repeat the feat and had crashed on the arctic pack in his identical airship, *Italia*. Amundsen had, on his own initiative, flown to the aid of the Italians. Though Nobile was rescued by others, then disgraced by the fact that he and his little pet dog were taken out on the first of the rescue planes to reach his stranded men, Amundsen had vanished.

Dr. Cook could not accept that Amundsen had lost his life, even when parts of his plane were found. He continued to maintain that once again, his great friend would emerge triumphant from his contest with the polar wastes. When so much time had passed that the sad truth could no longer be avoided, the doctor thought it a fitting end to an ideal life for his friend to have laid it down for his enemy.

By the summer of 1928, each new friend *The New Era* made contributed to the growing swell of pressure for its editor's release. In September it looked as though there was a chance of parole if authorities could be convinced that Cook's 16 months in the Tarrant County jail should be counted toward time served, as Judge Wilson had recommended. At least the doctor was optimistic. As he wrote to Dr. Thompson:

> I rather expect to be turned out in about 30 days, and I believe my chances are best without political pressure or publication of any kind. . . .
>
> If I get outside the walls—you will of course hear of it before I can send you news. So this may be my last letter but one is never out from here until he gets beyond the gates. I am in good health but tired of sunflowers and of Kansas.[80]

But his release didn't come. Outside antagonism against the doctor was still too great. So a new appeal for clemency was made on March 22, 1929, to the new president, Herbert Hoover. In his petition Cook said PPA had been operated according to "common business methods in the oil industry in Texas," that "the Government audit of the books showed that all money was spent to build up an Oil Company," and that Cook had taken nothing from the company for himself, but was owed "$21,000.00 for money advanced."

"To read a criminal intent into this kind of business enterprise with a seemingly undisputed record as above indicated, is at least a problem for further investigation," he suggested.[81]

On April 2 the petition was denied, just as the one put before President Coolidge had been. But at about this time new grounds for release presented themselves. Stories began to appear in the press about the fabulous wealth being made from the former holdings of the Petroleum Producers Association by those who had bought the properties for pennies in the government re-ceivership sale that disposed of its assets. The Pure Oil Company, which had bought half of PPA's assets in Howard County, was now listing them on its books at a value of $100,000,000.[82]

In Texas at least one former associate saw Dr. Cook's conviction as a con-spiracy to divest his company of its valuable holdings. "From what I see and hear," the man wrote to the imprisoned doctor, "it was, in my opinion, brought about by certain predatory interests who took advantage of your in-carceration to exploit and appropriate for their own selfish benefit, the results of what you discovered as a consequence of long and tedious research on your part. I understand that practically every claim you made in your literature, which was barred from the mails, has since been justified and was, therefore, warranted by your vision and foresight at the time."[83]

His friends urged Cook to seek a pardon based on these reports, but since he was due for parole in less than a year, he thought it best to make no more appeals that might bring outside pressure to prevent his release.

The problem that now weighed on Dr. Cook's mind was how he might earn a living once he gained his freedom. He professed to want only to return to medicine as an old-time family practitioner. Then, another answer seemed to come on August 8, 1929, when he received a visitor in the person of James R. Crowell of the *American Magazine*.

Crowell indicated that he wanted the doctor to write a series about his unusual career, intimating that the magazine had authorized him to offer $20,000 if the proposition was agreeable. Using the material already written for his memoirs, Cook began at once. In a subsequent visit he showed Crowell some of his chapters. Then Crowell stated what he was really after.

As Ben Hampton had years before, he wanted the doctor's reasons for making his audacious fake claim to the North Pole. Cook's reaction to Crowell's offer was much the same as it had been to Ray Long's suggestions nearly 20 years before: "I informed Mr. Crowell that I appreciated his offer and that I needed the money badly. However, I also told him I did not need money to the extent of telling an untruth, which any repudiation of my claim to the North Pole discovery . . . would really be. To a man in prison $20,000 is a lot of money. It was indeed a fortune to me, since I am without funds. But a million dollars would not be enough to cause me to waver from my claim to the discovery of the North Pole."[84]

After months of rumors, on February 5, 1930, the giant moving sign on the *Times* building at 42nd and Broadway ran the message THE GOVERNMENT BOARD OF PAROLES HAS RECOMMENDED THAT DR. FREDERICK A. COOK BE PAROLED IN MARCH.

It had been nearly seven years since his indictment in Fort Worth. In the space of time since that day in April 1923, both of his daughters had graduated from Cornell and married, and now he had two grandchildren. His brother Theodore, who had never ventured into the frigid zones of the earth, had accidentally frozen to death in a freezer plant of his own design in Callicoon. Many of the normal milestones in life had passed him by unwitnessed, and the doctor was just a few months short of 65, an age when men who had led ordinary lives normally settled into retirement.

The news of his impending release brought in a new flood of letters, many from unexpected sources. There was one from Sir Wilfred Grenfell, who had repudiated him in 1910. He now thanked Cook, belatedly, for the gift of dogs brought down from Greenland on the *Zeta* for his mission in Labrador in 1893. Another came from Samuel Beecher, who had sworn an affidavit against him for James Ashton, wanting to thank him for the kindness he had shown him and the rest of the party on the journey toward McKinley in 1906.

Correspondence came from people he had met only once. One letter was from a woman he had sat next to on a train in Illinois on his way to a lecture engagement. They had gone to a football game and had Thanksgiving dinner together and "had a lovely time." He had given her a copy of *My Attainment of the Pole,* and she still cherished it, she said.

Other letters were being written as well, by Professor William H. Hobbs, trying to persuade the authorities to deny Cook's parole. But it was useless. The doctor had an immaculate record.

The doctor's prison experience had not been, after all, a waste. As he later explained in a letter to former Secretary of the Interior Albert Fall, who was doing time in the Santa Fe federal penitentiary for his involvement in the Teapot Dome scandal: "I soon found that the damnable anticipation was worse than the realization of prison life. With scrupulous care to your mental and physical health you can come out years ahead in the game of life."[85]

As late as October 1929, Judge Killits had insisted that he would sign Cook's release papers only if some disposition of the $25,000 Cook owed the government was made. But now there was no threat of arrest in Ohio; even Judge Killits agreed that the doctor should be paroled. A visit from Leslie McKercher, who still believed in Dr. Cook, had turned the trick.

McKercher spent a whole morning in a heated conference with Killits and John Pratt. The judge still maintained Cook had his ill-gotten gains hidden away somewhere; the former PPA sales manager insisted Cook was penniless. McKercher, seeing he was making no headway, changed his approach. He told Killits if he was right, then sooner or later Cook would have to bring out those funds. Then the government could crack down on him and make him pay; besides, it would have him for perjury, since he had presented himself as a pauper, and could send him right back to prison. This point, McKercher thought, appealed to the judge, and he gave in;[86] Attorney General William D. Mitchell approved the recommendation of the parole board on March 8, 1930.

That evening, before Cook went "outside the walls," there was an extraordinary dinner in the hospital dining room attended by all the hospital staff and the physician-prisoners. Cook gave an eloquent speech in which he urged his prison comrades to obey the rules and support the officers in every possible way. Then he encouraged each of them to improve himself in the time he had remaining in prison. At the end of the dinner, many embraced the guest of honor as they said good-bye.[87]

At 10:30 the next morning, Cook's parole certificate arrived via registered mail, and his immediate release was ordered. But it took the doctor more than an hour to get out of the building and across the yard to freedom, since he was thronged by fellow prisoners who crowded up to congratulate him and wish him well.

Cook with reporters, March 9, 1930.

As he reached the gate with $60 in his pocket, after signing a pauper's oath that absolved him from paying his $12,000 fine and the court costs of his conviction, he found a small crowd of reporters waiting for him. Then he walked out in broad daylight with his head up, as he had said he would.

Unrepentant and still maintaining his innocence, he asserted that the riches obtained from some of his former holdings in Texas more than justified the claims for which he had been imprisoned. He did admit, however, that "the business methods of oil town booms deserve some regulation attention. I have received and taken my medicine in curing doses."

He did not believe that his experiences in prison had been a loss, he said; in fact, he called Leavenworth "an isle of rest." As he had written in a draft of a statement he planned to hand to the press: "No man is lost until he is lost to himself. With better understanding it sometimes happens that losses are gains."

He amplified this theme in the finished statement, which he now distributed to all the reporters:

> I am out of the jungle of Leavenworth, glad to leave, but grateful for an insight into human nature, not in my experience accessible anywhere else. Even an adventure in jail can be made profitable.
>
> The jungle-like atmosphere of Leavenworth has much to teach those with open minds. It has taught me about all the value of normal hunger. Hunger, not sex is the chief passion of life, and it includes all pulsating nature.
>
> Words only give ear to the voice of thought, and let us also remember that the tongue which engages hearing is also the first reach of the stomach; its music trend is like that of birds with the same purpose. Music voices hunger, the hunger of the whole heart of life. If we do not grasp this phase of experience, then we cannot understand the feeling cycle of thought. In jail or elsewhere, life is a winding trail. . . . Death is but another word for another trail.[88]

After a few pictures had been taken, Cook got into the car of Warden Thomas B. White and was driven to the National Hotel. There he was inevitably greeted by several more reporters. Ordinarily, a prisoner on parole would not be allowed to talk to the press, but Cook had received a special dispensation from Warden White. The doctor was still news.

He talked for nearly an hour and echoed the press's interpretation of the words of Roald Amundsen, saying that his claim to the North Pole was just as good as Peary's and that he still believed he had been within 20 miles of the Pole. When asked about PPA, he said he would "never, never" have anything to do with any more stocks as long as he lived, shaking his head for emphasis. Cook said he came to regard life in the prison, and its attendant monotony, as something abstract, from which he must stand aside mentally and regard as a thing apart. After posing for more pictures, he explained to the newsmen that he had been released into the custody of his "first friend," Dr. Frank Thompson, who "understands my strengths and weaknesses." Dr. Cook then got into an auto with several reporters and started for the station to catch the 9:00 train for Chicago.

One of the reporters who talked with him found him still possessed of considerable charm and optimism, despite the years of imprisonment. "At 60–5," he wrote, "Frederick A. Cook says he has no desire to submit himself again to the hardships of Arctic exploration; but there is nothing in his appearance to indicate that he would be incapable of it. His step is still firm. His carriage is erect and his head is up. His eyes—looking out of a face seamed with a 1000 wrinkles by the white glare of the ice fields—are clear. What is more important, there is a laugh in them."[89]

Upon his arrival in Chicago, he received the latest copy of *The New Era* and a note from one of his friends at Leavenworth: "You will probably never entirely realize how much those men loved and respected you, Dr. Cook. To even speak of it carries me away with emotion. Their trust and faith in you stand as an enduring monument to you and your wonderful kind heart."[90]

On the cover he read:

> Dr. Frederick A. Cook departed for HOME on the morning of March 9.
>
> Perhaps no more noted prisoner was ever committed to a Federal Penitentiary. None was ever held in higher esteem by officials and inmates alike. With his leaving on parole, Dr. Cook takes with him the best wishes of every man in the institution. Always ready to serve in any capacity, faithful and loyal to a fault, and with a heart full to running over with loving-kindness for the unfortunate shut-in, this man is sadly missed.
>
> We would not have Dr. Cook return to our midst. However much we love him . . . we are glad for his good fortune.
>
> Whatever the crime, in our humble opinion the debt has been paid. From the time of his polar claims controversy with Peary, to his fatal plunge into petroleum, Dr. Cook has been praised by some, condemned by others. All that is now history. His claims, along with those of Peary, must stand for future generations. The thousands of acres of Texas oil lands, both potential and proven,

still are there; some rich in production almost beyond belief, others condemned by the bit of the drilling machine. . . .

The world of freedom has reclaimed a man meek and loving, asking of nothing more than an even break with his fellow man, and aged far beyond his years by the empty existence of penaldom. His going is our loss![91]

Cook's release was occasion for comment all over the country. The *New York Times* felt compelled, once again, to try to explain the incongruities that seemed to mark the man's career, and to explain away his sterling prison record:

Under conditions of discipline and restraint Dr. Cook was always a ready worker, capable, helpful, well-behaved, cheerful and popular. It was only when left to his own devices and fancy that his moral principles took a queer twist, his imagination led him astray, and he fell.[92]

Dr. Thompson welcomed his old friend and saw to it that he was made the physical director of the Boys' Brotherhood Republic, where 900 underprivileged boys cheered him as they made him a lifetime member, an honor previously granted only to Mrs. Marshall Field and President Theodore Roosevelt. Dr. Cook wept as he stuffed the membership certificate into his pocket.

In Ann Arbor a bitter William Hobbs, who could find no one but himself willing to write a letter to keep the doctor in the penitentiary, commented, "Whether the great ex-president turned in his grave was not reported."[93]

CHAPTER 25

Was I One of Your Heroes?

BEFORE LEAVING LEAVENWORTH, DR. COOK HAD CAREFULLY BUNDLED UP HIS copies of *The New Era* and sent them off to Dr. Thompson, hoping to make use of their contents as the basis for future "literary efforts." They contained a record of his thoughts and dreams and his ambitions for the future. But what that future actually would hold was anyone's guess.

There were rumors that he had been offered a position as an assistant editor of a magazine or, perhaps facetiously, that he would enter the cold storage business in Dallas, but for the first few months he wanted just to rest and help Dr. Thompson in his office.

When he reached Chicago, he settled in at the Great Northern Hotel at Dearborn and Quincy Streets to readjust to normal society. Shortly after his arrival, word came that his brother Will had passed away, only emphasizing that he needed to get on with whatever remained of the rest of his own life.

His first income, $300, came from three articles containing an interview he had given to *Tower Magazine*. In reporting the doctor's future plans, the interviewer concluded, "He is thinking ahead now for himself—and it is quite possible that he may startle the world again with facts and theories drawn from his own experiences."[1]

The most immediate of those experiences was still his observation of life "behind the walls." He offered himself as a speaker on prison reform and the "dope peril" and sent the finished manuscript of his book on prison life, "Out of the Jungle," to a Philadelphia publisher for consideration.

His first speaking engagement was before the Milwaukee Kiwanis Club. Whatever doubts its president had entertained about making the offer were swept away by Dr. Cook's presentation:

> The enwrapped attention . . . and the comments to me after the meeting . . . were sufficient evidence that you have changed completely the attitude of many of our members toward yourself and your accomplishments and experiences in the past quarter century.
>
> While it was a mooted question with my program committee in advance as to whether we would get the approbation of our membership in booking you for the talk, now that it is over we

have no hesitation to recommend you to any service club in this
country or Canada. . . .[2]

But there would be no chance to speak on these subjects again. Cook was
informed by the Department of Justice that speeches on such topics were not
allowed under the terms of his parole; it ordered him to stop.

The reception of his manuscript was no more fruitful. "Literally and
from a standpoint of intrinsic worth it is excellent," the editor wrote, "but the
book is somewhat long and very serious in nature, and we are by no means
sure that it would have a sale which would reimburse the publisher or satisfy
the author."[3]

Though his first efforts to find gainful employment had been turned aside,
Dr. Cook was as persistent as ever. He wrote a long letter to Henry Ford recounting the useful work he had done in prison, then asked for a personal interview.
"I know that you are familiar with my capacity for work," he told Ford. "There
might be some place in your organization where my natural capacity might be
put to its best use."[4] But Ford's secretary had "nothing in the way of employment to offer a person of your capabilities."[5]

Still his ideas were not exhausted. While in Leavenworth, he had sketched
out a plan for "The Century Club"—a futuristic retirement village with all
the amenities of American small-town life and ample opportunity for health-
ful pursuits. It would be located on a square-mile tract of hill country 50 miles
from San Antonio. Its round houses of concrete and broken stone would have
big open fireplaces and be heated by concentrated reflected light and cooled by
forced air-conditioning. He hoped to interest Edison or Rockefeller in his concept, which he thought would help "not to prolong life but to prolong usefulness."
Cook also thought that such a facility might be adapted to rehabilitate first-time
offenders, drug addicts or the mentally ill. As he wrote to a friend, "I believe a
nice sum of legitimate money could be made and it would be an easy thing to
put over as well as a boon to humanity."[6] But there were no takers.

With his plans in abeyance, Dr. Cook took time to call upon his daughter
Helene, as she now styled herself, and meet her husband, Elliott Vetter, an executive of the National Lumber Company of Buffalo. It was the first of many
happy visits to the comfortable brick house on Bentham Parkway in Snyder,
where Cook took delight in Helene's garden, her chow dog, Chang, and her
Maltese cat, Bing. From Buffalo Cook took a boat to Detroit.

Sixty miles northwest of the city he looked over a narcotics farm where he
hoped to land a steady position. It had only 20 patients, and though a position was available, the doctor had bigger dreams.

In Detroit several reporters asked him about the sensational discovery of
the remains of the three members of Salomon Andrée's balloon expedition of
1897 in the Arctic. After a complete silence of 33 years, the world learned of
their fate through their diaries and the amazingly detailed photographs developed from films found frozen in the ice at their last campsite on White Island.

There were no clues, however, as to how death had overtaken them. Cook said he believed they had died in their improperly ventilated tent, asphyxiated by the carbon dioxide of their own breaths. But to him, it really didn't matter how they died, but why. "An explorer gives everything," he said. "His life belongs to the world." When asked about his own career, Cook assured them the Polar Controversy was over, but he was just as sure that future historians would justly appraise his work. He preferred to talk of other things now—the redistribution of the world's animals to provide more meat for mankind and the feeding of seaweed to cows to supply through their milk a ready source of iodine for people. As he spoke, one reporter noticed the doctor's still-remarkable eyes with their far-seeing look of an adventurer, but also that his clothes were badly in need of pressing.[7]

Dr. Cook found he still had a good number of old friends in Detroit, who, as he put it, had the advantage over those in New York of still being alive. The vice president of the S.S. Kressge Company took him for a river cruise, and he was invited to the theater every night and had to eat four dinners daily, despite his protests. "You know how I dislike high life but escape was impossible," he wrote to Helene. He was very impressed by a tour of General Motors' new Fisher Building with its elaborate decorations—"an art study which no book can give." He had planned to pay a personal call on Henry Ford, but he was not in Dearborn at the time.[8]

Still, for all that, he returned to Chicago without work. Writing was what he really wanted to do, but he could already see that it promised no guarantee of steady income, only subsistence. He had made a little money writing such articles as "How to Lower Taxes on Real Estate" for *The Apartment Owner* under the pseudonym "J.A. Addison" and had ghosted some articles on Dr. Thompson's African hunts and their trip to Borneo, but this was not the kind of subject matter he cared much about. With no other prospects, for a while he thought about returning to Texas and trying to "secure something from the wreck," but then gave the idea up.

Suddenly, the big break seemed to have come when he got an enthusiastic letter from the associate editor of the John Day Company, Critchell Rimington, who had heard about the doctor's efforts for *The New Era* from Mitchell Kennerley. Rimington had caught Kennerley's enthusiasm and now wanted the doctor to seriously consider doing an autobiography.

Dr. Cook immediately went to work to type up the memoirs he had written in prison. Before sending them off, he threw out the original dedication, "To my enemies from whom I have learned so much," and substituted "To Roald Amundsen, Companion, Co-Worker, Co-Defendant." When the editors at John Day read his manuscript, their enthusiasm cooled considerably; they asked for an extensive revision.

But when he finished it in July 1931, Cook was not at all sure what sort of reception his book would get, even though he had "taken out some of the heavy stuff." "To me the book is by no means satisfactory," he thought. "The theme lacks continuity but without rewriting the entire production I see no easy way of changing it."[9]

Discouraged by the slight prospects of publication, he again wrote to Henry Ford and the Danish premier trying to interest them in a plan he called "The Ark," which proposed transplanting penguins to the Arctic and hippopotamuses to the Amazon. He also offered his assistance as a special representative of the governor in the investigation of recent prison riots at Joliet and Statesville. In each case he was politely turned down.

At his new rooms at the Auditorium Hotel, the doctor continued to receive mail from old friends and people newly interested in his case. He resumed correspondence with Marie, who was living in San Francisco, and he learned that S.E.J. Cox had been all but "elected" for another term at Leavenworth.[10]

He also received letters from people claiming proof of his polar attainment. A psychic informed him that she had undergone a "mystical experience" on April 21, 1908, which proved that Cook was at the Pole. One persistent man wrote several times saying he had found predictions of his conquest in the Bible and pleaded with Cook to help him publish an article so that he could reveal this and other scriptural gleanings, among which were that the world would end in 1975 and that the sun and moon were the same size and equidistant from the earth—8,000 miles away.

Cook became acquainted with some other unusual people in person. Dr. Thompson introduced him to Dr. Ben L. Reitman, author of *The Second Oldest Profession,* a study of pimps. Reitman wrote from experience on both sides of the law. He had at one time been venereal disease inspector for the Cook County jail and "love doctor" for Al Capone's string of brothels. Reitman, the self-styled "King of the Hoboes" and a radical Socialist, specialized in studying and fraternizing with social outcasts. A huge coterie of underworld elements, both friends and subjects for investigation, congregated at his office at 32 North State Street. As they got to know Cook, Dr. Reitman and his latest "soulmate," Eileen O'Connor, were fascinated by his experiences, and Dr. Cook often was asked to take over Reitman's practice while he was away.

Managing Thompson's and Reitman's offices had convinced Cook that he could return to the practice of medicine if all else failed. But when he applied for a license to practice, he was turned down because his 1880s medical education was considered no longer sufficient for practice under Illinois law.

Making ends meet by occasional lectures on his polar experiences, the doctor filled his time by working on his manuscripts and maintaining an active correspondence with those interested in his career. His most regular correspondent was William Shea, who had written the articles about Peary that had so alarmed Stefansson.

Shea had started writing while Cook was still at Leavenworth. Although he admitted to associates that he had many questions about Cook's claims, he was willing to hear the doctor's explanations, since if he could sweep away the doubts surrounding Cook's polar trip and its aftermath, then Peary could be eliminated once and for all as the discoverer of the North Pole. As he listened by letter, his misgivings about Mount McKinley and Dunkle and Loose gradually lessened.

When Shea learned that Cook had written his memoirs, he asked to see them. After he had carefully gone over the carbon copy, Shea agreed with Critchell Rimington that the book needed extensive revision and offered to undertake the task, making a sample page to show what needed to be done. He also advised Dr. Cook that he should remove all invective against Peary. Shea, who had many literary contacts, obtained permission from Cook to show the manuscript to another publisher.

After looking it over, W.D. Howe of Scribner's told Shea that although the manuscript was perhaps publishable, he was not interested in it. "The unfortunate thing about it all," he wrote Shea, "is that Cook has rather put himself into a class by himself. You understand what I mean."11

Because of his conviction for fraud, publishers were convinced that anything he wrote would have no market. As Shea toyed with the idea that he perhaps might have enough material for a book of his own, another author appeared who was eager to write just such a book, though he had no material at all. His name was Andrew Freeman.

Felix Riesenberg, Walter Wellman's navigator on his attempt to fly to the North Pole in 1907 and one of Cook's former associates in the Arctic Club, had given Freeman his notes for a book he had once contemplated writing on the Polar Controversy. In reading them, Freeman had been enthralled by the human drama of the story and decided to write to the doctor. In response, Cook sent him his memoirs, which Freeman agreed needed "a tremendous amount of revision and elimination," but he proposed Cook take a different approach entirely. "It must tell more about you through action rather than through your philosophy of life," he suggested. "Your point of view, your reactions to the things that happened to you throughout your career will speak for themselves. It is better to let the reader draw his own conclusion rather than tell him what that conclusion should be."12

One day Dr. Cook received a letter with some unmistakable handwriting on it. It was T. Everett Harré's. His former literary associate had seen in the papers that he was living with his daughter and felt this chance finding of news of his whereabouts was "a sort of astral manna from the heavens of memory of better days and expectations." One thing was sure—T. Everett Harré had lost none of his verbal exuberance:

> Dear God, how I'd love to have a powwow with you! . . .
>
> . . . One thing, I think we're both Peter Pans!—despite the despites, we keep—mentally and physically—young! The truth is I feel no older (except for toxification of the bowels after alcoholic bouts) than in the gay 1910's. . . .
>
> After getting this clipping about you and wanting to celebrate, I acquired a good bottle of matured mountain whiskey, kept <u>in camera</u>, out of which I've had a stiff eggnog. Dost remember our

sessions at the Hotel Capitol in London, and the Martinis, the golden wine and English soda!

WHAT are you doing, how goes life, and what—for God's sake what, after the Pole and its aftermath—do you do for excitation?[13]

For Dr. Cook, life was not going well, and there was little in the way of "excitation." By the end of 1931, the doctor had settled into a routine. He spent three months each with his daughters in East Aurora and Snyder, New York, and the winters with his sister in Toms River, New Jersey, sometimes visiting his nephews on Long Island, one a medical doctor, the other a psychiatrist.

Dr. William Cook gave his uncle a thorough physical exam. He was in generally good health, but there were a number of chronic problems. His teeth were going bad, and his feet were troubling him, but the only serious thing was the condition of his eyes. They were starting to fail, and although he told his nephew that he would save six to eight months' salary from lectures to tide him over until he could establish a small practice, now even that little ambition had to be put aside. William Cook informed his aunt that Uncle Fred should give up any thought of returning to medicine, as he would soon be unable to see well enough to practice.

This was not the life Frederick Cook had hoped for when he had emerged from Leavenworth. His literary ambitions had been thwarted, and no one wanted to hear the visionary ideas of an ex-convict with a reputation of a lifetime of fraudulent schemes. In desperation, he looked north again for relief, considering the idea of spending a year at the magnetic pole and, like no other explorer before him, set about trying to find out whether such an expedition would violate his parole.[14]

With all his hopes shattered, Cook began to suffer from chronic complaints. Perhaps it was only the potassium iodide eyedrops Dr. Thompson had prescribed, which were known to sometimes cause mental depression, but by July 1932 his friend's condition so alarmed Thompson that he called in an associate, Dr. Max Thorek.

Dr. Thorek looked Cook over carefully:

> Great weariness was the most important malady we discovered when we examined the doctor. He wanted, he told me, just to "sleep for hours and hours!" It was a fortnight, therefore, before I ventured to draw my chair to his bedside one evening and talk with this puzzling man.
>
> "Do you know, Dr. Cook," I told him, "I'm a hero-worshiper?"
>
> There was deep sadness in his eyes, but a faint, courageous smile upon his lips, as he said:
>
> "Was I one of your heroes?"
>
> "Indeed, yes!"
>
> "But I am no longer?"

His eyes searched mine in quest of some hint that I still believed in him, or at least reserved judgment.

"Dr. Cook," I said, "the claims and counter-claims are difficult for a bystander to weigh. I only know that I would gladly do to help you anything that lies in my power to do."

He smiled an enigmatic smile.[15]

The weary explorer said he would like to tell him about his career, an offer Dr. Thorek eagerly accepted. During the telling, his patient seemed invigorated as he relived his journey to the Pole. But when he had finished, he sank back "with a look of defeat in his eyes."

"I don't expect you to believe me, Doctor," Cook said. "With the whole world convinced that I lied, I cannot hope that you will put your faith in my unsupported word. But I do want you to know that I am not without hope of vindication. . . . New discoveries have discredited page after page of the book which Peary wrote, but they have not touched the careful reports which I prepared in that Eskimo hut in that dark Arctic night."[16]

Eventually, Cook regained equilibrium. The man who had endured the dark arctic and antarctic nights, and had lived briefly in the limelight, survived his disappointments now as well. Once again he showed his elastic adaptability and settled into retirement, resigning himself to enjoy the simple pleasures left to him.

One of these was Helene's new summer cottage on the shores of Thunder Bay, Ontario, which he thought "the most restful place on earth." His parole officer let him leave the country to go there even though the terms of his parole restricted him to five states. When the Vetters purchased it, he suggested various Eskimo names for their dream home: *Tahkoo,* "Look here"; *Kissaut,* "the place where we anchor"; *Eemoo,* "milk," the symbol of life. The crisp, clear north air brought back the delight he had felt in the forests of Labrador so many years before.

He also took delight in his stays with Ruth and his two grandchildren, Betty Anne and Robert, and they took even more delight in him:

> After his release from prison Grampa lived with us for three months of every year. . . . We were precocious youngsters, but Grampa was always up to the challenge, not only playing with us but also keeping quiet vigilance when we were otherwise occupied. He rarely missed a trick. We delighted in his tales of eskimo life in igloos and on hunting/fishing expeditions in the frozen north. We saw the beauty and majesty of the polar bears and musk oxen through his reliving of his earlier years in the Arctic. He brought a spirit of adventure into our young lives and we loved him dearly for that. . . .
>
> . . . As I grew in understanding, Grampa's stories took on more expressions of his philosophy of life. After a tale of eskimo ingenuity

in fashioning hunting and fishing equipment he gave me what resembled an ivory arrowhead. Survival and quality of life depended on using your imagination with materials available. Eskimos made igloos out of blocks of ice; we made igloos out of sugar cubes. Grampa seemed to know so many alternative ways of doing things and we learned to risk the unusual methods. But you never said anything couldn't be done – some how, some way, some time. These were valuable lessons of living learned during the depression years, but with lifetime significance.[17]

During the summer, he still lived in Chicago, where he took comfort from his loyal and faithful friends. Dr. Thompson watched his eye problems closely, and Dr. Cook continued to watch Dr. Reitman's office when he had other business.

Reitman was writing a new book, "Living with Social Outcasts," and was characteristically ecstatic over his subject. He was confident it would be a success, as it was about "the things that I know something about—tramps, hoboes, bums, beggars, racketeers, criminals, fakers, charlatans, anarchists, socialists, free lovers, whores, pimps, preachers, professors, reformers and politicians."[18]

Reitman wanted Dr. Cook to write a chapter for the book based on his experiences in Leavenworth, which the doctor began at once. Reitman also wanted to include an essay about Cook himself in the book, but Dr. Thompson urged his friend to beware. "He is such an irresponsible damn fool," he told Cook, "that he is liable to say something that would do you great damage. . . . He was going to put you in among the class of felons (can you imagine that).

"Reitman loves you and would not for the world do anything to hurt you but he has the mind of a child and . . . so unintentionally he might do just the worse thing in the world."[19] Thompson persuaded Cook to prevail upon Reitman to strike any reference to him out of the book, which he did with regret.

Cook's days were now occupied with a new book of his own, "At the End of North." In it he would expand on his experiences of the winter he had spent at Cape Sparbo. At that time it seemed he had little to do but dwell on the harsh northern winter with all its monotony and vast isolation and hope for sunrise and spring. But now, in retrospect, he felt that perhaps his survival of that winter had been a greater and more meaningful experience than any other, and he would use it as the vehicle to express all the feelings that had accumulated since.

In the summer of 1933, when he visited the Century of Progress Exposition celebrating Chicago's centennial, he was struck by just how much of that progress he had witnessed. For the first time he began to think of himself as old, but when he wrote of "autumnal days" to Marie in his occasional letters to her, she would have none of it.

She wanted to stay young, she said, and so refused to even acknowledge that she was a grandmother. It was a brave, or irresponsible, snub of the reality of her present life—the reality of the Great Depression in which she had "been living on about nothing" for two years. She said she probably should have been looking for "a nice rich papa" but preferred to be independent. For comfort she had the little Boston bull terrier, Sunny Boy, that Helene had given her, on which she poured out all of her affection. "If I were a man I'd turn hobo and get somewhere," she declared, but if she wanted to travel, that would be how she would have to go, as she didn't even have money enough to go east to visit her daughters.[20]

The new year brought more disappointment for both Marie and Fred Cook. No longer able to make the rent, she was forced to move in with a friend in a little house in Redwood City. The Macmillan Company turned down his "At the End of North." They called it "a creditable and unusual production" but said they could find no room on their publication list in the tight book market caused by hard economic times.

Early in 1934 Dr. Cook thought about going back on the platform, but since the advent of radio and talking pictures, public speaking was now all but dead as a form of popular entertainment. An application to become resident physician at the old military prison at Alcatraz, which was being renovated and would soon reopen as a maximum security federal penitentiary, resulted in yet another rejection.

The mail also brought sad news about other old friends and associates. Leslie McKercher wrote that Cox was back in prison again, and word came that Captain Thomas Hall had died the previous year at 92, but without seeing the "unfolding of the truth" he had so ardently hoped for. Captain Hall's quest for it, however, had not been in vain. The discovery of his book was inspiring a new spate of attacks on Peary that grievously worried the admiral's old associates.

The first and most potent had been published in 1929, *Robert Edwin Peary*, by the Reverend J. Gordon Hayes. It owed much to Captain Hall but left out most of the repetitive arguments and anti-Peary rhetoric that weakened Hall's thesis though Hayes could not hide his own contempt for his subject.[21] In a more simple and straightforward analysis, though not free from error, Hayes had effectively dismissed all of Peary's achievements, one by one. Only reluctantly did he mention Cook and his claim, characterizing it as "most improbable," although "far less fantastic than Peary's."

Now the Reverend Hayes published in England a new effort, *The Conquest of the North Pole*. It briefly discussed evidence he had studied since his first book, and he now rated Cook's 1908 expedition "an attempt that cannot be dismissed in a few words." The narrative of that journey "as a whole bears the stamp of reality," he declared, and after a succinct recap of Cook's entire career, Hayes concluded that "Cook probably reached at least as high a latitude as that attained by Admiral Peary the following year" and that Cook's statements, "except in relation to his attainment of the North Pole and possibly his Glacial Island, may be accepted as substantially genuine, truthful and accurate."[22]

Another, slightly eccentric, book by Henry Lewin, *The Great North Pole Fraud,* was also being prepared in England. It would lambaste Peary's claims and reprint the very first anti-Peary book, *Did Peary Reach the Pole?* which Lewin had published anonymously as by "An Englishman in the Street" in 1911. More important, it also would include a monograph by Thomas Hall entitled "The Murder of Professor Ross G. Marvin," in which the captain strongly implied that Peary had ordered his favorite Eskimo to kill his private secretary.[23]

The onslaught against Peary continued with the publication of Henshaw Ward's article, "Peary Did Not Reach the Pole," in *The American Mercury.* Ward described to Stefansson, who had taken up correspondence with him as he had with all the earlier Peary critics, how he had felt when he discovered Captain Hall's book. "I felt sick at the stomach," he said. "It bored me and antagonized me. . . . But when I had finished reading it I had to admit that probably the arguments against Peary would never be met."[24]

From Ward, Stefansson also learned that even more damaging evidence against Peary might be forthcoming. One Lieutenant Commander Valentine Wood had told him that he had seen Peary's original workbook containing his astronomical sights. It had been given to his father, Commodore M.L. Wood, by Admiral Chester in 1913 to recompute. Both he and his father were convinced upon examination of the "very dirty book," covered with greasy fingerprints, that most of the sights it contained were either poorly made or out-and-out fakes.[25] Wood said that Chester had turned the book over to the National Geographic Society after his father had given it back, but all inquiries to the society by Ward went unanswered. A sympathetic contact at the society told him it was no use to pursue the subject. "There is none there who does not believe the Geographic infallible," she wrote, "furthermore, there is not a real scientist in the pot!"[26]

Ward had also interviewed Hudson Bridge Hastings, the astronomer from Bowdoin who had been kept at Eagle Island for more than a month after Peary's return from the Arctic in 1909. Hastings described what his duties had been—mostly checking for navigational and astronomical inconsistencies in Cook's public statements. But Peary had not only questioned him about Cook's astronomical figures; he had tried out his own on Hastings as well, asking him what positions they showed at or about the Pole. As Hastings talked about Peary's observations, it occurred to Ward that Peary had been seeking confirmation or refutation of their accuracy before he presented them to the National Geographic Society's subcommittee that was to rule on his polar claim.

Suddenly, Ward realized that Hastings had been Peary's Dunkle and Loose. When Hastings sensed by Ward's excitement the trend of his thought, and when Ward admitted it, he became incensed and would tell no more.

Ward had learned from Stefansson, in turn, about the true authorship of *The North Pole.* He wrote to A.E. Thomas. But Mr. Thomas did little beyond confirming that he was its author. He had already been grilled by Stefansson and Bowman and was sick of the topic entirely. "It is a damned dull book," he told Ward, "because Peary was a damned dull human being and it was impossible to extract much material from him that was not damned dull. . . . The whole subject bores me."27

Even Donald MacMillan's new book about the 1909 journey, *How Peary Reached the Pole,* seemed to further damage Peary's credibility. It contained many details at variance with Peary's accounts, and astoundingly, despite the book's title and the enormous emphasis laid on Peary's astronomical observations and their recomputation as the basis of proof of Peary's claim, MacMillan added his own emphasis to say: "An observation for latitude on the Polar Sea, or on any other sea, can be placed on a postal card. *And when placed there, or anywhere else, it is absolutely worthless as proof that a man has been there!*"

MacMillan then presented a set of fake observations "proving" that he was 250 feet from the North Pole on May 1, 1928, rather than at his actual location at the time, on the coast of Labrador, to demonstrate how easy it was to fake astronomical observations and how worthless they were as proof. "An astronomical observation for latitude is of the utmost value to the observer, as it proves to him that he has reached a certain spot, *but it is of no value to the world, for it can be easily falsified,*" he concluded with added emphasis.28

After sweeping away Peary's nominal basis for belief, MacMillan revealed why he believed his old commander had reached the Pole: "What proof had Peary to offer that he had reached the Pole? His word."29 Beyond that very unsatisfying answer, there was little else to explain "how Peary reached the Pole" between the book's covers.

For the Peary interests, the only positive in 1934 was the publication of *To the North!* a short history of arctic exploration by Jeannette Mirsky. Stefansson had written an introduction for it, in which he said he had been asked to go over Mirsky's manuscript but professed to have done little to it. He did do something, however.

In her finished book, Mirsky had praised Peary's epic journey to the Pole and dismissed his rival as "a great teller of stories." But as Stefansson told Marie Stafford, Peary's daughter, he had introduced Mirsky to Peter Freuchen, a raconteur in his own right, who provided her with "unpublished data" that persuaded her to radically change her text:

> The "unpublished data in the Cook-Peary controversy" referred to by Miss Mirsky in her note was what Freuchen told her about what the Cape York Eskimos told him. On p. x you find me saying that I was "asked by the publishers to go over the manuscript for possible corrections. There are several reasons why I could do little along that line." The "little" I did was confined to one chapter, that on the Cook-Peary controversy, but consisted in my getting her to rewrite that chapter and reverse her conclusions. The book was about to go to press with an adverse verdict approximately coincident with

Hall and Hayes. Freuchen's "unpublished data" helped to convince
Miss Mirsky where I might not otherwise have succeeded.[30]

Indeed, Freuchen's intervention had saved the day for the Pearyites. In her
original chapter Mirsky, rather than dismissing Cook as a "teller of stories,"
had said:

> The youthful Cook was a man of ability, of courage, and of con-
> siderable attainment. It is impossible to dismiss Cook by simply
> calling him a liar. . . . Cook did not reach the Pole, but that was
> a matter of mistaken calculation and insufficient observation for
> position—not a matter of intent. He tried to reach the Pole, he
> wholeheartedly thought he had reached the Pole, and the story of
> that effort is one of the most interesting and extraordinary on
> record. . . .
>
> In the face of Peary's announcement Cook was declared a hoax.
> . . . Yet . . . it is well to remember . . . that Cook made a trip which,
> when conditions and equipment are considered, stands unrivaled
> in the annals of Arctic exploration.[31]

Stefansson added that he had been careful not to tamper with the rest of
the text, even failing to notice factual errors about his own career until after
the book was published.

All of the anti-Peary activity worried Vilhjalmur Stefansson greatly. After
conferences with Isaiah Bowman and Captain Bartlett, he decided to ask the
Peary family to release the facts that *The North Pole* had been ghostwritten and
that Peary had ridden on the sledges for most of his successful polar journey.

Stefansson was convinced that these revelations, rather than hurting Peary,
would silence his critics by laying all of the book's errors and inconsistencies at
the doorstep of A.E. Thomas, who simply did the best "ghosting" he could
under difficult circumstances. And they would also explain Peary's fabulous
claimed speeds across the polar pack, by eliminating the need for the crippled
commander to walk, installing him, as Henson had said, on a swift sledge
across smooth ice for the disputed part of the journey.

When Stefansson approached Marie Peary Stafford for permission to disclose these as facts, she was shocked. She had always believed that her father
had written the book himself and, in any case, she stated Henson's remarks
could not be trusted. She dismissed Henson's book absolutely, saying he could
not have written it since he was "practically uneducated." As far as Stefansson's
plan was concerned, she told him that any publication of what he had discovered would be considered "an act of deliberate unfriendliness."[32]

William Hobbs was furious with Stefansson for wanting to publish what
he considered damaging allegations. Hobbs wished to meet the attacks by
writing favorable articles about Peary and hoped to be first to gain total access
to Peary's private papers, stored in his "bomb proofs" at Eagle Island, so that
he could end the debate once and for all in a definitive biography of Peary.

In response to Hobbs's request for access, Marie Stafford told him that her mother felt no obligation to make the admiral's papers available. Besides, she said, it would be different if no one had ever seen them. Hadn't they satisfied the "hostile committee" of the Congress in 1911? If her mother gave the records to anyone, Marie told Hobbs, it would be to the American Geographical Society, which, as the only major geographical society never to have honored Peary for the discovery of the North Pole, would be in a neutral position to examine them and publish its findings.[33]

Hobbs was adamant that publication of Stefansson's discoveries be stopped. He even had an old family friend of the Pearys', Henry Wise Wood, warn Jo against Stefansson. "I am familiar with the equivocal attitude of this gentleman towards the present controversy," he wrote, "and I neither believe he is a friend of Admiral Peary's nor that he is to be trusted by you or Marie. His efforts seem to be speciously directed to breaking down Peary's credibility and thus eventually to destroying him. . . . In view of his suavely destructive efforts, and Cook's attempts at a 'come back', and Hayes' embittered attack upon Peary, and the muckrakers' campaign which is on foot, I am convinced that the course suggested below is wisest for those who are protecting the Peary interests."[34]

The recommended course included maintaining a "dignified silence," suppressing what Stefansson wished to publish and giving Hobbs unlimited access to Peary's notes and records.

Stefansson was stung by this and wrote a long memorandum to his editor about the formidable "enemies" now lined up against Peary's claims, especially in England. He thought it a grave mistake that Peary's family was making. "These last days I have felt between grief and despair," he admitted, "though becoming the more convinced the more I looked into it that . . . the Peary family are . . . delivering the Admiral's reputation into the hands of his enemies."[35]

The announcement of the Nobel Prize for medicine for 1934 added a final touch of irony to a year that had gone so badly for the Pearys. It was awarded to three doctors for developing a therapy to control the disease that had killed Robert E. Peary. That therapy consisted of eating liver—the very prescription that Dr. Cook said he had urged upon Peary to rebuild his strength when he examined him aboard the *Windward* in 1901—a prescription Peary had rejected.

One of the reasons cited by Marie Stafford for keeping additional fuel away from the smoldering polar debate was the reemergence of Dr. Frederick A. Cook, who was once again very much in evidence and, in her opinion, "a menace and still to be reckoned with."[36]

Cook had, indeed, launched another attempt at vindication through the urging of his friend Ralph Shainwald, who now had legally changed his name to von Ahlefeldt. Ralph von Ahlefeldt had inherited his father's Rubberoid paint fortune and had plenty of money to back such a campaign. He had urged the doctor, as early as January 1934, to allow his lawyers to bring suit on his behalf against anyone who denied his claim so that its validity could be established in a court of law. Dr. Cook reluctantly consented to allow him to do so, but not until after his parole expired in April 1935. To simplify procedures Cook gave his friend a power of attorney to act in his behalf.

That spring Cook wrote to Jens Daugaard-Jensen, sending a list of questions for his two Eskimo companions to answer. But it was too late for that.

Etukishuk had died in the fall of 1934, and in April Ahwelah lay dying in his skin tent at Nerke with a torn picture of an angel over his head. His last wish was to taste the white man's food once more; his last request was that the stones of his grave be piled loosely so that the snow-buntings would nest among them and bring him the news of the world he would soon leave.[37]

But as Ahwelah departed, another old associate came back into Dr. Cook's life in support of his renewed efforts to prove his claim. She was Lilian Kiel, the *Hampton's Magazine* stenographer, who came to visit him at the Auditorium Hotel.

She had already been to Hendersonville, North Carolina, for an "inquisition" conducted by Henshaw Ward, who was now busily engaged in writing "The Peary Myth," his own full-length book debunking the Peary claims.

Dr. Cook took her to the hotel dining room for lunch, but Lilian Kiel could not keep her mind on the meal. "I can't remember eating anything," she wrote to Fred High. "I was so shocked and stunned at Dr. Cook's appearance. I tried very hard not to let him see how it affected me, – but I had not seen him for almost 17 years, and in that time his countenance had indeed changed! His face is sad, and at the same time heroic. But I fear that what the GOVERNMENT has done to him will never be undone until he has passed into the great Beyond. . . .

"The Doctor's 'Parole' finished that week, and he made an effort to be gay and lighthearted, BUT—the scars can never be erased. He seems quite well, physically, and very alert for his years."

Everywhere she went in Chicago, there were people eager to meet "the North Pole Stenographer," among them a man named Ted Leitzell, whom she met at a gathering of Cook's friends that evening.

The next day, April 21, a luncheon was given by Dr. Thompson to celebrate the twenty-seventh anniversary of Dr. Cook's discovery. The table was covered with red, white and blue flowers; first there was champagne, and ice cream shaped like Easter lilies finished off the good meal in between. Lilian Kiel thought the doctor, surrounded by his friends, looked too happy for words.

After a tiring day in which she heard for the first time of the work Dr. Cook had done at Leavenworth, she returned to her hotel to find a group of reporters waiting for her. After they left at 11:00, Miss Kiel cried herself to sleep. The reporters had said they would not be able to use her story because it was "too controversial" but that they would make up for it. As she told Fred High, "The reporter of the Herald-Examiner sweetly assured me that 'certain Chicago papers have very beautiful <u>obituaries</u> on file'! So that is what they plan to do? Give Dr. Cook a FINE OBITUARY! Isn't it terrible?"[38]

On April 23 von Ahlefeldt's lawyer filed suit against Peter Freuchen and his publishers for libelous statements about Cook in his book, *Arctic Adventure,* asking damages of $150,000.

Cook's own account in *My Attainment of the Pole* continued to win new friends for his claims as he distributed the last remainders to anyone who expressed interest. But Andrew Freeman knew that any attempts at further justification would have to come from another's pen.

Freeman had now finished his other literary commitments and renewed his requests for assistance in writing just such a book. "You know, of course, that I believe in you thoroughly," he told Cook, "and my approach to the subject will be strictly from a human angle tracing every event step by step that branded you so cruelly the world's most stupendous liar and faker. . . . Many persons have done studies on heroics. I wish to do a study of obloquy and calumny. . . . The story of what you suffered is so intensely dramatic and moving that the mere telling of it will go a long way toward winning the recognition that has been denied you for so long."[39] Cook did not have to be asked twice. Freeman's ideas fit in nicely with his renewed drive to have his case before the public.

In writing his prospectus, Freeman got the first hint of the difficulties that lay ahead. "The job is turning out harder than I anticipated. . . . I injected too much personal bias in it," he informed Cook, "and told things about Peary which are perhaps a little too sensational at this embryonic stage of the manuscript."[40]

By the end of the year, plans had been laid to make 1936 the year of vindication for Cook's polar claim. Soon he was again asserting that he had unanswerable proofs. "Before I die I must clear my name," Cook said. "After I am dead, I intend to have published posthumously the full scientific data of my explorations. It will be autobiography but will contain a mass of data never before collected in publishable form. It will establish irrefutably my claim to discovery of the pole."[41]

Later, the doctor would explain to William Shea the reason for his renewed efforts: "Lack of sustained interest is now my greatest difficulty. To fire ambition and keep it in line for specific action is not easy after 70. Last winter while in Chicago I resolved to bring the Polar Issues to a showdown. . . ."[42] Dr. Cook told Shea he had big hopes that when Henshaw Ward's book about Peary came out in January it would set the pace, but in October, shortly after completing the manuscript, Ward had died of pneumonia.

"Are you certain that the book will be published in January?" Shea wrote back. "After Henshaw died I had some correspondence with a professor at Yale who is acting as a sort of literary executor to Henshaw. I get the impression from this that the book might be suppressed. He said that he thought it should not be published and I gathered that he was hopeful that that would be the verdict of the Yale Press. I wrote them urging as strongly as I could that the book be brought out and I offered, as an old friend of Henshaw's, to read the manuscript. He replied saying that the publishers were getting opinions from geographers and others and that he would leave the decision to them."[43]

It had been Isaiah Bowman who had reviewed Ward's manuscript, and he advised Yale not to publish it. The Yale Press went one step further, advising Ward's widow not to solicit publication from any source. The book did not appear.[44] But Dr. Cook could wait no longer.

On February 19, the twenty-eighth anniversary of the day he had started for the Pole, he wrote a letter to Roland L. Redmond, president of the American Geographical Society, stating the merits of his case and concluding, "The time has come, therefore, when I demand a full and impartial investigation of my story. Because of its reputation of fairness and accuracy, I respectfully request that such an investigation be conducted by the American Geographical Society."[45]

The society's reply was a curt note saying his request would be referred to its council. Actually, the American Geographical Society had no intention whatever of giving any time to the matter. In reply to an objection to such an investigation by Belmore Browne, the secretary of the society refrained from even the mention of Cook's name. "Will you kindly keep it strictly confidential if I tell you that we hope that any further developments in this matter can be avoided," he wrote. ". . . The person referred to in your letter wrote to the president of this Society asking for such a re-examination and, since he had given a copy of his letter to both the Associated Press and United Press it seemed necessary to reply to it."[46]

On March 7, von Ahlefeldt filed against the Encyclopædia Britannica, Jeannette Mirsky and her publisher, Viking Press, and Houghton Mifflin Company, publisher of MacMillan's recent book. The damages asked against these defendants were $125,000. MacMillan and Stefansson were also sued, but no damages were asked, only a retraction of certain statements made about Cook in these books.

To Donald MacMillan, Peter Freuchen expressed amazement at Cook's resiliency, but he laughed off the suit and assured him that it would never come to trial, as the one Cook had filed against him never had.[47] In a way, MacMillan hoped his might. He was sure this would provide an opportunity to show what he believed to be Cook's total ignorance of navigational techniques and, in so doing, put an end to Cook's pretensions.[48]

Not everyone was so complacent about the Cook suits as Peter Freuchen, however. When their motions for dismissal on the basis that there was no substance to the charges of libel were denied, Mirsky and her publisher hinted at settlement, since they believed the cost of defense would exceed the damages that might be assessed if the verdict was unfavorable. They were willing to admit Cook's real achievements but maintained that their negative statements were merely a fair expression of their opinions on a historical matter and had no malicious intent. Von Ahlefeldt, however, advised his lawyers that Cook was not interested in money but sought vindication and so did not want to settle out of court.

While the court cases plodded along, additional avenues were being pursued. Cook made his first radio appearance on the Affiliated Broadcasting Company in Chicago on May 1, and the newspaperman Milton Lory, who remained a firm friend in Texas even though he had been called as a witness for the prosecution during Cook's trial, had begun to write a biography of the doctor. But the main hope for a revival of Cook's claims rested on Freeman's book.

On August 1, 1936, Freeman signed a contract with Doubleday, Doran and was advanced $2,000 for research. He sent the doctor the good news along with the bad:

> I had to let the publisher practically take my shirt in the matter of
> money arrangements in the contract. As a result I shall be forced,
> in order to live while the book is being written, to withdraw a sug-
> gestion I previously made to you regarding an arrangement in
> which I offered you a share in the earnings. Just how much the book
> will make is, of course, in the lap of the gods, but the opportunity
> [it] offers you in the way of public vindication is excellent. . . . It is
> certain to arouse a tremendous amount of attention and I have a
> plan by which I feel fairly certain your case will be reviewed by the
> American Geographical Society. Theodore Roosevelt, son of the
> ex-president, acted for Doubleday in the purchase of the rights to
> my book. . . . With his aid and the prestige of the publishing
> house, I think we can go a long way toward getting what you have
> deserved for so many years.[49]

At first Cook wanted Freeman to hold to his word that they would split the profits. When Freeman insisted there had been no formal agreement and that such an arrangement was now financially impossible for him, the doctor pledged to cooperate fully but warned him, "There will be a year of headaches."[50] Andrew Freeman quickly found those words more than prophetic.

Hardly into the project, he was coming to see he had taken on a task far larger than he had anticipated. Freeman moved to Brewster, New York, so that he could work uninterrupted on his manuscript with his wife, Mary Alice, assisting as editor, typist, adviser and fellow researcher. Throughout the summer he pleaded with Cook to send him material, but it was slow in coming. Together, the Freemans wrote scores of letters asking for information from people who had been involved in the momentous events of 1909. Most of these were greeted with stony silence.

At that very moment, another book was being readied for publication: a biography by William Herbert Hobbs entitled simply *Peary*. Before going to press, however, the Macmillan Company wanted to be satisfied that Hobbs's statements about Cook were true. Although he had not won any judgments, von Ahlefeldt's suits on the doctor's behalf had definitely had an effect, and everyone was leery about any mention of Dr. Cook for publication. Macmillan warned Hobbs that he would be financially liable for any judgment that might be rendered against it. In response to his publisher's warnings, Hobbs removed a gratuitous chapter entitled "Dr. Cook's Crime Record," concerning his Texas oil conviction, and the book went to press.

The main reason for his publisher's fear was a long and authoritative-looking rebuttal of Hobbs's articles written in support of Peary over the previous two years. It came from the man Lilian Kiel had met in Chicago, Ted Leitzell, and it was intended to show Hobbs's unreliability as a reporter on the competing polar claims. Leitzell had written four articles for the magazine *Real America* on the Cook-Peary feud and, in so doing, had become something of an authority on the subject. In his rebuttal, Leitzell accused Hobbs of flagrant distortions, including the redrawing or manipulating of maps to suit his purposes of defending Peary's exploratory claims.

When Hobbs's book appeared, it proved the accuracy of Leitzell's accusations. Of *The North Pole,* which Hobbs knew had been ghosted, he wrote: "Its literary quality is of a high order. Peary, like Captain Scott, if he had not chosen the career of an explorer, might have achieved a reputation as a writer."[51] Hobbs might have saved this observation, as the Reverend Hayes's latest book had already disclosed *The North Pole*'s true authorship.

Though Hobbs had never gained full access to Peary's papers, *Peary* contained several stories never before recorded that passed quickly into legend, to be endlessly repeated as indisputable fact.[52]

For William Hobbs, all unpleasantries in Peary's life were easily resolved. According to Hobbs, the Eskimos died that terrible winter of 1901 because Peary was helpless, "his physician having gone home on the *Erik.*" Dr. Dedrick, who had refused to go home and whose offers of help that winter had been rebuffed, was not mentioned by name anywhere in Hobbs's book. Even so, in the few letters he was allowed to quote, Hobbs unwittingly revealed something of the dark side of Peary's quest for fame.

Ironically, Dr. Cook was given an opportunity to review the book for the *Chicago Daily News.* After his very restrained evaluation appeared, von Ahlefeldt promptly sued Hobbs over his characterization of the veracity of Cook's Mount McKinley claim.

Hobbs's book was not the only one having difficulty coming to publication in 1936. The spate of lawsuits had made the entire subject of the Polar Controversy poison to publishers. Milton Lory's manuscript, "This Man I Know," received rejection slips from four big publishing firms. The last, Bobbs-Merrill, advised Lory to tone down statements about Peary to avoid libel and warned that the very zeal with which he defended Cook detracted from its credibility.

As the year drew to a close, Andrew Freeman could see that he could not possibly meet his February 1, 1937, deadline. Cook's responses to his written inquiries and in personal interviews had resulted in hundreds of pages of notes. He asked Cook tough questions and sometimes got puzzling answers that contained information contradicted by previous research. These raised disturbing conflicts that needed more study. Resolving them would take far more time than was left to him.

Little by little, Cook's biographer had assembled a file of documentation as the doctor turned over papers for him to study. Many of Freeman's queries to others remained unanswered, but he was able to find some who were willing to give their version of events.

In soliciting the help of T. Everett Harré, he expressed the thesis of his book as it was then developing. He felt that although Cook was a great explorer, he was also "a child and a foolish, head-strong one when it came to dealing with worldly realities. His enemies made him a victim of his own naive honesty." He told Harré it did not concern him who reached the Pole first, though he would show Peary had not. He was interested only in the human drama, he said, and "if the reader still chooses to believe that Cook is a faker, that is no concern of mine, but I have a hunch that no such impression will be found between the lines."[53]

By the time Doubleday gave him an extension to April 1, it was well known that Freeman was working on a Cook biography, and Helene Vetter had reason to worry about the security of the documentation in his possession at Brewster. Her vacation home at Ridgeville, Ontario, had been broken into twice, and each time, the intruders had gone through her father's things and left them piled on the floor, but she couldn't tell whether they had taken anything.[54]

As 1937 slipped away, and as all the intrigues, technicalities and details of his past career gave purpose and impetus to the lives of the people interested in gaining vindication for him, Dr. Cook's present life was gradually slowing down. He now gave lectures mostly to civic organizations and PTAs, where mothers brought cookies and children listened respectfully to the kindly looking old man's tales of polar bears and Eskimos. His vision was now fading badly, and he had to have an operation to correct the persistent problems with his feet.

But on December 9 Cook gained a national hearing over the CBS radio network when he appeared on Gabriel Heatter's "We the People" program in the studios of WABC in New York. He gave a brief résumé of his polar journey and at its end, in a fragile yet forthright voice, he appealed for belief in the claim he had made so many times before. "I have been humiliated and seriously hurt," he told the thousands listening, "but that doesn't matter anymore. I am getting old, and what does matter, to me, is that I want you to believe that I told the truth. I state emphatically, that I, Frederick A. Cook, discovered the North Pole."[55]

After extensions and more extensions, Andrew Freeman delivered his manuscript, all 250,000 words of it, with an additional 30,000 in notes, to Doubleday, Doran on December 13, 1937. It was still without a title. Dr. Cook thought it should be called "The Boreal Blast: Thunder at the Pole—the Polar Tumult and the Result," or at least one of those. But Freeman first inclined toward "Scapegoat in the Wilderness," then "Retreat from Glory," but finally settled on "The Great Hoax," with the ironic twist that it had been perpetrated by Peary and not by Cook.[56]

Dr. Cook was more than pleased with Freeman's book, saying, "For thoroughness it is a masterpiece," and as he settled in for the winter with his sister in New Jersey, he confidently looked forward to seeing it in print by spring.

Spring came, and with it came a letter from Andrew Freeman. It was about his book. After three months he had asked his literary agent to see what was holding things up. The agent informed him that Doubleday had said it would not publish the book because it was libelous toward Robert E. Peary.

Freeman was furious. He wanted an explanation, and he wanted his manuscript back if Doubleday had reneged. Cook's biographer paid a visit to Ted Roosevelt, who had acquired the book for Doubleday, but reported no satisfaction. "When I said I stood ready to make changes that would eliminate the libel," Freeman told Cook, "Roosevelt refused to point out the libelous passages and, at another meeting with my agent, finally confessed that he did not think when he agreed to take the book that I would 'attack' Peary and also that the book as it stands would embarrass him and his friends. So you see that old gang is still against you, doctor."[57]

Freeman said he was determined to publish the book just as it was and, in fact, he had Little, Brown interested in it, but the publisher would do nothing while the Doubleday contract remained in force. Theodore Roosevelt told Freeman's agent that his client would have to agree to reimburse Doubleday for the advance before it would release him from his contract. Things were at an impasse.

More bad news followed throughout the spring and summer of 1938. On May 27 the Encyclopædia Britannica case was dismissed. An engagement for another radio appearance was canceled. Freeman tried to sell his manuscript to other publishers without settling his dispute with Doubleday but got only rejection slips. Finally, he decided that he would have to remove all personal bias if he was to salvage anything from his labor. He asked to keep Cook's material in his files until the new version was ready so that he could check it for accuracy.

Ted Leitzell had almost fallen out with Cook when he learned that the doctor had agreed to help Freeman unreservedly. But when Helene convinced him that his past services were very much appreciated and valued, Leitzell had done more than stay on as Dr. Cook's advocate. That very summer he was in Alaska trying to retrace Cook's steps over the Ruth Glacier to the great mountain beyond. He had planned to make the trip with Hugo Levin, a friend of Dr. Reitman's, but not long before the planned departure, Hugo had a "fit of temperament" over accommodations and Leitzell decided to leave him behind.

On July 12, 1938, Leitzell had Johnny Moore of Star Airlines drop a cache far up the glacier for emergencies, then he and Joe Sertich, an Alaskan miner, were flown to Spink Lake near Alder Creek. While they were relaying equipment to the foot of Ruth Glacier, bears raided their camp. All they could salvage was five two-pound tins of pemmican, and a little flour, sugar and tea. But they were determined the expedition would not end this way.

Carrying all their camping and mountain gear, they hiked to the Coffee River, intending to raft it, but it was far too swift, so they started downriver along its bank, hoping the current would slacken. It was a miserable job chopping their way through the thickets of alder, and they made only two miles a day. Since the food supply was running low and no game was in sight, they cut over to the Chulitna. Ted Leitzell recalled that Cook had rafted it in 1903. Surely, he thought, it would be tamer than the Coffee.

On its banks the men felled a dead spruce and made a two-pole raft, binding the logs together with tent ropes, belts and pack straps. On the trip downstream they ground over submerged rocks, hit snags and were thrown in the water when the raft capsized. Sertich, who couldn't swim, nearly lost his life in the swift current.

When they finally drifted opposite Talkeetna, they had one pound of food left but had saved all their equipment. They were pulled ashore by its residents, who couldn't believe they had made the trip on such a flimsy craft. Only once since 1903 had anybody ever rafted down the Chulitna and lived to tell about it, they said. Some old pioneers at Talkeetna volunteered fabulous details of Cook's exploits in Alaska not mentioned in his book, and these, along with their recent experiences on the river, gave Ted Leitzell a new respect for the modesty and understatement of Cook's own narrative.

The harrowing experience had discouraged neither him nor Sertich, however, and after replenishing their food stores, they were flown back to Spink Lake by Estol Coll. With 75-pound packs and no experience traveling on glaciers, they still reached Glacier Point in three days. But the loss of their cache, which had sunk into an enormous natural tunnel of melting ice, prevented them from getting any farther than the Parker-Browne or Mazama parties of 1910 had. From what he could see from there, Leitzell thought there just might be a feasible route to the Northeast Ridge from the head of Ruth Glacier.

Though he could not confirm this, he was able to revisit Browne's Fake Peak and declared, absolutely, that Browne's claim that it was the same place as that shown in Dr. Cook's summit photograph was a fraud. He also ridiculed Browne's descriptions of the difficulty of the route up Ruth Glacier, and concluded that Browne and his party must have been very poor travelers.[58] But he also took a photograph from the site of the Fake Peak that exactly matched one of the doctor's. In *Harper's Monthly Magazine* it was labeled "the view from 16,000 feet," but Leitzell told Cook he would suppress it because "it would only give the opposition a chance to confuse the issue."[59]

Leitzell and Sertich decided to return by crossing both the Ruth and Tokositna Glaciers, even though their food was exhausted, so that they could reach a safe crossing place on the Tokositna River. An account of Leitzell's trip eventually appeared in the pulp magazine *Adventure,* which had earlier published an article by him about Cook.

In trying to relate Cook's route and photographs to his own experiences, Leitzell appealed repeatedly for clarifications from the aging explorer, but he got no direct answers. The doctor said that his eyesight was failing and that he had neither Belmore Browne's book nor even one of his own, so he could not make sense of Leitzell's questions about his 1906 pictures. Even when Leitzell wrote clarifications, the doctor remained vague and unspecific on crucial points of events that had happened more than three decades before.

As he had with all the others, Stefansson had taken up an active and disarming correspondence with Ted Leitzell and found, to his surprise, that this writer of pulp magazine articles possessed a deep and scholarly knowledge of arctic history. Indeed, Stefansson learned things that he did not know himself. By letter, they held lengthy discussions on historical geographical problems, and Stefansson, whether he was genuinely impressed with Leitzell's knowledge or simply to charm him, offered to sponsor him for membership in the Explorers Club.

Leitzell was flattered by Stefansson's offer and thought if he could bring Stefansson and Cook together, there might be a rapprochement.[60]

Stefansson's tactics so gained Leitzell's confidence that he admitted that his years of study had brought him no closer to the truth. "The further I delve into the affairs of Dr. Cook, the more perplexed I become," he told Stefansson. "It is impossible for me to believe that all of the men who have attacked him entered into a gigantic conspiracy, or that such men as you could be deliberately dishonest in attack. It is equally impossible for me to believe that all of the long string of erroneous attacks could be honest errors. Such a string of coincidences goes far beyond the bounds of probability."[61]

In spite of many letters of support for his petition, the American Geographical Society had failed to take any action on Cook's request for a hearing of his case. The society's secretary said that as long as stories about Cook appeared only in "unimportant" magazines, such as *Adventure,* there was simply no need to. "To give a man attention, pro or con, is to recognize him," he said. "To ignore him is to consign him to his proper place. . . . There is no better way of damning a person than to ignore him."[62]

Von Ahlefeldt's lawyer continued to press Cook's suits, but the one against Mirsky and Viking was decided in the defendants' favor in November. He now recommended that Cook settle for a simple apology from Professor Hobbs.

In Stefansson's case, the defendant was willing to make a statement: "When I wrote the said 'Introduction' [to Mirsky's book] Dr. Frederick A. Cook and the controversy about the discovery of the North Pole were not in my mind."[63] Dr. Cook modified the statement, adding a sentence saying that there was no intent to injure him and asked his lawyer to settle for that.[64]

The last two years had been just short of a total disappointment for the aging doctor. There were only two bright spots. In May 1937 the Soviets had announced they had landed planes at the North Pole. They described conditions similar to those Cook had published in 1909, but like Amundsen, they had ignored pleas, this time from Ted Leitzell, to make a detour and fly over Bradley Land. The other had come in July 1938, when Helene gave birth to his third grandchild, Janet.

In early 1939 Dr. Cook hoped he might go to Texas to see just what the oil lands the Petroleum Producers Association once held had produced and, on that basis, seek a pardon. But by then his health had declined too far to make the trip. Now he spent his time quietly with his daughters and their children, especially Betty Anne:

> Grampa got older and slower, even more gentle and kind, but his mind was always sharp and he could make people laugh. He attracted friends, people who joined in animated conversation, and I was not aware of the bitter animosity that raged against him outside my sheltered world. . . .
>
> But now his eyesight was failing. His explanation was "snow-blindness" due to eye damage from the Arctic brightness. He listened to the radio more and he listened to me more. As I approached my teenage years it was a special blessing to have someone who was attentive to my concerns, always affirming and encouraging me. And I would sit beside him ever more often reading Indian legends by the hour. . . . I became his eyes for much of his reading.[65]

By the end of summer, war had broken out again in Europe as Hitler overran Poland. Dr. Cook's dream that his generation would see an end to authoritarianism seemed another broken one. But the arctic dreams of others continued.

In November he met the explorer Sir Hubert Wilkins, who had done some flying in the Arctic and was now planning an expedition to reach the North Pole in a battered submarine. But Cook did not hold out much hope for Wilkins's chances. He knew from experience that war interferes with everything. Yet, he told Wilkins, exploration would go on, whatever the impediments, to the end of the world. It was a part of Man, he said, that he would always seek answers until no mysteries remained. He suggested to the Australian, however, that the greatest mysteries lay not at the North Pole. "This area here," said the old explorer as he put his fingers around his head, "that lies back of the eyes and between the ears. When that cranial sphere is fully explored we will have no reason to fight wars."[66]

Though his dreams of vindication had still not come true, there were occasional tiny victories. When the board of directors of the Explorers Club proposed hanging portraits of all its past presidents in the club's rooms, there was some argument over whether Dr. Cook's should be included. But the sitting president, Vilhjalmur Stefansson, insisted that it should. The portraits were arranged on the wall in order of succession: Dr. Cook's was hung just before that of Robert E. Peary.

But by the end of the year, Cook had given up the idea that any real recognition would ever come in the time that remained to him, and when Ralph von Ahlefeldt proposed yet another lawsuit, Dr. Cook wrote him a note. "You and I have had a good deal of experience in court action with other matter," he told his faithful friend. "The results have been worse than nothing. . . .

"We have figured with too much confidence that the trial would bring press reports which would result in favorable public opinion. On this I have positively changed my mind. The defendants will . . . read into the record as much as they can of what unfavorable matter has been published during the last thirty years . . . claiming that a man thus assailed cannot be greatly injured in a financial way by what is said now. . . .

". . . It does seem to me that we should have the attorneys, if we can do so, prepare to make a settlement out of court."[67]

More and more, the burning desires of the past had given way to the dying embers of the present, and in that changing light the priorities of life were changed as well.

"The big issues of early existence are but feeble stars in the blue dome of old age," he wrote. ". . . The eye of time gives a narrow distant view wherein the continuity of life's horizon is lost. Youth seeks to envision tomorrow in dreaming splendor with fight and dash. Old age has outlined dreams, but that electric glow, the halo of life's splendors, now becomes best defined. It is the after glow of autumnal sunsets. To me as the hibernating winter of the seeming end nears, every day is now a Thanksgiving day."[68]

His old friend had supported him faithfully, and when Ralph's wife, Ilse, fell gravely ill, Dr. Cook went to his home in Larchmont, New York, to attend to her personally. Night after night for three weeks he sat with her until she died on May 2. The doctor was so exhausted by his vigil that he could not even attend her funeral, and on May 5, 1940, Cook himself was stricken. He suffered a cerebral hemorrhage and, in a coma, was rushed to the United Hospital in Port Chester. Ralph von Ahlefeldt immediately petitioned President Franklin D. Roosevelt for a pardon for Dr. Cook.

Though his pleas for justice had been ignored while he was healthy, the news of Cook's illness made news all across the country. Letters came from many people who remembered years of friendship with him or a single small kindness.

May Kyle was one of those who had to explain why she wished him a speedy recovery. "I am that one time little girl to whom you gave a bouquet of roses from your garden on Bushwick Ave. Bklyn. on every Sunday afternoon to give to my Sunday School Teacher. That was about 47 years ago."[69] And another, Madeline Schorup Hicks, thanked him for the greatest gift of all. She had been delivered by him long ago in Brooklyn, and she told him how her mother had always spoken highly of him to her.

The coma was brief, and by May 9 Dr. Cook was able to recognize Helene and take some food, but his short-term memory had been erased.

Sir Hubert Wilkins, Ben Reitman, Lilian Kiel and other friends, including some members of the Explorers Club, joined in sending telegrams urging clemency for the doctor. On May 16 Cook received a full and unconditional pardon from the president. When told of it, the doctor answered feebly, "Yes, happy." When asked if he understood, he replied, "Yes—pardon," before lapsing from consciousness.[70] After that he seemed to rally and was moved to Ralph von Ahlefeldt's house on June 4.

Helene had given her consent only hesitantly to this, because she could not afford the expense of bringing her father to her home and feared he might not survive the trip to Harris Hill, where she now lived. Soon, however, Helene and the rest of the family had other reasons for concern.

"I do not fully understand Ralph's intense interest in Uncle Fred's affairs," Helene's cousin, Adah Murphy, wrote after visiting Larchmont to look over Ralph's arrangements. "He seems to have a strangle hold on everything. At any rate he is taking every advantage of Uncle Fred's condition to get things done. Whether it is all for the best I do not know. . . . It seems strange for a man to do so much on his own."[71]

Among the things von Ahlefeldt was trying to get done included securing a promise from Frederick A. Hartley, representative from New Jersey, to introduce a bill to reopen an investigation into Cook's polar claim. He also dispatched Dr. William Blake Burke, a Cook family friend, to Washington to confer with Daniel Lyons, the government pardon attorney, and to follow up with FDR's secretary, William D. Hassett, on whether accepting the presidential pardon would preclude a new trial to overturn the Texas mail fraud conviction.

The day Dr. Cook was moved to Larchmont, von Ahlefeldt initiated the formation of the Cook Arctic Club, with himself as president. The purpose of the club was to gain vindication for its namesake by outfitting an expedition to rediscover Bradley Land. Sir Hubert Wilkins agreed to lead the expedition, and several of Cook's friends, including Dr. Thompson, Hugo Levin, Eileen O'Connor, Ted Leitzell and Anthony Fiala, agreed to serve as the club's officers.

When Marie Cook heard of Fred's condition, she came up from Philadelphia, where she now resided. She was introduced as Mrs. Clarke, a friend of Helene's, to avoid publicity. Marie arrived on June 10, Fred's seventy-fifth birthday and 38 years since their wedding day. "Do you know me?" she asked. "Yes," he replied. "Well, what do you think of me?" she ventured. "Everything that is nice," Fred replied before drifting off into disconnected thoughts.[72]

When Helene came to visit, she became alarmed. She thought von Ahlefeldt's physician, Dr. Farel Jouard, had some peculiar notions about effective treatment. Jouard applied leeches and kept talking about diathermy, which sounded to her like an experimental procedure. When she had to leave, she was relieved that Marie had decided to remain and watch over the family's interests.

The stay was agony for Marie. She and Ralph clashed repeatedly over what was best for their patient, and she and Dr. Burke formed an alliance to check what they considered the excesses of Ralph and his physician. After a while, Marie Cook wanted Fred removed to Helene's house no matter what the consequences.

Marie suggested that things should not be done without the approval of a family member; when Ralph blew up, Marie appealed to Helene:

> For God's sake please do something quick as he may throw me out on my ear. If I don't agree with him I tell him so and then he starts a regular lecture—I listen and generally without commenting on it I do something else or go out. . . . There is no use trying to deal with anyone with his mentality he knows it all and knows that he does. So please drop everything else and devote your time to settling this matter. . . .
>
> He says the family are so suspicious of him and he doesn't want any dealings with them. Then he informed me that the power of attorney Dad gave him covers the libel suit as well as all his personal affairs that he is in reality completely in charge of Dr. Cook. . . .
>
> It looks to me as if there is some contrivance in the wind that he is going to take complete charge not only of his illness but all personal affairs. . . . Do you get my drift of his state of mentality? It is getting my goat believe me.[73]

Cook's close friends from Chicago began to arrive; first Doctors Thompson and Reitman, then Eileen O'Connor and Hugo Levin. Dr. Thompson urged Helene and Marie to have patience with Ralph von Ahlefeldt. He could see that whatever was done, no matter how odd, would make no difference now.

Dr. Cook's friends knew there was not much time left and sat up late into the night planning their strategies for his redemption. Someone recalled that in 1936 Cook had announced he was writing a document to be published posthumously that would clear his name. Dr. Thompson urged Helene to look for it and have it published at once to help defray her father's medical bills.

Cousin Adah continued to visit her Uncle Fred, even though she thought all the talk about polar expeditions and congressional investigations was wild nonsense. But the little group talked hour upon hour about how they would at last gain vindication for Dr. Cook at his eleventh hour. Hugo Levin spoke for all when he said, "Would it not be wonderful if we could clear the name of the Grand Old Frostmaster in the twilight of his life? All his life he has fought for justice—not, as he so often told me, for his own sake, but to leave a name for his children and relations."[74]

On July 24 Dr. Cook was taken to the New Rochelle Hospital, where the superintendent ordered that he be given a single room in the semiprivate wing at no charge. X-rays disclosed a possible intestinal blockage, slight pneumonia and a tumor on the lung. Cook was put on sulphopryreiden, and a colostomy was contemplated.

NDAY, AUGUST 5, 1940   TWENTY-EIGHT PAGES   PRICE THREE CENTS

Dr. Cook, Noted Explorer, Is Dead; Disputed Peary on Pole Discovery

Ralph wanted to keep his friend alive as long as possible "to give Doctor and his family the recognition of the world, create a demand for any manuscripts of his and restore to Doctor the dream of his life." He told Adah Murphy that he hoped to see Henry Ford at a dinner for Hubert Wilkins on July 30 and persuade him to sponsor the Bradley Land Expedition.[75]

But none of this was to be. The doctor slipped back into a coma, and two days later, on Monday, August 5, 1940, at about 8:05 A.M., Dr. Frederick Albert Cook succumbed at last.

He died absolutely alone, between the shifts of the nurses who looked in on him and before Ralph's daily visit. The official cause of death was listed as pulmonary edema.

Upon hearing the news, a friend of Eileen O'Connor's sought to console her:

> Dr. Cook was surely one hero to whom fate dealt a mean hand. One of God's noblemen, he deserved the best things in life, the honor and praise rightfully due one of his attainments, and instead, cruel enemies badgered him and harassed him unceasingly. After all, he lived to a good, ripe age, and until recently I know that he enjoyed life, even if it was hard, and I know few people who got so much out of life under distressing circumstances as did our good friend. . . .
>
> It is sad to think that he did not live to see his reputation vindicated. We who knew him never doubted him. . . .
>
> In Doctor Cook we lost a true and valued friend, and it is good to know that he had loyal friends all over America.[76]

One of those friends sent Hugo Levin a request, since she could not come for the funeral: "Will you put a small red rose-bud in the lapel of his coat for me—unless they decide to put the little red ribbon there—the one he wore so many years—I believe it was from the King of Denmark."[77]

Some of his friends suggested that Dr. Cook's body be cremated and his ashes scattered over the North Pole. Helene hesitated, not knowing whether her father would have wanted that. She listened, too, to advice from another friend of the family, who suggested cremation and interment in Buffalo. In the future, he said, when Dr. Cook was acclaimed as the discoverer of the North Pole, there should be a place for people to come and remember him. Though still uncertain, Helene accepted this plan. There would be no button-hole for the little red ribbon or for Lilian Kiel's rosebud.

Thirty-nine persons attended the services at New Rochelle for the man who had spoken to millions. They heard Ruth's father-in-law, the Reverend Charles E. Hamilton, praise Frederick Cook as a man possessed of "intellectual and moral honesty, charity, generosity and patience." "When we combine these elements, we have found a man of bigness," the Reverend Hamilton said, "a man who permits the truth to find its own approach."[78]

After cremation at Ardsley, New York, Dr. Cook's ashes were interred in the columbarium at Forest Lawn Cemetery in Buffalo on August 11. Sixty, including Rudolph Franke, who had pledged to stand by the doctor to the last that long-ago winter at Annoatok, witnessed the urn's placement behind a little brass door and the banking of flowers over it. Later, 35 friends helped plant a tree in Dr. Cook's memory on the cemetery lawn.

Cook's medals as displayed at Forest Lawn.

Cook's will assigned all his property, consisting mostly of notes, books, photographs and manuscripts, to Helene, including those still in the possession of Andrew Freeman, whose book remained unpublished. The entire estate was valued as a legal formality at the lowest possible figure—$500.[79]

The beautiful obituaries began to appear. Even the *New York Times* for once reserved judgment and forgot its enmity:

> Dr. Frederick A. Cook had one of the most unfortunate reputations in polar exploration: unfortunate because much of his excellent early work was overshadowed by his claims to having beaten Peary to the North Pole, and by his later jail sentence for oil stock frauds. He was recently pardoned by the President, but it brought little comfort to an old man embittered by years of disillusionment. . . .
>
> . . . There is something to support Cook's assertion that he went far toward that mathematical point where all meridians meet and one stands on the top of the world. Certainly he got some distance north, how far is not certain. . . .
>
> . . . It is sad that a life which opened with so much promise should have come to such an end.[80]

While looking through her father's effects, Helene came upon a little book of sayings he had bought. Among them were: "Personal magnetism can create beauty around you, can attract one, can make a person attractive to his fellow men. It is soothing. It is healing," and, "If your word is sweet you conquer the world."[81]

When the manuscript that Dr. Cook had said was to be published after his death finally came to light, it was found to be only a series of sketches, reminders, fragments and disconnected narrative passages:

> After this Post H. document appears in print it should be followed promptly by a book an elaboration of same with the appeal of a bleeding heart all throu. for a little understanding for a life intended as a service to humanity.

> Am anxious that Dr. Cook will go into history as a man who tried to see and do things in the light of day. cellular therapy energy & power theory.

> Greatest Joys
> Finding a key to Eskimo
> Discovery of cure for scurvy
> Escape from S. Polar Pack
> McK
> at P. & C. Sparbo
> Peace after torrid storm

> Remorse
> being doubted by organized thugs

> When you speak or write make the subject matter such as will entitle you to ask the whole world to listen.

> The sweetness & confidence of trusting and being trusted was for me the greatest discovery of the contact with primitive folk.

> The public creates heroes with a background of mystery instead of trying to appraise conduct to serve as precedents for others to study.

> White collar men seldom fit well into horse collar jobs.

> What did I get out of life what was put in Is life worth living Is there a purpose divine or . . . perhaps only that of better cellular perfection and organization.

> Companionship of self is a duty to be cultivated too much dependence for entertainment upon others.

> The more I see of the keen sense of animals the less respect I have, comparatively, for the supposed high intelligence of man.

How well nature manages the approach to the end. It seems ever a part of the mission of life to prepare for death. The joy of living and the shadow of the end follow regular cycles as surely and as regularly as night breaks the continuity of day. As the cycle of ages with its high lights and its darkness now merges with the dawn of a new life of better understanding. . . . The fruits of this life have been good, the beyond offers only what the mind projects. . . .

I have passed into the beyond, into the most profound unknown and there I am engaged in a new type of exploration. . . .

Something with form and color will eventually be resurrected to give me a place in history, but this will not be a true picture of the man whose affairs I have managed. No post-thumous portrait is ever drawn correctly. . . .

My life has afforded mere peeps into the beyond, Information thus obtained is never complete. . . .[82]

Frederick A. Cook

CHAPTER 26

The Pointed Finger from His Grave

IN THE WAKE OF DR. COOK'S DEATH THERE WAS A BRIEF REVIVAL OF INTEREST in the event that had been central to his life. In 1941 Warner Brothers announced plans for a film tentatively titled *Peary of the North Pole*. James Stephenson was slated to play the title role, with Lonelle Parsons cast as his enigmatic rival. Andrew Freeman even sent his manuscript to Hollywood to help writer Ray Schrock with background material. But like Freeman's literary portrayal of the Polar Controversy, the film never saw the light.

As often happens when the leader of a cause dies, the cause dies with him. So it seemed with the question of polar priority. With each passing year, the banner headlines of 1909 receded further into history and, as it seemed, disappeared forever. As for the grandiose plans of the Cook Arctic Club, they just melted away, as did the club itself.

Ted Leitzell was one who admitted that the subject of things polar had, for him, grown cold with Dr. Cook:

> When Dr. Cook died I vowed to myself that I was forever through with the problems of Arctic and Antarctic exploration, for my real interest through it all was to bring a few brief hours of happiness to a tired old man, and I did not really give a damn about establishment of historical accuracy for its own sake.[1]

> I lost contact with most of the people who had shown interest at the time I was active. . . .
> Among other things, I found that many of them were in this thing only for what they hoped to gain, and that they had no real interest in Dr. Cook. . . .
> What I say does not, of course, apply to Eileen O'Connor. I don't know of anyone who worked with greater devotion and sincerity than she to help set the record straight.
> Undoubtedly there were others in the group who were just as sincere, but I reached the point where I had my doubts about all except Eileen.[2]

One of those "others" was Hugo Levin, who kept in contact with the doctor's family. When given an opportunity to study Cook's writings, Levin believed "At the End of North" had commercial possibilities. In 1948, working from Cook's pencil manuscript, Eileen O'Connor made a good typed copy, and Levin set out to find a publisher. He was turned down repeatedly, but he persisted.

In 1950 he managed to interest Pelligrini & Cudahy in publishing it. To put the book into perspective and refresh long-faded memories, it wanted an introduction including a short biography of Frederick Cook. Helene Vetter was asked to help. Raising Janet and making a home for her husband had filled her life in the immediate years after 1940, and then she had begun a career of her own as a hospital dietician. But now she saw a way to restore her father's reputation; her interest in the controversy surrounding him reawakened.

She still had the papers he had willed her, but with his constant traveling, then his term in prison and all the demands made by prospective authors in the 1930s, much had been lost. What remained was in frightful shape, full of confusing and disjointed details. In looking through the material, a feeling bordering on despair, as she said, "that we somehow did not have the time for my father and I to talk all these things out," came over her.[3]

Pelligrini then decided it might be best to engage a professional editor to write the introduction. The publisher interviewed one after another, looking for an unbiased man, before settling on Frederick J. Pohl, a retired Brooklyn schoolteacher who seemed neutral on the subject of Cook and Peary. Pohl had authored *Amerigo Vespucci: Pilot Major,* a well-received effort to resurrect the controversial claims of the Italian navigator to the discovery of the continent that bore his name.

The first thing Pohl suggested was that the title should be changed to something less symbolic that would give more of an idea of the book's subject. After discussions with the Vetters, he decided on "Return from the Pole," and Pohl set to work researching material for his introduction.

As the project progressed, it fanned the smoldering embers of Helene Cook Vetter's memory of her father into a fire of enthusiasm at the thought that his name might be erased from the list of the infamous and rewritten on the roll of the immortals. In an echo of 1914, early in January 1951 she persuaded a representative from Maryland to introduce a resolution into the House of Representatives to reopen the case of Dr. Cook.

Using his papers as a sourcebook, Cook's daughter now tried to reestablish contact with people who had participated in the events of her father's life. One of the first she found, but only after persistent searching, was the North Pole stenographer, Lilian Kiel, who was living in retirement in Hollywood, Florida.

As militant a believer as ever, she was overjoyed to hear from her hero's daughter. Lilian Kiel soon became Helene's friend and confidante, and Helene told her about the book in progress: "Have an excellent editor. My only question is that the introduction is too long. His idea is to answer all controversial issues. Readers can tire."[4]

Pohl's introduction ran 41 pages, summarizing Cook's entire career, with special emphasis on the events surrounding the great dispute between him and Peary. Despite Helene Vetter's remark, to condense it as he did and still convey it accurately was no mean feat, but this he accomplished. Pohl then appended to the manuscript a formidable and useful bibliography for those who cared to explore more fully the fascinating questions it raised.

When the book was published that summer, Vetter and Pohl toured together to promote it. The reviews were good, and Pohl's introduction drew universal praise. After lying dormant for more than a decade, the voice of Frederick Cook stirred and spoke once more.

Return from the Pole dealt only briefly with Cook's controversial claim; instead, it told the story of the winter he had spent with his two Eskimo companions at Cape Sparbo, tempered and given new meaning by all that had come after. It embodied many of the ideas developed by long isolation, not only in that cold and bleak place where he, Etukishuk and Ahwelah had been the only human beings, but also when he had been, alone but for his memories, inside the equally bleak walls of Leavenworth, where he had discovered the ultimate terra incognita:

> Perhaps all intelligence and all knowledge is the result of exploration.[5]

> Our all-important discovery must be noted in that we found the greatest mystery, the greatest unknown, is not that beyond the frontiers of knowledge but that unknown capacity in the spirit within the inner man of self. In other words, all lasting good must be planted and nursed in that garden of life between the ears and behind the eyes. Therein is the greatest field for exploration.[6]

For many reviewers, his book revived the old ambivalence about Dr. Cook; they felt a need to reconcile his public acts with his private thoughts. "The writing is memorable for its intensity and for a certain nobility of sentiment," one wrote, "and it makes one doubt whether a man capable of such a book would also be capable of perpetrating the hoax he was accused of."[7] And with that doubt raised, others thought the doctor's claims, and Cook himself, should be given serious reconsideration:

> As human drama, as the fight of man against breath-taking odds, this book is heady stuff.
> Once again, and sadly, it must be admitted that men of Cook's salt are lost forever. The machine age has whittled stamina and even the Cook-Peary brand of courage from our present generation of adventurers. It is good to be reminded that men once ventured to earth's end with little more than a knife, a pack of dogs and large hearts. . . .

> . . . Frederick Cook was called a fraud and a passer of gold
> bricks. He was scorned and held to public view as a scoundrel. . . .
> Journals of the day attacked him. He was imprisoned for promot-
> ing worthless stock; perhaps unjustly. On reading *Return From The
> Pole,* you feel slightly uneasy over all this. The pointed finger from
> his grave is a bit too steady for comfort.[8]

But Vilhjalmur Stefansson did not agree. "Stef" was now the sage of arctic
exploration and the arbiter of all things polar. In his review for the *Saturday
Review of Literature,* he said of *Return from the Pole,* "As an attempted rehabili-
tation, it is most pathetic." Though he called it absolutely false, Stefansson
conceded that "its very pathos brings to mind the possibility that it may possibly be literature."[9]

One of the participants in the events the book portrayed felt otherwise.
Eighty-six-year-old John R. Bradley called the publishers. "That was written
by my friend!" he exclaimed, and he wrote to Helene that he was most pleased
when he had read it. Bradley encouraged her to continue her efforts so that
Dr. Cook at last would be vindicated.[10]

Helene Vetter was ecstatic at the book's success; she now quit her job to
devote her full time to salvaging her father's reputation. She and Hugo Levin
considered getting out a new edition of *My Attainment of the Pole.* Levin advised her to edit out all the references to the Polar Controversy and publish it
as a straight narrative of the expedition. Then, a translation of Rudolph Franke's
book was contemplated. A friend volunteered to help, but a sketch translation
showed little in it that suited their purpose of once again putting Dr. Cook's
name before the public in a favorable light.[11]

But if publication of *Return from the Pole* had reawakened the Polar Controversy, it also reawakened all the old suspicions. Helene Vetter began to
doubt even Frederick Pohl when he wavered in his support of her new efforts.
He seemed to her far too friendly with Stefansson, who had given Pohl access
to his extensive library and manuscript collection related to polar topics.

Her attempts to contact the people mentioned in her father's papers often
ended in disappointment. Most of the major figures in the controversy were
long dead, and more were dying every year; 1952 and 1953 claimed Franke
and Bradley. Helene Vetter determined to be bold before it was too late. She
arranged a meeting with Matt Henson, now 88, in New York City. The results
of her visit, as she told Lilian Kiel, were equivocal: "Just had to do it! He was
charming and talkative. His wife was a bit belligerent, afraid, uneasy, questioning. I may pay for my venture, but what did I have to lose? Personally I do
not think their throne is very secure. Time will tell."[12]

Helene Vetter then journeyed to Ann Arbor to read the collected correspondence of William Hobbs. Suddenly, she grasped the depth of the animosity that existed against her father. "His hatred, which shows up in the letters
I read, was certainly vicious," she told Lilian Kiel. "He was overjoyed when he

heard that Hayes was dying of cancer and would not be able to write any more about Peary. After reading these letters my thinking changed a bit. The whole situation is much deeper than any of us realized, even Dad. I did not realize the opposition had entered strong objections even to try to stop the presidential pardon."13

The "opposition" had, from the first notice of the resurrection of Dr. Cook, begun to remobilize. A series of articles had already appeared in *True* magazine by the American Museum's Roy Chapman Andrews, which closely toed the official Peary line about the discovery of the North Pole and its version of the truth about Dr. Cook. They soon took permanent form as part of a book called *Beyond Adventure,* which Andrews dedicated to the "eminent biographer" William Herbert Hobbs. Helene Cook Vetter sued Andrews for libel.

Other familiar tactics of old began to reappear. *Reader's Digest* paid Vetter more than $3,000 for the rights to publish a condensed version of *Return from the Pole,* then mysteriously failed to publish it, leading her to conclude that its editor had been influenced to suppress it. She even began to suspect that the Peary forces had systematically tried to remove Captain Hall's book from the inventories of the libraries he had sent it to in 1917.

Peary, after a long absence, began to appear again as a subject in the pages of the *National Geographic Magazine.* In 1951 an article about Donald MacMillan revived the story of Peary's 1908–09 expedition, on which he had served, and in 1953 Gilbert Grosvenor, still as firmly in control at the society as in 1909, flew to the North Pole and back, then used the trip to place a restatement of Peary's claims before its 2,000,000-plus members.

Another chance to recall the great explorer came when Josephine Peary officially presented his North Pole flag to the society, saying, "I know that in the Society's collection it will always have the care and place of honor it so rightly merits as a symbol of that momentous 6th day of April, 1909, when the dreams and aspirations and patriotic ambitions of one man's lifetime were realized.

"Please accept it with my deep appreciation of the Society's unfailing loyalty to Admiral Peary and my best wishes. . . ."14

Helene Vetter's previous efforts in Congress having come to nothing, in the fall of 1955 she appealed to the chairman of the Committee on Constitutional Rights to hear her pleas for justice for her father.

That same fall, she got a letter from the editor of *Life* asking permission to use her father's Mount McKinley pictures, for what purpose they did not say. But suspicion had seized her now; she remembered that *Life* had published an article about Peary not long before *Return from the Pole* was due to be released. "I realized that this was to forestall Cook's 50th anniv. of his McKinley climb," she later wrote to a friend. She was right.15

That summer, the foremost expert on Mount McKinley, Bradford Washburn, had taken some pictures of his own on Ruth Glacier. Washburn, the director of Boston's Museum of Science, had climbed the mountain three times, the first in 1942, and had made a comprehensive aerial survey of it with the financial support of the National Geographic Society in 1936. That survey had photographed Mount Hunter, the peak that had been named by Dunn for his aunt in 1903 and reported by Cook but had since been written off by many as just another of the doctor's outrageous fantasies.

Washburn was no friend of Dr. Cook's, however. He was by now a part of the geographical establishment that had spurned Cook and now supported his own projects. One of his old friends had been Belmore Browne, whom he admired greatly. Washburn was taking his pictures on Ruth Glacier to recall his friend's evidence against Frederick Cook and to counter the posthumous comeback Cook's daughter was hoping for.

Other plans to check any Cook revival were already in progress. The Houghton Mifflin Company was about to go to press with a verbatim reprint of Belmore Browne's 1913 book, *The Conquest of Mount McKinley,* with an affectionate remembrance of Belmore Browne by Bradford Washburn and a foreword by Vilhjalmur Stefansson, the entire subject of which was Cook's career of fraudulent geographical claims.

Late in 1955 Helene Vetter met *Life's* editor in New York City and was shown five of Washburn's pictures, which he said matched the ones published in *To the Top of the Continent* but were nowhere near the elevations or locations ascribed to them in her father's book. The copyright on Cook's pictures would expire the next year. What was she to do? Should she allow him to use them now, or have him use them then?

Frederick Pohl advised her to cooperate with Washburn. Pohl firmly believed that Cook had reached the North Pole but had not climbed Mount McKinley. He told her that he felt Washburn cared nothing for the "polar business" but only for the truth about the Alaskan mountain and even thought Washburn leaned toward his own position.

"If the Washburn proofs are presented, as they most certainly will be," he wrote Helene, "then in anticipation of that eventuality, those who believe Dr. Cook attained the Pole might better cooperate with a man who seems inclined to believe that the terrible strains of mountain exploring may have caused a temporary lapse. The public in its reading of biographies will forgive a lapse frankly admitted in the life of a genius or man of extraordinary accomplishment, and find the man all the more interesting.

"I know you are confronted with the most difficult decision that you have ever faced," Pohl continued. "We cannot change the past. The best we can do is to understand it with imagination and sympathy."[16]

But Helene Vetter had her own plans for the anniversary of her father's disputed climb. She was sponsoring an expedition to prove that the mountain was climbable over Cook's route. Her involvement was a recent development, however. The idea of the climb had started in 1948, when a group of three college students had been the fifth undisputed party to reach the summit of

McKinley. Among those young conquerors was Walt Gonnason from Falls City, Washington.

When Gonnason returned to the headquarters of Mount McKinley National Park, he met Harry Karstens, Archdeacon Hudson Stuck's climbing partner, who had been the park's first superintendent. Gonnason also met Adolf Murie, the park biologist, who showed him a picture of a mountaintop and asked him if he recognized it. Gonnason said he did: it was the summit of Mount McKinley. The picture was the alleged fake summit photograph Cook had taken in 1906.

When Murie told Gonnason the story behind the photograph, Walt was fascinated. He began to read about Cook's climb, and after studying maps and the aerial photographs of the mountain taken by Bradford Washburn, he thought he discerned a route from Ruth Glacier to the top that seemed to match Dr. Cook's descriptions in both its altitudes and terrain.

Gonnason studied Cook's pictures in *To the Top of the Continent* as well, and though some had been called into question and discredited, he was convinced of the genuineness of the one labeled as taken at 15,400 feet. Gonnason believed this picture, whose location had never been identified by the doctor's numerous critics, proved that Cook had at least climbed far beyond the point credited to him by Ed Barrill. In fact, he thought he could see the exact spot on one of Washburn's photographs where the doctor had taken this picture, at just about the altitude Cook had given in his book.

The question of whether Cook had actually climbed the mountain had by now became so overpowering that Walt Gonnason decided to do something about it.

"In February 1950," he recalled, "I left my home in Seattle to enlist the support of the National Geographic Society in Washington to settle this epic question in mountaineering."

When Gonnason made his proposal to Kip Ross, head of the Illustrations Division, Ross was enthusiastic. But when Gonnason had his interview with Gilbert H. Grosvenor, the editor seemed suspicious as he sat behind his big desk.

"Why do you want to climb that route?" he asked.

"To determine whether or not it was possible for Cook to have climbed the mountain," Gonnason replied.

At this Grosvenor's neck and face suddenly grew red, then he jumped to his feet.

"I don't know who the hell you are," Grosvenor said, shaking his finger at Gonnason, ". . . but we are not interested—we are not interested." He reinforced his repetition by slamming his hands down on his desk with such force that he shattered the plate glass covering it. The editor then stalked out of his office. The interview was over.[17]

Gonnason then went to New York City, where he tried to interest some of the popular magazines or a radio or television company in sponsoring the climb. He met with no better luck. While he was in the city, he looked up several of Cook's old supporters, including Anthony Fiala, who were enthusiastic about his project but could not afford to finance it. His money was already running low when a mugging took some more and convinced Walt Gonnason to seek his funding elsewhere.[18] He went west.

In Chicago he met Ted Leitzell and Dr. Thompson. They agreed that his proposed route looked climbable. Gonnason told them Bradford Washburn had conceded to him that the 15,400-foot picture was actually taken on the upper slopes but that Washburn would not admit to any possibility that Cook had climbed McKinley to the top. Gonnason also told Leitzell that while in Washington he had met with General Omar Bradley, who revealed to him that the Air Force had photographs of Bradley Land, and that it had even measured its height. The pictures, he said, were classified, however.[19] Leitzell and Thompson, though supportive, could not afford to help either, and Gonnason went back to Seattle empty-handed.

When Helene had located Ted Leitzell again in 1954, he had related the meeting with Gonnason to her. Now she remembered it and decided to use the money she had gotten from *Reader's Digest,* which had been put aside for her vindication campaign, to help fund Gonnason's dream.

Among the other contacts Vetter had reestablished was the one with Andrew Freeman, who, it turned out, still had the manuscript of "The Great Hoax," buried in his attic. She encouraged him to dig it out and consider publication. Helene invited Ted Leitzell and Andy Freeman to accompany her to Alaska to await the outcome of Gonnason's climb, but only Freeman accepted.

That same summer, another expedition was headed for Ruth Glacier, one led by Bradford Washburn to complete his dossier of photographic evidence against Dr. Cook.

On July 13, 1956, Don Sheldon airlifted Gonnason's party one by one to a point just seven miles short of the base of the East Buttress, which its leader believed Cook had used as his route to the summit. It was a beautiful day, just like the one exactly eight years before when Gonnason had stood at the top of the continent.

Gonnason, now 33 and a mining engineer in Seattle, had chosen three men with climbing experience to make the attempt: Otto Trott, a 45-year-old physician and surgeon from Seattle; Paul Gerstmann, 31, a pediatrician from Puyallup, Washington; and Bruce R. Gilbert, 25, a fruit grower from Yakima.

They moved camp up to the base of the ridge the next day, but there the weather closed in and prevented all further progress until July 20. That day they reached 10,000 feet in eight hours but were checked there by impossible ice conditions. They decided this could not have been the doctor's route and retreated to base camp. The weather then turned sour again.

On July 26 Helene Vetter arrived at Talkeetna, population 85, 60 miles from Ruth Glacier. She was met by Andy Freeman, who escorted her to the only accommodations in town, the Fairview Inn—dining room, bar, six bedrooms and one bath—where she would await news from her expedition.

The suspense was overwhelming. For relief she took a walk past a dozen dilapidated cabins to a sandy beach on the bank of the Susitna River. There she had her first glimpse of what had brought her to this remote spot:

> The clouds drifted away and revealed the great white monarch of the continent in full splendor. Standing alone, watching this breathtaking sight, many thoughts raced through my mind. I could understand the power that urged men like my father to conquer the unknown, but the aftermath, the intrigue, the hatred, the jealousy – all this seemed so futile and so devastating. . . .
>
> . . . The awe-inspiring view of Mt. McKinley was very brief. The fast moving clouds soon [covered] the mountain and hid the sun. I suddenly felt cold and shivered. It was [as] if the curtain was quickly drawn to preserve its mysteries.[20]

Andy Freeman met her in the road with disturbing news: Washburn was on his way to Talkeetna, and so were two reporters from *Life* magazine. He suspected the reporters wanted to document the dramatic moment when the two opposing sides met. If so, when Helene Vetter shook hands with Bradford Washburn in the small airstrip's hangar, the forced cordiality must have been disappointing.

Washburn packed his supplies and himself into Sheldon's tiny Super Cub, *Green Hornet,* and it taxied away, bound for his camp on Ruth Glacier. Several hours later the plane returned with news that the Gonnason party had been sighted below the East Buttress. Had it reached the summit? No, declared Washburn authoritatively; there were no tracks above their camp, he said.

It began to rain. The weather forced the two opposing camps into an uneasy closeness at the Fairview Inn that evening, where dinner at its one table now seemed an unappetizing ordeal. The *Life* photographer's camera was always in evidence, and its incessant clicking was getting on Helene Vetter's nerves. She soon retired for the night but could not sleep. A feeling of desperation sent her to Freeman's room, and once inside she broke down. There was still hope, he told her. Washburn might be wrong. They should wait for word from Gonnason.

Freeman's hopes were partially justified. The expedition had turned back, but it had achieved more than Washburn imagined. When the weather had cleared again on July 25, on their second attempt Gonnason's party reached 11,400 feet. The route up took them around numerous crevasses and seracs and required long traverses to avoid several near-vertical ice faces. Gonnason and Bruce Gilbert made the top of the ridge—the divide between the Ruth and Traleika Glaciers—in about two and a half hours. Farther on, the ridge became narrow, with too many overhanging cornices for assured stability. "This was the same type structure that had detoured us on the ridge only 2 or

3 days ago," Gonnason wrote in his diary. ". . . It is a very definite danger point that requires a belay! . . . This . . . prompted me to call an end to our attempt since I feel that we 'have' found a climbable route—'conditions favorable' for a strong party."[21] Two of the men had shown badly at relatively low altitudes, and that, more than anything else, persuaded Gonnason to abandon the climb.

When the others finally caught up, Otto Trott, from his vantage point on the ridge of the East Buttress, looked down on the scene of Parker and Browne's desultory attempts to reach its crest from Ruth Glacier in 1910 and called them "a ridiculous farce."

When the fog lifted on July 27, the *Green Hornet* shuttled more supplies to Washburn's camp and flew over the Gonnason party. In the snow they had stomped out the request "Land." When he returned to Talkeetna, Sheldon declared that he would be flying back to take the men out. But Washburn protested that he could not land in the national park without permission and insisted Sheldon would have to call park headquarters—a real chore on Talkeetna's one telephone line serving 16 parties. When permission came, fog was again forming. Washburn's domineering performance raised the specter of Robert E. Peary in Helene Vetter's mind. Peary, it had been said, acted as though he owned the North Pole; here was a man, she thought, who acted as though he owned Mount McKinley.

The wait for permission meant only one man could be brought out before nightfall, and that man, by prearrangement, would be Walt Gonnason. As Sheldon took off, another plane arrived. It carried a huge photo of the southern approaches to McKinley sent by *Life* and Mike Grehl, a reporter from the *Anchorage Times*. He got there just as the truce ended.

Freeman and Washburn were chin to chin in the roadway. "Why are you going out of your way after all these years to continue to stick knives in Cook?" demanded Freeman.

"If you hadn't released the publicity from New York City, we would not be here. Why re-open a controversy that has been dead for fifty years?" retorted Washburn.

"We have every right to bring out the truth which has been suppressed too long," shouted Freeman. "We are after the facts – you are not seeking them, merely tearing down."

"My ulterior motive is finding the truth," shot back Washburn, "and my only real regret about this study is what you guys are doing to the poor lady over there in the inn. You're taking her for a ride!"[22] The confrontation ended with Washburn's calling Freeman "un-American."

After this release of pent-up tensions, there was nothing to do but wait. Hour after hour dragged by. Dinner went untouched. Then, a little after seven, the drone of Don Sheldon's Super Cub brought the rival parties to the airstrip. When the plane stopped, Walt Gonnason had some trouble getting his six-foot-four frame out of the tiny cockpit, but when he had emerged, he enthusiastically greeted Helene Vetter, shaking her hand.

Gonnason wanted nothing but to wash and have dinner. When he had, everyone gathered around the table to hear his first report. "Our expedition was the first to traverse over Cook's route in fifty years," he began. "Even though we were unsuccessful in reaching the summit, I am convinced that Dr. Cook reached the peak from Ruth Glacier." A dead silence fell over the room.

After a moment he continued. "We called off the assault Thursday because of collapsing snow cornices and the rugged terrain. The party . . . lacked the balance necessary for the hazardous ice conditions we encountered."

"Then you and the men feel that Dr. Cook's route is possible?" asked Vetter hopefully.

"Absolutely," Gonnason replied without hesitation.

Turning to Washburn, Vetter remarked accusingly, "Apparently, the route is not an impossibility!"

"I never said it was an impossibility," snapped Washburn. "I merely said it was not Cook's route, his narrative is the account of a fictitious ascent."

As Gonnason continued his account, Bradford Washburn slipped out of the room. Several times one of the *Life* reporters prevailed upon him to come in and make comments as Gonnason traced his route on their huge photograph.

At least Mike Grehl was impressed. The *Anchorage Times* ran an eight-column banner the next day: GONNASON BACKS COOK CLAIM.

That morning Gonnason tried to get Washburn to draw what he thought Cook's route was on the photograph. But Washburn insisted, "Cook didn't have a route." Yet when pressed, though still insisting it was impossible, he drew with an impatient motion a rough route across the picture. But this was all theoretical, he insisted.

For hours the two sat and argued over the meaning of Cook's descriptions as Gonnason attempted to point out similar features on the photograph. Washburn stuck to his position: his photographs proved that Cook had never gone higher than 6,000 feet, he said. Washburn explained his points in great detail and with patience, but when challenged, he would jump up, pace the floor and then bang on the table to reinforce his view. He seemed particularly defensive whenever Belmore Browne's name was mentioned, and he invariably called any quote from Cook's narrative "nonsense" or "hogwash." Washburn argued that the granite slabs shown in Cook's summit photo did not exist. When Gonnason replied, "I say that's shadowed, packed snow," Washburn called this "rubbish."

Finally, Gonnason had had enough. "Hell, the man was there!" he exclaimed. "Why should there be an argument?"

The weather did not clear for four more days. On August 1 Don Sheldon picked up Otto Trott. After a meal and a refreshing bath, Trott was flown back to the glacier, and landed at Bradford Washburn's camp on one of its tributaries.

There Washburn pointed out a ridge identical to Cook's 15,400-foot photo that Gonnason had put so much store in. Washburn's camp was only 5,000 feet high.

There was not much time before the plane had to take off, but Washburn promised to meet Trott in Seattle to explain further. As the plane's motor warmed up, Washburn yelled over its roar to Trott in the cockpit, "I could not call Cook a damn liar in front of his daughter!"[23]

Yes, Gonnason had failed to reach the summit, as Washburn had predicted, but all the climbers seemed to believe that they had found Cook's route. This outcome did not reassure the Boston scientist. As a result of Gonnason's display of confidence, the *Life* reporters had shown signs of believing that there just might be something to Cook's claim after all. *Life* had rushed its article because of the publicity surrounding the new climb. Its writers had not indicated to Washburn what their editorial slant would be, and he was worried.

He urged Stefansson to write a letter to *Life*'s editor when the article appeared and to get prominent members of the exploring and geographical fraternity to do the same. Mrs. Vetter's energetic campaign to rehabilitate Cook's climb, he told Stef, "must be slapped down firmly."[24]

Washburn was careful to add that he was not trying to defame a dead man but to defend Browne, Stuck and a host of "splendid men" whom the "Cook crowd" had tried to cut down. All of the letter writers should confine themselves to the simple scientific facts, he said, since Mrs. Vetter's "facts" were simply an emotional rehash of claims discredited 50 years before by scientific investigators all over the world.

On August 15, 1956, Washburn had his promised meeting with Otto Trott and again said that Gonnason had taken his backer for a ride. Trott refused to listen to this, assuring him that Mrs. Vetter had asked Gonnason to make the climb, but he did listen to Washburn's explanation of why he believed Cook's climb was a hoax.

Trott, who now saw all of Washburn's photos, including a new one of Fake Peak, was staggered by what they revealed. But how could Cook's descriptions of conditions along his route be so accurate if he had not climbed the mountain? he asked. Washburn replied that they had been based on observations Cook had made in 1903, when he had a clear view of the route from the snout of the Muldrow Glacier. Although Washburn was willing to admit that an ascent of the East Buttress was possible, he insisted Cook never made one.

Though he still believed that not even Washburn and his photographs had actually proved Cook did not climb Mount McKinley, Trott left feeling that Cook had not really done it.[25]

Washburn's worries about the *Life* article proved baseless. He had shown his photos to *Life* as well, and its editors had come away even more convinced than Otto Trott. The article, titled "The Camera Eye vs. Dr. Cook," concluded that Cook's miscaptioned photographs, when displayed side by side with Washburn's, were convincing proof that Cook had faked his 1906 climb.

When Lilian Kiel saw the article, she was "completely stunned." "The old Hampton's tricks" leapt to her mind, and she sent Helene Vetter her sympathies. But Dr. Cook's daughter was determined to fight on. "I appreciated your wire and your kind thoughts," she told Kiel. "I am not discouraged or beaten. In fact, this gives me more ammunition. But how to present it is always a problem. . . .

". . . This summer's trip took great courage. The unexpected to have to live with my father's worst enemy and Life staff for one week was the worst ordeal that I ever expect to encounter. I still have faith that truth will eventually win. However we are so darn outnumbered."[26] If it was any comfort, the experience had been no more pleasant for Bradford Washburn, who called it "grotesque."

What Helene Vetter did not tell even Lilian Kiel was that she had made a startling discovery of her own about Mount McKinley. After returning from Alaska, she had asked her cousin, Adah Murphy, in Toms River, New Jersey, to see if there was anything dealing with Mount McKinley among some of her father's effects at the house on Lein Street, where he had spent each winter in the 1930s. It turned out that there was—the original diary of the 1906 climb, which had not been seen for 50 years.

It would not be seen again for another 33. After reading it, Helene Vetter put it away, telling only her family and Hugo Levin of its existence.[27]

In 1957 Helene Vetter formed the Dr. Frederick A. Cook Society to gain "official recognition for the scientific and geographic accomplishments" of her father. When the son of Adrien de Gerlache led a return of Belgium to the Antarctic as part of the International Geophysical Year, she sent him greetings and recalled the bond between their fathers.

But the cause she had taken up suffered a series of setbacks in 1959. Negotiations with Lord and Colbert to publish a revised *My Attainment of the Pole* were broken off. Her husband was stricken with a massive stroke that drained her energies and financial resources, and in November she learned of Lilian Kiel's death the previous September.

Her prodding efforts were still paying dividends, however, even though her attentions were turned elsewhere. Andrew Freeman had begun a drastic revision of his long-spurned manuscript.

In 1960 John Edward Weems's *Race for the Pole* was published, the first full-fledged book on the Cook-Peary controversy to appear since the 1930s. Weems took a decidedly pro-Peary stand, putting many episodes potentially embarrassing to the admiral in the best possible light and making, or repeating, a number of uninformed statements. Freeman's book made a good foil to it when it was published as *The Case for Doctor Cook* the next year—30 years after he first had the idea of writing the dramatic story of Frederick Cook's life.

Though he clearly advocated Cook's point of view, Freeman did not openly show vindictiveness toward Peary, nor did he denounce the admiral's claim as a fraud. Instead, he planted the seeds of doubt in the reader's mind, to germinate there later if they found fertile ground. What's more, in retelling the facts of the controversy, the book was free of significant error. Its weaknesses lay in its errors of omission and its scant attention to Cook's original polar narrative while emphasizing Peary's. With its publication, however, Cook's life achieved a semblance of permanent form at last. No longer could there be any fear of his being totally forgotten by history.

The North Pole became the goal of another surface expedition for the first time since 1909 when a party of Norwegians led by Bjørn Staib proposed to reach the Pole by dogsledge and then, if possible, to continue across the entire polar basin. They received partial funding in the form of a grant from the National Geographic Society.

Their light Nansen sledges disintegrated immediately during reconnaissance runs on the shore ice, so they had to build new ones, choosing a design similar in construction and weight to what Peary had used. Staib's party then set out from Alert on Ellesmere Island on March 29, 1964.

Though far more sturdy, their new sleds cut speed and load cruelly. On the first day in the rough coastal fringe, Staib struggled 14 hours to gain one mile. At the end of three weeks the Norwegians had progressed only 25 miles and could see they would never even reach the Pole. Once on the circumpolar pack, the sledges became mired in deep snow and could not be budged. Staib called in an airdrop of light plastic toboggans and abandoned his cumbersome sledges.

With the toboggans the pace picked up. Some days the expedition was able to cover more than ten miles. By now the goal had been reduced to reaching the ice island ARLIS II, where they arrived May 8. It had taken Staib's expedition 41 days to cover 300 miles.

In the autumn of 1964 Helene Vetter once again ventured into the enemy camp, paying an unexpected visit to Donald MacMillan and his wife. She was not greeted amicably by the last survivor of Peary's final expedition.

"Shortly after my 90th birthday," MacMillan wrote a friend, "Miriam and I were quite shocked to have a visit from Mrs. Vetter and her husband who had come over from Buffalo to talk with me. I suppose she thought at that age I had changed my opinion about her father and would then agree that he did reach the Pole. She soon found out I hadn't changed one iota from my original story. Miriam says she has never seen me quite so emphatic."[28]

When Helene Vetter persuaded State Representative Dorothy Rose to introduce a resolution asking Governor Nelson A. Rockefeller to proclaim

Thursday, June 10, 1965, as Dr. Frederick A. Cook Centennial Day in New York State, Rose and the proclamation office received letters against it. After the governor failed to sign it, a letter arrived from Donald MacMillan, who praised the decision, saying Cook should not be recognized, because "he was not an explorer. He did nothing of note whereby he should be called such."[29]

Helene Vetter was hurt and disgusted. "My purpose in visiting you last Fall," she wrote to MacMillan, "was to get your side of the story and to try to find out if there were any facts which others and I might have overlooked in our meticulous research. But I found that you had not bothered to update or check the facts; that you had lived your story for many years; that you are bent on your role as—accuser, jury, judge, and executioner."[30]

The centennial of the birth of Frederick Albert Cook passed largely unnoticed, except by a piece in the journal of the Arctic Institute of North America, which advanced some reasons why the doctor's claims should be reappraised and perhaps even taken seriously.[31]

The notice given him by the Arctic Institute worried some like Terris Moore, an old climbing partner of Bradford Washburn's. He wrote to MacMillan expressing his surprise at its defense of Cook and warned him that the Arctic Institute received too much support from the Canadian and U.S. governments to be simply ignored.[32] Moore was about to publish his own book, *Mt. McKinley: The Pioneer Climbs,* in which he wholeheartedly embraced the Sourdough Climb as established fact, while rejecting Dr. Cook's as a hoax. Moore dedicated the book to Bradford Washburn.

The Peary family had been so impressed with John Weems's *Race for the Pole* and so disturbed by Freeman's biography that they granted Weems Professor Hobbs's wish. Weems had started research in 1962 for his own biography of Robert E. Peary with full access to the admiral's personal papers. The manuscript that resulted quoted extensively from them in its effort to portray the explorer's life. But Weems often chose favorable passages while ignoring damaging revelations on the very same page. Even so, after reading the finished manuscript, Marie Peary Stafford sent Weems a number of specific "corrections" and also a list of "major objections."

"I am very much pleased with the casual, matter of fact way in which you have handled the Allakasingwah matter and your choice of the quotation from Mother's letter," she told Weems.

". . . I am pleased with the book and Robert is enthusiastic, both of these opinions, of course, being contingent on our corrections and, above all, our major objections being met."[33]

Some of these were met, but others weren't. When it appeared in 1967 under the title *Peary, the Explorer and the Man,* Weems's biography was unavoidably revealing, though many incongruities remained. The book seemed to waver between telling what he had found in Peary's voluminous letters and diaries and avoiding specific language that might have jeopardized his unique position as the only researcher ever allowed unlimited access to them. On the whole, his selections tended to perpetuate the image of Robert Peary as a noble and unusually single-minded man, but Weems's quotations implied much about Peary's personality and character that did not match the heroic portrait drawn by his earlier biographers.

For example, in quoting the 1908 letter in which Peary told Jo that he had landed two men "ostensively" for the relief of Dr. Cook, while actually establishing a station for himself to fall back on in case of the loss of his ship, Weems included Peary's admonishment near its end for Jo to be sure to tell their son "to remember 'straight and strong and clean and honest.'"

Because of his ambivalent methods, one reviewer said of Peary's career as portrayed by Weems, "It is sometimes uncertain whether [Peary] cared more for the land he sacrificed so much to reach, or for his own presence there. Was he serving the cause of great discovery, or was the Arctic serving his desire for acclaim? It is hard to tell."[34]

In 1966 Ralph Plaisted, a Minnesota insurance salesman, decided to try for the Pole using snowmobiles; he attempted to interest the National Geographic Society in backing him. Perhaps remembering the experience of the Staib expedition, the society granted him an interview, then did everything it could to discourage the venture. Plaisted tried anyway. But he was still 384 miles short of his goal when, after a heart- and backbreaking struggle with impossible ice, the pack went to pieces in high winds on April 29, 1967. On May 4 the attempt was abandoned, and the expedition's five members were flown to safety.

The rough reception he got from the polar sea made a connection in Plaisted's mind with his curt reception at the National Geographic Society. His month battling the polar pack had more than convinced him that Peary's claim was not only impossible but ludicrous.

The next year he tried again, and after a grueling journey, on April 19, 1968, Plaisted became the first man whose claim to have reached the North Pole over the surface of the Arctic Ocean was undisputed.

During the late 1960s Helene Vetter corresponded with two writers. One was working on yet another study of the Polar Controversy and the other a new Cook biography, but though both were published, they added little original to the unsolved puzzles of Dr. Cook's life.

A more important correspondence had begun in January 1965, when Vetter had received a letter from a California gardener, expressing interest in Dr. Cook. She sent him a copy of *Return from the Pole*. Hans Waale read the book every winter for years after, and then decided to look into the whole Cook affair. When he had, he became as obsessed with proving that Cook had climbed Mount McKinley as Captain Hall had been with proving Peary didn't discover the North Pole. He even opened up a lengthy correspondence with Bradford Washburn, who at first tried to dissuade him, then tried to dismiss him. But in the end the tenacious Waale, through his persistence and stubborn devotion to the subject, finally gained Washburn's grudging, if not affirming, respect. Waale soon became Helene Cook Vetter's new confidant, even to the point of her revealing the existence of her father's Mount McKinley diary to him.

In 1973 Dennis Rawlins, a college professor from Baltimore, published *Peary at the North Pole; Fact or Fiction?* reviving the arguments against Peary's claims. The book gave scant credit to its author's predecessors on the same ground, mentioning Captain Hall only in its cryptic notes, and contributed little that was really new to the subject beyond salvaging the unpublished work of Henshaw Ward. Nonetheless, it established Rawlins as the greatest living authority on the questionable aspects of Peary's claims. He called Peary's astounding navigational feat—traveling due north for 133 miles without any checks for position and landing smack on the North Pole—his "Pole-in-one" and termed the narrative of his polar journey a case of "temporary inanity." Such flippant remarks, and a general disdain for those who did not agree with him, put off many of Rawlins's readers and made them little disposed to hear the message that lay behind such rhetorical excesses.

Helene Vetter called Rawlins's effort "despicable" for its characterization of her father as a clumsy faker and for its description of how Rawlins had persuaded the Arctic Institute to drop its advocacy of Cook's claim. She confessed her despair to Hans Waale that nothing she had done had put her father any closer to vindication. But just before her death in 1977, she told her daughter that though she herself would not live to see it, surely it would come in Janet's lifetime. Janet now took up the cause.

Through the efforts of Janet Vetter and other members of the Frederick A. Cook Society, which had now been incorporated as a nonprofit educational organization in the state of New York, a major project was afoot that would set off a chain of events destined to unravel the perplexing questions still remaining about the rival polar claims of 1909. It came in the form of a made-for-television movie called *Cook and Peary: The Race to the Pole,* which was broadcast over CBS on December 13, 1983.

With the influence of the Cook Society, the script took the Cook-as-ingenuous-hero-martyr viewpoint, which was emphasized by Rod Steiger's tough-guy portrayal of Peary as a foil to Richard Chamberlain's naive Cook. After its airing, the National Geographic Society was flooded with indignant letters about its role in the controversy. This caused *National Geographic* to run a rare editorial, which called the film a "blatant distortion of the historical record, vilifying an honest hero and exonerating a man whose life was characterized by grand frauds."[35]

More important, the National Geographic Society then prevailed upon the Peary family to open to public view the admiral's long-hidden papers, which had been given to the National Archives in 1964 but had always been restricted. This was done, presumably, on the theory that their examination would vindicate Peary, refute the movie and set the matter to rest forever. Most of the restrictions were dropped on March 8, 1984.

Subsequently, the National Geographic Society commissioned Wally Herbert to examine the 225 cubic feet of Peary papers. Herbert, a noted British polar explorer who in 1969 had led the first successful dogsledge expedition to the Pole since Peary's attempt, was asked to make his report to the society's nearly 10.5 million members in time for its hundredth anniversary in 1988.

Herbert's report, though humane, theorized that Peary had missed the Pole by at least 30 miles and probably more, though it stopped short of accusing him of a deliberate fraud. When an article embodying Herbert's findings appeared in the September 1988 *National Geographic,* it prompted talk that the society had at last backed away from its blind adherence to what Henshaw Ward had called "The Peary Myth"—a myth, if it was such, that the National Geographic Society itself had played the key role in creating. But actually, the society was already quietly looking for others who might find errors in Herbert's analysis.

At this point, Dennis Rawlins again entered the fray. He announced he had discovered proof among Peary's papers that the explorer knew he had not reached the Pole and had perpetrated a deliberate fraud. The "proof" consisted of a piece of paper that had been kept in a safe-deposit box in Portland, Maine, with Peary's North Pole diary, Cook's seized Annoatok letters and other selected papers. The envelope in which it was kept bore an inscription in Jo Peary's hand describing the contents as the original observations made by Peary at the Pole in April 1909.

Rawlins took this label at its word and, working out the figures, concluded that instead of being at the Pole, Peary had been about 100 miles short of it. His discovery got wide press coverage in the *Washington Post* and other influential newspapers.[36] The National Geographic Society was stung by this revelation by the man who had so often sarcastically rebuked it for its role in what he called "the greatest scientific hoax of the century." The society asked the Foundation for the Promotion of the Art of Navigation, a private nonprofit organization composed mostly of retired Navy men in Rockville, Maryland, to check on Rawlins's findings.

The leader of the team from the Navigation Foundation, as it was called for short, retired Rear Admiral Thomas Davies, determined that the notes on the paper in question were probably made in 1906, not 1909, and represented a comparatively insignificant adjustment of instruments known as a time-sight check. Upon further consideration, Dennis Rawlins conceded that Davies was probably correct. But in admitting his mistake, Rawlins called on the National Geographic Society to admit its own error in hastily approving Peary's claim in 1909 without adequate examination or evidence. But the society would have none of it.

Fresh from this victory, the society cast aside Herbert's conclusions, which, it was rumored, had been published in *National Geographic* only when it became clear that they would come out in book form. Now it commissioned Davies and his organization to investigate Peary's papers again to settle the matter in an unbiased, independent report grounded in all of the navigational information they contained.

During the investigation, Admiral Davies did not inspire confidence in his impartiality when he announced that Peary's lack of observations for longitude and compass variation "didn't bother" him, or by his assertion that he would find the method Peary had used to stay on one meridian straight to the Pole without them. Nor were skeptics reassured by the appearance in the foundation's newsletter of letters from readers suggesting ways to bolster Peary's claim. One writer prefaced his offer of help with "you're going to need every argument you can muster."[37]

When the Navigation Foundation's report appeared in 1989 under the title *Robert E. Peary at the North Pole,*[38] it fell far short of the commendable goal set for it and in the end only deepened the controversy.

Like most writings on the subject, the report's review of Peary's career and the Polar Controversy was fraught with error, even as to easily verifiable facts. Furthermore, its language seemed anything but neutral, describing Peary as "mercilessly pilloried by a vociferous minority" and the latter-day victim of "one-sided negative publicity unsupported by any new or conclusive evidence whatsoever." In a note, the foundation's report called criticism of the 1909 examination of Peary's records by the subcommittee of its own sponsor, the National Geographic Society, "unwarranted."

Yet if nothing else, the report's analysis of Peary's data showed conclusively that there was nothing that could be scientifically accepted as hard evidence among Peary's voluminous papers to support his oft-doubted claim. At least Davies and his associates had not been able to find any, even though they were said to have read every paper in the Peary gift—this in itself, because of the gift's size and complexity, was a dubious claim.

Lacking any documentary proof, the Navigation Foundation attempted to create a basis for belief in Peary's polar discovery and his other controversial claims, including his "Farthest North" of 1906. An analysis of the Arctic Ocean sea bottom, for example, was advanced to corroborate Peary's line of incomplete soundings, allegedly made on the 70th meridian. The report also supplied the promised answer as to how Peary navigated.

Although he personally took no observations for latitude during the entire trip of 413-plus nautical miles—until the first that he took disclosed he had arrived at the very Pole itself, and this without having taken a single sight for longitude or a check of compass variation—the foundation maintained that Peary had indeed reached the North Pole.

Davies advanced as Peary's method of navigation the simplistic explanation that he used the sun's culmination at local noon (meridian altitude) to get his compass bearings. But even Davies's own report admitted that this method would have been inadequate for such purposes above 88° north latitude, where it might be in error by as much as 10° either way.[39] Moreover, that Peary used this method to find his way north was contradicted by documentary evidence from other members of the expedition and by Peary himself.[40] The center-piece of the foundation's evidence, however, lay not in his navigational method, but in an examination of Peary's North Pole photographs.

In the height of ironies, Davies tried to use for Peary the same basis that Cook had advanced to "prove" his own claim to have arrived at the North Pole—the length of the shadows cast by the men on the ice. His evidence was not gathered by an Eskimo holding a six-foot stick, however; it consisted of a mathematical analysis in which the altitude of the sun was determined by using shadows visible in Peary's photographs to determine the angle of the light rays that projected them. This method, known as photogrammetric analysis, was dependent on many critical parameters, including camera angle, focal length of the lens, time of day, and a determination of the true horizon in each photo-graph. Virtually none of these could be independently known with any cer-tainty, so to establish them, Davies relied on suppositions, apparently chosen to maximize a result favorable to Peary, drawn from Peary's own narrative. In other words, the Navigation Foundation seemed willing to accept the word of the very man whose credibility they were charged to test.

As a result of its investigation, the foundation was "pleased to announce" that Peary, Henson and the four Eskimos had been to within 1.6 miles of the North Pole on April 6, 1909, just as Peary, Mitchell, Duvall and the National Geographic Society's subcommittee had said they had.

In so doing, its report also disparaged Wally Herbert's findings, which had appeared in elaborated form in a book titled *The Noose of Laurels*. The report attributed Herbert's rejection of Peary's claim to a motive similar to the one Stefansson had imputed to Amundsen in 1926—trying to eliminate Peary as a claimant so that Herbert himself would be recognized as the first man to have led a dogsledge expedition to the North Pole. It also laid all the "un-warranted" doubts of Peary's credibility at the feet of Frederick A. Cook, saying it was he who had destroyed the scientific world's faith in real explorers by his "outrageous hoax."

In summing up their findings Admiral Davies, speaking for the Naviga-tion Foundation team, concluded:

> We should also like to say that after perusing hundreds of boxes of Peary's private papers, his correspondence and his journals, we are convinced of the man's integrity. . . .
>
> We sincerely hope that this report will help to set the record straight and perhaps put an end to the long process of vilification of a courageous American explorer.

The National Geographic Society trumpeted Peary's, and its own, vindi-cation at a full-dress press conference complete with elaborate press kits, which was followed by an equally elaborate *National Geographic* article in January 1990 repudiating Herbert's conclusions in his earlier article.

The society's president, Gilbert M. Grosvenor, defended his grandfather's backing of Peary and declared in an editorial that the Navigation Foundation's report was "unimpeachable." He also declared an end to the historic controversy at long last, with the decision in Peary's favor. It was a decidedly unilateral declaration.

Dennis Rawlins, for one, could not agree. He gave a counteranalysis that blasted the accuracy of Admiral Davies's methods. It also cast doubts upon Davies's general abilities at navigational analysis by citing his previous attempt to prove that Amerigo Vespucci had discovered the mainland of America, whose calculations Rawlins lampooned and which another astronomer called "amusing nonsense."

Though not in the same terms, a number of science writers raised doubts about both the objectivity and the accuracy of the methods used in the Navigation Foundation's report, calling attention to its lack of error analysis or any independent verification of its conclusions. The daily news media, however, generally accepted the findings that were so lavishly presented and upheld by the prestigious National Geographic Society in 1989, just as they had in 1909.

But where was Dr. Cook in all this? If he was barely mentioned beyond the standard vilifications, it was not for long. On August 10, 1989, his last lineal descendent, Janet Vetter, had died at the age of 51. Her will bequeathed to the Library of Congress the papers her mother had inherited and all that had been collected by the Vetters over nearly 40 years of diligent effort.[41]

For the first time in 80 years, the papers of Frederick A. Cook could be looked upon by whoever cared to see them. They were to reveal far more than anyone expected of them.

PART TWO

"A Knotty Problem."

Some truth there was, but dash'd and brew'd with lies,
To please the fools, and puzzle all the wise.
Succeeding times did equal folly call,
Believing nothing, or believing all.

—John Dryden

What is true in a man's life is not what he does, but the legend which grows up around him. . . . You must never destroy legends. Through them we are given an inkling of the true physiognomy of a man.

—Oscar Wilde

CHAPTER 27

A Matter of Veracity

A<small>FTER FINISHING A FAIR TYPED COPY OF HIS MEMOIRS</small>, F<small>REDERICK</small> C<small>OOK</small> penciled a sheet of paper and inserted it at the front of the manuscript. It was a strange preface to an even stranger life:

> This man Dr. Cook as we find him on the billboards of time is not the man I know. I am his manager and I have perhaps mismanaged his affairs but I have been in the foreground and the background of the panorama of his life also in his heart and in his mental reaches. If the Dr. Cook of public acclaim has a real existence I am the father of his destiny the progenitor of his worldly affairs. I know he is not as good as some friends rate him and I am sure he is not as bad as his enemies defame him. History will give Dr. Cook a place— this may be high, it may be low but a place is assured. . . .[1]

On more than one occasion Dr. Cook spoke of himself as he did in his preface—as a person apart—with himself looking on his public persona without a sense of recognition. So if we are uncertain what place in history Dr. Cook deserves, if we are still undecided how high or how low to place this man, that is understandable. The answer, many would argue, is simply a matter of veracity. But nothing about Dr. Cook is simple.

It would be tempting to read into both his early life and Peary's the roots of their destinies—to blame the peculiarity of the paths they chose on their fatherless childhood and the resulting emotional deprivation. That would be the modern thing to do, the comfortable, reassuring thing. Hindsight so easily justifies all that would never have been predicted. But of this there can be little doubt: although both Cook and Peary were deeply affected by the early loss of their fathers, many have been more unfortunate and turned out far differently. There can be no one event that results in such extraordinary consequences, even one so significant as this. No, the fates are much subtler than that, and beyond all powers of prediction or even afterthought.

Still, with the facts unknowable, we may be permitted our speculations, and it is therefore permissible to think that in the poignant remembrance of his father's funeral there might be a clue to all that was to follow for Frederick

Cook. Perhaps it was then that the boy-Cook decided he would leave more behind than a "mud colored suit left hanging on the wall after he was buried."

Life's chances are what we make of them, after all, and Fred Cook early showed a pattern that would mark his life's progress. He took circumstances as they were and turned them to his advantage. Forced early to be self-reliant, self-reliance became a lifelong habit, and this in turn instilled an early and unshakable confidence in himself. Every experience, whether gain or loss, was welcomed and searched for its lesson.

Late in his life, Cook wrote about the role of experience and self-confidence as the wellsprings of success:

> Experience is the greatest human asset and the most costly. It is of little use to those who by habit do not look backward and forward daily. The main difference between a man of self-acquired wealth and the one still in the treadmill of physical labor at forty is in the manner in which experience has been sought and used. Behind all this is intellectual alertness or inertia due mainly to the stamp of adolescent schooling. The man who succeeds, early finds and maintains a state of mind where he believes in himself—but continues to learn from others. The one who fails, too often lacks self-understanding—does not seek it—spends his spare time in figuring out other men's chances—fails in this and becomes lost in the darkness of his own intellectual inertia. All of this can be corrected at any age and stage of life—which proves that every man is his own paymaster. Intellectual inertia and empty pockets go together.[2]
>
> With this in mind, let us prepare to enter an old world in a new way. Every one of us has within, precious metal, power and capacity found in no other person. To find this is the first task. We may need means to test—perhaps a mirror, a hammer and a spike; but find it we must before the start is made. Now for paper and a pencil; then put down specific equipment. Of this you may have very little, but put down your best and your second best. Throw away the rest and re-equip for the special purpose which fits your capacity. . . .
>
> An abiding interest big enough to keep the machinery of life busy is most difficult to generate—most costly to maintain—but interest is the spark-plug of life and desire fires it—keep this ever before you.[3]
>
> When we thoroughly understand that self is all that we possess, then at any stage of life, we can remake self to fit that little notch in space and time allotted to all and, there, expanding with such power and glory as our genius for self-regeneration warrants. We get about all the reward that the intelligence of our effort is worth.[4]

> The only salable product that we have to offer will be ability, and ability is the result of well balanced intelligence. The kind of intelligence required must be the result of ideas that germinate in a mind well supplied with suitable information.
>
> Observation, study, and application will now supply the information. This plan of personal proficiency should fit us to the market of our future activities. Will we be ready when the door opens?[5]

> We know there is always room at the top. High altitudes are lonely places. Courage is lost in climbing. The back trail is always easiest— but only to those who keep going with a set determination to get to the top and win is the reward of victory.[6]

It is clear that Frederick Cook discerned the "precious metal" within at an early age and also developed the ability to "remake self to fit that little notch in space and time allotted." Intellectual inertia was never a fault he possessed, nor was a lack of capacity for work, either.

We have only to trace his progress from a rural one-room schoolhouse to the Medical College of New York or compare his vivid writings with his older brother's barely literate letters to see the disadvantages he overcame to rise to a respectable place in learned society. But Cook believed that any man was capable of doing this. "Though the birth right of a good family is valuable, and the handicap of low breeding is a great hindrance," he said, "in a final result, man is what he is mainly by his own choice of high or low habits of mind."[7]

While he cultivated the high habits of the mind, he never forgot to "look backward and forward daily" and so kept his perspective. By keeping in view where he had come from, he never lost the common touch ever so important in his relations with all manner of people, and as he would in Greenland, he filed away their qualities until he "could figure out reactions to all issues coming or going."

This perhaps was Cook's greatest achievement. He had a most extraordinary gift for grasping the essence of the psychological moment and anticipating the reaction to it of nearly everyone he met. Through his understanding of self and the qualities of his own mind, he recognized the common strand that runs throughout all of humanity. These characteristics made him unusually fitted to the life he chanced or chose to lead, and in the living, that life only enlarged and expanded his latent abilities.

That life started by chance on the fateful voyage of the *Kite* on which both his and Peary's destinies were sealed, both individually and collectively, but for different reasons. As a result of the North Greenland Expedition, Peary was, by his relatively easy success, seduced into entering a contest from which his nature, which could not bear defeat, also could never allow withdrawal, no matter how the losses mounted and no matter how unobtainable the prize, whereas Dr. Cook found that "abiding interest big enough to keep the machinery of life busy." In the Arctic he discovered the thing he loved and his purpose in life. But as Robert Dunn remarked in one of his novels, "It's always the thing we love that ruins us."

Just how much of Frederick Cook's life as he reported it is true? Did he reach the top of Mount McKinley or attain the North Pole? Unfortunately, the doubts raised by his opponents did their work too well. They have caused us to scrutinize every one of his actions for deception, to dissect each sentence he uttered or wrote for deceit, and to take a magnifying glass to every picture he exposed to, in turn, expose his dishonesty. They have centered our interest on answering these questions only and have diverted us from a far more important question—and a far greater mystery.

In the condemnation that followed the collapse of Cook's polar claim, all objectivity was lost. To destroy that claim, his opponents sought to discredit his entire life. But if we seek its deepest secrets, there may be things more valuable to learn from the life of Frederick Albert Cook than the answers to those two persistently asked questions.

As careful research has disclosed, no major character in our story has been able to stand such a minute examination as some have applied to Dr. Cook. If absolute truth is required to retain any honor, then all must fall. All made statements that were untrue. In some cases, these were deliberate lies, perhaps justified in the minds of those who spoke them as necessary to defend themselves or to achieve a greater good. So many little lies start out with such motives. But little lies require larger ones to hide behind, and these often grow so large that truth itself vanishes behind them, and vanishes from the mind as well, until the teller believes the lies himself.

Yet not all untruths are lies. Memories fade, but wishes persist; new information prejudices the way we remember or interpret the past. The thing we want to be true often replaces what actually transpired, especially when there is pressure to explain or justify our actions. Eventually, these private interpretations of reality become reality itself and are repeated in good faith—even sworn to. It is also well known that two observers may come away with totally different impressions of a single event based on their previous experiences. Then, too, subsequent events may distort and color what we observed as time strips the memory of details or gives it added meaning.

A small yet perfect example of these processes is found in the meeting of the *Belgica*'s scientists with the Onas near Harberton, when Dr. Cook reached into his pocket and gave a pinch of hard candy to each Indian. According to Lucas Bridges, writing long after the event, and at a time when he believed he had just cause for enmity against the "brisk young American surgeon," Cook expected this to adequately compensate the wary Onas for posing for pictures; "reckless hospitality," Bridges called it. But Lecointe, who also saw Cook's actions and recorded them shortly after the event took place, remembered that same little incident this way:

Cook took from a saddle bag some candy which he gave to the children. Then as if he were in a hospital he began to care for some small ones who had eye problems. Thanks to this system we were soon at ease and the Indians, reassured, permitted us to take photographs.[8]

So it is only when we have taken the time to examine all points of view that we can hope to regain perspective in such a passion-charged subject as is now before us. Many have staked out their ground and tied their personal reputation to one side or the other, and so, much is at stake.

Frederick Cook's life may be divided into two parts, and October 1907 marks the division. That was the month it became known that he had remained in Greenland and would try for the North Pole; thus he became Peary's mortal rival and an object of every suspicion. Only then did he become a controversial figure. And so it is our first task to look at the time before that date to see if there is any precedent for what so many believe came after. Is there a pattern of deceit, a latent dishonesty that might predict grand deceptions at McKinley and the North Pole? Or is Cook's record clean, and if so, are his narratives of his two greatest exploratory claims true? Or can a leopard really change his spots?

The place we must start is the moment of Cook's first meeting with Robert E. Peary in Philadelphia. At that instant in 1891, Dr. Cook's public life began, and the public man began to evolve who, in the end, seemed to be another person to the private man within. Here, immediately, we are confronted with something puzzling. We have read Cook's story: the grief over the loss of his wife and child, his lonely hours, with few patients, in a struggling medical practice, the chance window of escape provided by Peary's little newspaper notice. Yet according to a duplicate sent to replace the lost original in 1931, Dr. Cook's diploma was not issued until March 24, 1891, and he was licensed to practice medicine in New York County only in "March or April"—scarcely two months before he departed for Greenland and *after* his interview with Peary. Unless there is some mistake in the dates, he apparently inflated his experience both in his story and to gain a position with Peary's expedition.[9]

If he did, Peary seems never to have noticed. His letter to his mother as the *Kite* was about to return expresses absolute confidence in his young surgeon, and that confidence only grew as the expedition progressed. Dr. Cook proved himself capable in every way, medically and otherwise, though, as he acknowledged himself, his medical abilities were hardly tested when he sailed.

Peary's confidence in Cook as a doctor stemmed almost entirely from his human touch—what used to be called bedside manner. Peary's accident was no test of the doctor's abilities. Since Peary had suffered a "good break," no medical procedure was necessary, and so it is only one of many Cook-Peary legends that the man who became his hated enemy had "saved" Peary's leg and, by implication, his career as an explorer. This is not a reflection on Dr. Cook as a physician; it is simply a matter of fact.

In the nineteenth century, bedside manner, in many instances, *was* what it meant to be a doctor. A glance at Cook's educational requirements or into his medicine chest on Greenland's inland ice only emphasizes the importance to a doctor at that time of winning the confidence of his patients.

The example given by the Eskimo angekoks only held up, as if in a mirror, this attribute for Dr. Cook to reflect upon and confirmed in his mind that the power of suggestion was a more versatile medicine than anything that came from a vial of ox-gall, or even one of opium. In looking at the records of the North Greenland Expedition, despite the class-conscious comments of Jo Peary and Langdon Gibson, it can readily be seen that the power to instill trust in others was already present in Dr. Cook, fully formed.

Though this is the most thoroughly documented of Peary's expeditions, still, we might wish for more. Apparently, each expedition member's diary was returned to him. The Peary papers contain only the holographs of Peary's diary and a small portion of Mrs. Peary's. There is a partial typed copy of Astrup's diary and a full typed copy of Verhoeff's, but not a sentence of any other. There is not a word by Henson, who may have still been illiterate at the time.[10] Gibson's still exists, but there is no private journal of Cook's to consult, no contemporary thoughts about himself or others at this crucial time.

Could it be that he did not keep one? Perhaps; of all the expeditions he participated in, only two narrative diaries kept with any regularity seem to exist, and Cook's required reports to Peary that winter were consistently late and seem rather perfunctory. His ethnographic notes, for instance, run a mere nine pages of typescript and have hardly any depth. But it still seems incredible that the voluminous writer of the future did not start here.

All we have from him on this most important event in his life was written 40 years later, and it is clouded by time, discolored by all the unwelcome events that intervened and distorted by the memory and its wishes.

In the wake of so many later tragedies, Cook's memoirs show a somewhat sad tendency to view the North Greenland Expedition as a tragic event itself, rather than the amazingly harmonious and successful one it was. Certainly there were frictions, annoyances and stresses, but nowhere except in Cook's memory was there any terrible foreboding of what was to come. This is evident from each of the participants' surviving diaries.

From Peary's diary it seems that he considered Cook his second in command by October 1891 and that the tributes he paid him in his speeches and in his first book were genuine. But people like Peary can never abide the luster of a competing star for very long. As he had told his mother when only 24, "I cannot bear to associate with people, who, age & advantage being equal, are my superiors. I must be the peer or superior of those about me to be comfortable, not that I care to show my superiority, simply to know it myself."[11]

What was really in Peary's mind when he decided to take Eivind Astrup on the "Great White March"? Was it because Astrup was the best man for the job, or was he seen as the least threat, being only 20 and a foreigner? Peary's diary is silent on this matter.

Obviously, Peary had lost confidence in Gibson, and it seems that the reason for not taking Cook was that he wanted him to be at Redcliffe House to take care of Jo. But if his real reason for choosing Astrup was to have no competitor—as he would have none on subsequent expeditions—then his strategy failed badly, if not immediately. Astrup perhaps seemed dull because of his lack of skill with English, but he was intelligent, insightful and independent enough to disagree about what had been seen from Navy Cliff. From their contemporaneous diaries it is evident that Astrup's observations were the more accurate, and there can be no doubt that Peary knew, then and there, that his claim to having proven the insularity of Greenland was not true.[12] Though Astrup's version was dismissed in America, his report planted the first small seed of doubt that finally grew to overwhelm all of Peary's subsequent claims.

For Peary, this was only the first in the series of misstated and exaggerated claims that would emerge from every future expedition—the first little lie that would grow to obscure the truth. But like all that would follow, it was defended by Peary's backers until no longer defensible, then excused as an honest mistake and, finally, upheld against all rational evidence to the contrary. How different things might have been for both men had Peary chosen the first who stepped forward and taken Cook to Navy Cliff instead.

In 1911 Dr. Cook alleged in *My Attainment of the Pole* that Peary was responsible for the deaths of both Astrup and Verhoeff. Cook attributed Astrup's death to suicide resulting from the despondency he felt after being denounced by Peary's backers for his conflicting report from Navy Cliff and Verhoeff's to his determination to absent himself to avoid returning home with the Pearys.

Matt Henson once reported that on Peary's second expedition Astrup "cried and cried" to get away from Peary, and there is written proof that Astrup was insulted by Peary's letter to General Wistar alleging a plot to desert him in 1894, a letter that excused Peary for his own failure to adequately supply his expedition. Yet no evidence has been found that Astrup was ever despondent to the point of taking his own life. After all, he was supported in Europe, and his report on Melville Bay was most favorably received in his native country. Moreover, a letter written to Evelyn Briggs Baldwin contains Astrup's vow to return to Greenland and continue his life as an explorer: "I promise you . . . if we should not be successful next year, we are bound to be so one of the following 25 seasons"—not the kind of talk expected from a man contemplating suicide.[13]

In 1939 Mrs. Attwood R. Martin, John Verhoeff's stepsister, wrote to Jo Peary asking her what she thought had induced her brother to wander off to his death. She asked Mrs. Peary to write, as a memorial to him, her remembrances while she was alone with John when the rest of the party was on the inland ice. What her reply was, if it exists, is still sealed from view,[14] but it seems obvious that Mrs. Martin was not aware of how Josephine Peary had felt about the "very homely dwarf" or of the content of her brother's diary. But when Mrs. Martin wrote to Dr. Cook, he had no hesitation in saying that John Verhoeff hated the Pearys and refused to return on the same ship with them.[15]

It seems definite that Verhoeff inquired privately about the chances of remaining in Greenland alone, since other members of the expedition remarked on this at the time of his disappearance, as well as his odd behavior. Verhoeff was certainly an unusual person, but even his odd behavior had an explanation, though none of his fellow expedition members knew what it was.

Verhoeff had been expelled from Yale, just short of graduation, over an incident that was at once bizarre and characteristic. He and a fellow student had a disagreement about an article concerning a sporting event recounted in the pink pages of the *Police Gazette,* the popular "man's" magazine of the day. The two agreed to settle their dispute by having Verhoeff write a letter to the proprietor of the magazine, Richard K. Fox, and they bet $100 as to who would be declared correct in his opinion. Verhoeff naively relied on his adversary to mail the letter, but the other student kept it instead and forged a reply from Fox saying Verhoeff was wrong. Typically, Verhoeff was not satisfied and bet another $100 that if he wrote a second letter to a sporting authority in New York, he would be vindicated. Again he let his adversary mail it, and again the man forged a negative reply.

John Verhoeff then bicycled from New Haven to New York and there learned of his fellow student's deception; the men he had written to said they had not received his letters. When he returned, Verhoeff bought a gun. There was a violent argument, and Verhoeff managed to get back his $200 in the form of a personal check. His foe later entered his unlocked room at the college and destroyed the check, however.

Another bitter argument ensued, but since no one had seen the man enter Verhoeff's room, nothing could be proven. By now the incident had come to the attention of the Yale authorities, and Verhoeff was expelled for gambling, though the other man received no punishment because he was a graduate student and was not answerable to the same rules. After being expelled, Verhoeff vanished, and his friends worried that he had committed suicide. But actually he had gone to Oregon, then San Francisco.[16] From there he had written to Peary.

Although Verhoeff obviously resented the Pearys and was hurt by the reprimand he received for trying to rescue the dog caught on the cliffside, he expressed no bitter enmity for them in his diary. Far more bitterness against the Pearys can be found in the diary of Langdon Gibson than in John Verhoeff's.

Suspicions might be aroused by the fact that only a transcript of Verhoeff's diary remains, but a complete reading of it gives no reason, based on what is in other transcriptions in the Peary papers, to believe that the text has been altered, especially since the diary was copied in full, as none of the others were. This was probably done to protect Peary against any future allegations concerning the man's disappearance, just as Peary's correspondence with Verhoeff leading up to his selection for the expedition was reproduced in the later edition of Dr. Keely's book, *In Arctic Seas*.

Taking into account Verhoeff's personality, the logical inference is that the disgrace he had suffered at Yale made John Verhoeff determined to prove himself to the world. He would show his merit by doing some big thing, and if he didn't come back—as he mentioned in his application to Peary—well, what did he have to lose? Whether he actually intended to stay in Greenland is unknown, but given these circumstances it seems likely, considering that he hid his clothes and instruments. But there is nothing to indicate any plans to do so in Verhoeff's last diary entry—August 9, 1892—and we may be reasonably sure that this was the last entry because that is the last date he made an entry in his weather log as well, which, being a bound holograph, could not be tampered with without detection.[17]

One thing is sure, Verhoeff was not much concerned about risks, and it is probable this attitude led to his fatal experience crossing the glacier. In light of this history, it can be seen that Peary's public ridicule was an event likely to be magnified in John Verhoeff's mind, but it is far more likely that it was the incident at Yale, rather than Robert E. Peary, that drove Verhoeff to his death.

The honors he received after the return of the North Greenland Expedition seemed to have turned Peary's head, and his thoughts turned with it to nothing but his own further aggrandizement. In the aftermath of the expedition, the acclaim given to Peary, and the fantastic success of his subsequent lecture tour, opened Cook's eyes to the commercial possibilities of his now "abiding interest."

Whatever the reason for their break, Peary's denial of permission for Cook to publish his ethnological findings was so important to him that he resigned from Peary's second expedition. Even though Peary's tendencies were not nearly so pronounced as they would become later, Cook probably had already discerned the essence of Peary's character. And since he knew, through Gibson's fall from favor, Peary's need for absolute loyalty, he must have realized his resignation eliminated him from ever accompanying Peary again. But what good would it do him, he may have reasoned, if he could never gain financially from his experiences? It appears his split with Peary came as much over Peary's unwillingness to allow him to make himself "his own paymaster" as over matters of principle. Clearly, Cook already had enough self-confidence to go it alone and knew that he must, since he would never get the credit he deserved in a subordinate capacity to Peary.[18]

Once the break with Peary came, it did not take long for Cook to try to earn money from his experiences, and his transactions with Herbert L. Bridgman in 1893 show that he had not misjudged his ability to do so. Bridgman was obviously disappointed at Peary's refusal to allow him to publish his interviews with Dr. Cook, but the newspaperman was shrewd enough to make the immediate sacrifice for a longer-term gain when he invested in Peary's good will. Herbert Bridgman was always good at sensing where power lay and, by manipulating it, usurping the mantle of power for himself.

Although Cook did break faith with the contract he had signed, he may not have seen it that way. In his early lectures he laid little emphasis on the particulars of the expedition itself, and then always gave Peary the fullest credit. For the most part, his earliest lectures and published writings derived only from his own observations of natural phenomena and the Eskimos, which he probably reasoned he had never intended to sign away under the terms of that agreement. But Peary's reaction to Bridgman's interviews with Cook shows he did not agree.

Peary, however, at this stage in his life, was not yet embittered by defeat. Though disappointed by Cook's disloyalty, he no doubt genuinely regretted Cook's withdrawal from the Second Greenland Expedition. And their subsequent close cooperation in planning the equipment for that expedition, evidenced in several letters, shows they remained on amicable terms.

When Cook's lectures drew enough attention to enable him to chaperon Dr. Hoppin's retarded son to Greenland, the doctor made the most of it. In later years Cook spoke of this expedition as if it were his own brainchild, but contemporary newspaper reports show that he had little to do with its planning. According to these sources, the expedition was organized and the *Zeta* was chosen and fitted out by Captain James A. Farquhar of Halifax, Nova Scotia, the same man who later owned the *Erik*. It appears that Professor Hoppin simply hired Cook in the capacity of surgeon, guide and Eskimo interpreter.

There is a distinct conflict between Cook's statement at the time, that he went to Cape Breton with no idea of going to Greenland, and his memoirs' account, that he had met with Professor Hoppin and planned it all in advance. If the memoirs are correct, then the voyage of the *Zeta* offers a small prefigurement of the secret plans struck with John R. Bradley in launching the Bradley Arctic Expedition 14 years later. In each case, it was made to appear that the expedition had been a loose, almost casual affair, and in each case Peary's announced plans were anticipated.

Although Cook left a diary of this trip, and a rather full one, it is strangely silent on any background to the voyage, leaving out everything before departing Upernavik on August 19, 1893. It also is completely silent on the major event of the voyage: not a word can be found about how he induced the parents of Clara and Willie to let them return with him to the United States. Cook always was vague about this point, hinting that it, too, was a spur-of-the-moment decision. However, the letter published before he sailed in which he announced his plan to "bring back a family of Esquimaux" contradicts this.

He may have gotten this idea from Peary, whom Gibson records in 1891 as toying with the idea of taking Kyo with him when the *Kite* returned.[19] Why Peary did not carry through on this is not known; perhaps he thought that his successful journey of 1892 and his anticipated claim of proving the insularity of Greenland made this unnecessary to gain attention for his future plans. But Cook had the advantage of seeing Peary's success on his lecture tour and perhaps thought he could go one up on him by exhibiting something Peary had lacked.

Cook's letters to Peary in 1893 give an impression of good business sense and a fine grasp of showmanship. His uses of the Eskimo children and dogs later that year only add to the impression that he knew how best to present a proposition for the maximum effect—and economic gain. In any case, Cook consciously misrepresented Clara and Willie as examples of "wild people," the monetary advantages in this being obvious.

In 1894 his advertisements for the *Miranda* voyage were attractive and well placed, but his early flair for the impressive is best shown by his stationery's identifying his humble house at 15 Hart Street in Brooklyn as the "Official Bureau of the American Antarctic Expedition." The lessons of young Fred Cook's brief experience in the printing trade were never lost on Dr. Cook. This is just one of the first of many examples of Cook's profound understanding of the importance of appearances over substance.

Cook was a voracious reader of everything remotely related to his interests, and he absorbed most of what he read. In early 1894 he wrote: "The best vessels for navigation in the ice are wooden steamships, not too large, and strongly braced."[20] For his "tourist jaunt" to Greenland later that year, he had originally engaged the *Newfoundland,* then the *Algerine,* both just such ships. Why then did he end up taking the *Miranda,* a large iron-hulled vessel? One obvious possibility is that the *Miranda* was a bigger ship and could carry more paying passengers.

But even if Cook's motive was maximizing profit, his decision was not so reckless as it might seem. Though the 1894 season was very unusual for the amount of ice encountered, ice pressure—the great threat to iron-hulled ships—was not a serious factor at any time during the voyage. What did the *Miranda* in was her very size. No other ship that big had ever visited the town's harbor. A smaller wooden ship would have had no trouble clearing the reef that sunk her, but a wooden ship would probably not have survived the collision with the iceberg. So we are left with the remarkable twist that, just possibly, the "pleasure cruise" that Cook took to Greenland in 1894 might have met with disaster no matter what ship he had chosen, and ironically, his choice of an iron ship probably saved the whole expedition.

Other *Miranda* mysteries remain as well. What was behind the proposition he made to Russell Porter to have him cross Greenland west to east, which Porter thought it best not to write in his diary? Perhaps it had to do with making magnetic observations to better define the exact location of the North Magnetic Pole. In the March 17, 1894, issue of the Brooklyn *Standard Union,* Cook outlined such a plan and said, "I am very confident that scientific results of the very first importance would be achieved. . . . In competent hands a winter of investigation, such as is proposed, would be worth a great deal more than it would cost." But if this was all he had in mind, why the secrecy with Porter, since Cook had already announced it in the newspapers? Might it instead have had something to do with what Cook had heard from Astrup of Peary's "Independence Bay" claims? And did he want Porter to investigate them? The record is silent on these questions. Porter never mentioned the proposition again, nor did Cook in his sketchy diary.

Cook was evasive in his interviews after his return from Greenland, but in the aftermath of the ship's loss, naturally there would be a tendency to put the best face on things, since he hoped to mount another "pleasure cruise" in 1895. Perhaps his statements were no more than that, but there also appeared to be a desire to shift blame and divert attention from uncomfortable facts. His suggestion that Captain Farrell may have intentionally scuttled the *Miranda* to collect the insurance does not seem to have occurred to the other passengers. That they bore the captain no enmity is shown by Farrell's invitation as one of the guests of honor to the first dinner of the Arctic Club.

A close examination of the *Miranda's* history also sheds new light on the often-quoted story that Cook saved the expedition by leading a daring open-boat journey up the coast and returning with the *Rigel,* though in fairness, Cook never made this claim himself. The success of that trip to Holsteinborg owed more to the seamanship of the native crew and pilot. But Cook must be given credit as its guiding hand and for having the good sense to listen to his Eskimo navigator and follow his advice explicitly. Cook was adept at learning from others, and he had not forgotten his lesson in the natives' uncanny ability to predict the weather, taught him by the Eskimos he met on the *Zeta* cruise.

This willingness to "continue to learn from others" was part of his elastic adaptability and was demonstrated in Cook's published plans to attack the antarctic fastness. His grasp of the appropriateness of Peary's methods to the great frozen continent to the south was far ahead of its time, and Scott's failure to see this, as late as 1911, cost him not only the race for its Pole, but also his own life and those of his whole polar party. Two years in anticipation of Europe's call for an expedition to Antarctica, Cook's plan for reaching the South Pole varies surprisingly little from the successful strategy adopted by Amundsen 18 years later, though what Cook might have accomplished had he found a backer is an open question.

Cook's actual voyage to the Antarctic raises a number of interesting questions of its own. In his description of his last-minute appointment to the position of surgeon on that voyage, we have a dramatic parallel with the story of his chance reading of Peary's advertisement in 1891. Andrew Freeman's biography says Cook saw a notice in the New York *Sun,* on August 20, 1897, in which he learned that the *Belgica* was about to sail from Ostend minus her surgeon, and telegraphed Gerlache, who sent a favorable reply. He says nothing, and neither does Dr. Cook in *Through the First Antarctic Night,* about any previous contact with the Belgian expedition, when, in fact, Cook had already offered to join the expedition and had been turned down.

On August 6 he had telegraphed: "COULD I JOIN YOUR EXPEDITION AT MONTVIDEO WILL SUBSCRIBE BRING ARCTIC EQUIPMENT ALSO SOME ESKIMO DOGS ANSWER MY EXPENSE – DR. COOK."[21] And a small, unattributed newspaper article discovered among Cook's papers says that "Cook . . . was not disappointed to any very great extent when he learned by cable this forenoon that owing to lack of space in the explorer's vessel his offer to accompany the expedition to the Antarctic regions had been declined. The party is to sail shortly from Antwerp on the steamship Belgica. Several weeks ago, Dr. Cook offered his services, and the offer was taken under advisement."[22]

The content of this article dates it before August 16, 1897, the day the *Belgica* left Antwerp, and although Cook's telegram could be interpreted only broadly as falling within the time frame of "several weeks before," it still predates his first acknowledged official contact with Gerlache and contradicts his version of how he came to be the Belgian's surgeon.

Cook's rejection is confirmed by a letter sent from Rio by Gerlache in which he answered the criticism he had received for including so many foreigners in a supposedly Belgian national enterprise:

> I did not <u>intentionally</u> reject the candidatures of Belgian medical doctors, given that, on the contrary, I have done anything possible to provoke their candidatures; and . . . a Belgian doctor who was hired left us just before our departure. This doctor . . . told me that due to family affairs he could not accompany me, and it was only at the last moment of our departure that I sent a telegram to doctor Cook, to whose offer to participate I had first answered by a refusal.[23]

It appears, then, that it was Gerlache who invited Dr. Cook when he was left no other alternative by his surgeon's resignation. Although these bits of information may contradict only the exact manner and timing of Cook's appointment, there is other evidence that Cook may have sought the position long before August 6.

M.B. Ryan, an associate of the English inventor Hiram Maxim, reported that in August 1910 he had met Cook, who was at the time using the alias Mr. Coleman, in Munich. Ryan reported that he knew Cook on sight because in 1897 he had shared a stateroom with him on the liner *Paris* bound for Europe. Ryan stated that during the voyage Cook had told him he was on his way to apply for the position of surgeon to the Belgian Antarctic Expedition.[24]

There is some reason to believe that Cook did indeed make such a trip in 1897. The *Paris,* a ship in the American Line, was retired in 1899, so Ryan could not have confused the date with 1901, when Cook went to Europe to attend the conference on the scientific results of the *Belgica* voyage. Ryan's statement about the *Paris* is a small circumstance in a long article, the point of which has nothing to do with Cook's connection with the Belgian Antarctic Expedition. So it is difficult to conceive of why he would say this if it were not true.

Gerlache states explicitly in his book that he never personally had any communication with Cook before the exchange of telegrams that invited him to join the *Belgica* in South America. But Gerlache had been in Norway, where he was overseeing the refitting of the *Patria,* and did not return to Belgium until July 15, 1897, a bare month before sailing for the Antarctic. So he would have been absent during the time Cook would have been in Belgium.

But if Cook did make such a trip, why did he never acknowledge it? Perhaps at first Cook did not want it known that he was privately applying for a position with the Belgians while he was publicly trying to raise money for his announced plan of leading an American expedition into the Antarctic, or perhaps he did not want it known in case he was not chosen.

Subsequently, when he went to write the story of how he was chosen as the *Belgica*'s surgeon, the truth being hidden afforded him a far more interesting alternative. If this surmise is correct, perhaps it is only a continuation of something already evidenced in his story of how he was chosen by Peary and in his exhibitions of Willie and Clara as though they were "Arctic Highlanders": the flair for the dramatic—that slight turn on the prosaic that creates the extraordinary and raises the mundane to the fascinating.

Whatever the exact details of his commission as surgeon of the *Belgica,* as with Peary, he gained the genuine respect of those in command. His performance can hardly be faulted, and under those trying conditions—17 men living in cramped quarters, suffering from bad food and physical deprivation, all sick to death of each other and facing a questionable fate—he had every right to despair and no inducement to maintain a pleasant nature. Here we should see "men with their masks torn off" revealing every petty fault. And where are Dr. Cook's? It is a stage set on which only the most consummate actor could maintain a pose, yet the doctor never fails.

It is difficult to believe that Dr. Cook's sympathetic personality was anything but what it seemed, yet Georges Lecointe noted in his book: "In the beginning Cook was the most rigid American the New World has ever had; he could little enjoy our jokes 'à la française.'" But by the end of the voyage, he had to marvel at Cook's plasticity: "It is strange to note how his character completely changed during his stay amongst us. The calm, cold temper of this American became more cheerful with time and towards the end of the expedition, we had no more cheerful comrade on board than the American."[25] One characteristic that did emerge has been little remarked on or mistaken for something else in Dr. Cook: his tremendous degree of self-control.

Although Cook suffered along with the rest through the first antarctic night, he had an advantage over all the others, with the possible exception of Amundsen. His wondering mind filled up the dark emptiness and white spaces with thoughts, speculations and experiments, as he was filled, himself, with a rich inner life, while the others simply wished for an end. Though the experience was one he said he never wished to repeat, it taught him lifelong lessons. His tremendous willpower overcame the despair that seized his fellows, and his adoption of an optimistic attitude, even when he doubted his own medical recommendations, had the desired effect "to raise the patient's hopes and instil a spirit of good humor."

In the Antarctic Cook came to understand the power of human belief and hope and always tried to give the men something to believe in, whether it was his baking treatments, his assurances that raw penguin steaks would avert the scurvy or that his ditches would crack the iron grip the antarctic pack had on the *Belgica* and the minds of the men she bore.

The esteem they expressed for Dr. Cook was a result of true admiration. But contrary to many recent advocates' statements, Cook was not singled out for great praise on the expedition's return, and he was not the only non-Belgian to receive the Order of Leopold.[26] All of the scientific staff were treated equally, but his decoration by the King of the Belgians was no empty gesture. Gerlache had indeed been dealt a lucky hand when he accepted Frederick Cook's entreaties to be taken on the *Belgica*. And Lecointe agreed, "Without him, several of us would never have seen the civilised world again."

Amundsen was one who said that he owed his very life to Cook, and that is probably no exaggeration, though his praise should be tempered by remembering the Norwegian's relationship with the Belgian contingent. Amundsen had officially resigned from his post and even declined to go back to Europe with the *Belgica*. By crediting the American as the singular hero of the voyage, Amundsen could minimize the credit he gave the Belgians. He failed to mention, for instance, that it was Gerlache's route, not Cook's, that was used to cut the canal that freed the ship, and his later memories of the voyage, written in 1927, stray from recorded facts in contemporary sources in subtle ways with the same result. Though these might be only tricks of the memory, the generally bitter tone of Amundsen's memoirs justifies such suspicions.

On the *Belgica*, Cook had opportunities to mature talents only hinted at before. His photographs are a magnificent and very underrated achievement. Of the early antarctic photographers, only Herbert Ponting, Scott's professional photographer, with undoubtedly superior equipment and experience, surpasses his efforts. Cook's pictures are astonishing in quality and composition, even without considering the conditions under which they were taken and the limitations of the cameras then available. They remain a classic and valuable record of a virgin continent and the first evidence of a great photographic gift.

As a doctor, Cook's inquisitive mind and his willingness to look beyond the ordinary explanations also yielded new insights. In the Arctic he had been the first to describe the irregularity of the menstrual cycle in Eskimo women and their seasonal sexual urges.[27] But although he often implied as much, Cook was not the first to recognize that a diet of raw meat alone was sufficient to keep scurvy at bay. In 1857 Dr. Kane made several remarks in *Arctic Explorations* showing he was fully aware of the powers of uncooked meat as an antiscorbutic, even saying that if he had sufficient raw walrus he would "laugh at the scurvy."

Though he did not understand exactly why, Cook's supposition that tinned foods lacked some vital ingredient was correct, anticipating the discovery of vitamins by decades; it was recognized only much later that the flesh of sea animals is particularly rich in vitamins C, D and A.[28]

Cook's realization that the absence of light had a profound effect on men, both mentally and physically, is more original and perhaps the first clinical description of what has come to be called seasonal affective disorder. Observation was the key to both these discoveries; observation and the ability to look beyond the obvious would be the defining characteristics of Cook's ever-restless mind. But more than anything else, Cook's optimistic presence and his power to persuade his patients to believe in his unusual prescriptions gave hope to his dispirited comrades, and his "mad" scheme to free the ship, in the end, saved the Belgian Antarctic Expedition.

Dr. Cook was also able to apply what he learned from observation to construct ingenious camp equipment, his aerodynamic tent being the outstanding example. It was so far ahead of its time that Roald Amundsen did not hesitate to take one like it to the South Pole 13 years later.

But was this tent a completely original idea, as Cook implied? One wishes for a description of that "model of ingenuity" from the "fertile brain" of Robert D. Perry that had so impressed Dr. Cook on the *Zeta* voyage. Was Perry's tent anything like the *Belgica* tent? In the *Zeta* diary Cook left a place to describe or draw it, but that space is blank.[29]

As an explorer in Antarctica, Cook participated as fully as any man on the *Belgica*. He was among the first party to land on Brabant Island ("Two Hummocks Island"), an event now memorialized by a bronze plaque attached to a basalt boulder above Buls Bay. Placed there on July 21, 1984, by Commander J.R. Chris Furse, R.N., and François de Gerlache, grandson of the *Belgica*'s commandant, it bears Frederick Cook's name along with the others in the landing party—the only memorial to any of his specific accomplishments in exploration.

After that landing, he also took part in the first sledging expedition ever made in the Antarctic and helped establish the first camp ever erected there. As the only man with experience in camping in a polar zone, he must have been the guiding force in the preparation and execution of this pioneer journey.

Cook was also the instigator of the first sledging expedition on the antarctic pack ice, which used his unique equipment, and he volunteered to be left at Cape Adare for the winter. Today, in Gerlache Strait, the two tiny islands still named Brooklyn and Van Wyck attest to the very large role of Frederick Cook in the events of the Belgian Antarctic Expedition.

But it was in the literary field that Cook's participation in the voyage of the *Belgica* yielded its most astonishing accomplishment. *Through the First Antarctic Night* marked the beginning of his reputation, acknowledged even by his enemies, as a descriptive writer of unusual power. When one realizes that a bare ten years lay between the end of his formal schooling and his production of that book, it is more than astonishing.

Its republication in 1980 shows that it remains compelling, and a comparison with the Belgian accounts of the voyage confirms its credibility. It gives the reader an insight in the most subtle way into what made Dr. Cook the ultimate adaptable man and tells us as much about the author as about the Antarctic.

Although *Through the First Antarctic Night* has been used, by comparison, to deride Cook's subsequent books as fantasies, it has many elements in common with them. It is filled with details that others overlooked, and it contains often poetic writing that only a gifted writer could produce. Some of its passages tend to excess, but on the whole, they seem appropriate to evoke a land of excesses of cold and isolation. The book is nearly a perfect synthesis of observed fact and self-derived speculation. It conjures up the feel of high latitudes with vivid realism, yet it maintains an aura of the romantic and creates an atmosphere that allows the reader to experience things beyond normal experience—to make the extraordinary sound ordinary, and to make the ordinary fantastic.

The genesis of the book would be a fascinating study, but as yet, the journal from which it was derived has not come to light. Though the account seems too circumstantial for there not to have been a journal, there are hints that it may have been based merely on rough notes, filled out by memory—and enlarged by imagination.

Some of the dates Cook gives differ from those of other accounts. And Henryk Arctowski, in comparing his description of Alexander Island with one in a 1901 article by Dr. Cook,[30] said: "The only thing that I can say is that all my notes were written on the spot from day to day; that I have always made a point of giving correct descriptions and noting down exactly my first impressions."[31] In his article, Cook quotes from his "log" for February 18, 1898, describing the sighting, but Arctowski's statement seems to imply that Cook's observations were actually after-the-fact recollections, thus accounting for the variance.

One of the little unsolved mysteries stemming from the voyage of the *Belgica* is the report that Arctowski wanted to "kill" Dr. Cook when he came to Belgium. Could this have been more than a rumor, and if so, what could have been the motive for his anger?

Henryk Arctowski was a very ambitious man. Highly educated and fluent in several languages, he had published a number of scientific articles on his observations in the Antarctic. But these efforts earned him little attention outside the scientific community, and probably less money. Perhaps the phenomenal success of Cook's book and popular articles made Arctowski jealous.

When Cook was in Copenhagen, Herbert Bridgman wired Arctowski asking what he thought of the doctor's claims. Arctowski wired back that he should not take the doctor's story too seriously[32] and, in the days before Cook's proofs were to be decided upon at Copenhagen, he helped write material to discredit him. Perhaps Arctowski resented Cook's romanticization of the *Belgica* voyage and what he considered unscientific reportage for literary effect and saw in those reports the germ of Cook's later, questionable polar claims.

One feature of *Through the First Antarctic Night* that has often been pointed out, in the aftermath of those claims, is the book's extreme modesty. It was not until 1909, with the comments of Amundsen, that the important role played by Dr. Cook on the *Belgica* first came to public notice. Surely, no one could accuse Cook of being vainglorious from reading his book. However, this was not always the case.

In 1899 Herbert L. Bridgman received this telegram:

> MONTEVIDEO, S. A. April 4,— The *Belgica* arrived here this morning. All well. Our antarctic voyage has been a complete success. Much new land in Weddell Sea and open water to the far south discovered. Active volcanoes were also seen. I come home direct by early steamer. The *Belgica* will not return for another Winter, as originally planned. We lost men by accident, but none by disease.
>
> COOK.[33]

Jean du Fief, the general secretary of the Royal Belgian Geographical Society, pronounced the contents of this telegram "purely imaginary."[34] Indeed, there is no correct statement in it, nor was Cook even on the *Belgica* at the time it reached Montevideo, which was long after April 4.

In his book, Cook mentions that "an opportunity was found to send a cable message by steamer to Montevideo announcing our discoveries and the general results of our explorations." Was he referring to the Bridgman telegram? And if so, why would he send such a message when none of it was true? Could someone else have sent the telegram after tampering with it, perhaps to embarrass or even discredit him?

When he did arrive in the United States, in late June, Cook wasted little time publishing an account of the expedition. On July 2, 1899, a copyrighted account of the voyage appeared in the *New York Herald* under his name; it contained none of the inaccuracies of the Montevideo telegram.

Since the *Belgica* had not yet even reached Europe, this rush into print may have been viewed as unseemly. Cook was undoubtedly aware that Gerlache had agreed to publish nothing substantive on the voyage until after his first report to the Royal Society. At Punta Arenas the commandant had been offered 10,000 francs for his narrative and had been refused when he asked the society for permission to accept, even though he intended to apply the proceeds to refit his ship for further scientific studies in South America on his way home. All the other officers were bound by the same agreement, but Cook, having joined the expedition only after it sailed, may not have been so bound. In any event, Cook later felt compelled to say:

> In the notices of my return from the antarctic and in the story of the Belgian antarctic expedition, as published in the American newspapers, it has unintentionally been made to appear as if I desired to claim a major share of the credit for the results of this expedition. This I wish to disclaim. The credit of organizing the expedition belongs to its commander, Adrien de Gerlache; the honor of sending out the venture belongs to the enterprise of Belgian citizens. The fame and honor which are the result of a successful expedition belong to every member of the expedition.[35]

Perhaps the subsequent modest tone of his book resulted from criticism of such an appearance. But there now appears, on balance, little to fault in the story of Dr. Cook in Antarctica. On the contrary, it seems an indisputably glorious page in his career.

Even after the Copenhagen decision, while dismissing Cook as the "most audacious pretender in history," the *New York American* was willing to say of his antarctic experience: "Dr. Cook's behavior on this voyage is said to have been splendid. His courage never wavered and his surgical and medical skill repeatedly helped out the Belgians. On the return of the expedition he was decorated by the late King Leopold of Belgium."[36]

And so, even in the wake of Robert E. Peary's apparent victory, his backers were not satisfied. They feared that Cook's outstanding record aboard the *Belgica* might continue to be held up as a badge of an honorable character incapable of fraud. Surely something could be found, they thought, to show that the man who had dishonestly claimed the arctic Pole was a charlatan even then, in the midst of all that antarctic glory. They fixed upon the Yahgan dictionary.

Did Dr. Cook really attempt to represent the work of the Reverend Bridges as his own—to steal the missionary's life's work, as the *New York Times* reported on May 21, 1910?

The *Times* story was based on a letter of inquiry to Belgium by Dr. Charles Townsend, who had sat on the Explorers Club committee that had examined Cook's Mount McKinley claim as well as the one that had voted to drop his name from its membership. In his letter, Townsend protested that as he understood it, the dictionary of the Yahgan language was about to be published credited to Dr. Cook and asked that Thomas Bridges be acknowledged as its sole author.

But the response by Georges Lecointe, secretary to the *Belgica* Commission, showed that Townsend wasn't telling the commission anything new about the dictionary's authorship. On the contrary, Lecointe indicated that it not only knew who the true author was and intended to give him full credit, but that it had already gotten permission from Lucas Bridges for the right to publish his father's work.[37]

In saying that Cook victimized Bridges, the *Times* article contained a number of false statements. It alleged that the Reverend Bridges had asked for the manuscript back "again and again" but that Cook had never even written back. But Bridges had died nearly a year before the *Belgica* returned and the manuscript had been given to Dr. Cook. Moreover, Bridges's son acknowledged that Cook had written to him about the problems of transcribing the dictionary from his father's private alphabet, and Cook continued to write up until he left on his attempt to reach the North Pole.[38]

Rather than hiding the dictionary's true authorship, as it might be expected any potential usurper would do, there are at least three contemporary statements by Cook openly acknowledging that the dictionary was the work of Thomas Bridges and not his own.[39] Additionally, Adrien de Gerlache had cited Bridges as the dictionary's author in his book, and the proximate publication of the dictionary with the authorship ascribed to Thomas Bridges had been announced at an international conference in Vienna in 1908.[40]

It appears that Townsend, unaware of these pre-1910 published references to the dictionary's true authorship, based his allegation of Cook's dishonesty entirely on his interpretation of several announcements he had seen of the forthcoming publications of the scientific results of the voyage of the *Belgica*.

In Lecointe's book, for instance, there is a brief list of the volumes to be published by the *Commission de la "Belgica,"* including "A Yahgan Grammar & Dictionary, par F. – A. Cook." But in the first edition of Gerlache's book, and also in the publication announcement of the commission itself, we find:

> Volume X
> Physiologie, Anthropologie & Ethnologie
>   Medical report, par F. – A. Cook
>   Report upon the Onas, par F. – A. Cook
>   Grammaire et Dictionnaire Anglo-Yahgans, coordonnés et publiés
>   par F. – A. Cook, d'après les notes de feu le Rev. Thomas Bridges.
>   [Anglo-Yahgan Grammar and Dictionary, edited and published by
>   F. A. Cook, after notes by the late Rev. Thomas Bridges.] [41]

The closest Dr. Cook came to claiming authorship in a public statement was when he was quoted in the *New York Times* on February 21, 1901. Of the *Belgica* commission's report he said, "There will be eleven volumes in the record. One of them was contributed by me, and contains a vocabulary of 30,000 words of the Yahgan language, which is the tongue of the inhabitants of Tierra del Fuego." But since it is true that the volume by Cook, as announced, was to "contain" the vocabulary, and Cook does not say that he gathered the words or authored the dictionary himself, even this statement could be given a perfectly innocent interpretation.

In the *Times* article, Herbert L. Bridgman attested that Cook had shown him the dictionary and that "he always told me that he had made a special study of the Onas and had learned enough of them and their language to write a full report for the Belgian Commission." If Cook made such a statement, it would seem to have had nothing to do with the dictionary, which was Yahgan, not Ona, and a "Report upon the Onas" is listed as a prospective publication in itself.

Though Peary's backers might be easily dismissed, the account of Lucas Bridges must be seriously considered. He relates that he went to Belgium on an unspecified date, apparently in 1911, after hearing from a party of Norwegian travelers at Ushuaia that according to notices they had seen in the press, his father's dictionary was about to be printed there credited to one Frederick A. Cook, "Dr. of Anthropology." This he found to be true, he said, and he had the title page corrected.

In *My Attainment of the Pole,* Cook denied any attempt to steal the missionary's work and displayed part of an introduction he said he had written for the dictionary in 1900, acknowledging Thomas Bridges as its author.[42] The explanation of what Lucas Bridges found in Belgium may lie in this introduction that Dr. Cook says he wrote.

In the collection of papers owned by the Frederick A. Cook Society, there is a two-page typed copy of the complete introduction, of which only a part appeared in Cook's book. At the top of this copy is written in Dr. Cook's hand: "Copied from the printed copy from Belgium." Its heading is unclear as to who the author actually is:

Yahgan Grammar and Vocabulary
By
Frederick A. Cook,
Surgeon and Anthropologist of
The Belgium Antarctic Expedition.
Compiled during 37 years of missionary
work by

THOMAS BRIDGES

The text of the introduction, however, credits the work's origins and authorship to Thomas Bridges. Moreover, the circumstantial details of Bridges's life included in this full copy but not printed in Dr. Cook's book lend credence to his assertion that the introduction was written long before 1910, when they would have been fresh in his mind.

Perhaps in the translation of the introductory material Cook supplied in English to the Belgians, there was a misunderstanding of its ambiguous heading, and when the dictionary was set up, an assumption was made that Dr. Cook was its author or perhaps the French translator was confused by the title "Surgeon and Anthropologist" into interpreting "surgeon" as *docteur* rather than *médecin,* and thus Dr. Cook as a *Docteur d'anthropologie.*

Yet no trace of the proofs of the introduction, which Cook said were printed in 1906, has yet turned up. But with the subsequent extraordinary movements of Bridges's dictionary, which was thought lost in both World Wars and recovered only in 1946, this might be understandable.[43]

After a study of all the available evidence,[44] it seems incredible, considering the published acknowledgments of the true authorship of the dictionary, that Cook would seriously claim it as his work. Its very nature would have made it impossible for him to have amassed it himself in the short time available to him in Tierra del Fuego. And because it had no commercial value and little scientific interest beyond a tiny circle of specialists, it is hard to imagine what advantage he might have hoped to gain by making such a claim. No credible documentary evidence has been uncovered that Cook actually intended to claim credit for the dictionary, and this allegation would not have been entertained at all had not questions arisen about Cook's honesty during the debate over his claim to the North Pole.

Dr. Cook did considerable work on the manuscript on Bridges's behalf to ready it for publication. For this he has never been given any credit, since it all went for naught when the dictionary was eventually transcribed into a different system of orthography than the one he proposed. Perhaps this is why the introduction he wrote, in which he describes this conversion, was eventually discarded. He did, however, bring Bridges's work to scientific attention, and it is possible that had Cook not obtained the document and convinced the Belgians of its value, it might never have been published at all.

As for the announced volume X of the *Belgica* commission containing Cook's anthropological contributions and medical report, it was never published. But there is one published item that came out of the voyage that has definite negative implications for Cook's subsequent credibility. It is a little-known article that appeared in *Outing Magazine* in 1901,[45] in which Cook describes his adventures with a hunting party of Onas in pursuit of the guanaco, a llamalike animal.

This exciting South American interlude is found nowhere in *Through the First Antarctic Night* other than a brief and impersonal outline of Ona hunting techniques. Instead, we find there and in his earlier magazine articles, Cook's description of the warlike atmosphere that had taken hold in the year of the *Belgica*'s absence that necessitated his being taken down to the Indian missions by an Argentine gunboat for his own protection. It was open season on the Onas, and they retaliated in kind. "In the face of this hazard," Cook later wrote, "it was considered prudent for me, when I returned to continue my anthropological studies, to work with military representatives and with the still friendly mission Indians of the east and south."[46]

It therefore seems unlikely that Cook ever had the opportunity to persuade these Indians to take him into the interior. But in his 1901 article he explains how this was accomplished through the intervention of a nameless gaucho shepherd, who conveniently spoke not only Spanish and English but also Ona—a fantastically difficult language that few if any outsiders ever mastered. What influence this gaucho had over the hostile and suspicious Onas is never made clear.

The story is, on the face of it, preposterous and raises suspicion that the whole thing is a fabrication based on the information Cook picked up in his stay among the mission Indians after the return of the *Belgica* and in his previous talks with Thomas and Lucas Bridges. At any rate, this unique experience is never mentioned again in any of Dr. Cook's voluminous writings.

Another suspicious item is the portion of Cook's *Popular Photography* article of 1938 that describes his use of prussic acid as fixer for his photographs aboard the *Belgica*. This would be an incredibly risky procedure, since a closed room without proper ventilation would build up a concentration of hydrogen cyanide that could kill, as it would kill so many millions in the gas chambers of the war that was then about to begin, and such a story leaves us asking once more whether truth is being embellished for pure sensation.

Little has been written of Dr. Cook's employment as surgeon on the *Erik*. It is understandable that Peary's backers did not want it known that the man they were portraying in 1909 as an incompetent bumbler, had been hired by them in 1901 to be second in command of a relief expedition to render medical service to Peary and his family, who, for all the Peary Arctic Club knew, might be in the direst of straits.

Dr. Thorek recorded Cook's later reflections on the voyage of the *Erik,* in which he suggested that his medical examination of Peary might have been the beginning of the older explorer's enmity toward him:

> "Perhaps that was the point at which things broke. . . . I was shocked when I saw him. . . . When I examined him I found him suffering from early symptoms of pernicious anemia. I told him he must eat raw meat and liver. . . . He said he'd die before he swallowed such poison!"
>
> The smile on Dr. Cook's face now was one of sheer amusement, though it quickly gave place again to worried puzzled concern.[47]

Based on this and other accounts of Dr. Cook's 1901 diagnosis and prescription—exactly the therapy that was eventually proven in the 1920s to control the disease—some Cook advocates have suggested that he deserves credit for discovering the treatment for pernicious anemia and, by implication, the Nobel Prize that the acknowledged discoverers were awarded in 1934. However, no contemporaneous evidence has yet to be seen that Cook made a diagnosis of pernicious anemia in Peary in 1901.

The report he said he wrote for the Peary Arctic Club has not turned up, and all of Cook's accounts of his examination of Peary were written in the 1930s *after* the treatment had been described and, of course, long after Peary had died of pernicious anemia. Not even medical evidence supports Cook's account, since by the time the disease is diagnosed, without therapy it kills in two to five years, as it did Peary. Cook's alleged diagnosis came nearly 20 years before Peary's death. Even today, the early stages of the disease are unknown. Diagnosis before its characteristic physical manifestations, which generally do not appear until after the age of 50, can be done only by blood tests for certain antibodies—tests undeveloped and unavailable in Dr. Cook's day.

Of all the symptoms Cook describes in Peary, only anemia, lack of normal skin response and gastric malfunction match any of the common symptoms, of which others occur but are not mentioned by him. Even these symptoms could be the result of many more common causes and are not known to be present in patients far in advance of the appearance of the classic, chronic symptoms of the disease, such as Peary experienced just prior to being diagnosed in 1917.

Other contradictory evidence comes in the form of some fine pictures Cook took on the 1901 voyage. In them Peary does not show any of the symptoms described in Cook's memoirs, but rather looks quite good for a man of 45.

Finally, Dr. Cook told Max Thorek that "Dr. Dedrick had removed eight of his toes, leaving only the two small digits," which is not true, since Peary lost just seven toes to frostbite, the eighth being removed by Dr. Keen in Philadelphia only in 1902.[48]

The course of Peary's activities over the next eight years do not indicate a man wrecked in health. Upon his return in 1902 his feet were operated on in Philadelphia. No evidence has come to light that anything unusual was noticed during his hospital stay there. Peary was again hospitalized briefly in 1904, but the reason was not disclosed; perhaps he had an operation to correct his hernia, an affliction that he did not want to acknowledge publicly— and that Dr. Cook also fails to mention.

Dr. Louis Wolf, Peary's surgeon on the 1905 expedition, found his commander suffering from lumbago and an irregular heartbeat, but otherwise, it was his opinion that Peary was in perfect health. When Peary's subsequent medical history is considered, along with all of the errors and omissions in Cook's after-the-fact accounts of his 1901 diagnosis, it raises the distinct possibility that Cook never examined Peary at all.[49]

After the *Belgica* expedition, Cook's 1901 meetings in Europe with explorers and scientists broadened his horizons and established him as an important figure in exploration in his own right. There can be no doubt that men like Scott, Shackleton and Drygalski considered him a serious and practical man, just as Amundsen did, and listened respectfully to his advice. His record to this point deserved nothing less.

Cook's discussions with alpinists like Whymper and Conway must have aroused new interests, since three months after his return he helped found the American Alpine Club, and the next year he began to make plans to scale Mount McKinley.

As with his antarctic plans, the basic design of his attack on the mountain was borrowed, following Alfred Brooks's footsteps to its base. And though Cook filled in some blanks with ingenious solutions, the 1903 expedition failed to achieve any of its stated goals—even in being the first to try to scale McKinley. That honor fell to Judge Wickersham, whose camp they found. Nevertheless, it was an audacious attempt at barging into the unknown, and it settles some questions decisively.

The journey establishes Cook as the hardiest kind of traveler, able to endure every hardship that the harsh Alaskan wilderness dealt without the posturing and mock heroics of a Ralph Shainwald, the constant complaints of a Robert Dunn, or the quitting of a Jack Carroll. It also establishes Dr. Cook's optimistic self-confidence bordering on the irrational, his assertions that the unexplored mountain could be scaled "5,000 feet a day" and that he would spend a night on the summit and remarking, "I don't know why no one has done that before," being striking examples. These are not the first examples, however.

One companion on the *Miranda* recalled that the doctor nonchalantly remarked, after her bottom had been ripped out, that she could be repaired by simply keeling her over and putting in new plates. When the man pointed out that this would be impossible without a crane, and anyway, there were no plates to be had in Greenland, he reported that Cook thought for a moment and then simply said, "That's right." He described Cook as an "apt man, quick to observe, and quick to pass judgment . . . [but] entirely too impractical for me."[50]

Such anecdotes prop up the contention of Cook's proponents that he was in some ways childlike and unsophisticated—a man not equipped to deal with the wiles of the world. T. Everett Harré, who knew him well, once summed him up as "ingenious and impractical," and this was the impression he left with William Stead and the Danes at Copenhagen, especially in matters of money.

But perhaps the most significant incident of the *Miranda* voyage occurred after Cook arrived at Holsteinborg and met Governor Muller. It had to do with just such a matter, but it came out only in 1910, once again in the *New York Times*. Governor Muller had been persuaded by Cook to give him his collection of eider duck skins while the doctor was a guest at his house. According to Muller, Cook promised he would send $500 in gold that was aboard the *Miranda* in return but sent his check only—and that bounced. When Muller had the Danish consul in New York intervene in the matter, Cook is reported first to have refused to pay, then to have persuaded the Dane to settle for $200. Muller excused himself by saying, "He charmed me, as he did everybody he met before and after."

The *Times* reported that Muller wired Copenhagen about the incident shortly after Cook made his announcement that he had reached the Pole. As a direct result, it was alleged, King Frederick decided not to decorate the explorer with the Doonebog as he had planned.[51]

Lending credence to this report, in September 1909 the New York *World,* among other papers, reported that the award of the medal had been withdrawn at the last moment. It was speculated that this was in response to doubts being expressed abroad concerning the validity of the doctor's claims. Clearly, something persuaded the king to change his mind, but considering the way Copenhagen generally ignored the doubts raised elsewhere, it is reasonable to believe that there must have been some other reason for withholding the medal. But if the king withheld the Doonebog because of Muller's report, why did he permit his son to award Cook the Geographical Society's medal and approve, as president of the University of Copenhagen, the granting of Cook's doctorate? Perhaps the king did not see Cook's reported financial indiscretion as serious enough to bar these lesser honors but thought it did disqualify him for the Medal of Merit, the highest of honors he could have received, since it was reserved only for those who had done great deeds for humanity.

Could Muller's report have been another distortion planted in the *New York Times,* like the "theft" of the Yahgan dictionary, to destroy Cook's reputation as an honest man? This might be reasonable to suspect were it not for a number of other similar incidents involving Dr. Cook and money.

Cook's proponents have always maintained that his responses at Copenhagen to the fabulous offers he was receiving show he was not a shrewd man when it came to financial affairs and that they prove he did not premeditate a fraud to obtain money since in the end he practically gave his story away. These several other incidents, however, say something else again about the validity of this line of reasoning.

In 1896 Dr. Cook wrote to Peary asking whether he might include Ben Hoppin on his summer expedition aimed at removing the great Ahnighito meteorite from Cape York. The doctor suggested that Peary take the young man for $2,000. When Peary agreed to do so, but apparently for less money, Cook did not communicate Peary's offer to the Hoppin family but instead wrote Peary again, advising him to ask for the full $2,000 he had recommended— the Hoppins could afford it.[52]

We have also seen a number of instances in which Cook allegedly failed to pay others for services rendered. On the list are the members of the 1906 Mount McKinley Expedition, Dunkle and Loose, E.C. Rost, and various press agents of the Polar Publishing Company.

Some of these reports are mere hearsay; others were alleged by persons with bias against Cook or who had some other motive. We have Dunn's story, for instance, that the doctor suckered him out of his aunt's $1,000 by pretending to be thinking of taking Mrs. Cook into the interior of Alaska. But that story appeared only after Dr. Cook's fall. At least one came before October 1907, however, and it is well documented. That is the case of Russell Porter.

Porter was due $770 after the 1906 expedition for his services, which included drafting a topographical map. Since Cook pleaded the expedition had left him "hard up," Porter said he would settle for $550. Dr. Cook thanked him for being so understanding and made a definite agreement with Porter that he would pay him immediately upon selling the map to the Geological Survey in Washington. But Cook asked Porter for a receipt marked "paid in full," to be sent him before he had actually sent Porter the money.

Porter, naturally, did not understand this procedure, but obligingly sent him the receipt with a notarized stipulation that it was done at Cook's request and did not make any representation that Cook had actually paid him.[53] The doctor sold the map and then left for the Arctic without paying Porter anything. When Cook returned to the United States in September 1909, Porter had him served with legal papers, and the doctor then paid his debt in full.

Perhaps Cook needed all the funds he could muster and had put everything into the equipment for his polar voyage or simply forgot Porter in the rush to get ready. But the big checks made out to Cook that Bradley later displayed and the exchange of letters on the subject between Cook and Porter, not to mention Cook's strange request for an advance receipt, make both these arguments unlikely.

In the case of E.C. Rost, it seems that Dr. Cook got every nickel's worth and more of service that his lawyers said Rost had failed to deliver. The courts thought so, too, awarding Rost the full amount for which he had filed suit.

Even if we rule out the allegations made by Raymond Tarr of double-receipting Bradley for supplies bought at Gloucester as never-proven hearsay, there seems to be a certain suspicious pattern to Cook's financial dealings both before and after October 1907. Still, none of this is conclusive of anything larger. Had a matter of veracity never come up, it might all be dismissed as ordinary, if not trivial. But we are forced by those who insist on seeing Cook as an innocent or a naif to consider whatever evidence presents itself.

Robert Dunn saw Cook as an indecisive leader and scoffed at his "moves" and his plans to cross a pass no one knew existed. Yet Dr. Cook found the pass—the only one that a pack train could possibly get over in 140 miles of incredibly rugged, unexplored country. In this case, as in many others, it was Cook's self-confidence that led him to try something that others would not have even dared. The complete circumnavigation of the Alaska Range was his reward. It is a feat that has never been duplicated and ranks, perhaps, as the most underrated achievement in the early exploration of central Alaska.

In the past, Bradford Washburn gave most of the credit for that journey to Robert Dunn. More recently he has decided it was Fred Printz who was the leading light. Washburn's persistence in crediting anyone but Cook for the incredible journey of 1903 is one of the many unreasonable attempts to strip all legitimate accomplishments from the life of Frederick Cook. Anyone who reads Dunn's own book could not possibly believe such statements. Much can be learned from Dunn's "Shameless Diary," however, and those proponents of Dr. Cook who have dismissed it as cheap sensationalism risk undermining their own arguments.

Despite all its shortcomings, it remains the best source document on the trip, since no diary by Cook has come to light.[54] What's more, Dunn's observations of Cook were written four years *before* October 1907, so they cannot be a result of a conspiracy to discredit him.

Actually, when allowance is made for Dunn's propensity to criticize everyone, Cook does not come off badly. One searches Dunn's book in vain for a word of complaint or a criticism of others from Cook, unless utterly provoked.

What Dunn supposed to be a lack of leadership ability was perhaps a reflection of what Anthony Fiala called "the brotherly love plan," which, as Fiala learned from bitter experience and expressed with massive understatement, was "apt to fail" on the wild fringes of the world. Cook implied he endorsed this plan by saying "kindly helpfulness" and "heartfelt companionship" were his ideals of leadership. But by Cook's attempt to be just one of the boys, Dunn judged that he had no leadership ability at all, since he acted like "our sympathetic servant."

But even Dunn admitted to Cook's singular stamina and nerveless calm on the actual ascent and credited him fully with a real attempt to climb McKinley in 1903. Only after October 1907 would his opinion start to change.

After reading Dunn's book, L.C. Bement, who had gotten to know Cook on the voyage of the *Erik,* wrote to him. "Your description of him and his ways is so perfect that had I not known he was on the trip I could have named him," he told Dunn. "And since he is so real, the others must be. I trust you will not think that I am knocking on the Doctor, as I am very fond of him and consider him one of my best friends. But the Doctor's ways are his ways, and nobody could change them, not even him."[55]

But did he change them? Up to October 1907, Frederick A. Cook was a respected family man, a successful medical doctor, a valued citizen of his community and an active member of numerous civic, social and fraternal organizations. He was a founding member of the Arctic, American Alpine, and Explorers Clubs, and the sitting president of the last. He also sat on the board of the Geographical Department of the Brooklyn Institute of Arts and Sciences, and was a fellow of the American Anthropological Society and the Royal Belgian Geographical Society. He held the Belgian society's silver medal and the title of Chevalier of the Order of Leopold I. He was a published author with a very successful book and numerous articles to his credit, and two of his papers had been reproduced in the U.S. government's *Report of the Eighth International Geographic Congress.* It is sure that he was well liked by most of those who knew him. Nevertheless, he was neither rich nor generally famous.

If we exempt the revelations of his financial dealings, which came only after Cook had become a storm center of controversy and suspicion, there is little to criticize in his public life before October 1907 or to suggest that he would in two years be denounced as the most monstrous impostor the world had yet produced.

Still, the turning of the tide of public opinion that was about to sweep away his honored, if modest, reputation was driven as much by the events of September 1906 as those of September 1909. Although Professor Parker's initial skepticism about the truth of Cook's claim to have climbed Mount McKinley in 1906 seemed put to rest and the claim established as genuine before that year was out, it was really the doubt about McKinley that undermined the edifice of respectability Cook enjoyed prior to his polar claim and brought it crashing down to his total discredit. We must therefore return to Alaska and begin our search there on a great glacier for the origins of the calamity that was soon to overwhelm Frederick Cook.

Mystery is the lure that guides man to his destiny. For man is first and last a discoverer; civilization is built upon his discoveries. . . . Man travels from wonder to wonder, subduing the earth to his use, studying the laws that govern creation, racked, but not conquered, by hardship, until his progress across the face of the globe may be measured, not so much by milestones as by the mysteries conquered.

Not one . . . had penetrated the mystery that hung over the great mountain. But at last an explorer came a distance of 5,000 miles for the sole purpose of conquering the summit. Yet after two summers of terrible struggle along the avalanche-strewn highways to the mountain, a new element of mystery was added to the great peak. The riddle involved that most complex and baffling of all enigmas, the heart of man.

—Gertrude Metcalfe

CHAPTER 28

To the Top of the Continent?

"COOK IS A GOOD FELLOW, A GREAT SELF-ADVERTISER, BUT, IN MY OPINION, THE worst prevaricator in the world. He possesses great patience and is persevering, but he has not the executive ability of a school boy. He never reached the top of Mount McKinley. . . ."[1] That was the assessment of William N. Armstrong, one of the men Dr. Cook hired to help get his expedition into interior Alaska in 1906. But Armstrong, like the rest of Cook's critics in 1909, was nowhere near the great mountain at the time of Cook's attempt. Only Edward N. Barrill and Frederick A. Cook knew definitely whether the climb had been made. Barrill swore that it had not; Cook swore the opposite and maintained to his death that he had stood at the highest point in North America on September 16, 1906.

Who told the truth? Or perhaps a more accurate question would be, whose story is closer to the truth?

In 1903 Cook's self-confidence had been both his virtue and his defect, and it led him to believe he could accomplish things others said were impossible. During the actual climb, his confidence that he could overcome all obstacles made him press on so fearlessly that Robert Dunn called him foolhardy. But even Dunn did not fail to feel, after all his "mean pages," some respect for the man.

The descriptions of Cook's performance in 1906 show that he impressed others more favorably than the idealistic and hypercritical Dunn, who expected to find in others all the failings he perceived in himself, and they reinforce the impression that Dr. Cook did not lack the skills to organize or attempt any arduous task. It has been this impression that Armstrong and all of Cook's opponents have tried to obliterate.

Yet even after the first announcement of Cook's claim to having reached the Pole, Belmore Browne said of him:

> Dr. Cook is a born nomad and explorer. It is not the wanderlust in the ordinary sense of the word, but a desire to penetrate new regions and accomplish the apparently unobtainable. . . .
>
> I never looked upon him as a man of indomitable and colossal perseverance. . . . He impressed me however as a man above the average and a man of much but not unusual persistence. In physical strength, health and all around symmetrical development he is above the average, but not extravagantly so.

On such a trip as we took where great extremities are faced and the unexpected happens frequently, in the nature of things you expect a show of temper once in a while. But Cook always came up good humored, if not smiling, and during all my acquaintance with him in camp, on the mountain or in the comforts of civilization I saw nothing to indicate any streak of yellow in his make up. He was jolly, whole-souled, rather optimistic and cool-headed. He impressed me as being a man of broad humanity, but with no unusual ability but carrying around with him a great propensity for seeing the uninhabitable and unexplored portions of the globe.[2]

But Belmore Browne would soon change his tune. A little more than a month after he made this statement he would declare that this same man was so incompetent as a leader that the members of the 1906 expedition were fortunate to have escaped with their lives, and that in announcing himself the conqueror of Mount McKinley, Frederick Cook had perpetrated a gigantic hoax. This reversal would be scarcely believable had it not actually happened.

Perhaps, then, we should first look at Cook's accusers to see why there was such a radical shift of opinion. What were their motives, and on what basis were the allegations made that eventually disallowed his claim?

Immediately after Cook's announcement, the only contrary voice was Herschel Parker's, but he quickly moderated his tone, even lectured favorably on the doctor's feat and acknowledged its genuineness in a published article. Belmore Browne and Russell Porter appeared publicly with Dr. Cook in Seattle and shared in the congratulations he received there; the others were merely silent.

All of this changed in 1909 when Cook came under fire from Bridgman, Hubbard and other rich and powerful friends of Robert E. Peary. The members of the 1906 expedition, most of whom had still not been paid for their efforts, quickly realized there might be a way to recoup their losses—or finance new adventures. Barrill swore his famous affidavit and collected his "expenses."Armstrong said he simply disbelieved the doctor's story, while he quietly helped James Ashton gather evidence. Beecher, who said he was owed $825 by the doctor, claimed Barrill had told him the climb was a fake one month after the return of the expedition. Miller, who was also on Ashton's payroll, said he had learned of the fake in May 1908 from Barrill. Printz claimed $900 and, if the newspapers can be believed, dickered for payments to make affidavits supporting whichever side would pay him more.

Alfred Brooks called these men "incompetent judges and dishonorable witnesses" and dismissed all of them with the exception of Barrill. "As I see it," declared Brooks, "the matter lies purely between Dr. Cook and Edward Barrill. . . . Personally I prefer Cook's word. Barrill, by asserting that Cook bribed him, is a discredited witness, and consequently his unsupported testimony should not bear too much weight."[3]

That Barrill was paid a large sum of money for his affidavit is indisputable. It is not too harsh a word to say that he was bribed for it. But *bribe* suggests that the Peary Arctic Club paid to obtain a false statement. If Barrill's affidavit is true, and the money only made Barrill recant a former lie, what should it be called?

Barrill's veracity was discounted either way, however, and this is why, as Brooks predicted, his affidavit failed to have as much impact as its purchasers expected. Barrill lied either in the affidavit or when he told friends and acquaintances that he had climbed Mount McKinley with Dr. Cook and showed them his diary to prove it.

Some might argue that the latter was forgivable, especially since he was not under oath. But in October 1909, while he was in New York City to meet with General Hubbard, Barrill signed other affidavits that have not been made public. In one of them he swore that he had never told anyone that he had climbed the mountain but had simply avoided the subject. There is, however, considerable testimony by disinterested bystanders that contradicts this.[4] No, Ed Barrill lied, as everyone does at times. The problem is determining which of his statements are the false ones.

In the end, however, it was the testimony of Herschel Parker and Belmore Browne that destroyed Cook's claims of 1906, not Barrill's affidavit. Like the other members of the 1906 expedition, they eventually joined the chorus against Cook, but they were far more cautious in their initial public statements.

Browne's case shows the more radical shift. The climbing of Mount McKinley was much bigger news in the Pacific Northwest, as were all things Alaskan, than in the East. Only there did Cook receive any great acclaim for the titanic feat, and Belmore Browne wanted a piece of it. He made the doctor his guest at his home and made the most of Cook's notoriety. Later, when given an opportunity to have for himself all of the glory as conqueror of McKinley, Browne did not hesitate to doubt him. But in an article on the climb in 1907, Browne expressed his unreserved admiration for Cook's accomplishment, saying that his and Barrill's sufferings on the climb proved them to "be of the stuff men are made of."[5]

Immediately after Dr. Cook's announcement of reaching the North Pole, Browne was still singing the doctor's praises. Even when doubts began to surface about McKinley, Browne argued against giving the statements of anyone but Barrill consideration, since only he had been with Cook during the climb.[6] But by September 8 he had already conceded to a *Tacoma Tribune* reporter that "the fact is, I do not know whether Dr. Cook did or did not ascend the Peak." His first criticism of the doctor was reserved until September 20, when he declared his doubts, basing them on "no pictures" that could be verified as having been taken at a high altitude.[7]

In the wake of Barrill's affidavit, Browne appeared before the committee appointed by the Explorers Club to look into the climb. Now his story was that he and Parker had suspected the thing a fake from the first, and that this

Photograph 1. "SCENE OF GLACIERS, PEAKS AND CLIFFS." Photograph by Cook, 1906.'

Photograph 2. "THE TOP OF OUR CONTINENT." Photograph by Cook, 1906.

Photograph 3. "FIRST FIVE OF THE TWELVE NEW PEAKS OF RUTH GLACIER." Photograph by Cook, 1906.

had been confirmed by the photographs in Cook's published narrative. Later still, in 1913, Browne would relate how Barrill, while at Seldovia in 1906, had all but told him the climb was a fake.

This chronology raises questions about Browne's credibility and motives. In September 1909 a lawyer in Tacoma warned the Cook interests about Browne's shiftiness and cited the distinctly unfavorable local opinion it had caused. "They are justly righteously indignant at Browne's double dealing," he reported. "Some of them say they would not believe him under oath, and how could they, under the circumstances?"[8]

Late in his life, Belmore Browne acknowledged that he had a poor memory for dates and details. He made this remark in a memorial to his friend, Herschel Parker, who had just died. Browne immediately went on to prove it, as he remembered the man who had to be helped onto his horse and who balked at river crossings, even while wearing a huge inflatable vest, as having "physical elasticity and steadfast courage." Parker had made ascents in the Rockies and Europe, but he had never undergone anything like the approach to Mount McKinley, and it was more than he could endure. Even in his own diary Browne admitted that Dr. Cook turned back on the Tokositna glacier for Professor Parker's sake.

Parker himself was more cautious than Browne, even voting against the formation of the Explorers Club's committee to investigate Cook's climb. Once he was called before it, his testimony was less certain than Browne's: he at first "could not say definitely" whether Cook had pledged not to make another attempt on the mountain; then he admitted Cook had "announced" his intention to seek a route for the next year if Henry Disston failed to show up for the planned hunt.

Parker and Browne's testimony against Cook concentrated on three of the photographs that illustrated his book *To the Top of the Continent.* The first was captioned "Shoulder of Mt. McKinley" (photograph 1). The same picture in Cook's 1907 article for *Harper's Monthly Magazine* was labeled "The view from 16,000 feet." The two captions, taken together, implied that the picture was taken on the climb at that altitude.

The second was the picture of what Dr. Cook said was the summit of Mount McKinley (photograph 2). In the center of the right-hand margin of this picture was what Parker and Browne called a "distant peak." This feature of Cook's summit photograph, they said, had led them to doubt his veracity.

They pointed out what they believed was the same peak in the background of photograph 1, thus proving that Cook's summit picture had been taken close by. Furthermore, they attested, they had confirmed the location of photograph 1 because in a third picture the distant peak in question was shown opposite Cook's tent, pitched next to Ruth Glacier at a place he called Glacier Point (photograph 3). This camp, itself, was miles from the "top of the continent," so Cook's alleged summit was even farther away; they estimated 17 miles.

The interrelationship among these three pictures had convinced them as early as 1908, they said, that the climb was a fake, but they had not come forward then because Cook had already left for the Arctic and so was in no position to defend himself. But they claimed they had expressed their doubts privately as early as 1907.

The report issued by the Explorers Club as a result of the committee's investigation admonished its star witnesses, saying "that the so-called Cook controversy of the present year would not have arisen had Prof. Parker and Mr. Browne presented to the Board of Governors of the club in 1906 the same evidence which they have recently presented to this committee."[9] But even though the report said that Parker and Browne had in 1906 "unofficially expressed to the club their entire disbelief in Dr. Cook's alleged achievement," in light of their actions and statements after 1906, this seems most improbable.

When Cook's summit photograph was first printed in *Harper's Monthly Magazine* in 1907 (see page 287), the skyline was heavily retouched and the supposedly telltale distant peak was cropped out. The arguments made by Parker and Browne before the Explorers Club, therefore, would not have been possible before *To the Top of the Continent* was published in 1908 with a summit photo showing the "distant peak" for the first time. Since both Parker and

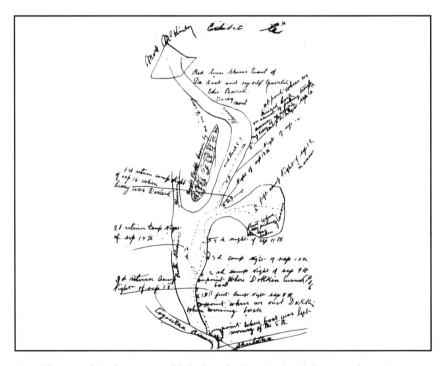

Barrill's map of Cook's route, published in the New York Globe, *October 14, 1909.*

Browne had published articles after 1906 that accepted Cook's climb as genuine, their "entire disbelief" cited by the Explorers Club report seems more a face-saving device for them than a statement of fact. More likely their disbelief arose only after the release of Barrill's affidavit, in which all the points they raised before the committee were first alluded to, including Barrill's warning to Cook that the peaks across the glacier would show in his summit picture and give the location away.

By November 30, 1909, with Cook having mysteriously vanished and again in no position to defend himself, the once fair-minded Parker was now ready to state publicly that Cook was a fraud—and more. "Nothing but stern necessity would prompt me to do this," he righteously declared, "but this is a case where truth and justice, as well as science and civilization, compel the step. Dr. Cook never made the ascent of Mount McKinley, as he has claimed. . . .

". . . My experience with Cook had demonstrated that he knew nothing about mountain climbing and had no scientific training. . . . In fact, I was in full charge of the expedition, as Cook seemed to realize his total incompetence for such work."[10]

Though the minutes of the Explorers Club committee show that at least some of its members were concerned with establishing the truth, the report that finally dismissed Cook's 1906 climb appeared only after things had gone against the doctor at Copenhagen, and it distorted Parker and Browne's testimony, stating as fact many things that they had been equivocal about. For instance, it said, "It was perfectly understood between Dr. Cook, Prof. Parker, and Mr. Browne that all attempts had been abandoned for the season," something that Parker "could not say definitely." The report also inflated the contributions of Parker and Browne while diminishing Cook's and Barrill's. "Dr. Cook and the guide Barrill were the ones who had shown themselves during the Summer's work least fitted for the arduous labor of mountain climbing at great altitude," it read, and it credited Browne's effort as the only reason the expedition got back without loss of life.

In light of such statements, the questions raised about Cook's organizational abilities and physical stamina need to be settled before we examine the arguments for and against his climb.

Cook's 1903 expedition was guided by Brooks's suggestions and Lieutenant Herron's inadequate map, which Judge Wickersham called a "geographic muddle." Though Cook started too late to have a real chance of success, the execution of his plan transcended being a mere copy of Brooks's accomplishment. He broke new ground, making discoveries that Brooks himself called "more important than the climbing of the great mountain itself."[11] The failure of the 1903 expedition to reach its stated goal and Dr. Cook's understated narrative have caused its real accomplishments to be generally underrated, however.

The 1906 expedition was boldly conceived but grounded in the experience Cook had gained in 1903 along with his evaluation of new evidence.

From his reading and his study of the problem, Cook assumed he would find a pass to the Kuskokwim for his pack train. Although both Parker and Browne later criticized this assumption, they also admitted that they had accepted Cook's plans at the time "without question." And there is no evidence in Browne's contemporaneous diary that the expedition's safe return had anything to do with his own leadership, that Parker was ever "in full charge" of anything or that Cook was incompetent.

Cook's specifications for the expedition's equipment were all carefully thought out. The design of the *Bolshoy,* the lightweight silk version of the *Belgica* tent and the interchangeable eiderdown and camel-hair ponchos and sleeping bags were all derived from previous experience, and none of them proved a misjudgment. Perhaps the best indication of the insincerity of Parker and Browne's verdict on Cook's ability to plan big enterprises is that they imitated Cook's methods and equipment in their own 1910 attempt to scale Mount McKinley, down to the last detail.

In 1906 as in 1903, Cook's overoptimistic assessment of his chances, not his executive ability, thwarted his first two attempts to reach the mountain. But it is known today that even had he discovered a pass to the Kuskokwim, he would not have found a workable route to the summit from that direction. In the end, his plan proved too visionary to find a route through territory that was largely a blank; blind luck would have been a better attribute.

There should be no doubt that Cook was fully up to the physical demands. Herschel Parker's unreservedly positive evaluation in 1910, when he called him "strong and enduring" and said "no man can go further on any trip than Dr. Cook," contradicts the Explorers Club's assessment of his being "least fitted" for such physical tests.

"Knowing Cook as I do personally," wrote Evelyn Briggs Baldwin, "and having seen him literally in the flesh, stripped for physical examination, I would be either stupid or untruthful were I to deny my belief in his physical or mental strength. . . .

"Many a trained athlete would indeed take pride in the muscular 'measurements' of Frederick A. Cook, —inherited from healthy parents, nurtured by a temperate life, and developed thru years of outdoor exercise."[12] This is well to point out, since Dr. Cook, dressed in street clothes, looked quite ordinary, yet his well-documented endurance testifies to the truth of Baldwin's evaluation.

That many attempts to answer the questions surrounding Cook's climb have been misled by such biased evidence as the Explorers Club's report is understandable. Until the 1980s most of the critical primary documents needed to fairly assess it were not available. But with the opening of the Peary and Cook papers, new light can be thrown on those unanswered questions.

His opponents have always maintained that Cook planned a conscious fraud when he set off with Ed Barrill in the *Bolshoy* toward the great mountain. As evidence, they cite his dispersal of the rest of his party on various assignments.

But at the time he sent them away, Cook still expected Henry Disston's arrival. If Disston had come, Cook would have been obliged to take him hunting, and there would have been no opportunity for any further exploration around Mount McKinley that season, much less an attempted climb. That Cook was committed to carrying out the hunt is evidenced by the deal he made with Bill Hughes for his pack train, which later brought him to grief in the Alaskan courts.

If he wished to get rid of witnesses, it was only Browne whom he needed to dispose of, the others already having been assigned to legitimate tasks to prepare Disston's hunt or conduct long-planned topographical studies. Browne insisted before the Explorers Club that he had wanted to go along if Cook had any intention of climbing the mountain. The doctor's promise that he would do no climbing was the only reason, Browne said, that he assented to going to the Matanuska Valley. Although Cook said he needed him to obtain some animal heads there for the Brooklyn Institute, according to Browne, Cook never once inquired after them when the expedition returned. This may be, but none of these assertions are recorded in Browne's contemporaneous diary, which, curiously, bears no record of his reaction to Cook's dramatic announcement that he had conquered Mount McKinley. Though he later said he knew it to be false even before he left Alaska, it contains not even a hint that Cook's claim was untrue.

In his 1913 book, Browne quoted the telegram Cook sent to Herbert Bridgman as evidence that despite his assurances, Cook had already decided to make another attempt. According to Browne it read: "Am preparing for a last, desperate attack on Mount McKinley."

But the crucial part of Cook's message actually read: "We are now arranging our final efforts, and I hope to wire you from Seward about our work in early October." There is nothing about a "desperate attack on Mount McKinley." This may be only an example of Browne's "poor memory for details," but it has been quoted as fact ever since.

Neither Parker nor Browne was able to confirm just what equipment Cook had with him for the climb. They said all but a few feet of climbing rope had been burned because it was defective, but they conceded there was ordinary pack rope, and perhaps a thermometer. When asked directly whether Cook had no instrument to measure the height of the mountain, Parker said he was "almost positive" but he "could not swear to it," and when asked whether he knew it as a matter of fact, he said no. He was sure, however, that there were no hypsometers. Parker said Cook did not know how to use one and that a barometer would have been useless, since Cook had no one to read the barometer at base camp for later correction of his readings. He was certain that the whole package of ice creepers had been lost along the way and that Cook could not have traversed difficult places without them.

Parker was incorrect about there being no one to read the barometer at base camp—Cook states in his book that John Dokkin had been assigned that task—but the rest of his testimony checks with Cook's own published list of his equipment. Cook didn't list any hypsometers or ice creepers, but he said he used a "horsehair lariat," indicating the packing rope.[14] Cook mentioned three aneroid barometers and later said he had a special barometer capable of registering 20,000 feet with supplementary markings to 20,500 feet, and another registering 16,000 feet, with a movable rim arranged to measure an additional 10,000 feet with approximate accuracy.[15]

Cook's lack of a hypsometer seems unimportant in hindsight, because Parker's 1912 attempts to determine the altitude of Mount McKinley using a hypsometer were far less accurate than Cook's 1906 report of its height without one—and this on the climb Parker asserted Cook had never made.

There are several things about Cook's equipment inventory, however, that suggest it was not adequate to the task. First is his lack of ice creepers. Though Claude Rusk in his 1910 attempt didn't try to scale anything like the slopes described in *To the Top of the Continent*, he said that he could not have done without them. And Ed Barrill's affidavit says that Cook turned back on September 15 because he thought it too dangerous to go on without snowshoes, much less ice creepers.

Today, the once "impossible" feat of climbing Mount McKinley is accomplished by hundreds of climbers every year. There is even a guidebook to advise potential climbers on what they will need; it calls ice creepers a "must." It should be remembered, however, that Cook did not use ice creepers at any time in 1903 yet climbed a treacherous ice and snow slope to an altitude of more than 10,000 feet and descended safely.

An even bigger obstacle would seem to be the lack of proper clothing. The outfits described by Cook made no provision to protect the hands and the head in temperatures as low as −16°, especially considering the increased feeling of cold experienced at high altitudes. It is difficult to believe, for instance, that a bandanna and a felt hat would adequately protect the ears under such conditions.

Furthermore, the fuel supply seems inadequate. Rusk reported using as much as a pint of alcohol to cook a meal. Even though the food Cook carried could be eaten without preparation, fuel would still be necessary to melt enough ice to make the four to five quarts of water per person now recommended for each day of the climb. This alone would seem to leave them very short, even if Ed Barrill's assertion that they left the stove running all night on September 14 to heat their igloo is not taken seriously.[16]

The food supply itself raises questions, considering present-day knowledge of the physiological reactions of the human body during high ascents. Though pemmican, which is about 30 percent fat, would supply the now-recommended 4,500 to 6,000 calories per day for such a climb, it would require far more oxygen to digest than the same amount of calories derived from carbohydrates—oxygen already in short supply at high altitudes. The experience of Parker and Browne, who copied Cook's food recommendations for their own attempts on Mount McKinley, supports its inappropriateness. They blamed their failure to reach the summit of the mountain in 1912 on their inability to digest the pemmican that was their chief mountain food.

Still, though these things raise doubts, they do not prove that Cook and Barrill did not make the ascent. Today's climbing guide to Mount McKinley lists among the skills requisite for an attempt: the ability to travel safely on a glacier, build igloos and snow-walled tent sites, read high-altitude weather and assess the stability of avalanche slopes and icefalls. The prospective climber, it says, also needs to know how to maintain his health in extreme cold through proper dress and how to recognize early signs of frostbite and pulmonary and cerebral edema. He must also know equipment and how to maintain it, and how to organize a big enterprise to the last detail.

It adds that previous experience at high altitudes is desirable but not essential and that an inexperienced climber can function well with a strong leader who is thoroughly familiar with the mountain. It recommends against teams of two, however, saying that although they can move quickly, they are extremely vulnerable if accident or illness should occur. But the bottom line, the guide states, is simply good judgment.

As physical conditioning, the guide recommends "hiking in the hills with a heavy pack for eight or ten hours a day" as probably the best training for McKinley—exactly what Cook and Barrill had been doing for the three months previous to their attempt. Even so, the *Mount McKinley Climber's Handbook* says that "determination and a willingness to suffer" are often more important factors in reaching the summit than physical fitness.[17] If any man ever possessed these two characteristics, it was Frederick A. Cook.

There can be little doubt that Dr. Cook's medical education, exploration experience and documented physical and mental attributes fulfill all of the suggested prerequisites but one: in 1906, *no one* was thoroughly familiar with Mount McKinley, though Cook probably knew more about it than anyone else at the time.

Nevertheless, Bradford Washburn has insisted that only a strong party of experienced climbers could have any chance of reaching the top of Mount McKinley by any conceivable route from Ruth Glacier and, even then, never within Cook and Barrill's time schedule. He has also pointed out that neither had any technical climbing experience. But Cook did have a few experiences to fall back on.

In 1903 he had reached 11,000 feet on the North Buttress, and he had also climbed several glaciers, including a vertical ice wall on Brabant Island, as well as the Needles in Antarctica. Cook was also absolutely fearless—or foolhardy, if you take Robert Dunn's viewpoint—and such a person may take risks that accomplish the impossible, if they do not kill him. Still, even if all doubts about logistical and physical probabilities can be put aside, inexperience is cited as the insurmountable barrier by skeptics like Washburn, who deny any possibility of Cook's having climbed the mountain in 1906.

Washburn's skepticism is well warranted, but before declaring the feat impossible for Cook and Barrill on a purely probable basis, consider the Sourdoughs' assertion that they climbed the North Peak in 1910.

They lost their only barometer; the rest of their "scientific" equipment consisted of one thermometer, a $5 Kodak and a watch. They carried no tent and no sleeping bags above 11,000 feet but remembered to take a hammer, nails and some boards to make a sign. They took no fuel and, for food, had six doughnuts and a thermos of hot chocolate each during the entire climb from that level. They did have crude ice irons but carried only long pikes instead of ice axes—another "must" according to today's guidebook; they claimed to have dug their steps in the ice with a common coal shovel. They had no rope other than to guy the 14-foot spruce flagpole they carried with them, but they never used it as lifeline while climbing. Yet, so equipped, they are credited with an ascent of 8,470 vertical feet to the summit of the North Peak and a return to camp at 11,000 feet in just 18 hours. Of this distance a 2,200-foot stretch was on inclines of 40 to 55 degrees.

Surely, if one believes their story, there is room for belief that Dr. Cook's equipment was adequate to his enterprise, despite its shortcomings.

Next, compare the Sourdoughs' climbing experience with Cook's. Their success has been attributed solely to their being hard-bitten pioneers with amazing grit and determination bred from a rugged outdoor life, which had taught them cold-weather survival techniques. Cook's grit and determination are legendary, and he had learned those same skills in both the Arctic and the Antarctic. Undoubtedly, except for portly Tom Lloyd, the Sourdoughs were in superb physical condition, though only one was under 40. But none had any technical mountaineering experience—not even so much as could be conceded to Dr. Cook.

If the Sourdoughs can be credited with starting from 11,000 feet and reaching the summit of the North Peak—a place considered far more inaccessible than the actual summit—and returning in less than a day, then Cook's story that he and Barrill could make the top of the South Peak from 12,100 feet and return to the same point in six days does not seem beyond the realm of the possible. Since the South Peak is 810 feet higher than the North, the vertical distance is roughly equal, and the South Peak is easier to reach than the North along their claimed routes. Once again, nothing in this comparison favors acceptance of the Sourdoughs and rejection of Dr. Cook. Yet the Sourdoughs' climb is treated by most authorities, including Bradford Washburn, as established fact, though Cook's is considered a fable.

Two more factors, however, deserve consideration. The first is Ed Barrill. Any party of climbers is only as strong as its weakest member. Barrill had no mountain-climbing or ice experience, but certainly he was a strong man. At six feet two inches and more than 200 pounds, he was a physical giant for the time, and he had proven his stamina in the field. If Cook did secretly plan to attempt Mount McKinley when he took leave of the other members of his party, then he may have chosen Barrill for exactly this reason.

The second is the possibility that the story of the Sourdoughs' climb is a fabrication. They certainly had a motive. There was a big forfeit bet at stake, and Tom Lloyd had a lot of crow to eat if he did not make good on his big bragging. As he admitted while claiming victory after his return, "Of course, after the papers got hold of the story we hated the idea of ever coming back here defeated."[18]

Since the possibility that Cook may have done just as he said has not yet been eliminated by an examination of his equipment or skills, nor is his story implausible when compared with the Sourdoughs' generally accepted accomplishment, the narrative of his climb will have to be examined in detail to see if it holds up.

From the point they started, Cook, Barrill and Dokkin carried about 150 pounds of equipment and supplies. They were then approximately 34 air miles from the summit at an elevation of 1,000 feet. To reach their goal, they needed to cover an actual distance greater than that, over very rough, unknown terrain, while ascending more than 19,000 vertical feet.

When Dokkin decided to turn back because he did not like the dangers of glacier travel, Cook and Barrill cached his equipment and continued up Ruth Glacier. From that point on we have the two men's conflicting accounts of what happened. But we also have their diaries.

Barrill's was published on October 15, 1909, the day after his affidavit appeared, in the *New York Globe.* Cook's was published only in September 1996 but, outside his family and a few of their intimate friends, was not even known to exist until the 1970s. Ed Barrill's actual diary apparently lay hidden until even later but has recently come to light as well. But are these the original diaries, written in 1906?

Belmore Browne testified that he saw Barrill keep a diary; Cook said he knew that Barrill made sketches but had never seen a diary. If Barrill kept one, Cook would have known it, since both men lived in the same tiny tent—the most likely place where entries would be made—and Cook was a very observant man. But an examination of Barrill's diary discloses that Cook signed his name and wrote his address in the book that he denied ever having seen. This fact alone seems to preclude any question of the diary's total fabrication.

Others said they had seen it prior to 1909. One who said it refuted the climb described it as having a red cover. Barrill's real estate partner, C.G. Bridgeford, who contended that it corroborated the climb, said its cover was black faux alligator. Bridgeford's was the correct description in both respects. He was also correct in saying that the 2½-by-5½-inch book had all the physical earmarks of hard usage such as it would have received on the journey it describes. Furthermore, it is a complete diary, not just of the climb, but of the whole expedition, having entries from May 18 through November 9, 1906, and in all the particulars it reports of events outside the climb, it is verified and confirmed by contemporary accounts. This would seem an impossibly elaborate forgery. And if it was forged in 1909, why would the forger make it agree with the 1906 story Cook's opponents were trying to contradict so far as the description of the climb?

Of course, Ed Barrill swore his diary entries from September 9 through September 18 were false, saying they were altered or dictated at Cook's direction. Whether we accept this or not, there seems no reason to doubt that Barrill wrote the diary in 1906. The only point in doubt is whether its description of the climb up Mount McKinley is true.

Cook's diary raises the same questions. It also contains more than a record of the climb but is less complete than Barrill's. The entries are very sporadic, but this is typical of Cook's extant diaries in general. The account of the climb itself is continuous but extremely sketchy. As with Barrill's, the events recorded outside the climb and Cook's continual references in the diary to Barrill as "Brill," the name by which he was known by members of the expedition, date it to 1906. (Belmore Browne's diary also refers to him as "Brill," as does Porter's.) It too, then, is contemporary with the events it describes. But as with Barrill's, the question remains whether its account of the climb itself is a fake.

By habit Cook wrote his narrative journals on the right-hand pages only, leaving the left-hand pages for notes and drawings, not necessarily in sequence with the events described on the facing page. His first entry on the climb begins on page 43:

> We pulled into the Tokositna and then Brill made a dock for the Bolshoy. John baked the bread and on the next day Sept 9 we started for the gl.[acier][19]

This entry runs onto page 45, which continues the narrative up to the time of its writing, saying that they took two and a half hours to reach the moraine of Ruth Glacier, four miles from the boat, and camped for the night four miles farther on, making eight miles' progress for the first day. By lunch the next day they had gone four miles farther, or a total of 12 miles. This entry is dated "Sept 9," though the "9" appears to be written over "10."

Barrill, in his diary, which he asserted was authentic up through September 8, says they started for the glacier that day, not September 9. At first, then, Cook's apparent readjustment of the date seems to be excused by his having simply lost a day. However, on page 47 of Cook's diary, the next entry is *again* dated September 9, and it is written over another figure—either 11 or 12. Its contents, however, indicate the passage of at least one more day, and possibly two:

> We have had a delightfully hard time to present good trail along old moraines. So good that horses could have been brought about to here. Last night and the night before we made superb camps beside the gl[lacier] got willows for fire and the temp has been somewhat warmer than in the river.[20]

Then, on page 51, the journey starts all over again on September 8. "We start with packs carrying 50 lbs," it says, but there is nothing about distances or camps.

Significantly, Barrill's diary for September 8 reads, "We reach the ice cliffs at 7-30 P.M. We are all tired out." The first September 9 entry in Cook's diary agrees with this, saying, "crossed a creek and camped along the first ice walls."[21]

In Cook's second account of September 9, he records that they camped at "2nd Lake"; he also records that "1st Lake" was 15 miles from the boat and that Dokkin returned from there "one day from the boat." Yet the first version records the first day's travel as eight miles, total, and Dokkin is still said to be making breakfast on the second day out. These various statements are irreconcilable as a record of a single trip. Already, suspicions have been raised as to whether they portray authentic events.

Claude Rusk strengthens those suspicions by telling us that the last place that willows could be gathered was 13 miles up the glacier. In Cook's second September 9 entry, he says that he cut the last willows between the 1st and 2nd Lake, which, if Rusk is correct, places Cook's camp at just about the spot he mentions in his first version of his diary as the second day of the trip—they were 12 miles from the boat at lunchtime, and if they made the same progress as the day before, they would have camped 16 miles out.

But why should there be any guesswork? And why are there two versions? Could the first version be true and the second the beginning of a fabrication?

On September 10 Cook's diary finds him camped at "Cerac pt.," a misspelling he preserved in his first article on the climb in *Harper's Monthly Magazine* for May 1907, further supporting the authenticity of the diary. But in a diary sketch of Ruth Glacier on page 44 there is a note "Sept 10" pointing to a spot much farther south and approximately the same place as their September 10 campsite shown on the route map drawn by Ed Barrill for the *Globe*. Barrill swore they camped at "Cerac Point" on September 13, not the 10th.

In his book Cook calls his "Cerac Point" campsite "Glacier Point," and he records its elevation accurately as being between 5,000 and 5,500 feet. In his diary he mentions he made "a scouting trip into ampth," indicating a side trip into the amphitheater containing Belmore Browne's Fake Peak, whose tributary glacier enters the Ruth adjacent to Glacier Point.

Barrill's diary for the same day says "moved camp up" in the morning "but I don't think we can go any higher in this direction," and it records the higher place as 7,700 feet—very close to his estimate of Fake Peak's altitude in his affidavit.

Possibly Cook thought he might be able to find a way to McKinley through this amphitheater, or at least get a better view of the terrain between him and the mountain by going away from its main massif. Doubtless, he was able to get a good view of the eastern ridge from a location near the head of the amphitheater and perhaps thought he could see a climbable route. From the same location in 1910, Belmore Browne noted, "The N.E. or E ridge is climbable from about 12,000 ft. up. Once on top of the Ridge it is an easy ascent to the S. summit."[22] Did this same view inspire Cook to concoct a fake account of his "easy ascent to the S. summit"?

In his affidavit, Barrill alleged that this was the very spot where the doctor told him to change his diary by erasing the real dates and altitudes and substituting dates two days earlier and altitudes 4,000 feet higher, the actual date then being September 12, according to Barrill. Barrill's diary clearly shows these features to have been erased, but that could have been done after the fact to support his version. He also said that Cook ordered him to stop keeping the diary entirely at this point and all the rest of the climb's entries were made at their return camps. It was here, also, that Barrill said the "summit" picture was taken at 10 A.M. on September 12 or 13, as he seems to contradict himself in the affidavit as to which date is correct.

Doubters of Cook's climb have pointed out that his book contains no mention of exploring the amphitheater containing Fake Peak, and they argue that the added time required for this side trip makes his claim of climbing Mount McKinley in a mere eight days even more fantastic.

There can be no doubt that Cook and Barrill reached the vicinity of Fake Peak. Photograph 1 that Parker and Browne pointed to at the Explorers Club was taken there and not at 16,000 feet, as it was captioned.[23] Moreover, both men's diaries mention the side trip into the amphitheater.

Though Belmore Browne stated in his 1913 book that this side trip would have taken Cook "at least a day's travel out of his course," it would have required a detour of only seven miles round-trip, and Browne's 1910 diary reports that he was able to make it from Fake Peak to Glacier Point "comfortably" in one hour and 40 minutes.[24] However, the shadows in the photographs known to have been taken in the Fake Peak amphitheater, according to Ted Leitzell's investigations on Cook's behalf in 1938, show that Cook spent most of a day there. Bradford Washburn confirmed this in the 1950s.

If Cook dictated the content of Barrill's diary for the next eight days' entries, there should be close similarity between the two accounts from this point on. Cook's diary for September 11 finds them camped at 8,300 feet at the base of the "N. ridge." Barrill says 8,000 feet, but both mention that their damp bags made sleep difficult.

From September 12 on, both diaries agree as to altitudes, which Barrill would naturally be dependent on Cook to supply. They also agree that they built a snow house at about 12,000 feet. Both diaries agree that the next day they dug into the side of the mountain for the night at 14,200 feet and that they built a second snow house at 15,600 feet on September 14. Here, however, differences begin to appear.

Cook mentions having a splitting headache, a common first sign of altitude sickness. He also mentions Barrill's having a nosebleed so severe that they decided to camp early. Barrill makes no mention of either but says they let the alcohol stove burn all night to keep the house warm.

Both diaries place the men at 18,200 feet, camped in the silk tent in the saddle between the mountain's two peaks on September 15,[25] and the next day they reach the summit.

Here is how each man recorded the conquest of Mount McKinley. First Cook:

> Sun Sept. 16. The top
> Exhausted – nearly frozen – not in shape to enjoy the scene – the slope, the snow, wind, clouds out of Pacific Japan current out of the Arctic clouds, both meeting & drifting north easterly 250 miles 50,000 sq. miles
>
> Alcohol stove inefficient
>
> Tube with date etc The hand shaking 20 minutes flag & names peculiar cloud effects no longer saw mirages

Now Barrill:

> Sun sept 16th 06
> we reach the top at last at about 11 a.m. to the gunsight [sharp pointed peak]. took some picture. They may not be good as it was cloudy stayed on top a short time then came down to camp 15600. we had a grait time shakeing hands on top. we could see a little of the top of foraker but there is to many clouds below us I had a nose bleed going up. the little snow house looks good to me as I am tired.

The rest of the two diaries agree with each other in all major details of the descent: the return on September 17 to 8,000 feet, and from there the next day to "caribou creek"; becoming snow-blind on the descent; the meeting with Dokkin on September 19; reaching the boat the following day.

There are two ways to view the close agreement between the two accounts of the climb: we might see Barrill's alleged joint forgery, or we might conclude that they record the same events because they are accounts of things that actually happened. If the diaries are intended as a joint forgery, however, the summit entries are most puzzling. If the diaries are a fraud, why, in this most important entry of all, should there be so much of a difference?

Barrill says they arrived at the summit at "about 11 A.M."; Cook's does not give the time. Strangely, although Cook gives no elevation for the summit or the time he reached it in his entry for September 16 on page 101, he gives both at the end of the previous entry on page 93, which is dated September 15. The pages between are blank. Cook was in the habit of putting the starting and ending point of the day at the head of each entry along with the weather conditions, so why this peculiar sequence?

An apologist might explain it away by "high-altitude stupidity"—the mental confusion at high elevations to which Hudson Stuck attributed his failure to make a critical reading of his thermometer at the summit in 1913. But why start on the same page as the entry for September 15, then skip seven pages and date the "continuation" of the entry there "Sept. 16"?

On page 93, Cook gives the time of arrival at the top as 10 A.M. and the elevation as 20,400 feet; he notes the temperature as –16°. In his book he says 10 A.M. also, but in his first lecture on the climb, given before the Mazamas in Seattle, he said "about noon." In his book, Cook says it was so clear he could see the Yukon and Tanana Rivers, the volcanoes on Cook Inlet and the Pacific Ocean beyond, though it was cloudy to the immediate south. His diary entry for September 16 seems to support this view, but page 93 mentions "some snow"—unlikely to be falling from the clear sky he was later to describe in his book as appearing almost black. However, Barrill says it was cloudy—period—but to the south "we could see a little of the top of foraker" peeking through the clouds.

In Hudson Stuck's book about his undisputed climb of the mountain in 1913, he says this of his view of Mount Foraker from the summit: "It was our first glimpse of her during the whole ascent. Denali's Wife [the natives' name for Foraker] does not appear at all save from the actual summit of Denali, for she is completely hidden by his South Peak until the moment when his South Peak is surmounted."[26] Stuck said this was the sight no man would fail to mention had he actually stood on the summit of Mount McKinley.

Though Cook never mentions it in either his book or his diary, astoundingly, Barrill says he saw "a little of the top of foraker"—the sight that could be seen only from the actual summit.

Just as the diaries taken together raise a number of suspicions about the story they tell, so does Cook's by itself. Helene Cook Vetter herself confessed to Hans Waale that it was its "mixup in dates" that led her to suppress her discovery of her father's diary.[27] But proponents, though admitting Cook's diary has problems, have pointed out some circumstantial features that they say authenticate its contents.

Under the brutal conditions described, its very sketchiness would seem natural, and the handwriting grows progressively worse as Dr. Cook climbs. The details of turning back his barometer to record heights above 12,000 feet and the medical notes have also been cited as badges of authenticity. But a clever, well-read man of Cook's medical and wilderness experience would certainly think to put such details in a forgery.

Moreover, there are other features that strain credulity, notably the absence of any record of the round of angles he claimed to have taken at the summit of the mountain, and the narrative conflicts with later accounts he gave before the Mazamas and in his article and book.

But there is one last thing that Barrill mentions in his summit entry that must be examined—Dr. Cook's photographs. This has been the linchpin of the arguments that Cook was a faker at Mount McKinley and, on the legal principle of "false in one, false in all," therefore a faker at the North Pole as well. Even Cook called his claim at McKinley "the key to the controversy," and Belmore Browne titled his chapter on finding Fake Peak, with finality, "The End of the Polar Controversy." But is it?

This line of attack started with Browne's photograph of Fake Peak printed in the newspapers in 1910 as "proof" that Cook was a faker. It was followed immediately by the remarks of C.E. Rusk on the illustrations in *To the Top of the Continent*:

> Practically every picture in the book purporting to represent places seen on the alleged "ascent," can be identified from the Mazama photographs as having been taken at a comparatively low altitude. His pictures of the "climb" were all secured on and around the tributary glacier, from fifteen to twenty miles from Mt. McKinley. He even has been unable to eliminate from the *sketches* well defined landmarks that are in reality miles from where he represents them to be.[28]

The truth of this statement was illustrated nearly 50 years later in a report by Bradford Washburn to the American Alpine Club of his investigations on Ruth Glacier from 1955 to 1957, an abbreviated form of which appeared in the 1958 number of the *American Alpine Journal*. Washburn was able to duplicate all but two of the photographs Cook had published, and each was close to the geographical limits Rusk had described. He also corrected the inaccurate locations and altitudes attributed to them in 1907 and 1908. None that were identified were found to be of places that fell outside the area Barrill's 1909 affidavit said he and Cook had visited. Most readers of Washburn's report concluded that it proved Cook never made the 1906 climb and convicted him fully of fraud in the matter.

On the other side, Cook's advocates have maintained that his photographs' false captions can be explained and that Belmore Browne's Fake Peak photo is a composite, manufactured to discredit Cook's summit picture, which is genuine. They have even used Washburn's photograph of the same place Browne photographed to support this position.

However brilliant, Bradford Washburn's work on Ruth Glacier does not prove that Cook did not climb Mount McKinley—something even Washburn admitted to Cook's daughter in 1955. What it does prove is that the captions given Cook's pictures misrepresented their true locations. Even the doctor's firmest supporters have been forced to concede that much about them, with the possible exception of his famous summit picture. But they blame this mislabeling of Cook's pictures on his absence during the production of his book, which did not allow him to read the galleys. However, Cook's 1907 *Harper's Monthly Magazine* article, over which he presumably had complete supervision, is no more accurate in identifying their true locations. Even though the magazine captions differ from those in the book, they also imply that some of the pictures were taken during the actual ascent.

A close look at the photographic evidence should decide the merits of these arguments. First, the quality and composition of Cook's photos taken on Ruth Glacier should be noted. Their reproductions in his book do not begin to realize the sharpness and detail of the original negatives that have survived. Dr. Cook's skill with a camera was remarkable, and his original pictures made on Ruth Glacier are a testament to his great photographic gift.

So, what significance can be attached to Barrill's remark about Cook's pictures—"they may be no good"? At the dinner of the National Geographic Society in December 1906, Cook was reported to have said that "he was afraid they would be failures because of the adverse climatic conditions," which matches Barrill's diary entry.[29] Aside from the obvious possibility that he was never there, what other reasons might explain why Cook had no authentic pictures taken from the upper slopes of McKinley to display?

The first was given by Cook himself when he told Admiral Chester and others in 1906: "Of course, you gentlemen can realize that you cannot represent a horizontal view of the highest pinnacle on the continent with a camera, for there can be no viewpoint from which a photograph can be taken. Furthermore, I had to leave my camera and all of the impedimenta at the foot of the slope to make the difficult climb to the top. Even overcoats were barred on this last march to the top of the mountain."[30]

This would explain the lack of pictures from the summit, but why then does Barrill say in his diary "took some picture," if there was no camera? And why are there no pictures from anywhere on the upper slopes? If it were not for the first question, Cook might have an alibi; if not for the second, he would probably have the credit for the climb and for reaching the North Pole as well.

A popular defense of Cook's mislabeled photographs has been that he did have his camera, but as Barrill feared, the pictures did not come out, so he used his lower-altitude photos as "substitutes."

Upon Cook's return from Copenhagen in 1909, Herbert Berri noticed several pictures in the *New York Herald*—labeled as having been taken on Cook's just-completed expedition—that looked very familiar. They had, in fact, been taken on the *Erik* voyage in 1901, during which Berri had snapped several of the same subjects, including drifting icebergs. When confronted by reporters, Cook calmly explained that an iceberg was an iceberg and that the old photos were used merely for "illustrative purposes." There was no intent to deceive, he said. And it should be noted that such substitution was not at all uncommon in the days when photography was an unsophisticated art and pictures often failed.

If Cook lacked a picture of the summit, he was not unique among early climbers. *No* successful picture of the summit was made until 1942, when Bradford Washburn took one. In all the other attempts, the conquerors' cameras invariably malfunctioned, even as late as 1932. Even so, most believers in Cook's claim are loath to concede his summit photograph is even a substitution, and therefore not genuine.

But since all of Cook's pictures were taken *in advance* of his climb, to believe that Cook just happened to have photographed features suitable for "illustrative purposes" *before* he even saw the features along his totally unknown route is implausible. And to think he "matched" them from memory after the fact seems unbelievable.

Even though there have been thousands of conquerors of Mount McKinley in recent years, all of whom have seen what its summit really looks like, the arguments over Cook's picture have been never-ending. It has been called "the most controversial picture in the history of exploration," and it has been defended by many of Cook's advocates to the last as, if not the true summit, then proof that Cook scaled the mountain as he said he did. Among these partisans was Hans Waale, who devoted many years of study to Cook's climb, starting in 1973.

Waale was convinced that Cook's photograph showed the so-called North Drift, a feature 70 feet northwest of the actual summit and nearly as high. From Denali Pass it appears to be the mountain's true summit. Waale theorized that Cook had mistaken it as such or photographed it as the summit for dramatic effect, the true summit being a rather flat, narrow ridge of solid, hard-packed snow, with a horseshoe-shaped depression a dozen feet deep with a hummock at either end.

Stuck's sketch of the summit of Mount McKinley.

This solid ice sheet covering the summit has always been advanced, even before the mountain was climbed, as proof that Cook's picture was taken elsewhere, since it clearly shows naked rock exposed at the top. But the permanency of the summit formation has been a matter of argument nonetheless. Stuck said the summit "looked as though every severe storm might change its shape," yet the next climbers to arrive, 19 years later, found it just about as Stuck had described it.

In 1947 Bradford Washburn stuck an eight-foot bamboo rod into the ice to mark the exact summit. Later climbers found the rod had canted only a little and migrated a few feet in the next ten years, even though exposed to constant high winds.

The apparent stability of the summit structure, and the fact that there was no possible angle from which the summit ridge could be photographed at 10 A.M. that could replicate the shadows in Cook's picture, seemed to rule out its actually being the top of McKinley.

Undissuaded, Waale placed ads in Alaskan newspapers and in climbing magazines for years, offering a reward or simply imploring climbers to do a systematic photographic survey to document any changes in the summit. He also gave specific instructions to photograph the North Drift by pointing the camera slightly southwest near the bottom of the commonly climbed ridge. His studies had led him to believe that such an alignment at 10 A.M. would fulfill the shadow requirements lacking in a picture of the true summit, duplicate Cook's photo and confirm his theory. He got no takers.

More than 70 years before Waale placed his ads, Belmore Browne and General Hubbard thought they had scotched all future debate by demonstrating conclusively that Fake Peak was identical to Cook's summit. But almost immediately others disagreed.

In 1914 Edwin Swift Balch, in his book *Mount McKinley and Mountain Climbers' Proofs*, superimposed outline tracings of the Cook and Browne photographs and found they did not match up at many points. The same year, in a 33-page booklet entitled *Mount McKinley, Its Bearing on the Polar Controversy*, E.C. Rost went Balch one better by reproducing the two pictures in the same scale and covering them with a grid corresponding to the major visible features. Again, they did not match at all points. Rost gave his own opinion, and that of several other "expert photographers," that Browne's picture was a clever fake—a composite of a real photograph and a painting—with the right-hand profile of rock filled in to approximate the Cook photograph's contours.

Of course, Rost was Cook's paid lobbyist at the time. Though one cannot expect an unbiased opinion from him, what of Balch? The year after Balch's book was published, Belmore Browne offered to put before the Philadelphia lawyer unpublished photographic evidence that he believed would convince him that the two photographs were of the same place. Much to Browne's surprise, Balch refused the offer.[31] Once again, Browne offered his photographs to Balch and any witness he cared to bring with him, but he was again angrily rebuffed by Balch, who challenged him instead to publish the "evidence" he possessed.

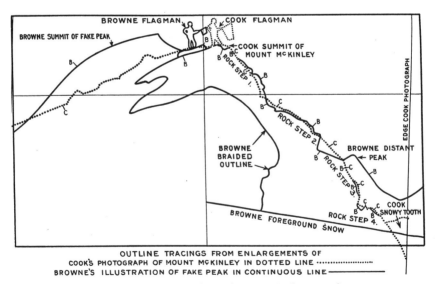

Balch's comparison of tracings of Cook's and Browne's photographs.

Browne couldn't understand why Balch refused. Perhaps Edwin Swift Balch, like so many players in the Polar Controversy before and since, did not want his conclusions upset. He was satisfied with his own arguments and his own answer. In defending Cook he had put his own credibility on the line; if Cook was ever conclusively proved a faker, he too would lose face.

Yet Balch's answer was based on the same faulty premise as Rost's. The only way two photographs of a subject taken at close range could ever be made to exactly coincide would be to take them from exactly the same location, with exactly the same camera and lens in the same lighting conditions, while tilting that camera at exactly the same angle. Even the first requirement could not be duplicated, as Browne explained to the press: "On account of the formation of the snow cornice it was impossible to photograph the rock from the exact spot where Dr. Cook himself stood. These cornices are shaped according to the whims of the winds that blow, and the formation varies from year to year. It will also be noted that there is more snow in the photograph I took. This is due to the fact that I was there in July, while Dr. Cook's photograph was taken in September." As a consequence, Browne estimated his picture of Fake Peak was taken seven feet to the right of Dr. Cook's position. But Browne still thought his photo absolutely convincing. "A considerable amount of snow naturally would melt away in two Summer months. But you can readily see that the photographs are of one and the same rock, and a very paltry rock it is at that," he said.[32]

Others who later visited that "paltry rock" would not agree with Browne's assessment. When Ted Leitzell arrived in July 1938, he declared baldly that Browne had lied about its being the same place. His reason was that the profile, which had been alleged by Rost to have been painted in, was missing! Washburn's photographs made in 1955–57 confirmed this, but Washburn argued that the rock profile had collapsed, and the place where it had broken away could be seen in Browne's 1910 picture as a fault or crack.

Cook's proponents maintained, however, that the rock profile on Fake Peak had never existed, the "crack" being the division where the actual photo stopped and the painting began.

Belmore Browne's diary of June 28, 1910, notes the condition of the rocks in the vicinity of Fake Peak as "rotten seamed cracked and disintegrated by the forces of nature . . . that look as if a breath of wind would send them crashing and rumbling to the glaciers far below." Given this, it is possible that the earthquake that shook the Northeast Ridge of Mount McKinley to pieces two years after Browne's description could easily have collapsed such a fragile structure. Counterbalancing this, however, modern photographs of the profile of the cliff on the left margin in Cook's photograph 1 still match Browne's in every detail. Why has the profile of Fake Peak disintegrated so badly while the similar-looking cliff, which is practically adjacent to it, remained intact? Could Browne's diary entry be a deception to excuse the differences future visitors would surely notice?

This seems unlikely, since there is photographic evidence to support Browne as well. One of his photographs taken below Fake Peak, head on, seems to show the missing rock profile as a narrow vertical ledge, and one long-distance shot also taken in 1910 by Browne's companion Merl LaVoy looking at Fake Peak from the other side, when magnified, suggests the profile seen in Cook's photo, reversed.

If it did nothing else, Washburn's 1956 visit to Fake Peak proved one thing beyond doubt. On its top his party found a written record by Belmore Browne, proving that there was no mistake, at least, that this was the place Browne had photographed in 1910.

Is Fake Peak the same place as Cook's summit? To this day no one has ever been able to take a picture from any spot near Fake Peak that exactly duplicates the alignment of the distant mountains across Ruth Glacier so that one coincides with the "distant peak" in Cook's summit photo. Even Washburn associate Adams Carter's elaborate attempts in 1957 to erect a 50-foot mast to compensate for the depth of ice and snow that had melted since 1906 fell several feet short of placing a photographer at the conjectural point where Cook stood when he took his picture. But even had Carter's experiment worked, if the rock profile had actually collapsed, there would be no way to make an exact duplicate. All we are left, then, is an examination of the photographs made before the time the collapse is alleged to have occurred. In effect, we must do what Belmore Browne invited Balch to do in 1915.

Browne's photographs, including their original negatives, are preserved among his papers at Dartmouth College. There are several unpublished views taken from slightly different points in both June and July 1910. In each, parts of the disputed rock profile are visible, though partially snow covered, and in each it looks the same as in Browne's supposedly retouched published photograph. The detail visible in the unpublished photographs shows the dividing line between the snow slope and the rock face—a detail said by E.C. Rost to have been painted in—to be a sharp shadow, and the snow slope's details are clearly natural and not painted.

We do not have the same opportunity to study the original negative of Dr. Cook's summit shot. It has vanished, though it may still exist. Even though Browne's photographs appear genuine, the fate of Cook's negative raises a nagging suspicion about Belmore Browne, since he once had the original Cook negatives, yet he apparently did not even keep copies.

In a letter to General Hubbard in 1914 he said he gave Evelyn Briggs Baldwin the "original negatives of Dr. Cook's fakes which I secured in 1910."[33] How Browne secured these negatives is not known. The Explorers Club asked Cook to write an order on Doubleday, Page for all materials used in *To the Top of the Continent*, including photographs, but there is no evidence that he complied. Perhaps Browne got them from the publisher, though it is doubtful that Doubleday, Page ever had the negative of Cook's summit picture.

In his 1958 article, Bradford Washburn lamented the loss of Cook's negative. As with Browne's photos, Washburn was convinced that additional detail could be brought out in enlarged prints made from it, and a comparison of these with modern photographs of Fake Peak would settle whether the two photos pictured the same place. Washburn was a friend of Browne's until Browne's death in 1954. That he apparently was never aware that Cook's negative had once been in Browne's possession raises further suspicion as to what Browne might have done with it.

After reading Browne's letter, the author obtained special permission to look through the uncataloged photographic materials of E.B. Baldwin at the Library of Congress, which had apparently lain undisturbed since their donation in 1935. Although two original pictures taken on Cook's North Pole expedition did turn up, none of his McKinley photographs were found. The only picture of Mount McKinley among Baldwin's material was a copy of the classic one made in 1910 by Merl LaVoy from Explorer's Peak from the east. Its presence hints that Baldwin did have contact with Browne about Cook's climb, since Browne is known to have kept copies of LaVoy's photograph for himself.

With the controversial negative still missing, we are left with the published versions of Cook's summit photograph to consider. These two differ greatly. The one that appeared in *Harper's Monthly Magazine* in May 1907 is cropped on the right and has a heavily retouched, bright sky. This contrasts with the version published in *To the Top of the Continent*, in which the picture has a very dark sky and is cropped on the left but unretouched, and the "distant peak" not seen in *Harper's* is visible at the right.

Cook's enemies have pounced on the differences between the two and have persistently cried "fake!" saying the *Harper's* version was Cook's attempt to disguise where it was taken, and the unretouched version was published only because Cook had left for the Pole without overseeing the final details of his book. But although Parker and Browne used this as the centerpiece of their evidence of Cook's fakery before the Explorers Club committee in 1909, there is another explanation for the differences in the published versions.

In 1931 an inquiry to Harper & Brothers by a student of the subject revealed that the magazine had never had the original negative and was displeased with the print provided by Cook.[34] "The sky in the photograph was very dark and had the appearance of being discolored," the *Harper's* correspondent replied. "To bring out the line of the Summit of Mount McKinley the photograph was given to a staff artist with instructions to carefully follow every detail of the form in the Summit and air brush a new sky. This was done, a plate made, then electros and printed.

"The reason I remember this distinctly," the man went on, "is because Dr. Cook complained about the sky having been retouched and stated that the sky at that altitude was black. We were all rather distressed for our intentions were simply to show clearly the line of the Summit, but as the Magazine was on sale, we could not make any change. Later when controversy arose, questioning various claims and statements of Dr. Cook, I naturally thought of this one photograph, the only one we had retouched and the complaint of Dr. Cook."[35]

But Cook himself asked to have some retouching of his Mount McKinley pictures done, according to another account. Edward Van Altena had done photographic work for Cook in the 1890s on his antarctic pictures. After returning to New York from Alaska, Dr. Cook brought him some 3¼-by-4¼-inch prints to be made into lantern slides. As he sorted through them, one came up showing a man with a flag on top of a peak. Van Altena asked whether that was the top of Mount McKinley. Cook, Van Altena said, looked flustered, as if he did not expect that picture to be among the prints, and laid it facedown on the table, saying, "Oh, we don't want that."

When another, different, picture of a similar pose came up and he asked the same question, Cook replied that it was the summit, remarking about the first picture, "Well, we thought we could not get any higher." Van Altena said it seemed clear to him that the doctor had intended to pass off the first picture as the summit if the higher one had not been made.

On one slide Van Altena made for Cook's lectures, the explorer asked him to take out a very small peak among the others in a mountainous skyline in the distance. The lantern-slide dealer complied with the request but thought it odd that he would want to "change nature." Later, he said, he discovered that the peak he had been asked to remove had been Mount McKinley itself.

Van Altena admitted that he was recalling incidents that had happened more than half a century before, but he said he was sure his memory of them was correct. Nevertheless, he was incorrect in at least one thing: Cook's 1906 McKinley photographs are not the dimensions Van Altena described; all measure 5 by 7 inches, something that could not be determined from their published format.[36]

A search through the photographic materials at the Frederick A. Cook Society in Hurleyville, New York, in 1991 turned up a number of original negatives and prints taken during the 1906 expedition. Though there are some unpublished views, none give any appearance of having been taken from the slopes of Mount McKinley, and most can be identified because of one picture that was published by Cook but has been overlooked ever since.

It appeared in the December 29, 1906, issue of *Collier's* magazine. In *Collier's* its caption is ambiguous but strongly implies that it was taken from the summit of McKinley. It can be deduced from the entire group of unpublished pictures, however, that they were all taken in the amphitheater of the tributary glacier containing Fake Peak, since taken together and along with the *Collier's* picture, they show a progressive sequence with common features that either overlap or can be identified in other published photographs, or they contain features that match sketches in Barrill's diary. The *Collier's* photograph was subsequently identified by Mount McKinley guide Brian

Okonek of Talkeetna as having been taken from the same location as the "15,400-foot" photograph that baffled Walt Gonnason and Bradford Washburn so long—one mile northeast of Fake Peak, but looking in the opposite direction toward the Coffee Glacier.[37]

Although there was no negative of Cook's summit picture, a print of it made from the original negative was uncovered in the Hurleyville search. This print, the sharpest ever seen, is uncropped and unenlarged, in the original 5-by-7 format; most important, it is unretouched. It appears to be a normal daylight exposure, not dark or underexposed; the sky behind Ed Barrill is quite bright. In this print the rock structures stand out boldly, and it cannot be doubted that they are identical to those of Fake Peak that still remain. Furthermore, more of the "distant peak" at the right is visible, and the top of the adjacent cliff, shown on the left margin of photograph 1, can be seen protruding over the left shoulder of Cook's "summit," doubly confirming that the places Cook and Browne photographed were, indeed, one and the same.[38]

Apparently, Cook's negative was intentionally underexposed when it was printed for publication to represent the "dark sky" encountered by Dr. Cook at the "summit" in his narrative. Or it may have been done to obscure the detail of the rocks and, therefore, lessen the chances of detecting the true location at which it was taken. If so, it has succeeded most admirably.

Perhaps we should not have had to belabor this issue. After all, there was already incontrovertible proof that Cook had been at Fake Peak, since photograph 1 was taken at or near the top of Fake Peak itself, and the picture drawn by Barrill and published with his printed affidavit in the *New York Globe* was drawn at this location and was practically duplicated by a sketch made by Belmore Browne in his diary from the same spot in 1910. But only conclusive evidence could ever persuade those who have had faith in Frederick Cook as an honest man to accept that he would have had the audacity to photograph this little rocky outcrop and pass it off as the highest peak in North America.

The few who have already conceded that Fake Peak is Cook's "top of the continent" have tried to justify this action in various ways. But even if we could accept the most innocent motive and concede that Cook might have photographed this spot as a backup in case his real photo did not come out, for him to have made the photograph with that intention *before* he even attempted the climb of Mount McKinley, which is what is evidenced from his own diary, seems odd indeed.

Though the picture is a fake, it still does not prove that Cook did not really climb Mount McKinley. That is a natural leap to conclusions, but not a logical one. It is understandable that, having represented it as the "top of the continent" in 1907, Cook could not afford to say it wasn't in 1909, considering the tremendous pressure he was under as a result of the Barrill affidavit. To admit to having faked the summit photo would have destroyed his credibility entirely, even if there was a reasonable excuse for his having used the photo to begin with.

Cook's unpublished photograph of Mount Barrille showing his tent pitched in the foreground.

But much more damaging than the original print of Cook's summit is another picture that turned up among the unpublished photographs in the Cook Society's collection. It shows "Mt. Barrille" and is taken slightly to the left of the position of a similar scene that appeared in *To the Top of the Continent.* Unlike the published photograph, which has been cropped at the bottom, in the foreground it shows Cook's silk tent pitched at this spot with Ed Barrill standing next to it. In his narrative, Cook says that after he left the camp at Glacier Point, he next camped at "8,000 feet, within a few miles of the northern ridge." This does not fit the location shown in this picture at all, being far beyond it and much higher. But it does fit the position of Barrill's "camp 8," exactly as drawn by Barrill on his map published in the *New York Globe*—the last camp Barrill says they made before turning back. This is also where Cook's photographic evidence runs out, published or unpublished. Therefore, this picture confirms Barrill's affidavit while contradicting Cook's narrative.

Still, there are unsettled questions, chiefly centering on the descriptions of landmarks along his claimed route, that Cook's narrative raises, which have led many to argue for its authenticity.

Cook's opponents downplay or deny the accuracy of his descriptions. They assert that the doctor's narrative becomes vague immediately after he reaches the point where Barrill says he turned back. Browne wrote that the mountain was easier to climb the way Dr. Cook did it—with pen and ink—than hand over foot. Or as Claude Rusk said after he followed Cook's route up Ruth Glacier, "However attractive his style may be from a literary standpoint, it is woefully lacking in detail to one who is trying to follow the events of that wonderful 'climb.'"[39]

Hudson Stuck, the acknowledged conqueror of McKinley, couldn't have agreed more:

> The descriptions in his book are clear and definite up to [10,000 feet]; he may be followed camp by camp; almost step by step. But in the chapter in which the ascent to the summit is narrated has nothing clear or definite at all. The whole chapter is a rhapsody of "icy infernos" and "heaven-kissed granite" and I have forgotten what extravagances of turgid rhetoric. The whole chapter is just such a chapter as a man would write who knew the lower levels, but was ignorant of the heights; he could not be more definite without danger; his vagueness leaves a loophole for defence. . . .
> . . . I will venture with all confidence this; that any man, who, having read Dr. Cook's book, shall himself climb to the top of the mountain . . . will never be convinced by all the special pleading in the world that the man who wrote that book had climbed where he climbed and stood where he stood.[40]

But in 1909 Alfred Brooks, who had seen Mount McKinley close-up even if he had not climbed it, had not been bothered by this lack of detail. He found Cook's "failure to be more specific . . . consistent," citing features he must have seen on the way to Ruth Glacier but did not report. Brooks said he knew of the rushed circumstances surrounding the publication of Cook's book. "Undoubtedly he can add much to his case by submitting all photographs now in his possession to some society," he added. "These with his complete observations will suffice to end the matter one way or the other. Scientists are entitled to this much."[41] But Cook never supplied those photographs or observations, even when given opportunities to do so.

Immediately after the publication of Archdeacon Stuck's descriptions of his own climb of Denali, however, students of the subject, including Edwin Swift Balch, noticed a number of similarities to Cook's "extravagances of turgid rhetoric." Cook described a natural camping place at 12,000 feet; Stuck camped at just that altitude, describing it in similar terms, and modern guidebooks say it is the *only* good campsite on the Northeast Ridge. Dr. Cook accurately described such features as a "huge rock" at the end of the ridge, a rock now named Browne Tower; a second natural campsite at 16,300 feet routinely used by climbers today; the relatively easy slope and snow conditions on the upper glacier between the peaks; "several miniature ranges running up to two main peaks about two miles apart"; and "rows of granite pinnacles," which can be seen in Stuck's photograph opposite page 94 in his book. Cook also mentions an "icy shelf" just below the summit itself, noted by other early climbers, including Grant Pearson, whose narrative of his climb in 1932 mentions "a fairly level plateau at the bottom of the summit dome."

Is it possible that Dr. Cook could have so accurately described such features on a route he never took? His critics have said yes, pointing out that Cook had been able to observe the mountain from all sides during his expeditions of 1903 and 1906. Bradford Washburn insists that Cook had a perfect opportunity to study the route up the Northeast Ridge from a point 30 miles off in 1903. He reminds us that Cook said of that view, "If it were not so very difficult to get at this side of the mountain, we reasoned that here the upper slopes might offer a promising route."

Stuck said Cook knew more about the mountain, up to 10,000 feet, than any living man. But can Cook's long-range observations account for the uncanny accuracy of his descriptions of features, all above that height, made six years before Stuck's climb and without any precedent to guide him?

Washburn accounts for Cook's generally accurate description of a climb along the Northeast Ridge by combining his 1903 observations with a theory first advanced by Belmore Browne in 1912. Browne said that Cook, approaching the mountain from Ruth Glacier, was confronted by the East Buttress and was confused by his view of three years before into believing that what was in front of him was the Northeast Ridge he had seen in 1903 from the north. Having made that misjudgment, Browne suggested, he then fabricated his ascent without knowing there was an intervening glacier and a dense tangle of peaks between him and his imaginative route along the true "northeast ridge."

Walt Gonnason, among others, obviated this difficulty by maintaining that Cook had climbed the mountain by the East Buttress. As evidence he quoted the passage in Cook's narrative that clearly states the ridge he was on was the divide between the Susitna and the Yukon watersheds, a description that could only mean the East Buttress. Cook's narrative, however, does not fit the East Buttress's physical description. It seems, instead, to indicate from its described topography, if not from all of the directions mentioned, that his route was the one eventually followed by all of the early parties who, climbing from Muldrow Glacier, went up the Northeast Ridge, known today as Karstens Ridge.

This problem has puzzled many who have looked into Cook's assertions hoping to prove the doctor did as he said: he seems to be claiming to have climbed one ridge while describing another, a situation Belmore Browne's theory fits exactly—unless he reached Karstens Ridge from Ruth Glacier.

Hudson Stuck recognized that possibility and tried to eliminate it:

> If Dr. Cook, approaching the mountain from the south, climbed to the summit by the northeast arrete (although my recollection is that the book is vague even on this cardinal point), he must have crossed at least two and probably three lofty icy ridges,

themselves high mountains, ascending to their crests, descending thousands of feet to the glaciers below and ascending the opposite sides; a task the mere physical distance and labor of which would be utterly out of the question in the two or three days he gives to the whole ascent.[42]

In the late 1950s, however, Hugo Levin, after studying Cook's diary, decided this must have been what the doctor had done and advanced the theory that Cook had actually climbed Karstens Ridge and not the East Buttress.

In an introduction Cook wrote to accompany Ralph Cairns's account of the *Fairbanks Times* Expedition of 1912, he said:

> We made the first ascent by the most eastern of the three north ridges in 1906. Hershell Parker, coming later, claimed that the northeast ridge was unclimbable, and that, therefore, our first ascent was impossible. In 1912 he started in from the north, reached the upper part of the same ridge upon which our climb was made from the east, and claimed to have reached the top. He has, therefore, disproven his own charge that we did not climb the mountain.[43]

The "most eastern of the three north ridges" is the East Buttress, but the one Parker climbed was not "the same ridge" but the center one, Karstens Ridge.

Then, in the 1913 edition of *My Attainment of the Pole,* Cook said of the two Parker-Browne expeditions:

> [in 1910] They balked at the north-east ridge, without making a serious attempt. This ridge—(the ridge upon which I had climbed to the top of Mt. McKinley)—was pronounced impossible. . . . During the spring of 1912 . . . [Parker and Browne] attacked the same ridge from the west and . . . a point near the top was reached.
>
> Mr. Parker now contradicts his former statement by saying, "The north-east ridge is the only feasible ridge."[44]

In this passage, the same confusion of the two ridges appears. It was the East Buttress (and then the South Buttress) that Parker and Browne balked at in 1910. Cook again states that this ridge, by which he ascended the mountain, was the "same ridge" that Parker-Browne climbed in 1912, when that was Karstens Ridge.

Both statements indicate that Cook actually made the mistake Washburn and Browne attribute to him. Both statements were made after his own attempt but *before* Stuck reached the summit and described what lay between the East Buttress and Karstens Ridge, and each shows that Cook did not realize at that time that the two ridges were not one and the same. Further supporting this is Claude Rusk's description of what he imagined a climb of the ridge before him would be like, as he stood at the head of Ruth Glacier and looked up at the East Buttress:

> The summit, seen from the upper [Ruth] glacier, is a very sharp snow point, although seen from the other sides of the mountain it has more of a rounded and dome-like appearance. The first part of the ascent of Mt. McKinley from this side would be a fierce battle with crags, steep gullies and avalanche-swept slopes, while the last few thousand feet would be a struggle up a long steep snow slope, broken by yawning crevasses. While through it all would be the handicap of rarefied air and bitter cold.[45]

This roughly equates to Cook's account of his own climb. What's more, on page 52 of Cook's diary there is evidence that Cook had this exact view, since he made a sketch of McKinley's top that corresponds to Rusk's description of a "very sharp snow point." His diary indicates he drew this picture at just about the same point that Rusk stood.

Some have argued that Cook would have seen the difference between the East Buttress and Karstens Ridge when he visited the snout of fidele Glacier with Dunn and Shainwald in 1903. In the February 1904 issue of *Harper's Monthly Magazine,* Cook clearly said of this view from the east: "Three spurs offer resting-places for glacier ice, over which a route to the summit may, perhaps, be found." (FAC, "America's Unconquered Mountain," *Harper's Monthly Magazine,* February 1904, page 344). But that none of his later statements reflect a recognition that the East Buttress and Karstens Ridge were not the same, suggests that the position he reached on Fidele Glacier's terminal moraine did not give a vantage point from which to make such a judgment, or at least that he did not recognize the "three spurs" as the same ridges he was dealing with when he was confronted with the East Buttress on Ruth Glacier.

Onto this much-debated scene belatedly stepped Hans Waale. Waale had gotten interested in Cook in 1940 when he purchased a copy of the 1909 pulp book *Discovery of the North Pole* in a Salvation Army bookstore shortly after he read of Dr. Cook's stroke. The juxtaposition of the book and the synopsis of Cook's subsequent career that appeared in newspaper obituaries had a powerful effect on him. "I could see apparent crookedness right away about his imprisonment," he recalled, "—and it filled me to overflowing with vengeance—I tell you—my fighting spirit was uncontrollable—I determined to lose all that I had if necessary and make enemies in every high place that I had to—with this vehemence I meant to fight like I was in a war—with all of my soul! For several years I could find out almost nothing any where besides what was in this book."[46]

Waale's ardor cooled, but in 1964 his interest was rekindled when he read *Return from the Pole* and obtained the Vetters' address from the U.S. Copyright Office. He wrote to Helene and began a correspondence with her and her daughter that lasted until his death in 1988.

"Providentially God is pleased for me to be [a] small man as much as I can—yet do my best for all," he told Helene Vetter early on. "I fit better with the underdogs usually, though I despise irresponsibility."[47] Waale described how his greatest interest was "the better comprehension of everything that is important" and said that for many years he had lost sleep over a prolonged study of the Bible—until he discovered Dr. Cook. Hans Waale then heard a new calling.

Agreeing with Cook that his expedition to Alaska's great mountain held the "key to the controversy," in 1973, at the age of 68, Waale took up the study of the doctor's climb in earnest. During the next ten years he spent more than $5,000 purchasing topographical maps and photographs of the continent's greatest peak, teaching himself the techniques of cartographic interpretation. His dedication was so great that Helene Vetter even gave Waale a copy of parts of Dr. Cook's long-hidden McKinley diary.

Inevitably, his studies brought him into contact with Bradford Washburn. His correspondence with Washburn was stormy, the Boston scientist threatening to break it off when Waale accused Cook's opponents of withholding information about the summit. Washburn, exasperated by Waale's refusal to accept his arguments, advised the 70-year-old gardener to go see the mountain for himself and then he would realize why "nobody who ever climbed McKinley has supported Dr. Cook's claim"—apparently forgetting about Walt Gonnason. Washburn also disavowed any real knowledge of the merits of Cook's claim to the North Pole, or of the rest of his ill-starred career.[48]

Waale's drawing of Cook's route.

Waale was sometimes discouraged, but he didn't give up, even though his pleas to climbers for summit photographs were all but ignored. "I feel more disgraced and humbled by climbers that simply will not answer," he told Janet Vetter, "than one who curses me like Washburn—but answers every time— and is generous with information that utterly goes against his repeated and unchangeable claims! This is science ethics on the part of Washburn—or at worst better politics than usual."[49]

By 1979, after prolonged study, Waale agreed with Hugo Levin that Cook had not climbed the East Buttress but neither did he think he had climbed Karstens Ridge. Instead, Waale proposed what he believed to be a route that matched the descriptions found in Cook's book in every particular— physical features, altitudes and directions: around Dan Beard mountain, over the East Buttress and down into the Traleika Amphitheater, over Karstens Ridge near Mount Koven, then across Muldrow Glacier and up Pioneer Ridge, across the north face of Mount McKinley onto Harper Glacier and then on to the summit.

After more intensive scrutiny of stereo views of the route, he was able to point out features along it that he thought matched the pictures that Cook had chosen to "illustrate" his route in the sequence he used them.

Bradford Washburn tried to disabuse Waale of his notion that such a climb was even possible, sending oblique photographs of Waale's proposed route. Although he agreed that parts of it were "perfectly possible" for Cook and Barrill to have climbed, he emphasized its circuitous characteristics and the difficult traverse required to go from the north face to Harper Glacier and other technical pitfalls that were "beyond" their abilities. He also declared a descent over this route in four days, even assuming perfect weather and modern equipment, "completely out of the question."[50]

But long study of Cook's diary materials strengthened and helped refine Waale's theories, and in October 1983 Waale revealed to Bradford Washburn the existence of the diary. Washburn was reluctant to believe it was genuine, but although he could hardly conceal his eagerness to see it, he simply called the fact that it existed, and its long suppression, "interesting and sad."[51]

Near the end of the year, Waale sent Washburn a detailed copy of the route he had developed during his studies, illustrating its progress using many of the aerial pictures Washburn had taken. After thoroughly looking it over, Bradford Washburn wrote back sympathetically that despite all the time Waale had put into it, he was sorry to say he still could not accept that he was correct. Although agreeing that the route "clearly follows the descriptions in the text of [Cook's] book and the diary," he continued to maintain his former objections, and given Cook and Barrill's time schedule, he said their "only prayer" would have been a route directly up the East Buttress. In the final analysis, he concluded, all factors considered, Waale's route was a "logistic impossibility."[52]

Waale considered it a huge victory that Washburn had admitted he had found a route that fit Cook's descriptions. "It ought to be on the news," he told Janet Vetter. St. Paul said faith could remove mountains; Hans Waale's faith had not done that, but it had, theoretically at least, moved Dr. Cook up Mount McKinley in harmony with every description in his narrative, and an untutored gardener had made the greatest living expert on the subject agree that this was so.

To understand Washburn's objections to Waale's ingenious mental climb requires a look at some real climbers' experiences on Mount McKinley since 1909.

A climb of the pioneer route taken by all the early parties from Muldrow Glacier averages 21 to 35 days round-trip, once on the glacier itself. The most popular route today is the one pioneered by Bradford Washburn in 1951— the West Buttress. An average time along this route is seven to 11 days to the summit and one to two days back to Kahiltna. Both routes are technically less difficult than the complex route outlined by Waale for Cook's climb—a climb that Cook said he and Barrill accomplished in 13 days from a base camp 34 air miles from the summit and back.

Before crying impossible, however, it should be said that the average expedition is heavily equipped and does at least some backhauling—that is, it relays supplies and has to retrace some of its route in so doing. Cook climbed in what is called today "alpine style"; he did no backhauling. To show the difference backhauling makes, we have only to look at Belmore Browne's diary for July 26, 1910: "Left camp 21 got to camp 15. . . . This shows the criminal side of relay work as with heavy packs we covered in all yesterday a distance equal to 6½ days relay packing."

Although Parker and Browne took weeks to cover the distance Cook claimed he covered in two days, Rusk and the Mazamas made it to Glacier Point in five, roughly the same as reported by Barrill in his affidavit. But Leitzell and Sertich took only three days with heavier packs. The next expedition up Ruth Glacier, in 1954, took five days to Glacier Point from 40 miles out.

Though it normally takes several weeks to climb Mount McKinley, it has been done in less time. Terris Moore climbed the Muldrow Glacier route in six days, eight hours as early as 1942, and in 1978 the two-man team of Galen Rowell and Ned Gillette made the summit in one day along the West Buttress, returned to 17,200 feet for the night and were back the next day. Even for these seasoned climbers, however, it was not easy. The rapid ascent caused Gillette a bout of mountain sickness, and Rowell developed signs of pulmonary edema, an often-fatal affliction for unacclimatized climbers who gain too much altitude too fast. What's more, the one-day climb was made from a starting elevation of 10,000 feet over a well-traveled route that was thoroughly familiar to both men.[53]

All expeditions that have traversed established routes have had that one important advantage over Dr. Cook. They were not striking out into totally unknown territory; they knew what was before them and, barring unforseen disaster, what to expect.

Another consideration must be the weather. During the prime climbing season, from May to August, weather confines climbers to their tents two days out of three, and only one day out of five is clear. The weather on the south side of the mountain begins to deteriorate after July, and September is especially poor, with the highest precipitation in Alaska. The weather typically runs in cycles, with good spells lasting three to six days, and ten days of bad weather is not unusual.

When all of this has been considered, although the rational side of the mind must accept Washburn's general objections against them, Waale's arguments in favor of Cook's claims have a very disturbing element. They *do* fit the descriptions in Cook's narrative to an almost eerie extent. With Waale's explanations Cook's sketchy narrative suddenly makes sense, especially when followed on Washburn's photographs. They leave the reader asking the question again—and this time much more seriously: how could a man describe a route, over which all the experts say he had never been, with such accuracy? And how much likelihood is there that *any* route, even one far more convoluted than Hans Waale's, could match, *in sequence,* at every major point, a totally, or even partially, fictitious narrative?

Belmore Browne insisted that "Dr. Cook's ability along topographical lines, his ability to report and make statements on the country traversed, and the country that we were going into, was notoriously inaccurate."[54] Is it really credible that this same man could remember with such accuracy so many

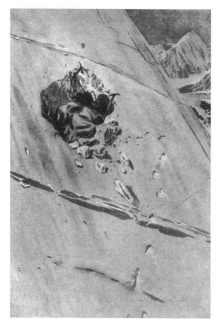

The icy ditch of terrors.

details of a route that he had seen just once three years before from 30 miles away through a pair of binoculars? This possibility seems incredibly remote.

But let us examine just a few points of Waale's reasoning to see whether the evidence for his route is sound.

The first has to do with two drawings made by Russell Porter for inclusion in Dr. Cook's book. One shows a snow house on a steep ridge and the other the "icy ditch" in which Dr. Cook said he and Barrill spent the terrible night of September 13, 1906.

In his desk copy of *To the Top of the Continent*, Cook made various corrections and comments. Of these two drawings the marginal notes say, "drawn from photograph." Without any evidence, Waale assumes that these "photographs" were "too poor to reproduce"; yet the drawings show distant topographical features in detail. In the "icy ditch" drawing, Waale identifies the background scene as a specific site on Peters Glacier and, using Washburn's photographs, proceeds to match it to a precise spot on his hypothetical route for Cook's climb. The evidence against Waale's conclusion here is overwhelming and exposes a sort of wishful thinking that undermines his entire structure.

Direct from Russell Porter comes a statement that he made these drawings not from photographs, but "conscientiously from minute word descriptions of the doctor himself."[55] This is only partially true. The background of the "icy ditch" drawing actually was drawn *from a photograph,* but not of the site Waale identifies.

The background comes from the view of Glacier Point in the distance of photograph 1 (see page 798). This was pointed out as long ago as 1910 by Claude Rusk:

> Having studied the last-described photograph, we are prepared to turn back to the thrilling scene [of the icy ditch]. . . . This picture is a modification of the one opposite page 239, previously mentioned [photograph 1]. In place of the cliffs at the left of the latter, we have the great, fanciful snow slope. But the position of the climbers would be nearly the same in the two, and, as a consequence they are at no point near the great mountain, no part of which appears in either picture.[56]

Photograph 1, detail.
"Icy Ditch" detail.

In a snow house on the northeast ridge, 12,000 feet.

The implications of Rusk's observations are grave. Because photograph 1 purports to be "the view from 16,000 feet," Porter's placing the climbers "from minute word descriptions by the doctor himself" on the slope with that same scene in the background suggests a deliberate attempt to deceive rather than an unintentional mistake, since the drawing implies that the photo was taken near this camping spot in the "icy ditch," which Cook placed at 14,300 feet in his narrative.

Likewise, the drawing of the snow igloo at 12,000 feet on the Northeast Ridge is also based on a photograph, this one among the unpublished views in the collection of the Frederick A. Cook Society (photograph 4). It shows the exact same scene the drawing does, including the ridges drawn at the right background and the pinnacle to the immediate right of the igloo's door. But it does not show the distant range, which apparently was intended to represent McKinley's summit in the distance. This area in the photograph is obscured by clouds. There is one other crucial difference: there is no igloo on the snow slope; it is perfectly blank.

Photograph 4. Glacier Point, cloudy shot. Photograph by Cook.

Photograph 5. Glacier Point, clear shot. Photograph by Cook.

That the distant range is a fantasy is shown by another unpublished photograph of the same scene (photograph 5), but with the sky clear of clouds. This reveals a completely different range close at hand. Even the odd-shaped pinnacle in the drawing is a deception, as in the cleared picture it proves to be only a portion of the side of one of the mountains in the distance. Perhaps Dr. Cook was giving the readers of *To the Top of the Continent* a hint when he wrote, "This supra-cloud world is a land of fantasy, of strange other-world illusions."

Like most of Cook's 1906 pictures, these photographs seem to have been taken in the tributary glacier's amphitheater containing Fake Peak. In fact, the rocks in the foreground and the odd-shaped pinnacle bear a striking resemblance to features in the drawing Barrill made of "Glasier Point" published in the *New York*

Globe along with his diary and make it a virtual certainty that photographs 4 and 5 were taken right next to Fake Peak and not on any 12,000-foot ridge. That Barrill was a very accurate sketch artist is shown by the close similarity of a sketch of the same place by Belmore Browne, who was a professional artist. Unfortunately, Browne's sketch does not include the crucial rocks and pinnacle of Barrill's drawing, which would be off the page to the right.

A second point deals with Waale's interpretation of Cook's McKinley diary. Waale places much emphasis on a drawing on page 52 of the diary. He asserts that this picture proves that Cook reached the Traleika Amphitheater. If he did, in Waale's words, "Barrill's affidavit lies," since it would put Cook over the East Buttress and on his way to Pioneer Ridge. But Waale's blind faith makes him see things at this point and makes other things on the very same page invisible.

The drawing on page 52 shows a sketch of a mountain and also another of a sharp peak, with various notes scribbled in the margins. Waale misinterprets Cook's problematic handwriting on the top of the page to read, "Sketch from top meter from N gl." He uses this and a vague description in Cook's book that he rose "out of an amphitheater with its crescentic walls

Barrill's drawing of "Glasier Point."

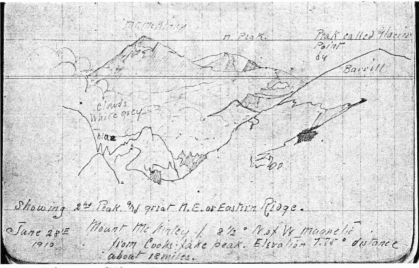

Browne's drawing of Glacier Point.

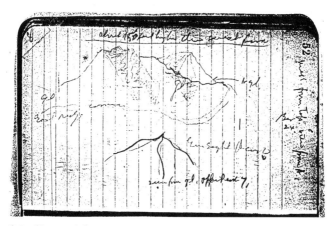

Page 52 of Cook's 1906 diary.

of granite . . . over tumbling blue-ribbed streams of ice" to show that Cook reached the Traleika Amphitheater and crossed Muldrow Glacier.

Actually, the note on page 52 of Cook's diary appears to read, "Mck. form. Top. view from N.," which when taken with the drawings could mean "McKinley formation. Top. View from North Glacier." Unlike Waale's interpretation, this makes sense. The sketch of the sharp peak, labeled "gun sight peak," also says, "seen from gl. opp. peak 7." "Peak 7" was what Cook called the last peak on Ruth Glacier before it turns southwest, and opposite it is the exact spot where Ed Barrill says he and Cook turned back. The "gun sight peak" is certainly the summit of McKinley, which as seen from this position looks exactly like the sketch by Cook and exactly as it was described by Rusk. And remember, Ed Barrill's diary entry for September 16 refers to the summit as "the gunsight." This is a unique view, since the summit looks rounded from other viewpoints.

The mountain at the top of Dr. Cook's sketch could be Mount Dan Beard, a mountain prominently visible from the glacier "opposite peak 7" and whose physical features correspond to elements of the sketch. More likely, it is the top of McKinley itself, viewed from farther up the North Fork of Ruth Glacier.

In correspondence with the author, McKinley guide Brian Okonek speculated that such a view of the summit could be had by climbing the ridges along the eastern margin of the North Fork—and Dr. Cook's note says "Mck. . . . top view from N." But Okonek could not be sure, he said, because the sketch was not very precise.[57]

Okonek's speculation seems to gain support from the affidavit of Walter Miller taken October 4, 1909, in which Miller stated he asked Barrill in May 1908 where they had actually been. He said Barrill replied, "We were on the first ridges, this side of the mountain." Further support comes from a sketch in Barrill's diary, which appeared on the pages between his entries for September 12 and September 13. (Permission to publish this drawing was denied.) According to Bradford Washburn, it appears to show, from left to right, the

Rooster Comb, the Northwest Fork of Ruth Glacier, the South Buttress of McKinley, Mount Dan Beard and a ramplike mountain to its right. These features indicate that it was made in the Ruth Ampitheater itself. The orientation of this drawing suggests it was made farther up the glacier, perhaps even on the North Fork itself, which runs between Mount Dan Beard and Explorer's Peak—the direction Belmore Browne took in his abortive attempt to scale the East Buttress in 1910. Browne tried this route because it seemed to him the natural approach to the ridge. Might Cook have felt the same? This point is slightly beyond that at which Barrill said they turned back. His own drawing seems to show that Barrill's affidavit, in this small respect at least, was not entirely truthful.

The "crescentic amphitheater" mentioned by Cook could describe the Great Basin of the Ruth as easily as Traleika Amphitheater, the identification Waale insists on. Witness Claude Rusk's description of it: "We had passed the last of the seven peaks, and had swung a short distance up a tributary glacier which turns abruptly around the seventh peak and sweeps southwesterly toward the southern face of Mt. McKinley. The head of Ruth Glacier is a great amphitheater, perhaps five miles in diameter, surrounded by high peaks from which come at least a dozen tributary feeders to form the main glacier."[58]

Another counterpoint to Waale's defense centers on a mismatch of altitudes, notes and observations in *To the Top of the Continent* to those in Cook's 1906 diary. Even Waale was puzzled by this. "No reference to McKinley Notes!" he exclaimed to Janet Vetter. "Just like they never existed – and no corrections or additions from them!! Mystery – Mystery – Mystery.

"All we have is Helene's remembrance [that] <u>Dr. Cook could not find them</u> – And Helene found them nearly 20 years after Dr. Cook's death! Astonishing."[59]

Waale could imagine no conceivable reason why Dr. Cook should not have used his 1906 notes in writing his finished narrative. Certainly, he still had them at the time he wrote the book in 1906–07. But Cook's book is not "practically a reproduction of the diary," as he later stated. In fact, the altitudes in Cook's long-lost diary match, in all meaningful ways, not his own 1908 book, but those in Barrill's diary *published only in October 1909*. It is this matching of the altitudes that conclusively proves that the two diaries are authentic and were both written in 1906.

That the altitudes in the original diaries do not match the ones given in Dr. Cook's finished narrative also suggests the reason for his failure to use the diary notes to write his book, of which Hans Waale could not, or would not, conceive. Perhaps after thinking over the climb a while, Cook decided that the diary, being nothing more than a fabrication anyway, was not plausible enough and so disregarded much of the specific information it contained to create a more convincing story for publication. As he told the persistent reporters in 1909, the record was "worked out better" in the book than in the diary. Surely, he did not envision ever having to produce the actual diary, and he certainly seemed reluctant when asked to do so.

If this supposition is true, it would have been logical to "lose" the diary permanently. Why, then, did he leave it to cause trouble later? We might as well ask why Peary kept the check James Ashton used to pay off Ed Barrill and the others. Perhaps Cook himself thought the diary *was* lost; it seems likely, at least, that he never personally had it in his possession after 1908.

Dr. Cook worked hurriedly on *To the Top of the Continent* and left for the North Pole without seeing it go to press. When Marie Cook's finances collapsed in the financial panic of fall 1907 and she was forced to sell the house on Bushwick Avenue, the household effects had to be put into storage, and Cook admitted in October 1909 that he had no idea where the diary was. With all that happened after his return from Copenhagen, he may have been too preoccupied to find it again, or perhaps did not want to. And Helene Vetter says she found it in "an unopened packing box" in New Jersey long after her father's death.

When Cook's descriptions of the summit of Mount McKinley and what he saw from it are examined, other features crop up that indicate that the final story of the climb was still evolving until it was set down in the May 1907 issue of *Harper's Monthly Magazine.*

Cook's critics have dismissed his description of edging "over the heaven-scraped granite to the top" because the summit is covered with ice. There are rocky outcrops, however, just northeast of a formation called Carter Horn at 20,220 feet and one a short distance down the domed snow ridge leading to Farthing Horn at 20,125 feet. In his published account in *Harper's,* Cook said he cached his record 200 to 300 feet below the summit in some rocks, which matches the position of the rocks near Farthing Horn. And strictly speaking, Cook's written description does not say that the top was bare rock, but that he edged "*over* the heaven-scraped granite *to* the top." But Cook then displayed his summit picture with Ed Barrill clearly standing on bare rock.

As we have seen, however, the picture is a fake, and what is more, Cook allegedly told Admiral Chester and others at the National Geographic Society dinner in 1906 that it was a fake and why. It is astonishing, then, to look at the account of Cook's first public description of the climb in Seattle on November 9, 1906, in which he was reported to have said:

> There were no rocks on the summit, only eternal snow, so no cairn
> could be built for the records that were left. The Stars and Stripes
> had been carried in a box in spite of all the difficulties of the ascent,
> and this box was placed against a granite cliff near the summit.[60]

Someone like Hans Waale might interpret this as a point in favor of Dr. Cook. But it would have been irrational for Cook to have changed the true description of the summit to fit his false picture had he genuinely accomplished the feat. And remember that in *Harper's* there was not only "heaven-scraped granite," but no mention of a box, nor is there one in Cook's diary, either. Instead, he speaks of depositing a metallic tube "in a protected nook" just below the summit. None of these details needed to be changed to fit anything, and they again suggest a still-evolving tale ungrounded in actual experience.

What of his figures that represent the height of Mount McKinley? Its true height is 20,320 feet. Cook came closer than Parker, who, not having reached the top, estimated it at 20,450 feet, and much closer than Hudson Stuck, the recognized conqueror who estimated 20,700. Cook is even closer than a 1908 survey that placed it at 20,467. How did Cook do better than the men who indisputably climbed or nearly climbed the mountain?

Cook's final figure of 20,390 feet was, as his speech before the Mazamas admitted, just about a perfect average of all the triangulations of the mountain that had been taken to that time, including the ones made by Russell Porter, which put it at 20,310 feet. It could have been just a very educated guess, and Dr. Cook published a lot of guesses: his diary says 20,400; the first report of his climb in the *New York Times* of October 3, 1906, says 22,800—probably a misprint; his lecture to the Mazamas says 20,300; his *Harper's* article says 20,391; his book says 20,390.

Cook's visual observations from the summit seem unimportant; having circumnavigated the entire McKinley group and looked back on the summit from all sides, he could easily assume what would be seen from it on a clear day. The only "scientific" observation Dr. Cook ever said he made was a round of angles taken with his prismatic compass, and these are not in his diary or his book, nor have they ever come to light.

Except for a considerable amount of hearsay evidence, which is interesting but useless to argue over, all the major arguments both for and against Cook's claim have now been considered. But as the endless arguments over the past 90 years have shown, it is a virtual impossibility to prove to everyone's satisfaction that Dr. Cook did or did not climb Mount McKinley. In the end, as Captain Hall said, people will believe what they want, regardless of all "evidence" or "logical argument." Readers are therefore welcome to their own opinion, as the author is entitled to his.

In Cook's favor, the ingenious analysis of Hans Waale and some of the descriptions by Barrill and Cook himself certainly give pause. But the route Waale proposes is far too difficult, based on the known powers of human endurance, even for a man like Cook, and the experiences of later climbers on the great mountain, who, even if not half so daring, would have had the advantages of a known route and the best modern equipment.

In the end, Cook himself failed to provide anything in his own support beyond his variously interpretable word, even to friends like Ted Leitzell, who had proven their dedication to his vindication unreservedly. He produced no photograph and, perhaps more important, no drawing of any feature above the place where Edward Barrill swore he turned back. He provided no verifiable scientific data that he could not have learned by observation or deduction. His equipment and timetable appear to have been inadequate, and his photographs are false. But the most convincing evidence of all comes from his own hand in the form of a diary that is more like Barrill's diary than his own finished narrative, and whose "mixup in dates," changes of dates, and two separate and different entries for the very same dates seem to support Barrill's contention that Cook's diary and his own were doctored and forged.

Cook's description of his climb of Mount McKinley appears to be a clever fake conceived and carried out by a most individual and brilliant mentality. If it is, then other questions arise—the deeper questions of human motives and the human mind. Belmore Browne said he believed Cook played on Barrill's sympathy to get him to go along with his version of events on Ruth Glacier. Barrill said that after John Dokkin, out of fear, turned back, Cook offered him $200 to "stay with him," but this does not necessarily imply a bribe, as some have assumed. Cook knew from Verhoeff's tragic experience that solo travel over an unknown glacier was close to suicidal.

Dr. Cook may have had every intention of attempting a climb of Mount McKinley, but an acute and resourceful observer is seldom a fool. When he reached Fake Peak on September 12, 1906, and looked out over the awesome spectacle of crags and peaks standing between him and his ambition, he knew the climb was impossible, given the time and equipment at his disposal.

Disston's change of mind had left him in a precarious financial position, as he later admitted, and if he didn't come back with the prize, he would not have enough money even to pay what he owed Barrill and the others. Ed Barrill, naturally, wanted his money and, even more naturally, didn't want to risk his life, especially since he would have gotten little of the credit for the mountain's conquest had they actually made it to the top. There was simply nothing in it for him, whether they succeeded or not, other than his paycheck.

In a different sense, Cook may have had this same thought, and anyway, no one would buy a book about another failed attempt. It is also possible that he considered the great mountain merely a stepping-stone to something bigger. There are indications, even in Dunn's narrative of the 1903 expedition, that he already was thinking about the North Pole. Perhaps he believed the renown produced by a conquest of the top of the continent would earn him the money to make a try for the top of the world.

That is exactly what Samuel Beecher thought:

> He was an excellent camp man, always good humored, ready
> to do his full share and more; courageous and simple, but not a
> man of good judgment in practical affairs. He seemed to have
> trouble whenever he had financial dealings. I think he claimed the
> ascent of McKinley, not so much through vanity and love of what
> glory might be in it, but because he hoped to establish a reputation
> that would give him backing for a polar expedition, which he
> always had in mind.[61]

If he could secure that backing, and if Peary did not come back with the Pole that fall, Cook would be in a position to take up the task, since Peary had loudly proclaimed before leaving in 1905 that this would be his "final attempt." Cook knew another attempt on the mountain the next year would be nearly impossible to finance, and even if it were not, another year would be lost to his competitors for the Pole, including Walter Wellman and his dirigible balloon, and to his own advancing age. And who could be sure that McKinley would yield even then?

Dr. Cook was already 41. If his youthful desire to accomplish "some splendid, sometimes spectacular aim" was to be fulfilled, if he did not want to be the "one still in the treadmill of physical labor," time was running out. Was it then that he decided to "prepare to enter an old world in a new way" and expand upon his real journey "with such power and glory as our genius for self-regeneration warrants"?

Standing on Fake Peak and looking upon that awe-inspiring landscape spread at his feet, crowned by the titanic uplift of McKinley that had defied all his efforts to scale its icy crest, he may have felt the frustrations he expressed five years later in *My Attainment of the Pole*. "I had no money. My work in exploration had netted me nothing, and all my professional income was soon spent. Unless you have felt the goading, devilish grind of poverty hindering you, dogging you, you cannot know the mental fury into which I was lashed."[62] And so, perhaps the result of that mental fury was his story of "The Conquest of Mount McKinley."

But why, if he chose this path, did he not take the time to provide the basis for a more convincing story? He and Barrill were alone on the glacier. They could have camped there another week or two without detection, living off the ptarmigan that Claude Rusk noticed were plentiful along the lateral moraines. Why, then, tell a story of climbing the formidable mountain in nine days and returning in four?

Perhaps it was simply that their supplies were exhausted. Cook talks about shooting ptarmigan and making a stew at Glacier Point, but his list of equipment includes no rifle. Then, too, John Dokkin had been instructed to start back to meet them in ten days, which put a limit on how long they might remain undetected if Dokkin could master his fear of crevasses. And if Dokkin did not come, the winter would, making their return difficult.

Or could it have been Dr. Cook's abundant self-confidence that gave the game away? Recall that in 1903 he repeatedly spoke of making the top in five days—5,000 feet a day—once he found a workable route. Wasn't that about what his final tale would average out to be?

But how did he think he would get away with it? Claude Rusk asked himself, "I wonder if Cook imagined that no other man with eyes and a camera would ever penetrate this region again?"[63] Certainly, Dr. Cook never imagined that anyone would so soon.

Cook knew from his studies of exploration that there is no place so lonely as the inaccessible place once attained. If the controversy over his polar claim had not sent expeditions swarming over Mount McKinley, it is highly unlikely that anyone would have visited the vicinity of Fake Peak for decades to come. By then its fragile rock face would have collapsed and with it all evidence of a fraudulent "summit" photograph. With no Barrill affidavit to guide them, there would have been no Parker-Browne to get there before it did. The true summit would have been left unseen, perhaps for decades, and by then the relentless forces of nature, as Archdeacon Stuck surmised, might have altered the summit, and none would have thought it unusual that Cook's picture no longer resembled it.

The record bears this out. After Stuck reached the summit, it would be another 19 years before another attempt at it would be made, and after Belmore Browne left it, Fake Peak would wait 28 years for another visitor. In fact, *every* man who *ever* visited Fake Peak for 50 years after 1906 went there to condemn or to vindicate Frederick A. Cook, and without Barrill's confession, the secret of that puny rock pile among the titans might have gone completely unnoticed forever. If we leave out Parker-Browne and the Mazamas, who also came because Cook had come, it would have been 48 years before another serious attempt would be made to climb McKinley from Ruth Glacier. By then, there might have been little thought devoted by anyone to the idea that Cook's climb had been a fake, just as there has been little devoted to questioning the authenticity of the Sourdough Climb.

The Sourdoughs: Charles McGonagall, Pete Anderson, Billy Taylor, Tom Lloyd (seated).

Some of that expedition's fantastic aspects have already been examined. In spite of them, it is now thoroughly accepted that two of its members reached the summit of the North Peak on April 3, 1910, and their exploit has been called the "most amazing accomplishment in mountaineering history." If true, it certainly deserves that appellation.

The case for their accomplishment is nearly parallel with Dr. Cook's, however. They brought back no photographic evidence from any high altitude on the mountain and no summit picture; neither did Cook. The account said to be taken from the diary of the expedition's leader embodies a narrative that, if not entirely false, contains highly questionable elements and suspicious inconsistencies; so did Cook's. They claimed to have accomplished a physical feat that seems beyond the powers of human endurance, despite little mountaineering experience and inadequate equipment; so did Cook. They provided no observations or physical evidence that can be verified as confirming their story; neither did Cook. They swore an affidavit that included material statements now believed utterly false; so did Cook. The details of the story of the climb were disputed by other members of the expedition's own party, some of whom said those details were untrue; so it was with Cook's. The record they said they left at the summit has never been recovered; neither has Cook's. No one has ever been able to duplicate their feat to this day; the same applies to Cook's.

Although the accuracy of Dr. Cook's descriptions has given hope to his supporters and baffled his critics, the Sourdoughs' descriptions are not even close. They said the summits were three miles apart; they are two miles apart, as Cook said they were. Billy Taylor, who claimed to have stood on the North Peak, said he didn't climb to the true summit on the South Peak because "it looked the same height" as the North Peak; actually it is more than 800 feet higher, a fact that has always been obvious to everyone else who has been there. Tom Lloyd estimated the height of the mountain at 21,000 feet, an estimate 610 feet worse than Dr. Cook's.

The Sourdoughs went the doctor one better, however. They claimed that because their pictures from their April climb did not come out, they ascended the mountain a *second* time, reaching the summit on May 17, 1910. They did this, they said, from the mountain's base in three days without camping once. No pictures from this even more marvelous second ascent have ever been seen, either.[64]

The sole piece of evidence by which the Sourdoughs' climb is credited is the Stuck party's sighting of their flagpole on the North Peak in 1913, when opposite it at 17,000 feet. Yet the year before, Parker and Browne had dismissed the Sourdoughs' claims when they failed to see any trace of it from the same position. Stuck explained this by saying, "It would never be seen with the naked eye save by those who were intently searching for it."[65] But Parker and Browne said they searched "each pinnacle" of the North Peak's summit ridge with their "powerful binoculars," and that the flagpole was not there.

Of their flagpole Tom Lloyd said, "We tramped it in, and filled in with rocks and built rocks up around it in a substantial, time-enduring monument to a height of fifteen inches above the surface, so that the flagpole is anchored in thirty inches of solid rock."[66]

In 1932 the Lindley-Liek expedition reached the North Peak by way of Denali Pass from 17,200 feet, becoming the first to climb both peaks. It took them 12 hours to cover the little more than 2,000 feet of elevation; the Sourdoughs claimed to have done 8,975 vertical feet and returned the same distance in 18 hours over a far more difficult route.

Albert Lindley looked down from the summit of the North Peak on the appallingly steep and icy route the Sourdoughs were reputed to have followed and thought if they had done what they claimed, "they must indeed have been giants."[67] As he sat there with Lindley, expedition member Grant Pearson thought about going down to the first rocks below the summit:

> We had intended to try to locate some sign of the fabulous flag-pole the sourdoughs had carried up to the last rocks on North Peak in 1910. "Perhaps we'll find a busted piece of the pole itself," I said, "or at least a piece of the rope they used to guy it, still lashed to a rock."
>
> But a storm wind began to howl down on us just after we started back; it was a long way to the last rocks where the pole might be, and we had lined out a different route back, avoiding rocks and sticking as much as possible to crusted snow. We left those relics of the expedition that started in McPhee's saloon for the next climbers.[68]

Yet no one has ever found a sliver of wood, a shred of guy rope or a trace of the "time-enduring monument" they erected that the newspapers said would be "plainly noticeable for centuries to come." Could Stuck have been mistaken? Certainly, a 14-foot flagpole would not be easy to spot from several miles off, even with binoculars.[69] Or did he lie to make the conquest of McKinley "all Alaskan"? After all, he had no designs on the North Peak, so perhaps he was willing to confirm their incredible story of scaling it. But he denied them the South, even though they said they had climbed it twice, thereby reserving for himself the glory of being first to ascend the higher of McKinley's two peaks. Harry Karstens's and Walter Harper's diaries say they saw the flagpole too . . . perhaps.[70]

Francis Farquhar, a longtime student of the early climbs, noted the difference in the reports of Parker-Browne and Stuck but excused it: "There are various explanations for the failure of the 1912 party to see the pole; but, after all, failure to see something is not conclusive proof that it isn't there, and the positive testimony of Karstens and Stuck that they saw it a year later must prevail.

"But even without this testimony the statements of the men themselves, leaving Lloyd out of the picture, should be sufficient."[71]

Why this is so, since these same men whose word "should be sufficient" swore to a false affidavit that all of them, including Tom Lloyd, had stood at the summit of the North Peak, Farquhar does not explain.

Considering the dubious aspects of the Sourdoughs' story and the absence of hard evidence—not even Lloyd's original diary has ever been seen—it is incredible that their story has been accepted without serious question. And though their unsupported claim to have scaled the South Peak is universally rejected as a lie, their equally unsupported conquest of the North Peak—a far more difficult climb—is held up as heroic by the same men who have sought to erase every trace of the indisputable accomplishments of Frederick Cook around Mount McKinley because they say *he* told the very same lie.

In private correspondence, Bradford Washburn called Cook "an intrepid explorer and a very great photographer," and his 1903 circling of the McKinley

Group "one of the most daring and extraordinary feats in the history of Alaskan exploration." He said he felt "infinite admiration for his early exploration of Mt. McKinley" and rated Cook's reaching even the point where his photographs on Ruth Glacier ran out in 1906 as "an almost equally amazing feat of courage and fortitude."[72] Although nothing like this has yet appeared in his published assessments of the doctor, it is all still true.

No history of the great Alaskan mountain can be complete without acknowledging Frederick Cook's real explorations and discoveries as well as mentioning his doubtful claims. But instead of any acknowledgment, there has been a systematic attempt to remove all evidence from Alaska's maps that the doctor ever passed that way.

Claude Rusk, even as he concluded that Cook's claim to the summit was false, anticipated this and argued eloquently against it:

> Undoubtedly there will be an effort to change the names bestowed by Dr. Cook. I fail to understand by what reasoning such a course is justifiable. He discovered the things that he named. We have no right to say that because he finally turned out to be a faker, he has no right to the fruits of his legitimate explorations. His offense has been very great; but who can say that his punishment has not been even greater? To my mind it would be as reasonable and as just to attempt to change the names of Mt. Hood, Mt. Rainier and Puget Sound because of some recently discovered shortcoming in the life of Vancouver.[73]

But changed they were. In Alaska today there is a Mount Tittman, a Mount Gannett and a Port Chester. There is a Mount Grosvenor, a Bartlett Island and even a Peary Creek. But all that remains of the pioneer explorer of the Alaska Range, Frederick Albert Cook, is a huge Alaskan glacier named after a little girl in Brooklyn and, ironically, a mountain beside that glacier named Barrille.

We have seen a host of characters step upon that grandiose stage of Ruth Glacier, and not one has left it with his integrity intact but Claude E. Rusk. He alone kept clear of all partisanship and maintained a balanced perspective.

When Rusk wrote to Cook asking to join the expedition that the doctor proposed to prove his claims after the release of the Barrill affidavit, he closed by telling him, "I might add that, from the first, I have believed in you, and take no stock in those who are trying to rob you of the glory of your achievements."[74] It was, no doubt, with much disappointment that he came to the realization that his belief had been misplaced and that the glory of Dr. Cook's achievements did not include standing atop Mount McKinley. But Claude Rusk was one of those rare individuals, in an all-too-common story of human failings, who could face the truth and retain compassion.

As we turn from Mount McKinley, we could do no better than to listen to the words of Claude Rusk:

And what of Dr. Cook? During my sojourn in Alaska, I talked with many men concerning him. All—with a single exception—were united in the belief that he did not reach the top of Mt. McKinley. Of his courage and his resolution there can be no doubt. He is described as absolutely fearless. He was also considered as always willing to do his share and as an all-round good fellow to be out with. Had he been content to rest his laurels upon the things he had actually accomplished—to say nothing of the possibilities of the future—his fame would have been secure. His explorations around Mt. McKinley were extensive. They were of interest and of value to the world. He discovered a practicable route to the great mountain from the southeast side. Had he persevered, he doubtless would have reached the summit on some future expedition. He was the first to demonstrate the possibility of launch navigation up the Susitna and the Chulitna. That one trip alone—when with a single companion he braved the awful solitude of Ruth Glacier and penetrated the wild, crag-guarded region near the foot of McKinley—should have made him famous. But the Devil took him up onto an exceeding high mount and showed him the glories of the icy alpine world and—the doctor fell. Let us draw the mantle of charity around him and believe, if we can, that there is a thread of insanity running through the woof of his brilliant mind.[75]

WHAT THE NORTH POLE LOOKS LIKE ACCORDING TO DR. FREDERICK A. COOK

There can be no conquest to the man who dwells in the narrow and small environment of a groveling life, and there can be no vision to the man the horizon of whose vision is limited by the bounds of self.

— found among the papers of
Matthew A. Henson

CHAPTER 29

Return to the Pole

WHEN DR. COOK WENT TO ALASKA IN 1906, HE HAD EVERY INTENTION OF actually climbing Mount McKinley. His decision to fake the climb, if that supposition is correct, came only when he was faced with financial embarrassment. And if McKinley was only the means to try for the "End of North," then he probably had every intention of reaching the Pole if given a chance.

When he got that chance from John R. Bradley, he may have reasoned that the mountain had served its purpose, and whatever wrong was done in Alaska would be put right when he reached the top of the world. There is no doubt that the doctor believed it could be done. In 1900 he wrote, "To the man who understands polar conditions and is willing to bunk on snow and feed on frozen meat for three months or three years . . . there is absolutely nothing impossible in crossing this five or ten degrees of latitude."[1]

In 1902 Cook told the *Brooklyn Daily Eagle* that there was less danger to be faced in the Arctic than in New York City and that "the food question is really after all the cul de sac that closes up the way to the Pole. . . . If any way can be suggested whereby the food question can be solved the difficulty of reaching the Pole would be reduced to a minimum."[2] If Cook sincerely believed he was the man who could solve that problem, then leaping to conclusions based on Mount McKinley is neither logical nor just. Dr. Cook's Bradley Arctic Expedition of 1907–09 must be judged on its own merits, whatever may have happened in Alaska.

Once stripped of the complexity that accumulated as his dispute with Peary deepened, there are really only a few questions to consider. Did Dr. Cook reach the North Pole in 1908? If the answer is yes, then all is settled. But if it is no, other questions arise: was his expedition a premeditated fraud or a serious attempt? If he made a serious attempt, is it possible that Cook did not reach the Pole but believed that he had? If he was mistaken, just where did he go instead? Though the questions are few, there is much to consider.

PEARY'S PLAN

John Bradley's announcement that Cook had stayed in Greenland to try for the Pole came as a complete surprise to Peary. But his friends took comfort in thinking that Cook, on his first attempt, with little experience and no equipment, had not the slightest possibility of getting even close to the goal that had eluded Peary during 14 years in the Arctic, the last six with the almost unlimited resources of the Peary Arctic Club at his disposal. Peary himself thought, "The Almighty has not made the man yet who can sledge from the 79° parallel to the pole.

"As to Dr. Cook's proposed route it is the merest rot & should he even (which I doubt) reach the northern extremity of Nansen strait . . . he will then be as far from the Pole [as] Cagni when he started. . . ."[3] To Peary's friends, Cook's expedition seemed a "joke," and if Cook did claim the Pole, it would be something worse—a conscious and premeditated fraud.

Then and there, in 1908, plans were laid to discredit Cook should he dare return claiming success in a venture Peary was sure was an impossibility. The preexistence of these plans is shown in the statements of Herbert L. Bridgman and Jo Peary about Cook's claim in the first days of September 1909, before Peary emerged from the Arctic. They anticipated each line of attack on Cook's credibility that Peary and his allies pursued in the last four months of 1909, until it dissolved in the wake of the Copenhagen decision.

Peary's plan to skewer his rival's claim had six prongs: 1, that Cook was not an honorable man, having acted dishonorably in usurping Peary's plans, methods, Eskimos and dogs; 2, that he had neither the equipment nor the experience to carry off such a feat; 3, that he must produce the record left by Peary at Cape Thomas Hubbard in 1906 to prove he got that far; 4, that the Eskimos' account of the journey would contradict Cook's story; 5, that Cook had no ability with navigational instruments and that his observations would fail to prove he had reached the Pole; and 6, that there were credible doubts about Cook's Mount McKinley climb and therefore was precedence for his making fraudulent claims. Every single piece of "evidence" brought against Cook in 1909 from any source fell into one of these six categories. The last has already been dealt with and, as we have seen, had merit, but what of the remaining five?

Polar Etiquette

Even more than in the case of Sverdrup, Peary's cries of a violation of "polar etiquette" by Dr. Cook were nonsense, since Cook took his inspiration from Sverdrup, not Peary. That Cook kept his plans close to the vest indicates that he had learned the lesson in Peary's treatment of his rivals, and he may have decided that Sverdrup's route across Ellesmere Land to his jumping-off point would minimize any moral or physical conflict with Peary, as well as take advantage of the gamelands Sverdrup had discovered.

But nonsense, too, was Cook's insistence that the polar trip was only a contingency plan in case everything was found to be propitious. "We prepared our plans quietly and thoroughly," said John Bradley, and Cook's polar expedition gives every indication of having been thought out down to the last detail long before he arrived at Annoatok.

In October 1907, two years before Cook returned, Bradley accurately described Cook's program as he later claimed to have carried it out in almost every respect, including the exact route he followed. He even mentioned the "house sledges" Cook planned to live in along the way—something Dr. Cook himself never referred to in any of his own accounts of the trip.[4] And in an interview that appeared in the *New York Herald* on September 2, 1909, Bradley even indicated Cook expected to be away two years when he said, "I fully expected he would return this fall, according to the plans."

As they had been in Alaska, Cook's plans were firmly grounded in the experiences of his predecessors, with a visionary approach to what could not be known in advance. He even planned for a contingency that neither he nor Bradley ever mentioned—that Peary might arrive in north Greenland in 1907. It is evident from the Bradley interviews that the two men had considered this possibility, had also weighed the consequences if Peary did not get away that summer, and that the gambler rather enjoyed the thought that they might beat the "expert" at his own game. "Perhaps he'll have the satisfaction of telling Peary he has found the Pole," Bradley said of Cook.[5]

Bob Bartlett admitted he had told the doctor "everything" about Peary's plans, so Cook probably knew the *Roosevelt* would not be ready in time. Then Peary wrote to Sam Bartlett in Brigus on June 30, 1907, that he had decided to postpone the expedition until 1908 but would still send the *Roosevelt* on a "flying trip" to Etah in August to deposit a load of coal.[6] The *Bradley* sailed July 3. It is reasonable to assume that by then Sam Bartlett may have passed this information to Moses Bartlett, the *Bradley*'s captain, and that it became known to Bradley and Cook through him.

It is also probable that Cook chose Annoatok as his winter quarters instead of Etah to avoid being accused of occupying Peary's traditional northern base. The choice also placed him out of the way, just in case Peary did arrive at Etah. But when the *Roosevelt* did not appear by the end of August, Cook could be sure she had not sailed, and it will be noticed that in his winter diary he never considered the possibility that the ship wreckage that so concerned him could have been part of the *Roosevelt*.

Equipment and Experience

The contention that Cook was not properly equipped for a try at the Pole cannot be supported from contemporary evidence. Several independent eyewitnesses testified that the *Bradley* was crammed to the hatches with appropriate supplies for a prolonged polar journey.[7]

A look at the inventory of goods listed by John R. Bradley in his interviews and by Cook in his winter diary should convince anyone that he was luxuriously fitted out for the winter of 1907. That Murphy, Pritchard and Whitney lived off his supplies a second winter further testifies to the adequacy of his provisions. Cook's supplies at Annoatok were also supplemented with a cache of two dory loads of dry stores, food and kerosene, which Moses Bartlett landed at Etah.[8] John R. Bradley was just not the sort to go second class or leave short the one whom he was betting on winning the big prize and, in Peary's words, "writing his name where it would endure until the scroll of the Heavens withers" as the man who backed the discoverer of the North Pole.

The one necessary item in short supply was pemmican. The *Bradley* carried only 200 pounds of it, perhaps because there was no time to have large quantities of this specialty item prepared commercially, or perhaps by design, to allay suspicions of Cook's intention to essay the Pole, which the ordering of tons of pemmican might have aroused in the Peary camp. But whatever the reason, the making of his own pemmican gave Cook's expedition an advantage over every other that ever attempted to reach the Pole by dogsledge.

Tainted pemmican had incapacitated Astrup in 1894, as well as Anthony Fiala on Ziegler's 1903 expedition. The stuff produced by Armour for the 1908 Peary expedition included tacks, ground glass and caustic soda.[9] And MacMillan's pemmican was so full of salt that it almost aborted his attempt to locate Crocker Land in 1914.

In 1937 David Haig-Thomas, a British explorer whose sledge trips took him over a portion of Cook's route, reported that the Eskimos thought pemmican was bad for dogs, as they had difficulty digesting the rich concoction. They recommended half-dried walrus meat instead. Haig-Thomas thought he knew what would be ideal. "A future expedition might make its own pemmican of ground dry walrus meat mixed with different sorts of blubber: seal fat for the cold weather, and walrus blubber for the warm weather," he suggested.[10] Little did he know that his idea had been anticipated exactly 30 years before in Cook's box house at Annoatok.

Annoatok was, indeed, very far south for a winter base, but the route Cook chose from it allowed him to feed his dogs exclusively on fresh meat, their ideal diet, as well as to conserve his sledge supplies for the time when there would be no more game.

Other dogsledge expeditions, before and since, have learned that when dogs have not been worked over the winter, some invariably play out in the first few days of hauling heavy sledges. The trek across Ellesmere Land gave the dogs a hard test in the field for four weeks before venturing onto the polar sea, putting them in top condition, and Cook could be sure of selecting the best 26 for the arduous journey still before him. After such a trip, when he finally jumped off for the Pole, the attrition experienced by other expeditions would have been minimized.

Arguments like George Kennan's that Cook's sledge rations were insufficient for an 80-day unsupported round-trip to the Pole ignore the nearly parallel feat of travel and food economy in Nansen's 1895 attempt from the *Fram*. And all the arguments that the amount of food Cook included in his sledge loads was inadequate have miscalculated. In *Has the North Pole Been Discovered?* Captain Hall exhaustively compared Cook's food supply with that of Nansen and reasonably concluded that there was nothing impossible about any aspect of Cook's story in regard to food.[11]

That epic journey of Nansen's, in fact, is the only reliable yardstick by which to measure other early claims of long, unresupplied journeys over the polar sea, all others being doubtful in some respect. It alone is fully documented with a complete narrative journal, adequate and consistent scientific observations and independently confirmed by two fully literate witnesses, though there were no shared sextant observations for position. It could even be argued that the narrative of Nansen's polar adventures was a ready-made sourcebook for anyone who might be tempted to fraudulently represent a journey beyond his own "farthest north" to the very Pole itself.

When considering Peary's argument that Cook had no experience on the polar sea ice and therefore could not have done what he said he did, one has only to remember that Nansen and Johansen had none whatever to dismiss it. Cook, at least, had done some traveling on the antarctic pack.

Having thoroughly digested Nansen's book, Cook knew what was required of the prospective polar traveler. "The man who succeeds in reaching the North Pole," he said, "must be one who, by habit and occupation, has given the greatest possible care to the minor details of daily life and work. One who is certain to make sure of big things, but neglects little ones, will quickly fail in his effort. . . . It is a path full of obstacles, hardships and difficult, dogged work, with no pleasures except those which are mingled with a thousand little incidents as the elements of nature and the failings of man are overcome. . . . It will be very complex with little details."[12]

Anthony Fiala thought Cook had a better grasp of the complexities of arctic equipment than Peary did,[13] and Professor Steensby, the anthropologist who met Cook aboard the *Hans Egede,* perceived a far more important difference between the two men. Peary, he said, "travelled in the most old-fashioned manner, and would bring his own civilization with him," and that was why he made so many unsuccessful attempts. But "the more far-seeing Cook," Steensby said, "who went in apprenticeship to . . . the poor, 'savage' polar Eskimos," succeeded on the first attempt.[14] This statement may seem surprising, since Peary attributed his ability to reach the Pole almost solely to experience that had caused him to adopt the techniques of the Polar Eskimos. But a careful study of his expeditions shows that Professor Steensby was correct. Peary was very selective about what he adopted from the Eskimos, and then it was only out of necessity.

True, Peary wore Eskimo attire in the field, but never in the summer while around camp. Even so, in 1899 Peary suffered the loss of seven of his toes—a severe injury—though no one who was with him at the time suffered any injury at all. Perhaps his much vaunted experience for once played him false. Or could he have overlooked one of those "little details" that he had considered unimportant, like changing the moisture-absorbing grass in his kamiks every day?

Peary, in his writings, often expressed his feelings of superiority to the Eskimos and contempt for their ways. "I had come to regard them," he said in *The North Pole,* "with a kindly and personal interest, which any man must feel with regard to the members of any inferior race." He detested sleeping in igloos, saying that they were "an offense to every civilized sense" and he "tried to forget the experience as soon as possible." He always lived in a "civilized" house while in the Arctic until 1902, and on his last two expeditions he spent most of his time in his warm cabin on the *Roosevelt*, with electric light and steam heat, furnished and equipped with a player piano, a bathtub, a cellarette and a big sign at the door reading Positively No Admittance, where he enjoyed whatever other pleasures were available. He never ate blubber or raw meat if he could help it, and he always had a good supply of wine and liquor on hand. There is no evidence that he was ever a good dog driver, and after he lost his toes, he never drove dogs at all.

He may have been the stuff of legends to his collegiate assistants in 1909, but in truth, the field abilities of the physically fit man who in 1895, at the age of 39, had said he was too old for arctic work were severely diminished by his physical incapacities after 1899. By the time of his last attempt at the Pole, ten years later at 52, those abilities were themselves the stuff of legends— literally—and as Henson attested, he was not much more than a load of freight.

Dr. Cook also loved the civilization of his box house. Neither did he drive dogs, leaving that to the Eskimos, and he also probably rode whenever he could—as the Eskimos always did. But he was far more adaptable than Peary. He never tried to forget *any* experience, no matter how "offensive," and when in the field, he adopted the Eskimo lifestyle completely—and even enjoyed it. When he returned to Annoatok in 1909, only by the way he walked could even an Eskimo discern that he was not one of them.

As already established, Cook's physical abilities cannot be doubted. He also had the additional advantages of being nine years younger and having none of Peary's physical impairments.

In his choice of equipment, Cook was ready to take the best ideas from others, but often the best ideas proved to be his own. He also tested everything and rejected what did not work, like his louvered socks and house-sleds. In response to the failure of his blue-lensed glasses at McKinley, he invented his yellow ones. With their vented visors to keep them from fogging, they were the forerunners of today's modern ski goggles. Amundsen used them without modification on his trip to the South Pole, just as he used Cook's tent design and sledges that were virtually copies of the pattern adopted by the doctor for his North Pole journey—a McClintock-style sledge with a light elastic framework of hickory.

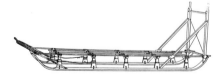

McClintock-style sledge, used by Cook.

Peary bragged about his "clipper-built" sledges, and though he credited them with his ultimate success, these 95-pound monstrosities began to go to pieces on the very first day out.[15] Only five of the original 28 survived any part of the trip intact, and 14 were totally destroyed; of the five he took to the Pole, all had been rebuilt from the shards of others.

Compare this record with that of the sledges made by Theodore Cook to his brother's specifications. Wilfred Grenfell used them exclusively in his missionary work in Labrador and related that an associate had used one to travel more than 2,000 miles one winter without a single mishap. Theodore Cook also made all the sledges for the Ziegler expeditions. These sleds weighed an average of 85 pounds and carried loads of about 600 pounds, so they were a good deal heavier than his brother's 52-pound polar sledges. But in his letters to Peary, Theodore Cook rated his 44-pound sledge at 800 pounds' capacity. Amundsen's sledges weighed 53 pounds and hauled loads of 880 pounds.

Anthony Fiala said that during two years' use, none of the Cook sledges broke down through a fault of design, and on his brief trip into the extremely rough ice north of Franz Joseph Land, they proved fully up to the task. Though their drawbars were often bent flat in a collision, the elastic hickory always jumped back to its original shape without breaking, causing one of Fiala's assistants to exclaim, "Mr. Fiala, these sledges are made of India rubber!"[16]

Ironically, Peary turned down T.A. Cook's design on sight and, most telling, even declined purchase of Cook's superior lumber, opting instead to save a few pennies by using brittle oak. Peary himself, in his polar diary, admitted the shortcomings of his sledges by noting: "Modifications in 'Peary' type sledge. <u>All Hickory.</u>"[17]

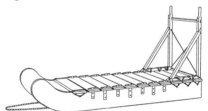

Eskimo-style sledge, used by Peary.

Peary's 1909 sledges were based on the traditional native model, which was not designed for travel over sea ice, since the Eskimos feared it greatly. That Peary took these sledges on his most important trip untried is amazing; he had used only native-type sledges in 1906. It is also puzzling that Peary took no boat, since he was nearly prevented from returning in 1906 by open water. Nansen and Johansen owed their lives to the kayaks they laboriously hauled; Cagni also carried kayaks, and Baldwin and Fiala both carried specially designed canoes. And as early as 1894, Dr. Cook had advanced the idea he used in 1908—a skin covering that could turn a sledge into a boat for crossing leads.[18]

Why didn't Peary ever build on his highly touted experience? Perhaps he had much less experience on sea ice than he claimed. His attempt at the Pole in 1900 was absolutely negligible, making a mere 12 miles. The 1902 attempt claimed a northing of 87 miles and has never been seriously questioned. But considering that Peary still had painful and vulnerable stubs left of his toes that required an operation immediately after his return from the Arctic that fall, and also a hernia, which Dr. Dedrick described as "of a nature easily strangulated and inflamed," for which he had no truss, there is room for doubt of its authenticity. Peary's pattern of exaggerated claims, both before and after 1902, make it possible that Peary's fear of Dedrick's revealing "medical secrets" lay in his realization that if his true physical condition were known, even his modest claim of 1902 would be very difficult to credit.

Captain Hall and J. Gordon Hayes have made strong cases that the 1906 "Farthest North" was a hoax, and evidence among the Peary papers tends to confirm their belief that Peary never came near the Italian record of 1900, which itself is highly doubtful. Peary gave no estimate of distances traveled for 28 of the 34 days. He apparently doubted the readings his sextant indicated because it had been damaged. The original diary has disappeared, but the typed transcript of it stops the day before he reached "Farthest North," at a position 36 miles away from his claim of 87°6'—too far to enable him to reach it in a single day.[19]

Peary's advocates have often said that only he could induce Eskimos to follow him over the dreaded sea ice to the Pole, and that this stemmed from their great love for *Pearyaksoah.* Although Peary recognized the Eskimos as indispensable, telling MacMillan, "Never let your eskimos get away from you," he refused to acknowledge their actual superiority on their own ice. He depended on the stick of intimidation to gain their allegiance, combined with the carrot of a monopoly on the trade goods they desired.

MacMillan admitted that despite more than 20 years of association with them, "There was [not] even a deep feeling of friendship between [Peary] and a single member of the Smith Sound tribe, but he was certainly admired and deeply respected by every man, woman, and child, even to the point of fear."[20] That they did follow him and even respected him is a tribute not to Peary's winning ways but to a real terror of the man, whom some Eskimos were still calling "the great tormentor" as late as the 1950s.

Perhaps the greatest advantages Cook had over Peary were his own greatest assets—his pleasing personality and ability to understand human nature. Cook's winter diary reveals his firm grasp of the Eskimo mentality and why they were willing to go with him without threats. They followed Cook partly because they genuinely liked him, but most of all because he promised to show them what must have been an Eskimo's vision of heaven—the musk ox lands to the west. "Tell them that the North Pole is the throne of the hunting god," Cook said, "and that there are plenty of walrus and polar bear there and wild sea fowl to be shot there. Tell them anything that promises a picnic and they are all agog."[21]

Cook needed the help of the Eskimos, but why did he not take Rudolph Franke with him on his journey as he promised? Cook detractors have seen in the sending back of his only white companion an act parallel to his attempt to "get rid of witnesses" at Mount McKinley. There is merit in this belief, based on what Franke would innocently reveal about Cook's expedition later. He would have betrayed any attempt to concoct a fraudulent polar journey, but as before the seemingly easy answer is probably wrong.

John R. Bradley reported that Cook wanted a white man to stay the winter "mostly for the companionship," and also that Cook never planned to take this companion to the Pole: "From the Polar sea there will be only two sturdy young eskimos and their dogs," Bradley said in 1907.[22]

Anthony Fiala, musing on his own inability to get more than ten miles toward the Pole, blamed it on his failure to find a test that would identify men suitable to the task and all its hardships. In choosing two Eskimos, Cook needed no such test. He knew that the hardships of a polar journey were just part of their ordinary life, and despite his warm affection for Franke, he based his decision on cold reality. "I knew no white man could match the Eskimo adaptability to this kind of task," he said. "Francke could have been small help to me and might have been a serious handicap, not through any personal deficiency of his, but through his inevitable racial unfitness for this terrible task."[23]

This is a reverse twist on why Peary said he did not send Matt Henson back and take Bob Bartlett to the Pole. He said of Henson: "He had not, as a racial inheritance, the daring and initiative of Bartlett, or Marvin, MacMillan, or Borup. I owed it to him not to subject him to dangers and responsibilities with which he was temperamentally unfit to face."[24]

That Franke became so despondent at having to turn back that he neglected his physical well-being might indicate his mental unfitness for a polar journey. But there is actual evidence that Franke would not have performed well in the field. This comes from his own ill-fated 1914 attempt to visit Bradley Land, which cost the life of his friend Arthur Haark.[25] Franke's book and other writings mark him as a naive dreamer who, although good-hearted and honest, was not well suited to the hardships and complexities of arctic exploration.

Moreover, taking Franke would have meant *not* taking one of the Eskimos. For psychological reasons, two Eskimos were necessary to keep each other company, and Cook knew that three was the most practical traveling unit. Three men could just handle a 700-pound sledge over rough spots, and the standard snow igloo was designed for three men, as was Cook's silk tent. Franke, as a fourth man, could have added nothing to the efficiency of the party and would have required just that much more food and weight on a trip where every extra ounce would tell.

Cook, in all his writings about his polar journey, emphasized the advantages of traveling with Eskimos. This is certainly so on land ice or the ice foot along shore. But what of taking Eskimos onto the treacherous moving pack ice of the Arctic Ocean where they never ventured themselves if they could help it? Cook hadn't always considered this good strategy. "Lieutenant Peary has been handicapped in my opinion more or less by having only natives with him," he told the *Daily Eagle*'s reporter in 1902. "Native guides are good in their place, but they cannot be relied on for serious adventure. . . . You can set this down as incontestably true, that no one white man, accompanied only by natives will ever reach the Pole."[26]

Did Cook still have this startling view in 1908, or had he by then changed his mind? If so, what made him change it, since he had no further experience with Eskimos between 1902 and 1907? Yet in 1909, he credited them fully in

Etukishuk and Ahwelah.

his success. It might be surmised that his daily observations of them over that winter at Annoatok convinced him of their superiority as traveling companions—if they could be persuaded to go onto the polar pack. But Bradley said in 1907 that it was Cook's plan to take only two Eskimos with him *from the start.*

Since Peary also relied on natives to get him to the Pole, Peary's supporters did not attack their general reliability, but they tried to characterize Cook's companions as "mere boys" and therefore poor choices for such a journey. But an Eskimo at 19 is no boy; he knows all the skills needed to survive. Only someone with Peary's arrogance could say that he taught an Eskimo anything about traveling over ice. What's more, Peary had thought enough of Etukishuk, the "mere boy" of 1909, to take him over the sea ice all the way to the "Big Lead" three years before—at age 16, if his age has been recorded correctly.[27]

The subsequent histories of Cook's Eskimo companions show that his judgment of their abilities was very accurate. Just after Cook left for Upernavik, Harry Whitney took the two men hunting in Ellesmere Land and found both highly capable and able to "get their sledges over the ice faster than any other drivers, pushing, lifting and jumping them."[28] Both became legendary hunters. Donald MacMillan praised Etukishuk as the finest Eskimo in the whole tribe, and Edward Shackleton called Ahwelah the foremost Eskimo in Nerke.

On the basis of his winter diary, the preparations made, the kinds and quantity of food and equipment taken, the condition of his dogs and his choice of companions, there is every indication that Cook's expedition was superbly equipped, fully intended to attempt the Pole, and contrary to Peary's second objection, nothing indicates it lacked any requirement to do so but a favorable chance.

Anthony Fiala said of this uncontrollable factor, "The element we call Chance has much to do in the giving of success or failure, but the human elements of endurance and courage are the most important of all. . . . The Polar explorer has a hard, cold, and lonely way in which patience, more patience, and still more patience seem to be the cardinal requirements."[29] And as for those human elements and that requirement, we have already seen that Frederick Cook possessed them in abundance.

The Missing Record

The third prong of Peary's plan to discredit Cook can be quickly dispatched. Even MacMillan had difficulty locating Peary's cairn, though he made a deliberate effort to do so. Cook's failure to retrieve its record should not raise any suspicion. He could not afford to waste time in getting away for the Pole. And everyone, including Peary, has conceded that Cook really did reach the tip of Axel Heiberg Land.

Very odd, however, is the fact that Cook failed to leave a cairn of his own at Cape Thomas Hubbard or at any place along his return route, especially at his point of return to land from the Pole, announcing his triumph. Though this should have raised questions, it was never mentioned by Peary.

If Cook's intent was to make a fraudulent claim, he may have left no cairns because the requisite message would have to be dated. Cook would not have wanted to be tied, as Peary's story tied him, to an inadequate time schedule or one that might limit the possibilities of any later fictitious story he might choose to tell.

Eskimo Evidence

Peary's fourth prong of attack, his long-awaited evidence against Cook, consisted of the Eskimos' account of where the doctor had gone after he sent Franke back to Annoatok. Not only did their initial account have little immediate impact, but the subsequent conflicting versions of what they said and the biased witnesses who reported their statements largely destroyed its value as evidence.[30] Rasmussen alone, who understood the Eskimo language well, gave two diametrically opposed stories from the tribe: the first, before the Cook proofs went to Copenhagen, refuted Peary's report of what the Eskimos said without Rasmussen's ever having seen it, and the second, after the Copenhagen decision, corroborated Peary's account.

Peary never learned even the pidgin-Eskimo that Inuit speak before a qallunnat. Only Matt Henson could have understood what the Eskimos said, and Peary seemed fearful that "Henson's version" of the Eskimo story would get out. Peary also gave specific instructions to Bridgman that no member of the expedition should comment on the report once it was published: "The statement is absolutely true, nothing to be added or taken from it," he telegraphed.[31] This seems to indicate that there *was* something false or something more in the Eskimos' report.

Remember, Henson said that the Eskimos had initially told him they had been to the Pole but changed their story under questioning, at first repeating what Cook had told them but then, as is the Eskimo habit, changing it when they perceived this was not what Henson or Peary wanted to hear.

Dr. Goodsell, who requested an interview with Cook's two companions in private, was refused this privilege. Peary can be forgiven, perhaps, after Cook, Vincent and Dedrick, if he did not trust his doctor. Goodsell alone among the expedition's major members did not sign the statement attesting to the truth of the Eskimos' story that appeared in the *New York Times*. Instead, he left the two pages blank in his diary where he had hoped to record his Eskimo interview, "as a mute white protest."[32]

Oddly, Peary appears never to have asked the Eskimos the direct question "Did Dr. Cook say he reached the Big Nail?" Perhaps they told him what they had been instructed to tell—that Cook went beyond Peary's "Farthest North," or as they told Billy Pritchard, that they had gone "way, way, north," but Peary wanted to play it down until he definitely heard that Cook was claiming the Pole. He had already heard rumors at Nerke, but there is every indication that Peary did not receive definite news of Cook's claim until he read Captain Adams's letter on August 25. Peary then put on full steam for the nearest telegraph station.

A New Basis for Judgment

Though Peary declared Cook's journey a fake from the start, Peary and his allies never possessed any hard evidence that Cook had not done as he said. All of the evidence they advanced was circumstantial, at best, and aimed at undermining Cook's credibility. Peary was certain that Cook lacked the scientific knowledge necessary to locate the North Pole. But the repeated mathematical analyses by various astronomers "proving" that Cook, based on the evidence he presented in his narrative, could not have been where he said he was, if they had any validity, went over the heads of most of their intended audience. Even the down-to-earth testimony of Captain Loose that Cook had not the slightest idea of celestial navigation was negated by Cook's failure to use any of the observations Loose provided in his report to Copenhagen. It was only the complete absence of observational data in the proofs rejected by the Danes that convinced most people that Peary was right at least on this point, although many still refused to believe that Cook had intentionally tried to hoax the entire world when he initially claimed the Pole.

As one observer summed up the results of Peary's plan in the wake of the Copenhagen decision, he found that all his backers' exertion of power and expenditure of money had amounted to very little:

> Dr. Cook has not been exposed. He has exposed himself . . . culminating with his failure to furnish [the Danes] with any competent observations, not even such a plausible set as could easily have been fabricated. It is interesting to see how futile have been most of the attempts to discredit his claim by criticism of his narrative. The objections brought forward when his announcement was made, that the ice was too smooth, that the speed was too great, that he had no scientific companion with him, etc., were found a few days later to apply also to Peary's narrative. The testimony of the Eskimos as reported was conflicting. The charge that he did not intend on the start to make a dash for the Pole, and was not outfitted for it, was at once disproved by his backers. In the calculation of

his pemmican his critics used arithmetic as faulty as his own. Most of the discrepancies, slips and self-contradictions detected in his narrative he found it easy to explain away with more or less plausibility. The three witnesses brought against him—Barrill and Loose and Dunkle—had been content to testify for him so long as they were satisfactorily paid. The last and most skillfully arranged plan for his exposure was a most ludicrous failure, for the series of observations manufactured by Captain Loose and brought forward in New York after Dr. Cook's report had been deposited in the safe at Copenhagen, were not included in the evidence submitted to the committee. The lesson of this is that it is almost impossible to prove a negative by circumstantial evidence.[33]

Whole books have been written on the premise that Cook's claim was defeated by a conspiracy of the Peary Arctic Club, which expended its limitless resources to discredit him—a plot he was powerless to resist, both by temperament and by physical resources. But this is not true.

Undeniably, there was a monied, organized effort against Cook. But our observer is entirely correct. It was not the Peary Arctic Club's "conspiracy" that denied Cook his title to the North Pole. Dr. Cook's claim failed because, as with Mount McKinley, he never offered anything in its defense except his bare word. That is the fact of the matter, but it does not prove that Cook did not reach the North Pole.

The Peary Arctic Club's tactic of demanding proof of Cook put Peary in the uncomfortable position of having his own claim opened to the same kind of scrutiny. Given his public reputation prior to 1909, Peary's claim would have been accepted without question had he not raised questions about Cook's. His attempt to discredit his rival, however, revealed not only Peary's lack of hard evidence against Cook, but also the inadequacy of his own proofs. It also brought down the carefully constructed facade his backers had contrived for Peary over many years; the real Peary was exposed, and many recoiled from what they saw. It was as much this dislike of Peary and the wish to see him defeated that drove the Polar Controversy as it was the merits of Cook's claim, and the palpable animus of men like Captain Hall and Representative Macon set in motion the inevitable destruction of Robert E. Peary's cherished dreams of fame and an honorable name.

The difference between the acceptance of the two men's claims today still rests solely on the equal acceptance of the two separate judgments of them handed down in 1909. But the National Geographic Society's judgment had all but been decided in advance, whereas the University of Copenhagen judged the material it was presented on its merits. It is most ironic, then, to look at the *New York Times*, an institution, like the National Geographic Society, that profited mightily from Cook's destruction, as it editorializes in the wake of the Copenhagen decision:

Finally, in bidding this strange story good-bye, there is one reflection that must be of great comfort to all Americans—that the fount and origin of these woes was not in the action of any half-baked institution of our own country, but in the ill-considered impulsiveness of the authorities of an ancient European institution of learning, in whose discretion we are not to be blamed for having reposed some degree of confidence.[34]

As so often happened in the Polar Controversy, reality had been stood on its head. But another *Times* editorial contained one valid question that remained unanswered: Why had Cook apparently failed to master the one skill necessary to locate the Pole, or even fake a trip to it—the use of a sextant?

His failure to submit any observations at all, even after consulting with Dunkle and Loose, seems to indicate that he was incapable of handling the calculations involved. And this has led many to assume that his claim must therefore have been a premeditated fraud and he the clumsiest sort of faker, in the proposition for a quick killing before he was found out, while fully aware that his claim would never have a chance of being established as fact.

Yet there is no indication that Dr. Cook did not actually intend to try for the Pole. And if he hoped only to cash in on his moment of fraudulent fame, why then did he not return in 1908 and establish his claim a year before Peary could possibly have reached the Pole? If quick money was his only motivation, why did he pass up huge sums for his story and practically give it away instead to the *New York Herald*? These points have baffled many, since they obviously conflict with the idea of Cook as opportunist. They suggest instead that Cook's actions are not so simple as they seem, and to be understood would require patient study.

Since none of the points of Peary's plan, not even Hubbard's attempts to prove Cook's fakery in Alaska, proved his fakery at the Pole, we must turn elsewhere for a new basis on which to judge Cook's claim.

In an analysis he wrote of the Cook and Peary claims, Walter Wellman, with admirable logic, suggested:

> There are three ways to test the good faith of one who claims to have been to the pole—first, by his character; second, by his narrative; third, by his astronomical observations.
>
> The first and second are much more important than the third. If both character and narrative are above suspicion, as in the cases of Nansen, Abruzzi, Shackleton and others, the astronomical observations are real matters of course, important from the scientific point of view but negligible as proof, because no proof is required. On the other hand, if character and narrative be impeached, a traveller's alleged astronomical observations are of no value, for the simple reason that, having concocted a story, such a man would

not hesitate to concoct astronomical observations to match it—
something very easily done.[35]

Unfortunately for Wellman, he failed to apply these sound premises without bias, weakening the force of his conclusion that Cook was an impostor
and Peary was the real discoverer of the Pole. But his premises *are* sound, and
they shall now be applied to Cook's claim in their reverse order.

COOK'S OBSERVATIONS

Suspicions were voiced by Robert Dunn as early as 1904 that Cook was not
capable with instruments, even though he dragged his "junk box" all over
Alaska and back again. To Dunn, his useless instruments were simply a sop to
the "iron crown of science," excusing the adventurer's inexplicable passion "to
win the Impossible, to learn the Unprofitable." Parker and Browne expressed
similar doubts in 1909, and Captain Loose found Cook just this side of complete ignorance on the subject of celestial navigation.

Some will argue that Loose was bought, and though Parker and Browne
could certainly be considered biased, so too might Rudolph Franke's statement
that he saw Cook use a sextant to navigate the *Bradley*. Franke called Cook
marvelously proficient in handling celestial mathematics, but because Franke
was Cook's loyal companion, and his own schooling never took him past primary school, he might have been easily deceived.[36]

The only relevant testimony written before the Polar Controversy began
is that of Dunn, and even the Peary Arctic Club wouldn't touch his "shameless
diary" as evidence. How, then, can these conflicting claims about Cook's navigational abilities be settled?

There appears to have been nothing inadequate about Cook's complement of scientific instruments. He took a glass artificial horizon rather than a
mercurial one, but others, including Greely, had done so before him. But the
doctor's own statements about his most crucial instrument raise suspicion.

Franke described Cook's sextant as a fine aluminum instrument made in
France, and Bradley confirmed this. Cook, however, told William Stead it was
not aluminum, but "the heaviest thing we had to haul." On at least two occasions he could not recall the name of its maker, a lapse several fellow explorers
called extraordinary, and he was equiv-
ocal that the instrument recovered
from Etukishuk and put on display
by Peter Freuchen in Copenhagen in
1911 was, in fact, his.

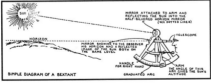

Suffice it to say that his instru-
ments were theoretically adequate. The important question is, could he use
them?

Evidence of Cook's ability with instruments should be found in the latitu-
dinal sights printed in *My Attainment of the Pole,* the only observations he ever

published and, apparently, the only ones in existence. An unpublished paper by Hugh Mitchell, Peary's "expert calculator," points out the problem these observations pose:

> We have [in Dr. Cook's book] two sets of so-called observations of the double altitudes of the sun's upper and lower limbs, in each of which the double altitude of the two limbs differs by approximately once the diameter of the sun. It is clearly evident therefore that the author of these original field notes believed that double altitudes of the sun's upper and lower limbs should differ by about once the diameter of the sun.[37]

In actuality, the difference should have been about twice the diameter.

Before we dismiss Mitchell as Peary's paid agent, we should note that a German astronomer, Dr. A. Wedemeyer, noticed the identical problem while analyzing one of the double-limb observations printed in the first edition of *My Attainment of the Pole.* Wedemeyer attributed the inaccurate result to either an unreliable instrument or an observer who "wasn't capable of making the observations correctly." Yet he noted that Cook's measurement of the shadow of his tent pole was almost exactly what it should have been at the latitude stated for April 14, 1908—11° 7.8'—even though his celestial observation for the same day was mathematically incorrect. "The suspicion that the observation of the latitude 11 degrees 6.6' is calculated and not observed must be automatically evident to the experienced reader," the astronomer concluded, "and it is unnecessary to delve more deeply into the contents of Cook's book."[38]

The 1912 German edition repeated these errors, but when Mitchell Kennerley brought out a new edition later in 1912, the calculations in these two particular latitude sights were altered: one was totally revised; the other had the new figures printed beside the old figures, although another new plate was subsequently produced for the 1913 edition.

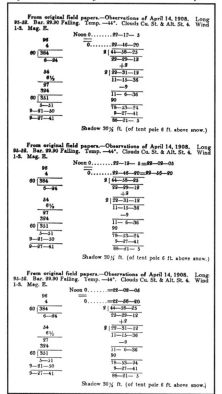

Cook's observations for April 14, 1908, from My Attainment of the Pole: *1911 edition, 1912 edition, 1913 edition.*

In writing Representative Helgesen's 1916 speech attacking Cook's claim, E.C. Rost pointed out that although there were changes in the internal calculations of the two double-limb observations between the editions of Cook's book, their results remained the same. These changes neatly solved the problem observed by Mitchell and Wedemeyer while maintaining the same necessary resultant latitude. "If Dr. Cook was as clever in making observations as in correcting the errors after they were brought to his attention," Rost summed up, "he would be able to more convincingly demonstrate that he really knew anything about his geographical position during the various stages of his so-called 'Polar journey.' As his observations prove that he was either deplorably ignorant or inexcusably careless in making his observations, we can place no more reliance upon them than we can upon Peary's. . . ."[39]

Dr. Cook's papers contain thin tissue sheets on which these observations are written. The penciled figures are smudged, and reading them is further complicated by wrinkles in the papers, some of which may easily be taken for lines. The one recording the first double-limb altitude, April 8, appears to match the original, 1911 edition of *My Attainment of the Pole* and not the later "correction." The observation for April 14 defies absolute interpretation, but it appears to match the 1912–13 "correction," with its original numbers modified but not erased.

Whatever the figures on the papers actually may be, Rost's clever analysis is a hard blow to the belief that they are really originals taken down on Cook's way to the Pole. And Rost's contention that these observations are forgeries is strengthened by the apparent match of Cook's "original" sheets to only one of the printed observations as first published in 1911.

Just as Peary had mortally feared, other aspects of Cook's observations suggest they were modeled on the observations published in *The North Pole* in 1910. Cook makes Peary's mistake of applying a correction for refraction after semidiameter correction, when it should actually be applied before. Also, Cook uses a 9-minute correction for refraction, the same as Peary obtained from a standard table. Refraction, however, is a function of the altitude of the sun; the higher the sun is in the sky, the less correction is needed. Since the sun would have been almost twice as high for Cook (12 degrees) as it would have been for Peary (7 degrees), the correction figure should have been much less—approximately 5 minutes according to the standard formula used to compute refraction.

Further supporting the notion that these sheets and the data they contain are after-the-fact fabrications is the failure of Dr. Cook to submit them to the University of Copenhagen in 1909. Although Minister Egan quoted Captain Schouby of the *Hans Egede* as having looked at "sheets" that contained calculations that "amazed" him, Cook's letters say something quite different.

In 1909 he wrote to Professor Torp, "When in Copenhagen I told you that I had with me *only the worked up observations as published,* otherwise I would then have left the papers for immediate examination." In 1911 he wrote to Professor Salomonsen, "As indicated in my letter to Rektor Torp in November of 1909, *my field data is incomplete,* and therefore I preferred to rest my case upon a report and reduced observations." These letters taken together imply that in neither September 1909 nor January 1911 was Cook claiming to have these original field papers. In fact, he was using as the reason for his nonsubmittal of data while in Copenhagen, and his acceptance of the University's verdict of "not proven," that he had left his observational field data in Greenland with Whitney. Yet in August 1911 these very data appeared in *My Attainment of the Pole,* albeit in mathematically incorrect form.

On this basis, we might take the view of Dr. Wedemeyer and not look further into Cook's polar claim, yet ironically, Dr. Cook's apparent ignorance of navigational mathematics leaves a door open through which he might escape the ignominy of being judged a deliberate faker and makes the authenticity of these calculation sheets a moot point.

THE MAGNETIC MERIDIAN

There is convincing evidence that Dr. Cook believed he could reach the North Pole without taking *any* navigational sights. He said this could be done by compass alone, if an explorer were traveling on what he called the "magnetic meridian."

Loose, in his affidavit, reported that Cook twice advanced this theory as the method by which he navigated to the North Pole. Before dismissing this as a fabrication to make Cook look unschooled in navigational techniques, it should be noted that as late as the 1930s, Cook said that following the magnetic meridian made it easy for him to find the Pole.

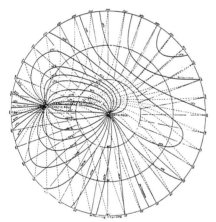

The magnetic and geographic North Poles, showing lines of equal declination (solid) and magnetic meridians (dotted).

"Not far to the west of Sverdrup's farthest North was the magnetic meridian," he wrote in one unpublished item. "Reasoned from every angle I now came to the following conclusions. . . . Instrumental correction for position and for compass was possible on this line. And [if] we could leave from a known fixed point at Svartevoeg move westerly and hold the 97th of longitude where the compass points south to the magnetic pole the reverse end of the needle would take us with some degree of accuracy to the geographical pole. No such advantages were offered from any [other] one of the possible approaches to get to the Boreal Center."[40]

There are many other mentions of the magnetic meridian scattered throughout Cook's unpublished writings, and even one in the author's note published in *Return from the Pole*. And Dr. Thorek quotes Cook as telling him, "Navigation was not difficult. We were almost constantly on the magnetic meridian, with our compass pointing due south."[41]

Though such concepts as *magnetic meridians* exist—imaginary lines, though not necessarily straight ones, drawn on maps to represent the direction of the horizontal component of the earth's magnetic field at each point along them—they converge at the magnetic pole but not at the geographic pole. Cook never claimed to have any apparatus necessary to measure horizontal intensity on his polar journey, and since they do not, by their nature, converge at the geographic pole, true magnetic meridians would have been of no help in themselves in navigating toward it.

What the doctor meant by "magnetic meridian" was the isogonic line—an imaginary line, the points along which represent a constant declination of the magnetic compass—on which the declination was always 180 degrees. Isogonic lines, since they represent constant declination, by definition, must converge at *both* the magnetic *and* the geographic poles.

Such a line curving away from the magnetic pole on which the compass would constantly point 180 degrees could be plotted today, but it is unknown whether it exactly coincided with the 97th parallel of longitude in 1908. Where it lay that year can only be speculation, since only by a series of celestial observations could its location have been established definitely.

Since a magnetic field's characteristics can change unpredictably, sometimes within moments, because of magnetic storms on the sun and other factors still not completely understood, it is impossible to reconstruct past magnetic force fields with any certainty, unless data exist on which to construct them. In 1908 magnetic data in the region through which Cook said he traveled were virtually nonexistent. Therefore Cook could not have predicted where his magnetic meridian lay; without data its position would have been guesswork, though he may have chosen the 97th meridian because it was the approximate one on which the North Magnetic Pole was located by Amundsen.

What is lacking, then, is just what Dr. Cook never provided. Without celestial observations to establish where it lay, his magnetic meridian could never be located, and without frequent checks via his sextant, it would soon be lost.[42]

Did Cook really believe he could make such a precise determination of his magnetic meridian without observations? It is likely that he had read geomagnetic theories along this line, since he read everything he could find on polar subjects, but there are many indications that he only half digested their technical details or failed to understand many of their underlying principles. Other examples of his difficulty with far more obvious scientific facts exist, only one of which needs to be given here.

After his return from the Arctic in 1909, Cook faced tough questioning regarding his statements that he could see 15 miles on either side of his route. When it was pointed out to him that because of the curvature of the earth, he could not have seen more than three to four miles at sea level, he changed the subject. In his papers there is this remarkable statement:

> For every rise of 300 feet in altitude, the range of vision is increased 200 miles.
>
> At 1800 feet which is about the height of Svartevoeg one should see 1200 miles—or to the pole and 680 miles beyond the Pole—on the basis that a man 6 ft high can see 4 miles at sea level.
>
> From a hummock 24 ft high it should not be difficult to see 16 miles, the horizon therefore should be 32 miles wide.[43]

Not only does Cook show no knowledge of the formula used to compute the apparent horizon, remarkably, he makes no allowance for the earth's being a sphere, but treats the world as if it were flat.

This passage, perhaps more than anything else, shows Cook's inability to grasp mathematical concepts and raises doubt that he could even have handled the relatively simple mathematical calculations necessary to compute latitudes by meridan altitude using a sextant, much less the more complicated calculations involving spherical trigonometry necessary to determine longitude and magnetic variation.

No doubt, he arrived at the location of his magnetic meridian just as he told Captain Loose—after studying the journeys of Sverdrup and Nansen as they approached the geographical North Pole from opposite hemispheres. He may have seen in this idea a way of making up for his lack of navigational skill. "Then it was only a matter of latitude," he is alleged to have told Captain Loose, "and I could rely on my dead reckoning for that." It was simple—"ingenious and impractical," as T. Everett Harré might have said.

"When one realizes that Dr. Cook evidently knew nothing about the variations of his compass or the methods to control them and yet set his course to the pole by the compass, the most fantastic suppositions as to his wanderings are possible,"[44] concluded I.A.D. Jensen, a member of the Danish Konsistorium, which analyzed Cook's field notes in the notebook he belatedly sent to Copenhagen. Yet this is what Dr. Cook said he did. Of his return from the Pole he writes: "Compass in hand, my lonely march ahead of the sledges continued day by day."[45]

If Cook did act upon his theory of a magnetic meridian, he may have followed a course set solely by compass, made a very long journey to what he believed to be the North Pole and then turned around and retraced his course by the same method. Barring a disruption in the magnetic field while he was out of sight of land, he theoretically could have returned to somewhere near his starting point using this method. But if this is what he actually did, at least one thing is sure: he never could have reached the North Pole by this method combined with dead reckoning alone, except by the very slightest of infinitesimal chances, and he never would have known it if he had done so without making checks for his position using his sextant.

In his *Hampton's* series, Cook took great pains to say why he might have missed the Pole: "We were compelled on our journey to go in various directions to find a way. We made wide detours, at other times we had to retreat and find new passages. Perhaps, in so doing, I did become confused and overestimated my progress. If that is so, it is a fact neither I nor anyone can settle now. Wherever I went, however, I maintain it was northward and I did reach a spot which I believed to be the Pole."[46]

This could be interpreted as supporting the idea that Cook relied solely on dead reckoning, since he speaks of "overestimating" his progress. Yet his dead reckoning estimates are allegedly confirmed by his observational data in his field notes to an impossibly accurate degree, and his reported calculations of longitudes down to the arc-minute, which are unsupported by any observational data, are impossibly precise that near the geographical pole, where all longitudes meet. Moreover, estimation would not be necessary with a sextant.

Cook stated that he took observations for latitude and longitude, but he never furnished any data to support his positional sights until two years after his return. Even then, the changes introduced in them between the first and second editions of *My Attainment of the Pole,* as already seen, make their authenticity suspect.

SHADOWS

In his 1911 *Hampton's* series, Dr. Cook first advanced the reason he felt sure he had reached the Pole despite his doubts about his estimations: observation of shadows. This also suggests that he did not rely on his sextant. In one of his brief lapses of faith, even Captain Hall, who was puzzled by Cook's lack of any magnetic variation data, said he thought Cook "invented these shadow ghosts" to counter "the Peary conspirators in their dastardly misrepresentations" concerning his lack of navigational data. "Had Cook lost his sextant this method of measuring shadows would have been an ingenious substitute," Captain Hall reasoned. "But having a sextant and using it, it seems unlikely that he would consider it advisable to measure shadows."[47]

There is reason to believe that Hall's surmise is correct, except for his assumption that Cook used his sextant. There is no mention of shadows in Cook's *Herald* series, which ended on October 7, 1909. However, in its October 24, 1909, issue, the *New York Times* published excerpts of an article entitled "Easy Tests to Show if Cook Found Pole," by the French astronomer Guillaume Bigourdan, which had appeared in the Paris daily *Le Matin.*

Bigourdan cited several means whereby the Eskimos accompanying Cook could have been made to comprehend when the Pole was reached. Among these were the unchanging altitude of the sun and the unchanging length of shadows cast upon the ice during every hour of the day. "These phenomena and their meaning could easily be grasped by the most untutored minds, even those of savages," he wrote.

"If, as Dr. Cook asserts," said the astronomer, "he was at the pole on April 22, 1908, the sun remained for him and his party constantly at a height of about twelve degrees, and the length of the shadow of each of them standing upright was four and a half times his height. If Dr. Cook really reached the pole he must certainly have drawn the attention of his companions to this phenomenon, the novelty of which would have stamped it indelibly on their memory. Those primitive men surely would have felt the greatest astonishment on perceiving that they had reached a point where time was at a standstill."

This is exactly the evidence that Cook later advanced in *Hampton's* and used successfully to impress the "untutored minds" of the millions who heard him lecture during the next six years. Yet before *Hampton's,* Cook had said "the position of the pole is determined by the altitude of the sun. That is the only general way"—whatever that meant. It is likely that Cook read the *New York Times* article, as he read everything else on the subject, and adapted it to his purposes, since there is no evidence that Cook ever made observations of shadows during his polar trip.

In *My Attainment of the Pole* a transcript of his field notes is appended at the back. Several of these entries record the length of the observed shadow, but these are always noted as "copied from other field papers" or "from observation paper." There is no mention of measuring shadows, even at the Pole, in the notebook that contains the originals of these field notes. Certainly, if this were the method by which Cook convinced himself that he had reached the North Pole, it would have appeared in the original field notes.

Though Cook never mentioned measuring shadows until 1911, he had already, in December 1909, submitted his notebook containing his original field notes to the University of Copenhagen. Since that notebook did not contain any shadow measurements, Cook could not afford to add them later, and

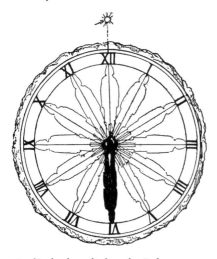

Cook's shadow dial at the Pole.

so they are not there to this day.[48] But they *are* on those "original" observation sheets that appeared only *after* Dr. Cook had advanced his shadow measurement method of verifying his arrival at the Pole. That nowhere else in Cook's papers could be found any references or notes on the length of shadows, except on the sheets containing the celestial navigation sights for latitude, only strengthens the supposition that those sheets are fabrications.

Calculations of the length of shadows anywhere, including the North Pole, for a given day do not require the observer to have been there. All that is needed is a table showing the altitude of the sun at a given position and time and a common protractor. Such data would not be proof of Cook's arrival at the Pole if they existed, and his later advancement of them combined with their absence from his original notes suggests their invention after the fact, as well.

Another indication that Cook never actually measured shadows is the illustration of a "shadow dial" on page 308 of *My Attainment of the Pole*. A sharp-eyed reviewer noticed the mistake: "That diagram shows the shadow coming back to the same position after twelve hours, not twenty-four. The man was so supremely careless in preparing the book by which he desired to be judged that he actually allowed a blunder of this sort to pass. We can hardly believe that he could have allowed it to pass if the shadow game had ever been played."[49]

DR. COOK AT COPENHAGEN

Despite all this, could it be that Cook believed that he had reached the Pole itself? After considering the many baffling questions that surround his 1909 claims, many have surmised that he must have, and some logical arguments can be made that he did. At Copenhagen he was so convincing to those he met that he was almost universally felt to be absolutely sincere in his statements. One glaring exception was Philip Gibbs.

Gibbs's account of how he unmasked Dr. Cook is another good example of how time and wish distort memory. Of that moment of realization on the *Hans Egede* that Cook was a fraud, Gibbs said in 1946:

> Suddenly he became very angry and said: "Don't you believe me? Do you doubt my story? Haven't other explorers come back and given their word which has been believed? Why do you disbelieve me?"
>
> Those may not have been his exact words but that was the gist of his defence, shouted out with violence.[50]

Gibb's story in 1923 was somewhat different in detail, though basically similar. But his original account, published in September 1909, said,

> I had asked Dr. Cook many seemingly impertinent questions, but he had answered all of them with great good humor, with perfect readiness and with a frank look in his blue eyes.[51]

So it was not the original interview that made Gibbs suspicious of the doctor; the violent outburst was a later addition imposed by his mind to justify a young reporter's rash conclusion. But Gibbs soon was publishing more and more negative stories about Cook, nonetheless. What then was the real source of his suspicion? The answer is Peter Freuchen.

It was Freuchen's doubts expressed to Gibbs and, later, his incorrect translation of Knud Rasmussen's letter to his wife that persuaded Gibbs to denounce Cook. Freuchen had translated Rasmussen's words to read, "My first impression when I heard about Dr. Cook was an enormous disappointment, and

I am sorry." But Rasmussen's disappointment stemmed from Cook's having left him no opportunity to make an attempt on the Pole himself. "I never was so much moved in my life as by the success of Cook, for I hoped to carry off this triumph myself," the letter actually read. Freuchen later admitted, "My knowledge of English was so poor that I gave Gibbs just the opposite impression of what I intended."[52]

Based on Freuchen's mistaken translation, Gibbs had put in print that Rasmussen had changed his mind about Cook's claim. By then he was in too deep to retreat and had no choice but to maintain the position he had impulsively taken and hope for the best. As he later admitted, "There were moments when I had frightful doubts about the line I was taking. Supposing after all Cook had been to the North Pole? Supposing I was maligning an honest and heroic man?"[53]—and ruining his own career.

Luckily for Gibbs, events converged with his misguided course; he went on to become a distinguished reporter and was even knighted. But in his later account of the event that launched his illustrious career in journalism, you can almost see him mopping his brow in relief at the ultimate outcome: "I took a big chance, and looking back on it one which was too dangerous and not quite justified. I had no proof whatever that he was a fraud."[54]

As was often remarked during those days in Copenhagen, Cook's apparent confidence in his claim and his simple directness dispelled all doubts in most people's minds that he was telling the truth. Gibbs noted this reaction and attributed it to Cook's personality, "so strange and so powerful." When one looks at the record of Dr. Cook at Copenhagen, it shows that Gibbs, at least on this point, had not underestimated the man. There were points on which doubts could have been raised but none were. That Cook obtained high honors without proof of any kind can be attributed to the kindness of the Danish people, a characteristic every explorer who had visited Greenland was familiar with, and to the international tradition, up to then, of taking an explorer at his word. No proof had been demanded of anyone else, ever. Why demand it of Dr. Cook? Peary's outbursts upon his return were considered, in Denmark as elsewhere, bad form and were resented even more in Scandinavia because of his unjust accusations against Sverdrup. But in America some believed Cook had gone to Denmark first to take advantage of the Scandinavian dislike for Peary, establish his claim there, then rely on the American propensity to bow to the superiority of European culture to carry him through. William N. Armstrong advanced this scenario:

> The psychological moment arrives, he lands in Europe and sets the world afire—he had made it ready to burn; he now applies the match. It might have been smothered at first, but it got too great a start in Europe. It never would have gained such a sweep if it had been started first in this country, which no one knew better than Cook. . . .

> All sought a hero. He came to them meekly, worn out, and in rags. They embraced him in a frenzy of worship. Peary abused him, called him a liar. Cook returns a soft answer, saying he believes Peary is honest, and if Peary claims to have reached the pole, he (Cook) believes he did. Peary continues his abuse until our meek and lowly hero declares he is willing to divide the honor with his persecutor. Can you beat that sort of stuff? It never was known to lose, and Cook is a past master at handing it out. . . .
>
> Still the people will not listen. All they are willing to comprehend is that their long-suffering hero is again being abused. . . .
>
> Too bad! When a man is capable of perpetrating such a huge joke on the American people, isn't it a shame to spoil it?[55]

But spoil it Armstrong and all the other Peary allies did. Still, it took a tremendous effort to overcome the tactless display of pique in Peary's "Gold Brick" accusation compared with Cook's master stroke of adopting a dignified and gentlemanly reserve in response to his rival's excesses, even though, as his notes made in Greenland show, he was livid over "Peary's bunglesome hindrance."

This tactic won over many who had no interest in the arcane technical arguments advanced to disprove Dr. Cook's story and brand him an impostor. Cook received scores of letters, perhaps hundreds, like one from Frank D. La Lanne, the president of the National Board of Trade, who saw him speak at the Academy of Music in Philadelphia, in which he said, "Your honest, sincere and genuine method of putting everything, made all your listeners your lovers."[56]

It was that characteristic of his speech, and his ever-present smile, that won Cook so many admirers. He seemed a common man like themselves, not an arrogant, icy hero like Peary, and they wanted him to win.

"That smile of Cook's! I shall never forget it," exclaimed one man even after the rest of the explorer had disappeared without a trace. "He smiled as he waved his cap above his head, imitating the honest bluster of a schoolboy, when the steam launch dropped him at the quayside. He smiled at the newspaper interviewers, which is unusual; at the professional photographers, which is still more unusual; when he was squeezed in the shrieking crowd between the crown prince and Mr. Stead—who helped to welcome Cook, and who confessed to me the other day that 'Cook had me nicely'; . . . But his most audacious smile was when the king and queen and hundreds of men of learning—professors, explorers, geographers and mathematicians—hanging in hushed silence on his words as he told the precious story of his dash across the ice ridges. . . . I doubt not that if you could find Cook now he would be smiling to himself at what was perhaps the only real success he has ever had. . . .

"How different Peary! . . .

"Peary strikes me as a man who never smiles except when he thinks it would be rude not to do so."[57]

That Dr. Cook fully understood the import of his reception in Copenhagen is indicated by the statement of his friend Charles Wake, who asked the doctor what proofs he had of reaching the Pole. "So long as I live," said the insurance man, "I cannot forget the degree of nonchalance with which he waved his hand toward the beautifully engraved degree and the handsome gold medal that had been conferred on him by Copenhagen and dramatically replied: 'There is the best evidence.' Perhaps in this he was telling the truth."[58]

SIMPLE HERO OR SIMPLE EFFECT?

Already, at Copenhagen, people wondered what to make of Dr. Cook. To many, like William Stead, he seemed a simple, honest, even guileless man who had by terrific grit accomplished a great thing but was too limited to have conceived the fraud of which he was being accused. To others, like William Armstrong, he was a clever faker who had plotted to "set the world afire" and then bask in the glow of fame and money that resulted from the conflagration.

Let us try these two images on the events that followed to see which makes the better fit. First we will assume that Dr. Cook was the "Simple Hero" that Georg Brandes and so many others thought him to be, who honestly believed he had been to the Pole but might have been mistaken. We will try to explain all of his subsequent actions while keeping this assumption intact.

As we have seen, everything indicates an honest effort on Cook's part to mount a genuine expedition to the Pole, so we are off to a good start. He makes a long trip along his magnetic meridian and convinces himself that he has reached the Pole by measuring the length of shadows, as he explained in his *Hampton's* articles. He arrives in Denmark and declares he has done the deed. He is perfectly convincing because he is convinced of it himself. After his long isolation from the civilized world, he is unprepared for his unexpected hero status and bewildered that he has achieved such notoriety and is the subject of such frenzy. Against all advice, he bypasses huge offers of money and out of loyalty practically gives his story away to the *New York Herald*. Beleaguered by Peary's unfounded attacks, he cuts short his plans and departs Europe to defend his honor in America.

When he arrives in the United States, he learns that Harry Whitney has been forced by Peary to leave his crucial records in Greenland. He knows that without them his proofs are incomplete and may be rejected. He starts a letter to Rector Torp, asking the university to put off judgment until he can recover his data, but then reconsiders and does not send it. After all, he reasons, he reached the Pole, and Peary's charges are absurd and baseless, anyway.

Then, the Barrill affidavit brings up serious questions about his former veracity. As doubts mount in the press, increasingly he feels his case may be lost without his records. His hostile reception in Hamilton, Montana, convinces him that he now must provide convincing evidence that he has been to the Pole or he will be declared a fake, even though he has told the truth. He must take a risk or all will be lost.

He seizes on Dunkle's offer to assist him in checking his calculations for accuracy. In talking to Captain Loose about navigational matters, he learns he was mistaken about how to make astronomical observations; even if recovered, his sextant data are worthless because they are in error. He suddenly realizes that he cannot prove his claim, and he thinks in chagrin of how all those who have expressed belief in him will react when he is unable to do so.

He now recognizes that he could not have actually reached the exact Pole, but to admit that would brand him as a shameless impostor, even though he had made a real and honest journey to a spot he believed to be the Pole; he even tells himself he might have been there by chance—who knows? But faced with this realization, his previous self-assurance and calm demeanor desert him. Nothing he has can prove he reached the Pole, but unwilling to submit the false calculations provided by Loose and unable to create a set himself, he turns in his incomplete data with his letter asking that a final decision not be rendered until he can recover his lost data.

He is already unable to face the strain and the embarrassment of his situation; the added worries over rumors of threats on his very life bring him to the edge of nervous collapse. He disappears to recover his mental balance and let time lend perspective to matters.

When given the chance to vindicate himself in *Hampton's,* he naively hopes to explain his seemingly inexplicable actions. But upon his return from exile, he finds the magazine he hoped would help him reestablish his good reputation emblazoned with "Dr. Cook's Confession." He is at first heartbroken, but then he decides that Peary and his allies are without shame and no longer worthy of gentlemanly respect; fire must be met with fire.

With great distaste, he begins a campaign for his personal honor, sets aside his courteous inclinations, and attacks Peary with the sole purpose of restoring his good name. He travels ceaselessly across the country and in Europe telling his story, but in the end, the Peary interests block all attempts at a hearing before Congress through vast expenditures of cash and political influence.

If we accept that Dr. Cook was the Simple Hero, then all of the interpretations of the incidents we have selected here seem to fit very well and safely explain away a number of distressing facts without imputing any fraudulent intent. In fact, this is basically the explanation Dr. Cook gives for his actions in *My Attainment of the Pole.*

But what if Dr. Cook was something more complex than the Simple Hero? Another man who observed him at his lecture in Philadelphia looked hard trying to decide:

> Dr. Cook does not look nor talk like a man who is a liar or a charlatan. There is nothing in his manner or his utterance which betokens the mind of a trickster. Throughout his entire discourse there ran a simple and manly strain of sincerity. His face denotes lines of shrewdness; his eye is keen, and there is something in the

countenance and the bearing which indicate that he is a man of
stuff that is not to be trifled with when he is fully aroused for action.
But it is not at all easy to discern the nature of a sly and subtle
schemer, or the facile aptitude for devising a fabric of chicanery
that would need to be sustained not simply by the resources of a
fertile and unscrupulous imagination, but by the wariest and
adroitest ingenuity. . . .

    Nor was there any trace of egotism in the tone or expression of
Dr. Cook as he stood on the Academy stage and gave his recital
of some of the things he had seen and done. . . . Dr. Cook is not at
all an eloquent speaker; there is no posing in his mannerism, and
his talk itself is equally free of affectation. . . .

    . . . What he thus disclosed unconsciously—unless we are to
assume that he is really a consummate actor in the artifices of simple
effect—must strengthen a reasonable presumption of his honesty
in claim and statement. . . . It would require, indeed, extraordinary
skill in subterfuge or a Jekyll-Hyde duality, to be an inventor of the
yarn which he is charged with as a deliberate falsifier, to live up to it,
and to take on the seeming or external character of a man of decency
and at least ordinary honor.[59]

    But what if he *were* possessed of that extraordinary skill? Let us assume
Dr. Cook was really a "Consummate Actor" in the artifices of simple effect.
    When he returns to Annoatok, he is furious at Peary's seizure of his furs
and stores and makes careful notes he can use against Peary should he dare to
challenge his claim. But then he resolves to say nothing, knowing that if Peary
claims the Pole, so much the better, since he probably will not have been there
himself. He is encouraged by the way his story of how he reached the North
Pole is readily accepted in Greenland and, after slight adjustments, is assured
that the outline is convincing.
    He comes from the North with his fraudulent story and carries out his
plan to land first in Denmark. He has the outline settled but is reluctant to give
details, even at his grand lecture before the Geographical Society. He determines
"to confine himself to what he had already said, and to say no more." His self-
control is nearly superhuman, and he good-naturedly answers all questions
with lies, without blinking, knowing that most will not understand enough to
know whether his answers are correct and that his total self-assurance and disarming manner will count for much more than the words themselves. As he
hopes and expects, his word is accepted without much question by the kindhearted Danes and he is given high honors; these he assumes will pave the way
for his claim's acceptance in the United States and elsewhere.
    When Peary announces his own claim and then intemperately blasts him
as a fake, Cook keeps a gentlemanly bearing and only wins more support for
his dignity under trying circumstances. But he sees that there is going to be a

death struggle with Peary, and so he gives his story to the prestigious *New York Herald*, even though he has other extravagant offers for it, gambling on trading a short-term loss for a long-term gain should he be victorious with the help of the *Herald*'s considerable power.

He returns to the United States and discovers that Whitney has not been allowed by Peary to bring back his records—just as he knew Peary would do, if the chance arose, from his own and others' experiences in the past when Peary was faced with a rival. By burying his belongings, Peary has given him the perfect excuse should his claim fail a scientific examination.

When he hears that Barrill may be planning to betray his fraud at Mount McKinley, he invites his climbing partner to come and meet him, sending him $200, because if Barrill tells of his previous fake, the game could well be up. When Barrill is paid thousands by General Hubbard and confesses that he lied originally, he simply denies everything. But when the Explorers Club calls him to task, and after his mixed reception in Montana, he can see the Mount McKinley climb will be his undoing unless his polar claim can be irrefutably established.

He accepts the offer of Dunkle and Loose to manufacture conclusive proof that he reached the Pole, all the while maintaining to them that he is only interested in checking his original observations. He suspects this is probably a trap, but he cannot dare ask someone himself to make up a set of observations under the circumstances, so he will play along and see how things fall out, confident that he might yet turn the situation to his own good. When he senses the pair may turn on him, or even be a plant by the Peary forces, he dismisses them without paying what he agreed. To use Loose's figures would be suicide, but he has no intention of dying—though he knows nothing can sustain his original claim any longer. He will buy time while maintaining interest and adapt to future circumstances as they arise.

He has letters written to himself threatening his own life and makes sure witnesses notice that he is genuinely being followed by Hubbard's agents. He medicates himself so that he cannot sleep, to simulate a convincing state of acute anxiety. Under this pretext, he flees the country after submitting inconclusive proof of his polar journey to Copenhagen, explaining that Peary had prevented the return of his critical records from Greenland.

After setting the press on edge in its futile attempts to find him for nearly a year, he suddenly reappears to announce to the world that in due time he will have a "full answer to everything." When *Hampton's* offers to run his story and its editors suggest that he confess to having perpetrated a North Pole hoax, he correctly guesses that they are in collusion with Peary and that they will tamper with his story to that effect.

Since he has determined to take on the role of the well-intentioned-man, made martyr to explain his actions, he allows them to have it with "no editorial guarantees whatsoever." He writes a story that allows room for doubt in his own mind that he actually reached the Pole but denies any scheme to fake, leaving the door open for a reassertion of his claim if circumstances warrant.

When he returns from exile, he finds that he is not vilified, despite *Hampton's* distortions. Having always realized the vulnerability of Peary's claim, when he reads its details in his rival's *Hampton's* series, he knows Peary never reached the Pole, either. With this knowledge, along with that of Peary's previous false and exaggerated claims, which he has learned through explorers' inside gossip, plus the secrets he knows about Peary's personal life, he decides to mount an organized campaign to reassert his own claim. This includes a film, lectures and the publication, at long last, of his book, all viciously attacking Peary, knowing that Peary has too many skeletons in his closet to strike back without condemning himself.

Though he hopes to reestablish his polar claim, at least in the popular mind, his actual aim is nothing more than to make money, and he finds willing aides in men like T. Everett Harré and Fred High, who have the same aim themselves and see in his exotic story a great potential to do so. All the actions that seem directed at putting his claims before Congress are merely to boost his controversial lectures, and for six years the plan works well.

This second scenario with all its assumptions fits just as well as the first. That is the perplexing problem of Dr. Cook. To his defenders he is the "Simple Hero," an innocent unfortunate who achieves great things, becomes enmeshed in the inexplicable ways of the world of big power and money and is destroyed. To his opponents he is the "Consummate Actor," preying on the propensity of most people to look no deeper than the surface and, seeing its earnest smile, believe.

If he was either, he was a most extraordinary man. But in all probability, he was something between these extremes, as "the manager of his affairs" so aptly observed. No doubt, neither of these scenarios is entirely correct.

The only way to resolve this duality is to consider Walter Wellman's second test and follow Cook's course to the Pole step by step, because it is on the basis of whether his narrative is truthful that we will know whether he was more of a hero than an actor, or vice-versa, and as a result be able to test Wellman's all-important first criterion: character.

PEARY AT THE POLE?

Before beginning, however, the journey of Robert E. Peary toward the Pole in 1909 must be considered, since it may influence what we believe about Cook's journey.

Dr. Cook himself was careful, for the most part, not to question the authenticity of Peary's account, even though he expressed doubt privately and all but dismissed it in his New York *World* interview in 1910. There was a good reason for his having taken this position.

When Cook returned from his polar trip, he was accused of claiming incredible speeds over the polar pack—until Peary returned claiming impossible speeds. This "proof" against Cook's story was then dropped, since to raise it was to bring Peary's statements into question as well.

As Peary's full story appeared, many noticed that it bore a remarkable resemblance to Cook's in all important aspects, including the description of the Pole itself. Some said that either the two stories were corroborations of each other or one had been copied from the other. The conventional wisdom has been that since Cook's original report was published first, there was no doubt who copied whom. Certainly, Peary read Cook's original dispatch as published in the *Herald* before giving out his own first account.[60] However, Peary's *Hampton's* series and his book preceded Cook's parallel accounts by a year each, and even Cook's 1909 *Herald* series was published after Peary's three-part narrative in the *New York Times*. If these various items are read in sequence as they appeared, there are a number of details that could be alleged to have been copied by Cook from Peary, though the general descriptions of Cook's journey and his specific description of the Pole did, indeed, precede anything that Peary published.

The immediate acceptance of Peary's account without much question, then, actually helped Cook. If Peary were to be discredited, Cook's story would have to stand on its own merits, and without Peary's it would seem much more fabulous in its claims.

If Cook was the Consummate Actor, it might even be reasoned that he stopped funding E.C. Rost's brilliant efforts in Congress because his lobbyist was on the verge of totally destroying Peary's claim, just as Lucien Alexander feared, and Cook realized the implications for his own story if that was done. Even as late as the 1930s, Cook asked Andrew Freeman to treat Peary with "respect" in his book and said that he had no desire to say anything against his claim, though at about this same time he was reported by Dr. Thorek as saying he didn't believe that Peary was even second to the Pole.[61]

The dispute over Peary's claims continues. But despite efforts of the National Geographic Society and others to prop up Peary's credibility, there seems to be no evidence that proves Peary reached the North Pole in 1909. In fact, based on his own papers, there is compelling circumstantial evidence that he did not. These documents and all of his actions in connection with his polar claim indicate that he was a man with big secrets to hide.

He said hardly a word to Matt Henson on the return journey from the Pole and then all but cut his contacts with his long-time servant and companion for the rest of his life.[62] Upon his return to the *Roosevelt*, Peary apparently told no one except Bob Bartlett that he had achieved his lifelong ambition.

The only person to ask him directly whether he had been to the Pole was Dr. Goodsell, to whom Peary replied, "I have not been altogether unsuccessful." Matt Henson told Goodsell that they had raised the flag at a place where the sun uniformly circled the horizon, but hastily added, "It might have been a little higher in the north."[63] If this was so, Peary was not at the Pole.

Pages torn from a Peary notebook and neatly pinned at the corner appear to contain calculations trying out the plausibility of the claim he was contemplating, given the unavoidable facts of the time of his departure and return to the *Roosevelt*. One of these memoranda reads, "Goodsell returned to ship from 84° 29' in 12 days. MacMillan in 11 days, . . . Borup returned from 85° 23' in 23 days . . . Marvin's men came in from 86° 38' in 23 days. Captain came in from 87° 47' in 24 days. Self came in from   in 20 days"—leaving the farthest northern latitude he was to claim blank, just as he had left the same information blank on the cover of his diary. Peary waited 53 days before making a public claim by erecting a monument at Cape Columbia on June 12, 1909; though one of its arms was inscribed "North Pole, April 6, 1909, 413 miles," the monument's typed record of the expedition posted on it said only that the Pole had been attained "in the spring of 1909."[64]

Peary was wary about submitting his original records even to the National Geographic Society and did so only after checking his calculations in conversations with Professor Hastings at Eagle Island. When he did submit them and got the society's approval with only a superficial examination, he refused ever again to allow his "original" observations or diary to be examined by any scientific society that could verify them. He refused even to leave them overnight with the congressional subcommittee in 1911.

When he appeared before Congress, he submitted a diary that Representative Robertson noted was "a very cleanly kept book," without a smudge on it. This raised suspicions that it was not authentic, and nothing was seen of the "very dirty book" later alleged by Commodore Valentine to have been Peary's original workbook, whose navigational sights seemed to him fraudulent.

Walter Wellman, speaking from his own experience, said, "The public should know that if Dr. Cook has any adequate records, they are dirty, greasy, grimy notebooks kept from day to day, poorly written, in places almost illegible, penned with frost-bitten fingers by a weary man lying in the half darkness of a reinskin bag within a snow hut or tent. . . .

"Even the grime and grease have their worth. So-called copies will not do. Alleged copies may be made anywhere; the grimy originals must be produced."[65]

Dr. Cook's diaries and records stand up to this test; they have many of these attributes. But Peary's diary has none of them, though Otto Tittman said the one he saw at the National Geographic Society's examination "had all the earmarks of being the original." The diary preserved at the National Archives could not be cleaner and neater, nor could it contain more perfectly formed and even writing if it had been written at leisure while sitting at a comfortable desk in a heated ship's cabin in the Arctic or on an island in Casco Bay.[66]

That Peary was sensitive about the doubts raised by his diary's immaculate condition is evidenced by a one-page typed memo in his papers defending the book against this criticism. It is not very reassuring or convincing.[67]

But if it is a fake, why does the diary preserve 32 pages of egotistical statements and crass, money-making propositions detailing ways to cash in on the discovery of the North Pole—and this in a book that devotes only 59 pages to the record of that task's accomplishment? And why are the most crucial pages left blank or written on loose slips when they could easily have been fabricated along with the rest?

There is an explanation for this that would be plausible to anyone who has spent hundreds of hours studying the papers of Robert E. Peary. The man had difficulty throwing away anything that contained a word about himself or his history. He kept everything right down to the receipts for thermos bottles, memos of his secret thoughts and even the check that paid Barrill's bribe—everything except those things that told the truth about things he had lied about publicly.

His diary entry for July 5, 1891, where he records his "puny discovery" of a Greenland fjord instead of the "N. Cape" or the "East Greenland Sea," survives only in a heavily crossed-out stenographer's typescript; the original diary page is nowhere to be found. The crucial pages documenting his "Farthest North" of 1906 apparently don't exist at all, in any form, and the pages of his 1909 diary are blank on the days he claimed to have been at the North Pole.

These are the facts. The rest is only speculation.

Peary certainly knew that in calling for Cook's "proofs," he would have to present his own complete, original diary. There would be no excuse for missing pages this time. However, the original may have contained something that he wanted to suppress. So he carefully copies over the greasy, grimy original and presents the copy as the original, leaving out what he wished to suppress and leaving in everything else.

Why? Because, as the puzzlement over what the diary contains or does not contain versus its physical condition proves, *nothing could be more convincing than the original thoughts as written in the original diary;* the idea was not to tamper, but to edit. Perhaps he intended to fill in the blanks he left, but then decided not to risk making any commitment about the Pole that later visitors could call into question.[68]

Peary's testimony before Congress was full of prevarications, contradictions and incredible lapses of memory on crucial points. It was a disaster for Peary, and it set in motion all the doubts that plague his claim to this day.

Peary never presented any verifiable evidence to support his bare word—no variations of the compass, no soundings that found bottom beyond the continental shelf, no shared sextant data. In fact, he seems to have consciously avoided taking any observations personally, though he was well acquainted with the techniques of celestial navigation. Ironically, therefore, this fact tends to condemn Peary's claim, since unlike Cook, if he did not reach the Pole, he surely would have known that he had not.

During the 1989 Navigation Foundation study, a thorough search of Peary's papers by a supposedly neutral party with the avowed purpose of proving or disproving his claim from the evidence they contained failed to produce anything concrete in support of Peary's claim that does not rely on Peary's own reports for crucial missing data. However, after the foundation had, according to its account, examined every item in the immense Peary gift, an independent researcher discovered two unpublished pictures showing the sun above the horizon—something that not a single published picture ever showed—at just the altitude it should have been at the time Peary said he was at the North Pole. And there could be no doubt that one of them was taken at the location Peary claimed to be the North Pole, since it shows his flag flying from a distinctive ice hummock he used as a backdrop in several of his published North Pole pictures. Here, at last, was concrete evidence of the truth of Peary's claim—or was it?

These pictures would confirm Peary's story *if* they showed some overlapping feature that would also show that the sun was at about the same altitude at widely differing times of the day. This the pictures do not show, though such pictures could easily have been made at the Pole. If they had been made, they would have been irrefutable proof that Peary was actually there. That no such pictures exist, then, is a strong indication that these two pictures were not taken at the Pole, because it is just as easy to wait at a more southerly latitude on any day of the year that the sun would reach the required altitude and then photograph it. Since the polar pack is devoid of permanent features, any such picture would look the same as one taken at the Pole.[69]

All of Peary's actions after April 6, 1909, as well as the actions of those who have defended him since, give every indication of a guilty man trying to shield his greatest deceit from the unwelcome spotlight of any impartial investigation. Moreover, evidence preserved by Peary himself shows that all his expeditions before 1909 had produced exaggerated or false claims, and it is also now evident that his personal conduct was not as heroic as the public was led to believe. Therefore, Peary fails the most important test that Walter Wellman set for the veracity of a claimant to the North Pole—the test of character.

Peary also fails Wellman's second test. Five major books have devoted themselves to showing that Peary's narrative does not hold up on its own internal evidence. Though one may differ on their authors' individual points, it is difficult to deny their common conclusion: Robert E. Peary did not reach the North Pole.

On the other hand, there has never been an attempt at analysis advocating Peary's claim based on his narrative, not even the recent, highly publicized examination by the Navigation Foundation, which critics have said is in many ways no more than bad science and wishful thinking, if not outright invention.[70]

The reason for this is the impossibility of doing so and still defending Peary. As Captain Hall rightly observed: "Interested persons with mercenary ends to accomplish; or implicated partisans desiring to sustain themselves, may by sophistry and personalities attempt to divert attention from the astounding revelation [of the imaginary character of Peary's narrative] and thereby break its force. But I venture to say no reasoning from the narrative itself will be resorted to. No reviewing of the facts, or attempts at elucidation will be indulged in, for the sufficient reason, that more light would be thrown thereby upon actions which are now exposed."[71]

"To make the course he claims he did make, in a direct line over acknowledged drifting ice floes, and return in the tracks of the outward march to the point of departure would be a travesty on natural and physical laws," the captain added for good measure.[72] All that is left to us, then, is Peary's navigational observations, which as Wellman observed are worthless without passing the first two tests, and if the story of Commodore Valentine can be believed, they are forgeries.[73]

In a remarkable interview published by the *New York American* on September 7, 1909, Jo Peary is said to have asked her husband after his return from an earlier attempt to reach the Pole, "Why don't you tell them that you have found it and let it go at that?" To which she said he replied that "there were a hundred ways in which he would be found out." How right Peary was. We will, therefore, for purposes of this discussion, consider Robert E. Peary's claim to have reached the North Pole on April 6, 1909, a hoax and any comparisons with that journey to support or contradict the journey claimed by Frederick A. Cook to be without merit.

COOK'S SPEED

Without Peary, Dr. Cook's time schedule to the Pole, at an average of more than 15 miles a day, now looks impossible. Disallowing Peary's, no dog sledge journey to the Pole, before or since, even ones that were resupplied en route and did not need to haul all supplies from land and back again, has ever approached anything like it. Until 1995 no surface expedition had ever reached the North Pole and returned to any point of land unresupplied in any amount of time—if Cook did not do it.[74]

Cook's journey to the North Pole was not a matter of simply traveling 520 air miles from Cape Stallworthy, the modern name for Cape Thomas Hubbard, to his goal at a rate of 15.3 miles per day. Nansen, because of unavoidable detours, estimated he had to travel 1.4 total miles to make 1 mile north. Both Wally Herbert and Ralph Plaisted estimated that they had to travel 1.75 miles for every mile in the direction of the Pole.[75] Even if we accept only 1.5 as the true figure, this would add 260 miles to Cook's journey and nearly 7.7 miles to his daily average of *actual* miles traveled. If Cook's narrative is accepted, then his speed must have averaged 23 *total* miles per day en route. Surely that is an impossible speed over arctic pack ice for 34 consecutive days.

As Walter Wellman pointed out: "Arctic sledging is . . . wholly a question of physical laws of mechanical forces. No miracles are to be expected; one may

Struggling over the polar pack.

perfect and improve, and do a little better, but he cannot revolutionize, cannot perform prodigies. Every pretended sledging feat must be tested by its inherent probability, its approximate conformity to the standard. If it greatly exceeds all past performance, a good reason for the superiority must be given."[76]

On Nansen's journey, that best yardstick of early unresupplied polar travel, he gained more than 20 miles in a single day only twice and, on average, gained four to five miles per day in actual latitude over the entire trip.

Dr. Cook, in his fateful September 18, 1902, interview with the *Brooklyn Daily Eagle,* hypothesized a 1,200-mile round-trip to the Pole. He allowed an additional 300 miles "at least" for detours and said, "Since it is impossible to average more than ten miles a day, it would require 150 days to cover the 1,500 miles." In 1909 he claimed to have traveled, using his formula for detours, 1,248 miles in 88 days at an average speed of slightly more than 14 miles per day. Yet Cook never gave any plausible reason for his ability to exceed all past performance by such a wide margin.

With the exception of Peary's, only one sledge journey on the polar sea has claimed a faster rate of travel than Cook's. That was Donald MacMillan's 1914 trip toward Crocker Land. MacMillan averaged 16.6 miles going out and 37.5 coming back, or about 20 miles per day. But the differences between MacMillan's journey and Cook's are marked.

Ensign Green reported that at 105 miles out "we cached most of our food and ran for it." MacMillan turned back when he hit the first really rough ice, and on the way back, according to Green, "With empty sledges we double-marched back to land. . . . Four hours sleep, 40 miles hike, four biscuit, and a bit of meat, was our program."[77]

MacMillan's journey confirms ice conditions across the first portion of Cook's route, where he reported his greatest speed. But since MacMillan's sledge loads were considerably lighter, though his dogs were in poor shape, it cannot confirm Cook's average speed and corroborates nothing beyond the point MacMillan turned back. Nor does it compare with an expedition to the Pole, which would have to carry everything needed to sustain life for the entire journey.

DR. COOK'S NARRATIVE

Dr. Cook maintained that the proof of his claim lay in the narrative content of *My Attainment of the Pole*. Captain Hall found Cook's narrative consistent and pronounced it "unimpeachable." But a comparison of the speech on the floor of the House of Representatives, delivered by Representative Macon during the debate over the Peary Bill, with Hall's book shows that Hall took a direct and active role in the attempt to thwart Peary's recognition by Congress. Such a comparison discloses a number of *identical* passages between the two and shows that Hall's "mare's nest," which Bridgman feared, was the basis of Macon's speech, a speech aimed at discrediting Peary—hardly the action of an impartial analyst.

Moreover, there is a letter showing that Hall consulted with Cook personally on more than one occasion about the material content of *Has the North Pole Been Discovered?*—before it was published. Hall even asked Cook to restate suggestions that he had made, which the captain wanted to include in the text but had forgotten—a mortal blow to those who contend that Hall was truly impartial.[78] No, Captain Hall wanted Cook to win or, perhaps more, wanted Peary to lose. Yet Cook partisans continue to cite Hall's book in Cook's favor, as if it were unbiased analysis.

But unlike Peary's, most of the defenses of Cook's claim do center on his polar narrative. Its defenders contend that, like his Mount McKinley descriptions, it refers to physical features that only a person who had actually made the journey could have known about, since no one had ever been there before. Therefore, it is argued that Cook had observed these things firsthand and must have at least reached the near vicinity of the Pole. These descriptions can be divided into four major items.

Bradley Land. Captain Hall said that if Bradley Land did not exist, Cook's claims would fall. Edwin Swift Balch agreed with the statement of J.M. Wordie, a British polar traveler and historian who said, "The existence or non-existence of 'Bradley Land' is the touchstone for testing Dr. Cook's claims to have reached the North Pole. If land does not exist, his case is demolished forever. A photograph of what is undoubtedly high mountainous land is given in Dr. Cook's book and is labeled 'Bradley Land'; and the letterpress is equally unambiguous. Judgment on Cook should therefore be reserved till his statements have been confirmed or refuted."[79]

Bradley Land does not exist, yet today's partisans have not admitted that Cook's claims are thereby "demolished forever." Instead, they have tried to resuscitate them by linking Bradley Land to a discovery made in the Arctic only after Dr. Cook's death.

Despite Walt Gonnason's contention, the Air Force had no classified pictures of Bradley Land, but after World War II aerial reconnaissance did reveal a number of large tabular bergs drifting slowly clockwise in the arctic basin north of Ellesmere Island. Several arctic researchers and scientists have suggested these so-called ice islands—breakaway pieces of the ancient ice shelf—

are probably what Cook mistook for Bradley Land, and Cook's advocates have repeated these statements to support the doctor's claim.

Cook gave this description of Bradley Land: "The lower coast resembled Heiberg Island, with mountains and high valleys. The upper coast I estimated as being about one thousand feet high, flat, and covered with a thin sheet ice."[80] According to his published field notes, Bradley Land consisted of two islands, the southern one being 1,800 feet high.

Ice islands are no more than 100 to 200 feet thick, total. They are nearly flat with only rolling undulations and rise only about 25 feet above sea level. Cook's Bradley Land therefore does not remotely resemble an ice island, or even an ice island magnified by mirage. And Cook published two pictures of the high, mountainous land he called Bradley Land.[81]

Cook's Eskimo companions are reported to have said these pictures were of two small islands off the northwest coast of Axel Heiberg Land; others believe they are of the coast of Axel Heiberg Island itself, though the pictures have never been duplicated.

But why would Cook take the chance of saying there was land between 84° and 85° north if there wasn't any, then publish a picture of some other place and label it as a land he could not be certain even existed?

The answer to the riddle of Bradley Land follows the precedent set at Mount McKinley, where Cook appears to have successfully described actual features along his imagined route based on his own observations supplemented by a thorough knowledge of other explorers' reports and the existing scientific literature. From these, Cook was led to believe that it was likely that he would discover land at about 85° north. In 1900 he wrote, "It seems reasonable to expect some rocky islets north of Greenland as far as the 85th parallel, surely to the 84th. If stations were placed here there would be only 360 miles to cover [to the Pole]."[82]

That Cook still expected this in February 1908 is shown by the two letters that he left at Annoatok, in which he mentions the same possibility as "very likely." From his reading of Dr. Harris's paper, he thought he had good reason to believe a body of land existed near where he placed Bradley Land. And Cook was by no means alone in believing this. Harris's paper had already prompted several expeditions to look for a "new Arctic Continent" where Harris postulated it. Furthermore, Cook revealed how he may have arrived at Bradley Land's description without having seen it when he told reporters at the news conference at the Waldorf, "Well, if there is any land up there it is always at a considerable altitude—at least 1,000 feet."

If Cook possessed the self-assurance to come back without any proof and yet calmly assert that he had discovered the Pole, he certainly would have been willing to take a calculated risk that there was land in the vicinity of 85° north. Even if his initial claim was doubted, he may have reasoned, if this land was eventually determined to exist, he would ultimately be given the credit of reaching the Pole, just as Hall, Balch and Wordie later asserted he would.

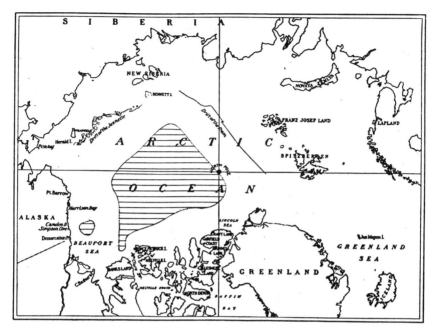

Rollin A. Harris's 1904 map, showing hypothesized land near the Pole.

Cook's faith in Harris's paper may have been reinforced by Peary's mistaken or fraudulent claim of seeing Crocker Land to the northwest of Axel Heiberg Land in 1906, and if Bradley Land proved nonexistent, he could fall back on confusing a mirage of Crocker Land with it.[83] Indeed, some Cook apologists have seized on MacMillan's excuse of mirage for Peary's "discovery" of a land that does not exist to excuse Bradley Land's nonexistence. Cook's failure to visit Bradley Land, even though he said he came within a few miles of its claimed position on his return route, gave all of these possibilities life, which would have evaporated like MacMillan's mist had he claimed to have set foot there.[84]

The Glacial Island. A far better candidate for an ice island is the "Glacial Island" that Cook said he crossed between 87° and 88° north. His description of it fits almost exactly the ice islands now known to drift within two degrees of the Pole—exactly where Cook says he crossed it. But his photograph of it, like that of Bradley Land, has proven fraudulent.

That it was fake was first made public by Wally Herbert in his 1989 book, *The Noose of Laurels,* and seems to be the main reason he concluded that Cook was a liar after years of believing there was at least some possibility he might be truthful. An uncropped lantern slide Herbert found among Cook's photographic material donated to the Library of Congress by Helene Cook Vetter in 1973 shows rocky land attached to the right-hand margin—an impossibility at the reported position of the Glacial Island.

Herbert probably did not realize that this was not his original discovery. J.M. Wordie stated in private correspondence in the 1920s that the ice in the picture seemed to have a distinct rise to it, indicating it was taken along the ice foot of some island, and it was the discovery of this very lantern slide among Cook's materials by Evelyn Briggs Baldwin in 1913 that led to his renunciation of Cook. This is the picture Baldwin took the Shainwalds to see at the Prince George Hotel. Among Baldwin's papers are several photographic copies of this slide labeled "Exhibit A."

But how could Cook have dreamed up an ice island before any had been discovered? Again there were precedents. Nansen mentioned in his book, *Farthest North,* that he passed over undulating country covered with snow far at sea. In *Nearest the Pole,* Peary described crossing "several large level old floes, which my Eskimos at once remarked, looked as if they did not move even in summer," and "several berg-like pieces of ice discolored with sand were noted."[85]

Dr. Cook's published indecision as to whether his Glacial Island was genuine land or floating ice may have served as a hedge that some such feature might be discovered—since this part of his route lay across the zone Dr. Harris had indicated might hold an unknown continent—and still have left open an excuse for its absence if it wasn't there.

Unfortunately for Cook, he left for Greenland in 1907 without having seen another important paper, "On North Polar Problems," in which Nansen systematically demolished Harris's theories and cited convincing evidence that the Pole was surrounded by a deep abysmal sea for hundreds of miles in every direction. Had he read it, Cook might have thought twice about reporting any land along his claimed route.[86]

Polar Precedents. Many of the features and incidents described along Cook's route from Svartevoeg to his Glacial Island will sound familiar to anyone who has studied the previous writings of Cook and Peary. The distortions of the sun at low altitudes and the descriptions of ice flowers forming along new ice can be found in *Through the First Antarctic Night.* The sudden storm on the pack has a close parallel in the "hurricane" at Annoatok described in Cook's winter diary of 1907–08. The collapse of the igloo on the arctic pack is very similar to the collapse of the igloo at Sunrise Camp in 1892, as described in *Northward over the "Great Ice,"* and Cook's crossing of the Big Lead shares much with Peary's description of that same accomplishment in *Nearest the Pole.*[87]

As for conditions at the Pole itself, though not definitely known in 1908, there was general agreement after the discoveries of Nansen aboard the *Fram* that there was no land in the immediate vicinity of the Pole. Dr. Cook held this view himself. "The north pole is in the center of an imprisoned sea of ice," he wrote in 1904; this may have been reinforced the following year by another widely available paper entitled, "On the Physiographic Improbability of Land at the North Pole."[88]

At the Pole, Cook set the thickness of the ice at 16 feet, a very common measurement in the central polar basin cited in other narratives, including

Nansen's. Cook correctly said the ice drifted southeast over the Pole, but this might have been deduced from the course of the *Fram,* Siberian driftwood and the wreckage of the *Jeanette.* In keeping with his magnetic meridian theory, Cook said the compass pointed south toward the magnetic pole along the 97th meridian. This is the same opinion he held in 1902, when he was asked, "How would you know when you reached the North Pole?" by the *Brooklyn Daily Eagle*'s reporter. He replied, "The compass would point exactly south."

This naive reply, coupled with his 1894 comment that he was on the "wrong side" of Greenland to take any magnetic observations, gives some insight into Cook's simplistic misconceptions about geomagnetism. However, his observation that the magnetic compass points in the direction of the magnetic pole, which would be in the direction Cook indicated, is certainly a safe general assumption in the absence of data, though the exact direction it would have pointed in 1908 is speculative.[89]

Dr. Cook also places the temperature at the Pole ten degrees higher than south of it, in line with a long-held contemporary scientific theory that the temperature would rise as the Pole was approached because of the constancy of sunlight.

Cook's familiarity with scientific theories of his time led him to believe that each pole was depressed about 13 miles to compensate for a perceived equatorial bulge of 26 miles.[90] On September 22, 1909, the *New York American* quoted him as saying "there were peculiarities of the horizon that distinguished the top of the earth from any other spot I have ever seen." He also expressed to Captain Loose his ambivalence over whether there was a flattening at the Pole, and as late as the 1930s, he continued to try to support his claim to the Pole by somewhat vague discourses in his memoirs on the strange appearance of the sky and a "widened horizon" there. He said the movement of the clouds and other phenomena indicated a "dead center" at the Pole, an idea based on a once-popular theory of the effects of centrifugal motion, now discredited.

Today, satellites have revealed that instead of a depression, the earth bulges slightly at the North Pole—62 feet higher than if the earth were a perfect sphere. Given the theories of his time, however, perhaps Cook's only obvious gaff came in his description of the movements of the sun at the Pole—again, a problem requiring a grasp of mathematical concepts.

Professor de Quervain, a fellow passenger on the *Hans Egede,* said that in a conversation with the doctor when the ship was off Cape Farewell, Cook had told him that the altitudes of the sun at midnight and noon at the Pole were "very different." When de Quervain pointed out that the sun should appear to circle the horizon at a uniform elevation, Cook then accepted his suggestion that he must have been confused when he made his observations at the Pole.[91]

Perhaps as a result of this conversation with de Quervain, in *Petermanns Mitteilungen* for October 1909, Cook stated: "In two days' observations it was determined that the sun circled the horizon always at the same elevation, from which resulted the only possible proof that the pole was actually reached."

Of course, the sun does not do this at all, but actually rises spirally, higher and higher, until June 21, then it begins to sink spirally until September 22, when it sets. On April 21 and 22 the sun would have appeared to rise, respectively, 20' 33" and 20' 21" daily, but Cook did not include this in his reports until the publication of his book in 1911.[92]

In 1914 the *Scottish Geographical Magazine* summed up all the observations of Cook's polar narrative and found in them nothing startlingly original:

> With a knowledge of Peary's Crocker Land, found in 1906, Peary's land ice near 86° N., found the same year, and the experience in polar travel, which Dr. Cook certainly had, both in the Arctic and Antarctic, we submit that an imaginative man, taking into account probabilities, had an easy task in writing the story, and surely any man of even average education could write of the pole as "an endless field of purple snows. No life. No land."

> The more plausible hypothesis is that Cook never traveled as far north as the alleged Crocker Land, but turned back at or about the Big Lead and unwilling to admit defeat in the project which he asserts was his life's ambition, proceeded to write his story from the data previously outlined by Peary.[93]

Cook's description of "purple snows" at the Pole was much ridiculed, but on the Baldwin-Ziegler Expedition, Russell Porter noticed similar color effects after the prolonged darkness of a polar winter. "As time went on, and the sun stayed up for longer intervals during each twenty-four hours," Porter observed, "this color changed to lavender, violet and purple, and then, strange to say, this weird mono-chrome slowly disappeared. The effect of this predominance of colors at the violet end of the solar spectrum is shown in the 'color notes' or sketches made by the writer in the spring of 1902, when the temperature ranged between thirty and fifty below zero."[94] If Cook's only experience with the arctic pack was a short trip not long after the rising of the sun, as the Scottish journal suggests, he may have experienced this same phenomenon and used it as the basis of his descriptions of the Pole itself, which after all looks like any other part of the pack.

Cook said he never sighted a single living thing on his polar journey, though Peary said he saw a seal as well as bear tracks near the 86th parallel going north and fox tracks near the 87th both going and coming. But their language in describing an absence of life at the Pole is nearly identical. Cook said, "We were the only pulsating creatures in a dead world of ice," and Peary, "We, the only living things in a trackless, colorless, inhospitable desert of ice."[95] This was the popular view at the time, but the central arctic pack is not a "sterile sea," nor has it been so reported by travelers toward the Pole since 1909.

Amundsen noted a flock of birds at his landing place within three degrees of the Pole in 1925, and Wally Herbert in 1968–69 saw not only birds but also five seals and six polar bears in the supposedly sterile area above the 85th degree of latitude. One of the bears was seen above the 87th parallel. In 1990 two Norwegians skiing to the Pole were attacked by a polar bear above the 88th. Since bears sit at the top of the Arctic's food pyramid, their presence implies a complete chain of life below them.

The Westerly Drift. Today it is known that the Beaufort Gyre passes through the area that Cook traversed on his described return route. How can Cook's western drift on his return be explained, when no such current was then known to exist? It might be discovered by a journey of less than 100 miles to the northwest. Recall Donald MacMillan had his pick ax swept away by a strong current during an attempted sounding on just such a journey in 1914, and he noted a strong tide or current at the place he turned back. Or it could have been just a lucky expedient, since if Cook's story is false, it was necessary that he be carried west to explain his inability to reach Axel Heiberg Land and his subsequent absence over the next winter.

POLAR PICTURES

Opposite pages 300 and 301 in his book, Dr. Cook printed two pictures with practically no detail and no discernible shadows. Each shows an igloo representing his camp at the North Pole. Like his underexposed picture of the "top of the continent" whose "dark sky" does not allow the viewer a clear look at the details of the summit, these pictures appear to be overexposed, to the same effect. Cook attributed their washed-out appearance to the actinic light at the Pole, which caused a "blue haze over everything" and a diffuse effect on the film.[96] When the picture opposite page 300 was published ("Suitable for Framing") in the *New York Herald* on September 22, 1909, it was, as the *Sun's* correspondent noted at Cook's Carnegie Hall lecture, heavily retouched.

The retouched version shows a pile of ice debris, apparently left from the construction of the igloo, at its entrance. But the features retouched in the *Herald* version of this photograph are not fantasies of the airbrush artist. A photograph in Rudolph Franke's book, opposite page 49, shows an almost identical view of the same igloo, though it makes no representation of

Retouched photo of Cook's snow house at the Pole.

having been taken at the North Pole but is used simply as an illustration of an igloo. Its snow blocks are configured the same, the Eskimos are posed in the same positions on either side, one holding a saw knife, and there is debris in front of the doorway as in the *Herald*'s retouched version. But in Franke's book there is no flag on the igloo, the image is reversed and the ice blocks and debris are not touched in. Moreover, the picture is not overexposed by "actinic light" and is much clearer than those Cook published. The existence of a clear photograph of this igloo tends to show that the "North Pole igloo" picture, too, is a fake, since it destroys the reason Cook gave for the lack of definition in the ones he printed.

MacMillan reported that Etukishuk told him that this "polar igloo" was built near Cape Faraday on the eastern shore of Ellesmere Land in the spring of 1909. By that time Cook had abandoned one of his sledges and all of his dogs. No dogs and a portion of only one sledge are visible in either of Cook's polar igloo photographs.

Other photographs in *My Attainment of the Pole* indicate misrepresentation as well, when compared with original prints now in the Library of Congress. In one of an igloo displayed opposite page 172, the original shows definite shadows of measurable objects, none of which are long enough for even the highest sun angle Cook would have experienced on the outward trip—12 degrees. This picture must have been taken much later, when the sun would have been at a far higher angle than implied by its position in the text.

The best near-contemporary pictures of what shadows look like at polar dawn can be found in Anthony Fiala's *Fighting the Polar Ice*. The difference between Fiala's photographs and Cook's is immediately striking, Fiala's shadows stretching to immense lengths because of the very low angle of the sun, would be similar to what Cook should have seen in March.

Proponents have often pointed to one of Cook's photos as evidence in his favor. The one opposite page 269, labeled "Mending near the Pole," has shadows appropriate to a sun angle of 12 degrees, but the same could be said of this as has already been said of Peary's alleged pictures of the sun at the Pole.

The negative conjectures about Cook's narrative presented so far may seem to some no more valid or convincing than many of the positive conjectures that have been made in his defense. The testing ground of which conjectures are the more valid, then, must be the contents of the book by Cook's only literate witness and the notebooks written on the journey and preserved by Dr. Cook himself. Since these constitute the other primary documents of the expedition, we must now open them, translate Franke's gothic type and puzzle over the tiny pencil marks on the pages of Cook's diaries to confirm or reject our suppositions.

A DEFECTIVE DIARY

A comparison of Cook's account with Franke's presents an immediate contradiction. Franke declares in his book that the expedition stood ready to leave Annoatok on February 25, 1908, and he told the New York *World* on October

14, 1908, that it left the next day, yet Cook says he started one week before, on February 19. Which is correct?

Franke admits that he was confused as to the date when he returned to Annoatok after parting with Cook, and his statements about the time the expedition started for Ellesmere Land might be dismissed on that account. But he should have had the correct day at least up until the day of departure, since Cook kept track and would surely have told him, or at least they would have believed it to be the same incorrect date.

Peary's notes state that Franke told him they left on February 26, as does Dr. Goodsell's diary of August 10, 1908, so Franke's impression of the date the expedition started could not be due to a lapse of memory caused by too much time having intervened before he wrote his book.

According to Franke's account, the sun rose the day after he and Cook started, ending an absence of 128 days. This would be correct for February 29 if the sun set on October 24 as recorded in Dr. Cook's diary. In the *New York Herald* of September 3, 1909, Franke says he left Cook on March 3, 1908, to return to Greenland, and at that time they had been four days on the way to the Pole. That would indeed make the date of departure February 29.[97]

Since the sun rose officially at Annoatok in 1908 at noon on February 19, though the sight of it might have been advanced or retarded a day either way by extreme refraction, should Franke's testimony be dismissed as simply mistaken? Perhaps not.

Besides his several statements that the expedition left on February 26, Franke says on page 66 of his book that the advance party was sent across Smith Sound "in the second week of February" and that he did not accompany it "because during the last eight days before the main expedition was to start much work remained to be done." Counting back eight days from February 26 gives February 18 for this party's departure, which does not match "the second week in February," though eight days before February 19 does. But in *My Attainment of the Pole,* Cook gives the date the advance party left as February 5, which doesn't match either. However, in his diary, Dr. Cook says on February 17: "We had planned to send a party to-day to Ellesmere Ld. but there is a gale blowing out of the Sd. which makes this start impossible, and since this start cannot be made to-day we must wait a few days and all start together."

Obviously this didn't happen, since he reports in both his book and his original diary meeting the advance party in Ellesmere Land later, and his diary entry states that the advance party had not left as of February 17. In his book Cook places the trip that Franke made to Cape Veile at "the end of January," but his diary states that Franke left on January 14 and was back the 19th. With that single exception, a pattern emerges from this confusion: all of Cook's published dates have been shifted *backward* in time for some reason.

All of Franke's statements, though not consistent as to what the day of departure actually was, *are* consistent in indicating a date *after* February 19.

This discrepancy is critical to the consideration of Dr. Cook's narrative of his polar journey.

Cook's diary entry for February 9 indicates he expects to leave in ten days to two weeks, but on February 13 he says he is still without enough dogs. Though he wrote to Herbert Bridgman in December 1907 that he already had a hundred, his diary says he is waiting for the Eskimos to return from the walrus grounds to bring him more. On February 17 he says he expects to leave "in a few days." But the two letters he left at Annoatok are dated February 20, 1908, the day *after* he later claimed to have left, and in them he says he will be leaving for the Far North "in a day or two." Therefore, everything points to a date of departure that has also has been moved back in time, so Franke's may be correct.

Since Cook's original field notes state that he did not leave Cape Thomas Hubbard until March 18, and they account for each day between then and February 19 (not all of his notes are printed in *My Attainment of the Pole*— those entries from February 19 to March 17 are omitted but exist in his original notebook), if he actually left a week later, as Franke said, he would have arrived at Svartevoeg a week later, or on March 25. To reach the North Pole from there by April 21, he would have to cover 520 miles at a pace of nearly 19 miles per day straight-line distance, and nearly 30 miles per day if we apply our formula for detours. So unless Cook traveled at incredible speed or arrived at the Pole on April 28, his story cannot be true if we accept Franke's date. But he cannot have arrived on April 28, because his reported observations at the Pole are valid only for April 21. Either way there is a problem.

How can this difference of reported departure dates be resolved? Both Franke and Cook agree they saw the sun for the first time the day after they left Annoatok for the Pole. Dr. Cook says the date was February 20; Franke, February 27. Is it possible that the sun had risen some days before and they had not noticed it? For men who longed for the return of its light, this might at first seem incredible; however, it is possible.

Peary was also very concerned about Cook's timetable. In a memorandum he pointed out how easy it would be to miss sunrise at Annoatok, which has a northern exposure, with high cliffs to the south. Since the sun would rise at about noon and thus be due south, it would not have been visible directly from Annoatok. What is more, as Cook noted in Antarctica, a low-lying ice mist often obscures the polar horizon even on clear days, and Cook reported the period before he started as extremely stormy, implying cloud cover.[98]

Not until they got out on the ice of Smith Sound and clear of the land could they have looked directly south toward the rising sun. The day of their departure for Ellesmere Land, Dr. Cook described the sky as gray before noon, so the next day—the day both men report they first saw the sun—was the first time they would have had a clear horizon without obstruction or cloud cover to the south. So it may well be that the first sight of the sun was not "sunrise" at all, leaving open the possibility that Franke's date of departure is actually correct.

When Dr. Cook's reasonably well-kept narrative diary is examined to see what happened on February 18–19, there comes a startling discovery. Not only do the diary entries end at February 18 without indicating any imminent departure for the Pole, but there is a signature missing from the diary at this point, leaving no place to record the events for the next 11 days in sequence. The diary is complete, and no pages have been removed; it is simply defective— the signature having been left out. So if Cook's account is false, the choice of February 19 as the starting date of the trip may stem from this chance of fate that Cook purchased a defective diary.

Among the notebooks at the Library of Congress, however, was an even more amazing discovery. Although there were two notebooks that purported to cover the time from when Cook left Annoatok to when he went into winter quarters at Cape Sparbo in September 1908, neither contained a consecutive account of events as they happened. There was no contemporaneous diary of Cook's polar journey.

THE POLAR NOTEBOOKS

There are four polar notebooks preserved with Cook's papers in the Library of Congress. Three are miniature memorandum books and one is a pocket diary. (See the end notes for a detailed description of each of these books.) [99] One of the memorandum books (notebook 1) contains what was published, in part, in *My Attainment of the Pole* as Cook's "original field notes." It has notations from February 19 to September 4, 1908, but bears the heading "copied at Sparbo winter," indicating that it is not the original but a copy of the original. The pocket diary (notebook 4) contains an account of the expedition, starting with a record of the journey across the ice from Svartevoeg, the first date given as March 20, 1908, apparently reporting events as they happened or just after they occurred. But after five days the writing, initially in a large hand (though not as large as Cook's "hunting diary" kept in the field during the winter of 1907–08), becomes smaller, and the text thereafter uses the past tense exclusively. Furthermore, some of the statements made on those first few pages are crossed out and modified in a way that makes them irreconcilable with what was originally written.

This pattern is similar in its inconsistencies and changes to Cook's Mount McKinley diary, and the suspicion again arises that an apparently original and accurate record has once again become a fabrication. If Cook's eventual story is not a record of facts, then a careful examination of the internal evidence in his polar notebooks should disclose a story "in the making," since a single record of actual events cannot vary. Such an examination requires a thorough familiarity with Cook's difficult handwriting and a good magnifying glass, because as the reporters at the Waldorf-Astoria observed when he showed them one of his notebooks, the writing is often minute, with as many as 12 lines to the inch.

With magnifying glass in hand, let us now look at a few excerpts. On page 31 of Cook's notebook 4, our suspicion about the starting date is supported when we see "the start was made early in March" crossed out in favor of "the middle of February." Page 15 records: "We did not actually see land until 30 [of March]. This proved to be Crocker Ld." Cook goes on to describe it in detail, but his field notes make no mention of Crocker Land, and he later said that he saw only what he thought were indications of land near the reported position of Crocker Land. He eventually claimed to have discovered Bradley Land on March 30. Yet in the notebook this does not appear until the entry on page 17, dated April 4: "At noon however we saw actual land to the west. It was a low ice sheeted country about 1000 feet high and about 60 miles away. . . . Our obs. on the 5th placed us at 85°16' long 96°11'. We had drifted east more than we had calculated in our reconing." In Cook's published field notes, no land is mentioned as being seen this day, and no observations for position are given for April 5. On page 19: "April 11 Close to the 87th ["87th" written over an erasure] we passed over a surface suggestive of land For a distance of 15 miles the ice was slightly raised free of hummocks and crevices with only the rolling irregularity of old ice and ever present cestrugi or drifts. The cracks and leads, the pressure ridges of hummocks were absent." This appears to be the Glacial Island that Cook's published field notes record as being traversed on April 13, not April 11. In his published field notes, Dr. Cook gives his position on April 11 as 87°20' north latitude, 95°19' west longitude. In the notebook he gives 86°40.5' and 97°8'.

Also on page 19, after the heading "at the pole," there is a blank space. The next entry is clearly dated "April 28," but this is written over with a "22" and followed by "We turned our backs to the pole. . . ." Several notations elsewhere indicate that Cook left the Pole on April 24.

April 22 tallies exactly with the earliest reports Cook made about the date of his arrival at the North Pole, and the notations about leaving on April 24 would be consistent with the time he claimed to have spent there, *if* he arrived on April 22.

In the letter Captain Adams wrote to Peary, he says that Cook reached the Pole on April 22, 1908.[100] In Cook's own letter to Captain Bernier, he also says he arrived at the Pole on April 22, though when the letter was printed in the *New York Herald,* this was changed to the then-standard April 21.[101]

On page 22 we find "Here on the 24 [of May] we had one clear day during which we got fair observations & a peep at both Bradley & Crocker Lands." In Cook's published field notes, he says that he did not see the land discovered on the way up again, but the Eskimos did, while he was sleeping. And, of course, neither Bradley Land nor Crocker Land actually exists.

These discrepancies and the written-over date of April 28 in the notebook, as well as other adjustments that seem to have been made to latitudes and dates, suggest that Cook was improving his story as he went along, originally computing his arrival at the Pole one week later than he eventually claimed. This fits in with a one-week-later departure, just as Franke reported.

That none of these changes are intended as corrections to inadvertent mistakes is confirmed by a notation marked "Apr. 19-27 88-90," implying that he was still traveling *toward* the Pole on April 27. This occurs in notebook 3, which was used as a sketchbook for the full-length book Cook planned to write. Most of what was written in this book has been erased. There remains, however, an outline of the book in 26 chapters. Chapter 17 is titled "about the pole." Turning to where this should be in the notebook, we find nothing was ever written on the page except a date that, although erased, is still clearly visible as "April 28." The corner of this page, which following the pattern of the other pages should bear the chapter's title, is torn away.

Returning to notebook 4, we find what is apparently a set of narrative comments to accompany a lecture illustrated by 100 lantern slides, scattered on nonconsecutive pages, but with each caption numbered in sequence. This narration is similar to the 2,000-word dispatch Cook sent from Lerwick; however, it, too, shows differences from his eventually published story.

In the introductory remarks on page 52 can be found the magnanimous man as he appeared at Copenhagen: "But let us be liberal since our success is built upon the failure of our predecessors. . . . Let us share the present glory . . . especially with Peary." On page 57 appears the original intention to claim the sighting of Crocker Land in nearly the same words he wrote to Captain Bernier: "We saw Crocker Ld. and beyond a new land was discovered." On page 72 he notes that he made two rounds of observations at the Pole but does not record them, and this statement is written over an obvious erasure of a previous statement. In the entire lantern slide narration, all the latitudes and longitudes have been erased or rewritten and their values changed.

Two pages of notebook 3, perhaps inadvertently, were not erased along with the rest. They contain an outline of chapter 13 entitled "Adrift with the ice of the Circumpolar sea," covering March 25 to April 4. Its contents do not match the published field notes, either.

There can be no legitimate justification for these discrepancies, especially the failure of the dates and latitudes to match the original field notes, if those notes were genuine. We must now recall Captain Hall's admonition about Peary:

> But it was not the falsehood itself that was significant; it would not have been significant even if he had falsified every sentence in his story. But the significance rested in the FACT that the falsehood proved INVENTION, and proving invention, SOLVED THE PROBLEM.
>
> When anyone can catch Cook at business of that character it will be Cook's undoing.

Judge Killits couldn't have agreed with Captain Hall more, and we should also recall his admonishment to the Texas jury:

> Self deception is a perfect defense to any charge of fraudulent con-
> duct, and conviction cannot be had so long as a reasonable doubt
> of its absence exists.
>
>   You will note, however, that when the charge is that fraud was
> committed by and through deliberate misrepresentation of material
> existing facts, there is no room for reasonable doubt on the subject
> of self deception. When it is clearly proven that a conscious lie has
> been uttered, there is an end to any valid claim of self deception.

By the inconsistency of his own account of the events of his expedition,
written in his own hand in his contemporaneous notebooks kept on his polar
journey, Dr. Cook has been undone, and the end to any valid claim of self-
deception has arrived.[102]

A MISSING NOTEBOOK

In his surviving notebooks, Dr. Cook made what appeared to be numerous
cross-references—notations such as "N. I page 96," where he listed the topic
"dog comfort." There were also references to "N. II." The largest of the Polar
notebooks (notebook 4) is labeled "N. III." At his press conference at the Waldorf, Cook displayed a notebook that was reported to contain 173 pages and
told the reporters that he had two more of these, which could correspond to
"N. I" and "N. II."

Cook said that he wrote more than 150,000 words at Cape Sparbo, but
the narrative content of his tiny memorandum books along with N. III,
which are all now in the Library of Congress, do not appear to have nearly
that many words despite their minute print. Furthermore, that there were
three larger notebooks is supported on page 416 of *My Attainment of the Pole*,
where Cook wrote: "My three notebooks were full, and there remained only a
small pad of prescription blanks and two miniature memorandum books."
Actually there are three miniature memo books. Perhaps he never intended
anyone to see the one he had erased (notebook 3). There were also seven prescription blanks, but nothing else used as writing material could be found
among Cook's papers.

All of this consistently pointed to two missing notebooks. But where were
they?

By way of Walter Lonsdale, Dr. Cook had submitted a notebook in support of his claim to the University of Copenhagen in January 1910; it was
returned to Cook in February 1911. But unbeknownst to him, the Danes
had made a photographic copy. An inquiry to Denmark by the author turned
it up, apparently undisturbed and forgotten, in the Royal Astronomical
Observatory Library in Copenhagen.

After a long wait, a copy arrived. The book proved to be "N. I," so often
referred to in the notebooks already examined. It said so—"Notes I"—on the
flyleaf, and "dog comfort" was indeed on page 96. Most important, the book

was titled "From Annoatok Northward and Return." Here then was a photo-copy of the actual diary of Dr. Cook's polar journey, containing its complete narrative, including the field notes Cook eventually published.

But where was the original? Why did Cook retain his copy of the field notes as in notebook 1 but not the original itself? Was there something in the book that, like Peary with his original diary, he wanted to suppress?

It was an exciting find. And coming years after the original analysis of Cook's other diaries, a careful examination of the contents of this missing notebook would serve as a test of all the speculations already made.

The photocopy was of variable quality, and this, combined with Cook's difficult handwriting, made deciphering every word of it impossible. Grudg-ingly, however, the diary gradually gave up its secrets.

The book is physically identical to Dr. Cook's Mount McKinley diary in size and format, except that it has only 158 pages, whereas the McKinley book has 176. But the polar diary has an index indicating entries as high as page 177. The pages after 154 are renumbered, however, the original numbers printed on the corners having been torn off. The inside of the back cover was numbered 159.

Since these books each had 176 numbered pages originally, some pages from N. I had been removed at some time before the book was sent to Denmark. Index entries for the missing pages indicated that they may have once held pro-motional material. For instance, page 177 (probably the flyleaf) once contained a "Syndicate Script." It may be that Cook, no less than Peary, was squeamish about having his schemes for profiting from his polar quest made public. But what the renumbered pages contain is far more important than what is known to be missing—and may explain why the original probably no longer exists.

A now-familiar pattern emerges. The bulk of N. I appears to be the original record of each day from Cook's departure from Annoatok to his near approach to Svartevoeg. All these entries are in a large hand, as if written in the field, filled with circumstantial detail and unimportant incidents as they happened. However, when the polar party sets off over the ice, the writing suddenly grows small. These entries are far more neat in penmanship and consistency of layout and are nearly identical to the field notes Cook later published, though there are occasional unimportant differences.

More important is the layout of the book. Cook habitually, and without exception in his Alaskan and polar diaries, wrote his narratives only on the right-hand pages, reserving the left-hand pages for notes. The entries in N. I follow that pattern to the place where the pages are renumbered. Then the narrative continues as the published field notes but is written consecu-tively on *both right and left pages* until the inside of the back cover, where the reader is referred to page 154. There they continue on the left-hand pages back to front.

Can this very peculiar arrangement be explained in the context of our former analysis? Suppose it was an attempt to make the fictitious field notes appear to be a continuation of the actual original notes that occupy the bulk of N. I, and it was Cook's dissatisfaction with the result, which differed significantly from the original diary entries in size, style, content and format, that caused him first to recopy its contents in a consistent, consecutive format, and eventually to discard the original entirely.

Up to the renumbered pages, N. I seems to be the actual record of Cook's journey from Annoatok, but the headings, because they summarize the entries that follow, were obviously written after the fact, and their dates look as if they have been adjusted. Originally, N. I must have held the complete record of the journey up to his actual arrival at Svartevoeg, and being near the end of the book at that time, he started a fresh book to record his polar attempt (notebook 4), whose first date is given as March 20.

But when he went to write the "field notes" of his fictitious journey, he had to make some adjustments. Since he left a week later than his eventual story, the missing pages probably held the descriptions of the missing week,[103] so he would have had to remove the pages covering the events of the days after March 17, the day before he said he started for the Pole. This would necessitate renumbering the remaining unused pages to make the following entries appear continuous and readjusting all the dates on the original entries.

This explanation of N. I's arrangement is supported by its content. On page 145 Cook states that "we must rest – and recuperate." All the material between pages 145 and 155 is dated March 16, and it all appears to have been written at the "rest" camp, which is definitely south of Svartevoeg, since it describes the ice in Nansen Sound in detail. On this span of pages is a chronology of events that clearly could not have happened on a single day, yet the first renumbered page (155) begins with Cook's arrival at Svartevoeg on March 17. All succeeding entries match the published field notes.

In *My Attainment of the Pole,* Cook says of his first sight of the sun on February 20: "A great ball of fire rose along the icy horizon." The entry on page 9 of N. I for that date reads: "The sun. What joy. At 1 [this clearly written over "2"] pm the frosty haze lifted and we saw the sun a huge distended ball of fire—the first which we saw of it for nearly 5 months though at this latitude it should be absent for only four months. It remained with us for about 2 hours the icy haze lifting it by refraction." In other words, the sun had already risen some time before 1 P.M., or possibly 2, and remained visible until 3 or possibly 4 P.M. Since the sun at this time of year at Cook's location was rising approximately two thirds of its apparent diameter each day, on the day after sunrise, February 20, the day Cook says he first saw it, the sun should have risen at 11:40 A.M., and at apparent noon, the disk of the sun should have cleared the horizon by about half its diameter. It would then start to settle and would set at 2:03 P.M. On the day Franke claims it was, February 27, the sun would have risen at 10:01 A.M., ascended well clear of the horizon and would not have set until 4:04 P.M. In making such calculations a number of assumptions have to be made in the absence of hard data. The position of the expedition's first sight of the sun can be deduced within a few miles from Cook's statement in *My Attainment of the Pole* that at the end of the first day's travel he had gone 20 miles north, but was still 30 miles from Cape Sabine. This would place him at approximately 78°50' N., 72°W. What time Cook was keeping is important. The assumption is made that he kept Atlantic Standard Time (60°W). The setting back of one hour in the entry supports this, since at the location of Annoatok his watch would have been nearly an hour fast compared with the sun. The temperature and pressure are of less importance and have been arbitrarily set at standard pressure, 1016 millibars, and –40°F.

Therefore, although Cook's entry could not possibly be describing the expected movements of the sun on February 20, 1908, it fits very well with Franke's date of February 27, one week later. This entry thus tends to confirm Franke's date of departure and the idea that a week is missing from Cook's polar narrative.

Cook wrote a rare elaboration on page 8 directly opposite it: "The sun returned to-day after an absence of 4 months, Oct 24 to Feb 20 [three illegible words follow, possibly "some 120 days"] but to us with high cliffs Eastward the sun has not been seen for nearly 5 months and I suppose it will be many days before [we?] see it over our old camp," thus confirming Peary's belief that the returning sun could not be seen from Annoatok for a considerable period after it actually rose.

That N. I has been adjusted backward is also supported by other internal evidence: there are several more sets of consecutive entries given the same date, yet they describe events on more than one day, and the entry for "March 12" says, "These are cold days curious that we should have our coldest days in the end of March."

After entering his "original field notes" into his diary on the still available pages to the inside of the back cover and then continuing them backward on the left-hand pages, Cook must have had second thoughts. He must have seen the suspicions the physical arrangement and appearance of the book might raise and decided to copy it over in consecutive order. In the copy he substituted an entirely consistent format—short telegraphic phrases with little detail—similar to the field notes he eventually published for the whole journey. So the "copy" (notebook 1) is not a copy at all up through March 17, but a severe condensation, even leaving out many events that would be the "highlights" on those days. When called upon to present his original record at Copenhagen, he had no choice but to hand over N. I, but he could take comfort in the knowledge that these differences between it and the copy would not be known to the Danes.

In publishing his field notes in *My Attainment of the Pole*, he was careful to leave out the days that record events before March 18 because they differed between N. I and notebook 1, and probably he eventually suppressed N. I altogether so that the conflict would never come to light. But the Danes had made a complete photostat, and so the deception is revealed.

The whereabouts of "N. II" are a complete mystery, but it seems illogical to suppose that Cook kept N. I and N. III but abandoned N. II. Perhaps it contained the draft of the story of his journey to the Pole that appeared in the *New York Herald*, since the September 26, 1909, *New York American* quotes an interview with a New Haven paper in which Cook mentioned a "manuscript" of his journey. N. III is badly mutilated, having had 101 pages removed from it since the reporters saw it at the Waldorf. Therefore, only a few of the original pages written by Cook on his journey toward the Pole seem to have been preserved by him.

The contents of N. I, then, neatly confirm every speculation previously made that was relevant to it without conflicting with a single one, adding to the confidence we can feel in being close to the truth.

VISIONING THE UNIMAGINABLE

Of the many original pictures now in the Library of Congress that Cook made on his 1907–09 expedition, only two show really rough ice. Both appear to have been taken at the same location. One was published opposite page 172

Rough ice. Photograph by Cook.

in his book, and the other, unpublished, shows to better advantage the ice visible in the published picture, thrown up in all directions as far as the eye can see. Looking at the utter chaos of ice in that picture, it is easy to imagine what might have happened that day in late March 1908.

As he looks out upon those jumbled blocks, Dr. Cook knows, just as he knew standing on Fake Peak and looking out upon the great uplift of McKinley, that his dreams are unobtainable, yet he still longs for them:

> Beyond and above me I visioned the unimaginable, blinding white regions of ice and cold, about which, like a golden-crowned sentinel, the face of flame, the circling midnight sun kept guard. Upon this desolate, awe-inspiring stage—unchanged since the days of its designing—I saw myself attempting to win in the most spectacular and difficult marathon for the testing of human strength, courage and perseverance, of body and brain, which God has offered to man. I could see myself, in my fancy pictures, invading those roaring regions, struggling over icy lands in the dismal twilight of the Arctic morning, and venturing, with a few companions, upon the

lifeless, wind-swept Polar sea. A black mite, I saw myself slowly piercing those white and terrible spaces, braving terrific storms, assailing green, adamantine barriers of ice, crossing the swift-flowing, black rivers of those ice fields, and stoutly persisting until, successful, I stood alone, a victor, upon the world's pinnacle![104]

But it is already nearly April, and he is still more than 400 miles from the Pole. He is 42; there will be no more chances, no more youth. Dr. Cook must have realized then that it was impossible to reach the Pole, not only for him but for anyone attempting it by dog sledge.

Captain Hall imagined what might have gone through Peary's mind as he confronted that terrible realization:

> One of three things he must do, his decision must be instant and final. First: Openly to acknowledge failure. . . . Second: To proceed to certain death in a futile attempt to encompass the impossible. Third: Imposture, with riches and glory. The temptation is colossal. Less than this has wrecked greater men. . . .
>
> The price is enormous. It is, moreover, an opportunity never again to be presented. He casts the die! Conscience is easily soothed. The record to the Pole, even though successful with all the trials, risks, physical and mental strains—what is it after all in the last analysis but entries in a diary?[105]

And how much more would that thought appeal to a man like Dr. Cook?—"what is it after all . . . but entries in a diary?" He may have reasoned that to be able to write the account of such a journey without having actually done it—one that would convince the world—would be a greater accomplishment than the journey itself. There was nothing but more ice at the North Pole anyway; given the reality he now sees for himself, a man would prove himself a fool who even made the attempt! He does the prudent thing and turns back. As he said, "No man has any right to take such chances as that."

When Dr. Cook decided to concoct the story of his journey to the Pole is unknown. Though there is nothing to indicate that he did not intend to make an honest try, his optimistic dreams and practical preparations were quickly crushed in the grinding pack of the Arctic Ocean. Perhaps it would be charitable to think that the terrible winter at Cape Sparbo had turned the doctor's mind and, as Amundsen wished to believe, "some physical misfortune must have overtaken him to change his personality, for which he was not responsible." But the thing cannot be so innocent as that.

If he had no intention to foist a fraud, Dr. Cook could have returned rapidly to Greenland and gone home. Why all the wandering in uninhabited lands and the overwintering at Sparbo? It was that portion of his journey that convinced many of the truth of Cook's polar claim, since this detour seemed to them unnecessary for anyone bent on making an untruthful report. Captain Hall's reasoning was typical:

> With an apparently aimless purpose, [he] wandered a year in a pre-
> viously explored country to inevitable destitution, possibly for all
> he could have known, to starvation and ignominious death; that
> he voluntarily marched 500 miles away from his caches of supplies
> to crawl into an underground den at Cape Sparbo to stay there
> through an Arctic night without food and practically without
> ammunition, and deliberately by hunger reduce himself and his
> two Eskimos to the skeletons that Whitney met at Annoatok, on
> their return in 1909. Are we convinced that this is a true version of
> a sane man's proceedings and can we accept it without a scintilla
> of worthy evidence to accompany it?[106]

Captain Hall believed that such a course would be nothing short of "down-right hopeless imbecility" and that it would have been more advantageous for Cook to go directly back to Annoatok and get the jump on Peary by establishing his claim a full year in advance of his rival's return. "It would take a Jules Verne to concoct a plausible yarn of the Sparbo trip," Hall concluded.

Even so, the captain left open the possibility that Cook may have had some hidden purpose. "Suppose that Cook with his acknowledged brilliant mind is also actually possessed of surpassing ingenuity," he proposed, "and that unknown, unexplained, and unsuspected by any one else, he knew of good reasons for the Jones Sound trip, and the night at Sparbo to perfect his fraud."[107]

Indeed, and Captain Hall very much overestimated the illogic of such a course of action. The flaw in the captain's reasoning was that he assumed the rest of the doctor's story was true even if he had lied about reaching the Pole. If, however, Dr. Cook gave up less than a week after he started across the polar pack ice, as his diary seems to indicate and as the Eskimos are alleged to have said, then the broad themes of the rest of his story are *necessarily untrue,* if not all of it.

SPARBO SCENARIO

The journey that ended at Cape Sparbo can be reasonably explained if we are willing to indulge in more speculation. Let us imagine Dr. Cook has made an honest attempt and failed to reach the North Pole. On the way back to land he thinks about Mount McKinley and how his claim to "the top of the continent" had been accepted without serious question. He now decides to claim the top of the world.

It has been only about a week since he parted with his two extra Eskimo helpers on the march north over the ice. He can't go back the way he came; he does not want to risk running into any of the Eskimos he has left in Ellesmere

Land, who are likely slaughtering musk oxen and feasting there. To do so would give away the game; he must stay away long enough to simulate a journey to the Pole. He returns to land and camps at Svartevoeg for a couple of days; still loaded with supplies, he has no wants and does not need the caches he so carefully laid on the outward journey.

He starts down the uninhabited west coast of Axel Heiberg Land, intending to go not back to Greenland but to Lancaster Sound. He knows that the Dundee whaling captains Adams and Milne regularly visit the sound every summer. If he can catch a whaler back to Scotland, he will be in a position to go to Europe and pick up honors to fortify his claim before returning to the United States and *still* get a year's jump on Peary.

When the advancing summer makes snow conditions unfavorable for sledging, he abandons his dogs against the Eskimos' vigorous protests and takes to his folding boat to reach Lancaster Sound. Unfortunately for his plan, he fails to make connections with the whalers and is compelled to winter, as it is now too late in the season to return to Greenland. Although it was not his intention to winter, he knows no Eskimo ever starved in a gameland and remembers that Cape Sparbo, which they passed on their journey south, was a paradise of birds, bears, walrus, seals and musk oxen. The ever-adaptable doctor decides it is all to the good, as it will give him time to perfect the details of his "polar dash." They turn back for Sparbo.

He still has plenty of ammunition but does not want to waste it. He slaughters the ample game at Cape Sparbo, shooting the bears but letting the Eskimos take musk oxen with stones, lines and lances, birds and hare with slingshots, and walruses with harpoons. He helps the Eskimos build a snug rock igloo covered with sod over whalebone rafters and lines it with animal skins.

Once comfortably situated, he begins writing his fictitious journey to the Pole. He outlines his book to come, chapter by chapter, in his little notebooks; he tries out various dates and computes his latitudes again and again to make the speed and distances reasonable, adjusting them as he goes. At first he sets his arrival at the Pole for April 28, but after some consideration, that seems too late to assure a plausible date for safe return to land before the pack breaks up. He adjusts the date backward a week. He feels safe in doing this, remembering there are no entries in his winter diary after February 18 because of the diary's defect. Since Franke has this diary, he therefore settles on February 19 as the earliest possible departure date he can claim.

He fills the time fine-tuning his story, modifying the circumstances as he thinks over every detail, filling it out from his real polar experiences and the things he has read. As the winter passes, he feels more and more confident that he can pull it off convincingly.

He starts to work on a set of "original field notes" to match his now fully developed story. At first he writes it in his original notebook, then has misgivings and recopies it in a small memorandum book. He varies his daily routine by modifying his equipment for the return to Greenland when the sun rises.

A few days after the polar dawn, he sets out for Annoatok. The snow is deep, the going is slow, and man-hauling the sledge is incredibly strenuous. Now he knows why the Eskimos so value their dogs! He experiences the first real privation of the entire trip. He nearly runs out of ammunition; he really almost starves and is saved only by the ingenuity of his native friends and a putrid seal left by Panikpa at Cape Sabine. When he arrives at Annoatok in April, he has experienced the real, near-death exhaustion of what an actual polar dash would have been like. No longer does he need imagination to fill in the bone-numbing fatigue and starvation that such a journey would have involved.

When he discovers Peary's "grab" of his supplies and furs, he realizes Peary's fury and knows he must beat Peary back and make his claim first. This will be his revenge. He has resented the way Peary has gotten everything and he nothing, especially since Peary, despite his reputation, actually knows less about polar travel and Eskimo ways than he does. He also dislikes Peary's treatment of the Eskimos, whom he genuinely admires. He knows, after his own experience on the pack, that if Peary claims the Pole, it will probably be a fake, too, as he has seen the impossibility of the task first hand and knows Peary's infirmities by heart. He feels almost justified in seeing Peary deprived of the honor of his own false claim of being first to the Pole. He reasons that Peary will not dare challenge his claim without a genuine one of his own, since his rival knows his "polar secrets," and at the very worst he will be forced only to share the glory. But of course, he will retain priority, since he will claim to have been at the Pole a full year earlier than Peary could have been there.

IMMOVABLE ICE

Just where did Cook go if not to the Pole? The Eskimos' evidence was conflicting, but once again, Cook's own writings are the most reliable evidence against him.

Until Cook passed down the Crown Prince Gustav Sea, only Sverdrup's parties had ever been over the area. Even so, Captain Sverdrup, who traveled there earlier than June, noticed that the pull of the moon had no effect on the ice between the Ringnes Islands and Axel Heiberg Land. Peary's observations in the area in late June 1906 led him to believe that the ice never broke up between these islands and attributed the good condition of Cook's surviving sledge to his having traveled most of the way over this comparatively smooth ice.

Those who traveled that way in the 20 years after 1908 reported the ice never broke up even late in the summer. Stefansson journeyed extensively over the area in 1915–16 and said that although the surface melted into slush that impeded travel and deep ravines developed in the ice, it never broke up. He was able to cross over to Amund Ringnes Island from Heiberg Land in late July 1915.

Dr. Cook described "open water and impossible small ice as a barrier between us and Heiberg Island" in the same area in June 1908. But the Eskimos told Rasmussen they did not reach Heiberg Land because of "deep crevices" in the ice.

Regular ice surveys during the last few decades indicate that the ice is solid between these islands at least until August and starts to break, even in the extreme south, only in September. These aerial surveys document that during June the ice between the Ringnes Islands and Axel Heiberg Land for every year from 1961 to 1978, without exception, was totally consolidated, with ridging and hummocking averaging only one to two tenths of the surface. Moreover, this ice is almost always multiyear ice—ice that has not moved in at least two years—meaning it never melts in an average year. And climatic records and the oral traditions of the Eskimos, who have infallible memories in such matters, indicate that if anything, arctic winters were colder prior to 1920.

If Cook was actually above Amund Ringnes Island and 50 miles west of Axel Heiberg Land on June 13, 1908, as he said, it seems extremely unlikely that he would have been unable to return to his caches in Heiberg Land. On the contrary, all evidence indicates that by June 13 Cook was far south of his reported location and simply guessed at the ice conditions where he claimed to have been based on his experience with the ice in Smith Sound and Melville Bay. Open water and thin, cracked ice in June do not occur in the region through which he said he had traveled, even today.

Cook also stated that his route was down Hassel Sound between the Ringnes Islands, but he failed to correct the error of Sverdrup, who said that Hassel Sound is only three miles wide; it is actually 16. Cook was a meticulous observer of what he actually saw. A case in point is Sverdrup's "Shei Island," which Cook said was a peninsula. Though this was lost on MacMillan in 1914, later surveys confirmed Cook's observation. If he actually passed down Hassel Sound, he surely would have reported Sverdrup's error there as well. The inaccuracies of Cook's observations of both physical and ice conditions tend to support the Peary version of the Eskimos' story, which placed Cook's route east of Amund Ringnes Island and his mid-June location as much farther south.[108]

The arguments over whether Cook visited Meighen Island before it was officially discovered by Stefansson are irrelevant, since he could have discovered it after his return from the North Pole without disqualifying his claim. He may never have seen it, since it is hidden most of the summer by fog, but the fact that the Eskimos located it almost precisely on their 1909 map for Peary indicates that he probably did. His failure to announce its discovery could be linked to his ignorance of the use of a sextant. Any description of a new island would have required Cook to state its coordinates. If he was as inept with a sextant as he appears to have been, he would have been unable to locate Meighen Island precisely, thus providing conclusive evidence of his incompetence as a navigator capable of locating the North Pole.[109]

If Cook's story of the timing of his return to land is not true, then it not only strikes down Cook's claim to the Pole but also destroys the credibility of his account of the winter he spent at Cape Sparbo. That story captured the imagination of many, including that of John R. Bradley, who exclaimed, "He started out simply to make a dash for the pole. He made it. He won. I call it a good sporting performance—the greatest ever. Think of that trip back. That means more to me than finding the pole. What an exploit it was! What a man to do it! To win out—that's the thing! Why, it ought to put new life into every boy in America"[110]—as it did some old men as well.

Captain Hall marveled, "He had already survived a winter as probably no other man in written history had, without food, fuel, or ammunition. With nothing but his hands and one sled, he faced the approaching Arctic winter at Cape Sparbo on Jones' Sound. With part of a sled runner, he made the only weapon with which he could supply food and fuel for three men, and made a den into which they crawled till the six months winter was passed."[111]

Professor Steensby predicted that when the world learned of Cook's desperate winter at Sparbo, everyone would understand how easy it was for such a man to reach the Pole. And for many, that it has done and more. This survival of reliving the Stone Age with his two Eskimo companions, bereft of all vestiges of civilization, is something even many of those unsympathetic to Cook's polar claims have been willing to give him credit for. And Dr. Cook thrilled millions at his lectures with his account of that grim winter in the dank underground den. Yet, again, we must turn to the product of Cook's own hand to glimpse the truth.

JUST HOW IT FEELS TO BE A SAVAGE

An account of that winter is contained in two notebooks. Notebook 4 is largely filled with sketches for Cook's book, neatly organized by chapters and written in the past tense. Among the topics it lists for discussion is "Just how it feels to be a savage." Notebook 2, one of the tiny memorandum books, though, does contain a narrative diary appearing to have been written contemporaneously with actual events. The book is sketchy but gives enough to judge the accuracy of the fabulous story Cook told of that winter of 1908–09.

Of the very day he arrived at Sparbo, he writes: "Sep. 1 Got our first Walrus—great rejoicing." The next day he records: "Sep. 2 got 3 musk ox 1 with the lance 2 with lines and stones." This may sound daring, but in newspaper interviews George Borup told how easy musk oxen were to take with a lance and how hunters practically had to shoo away those they didn't wish to slaughter. Stefansson, too, noted they were easy victims, since they rarely fled from their enemies.

The next day there was an unwelcome dinner guest: "Sep. 3 1908 Bear stole one ox cache & wasted a cartridge on him and he took that also," indicating

Cook still had ammunition, though he later reported to the world, "We were beset on the shores of Baffin Bay with neither food, fuel nor ammunition."

Instead of a barren wilderness, he records in his diary, "Loons and Eiders passing in great flocks," and Bob Bartlett confirmed the abundance of birds in the marshy areas south of the headlands in 1910. Later, Dr. Cook writes matter-of-factly of more slaughtered musk oxen: "got 3 wounded 2 others." Cook even publicly contradicted his story by saying, "I tell the world . . . that the future happy hunting ground of the Eskimo is in Jones Sound where we wintered."[112]

No doubt the house they built was as good as any standard Eskimo winter shelter in Greenland, and its being much farther south, the weather was not so severe. Captain Bartlett noted that he found Cook's house still snugly lined with skins when the *Beothic* called in 1910.

On September 24 Dr. Cook's diary reports that they found a hatch cover and three planks, each nearly eight feet long, washed up on the shore, which they fashioned into harpoons, negating Cook's report of having had to make weapons from their sledge. By September 25 Cook feels secure enough to say that he has begun working up his notes. By October 4 he is apparently so well situated that he is longing not for daily sustenance but for such luxuries as coffee, potatoes and turnips, which he didn't even like before he left, and he records, "Slept 10 hours wonderful dreams 4 hours eating & exercising together 6 hours writing 4 hours."

None of this sounds like desperate men battling with Stone Age implements to eke out subsistence from a barren arctic wasteland. The diary does, however, have some interesting additions to the published narrative of his experiences. For instance, he notes that he posted dummies and kept his big United States flag flying over the igloo to ward off bears.

Another apparent exaggeration is Cook's report of the shortage of paper he had for writing. Though he said he used even film wrappers and toilet paper to write upon, of the notebooks he brought back with him, not one of them is filled. One is almost completely blank, having been erased, and each of the others has at least one blank page.

It is undeniable that Dr. Cook suffered greatly on his journey to Annoatok in the spring, but his condition upon arrival there was the result of that desperate march and not the privations of the winter or the "trip to the Pole," as Captain Hall and others have illogically assumed. By arctic standards, it was probably a luxurious winter in that stone igloo on the shores of Jones Sound, just as he told Marie in his letter from Greenland: "We finally made ourselves very comfortable in an underground den." The hardest thing must have been the isolation. Few civilized men could have dealt with that. But Dr. Cook was not like many civilized men.

He had enormous willpower, an amazing capacity for work, a rich inner life and an infinitely curious mind. These sustained him throughout his entire life with all its peculiar trials. No doubt he took great interest in "just how it feels to be a savage."

One anthropologist has said that an Eskimo struck him not as an Eskimo at all, but rather as a man with a mask playing the part of an Eskimo—all of his true motives, thoughts and emotions suppressed and hidden, devoted to the grim task of group survival. It is tempting to think that Dr. Cook and the Eskimos had very much in common in this respect. He, too, seems a man with a mask, and there can be little question that he was well suited to the part of playing an Eskimo. For a man who was "naturally reticent"—Robert Dunn said you had "to be a mind-reader to draw him out"—and who, as another acquaintance said, found it difficult to be intimate with anyone despite the numerous clubs and organizations to which he belonged, it is not hard to imagine that he was content that winter to create the fanciful record of his recent experiences without distraction.

In 1937 J.M. Wordie visited the site of Cook's winter igloo at Cape Hardy.[113] He found the skulls of musk oxen scattered over an area within three miles of it. That the skulls had been separated from the bodies showed they had been killed for food, not sport.

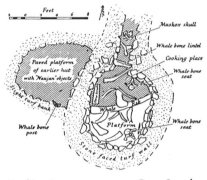

He confirmed the house would have been a comfortable shelter and found pieces of wood, canvas, several rifle cartridge cases, parts of an American drill, knives, steel files, shell trouser buttons, corn, objects made of oak, and tin cans with screw necks but no papers or other documents.[114] Wordie found the area still rich in game, with 80 head of musk oxen within a three-mile radius of the house.

Cook's winter quarters at Cape Sparbo.

MISSING PAPERS

The visit of the *Beothic* to that same house in 1910 is an episode still shrouded in mystery. No diary or logbook of that voyage is among Bob Bartlett's papers at Bowdoin College, and little could be found elsewhere. Though there is a brief record of his visit to Cape Sparbo, there is no record of what transpired at Etah, when the *Beothic* was the first ship to touch there after the *Roosevelt* sailed home in August 1909.

It was widely speculated in the press in 1910 that the real purpose of that "hunting trip" was to hunt down and retrieve the records and instruments Cook said he left with Harry Whitney. Yet Peary had refused to take them with him when he had a chance. That Bartlett, Peary's right-hand man, captained the ship can hardly be considered an innocent coincidence, and the presence of Whitney only reinforces the probability that the *Beothic's* mission was not to bring the papers and instruments back but to dispose of them.

Harry Whitney comes off as a pathetically shallow figure in this story. When Captain Sam Bartlett of the *Jeanie* wanted to return to Etah to retrieve

Cook's belongings in 1909, Whitney insisted on going on another hunt instead, even though, as he told Wilfred Grenfell when he reached Labrador, he thought they "would be interfered with."[115] Being incredibly rich and careless, he said he never gave a thought to the value of Cook's instruments as proof of his claim and didn't trouble to return for them when he transferred to the *Jeanie* from the *Roosevelt* in North Star Bay. He thought he would just buy Cook a better set when he got back. Though he dutifully buried Cook's instruments at Etah as Peary directed, he brought home, according to Dr. Cook, a special .22 caliber rifle despite "his word as a gentleman" not to take a thing aboard the *Roosevelt* that had belonged to Peary's rival.

There is every indication that Whitney wished he had never gotten mixed up in the increasingly nasty polar dispute. He did not like the publicity, and the Peary interests soon put pressure on him to come over to the "right" side of things. It appears that General Hubbard had a talk with young Whitney, and Bob Bartlett even offered him a berth on Peary's abortive antarctic expedition. The Cook side vied for Whitney's allegiance as well, Dr. Cook and H. Wellington Wack visited him in late October, but Whitney by then seems to have made his choice, and it appears that choice was squarely for his own comfort.

Though a man like bo'sun Murphy might have enjoyed lording it over a pretty boy, Whitney's treatment at Etah was probably much exaggerated by Cook.[116] His notes on the Peary "grab" show Cook was somewhat confused over what had transpired at Etah during his absence; for instance, he erroneously placed Bridgman aboard the *Erik*. Even so, there is evidence that all was not smooth between Whitney and Peary's crude boatswain. Whitney seemed to acknowledge this and the trend of his thought when he said, "Something has been said in this controversy about my experience in the North which was not too pleasant. I cannot say too strongly that I do not hold Commander Peary in any way responsible for this and when I told him about it I am sure he sincerely regretted those things which I have forgotten in the keen pleasure I had in my arctic winter."[117]

Peary thought Whitney had been lax as his "guest" and lacking in judgment and "gentlemanly feeling" to have had anything to do with his rival, and it probably did not take much to convince Whitney, after he learned of Peary's attitude, that there was nothing to be gained by sticking up for Cook. Whitney's big interest in life was "keen pleasure." And what did a man like Dr. Cook have to offer him, anyway? Whitney's presence on the *Beothic* proved he placed his own comfort above principle, as he stood by and watched while the things Cook had entrusted to him to deliver safely to the United States were dug from their cache on the beach at Etah. No longer could there be any doubt as to where Harry Whitney's allegiance lay. On a list of "arctic explorers" who Cook said supported his claim in 1914, Peary penciled in an emphatic "NO" next to Harry Whitney's name.

That Cook's cache at Etah was opened can hardly be doubted. T. Everett Harré reported that in 1910, "One of [Peary's] closest associates came frequently to the Hampton Magazine offices to supply details, which Peary couldn't remember." This "associate" said he had been present when Cook's box at Etah was opened, and that there were instruments, including an artificial horizon, in the box.[118] That associate could not have been anyone but Captain Bob Bartlett.

Upon his return to America, Captain Bartlett was reported to have said, "What use can Dr. Cook have in going to Etah for 'proofs,' when there are none? The only articles belonging to Dr. Cook at Etah are some clothing and such like and possibly a sextant. But as for records, you can stake your life that none are there. As for what belongs to him, they have been divided up among the Eskimos. . . ."[119] Indeed, the sextant that Cook was alleged to have used was sent back to Copenhagen by Peter Freuchen, who discovered it, bent and missing an eyepiece, in the bottom of Etukishuk's toolbox. But none of Dr. Cook's written records, which he said had been buried with it, have ever been recovered.

If there were any, what happened to them? An easy answer is that Bartlett had them. Perhaps that was why he so badly wanted to see Peary when he met Peary's lawyer in the train station in Boston. If they were the rough notes for the story Cook eventually told, they would have *appeared* to support his story, even if Peary and Bartlett were convinced they were fakes. The natural thing then would have been to destroy them, but Peary kept so much else, why not these?

There is, in fact, evidence that Cook *did* leave some papers with Whitney. Though Whitney said publicly he was not sure that he had, since he had not looked in all the boxes, a letter from Whitney's mother mentions she received a letter from Greenland in which her son said Cook had left some "valuable instruments and records" in his care.[120]

So what did Cook leave with Whitney? When asked, Cook stated: "I gave Mr. Whitney one sextant, one or two compasses and a few sheets of paper. That is all. I simply left with Mr. Whitney memoranda that seemed best at the time."[121]

Besides denying that there were any notes at Etah, Captain Bartlett denied that the *Beothic* was the source of the "joke," reported in the *New York Times,* that the captain of the *Hans Egede* had fallen in with "a yacht" and that someone on the yacht reported she had on board John R. Bradley and Harry Whitney, who were on the way to retrieve Dr. Cook's records.

But perhaps that is close to what actually happened. The *Beothic,* a big steel-hulled sealer, would not likely be described by a sea captain as "a yacht." What's more, the New York *World* of September 18, 1910, reported that John R. Bradley had gone north on the schooner *Beauty* that summer. Could the *Beauty* have been the yacht the Danes met, and did Bradley get to Etah before the *Beothic?*

Bradley had been publicly embarrassed by the Polar Controversy but privately continued to believe in Dr. Cook; if he could retrieve Cook's records, he might vindicate both Cook and himself. And Cook told the *World*'s correspondent in October 1910 that he was expecting "corroborative evidence" before he made his full "answer to everything." It seems likely that Bradley was on the yacht hailed by the Danes but failed to reach Etah before the *Beothic,* and by then it was too late.

Perhaps Dr. Cook was the least interested of all in his lost records. At first he said that they were not important because he had copies of them; then he said his claim could not be made good without them; then he asked Rector Torp to suspend judgment on his claim until he retrieved them. But Charles Wake said Cook had told him that the material left in Greenland dealt only with his return to land and his winter at Cape Sparbo. "Whitney has no records of mine that would or would not tend to prove my case," Cook declared, and two days later stated unequivocally, "The records are not of the slightest importance since I have copies of all of them. . . . Anyway, I don't care anything about them."[122]

It is likely that there were papers, but the fact that he never made any attempt himself to retrieve them, though he certainly had the money to charter a ship for the purpose, indicates that they contained nothing vital or that he did not wish them retrieved. The "lost" records, he must have realized, conveniently excused why he was never able to credibly establish his claim, so it is possible that they were more valuable as an excuse than as a proof.

This theory seems reasonable, especially after reading Cook's 1911 letter to the University of Copenhagen in which he accepted its verdict on his records as "not proven." The date of that letter is just after his return to America from exile, and it shows that he was apparently very content, perhaps even relieved, at the restrained language of the Copenhagen decision.

DENMARK'S DECISION

The Danes' temperate language was probably designed to get the university out of an embarrassing situation while avoiding all official imputation of fraud on Dr. Cook's part. Indeed, when the university convened a second Konsistorium in 1914 to take up what to do about Cook's diploma, it considered many alternatives but did nothing, not wanting to become reenmeshed in the ongoing dispute. All of the Konsistorium's statements were couched in very diplomatic language so as not to offend anyone or open any old wounds.[123]

Some of the extreme statements attributed to members of the 1909 Konsistorium seem to have been press exaggerations. Certainly the comment attributed to Rasmussen, that he had examined Dr. Cook's observations and said, "No school boy could make such calculations," is one of these. There were no "calculations" in them, and besides, according to Peter Freuchen, Rasmussen had a severe aversion to mathematics of even the simplest kind and could not take observations himself.[124]

Professor Strømgren specifically denied that he had ever used the term *hoax* in connection with Cook's claim or that he had called Cook a swindler.[125]

However, some comments seem authentic and reveal how some of the men who sat in judgment of Cook's polar claim actually felt when they were compelled to hand down a "geographical assassination" of the man whom they had so recently feted and who had charmed them so completely. As the Danish minister intimated, Cook had the gold medal but he was never placed on the official list of recipients.

HOW A MAGAZINE MADE HISTORY

In *Return from the Pole,* Dr. Cook was to expand upon his experiences of that winter at Cape Sparbo with his two Eskimo companions. In that book he used the long philosophical discussions he says he had with them to expound upon many ideas he had developed in his far longer period of isolation at Leavenworth prison. Yet in *Hampton's Magazine,* Cook said of that time, "I cannot describe the utter loneliness of existence. I had been so long with my Eskimo companions that they had ceased to arouse interest. We spoke little. About what could I talk with these savages?"[126]

Of course, the *Hampton's* articles have been dismissed by supporters of Dr. Cook because of Lilian Kiel's disclosure of how the series was tampered with. But the "faked confession" is perhaps the most overrated episode in the entire Polar Controversy.

Lilian Kiel herself said that exclusive of editorial excisions, only the first article was altered substantively:

> By the successful injection of "INSANITY" into the first installment, it was hardly necessary for us to bother ourselves about the other three issues. Consequently, with the exception of the OMISSION of such material as would have incriminated Robert E. Peary, the February, March and April issues of Hampton's "Dr. Cook's" story went to press about as he had really written it—with the usual "editorial corrections" etc.[127]

In denouncing the *Hampton's* series in 1911, Dr. Cook confirmed this: "The articles that eventually appeared in Hampton's, with the exception of unauthorized editorial changes and excisions of vitally important matter concerning Mr. Peary, were practically the same as planned in London."[128]

Some have wondered why Cook never identified which parts were inserted. But anyone who reads through the first article will have no trouble telling the insertions from the original text. As Elsa Barker noted, it is easy to distinguish different authors' styles. Furthermore, the content of much of this article, and most of the rest of the series—with the exception of the last installment, which was never used again—is either identical to passages in *My Attainment of the Pole* or only slightly different, and what isn't the same matches the book in content, if not in wording.

T. Everett Harré was the man Lilian Kiel identified as the author of the insertions, but this assertion raises a number of problems. Though Harré had once wished to boil in oil "this abomination from Brooklyn" and put the "tumbscrews" to his backers, Cook employed him as the manager of his Polar Publishing Company in 1911 and was friendly with Harré long after that. Why would Cook have hired Harré if Kiel had told him he was the author of the infamous "confession"? When Harré moved to the Polar Publishing Company from *Hampton's*, Kiel's moral indignation did not prevent her from moving there with him, and Harré also later obtained a position for her with his publisher, Mitchell Kennerley, in 1913. If Harré was truly the architect of the confession that so outraged Kiel, would any of this have happened? There seems to be something amiss here.

That Lilian Kiel was not the innocent she professed to be is indicated by her statement before the House Education Committee in 1915 that she was disinterested in who was the true discoverer of the Pole. On the contrary, everything indicates that she was working for Cook's vindication, was not above deceptive tactics to establish his claim and, in fact, was at least infatuated with him.

In a letter from Etta Rost, we read of several "stunts" Lilian Kiel had thought of, including "that 'reporter' trick," which Etta thought "the very brightest, most telling thing that has been done in the whole Cook case." In a second letter, she writes of another of Kiel's "stunts" admiringly: "I am all consumed with curiosity to know what kind of a 'message' you will receive from Marvin. You certainly do have the most original ideas! No one else would have thought of that."[129]

Many people other than Etta Rost would be curious about a message from the long-departed Ross Marvin and, though nothing else has come to light, would also like to know the details of Kiel's other "original ideas." The implications are clear, nonetheless.

Lilian Kiel's various statements are not consistent—another bad sign for her veracity. Although she accused Harré and expressed her interest in truth and justice before the Education Committee in January 1915, in April 1914 she was quoted as saying, "I helped write some of those 'insanity' paragraphs which were inserted after Dr. Cook had O.K.'d the galley proofs of his story for *Hampton's*." She also told the committee that she had forced Dr. Cook to read the articles, in full, only "last October," that is, October 1914, although Cook clearly was aware of their full content when he denounced them in September 1911.

Kiel asserts in her letters that on April 15, 1916, she deposited in a box her four stenographer's notebooks of original notes as dictated to her for Peary's magazine articles by Elsa Barker, along with other items, including Edward Brooke's pictures of Peary's Eskimo children taken on the Crocker Land Expedition and letters from Barker to Peary about his observations on his polar journey. This box was placed in storage at the Prince George Hotel in New York, the doctor's residence at the time. The two of them cosigned the deposit slip.

In the 1930s, after she had gone to see Dr. Cook in Chicago, she routinely addressed him in her letters "My Dear One," and when Cook was on his deathbed, she instructed Ralph von Ahlefeldt to "place a kiss upon his lips for me, and just whisper the word—'Auf Wiedersehen.'"[130]

Harré's role is far less clear. He denied that he wrote the "insanity" insertions, then placed the blame on managing editor Ray Long, and even said he protested the incident to Ben Hampton. Harré said he had "collaborated" with Cook to write the *Hampton's* series, and if he did, this supports the notion that the insertions were not Harré's, as their style is not consistent with the rest of the article. He later asserted he knew more about the inside story of the Cook-Peary affair than anyone, having worked with both, but he never gave more than tantalizing hints of what those details were.

Although the plea of "insanity" to explain Cook's actions does seem to have been inserted, the whole series has frequent recourse to psychological imagery. This may have been part of Harré's collaboration, since the 1914 edition of *Who's Who in America* says that Harré was "interested in psychic phenomenon," and the numerous references to psychological concepts and the workings of the unconscious mind provide the link between the "confession" and the balance of the Cook series.

MY ATTAINMENT OF THE POLE

Dr. Cook proclaimed in his original introduction to *My Attainment of the Pole*, "I was relieved of much of the routine editorial work by Mr. T. Everett Harry. By his ceaseless study of the subject and his rearrangement of material,

T. Everett Harré.

a book of better literary workmanship has been made." This was changed in subsequent editions to read, "by whose handling of certain purely adventure matter a book of better literary workmanship has been made."[131] This change—one of the few made to the text among the three editions—is curious, and perhaps significant. Is it designed to obscure Harré's true contribution to the book's content by limiting his role in its creation to "purely adventure matter"?

One reviewer of *My Attainment of the Pole* suspected that Harré's contribution explained a number of the book's peculiar features when compared with Cook's former writings. He objected to its turgid style and to the ignorance or misuse of the English language it contained, remarking that if Dr. Cook's claim that "a book of better literary workmanship has been made" was true, then "what its earlier embryonic condition must have been staggers the imagination, for even after all Mr. Harry's care the literary workmanship not unfrequently suggests the collaboration of a learned Babu."[132] The reviewer characterized the book as "at best what Tennyson called 'confessions of a second-rate sensitive mind.'"

Along with these crudities and excesses, he noticed a number of errors not to be expected of an experienced arctic explorer or well-schooled physician: a "walrus" was described as if it were a narwhal and there were such physiological absurdities as "the iris was reduced to a mere pinhole." The reviewer also noted a curious lack of any personae for the two Eskimos; the only other companions on that brain-numbing march to the Pole, the sledge dogs, got hardly a notice, none being mentioned by name or lamented with the slightest regret as they were sacrificed to the ultimate goal.

That the book contained instead "an unfailing stream of that fervid enthusiasm, that gushing rhetoric, those iridescent descriptions, which have always furnished such convincing proof of the sterling purity of the doctor's soul," made him conclude:

> It is impossible, except on the hypothesis of a rapid breaking-down of his faculties, to reconcile his clear scientific description of the Antarctic voyage of 1898 with the wordy rubbish to which he has put his name for the Arctic journey of 1908. . . . The vagueness as to dates and times convinces us that there can have been no systematic diary. The voluntary separation from instruments and notes on the author's return was not the action of a sane explorer; and the failure to take any steps to recover them is inexplicable if they existed. The efforts in this book, published long after the events, to make out a plausible case, have failed, and so egregiously as to inspire a doubt whether they are actually the work of the man who figures as the explorer and author.

By implication, Harré was the man responsible for the "wordy rubbish" to which Cook signed his name. Could Cook, like Peary, have entrusted the book on which his claim would hinge to a ghost writer?

Harré characterized his part by saying he "undertook the editorial revision of all [of Cook's] material on his Polar exploit for book publication."[133] His 1913 "Eskimo Romance," *The Eternal Maiden,* gives evidence of Harré's "ceaseless study of the subject," even having a brutish character named "Olafksoah" modeled on Peary himself, and a fair grasp of arctic "atmosphere," much of it obviously gained from his association with Cook.

A brief passage from Harré's next book, describing its biblical heroine, will convince anyone that Harré was capable of the sort of literary excess that dismayed our perceptive critic:

> Her skin browned with the juices of nuts, swathed in the fantastic
> garb of elder Egypt, close-clinging as sumptuous cerements, Mary
> resurrected the beauty of those dead princesses of elder times whose
> mummies lay in the tombs and whose ghosts moaned unrequited
> love laments on moonlit nights to the monks who inhabited their
> graves. Her eyes were painted until they resembled glazed beads of
> agate; the brows and lashes were dyed to a bitter black with attar of
> roses and kohl. . . . Strange musty odors, suggestive of dried dead
> flowers, exhaled from her robes. From her knees to her ankles was
> painted a fluttering fall of flower-petals. On her breasts great
> scarabaei clustered.[134]

Nevertheless, most of the main elements of *My Attainment of the Pole*
originated with Dr. Cook. Many were outlined in practically the same terms
in the extant Cape Sparbo notebooks, including a list of many of the vivid
color images that mark the book's descriptions.

Despite our reviewer's unfavorable comparison of the two books, at least a
few passages in *Through the First Antarctic Night* might also be described as
"wordy rubbish," and showed the same tendency to excess. And there are a
number of other points by which a common author of the two books can be
recognized. Little of the substance, then, and certainly not all of *My Attainment of the Pole*'s extravagance are the work of T. Everett Harré.

Dr. Cook knew that to be successful, a story had to capture the imagination of its intended audience. "Apply as far as possible principles of experience
in such a way that the common man grasps it," he advised. "A book must live
by the emotional impress it delivers," he believed. "If it fails to blend with the
reader's mentality and does not supply a ferment to produce a wine of action it
is itself potentially dead. How can the printed page live is ever the author's
study."[135]

In Harré, Dr. Cook found an editor in tune with his ideas about writing,
who had a knack for sometimes excessive but sometimes mesmerizing descriptions. Surely, if Cook was the unscrupulous knave some have made him out to
be, he would not let a little thing like the authorship of "Dr. Cook's Confession," or even thumbscrews and boiling oil, stand in the way of obtaining
the services of such a man.

If there is some question as to just how much of the book's literary style,
which has either enthralled or appalled its readers, is Cook's responsibility,
there can be no doubt that the considerable portions of the book devoted to
the Polar Controversy are his alone. Many have scoffed at *My Attainment of
the Pole* for its color-drenched descriptions and its aggressive attacks on
Robert E. Peary and the exploring establishment that ostracized Dr. Cook.
But those who have proclaimed Cook's narrative an outrageous fraud while
embracing Peary's *The North Pole,* with its far more implausible story, have
missed the true intent of Cook's book.

Even though it professes to be "the final proofs of Dr. Cook's [polar] attainment," *My Attainment of the Pole* was not in any way intended to convince the scientific community, which had already rejected his claims. The book was aimed squarely at supplying "a ferment to produce a wine of action" to intoxicate the minds of the masses and raise the possibility in those minds that Dr. Cook actually had reached the Pole, in spite of what the scientists thought.

As he said on its closing page, "My case rests, not with any body of armchair explorers or kitchen geographers, but with Arctic travelers who can see beyond the mist of selfish interests, and with my fellow-countrymen, who breathe normal air and view without bias the large open fields of honest human endeavor.

"In this book I have stated my case, presented my proofs. As to the relative merits of my claim, and Mr. Peary's, place the two records side by side. Compare them. I shall be satisfied with your decision."[136]

Remember what Cook said of an Eskimo's central desire of life: "The real pivot upon which all his efforts are based is the desire to be rated well among his colleagues. . . . Is not this also the inspiration of all the world?" Dr. Cook knew the truth about human immortality: that as long as just one living person remembers you, you are immortal, and as long as that one believes in your goodness, you are in heaven, not hell. And there are good reasons, based on the content of *My Attainment of the Pole,* for belief in Frederick A. Cook and his ultimate salvation—if one only makes the right interpretations and has faith.

Lending additional strength to those who still believe today are those harsh charges leveled against Peary on the pages of Cook's book, which convinced many of its original readers that a monied conspiracy had robbed Cook of his honor and which blurred the fact that his own lack of proof was actually the reason his claims were rejected. Some of these charges, widely dismissed at the time of their writing, now have been shown to be true, and most of the rest have at least some plausible basis.

My Attainment of the Pole is, then, a polemic—not for scientific vindication but for popular belief—and a magnificent one, couching its true intent in the beguiling story at its core. Dr. Cook had no fear of a comparison between his own narrative and Peary's, since he knew Peary's claim was false and far more implausible than his own. It was perhaps this knowledge—that Peary's story was no truer than his—that justified in Cook's mind his bitter attacks upon Peary, convinced him that Peary would never fight back and assured him that he would be allowed to live comfortably as a lecturer denouncing the limitless conspiracy of the "Arctic Trust."

PEARY'S FRIENDS

It may have been his reading about the forced resignation of Admiral Edward B. Barry from the U.S. Navy by President Taft in February 1911, as an "outgrowth of charges affecting the moral character of the naval officer," that prompted Cook's first attack on Peary's own morality. At the time, however, few openly believed the charges Cook made against Peary, and this part of his book was rejected out of hand as false. As the reviewer of *The Living Age* saw it, "Cook has now revealed to us . . . his animosity against Peary. We know that it is universally recognized that, whatever may be his faults of taste, Peary is a man of high character and honorable conduct; and the malignant and unjustifiable attack made upon him recoils upon his assailant."

In the aftermath of the Polar Controversy, it was said that the admiral couldn't even stand to hear Cook's name mentioned. Actually, he was obsessed with Cook and had his every movement watched. The most minute notice about him was clipped from the newspapers, and Peary was one of the first to read *My Attainment of the Pole*. He not only read it but constructed lists of the criticisms it made of him and his backers. Though he minimized its contents to his intimates, Peary was obviously stung by how close it hit to home.

As usual, he took out his frustrations in memoranda he wrote to himself. In one he asserted the stories of his alleged "immorality among the Eskimos" were the products of Dr. Dedrick's "drug crazed imagination." Peary then combined his old and new antagonists, saying that before Cook left on the *Erik* in 1901, he had supplied Dedrick with a large quantity of morphine. Such ravings tell less about Cook than Peary, and the terrible result of his own self-imposed destiny.

This is the saddest feature of the history of Robert E. Peary—the story of a potentially brilliant but hopelessly romantic mind dissipated by an irrational ambition to achieve an impossible and useless dream. Peary realized too late the truth of Jo's refrain: "life is nearly over and we have missed most of it."

At first, General Hubbard was willing to leave the fight over the Pole to Peary. But he quickly realized that Peary was not capable of a rational approach to the problem of Dr. Cook. He soon issued a "gag" order, and Peary willingly put his case into the corporate lawyer's hands. After that, Peary's role seems to have been confined to almost daily letters to Hubbard filled with his fears, petty worries and endless trivial suggestions.

Among these are Peary's startling letter of December 1910, in which he said he believed that Cook could, under the proper influences, be induced to "confess" his imposture. But it is amazing how little Peary himself seems to have had to do with discrediting Cook once he had placed the process in motion by hurling his "gold brick."

Peary's suggestions were, in effect, a wish list, and General Hubbard was willing to play fairy godfather to Peary: bankrolling Ashton's payment of "expenses" to Barrill and anyone else who swore out an affidavit against Cook's Mount McKinley climb, then headlining them in his own newspaper; underwriting Parker and Browne's expedition to bring back photographic evidence against Cook from Alaska; picking up the bills for the distribution of *Veritas* and Fess's speech; paying for Burns's detectives and a private lobbyist; even approving Peary's expensive bauble, the Polar Star.

Hubbard may have originally believed in Peary, but there are indications that by 1912 he had doubts. Once pledged, however, there was no way a man like General Thomas Hamlin Hubbard would recant his loyalty. Hubbard was used to winning, and despite his fine rhetoric at Bowdoin, his tactics did not always consist of fair play. Then, too, the Peary Arctic Club was not about to desert the man in whom it had invested half a million dollars—not when he claimed to have brought home the polar prize at long last.

When Peary emerged from the North just five days after Cook and claimed that prize for himself, Herbert L. Bridgman sent Jo Peary a telegram saying that he would surely have to open the "Greely Chartreuse" now. His reference was to a bottle of liqueur left in the Arctic by General Greely in 1884 and discovered at Fort Conger by Peary, who gave it to his old friend in 1902. Bridgman had vowed that he would not drink the despised Greely's bottle until Peary reached the Pole. This was just the kind of gesture Bridgman enjoyed thinking up, but he went his original idea one better when Peary actually made his claim. "We shall have to invite Dr. Cook and General Greely to make the festivities complete," he gloated.[137] He liked nothing better than rubbing it in. With such a mind as his, it is virtually certain that the real driving force behind the campaign to demolish Cook was Herbert L. Bridgman.

In 1908, after failing to convince Peary that Cook might be up to something, Vilhjalmur Stefansson went to see the man he described as "Peary's manager and best friend, the man who above all other associates was responsible for Peary's successes." "I stated my case much more forcibly, because he was more receptive," Stefansson recalled. ". . . Bridgman immediately began gathering information, but, as he later told me, without informing Peary. . . . Bridgman, therefore, had in his files long before the press opening of the controversy most of the evidence later used to attack Cook's reputation with regard to Mount McKinley. He had gone farther back and dug into the unpublished records of the Gerlache Antarctic Expedition, unearthing the charge, among others, that Cook had attempted to publish as though gathered by himself a vocabulary of a South America dialect which had really been gathered by a missionary. . . ."[138]

Bridgman seems to have gotten personal pleasure out of being the power behind the throne. He was not content to manipulate only the rich and powerful, however, but also little people like Mene Wallace and his guardians. He had practically singlehandedly created Peary's heroic image, and he tenaciously protected it against all attacks. He needed no publicity; his satisfactions were entirely private. Bridgman was so self-effacing that when he died in 1924, his wife was shocked to discover that he was a near millionaire.[139]

Without Bridgman's unscrupulous brains and Hubbard's munificent wallet, Robert E. Peary would not have gotten far in the Polar Controversy against Frederick A. Cook, a man he continually underestimated and never understood. Peary was rarely more truthful than the time he said, "Never was a man more fortunate in his friends than I."

However, a fully knowledgeable examination of the statements of Peary's friends in support of his claims only adds to the assurance that those claims are false, since it is never necessary to defend truth with falsehoods, as falsehood can never be defended by truth. And there is little that is not false in the statements of Peary's friends.

One exception is Donald MacMillan, who admitted that there was no other proof of Peary's claim than his word. In his book, *How Peary Reached the Pole,* MacMillan makes many honest and candid admissions. MacMillan, among all of Peary's friends, didn't lie for Peary, but neither did he really defend him, either. He simply believed.[140]

Those who have tried to defend him have had no recourse but to lies. If Peary had a "co-conspirator" in his fraudulent claim to the North Pole, it was Bob Bartlett, and his autobiography shows that he either was a clumsy liar or had an incredibly poor memory. It contains amazing factual blunders, like a supposed conversation with Peary in 1906 in which they discuss Shackleton's journey toward the South Pole, which did not take place until 1909, and statement after statement about Peary that is contradicted by documentary evidence. But of all the absurd statements that the *Log of Bob Bartlett* contains, the most absurd is "I had learned from Peary a spirit of generosity towards Arctic travelers."[141]

Even Bartlett was outdone by men like Henry Rood who attached themselves to Peary simply to make money. His article, "The Coming of Cook,"[142] is a notorious example of the kinds of lies and distortions printed in connection with the dispute over the discovery of the North Pole.

Others, like Peary's first biographer, Fitzhugh Green, traded on their association with Admiral Peary to maximize their minimal accomplishments. Green may have exceeded his hero in lack of candor, however. Of his journey back to Etah in 1914 after he and MacMillan had discovered that Peary had not discovered "Crocker Land," he wrote, "Next morning we separated, [MacMillan] with Etukishuk towards land in the east, and I with Pewahto down the unknown shores in the southwest. The balance of the trip, though long, was without noteworthy event."[143] Apparently, Green's murder of his Eskimo companion on that trip was not considered a "noteworthy event."[144]

In speaking well of Peary, MacMillan and Bartlett, at least, can be excused as defending their own reputations, since their main claim to fame was their contribution to his "discovery of the North Pole." But Vilhjalmur Stefansson is more difficult to fathom and appears to have been more mercenary—and wily. And it paid him handsomely in expedition finances, gold medals, honorary degrees, book contracts—even "an honorable name and fame"—though his actual exploratory achievements don't measure up to Dr. Cook's substantiated exploits.

Stefansson also shared some things with Dr. Cook beyond his wide fields of interest and infinitely charming personality. He, too, was prone to "scientific speculations," such as his now thoroughly discredited view of human history that great empires in northern climes had supplanted lesser ones in the south and his advocacy of the efficacy of a high-fat diet to prolong life, along with such exaggerations and embellishments as his "Blond Eskimos" and "Friendly Arctic." Yet "Stef's" visionary ideas made him in his later years "The Prophet of the North," a role Dr. Cook would have been well suited to had he not fallen into dishonor. There can be no doubt, however, that since it served his own ends, Stefansson always was a good friend to Robert E. Peary.

And Peary has had friends willing to take his part generation after generation since. Peary's elevation to "Discoverer of the North Pole" made him a locus for the power and money needed to mount future expeditions through his connections and influence with the American geographical establishment. Those institutions and organizations that hastily approved Peary's unsupported polar claim have never been eager to have their judgment reexamined. Some have just "let sleeping dogs lie," though some have actively worked to preserve the status quo, since by placing their own credibility on the line in certifying Peary's claim, a defense of his claim became a defense of their own credibility.

As late as 1957 the National Geographic Society's patriarch, Gilbert H. Grosvenor, continued to trumpet Peary's accomplishments as "a glorious chapter" in the society's history and to tell how its subcommittee's "careful, scholarly vindication of Peary's claims won world-wide approval and clearly established The Society as a potent force in the fields of exploration and scientific research."[145]

The nonprofit society's association with Peary was so profitable that it, by some accounts, attempted to repeat this success by equally dubious approval of Commander Richard E. Byrd's flight to the North Pole in 1926—a flight many scholars now believe never took place—for which the only basis of "proof" is the National Geographic Society's certification of it after a recomputation of Byrd's navigational data by Hugh C. Mitchell—the very same "expert calculator" who "proved," and improved, Peary's observations at the "Pole."[146]

Those who have wished to obtain financial backing or other advantages of the prestige associated with the "potent force" the National Geographic Society and other geographical organizations have wielded have been willing to swallow Peary's impossible story whole to get them.

Men like MacMillan, Bartlett and Stefansson used their support of Peary to gain backing for their own exploratory enterprises, and there are still men today, including active arctic explorers and experts on Alaskan mountains, who can attest to the advantages of supporting the claims of Robert E. Peary or rejecting Frederick A. Cook's. Then there are men like Walt Gonnason, Wally Herbert and Ralph Plaisted who can tell what it is like to come down on the wrong side of the conventional wisdom about Peary's polar exploits.

DUNKLE AND LOOSE

But other men's motives are less easily explained. They are dark and personal. The largest unknown factor in the Polar Controversy's equation is certainly

William C. Reick and his hatred for his former boss, James Gordon Bennett. His management of the news in Peary's favor at the *New York Times* was skillful and unprincipled, though Bennett was not above his own distortions and manipulations, either.

Although Bridgman and Hubbard forwarded all correspondence concerning Peary to the explorer, and Peary dutifully and sometimes foolishly kept it, Reick's extant correspondence with him is not extensive. Yet Peary wired Reick after the Copenhagen decision congratulating him for the great victory he and the *Times* had "won." But if Reick did anything beyond the editorials and manipulations of the news in the *Times*, which were not inconsiderable in themselves, the hard evidence has yet to be seen.

Cook advocates have dismissed the Dunkle-Loose affidavits, as they have that of Edward Barrill, as bought and therefore transparently false. However, Barrill's account of what happened on Ruth Glacier appears to have much more merit and plausibility than Cook's, and a careful reading of Dunkle and Loose discloses a number of details that could not have been made up. This does not mean that every word they swore to is true, but only that their statements are substantially based in fact.

"The affidavits are so circumstantial that it is difficult to doubt their truthfulness," one editor commented; "but why did Cook fail to pay them their price, when the betrayal of the secret was sure to follow? There is more in all this than is natural. Even the very names involved in the Cook affair are so strange as to seem to belong to the world of fiction rather than of fact. Not content with Wake and Wack, he must consort with Dunkle and Loose, regardless of the suggestion of ways that are dark and tricks that are vain which the conjuncture can hardly fail to provoke."[147]

The story their affidavits discloses does indeed seem utterly remarkable behavior for a man in Dr. Cook's tenuous position. But even if we accept Dunkle and Loose as substantially telling the truth, an explanation can be made to harmonize with the "Simple Hero" defense that neatly explains it— and everything else – about Cook's association with them—away.

Our editor placed his tongue firmly in cheek when he said:

> On the face of it, the matter looks very bad for the doctor, and it seems almost a duty of charity to point out a way of escape for him if the net tightens. . . . Cook, let us suppose is a perfectly honest and exceptionally guileless man. He has reached the Pole; he knows it himself beyond a doubt, and he is pained to find himself in a difficult position owing to the perverse skepticism of an unkindly generation. This difficulty, he feels, cannot be removed by the presentation of his genuine observations, which, though good enough for all practical purposes, will be picked to pieces by coldhearted scientists because he is not enough of a nautical expert to have made them with the requisite accuracy. What more natural

than that he should accept the aid of a kind navigator who will give
him a better set of observations? He doesn't want them for the purpose of deceiving anybody, but simply in order to establish what he
knows to be the truth. And the very fact that he is not afraid to do
all this in the dark, and thus run the risk of the most cruel accusations of fraud, only brings out the simplicity of his nature. . . .

It is interesting to notice the delicacy of the language employed
on both sides throughout. Never was there anything more than an
implication that the observations of Dr. Cook himself might be
non-existent or worthless.[148]

Indeed, some of Cook's closest associates including Walter Lonsdale, Charles
Wake and Anthony Fiala were aware that Cook had met with Dunkle and
Loose yet felt the meetings were essentially innocent.

Nevertheless, many of the details related in the affidavits lend credibility
to Dunkle and Loose's story. Mention is made that Loose wrote articles in
favor of Cook for the *Berlingske Tidende,* which he did do. Dr. Cook's papers
contain a copy of the same solar ephemeris that Loose said he bought for
him—and it shows little use. Loose mentions that he asked Cook what the
weather was on January 15, 1908, to support his observation of the star
Capella, and says that the doctor consulted his diary and told him that it was
clear. Dr. Cook's long-hidden diary entry for that day shows the barometer
to have stood at 29.51 and the temperature at −38°, indicating fair weather.
And these figures are exactly the ones recorded for that date by Loose in the
New York Times—81 years before the content of Cook's diary was publicly
available—and could not have been guessed at by Captain Loose. That Loose
said some of the latitudes from Cook's notebook did not match those given in
Cook's *Herald* story is also accurate, since, as has been seen, there are differences between his notebooks and his published account. However, Loose's
description of the notebook from which Cook read them does not match that
of any of his extant notebooks.

That Cook followed his magnetic meridian, did not correct for magnetic
variation and was equivocal about a depression at the Pole were all ideas Cook
held and maintained till the end of his life, showing that Loose must have
discussed these matters with him substantially, as he reports, and that his
memory, or notetaking, was accurate.

The only glaring discrepancy in the affidavits is that Loose said he lost
Cook's copy of *New Land,* while Dunkle has him returning it when their business had been concluded.

Of course, none of this precludes that Dunkle and Loose were someone's
paid agents. In fact, their affidavits contain minute details that are more than
ordinary memory would retain and indicate that Dunkle and Loose kept precise notes of their dealings with Cook, something that might be expected if
they had been hired to place the doctor in a compromising position.

The principal suspect as their employer would have to be William C. Reick, whose letters and telegrams to Peary about identifying "Black's" handwriting could have been just a cover for himself. After all, Herbert Bridgman, who knew a lot of things in advance, said he was sure Reick and the *Times* could "lead the procession effectively" just before Dunkle and Loose made their debut in the *Times*'s pages. As usual, Peary seems to have had nothing to do with it.

That it was the *Times* that got the exclusive Dunkle-Loose story was not lost on the competition, one of whom remarked, "It must not be forgotten that the paper publishing the story has been bitterly opposed to Dr. Cook from the beginning. We do not insinuate that the *New York Times* would deliberately print a false story against Dr. Cook, but under the circumstances it is conceivable that the paper might fall a victim to such adventurers as Dunkle and Capt. Loose. If the story prove false, then there is some truth in secretary Lonsdale's charge that a conspiracy is at work against the explorer. If it prove true, then the most charitable conclusion would be that Dr. Cook is a madman."[149]

But the fact remains that the reportage of these events seems to "prove true," and it is also a fact that Dr. Cook later claimed insanity, if not to explain his mistaken claim to the North Pole, then to justify his seemingly irreconcilable actions after his return to civilization.

AN INSANITY DEFENSE

In *My Attainment of the Pole,* Cook said that he had delivered his lectures, answered questions rationally and smiled constantly and pleasantly without knowing just what he was doing. But among all his controversial claims, this one of helpless puzzlement upon reaching civilization after nearly two and a half years in the Arctic, and acting like an "automaton" or "a machine," is most implausible and is impossible to accept.

On the contrary, what almost everyone observed during that time was not a desperate man struggling to readjust but, rather, a man in such total possession of himself that it was his most striking characteristic. And this characteristic was observed in Cook long before the Polar Controversy.

Yet in *My Attainment of the Pole,* Cook tries to convince his readers that he was not a well man. He tells them that on his lecture tour his laryngitis grew so bad that he could hardly be heard by the time he reached St. Louis. But the newspapers said that by then his voice was back in trim and he could be easily heard. He said that after a few weeks he began to feel persecuted and that the sight of crowds began to fill him with terror. But nowhere is there an indication that he shied away from the crowds that cheered him wherever he went, except momentarily at the St. Louis railway station mob scene, and then he chose to plunge into its midst. Nor is there any evidence of paranoia. Asked whether he felt people believed in him, Cook replied, "I must say that the generous attentions which have been bestowed upon me should satisfy any man of the good will and fairness with which the American People are inclined to hear my story."[150]

He seemed in control at all the inquisitions staged by the press. Cook even told Andrew Freeman that some "good samaritan" had sent him the questions the *Times* would ask in advance of his crucial meeting with the newsmen at the Waldorf. Yet even without advance warning, he defended himself confidently against the Peary Eskimo testimony and seemed only slightly ruffled as he read Barrill's affidavit while reporters looked on.

Of his reception at Hamilton, Montana, he wrote in *My Attainment of the Pole*, "Disgusted, with a heavy heart I left the hall. The oppression of my loneliness, defenselessness, and hopeless confusion rendered all sleep impossible that night." Yet an eyewitness reported that after the confrontation with Barrill, he chatted until a late hour with partisans and said the whole thing did not matter and that he was not disturbed by it in the least.

These and a hundred other little things undermine belief in Cook's story of incapacity or of acting involuntarily under great strain as an explanation for his inexplicable later actions.

When the very subject of his sanity came up in Copenhagen, he replied, "I hope I am not crazy, but from the hysterical and foolish telegrams I am getting I should judge there are plenty of lunatics at large."[151]

There were accusations that Cook's personal representatives attempted to bribe Fred Printz in Montana. There also reports that Dunkle and Loose, after their affidavit was published, were similarly approached with a bribe to retract their story. A man named George Lightfoot was identified as having offered Loose $5,000 to do so. B.S. Osbon alleged that Dunkle had admitted the affidavit was a lie, but Osbon's pro-Cook articles, which appeared in *Tourist Magazine* in 1910, were filled with unsupported statements. Though nothing came of Osbon's allegations, they contained the interesting fact that one of the letters threatening Cook's life was written on the stationery of the mining company with which Lightfoot was associated, raising the possibility that Osbon or Lightfoot, both friends of Dr. Cook's, had something to do with those letters, which the doctor later said contributed to his nervous prostration and subsequent flight into exile.

Anthony Fiala reported he had heard that Dunkle and Loose were paid $1,000 by the *Times* for their affidavits, but neither seems to have done himself much good beyond that by having sworn to them. Dunkle was quickly dismissed from his job at the Travelers Insurance Company because of the press notoriety. As for Loose, he wrote to Bridgman:

> I have finished Dr. Cook in the American press, but more so in the Scandinavian, and I am ready to face him again should he dare come forth. . . .
>
> Mr. Peary, of course, do not owe me anything for this, but he might know of an old navy tug or something, or a yacht of some

kind in need of a fully competent and strictly sober master,—so if you kindly will remember me when you see the Commander, I shall very highly appreciate it.[152]

But Loose apparently got nothing. Just after Cook "came forth" from exile, Loose left for Norway in January 1911, proclaiming he had done nothing dishonest.[153] The only big winner in the Dunkle-Loose affair was the *New York Times.* As an observer of the industry remarked,

> The great victory won by the *New York Times* in the polar controversy which for so many weeks raged furiously through the columns of the American press is recognized by scientists the world over and the public generally as making more firm the reputation of *The Times* as a newspaper that does things.[154]

Just what it did, as opposed to what it reported, remains open to speculation. However, it would not be too much of an exaggeration to say that the downfall of Dr. Cook marked the beginning of the rise of the *Times* to the powerful institution it was to become, and the decline of the once preeminent *Herald* into oblivion.

Whether he simply reported the news or helped create it, one thing is sure: William Reick got his revenge.

A man so various, that he seem'd to be
Not one, but all mankind's epitome:
Blest madman, who could every hour employ,
With something new to wish, or to enjoy!
But wild Ambition loves to slide, not stand,
And Fortune's ice prefers to Virtue's land.

We loathe our manna, and we long for quails;
Ah, what is man, when his own wish prevails!
How rash, how swift to plunge himself in ill;
Proud of his pow'r, and boundless in his will!

His memory, miraculously great,
Could plots, exceeding man's belief, repeat;
Which therefore cannot be accounted lies,
For human wit could never such devise.
With little pains he made the picture true,
And from reflection took the rogue he drew.

Some future truths are mingled in his book;
But when the witness fail'd the prophet spoke;
His judgment yet his memory did excel,
Which piec'd his wondrous evidence so well.

Great wits are sure to madness near allied,
And thin partitions do their bounds divide;
But charming greatness since so few refuse
'T is juster to lament him than accuse.

It looks as Heav'n our ruin had design'd,
And durst not trust thy fortune and thy mind.
Now, free from earth, thy disencumber'd soul
Mounts up, and leaves behind the clouds
and starry pole.

—John Dryden

CHAPTER 30

To Dream and Not to Count the Cost

IN THE WAKE OF THE DUNKLE-LOOSE AFFIDAVITS, THE EDITOR OF THE Richmond *News-Leader* marveled at the fabulous, if fleeting, triumph of Dr. Cook's apparently fraudulent claim to have discovered the North Pole:

> Dr. Cook imposed on most of the world the most enormous, tremendous, gigantic, complicated, circumstantial, complete, and plausible lie of all history. The performance will stand in a class by itself. In many respects it is more remarkable and interesting even than Peary's real expedition to the pole. . . .
>
> His skill, his audacity, his quickness, and his nerve are almost beyond belief. He faked the Danish Nation, scientific and learned, and simple and unlettered alike. He underwent successfully the most rigid examinations and cross-examinations by battalions of the keenest and most skeptical and suspicious of all inquisitors. With strong and steady eyes and clear voice he met all objection and piled lie on top of lie with the unhesitating facility of a master builder. He deluded the doubters and won over the skeptics and those who had derided him most scornfully.
>
> No longer can the devil hold his job and eminence as the father and prince of liars. He is down and out. He is a back number. He is overthrown by this wandering, long obscure, and poverty stricken American who faced single-handed the world of science and came from the lonesome and silent vastness of the frozen North to dazzle and astound the world.[1]

Another editor shuddered at the thought of what might have happened had Cook been more skilled in navigational methods. No doubt the backers of Robert E. Peary heaved a sigh of relief that he was not. They would have been content to let the matter rest at that point, as a shameless fiction finished with its exposure at Copenhagen, had Dr. Cook not forced them to do otherwise.

While Cook toured the country spoiling for a confrontation with Peary, he was met only with stony silence and unsigned propaganda. In later years, any discussion of this period of the Polar Controversy would have necessarily brought up the thrust of Cook's attacks and drawn unwanted attention to the critical question of Peary's character. It would also have exposed the shallow foundations on which Peary built his near-universal recognition as discoverer of the North Pole. For these reasons, the life of Frederick Cook after his rejection at Copenhagen has never been dealt with in depth by his detractors. The doctor's postexile lectures and congressional campaign have therefore been all but ignored, and even his conviction for mail fraud has been mentioned in only a general way as proof-positive of his dishonest nature.

Cook's proponents, on the other hand, in depicting his six years as a lecturer have omitted the ungentlemanly details, portraying them as a noble and desperate struggle of a wronged man to regain his good name, an effort ultimately crushed by the powerful forces and vast resources arrayed against him. For them, his trial and imprisonment were just the ultimate plot of the "Arctic Trust" conspiracy to destroy Cook's reputation forever.

But Cook's later career should be neither ignored nor distorted. If we are to come to a conclusion about the basic motivations behind his seemingly paradoxical actions, if we are to determine whether they were part of the plan of a ruling mind, then there, if anywhere, the answer must lie.

William Stead said that although Cook got only three and a half hours of sleep a night, he was always "perfectly cool" and never changed demeanor the whole time he was in Copenhagen. Yet, just before his disappearance Cook was described by his friends and family as a distraught man on the verge of physical and mental collapse. But Dr. Thomas Dedrick, for one, failed to notice it. In all his meetings with Cook in the months after his return from the Arctic, he was struck most by his remarkable calm. "I have never met him when he was not in the best spirits and health with a remarkable grasp of the subjects under consideration," Dedrick said. "Each time I met him he seemed more rested from his wearisome labors. I never saw any of the irritation which explorers have sometimes shown when engaged in literary work on their return to civilization."[2] Here, as in so many other instances before, there are two irreconcilable views of Dr. Cook.

Before departing without notice on November 24, 1909, Cook gave Walter Lonsdale a different alias and traveling route than he gave Charles Wake. He also stopped at the office of the Arctic Club's secretary, Rudolph Kersting, telling him he was bound for Toronto on the West Shore Line, and made arrangements through him to forward letters there. Kersting received a letter from Cook on November 27 posted at Toronto the day before.[3] Such actions seem to favor Dedrick's evaluation and indicate Cook's disappearance was something other than the spur-of-the-moment decision of a desperate man to elude his pursuers. Just where he went from New York is not known; he made several conflicting statements.

In the 1930s he gave Andrew Freeman a circumstantial account of going to Albany to see Clark Brown. Cook said he had met Brown at a lecture, where they discussed the engineer's intense interest in terrestrial magnetism. According to Cook, Brown recommended he drop out of sight until the press sensation over the Polar Controversy eased. Cook said he told Brown he was thinking about going to rural New York to rest, but Brown insisted that he would never be safe from the press there and advised him to leave the country. Cook then took a train north, he told his biographer, and followed Brown's advice.

But this meeting never happened. Cook did not even receive his first letter from Clark Brown until December 1910, to which he replied on December 25: "I want to thank you for the fine friendly stand you have taken for me, and some day in the near future I hope to have the pleasure of meeting you."[4] Why, then, this elaborate "recollection" to Freeman about a meeting with a man he would not meet for more than a year?

The story is in keeping with Cook's explanation in his own defense. It allows him to blame Clark Brown for his fleeing in the face of mounting criticism and adverse evidence, which looked to many like an admission of guilt and makes him seem like a confused and desperate man unable to decide what to do for himself.

But Michael Ryan, the man who recognized him at the Hotel Stachus in Munich in 1910, could not get over the demeanor of the fugitive who was then being sought far and wide by the world's press. "The assurance of the man took my breath away," Ryan recalled. "Here was the hotel crowded with Americans, who had either come to see or had seen the passion play [at Oberammergau]. Cook wandered about the lobby of the hotel the most unconcerned person in it, save Mrs. Cook, who is a large woman, and has all the nerve of her husband."[5] Ryan's observations show that at least by August 1910, Cook had regained the total self-control that so many had remarked upon earlier as his outstanding characteristic. Perhaps he never lost it.

In his writings, Cook recorded his own definition of what it meant to be a gentleman:

> They are men who fit into the picture where they're found. A gentle man works into and with life's splendor. While the social mill grinds with complaining wheels, he is there with oil and water and a mop. In the drawing room or in the slums, in the agitated mob or alone with his dog, he is ever the man that he should be. Whether in jail, in church, the White House, he is unruffled in the trouble and excitement that others feel.[6]

Except for his "nervous breakdown" of November 1909, or in the eyes of Jo Peary and Robert Dunn, this was always the man Dr. Cook was described as being—the man who endeared himself to all who met him by his dignity and total self-assurance. But even the trusting Charles Wake came to suspect that the "plot" against his friend's life, the threatening letters and his subsequent nervous collapse were really only masterly deceptions.

If his disappearance was a conscious plan to tantalize the world and maintain his newsworthiness in the face of the imminent rejection of his claims in

Denmark, it worked marvelously well. And, whether plan or chance, it prolonged Cook's ability to earn money from the lecture platform for years after he would have been vilified and forgotten had he remained to answer questions about his claims immediately after their dismissal. So rather than a tragic mistake of a desperate man on the verge of nervous collapse, his flight could have been the conscious plan of a coolly calculating and supremely self-possessed charlatan.

Despite his statements that he did not know what he would do for a living when he returned to America, he already had in mind "a full answer to everything" long before he returned to New York and discovered the *Hampton's* cover emblazoned with "Dr. Cook's Confession." In a letter to an associate only four days after his return, Cook outlined the theme he would drive home during the next six years on the platform: "I am all alone against an organized army of rival interests, oiled and fed by unlimited funds; every charge put against me is false, and if my health and money will hold out, in the end all this will be proven."[7]

Cook's lectures were part of an extremely shrewd plan to reestablish his case in the court of popular opinion by means of a melodramatic movie, shocking accusations against Peary's character, and his book, all designed to keep the polar dispute alive as long as it could be made to pay.

Dr. Cook explained his change in tactics this way: "When friendship is not active or in the minority make capital out of enmity. . . . In the polar scrap I tried first the respectful attitude of true sportsmanship. When this failed and was used against me—I used enmity—to put opposing forces on the defensive. An attack is the best means of defense."[8]

Cook rarely underestimated his enemies as they always did him. They apparently never understood that money and influence could not overcome the most dominant of human motivations or appreciated the consequences of a merciless victory. "Among the basic values of human conduct is to be rated the ever-present danger of a defeated enemy," Cook wrote. "You may whip a boy, but he does not stay whipped. He plans for the rest of his days to come back. Thus the cost of defeat falls mainly upon the victor."[9]

Dr. Cook also understood the value of persistence and confrontation: "We call it good to see the backs of our enemies, but it is better to watch the imprint of their faces over a period of years. Many, you will find if encouraged, will fall in line to become double boosters. Enmity is most often the result of envy and it is a law of nature to become like the things we want."[10]

Far from being the helpless little man, through his persistence and by confrontation, Cook managed to confound the Arctic Trust's every move. With the help of the ruthless propaganda of Fred High and the masterly political manipulations of E.C. Rost, he was more than a match for all its money and professional hirelings like Lucien Alexander; he managed to purloin hearing minutes from the very offices of congressmen and even infiltrated the enemy camp by placing a confederate on MacMillan's Crocker Land Expedition.

Peary was extremely frustrated by Cook's constant attacks. He believed that *The Platform* was run off the proceeds from Cook's lectures and that Cook, not Fred High, was the author of its screeds against him. There is every indication that High worked closely with Cook, E.C. Rost, B.S. Osbon, Clark Brown, and G.W. Baker to obtain his material. Whether Cook wrote them or not, the themes and the language found in High's magazine were delivered from the stages of the lyceums and vaudevilles by Dr. Cook himself. Hindered by his own personal secrets, Peary found himself at a distinct disadvantage. He could make no reply and was forced to avoid open confrontation with Cook, and in the end, the campaign for Cook's vindication planted the seeds of Peary's destruction deep in the pages of the *Congressional Record,* and forever in the public domain.

By 1916, when revenues began to fade, Cook moved on to other means of livelihood, the first being the Orient Film Company, whose prospectus guaranteeing huge, can't-miss profits was a tiny pre-echo of things to come in Texas. Although this promotion was such a failure that he could not even raise enough money to finance his proposed trip, Dr. Cook had no compunctions about stating to the press that $175,000 had been subscribed for the venture.[11]

Careful study of Cook's account of his world trip reveals many of the same doubtful characteristics as the narratives of his more famous expeditions. Even though it was written in 1916, it is at considerable variance with the dates recorded in his sketchy 1915 diary, and his articles recollecting it in *The New Era* show what a master of embellishment Dr. Cook had become.

In recounting the events of the trip to Andrew Freeman in the 1930s, the Dyaks were made very fierce, despite his contemporaneous statements that they were disappointingly tame, and his two-day visit to a single village to film their way of life became "several months" of serious anthropological study among "the tribes."

Likewise, many of the dramatic aspects of his entry into Leavenworth, which he reports in "Out of the Jungle," are at odds with the recorded facts. However depressed he was at the loss of his freedom, the evidence shows he knew, even before he arrived at the penitentiary, that he would be assigned to the hospital. He paints a dark psychological picture in his memoirs, but at the time of his incarceration he said that some hoped "perhaps it was Dr. Cook's farewell that ended within the high walls of the Federal penitentiary, but I prefer to think otherwise."[12] Even then, despite later talk of his "blackest hour," his self-confidence had not deserted him completely.

After the collapse of his polar claim, he increasingly seems to have convinced himself that he had actually accomplished a feat that was at least its equivalent. Though in October he could not recall the date he had claimed to have attained the Pole, his real experiences were as vivid as ever when he told the *World's* reporter, "To travel from Sparbo to Annoatok, in the Arctic night with no dogs and no food, dragging my own sledge, is a more difficult performance than going to the Pole."

Perhaps this was the justification for his future claims and the first sign in Dr. Cook of the sometimes irrational adjustments the human mind makes to preserve sanity when faced with a too-painful reality—as one writer put it, "the magnifying-glass which distance often lends to facts and motives and the mirror of distortion that repetition almost invariably holds up to truth."[13] In his private writings, Cook reinforces the suspicion that he was either a man increasingly incapable of separating fantasy from reality, or one for whom fantasy was infinitely preferable.

We find in his postprison jottings observations he said he had made in sub-Saharan Africa, one place he had never set foot, and a note that "in disgrace [Peary's] body has been removed from Arlington under circumstances not yet publicly explained."[14] Such fantasies allowed the wish to replace reality, and they also allowed Dr. Cook to justify his story to himself to the point that it culminated in his passing a polygraph test in 1938, during which he declared himself the discoverer of the North Pole.

But although there seems to be a pattern of deception in some aspects of Cook's later career, what can be said of its central event—his trial and conviction for mail fraud?

No doubt the government mobilized its full might to make an example of the Petroleum Producers Association, and it spared no expense in assembling hundreds of witnesses and many more hundreds of exhibits. Some have suggested the trial was a political ploy to divert attention from the Teapot Dome scandal that was about to savage the reputation of President Harding and his Ohio Gang. But although there were rumors, the depths of the deal Secretary of the Interior Albert Fall made with Harry Sinclair had not yet been plumbed when Cook went to trial in October. A case could be made, however, that the oil fraud prosecutions of 1923 in Fort Worth were a general reaction to investigations into improprieties at the Veterans Bureau, which resulted in the imprisonment of Colonel Forbes at Leavenworth and, ironically, his emergence as a vocal Cook advocate after meeting the doctor there.

Several conspiracy theories loosely alleging that the government specifically and unjustly targeted Cook for prosecution have been advanced, with the insinuation that Peary's old cadre inspired it, but the judicial records at the National Archives regarding the Texas oil prosecutions are too sparse to support such theories.

Some things that have been insinuated are untrue, such as that John Killits was a "hanging judge" hand picked by the prosecution to assure Cook's conviction. On the contrary, Justice Department correspondence shows that Judge Killits was brought in originally to hear the Pilgrim Oil case and was invited by Judge Wilson to hear Cook's case only after a string of unforeseeable circumstances. And Wilson later showed sympathy for Cook at every turn.

Nothing in the judicial records indicates anything more than a natural desire to win the Cook case as an example to all fraudulent promoters. As for illegal maneuvering, there is no solid evidence. Implications made to the contrary, drawn from this material, have been, like so much else in the Polar Controversy, based on selective quotation and deliberate distortion.[15] However, in such an expensive and important show trial as Cook's, the scarcity of correspondence may itself raise suspicions that the full story behind Cook's prosecution will never be known.

Dr. Cook maintained that in his oil promotions he was simply following established business practices of the time. His defenders have proclaimed him innocent of fraud because of the subsequent discovery of oil on PPA's former holdings. Like Senator Bailey, they argue he was a guileless man who was on trial because he failed to strike oil. Why, for instance, they ask, did Cook open his files and books to the postal inspectors and the government's accountant if his business dealings were obviously fraudulent?

The answer to that question may be likened to his behavior upon his return from the Arctic in 1909. His open and innocent-appearing actions while at Copenhagen convinced many then that he was honest in his claim of polar attainment and still do to this day.

There is no doubt that many of the properties once owned by PPA did eventually produce petroleum, and a recent attempt to vindicate the doctor by the Frederick A. Cook Society has shown that approximately 70 percent of the 90 parcels of land in which PPA held fractional royalties eventually were producers. From 1934 to 1990 these yielded 4,000,000 barrels of oil.[16] But this is not a great deal of oil for 90 properties over a 56-year period—an average of just slightly over two barrels of oil per property per day. And PPA had only fractional royalties on even this minute amount—some as low as .00632 percent. However, no records exist for these properties before 1934, and what they may have produced in the period immediately following PPA's ownership, if anything, is unknown and unknowable. But with oil selling below $2 per barrel in the 1930s, this would probably not represent vast wealth.

Although oil was eventually produced, at the level of operations being pursued by PPA at the time of its indictment, many years might have passed before it found oil in profitable quantities. Considering how little capital the company had, it might never have had enough to develop its holdings.

Furthermore, much of the oil since produced was found and extracted by using technology that did not exist in 1923 or was not commercially feasible until the price of oil had soared. To say that the properties once held by PPA eventually produced commercial quantities of oil, or even vast quantities, then, is deceiving unless measured against the probabilities of PPA's finding it with the technology and capital at its disposal in the 1920s.

Even if further research can establish that other PPA assets eventually produced immense wealth, this would not relieve Cook and his associates of the entire scope of the 12-count indictment brought against them in 1923. The claims that PPA made in its literature went far beyond promoting its holdings' potential. They led investors to believe PPA already had substantial actual returns from oil when, in fact, those returns were negligible. PPA enticed investors with guaranteed 2 percent monthly dividends and then withdrew the promise to pay. Though the defense argued that the dividends PPA did pay derived from legitimate revenues other than oil runs, it is clear that they came almost exclusively from the sale of stock—an illegal practice, itself.

PPA claimed gushers, but they weren't gushing, and oil runs, but they weren't flowing. That PPA made no attempt even to gather in the stock certificates of the companies it claimed to be merging indicates that there was no real interest in the properties, that the term "merger" was meaningless, and that PPA's interest lay solely in the 25 percent fee obtained on each share exchanged. PPA never actually merged, in any real sense, with more than a few of the hundreds of defunct companies whose stockholders it approached. That in itself was a huge deception, since PPA's literature stated it would manage the assets of these companies more efficiently, once acquired.

Certainly, PPA had field operations and producing wells, though they produced mere trickles of oil, but that the cost of postage, envelopes and lists of names far exceeded the expenses of those field operations confirms the prosecution's contention that PPA was far more interested in stock exchange fees than in oil production.

Though it could be argued that the evidence did not convincingly prove several of the 12 charges against PPA, the hundreds of exhibits were so full of fraudulent claims that the jury did not bother to consider the vicissitudes of the oil business or look at the finer points of law too closely. Their brief deliberations, despite the number of counts and the complexity of the case, show that they were so convinced by the mountain of physical evidence that they had little trouble reaching their verdict.

Senator Bailey had the good sense to realize that there could be no defense against such massive documentary evidence. In fact, he made none beyond the rhetorical, banking everything on having the case thrown out on technicalities or judicial error. But not even Judge Killits's bias against the defense or his remarkable and sometimes unwarranted clashes with Bailey could outweigh the endless parade of prosecution witnesses with their reams of sensational PPA literature.

Dr. Cook's testimony at the trial did nothing to help his case. On the contrary, it was as devastating to his credibility as was Peary's before Congress and showed that he, too, was a man with much to hide. He tried to avoid a direct answer to incriminating questions, pleaded an astounding ignorance of the inner workings of the company of which he was the president and sole trustee, or simply denied the conflicting testimony of others. Like Peary, Cook also showed an amazing lack of recall of key events.

His later appeals based on statements by the government's accountant that the PPA books were in perfect order are misleading. Matheny said what was in the books showed no attempt to cover up wrongdoing, but he never said they balanced and were in perfect order, as Cook later claimed. Instead, Matheny noted considerable errors of omission, the significance of which, of course, could not be judged, and characterized PPA's books as "irregular and complicated."

The jury had no choice, based on the evidence, Dr. Cook's own testimony and Bailey's weak defense, not to mention the judge's detailed charge, but to bring in the verdict they did, and no one who has read the entire 12,000-page transcript of the trial can doubt that the verdict was just. Even Cook was willing to say, "The charge [of exaggerated prospects for PPA assets] was probably true, but only in the sense that a farmer puts the largest potatoes on the top of the basket."[17]

Though the verdict was just, the sentence was wickedly excessive. Judge Killits's address to Cook revealed personal animus and more than hints that the sentence's severity was partially the result of his fake geographical claims. No doubt it was also motivated by a desire to humiliate Joseph Bailey.

In the 1930s Killits tried to justify himself by attributing his "verbal explosion" to what John Pratt had alleged: Cook's nefarious scheme of paying for most of the defendants' legal counsel to put them at his mercy, and then the defense's encouraging most of the defendants' absence from the trial so that they could not testify against Cook. Killits called this "disgusting perfidy" on the defense team's part, and as proof he offered that Senator Bailey made practically no defense of anyone's actions but Cook's.[18]

The trial record does not support this. It was Judge Killits himself who allowed the defendants to be absent during the testimony, and during the trial he agreed that if Cook was not guilty, no one else was. Naturally, then, the defense of Cook was of paramount importance, and all of the defense's energies had to be directed to proving him innocent.

As for Killits's skepticism about Cook's lack of funds, there is no accounting for the money Cook received from the promotions of the Vitek and Ray oil syndicates. Records show that Cook personally received $125,271.05 from these promotions and never reimbursed PPA even the agreed 6 cents per letter for sending them out. Yet neither he nor his wife had large amounts of money at any time in their lives after the collapse of PPA.[19]

There are several parallels between Cook's careers in oil and exploration. In both he tended to maximize his image through expert and professional advertising, while embellishing the basis of his statements to get the very best publicity and financial advantage. As at the foot of Ruth Glacier or at the edge of the Arctic Ocean, there are many indications that Dr. Cook may have had only good intentions at the outset in Texas as well, but in all three cases he seems to have entered an unknown field with overly optimistic prospects of success, which resulted in his ultimate failure despite his best efforts.

During the trial, Cook testified that he wanted to leave "a lasting monument to my name and memory"—the same motivation that drove Peary. This was something that had escaped him in his previous adventures. When his grand dreams once again fell through in Texas, he again attempted to shift blame, as

he had in the wake of the *Miranda* disaster and when he said his unpaid
Alaskan bills must have been overlooked by the society that sponsored the
trip—a society that did not exist. Once again confronted with others willing
to swear against him, he again denied everything or pleaded ignorance, just as
he had after the publication of the Eskimos' story and the Barrill affidavit.

Still, perhaps we could be permitted to imagine that like many oil speculators of his time, Cook simply got caught up in his own rhetoric and the boom
mentality prevailing in Texas. He may have actually believed so thoroughly in
the future that he felt justified in cutting legal corners in the present. When he
struck oil, he may have told himself, all his marginal practices would be vindicated, as he may have told himself that his false claim at McKinley would be
justified by his genuine conquest of the Pole.

The demise of Texas Eagle, which virtually wiped out his personal capital,
seems to indicate both his initial honest intention and his lack of experience,
and that failure may have forced him to try to recoup his losses, as he did at
McKinley, by whatever means possible. As one witness swore at his trial, he
may have decided from that point on "he was working for F.A. Cook."

This time, however, his false claims violated the law, and by chance, the
seating of Judge Killits resulted in the stiffest sentence ever handed down for a
similar crime in Texas. But even in prison Cook proved more than a match for
the situation. Through his public writings he regained most of his lost esteem.
His performance as a model prisoner and Amundsen's public defense of him
managed to reestablish, in spite of everything, the possibility that he just might
have been to the Pole after all, or at least that he may have been honestly mistaken, as once again, he seemed a man incapable of such a grand deceit.

Given Cook's amazing resiliency and his ability to turn every catastrophe
to some advantage, the Norwegian explorer's evaluation of his old friend from the
Belgica as "a genius" seems not to have been misapplied. Cook's own evaluation
of Amundsen, which he wrote after his friend's death, is also enlightening.

In his memoirs Cook recounted their meeting in the warden's office, and
there, too, he embellished some details. The words he puts into Amundsen's
mouth are too close to his own recorded thoughts, and he tangles his chronology, but in his retelling of Amundsen's magnificent career as an explorer, the
feeling is inescapable that Frederick Cook thought Roald Amundsen had led
the life he had hoped for himself: first through the Northwest Passage, first to
the South Pole and, it now seems, first to the North Pole as well. Yet he recognized Amundsen's one great weakness, since it was his own great strength:

> It often happens that a man who knows the big events of life
> best, is most thoroughly absorbed in the subject, has lived nearest
> to great happenings, is least able to describe the most thrilling
> experiences. Few great generals are able to report graphically their
> battles. Amundsen belongs to this type. Under his eyes were the
> most wonderful discoveries of our time, but you may look in vain

through his books for a suitable description of his remarkable experiences in his own words. Between all his lines there is the result of man's greatest tortures and his greatest glory in life. He was surcharged with the power to do things, but undercharged with the capacity of self expression.[20]

For Frederick Cook, self-expression was effortless, though his deeds fell short; perhaps he wished at that moment more for Amundsen's shortcomings than his own strengths:

> The men who get behind bars are, usually, of a type that could be made into good writers—by careful study and practice. They have had exciting experience—perhaps, too much of it—The spirit of romance is their main incentive in life. The lure of song and story is, too often, the cause of their downfall. It is just these qualities, with far-reaching powers of observation, that must be the background of all literature.[21]

But it seems that Amundsen, despite his heroic deeds, died an embittered man. Can we say the same of Cook?

In prison, Cook's restless nature was for the first time restricted. He had time to think, review the past and come to terms with all that had gone before. Looking back through prison bars gave him a new perspective on his life, though he still believed that a man's destiny was ultimately in his own hands:

> In spite of our finely spun philosophy, man is and always will be self-made. Success or failure is mainly of his own making.
>
> Our greatest asset, therefore, is that which we have within ourselves—and so why not get next to self? All this is self-evident, but few get to this angle of wisdom until the fruits of life begin to fail, then it is too late. Perhaps it is never too late to mend, but it is also never too early to prepare for better days. Too long do we linger in sowing wild oats, only to find that the hardest work, the greatest suffering, is the reward of our efforts to fill the nothingness of empty desires.[22]

It was then, at Leavenworth, that he spoke of "capitalizing calamity" with the confidence that he could, by his own intelligence, still conquer every obstacle and redeem his empty desires. As he had always done in the past, he evaluated his position and turned it to his good. This was his genius, and in this, at least, he never failed.

In 1932 Robert Dunn published a book that was almost an autobiography—almost, because he allowed fictional characters to enter and comment upon its real events. In the book Dunn called himself Rupert. One of his fictional characters was named Sydney, a sort of alterego to Rupert—a device by which he could have dialogue with himself. In one scene, Rupert and Sydney are sitting in the bar at the Waldorf-Astoria late in 1909, discussing the aftermath of Dr. Cook's downfall. Sydney goes directly to the root of the matter:

"Integrity's the point. Personal character."

"Exactly. And the Doc's is not so good. But he couldn't take a notary along with affidavits.". . .

"Some say his whole life's been aimed for this hoax. Never," Rupert defended. "The Doc's incapable of deep scheming. He hasn't the brains or imagination. Only tenacity, which he hides under vowing he always, 'Follows the line of least resistance.'"

"That doesn't match up. He's bucking the world."

"Yes, there's the broken circuit somewhere, which makes your man of mystery."

"Controversies rage around Cook's sort, as though they were fated to baffle the world." Sydney rarely echoed him so. Rupert went on—

"He belongs in fiction. He has the divine itch to explore, for the thrill of first beholding a new, untrodden valley. But you'd never grasp that, finding one with him as I have. Then you feel only his pig-headedness, and a thick hide. His tireless physique, that belongs in the stone age, or on Olympus. Add and mix well the dominant vanity that pervades his every pore and fibre. You get a man who can go to ends callous, brutal and even horrible, beyond our perception."

"But Cook hasn't—yet."

"He never actually will." Rupert paused. "Thousands believe in him, but he has no organized following, like a pacifist or a Baconian. He's not that kind of freak. He'll never sniff incense from acolytes upon some adventurer's dream-Elba. Because his real enthusiasm is unsteeled by ideality, he's too irresponsible toward the sacred cow of science, too unresilient to counter-attack."

"What really has he done?"

"One thing, harder than to find the Pole. He was alone for eighteen months in the Arctic, without another white man. Any normal, civilized being would have gone mad. His nervous system couldn't have stood it—but I tell you that the Doc has none. Nerve—colossal—but no nerves!"

"He just misses the heroic."

"Just." Rupert laughed, tonguing a cheek. "Instead, he's the true romantic. . . ."

"When he first sprang the Polar coup, I doubt that he was aware how he'd jolt our hero-racket-loving world, and the jealous little scientists."

"Couldn't he have thought that he really reached the Pole?"

"Maybe, though I doubt it. And what odds whether he did, if it wasn't the fact?"

"Proves his good faith," reminded Sydney.

"How? In one with no moral sense, whatever."

"I'd like to look inside his mind."[23]

That was a wish Frederick Cook never consciously granted.

In *Hampton's,* Dr. Cook—or perhaps it was T. Everett Harré or Ray Long— wrote, "I shall try to open the most secret chambers of my mind, and show my mental processes during the past several years; how my ambitions, my discouragements, my thoughts, my illusions, played their part in this drama of my mental life; and prove how inevitable, psychologically, as I see it now, was my triumph and my tragedy."[24] But just as there is some doubt as to who wrote this passage, there is also some doubt that the explanation he made was true. And anyone who ever believed he had a handle on the mental life of Frederick A. Cook always lost his grip.

Many thought they had the measure of the man at first sight. A.C. Miller, who met him in Alaska, was sure of it. "I shall never forget my first meeting with him," Miller recalled. "He had come up the Susitna River in a launch. . . . I could see at once that here was a man whose nerves were in perfect control; the poise and the dignity of the man and a certain air which showed a great reserve force impressed me. . . .

"I could see by the way that he acted that, calm as he was, he was not the kind of a man to ever give up anything which he had attempted."[25]

Dr. Cook struck many who met him just once that way. His poise and self-assurance lingered in the mind, as did the directness of his speech and the gaze of his clear blue eyes. Typical was the New York *Sun* reporter who recorded, "Conversation with him alone and in the company of others gives the impression that he is stating simple truths, so much so that he makes statements of facts that when thought over are deeply stirring, but which sound at the moment almost ordinary, everyday things."[26]

William Stead and the others who met him in Denmark thought him not only sincere in his statements but incapable of weaving such an intricate fabrication as a fanciful trip to the North Pole. "Such a flight of ambitious imagination was beyond any but the champion Criminal of the world," thought Stead.[27] And Minister Egan said Cook impressed the Danes "as a slow thinking, rather unbusinesslike man, not very well educated, and having hardly enough sagacity to perpetrate a hoax of the colossal proportions he did."[28]

Yet Professor de Quervain, who met him in Greenland, had quite a different impression and a greater insight, as one who had come from the same common stock: "The plastic expression of Cook corresponds to the make-up of a man who in the most difficult circumstances soberly and judiciously sees the reality of things and takes his measures accordingly."[29]

Some residents of Sydney who knew both Cook and Peary had no doubts about whom they preferred. "Dr. Cook is a splendid character," one asserted. "He is a gentleman clean through; brave, generous to a fault, always thinking of the comfort of others, and never for one moment sparing himself. . . . No circumstance, however tiring, ever seemed to ruffle his genial spirit. He was an Arctic enthusiast, and studied everything. When he went North with the Hoppin Expedition in 1894 *[sic]* it was the spirit of the North that enthused him. . . .

". . . Peary is more reserved and carries the habit of discipline and conquest with him. When we were with him we could not take a picture, converse with the natives, or pick up a walrus tooth without his permission. In his mind he owned the road to the Pole; he appeared to own the natives, the dogs, the game; the whole horizon was his and all for his own glory."[30]

Dr. Jackson Mills, who met Cook on the Peary Relief Expedition in 1892 and knew him professionally afterward, thought he had proof of Dr. Cook's true personality. "A man can easily gain an estimate of another's character in the monotonous solitude of the Arctic regions, where men are cooped up together during the long nights, which are wearing on mind, nerves and temper," thought Mills. "Dr. Cook had a remarkably even disposition and in all that time I do not believe I ever saw him get into a temper once.

"He was absolutely reliable."[31]

Certainly, most members of the Belgian Antarctic Expedition would have agreed with Mills's estimate. But then, even his most intimate acquaintances acknowledged that "he has never truly been known," and what they thought they "knew," they eventually doubted.

"A man must know himself before he can understand others," Dr. Cook had said, "must know himself before he can wield a power over others, and eventually must know himself, or die unknown." There is every reason to believe that Frederick A. Cook, at least, knew himself.

Charles Wake said he had a "magnetic personality" and termed him "sincere, modest, and very much of a man." Leslie McKercher called him "the strongest personality I have ever known." Yet Lotta Davidson, when asked for an anecdote about her friend, could not think of any, though she agreed he was a very fine man.

That man who had seemed so genial and honest, however, was now said to be capable of lies, coldly calculated. Yet Dr. Cook's friends were loath to believe him capable of monstrous fraud. It just couldn't be, they reasoned. As Amundsen said, "Peary denounced as a lie his fellow-countryman's renowned exploit. . . . This weakened to a great extent the belief in the reliability of Cook's statements among people who didn't know him, but among us who know him as a spotless, worthy man the charge fell harmless to earth."[32] No, it was much more comfortable to believe in their previous evaluation derived from everyday experiences.

It is just this point—that this man who had so many fine qualities was not, apparently, what he seemed—that has disturbed so many on both sides of the argument about Cook and what he really accomplished.

The *New York Globe* was right to point out that "Cook is an extraordinary person, and is not to be judged by the ordinary standards."[33] It was that recognition of the extraordinary in Dr. Cook that drove Herbert Bridgman and all the others who attempted to destroy Cook's reputation completely and finally to submerge any chance that his polar claim could ever resurface.

The human mind likes to think in absolutes, not uncertainties; it likes to pin a label on everything and place it in a category and, in so doing, often uses its reasoning ability to impose order that does not necessarily exist. The complexities of reality are more difficult to deal with than a story to which the ending can be written to order.

It is to that orderly side of the mind that the positive image of Dr. Cook appeals most strongly. Many refuse to believe that the divergent views of what Cook was could be true of one and the same man. To see only the good qualities in someone, or even only the evil ones, is far more comfortable; to admit that both are present is somehow vaguely threatening. That is why, since the beginning of time, the idea of a Pure Victim has held a lasting fascination. It is not surprising that he has aroused an almost evangelistic zeal in men like Hans Waale, who have seen only the good in Dr. Cook, and it is not without reason that Cook was occasionally compared to Christ.[34]

Even Captain Hall, as he imagined Frederick Cook's vindication, elevated the doctor close to the realms of the divine:

> There will surely arise in history, a gigantic figure; towering, like Chimborazo above the clouds. Then all the world will likely say, "Go take your kingdom. You have conquered all. You have won a victory, even over death. The trail that you have described over that trackless crystal solitude, will be a familiar scene in the thoughts, and in the day dreams, of ages and ages of admirers."[35]

Others, not so enraptured with the idea of Dr. Cook as a pure victim, only marveled at the naïveté of men like Captain Hall. "Any study of the psychology of Dr. Cook's rascality," one maintained, "would in no wise be complete without a study of the psychology of those who, contrary to all evidence, still maintained (and perhaps some still do maintain) the belief that this adventurer reached the Pole. Certainly the promoters of fraudulent oil stock who saw value in the name of Dr. Cook as an advertisement of their project must have placed a cynical reliance upon the power of the human mind to ignore reality. . . .

"Among the great knaves of history, if that is any comfort to him, Dr. Cook has won a front place. His story will not soon be forgotten."[36] Nor has it been. Even today, for every discrepancy revealed, for every argument brought to bear against his claims, which now seem irrevocably shattered by the contents of his own diaries, there have been defenders and counterexplanations. But even in 1909 this was recognized as inevitable.

"There will be a 'Cook party' to the end of time," one editor declared, "no matter how strong the evidence brought against him in the future, no matter if he made public confession to fraud. . . . This sentiment of personal devotion and championship once aroused is one of the most powerful and indestructible of human motives."[37] Although it was a matter of simple justice that the proper man should get credit, he said, who had reached the Pole first, or at all, was "a question of no importance."

J. Gordon Hayes agreed. "There is no reason for anyone to lose his sanity because the North Pole was not attained on foot," he said; "the matter was of very little importance."[38] But for anyone who has become deeply involved in the story of Frederick Cook, it matters very greatly indeed.

Some of these are simply true believers in the goodness of human nature and have been attracted to Cook's cause hoping to right what they perceive as a grievous wrong. As Ben Reitman wrote to Dr. Cook, "I think Frank Thompson would gladly go bankrupt if he could be able to get the world to accept your priority contest to the Pole. And many people feel the same about it. And, my dear Cook, this should make you very happy. To have provoked loyal friends such as you have one indeed needs to be a great soul."[39]

Even if the subject of such loyalty is not worthy of it, such men should be admired, not pitied. If they believe in the best in human nature, who can fault them for that? As Lord Chesterfield said, "It is the man who tells and who acts the lie who is guilty, and not he who honestly and sincerely believes the lie."

But most are not in so exalted a class. Many who have advocated most strongly Cook's total innocence have been willing to believe anything bad of Peary, seeing in him a symbol of something larger.

"The very invincibility of Peary's position was the main cause of the hostility to him," one observer believed. "Peary was a man of established reputation, an officer of the navy, a member of learned societies, backed by all the authority of science and education and of the whole social organization. Cook on the other hand, was a solitary adventurer outside the pale of official recognition, who all alone had snatched away the prize which the other could not have failed to grasp. Thus all the restless souls who live in perpetual revolt saw in Cook a martyr-hero and in Peary only a representative of authority, which is always to be opposed."[40]

No doubt such sentiments lay behind the obsession of Captain Hall and the efforts of Andrew Freeman, William Shea, Ted Leitzell and others. Of them Dr. Cook exclaimed, "I spent a half million and 10 years to prove that I had been to the pole—went to jail sat down [and] others did it for me!"[41] But it was not until Farley Mowat's vision of Cook as an antiestablishment figure in his book *The Polar Passion,* published at the apex of the antiestablishment 1960s, that this image became nearly the standard portrayal of Cook, and the one taken up by his recent biographers.

Yet Dr. Cook, however unique an individual, worked with and within the geographic and exploratory establishments and, in fact, helped create them. Only when he had been rejected by them did he say they were infested with "kitchen geographers." But none of the authors who saw Cook as an antihero dug deep enough to disturb the legend of "The Man against the System" or to ruin the riveting story of, as one dubbed him, "The Prince of Losers."

Then there were men like E.B. Baldwin, who saw Cook as a means of squaring old grudges with Peary, and Clark Brown, who sought his own immortality through proving Cook's claim. There were opportunists like T. Everett Harré, willing to work for either side as long as the story they wrote put money in their pockets, and whom Cook was just as willing to use to the same end. Even Fred High apparently regarded Dr. Cook as no more than a moneymaking machine. After years of his vociferous pro-Cook propaganda, he told Henshaw Ward, "Understand my position has always been this. I never felt that I knew enough about the North Pole to say whether Cook, Peary, both or either or neither of them were there."[42]

Those like Ed Barrill and the Rosts were content as long as they were paid but stood ready to reverse themselves as soon as they were not. Today there are those who, like many on the Peary side of the question, continue to defend Cook because they have bound up their own credibility with his. To these, the preservation of their own ego or their own fantasy is preferable to the restoration of truth.

Of all but the true believers, it might be said, as Dr. Cook once did, "Sincerity is seldom more than the aspect of a well grounded ambition."[43] Yet, regardless of motive, Cook willingly accepted aid from any source because, as he also said, "It is not what you have actually done but what others . . . desire to say good or bad about you. Even the flowers on the grave do not count. It is the verdure which others give to your world—which makes history."[44]

The life of Frederick Cook was so unusual, and his good qualities so appealing and undeniable, that it seemed impossible for even those who had no belief at all in him not to feel a sense of loss at what might have been when he fell:

> Except for one fatal quirk this man appeared to have most of the essential qualities which go into the making of a useful and respectable citizen. He was industrious, he was intelligent, he was ambitious, he was capable. Yet all of them were irreparably damaged by a moral weakness which made it impossible for him to be honest with himself or with anybody else.[45]
>
> The whole history of Dr. Cook affords an amazing and an absorbing chapter in the study of human psychology. Dr. Cook, when he came back from his venture near Mount McKinley, and

when he returned from his more northern exploit, must have
known that discovery of his fraudulent claim was as inevitable as
the rising of the sun. The weight against this consideration was the
hope of immediate financial gain and of international notoriety. A
strange mind, indeed, which in the face of such facts could make
the decision chosen by Dr. Cook![46]

Robert Dunn was right. Cook *was* the true romantic. But he did understand the consequences when romance supersedes reality.

"One who is not honest with himself is never honest with others," he
wrote. "If crime ever has a beginning—in shameless lies of this kind is where it
starts.

"Every time a resolution is broken, the bar of personal restraint becomes
weakened and at the same time a hundred doors to waywardness open."[47]

Not even his own wife seems to have been able to understand the "strange
mind" of Dr. Cook. T. Everett Harré, who knew both Jo Peary and Marie
Cook, remarked that though it might not be gallant to say so, he thought the
real reason their husbands sought the North Pole was to get as far away from
them as possible. He was fond of relating this story about Mrs. Cook:

> She drew her chair close to my desk. "I've been married to Dr.
> Cook for years, and he's still a stranger to me," she began, rather
> wistfully. She told me that at the time the Controversy was raging,
> Dr. Cook believed that Peary's spies or detectives were watching
> him and wanted to steal his notebooks. They were then staying at
> the Gramatan Inn above New York. "Dr. Cook was exceedingly
> nervous, and when a window would rattle would rush to the win-
> dow and look out. As he felt sure that spies were after his papers, he
> insisted that I carry them inside my corset." As Mrs. Cook was an
> exceedingly buxom lady, I could imagine how she came to feel
> something of a martyr by being the secret cache for Cook's polar
> observations!
>
> Finally Mrs. Cook leaned closer, and in a low confidential voice
> went on, "My husband has come to trust you, I think, more than
> he had ever trusted anyone in the world. Tell me—do you think
> that Dr. Cook believes that he got to the North Pole?"[48]

Mrs. Cook, according to Harré, wanted him to intervene with her husband
to give her $700, her own once-ample funds having been dissipated. Harré
related that Cook declined, saying that she had refused to aid him in the outfitting of his North Pole expedition.

Though it might be a cruel leap to conclusions to think that Dr. Cook
married Marie Hunt for her money, there are undeniable hints in several surviving letters to her, besides the one he wrote to her from Greenland in May
1909, that their relationship was strained, at best. Still, long after their divorce,

Marie Cook wrote to her former husband of the predicament in which he had placed her:

> I meet a lot of men, but they never register with me, perhaps because I compare them mentally with what I wanted you to be, and [what] you were when I first met you. You hypnotized me and then dehypnotized me so many times that my mind is not entirely clear just how you would appear to me now, altho I think at times I've never lost the first impression you made with me, and presume that is the reason I compare all men with you. . . .
>
> Perhaps you have found someone in whom you are interested, and if you have and are happy, I shall be happy too, but that's no reason why you should entirely forget me, is it? . . . I have only been a part of your life, but Not <u>in</u> your life.[49]

Was Dr. Cook the same man in 1901 that he was in 1909? And if not, what changed him? In the wake of the Copenhagen decision, the *New York Times,* which periodically tried to explain away Cook's good and admirable qualities, said it thought it perceived a pattern in his behavior:

> The present exposure, while by far the greatest, is by no means the first which he has suffered. Of the others, that which followed his claim to have climbed Mount McKinley is best known, but the difference between that and half a dozen more seems to be that it has been more carefully investigated. Far back in the mists of time are stories of a museum exhibition of dubious Eskimos, the Miranda cruise made a lot of unpleasant talk as to the methods of its manager, and when, after the antarctic expedition in which Dr. Cook took part, he managed to get ashore at a South American port and cabled widely the news of the voyage, his companions thought they had reason to accuse him of violating an agreement which left the privilege of doing this to his chief.
>
> There has been a curious likeness in all these episodes—in each there was the desire to make money, combined with a yearning for personal glory, and in each appeared the same unscrupulousness as to the means used in attaining them. Always, too, there was the same inability to foresee exposure—or the same indifference to it.[50]

Yet Lotta Davidson, who knew him for many years, had no inkling in 1909 that a change had come over him. "I am certain that Dr. Cook has discovered the pole or he never would make the statement," she said. "I feel confident in him, not only because I know him so well, and have such perfect faith in him, but because no man would willfully state such a thing if it were not so. Think of the terrible consequences that would follow."[51]

But at McKinley "the door to waywardness" had swung full open, and the terrible consequences did follow, not only for him but for his daughter and granddaughter as well. It must have been truly blind faith that kept Helene Cook Vetter from noticing in that lantern slide she gave to the Library of Congress the solid land attached to her father's "Glacial Island," described by him as hundreds of miles from any shore. It must have been only the highest ideal of her father as an honest man that kept her from admitting that the tiny words and figures in his diaries could not be interpreted in any way except that his journey to the North Pole was a fabrication.

There is no other way to explain it. Surely she and her daughter must have read every word Dr. Cook had written. Perhaps they knew; after all, they held the diaries back for nearly 50 years, and then only death released them. Perhaps they simply could not bring themselves to admit the truth, or hoped that some new evidence would turn up. That the answers were in their hands and before their eyes and yet they seemed to have no doubts and spent most of their lives seeking vindication for Dr. Cook is at once amazing, admirable and very sad.

If the psychology of his descendants is puzzling, Dr. Cook's remains even more baffling. Others who had no opportunity to read his diaries persisted in feeling, like Robert Dunn, that there might be something to learn if only the unfathomable mind of Dr. Frederick A. Cook could be even momentarily revealed.

But whatever the complex secret details of his thoughts may have been, it seems inescapable that Dr. Cook, at base, was not the man his wife, daughter, friends and acquaintances thought they knew in 1901, 1909 or any other time.

Many who thought they knew him thought him naive and unworldly, humble, modest and even a bit shy, but no one who reads his private prison writings can believe this, nor could they believe that he lacked "the brains or imagination" to concoct a story of how he attained the North Pole or the cool reserve to tell the world that he had. No one who reads even the material he published in *The New Era* should have any doubts that an imaginary trip to the North Pole or the top of Mount McKinley was well within his capabilities.

These writings reveal him as extremely sagacious. They contain many profound and insightful thoughts and bear witness to an exceedingly rich inner life. Though he may have gotten his science tangled occasionally, they show a deep understanding of human nature that approaches genius.

The closest he ever came to allowing that coveted look inside his mind was through those unpublished writings now in the Library of Congress, especially "Out of the Jungle." In that book, ostensibly an argument for prison reform, we may best glimpse the hidden thoughts of Frederick A. Cook and, through them, the justification of all that transpired in his life.

Though he never says so directly, it is impossible, if only through its metaphors, to escape the feeling that his musings on the psychology of criminals and the society that creates them come from "the greatest human asset and the most costly"—the pages of his own "book of experience":

Idleness is the false lure of the wayward. Most boys early develop an all-absorbing ambition. If the mind and body is put to work on the path fired by this inspiration, there will be developed a capacity for a prodigious amount of work; and this rule follows along all through the successive stages of man's existence, for the adult is always a boy.[52]

The young man of our day early dreams of a spectacular purpose in life, but this purpose has rubber qualities. It is easily stretched to meet the call of the wilds. To him all the world is still unknown. He lives at the edge of the beyond, with the lure of wonderlands ever over the far horizons.[53]

The compass course of where to go, the book of experience which tells us what to do, the joy of contentment in art of work best done, the spirit of pleasure in full clean living, these are only adjuncts to a better wisdom of late life.[54]

Contentment, and only contentment, anchors life; but it takes most of us half a life-term to learn that important lesson. We are prospectors until 40, and mostly claim jumpers after that. If a gold digger comes along who has seen somebody who has heard of somebody who told of the glitter of gold in some remote nowhere, it is the nature of man to pack up and go. . . . You may ask, "Why follow the fool's bugle." The reply comes, "It has been done before. I am off." And this is true, it has been done before—once in a million times—and so we're off on that once-in-a-millon chance. If there were no fools there would be no millionaires, and no jails.[55]

Instead of foresight being the very groundwork of human planting, the lure of adventure pulls at an age when the eye is open mainly to a comedy of thrills. Why stay in the cold monotony of white collar jobs when the road of far off plenty is open and free for all. . . . The price of a fool's adventure is high.[56]

A job in which there is leeway for a creative mind to expand is man's greatest blessing, and such a position is open to all, every-where, in every strata of human culture. Mental vagrance leads to over-reaching and then the stream of crime begins.

Man is always seeking an altitude from which he can observe the passing and the coming events of his travels in the trail of life. Occasionally he gets into a ditch and then in darkness and often under duress begins a struggle for light to determine the direction of right and wrong. All of human adventure is up and down, over hills and gullies. Fortunate indeed is he who can find a footing along the ridges to ever higher planes of endeavor.[57]

In the sum-total of individual endeavor, it is the main direction which counts. Right and wrong is in the high lights and shadows—the side scenes in passing. The main trend of life is like that of the animals of the wilds; to make the best use of nature in harmony with the conditions encountered. An eye trained to high attainment may lose its way in vallies of indecision, but this waywardness is only an experience to improve the direction of the ultimate aim. When we go onward, ever onward to a higher plain, we need not worry about mistakes that gave us pain; these are in the plans of Sublime Creation.[58]

Intelligence is a marketable product, changed, recast and decorated to suit price, supply, demand and desire.

Most people get a taste of what they desire but their desires are not often in accord with the source of supply nor with the market of demand. . . .

. . . In the child there are other responsibilities but fully grown men and women are mainly the product of their own making by conditioned desires.[59]

A salesman must come with a smile on his face. . . . He must wear the clothes and manner of a gentleman and . . . he must talk fluently on any subject from peanuts to aeroplanes. . . . These are the faces that smile without a heart.[60]

In the face that smiles without a heart there is the surest sign of stupidity, moral disease and ethical degeneration but it is just this face that the artifice of social culture demands.[61]

All life is but an adventure to give advantageous use to the function that nature has provided for every man. Even the hardship of jail can be made an experience of great value. If we will but keep in mind that we must assure the consequence of every act; that we must do our best with the material at hand and direct all our interests to a worthy purpose—the time becomes useful everywhere. . . .

We can see from prison bars a world of reflective grandeur that others never see. We can see, in the darkness and the depths, a great unknown, where the mind must be geared to deeper thoughts to pierce the mysteries. We envisage mankind from a new angle—examine the economic fabric with microscopic eyes—see the social storms from sound-proof booths—get the thunder of political seas under the protection of a dark jungle. Safely tucked away in a well stocked winter den, we may not gain strength to move mountains, but we can recondition courage and perception to find stepping stones to a bigger, better life.[62]

The necessities of life are those that nature supplies. Evil is the period that follows thou shall not! It has no other existence. Evil is a violation of the agreed local custom of inter-relations. The chief use of the word seems to be to express an opposing quality to good.[63]

All that is really good or bad or culturally acquired is an appendage to the brain, a by-product of recent acquisition as anthropologic time is rated.

Since this is true why expect a perfect man, when but one percent of his brain capacity is used for the work by which we rate the individual. . . .

That little one percent of the brain which to our misunderstanding is all there is to men, cannot promote all good and check all evil while the 99% is desperately busy in the main business of life which business has no relation to morality or immorality. Herein is the source of all our so called misconduct.

And it is for this reason that we rise or fall to the lure of the moment. The deep seated tendencies like love of parents and home, love of wife and children, soul companionship of playmates or friends, these and other passions have an abiding place in that one percent of the mind; but this is suppressed by the lure of the moment, as must be the case, for conscious life is mainly stirred by mental stimuli that come and go like the heart beats, only very few of these thought waves are recorded in the fabric of memory.[64]

Right and wrong are but a point of view very much influenced by the ever present demands of the body.

The main hope of a change for betterment as demanded by civilization in a large way for the masses is by carefully guarded reactions in early life, to be later conditioned into regular habits by subconscious direction.[65]

When, by mistakes, we find ourselves adrift enroute to bread and water, it is time to sit down and face the world in the full light of noon. . . . A chance acquaintance may be a liability or an asset. He may make or break your career for life.[66]

Peary was that chance acquaintance for Dr. Cook, and as chance would have it, he returned the favor to Peary. But what was the two men's true relationship? Was there a dislike of each other even before their confrontation in 1909?

Thomas G. Scott, the promoter who had charge of the Chicago World's Fair Eskimos whom Dr. Cook brought to New York, said Cook told him differences arose on the 1901 expedition because Peary desired to control everything, including Cook's Eskimo studies.[67]

Perhaps the break came in 1902 when Cook failed to secure the post as leader of the second Ziegler Expedition. Herbert Bridgman is alleged to have told Baldwin in 1913 that Cook, while secretary of the Arctic Club in 1902, had "exceeded his authority" in trying to turn Ziegler against Baldwin in the hope of securing for himself the leadership of the expedition.[68] And in a letter, Jo Peary even mentioned "the Ziegler-Cook Expedition."[69] Did he come that close? And if so, what caused William Ziegler to change his mind? Was some influence applied from the exploring fraternity to drop Cook from consideration, and was that influence inspired by Bridgman or by Peary himself?

The day after his brother's claim to the Pole was announced, William Cook possibly hinted at this: "It is my opinion that my brother so far as his polar explorations are concerned has been treated in a manner I would describe as mean—very mean. How I will not say."[70] And Ivar Fosheim, Sverdrup's hunter, recalled getting a letter from Cook in the fall of 1902 complaining of Peary's treatment of him.[71] Perhaps the appointment of a man like Cook by the incredibly rich Ziegler had to be averted, since such a combination would have created too dangerous a rival to Peary.[72]

That Peary sequestered his eldest Eskimo son on the *Roosevelt* "to prevent Cook from taking him back" shows that Peary, by 1908, thought Cook capable of doing such a thing, and perhaps anything. And though Cook seems to have been on amicable terms with the Pearys and Herbert L. Bridgman at least through 1903, Marie Cook was reported to have said on the same day as William Cook's dark hint, "My husband never believed in sensationalism and his feeling against Peary was pronounced. He saw Peary's work in Greenland and didn't like the way he treated the natives. . . .

"He said that one man, with determination and genuine love and regard for the natives, could do more than whole expeditions."[73]

Did Cook hate Peary? Perhaps the answer lies in the recollection of a fellow passenger aboard the *Hans Egede* who recalled the doctor's exclaiming, "If Peary ever reached the Pole before me, I would take a revolver and kill myself."[74]

As Peary read in Cook's letter to Franke from the polar sea that he had reached Cape Thomas Hubbard and was striking out for the Pole itself, when he had been so sure that Cook hadn't the ability to get even that far, he could not escape recognizing that his former surgeon was an explorer of more than average ability and also what he most feared—a real and dangerous rival. That realization must have chilled Peary with the awful possibility that Cook might actually succeed, and it may have caused him on his own journey to risk nothing, so as to be sure to return with a claim of his own. If it did, it robbed Peary of even the small chance that he could have carried off the feat himself.

That Cook was an explorer of actual ability was something the Peary forces knew but took pains to deny. Long after the doctor's downfall, Isaiah Bowman told Edwin Swift Balch privately, "There is no doubt that Cook has done some remarkable things in the way of exploration. . . .

"I have always labored under the suspicion that Cook accomplished very much more than he has been given credit for, in spite of the fact that . . . I do not believe that he actually reached the North Pole."[75] And though Donald MacMillan denied Cook the title of explorer on his centennial, at an earlier time when Cook's claim had seemed irrevocably crushed, he admitted that Cook had a rightful claim to a very high place in the history of arctic exploration but that the public indignation that followed the exposure of his false claims had robbed him of credit for his true exploits. Though this is true, is there any reason why what is rightfully his should not now be returned to Dr. Cook?

In a thoughtful little book about the motivations of explorers called *The Springs of Adventure,* Wilfrid Noyce discusses the urges that send men forth to the wild places of the earth. He tells us that many explorers' prime motive lies in seeking to accomplish the impossible to "prove themselves to themselves," and so become master of themselves. In *My Attainment of the Pole,* Dr. Cook wrote of his impossible accomplishment of reaching the Pole:

> I felt that I, a human being, with all of humanity's frailties, had conquered cold, evaded famine, endured an inhuman battling with a rigorous, infuriated Nature. . . . I had proved myself to myself. . . . Over and over again I repeated to myself that I had reached the North Pole, and the thought thrilled through my nerves and veins like the shivering sound of silver bells.[76]

Some explorers, Noyce tells us, find in the mere survival of incredible hardships an approach to the central mystical experience of life itself: "The state of awe is difficult to come upon . . . the kind of awe that I mean, the awe in which self is for the time lost and consciousness absorbed in a greater consciousness normally incomprehensible to it. . . . We reach the physical state needed for the spiritual experience. The moments are fleeting and tenuous but the memory of them remains all the more wonderful for that. . . .

"Some find it in the lonely places of the earth, to which they escape."[77]

It is not necessary to look far in Dr. Cook's writings to see that the quest for that central mystery was a potent drive for him:

> The white lights and dark shades entering into the soul make life a long dream—the spirit now effervescing, then smothered again, almost frozen, only to be thawed out for an ascent into an atmosphere of heavenly purity.
>
> In my judgment, polar grandness lifts the mind's horizon, and as a whole the experience affords a wild, weird, and poetic existence long to be remembered. It fires the soul with new flames and instills the body with renewed action. The dayless nights and the nightless days and fierce storms are bewildering, but these maddening contrasts are productive of clear and forcible intellects. . . .

> There the strong relentless conditions incite the mind, but throw it
> back upon itself. They inspire the imagination without satisfying
> its curiosity.[78]

The true explorer must look upon the mysterious unknown and, in seeing it, gain the opportunity to glimpse the greatest mystery that lies within. Science is always secondary to the great but useless object that fires his mind.

Escape, itself, is often the driving force—escape from menial existence—and in Peary's little ad for a surgeon in 1891, Dr. Cook found the relief he sought. "I cannot explain my sensation," Cook said of that moment. "It was as if a door to a prison cell had opened. I felt the first commanding call of the Northland. To invade the Unknown, to assail the fastness of the white frozen North—all that was latent in me, the impetus of an ambition that had been stifled and starved, surged up."[79]

To such men, the future accomplishment of some large task seems more meaningful than the thousand little details of the present. They long to get away, impelled by dreams of some great accomplishment, as Noyce says, "losing themselves in the sublime idea ahead, not aware that they are neglecting home or work or the opportunity of everyday . . . to dream dreams of an escape toward some glorious and useless goal. Yes, there is a streak of madness about them. But it has descended from the stars on which they fix their eyes. It is a divine madness."[80]

"The world needs men with a distant vision," wrote Frederick Cook, "men who can give the world great dreams. To dream and not to count the cost."[81] But as Wilfrid Noyce observed, "The trouble with dreams is that they tend to get in the way of other necessary things in life."

After the dreams lie shattered or, sometimes worse, fulfilled, explorers often, like Dorothy waking up in Kansas, look upon home with new eyes and realize, too late, the opportunities of everyday are gone and were not so worthless as they seemed to them while dream-possessed.

Late at night, from his prison room in Kansas, a wakeful Dr. Cook wrote this advice to other dreamers:

> The world of every man is composed of about six people. We speak
> of society, state, country and a host of friends, but, in the final
> analysis, there are just about a half dozen individuals that really
> count in the life of one—and in the circle of every one—these
> should be near. Peace of mind, freedom of heart and soul—the
> very essence of the power that is within you, cannot expand in the
> isolation of self from those who pull the heart strings. . . .
>
> These are a part of your own mental mechanism. Without
> them no part of the earth will be quite satisfactory. Necessity may
> force you to break the circle, but do it cautiously, for here is likely
> to be your most lasting source of regrets.[82]

As he penned a letter to Ruth from that prison room, he now saw from a new perspective everyday things that once had been:

> You were about four years old. . . . [It was early spring and] we sat around a big mahogany table, in a big room with gas lights burning and [you] kissed each of the strawberries before I was allowed to eat one. In the season that followed I ate a lot of strawberries. Those kisses and those strawberries are to this day among the sweetest fruits of all time.
>
> Then things began to happen in which you had no part. I was much away from home. This will always be the most tragic period of my life, for there after home had little lure for me. This was my mistake not yours nor mother's, but let it stand as a lesson.[83]

But the "divine madness" of the true explorer, even if the impossible is obtained, must someday be subjugated to the mortal madness of ordinary life when physical powers fade below the level necessary to challenge the more impossible. Then the explorer must find his way back into and through the complex wilderness of civilization.

This is a difficult task for the genuine explorer, Noyce tells us, since he craves the primitive life obtainable only in places of great solitude, "the savage returning to his wild and native habits," as Darwin put it. For a brief time the explorer might become a "natural man" undistracted by civilized irrelevancies. "Only by looking *inward,* rather than outward at the contemporary scene, men are likely to solve the contemporary world's problems," wrote Noyce. "Burrowing into themselves, trying to bring to their aid some of that massive subconscious which is at the root of their actions—all this involves going back also to the early man and trying to feel, as well as to understand, his myths and mysteries."[84]

That Dr. Cook realized all this and even relished it, there can be no doubt. After all, in his little diary that he kept on the bleak shore at Cape Sparbo, didn't he wish to write a chapter in his book of experience entitled "Just how it feels to be a savage"?

But as for Robert E. Peary, if he ever felt those wild pleasures, they all but vanished in the terrible hardships and failure of the Second Greenland Expedition and the permanent physical impairment that he suffered at the very beginning of the next. After

Frederick A. Cook, 1898.

that, Peary simply endured "this Black Hole" of the Arctic, using it; unwilling or unable to withdraw from it until he had gained what he most desired—not the North Pole, – but the adulation, fame and money that would result from the assertion of its conquest.

To say that a true explorer is not interested in these things at all would be foolish. But for Peary they were an end in themselves. He needed money to gain his true object, Fame, and Peary said he would do anything to gain it. "If I had the money myself," he wrote to the editor of *Collier's*, "or could earn it even by such a bargain as used to be effected in the good old times when souls were a marketable commodity and always in demand by the devil, I would put the thing through single-handed."[85]

For Peary, while money was necessary to gain fame, fame was a means to get more money. To him the accomplishment was always secondary to the reward. But for Dr. Cook, the attraction of these other motivations of an explorer—fame and money—is less certain.

As Belmore Browne realized, he carried around with him the innate desire to see the unknown places of the earth, and as Herschel Parker said, "He liked the life." Money was necessary to continue that life, and fame and money would be necessary to lead any life at all when he could no longer even dream of accomplishing the great goals that had eluded his physical grasp.

In the gripping story Cook created about his attempt to reach the North Pole, he was not satisfied with his real experiences, remarkable as they were. There would be for him not just a taste of what he desired when he returned. Years before, he had realized, "The public wants the pole and nothing short of it. People will hail the man whose foot has been on the exact spot, but they will condemn all efforts short of that,"[86] so he took those real experiences and presented them "changed, recast and decorated to suit price, supply, demand and desire." Was it not the law of Nature that every creature be allowed to profit by its own intelligence? Who would have endured what he had endured in those two and a half years just past, even to reach the position in which he now found himself as a result? Who was there to say "Thou Shall Not!"?

How much Dr. Cook profited initially from his claim to have discovered the North Pole is not known. Estimates range from $30,000 to $100,000, with his secretary placing him $69,000 to the good before his disappearance. That the average yearly salary of a New York physician in 1909 was $1,500[87]— just half of what Cook earned for less than three hours' work at Carnegie Hall in his first lecture on his "Discovery of the North Pole"—gives some perspective on the tremendous amount that even $69,000 then represented. But Cook's advocates have argued that his not making more than this only proves his good faith and his honest intentions.

Like one who met him in Copenhagen, they have said: "He could discover the Pole, but he did not know how to sell a book recounting this discovery. A man who thus lets thousands of dollars slip carelessly thru his fingers is not likely to be a party to a huge deception such as would be simply discovering the North Pole on paper."[88]

Dr. Cook used this argument himself as evidence that he was an honest man. "As a matter of fact," he said, "at no time did I plan to make money. On returning to civilization I had no remote thought that I would be the object of such attention, or that my lectures or writings could earn any great sums. Had I worked out a huge scheme to exploit my achievements—as some of my enemies have alleged—I would have cleared a million dollars or more."[89]

Though Cook could have gotten far more money by taking Hearst's offer to double anyone else's—something he later said he regretted not having done—or by fulfilling the $104,000 worth of lecture engagements he canceled to prepare his report to Copenhagen, there is little evidence that he was as naive as he claimed.

In 1900 he had written, "The hero-worshipers are ready, but who is the hero to be made? By what route can he climb the ladder of popular fame?"[90] Ten years later he is that man but tells us he "had no remote thought that I would be the object of such attention."

As we have seen, Peary's polar diary devotes 32 pages to the ways that he should profit from "the discovery of the North Pole." Though far less grandiose, scattered through notebook 2, kept at Cape Sparbo, can be found Cook's own plans to cash in on his claim:

> Book of 50 pictures for news stands
> Posters, book and lectures
> 25 enlarged pictures for travelling exhibit
>
> His private soc. or an inst like B'klyn
> 1000 miles in an Arctic Boat (over frozen seas)
> A Vaudeville lecture
> Comedies and Tragedies of the People of the N.P.
> A School geog. . . .
>
> An automobile coat made of light seal skins
> Eider down carriage auto and baby carriage robes
> picture frames of narwhal and walrus tusks
>
> News 2000 also 5000
> Weekly 2000 page of pictures
> Magazine 10000

At other places in his diaries we find the sketches for several magazine articles, the complete text for an illustrated lecture tour, and the outline of a booklet of pictures entitled "The Conquest of the North Pole," to be sold for 50 cents a copy at those lectures.

It is the chilling similarity of these passages in Cook's diaries to those in Peary's that gives one pause to think that perhaps the two men were not so dissimilar as they appeared. Those who wince at Peary's hopes of being one of the "World Men" and rejoice in Cook's simple humility should not forget what Frederick Cook wrote to Thomas Laity from Texas about himself and his treatment by the world: "They cannot kill his ambition or his soul or the determination of his will, or the wonderful brilliance of his mind, if he is made of the stuff from which the world's leaders are moulded."

When Dr. Cook started to drive a bargain for his book, the man who supposedly "did not know how to sell a book recounting about this discovery" demanded an advance of $30,000 of Doubleday, Page, which turned it down as excessive.[91]

Though Cook released Harper & Brothers from a contract said to total $300,000, we should never make the mistake of judging Dr. Cook by the yardstick of ordinary logic. Cook was not in the game for quick profits, but rather for steady, lifelong gain. In his memoirs he tells us, "The story went to the New York Herald. If the work had any earning power, I would collect the millions anyway. I would fight my battle alone. What had I to fear!"[92]

Cook was truly fearless, even in the big risks he took financially. As an object of adulation, he maintained an unfailing simplicity and directness that most took for sincerity. Assailed by an outraged rival, he held to his gentlemanly reserve and won still more friends. Faced with frenzied crowds, he affected no emotion whatever. Bombarded with difficult questions, he coolly answered all with assurance. Indeed, what had such a man with such complete self-control to fear?

Rather than being a clumsy short-term hoax that he knew would be exposed, all of Cook's actions point instead to his belief that he could actually establish his claim, or if he could not, that his personal resourcefulness was sufficient to turn any notoriety that resulted to his good anyway. And how superbly he succeeded! His "capitalization of calamity" between 1911 and 1916 easily exceeded the amount he gained before he was discredited.

Cook's impoverished upbringing taught him the necessity of money as security, not the luxury of it. We have already seen that his dealings with others over money, even petty sums, were not always honest, that he married money, if not for it, and that he knew how to use money when he had it.

After each adventure he worked, scrounged and flattered to obtain financing for the next.[93] In the field, he was difficult to tell from the natives, but after his return to America in 1909, he always went first class: the Waldorf-Astoria, the *Mauritania,* the Adion. He wore fine suits, was known as a big tipper and was regarded as a perfect gentleman—"ever the man that he should be"—everywhere.

It might be said that Cook took the long view—that he did not desire fleeting fame, and that he desired limitless money even less than that. What he desired was what every man desires—immortality—a place for Dr. Cook in history, whether high or low. When that place was still in doubt, one newspaper editor mused upon Cook's fate:

> Dr. Cook's experience was tragic. He was an explorer of ability and courage. No one could have fought his way as far north as he did if he had not had ability and courage. If he deliberately faked the story of his discovery of the pole, he has paid a steep price for his folly; if he really believed he had reached his goal when he had not, he is to be greatly pitied; and if he actually did discover the pole, as he still claims, then a great injustice has been done him.[94]

Since it now seems certain that the first of these three possibilities is true (though those who wish it otherwise will deny it forever), we should ask ourselves just how tragic the fate of Dr. Cook really was.

In his classic essay, "The Essence of Tragedy," Maxwell Anderson tells us that to be a truly tragic figure, the hero of a successful tragic play must come to a moment of realization that in the end makes him a better man, no matter how complete his defeat. Did that "Consummate Actor," Frederick A. Cook, ever reach the "essence of tragedy"—that point of self-revelation that makes the play worth the candle? Did he ever realize his error? Did he ever really confess? "Dr. Cook's Confession" was no real confession at all, so let us examine another:

> Analyzing my own actions in retrospect, I don't believe I ever had any basic desire to be dishonest. One of the motivating factors in my actions was, of course, the desire to acquire money. The other motive was a lust for adventure—and this was the only kind of adventure for which I was equipped. . . .
>
> . . . Every swindle I ever developed had a hole in it somewhere, but I made everything plausible—to anyone who did not dig too deep or ask questions.
>
> Lies were the foundation of my schemes. A lie is an allurement, a fabrication, that can be embellished into a fantasy. It can be clothed in the raiment of a mystic conception.
>
> Truth is cold, sober fact, not so comfortable to absorb. A lie is more palatable. The most detested person in the world is the one who always tells the truth, who never romances.
>
> If a lie is told often enough even the teller comes to believe it. It becomes a habit. And habit is like a cable. Each day another strand is added until you have woven a cable that is unbreakable. . . .
>
> . . . Some small gesture that was out of character in the role I was portraying, or the wrong answer to a question might have betrayed me. Fortunately for me, I always had the right answer and carried off convincingly the role I played.
>
> To do this successfully—as I did for about half a century— I had to possess, first of all, a vast store of general information. Besides that, I had to know the rudiments of many professions. If

I played the role of a physician, I had to be in a position to use medical terms accurately. As a mining engineer, I had to know geology and mineralogy. As a broker or investment banker, I had to be up on the latest and most intricate financial matters. . . .

. . . People will tell you that crime does not pay. Perhaps that is right. But it paid me handsomely. I feel that I have lived a thousand years in seventy. Those periods of incarceration —well, they were not always what I would have chosen, but they gave me time to relax, reflect, and catch up on my reading. . . .

. . . I am now seventy years old and I look back over my career with mingled feelings. I have retired and I want to do what I can to promote harmony among my fellow men. For this reason, I de-cided to tell the inside story of my long and, I must admit, dishon-orable career.[95]

These are the words of Joseph Weil, Dr. Cook's secretary at Leavenworth's hospital. Joe Weil proclaimed himself "The World's Greatest Swindler" but said he believed in Dr. Cook absolutely. Yet how uncannily his words seem to fit the object of his belief! If Joe Weil was sincere in that belief, he must surren-der his crown.[96]

No, Dr. Cook never confessed. But there is some evidence that he realized, as he looked out over the great walls of Leavenworth that denied him the far horizon but could not limit the brilliance of his mind, when he turned his thoughts inward to that mind itself, he discovered the greatest and most impenetrable of all fields of mystery in need of exploration.

In confinement, some hidden truths he never grasped before emerged that dwarfed even those in his most grandiose dreams of the past:

We are but microscopic units in a universe of power so nicely organized that we are not necessary to the forces that guide nature. . . . In all probability, the demise of all humanity would greatly improve nature for future generation of other life. Man is a liability, not an asset to the universe as a whole.[97]

Perhaps man may be excused for the ego by which he gives himself great importance for out of his feeling comes that knowledge which enables a grasp of creation and pre-creation.[98]

He also realized finally that a dreamer who is mastered by the slavery of the lies he creates to preserve his dreams can never truly be a free man:

We need to have a clear conception of what REAL freedom is. . . . It is not a state of things by which every man does exactly what he likes. It is rather a state of mind in which men like to do what they can; what they may and what they should do.

> To enjoy REAL freedom, a man must have some knowledge of his natural powers, his civil privileges and his moral duties; and by knowing and accepting these he becomes free to realize his best self as a member of mankind.[99]

Among the things Dr. Cook clipped and saved at Leavenworth were several poems. One was Kipling's "If":

> If you can dream—and not make dreams your master;
>   If you can think—and not make thoughts your aim,
> If you can meet with Triumph and Disaster
>   And treat those two impostors just the same;
>   . . . .
>
> If you can make one heap of all your winnings;
>   And risk it on one turn of pitch-and-toss,
> And lose, and start again at your beginnings
>   And never breathe a word about your loss;
>   . . . .
>
> If you can talk with crowds and keep your virtue,
>   Or walk with Kings—nor lose the common touch,
> If neither foes nor loving friends can hurt you,
>   If all men count with you but none too much;
> If you can fill the unforgiving minute
>   With sixty seconds' worth of distance run,
> Yours is the Earth and everything that's in it,
>   And—which is more—You'll be a Man, my son.

Another was an anonymous poem called "The Man Who Has Won":

> I want to grasp the hand of the man who has been
>   through it all and seen,
> Who has walked with the night of an unseen dread and
>   stuck to the world-machine;
> Who has bared his breast to the winds of dawn and
>   thirsted and starved and felt
> The sting and the bite of the bitter blasts that the
>   mouths of the foul have dealt;
> Who was tempted and fell, and rose again, and has gone
>   on trusty and true,
> With God supreme in his manly heart and courage burning
>   anew. . . .

Finally there was this:

> I would like to be a could-be if I could not be an are
>   For a could-be is a may-be with a chance of reaching par.
> I would rather be a has-been than a might-have-been by far
>   For a might-have-been has never been but a has-been was an are.

Anthony Fiala, the man who got and failed miserably at the job of heading the second Ziegler Expedition that, had he been given it, might have written a different end to Frederick Cook's book of experience, observed prophetically: "Even after the final decision has been given by the scientists who are to examine the proofs presented by Dr. Cook there will probably be thousands of people all over the world who will not be convinced. There will be doubters that no scientific criticism or approval will sway. It will probably be the same way with Mr. Peary, although the general impression seems to be that he reached the pole.

"There may be two sides to this controversy forever, unless in the future world the two explorers occupy separate spheres, their discussion will probably be continued without interruption. As Dante's conception of the lowest circle is one of ice, it may be that the two will have it out there."[100]

"At all events," Captain Hall remarked in his book, "the whole truth as to both explorers will in time undoubtedly be known." One part of the truth about Dr. Frederick A. Cook is that he failed to reach the North Pole. But about the whole truth, Captain Hall was wrong.

Robert Dunn was closer to understanding the whole truth when he wrote:

> It is insincere to deny a man responsibility for his acts, dishonorable to pervert by gloss or omission the significance of any of his deeds, noble or ignoble. . . .
>
> The world dwells mostly on the sensational fact of winning pole or peak, oblivious to that the long human struggle, inspired by that master motive which mitigates endurance and suffering, are to the explorer his real end, consciously or not. . . .
>
> . . . I know that the whole truth is always beyond reach. Sometimes you think that there cannot be such a thing. . . . To tell the truth about other people is hardest of all. . . .
>
> . . . Failure is more than the average lot of any venture. It is typical, and through this dark glass human nature appears more colorful and more complex than in the raw light of achievement. So I think that failure, more than less, helps the significance of this record. . . . The fiascos could reveal more of the big perspective than the successes of exploration, and give it more honest touch and a brighter future with all men.[101]

The whole truth about Frederick A. Cook can never be told, though this book had hoped to tell it. At least the record of his life stands at last for us to ponder, asking us for an understanding of it and, through it, something of the imponderable in ourselves as well. And if we look deep enough into both, we will pause before we condemn it.

We must realize, with Dr. Cook, that it is only by looking into the hidden recesses of Self that understanding and forgiveness of others could ever be made possible—even for one who deceived millions so magnificently:

> In nine cases out of ten, the man hated is to us a man unknown. No one is quite as good or as bad as our unreliable sense of perception indicates. The best neutralizer of discord is understanding. If you really know a man thoroughly you cannot hate him.[102]

> Self [is] usually loyal to self, but sometimes fails itself. Self tries to deal fairly with self, but self-cheating is a common form of wrong doing. The laws of the universe of self are more numerous than the laws of State and harder to obey. There are no courts or juries or legal tribunals. The laws of self, when violated, bring automatic, autocratic punishment, with long suffering. . . .
>
> The greatest defect of self is its inability to understand that which it has not tried. Its defective perception in hearing the unheard, seeing the unseen or feeling the unfelt. It is mainly this which prevents self from becoming complete master of self.[103]

> Life begins in a mirage of illusions– it ends in long shadows of delusion– and yet in the unknown between the beginning and the end must appear all that living implies. We all enter an undiscovered world and promptly become explorers. Nothing is real– nothing has any existence whatsoever to any individual until it has passed through the feeling perception of thought.[104]

> I know of no better theme to test this feeling capacity of the brain than the delusion of polar conquest. Here in the blinding dazzle of day which endures months and in the dead gloom of long-continued dayless nights we deal with a condition which gives sanity and insanity a co-relation in the normal thought stream. . . .
>
> Our hindsight is better than our foresight and always will be, but the sum total of the power within us is delivered in response to the feeling connections which we maintain between the past and the future. From this there is no escape– We are good, bad or indifferent, as judged from every realm of endeavor in direct proportion to the degrees of usefulness which we give to the lessons of experience.

My trail to the North Pole has in it all the shadow of miscon-
ception above indicated. Every step and every misstep in this icy
path is but the responsive gesture of a brain that must feel its way
into a dark unknown.[105]

Our hardest death is the death that we live in fear of death. Life
is good and true to those who try with the sunshine of better days
ever before them. The world and stars and all the universe has to
offer is but the birth of thy own thoughts.[106]

If by this new understanding I am enabled to deliver a message to
others which will enable them to envision the unknown ever before, then in spite of my many mistakes some credit for original
discovery should go on my grave.[107]

The world has important use for dreamers, even if they fail.[108]

The voice of praise is stilled, the wreaths of roses have withered. I suppose the worst has been said of me.
—Frederick A. Cook

Cook Summit

IN 1986 COMMANDER CHRIS FURSE, R.N., OF THE FIFTH JOINT SERVICES Expedition, which spent 1984 on Brabant Island, submitted six names for features on the island to the Antarctic Placenames Committee.

Among them was one for the higher of the two hummocks that Frederick Cook, accompanied by either Henryk Arctowski or Roald Amundsen, attempted to reach during the *Belgica's* camping expedition there in 1898. The name proposed for this spot was Cook Summit. It was approved by the board and later that year was adopted by the United States Advisory Committee on Antarctic Names as the peak's official name.

There could be no more fitting memorial to Frederick Albert Cook. The highest point in the Solvay Mountains, Cook Summit towers 5,217 feet above the scene of the high point of his spectacular career, when his calm presence and restless imagination ensured the safe return of the Belgian Antarctic Expedition. But as with the North Pole and, probably, the crest of Mount McKinley, Dr. Cook never actually stood on Cook Summit; he reached only the lesser peak below it.

In the bright antarctic day it is "golden with the Beauty that is ever desired, the Ideal never attained," and through the long antarctic night it stands "softly silver with the melancholy and eternal hope of the deathless love that eternally desires, eternally pursues, and is eternally denied"—the silent symbol of a man who was the true romantic and of life spent in the mad quest of prodigious dreams that he hoped would fill the nothingness of his empty desires. A life that by choice and by chance, just missed the heroic.

An Impertinence

Nullam tam imprudens mendacium est ut teste careat.
There is no lie so reckless as to be without some proof.

—Pliny the Elder

IN HIS AUTOBIOGRAPHY, *LIVING AGAIN,* FELIX RIESENBERG RELATES THIS STORY:

> Rudolf Kersting . . . took me to meet the doctor at luncheon at the hotel Prince George in New York. . . . Two charming women, one of them a countess, graced the luncheon. Dr. Cook, then the prosperous oil promoter, looked benign; his face was pale but filled out like the skin of a well-fed seal. . . .
>
> The countess chided Dr. Cook on his riding through the crowded streets of Brooklyn decked with wreaths of flowers. The cocktails were strong; we felt uplifted and at peace, for the polar war had been almost forgotten. It occurred to me that I might gain first-hand information as to the facts. I said, "Doctor, I would like to ask you a question."
>
> "Certainly." He spoke after a moment and beamed upon me. All paused in their talk. A question, always an impertinence, arrests the minds of all of us; we have an instinctive dislike of the quiz. "What is your question?" Dr. Cook had a question of his own. Conversation stopped; glasses were poised; all looked at me and then at Dr. Cook.
>
> *"Did you get to the North Pole?"* I asked.
>
> A pause followed that seemed long. Dr. Cook looked at me, his eyes unblinking, his face serene with the calm of an unperturbed conscience. He placed his fingers flat on the edge of the table and said, "I'll answer your question in this way. My claims and records were presented to a committee of the Congress of the United States, and they found that I had reached the North Pole."[1]

Of course nothing of the kind ever happened. But if not to the North Pole, just how far north did Dr. Cook go in 1908?

Perhaps the answer to that impertinence lies on the first few pages of Dr. Cook's notebook 4. Those pages have a number of deletions and interlineations. In the transcript that follows, "x" indicates a deletion—a passage crossed out; "z" indicates an interlineation—a passage written into what appears to have been originally written or added above the line; ("?") indicates that this is the author's interpretation of a marginally legible word or phrase. To read what was originally written, read the "x's" and omit the "z's"; to read the revision, do the opposite. Those items noted as written in ink are apparently from an earlier date, as all the other entries, which are in pencil, are written around them.

With the exception of some reminders and titles added at the tops of the pages at a later date, here are these pages reproduced in full:

[p. 1] Mch 20   1908   We are at last over the crushed ice of the pack edge - These 3 days have been difficult [x beyond any] [z of the (written above "any")] ice conditions [x which I have before experienced]. Great paleocrystic floes interrupted by wide areas of young ice and miles of huge boulders and small ice the result of the grinding pack against the land. [x I hope however] we are [x beyond this miserable (tearing?) surface] Beyond [z however] are beautiful smooth floes with little snow and few hummocks. In spite of these [x hopeless] [z difficult] ice conditions we have made good progress. Fortunate in having many dogs experienced helpers and strong sledges we have dragged our equipment [x over] [z along] about 50 miles. We are therefore by dead reconing at about 82.10 Lt Long 95 W. The supporting party - Koolootingwah & Inguito left us here to-night and with light sledges they aim to make the land in 36 hours. [x with] no dog food [z was given them] for we want all we can possibly carry. The returning party helped to construct the snow house waited for a cold piece of M[usk]O[x] and with a bit of butter and frozen meat for them in case (of an?) emergency left us with the land behind the cld.

[p. 2]which hung over the loom of Heiberg Is. Their dogs rushed as if they knew there (would?) be no food until land was reached.

As we awoke on the following morning and peeped out of our eye port, we saw the sun edging along the N.E. throwing an orange glow ["an orange" written over two other words] over ice that gladdened our hearts. The temp was [z -63] - the (Bar. ?) - not a cloud [x on the] to mark the dome of pale blue.

After 3 cups of tea each 3 biscuits and about 2½ lbs of MO meat par-boiled we crept out of our bags pushed our legs into the bearskin cylinders which answer as trousers - worked our feet into frozen boots climbed into the fur coats and then with a big knife a door was cut so we could walk out and quickly toss our household furniture on the sledges.

As we gathered in the traces of the dogs and set our course we said to one another (ume-noona-ter-ronga-disangas-guil?) - land out of sight to-day. We therefore left the northernmost land - the fringe of the little known and plunged into the mysteries of the unknown polar basin. Heiberg land was already only a

[p. 3]a dull purple blue haze and Grant land was making fantastic figures of its peaks and ice walls - a curious mirage made some of the peaks seem like active volcanoes others had huge spires piercing the skies and altogether this unexplored upper surface of Grant land gave us considerable entertainment. at every breathing spell the heads were turned to the [x last sight of land] ["Etah 80." written here in ink] [z land as if we were leaving home and friends there]In the afternoon a purple haze screened the land [x and we never again saw Grant Land] [z but we saw it repeatedly for brief spells for several days following]

We made a long march this [z (with it)] day dogs well fed sledges though heavily loaded about 600 lbs [x "600" written over 550] each went easy and the Boys were enthusiastic. Everything was in our favor. The few cracks in the ice which we crossed gave very little trouble. Continued marching for 12 (over 10?) hours made about 32 miles. I hope such luck will fall to our lot often.

We were too tired to begin the construction of the s[now]-h[ouse]. at once. For a brief spell we threw ourselves down on the sledges ["Food. 14" written in ink] and fell asleep. When I awoke in about a half hour a strong wind (came?) from the west and a black sooty vapor

[p. 4] ["Names. Glouscester 12" written in ink] was hurrying towards us. We were on an old floe with many big hummocks and we quickly sought a bank of hard snow in the lee of one and erected our snow dome. That night it blew fiercely but before (dawn?) it cleared and an easy wind followed which cut like a knife many new cracks formed near us but we found a way around all easily. Beginning our march ["Literary sug. 160" written in ink] at noon we moved along at a good pace until about 6 pm [z (22) above line] when we saw before us much troubled ice several floes, many hummocks much crushed ice and all signs of a vigorous pack (movement?) Soon after a broad [x black] [z yellow] band of young ice with steam like vapor rising above it. This proved to be the big lead which runs parallel to the general coast of northermost land extensions

For a time this [x a time] this huge separation in the pack was a mystery to me. At first sight there seems to be no good reason for its existence but [p. 5] ["Returns 168" written in pencil] it is precisely what one finds ["Rx 6" in pencil] on a smaller scale whenever two packs come together such as a land pack and a central pack. The movement of the land pack is intermittent and usually along the (west?) the movement of the central pack is usually constant in almost every direction with the tide currents and winds. This lead is [x serves] the breaking line between the two bodies of ice. It widens as the pack separates narrows as the central ["Schooner. 10" written in ink] pack presses landward but in low temperatures new ice forms rapidly [z is narrower early in the season wide later] and this offers an obstruction to old ice as it comes together. The grinding of this young ice, the fractured corners of the old floes and the new ice constantly forming make a line of troublesome irregular ice to both sides of the lead. Here and there a few floes have been pushed through this broken debris and to find a place where these make a safe crossing is now our

Here there are two intervening pages, which contain other material; on page 6 is the "Rx 6" referred to above, which reads:

The journey on the sledges in detail [this is written up the left margin and underlined]. Rx. View pt. Key, Color. Style Intro Effect. Outline, Perfect, Retrospect is it to be descriptive or narrative. Divide into measured stages. The Daily Routine. The Special Observations. The Regular Tabulations. Maintain Viewpoint. Sum up Gen. view & Impressions. The most imp[ortant] result of day.

Page 7 contains an entry for May 25 and 26, 1907, then the narrative continues:

[p. 8]mission. Etuk went E and I went West to seek a crossing. We found several places where we might cross after the young ice strengthened.

A small "22" is written here in margin, perhaps indicating the date March 22.

So we camped. We selected a strong old floe with several large hummocks. We had two important reasons for this the first was that only in the lee of big hummocks did we find snow of the proper hardness to cut blocks for our igloos and the second reason was our aim to camp on ice that would not easily break. This night (Mch 24)? was a beautiful one. The sun settled into a purple haze and soon we saw 3 suns - and as they all sank they left a bright zone extending from NW to NE from which there came a strange glow which light up the pack magnificentlynow it was violet then (laven?) then purple again pale blue. The lead looked like a huge river with banks of marble and the young ice at times was dark at other times very light now green again yellow and again dark blue.

[p. 9]["Wednesday 28" crossed out in pencil] The dogs were restless they howled all night and sniffed the air pointing their noses to the land as if they scented game. The temp was -40—somewhat warmer—but it increased [*sic*] in the morning to -55 with a wind the direction of which was scarcely perceptible by its force but it was piercing.

At about noon [z 23] we found a place which we believed would offer us a safe crossing and we quickly broke camp and started. The sledges went hard on the young ice and in places the surface (waved?). If I had not crossed such ice many times before I should have hesitated long before attempting but by keeping the sledges widely separated and a line always ready to throw to any one breaking through the thing was safe enough. We had our greatest difficulty with the ice of the op. shores. It was a jumble of broken ice through which we were compelled to cut a trail in many places. It was midnight before we camped and

The intervening page 10 has old notes in ink about the yacht *Bradley* and its cost.

[p. 11]I hardly think we made 10 miles. Before us is the [z purple] [x blue] glow of midnight the ice northward looked smooth.[2]

All the foregoing material is written on the lines of the notebook and is rather large but smaller in scale than the notes in the "hunting diary" kept by Dr. Cook during the winter of 1907–08 while he was in the field—something one would expect of writing done with gloved hands. But at this point the writing gets suddenly half this size, with two lines written between each rule on the paper, and it shifts to the past tense exclusively. Instead of running observations, it gives summaries of past events. Later in the notebook, three written lines are crammed between the printed rules.

It is instructive to compare the passage quoted from Cook's diary with the narrative of the same time period in *My Attainment of the Pole,* between pages 200 and 225. The book has many things in common with these eight diary pages and illustrates how Cook filled out his story from his notes. Several differences should be noted, however. The diary seems to indicate the passage of five days since leaving land, and if the mileages are added up, the expedition was at that time 92 miles offshore, at approximately 82°52' north latitude. This is much farther than later accounts, attributed to the Eskimos by the Peary interests, credited his entire journey north, but shorter than that recorded in his published narrative for the first five days. Once again dates and distances do not match the final narrative. In *My Attainment of the Pole,* for the first three days, Dr. Cook records a progress north of 63 miles, not 50; he crosses the "Big Lead" on March 23, the sixth day out, not the fifth, and by the end of that day he is 102 miles from land, not 92.

Interestingly, this is the exact distance that Captain Hall in *Has the North Pole Been Discovered?* decided that Dr. Cook had gone at a minimum:

> Even though he went no farther north from Heiberg Land than 92 miles, it is a greater distance than any explorer in arctic history had succeeded in reaching, excepting Nansen, Cagni and possibly Peary. It lacks only 37 miles of equalling the northing made by Nansen after he left his ship. Therefore, if we admit for this purpose, that Cook did not go to the Pole, can it be the history of polar exploration, to omit his acknowledged exploits?[3]

This passage raises the question of how Hall decided on this figure. It corresponds to Cook's mileage total for the first four days of his journey as recorded in his narrative—the same mileage recorded for the first five days in his diary—but since nothing in Cook's book even hints this to have been his stopping point, why choose it as the extent of Cook's journey? Could Captain Hall have seen Cook's notebooks?

In the notes Baldwin prepared for his abortive "On the Trail of the Pole Seekers," he counts pictures of five different igloos in *My Attainment of the Pole,* indicating at least five days of travel on the ice, and points out that these were photographed soon after the return of the sun, when snow was still lying on the pack. He also notices that the igloos were freshly built when the photographs were taken because there is no drift at their bases.

Baldwin, working from Cook's notebooks, also noted that the periods in which Cook reported disturbances in the pack correspond well with the phases of the moon for 1908. This is particularly interesting because Peary, in his extensive notes on *My Attainment of the Pole,* states as evidence against Cook the lack of any mention of the moon's effect on ice conditions.

Finally, actual physical conditions now known to exist in the areas through which Cook said he passed support the authenticity of Cook's diary to this point. Cook's route crosses what is known today as a "current null area"—an area that is disturbed by little or no current during the early spring months—which would account for his long mileages once he cleared the ice thrown up against the coast of Axel Heiberg Land. Likewise, his descriptions of "grounded icebergs" appear accurate since bergs congregate in the null current area.

His description of the location of the "Big Lead," which he thought separated the central pack from the land-adhering ice, corresponds almost exactly with a southwesterly shear zone caused by the westerly movement of the Beaufort Gyre against the shorefast ice along Axel Heiberg Island and the Ringnes Islands. This zone occurs about 95 miles offshore along Cook's route—matching well with the conjectural point where he turned back. This also accounts for the pictures that show his party passing nothing but level fields of ice, and also the two that show a camp at the edge of a zone of chaotic hummocks and pressure ridges.

All of these physical descriptions support every feature of these eight pages of Cook's diary. And unlike Cook's descriptions of Bradley Land, the Glacial Island and conditions at the North Pole, such details merit the argument that he must have reached this point to have described these unknown features, since he had no precedent to give him guidance other than Peary's general speculations in *Nearest the Pole*. This also would account for his discovery of the unknown westerly current that he later blamed for his inability to return along the route of his outbound caches.

Further evidence that Cook traveled at least as far as notebook 4 indicates comes from the results of a secret study reported in *Politiken* on January 28, 1911. Conducted by a Mr. Lacour of the Danish Meteorological Service working under the Carlsberg Fund, this study of the weather along the fringe of the arctic basin during the time of Cook's reported journey corroborates descriptions of the meteorological conditions up to the 84th parallel. This would be nearly the exact period Cook would have been on the polar pack in a trip to approximately 82°50' North and back to land again. This same Danish study indicated that no such data reported by Peary seemed to match actual weather conditions in 1909.

Finally, there is the independent and completely confirming evidence of a pro-Peary witness, one who always maintained that Cook's journey amounted to no more than an advance of 15 miles across the polar pack. This witness was Donald B. MacMillan, who made this summary of his sledge journey in search of "Crocker Land" in 1914:

> Our eight days' travel out from Cape Thomas Hubbard was over ice which had not been subjected to great pressure. . . . At our farthest north, 82°, all was suddenly changed. The long, level fields ended in a sharp line going east and west; beyond this line there was the roughest kind of ice.[4]

All this evidence seems to support the conclusion previously advanced: that Frederick Cook did indeed make an honest attempt to reach the North Pole in 1908 but was turned back by the impossibility of the task.

IN MOST RESPECTS *COOK & PEARY* HAS BEEN THE SOLE CREATION OF ITS author. He did all research and transcriptions from handwritten sources, and the suppositions it contains are entirely his own. Therefore he is responsible for whatever errors the book may contain—whether of fact, lack of care or logic. Such errors, however, are inadvertent, stemming from the magnitude of the task, or from trust placed in erroneous sources of information, and are not the result of any wish to distort or bend the facts to any preconceived aim. The book's conclusions evolved only as research revealed their inevitability.

Though any errors are the author's, this project could not have been completed without the aid of many other persons. They include the staffs of all the repositories of manuscript material visited during the research for the book. Among them I would particularly like to thank Mary Allison Farley, of the Frederick A. Cook Society, who helped me more than she realized; Philip N. Cronenwett of Dartmouth College, whose professionalism is above reproach; Dianne Gutscher of Bowdoin College, who not only provided research material but also effected my escape from Brunswick as Hurricane Bob approached; Marjorie Ciarlante, of the National Archives, who very efficiently managed my requests for the hundreds of boxes of Peary material I consulted; Karen Stuart of the Library of Congress, who provided me with the transfer files of Dr. Cook's papers while she was still in the process of preparing them; and Margaret Schmidt-Hacker, of the National Archives, Southwest Branch, who not only guided me through the legal records of the Cook trial, but also suggested further lines of pursuit in Washington and helped me navigate around Fort Worth.

Among others, I would like to acknowledge Bonita Favin of the Montgomery College interlibrary loan department, who executed hundreds of interlibrary loans on my behalf, and the hundreds of anonymous librarians and library assistants who filled them; Debbie Brodey, who dispatched hundreds of reels of microfilm for examination on the microfilm reader generously lent to me by Randy and Patty Troth. Also deserving acknowledgment are my translators, Bette Hurst, Jack Suruda, Marion Smith, Terry Tamer and Dr. Thomas Walker, my photographic technician, Rob Williams, and Paul Leech, who kept the computer running.

Dr. David Zipoy of the University of Maryland Astronomy Department helped with things astronomical; Norman Peddie of the U.S. Geological Survey explained the mysteries of geomagnetism; Keith Pickering supplemented both and reviewed the technical points of each. Dr. Jozef Verlinden reviewed the chapters on the Belgian Antarctic Expedition and provided much useful material.

Then there was my reader, Karen Catlett, inscrutable as Dr. Cook, who listened endlessly to my theories, read every word without complaint and had all the hoped-for reactions, all for the price of an occasional potato, then vanished without a word.

A great amount of credit must also go to my editors, Sally Atwater and Val Gittings, whose suggestions improved the book but left it the one I had written.

And, of course, *Cook & Peary* would not have been possible in its present form without the cooperation of the many individuals and organizations who gave me access to the materials in their possession or who allowed me to quote from those they controlled, especially Silas H. Ayer III, who was most generous with his time and in allowing me the use of some of his unpublished photographs from the *Erik* voyage.

Finally, I wish to extend my thanks to the many stout supporters of Dr. Cook, chiefly Sheldon Cook-Dorough, who spent many hours writing me his thoughts and supplying me with positive evidence on the doctor's behalf; the ever-kind Warren B. Cook, Sr., President of the Frederick A. Cook Society and grandnephew of the explorer; and Bette Hutchinson, Dr. Cook's admirable stepgranddaughter, for her personal recollections of her Grampa and for many other kindnesses. It is these last, and others who believe in Dr. Cook absolutely, who might be most disappointed by my book. I hope, nonetheless, that they may find some merit in it they did not expect.

ANYONE WHO WISHES TO CORRESPOND WITH THE AUTHOR, ESPECIALLY AS TO factual errors, is welcome to do so and will receive a response if a self-addressed stamped envelope is included. The author declines, however, to debate points and theories based on hearsay evidence, or his own clearly labeled opinions and speculations, unless the correspondent has documentary evidence to the contrary.

Address correspondence to Robert M. Bryce c/o Stackpole Books, 5067 Ritter Rd., Mechanicsburg, PA 17055.

This list contains all of the published writings of Dr. Cook that are known to the author. It does not include literal reprints of his books in England that do not have additional material written by him, but does list foreign language versions that may contain different or additional material.

1893

"The Most Northern Tribe on Earth," *New York Medical Examiner,* vol. 3 no. 2: 23–24.

1894

"The Antarctic's Challenge to the Explorer," *The Forum,* v. 17 (June), pp. 505–512.

"The Arctic Regions as a Summer Resort," *Home and Country,* October, pp. 257–264.

"Gynecology and Obstetrics among the Eskimos," *Brooklyn Medical Journal,* vol. 8: 154–169.

"How Polar Expeditions Are Equipped," *Harper's Young People,* June 19, pp. 565–568.

"Medical Observations among the Esquimaux," *New York Journal of Gynæcology and Obstetrics,* v. 4: 282–286.

"Peculiar Customs Regarding Disease, Death, and Grief of the Most Northern Eskimo," *To-Day,* June, pp. 225–229.

Plans for Dr. Cook's Antarctic Expedition and Story of the Eskimos and Dogs. Undated Pamphlet.

"A Proposed Antarctic Expedition," *Around the World,* vol. 1: 55–58.

1895

"The South Pole and Its Problems," *Boston Commonwealth,* March 16, pp. unknown.

1896

"The Greenlanders." *In:* Walsh, Henry Collins, *The Last Cruise of the Miranda.* New York: Transatlantic Publishing Co., pp. 172–177.

1897

"Some Physical Effects of Arctic Cold, Darkness and Light," *Medical Record of New York,* vol. 51, (June 12): 833–836.

1899

Dr. Cook's first account of the Belgian Antarctic Expedition was published in a copyrighted story in the *New York Herald* on July 2.

"La 'Belgica' dans les glaces antarctiques," *Crédit public,* Brussels, no. 135.

"The Frozen South," *Harper's Weekly,* July 22, pp. 714–717.

"Life in the Antarctic Ice on the Belgica," *Review of Reviews,* November, pp. 606–607.

"The Possibilities of Antarctic Exploration," *Scribner's Magazine,* December, pp. 705–712.

"Through the First Antarctic Night," *Buenos Aires Christian Advocate and the Epworth Herald,* vol. 6 no. 5, pp. unknown.

"Two Thousand Miles in the Antarctic Ice," *McClure's Magazine,* November, pp. 3–18.

"Le voyage de la Belgica à 3300 kilomètres dans les glaces antarctiques," *Le Petit Bleu,* November 16–22. Half a page of small print every day.

1900

"The Belgian Expedition: Two Thousand Miles in the Antarctic Ice," *Windsor Magazine (London),* May, vol. XI, p. 719; vol. XII, p. 468.

"The Giant Indians of Tierra del Fuego," *Century Magazine,* March, pp. 720–729.

"The New Antarctic Discoveries," *Century Magazine,* January, pp. 408–427.

"A New Tent for the Snow Line," *Outing Magazine,* December, pp. 333–335.

"The Possibilities of Human Life within the Antarctic," *Independent,* May 24, pp. 1245–1248.

Through the First Antarctic Night. New York: Doubleday, McClure & Co.

"A Walk to the North and South Poles," *Canadian Magazine,* September, pp. 418–425.

1901

"The Aurora Australis, as Observed from the Belgica," *Popular Science,* May, pp. 21–33.

"Captain Fabian Gottlieb von Bellingshausen, 1819–1821. The Discovery of Alexander I., Peter I., and Other Islands," *Bulletin of the American Geographical Society,* vol. 33: 36–41.

"With Fuegians on a Guanaco Hunt," *Outing Magazine,* February, pp. 576–580.

1902
"The Daily Work of an Arctic Explorer." *In:* The White World, ed. by Rudolf Kersting. New York: Lewis, Scribner & Co., pp. 135–144.

"Die erste Ueberwinterung in der Antarktis," Supplement to *Allgemeinen Zeitung (Munich),* no. 40.

"The People of the Farthest North," *Everybody's Magazine,* January, pages 19–32.

Vers le Pôle Sud. L'expedition de la "Belgica" 1897–1899, Adaptation française par A.-L. Pfindler. Brussels: Falk fils, 320 pages. Reprinted as *Vers le Pôle Sud. Premier récit avant la découverte du Pôle Nord.* Brussels: Falk fils, 1910, 320 pages. French language version of *Through the First Antarctic Night.*

1903
Die erste Südpolarnacht 1898–1899. Bericht über die Entdeckungsreise der "Belgica" in der Südpolarregion. Kempten: J. Kösel, 415 pages. German language version of *Through the First Antarctic Night.*

1904
"America's Unconquered Mountain," *Harper's Monthly Magazine,* January–February, pp. 230–239; 335–344.

"A Comparative View of the Arctic and the Antarctic": Abstract. *National Geographic Magazine,* vol. 15: 460–461. See 1905 for full paper.

"Factors in the Destruction of Primitive Man," *Brooklyn Medical Journal,* vol. 18: 333–335.

"Round Mount McKinley," *Bulletin of the American Geographical Society,* vol. 36: 321–327.

1905
"A Comparative View of the Arctic and the Antarctic." *In: Report of the Eighth International Geographic Conference, Held in the United States, 1904.* Washington, D.C.: GPO, pp. 705–709.

"Results of a Journey around Mt. M'Kinley." *In: Report of the Eighth International Geographic Conference, Held in the United States, 1904.* Washington, D.C.: GPO, pp. 768–762.

"The Voyage of the Belgica": Abstract. *In: Report of the Eighth International Geographic Conference, Held in the United States, 1904.* Washington, D.C.: GPO, p. 710.

1907
"The Conquest of Mount McKinley," *Harper's Monthly Magazine,* May, pp. 822–837.

"Why Not Conquer the South Pole?" *Harper's Weekly,* May, pp. 674–676.

1908

To the Top of the Continent. New York: Doubleday, Page & Co.

1909

Dr. Cook's 2,000-word dispatch from Lerwick, which originally appeared in the *New York Herald* of September 2, was reprinted in several places, including "The North Pole at Last," *Outlook,* September 11, pp. 61–64; "The Discovery of the North Pole: First Report by Dr. Frederick A. Cook, Sept. 1, 1909," *National Geographic Magazine,* vol. 20: 892–916. The same text can be found in *World's Work,* October, pp. 12104–12107, and *Harper's Weekly,* September 11, p. 7.

"The Conquest of the North Pole," *New York Herald* and other papers controlled by the *Herald.* Serial narrative in twelve installments, every other day from September 15 to October 7.

"How I Reached the North Pole," Victor record #31755, two sides, approximately five minutes. Camden, New Jersey: Victor Talking Machine Company, recorded in October.

Through the First Antarctic Night and *To the Top of the Continent* reprinted by Doubleday, Page & Co.

"Two Midnights in the Arctic. An Account of Certain Events and Experiences in the Quest of the Pole," *Circle,* December, pp. 303–304.

1911

"Dr. Cook's Own Story," *Hampton's Magazine,* January–April, pp. 51–66; 162–177; 295–308; 493–502.

My Attainment of the Pole. New York: Polar Publishing Co. 604 pages.

1912

Meine Eroberung des Nordpols, übersetzen von Erwin Volckmann. Hamburg: A. Janssen. German language version of *My Attainment of the Pole.*

"Mount McKinley," introduction to Ralph Cairns's article entitled "Hazards of Climbing Mount McKinley," *Overland Monthly,* February, p. 106.

My Attainment of the Pole, 2nd Edition. New York: Mitchell Kennerley. 604 pages. Slight revisions to 1911 edition.

1913

My Attainment of the Pole, 3rd Edition. New York: Mitchell Kennerley. 610 pages. Slight revisions to 1912 edition plus new material added at end.

c. 1918

What About the Future? Rocky Mountain Sheep Association, Bulletin A, undated, 4 pages.

1925

"Dr. Cook, 'The Prince of Liars,' Writes from His Prison Cell," *American Weekly,* in four parts: July 19, July 26, August 2, August 9.

1926–1930

Numerous essays, editorials and descriptive pieces for *The Leavenworth New Era;* later issues entitled *The New Era,* most unsigned.

1928

Zum Mittelpunkt der Arktis; Reiseberichte ohne die Pol-kontroverse. Braunschweig: Georg Westermann. German translation of *My Attainment of the Pole,* omitting all material in reference to the Polar Controversy.

1930

"Clouds," *Photo Era,* April 30, p. 215.

1931

Various articles for *The Apartment Owner* under the nom de plume J.D. Addison.

1938

"My Experiences with a Camera in the Antarctic," *Popular Photography,* February, pp. 12 and following. This item was written in collaboration with Ted Leitzell.

1951

Return from the Pole. New York: Pelligrini & Cudahy.

1953

Wo Norden Süden ist. Hamburg: Hoffman und Campe Verlag, 1953. German language version of *Return from the Pole.*

1980

Through the First Antarctic Night. London: C. Hurst & Co. Facsimile reprint of the 1900 edition with an additional introduction by Gaston de Gerlache.

1996

To the Top of the Continent. Edited by Russell W. Gibbons. Mukileto, Washington: AlpenBooks. Reprint of Cook's 1908 edition with the exception of the material in the original appendixes and some of the illustrations. It also contains a full transcription of the text of Cook's 1906 Mount McKinley diary, edited by Sheldon Cook-Dorough, but does not reproduce all of the drawings it contains. A partial text of Edward Barrill's diary is also reproduced from the facsimiles that appeared in the *New York Globe* on October 15, 1909. Both of these diary transcriptions contain transcription errors. Two new appendixes consisting of explanatory or argumentative material and an article by Russell W. Porter are added.

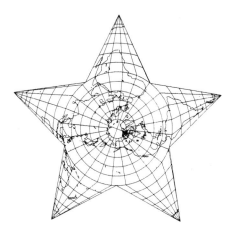

Sources

Much of the information in this book is from unpublished sources. They repose in several major manuscript collections in the National Archives II, College Park, Maryland, the Library of Congress in Washington, D.C., and other, smaller collections around the country. To avoid needless repetition the following abbreviations have been adopted:

BBD   The papers of Belmore Browne, Dartmouth College, Hanover, New Hampshire

BCV   The Balch Family Papers (#4634), Special Collections Department, University of Virginia, Charlottesville, Virginia

BLC   The papers of Evelyn Briggs Baldwin, Library of Congress

CFD	The papers of Charles W. Furlong, Dartmouth College, Hanover, New Hampshire
CSC	The collection of the Frederick A. Cook Society, Hurleyville, New York (In 1996 the bulk of this collection was transferred to the Byrd Polar Research Center Archives at Ohio State University, Columbus, Ohio)
DMB	The papers of Donald B. MacMillan, Bowdoin College, Brunswick, Maine
FCC	The Frederick Cook Collection, Library of Congress
FCD	The papers of Frederick A. Cook, Dartmouth College, Hanover, New Hampshire
HWA	The papers of C. Henshaw Ward, National Archives
LGB	The papers of Langdon Gibson, Bowdoin College, Brunswick, Maine
PFC	The Peary Family Collection, National Archives
RBB	The papers of Robert A. Bartlett, Bowdoin College, Brunswick, Maine
RDD	The papers of Robert S. Dunn, Dartmouth College, Hanover, New Hampshire
RPA	The papers of Russell W. Porter, National Archives
SBA	National Archives, Southwest Branch, Fort Worth, Texas
SCD	The Vilhjalmur Stefansson Collection, Dartmouth College, Hanover, New Hampshire
THA	The papers of Thomas H. Hubbard, National Archives

All manuscript material from Bowdoin College is reprinted courtesy of Special Collections, the Bowdoin College Library.

Transcriptions

These materials are often handwritten and, of course, unedited for publication. Dr. Cook's writings are especially problematic since his handwriting has many odd features and requires some practice before it can be interpreted properly. Despite the author's best efforts, a few words defied being deciphered; these have been noted as "illegible." If the identity of a word was questionable, it has been enclosed in parentheses followed by a question mark (?) to indicate that this is the author's interpretation of what appeared on the page. In all other cases the author believes that he has transcribed the words correctly.

Though in no case have any words been added or changed intentionally, punctuation is a different matter. In Cook's writings, especially his diaries, he often failed to use any punctuation. Sometimes he capitalized or lowercased words irrelevantly. Complicating matters further, those items written in ink have a dot at every point where he rested his pen between words. These are indistinguishable from periods. Therefore, the punctuation has been edited slightly whenever the passage, as written, might cause misunderstanding or make the thought unintelligible. This has been done very sparingly, however. In all cases, quoted passages have been identified so that the reader may locate the originals. In general, the reader should assume that any errors of spelling or grammar within quotes are faithful transcriptions of the originals.

Personal Names
Persons referred to frequently are represented by their initials as follows:

AF	Andrew Freeman, first biographer of Dr. Cook
BB	Belmore Browne, member of Cook's 1906 Mount McKinley Expedition
CJN	Charles J. Nichols, Peary's attorney
DBM	Donald B. MacMillan, member of Peary's 1908 North Pole Expedition
EA	Eivind Astrup, member of the first two Peary expeditions to North Greenland
EBB	Evelyn Briggs Baldwin, meteorologist of Peary's Second Greenland Expedition
FAC	Frederick Albert Cook
HA	Henryk Arctowski, geologist of the Belgian Antarctic Expedition
HCV	Helene Cook Vetter, the explorer's natural daughter by his second marriage
HLB	Herbert L. Bridgman, business manager of the Brooklyn *Standard Union* and secretary of the Peary Arctic Club
JDP	Josephine D. Peary, the explorer's wife
JMV	John M. Verhoeff, meteorologist of Peary's North Greenland Expedition
LA	Lucien Alexander, Peary's personal lobbyist
LG	Langdon Gibson, hunter of Peary's North Greenland Expedition
LK	Lilian Kiel, stenographer
MKJ	Morris K. Jesup, philanthropist and first president of the Peary Arctic Club
MWP	Mary Wiley Peary, the explorer's mother
RA	Roald Amundsen, mate of the *Belgica*; discoverer of the South Pole
RD	Robert S. Dunn, member of Cook's 1903 Mount McKinley Expedition
REP	Robert Edwin Peary
RWP	Russell W. Porter, topographer of Cook's 1906 Mount McKinley Expedition
TSD	Thomas S. Dedrick, surgeon of Peary's 1898–1902 expedition

| THH | General Thomas H. Hubbard, owner of the *New York Globe* and president of the Peary Arctic Club from 1908 to 1915 |
| VS | Vilhjalmur Stefansson, arctic explorer |

Newspapers

Newspapers are abbreviated as follows:

BDE	*Brooklyn Daily Eagle*
BSU	Brooklyn *Standard Union*
FWP	*Fort Worth Press*
FWST	*Fort Worth Star-Telegram*
NYA	*New York American*
NYG	*New York Globe*
NYH	*New York Herald*
NYS	New York *Sun*
NYT	*New York Times*
NYW	New York *World*

All others newspaper titles are written out.

Frequently Cited Books

Several books are quoted occasionally throughout the text. They are abbreviated as follows:

CDC	Freeman, Andrew A., *The Case for Doctor Cook*. New York: Coward-McCann, 1961.
CMM	Browne, Belmore, *The Conquest of Mount McKinley*. New York: G.P. Putnam & Sons, 1913.
HNPBD	Hall, Thomas F., *Has the North Pole Been Discovered?* Boston: R.G. Badger, 1917.
MAP	Cook, Frederick A., *My Attainment of the Pole*. New York: Mitchell Kennerley, 1913. It is this edition of MAP that is being cited unless specifically stated otherwise.
MLE	Amundsen, Roald, *My Life as an Explorer*. Garden City, N.Y.: Doubleday, Doran & Co., 1928.
NTP	Peary, Robert E., *Nearest the Pole*. New York: Doubleday, Page & Co., 1907.
PEM	Weems, John Edward, *Peary, the Explorer and the Man*. Los Angeles: Jeremy P. Tarcher, 1988.
SDE	Dunn, Robert, *The Shameless Diary of an Explorer*. New York: Outing Publishing Co., 1907.
TFAN	Cook, Frederick A., *Through the First Antarctic Night*. New York: Doubleday, McClure & Co., 1900.

TSP   Amundsen, Roald, *The South Pole.* London: John Murray & Co., 1912.

TTC   Cook, Frederick A., *To the Top of the Continent.* New York: Doubleday, Page & Co., 1908.

UPE   Bridges, E. Lucas, *The Uttermost Part of the Earth.* New York: E.P. Dutton & Co., 1949.

WPNP   Astrup, Eivind, *With Peary Near the Pole.* Philadelphia: J.B. Lippincott Co., 1898.

Place Names

The names of many of the places mentioned in this book are variously spelled in the original narratives because of uncertainty as to how to transliterate native names. To avoid confusion, the names have been standardized to the spellings used in these authorities:

For Greenland: Laursen, Dan, *The Place Names of North Greenland.* København: C.A. Reitzels Forlag, 1972. There is one exception to this rule. Instead of Laursen's "Anoratoq," "Annoatok," the spelling favored by Dr. Cook, is used.

For Alaska: Orth, Donald J., *Dictionary of Alaska Place Names.* Geological Survey Professional Paper 567. Washington, D.C.: GPO, 1967.

Money

Throughout the text sums of money are mentioned. The amounts quoted are expressed in the actual amounts exchanged at the time. This can be deceiving unless the reader keeps in mind the huge devaluation of the dollar since the turn of the century. To get a clear idea of what the amounts would be equivalent to in terms of the buying power of a 1996 dollar, apply the following formulas:

For 1890–1900 multiply by 16.85; for example, $100 = $1,685.
For 1901–1910 multiply by 16.16; for example, $100 = $1,616.
For 1911–1915 multiply by 14.77; for example, $100 = $1,477.
For 1916–1918 multiply by 11.23; for example, $100 = $1,123.
For 1920–1925 multiply by 8.19; for example, $100 = $819.
For 1926–1929 multiply by 10.47; for example, $100 = $1,047.

At the time of the Belgian Antarctic Expedition and its aftermath, 1897–1901, the Belgian franc was worth 20 cents, or five to the dollar.

Mileages and Temperatures

All mileages for travel across the sea, including over the ice of the Arctic Ocean, are in nautical miles. Nautical miles are 15 percent longer than statute miles, the miles generally used for distances over land. One nautical mile equals a minute of latitude, and 60 nautical miles equal a degree of latitude. All temperatures are in degrees Fahrenheit.

Notes for Preface
1. NYT, December 1, 1910.
2. Winchester, J.W., "Dr. Cook, Faker," *Pacific Monthly*, March 1911, page 256.
3. NYT, September 11, 1909.
4. MAP, pages 286–287.
5. FAC, "Dr. Cook's Own Story," *Hampton's Magazine*, February 1911, page 162.
6. NYH, September 11, 1909.

Notes for Chapter 1: The Sunrise of Ambition
1. FAC, "The Prince of Liars," *American Weekly*, July 19, 1925.
2. HCP. This passage comes from one of several items labeled "Preface." This particular one bears the title "Back to Inscription," page 2. FCC.

A note about Dr. Cook's "memoirs"

While in Leavenworth, Cook worked on a number of ideas for books, including "Twilight of the Unknown," "Wild Men and Wild Women," "Opianna," "Coming of the Pygmy Age," "Peeps into the Beyond," "Memoirs of Polar Adventure" and "Amundsen, the Indomitable Pathfinder," which exist only in fragmentary or unfinished form. Two, however, exist in good drafts: "At the End of North" and "Out of the Jungle." Cook also worked on a set of memoirs called "Hell Is a Cold Place." These memoirs exist in a draft typescript with some parts in several versions and with some emendations and variations among the versions. There is also a handwritten manuscript for these memoirs, which is more extensive and in many places different from the typescript as to details. Quotations have been taken from all of these materials as seemed appropriate to the narrative, and they are distinguished in these notes as HCP (Hell Is a Cold Place) for the typescript and NFM (notes for memoirs) for the pencil manuscript. The paging is sometimes confusing, there being many deletions and additions, including cut-and-paste sections from other sources. The pencil holograph is often unpaged and there are disconnected unpaged notes. For NFM, the paging and chapter have been identified where possible.

3. NFM, labeled "Genesis of the Poleward Urge III," page 1. FCC.
4. There is a drawing of Theodor Koch in the NYH, September 4, 1909. The details of Cook's early life not otherwise noted are taken from typed notes by HCV or AF. The HCV notes are labeled "dictated in 1934." FCC. They are on small sheets of paper and in telegraphic phrases. Throughout, Dr. Cook is referred to as "Dad" or "D." All references to these notes are listed here as "HCV notes." The AF notes were taken during personal interviews with FAC, and all citations are from Freeman's working typescript. CSC.

5. The petition, written in German gothic script, detailing the sequence of events after Theodor's father's death is in the FCC. Translation by Dr. Thomas Walker.

6. Dates are not always consistent in the various extant sources. Dates in this chapter are taken from a clipping from the *Callicoon Echo,* dated to September 1909 by content. The information in this article appears to have come from an interview with Theodore Cook; additional dates are from a family tree; typescript. FCC.

7. NYH, September 3, 1909. The article states that "the entire population of Callicoon and ten miles within its radius is of German origin"; however, a check of the 1870 census for Sullivan County showed many names of English origin as well. Many of the Germans in the area were lured there by unscrupulous land speculators. After the railroad reached Callicoon Depot in 1850, the speculators bought up the nearby worthless rocky hillsides and promoted them heavily in Germany to unsuspecting immigrants. Whether Koch was one of their victims is uncertain.

8. Magdalena Lang (the family's original name) was born, according to a baptismal certificate for her son August, on June 24, 1836, at Nuhsbach in Rheinbainen. FCC.

9. The Cook birth order is problematic. Lillian maintained that she was born on May 15, 1868. This is not likely, since August was definitely born on October 24 of the same year. According to other documentation, Lillian was born in 1862 (NYH, September 4, 1909). A check of the 1870 census did not turn up any Cooks or Kochs in Callicoon Depot or Jeffersonville, where they might have been staying after Dr. T.A. Koch's death, and so her birth year could not be confirmed. The placement of the dead infant, mentioned in a letter from Elliott J. Vetter to Trevor Lloyd, dated July 20, 1956, CSC, could not be verified absolutely. Apparently, no one has compiled an accurate genealogy of the family. That the family knew little of its own history is indicated by a photocopy of a letter from FAC to his cousin, William Koch, dated April 24, 1891, FCC. In this letter FAC wrote that he was surprised to learn that Theodor had been the last born and not the first son. Yet in later life, FAC associated his father's decision to leave Germany with the ideals of Carl Schurz and the liberals who fled to America after the failed revolution of 1848. The success and influence of Schurz as a social and political leader was the pride of every German in America, but other than the timing of Dr. Koch's arrival, there seems to be no evidence of any connection between Theodor Koch and Schurz.

10. This is the family tradition. It is possible that the Kochs changed their name only after they moved to Port Jervis in 1878. One account has it that the name became Cook only in 1880, or after their arrival in New York City (*New Jersey Courier* [Toms River], August 9, 1940). August's baptismal certificate lists both parents' names in their German spellings, though this

may have been only a formality, since the text is in German script. Dr. Koch's original tombstone at Hortonville is inscribed "Dr. T.A.L. Kook"; a later replacement says "Dr. T.A.L. Cook" but misspells his place of birth, so the stone cutters may have simply spelled unfamiliar words phonetically—a common sight in many old graveyards. Since the family could not be found on the 1870 census rolls, the time of the name change could not be verified. Curiously, both tombstones for Theodor Koch are still standing in the Hortonville cemetery but are about fifty feet apart.

11. HCP, chapter 1, pages 5–7. FCC.

12. HCP, chapter 1, page 6. FCC.

13. NFM, III, pages 2–3. FCC.

14. FAC, "Dr. Cook's Own Story," *Hampton's Magazine,* January 1911, page 52.

15. All statements in this chapter attributed to William Cook are from the NYH, September 2 and 4, 1909.

16. FAC, "Seeing the Unseen," *Leavenworth New Era,* September 1927.

17. NFM, III, page 3. FCC.

18. MAP, page 26.

19. NFM, III, page 4. FCC.

20. The requirements for becoming a doctor at NYU in 1890 are in a letter, Edgar S. Tilton to AF, dated March 2, 1937. CSC.

21. NFM, III, page 5. FCC.

22. NFM, III, page 6. FCC.

23. *Saturday Review, London,* November 22, 1856, pages 660–662.

24. Perhaps not. Among Cook's papers is a serial newspaper story, entitled "Life in Arctic Seas. The Diary of a Peterhead Whaling Captain," pasted in a small notebook. The story is dated 1889.

25. WPNP, page 10. This is the notice Astrup saw in the Philadelphia press. No doubt the item in the New York *Telegram* was similar in nature.

26. NFM, III, page 8. FCC.

27. WPNP, pages 14–15. This is a slightly adapted version of the plan as outlined to the Academy of Natural Sciences of Philadelphia and quoted in *Harper's Weekly,* May 23, 1891, pages 335–336, where it is not written in conversational English.

28. HCP, labeled "add to end of Chapter 1," unpaged typescript. FCC.

29. FAC, "The Prince of Liars," *American Weekly,* July 19, 1925.

30. NFM, III, page 8. FCC.

Notes for Chapter 2: I **Must** *Have Fame*

There are four book-length narratives dealing at least in part with Peary's North Greenland Expedition of 1891–92. All incidents not specifically noted can be found recorded in one of these books, which are abbreviated as follows:

IAS   Keely, Robert N., Jr., and G.G. Davis, *In Arctic Seas: The Voyage of the "Kite" with the Peary Expedition.* Philadelphia: Edward Stern & Co., 1892. An expanded version of this book embodying its text and additional material, including the Peary-Verhoeff correspondence, appeared the next year as *In Arctic Seas: The Voyage of the "Kite" with the Peary Expedition, Together with a Transcript of the Log of the "Kite."* Philadelphia: Rufus C. Hartranft, 1893. Unless otherwise noted, all quotes are from the 1892 version.

MAJ   Peary, Josephine Diebitsch, *My Arctic Journal.* New York: Contemporary Publishing Co., 1893.

NOGI   Peary, Robert E., *Northward over the "Great Ice."* New York: Frederick A. Stokes Co., 1898. 2 vols.

WPNP   Astrup, Eivind, *With Peary near the Pole.* Philadelphia: J.B. Lippincott Co., 1898.

Unless otherwise noted, incidents from Peary's early life are mentioned in:

PEM   Weems, John Edward, *Peary, the Explorer and the Man.* Los Angeles: Jeremy P. Tarcher, 1988.

Whenever possible all quoted material that coincides with PEM has been checked against PFC material for context and accuracy. Citation from this book has been resorted to *only* when the original could not be located. Such an instance is characterized in these notes by the phrase "not located in." The author assumes that the item thus described is somewhere in the PFC, but the use of this phrase indicates he was unable to locate it there.

A note on the papers of the North Greenland Expedition
The PFC is very rich in the papers of this expedition. There are diaries of Verhoeff, Peary, Astrup and Mrs. Peary. There is no diary by Cook, but there are a number of reports and other documents in his hand. Peary's diary is incomplete, but there are a few pages of typed transcript from it that apparently no longer exist in manuscript. Peary's diaries have been rebound, and some of the pages are not in the correct order within them. Mrs. Peary's diary is only fragmentary, consisting of entries, some on loose leaves, for the following dates: 1891: June 6 to July 17; a letterlike set of entries for July 18–28; July 21–29; October 10 to November 21. 1892: January 19 to February 16. Verhoeff's and Astrup's diary entries are present only in typescript copies. Verhoeff's is complete, Astrup's is a partial copy. Other papers are noted below.

1. A copy of Astrup's three-page letter dated March 15, 1891, is in the PFC. In it he mentions knowing Fridtjof Nansen.
2. WPNP, pages 10–12.

3. Henson's early biography is uncertain since its sources are contradictory. These details are from *Dark Companion,* by Bradley Robinson, published in 1947. Its accuracy is extremely doubtful, even though the author says he wrote it with Henson's collaboration. Many of the incidents it describes cannot be reconciled with Henson's *A Negro Explorer at the North Pole,* published in 1912. How much of his own book Henson actually was responsible for is unknown. When compared with documentary evidence, many of the events portrayed in *Dark Companion* seem to be embellishment or pure fantasy, not to mention page after page of quoted conversations with no documentation. Even Henson's birthdate is questionable. According to Henson's marriage license, issued April 13, 1891, he was born in 1868, not 1866 as usually cited. John Verhoeff's diary lists the birthdays of all the expedition members; it gives Henson's as August 8, 1869.

4. Among the letters in Cook's papers is one of this sort. (Letter, Ernest Gilkes to FAC, dated September 20, 1909. FCC.) Dr. Cook, after his marriage in 1902, had a black servant. This man is mentioned in the NYT, November 20, 1904. He did not accompany Cook on any expeditions.

5. Letter, REP to May Kilby, dated May 6, 1877. PFC.

6. REP, manuscript, dated 1881. PFC.

7. Typescript among Peary's letters; no holograph was found. PFC.

8. Typescript included with a typescript of Peary's diary entries for June 1879. PFC.

9. REP, Diary entries: October 7; December 10; December 30, 1879. PFC. None of the letters mentioned in the diary were found among Peary's papers, but a description of May's last letters are in a letter, REP to MWP, dated December 7, 1879. PFC.

10. Letter, REP to MWP, dated December 7, 1879; typescript. PFC.

11. Draft of a letter, REP to MWP, dated August 16, 1880, cited in PEM, page 3. Not located in PFC.

12. Letter, REP to MWP, dated October 10, 1880. PFC.

13. Rough draft of note, cited in PEM, page 51. Not located in the PFC.

14. Letter, REP to May Kilby, dated June 12, 1878; typescript. PFC.

15. NOGI, vol. 1, page xxxiv.

16. REP, Diary, 1885; quoted in PEM, page 73. Not located in the PFC.

17. An account of this trip can be found in NOGI, vol. 1, pages 3–38.

18. Letter, REP to MWP, dated July 29, 1886. PFC.

19. Letter, REP to MWP, dated February 27, 1887. PFC.

20. Letter, REP to MWP, dated June 30, 1887. PFC.

21. Letter, REP to MWP, dated July 30, 1889. PFC.

22. Green, Fitzhugh, *Peary, the Man Who Refused to Fail.* New York: G.P. Putnam's Sons, 1926, page 58.

23. Letter, REP to MWP, dated February 26, 1891. PFC.

24. Letter, REP to MWP, dated February 1, 1891. PFC.

25. Letter, REP to MWP, dated March 15, 1891. PFC.

26. Letter, REP to MWP, dated April 7, 1891. PFC.

27. Form letter, REP, 1891. PFC.

28. Letter, LG to REP, undated, inscribed "answered 3/18," [1891]. PFC.

29. Letter, JMV to REP, dated March 16, 1891. PFC. This letter expresses none of Verhoeff's intense desire to go north. According to acquaintances' and family members' reminiscences of him preserved at the Filson Club in Louisville, Kentucky, as a child he too had read Dr. Kane's book and had long dreamed of discovery in the Far North.

30. Letter, JMV to REP, dated March 30, 1891. PFC.

31. Letter, REP to JMV, dated May 3, 1891, both quotes. PFC. Verhoeff sent Peary the money by telegraphic transfer May 6, 1891. Peary gave Verhoeff a receipt for the $2,000 on June 6, 1891, the day the *Kite* sailed for Greenland: "Rec'd of Jno M. Verhoeff the sum of two thousand dollars ($2,000.–) towards the expenses of the Expedition." Copy in PFC.

32. Contract between REP and FAC, signed June 4, 1891. PFC. Other such contracts are present for Astrup, Gibson and Henson. Verhoeff's was not located in the PFC.

33. NYT, June 7, 1891. This story mentions that the names of the other members of the expedition were secrets.

34. Letter, FAC to William Koch, dated June 3, 1891; photocopy. FCC.

35. JDP, Diary, June 6, 1891. PFC.

36. HCP, labeled "add to end of Chapter 1;" unpaged typescript. FCC.

37. JMV, Diary, June 16, 1891. All quotations of JMV diary are from a typescript of his diary. PFC. Verhoeff had this to say of his arguments with Dr. Cook: "He seems to have a pretty good opinion of himself and does not mind asserting his opinions in a positive way. However instead of convincing me it is very liable to cause me to elevate my voice and contradict him, so we are even. However it is not often this happens and we are good friends." (Letter, JMV to Mattie Verhoeff, dated July 30, 1891. Collection of the Filson Club, Louisville, Kentucky.)

38. JMV, Diary, June 27, 1891. PFC.

39. IAS, pages 72–73.

40. JDP, Diary, June 28, 1891. PFC.

41. JDP, Diary, June 30, 1891. PFC.

42. JMV, Diary, June 28, 1891. PFC.

43. JDP, Diary, loose pages: page 62 (c. July 1, 1891). PFC.

44. JMV, Diary, July 5 and 7, 1891. PFC. Verhoeff had a fair-sized personal inheritance from his father, who had made his money in the steamboat business.

45. JDP, Typescript labeled "32 page letter to the New York Herald," undated. PFC.

46. MAJ, page 27.

47. JDP, Diary, July 21, 1891. PFC.

48. JDP, Diary, July 23, 1891. PFC.

49. FAC, Report to REP, dated December 29, 1891; holograph. PFC.

50. Letter, REP to MWP, dated July 2, 1891. PFC. Obviously, from the content, this date is incorrect. Three weeks from July 11 would make the date of the letter August 1. Since the *Kite* left on July 30, this must have been written on or slightly before that date.

51. IAS, pages 142–143.

52. WPNP, page 20.

Notes for Chapter 3: The Inspiration of All the World

1. HCP, chapter 2, pages 2–7. FCC.

2. JDP, Diary, November 9, 1891. PFC.

3. LG, Diary, August 10, 1891. LGB. Gibson's holographic diary is preserved along with his ornithological records at Bowdoin College in Brunswick, Maine. It is a legal-sized ledger book with "Record" inscribed diagonally across the cover, bearing the inscription "L. Gibson North Greenland Expedition 1891–1892." The diary is finely written on 145 of its 200 pages. The rest are all blank except for a scrapbook at the back. The diary once contained photographs, but these have all been torn out. It does, however, preserve some unique mementos, including drawings by Astrup, seal whiskers, pressed flowers and paper money from Greenland.

4. HCP, chapter 2, pages 3–6. FCC.

5. A copy of this order dated August 12, 1891, exists in a typescript in the PFC. It varies somewhat from the text printed in NOGI, vol. 1, pages 100–101.

6. LG, Report to REP; undated holograph. PFC.

7. Ibid.

8. FAC, Report to REP, dated December 30, 1891; holograph. PFC. The text varies somewhat from that printed in NOGI, vol. 1, pages 114–121.

9. HCP, chapter 3, pages 9–11. FCC.

10. FAC, Report to REP, dated December 30, 1891; holograph. PFC.

11. Ibid.

12. WPNP, pages 23–24.

13. MAJ, pages 49–52.

14. WPNP, pages 124–125.

15. WPNP, pages 22–23.

16. FAC, Medical report to REP, dated September 1, 1891; holograph. PFC.

17. LG, Diary, September 11, 1891. LGB.

18. LG, Diary, September 15, 1891. LGB.

19. LG, Diary, September 21, 1891. LGB.

20. REP, Diary, September 10, 1891. PFC.

21. REP, Diary, September 17, 1891. PFC.

22. FAC, "Peeps into the Beyond," chapter 4, page 7; unfinished pencil manuscript. FCC.

23. WPNP, page 24.

24. These instructions are preserved in a typescript. PFC.

25. NOGI, vol. 1, page 175.

26. MAJ, page 41.

27. MAJ, page 89.

28. MAJ, page 90.

29. JMV, Diary, January 13, 1892. PFC.

30. JMV, Diary, July 20, 1892. PFC. *Kunik* is the Eskimo word for "kiss."

31. LG, Diary, December 1, 1891. LGB. *Inuit* is what the "Eskimos" call themselves. The word means "the people." The word *Eskimo* is an uncomplimentary term coined by the Labrador Indians that means "one who eats raw meat."

32. LG, Diary, November 23, 1891. LGB.

33. Taken from a typescript of the order by REP, dated October 1, 1891. PFC.

34. JMV, Diary, October 1, 1891. PFC.

35. HCP, chapter 7, pages 7–8. FCC.

36. LG, Diary, January 9, 1892. LGB.

37. JMV, Diary, December 1, 1891. PFC.

38. LG, Diary, January 19, 1892. LGB.

39. JDP, Diary, November 15, 1891. PFC.

40. JMV, Diary, March 6, 1892. PFC.

41. HCP, chapter 7, page 5. FCC.

42. REP, Diary, December 23, 1891. PFC.

43. Ibid.

44. Verhoeff reported that they cast dice for the books (JMV, Diary, December 26, 1891). Matt Henson got a harmonica instead of a book (REP, Diary, December 26, 1891); both. PFC.

45. MAJ, pages 93–95.

46. REP, Diary, December 26, 1891. PFC.

47. NOGI, vol. 1, pages 183–184. Evidently, Peary was very superstitious. His diary contains numerous references to omens, evil eyes, luck and spiritual interventions by his mother.

48. MAJ, pages 95–98.

49. LG, Diary, December 31, 1891. LGB.

50. WPNP, page 26. Astrup's reference to this incident as happening "Christmas Eve" instead of New Year's Eve is an error of memory or otherwise.

51. JMV, Diary, January 1, 1892. PFC. Verhoeff's changing attitudes toward Matt Henson can be seen in the way he addresses him in his diary: at first, "Matt," later, "the nigger," still later, "the negro," and then again as "Matt."

52. FAC, "The People of the Farthest North," *Everybody's Magazine,* January 1902, pages 19 and 32.

53. LG, Diary, February 2, 1892. LGB.

54. NOGI, vol. 1, page 207.

55. NOGI, vol. 1, pages 209–210.

56. JDP, Diary, February 16, 1892. PFC.

Notes for Chapter 4 : A Permanent Drawing Power for Life

1. FAC, Medical Report to REP, dated September 1, 1891, holograph. PFC.

2. NOGI, vol. 1, pages 222–223.

3. LG, Diary, February 19, 1892. LGB.

4. This quote and the account of this episode are from JMV, Diary, February 20, 1892. Peary does not give an account of this incident in his diary, stating only, "Note Verhoeff's escapade and my lecture to him." PFC.

5. NYT, September 24, 1892; also AF notes. CSC.

6. MAJ, pages 125–128.

7. JMV, Diary, April 26, 1892. PFC.

8. REP, Diary, May 8, 1892. PFC.

9. REP, Diary, May 6, 1892. PFC.

10. Letter, JDP to REP, dated May 7, 1892. PFC.

11. HCP, chapter 4, page 4. FCC.

12. LG, Diary, page 127, writing of May 11, 1892. LGB. Gibson apparently kept a field diary on the trip across the ice cap. When he returned to Redcliffe, he wrote up all the days he had been away in a running narrative in his regular diary, though designating each day as if it were a sequential entry.

13. WPNP, pages 192–193.

14. WPNP, page 194.

15. REP, Diary, May 22, 1892. PFC.

16. EA, Diary, May 25, 1892. PFC.

17. Holograph. PFC.

18. LG, Diary, page 129, writing of May 25, 1892. LGB.

19. WPNP, pages 198–199.

20. LG, Diary, page 131, writing of May 28, 1892. LGB.

21. LG, Diary, page 132, writing of June 1, 1892. LGB.

22. JMV, Diary, May 11, 1892. PFC.

23. MAJ, pages 157–158.

24. JMV, Diary, June 21, 1892. PFC.

25. JMV, Diary, June 29, 1892. PFC.

26. NFM, chapter XIII, "Death Disease and Elusive Glory in Poleward Adventure," page 3, pencil manuscript with typed insert. FCC. Cook made some emendations on this passage. These, however, have been ignored.

27. Verhoeff had not even been able to take a gift from Peary without remarking in his diary, "I have not felt friendly towards him since [the reprimand]." (March 8, 1892.)

28. HCP, chapter 4, page 6. FCC.

29. JMV, Diary, July 11, 1892. PFC.

30. MAJ, pages 165–166.

31. NOGI, vol. 1, pages 166–167. Kyo became so feared that in 1902 his tribesmen did away with him while on a hunting trip. REP reported his death to JDP in a letter dated March 5, 1902. PFC.

32. HCP, chapter 10, page 9. FCC.

33. MAJ, page 181.

34. Heilprin, Angelo, "The Peary Relief Expedition," *Scribner's Magazine,* January 1893, page 16.

35. MAJ, pages 176–177.

36. Note, JDP to REP, dated August 28, 1892. PFC.

37. Heilprin, Angelo, "The Peary Relief Expedition," *Scribner's Magazine,* January 1893, pages 22–23; all quotes.

38. MAJ, 182–183.

39. WPNP, pages 213–214.

40. EA, Diary, July 5, 1892. PFC.

41. WPNP, pages 243–244.

42. FAC, Medical Report to REP, dated September 20, 1892, holograph. PFC.

43. MAJ, page 204.

44. This account of Verhoeff's movements is taken from LG, Diary, August 12–18, 1892. LGB.

45. IAS, 1893 edition, pages 471–472.

46. Holograph. PFC.

47. WPNP, page 33.

48. Holograph. PFC.

49. MAJ, page 207.

50. HCP, chapter 4, page 7. FCC.

Notes for Chapter 5: The Conditions of Happiness

All incidents in the voyage of the *Zeta* are taken from Cook's unpublished diary unless otherwise noted. This is referred to below as ZD. The diary is in a notebook 4¾ by 7¼ inches, bound at the top, with a green paper cover, now covered with reinforcement material on its face. There are no entries from July 10 to August 18. Information on this part of the trip is from contemporaneous newspaper accounts. The entries begin on August 19, 1893, and run through October 5, 1893. For a portion of the diary the dates are incorrectly entered as August when they should be September. The dates thus entered have been corrected in the notes below. There are no other published descriptions of the voyage beyond newspaper accounts.

1. MAJ, page 227.

2. REP, Diary, June 30, 1892, typescript. PFC.

3. REP, Diary, July 5, 1892, typescript. PFC. The typescript says "Ballicas," but in context this must certainly be a transcription error for "Balboa's."

4. NYT, September 13, 1892.

5. NYT, September 24, 1892.

6. *North American* (Philadelphia), September 25, 1892.

7. Letter, REP to MWP, dated December 22, 1892. PFC.

8. BDE, October 17, 1892.

9. Letter, FAC to REP, dated October 8, 1892. PFC. This letter emphasizes the untrustworthiness of Henson's autobiographical accounts. All official
biographies say he was single until 1906, when he married Lucy Ross. However,
this letter mentions "his wife" in 1892. Henson was married in April 1891, to
Eva Flint in Philadelphia. The only published contemporary reference to her
came in Peary's report to the Philadelphia Academy of Natural Sciences: "Matt,
my colored boy, . . . deserves more credit, perhaps, than any other in joining
the expedition, belonging, as he did, to a race supposed to be ill fitted for cold
regions, and leaving behind him a young bride." (*Proceedings of the Academy of
Natural Sciences of Philadelphia,* vol. 52 [1892]: 349.) Henson left her in 1897
when she gave birth to a child only seven months after his return from Peary's
1896 meteorite expedition; she sued for divorce.

10. Quoted in *Journal of the American Geographical Society,* vol. 26
(1894): 76. Translated from the original French in *Nouvelles Géographiques,*
January 6, 1894, page 13. Dr. Isaac Hayes was surgeon to Kane's Second
Grinnell Expedition. He claimed that while exploring independently, he
reached the edge of the "Open Polar Sea," and he wrote a book by that title
about the journey in 1867. Of course, that long-held theory was soon
exploded.

11. Pond, J.B., *Eccentricities of Genius.* New York: G.W. Dillingham Co.,
1900, page 296.

12. Letter, JDP to REP, dated January 31, 1893. Quoted in PEM, pages
132–133. Not located in PFC.

13. Letter, REP to MWP, dated January 1, 1893. PFC.

14. Letter, REP to F.W. Putnam, dated January 28, 1893. PFC. The
ethnographic items Cook collected are still in Chicago at the Field Museum
of Natural History. For details of the 280 specimens see Van Stone, James W.,
"The First Peary Collection of Polar Eskimo Material Culture," *FIELDIANA
Anthropology,* vol. 63, no. 2, December 27, 1972. Field Museum of Natural
History Publication 1156.

15. Letter, FAC to REP, dated January 30, 1893. PFC.

16. Letter, FAC to REP, dated February 3, 1893. PFC.

17. REP, "Report of the Operations of the North Greenland Expedition
of 1891–1892," *Proceedings of the Academy of Natural Sciences of Philadelphia,*
vol. 52 (1892): 349.

18. NOGI, vol. 1, page 423.

19. Letter, FAC to REP, dated March 9, 1893. PFC.

20. Letter, REP to FAC, dated March 21, 1893. PFC.

21. Letter, HLB to REP, dated April 1, 1893. PFC.

22. Letter, HLB to REP, dated April 5, 1893. PFC.

23. FAC, "The Most Northern Tribe on Earth," *New York Medical Examiner,* vol. 3, no. 2 (1893): 23–24.

24. HCP, chapter 5, pages 1–2. FCC.

25. Letter, FAC to REP, dated April 26, 1893. PFC.

26. Letter, REP to HLB, dated May 1, 1893. PFC.

27. Letter, HLB to REP, dated May 2, 1893. PFC.

28. Letter, REP to FAC, dated May 9, 1893. PFC.

29. Letter, FAC to REP, undated, but probably, based on content, early June 1893. PFC.

30. Letter, REP to FAC, dated June 15, 1893. PFC.

31. JDP told Judge Charles P. Daly of her changes of heart in a letter to him dated October 5, 1894. PFC.

32. EBB, Diary, August 20, 1893. BLC.

33. HCP, chapter 5, pages 2–4. FCC.

34. HCP, chapter 5, page 4. FCC.

35. FAC, "Peeps into the Beyond," pencil manuscript sketches. FCC.

36. BSU, July 11, 1893. That Perry paid $1,000 is from the *Sunday Telegram* (Worcester, Massachusetts), August 1, 1937. The story about Jack of Diamonds that follows is also from this source.

37. Unattributed newspaper clipping, undated, but before July 7, 1893. CSC.

38. ZD, August 20, 1893. FCC.

39. ZD, undated entry c. August 23, 1893; both quotes. FCC.

40. ZD, August 29, 1893. FCC.

41. ZD, September 4, 1893. FCC.

42. Ibid.

43. ZD, September 5, 1893. FCC.

44. Ibid.

45. ZD, September 6, 1893. FCC. All entries for September 6–28 are erroneously dated August in the diary.

46. ZD, September 8, 1893. FCC.

47. Ibid.

48. Ibid.

49. ZD, September 12, 1893. FCC.

50. NFM, chapter XIII, page 10. FCC. That Cook was already contemplating a voyage to the Antarctic during the *Zeta* voyage is indicated by several reminders in marginal notes in the ZD to look up information about Antarctica.

51. *Cape Ann Breeze,* October 6, 1893; *Boston Globe,* October 5, 1893.

52. BDE, October 8, 1893.

53. NYW, December 11, 1893.

54. NYT, September 10, 1909.

55. FAC, "A Proposed Antarctic Expedition," *Around the World,* vol. 1 (1894): 55–58.

56. HCP, chapter 7, page 5. FCC.

57. HCP, labeled "Incorporate into Chapter 2, etc.," page 6. FCC.

58. Nansen, Fridtjof, *Farthest North.* New York: Harper & Bros., 1897, vol. 2, pages 3–4; both quotes.

Notes for Chapter 6: Will You Kindly Come to Our Rescue?

The main published source of information about the *Miranda* expedition is the "official history" by Henry Collins Walsh. This book also contains firsthand accounts by other passengers of the *Miranda.* Unless otherwise indicated, the author is Walsh.

A book of articles written by members of the Arctic Club entitled *The White World* was released in 1902. This book contains articles by five "survivors" of the *Miranda.*

Also, there are the published reminiscences of Russell W. Porter. A very full holographic diary kept on the expedition by Porter is in the National Archives. The diary is hardbound, 7¼ by 8¾ inches, with "Record" printed on the spine. It has many interesting photographs taken during the voyage pasted into it.

Cook wrote a chapter on the *Miranda* for NFM but did not use it in HCP. He also kept a diary on this voyage, which is now in the library of the Explorers Club in New York City. It is a 5-by-8-inch notebook of 193 pages but has narrative entries for only July 28 to August 12, 1894, containing sketchy information, none of it unique.

These books and diary are referred to as follows:

ADRP	Porter, Russell W., *The Arctic Diary of Russell Williams Porter,* edited by Herman Friis. Charlottesville: University Press of Virginia, 1976.
LCM	Walsh, Henry Collins, *The Last Cruise of the Miranda.* New York: Transatlantic Publishing Co., 1896.
PMD	Porter's *Miranda* Diary, holographic diary. RPA.
TWW	Kersting, Rudolf, ed., *The White World.* New York: Lewis, Scribner & Co., 1902.

1. NYS, December 11, 1893.

2. BSU, December 2, 1893.

3. *Plans for Dr. Cook's Proposed Antarctic Expedition and Story of the Eskimos and Dogs.* This appears to be the program for the lecture series of 1894. FCC.

4. FAC, "My Eskimo Children," in *Plans for Dr. Cook's Antarctic Expedition and Story of the Eskimos and Dogs.* FCC.

5. Of the Chicago World's Fair Eskimos, Cook had said: "The Chicago Esquimaux should not be in any manner confounded with those with whom [I] spent sixteen months at Whale Sound, as they are but remotely connected.

The home of the World's Fair colony is, indeed, south of the Arctic circle, and they have but few of the characteristics in common with those of the genuine Highlander." Clipping, BSU, exact date unknown, but dated by content to March 1893. CSC.

6. ADRP, page 6, states: "The Eskimos he was exhibiting had been left stranded by some promoter at the World's Fair in Chicago, and the doctor, out of the goodness of his heart, was taking care of them and seeing that they were returned to their home in Labrador."

7. NYT, September 10, 1909.

8. FAC, "Medical Observations among the Esquimaux," *New York Journal of Gynæcology and Obstetrics,* vol. 4 (March 1894): 282–286. Cook appeared before this society January 16. He addressed the Brooklyn Gynæological Society on January 4, 1894.

9. "Dr. Cook among the Esquimaux," *New York Journal of Gynæcology and Obstetrics,* vol. 4 (March 1894): 289.

10. Letter, FAC to Robert Stein, dated January 24, 1894. FCD.

11. ADRP, page 6.

12. PMD, August 22, 1894. RPA.

13. NYT, July 8, 1894.

14. PMD, July 8, 1894. RPA.

15. Ibid.

16. NYT, July 25, 1894. Letter by an unidentified passenger.

17. PMD, July 22, 1894. RPA.

18. PMD, July 17, 1894; both quotes. RPA.

19. PMD, July 22, 1894. RPA.

20. LCM, page 36.

21. Letter, Philip Safery Evans to his parents, dated July 24, 1894, photocopy. FCC.

22. NYT, September 12, 1894.

23. PMD, July 31, 1894. RPA.

24. NFM, chapter IX, "The Last Voyage of the Miranda, 1894," pages 13–14. FCC.

25. ADRP, page 14.

26. PMD, August 10, 1894. RPA.

27. NFM, chapter IX, pages 16–17. FCC.

28. NFM, chapter IX, page 18. FCC.

29. PMD, August 10, 1894. RPA.

30. RWP, "The Finding of the Rigel," in LCM, pages 196–197.

31. Ladd, Maynard, "The Trip to Holsteinborg," in LCM, page 204.

32. The drawing of lots is mentioned in Walsh's book but not in Porter's diary, which describes the meal.

33. LCM, page 135.

34. PMD, August 21, 1894. RPA.

35. Ibid.

36. Dyche went the next year and returned with Peary's relief ship. He collected 4,000 birds, eggs and mammals.

37. Brewer, William, "Wrecked on the Coast of Greenland," in TWW, pages 216–217.

38. PMD, August 22, 1894. RPA.

39. Wright, G. Frederick, "The Last Trip of the Miranda," *Congregationalist,* September 13, 1894, page 348.

40. PMD, August 23, 1894. RPA.

41. Ibid.; both quotes. RPA.

42. PMD, July 24, 1894. RPA.

43. ADRP, page 14.

44. PMD, September 4, 1894. RPA.

45. PMD, August 29, 1894. RPA.

46. PMD, September 6, 1894. RPA.

47. PMD, September 10, 1894. RPA.

48. Walsh, Henry Collins, "The Unfortunate Miranda," in TWW, page 292.

49. NFM, chapter IX, page 27. FCC.

Notes for Chapter 7: This Vanishing of the Pole Star

There are three book-length published accounts of the *Belgica* expedition. Commandant de Gerlache's "Fifteen Months in the Antarctic" and Captain Lecointe's "In the Land of the Penguins" are in French and have never been translated into English. The translations used here were prepared by Terry Tamer and Bette Hurst. The only account in English is Cook's. The original diary he kept on this expedition has not been located. The author's inquiries to the major archival institutions of Belgium yielded no trace of it. These and other frequent references are as follows:

APM   Lecointe, Georges, *Au pays des manchots.* Bruxelles: Société Belge de Librairie, Oscar Schepens & Cie., Éditeurs, 1904.

AVB   Arctowski, Henryk, "The Antarctic Voyage of the 'Belgica' during the years 1897, 1898, and 1899," *Geographical Journal,* vol. 18 (1901): 353–394.

MLE   Amundsen, Roald, *My Life as an Explorer.* Garden City, N.Y.: Doubleday, Doran & Co., 1928.

QMA   Gerlache, Adrien de, *Quinze mois dans l'Antarctique.* Paris: Hachette & Cie., second edition, 1902.

TFAN   Cook, Frederick A., *Through the First Antarctic Night.* New York: Doubleday, McClure & Co., 1900. The spellings in this book are British, e.g., "colour," "honour," etc. These spellings have been converted to American usage in the quotes.

TSP   Amundsen, Roald, *The South Pole.* London: John Murray & Co., 1912. 2 vols.

UPE   Bridges, E. Lucas, *The Uttermost Part of the Earth*. New York:
           E.P. Dutton & Co., 1949.

Some unpublished details were provided by Dr. Jozef Verlinden, whose thorough study of the Belgian expedition is documented in *Poolnacht,* Tielt, Belgium: Lannoo, 1993. For additional foreign language references not used, see the extensive bibliography of writings by the expedition's members in this book.

1. NYT, September 12, 1894; including the quotes.
2. NYT, September 15, 1894.
3. Gilder, W.H., "Arctic Lorelei Still Unconsenting," *Illustrated American,* October 13, 1894, page 456.
4. Letter, FAC to Albert White Vorse, dated January 1, 1895, printed in the New York *Sunday Advertiser,* February 10, 1895.
5. WPNP, pages 44–45.
6. Stokes, Frederick W., Diary, April 20, 1894. BLC.
7. WPNP, pages 45–46.
8. Stokes, Frederick W., Diary, April 20; April 26, 1894, copy of extracts. BLC.
9. Details of the expedition members' complaints are from unattributed Philadelphia newspaper clippings, September 1894. CSC.
10. WPNP, page 46.
11. Lee's diary of August 7, 1894, states: "Mr. Peary assures me that I shall not lack opportunities for having good positions in the States if everything here is successful or if it is not. And I really believe it is the best for me." Lee was appointed as a deputy U.S. marshal when he returned. Papers of Hugh Lee, National Archives.
12. Affidavit of W.T. Swain, dated January 20, 1911. BLC.
13. Unattributed newspaper clipping, dated September 27, 1894. CSC.
14. Letter, EA to EBB, dated October 18, 1894. BLC.
15. *Journal of the American Geographical Society,* vol. 27 (1895): 60–62; both quotes. The first quotes Charles Rabot in *Comptes Rendus,* 1894: pages 428–437.
16. *Journal of the American Geographical Society,* vol. 27 (1895): 61.
17. Letter, EA to EBB, dated December 1, 1894. BLC.
18. Pond, J.B., *Eccentricities of Genius.* New York: G.W. Dillingham Co., 1900, page 298.
19. Letter, JDP to REP, dated "begun June 2 finished June 21" [1895]. PFC. The "no 1," before fame dislodged her, to whom Jo alludes is Bert's mother. In this same letter Jo mentions how much she resented that he assigned half of his salary to her mother-in-law. During his absence in Greenland in 1891–92 he had assigned his entire salary to his mother.
20. NOGI, vol. 2, page 294.

21. These dreams are mentioned in Peary's diaries for 1901–1902. PFC.

22. Letter, REP to JDP, dated March 31, 1895; all quotes. PFC.

23. NOGI, vol. 2, page 533.

24. NYT, October 2, 1895; the Dyche quote is from the same source.

25. Letter, JDP to MKJ, dated October 16, 1895. PFC.

26. Letter, William Johnson Hoster to EBB, dated October 2, 1895. BLC.

27. Letter, FAC to Samuel Entrikin, dated September 25, 1895; printed in *Tourist Magazine,* November 1910, page 454.

28. NYT, March 10, 1895.

29. NYS, January 22, 1896.

30. Details of Nansen's expedition are taken from his book, *Farthest North,* vol. 2.

31. Letter, FAC to EBB, dated October 19, 1896. Printed in a circular for one of Baldwin's lecture tours. BLC.

32. Mill, Hugh R., *The Siege of the South Pole.* New York: Frederick A. Stokes Co., 1905, pages 384–385.

33. Cook states in his memoirs that this interview was with Andrew Carnegie himself. But in his talks with AF he identified the Carnegie as one of his nephews. This seems more likely. Dialogue is taken from HCP, chapter 5, pages 5–6. The material describing Cook's plans is from a contemporaneous interview with Cook in the NYT, April 11, 1897.

34. Before Cook was accepted, Gerlache had been through three doctors. The first was a Dr. Massart, who resigned. The second, Dr. Arthur Taquin, had been involuntarily dropped in favor of the unnamed Flemish doctor who left at Antwerp, and made Gerlache's life miserable upon his return by claiming to have been cheated of his glory. In a letter written from Rio on October 23, 1897, to Gerard Harry, an influential publisher of several Belgian newspapers, Gerlache explained his extreme reluctance to hire Dr. Cook, as he had already received scathing criticism in the Belgian press for taking so many foreigners on his "Belgian" antarctic expedition. A photocopy of this letter was provided to the author by Dr. Jozef Verlinden of Heverlee, Belgium.

35. This is the way the telegram is reproduced in TFAN, page 47. Actually, it should read, "Pouvez rejoindre Montevideo mais hivernerez pas." Literally, it reads, "You can join Montevideo but will not overwinter."

36. BDE, September 4, 1897. The details about Anna Forbes are from HCV notes. FCC.

37. TFAN, page 48.

38. HCV notes. FCC. Bahia is known today as Salvador.

39. A complete description of the expedition's plan can be found in du Fief, Jean, "La zone australe et le projet d'une expédition antarctique belge," *Bulletin de la Société royale belge de Géographie,* 1896, pages 5–28, and Delaite, Julien, "Intérét scientifique de l'expédition antarctique belge," *Bulletin de la Société royale belge de Géographie,* 1896, pages 93–122.

40. APM, page 72.

41. TSP, vol. 1, pages 18–19.

42. QMA, pages 55–56. Actually, the first engineer, Henri Somers, was older—34.

43. HCP, chapter 14, page 11. FCC.

44. HCP, chapter 13, page 4. FCC.

45. TFAN, page 8.

46. TFAN, pages 17–18.

47. TFAN, pages 63–64.

48. FAC, "Factors in the Destruction of Primitive Man," *Brooklyn Medical Journal,* vol. XVIII, no. 9 (September 1904): 334.

49. AVB, page 359.

50. TFAN, page 93.

51. TFAN, pages 96–97.

52. UPE, pages 226–227. Bridges mistakenly states the date as New Year's Day; it was actually January 2, 1898.

53. These details are given in Lecointe's book in chapter 11: "En detresse," APM, pages 104–112.

54. UPE, pages 227–229.

55. FAC, "The Giant Indians of Tierra del Fuego," *Century Magazine,* March 1900, page 729.

Notes for Chapter 8: An Unimaginable Dream

1. FAC, "The New Antarctic Discoveries," *Century Magazine,* January 1900, page 414.

2. Ibid., page 418.

3. Ibid., pages 422–423.

4. HA, "Exploration of Antarctic Lands," in *The Antarctic Manual for the Use of the Expedition of 1901,* edited by George Murray. London: Royal Geographical Society, 1901, page 470.

5. RA, Diary, February 4, 1898, quoted in Huntford, Roland, *Scott and Amundsen.* New York: G.P. Putnam's Sons, 1979, page 60. Reprinted by permission of A.P. Watt, Ltd., and Anne-Christine Jacobsen.

6. FAC, "My Experiences with a Camera in the Antarctic," *Popular Photography,* February 1938, page 92.

7. Gerlache, Adrien de, "The Belgian Antarctic Expedition," *Geographical Journal,* vol. 13, (1899): 651.

8. TFAN, page 151.

9. TFAN, pages 176–177.

10. TFAN, pages 181–182.

11. TFAN, pages 187–188.

12. TFAN, pages 191–192.

13. TFAN, page 200. According to the scholar of the voyage, Jozef Verlinden, Gerlache may have decided to overwinter for practical reasons. After the discipline problems he had had with his crew whenever he touched

land, he feared returning to civilization. If the crew deserted or became unruly, he despaired of finding any suitable replacements among the riffraff he had seen in the far South American ports.

14. TFAN, page 207.
15. AVB, page 377.
16. TFAN, pages 216–220.
17. TFAN, pages 212–215. For Lecointe's amusing account of this incident, see APM, page 202.
18. TFAN, pages 231–233.
19. TFAN, pages 237–238.
20. TFAN, page 243.
21. TFAN, pages 250–251.
22. APM, page 228.
23. TFAN, pages 254–255.
24. APM, page 331.
25. TFAN, pages 282–283.

Notes for Chapter 9: A Year, a Month, and a Day

1. TFAN, page 289.
2. TFAN, pages 290–292.
3. QMA, page 197.
4. HCP, chapter 14, pages 1–2. FCC.
5. APM, page 255.
6. TFAN, page 304.
7. QMA, page 208.
8. APM, pages 246–247.
9. The details of Danco's death not mentioned in TFAN and not specifically cited are taken from the chapters on this event in APM and QMA.
10. APM, pages 251–252. TFAN, page 313 quotes this in a slightly cleaned-up form.
11. APM, page 252.
12. QMA, page 213.
13. MLE, page 27. In this quote, Amundsen says that he and Cook knew from their readings that eating raw meat would prevent scurvy. However, contemporary entries from Amundsen's diary show that he himself did not know this in 1898.
14. HCP, chapter 13, pages 16–18. FCC.
15. AVB, page 381.
16. TFAN, page 332. Although Cook does not mention serving raw meat specifically in TFAN, APM states that Amundsen, at least, ate raw penguin.
17. MLE, page 28.
18. AVB, page 381.
19. TFAN, page 334.
20. APM, pages 286–287; see also QMA.

21. APM, page 257.

22. TFAN, pages 339–342.

23. TSP, vol. 1, page 23.

24. APM, page 278; also, information provided the author by Jozef Verlinden, scholar of the voyage.

25. APM, page 262.

26. TFAN, pages 351–352.

27. APM, page 263.

28. TFAN, pages 354–355.

29. RA, Diary of first sledging journey on the Antarctic Pack, quoted in Huntford, Roland, *Scott and Amundsen.* New York: G.P. Putnam's Sons, 1979, page 66. Reprinted by permission of A.P. Watt, Ltd., and Anne-Christine Jacobsen.

30. APM, page 265.

31. TFAN, page 366.

32. APM, pages 331–332.

33. APM, page 274.

34. APM, pages 272–273; see also QMA.

35. RA, Diary, November 19, 1898, quoted in Huntford, Roland, *Scott and Amundsen.* New York: G.P. Putnam's Sons, 1979, page 66. Reprinted by permission of A.P. Watt, Ltd., and Anne-Christine Jacobsen.

36. APM, pages 300–301.

37. TFAN, pages 392–393.

38. MLE, pages 28–29.

39. MLE, page 30.

40. Ibid.

41. MLE, pages 30–31.

42. TFAN, page 401.

43. TFAN, page 403. In his memoirs, Cook dared to write some of this spicy poetry. He tells two stories related to the sudden rediscovery by the Belgians of the charms of the feminine sex.

44. NYT, May 6, 1899.

45. UPE, page 239.

46. UPE, pages 239–241.

47. FAC, "My Experiences with a Camera in the Antarctic," *Popular Photography,* February 1938, page 14.

48. BDE, July 9, 1899.

49. Details of Cook's return through South America are from HCV notes. FCC.

50. NYT, June 24, 1899.

Notes for Chapter 10: You Have Chosen the Happier Lot
There is no full published account of the voyage of the *Erik,* though there are a number of incidental accounts. A brief outline of the voyage can be found in

Bridgman, Herbert L., "Peary's Progress to the Pole," *Bulletin of the American Geographical Society,* vol. 33 (1901): 425–431.

There is an unpublished diary by Clarence Wyckoff in the possession of his daughter, Betty Wyckoff Balderston. The quotations below are from a full but slightly edited typescript. The original was not seen, but the author was assured that the typescript was factually the same as the original, though differing somewhat in language. Many details and dates, and all incidents involving Clarence Wyckoff himself, come from this typescript. Of other unpublished documents, the most important are those related to the Dr. Dedrick dispute in the PFC and two sets of penciled notes for his memoirs written by Cook long after the fact. These notes were, for the most part, not used in the typed draft of HCP. These have been used here very selectively, however, since some of the details reported are suspect when compared with other documentation. There is also a diary by Louis Bement in the possession of his heirs, but it contains entries only for July 7–29, 1901, and thus contains nothing about the voyage's key events.

Information on Peary's expedition of 1898–1902 is taken from:

NTP   Peary, Robert E., *Nearest the Pole.* New York: Doubleday, Page & Co., 1907.

1. *Brooklyn Citizen,* November 24, 1899.
2. *Boston Herald,* November 7, 1899.
3. UPE, page 533, mentions the correspondence from Cook.
4. TFAN, page 468.
5. Pond, J.B., *Eccentricities of Genius.* New York: G.W. Dillingham Co., 1900, pages 293–294.
6. Ibid., page 548. Cook was not the first to set foot in Antarctica. That honor belongs to Carstens Borchgrevink.
7. The official reception was held at the Théâtre Communal in Brussels, three days after the *Belgica's* arrival in Antwerp, on November 15, 1899. With Prince Albert in attendance, Adrien de Gerlache gave his first account of the expedition before an invited audience. Cook is listed as one of the 17 members of the Commission in "Note relative aux Rapports Scientifiques." Anvers: J.E. Buschmann, 1902, 16 pages.
8. Material on the European trip is from HCV notes. FCC. Some dates and a few additional details are taken from the notes that AF took for his projected book in the 1930s. Some of these eventually appeared in CDC. Freeman worked with Cook personally from 1931 to 1937, conducting many interviews with him that resulted in scores of pages of typed notes. CSC. Cook's memory of his trip to Europe is inaccurate. Though consistently stated as 1900 in both of these sources, it actually was made in 1901. Both HCV's notes and AF's book give the incorrect date.

9. Mentioned in FAC's fragmentary "Peeps into the Beyond," pencil manuscript. FCC.

10. HCV notes. In NFM, Cook has this same conversation with Rudolf Virchow.

11. That Cook already had been sent the other medals is mentioned in the NYT, December 30, 1900. All of these medals are on display at Cook's burial place in Buffalo.

12. The certificate of award of the order, dated October 19, 1899, is in the FCC. This order, established in 1832, was awarded to civilians and military officers who had distinguished themselves through service to Belgium. Cook's medal was the civilian award, without crossed swords.

13. TSP, vol. 1, page 24.

14. NYT, February 21, 1901; both quotes.

15. The substantially complete draft typescript of this 200,000-word manuscript is in the CSC. In the introduction Cook says that he finished it aboard the *Belgica,* but because of the breadth of information it covers, it seems more likely that it was finished sometime in 1901. It was never published.

16. Hints of their first meeting are in a letter, Marie Cook to FAC, dated June 16, 1931. Cook in HCV notes said that he met Marie when he went to deliver Jo Dudley's twins, but according to his step-granddaughter, Bette Hutchinson, Jo did not have twins.

17. This feat was somewhat of an exaggeration since the true weight of the meteorite is only 34 tons. Though Peary insisted on 100 tons, the weight was estimated at 40 tons in a contemporaneous article that appeared in the NYT. Peary exchanged letters with Professor Henry A. Ward of Chicago, defending his estimate of the weight of the meteor. Professor Ward, from his own experience and mathematical computation based on the bulk and composition of other large meteorites, including the Bacubirito in Mexico, estimated it at 50 tons. Peary missed two other large meteorites at Cape York: "The Man," weighing 3.5 tons, and the "Agpalik," weighing 20.5 tons.

18. NTP, page 285. During a deposition for a lawsuit, Robert A. Bartlett swore that it was Peary's "invariable and inflexible rule to forbid any member of his expedition to take out of the Arctic any furs, ivory or any supplies that in any possibility could be of any use to any future Polar expedition." But he did not include Peary, himself, in his statement. (Letter, CJN to Victor Schneider, dated June 26, 1912. PFC.)

There is much indirect evidence of Peary's activities in the fur and ivory trade in the PFC. There are bills from furriers and instructions about bundles of furs and skins. For a discussion of how the Peary Arctic Club "laundered" its furs and ivory through the American Museum of Natural History, see Kenn Harper's book, *Give Me My Father's Body,* pages 74–81. Benjamin Hoppin, who accompanied Peary on his meteorite expedition of 1896, had this to say of Peary's preparations to return to the United States: "Work has been going on now for a good many days in boxing up articles and preparing bundles of skins, etc., for the exhibition at the American Museum, and for different persons." (*A Diary Kept While with the Peary Arctic Expedition of 1896.* Privately published, no date or place of publication, page 59.)

19. *Bulletin of the American Geographical Society,* vol. 29 (1897): 120–121.

20. Ibid., pages 117–118; both quotes.

21. Letter, REP to Otto Sverdrup, dated November 4, 1897. Printed in *Bulletin of the American Geographical Society,* vol. 31 (1899): 92.

22. Hurlbut, George C., "Mr. Peary's Plan and Capt. Sverdrup," *Bulletin of the American Geographical Society,* vol. 29 (1897): 453.

23. Letter, REP to Otto Sverdrup, dated December 25, 1897. Printed in *Bulletin of the American Geographical Society,* vol. 31 (1899): 93.

24. Letter, REP to MKJ, dated January 29, 1898. Cited in Rawlins, Dennis, *Peary at the North Pole; Fact or Fiction?* Washington, D.C.: R.B. Luce, 1973, page 39.

25. NTP, page 90.

26. Sverdrup, Otto, *New Land.* London: Longmans, Green & Co., 1904, vol. 1, pages 59–61.

27. Ibid., page 116.

28. Letter, REP to JDP, dated August 27, 1899. PFC. This letter contains the doubts expressed about Baumann's motives in visiting him as well.

29. Letter, JDP to REP, dated August 28, 1900. This letter is cited in PEM but apparently is no longer in the PFC. How it was separated from the Peary papers is unknown. It came up for auction in the catalog of Brian Riba Auctions, Inc., of South Glastonbury, Connecticut, in the summer of 1990, where it was listed as item 155. This quote and the synopsis of Jo Peary's reaction to Allakasingwah's revelations are from excerpts of the letter printed in the auction catalog in which it was offered for sale. Requests to obtain a copy of the complete letter for study purposes from its current owner were refused.

30. NFM, "Voyage of the Eric 1901 for the Relief of Peary," unpaged. FCC.

31. HLB, Printed memorandum, dated June 12, 1901, to the members of the Peary Arctic Club; both quotes. PFC.

32. Wyckoff, Clarence, Diary, July 23, 1901. Most of the unattributed incidents of the voyage of the *Erik* not having to do with Wyckoff are from NFM. However, dates and some other details are from contemporary newspaper accounts, the Bridgman article cited above and the Wyckoff diary, with the diary the preferred source when there was a conflict.

33. JDP, Account of the arrival of the *Erik,* August 4, 1901. A single sheet of paper in Josephine Peary's hand, mixed with her correspondence. PFC. That Mrs. Peary was not actually so overjoyed at the sight of the party that had come to rescue her is evidenced by a note in her little leather-bound datebook in which she wrote, "Aug. 4 4 PM 'Erik' arrived Bridgman, Cook, Wyckoff, Bement, Church, Stone, Berri 'Peuke nahme'" (Eskimo for "no good".) PFC.

34. HCP, chapter 5, pages 8–9. FCC. Oddly, Cook does not mention another medical problem in his recollection of Peary's condition. Peary had a hernia, and he had broken his truss. Before the *Erik* sailed, Dr. Dedrick left Dr. Cook a written reminder to measure him for a new one to be sent up on the ship expected in 1902. PFC.

35. HCP, chapter 5, page 12. FCC.

36. NFM, "Voyage of the Eric," page 2. This is a separate account not to be confused with note 30 above. FCC.

37. Letter, TSD to REP, dated August 21, 1901. PFC. The attached memorandum declared, "My salary of course ceases from date." It went on to ask for an order on the Peary Arctic Club for his full salary to date, excepting the times when he was out of service because of resignations, and offered to fulfill any other obligation included in his contract. PFC. Part of the letter appeared in the NYT, November 10, 1902.

38. Wyckoff, Clarence, Diary, August 24, 1901. A somewhat different account, as to detail, can be found in NFM, "Voyage of the Eric," pages 6–7. FCC.

39. HLB, Memorandum, dated August 25, 1901; holograph. PFC. Details of the conversation with Dedrick are from this as well.

40. HLB, "Three Farewells to Peary," in TWW, page 197.

41. NYT, September 22, 1901; both quotes.

42. Letter, Cora Dedrick to HLB, quoted in letter, HLB to JDP, dated September 17, 1901; both quotes. PFC.

43. Letter, REP to Charles A. Moore, dated August 25, 1901. PFC.

44. Peary's diary contains many references to what he considered miraculous interventions by his dead mother.

45. Four days is the traditional period of Eskimo mourning when they do not leave the igloo after a death.

46. All diary entries are from the typed copy. PFC.

47. Letter, REP to TSD, dated October 1, 1901. PFC.

48. Letter, TSD to REP, dated November 28, 1901. PFC.

49. Letter, FAC to JDP, dated November 21, 1901. PFC.

50. A copy of the announcement is in both the PFC and the FCC.

51. In the FCC is a little remembrance book, "Wedding Chimes," but other than the names of Dr. Cook and Marie and the date and the signature of the pastor, it is blank.

52. Letter, J.M. Mills to FAC, dated June 17, 1902. FCC.

53. The automobile may have been purchased with a $3,000 loan Marie gave Cook on April 28, 1902. Although Cook signed the agreement to pay $2,000 a year to Lipsius's widow on a mortgage of $18,000, the title, signed by Marie Hunt on May 1, 1902, was in her name. She put $6,000 down on the house and took possession on June 8, 1902. Documentation of these transactions is in the CSC.

54. BSU, September 5, 1909.

55. Although Dedrick had been threatened with being marooned in Greenland, he was transported home free of charge.

56. NYT, September 22, 1902.

57. Letter, REP to JDP, dated March 5, 1902. PFC.

58. Quoted in Green, Fitzhugh, *Peary, the Man Who Refused to Fail.* New York: G.P. Putnam's Sons, 1926, page 229. The date is not attributed but placed at "about March 3, 1902" by Green.

59. NTP, page 344.

60. Such an examination might have vindicated Dedrick. What evidence that remains leans in that direction, but the diaries he kept are now incomplete—pages torn out, their writing smeared and difficult to decipher. Some passages on certain pages have been clipped out with scissors. See also the note below.

61. NYT, September 22, 1902; both quotes.

62. NYT, September 25, 1902.

63. NYT, November 10, 1902.

A note on the disagreement between Dedrick and Peary

Dedrick would not give the reason for his break with Peary and neither would Peary. The only person to write about the cause of their differences in any detail is John E. Weems in his book, *Peary, the Explorer and the Man.* Weems was the first and, for many years, the only researcher allowed unlimited access to Peary's papers. In his discussion of this dispute he strongly implied that the basis of the trouble was what Bridgman and Cook had supposed, that Dedrick resented being placed under Henson. He used as a basis for this a quote from Dedrick that the doctor had overheard the Eskimos remark that Peary was the "middle finger," Henson the "ring finger" and Dedrick the "little finger" and had complained to Peary about it. Though Peary explicitly states that Dedrick was jealous of Henson in a memorandum dated April 13, 1901, this explanation is highly misleading, but considering the other documentation that has survived, certainly it is the explanation that lets Peary off with the least blame.

Understanding the problems that arose between the two men requires a careful reading of Dedrick's diary material and notes and memos given by him to Peary both before and after the two broke with each other in the spring of 1901. There are also a number of memoranda in Peary's hand on this matter, but, unfortunately, Dedrick's diaries are incomplete. Some of the pages have had certain passages cut from them with scissors—the only such mutilation observed in any of the thousands of papers examined by the author in the PFC.

Although the two men did have some differences before, until April 1901 Peary and Dedrick had been on generally friendly terms. In fact, the letter of August 27, 1899, already quoted, indicates that Peary thought fairly well of him at that time. In the fall of 1900, Dedrick told Peary explicitly that he resented Peary's doing all the exploring himself, as well as keeping him from sharing in other meaningful work. In the winter of 1900–1901 the whole party at Fort Conger, where Peary had torn down Greely's large winter quarters and constructed several smaller buildings out of it, was suffering from the early signs of scurvy. Henson was practically incapacitated and Peary showed symptoms as well. Dedrick was the strongest of the three and gave precise and professional medical instructions to Peary on how to care not only for himself and Henson, but also for the Eskimos while he was away hunting to keep them in fresh meat. He also gave a number of valuable suggestions on how to combat mental despair in a long memorandum dated February 21, 1901, which is preserved in the PFC. Peary did not want to believe that scurvy was coming on but showed the diagnosis was correct by several passages in his memoranda, one noting the unmistakable rash about the ankles associated with scurvy ("I suppose the Dr. would call this the scurvy mark. God knows, I hope not." March 16, 1901).

Trouble had been brewing since September 1900 but came to a head only on March 8, 1901, when Dedrick had a long talk with Peary and made the following complaints, according to a memorandum in Peary's hand:

1. That Peary never gave him liquor unless asked for.
2. That Peary had given the good liquor to the natives.
3. That there should be separate houses for men and women.
4. That not enough hunting had been done in the fall to sustain life.
5. That he had been debarred from the work of exploring.
6. That the stores were not fairly distributed.

Peary denied all this and in so doing revealed the somewhat sordid goings-on in his camp. He implied that liquor was available to Dedrick whenever it was wanted "for his own use or medical purposes" and that he had not given the natives the "good liquor" but only "the alcohol & molasses." Of separate quarters he noted, "He found it agreeable enough last Fall when the girl Saune was enduring him, & consenting to live with him." He enumerated all the game slaughtered in proof that it was adequate. As to the doctor's being misused and kept from important work, Peary stated that he had explained to Dedrick before he signed the contract that there was nothing in the work except the money. He also had explained that he, as commander, had special privileges: "That I had spent the best years of my life & a great deal of money & hard work in Arctic work & I felt all the credit of the work should be properly mine." A long, comparative explanation then sought to justify the adequacy and equal distribution of the rations, but revealed that they were indeed very short—something the "deserters" of 1894 had also complained of.

In effect, he was defending his leadership, which was being challenged by someone who seemed to wish to take charge, and this was something Peary could never tolerate: a rival. Even so, on April 4, 1901, just before starting on his spring attempt at the Pole, a trip the doctor advised against because of

Peary's and Henson's condition, Peary wrote a memorandum to the Peary Arctic Club recommending Dedrick be paid his bonus, saying, "His services, professionally; as a hunter; & in other ways have been very valuable.

"Were the work of the Expedition to end today, I should unhesitatingly pay him the bonus specified in his contract with me of Aug. 1898." And before leaving for the North, Peary wrote to the doctor: "I have full confidence in your experience ability & discretion." (Note dated April 4, 1901.)

Many of the notes Peary wrote at that time refer to his possible "non-return" from the northern trip, so perhaps these expressions of confidence in his doctor were just for posterity. There is a sense about these notes that is similar to his feelings expressed in the will-like letter he had written to Jo in 1895. "How blind, blind, blind, I was & how clearly you saw it all," he now wrote her. "A great slice out of our lives, apart from each other & for what — a little fame. I would exchange it all for a day with you. . . ." (Note dated April 4, 1901.)

About the advisability of his trip, the doctor was right, and Peary admitted later, "On reaching Lincoln Bay it was evident to me that the condition of men and dogs was such as to negative the possibility of reaching the Pole, and I reluctantly turned back." (NTP, page 334.) He returned just eight days after he launched his spring campaign. It seems to have been bitterness at this abject failure that led directly to the split with Dedrick.

The incident that irrevocably divided the two happened the day Peary returned to Conger. Dedrick objected to Peary's saying in his message to the Peary Arctic Club, to be taken south by the whalers, that everything with the expedition was "all well." Dedrick remarked, "All well that are not sick." Dr. Dedrick wanted to go north instead; Peary refused, and Dedrick resigned.

Peary carefully copied Dedrick's long resignation letter of April 13, 1901. One passage referring to Peary's desire to have a monopoly on credit for the expedition's work is particularly revealing:

> By the shades of the immortal Kane, whose discovery & exploration of Grinnell Land by his surgeon Hayes, & of the most northern point ever visited, Cape Constitution, by his steward Morton (while Kane was incapacitated) this no American would submit to.
>
> It prostitutes the enlargement of scientific & geographical knowledge to personal vanity & desire for adulation. . . .
>
> By your attitude self aggrandizement must accompany this or it remains unaccomplished.
>
> Never will I hold any official connection with such an expedition. . . . Even your probable effort to deprive me of [my bonus] will not prevent my asserting my manhood & stigmatizing your expedition.
>
> Twere enough that every member of this party this Spring has suffered incipient scurvy (Henson decidedly) because of your mis-

management, your love of pleasure & of private quarters . . . but the
"I" permeates even the hunting. . . .

Peary not only resented this challenge to his authority, he may also have
begun to fear that Dedrick might disclose the secrets of his camp and attempt
to destroy his reputation. Peary now turned bitterly against Dedrick and wrote
a long memorandum detailing all of the doctor's faults, including "a strong
tendency to megalomania," "disquietude at the slightest physical significance
in himself or others," "unprofessional garrulous loquacity" and "a very exaggerated idea of his own relative importance." (Undated memorandum.)

After the doctor had refused to go home, in another memorandum, Peary
accused Dedrick of child molestation, repeated rape of women patients under
his care and causing the death of an Eskimo woman by throwing her to the
floor. (January 28, 1902.)

During the winter of 1901, Peary took to writing memoranda in the third
person threatening legal action: "We also beg to say that we have been commissioned by our client Commander Peary to inform you that he has submitted
the matter of your recent publication of medical secrets learned by you in the
course of your work as surgeon of the expedition to eminent medical & legal
authorities & acting upon their advice he has had preferred formal charges against
you as a man & a physician." Perhaps this is what Peary feared the most—that
Dedrick would disclose his bodily decline, which left him in no condition to
undertake the gigantic physical effort needed to reach the North Pole.

Dedrick shows in his diary his own private hell. His predicament could be
summed up in a motto he scrawled in his diary of 1900: *"La glorie des méchants
ne dure pas, mais la paix intérieure des bons est permanente."* (The glory of the
evildoers does not last, but the inner peace of the good is permanent.) Dedrick
was struggling with his conscience. In the extreme loneliness of Fort Conger,
he, like Peary, had sought the comfort of a native woman, but apparently, unlike Peary, he regretted his unfaithfulness. Perhaps his resolve to stay in the
North was his way of doing penance for what he perceived as his sins, and
even though Peary no longer wanted him, the desertion of his duty would
have been just more guilt weighing down upon him. He had vivid dreams of
having breakfast with his wife and looked back fondly on days of struggle in his
youth "against poverty & temptation," though he admitted, "I seldom get near
the plane of my ideals." (TSD, Diary, September 26, 1901.) After separating
from Peary, he said that he felt his "better self" emerging once more and was hopeful that his staying North would somehow atone for his moral transgressions.

A reading of the material that remains among Dedrick's papers shows that
his motivations were far more complex than a jealous pique at Matt Henson.
The Eskimos' description of his place as below Henson's was evidence that his
position was being undermined in the natives' eyes. Since Dedrick was the
most able of the three expedition members to hunt, he needed to command
their respect to gain their assistance in the field.

For similar reasons, Dedrick worried over Henson's continually demeaning him in front of the Eskimos. When he confronted Henson, he quoted him as saying, "Yes it is true—what are you going to do about it? It is no use to go to Lt. Peary. He sits in the igloos every night and listens to us. He will do nothing." (TSD, Diary, April 16, 1901.)

Even so, there is little animosity in Dedrick's diaries toward Henson personally, let alone indication of real racism. The author saw no racist remarks in Dedrick's diary that have survived, and in fact, he seems to have taken a real interest in helping Henson in a number of ways. For instance, Dedrick gave careful instructions to Peary about helping Henson's mental outlook in other ways than simply letting him drink, and the doctor notes his pleasure in teaching Henson arithmetic and to read, write and spell. (TSD, Diary, October 12, 1900.)

A note among Henshaw Ward's papers indicated that at one time Dr. Dedrick's personal papers were stored in the Washington, New Jersey, public library. They were restricted, but Dr. Cook was specified as being allowed to look at them. According to correspondence by the author with Carol H. McNeil, the senior library assistant there, the papers might have been destroyed by a fire that consumed the Scout Club House in the town, where some of Dedrick's possessions were stored after his death in France in the 1920s.

64. *Macon* (Georgia) *Telegraph.* November 10, 1902.

65. Letter, REP apparently sent copies to both MKJ and H.W. Cannon, another member of the Peary Arctic Club, dated October 27, 1902. PFC.

66. NYT, November 14, 1902.

67. Peary was operated on in Philadelphia by Dr. W.W. Keen. A letter from him to REP, dated September 30, 1902, details the operation. PFC. One of the two remaining toes on the left foot was removed, leaving only the little toe on each foot. On the right foot he removed the scar tissue and shortened the bones of the first and second toes by beveling them. Dr. Keen estimated Peary would be in the hospital for ten days and could be back on duty in thirty days.

68. NYT, November 19, 1902.

69. NYT, November 30, 1902.

Notes for Chapter 11: Between the Forbidden Tundra and the Smiling Snow
There are several published sources of information about Dr. Cook's first attempt to climb Mount McKinley. Cook published three accounts of the trip in 1904, cited individually in the notes below and the appended bibliography of Cook's writings. An account of this expedition is also included in his 1908 book, *To the Top of the Continent.* There is very little information about this expedition in any of Cook's later writings, and nothing that adds anything of significance to these accounts. No original field notes or diary from this expedition were seen among Cook's papers, though in Dunn's unpublished autobiography he mentions that Cook kept one.

A series of five articles was published by Robert Dunn that appeared in *Outing Magazine:*

"Across the Forbidden Tundra," January 1904, pages 459–471.

"Into the Mists of Mt. McKinley," February 1904, pages 535–545.

"Storm-wrapped on Mt. McKinley," March 1904, pages 697–706.

"Highest on Mt. McKinley," April 1904, pages 27–35.

"Home by Ice and by Swimming from Mt. McKinley," May 1904, pages 214–219.

These were followed by Dunn's book in 1907. It should be noted that Dunn's magazine account and book differ in some significant details. Wherever a variant account of the same incident is given, the earlier account has been used. Both versions have incidents that are mentioned in only one or the other. Dunn's original "shameless diary" was not located at Dartmouth College.

These sources are abbreviated as follows:

DOS   Dunn's *Outing Magazine* series. See above for the dates and titles of individual articles.

SDE   Dunn, Robert, *The Shameless Diary of an Explorer.* New York: Outing Publishing Co., 1907.

TTC   Cook, Frederick A., *To the Top of the Continent.* New York: Doubleday, Page & Co., 1908.

1. Dickey's description of Mount McKinley appeared in the NYS, January 24, 1897.

2. Brooks, Alfred H., and D.L. Reaburn, "Plan for Climbing Mt. McKinley," *National Geographic Magazine,* January 1903, pages 33–35.

3. FAC, "Round Mount McKinley," *Bulletin of the American Geographical Society,* vol. 36 (1904): 321.

4. Letter, FAC to REP, dated March 30, 1903. PFC.

5. NYT, September 3, 1909.

6. Steffens, Lincoln, *The Autobiography of Lincoln Steffens.* New York: Harcourt, Brace & Co., 1931, page 323.

7. Ibid., pages 325–326.

8. DOS, page 459.

9. Dunn, Robert, *World Alive.* New York: Crown Publishers, 1956, page 99.

10. SDE, page 18.

11. Dunn, Robert, *World Alive.* New York: Crown Publishers, 1956, page 101.

12. Letter, REP to HLB, dated May 21, 1903. PFC. That the AGS did not help is in a letter from FAC to REP thanking him for his efforts, dated April 15, 1903. PFC.

13. DOS, page 460

14. Ibid.

15. SDE, page 20.

16. DOS, page 460.

17. DOS, page 461.

18. Dunn, Robert, *World Alive*. New York: Crown Publishers, 1956, page 99.

19. DOS, page 461.

20. TTC, page 9.

21. Cook remembered this horse's name as "Ronzo."

22. SDE, page 36.

23. DOS, page 462.

24. DOS, page 464.

25. DOS, page 462.

26. DOS, pages 465–466.

27. DOS, pages 463–464.

28. DOS, page 468.

29. Ibid.

30. DOS, page 469.

31. SDE, page 86.

32. DOS, pages 469–470.

33. DOS, page 535.

34. DOS, page 538.

35. DOS, page 540.

36. DOS, pages 541–542.

37. DOS, page 543.

38. DOS, page 542.

39. DOS, pages 544–545.

40. FAC, "America's Unconquered Mountain," *Harper's Monthly Magazine*, January 1904, page 238.

41. DOS, page 699.

42. Ibid.

43. DOS, page 700.

44. DOS, pages 703–704.

45. DOS, page 705.

46. SDE, page 189.

47. Wickersham left Fairbanks on May 16, 1903, on the *Tanana Chief* with two mules, appropriately named Mark and Hanna, and three companions. The steamboat took them down the Tanana and up the Kantishna to the limit of navigation. There they found an abandoned boat, which they dubbed "Mudlark." In it they proceeded up the Kantishna, cached the boat, and crossed the Chitsia Hills toward Mount McKinley, arriving at the camp later visited by Cook at the foot of the glacier on June 18. Two days later they reached an altitude of something over 10,000 feet on the wall of the mountain that now bears the judge's name, then turned back for home, satisfied they

had accomplished so much with so little. A full account of Judge Wickersham's journey can be found in his book, *Old Yukon Tales, Trails and Trials.* Washington, D.C.: Washington Law Book Company, 1938.

48. DOS, page 27.

49. SDE, page 197.

50. SDE, pages 197–198.

51. DOS, page 28.

52. DOS, page 31. Dunn named the big peak he saw Mount Hunter, after his aunt. However, Bradford Washburn, the recognized authority on the topography of the Mount McKinley region, has stated that it would be impossible to see today's Mount Hunter from Dunn's position on the Northwest Buttress of McKinley. Dunn's name, "Mount Hunter," was applied to the 14,570-foot mountain that bears it today by surveyors in 1906. Washburn believes that what Dunn saw and named after his aunt was what is now called Kahiltna Dome, 12,525 feet high.

53. DOS, page 32.

54. DOS, pages 31–32.

55. DOS, page 32.

56. DOS, pages 33–34.

57. DOS, page 34. The route that stymied Cook's party on the Northwest Buttress was not climbed successfully until May 1954. It required pitons to be placed to get over the pink cliffs.

58. DOS, page 34.

59. DOS, page 35.

60. DOS, page 214.

61. DOS, pages 214–215.

62. TTC, pages 76–77.

63. DOS, page 216.

64. SDE, page 265.

65. DOS, page 216.

66. Ibid.

67. SDE, page 281.

68. FAC, "America's Unconquered Mountain," *Harper's Monthly Magazine,* February 1904, page 344.

69. DOS, page 218.

70. DOS, page 219.

71. FAC, "America's Unconquered Mountain," *Harper's Monthly Magazine,* February 1904, page 344.

72. DOS, page 218.

Notes for Chapter 12: And Therefore to the Top of the World

There are published and unpublished accounts of Dr. Cook's second expedition to Mount McKinley. They are abbreviated as follows:

BMD   Diary of Belmore Browne, 1906, holograph and typescript, Dartmouth College, Hanover, New Hampshire.

CMM   Browne, Belmore, *The Conquest of Mount McKinley.* New York: G.P. Putnam & Sons, 1913.

ADRP and TTC also have accounts of this journey. There is a diary by Russell Porter, which, unfortunately, contains entries only up to June 1906. There are also diaries by Cook and Edward Barrill, one of the packers. Cook also wrote an account of the climb in 1907 for *Harper's Monthly Magazine.* Cook's later writings have some material about this expedition, but they add little to the published accounts. Considering the span of time that had elapsed and the wealth of contemporary documentation, these were eliminated from consideration as sources of information.

1. Letter, REP to FAC, dated December 14, 1903. PFC.
2. The details of Dunn's expulsion from the Arctic Club are taken from his unpublished autobiography, pages 354–356. The letter from Steffens to Kersting is quoted on page 355. RDD. Although Cook defended Dunn at the time, in his account of the 1903 expedition he referred to Dunn, without naming him, as "the haphazard chap who has run the life of a literary hack bewails his misfortunes, makes copy, secrets his observations of interesting things, and makes life tiresome by his egotism." (TTC, page 41.)
3. *National Geographic Index,* 1888–1988. Washington, D.C.: National Geographic Society, 1989, pages 17–23.
4. Mentioned in a letter, HLB to REP, dated November 24, 1902. PFC.
5. According to an internal memo of the Peary Arctic Club, the cost of the ship was as follows: construction, $91,488.59; equipment, $10,489.77; stores, $28,025.57. The ship was designed by naval architect William E. Winant; her builder was Captain Charles B. Dix. PFC.
6. REP, "My Plans for Reaching the Pole," *Harper's Weekly,* July 9, 1904, page 1054.
7. At first there was an attempt to buy the *Gauss,* Drygalski's antarctic steamer, which was on the market. Peary recommended her to Jesup on January 9, 1904. The price was $85,000, but he wanted more powerful engines installed that would raise the cost to $150,000. Canadian Captain Joseph E. Bernier bought the *Gauss* for $75,000, however, on behalf of the Canadian government, which renamed her *Arctic.* When an attempt to get Congress to appropriate $50,000 toward Peary's new ice vessel failed, Jesup agreed to order his steamer in June. The design had a pronounced raking stem and a wedge-shaped bow. A very sharp rise of floor afforded a form of side that it was hoped could not be grasped by the ice, and a big overhang at the stern was devised to protect the propeller. Screw tie-rods were used to bind the ship together, and the bow was almost completely filled in to meet the impact of the ice. Other peculiarities included a massive and unusual reinforcement of the rudder post

to prevent twisting and a rudder that could be lifted out of the water. Besides her steam power, the schooner-rigged vessel carried 14 sails. She was launched on March 30, 1905, and taken on her shake-down cruise by Captain Frank A. Houghton.

8. Peary wanted to name the ship after Jesup, who declined, offering the name "Roosevelt" instead. Letter, MKJ to REP, dated February 15, 1905. PFC.

9. *Report of the Eighth International Geographic Congress Held at Washington, 1904.* Washington, D.C.: GPO, 1905, pages 79–80.

10. Letter, REP to FAC, dated April 14, 1904. PFC.

11. When the proceedings of the congress were printed in 1905 by the Government Printing Office, many papers were abstracted, but two of the three by Cook appeared in full.

12. Memorandum, REP to HLB, dated October 6, 1902. PFC.

13. This account of how Cook met Parker is taken from AF notes. CSC. Professor Parker had delivered a paper at the recent geographic congress, and both men were founding members of the American Alpine Club and the newly formed Explorers Club, but, according to Cook, they had not met before.

14. This anecdote is in HCV notes. It is confirmed by an interview with Wallace that appeared in the NYH, September 3, 1909.

15. Holograph, dated July 1, 1905. CSC.

16. From the letterhead of T.A. Cook's stationery. PFC.

17. Letter, T.A. Cook to REP, dated September 7, 1903. PFC. All the grammatical errors and misspellings in this quote are reproduced from the letter.

18. In correspondence between REP and T.A. Cook, dated June 7, 10, 14, 16, 23, 1905. PFC.

19. TTC, pages xi–xii.

20. Letter, FAC to RWP, dated March 14, 1906. RPA.

21. Fiala made a mere ten miles toward the Pole before giving up.

22. ADRP, page 156.

23. Letter, Alfred Brooks to FAC, dated March 14, 1906. RPA.

24. RWP, Diary, May 18, 1906. RPA.

25. Ibid.

26. RWP, Diary, May 24, 1906. RPA.

27. TTC, pages 110–112.

28. Browne, Belmore, "The Struggle up Mount McKinley," *Outing Magazine,* June 1907, page 264.

29. ADRP, page 159.

30. BMD, June 14, 1906. BBD.

31. The details of the return are from Browne's diary.

32. NYT, October 16, 1909; both quotes. That Parker wore an inflatable vest was mentioned here by Armstrong.

33. BMD, July 1, 1906. BBD.

34. BMD, July 19, 1906. BBD.

35. Ibid.

36. CMM, page 55. That Cook turned back for Parker's sake is recorded by Browne in his diary entry for July 22, 1906. BBD. Browne's book reverses the events of two days. It has the windy night in the tent occurring before the attempt to get onto Ruth Glacier. The diary has been taken as the authority.

37. BMD, July 28, 1906. BBD.

38. ADRP, pages 159–160.

39. BMD, July 31, 1906. BBD.

40. Letter of J.A. MacDonald, reproduced in MAP, page 533.

41. FAC, Diary, 1906. FCC. Undated entry on page 37.

42. NYT, October 7, 1906.

43. ADRP, page 160; both quotes. Porter mixes up the glaciers here. It was the Ruth that Cook ascended, not the Tokositna.

44. NYT, October 3, 1906. The telegram, dated September 27, arrived October 2.

45. Letter, HLB to JDP, dated October 12, 1906.

46. NYT, November 28, 1906.

47. *Tacoma Daily Ledger,* October 26, 1906.

48. NYT, November 10, 1906.

49. NYT, October 7, 1906.

50. NYT, October 31, 1906.

51. Quote from *Seattle Post-Intelligencer,* November 8, 1906; the itinerary is from HCV notes.

52. *Seattle Post-Intelligencer,* November 10, 1906.

53. The description of Cook's climb, including all quotes, is from FAC, "The Conquest of Mount McKinley," *Harper's Monthly Magazine,* May 1907, pages 825–837.

54. *Seattle Post-Intelligencer,* November 10, 1906.

55. Parker, Herschel C., "The Exploration of Mt. McKinley: Is It the 'Crest of the Continent'?" *Review of Reviews,* January 1907, page 58.

56. Letter, Hudson Stuck to Alfred Brooks, dated December 14, 1906. Photocopy of letter courtesy of David M. Dean.

57. Letter, Alfred Brooks to Hudson Stuck, dated January 30, 1907. Photocopy of letter courtesy of David M. Dean.

58. When Peary reached New York, 30,000 people attended the public reception given to him by the American Museum of Natural History. The crush was so great that the 25 police at the museum found it useless to try to control the crowd. The hero was forced to seek refuge in the director's office.

59. All quotes from speeches made at this dinner are from "Honors to Peary," *National Geographic Magazine,* January 1907, pages 49–60.

60. Amundsen's voyage: He left Norway in July 1903 aboard the *Gjøa.* After spending two years in the vicinity of the North Magnetic Pole, on August 30, 1906, he finished navigating the Northwest Passage. Amundsen

was honored by the Norwegian Club of America in November 1906 before sailing for Europe. Cook still had not returned from the West and did not attend. When Amundsen tried to collect the long-standing prize offered in Great Britain for the first explorer to navigate the Northwest Passage—100,000 pounds sterling—it was declared to have been withdrawn and therefore null and void. Amundsen was, however, awarded medals by the Royal Geographical Society, London, and the National Geographic Society and decorated with the Grand Cross of St. Olaf by Haakon VII, king of Norway.

61. Peary had already had an audience with Theodore Roosevelt at the White House, where he met Walter Wellman, who was also waiting to see the president. Wellman discussed with Peary the difficulties he had had with his attempt to fly to the Pole in the *America*. Bad weather and technical problems had forced him to put off the flight until the next year.

Notes for Chapter 13: The Wind-Loved Place

Much of the material for this chapter is taken from Cook's unpublished diary of his winter at Annoatok. The book is a 5¼-by-8¼-inch, leather-bound book. On its cover is engraved in gold, "Graves' Double-Indexed Diary." The diary contains entries from July 3, 1907, to February 18, 1908. Since the pages in the diary are predated, the first entry begins in the middle of the book and "wraps around," using the pages for January and February for 1908. The paper is quadrilled. The entries are continuous (though not every day has an entry), generally written in ink, with the back of each page left blank. Some of these left-hand pages have been used for other notes, apparently discontinuous, and there are a few notes by a hand other than Cook's—perhaps HCV—written in at a later time. There are gaps in the diary whenever Cook was away from his winter quarters. These days were kept in a separate diary. This "hunting diary" contains discontinuous entries dated between May 25, 1907, and December 11, 1907. It is a 4½-by-6¾-inch, leather-bound book, with "Day Book" printed on the cover. It contains scattered records, apparently written when Cook was in the field. This is suggested by the use of pencil rather than ink for the entries, since ink would freeze, and by the larger size of the handwriting, probably done with a gloved hand.

The translation of the passages from Franke's book, entitled "A German's Experiences in the High North," were prepared by Dr. Thomas Walker and Marion Smith.

These sources are abbreviated as follows:

AWD   FAC, Annoatok Winter Diary, 1907–1908. FCC.

EDHN   Franke, Rudolph, *Erlebnisse eines Deutschen im hohen Norden.* Hamburg: Alfred Janssen, 1914.

1. Letter, FAC to RWP, undated. RPA. There is a reply to this letter from Porter dated February 28, 1907.

2. In the above letter, Cook tells of his money troubles, including the borrowed $1,000 and his nonpayment of his packers. A letter from Rose Daly, *Harper's Magazine's* financial secretary, dated February 28, 1957, cited by Bradford Washburn in his 1991 book, *Mount McKinley: The Conquest of Denali,* states that Cook had been paid $1,000 in two checks dated May 15, 1906, and February 26, 1907, for his article, which appeared in its May 1907 issue. Cook may have used this last to ensure domestic tranquility by paying his wife back part of her money. There is a series of letters dealing with Cook's financial arrangements with Russell Porter in the RPA.

3. John R. Bradley, "My Knowledge of Dr. Cook's Polar Expedition," *Independent,* September 16, 1909, page 636.

4. FAC, Diary, dated May 25, 1907, one of three entries from May 1907 recorded in a separate book from the sequential diaries referred to above. This diary for the most part was apparently written in the fall and winter of 1908. These entries are on page 7.

5. EDHN, pages 11–12.

6. EDHN, pages 13–14.

7. John R. Bradley, "My Knowledge of Dr. Cook's Polar Expedition, *Independent,* September 16, 1909, pages 637–638.

8. The account of Cook's meeting with Bradley and Marie's reaction are adapted from AF notes. CSC.

9. The flag design is on the back of a letter to Marie sent from Gloucester on June 12, 1907. CSC. The design was used on the stationery of the Bradley Arctic Expedition.

10. AWD, July 3, 1907.

11. Letter, FAC to Edward N. Barrill, dated June 15, 1907. PFC.

12. This was Cook's recollection in the 1930s. That Grosvenor was in Baddeck at this time is supported by a letter, Gilbert H. Grosvenor to REP, dated June 18, 1907, in which he says that he will be going to Cape Breton on July 1.

13. Details having to do with Franke alone or his recollections, not otherwise attributed, are contained in his book.

14. EDHN, pages 19–21.

15. AWD, August 14, 1907.

16. NYH, September 17 and 19, 1909.

17. NYH, September 17, 1909; both quotes.

18. EDHN, page 27.

19. EDHN, pages 27–28.

20. Photographic copy of holographic letter, FAC to Henry Collins Walsh, reproduced in the NYT, September 5, 1909.

21. Holograph. FCC.

22. AWD, August 27, 1907.

23. AF notes. CSC.

24. EDHN, page 28.

25. EDHN, page 30.

26. AWD, September 7, 1907.

27. NYH, September 19, 1909.

28. AWD, September 10, 1907.

29. Cook's diary says "the *Gauss* or the *Arctic.*" This is the same ship. See Chapter 12, Note 7.

30. AWD, September 14, 1907.

31. AWD, September 16, 1907.

32. AWD, September 17, 1907.

33. AWD, September 18, 1907.

34. AWD, September 21, 1907.

35. EDHN, page 49.

36. EDHN, pages 45–46.

37. AWD, September 28, 1907.

38. AWD, October 7, 1907.

39. AWD, October 11, 1907.

40. AWD, October 13, 1907.

41. AWD, October 25, 1907. In his book Franke says his birthday was July 3, not in August.

42. AWD, October 27, 1907.

43. AWD, November 16, 1907.

44. FAC, Hunting Diary, November 19, 1907. FCC.

45. FAC, Hunting Diary, December 1, 1907. FCC.

46. Letter, FAC to HLB, dated December 6, 1907. PFC. There are two copies of this letter. They vary slightly in text.

47. AWD, December 11, 1907.

48. EDHN, pages 50–51.

49. EDHN, pages 51–52.

50. EDHN, pages 54–55.

Notes for Chapter 14: I Have Been to the Pole!

1. AWD, January 7, 1908.

2. AWD, January 15, 1908.

3. AWD, January 16, 1908.

4. AWD, January 17, 1908.

5. EDHN, pages 61–62. In his book, Franke added a postscript to this account: "I was filled with shudders and disgust, but at that time I did not know that I would make the acquaintance of this beast in the form of a man." It is possible, however, that some if not all of the human bones Franke saw at Cape Sabine were not from the dead Eskimos but from some of Greely's men who died there in 1883–84. On page 50 of his book, *North to the Horizon,* Dr. Harrison J. Hunt of the Crocker Land Expedition remarks on what he found

at Peary's house in 1914: "There were some wooden coffins outside, with dead Eskimos inside, dead for many years. No one objected when I pried one open, and finding only a skeleton, chopped up the wood of the coffin for kindling."

6. AWD, January 21, 1908.

7. AWD, February 9, 1908.

8. AWD, February 10, 1908.

9. Peary authorized a fund-raising drive among Oregon schoolchildren to contribute 1 to 5 cents to help make up his deficit. The Associated Press published an account of this scheme including a telegram from Peary endorsing it. A typewritten copy of the AP story is in the PFC. At this same time Peary was buying up many of the islands in Casco Bay for cash through his agent, a Captain Morrill. There are a number of letters at Bowdoin College of this nature up to July 1907, the month Peary gave up his plans to head north that year. In these letters he cautions the captain to keep the transactions quiet and the name of the buyer secret. Records in his papers also show that at this time Peary was speculating in Japanese imperial bonds at $1,000 each.

10. Bartlett, Robert A., *The Log of Bob Bartlett*. New York: G.P. Putnam's Sons, 1928, page 203. This may not be an accurate account. In the PFC there is a note from Bartlett in which he says he was informed by his mother in September 1907 that Cook had stayed north to try for the Pole, though he could scarcely believe it. No doubt his mother had the news from Moses Bartlett.

11. Morris, Charles, *Finding the North Pole*. (Philadelphia)?: W.E. Scull, 1909, page 120.

12. NYT, October 4, 1907.

13. VS, "Cook and Peary," unpublished paper, pages 2–3. Undated typescript, but content dates it to after 1934. SCD.

14. Letter, said to have been seen at the offices of the International Polar Commission in 1912 by Cook; cited in CDC, page 101. There can be little doubt that Peary sent one. Lecointe referred to a letter to the Polar Commission, which it had received from Peary in 1908, in newspaper stories that appeared in September 1909 but he did not disclose its contents. Bridgman also referred to this letter in a letter to Mrs. Peary, dated October 15, 1908, the day after the New York *World* printed an article containing the text of Cook's letter to Franke from the polar sea. (See note 28 below.) It said in part: "Perhaps you have not seen the enclosed in yesterday's 'World,' copy of which I sent yesterday to Secretary Lecointe of the Polar Commission, saying that, perhaps, Cook's letter, Mar 17, might throw light on Peary's note to the President of the International Polar Commission." PFC. The author was unable to locate a copy of Peary's original letter in the PFC, but Lecointe is quoted in the NYH, October 22, 1909, as saying of it, "As for Commander Peary, he has shown himself farseeing in every respect. One act of his foresight is a document sent by him in May, 1908—that is, before he left on his last voyage— to the International Polar [Commission], consisting in advance of an anticipatory detailed statement against Dr. Cook's supposed enterprise."

15. NYT, September 9, 1909.

16. Letter, REP to Theodore Roosevelt, dated July 15, 1908. Quoted in PEM, page 239, not located in PFC.

17. Letter, JDP to REP, dated November 17, 1907. PFC.

18. There are several letters of this nature from JDP to the Navy Department written in 1906. PFC.

19. Letter, REP to Alexander Graham Bell, dated January 1, 1907. PFC.

20. Two undated drafts of letters by REP; no addressee. PFC.

21. AWD, February 13, 1908.

22. AWD, February 16, 1908.

23. AWD, February 17, 1908.

24. The Ziegler Polar Expedition established a supply base with a large cache of food on Shannon Island in 1901. In November 1902 Ziegler offered to put this at Peary's disposal, but Peary rejected the offer.

25. Holographic letter kept with Peary's most important papers. Original restricted; microfilm examined. PFC.

26. EDHN, page 68.

27. EDHN, page 71.

28. There are slight variations in the several published versions of this letter. Since Franke had the holograph, this has been copied from his book, where it is reproduced in English on pages 127–128. There is a typed version of it in the PFC, which varies considerably. However, most of the differences appear to be transcription errors, possibly because of Cook's problematic handwriting. Several obvious transcription errors in the letter as it appears in Franke's book have been corrected in the quote.

29. EDHN, page 188.

30. Letter, Rudolph Franke to REP, dated August 13, 1908. PFC. The letter appears to be a copy in Ross Marvin's hand.

31. A copy of this in Ross Marvin's hand is in the PFC.

32. Letter, Ross Marvin to L.C. Bement, dated July 30, 1908. In possession of Silas H. Ayer III.

33. Letter, Ross Marvin to L.C. Bement, dated August 13, 1908. In possession of Silas H. Ayer III.

34. Henson, Matthew A., *A Negro Explorer at the North Pole.* New York: Frederick A. Stokes Co., 1912, pages 29–30.

35. Instructions to John Murphy from REP, holograph, written in Marvin's hand, signed by Peary, dated August 17, 1908; both quotes. PFC. John E. Weems, on page 238 of PEM, quotes these instructions from "either the original or a copy," noting that they had been quoted "in varying versions." The short, five-paragraph version he uses has nothing about skins. The original order has 27 paragraphs handwritten over its six pages, only 12 of which have anything to do with Cook.

36. Letter, REP to JDP, dated August 17, 1908. PFC. The nature of these letters on the "Cook affair" that Peary mentions is unclear, unless they

were the ones Franke turned over to Peary. No others were located in the PFC. "Sammy" was Peary's pet name for his first Eskimo son.

37. In his book Franke gets the Bartletts confused and refers to the captain of the *Erik* as Bob Bartlett. Bob was on the *Roosevelt* at this time, heading north with Peary; the captain of the *Erik* was Sam Bartlett.

38. Greely, Adolphus W., "Polar Exploration during the Year 1908," *Independent,* April 1, 1909, page 687.

39. A photographic copy of the program for the benefit performance is in the CSC.

40. Letter, Marie Cook, addressee not given, but probably John R. Bradley, as she asks him to pay some bills from the expedition. The letter is undated but is on stationery from a hotel in North Sydney, CBI, indicating it was written some time after October 1907. CSC.

41. *Tacoma Daily Ledger,* September 2, 1909. Since Mrs. Cook gave no interviews before September 5, 1909, this must have been information obtained earlier.

42. NYT, October 5, 1908.

43. Letter, JDP to REP, dated March 23, 1909. PFC. According to an interview Andrew Freeman had with Franke in the late 1930s, Herbert Bridgman tried to buy Franke off by offering him a job. Franke, according to Freeman, told Bridgman "to go to hell" and left for Palm Beach, Florida, where Bradley had a job waiting for him at the Beach Club. AF notes. CSC. There were later attempts to trace the furs Franke turned over to Peary, but they were unsuccessful. In 1910 Peary wrote to his lawyer: "I do not understand how anybody can know what the 'Erik' brought home; and certainly the bills of lading on the 'Rosalind' which brought all the 'Erik' stuff from St. Johns to New York are the only evidence, and those are, I presume, in regular routine in the Custom House. To the best of my knowledge and belief, there were no furs." (Letter, REP to CJN, dated November 3, 1910.)

44. Records of all these transactions are in the PFC. The museum was to pay in five installments through 1911, the first $20,000 to be delivered by July 1909, paying 5 percent additional in interest on the rest. Letter, H.C. Bumpus to JDP, dated February 16, 1909. PFC.

45. For the full story of Mene's tragic life, see Harper, Kenn, *Give Me My Father's Body.* Toronto: Blacklead Books, 1986. The *San Francisco Examiner*'s story appeared in its magazine section on May 9, 1909, following other stories in April in the NYW, NYS and the New York *Evening Mail.*

46. Letter, HLB to Charles D. Dickey, quoted in a letter, HLB to Sam Bartlett, dated May 12, 1909. PFC. Details of the meeting with Mrs. Cook are in a memorandum from Bridgman dated July 2, 1908. PFC.

47. Agreement between NYH and owners of the *Jeanie,* undated; before July 15, 1909. PFC.

48. Letter, HLB to JDP, dated July 15, 1909. PFC.

49. Letter, HLB to REP, dated July 21, 1909. PFC.

50. Letter, HLB to JDP, dated July 14, 1909. PFC.

51. Letter, JDP to REP, dated July 16, 1909. PFC.

52. Letter, JDP to REP, dated July 17, 1909. PFC.

53. Whitney, Harry, *Hunting with the Eskimos.* New York: Century Co., 1911, pages 267–269; both quotes.

54. FAC, "Dr. Cook's Own Story," *Hampton's Magazine,* February 1911, pages 168–169.

55. Morris, Charles, *Finding the North Pole.* (Philadelphia)?: W.E. Scull, 1909, page 44.

56. FAC, notes taken down, apparently, by the events recorded, between April and August 1909, while in Greenland. They are written in pencil on loose sheets of quadrilled paper torn from a notebook. FCC. Some of Cook's charges are lent support in Dr. Hunt's book, *North to the Horizon,* page 21, where he states: "When Peary was last north, he took a younger woman on his trip, but when he returned he went off in the hills with his former wife. . . ." Peary had one other Eskimo son besides "Sammy," named Kali, who was born in 1906, the same year as Matt Henson's Eskimo son, Anaukaq. According to the Eskimos, Cook had no Eskimo children.

57. FAC, Draft of letter to REP. Apparently, from the quadrilled paper, written in the same notebook as the notes cited as 56 above, and torn out.

58. Typewritten copy is in the PFC.

59. CDC, page 127. That he took Pewahto is in a memorandum by REP in the PFC.

60. Some accounts state that the Eskimos called the Pole the "Big Navel," since on maps it seemed to them to be a point at the center of concentric rings. But "Big Nail" is by far the more common term, even though it may be based on a misunderstanding.

61. Letter, FAC to Marie Cook, dated May 8, 1909, holograph. FCC. "Mary" was Cook's address for his wife when at his most intimate.

62. Morris, Charles, *Finding the North Pole.* (Philadelphia)?: W.E. Scull, 1909, page 45.

63. Helgesen, Henry T., "Dr. Cook and the North Pole," Extension of Remarks, *Appendix to the Congressional Record,* 64th Congress, 2nd session, September 4, 1916, page 54. The version of this letter published in the NYH, October 6, 1909, has some significant differences.

64. NYT, October 21, 1909.

65. Egan, Maurice Francis, "The Witnesses for Dr. Cook," *Rosary Magazine,* November 1909, page 493; quoting Rasmussen.

66. The account of the dinner is from AF notes. CSC.

67. Egan, Maurice Francis, "The Witnesses for Dr. Cook," *Rosary Magazine,* November 1909, pages 492–493; both quotes. Egan says this article was written on October 16, 1909—after the Eskimo testimony appeared in the New York papers—see chapter 17.

68. New York *Evening Telegram,* September 16, 1909; quoting an interview with de Quervain that appeared in the *Cologne Evening News* on September 6, 1909. The *Evening Telegram* was controlled by James Gordon Bennett.

69. Steensby, Phil. H.P., "The Polar Eskimos and the Polar Expeditions," *Fortnightly Review,* November 1909, pages 893, 901–902.

70. AF notes. CSC.

Notes for Chapter 15: I Show You My Hands

1. NYT, September 2, 1909.

2. NYS, September 5, 1909.

3. NYH, September 2, 1909.

4. Egan, Maurice Francis, "Dr. Cook in Copenhagen," *Century Magazine,* September 1910, page 759.

5. NYT, September 2, 1909.

6. Egan, Maurice Francis, "How Cook Came and Went," *Benziger's Magazine,* October 1909, pages i–ii. Holger Dansker is the national hero of Denmark in the form of a seated statue in the lower vault of the castle. Legend has it that he will come to life and rise up to save the Danish nation should it ever be threatened with destruction.

7. Crockett, Albert Stevens, *When James Gordon Bennett Was Caliph of Bagdad.* New York: Funk & Wagnalls Co., 1926, page 11.

8. Quoted in a letter, A. Cunningham Hay, vice-consul at Lerwick, to FAC, dated September 2, 1909. FCC.

9. NYH. September 2, 1909.

10. Ibid.

11. NYT, September 4, 1909; both quotes.

12. NYT, September 2, 1909; all comments.

13. NYH, September 3, 1909.

14. NYA, September 4, 1909.

15. NYT, September 3, 1909.

16. Ibid.

17. NYT and NYH, September 2, 1909. The wording of Cook's telegram to Marie implies that she had informed him in her letter delivered by Captain Bernier that she had lost the house and her address was indefinite.

18. NYT, September 2, 1909.

19. NYT, September 3, 1909. Lord Northcliffe was the title bestowed in 1903 on Alfred Harmsworth, the man who had given Peary the *Windward.*

20. Telegrams, James Gordon Bennett to FAC, dated September 3, 1909, and September 6, 1909. FCC.

21. The gumdrop story appeared in the NYT, September 3, 1909. The slogan is taken from FAC, "The Prince of Liars," *American Weekly,* August 9, 1925.

22. These details do not match Gibbs's account of his first meeting with Cook. They are from a translation of an article that appeared in the Danish *Illustreret Tidende,* September 12, 1909. CSC.

23. Gibbs, Philip, "Adventures of an International Reporter," *World's Work,* March 1923, page 481.

24. Ibid., pages 482–483.

25. Egan, Maurice Francis, "Dr. Cook in Copenhagen," *Century Magazine,* September 1910, page 761.

26. Gibbs, Philip, "Adventures of an International Reporter," *World's Work,* March 1923, page 483.

27. Egan, Maurice Francis, "How Cook Came and Went," *Benziger's Magazine,* October 1909, page ii.

28. Stead, W.T., "Dr. Cook: The Man and the Deed," *Review of Reviews,* October 1909, page 434.

29. Miller, J. Martin, *Discovery of the North Pole.* (Chicago)?: J.T. Moss, 1909, page 78.

30. Ibid.

31. Morris, Charles, *Finding the North Pole.* (Philadelphia)?: W.E. Scull, 1909, pages 174–175.

32. NYW, September 5, 1909.

33. NYT, September 5, 1909; these are two separate quotes.

34. Ibid.

35. NYW, September 5, 1909.

36. Miller, J. Martin, *Discovery of the North Pole.* (Chicago)?: J.T. Moss, 1909, page 80.

37. NYH, September 5, 1909.

38. NYT, September 7, 1909.

39. *Aarbog for Københavns Universitet, Kommunitetet og den polytekniske Læreanstalt, indeholdende Meddelelser for det akademiske Aar 1909–1910,* published in 1914, pages 1244–1248. Translation in PFC.

40. NYT, September 6, 1909.

41. NYH, September 5, 1909.

42. NYW, September 5, 1909.

43. HCP, chapter 13, pages 19–21. Amundsen's plans to drift to the North Pole were not confidential, as Cook implies here. He had already presented them fully before the Royal Geographical Society of London on January 25, 1909.

44. NYT, September 7, 1909.

45. Telegram, Marie Cook to FAC, dated September 2, 1909. FCC.

46. Letter, Curtis Brown to FAC, dated September 3, 1909. FCC.

47. Letter, Benjamin Hampton to FAC, dated September 3, 1909. FCC.

48. Letter, H.M. Lyon to FAC, dated simply "Sunday" (probably September 5, 1909). FCC.

49. Letter, Ralph Shainwald to FAC, undated. FCC.

50. *Collier's,* October 2, 1909, page 11.

51. Gibbs, Philip, "Adventures of an International Reporter," *World's Work,* March 1923, page 486.

52. NYH, September 8, 1909. Cook's reference was to the once-celebrated controversy between Commodore Winfield Scott Schley and Rear Admiral

William T. Sampson over who should have credit for the great victory over Spain's Atlantic fleet in the Spanish-American War. The Spaniards had been bottled up in the harbor at Santiago, Cuba, for weeks. Admiral Sampson, the commander of the blockading American fleet, had departed with the USS *New York* early on the morning of July 3, 1898, for a conference with General Shaftner, who was in command of the siege of the city. At 9:30 A.M., the Spanish fleet unexpectedly made a run for the open sea and was cut to pieces by the superior American ships, which had been left in charge of Commodore Schley. Sampson, who had put about at the first sign of the engagement, arrived just at the end of the action that virtually destroyed every one of the Spanish vessels, but claimed credit for the victory because he was the ranking officer. Of course, Schley did not agree with this assessment.

53. NYS, September 7, 1909.

54. NYT, September 7, 1909. Dr. Stebbins was a dentist who had been a passenger on the *Miranda*.

55. NYT, September 7, 1909.

56. NYH, September 8, 1909.

57. NYT, September 7, 1909.

58. NYT, September 8, 1909. The London *Post* of the same date counted the words.

59. Stead, W.T., "Dr. Cook: The Man and the Deed," *Review of Reviews*, October 1909, page 438.

60. Egan, Maurice Francis, "Dr. Cook in Copenhagen," *Century Magazine*, September 1910, page 762.

61. NYS, September 8, 1909.

62. NYT, September 8, 1909.

63. Gibbs, Philip, "Adventures of an International Reporter," *World's Work*, March 1923, page 484.

64. NYT, September 9, 1909; both wires.

65. NYT, September 8, 1909; quoting *Le Temps*.

66. Telegram, FAC to John R. Bradley, undated. FCC.

67. NYT, September 9, 1909.

68. NYT, September 7, 1909.

69. NYT, September 9, 1909.

70. Morris, Charles, *Finding the North Pole*. (Philadelphia)?: W.E. Scull, 1909, page 176.

71. Ibid.

72. The original degree is now in the FCC.

73. Morris, Charles, *Finding the North Pole*. (Philadelphia)?: W.E. Scull, 1909, page 177. The last line is found in Miller, J. Martin, *Discovery of the North Pole*. (Chicago)?: J.T. Moss, 1909, page 81.

74. Huntford, Roland, *Scott and Amundsen*. New York: G.P. Putnam's Sons, 1979, pages 218–219. In correspondence with the author, Huntford said that he identified the note as on Dr. Cook's stationery because Cook's name was printed at the top.

75. NYT, September 9, 1909.

76. Stead, W.T., "Dr. Cook: The Man and the Deed," *Review of Reviews,* October 1909, pages 437–438.

77. Egan, Maurice Francis, "Dr. Cook in Copenhagen," *Century Magazine,* September 1910, page 763.

78. Both these telegrams are dated September 8, 1909. FCC.

79. NYT, September 11, 1909; all quotes.

80. Egan, Maurice Francis, "How Cook Came and Went," *Benziger's Magazine,* October 1909, page iv.

81. *Nord Atlanterhavsposten* (the ship's magazine), September 17, 1909. Copy in FCC.

82. Stanton, Theodore, "Dr. Cook at Copenhagen," *Independent,* October 7, 1909, page 817.

83. Stead, W.T., "Dr. Cook: The Man and the Deed," *Review of Reviews,* October 1909, page 448; both quotes.

84. Gibbs, Philip, "Adventures of an International Reporter," *World's Work,* March 1923, page 486.

Notes for Chapter 16: We Believe in You

1. NYS, September 7, 1909.

2. NYH, September 7, 1909.

3. Ibid.

4. Ibid.

5. Ibid.

6. NYH, September 9, 1909.

7. NYH, September 10, 1909.

8. Ibid.

9. Ibid.

10. NYH, September 11, 1909.

11. NYH, September 13, 1909.

12. Ibid.

13. NYH, September 11, 1909.

14. NYH, September 10, 1909.

15. NYH, September 15, 1909.

16. NYT, September 11, 1909.

17. NYT, September 12, 1909.

18. Letter, JDP to REP, dated September 12, 1909. PFC.

19. Telegram, REP to THH, dated September 13, 1909. PFC.

20. Burrage, Henry S., *Thomas Hamlin Hubbard.* Portland, Me.: Printed for the State, 1923, page 60. The associate quoted was Judge Holt.

21. Ibid., page 54.

22. Letter, THH to REP, dated September 9, 1909. PFC.

23. NYT, September 12, 1909.

24. NYH, September 15, 1909.

25. NYH, September 16, 1909.

26. NYH, September 13, 1909.

27. NYT, September 20, 1909.

28. Ibid; all quotes.

29. NYT, September 17, 1909.

30. Letter, HLB to Franklin Hooper, dated September 20, 1909. PFC.

31. NYT, September 18, 1909.

32. NYT, September 20, 1909.

33. NYT, September 21, 1909.

34. Morris, Charles, *Finding the North Pole.* (Philadelphia)?: W.E. Scull, 1909, page 182. The details of Cook's New York reception not specifically attributed are taken from this book, which was written quickly to take advantage of the great interest in the subject and issued in November 1909. It used New York newspaper accounts, most of which can be found, nearly word for word, in the September 22, 1909, issues of the NYT, NYH, NYS and NYW.

35. NYS, September 22, 1909. Coler and Mayor McClellan were political enemies. Coler had asked Governor Charles Evans Hughes to remove the mayor from office for misuse of funds.

36. A typewritten draft of this speech on the Scandinavian-American Line's stationery is in the FCC.

37. NYS, September 22, 1909.

38. Ibid.

39. NYW, September 22, 1909.

40. NYS, September 22, 1909.

41. NYW, September 22, 1909. What the doctor is reported to have said varies considerably from one account to another.

42. NYS, September 22, 1909. A typewritten draft of this speech on the stationery of the Scandinavian-American Line is in the FCC. It varies slightly from the text as reported.

43. NYW, September 22, 1909.

44. NYW, September 21, 1909.

45. Details of Peary's arrival are from Kennan, George, "Commander Peary's Return," *Outlook,* October 2, 1909, pages 252–254. According to Marie Peary Stafford, Peary never let his son kiss him. "Men don't kiss," he told him, and taught him to salute instead. (Letter to J.E. Weems, dated April 26, 1966. PFC.)

46. NYW, September 22, 1909.

47. Attributed to NYH, September 22, 1909, by AF, but could not be verified from that source; both quotes. AF's transcript. CSC.

48. NYW, September 22, 1909.

49. Ibid.

50. NYT, September 22, 1909.

51. NYH, September 15, 1909.

52. NYT, September 22, 1909.

53. NYW, September 23, 1909.

54. NYH, September 23, 1909.
55. Ibid; all quotes.
56. NYW, September 23, 1909.
57. NYH, September 23, 1909.
58. NYW, September 23, 1909.
59. Ibid.
60. Ibid.
61. Ibid.
62. NYH, September 24, 1909; all quotes from Cook's speech.
63. Ibid.
64. Letter, Edwin Andrew to FAC, dated October 14, 1909. FCC.
65. NYT, September 27, 1909.
66. Ibid.
67. Lonsdale, Walter, "The Real Story of Dr. Cook and the North Pole," *Travel Magazine,* June 1910, pages 451–452.
68. Quoted in the NYH, September 17, 1909.
69. NYH, September 28, 1909.
70. NYH, September 25, 1909; all quotes since last note.
71. NYH, September 27, 1909; all quotes since last note.
72. NYH, September 29, 1909.
73. NYH, October 1, 1909; all quotes since last note.
74. NYH, October 3, 1909; all quotes since last note.
75. NYH, October 5, 1909; all quotes since last note.
76. NYH, October 7, 1909; all quotes since last note.
77. NYS, September 28, 1909; both quotes.

Notes for Chapter 17: Into the Hall of Bribery
1. NYT, September 29, 1909.
2. *St. Louis Star,* quoted in the NYH, October 1, 1909.
3. *Detroit Free Press,* quoted in the NYH, September 29, 1909.
4. Detroit *Journal,* quoted in the NYH, September 30, 1909.
5. Philadelphia *Evening Telegraph,* September 30, 1909.
6. NYT, September 24, 1909.
7. NYH, September 28, 1909.
8. Chicago *Journal,* quoted in the NYH, September 29, 1909.
9. Telegram, Henry Rood to REP, dated September 29, 1909. PFC.
10. NYT, September 30, 1909.
11. NYT, October 2, 1909.
12. NYT, October 3, 1909.
13. Letter, REP to THH, dated October 4, 1909. PFC.
14. Letter, REP to HLB, dated October 7, 1909. PFC.
15. Letter, THH to REP, dated October 7, 1909. PFC.
16. Letter, REP to THH, dated October 12, 1909. THA.

17. REP, undated memorandum. PFC. This is on Sydney Hotel stationery, which dates it to probably no later than October 1909, since no other pieces of this stationery are present after that date, though there are many before dated in either September or October.

18. NYT, October 3, 1909.

19. Letter, REP to THH, dated October 8, 1909. PFC.

20. Letter, J. Selwin Tait to THH, dated October 4, 1909. PFC. Great Falls is a large cataract on the Potomac River above the city.

21. NYT, October 5, 1909.

22. NYT, October 8, 1909.

23. NYT, October 11, 1909.

24. NYH, October 11, 1909.

25. NYT, October 13, 1909.

26. Ibid.

27. Dedrick's and Dyche's statements are in the NYH, October 14, 1909.

28. Quoted in the NYH, October 14, 1909.

29. NYT, October 13, 1909.

30. NYG, October 13, 1909.

31. NYS, September 5, 1909.

32. NYT, September 9, 1909.

33. Letter, J.E. Shore to HLB, dated September 9, 1909.

34. Whitney, Caspar, "Who's the Liar?" *Collier's,* October 16, 1909, page 15.

35. NYT, October 14, 1909. Whatever his ancestry, according to his affidavit, Edward N. Barrill was born in Buffalo on April 9, 1864.

36. Ibid.

37. NYH, October 12, 1909.

38. Letter, Albert E. Joab to M.T. Hitchcock, dated September 21, 1909. CSC.

39. Telegram, FAC to Edward N. Barrill, dated September 21, 1909. PFC.

40. Letter, FAC to Edward N. Barrill, undated. PFC.

41. Cook's phone call is mentioned in a letter, H. Wellington Wack to FAC, dated September 23, 1909. FCC.

42. NYT, October 14, 1909.

43. This series of telegrams as well as others dated October 6 and 7, which tell of Ashton's arrangements to come east, are in the PFC as well as the original draft drawn by Ashton.

44. Letter, REP to THH, dated October 7, 1909. PFC.

45. Letter, William Reick to REP, quoted in a letter, REP to THH, dated October 5, 1909. PFC.

46. Crockett, Albert Stevens, *When James Gordon Bennett Was Caliph of Bagdad.* New York: Funk & Wagnalls Co., 1926, pages 305–306.

47. NYH, October 12, 1909.

48. Ibid; both quotes.

49. NYH, October 16, 1909.

50. NYT, October 15, 1909.

51. Ibid; both quotes.

52. NYH, October 15, 1909. In a separate interview, Ashton said that he thought he had paid Barrill $100 to $200 for expenses but would have to look it up on his expense books to be sure. (NYT, October 30, 1909.)

53. NYG, October 14, 1909.

54. NYT, October 15, 1909.

55. Letters, REP to HLB, dated October 30 and November 14, 1909; REP to William Reick, dated October 28, 1909. PFC.

56. Kennan, George, "Arctic Work and Arctic Food," *Outlook*, November 20, 1909, page 625.

57. NYH, October 16, 1909.

58. This scroll is preserved at the Frederick A. Cook Society in Hurleyville, New York, and is pictured in the NYH, October 16, 1909.

59. NYH, October 16, 1909.

60. NYT, October 16, 1909.

61. NYT, October 17, 1909.

62. The account of the Explorers Club committee meeting and all the quotes of testimony given there are taken from an uncorrected, typed set of the minutes of the meetings of October 15 and 17, 1909. PFC.

63. NYT, October 21, 1909; both quotes.

64. NYT, October 22, 1909. Actually, the map alone was mailed out to the Associated Press by the Peary Artic Club, confidentially, the first week in October.

65. Letter, REP to HLB, dated October 19, 1909. PFC.

66. Letter, Matthew Henson to REP, dated October 9, 1909. PFC.

67. Brady, William A., *Showman.* New York: E.P. Dutton & Co., 1937, pages 250–251.

68. Letter, REP to H.C. Bumpus, dated October 14, 1909. The asterisks indicate a section of this letter that is physically missing. A number of Peary's letters and papers were damaged by the wet storage conditions at Eagle Island.

69. Telegram draft, REP to HLB, dated October 17, 1909. PFC.

70. Brady, William A., *Showman.* New York: E.P. Dutton & Co., 1937, page 251. No such picture has ever turned up, and most of the Henson pictures have disappeared with it. Henson said he exposed 110 or 120 pictures on the polar journey, but only the few that were printed in a magazine article and his book have been seen, in addition to those used by Peary in his own book. There are some lantern slides among the small collection of Henson memorabilia at the Morgan State University library in Baltimore, none of any significance. Documentary evidence in the PFC, however, shows that the American Museum of Natural History once had two sets of slides made from Henson's negatives in its possession. (Letter, REP to DBM, dated November 15, 1909. PFC.) It says in part, "I should particularly object to you or anyone else using the slide said to [be] the North Pole." Perhaps Henson's pictures may yet be

recovered. Henson's pictures were evidently quite good. Peary received a letter from an editor at *Hampton's* complaining that the Henson pictures which Mac-Millan was displaying at his lectures "were exactly what we wanted to get" and "apparently better than anything we have." (Letter, W. Curtis to REP, dated January 14, 1910. PFC.)

71. NYT, October 18, 1909.

72. Brady, William A., *Showman.* New York: E.P. Dutton & Co., 1937, pages 251–252.

73. Letter, REP to HLB, dated October 15, 1909. PFC.

74. Letter, REP to Benjamin Hampton, dated March 27, 1910. PFC.

75. Letter, REP to HLB, dated October 19, 1910. PFC.

76. The telegram is dated October 21, 1909, and went through several cities trying to catch up with Cook, finding him at last on October 24. FCC.

77. NYT, October 27, 1909.

78. NYT, October 29, 1909.

79. *Anaconda* (Montana) *Standard,* October 30, 1909. All of the quotes and the details of the meeting in Montana are from this issue.

80. *Helena* (Montana) *Independent,* October 29, 1909.

81. NYT, November 1, 1909.

82. There are two letters from Ashton to Hubbard indicating that the search was being made, dated November 13 and 20, 1909. PFC.

83. NYT, November 1, 1909.

84. *Helena* (Montana) *Independent,* October 31, 1909.

85. On October 4, Peary asked Hubbard: "Will it not be good move for you representing the club, or I, standing above (whichever you think best) to go on record (taking the initiative as it were) in a brief open letter or telegram to the National Academy or the National Geographical Society, suggesting a composition of the committee as discussed in our conversation at Bar Harbor?" On October 7, Hubbard replied: "Mr. Raven, Mr. Bridgman, Mr. Bumpus and Mr. Huntington have just now been here [these were officials of, respectively, the National Academy of Sciences, the Peary Arctic Club, the American Museum of Natural History and the American Geographical Society]. The conclusion reached is that the assent of the Geographical societies and the American Museum of Natural History should be given, to the effect that Dr. Remsen, as President of the National Academy of Sciences shall select a committee of impartial experts. . . . I advised the gentlemen that the actual selection should be deferred for two weeks, and that you should be consulted as to bodies from which the selection should be made." Hubbard had already wired Henry F. Osborn, close friend of Morris K. Jesup and his successor as president of the American Museum of Natural History, asking him to "defer final arrangements of Committee until you see Peary." (THH to Henry Fairfield Osborn, dated September 29, 1909, cited by Dennis Rawlins in *Peary at the North Pole; Fact or Fiction?,* p. 170). Osborn responded on October 6: "I could, however, explain in person better than by letter why I think the Academy

[of Sciences] would accept with pleasure a decision of the Peary Arctic Club to refer the matter to other scientific bodies." All letters are in the PFC.

86. Letter, Gilbert H. Grosvenor to REP, dated March 8, 1907. PFC.

87. Letter, Gilbert H. Grosvenor to REP, dated October 5, 1909. PFC.

88. Telegram, Gilbert H. Grosvenor to REP, dated October 12, 1909. Cited in Rawlins, Dennis, *Peary at the North Pole; Fact or Fiction?* Washington, D.C.: R.B. Luce, 1973, page 191.

89. Telegram, REP to Gilbert H. Grosvenor, dated October 13, 1909. Cited in Rawlins, Dennis, *Peary at the North Pole; Fact or Fiction?* Washington, D.C.: R.B. Luce, 1973, page 191.

90. Letter, REP to THH, dated October 14, 1909.

91. Letters, REP to THH, dated October 12 and 13, 1909, are just two of many examples in the PFC.

92. Letter, REP to CJN, dated October 18, 1909. PFC. The list of what Peary originally sent to the NGS is also in this letter.

93. Letter, REP to CJN, dated October 29, 1909. PFC.

94. NYT, November 4, 1909.

95. Ibid.

96. Letter, James Ashton to THH, dated November 4, 1909. THA.

A note on the "Chunk of the Pole" letter

During Ed Barrill's brief visit to New York on October 14, 1909, he and his wife, Fannie, swore out affidavits about this letter. These are possibly the affidavits Ashton refers to here. In her affidavit, Mrs. Barrill contended that she had seen the letter and that it had the language in it that her husband would allege before the audience in Hamilton, Montana, later that month, but that it had been lost or mislaid in one of "my periodical house cleanings."

Barrill affirmed his wife's statement in his own affidavit, and swore a second in which he stated he had received six letters from Dr. Cook since his return from Alaska. He numbered and attached five of the letters to the affidavit, saying the one that was missing was the fifth in the sequence and was the one to which his wife made reference in her affidavit.

It was that letter number five that allegedly contained the statement about "a chunk of the pole." The Barrills looked high and low—and they eventually found it. This is what it said:

July 15, '07
Battle Harbor, Labrador

Dear Barrille

I am very much surprised at the tone of your letter. The whole thing has been to me a drag and a loss. Your money and that of the others I have picked up dollar after dollar by hard work but Printz more than the others has been hired by Disston and I know he will pay in time. If not when I come back in Oct. I will go to Philadelphia and sit down until I get it. I have no more money in sight. I am trying to make up for my losses this summer by a trip to Labrador and Greenland, whether I succeed or not I will not know until I return in October.

By this same mail I am writing to a friend who owes me a hundred dollars to send it to Printz. This will reach him soon after this letter but do urge Printz to write to Disston often. I am also writing Disston by this mail to send Printz $400 and thus close the account. I can do no more — until I return.

I will write you at once when I get back and will expect you to tell me about it then but during my absence do not write [here the word "about" is written and crossed out] as the letter will not get to me and only go from place to place and will be opened by others.

We go from here to Greenland into the arctic ice and if all goes well the party will return in about 3 months.

Yours very truly,
F. A. Cook.

Holograph. PFC.

There is not only no mention of "a chunk of the pole," but Dr. Cook gives no hint that he has any intention of even trying for the North Pole, instead saying twice that he expects to return in October. But what subject did Cook not want Barrill to write about in a letter that might "be opened by others"?

This must be the letter in question, since it fits in by place and by date with the other five, and it is unlikely that Dr. Cook would write another letter to Barrill from Battle Harbour—the last place visited before leaving for Greenland—on the same day he sailed for the Arctic. And Barrill himself said there was only one letter missing. Therefore, there does not seem to have been a "chunk of the pole" letter at all.

As for Dr. Cook's claim at Hamilton that he had a letter from Printz saying that for $350 he would swear that Barrill's affidavit was not true, that claim is also suspect. There is a handwritten letter that says this in the papers held by the Frederick A. Cook Society, but it clearly says "copy" at the top. It is signed "Fred Printz," but this signature, although similar, does not compare in many points to the signature on the affidavit Printz signed for James Ashton, now preserved in the Peary papers along with the affidavits of Fannie and Ed Barrill. Also, the letter is written on letterhead stationery of the Chittenden Hotel in Columbus, Ohio. No contemporary account gives any reference to Fred Printz being in Ohio during the period of the Polar Controversy. So, the countercharges made at Hamilton as to these correspondences seem to mean nothing as far as settling the question of whether Cook planned to fake his polar journey before he even started it.

97. NYT, November 8, 1909.

98. NYT, November 9, 1909.

99. "Mr. Peary's Own Story," *Review of Reviews,* December 1909, page 660.

100. NYT, November 27, 1909.

101. NYT, November 28, 1909.

102. Ibid.

103. Ibid.

104. Letter, REP to William Reick, dated November 27, 1909. PFC.

105. Letters, REP to HLB, dated October 30, 1909; REP to William Reick, dated October 28, 1909; REP to THH, dated October 26, 1909; REP to THH, dated November 14, 1909, are four examples. PFC.

106. Letter, HLB to REP, dated November 24, 1909. PFC.

107. Letters, Peter Freuchen to HLB, dated November 30, 1909, SCD; HA to HLB, dated November 24, 1909. PFC.

108. Letter, THH to REP, dated November 15, 1909. PFC.

109. NYT, November 19, 1909.

Notes for Chapter 18: Tell It to the Danes!

1. NYT, December 27, 1909.

2. Lonsdale, Walter, "The Real Story of Dr. Cook and the North Pole," *Travel Magazine,* June 1910, page 427.

3. Ibid.

4. NYT, December 10, 1909. The envelope from Wack is in the CSC. It contained several letters including one dated October 25, 1909, to Cook from C.O. Anderson, a lawyer in Kennewick, Washington, who had interviewed an eyewitness to the payoff of Barrill "in large bills" at a Tacoma bank. The witness alleged Barrill was paid about $1,500. Wack went to Valparaiso, Indiana, on November 11, 1909, to visit the witness, J.D. Burke, who confirmed Anderson's account in every detail. (Letter, H. Wellington Wack to FAC, dated January 14, 1911.)

5. Telegram, William Reick to REP, dated December 3, 1909. PFC.

6. All information in reference to the Dunkle-Loose affidavits and all quotes from them are from the NYT, December 9, 1909.

7. Editorial in the *Philadelphia Record,* quoted in the NYT, December 13, 1909.

8. Editorial in the *Springfield* (Massachusetts) *Republican,* quoted in the NYT, December 13, 1909.

9. NYA, December 10, 1909.

10. Lonsdale, Walter, "The Real Story of Dr. Cook and the North Pole," *Travel Magazine,* May 1910, page 374.

11. Bartlett, Robert A., *The Log of Bob Bartlett.* New York: G.P. Putnam's Sons, 1928, page 210.

12. All information on the Copenhagen decision is taken from the official report printed in *Aarbog for Københavns Universitet, Kommunitetet og den polytekniske Læreanstalt, indeholdende Meddelelser for det akademiske Aar*

1909–1910, published in 1914. All quotes are taken from a translation of this item. PFC.

13. Lonsdale, Walter, "The Real Story of Dr. Cook and the North Pole," *Travel Magazine,* June 1910, page 451.

14. NYT, December 22, 1909.

15. NYW, December 22, 1909; all quotes.

16. NYT, December 22, 1909; both quotes. While the Cook serial was running, the NYH ran an editorial that sounded almost apologetic that Cook had let it have the story so cheaply. No doubt, Bennett got his money's worth.

17. Letter, Georges Lecointe to HLB, dated December 29, 1909. PFC.

18. NYT, December 22, 1909.

19. NYT, December 23, 1909.

20. Editorial in the *Newark Evening News,* quoted in the NYT, December 23, 1909.

21. NYT, March 31, 1910. Chauncey M. Depew, U.S. senator from New York and well-known wit, speaking before the Transportation Club on the occasion of a welcome to Ernest Shackleton. This quip has been repeated endlessly and erroneously attributed to Peter Freuchen.

22. "An Historic Swindle," *Nation,* December 23, 1909, page 616.

23. NYT, December 22, 1909.

24. Letter, REP to THH, dated December 24, 1909. PFC.

25. Quoted in *Appendix to the Congressional Record,* January 25, 1916, page 295.

26. Lonsdale, Walter, "The Real Story of Dr. Cook and the North Pole," *Travel Magazine,* May 1910, page 374.

27. Letter, REP to THH, dated December 16, 1909. PFC.

28. Letter, THH to George Little of an unknown date, quoted in a letter, George Little to Herschel Parker, dated December 13, 1909. PFC. George Little, the librarian in Hubbard Hall, was first in Peary's class at Bowdoin; Peary was second.

29. Letter, Herschel Parker to George Little, dated December 11, 1909. PFC. Before the Explorers Club committee just three months before, Parker had said, "Both Mr. Brown and myself intended to return to Mt. McKinley at some future time to make another attempt on the mountain, and we would not have considered for an instant the possibility of approaching the mountain from the South." (Minutes of the committee meeting, October 15, 1909. PFC.)

30. CMM, pages 113–114. That they had actually written to the packers is confirmed in a letter, BB to THH, dated March 2, 1910. PFC.

31. Letter, Hudson Stuck to REP, dated January 21, 1910. PFC.

32. NYT, June 5, 1910.

33. Letter, Elsa Barker to REP, dated September 5, 1909. PFC.

34. Letter, Elsa Barker to REP, dated September 13, 1909. PFC.

35. Harré, T. Everett, "From Pole to Prison—The Mystery and Tragedy of Dr. Cook." Unpublished article, 1940; all details and quotes, CSC, except the telegram, dated September 14, 1909. PFC.

36. Letter, T. Everett Harry to REP, dated October 23, 1909. PFC.

37. Barker, Elsa, "Peary: The Man and His work," *Hampton's Magazine,* December 1909, pages 814d–814f.

38. Letter, REP to Frederick A. Stokes, dated February 5, 1910. PFC.

39. Letter, Frederick A. Stokes to REP, dated February 14, 1910. PFC. A.E. Thomas later told Vilhjalmur Stefansson and Henshaw Ward how he obtained his materials. See their correspondence. SCD and HWA.

40. NYT, February 12, 1910.

41. Ibid.

42. Helgesen, Henry T., "Analysis of 'Evidence' Presented by Robert E. Peary to Committee on Naval Affairs, 1910–11." Extension of Remarks, *Appendix to the Congressional Record,* 64th Congress, 1st session, January 25, 1916, page 296. A complete transcript of the so-called Peary Hearings is in this issue. All information about these hearings is drawn from this source, as are all the quotes.

43. Ibid., page 298.

44. NYT, March 16, 1910.

45. Letter, Robert E. Ely to CJN, dated March 17, 1910. PFC. The NYT implied that Peary's rejection in the South was racially motivated because of his association with Matt Henson.

46. Letter, Elsa Barker to REP, dated March 26, 1910. PFC. Barker was not the first choice to write "Peary's Own Story." It was originally thought improper for a woman to do the writing since she might have to travel with the explorer on his anticipated lecture tours while the work progressed. H. Merton Lyon was the first choice, but he failed to produce acceptable copy, so Barker was called in.

47. Letter, Elsa Barker to REP, dated April 1, 1910. PFC. Barker worked from typed copies of Peary's diaries, not the originals.

48. Ibid; anonymous attachment to this letter, undated.

49. Letter, William Morrow to REP, dated April 15, 1910. PFC.

50. *Emporia* (Kansas) *Gazette,* undated clipping. PFC.

51. W.F. Thompson in August 1910, quoted in Cole, Terrance, *The Sourdough Expedition.* Anchorage: Alaska Northwest Publishing Company, 1985, page 9.

52. Unattributed news clipping, dated December 25, 1910. PFC.

53. BB, Diary, June 22, 1910. BBD. "Glacier Point" was Cook's appellation used in his book for the camp on the mossy shelf above the glacier, though in his diary he called it "Cerac pt." Ed Barrill named the snow-drifted hillock in the saddle next to Fake Peak "Glasier Point," misspelling it and drawing a picture of it in his diary, which appeared in facsimile in the NYG along with his diary on October 15, 1909 (see page 833).

54. BB, Diary, June 28, 1910. BBD.

55. CMM, page 169.

56. Rusk, C.E., "On the Trail of Dr. Cook," *Pacific Monthly,* January 1911, page 48.

57. Rusk, C.E., "On the Trail of Dr. Cook," *Pacific Monthly,* November 1910, page 483.

58. Letter, THH to REP, dated October 26, 1910. The peak Browne said Cook photographed is actually 19.48 miles from the summit of Mount McKinley.

A note on the financial arrangements of the Parker-Browne party

There are receipts for $4,511.40 in the PFC for this expedition and originals of several checks drawn by Browne on Hubbard's account at the Brooklyn Trust Company. The entire expedition cost approximately $8,000. Browne indicates this and that Hubbard paid $5,000 of it, in a letter, BB to THH, dated November 5, 1910. PFC. As to the balance, no records were seen other than a letter saying that Parker and Browne expected to pay for their own travel and personal expenses. Bridgman had pledged $3,000 to the Explorers Club expedition in 1909; perhaps he paid the difference.

59. The dialogue is from an unattributed newspaper article, dated April 23, 1910. PFC. Parker's remarks about Lloyd and his description of Cook's climb as "a glorious failure" are from another unattributed clipping of remarks made before the Explorers Club, rubber stamped "Oct.8.1910." PFC.

60. Rusk, C.E., "On the Trail of Dr. Cook," *Pacific Monthly,* November 1910, page 486.

61. Rusk, C.E., "On the Trail of Dr. Cook," *Pacific Monthly,* January 1911, pages 61–62.

Notes for Chapter 19: I Suppose I Am

1. Letter, Theodore Roosevelt to REP, dated December 23, 1910. PFC.

2. Letter, REP to THH, dated December 29, 1910. PFC.

3. NYT, March 6, 1910.

4. Letter, Frederick A. Stokes to REP, dated May 3, 1910. PFC.

5. Letter, REP to Frederick A. Stokes, dated July 12, 1910. PFC.

6. Letter, Frederick A. Stokes to William P. Northrup, quoted in letter, Frederick A. Stokes to REP, dated October 1, 1910. PFC.

7. Memorandum containing reports of Stokes's salesmen, dated November 15, 1910. PFC.

8. Letter, THH to REP, dated December 24, 1909. PFC.

9. Letter, Henry Gannett to THH, dated February 28, 1910. PFC.

10. Letter, Henry Gannett to THH, dated June 8, 1910. PFC.

11. NYT, February 10, 1910.

12. Quisenberry, A.C., "Dr. Cook. A Prophecy," unattributed newspaper clipping, undated. PFC.

13. What Bartlett found at Cape Sparbo is from a remembrance of Rainey contained in a logbook kept by Bartlett, Box 15. RBB.

A note on the Beothic

Every major source but one lists the name of this vessel as *Boethic,* including the contemporary newspaper accounts. This is incorrect. The ship is pictured in the NYT, September 17, 1910. In the photo the name can be seen on her bow, BEOTHIC, even though the caption reads "Boethic." The sealer was named *Beothic* after an extinct Indian tribe of Newfoundland, now commonly spelled Beothuk. Beothic is a variant spelling used in earlier times.

14. NYH, September 8, 1910.

15. Letter, CJN to REP, dated October 24, 1910. PFC.

16. Rainey, Paul J., "Bagging Arctic Monsters with Rope, Gun and Camera," *Cosmopolitan Magazine,* December 1910, pages 91–97. Of course, Cook had nothing to do with where his records were cached by Whitney and Bartlett.

17. In the *Chicago Daily News,* February 20, 1910, a story appeared saying Cook's records had been sent to the Police Museum in Copenhagen and filed there under "grand forgeries." This story was undoubtedly a press fabrication. In personal correspondence with the *Politihistorisk Selskab,* the police historical society, which operates the Police Historical Museum in Copenhagen, its detective superintendent found no record of ever having them. The *Rigsarkivet,* the Danish National Archives, assured the author that there was no evidence that any possibility regarding Cook's "proofs" considered by the University of Copenhagen suggested "even remotely, that the matter or the documents be handed over to the police." (Letters, H. Winther-Hinge to the author, dated February 16, 1993; Wilhelm von Rosen to the author, dated March 1, 1993.)

18. FAC, "Dr. Cook's Own Story," *Hampton's Magazine,* April 1911, pages 494–495.

19. NYT, March 13, 1910.

20. FAC, "Dr. Cook's Own Story," *Hampton's Magazine,* April 1911, pages 496–497. On July 10, 1910, the New York *World* gave its readers the first glimpse of the explorer in eight months when it printed a photo of the doctor taken by a patient reporter who had lain in wait outside his Santiago hotel, but that was the last to be seen of the elusive "Mr. Craig."

21. FAC, "Dr. Cook's Own Story," *Hampton's Magazine,* April 1911, page 499.

22. Letter, FAC to Marie Cook, dated April 19, 1910. On the stationery of the African Steamship Company; the ship's name appears to be the SS *Torquah.* FCC.

23. FAC, "Dr. Cook's Own Story," *Hampton's Magazine,* April 1911, page 500.

24. NYT, December 1, 1910; both quotes.

25. FAC, "Dr. Cook's Own Story," *Hampton's Magazine,* April 1911, page 501.

26. NYW, October 2, 1910. All details and quotations of the London interview come from this source.

27. Letter, J. Scott Keltie to REP, dated October 12, 1910. PFC. Besides Wack and Lonsdale, Cook had other visitors in London, including Ralph Shainwald and Rudolph Franke, who obtained an affidavit for his suit against Peary saying that the furs he claimed Peary had taken under duress were to be split 50-50 between him and Cook.

28. Letter, Ernest Marshall to William Reick, dated October 14, 1910; on London Office of the NYT stationery. PFC.

29. Memorandum from T. Everett Harré to AF, quoted in CDC, page 221.

30. Ibid.

31. Letter, Benjamin Hampton to REP, dated October 20, 1910. PFC.

32. FAC, "Dr. Cook's Own Story," *Hampton's Magazine,* January 1911, pages 51–52.

33. Miss Kiel's recollections of the events at *Hampton's Magazine,* including all of her transcribed quotations, are from an unpublished article by her entitled "The Faked 'Confession' or How a Magazine Made History!"; a 47-page typescript, dated February 14, 1916. FCC.

34. Letter, REP to CJN, dated December 6, 1910. PFC.

35. Letter, HLB to CJN, dated December 28, 1910. PFC.

36. NYW, December 23, 1910.

37. NYT, December 23, 1910.

38. Ibid; all quotes.

39. NYT, December 2, 1910.

40. *Detroit Free Press,* quoted in the NYT, December 3, 1910.

41. *Pittsburgh Gazette-Times,* quoted in the NYT, December 3, 1910.

42. *Current Literature,* January 1911, pages 18–20.

43. All details and quotations from the so-called Peary Hearings are taken from Helgesen, Henry T., "Analysis of Evidence' Presented by Robert E. Peary to Committee on Naval Affairs, 1910–11," Extension of Remarks, *Appendix to the Congressional Record,* 64th Congress, 1st session, January 25, 1916, which contains a verbatim transcript of the hearings, pages 268–327. These brief excerpts represent only a small portion of the testimony taken. In the quotations cited, a break in the text indicates a missing section of the testimony. Anyone concerned with the question of whether Peary really reached the North Pole should read this testimony in full.

44. A receipt for $280, dated March 18, 1911, paid by Peary to Mitchell for his services, is in the PFC. Mitchell conferred with Peary on a number of occasions at the Dresden on Connecticut Avenue in Washington, D.C., during the winter of 1910–11. Apparently, Peary worried over how their meetings might appear if they became known. "Not knowing what turn questioning might take in future hearings before the Congressional subcommittee," Mitchell said, "he would sometimes at the end of a conference caution me to think carefully over the facts of our visit and establish a clear mental record

thereof." On the day he testified, Mitchell says, Peary called him personally to thank him. Mitchell, Hugh C., "Peary at the North Pole," *U.S. Naval Institute Proceedings,* vol. 85, no. 4 (April 1959): 68–69.

The Royal Geographical Society's approval of Peary's "proofs" in the form of copies of the latitude observations taken on his polar journey was given only after the award of its special gold medal. It was hardly unanimous. After examining Peary's copies, a vote was taken on whether a letter of support should be sent to Peary by Leonard Darwin, the society's president. Of the 35 members of the RGS Council, 18 were absent, two abstained, and the letter was approved by a vote of eight to seven.

45. Letter, REP to THH, dated January 26, 1911. PFC.

46. "Recognition of Robert E. Peary, the Arctic Explorer," House of Representatives Report no. 1961, 61st Congress, 3d session. Washington, D.C.: GPO, 1911, page 22.

47. Macon, R.B., Speech before the House of Representatives, February 16, 1911, *Congressional Record,* 61st Congress, 3d session, vol. 46, part 3, pages 2701–2725; all quotations.

48. Letter, FAC to George E. Foss, dated January 10, 1911. BLC.

49. Letter, REP to THH, dated January 26, 1911. PFC.

50. Letters, REP to HLB, dated March 1, 1911; HLB to REP, dated March 2, 1911. PFC.

51. MAP, page 602.

52. Telegram, REP to THH, dated March 4, 1911. PFC.

53. NYT, December 26, 1910.

54. Letter, FAC to Carl Salomonsen, dated January 17, 1911. Quoted in *Beretning angaaende Cook-Sagens ydre Forløb,* copy of unpaged typescript obtained by the author from the University of Copenhagen. The notebook was returned to Walter Lonsdale on January 30, 1911, under a power of attorney granted to him by Cook on December 13, 1910, but whether the other material was returned is unknown. Inquiries to Denmark turned up no trace of them in the Police Historical Society, the National Archives, the Royal Library, the Astronomical Observatory Library, the Library of the University of Copenhagen or its archives. However, the Danes made a copy of Cook's notebook before returning it to Lonsdale. The original has not turned up. (Letter, Wilhelm von Rosen to the author, March 1, 1993.)

55. Letter, REP to THH, dated January 26, 1911. PFC.

56. All descriptions and all quotes are taken from the anonymous stenographer's record and critique of Cook's lecture at the Manhattan Theatre, dated February 13, 1911. PFC.

57. Letter, THH to REP, dated February 16, 1911. PFC. On the same day, Peary wrote to Hubbard about reports that Rudolph Franke was in New York. The *Herald* had it that he would lead an expedition to Greenland. Peary suspected this was more of Bennett's propaganda and that if Franke went north at all, it would be to "discover" Cook's lost records and "bring down, for

purposes of exhibition, certain of the eskimos." Peary was sure the ultimate purpose was to derail his recognition by Congress. PFC.

58. Letter, REP to HLB, dated April 1, 1911. PFC.

59. Typescript of this letter labeled "copied April 12, 1911." PFC.

60. Letter, REP to HLB, dated April 5, 1911. PFC.

61. FAC, Signed typescript of lecture, undated, but contents date it to early 1911. FCD.

62. Letter, THH to REP, dated March 2, 1911. PFC.

63. "The Wonderful Adventures of Dr. Cook," *Living Age,* July 6, 1912, pages 30–36.

64. Letter, REP to HLB, dated November 2, 1911. PFC.

65. Letter, CJN to REP, dated February 7, 1911. PFC.

66. Stokes-Peary correspondence, 1911. PFC.

67. NYT, September 3, 1911.

68. All quotes are from "Cook's Big Success," translation of an article from *Dagens Express* (Copenhagen), October 25, 1911. Translation attached to original newspaper. CSC.

69. Letter, Thorvald Mikkelsen to HLB, dated October 24, 1911. PFC. Which version of Cook's performance is true? Of this incident Maurice Francis Egan said in his memoirs, "His lecture occasioned a very unpleasant fracas, although his friends were in a majority in the lecture hall." Egan went on to assert that the crown prince still did not think Cook a faker, and many ordinary Danes still believed in him as well, but his failure to return to Etah to retrieve his evidence eventually eroded their confidence. (Egan, Maurice Francis, *Recollections of a Happy Life.* New York: George H. Doran Co., 1924, page 272.) It will also be noted that Cook had no need of a carriage to reach his hotel, which was just across the street from the hall.

70. NYT, October 26, 1911.

71. Letter, THH to REP, dated November 18, 1911. PFC.

72. Letter, REP to CJN, dated November 21, 1911. PFC.

Notes for Chapter 20: Veritas

1. High, Fred, "The Man against the System," *Platform,* vol. ii, no. 12, April 1912, unpaged.

2. *Arizona Republican* (Phoenix), April 25, 1911.

3. *Red Oak* (Iowa) *Express,* August 16, 1911.

4. *Kansas City Times,* August 3, 1911.

5. *Evening Republican* (Columbus, Indiana), August 12, 1911.

6. Letter, E.C. Stellhorn to William Koch, dated July 27, 1911. FCC.

7. *Yankton* (South Dakota) *Press and Dakotan,* July (date unknown) 1911.

8. Letter, REP to HLB, dated March 13, 1912.

9. All these comments are from Peary's North Pole Diary. The diary is a notebook, bound at the top. The lower pages are filled with the journey's running narrative; the upper pages are devoted to notes. More than a third

of all the writing in the diary is devoted to such notes as these. Original restricted, microfilm copy examined. PFC.

10. Letter, REP to HLB, dated April 4, 1912. PFC. Peary's original sketch for the medal is also in the PFC.

11. Letter, REP to THH, dated March 11, 1912. PFC.

12. Letter, REP to HLB, dated March 21, 1912. PFC.

13. Letter, REP to HLB, dated March 29, 1912. PFC.

14. Letter, HLB to REP, dated December 21, 1912. PFC.

15. Letter, REP to HLB, dated March 16, 1912. PFC.

16. TSP, vol. 1, page 24.

17. Letter, THH to HLB, dated February 27, 1912. PFC.

18. Letter, DBM to HLB, dated November 25, 1909. PFC.

19. Letter, REP to THH, dated April 29, 1912. PFC.

20. Undated review excerpt from the *Wesphalian Merkur*, printed at the back of Franke's book. Translation by Dr. Thomas Walker.

21. Undated review excerpt from *Das Wissen*, printed at the back of Franke's book. Translation by Dr. Thomas Walker.

22. The information about Cook's 1912 European tour is from the NYT, May 5, 1912; the itinerary comes from AF notes. CSC.

23. "Honors to Amundsen and Peary," *National Geographic Magazine*, January 1913, pages 113–130.

24. Cook's letter, dated September 26, 1912, is printed in a 1913 interview of Clark Brown by Thomas C. Stowell, in a Sunday magazine of an unidentified Albany newspaper, probably the *Albany Knickerbocker*. The account of the Bridgman interview also comes from this source. Typescript copy in CSC.

25. *Los Angeles Times*, February 11, 1913.

26. Letter, Raymond P. Tarr to HLB, dated January 24, 1913. PFC. The description of Cook's lecture is also from this letter. He had written to Bridgman with a similar proposal in October 1909.

27. Letter, Melville E. Stone to HLB, dated February 5, 1913. PFC.

28. Los Angeles *Record*, February 10, 1913.

29. *Los Angeles Times*, February 11, 1913.

30. Los Angeles *Record*, February 10, 1913.

31. Telegram, HLB to REP, dated February 11, 1913. PFC.

32. Letter, THH to HLB, dated April 19, 1913. PFC.

33. Hubbard, Thomas H., "To Students of Polar Exploration." Reprinted from *Acts of the 10th International Congress of Geography, Rome, 1913*, pages 683–684.

34. Letter, REP to THH, dated June 13, 1913. PFC.

35. Letter, Robert A. Bartlett to REP, dated July 16, 1913. PFC.

36. Letter, REP to THH, dated November 12, 1913. PFC.

37. Letter, REP to HLB, dated July 4, 1913. PFC.

38. Stuck, Hudson, *The Ascent of Denali (Mount McKinley)*. New York: Charles Scribner's Sons, 1914, pages 165–166. In his private correspondence

Stuck called Cook "the great fraud," "the monumental liar and faker" and "that rascal" and during the Polar Controversy railed against his "impudent attempt to filch the last great prize of geographical exploration," which "belonged to another." (Correspondence of Hudson Stuck with John Wilson Wood: Domestic and Foreign Missionary Society, Alaska Papers, Archives and Historical Collections, Episcopal Church, Austin, Texas, cited in Dean, David M., *Breaking Trail: Hudson Stuck of Texas and Alaska.* Athens: Ohio University Press, 1988.)

39. *Fairbanks Daily Times,* June 21, 1913. Karstens was not on the best of terms with Stuck during the climb, but as Stuck admitted in his diary, "I am so dependent upon him in this expedition that I have to put up with any bad temper he may show." Stuck had to be literally hauled up the last approach to the summit and upon reaching it blacked out. After the climb, Karstens was bitterly jealous of all the attention Stuck got, and although Stuck divided the profits from his lectures and book with Karstens and acknowledged his role in their success, this did not satisfy Karstens, who called him a "liar" and a "sneak." Soon after the climb, in August 1913, Karstens lamented to the naturalist Charles Sheldon, with whom he had explored the northern slopes but whom he could not persuade to attempt an ascent, "Sheldon 'O' Sheldon, why dident you come . . . why shouldent I have a *man* with me one worthy of the [ascent] and not an absolute paresite and liar." Perhaps Karstens was put off by Stuck's bookishness or noticed his homosexual and pedophilic tendencies, which Stuck repeatedly reveals in his diaries, but which the archdeacon's biographer, David M. Dean, maintains were strictly unconsummated. These excerpts of Karstens's correspondence and Stuck's diaries can be found in Dean's book, *Breaking Trail: Hudson Stuck of Texas and Alaska,* Athens: Ohio University Press, 1988.

40. High lampooned the National Geographic Society, saying that although it boasted of a committee that approved each applicant for membership, in fact, anyone with $2 was welcome to join this "society." To prove it he signed up a dog named Bronte, Balsamo the "talking skull," and John Walrus, a stuffed head on the wall of his office in Steinway Hall in Chicago. This exposé appeared in *Platform,* vol. vi, no. 1, December 1915.

41. *Benton Harbor* (Michigan) *News-Palladium,* November 19, 1913.

42. *Daily Leader* (Benton Harbor, Michigan), November 19, 1913.

43. Ibid.

44. Letter, Victor M. Gore to REP, dated November 21, 1913. PFC.

45. *St. Joseph Evening Herald,* November 25, 1913. There is a paper, dated at Annoatok, April 21, 1909, signed by Cook in the PFC. It lists goods "taken from my supplies – and Mr. Murphy – has returned similar goods of like amounts from his supplies." Whether this constitutes a "receipt" is a matter of semantics.

46. Letter, REP to THH, dated December 5, 1913. PFC.

47. Letter, Victor M. Gore to REP, dated December 16, 1913.

48. *Benton Harbor* (Michigan) *News-Palladium,* November 19, 1913.

49. Telegram, REP to THH, dated December 16, 1913. PFC.

50. Numerous bills for services of the Burns Detective Agency are in the PFC. Apparently, Hubbard paid all of them. A typical charge would be that of July 1914—$290.52.

51. Letter, Ralph Shainwald to Miles Poindexter, dated December 31, 1913; photostat. CSC. Shainwald said that 60 pages had been clipped from one notebook and 15 from another. In a contemporaneous press interview, Bridgman denied he had seen Baldwin recently.

52. *Minneapolis Journal,* December 20, 1913.

53. NYT, December 28, 1913. No trace of the copy of Baldwin's manuscript marked up by Cook was located in the BLC, though there was a clean copy.

54. NYS, December 23, 1913; both quotes. According to a letter from G.W. Baker to Clark Brown, dated January 8, 1914, the whole scene between Cook and Baldwin at the Prince George was secretly being recorded: "We have a record of his conversation with Dr. Cook which was taken by means of stenographers connected by secret wires to the Doctor's room. This and other evidence will be brought to light whenever we deem it advisable." This record has yet to see that light. CSC.

55. NYS, January 1, 1914.

56. Washington *Evening Star,* January 26, 1914.

57. *Washington Post,* January 4, 1914.

58. Letter, REP to THH, dated January 11, 1914. PFC. Baldwin said the report of his remarks about Cook was inaccurate in a letter to the NYT that appeared in its pages on December 29, 1913, and insisted that he still intended to give Cook a fair shake: "Perhaps no one better than myself fully understands what it means to give an impartial expression of opinion, owing to the pressure of politics or personal prejudice, and yet this I shall do. I believe in giving even to the devil his dues." In the NYT of December 31, 1913, Baldwin made good his promise: "The comparative evidence would seem to indicate that Dr. Cook reached latitude 88 degrees 21 minutes north—the northern termination of the 'glacial ice,' as described in his original dispatch."

59. Letter, REP to THH, dated February 23, 1914. PFC.

60. *Pittsburgh Leader,* April 26, 1914.

61. Letter, Constantin Brun to THH, dated April 11, 1914. PFC.

62. Letter, FAC to members of Congress, dated May 20, 1914. FCC.

63. New York *Morning Telegraph,* May 25, 1914. Cook filed suit May 23, 1914.

64. Letter, REP to THH, dated May 22, 1914. PFC.

65. Letter, Rudolph Franke to the secretary of the Department of Justice, dated May 19, 1914. FCC.

66. Letter, Josephus Daniels to Charles B. Smith, undated, printed in *Appendix to the Congressional Record,* March 5, 1915, page 838.

67. Letter, Edward S. Brooke to Miles Poindexter, dated March 9, 1914. FCC.

68. Letter, Ejnar Mikkelsen to FAC, undated. FCC. Ejnar was Thorvald's brother—the man who had sent the negative report on Cook's 1911 performance in Copenhagen to HLB.

69. Letter, Miles Poindexter to LA, dated June 12, 1914. PFC.

70. Letter, LA to Luke Lea, dated June 5, 1914, quoting Cook's advertising matter "from two or three years ago." PFC.

71. Letter, REP to THH, dated July 8, 1914. PFC.

72. Letter, LA to THH, dated July 11, 1914; both quotes. PFC.

73. These letters are dated July 20, 1914. PFC.

74. Many such messages in cipher from Burns's New York office can be found in the PFC.

75. From existing Peary files a detailed, and almost daily, itinerary of Cook's movements for the period July to December 1914 can be constructed; see Peary-Hubbard correspondence. PFC.

76. Letter, Hugh J. Lee to THH, dated August 2, 1914. PFC.

77. Details of his route are contained in a letter from DBM to "Mr. Brainard," dated August 25, 1914. DMB.

78. In his diary MacMillan tells of the condition of his dogs as growing worse from April 14 onward. DMB.

79. Details of the journey toward Crocker Land are taken from MacMillan's original diary, not his published articles or subsequent book, which differ as to distances and other details. DMB.

80. DBM, Diary, April 21, 1914. DMB.

81. DBM, Diary, April 23, 1914. DMB. Green placed them by sextant reading at $82°11'1.25"$—120 miles true west of north from Cape Thomas Hubbard. At this point, the magnetic variation was 178 degrees westerly.

82. Ibid.

83. Letter, REP to THH, dated August 3, 1914. PFC.

84. REP, Memorandum, dated October 17, 1914. PFC. Actually, Cook was not expelled from the Explorers Club. His name was dropped for nonpayment of dues.

85. Newark *Star and Advertiser,* September 14, 1914, lists the bill.

86. Letter, DBM to THH, dated December 11, 1914. PFC.

87. Letter, REP to DBM, dated July 7, 1915. PFC.

Notes for Chapter 21: A Perversion of History

An account of the world trip of 1915–16 is contained in "Battling around the World in War-Time," which Cook apparently wrote in 1916. All details of this trip not directly quoted are from this lengthy typescript. A number of the details and dates have been adjusted, however, using the sketch diary Cook kept on the trip. The diary has entries from June 8, 1915, to December 12, 1915. It is a leather-bound $3\frac{1}{2}$-by-6-inch Bee-Vee diary with "1915" printed in gold on its dark green cover. The entries are very sketchy, mostly in telegraphic phrases and reminders. Details between the diary and the manuscript vary considerably. Where there was a choice, the diary was taken as the authority. Cook later wrote articles about this trip for the prison newspaper at Leavenworth in the 1920s. Frank P. Thompson wrote a summary of the trip for Mr. and Mrs. Thomas Aspell in a letter, dated February 26, 1953. FCC. This gives a few additional details but also conflicts with other accounts, perhaps due to the passage of time.

BAW   FAC, "Battling around the World in War-Time." Typescript in six parts, c. 1916 by content. FCC.

1. H. Resolution 709. 63d Congress, 3d session.
2. Caraway, Thaddeus H., "The Attack on Dr. Frederick A. Cook," Extension of Remarks, *Appendix to the Congressional Record,* 63d Congress, 3d session, March 4, 1915, pages 670–685, reprints the minutes of this hearing. All details and quotes are taken from this source.
3. Letter, LA to THH, dated February 2, 1915. PFC.
4. Letter, LA to THH, dated March 4, 1915. PFC. This letter contains all the details of Alexander's dealings with Fess, how he wrote the speech and all of the quotations.
5. Letter, LA to THH, dated April 9, 1915. PFC.
6. How the minutes were obtained is taken from AF notes. CSC.
7. Alexander's plan was sent to General Hubbard in a letter dated April 27, 1915. PFC.
8. Letter, LA to THH, dated April 22, 1915. PFC.
9. A copy of Peary's sworn statement, dated December 9, 1912, is in the PFC. It reads: "I, ROBERT E. PEARY, the defendant herein, swear before God, the Almighty and Allknowing that: "I did not tell the plaintiff in August 1908 at Etah, that I would only take him onto my ship "Eric" and return him to New York provided he would give me his entire collection of blue fox skins, navalhorns and walrus' teeth, which the plaintiff and Dr. Cook co-jointly had collected, without any pecuniary consideration. SO HELP ME GOD."
10. A commission had been sent to Canada and the United States to hear testimony from various witnesses, including Cook himself. During his interview on June 15, 1911, Peary's lawyer reported, he had gotten Cook to say under oath, after some reluctance, that he was the Cook who claimed to have reached the North Pole in 1908, adding, "And I did go there," much to the lawyer's delight. (Letter, Mr. Griffith of Joline, Larken & Rathbone, lawyers, to CJN, dated June 15, 1911. PFC.)
11. Letter, LA to REP, dated April 17, 1915. PFC.
12. Letter, LA to REP, dated April 9, 1915. PFC.
13. *Chicago Tribune,* undated clipping c. April 1915. FCC.

14. Letter, LA to REP, dated May 11, 1915; both quotes. PFC.

15. Letter, LA to REP, dated June 3, 1915. PFC.

16. Prospectus for the Orient Film Company. FCC.

17. FAC, "The Call of the World's Highest Peak," page 1; typescript. FCC.

18. An accounting of the Orient Film Company's finances was obtained from legal papers in the FCC.

19. BAW, part 1, pages 7–9.

20. Letter, Frank P. Thompson to Olivia Thompson, dated August 15, 1915. FCC.

21. BAW, part 3, pages 8–9.

22. BAW, part 4, pages 6–7.

23. FAC, "Wild Men and Wild Women," *Leavenworth New Era,* November 1927.

24. BAW, part 4, page 13.

25. BAW, part 6, pages 3–4.

26. ———*Advertiser, Tokyo,* November 27, 1915. The clipping does not have the complete name of the paper. FCC.

27. BAW, part 6, page 13.

28. NYT, December 19, 1915.

29. NYT, December 29, 1915.

30. BAW, part 6, pages 13–14.

31. Letter, LA to HLB, dated January 27, 1916. PFC.

32. Ibid.

33. Letter, Adolphus W. Greely to Henry Helgesen, dated February 17, 1916, printed in *Appendix to the Congressional Record,* 64th Congress, 1st session, July 21, 1916, page 1645.

34. Letter, A.A. Veblen to Henry Helgesen, dated April 3, 1916, printed in *Appendix to the Congressional Record,* 64th Congress, 1st session, July 21, 1916, page 1646.

35. Letter, Julius Meyer to Henry Helgesen, dated January 24, 1916, printed in *Appendix to the Congressional Record,* 64th Congress, 1st session, July 21, 1916, page 1645.

36. Goodsell protested Cook's lecture when he visited Goodsell's hometown, New Kensington, Pennsylvania, in 1912, saying Cook's version of Franke's treatment at Peary's hands was false, but he later furnished Franke with material for his book after he fell out with Peary in 1914. Goodsell also corresponded with Cook directly, after this date, and asked Cook to use his connections to get him a position on another arctic expedition.

37. Letter, Etta Rost to "Girlie" (possibly, but not certainly, from content, Lilian Kiel), dated February 20, 1916; both quotes. FCC. Some confusion may result from the dates mentioned. Helgesen's speech is dated January 25, 1916, but was printed in the February 12, 1916, *Congressional Record.*

38. Helgesen, Henry T., "Peary and the North Pole," Extension of Remarks, *Appendix to the Congressional Record,* 64th Congress, 1st session,

July 21, 1916, page 1646. Like the previous speech, this one is dated earlier than the issue of the *Congressional Record* in which it originally appeared—August 3, 1916. Ross never approached closer than five miles to Meteorite Island and did not describe the meteors there, though he suspected a meteor might have been the origin of the iron knives the natives had.

39. Letter, LA to REP, dated September 23, 1916. PFC.

40. *New York Tribune,* September 22, 1916.

41. Letter, LA to REP, dated September 23, 1916. PFC.

42. From blurbs along the left-hand margin of the stationery printed for the Orient Film Company. FCC.

43. Letter, John W. Ruskin to FAC, dated October 8, 1916. FCC.

44. Circular, after November 8, 1916, dated by a testimonial it contains. FCC.

45. *New York Tribune,* October 24, 1916.

46. Helgesen, Henry T., "Dr. Cook and the North Pole," Extension of Remarks, *Appendix to the Congressional Record,* 64th Congress, 2nd session, September 4, 1916, page 42.

47. Ibid., page 43.

48. Ibid., page 70.

49. Letter, LA to REP, dated December 14, 1916. PFC.

50. See Mitchell, Hugh C., "The Discovery of the North Pole," 44-page typescript, inscribed "Washington, 1916." PFC.

51. Letter, LA to REP, dated March 3, 1917. PFC.

52. Letter, REP to Simeon D. Fess, dated March 8, 1917. PFC.

53. REP, Memorandum, dated September 10, 1916. PFC.

54. REP, Memorandum, dated September 23, 1916. PFC.

55. Letter, Congressman Helgesen's secretary to Mene Wallace, dated October 26, 1916, quoted in Harper, Kenn, *Give Me My Father's Body.* Ontario: Blacklead Books, 1986, page 212.

56. On September 2, 1910, Mene had written to his friend Chester Beecroft, telling of his life since leaving civilization: "Peary had them land me at North Star Bay along way south of my home. We had to sign their agreement, you remember, that I would land when Peary said, but they promised in return for the black-hand papers they made you sign, to take me back to Etah.

"But as they had broke faith and human rule with me when I was there stolen gest I was not surprised when they dump me off, by Peary's orders, in a strange part of Greenland, with no furs, gun, sleg dogs, or equipment to battle for life in the desolit ice. . . .

". . . I know you will expect something about Cook. Well, Dob, I have gone to the bottom of the matter. No one up here believes that Peary got much farther than when he left his party. His name up here is hated for his cruelty. Cook made a great trip North. He has nothing in the way of proofs here that I can find. I believe that he went as near as anyone, but the pole has yet to be found. Cook is loved by all, and every Eskimo speaks well of him and hopes that he has the honor over Peary—has he? I will know all soon and will let you know.

"I don't think both ends and the middle of the earth are worth the price that has been paid to almost find one pole. See all the white bones. Where is my father? Why am I no longer fit to live where I was born? Not fit to live where I was kidnapped? Why am I an experiment there and here—and tormented since the great white Pirat interfered with nature and made a failure and left me helpless orfin—young, abandoned 10,000 miles from home?"

The letter was read into the testimony of the Peary hearings and published in the *Appendix to the Congressional Record* for January 25, 1916, pages 323–324. The letter originally was published in the NYW, December 23, 1910.

True to his deal with Herbert Bridgman, Royal Fuller, the *Herald* reporter on the *Jeanie,* in exchange for "the rights," published just what Peary approved—that Mene had been put ashore after being generously supplied with a fine set of equipment.

Today, from one of the shelves in the Tower storage room in the American Museum of Natural History on Central Park, the life masks of the dead Mene and his long-lamented father stare back with unhappy expressions.

Notes for Chapter 22: *The Meanest Men in the World*

HNPBD   Hall, Thomas F., *Has the North Pole Been Discovered?* Boston: R.G. Badger, 1917.

1. The details of Cook's experiences in Wyoming are taken largely from AF notes, which he made from interviews with Cook in the 1930s. Most of these are unverifiable and are used advisedly in the absence of any more reliable information. A few additional details are taken from Cook's trial testimony contained in CR 2273, *United States v. Frederick A. Cook, et al.* SBA. A copy of the four-page Rocky Mountain Sheep Association tract entitled "What About the Future?" is, like the Freeman notes, in the CSC. Wool was needed in vast amounts for uniforms during the war. It was estimated that over 750,000 yards would be required just to make the rank chevrons through the end of the 1919 fiscal year.

2. *Chicago Daily News,* October 18, 1917.

3. HNPBD, page 460.

4. HNPBD, page 461.

5. The local color of Fort Worth during the oil boom is depicted in "Sudden Wealth and Other Troubles Where Oil Makes or Breaks Men," *Literary Digest,* April 10, 1920, pages 59–60.

6. *Wichita Falls Times,* May 19, 1919. Written on by Robert A. Bartlett. PFC.

7. Quoted in REP, *Secrets of Polar Travel*. New York: Century Co., 1917, page 274. The letter is said to have been written in September 1917; date and addressee unspecified.

8. Letter, REP to "Mrs. Bates," dated May 28, 1918. PFC.

9. This quote and all the other information on the history of the Texas Eagles, unless otherwise indicated, are from the FWP, February 24, 1923. A typescript of the annual report is in the CSC.

10. The information on oil promotion schemes comes from the personal recollections of participants in the oil boom recorded in *Research Data for Fort Worth and Tarrant County, Texas,* Texas Writers Project, Fort Worth Public Library Unit, 1941, pages 1883–1894, preserved at the Fort Worth Public Library. Stamps's recollections are on page 1894.

11. *Seattle Daily Times,* September 9, 1912.

12. VS, *Discovery.* New York: McGraw-Hill Book Co., 1964, page 137. Amundsen made various criticisms of Stefansson in his memoirs published in Norwegian. Some of these were cut out or softened in the English version of MLE.

13. Letter, REP to Henry Bryant, dated January 9, 1919. PFC.

14. HLB, "Peary," *Natural History,* vol. 20 (1920): 11.

15. HLB, Remarks at the Peary Memorial Meeting of the Explorers Club, March 12, 1920; quoting Kenneth Sills. PFC.

16. Philadelphia *Evening Bulletin,* February 21, 1920.

17. The dealings with Ferry are contained in a letter, FAC to Frank P. Thompson, dated October 21, 1920, which attaches a letter, LeRoy Ferry to President, The Texas Eagle Oil & Refining Company, dated September 1, 1920, proposing the deal, and also Bradstreet's report. CSC.

18. Letter, FAC to Frank P. Thompson, dated March 23, 1921. FCC.

19. *Fort Worth Record,* January 20, 1922.

20. "A Memorial to Peary," *National Geographic Magazine,* June 1922, pages 641–643.

21. Letter, FAC to Frank P. Thompson, dated March 15, 1922. CSC.

22. CR 2273, vol. 23, pages 165–166. SBA.

23. The information on Cox's history is taken from Washburn, Watson and Edmund S. DeLong, *High and Low Financiers.* Indianapolis: Bobbs-Merrill Co., 1932.

24. From personal recollections of the oil boom preserved in *Research Data for Fort Worth and Tarrant County, Texas,* Texas Writers Project, Fort Worth Public Library Unit, 1941, page 1894.

25. Quoted from Howard, Sidney, "Oil Crooks," clipped from an unidentified magazine, page 33. Dated by content to 1923. CSC.

26. Barnes, John K., "Doctor Cook's Discovery of Oil," *World's Work,* April 1923, pages 614–615.

27. *Texas Oil World* (Fort Worth, Texas), January 25, 1923.

28. NYT, January 11, 1923.

29. Letter, FAC to C.H. Delander, dated January 31, 1923. CR 2273, vol. 13, pages 7–12, Government exhibit 564. SBA.

30. FWP, November 16, 1922.

31. *Fort Worth Record,* January 30, 1923; FWP, February 1, 1923. A check of the Tarrant County Records Office failed to disclose any stated grounds for the divorce. It was uncontested, and the file contained only routine paperwork and a copy of the decree. The number of the decree is 62669, granted March 8, 1923, and issued April 3, 1923.

32. FWP, February 2, 1923.

33. FWP, February 8, 1923.

34. FWP, February 9, 1923.

35. FWP, February 17, 1923.

36. All details of the hearing are from the FWP, February 17, 1923.

37. FWP, February 23, 1923.

38. Letter, FAC to Frank P. Thompson, dated February 23, 1923. CSC.

39. From the indictment against the officers of PPA. SBA.

40. FWP, May 15, 1923.

41. Joseph Bailey's career is covered in Acheson, Sam Hanna, *Joe Bailey, the Last Democrat.* New York: Macmillan Co., 1932.

42. Letter, John S. Pratt to John H.W. Crim, dated May 26, 1923. RG 60, File 36-194. National Archives.

43. Letter, David Cahill to John H.W. Crim, dated May 26, 1923. RG 60, File 36-194. National Archives.

44. Letter, Henry Zweifel to John H.W. Crim, dated July 28, 1923. RG 60, File 36-194. National Archives.

45. Coded telegram, Henry Zweifel to John H.W. Crim, dated August 16, 1923. RG 60, File 36-194. National Archives.

46. The account of the pretrial maneuvers are from the testimony of Henry Zweifel, CR 2273, vol. 30. SBA.

Notes for Chapter 23: At the Head of the Fraudists

Unless noted otherwise, every incident in the trial itself is taken from the trial record, Federal District Court, Northern District of Texas, CR 2273, *United States v. Frederick A. Cook, et al.* The record is preserved at the National Archives, Southwest Branch, Fort Worth, Texas. It consists of approximately 12,000 typed, legal-sized sheets in 31 volumes, one for each day of the trial.

The trial record is incomplete. Missing from it is volume 2, which contained the first government exhibits including, most unfortunately, exhibit 1, which was the Declaration of Trust of PPA. What is known of this document comes from references to it in the rest of the trial, particularly the charge to the jury, and Judge Killits's private correspondence. Volume 2 also contained the defense's opening arguments. Excerpts of these are found in the local newspapers, but a comparison of the reports of the trial with the actual transcript shows that the newspaper quotes are only approximations or paraphrases of the actual testimony. Volume 2 was missing when the record was transferred to the Archives from the Federal Record Center in 1953, and its disposition is unknown. Also missing are the closing arguments. The reason for this is not clear, but they may have been felt to have been irrelevant to any appeal and were not reproduced in the full typescript from the court stenographer's notes. For whatever reason, volume 31 consists only of Judge Killits's 98-page charge to the jury.

The following abbreviations are adopted below:

DE   Defense exhibit
GE   Government exhibit

1. FWP, October 15, 1923.
2. FWST, October 16, 1923. Reprinted by permission.
3. From the indictment against the officers of PPA, page 12. SBA.
4. CR 2273, vol. 3, pages 19–20. Undated circular, GE 15-A.
5. CR 2273, vol. 3, page 41. Undated circular, GE 18.
6. CR 2273, vol. 3, pages 58–60. Letter, dated October 28, 1922, GE 19.
7. CR 2273, vol. 3, pages 77–79. Letter, dated November 4, 1922, GE 21.
8. CR 2273, vol. 3, page 108. Letter, dated December 12, 1922, GE 26.
9. CR 2273, vol. 3, pages 121–127. Letter, dated December 22, 1922, GE 28.
10. CR 2273, vol. 3, pages 131–132. Letter, dated January 6, 1923, GE 29.
11. CR 2273, vol. 3, page 140.
12. CR 2273, vol. 3, pages 151–152. Letter, dated January 18, 1923, GE 31.
13. CR 2273, vol. 3, pages 170–173. Circular, dated January 16, 1923. GE 47.
14. CR 2273, vol. 3, page 104.
15. CR 2273, vol. 4, page 28.
16. CR 2273, vol. 5, pages 96–99. Letter, dated February 20, 1923, GE 83.
17. CR 2273, vol. 5, page 234.
18. CR 2273, vol. 5, page 237.
19. CR 2273, vol. 5, page 238.
20. CR 2273, vol. 5, page 240; both quotes.
21. Letter, John M. Killits to George Hahn, dated October 19, 1923, partial typed transcript. SCD.
22. CR 2273, vol. 7, page 225.
23. CR 2273, vol. 8, pages 22–23.
24. Telegram, Henry Zweifel to John H.W. Crim, dated October 25, 1923. RG 60, File 36-194, National Archives.
25. CR 2273, vol. 12, page 84.
26. CR 2273, vol. 12, page 149.
27. CR 2273, vol. 14, page 17.
28. CR 2273, vol. 14, page 28.

29. CR 2273, vol. 14, pages 28–30.

30. CR 2273, vol. 14, pages 105–107.

31. CR 2273, vol. 14, page 111.

32. CR 2273, vol. 14, page 117.

33. CR 2273, vol. 14, page 272.

34. The judge must have been a great admirer of Dickens's. Pecksniff was the notorious hypocrite from *Martin Chuzzlewit;* the rest are from *David Copperfield.* Spenlow and Jorkins were lawyers, Spenlow using Jorkins's obdurate and ruthless reputation to excuse his failure to act. Uriah Heep was Mr. Wickfield's swindling clerk, described as a cadaverous, red-haired, ostentatious hypocrite.

35. Letter, John M. Killits to George Hahn, dated November 5, 1923, partial typed transcript. SCD.

36. CR 2273, vol. 18, pages 393–395.

37. CR 2273, vol. 19, page 75.

38. FWST, November 7, 1923.

39. CR 2273, vol. 21, page 133.

40. All of these figures can be found in the tables presented in volume 22 of the trial record.

41. CR 2273, vol. 22, page 165.

42. CR 2273, vol. 22, page 166.

43. CR 2273, vol. 22, page 177.

44. CR 2273, vol. 23, pages 165–172.

45. CR 2273, vol. 23, page 172.

46. CR 2273, vol. 23, page 198.

47. CR 2273, vol. 25, page 2, DE 16.

48. CR 2273, vol. 25, page 10.

49. CR 2273, vol. 25, page 46.

50. CR 2273, vol. 25, pages 47–51.

51. CR 2273, vol. 25, page 58.

52. Ibid.

53. CR 2273, vol. 26, page 21.

54. CR 2273, vol. 26, page 38.

55. Ibid.

56. CR 2273, vol. 26, page 45.

57. CR 2273, vol. 26, pages 58–59.

58. CR 2273, vol. 26, page 106.

59. CR 2273, vol. 26, page 177.

60. CR 2273, vol. 27, page 18.

61. CR 2273, vol. 27, page 75.

62. CR 2273, vol. 28, page 242.

63. CR 2273, vol. 28, page 244.

64. CR 2273, vol. 28, pages 250–252.

65. Letter, John M. Killits to George Hahn, dated November 16, 1923, partial typed transcript. SCD.

66. CR 2273, vol. 30, pages 42–43.

67. CR 2273, vol. 30, pages 44–47.

68. The accounts of the closing arguments are from the FWST, November 19–20, 1923, and the FWP, November 21, 1923.

69. CR 2273, vol. 31, pages 24–25; both quotes.

70. CR 2273, vol. 31, page 27.

71. CR 2273, vol. 31, pages 48–52.

72. CR 2273, vol. 31, pages 55–56.

73. CR 2273, vol. 31, page 61.

74. FAC, "The Prince of Liars," *American Weekly,* August 9, 1925.

75. Accounts of the sentences are from *Dallas Morning News,* November 22, 1923; FWST, November 21, 1923; FWP, November 22, 1923. Killits's speech to Cook as presented here is a synthesis of all three of these accounts, which vary considerably, plus material contained in CDC. What, exactly, the judge did say is unknown. The trial transcript does not contain it, and the author was assured by letter that it is not elsewhere among the holdings of the SBA.

76. FWP, November 22, 1923.

77. Ibid.

78. Ibid.

79. NYT, November 23, 1923; both quotes.

80. FWST, November 22, 1923.

81. *Beaumont* (Texas) *Enterprise,* date unspecified, quoted in "Dr. Cook's New Usefulness," *Literary Digest,* December 8, 1923, page 10.

82. "Barnum and Cook," *Nation,* vol. 117, December 5, 1923, page 624. © 1923, 1951, The Nation Company, Inc.

Notes for Chapter 24: The New Era

Cook's experiences in Leavenworth are drawn from his extensive prison writings. Chief among these are his finished manuscript, "Out of the Jungle," and its drafts and notes. Incidents not specifically attributed can be found in these materials. "Essay for *The New Era*" refers to typed or handwritten drafts intended for the prison's paper but not necessarily published there.

OOJ   FAC, "Out of the Jungle," finished typescript. FCC.

1. FWP, December 5, 1923.

2. Letter, FAC to Helen Cook, dated December 20, 1923. FCC.

3. Letter, FAC to Ruth Cook, dated December 20, 1923. CSC.

4. FWP, June 6, 1925.

5. HCP, chapter 1, pages 2–3. FCC.

6. *Research Data for Fort Worth and Tarrant County, Texas.* Texas Writers Project, Fort Worth Public Library Unit, 1941, page 1185.

7. Barnes, John K., "Doctor Cook's Discovery of Oil," *World's Work,* April 1923, page 615.

8. Letter, Henry Zweifel to Attorney General Donnovan, dated March 4, 1924, appending a letter from J.A. Feagin to Henry Zweifel of the same date. RG 60, File 36-194. National Archives.

9. Letter, John S. Pratt to Earl J. Davis, dated March 7, 1924. RG 60, File 36-194. National Archives.

10. *United States v. Frederick A. Cook, et al.,* Opinion of the Court, May 7, 1924, page 10. SBA.

11. Ibid., pages 4–5. SBA.

12. FWP, May 7, 1924.

13. FWP, June 10, 1924.

14. FWP, August 23, 1924.

15. Letter, James C. Wilson to Harlan F. Stone, dated September 16, 1924. RG 60, File 36-194. National Archives.

16. Letter, Henry Zweifel to Seymour Johnson, dated September 15, 1924. RG 60, File 36-194. National Archives.

17. CR 4382, *Frederick A. Cook, Plaintiff in Error vs. United States of America, Defendant in Error,* page 38. SBA.

18. Judgment 4382, 5th Circuit Court of Appeals, 4 Federal Reporter (2nd series): 518.

19. FWP, February 25, 1923.

20. NYT, April 6, 1925.

21. Ibid.

22. OOJ, page 9. FCC. The typescript gives the date March 6, which is incorrect.

23. OOJ, page 2. FCC.

24. OOJ, pages 7–8. FCC.

25. NYT, April 7, 1925.

26. OOJ, page 9. FCC.

27. OOJ, pages 18–19. FCC.

28. OOJ, pages 19–20. FCC.

29. OOJ, page 75. FCC.

30. OOJ, page 82. FCC.

31. OOJ, page 89. FCC.

32. OOJ, pages 27–28. FCC.

33. FWP, December 9, 1925.

34. Letter, Thomas F. Hall to Edwin Swift Balch, dated January 19, 1926; all details and quotes. BCV.

35. Letter, Thomas F. Hall to Stewart Beach (managing editor of *Independent*), dated March 17, 1926. Harriet Tidd Collection (#6828), Special Collections Department, University of Virginia, Charlottesville.

36. Letter, Thomas F. Hall to Edwin Swift Balch, dated January 19, 1926. BCV.

37. MLE, page 74.

38. HCP, chapter 15, pages 11–12. FCC.

39. HCP, chapter 15, pages 7–8. FCC.

40. Unattributed clipping datelined January 25, 1926. CSC.

41. Washington *Evening Star,* January 24, 1926.

42. Letter, Adolph S. Ochs to JDP, dated February 1, 1926. PFC.

43. NYT, March 4, 1926.

44. Letter, Thomas F. Hall to Stewart Beach, dated March 17, 1926; both quotes. Harriet Tidd Collection (#6828), Special Collections Department, University of Virginia, Charlottesville.

45. Unattributed newspaper clipping, undated. FCC.

46. McConnell, Burt M., "The Peary Side of the North Pole Controversy," *Independent,* April 3, 1926, page 385.

47. Ibid., page 384.

48. Letter, VS to J. Gordon Hayes, dated February 5, 1927. SCD.

49. Letter, Thomas F. Hall to VS, dated October 7, 1926. SCD.

50. Letter, Thomas F. Hall to VS, dated October 19, 1926. SCD.

51. Memorandum, VS to Isaiah Bowman, dated January 26, 1927. SCD.

52. VS, "Memorandum on Henson Interview," dated June 11, 1926. SCD. In his address before the American Geographical Society in 1897, Peary himself had said, "No successful polar party can be led from the rear." (*Bulletin of the American Geographical Society,* vol. 29, no. 2 [1897]:120.)

53. Green, Fitzhugh, *Peary, the Man Who Refused to Fail.* New York: G.P. Putnam's Sons, 1926, page iv.

54. Ibid., pages 18–19.

55. Ibid., page 392. Among Peary's papers is his will, but since he left everything to his wife and son, there is no accounting of his net worth as a whole. There are hints, however, that Peary was far better off than his biographer imagined. One memorandum shows that at the time of his death, Peary's holdings of stock in just two companies, Republic Steel and U.S. Steel, amounted to $90,571.25.

56. Ibid., page 397.

57. Letters, Gilbert H. Grosvenor to Fitzhugh Green, dated May 24, 1926; Fitzhugh Green to Gilbert H. Grosvenor, dated May 27, 1926. PFC.

58. OOJ, page 27.

59. Brannon, W.T., *"Yellow Kid" Weil.* Chicago: Ziff-Davis Publishing Co., 1948, pages 236–237.

60. Ibid., page 238.

61. Letter, FAC to William Shea, dated May 20, 1927. FCC.

62. Decision 308 of the United States Supreme Court, January 3, 1928.

63. *The New Era,* April 1927, quoted in the *New York Evening Graphic,* Magazine Section, May 28, 1927.

64. FAC, "Application for Executive Clemency," dated February 20, 1928, quoted in CDC, page 253.

65. Letter, John M. Killits to C.J. Stillson, dated October 7, 1926. RG 60, File 36-194. National Archives.

66. FAC, "We See Only Through the Eyes of Experience," essay for *The New Era*. FCC.

67. FAC, "We Begin Somewhere, End No Where," essay for *The New Era*. FCC.

68. FAC, "The Feeling Face of Friendship," essay for *The New Era*. FCC.

69. *The New Era,* April 1929, pages 1–3.

70. Undated typescript, page 8. FCC.

71. FAC, "Do We Subdue Nature?" essay for *The New Era*. FCC.

72. FAC, "Man's Place in Nature," *The New Era,* January 1930, page 5.

73. FAC, "Stop the Whale Killers," essay for *The New Era*. FCC.

74. OOJ, page 242.

75. FAC, "The Social Heritage is a Smoke Screen between Man and Woman," essay for *The New Era*. FCC.

76. FAC, "Caravancia," essay for *The New Era*. FCC.

77. FAC, Miscellaneous notes for *The New Era*. FCC.

78. "Go to the Best Jail Says Dr. Cook," *Literary Digest*, February 1, 1930, page 37.

79. OOJ, pages 133–134. FCC.

80. Letter, FAC to Frank P. Thompson, dated September 17, 1928. FCC.

81. FAC, "Petition to the President," dated March 22, 1929. CSC.

82. *Research Data for Fort Worth and Tarrant County, Texas.* Texas Writers Project, Fort Worth Public Library Unit, 1941, page 1885. Mack Taylor, assistant district attorney for mail fraud cases at the time, confirmed this.

83. Letter, Ennis Nichols to FAC, dated January 14, 1930. FCC.

84. *Kansas City Star,* March 10, 1930.

85. Letter, FAC to Albert Fall, dated July 16, 1931. FCC.

86. Letters, L.A. McKercher to Ted Leitzell, dated April 16, 1938, and June 15, 1938. CSC.

87. Undated news clipping c. March 10, 1930, which simply says "Times." CSC.

88. FAC, Statement to the Press, printed in the *Kansas City Star* and elsewhere, March 10, 1930. FCC.

89. McGarry, William A., Interview with Cook for *Tower Magazine.* Typescript of the interview. FCC.

90. Letter, Lucy O'Connell to FAC, dated April 11, 1930. FCC.

91. "Our Friend, Dr. Frederick A. Cook, Leaves on Parole!" *The New Era,* March 9, 1930, page 1.

92. NYT, March 11, 1930. © 1930, 1958, The New York Times Co. Reprinted by permission.

93. Hobbs, William Herbert, "The Crime Record of Dr. Cook," suppressed chapter for his book, *Peary.* SCD.

Notes for Chapter 25: Was I One of Your Heroes?

1. McGarry, William A., Interview with Cook for *Tower Magazine*. Typescript of the interview. FCC.

2. Letter, Huron H. Smith to FAC, dated April 9, 1930. FCC.

3. Letter, Dorrance and Co. to FAC, dated July 14, 1930. FCC.

4. Letter, FAC to Henry Ford, undated draft, before April 14, 1930. FCC.

5. Letter, V.L. Shevlin to FAC, dated April 14, 1930. FCC.

6. Letter, FAC to C.C. Peters, dated July 18, 1930. FCC.

7. Unattributed newspaper clipping, dated October 1930. CSC.

8. Letter, FAC to HCV, dated October 17, 1930. FCC.

9. Letter, FAC to William Shea, dated July 14, 1931. FCC.

10. In May 1930 Cox, his wife and seven others were indicted for criminal activities in connection with Universal Oil and Gas. They came to trial in November 1931 and were convicted January 4, 1932. Cox was sentenced to ten years, and his wife, 36 months.

11. Letter, W.D. Howe to William Shea, dated August 2, 1931. FCC.

12. Letter, AF to FAC, dated October 1, 1931. FCC.

13. Letter, T. Everett Harré to FAC, dated May 23, 1932. FCC.

14. Letter, D.E. Lamb to FAC, dated March 19, 1932. FCC.

15. Thorek, Max, *A Surgeon's World*. Philadelphia: J.B. Lippincott Co., 1943, page 279.

16. Ibid., page 288.

17. Hutchinson, Bette, memories of Dr. Cook written for the author, dated May 1, 1990.

18. Letter, Ben L. Reitman to FAC, dated May 9, 1933. FCC.

19. Letter, Frank P. Thompson to FAC, dated May 24, 1933. FCC.

20. Letter, Marie Cook to FAC, dated May 14, 1933. FCC.

21. The polar authority H.R. Mill described Hayes, in terms that might also describe Captain Hall, as "a man of strong opinions, little knowledge but enormous diligence." Mill said he had tried to "control his expression" in *The Conquest of the North Pole* and "succeeded to a quite considerable extent." (Undated letter to William H. Hobbs in answer to Hobbs's letter of February 12, 1935. CSC.)

22. Hayes, J. Gordon, *The Conquest of the North Pole*. New York: Macmillan Co., 1934, pages 45–48.

23. The evidence of this is enough to raise suspicion but is inconclusive. See Captain Hall's monograph, "The Murder of Professor Ross G. Marvin," in Lewin, W. Henry, *The Great North Pole Fraud*. London: C.W. Daniel Co., 1935, pages 155–177.

24. Letter, Henshaw Ward to VS, dated "Sep 23" [1934]. SCD.

25. Statement, Valentine Wood to Henshaw Ward, dated September 12, 1934. HWA.

26. Letter, Muriel Wood to Henshaw Ward, dated May 23, 1935. HWA.

27. Letter, A.E. Thomas to Henshaw Ward, dated June 20, 1935. HWA. Thomas told William Shea that he had written 80 percent of *The North Pole*

and that "certainly, Mrs. Elsa Barker had nothing to do with the writing of the book." (Letter, A.E. Thomas to William Shea, dated May 25, 1928. FCC.) However, a direct comparison of Peary's book and the *Hampton's Magazine* articles authored by Barker shows that at least 80 percent of the book's material is absolutely identical to the *Hampton's* articles, and the great majority of what is not identical could be termed no more than editorial changes, many of them slight. Considering this, how Thomas could claim any part of *The North Pole's* authorship is puzzling—unless he wrote the magazine articles, and there is no evidence of that whatsoever. Ward's meeting with Professor Hastings on June 11, 1935, is detailed in a memorandum on the meeting, dated June 14, 1935. HWA. In *Peary,* William H. Hobbs, who probably learned of Hastings's role through Stefansson, said in a note on page 400 that Hastings had made an unofficial but very careful recomputation of all Peary's observations on the route to and near the Pole. Whether he got this information directly from Hastings is not disclosed, but if he did, it confirms Ward's suspicions.

28. DBM, *How Peary Reached the Pole.* Boston: Houghton Mifflin Co., 1934, pages 282–283.

29. Ibid., page 290.

30. Letter, VS to Marie Peary Stafford, dated September 28, 1934. SCD.

31. Quoted in a letter, VS to Marie Peary Stafford, dated October 15, 1934. SCD.

32. Letter, Marie Peary Stafford to VS, dated January 11, 1935. SCD.

33. Letter, Marie Peary Stafford to William H. Hobbs, dated March 31, 1935. SCD.

34. Letter, Henry A. Wise Wood to JDP, dated January 11, 1935. SCD.

35. Letter, VS to Edwin Balmer (editor of *Redbook*), dated January 15, 1935. SCD.

36. Letter, Marie Peary Stafford to William H. Hobbs, dated March 31, 1935. SCD.

37. Shackleton, Edward, *Arctic Journeys.* New York: Farrar & Rinehart, 1938, page 290; Haig-Thomas, David, *Tracks in the Snow.* London: Hodder & Stoughton, 1939, page 49.

38. Letter, LK to Fred High, dated June 25, 1935; both quotes and the details of her visit to Chicago. CSC.

39. Letter, AF to FAC, dated October 22, 1935. FCC.

40. Letter, AF to FAC, dated November 19, 1935. FCC.

41. *Chicago Daily News,* March 7, 1936.

42. Letter, FAC to William Shea, dated August 22, 1936. CSC.

43. Letter, William Shea to FAC, dated December 23, 1935. CSC.

44. Through the efforts of Dennis Rawlins, the manuscript of "The Peary Myth" was recovered from Ward's widow and is now in the National Archives.

45. Letter, FAC to Roland L. Redmond, dated February 19, 1936. FCC. Cook's optimism at this time might be judged by his writing to R. Russell

Smith in Gloucester on February 28, inquiring as to a suitable schooner to execute his plans for animal transfers between the Arctic and Antarctic. Cook's letter of appeal was written with Ted Leitzell's help.

46. Letter, Raye R. Platt to Belmore Browne, dated March 14, 1936. BBD.

47. Letter, Peter Freuchen to DBM, dated March 21, 1936. DMB.

48. Letter, DBM to George Treat, dated June 6, 1936. DMB.

49. Letter, AF to FAC, dated August 1, 1936. FCC.

50. Letter, FAC to AF, dated August 17, 1936. FCC.

51. Hobbs, William Herbert, *Peary.* New York: Macmillan Co., 1936, page 407.

52. Hobbs gives Hugh Lee's diary of 1893–1895 as the authority for some of these stories. The original diary is among Lee's papers at the National Archives along with a typescript written in narrative form, made in the 1930s. The typescript contains all of the stories attributed to Lee by Hobbs. The original handwritten diary mentions none of these, even in other terms. Is the "diary" Hobbs quotes the typescript? And is it apocryphal? For instance, Hobbs has Peary say, dramatically, on hearing of the disastrous tidal wave on October 31, 1893, "The fates and all hell are against me, but I'll conquer yet!" This story is in the Lee typescript, but Lee's original diary for the day closest to it, November 1, 1893, has no mention of it. In his earlier biography, Fitzhugh Green quotes Peary as having said this at least three different times; he gives no source.

53. Letter, AF to T. Everett Harré, dated February 15, 1937. FCC.

54. Letter, HCV to FAC, dated February 21, 1937. FCC.

55. Transcribed from a tape of the radio transcription disc. CSC.

56. Letters, AF to FAC, dated January 2, 1938; FAC to AF, dated January 28, 1938. FCC.

57. Letter, AF to FAC, dated May 21, 1938. FCC.

58. Letter, Ted Leitzell to VS, dated November 29, 1938. SCD. Leitzell published an account of his trip in *Adventure Magazine,* October 1939, pages 106–110. The details are taken from this article and stories in the *Anchorage Daily Times,* July 13 and 25, 1938.

59. Letter, Ted Leitzell to FAC, dated September 6, 1938. CSC.

60. Letter, Ted Leitzell to VS, dated April 29, 1938. SCD.

61. Letter, Ted Leitzell to VS, dated May 23, 1938. SCD.

62. Letter, Raye R. Platt to William H. Hobbs, dated July 26, 1937. SCD.

63. Letter, VS to Stanley Boriss, dated November 5, 1938. FCC.

64. Letter, FAC to Stanley Boriss, dated November 17, 1938. FCC.

65. Hutchinson, Bette, memories of Dr. Cook written for the author, dated May 1, 1990.

66. NYT, November 21, 1939. © 1939, 1967, The New York Times Co. Reprinted by permission.

67. Letter, FAC to Ralph von Ahlefeldt, dated December 15, 1939. FCC.

68. HCP, chapter 18, page 22.

69. Letter, May Kyle to FAC, dated May 22, 1940. FCC.

70. NYT, May 18, 1940.

71. Letter, Adah Murphy to HCV, dated June 8, 1940. FCC.

72. Letter, Marie Cook to HCV, dated June 10, 1940. FCC.

73. Letter, Marie Cook to HCV, undated. FCC.

74. Letter, Hugo Levin to Adah Murphy, dated July 23, 1940. FCC.

75. Letter, Ralph von Ahlefeldt to Adah Murphy, dated July 29, 1940. FCC.

76. Letter, Russell T. Neville to Eileen O'Connor, dated August 5, 1940. FCC.

77. Letter, LK to Hugo Levin, dated August 5, 1940. FCC. The ribbon was emblematic of the Order of Leopold I, given by the king of the Belgians.

78. NYT, August 8, 1940; *New York Herald-Tribune,* August 8, 1940.

79. Cook's will is in the form of a one-page letter to HCV, dated October 4, 1937. CSC.

80. NYT, August 6, 1940. © 1940, 1968, The New York Times Co. Reprinted by permission.

81. MacDonald, Mary Greer, *Beautiful Thoughts for Every Day.* No place of publication: 1932. FCC.

82. FAC, Post-Thumous (1935), unpaged pencil manuscript fragments; all quotes. FCC.

Notes for Chapter 26: The Pointed Finger from His Grave

RFP   Cook, Frederick A., *Return from the Pole.* New York: Pellegrini & Cudahy, 1951.

1. Letter, Ted Leitzell to VS, dated September 30, 1941. SCD.

2. Letter, Ted Leitzell to HCV, dated April 16, 1954. CSC.

3. Letter, HCV to Hans Waale, dated November 18, 1973. CSC.

4. Letter, HCV to LK, dated April 26, 1951. FCC.

5. RFP, page 315.

6. RFP, page 312.

7. Review of RFP, *New Yorker,* September 29, 1951, page 121. © 1951, 1979, The New Yorker Magazine, Inc. Reprinted by permission.

8. Review of RFP, *Our Navy,* January 15, 1952, page 16.

9. Review of RFP, *Saturday Review of Literature,* December 8, 1951, page 26.

10. Letter, HCV to LK, dated October 16, 1951. FCC.

11. Letter, HCV to Nora High, dated December 8, 1953. CSC.

12. Letter, HCV to LK, dated October 6, 1954. FCC.

13. Letter, HCV to LK, dated December 19, 1954. FCC.

14. JDP, draft of letter to the National Geographic Society, dated April 22, 1955. PFC.

15. Letter, HCV to Hans Waale, dated March 5, 1973. CSC.

16. Letter, Frederick J. Pohl to HCV, dated January 11, 1956. CSC.

17. Gonnason, Walter, unpublished statement given to *Life* magazine, dated July 29, 1956. CSC. Gonnason's account of his meeting with Grosvenor is from the *Arizona Daily Star* (Tucson), September 22, 1994. That Grosvenor broke the glass was also told to the author by Gonnason in a telephone conversation on February 14, 1994.

18. NYW, April 14, 1950.

19. Letter, Ted Leitzell to HCV, dated April 16, 1954. CSC.

20. Unless otherwise noted, all the details of the confrontation between the two parties at Talkeetna, including this quotation, are from HCV's unpublished article, "Talkeetna Encounter," written for *Esquire*, c. 1956. CSC.

21. Gonnason, Walter, Diary, July 25, 1956, typed transcript. CSC.

22. "The Tale of a Wayside Inn," *Sports Illustrated*, August 20, 1956, page 16. Other dialogue from HCV article, "Talkeetna Encounter." CSC.

23. Trott, Otto, Diary, August 1, 1956, typed transcript. CSC.

24. Letter, Bradford Washburn to VS, dated August 12, 1956. SCD.

25. Several letters from Trott to HCV in 1957 indicate that Washburn convinced Trott that Cook was dishonest by presenting evidence of his "theft" of Bridges's Yahgan dictionary. CSC.

26. Letter, HCV to LK, dated September 30, 1956. FCC.

27. A statement attesting to the discovery of the diary, dated March 11, 1974, is attached to the diary. FCC.

28. Letter, DBM to Terris Moore, dated September 16, 1967. DMB.

29. Letter, DBM to Louis Sherwin, chief of the Proclamation Office of New York State, dated June 21, 1965. CSC. Cook Centenary Day was proposed in New York State Resolution no. 165, dated April 13, 1965.

30. Letter, HCV to DBM, dated July 25, 1965. DMB.

31. Euller, John, "The Centenary of the Birth of Frederick A. Cook," *Arctic*, vol. 17 (December 1964): 219–221.

32. Letter, Terris Moore to DBM, dated August 19, 1967. SCD.

33. Letter, Marie Peary Stafford to John Edward Weems, dated April 26, 1966. PFC. The letter referred to is the one in which Jo poured out her outrage and heartbreak at her husband's infidelity. See chapter 10, note 29.

34. Franks, Bruce, Review of paperback republication of PEM, *Backpacker*, November 1988, page 74.

35. Grosvenor, Gilbert M., "The Truth about the North Pole," *National Geographic*, March 1984, unnumbered page at front.

36. Rawlins was led to this paper by a reference to it in a long-sealed file of Isaiah Bowman's at Johns Hopkins University. Bowman had gone to Eagle Island in 1935 in response to Marie Peary Stafford's offer of assistance in fighting the resurgence of Cook's claim. While there, Bowman learned of the existence of this paper from Jo Peary and asked for a copy. Bowman noted, "Mrs. Peary has in the safe deposit box in Portland a slip of paper given her by Admiral Peary with the remark that she should treasure it as her most precious posses-

sion and never let it out of her hands unless it was to silence 'that G——
d—— s—— of a b—— Cook.' Marie will go over to Portland and copy off
and send to me whatever is on the slip." (*Washington Post,* October 12, 1988.)

When he got the copy, Bowman could make no sense of the figures
and sent it to Harry Raymond, an astronomer at the Carnegie Institute of
Washington. Raymond's analysis of the figures, which he took to be sextant
readings of the sun, placed Peary 200 nautical miles from the Pole. Bowman
recommended to Mrs. Stafford that the paper be sealed for 50 years. But also
among the Bowman papers was a letter in which Marie Stafford told Bowman
that her mother admitted she may have made a mistake when she dated the
worksheet April 7, 1909. How this could have happened and why Peary
allegedly described this paper as Jo's "most precious possession" remain
mysteries.

37. Letter, William E. Molett, published in "Reader's Forum," *The Navigator's Newsletter,* issue 25, Summer 1989, page 2. Molett, a retired Air Force
lieutenant colonel and authority in high-latitude navigation as a result of
being a veteran of many polar flights, went so far as to offer the Navigation
Foundation a method by which Peary could have navigated based on a discussion presented by Arthur Hinks before the Royal Geographical Society in
November 1909. (Hinks, Arthur R., "Notes on Determination of Position
near the Poles," *Geographical Journal,* vol. 35 [1910]: 299–312.)

At first, Admiral Davies was enthusiastic, but later he phoned Molett to
say that "he had found a marvelously simple way for Peary to navigate" and
wouldn't need to make use of Molett's method. Molett warned Davies that he
knew of no other method that would work and cautioned Davies that he
might be mistaken.

When the Navigation Foundation study was published, Molett protested
to Gilbert M. Grosvenor, president of the National Geographic Society, that
the Navigation Foundation had confused lower latitude navigation methods
with polar navigation, where the "marvelously simple" method of using
meridian altitudes to get an accurate compass bearing would be impossible.
Molett complained that instead of using his method of explaining how Peary
reached the Pole, the Navigation Foundation had used "an impractical system
they dreamed up as a solution to the problem." Molett dismissed the Navigation Foundation's explanation of how Peary navigated by saying, "It absolutely
cannot be done." The National Geographic Society brushed him off.

But Molett did not give up on his idea. He presented it at a U.S. Naval
Institute symposium on Peary at Annapolis in 1991, but his undemonstrative
explanation made little impression on his audience. Eventually he published it
in a vanity press book in 1996.

Though Molett's book was intended to bolster Peary's claim to the Pole, it
actually harmed it by very effectively destroying the credibility of the Navigation Foundation's explanation of how Peary navigated. But the more plausible
method that Molett explained in detail as his alternative was not available to

Peary at the time of his last polar expedition. It had not even been advanced by Hinks until months after Peary's return from the Arctic in 1909 and had not been published until 1910. And like Molett's explanation of it in Annapolis, Hinks's original idea had been totally lost on even the distinguished scientists of the Royal Society then. Hinks later admitted that he was unable to persuade even Robert Scott to make use of it on his journey to the South Pole the next year. Therefore, it seems improbable that Peary could have known anything about Hinks's method or that he would have understood it if he had.

In *Hampton's* (August 1910, page 179) Peary took pains to minimize the difficulties of Arctic observations and then explained the reason he did not take more of them was to save his eyes from the strain inherent in taking celestial observations with an artificial horizon. This would have seemed the perfect place for him to have mentioned why he did not *need* to take any by explaining how he navigated without taking them, but Peary said not a word of the method Molett proposed nor advanced any other that would have allowed him to dispense with them.

Nevertheless, based on several pieces of circumstantial evidence from Peary's reports, Molett argued that Peary had somehow independently grasped the key part of Hinks's coming theory and used it on his polar journey. Molett's evidence was by no means conclusive, however, and, in fact, some of Peary's statements, including those cited by Molett, could just as easily be taken as proof that Peary knew nothing whatsoever of any such navigational method. Furthermore, the Navigation Foundation informed Molett that it had uncovered no evidence during its examination of Peary's papers that Peary used Hinks's method.

Molett and Davies had thus neatly canceled each other's theories out; therefore, Molett's book was actually a net loss for Peary's case.

All quotes are from Molett's book, *Robert E. Peary and Matthew A. Henson at the North Pole,* Frankfort, Ky.: Elkhorn Press, 1996.

38. Davies, Thomas D., *Robert E. Peary at the North Pole.* [Rockville, Md.]: Foundation for the Promotion of the Art of Navigation, December 11, 1989. See also the Supplement to this report, dated April 16, 1990. All quotations are from the main report.

39. This is because it is notoriously difficult to determine transit of the sun—the moment in time when it crosses a given meridian—by observation alone in very high latitudes. At the time of the year Peary made his observations, the point of transit (when the sun would be due south) is so low that it would appear to the observer to neither rise nor fall for as much as 30 minutes, even leaving out the distortions that the extreme refraction possible at such low sun altitudes might introduce. By the time the "dip" of the sun—the point when it was observed to be falling—was recognized, it would have been pure guesswork as to when transit had actually occurred.

40. In Peary's book he gives the time of his observations in reference to "Columbia Meridian Time." For instance, he says of his observation of April 6,

1909, "After the usual arrangements for going into camp, at approximate local noon, of the Columbia meridian, I made the first observation at our polar camp" (*The North Pole,* p. 287). This implies reliance on his watch to determine when the sun reached its meridian altitude, with the assumption that he was still on the 70th meridian after 410 straight-line miles of travel. Although Peary later signed a statement saying that after he left Bartlett he "made five long marches due north along the meridian of Columbia" ("Certificate of Peary as to the movements of the Expedition from April 1st, 1909, to Apr. 7th 1909." PFC.), Peary took no longitude sights on his entire trip, so he would have had no way of knowing exactly where due north was or how far from the 70th meridian he was at this time or any time during the entire journey, so this method could not have been accurate either.

41. The Library of Congress apparently did not exercise its rights to all the materials accumulated by HCV and Janet Vetter. As a result, many important documents, letters, papers and photographs went to the Frederick A. Cook Society in Hurleyville, New York. On what basis the material was divided between the Cook Society and the Library of Congress defies explanation. Documents intimately related to one another were separated, and in one case parts of the same manuscript were divided.

The state of organization of the Cook Society Collection at the time the author visited it in 1990–91 precluded a systematic search. The author subsequently studied the collection at the request of the Frederick A. Cook Society in October 1994, and was able to produce a detailed report on its content and state of preservation. (Bryce, Robert M., *The Collection of the Frederick A. Cook Society Housed at the Sullivan County Historical Museum, Art and Cultural Center, Hurleyville, New York,* 1994, 33 pages.) As a result of this survey the author recommended that the papers received from Janet Vetter's estate be given to the Library of Congress, where all of the material assembled by the Vetters could be reunited in one sequence. Barring this, it was suggested that they should be given to some other professionally managed manuscript repository for arrangement and preservation.

After studying the report and its suggestions, the Cook Society negotiated the transfer of a substantial portion of its holdings to the Byrd Polar Research Center Archives at Ohio State University in Columbus, Ohio, in June 1996. The center had hosted a two-day symposium on Dr. Cook in October 1993.

Many important discoveries among the approximately 40 linear feet of material are sure to be made as it is reorganized and classified.

Notes for Chapter 27: A Matter of Veracity
1. Pencil preface inserted at front of the typed manuscript of HCP. FCC.
2. OOJ, page 300. FCC.
3. OOJ, pages 306–307. FCC.
4. OOJ, page 326. FCC.

5. OOJ, page 251. FCC.

6. OOJ, page 308. FCC.

7. OOJ, notes. FCC.

8. APM, page 115.

9. The diploma copy is in the FCC. It states the dates quoted.

10. A careful examination of what evidence exists strongly suggests that Matt Henson was never fully literate.

First there is the circumstantial evidence:

In 1891 he received a harmonica for Christmas when all the other men received a book, suggesting he could not read at that time. Though he says in his coautobiography, *Dark Companion,* that as a boy he was taught to read by Captain Childs, Dr. Dedrick states in his diary that he was teaching Henson to read in 1900. A newspaper account of Henson's first lecture in 1909 has him fumbling with his bulky manuscript and having to be prompted constantly from the wings while trying to read it, only to abandon it completely and talk directly to the audience. When Isaiah Bowman and Stefansson asked Henson in the 1920s why he had never read Peary's *The North Pole,* Henson replied that if a man had lived something, he didn't need to read about it.

There is then the physical evidence, or the lack of it:

Letters from Henson are scarce, but a comparison of the handwriting on the ones that do exist demonstrates that they were written by more than one person, depending on where Henson was at the time. Though he accompanied Peary on all his major expeditions, there is not a trace of any narrative diary by Henson from any of them, nor are there even any rough notes or anything else recording Henson's experiences, not even a typescript of them, among Peary's papers. Why would Peary, who kept originals or copies of practically everything, have nothing written by Henson?

Some Henson revisionists have taken him at his word and credited him with the ability to take celestial observations. When one recalls Dr. Dedrick's 1900 diary entry in which he describes teaching Henson arithmetic starting with addition, this seems unlikely. Peary told Hubbard flatly, "Henson has previously stated that he could take observations, which is erroneous." (Letter REP to THH, dated February 28, 1911.) And not a scrap of physical evidence in Peary's papers was seen that would contradict this statement.

All this does not mean that Henson was illiterate. It appears that he could read and write to a degree but never mastered either and, finding them slow and painful, avoided both whenever possible. Though he could readily sign his name, he sometimes misspelled it. There is only one letter that the author examined, dated September 5, 1906, that seems to have been written by Henson without assistance. This letter is in the papers of the 1906 expedition. It is in a neat hand matching his characteristic signature, but it is full of spelling and grammatical errors. ("I have never caried you any tailes and it is to late to began now, I can only say all the tailes that have been caried to you abot me is falce.") Henson's other letters are generally free from such errors.

Although he may have dictated at least parts of *A Negro Explorer at the North Pole,* there seems little reason to believe Henson wrote any of it, and one source states it was derived from the diaries of Dr. Goodsell, as were substantial parts of Peary's *The North Pole.* No trace of any original manuscript of Henson's book has ever been found. In a letter to Peary dated April 10, 1911, Henson states, "My wife and I are writing a book," so perhaps Henson dictated his recollections to his wife, who wrote them down for him; the finished book may have been written by a ghostwriter working from these, with Goodsell's diary supplying the chronology and additional material.

Henson, no doubt, did not want to advertise his lack of education. As his "word jamborees" in Greenland demonstrated, he wanted to be taken seriously and was hurt when he was not. Like many others with good native intelligence but severe educational shortcomings, he probably tried to cover them up by inflating his abilities, even boasting in his book that he liked to read Shakespeare and to reporters that he knew "all about" celestial navigation.

Jo Peary described him as a "vainglorious braggart." Marie Peary Stafford dismissed the idea that Henson could have authored *A Negro Explorer at the North Pole* as ludicrous, calling him "practically uneducated." In a letter to Floyd Miller, she expressed her great displeasure at Miller's portrayal of Henson at her father's expense in the manuscript of his book *Ahdoolo!:* "With complete appreciation and gratitude to Matt's usefulness to Dad in the field, I still maintain that except for his extraordinary ability as a dog driver and the fact that as a negro, he could not only endure but actually enjoy work in the Arctic, there was nothing remarkable about him." (Letter, Marie Peary Stafford to Floyd Miller, dated July 18, 1962. PFC.)

None of this should take away from the fact that Henson was a durable traveler and expert dog handler. He probably knew more about the Eskimos and their culture than Peary ever dreamed there was to know. There can be little doubt that whatever Robert E. Peary achieved in the North after the loss of his toes could not have been done without Matthew A. Henson. Unfortunately for Henson, as a black man in his time, he was given little credit then for what he did. Dependent on Peary for his livelihood, he was inextricably linked to Peary's successes—or failures.

But recent attempts at revisionism on his behalf can be little more than guesswork, and the guesses have generally strayed from what little is known for certain. In attempting to embroider his past and enlarge his own role in the Peary expeditions, Henson told conflicting stories at every turn, and the truth about Matthew Henson can now never be known.

11. Letter, REP to MWP, dated October 10, 1880. PFC.

12. Peary's original cairn record was retrieved from Navy Cliff in 1912 by Peter Freuchen. It reads in part: "I have named this Fjord 'Independence' in honor of that day, July 4th, dear to all Americans, on which we looked down into it." There is no mention of a "bay." The record is in the PFC.

13. Letter, EA to EBB, dated October 18, 1894. BLC.

14. Under the terms of the gift, the bulk of Mrs. Peary's correspondence from 1900 to 1955, the year of her death, is restricted until 2000, though scattered letters from this period are available. The year 1900 was when she discovered her husband's infidelity.

15. Letters, Mrs. Attwood R. Martin to JDP, dated June 12, 1939. PFC. FAC to, presumptively, Mrs. Attwood R. Martin, dated June 19, 1939. FCC. This letter is not addressed to Mrs. Martin, or anyone else, specifically, but the coincidence of the date of Martin's letter to JDP on this very subject makes it almost a certainty that Cook's account was written in response to a letter from her.

When Mattie Verhoeff had written to Cook in 1894 regarding her brother's disappearance, his reply did not even hint at his later accusations against Peary. But he ended his letter by trying to interest Miss Verhoeff in going on his upcoming excursion to Greenland on the *Miranda.* (Letter, FAC to Mattie Verhoeff, dated March 20, 1894. Collection of the Filson Club, Louisville, Kentucky.)

16. All these details were given by an unidentified friend of Verhoeff's from Yale in the Philadelphia *Public Ledger,* September 25, 1892. It was a family tradition for Verhoeff men to go to the Sheffield Scientific School at Yale and for the women, like his sister, to attend Vassar. Verhoeff's expulsion would therefore have been just that much more of a serious matter to him.

17. Verhoeff's meteorological entries stop at August 9, but they are dated ahead to August 15. These dates are all blank.

18. Peary failed to publish either Cook's ethnographic study himself or any of the other scientific results of his expedition in full detail. A.E. Thomas had described Peary as a man to whom a few things mattered much and to whom nothing else mattered at all. Science, though he tried to give the opposite impression, was not among those that mattered much. And Peary couldn't understand anyone to which it did. He wondered why Nansen never tried to drift over the Pole again. "You know as well as I that [Nansen's] talk of having secured all the scientific information that is desirable, and not considering the Pole alone of any especial value, is all rot," he told Henry Bryant. "We both know that no man would give a few facts of so-called scientific information the slightest weight, if balanced against the Pole." (Letter, REP to Henry Bryant, dated January 17, 1903. Quoted in Green's *Peary, the Man Who Refused to Fail,* page 239.)

The extremely thorough ethnological measurements of the 75 Eskimos Peary photographed have never been published, either. When these photographs were turned over to the National Geographic Society by Jo Peary, they were thought so little of that their order was not even maintained. It was only in 1972 that a researcher was able to devise a system of matching the photos with the data written down by Dr. Cook. (Letter, Betty Kotcher to Andrew Poggenpohl [art editor of *National Geographic*], dated July 3, 1972, inserted in the Peary papers' finding aid [RG 101]. National Archives.)

As for Verhoeff's faithfully kept meteorological records, which Peary told him would be a major part of the expedition's data, Peary implied in *Northward over the Great Ice* that they were lost with Verhoeff. Yet, they are preserved today at the National Archives, carefully written in tiny print in Verhoeff's log book, a futile monument to his singular determination.

19. LG, Diary, November 24, 1891. LGB.

20. FAC, "How Polar Expeditions Are Equipped," *Harper's Young People,* June 19, 1894, page 566.

21. A copy of the original telegram was furnished to the author by Gaston de Gerlache, Adrien's son. It appeared in the reprint of *Through the First Antarctic Night* (London: C. Hurst & Co., 1980) in slightly different form.

22. Unattributed newspaper clipping, undated. CSC.

23. Letter, Adrien de Gerlache to Gerard Harry, dated October 23, 1897. Private collection. Translation from the French by Dr. Jozef Verlinden.

24. NYT, September 24, 1910. The author made a cursory search of incoming ship rosters at the National Archives but did not turn up Cook coming back from Europe in 1897. In any case, some of these handwritten records are damaged or no longer legible. A number of inquiries to Belgium failed to discover any correspondence sent by Cook to officials of the expedition, though a major effort to catalog the correspondence held in the Royal Observatory has not reached the time period in which he might have written.

25. In an interview given to *Le Messager de Bruxelles,* October 20, 1899, quoted in a letter, Jozef Verlinden to the author, dated November 20, 1994.

26. The official government publication, *Moniteur Belge,* for November 7, 1899, announces that the Order of Leopold will be given to Gerlache, Lecointe, Amundsen, Racovitza, Arctowski, Cook and Dobrowlski. Mélaerts received the Civil Cross 1st Class; he was the only officer (second mate) who received a lesser decoration.

27. One recent writer, in his zeal to show that Cook was a lifelong teller of tall tales, called Cook's observations of the Eskimos' menstrual cycle, seasonal sexual desire and other peculiarities associated with the absence of the sun "a fascinating blunder" and an "amazing gaffe." Though he incorrectly stated Cook's observations, in reality, these seasonal cycles are well-established facts, noted by many subsequent anthropologists who have studied the Smith Sound Eskimos' reproductive cycles. They have an actual physiological basis, as well, thought to be linked to the pineal gland, which produces the hormone melatonin at night and plays a role in regulating the seasonal cycles of animals in response to changes in the amount of light. It is theorized that the use of artificial lights has moderated these cycles in most humans, and recent experiments have shown that humans deprived of artificial light have marked changes in their sleep cycles and other biological rhythms.

28. Skin of the narwhal, so much prized by the Eskimos, is very rich in vitamin C. The liver and kidneys of the walrus and seal, which they eat raw, are also high in C. The intestines have vitamins A and D.

29. The tent is described in detail in FAC, "A New Tent for the Snow Line," *Outing Magazine,* December 1900, pages 333–335. All attempts to trace specifics about Robert D. Perry's tent failed. Perry made a donation of artifacts to the Worcester, Massachusetts, Natural History Museum, now the New England Science Center. The curator of collections, Duke Dawson, informed the author that apparently Perry donated only a number of big game heads, of which the museum still has only one, a walrus. (Letter to the author, dated June 21, 1995.) Dawson enclosed a feature article about Perry that appeared in the *Sunday Telegram* (Worcester, Massachusetts) on August 1, 1937, in which Perry reminisced about his association with Cook and Peary but gave no hint that Cook had appropriated his tent design.

30. FAC, "Captain Fabian Gottlieb von Bellingshausen, 1819–1821. The Discovery of Alexander I., Peter I., and Other Islands," *Bulletin of the American Geographical Society,* vol. 33 (1901): 36–41.

31. HA, "Exploration of Antarctic Lands," in *The Antarctic Manual for the Use of the Expedition of 1901,* edited by George Murray. London: Royal Geographical Society, 1901, page 496.

32. Telegram, HA to HLB, dated September 4, 1909. PFC.

33. NYT, April 5, 1899.

34. NYT, April 7, 1899. Cook later said that "press rivalries" had resulted in the telegram's becoming "garbled."

35. FAC, "The Frozen South," *Harper's Weekly,* July 22, 1899, page 714. A similar statement to this also appeared in *Through the First Antarctic Night.* Cook's version even beat Gerlache's into print in Europe, however, as "Le voyage de la Belgica à 3300 kilomètres dans les glaces antarctiques," *Le Petit Bleu,* November 16–22, 1899. Cook's narrative covered half a page of small print every day.

36. NYA, December 22, 1909.

37. A portion of Lecointe's letter was published in the NYT, May 21, 1910.

38. Furlong, Charles W., "Into the Unknown Land of the Onas," *Harper's Monthly Magazine,* August 1909, page 444, says: "In my pocket I had a letter given me by that courageous explorer, Dr. Frederick Cook, at the present time lost somewhere in the great ice-fields of the Arctic." Lucas Bridges's acknowledgments are in UPE. Furlong, who had been a traveler in Tierra del Fuego in 1908, later said he was the one who brought the matter of the "stolen" dictionary to Townsend's attention.

39. NYT, June 24, 1899; BDE, July 7, 1899; *Harper's Weekly,* July 22, 1899.

40. QMA, page 88; Denuce, Jean, "Note sur vocabulaire complet de la langue Yahgane," in *Verhandlungen International Amerikanisten Kongress,* Vienna, 1908, vol. XVI. Vienna: 1910, pages 651–654.

41. QMA, page 299, first edition, Brussels: Imprimerie Scientifique Ch. Bulens, 1902; see also *Liste des Rapports Scientifiques publiés sous la direction de la Commission de la "Belgica."*

42. MAP, pages 497–498.

43. For a history of the dictionary's travels, see Moeller, Rosemary H., "The Case of the Wandering Dictionary," in UPE, pages 529–537.

44. Bryce, Robert M., "Dr. Cook and the Yahgan Dictionary." Special supplement to *Polar Priorities,* vol. 14 (1994), 12 pages.

45. FAC, "With Fuegians on a Guanaco Hunt," *Outing Magazine,* February 1901, pages 576–580.

46. FAC, "My Experiences with a Camera in the Antarctic," *Popular Photography,* February 1938, page 14. Ted Leitzell anonymously coauthored this article.

47. Thorek, Max, *A Surgeon's World.* Philadelphia: J.B. Lippincott Co., 1943, pages 282–283.

48. These pictures can be viewed in Rand, Sturgis B., "Robert E. Peary and His Campaign for the Pole," *McClure's Magazine,* January 1902, pages 354–363. Prints of some of them are in the FCC and PFC. One appears on the dust jacket of this book. There should be no doubt that Peary lost only seven toes in the Arctic, though the secondary literature has confused the issue. The BDE for September 18, 1902, reproduces verbatim Peary's message to the Peary Arctic Club, dated April 4, 1901. After enumerating his accomplishments, he has this to say: "Considering that I am an old man, have one broken leg and only three toes, and that my starting point was Etah, I feel that this was doing tolerably well."

49. Louis Wolf's evaluation of Peary's condition in 1905–06 is from remembrances of him written for Herbert L. Bridgman's projected biography. PFC. Of all the surgeons Peary ever employed, only Dr. Wolf did not come into conflict with him. He admired Peary greatly and badly wanted to accompany him in 1908 but was unable to do so.

Dr. Dedrick's 1901 note regarding Peary read: "Dr. Cook—Be sure measure Peary for truss for his rupture & send next year. I would suggest some Port Wine & any such tonic & strength builders as you may think for him to build up." PFC. Port wine was a common prescription for simple anemia (like that associated with incipient scurvy) in the nineteenth century.

Cook's claim to have diagnosed Peary correctly and to have recommended the proper treatment years before it was discovered brings to mind a parallel claim in regard to one of his pet theories, which he called "Power Theory." This idea bears some similarity to Einstein's theories concerning the interchangeability of matter and energy. In his memoirs, Cook says that he thought of it and put it down in his journal on the North Greenland Expedition in 1891—a journal that has not come to light—which would place it well in advance of even the first of Einstein's theories along these lines. However, in the November 1929 issue of *The New Era,* he claimed "priority" for this idea as one developed "within these walls," that is, in Leavenworth.

50. NYT, September 15, 1909. By all accounts Theodore Cook had some of these same characteristics. He was remembered as a "rustic genius" but with an impractical streak that led him to go bankrupt on several occasions when his "ingenious and impractical" schemes failed.

51. The full account of this incident is in the NYT, January 9, 1910.

52. Letters, FAC to REP, dated May 20 and 22, 1896. PFC.

53. The letters and documents referred to are in the file of correspondence between FAC and RWP. RPA. In an affidavit dated December 9, 1909, Porter said, "Cook neglected and refused to pay the same or any part thereof." PFC.

54. In his unpublished autobiography, page 334, Dunn mentions that Cook kept a notebook on the trip. RDD.

55. Letter, L.C. Bement to RD. Quoted in Dunn's unpublished autobiography, page 356; no date is given. RDD.

56. Peter Freuchen indicated he knew of this incident in 1909: "The first time I was in Greenland I saw some men who had been deceived by Cook on his 'famous' Miranda-expedition." (Letter, Peter Freuchen to HLB, dated November 30, 1909. PFC.)

Notes for Chapter 28: To the Top of the Continent?

Cook's Mount McKinley diary is a 4¾-by-6¾-inch leather-bound book with "Record" printed on the cover in gold. It contains 176 numbered pages with sporadic entries from July 17, 1906, to September 20, 1906. In September 1996 a transcript of this entire diary was published (see 1996 entry in the Bibliography of the Published Writings of Dr. Frederick A. Cook in this volume). However, the transcription contains a number of errors, many of a nature that severely compromises the value of the transcription. For instance, on page 55 the word "lake" is twice transcribed as "fork" which completely destroys the significance of the passage. The transcription also fails to reproduce the two crucial maps on pages 44 and 46 which show the two lakes being referred to and some other crucial elements necessary for correct interpretation of the diary's text. All quotes from the diary in this chapter have been checked for accuracy against the original and crosschecked against a partial typed copy made by HCV.

1. NYT, October 15, 1909.

2. *Seattle Post-Intelligencer,* September 3, 1909.

3. NYT, October 23, 1909.

4. One such example can be found in the NYT, October 26, 1909, which reported that Dr. Henry L. Williams, coach of the University of Minnesota football team, declared that when he was in an inn at Darby, Montana, in February 1909, he heard Barrill hold forth on the story of the climb of Mount McKinley and that Barrill said at that time that he and Cook had reached the summit. There are also a number of letters in the CSC from others who had heard Barrill tell the same story.

In 1988 Bradford Washburn received a letter from Marjorie Barrill, Ed Barrill's daughter, giving an account of what her father had told her about his dealings with Cook. In her letter Marjorie Barrill quoted her father as saying of Cook's announcement that he had climbed Mount McKinley, "I didn't think he would really lie about it. *But he did.*" He also was reported by her to have said that Cook never paid him his wages from the trip and that at their confrontation in Hamilton, Cook "stalked off the stage in a rage."

Yet Cook was described in all accounts as perfectly calm throughout the entire Hamilton ordeal; there is also documentary evidence that Barrill got his wages and $200 besides. And of Barrill's statement that he "didn't think he would really lie about it," if Cook's claim is false, Ed Barrill was fully complicit in the fraud, since according to his own testimony, he copied the false entries that Dr. Cook dictated to him into his own personal diary. Marjorie Barrill's letter appeared in the 1988 number of the *American Alpine Journal,* pages 80–82. Barrill's unpublished affidavits are in the PFC.

5. Browne, Belmore, "The Struggle up Mount McKinley," *Outing Magazine,* June 1907, page 276.

6. NYT, September 10, 1909.

7. *Tacoma Tribune,* September 20, 1909.

8. Letter, Albert E. Joab to M.T. Hitchcock, dated September 21, 1909. CSC.

9. NYT, December 25, 1909.

10. NYT, November 30, 1909.

11. New York *Evening Post,* October 26, 1903.

12. EBB, "On the Trail of the Pole Seekers"; section entitled "Adequacy of Cook's Supplies," pages 4–5, unpublished manuscript. BLC. It was said that Cook at age 26 had a five-inch chest expansion.

13. All information on the testimony of Parker and Browne is taken from an uncorrected set of the minutes of the meetings of the Explorers Club committee, October 15 and 17, 1909. PFC.

14. FAC, "The Conquest of Mount McKinley," *Harper's Monthly Magazine,* May 1907, page 827.

15. FAC, "Dr. Cook's Own Story," *Hampton's Magazine,* March 1911, page 304.

16. Edward N. Barrill, Diary, September 14, 1906. PFC. In the 1950s Bradford Washburn said he found half of the one-pint alcohol containers Cook had taken up Ruth Glacier discarded in the area near Glacier Point and on the tributary glacier containing Fake Peak, though these have never definitely been identified as Cook's.

17. Randall, Glenn, *Mount McKinley Climber's Handbook.* Talkeetna, Alaska: Genet Expeditions, 1984. Fitness by itself, however, is no guarantee of success in high-altitude climbing. Naomi Uemura, the first man to make a solo journey to the North Pole, died of hypothermia and exhaustion on Mount McKinley in 1984 at 17,200 feet on his descent after reaching the summit on his winter solo attempt.

18. NYT, June 5, 1910.

19. FAC, Mount McKinley Diary, page 43. FCC.

20. FAC, Mount McKinley Diary, page 47. FCC.

21. FAC, Mount McKinley Diary, page 45. FCC.

22. BB, Diary, June 28, 1910. BBD.

23. Washburn states that photograph 1 was taken from the top of Fake Peak itself. By the angle of the shadows, he estimated that Cook's summit photograph had been taken between 10 and 11 A.M. This matches Barrill's affidavit well.

24. BB, Diary, June 28, 1910. BBD.

25. Randall's *Guide* warns against camping here, at Denali Pass, because of excessive winds. The altitude is interesting when connected with a piece of hearsay evidence in which a man purported to have interviewed Hudson Stuck after his climb. He alleged Stuck to have said at that time that he had found traces of a camp at that altitude, and that perhaps Cook had climbed a spur in the fog and thought he had reached the summit. (Letter, George Kilroy to FAC, dated September 19, 1929. CSC.) Cook's is the only expedition before Stuck's to claim to have camped at this altitude, though the "second" Sourdough expedition said they reached this point and took photographs of the summits in 1910. This is just one of many unconfirmable anecdotes surrounding Mount McKinley.

The diary of Walter Harper, one of Stuck's companions on his climb, mentions finding Parker and Browne's camp at the top of the Northeast Ridge, despite the earthquake, looking as though they had left it the day before, and seeing the footprints of Parker and Browne from 1912 higher up. (Harper Diary, May 27; June 2, 1913.) Karstens's diary also mentions the camp at the top of the Northeast Ridge. Neither has anything about a higher camp. Would they not have mentioned Cook's camp had Stuck's party come across it?

Walt Gonnason said Harry Karstens had told him in 1948 that Merl LaVoy had told *him* that he had actually reached the summit of Mount McKinley in 1912, but that they had agreed that unless all members of the Parker-Browne party reached the top none would claim it. Later, Gonnason said, Belmore Browne told him the same thing, only that, instead of LaVoy, it was *he* who had reached the summit. Gonnason speculated that Browne's party had actually suppressed the fact that they had conquered McKinley because what they found there confirmed that Cook had told the truth. (Gonnason, Walter, "The Mountain in the Clouds," typescript of unpublished article, undated. CSC. Repeated nearly word for word by Gonnason to the author in a telephone conversation on February 14, 1994; author's notes.)

26. Stuck, Hudson, *The Ascent of Denali (Mount McKinley)*. New York: Charles Scribner's Sons, 1914, page 101. Though this may have been true of the route Stuck took, Mount Foraker is visible from Denali Pass and also from along the commonly climbed summit ridge used by most climbers today.

27. Letter, HCV to Hans Waale, dated November 18, 1973. CSC. There is a statement attached to the diary dated March 11, 1974, attested to by the

three Vetters and Hugo Levin that "this diary was found in an unopened packing box by Adah Murphy and me [Helene Cook Vetter] during Fall 1956." However, in a letter to Hans Waale dated October 16, 1973, she said, "I accidentally found it after his niece's death in 1959."

28. Rusk, C.E., "On the Trail of Dr. Cook," *Pacific Monthly,* November 1910, page 486. In a letter to Clark Brown as early as July 28, 1911, Cook admitted that *To the Top of the Continent* was "full of mistakes," and said that a whole chapter had been left out and "the pictures have the wrong captions." CSC.

The last unidentified photo in Cook's book, labeled "Clouds and Cliffs, 13,000 feet," was located by Brian Okonek in 1995 as having been taken in the Great Gorge just north of Cook's photo of Mount Barrille, but looking back down the glacier; its true elevation is 4,800 feet.

29. Decker, Karl, "Dr. Frederick A. Cook—Faker," *Metropolitan Magazine,* January 1910, page 422. The most curious thing about this article is a map it contains purporting to show the location of the peak Cook photographed as his top of the continent. The map says it was based on a drawing by Belmore Browne, yet it shows Fake Peak, which Parker and Browne located up a tributary glacier east of Ruth Glacier, as being on the *west* side of Ruth Glacier, and the "distant peak" they pointed out before the Explorers Club is shown on the east side. Since, according to the article itself, it was written on November 28, 1909, 45 days after Cook's meeting with the Explorers Club, it seems logical that the map was prepared well in advance of the text. Before the committee, Browne said that the mountain Cook had climbed and photographed as the summit of Mount McKinley was "the gun sight peak" "on the extreme left hand side in the foreground of" photograph 1, later named by Browne "McKinley Cliff," or one very close to it. (Browne's testimony before the Explorers Club committee, October 17, 1909, page 14.) Although Fake Peak is close to it, Browne's map indicates that he was confused about exactly where this cliff was in relation to Mount McKinley when he drew the map, and that his testimony before the club was possible only after he read Barrill's account and saw the approximate correct location of Fake Peak on the map Barrill drew for the *New York Globe* to accompany his affidavit. Browne admitted his confusion and tried to explain it on page 113 of CMM. He wrote: "We were also influenced to some degree by the map of this glacier shown in Edward Barrill's affidavit, in which he shows that Dr. Cook's photographs were taken on this [more easterly] glacier." But Browne says he realized his mistake only when he arrived on the actual scene of the two glaciers in 1910.

In his testimony, Browne said that he had seen the original of Cook's summit picture. But though he could not remember where or when he had seen it, he was willing to say of the picture itself that it "would correspond identically in the distance with the mountain ranges shown across the Ruth Glacier on [photograph 1]." Apparently, in this one instance, Browne's "poor memory for detail" did not prevail. (Explorers Club testimony October 17, 1909, page 16. PFC.)

30. Ibid.

31. The exchange of letters between Browne and Balch in March 1915 is preserved in the BBD and BCV.

32. NYT, November 11, 1910; both quotes.

33. Letter, Belmore Browne to THH, dated January 21, 1914. PFC.

34. Letter, William E. Mears to E.A. Murphy, dated October 14, 1931. FCC.

35. Letter, William E. Mears to E.A. Murphy, dated October 26, 1931. FCC.

36. Affidavit, Edward Van Altena, dated April 6, 1962. CFD. Van Altena was reluctant to put this account in writing and did so only after years of requests by Charles Wellington Furlong, one of those who sought to prove that Cook stole Bridges's Yahgan dictionary. Coincidentally, Robert Dunn's pictures of the 1903 climb are exactly 3¼ by 4¼ inches. Might it have been some of these that Van Altena confused with the 1906 pictures? As for the "removal" of Mount McKinley that he reports, there is one 1906 picture that would fit that bill exactly. It would be the one opposite page 196 in *To the Top of the Continent,* which should show Mount McKinley on the right margin of the film. However, there is a nearly identical unpublished picture of this same scene, and McKinley is not visible in it, either, because of low clouds. The other summit picture Van Altena alludes to has not come to light.

37. The time Washburn assigns to the "15,400-foot" photograph does not match Barrill's affidavit. Barrill said it was taken two or three hours before the summit picture was taken. Washburn, however, had deduced from its shadows that it was exposed "in the afternoon." Because Washburn did not see Barrill's full affidavit until 1988, he was mystified by this photograph's location until 1956. He had still not seen any part of Barrill's original diary or other crucial evidence when the author brought them to his attention in 1992. Fake Peak is clearly visible in the "15,400-foot" photograph. It is the small-rounded point second from the right.

38. That the photograph is indeed from the original negative was confirmed to the author by the historian of the Frederick A. Cook Society, Sheldon Cook-Dorough, in a letter dated June 25, 1993. He noted that it was described as such in Cook's hand on the reverse. The author saw the print personally in 1991, but repeated attempts to obtain a copy over a two-year period failed. The author finally received photocopies of this picture in May 1994. However, the copies were made from a *second* print, not the one originally seen. It was distinguished by a different inscription on its reverse. In October 1994 the author made a survey of the Cook Society's collection. There he saw the print that had been used for the copies. Though yellowed and faded, it was definitely from the original negative. But the photocopying process brought out its contrasts very vividly when set to a darker copy position. Though a

thorough search was made by the author, the clearer copy seen in 1991 could not be located among the society's photographic materials in 1994.

Actually, even in the absence of this print, there are two key points in the original published version of Cook's photograph in *Harper's Monthly Magazine* that show that it is the same place as Browne's Fake Peak. One is a cavelike structure at the extreme left of the photograph with its dark vertical recess. This same structure is covered by snow in Browne's photograph, but it is clearly visible in Washburn's and Adams's later photographs from the 1950s. Also, in the *Harper's* photograph, and in no other, the telltale top of McKinley Cliff can be seen peeking up over the left-hand side beyond Cook's "summit."

39. Rusk, C.E., "On the Trail of Dr. Cook," *Pacific Monthly,* January 1911, page 59.

40. New York *Evening Post,* March 30, 1915.

41. NYT, October 23, 1909.

42. New York *Evening Post,* March 30, 1915.

43. FAC, "Mount McKinley," *Overland Monthly,* February 1912, page 106, serving as an introduction to Cairns's article, "Hazards of Climbing Mount McKinley."

44. MAP, page 534.

45. Rusk, C.E., "On the Trail of Dr. Cook," *Pacific Monthly,* January 1911, page 54. In his diary, Cook notes he built his first snow house "bet[ween] peak 12 and the fall of the cornice." On the sketch map of Ruth Glacier in his diary, "peak 12" is the fourth peak in a row *north* of Ruth Glacier, most probably placing it on Karstens Ridge or Pioneer Ridge, certainly not on the East Buttress.

46. Letter, Hans Waale to HCV, dated May 1, 1975.

47. Ibid.

48. Letter, Bradford Washburn to Hans Waale, dated September 20, 1973. CSC. In 1991 Washburn, in a lengthy phone conversation, raised each of these points with the author but after realizing he had not persuaded his listener to his way of thinking, termed Cook a "convicted felon," who tried "to steal two men's life work." As far as his remark about no one who had ever climbed the mountain believing in Cook, when reminded of Gonnason, Washburn admitted Gonnason had gone for Cook's story "hook, line and sinker" (author's notes of the conversation). Gonnason adamantly reasserted his full belief in Cook's claim in a phone conversation with the author on February 14, 1994.

The author made several written inquiries to Washburn concerning aspects of Cook's disputed climb but received no substantive answers to any of his specific questions. Finally, after having his motives and biases questioned, Washburn recommended to the author Brian Okonek, a Mount McKinley guide, for help in identifying the picture that appeared in *Collier's* and two drawings from the original diaries of Cook and Barrill. When Okonek wrote to Washburn identifying the three items as not being supportive of Cook's claim, Washburn then called the author and was very forthcoming in identifying the places shown in these drawings, then followed up by sending topographical maps indicating their exact locations. He enclosed the letter from Okonek identifying Cook's photograph from *Collier's* as being taken on the tributary glacier at the same location as the "15,400-foot" photograph, but looking north-northeast toward the north fork of the Coffee Glacier, instead of south toward Fake Peak. (Letter, Brian Okonek to Bradford Washburn, dated November 22, 1992.)

49. Letter, Hans Waale to Janet Vetter, dated March 9, 1980. CSC.

50. Letter, Bradford Washburn to Hans Waale, dated August 16, 1979. CSC.

51. Letter, Bradford Washburn to Hans Waale, dated October 27, 1983. CSC.

52. Letter, Bradford Washburn to Hans Waale, dated December 5, 1983. CSC.

53. Rowell, Galen, *High and Wild.* San Francisco: Sierra Club Books, 1979, pages 141–150. In July 1986 Gary Scott, an Australian park ranger, made the ascent of the West Buttress and returned in a single day. The author could find few published details of this climb other than that Scott was already acclimatized from spending five weeks at a medical camp at 14,300 feet and that he reached the summit from base camp in 18½ hours. For descriptions of the various routes up McKinley see Waterman, Jonathan, *High Alaska.* New York: American Alpine Club, 1988. It should be noted that this book's discussions of the early climbs, including Cook's and the Sourdoughs', have some historical inaccuracies.

The first credited ascent of an unknown route up the East Buttress was made in 1963; it took 24 days just to reach the summit. But the most likely route Cook might have taken from Ruth Glacier, Catacomb Ridge, was not climbed until 1969. A party led by Joseph K. Davidson took 21 days to gain the summit and had to place 10,500 feet of fixed rope, 74 pickets, three rock pitons, six ice screws and two ice pitons to do it. Waale's hypothesized route is far less direct than either of these and technically more difficult in some places.

54. Transcript of testimony before the Explorers Club committee, October 15, 1909, page 11. PFC.

55. NYT, December 10, 1909.

56. Rusk, C.E., "On the Trail of Dr. Cook," *Pacific Monthly,* January 1911, page 60.

57. Letter, Brian Okonek to the author, dated January 13, 1993. In the summer of 1994 the Frederick A. Cook Society sponsored an expedition headed by veteran climber Vern Tejas. Several of the team reached the crest of the East Buttress and made a photograph of Pegasus Peak, which they believed matched Cook's drawing on page 52 of his diary. This was fresh proof, the society said, that Cook climbed the East Buttress. However, the expedition

accomplished nothing more than Walt Gonnason's 1956 attempt. It climbed no higher, and Gonnason had already photographed this same scene in 1956 from a very similar position. See *Polar Priorities,* v. 14 (October 1994), page 24 and back cover.

58. Rusk, C.E., "On the Trail of Dr. Cook," *Pacific Monthly,* November 1910, page 483.

59. Letter, Hans Waale to Janet Vetter, dated June 11, 1979. CSC.

60. "The Conquest of Mount McKinley," *Mazama,* March 1907, page 58.

61. Metcalfe, Gertrude, "Mount McKinley and the Mazama Expedition," *Pacific Monthly,* September 1910, page 262.

62. MAP, page 29. The idea that Cook thought Peary out of the running is upheld by the recollection of whaling Captain George F. Comer, who talked to Cook before he left for Gloucester in 1907 about the possibilities of reaching the Pole. Comer said: "I remember distinctly Dr. Cook's telling me that as long as Peary was in the arctic field he would not search for the pole, and at that time, if you remember, there was some doubt about Peary's getting the money to finance an expedition. I imagine that was why Dr. Cook started at that time, thinking he would have the field to himself." (NYT, October 7, 1909.)

63. Rusk, C.E., "On the Trail of Dr. Cook," *Pacific Monthly,* January 1911, page 60.

64. The only account ever published of the "second" Sourdough climb appeared in the *Fairbanks Daily Times,* June 9, 1910.

65. Stuck, Hudson, *The Ascent of Denali (Mount McKinley).* New York: Charles Scribner's Sons, 1914, page 173.

66. NYT, June 5, 1910; both quotes.

67. Lindley, A.D., "The Ascent of Mt. McKinley," *Canadian Alpine Journal,* vol. 21 (1932): 119.

68. Pearson, Grant H., *My Life of High Adventure.* Englewood Cliffs, N.J.: Prentice-Hall, Inc., 1962, page 157.

69. When Parker met Charles McGonagall, one of the Sourdoughs, at a mining camp in 1912, he told Parker that they had left their shovel to mark their arrival at the summit of the North Peak. He didn't mention a flagpole.

70. Karstens's entry for June 3 reads: "Windy & cold. Moved camp very near to top of 1st Serack making 2 trips very near 17000 ft. basin where Parker climbed from though something must have been rong to climb from there 'Hurrah' everyone sees flag staf on North Peak Perfectly clear through glasses." (Karstens's complete diary appeared in the 1969 number of the *American Alpine Journal,* pages 339–348.)

Walter Harper's diary for the same day reads, "While resting we began to talk about the flag staff that was supposed to have been put up on the north peak of Denali by Anderson and Taylor, and as we were talking about it I suddenly looked up to the ridge that was running down the north peak and to our great surprise I saw it standing out against the blue sky. The pole was about twelve or fourteen feet long. It has been there for three years." (Harper Diary, June 3, 1913.)

Francis P. Farquhar's article on the first ascents of McKinley also quotes an interview with one of Stuck's other companions, Roger B. Tatum, that appeared in the *Knoxville News-Sentinel,* May 22, 1932: "They were able to see the flagpole on top of the north peak of Denali that a previous expedition had planted." (Farquhar, Francis P., "The Exploration and First Ascents of Mount McKinley," part 1, *Sierra Club Bulletin,* June 1949, page 103.)

Notice that while Karstens says "everyone" saw the flag staff, and Harper says "to *our* great surprise *I* saw it," Tatum says "they." Harper's diary is reproduced in the 1977 reprint of Stuck's book published by The Mountaineers, Seattle.

71. Farquhar, Francis P., "The Exploration and First Ascents of Mount McKinley," part 1, *Sierra Club Bulletin,* June 1949, page 104.

72. Letter, Bradford Washburn to HCV, dated September 13, 1955. CSC.

73. Rusk, C.E., "On the Trail of Dr. Cook," *Pacific Monthly,* January 1911, page 59.

74. Letter, C.E. Rusk to FAC, dated October 26, 1909. CSC.

75. Rusk, C.E., "On the Trail of Dr. Cook," *Pacific Monthly,* January 1911, pages 58–59.

Notes for Chapter 29: Return to the Pole

1. FAC, "A Walk to the North and South Poles," *Canadian Magazine,* September 1900, page 422.

2. BDE, September 18, 1902.

3. Undated memorandum. PFC.

4. Unattributed newspaper article, dated October 1, 1907. CSC. Also, Bain, George Grantham, "Alone in the Arctic," unattributed article, copyrighted 1908. CSC.

5. Bain, George Grantham, "Alone in the Arctic," unattributed article, copyrighted 1908. CSC.

6. Letter, REP to Sam Bartlett, dated June 30, 1907. PFC.

7. See the statements of Joseph MacDonald, NYT, September 16, 1909, and Allen Whitten, NYT, September 14, 1909. Dr. Cook's brother confirmed all of this when he was reported to have said: "The expedition was planned and was well fitted out and there was no necessity of sending any relief expedition. . . . Theodore was, however, bound to keep the details secret." Undated clipping from the *Callicoon Echo,* dated by content to September 1909.

8. NYH, September 11, 1909.

9. Peary took nearly 30,000 pounds of pemmican in 1908, three-quarters destined for the dogs. Allen Whitten, boatswain of the *Erik,* attributed Peary's constant failures in the Arctic to his never taking enough provisions north. There are hints that Peary may have skimmed off some of the money his backers

contributed to provision them. In any case, he seemed oddly frugal in supplying his expeditions with absolute necessities.

In a letter to MacMillan, Peary related that he settled on Armour's product solely because it cost 5 to 10 cents a pound less than that made by Kemp Day & Co., even though he had already had several bad experiences with Armour's pemmican. (Letter, REP to DBM, dated March 22, 1912. DMB.) In 1905 he literally poisoned most of his dogs with rotten whale meat that he got for pennies a ton in Labrador.

10. Haig-Thomas, David, "Expedition to Ellesmere Island, 1937–38," *Geographical Journal,* vol. 95 (1940): 272.

11. HNPBD, pages 407–409.

12. FAC, "A Walk to the North and South Poles," *Canadian Magazine,* September 1900, page 420.

13. Letter, Anthony Fiala to William Shea, dated September 30, 1926. FCC.

14. Steensby, Phil. H.P., "The Polar Eskimos and the Polar Expeditions," *Fortnightly Review,* November 1909, page 901.

15. Borup, George, *A Tenderfoot with Peary.* New York: Frederick A. Stokes Co., 1911, page 301. Later users of Peary-type sledges varied in their opinions of them. MacMillan used these on his trip toward Crocker Land in 1914, but said nothing as to their performance. Fitzhugh Green, however, said that when the sledges were heavily loaded on the early part of the trip, rough ice "smashed many." Peary-type sledges were also used on the disastrous *Karluk* voyage with mixed feelings. William Laird McKinlay, the *Karluk*'s meteorologist, preferred them to Nome-type sledges, but other crew members differed. Bjarne Mamen considered them too heavy and too frail, and John Hadley said, "They are only good to be photographed." (McKinlay, William Laird, *Karluk.* New York: St. Martin's Press, 1976, pages 45–46.) Wally Herbert took an exact copy of the Peary sledge preserved at the National Geographic Society's headquarters with him over Ellesmere Land in 1967. How it fared he does not say in his book, *Across the Top of the World.* When the author asked Herbert in October 1993 how it held up, he said it broke up quickly and agreed with Hadley's assessment. But a copy of a Stefansson sledge broke up even more quickly, he added. It was a McClintock-style sledge made of hickory, but how closely it matched T.A. Cook's design, materials and craftsmanship is unknown.

16. Fiala, Anthony, *Fighting the Polar Ice.* New York: Doubleday, Page & Co., 1907, page 171. According to an article published in September 1909 in the *Sullivan County Democrat,* Theodore built more than 200 sledges. It also published a picture of one of his very graceful designs made of white hickory with rawhide lashings and shod with lignum vitae shoes. On pages 61–63 of his original polar diary Dr. Cook says: "In the rough and tumble work overland [Ellesmere Land] we have had a good test of the sledges and the relative strength of the Eskimo pattern and our own. Most of the Eskimo sledges are badly broken, some beyond repair, but ours handled by the same people and

the dogs have to the present had no important break." He notes a defect, however, saying that because their runners had not been put on with bolts when first bent, they would not stay straight.

17. REP, Diary, opposite entry for March 8, 1909. PFC.

18. BSU, March 17, 1894.

19. REP, Diary, April 20, 1906; typescript. PFC. The entry gives his position as 86°30'N.

20. DBM, *How Peary Reached the Pole.* Boston: Houghton Mifflin Co., 1934, page 57.

21. BDE, September 18, 1902.

22. Unattributed newspaper clipping, dated October 1, 1907. CSC.

23. FAC, "The Prince of Liars," *American Weekly,* August 2, 1925.

24. REP, *The North Pole,* page 273. In *Hampton's* he had been more blunt; instead of the names, he wrote, "my Anglo-Saxon friends." Considering Henson's reputed ability with dogsledges, Cook's remark probably has far more merit. In Cook's original polar diary, he says he left Franke because he *couldn't* handle a sledge. Peary gave several different reasons for taking Henson, including that he was the best ice traveler. But this is not supported by remarks about Henson recorded in Peary's typed transcript of his diary kept on his 1906 attempt to reach the Pole. There he says on April 2, "Henson not turning out as expected"; on April 5, "He is as bad as any of them, though of course will not admit it. . . . [Henson has] fallen down badly on his job and if he does not do better very soon I shall make a change." On April 6 he calls him "sluggish," and on April 15 says, "He is worse than the Eskimos in being frightened to death with these leads."

On page 5 of his original diary, Cook made a list of supplies "for 4 men for 3 mo." so he may have originally actually intended to take Franke but decided not to after watching his performance in the field.

25. Franke's trip was aided by Edwin Swift Balch, not Bradley, as Franke's neighbor told Lucien Alexander. Balch was interested in the rediscovery of Bradley Land to prove the theories he had advanced in his book, *The North Pole and Bradley Land,* the year before. He encouraged the expedition and even supplied Franke with navigational and scientific instruments.

Franke and Haark left on June 29, 1914, aboard the SS *Guide* under Captain Bernier. Since, technically, the captain could not accept passengers, he employed them at 25 cents a month. The *Guide* was unable to reach Etah as planned and was frozen in for the winter far to the south at Arthur Bay in Lancaster Sound.

From there, Franke, Haark and one Eskimo set off on February 18, 1915, with two sledges and 16 dogs. A few days out, they broke Peary's dictum and let their Eskimo get away from them, and when he left he took most of their provisions, leaving the two white men to fend for themselves. They tried to continue their journey toward Axel Heiberg Land, but Haark did not return after going in search of game on March 13.

With a trapper named Vigman, whom they had met earlier gathering arctic foxes along those desolate shores, Franke went searching for his lost companion and, on April 22, found Haark, frozen to death.

Taking the body, Franke returned to the *Guide,* arriving there on April 30. At the end of the voyage, Franke, because he was a German, was interned at Quebec as a prisoner of the war that had broken out since he had left. Franke sent an English synopsis of his diary, the original having been written in German, to Edwin Swift Balch. The story of his sad trip is from that synopsis. BCV.

26. BDE, September 18, 1902.

27. Considering that they died within a short time of each other in 1934 and 1935 of natural causes, it is possible that Etukishuk and Ahwelah may have been older than they looked. An Eskimo did not keep track of his age after he reached twelve. But there cannot be much question in the case of Etukishuk that he was about 20 years old in 1908, since there is a picture of Panikpa and his wife with Etukishuk in her hood taken in 1891, making him no more than three at that time.

28. *Philadelphia Record,* October 1, 1909.

29. Fiala, Anthony, *Fighting the Polar Ice.* New York: Doubleday, Page & Co., 1907, pages 3–4.

30. The PFC contains a set of notes in Borup's hand about the Eskimo interviews, apparently taken down in Greenland. These notes, from the use of the past tense, appear to have been dictated by Peary, rather than taken down at the interview itself. They are written in a notebook identical to the kind Peary used for his North Pole Diary. They differ in some details, but are generally the same as the report published by the NYT, October 13, 1909.

31. Undated telegram draft. PFC.

32. Goodsell, John W., *On Polar Trails.* Austin, Texas: Eakin Press, 1983, page 156.

33. "The Psychology of the Cook Fake," *Independent*, December 30, 1909, page 1514.

34. NYT, December 22, 1909.

35. NYT, November 29, 1909.

36. NYH, September 3, 1909.

37. Mitchell, Hugh C., "A Dilemma," unpublished paper, dated March 2, 1915. PFC.

38. Wedemeyer, A., Review of MAP in *Zeitschrift der Gesellschaft für Erdkunde zu Berlin,* no. 3, 1912, page 232. Translation by Dr. Thomas Walker.

39. Helgesen, Henry T., "Dr. Cook and the North Pole," Extension of Remarks, *Appendix to the Congressional Record,* 64th Congress, 2nd session, September 4, 1916, page 56. One of the criticisms that was brought up persistently against the authenticity of Cook's observations was that he expressed his reduced results down to seconds of arc. In *Peary,* as late as 1936, William H. Hobbs was still using this criticism, saying, "every Polar explorer should

know that it is quite impossible to fix the polar position astronomically with any accuracy," yet he gives a reduction of Peary's first sight down to .01 of a second of arc in the same book. It should also be noted that Bartlett's sight and *all* of Peary's observations at the Pole, which were reproduced in facsimile in *The North Pole,* were expressed down to seconds. Of this Hobbs certainly was aware.

40. FAC, "Memoirs of Polar Adventure," chapter 30, page 10, pencil manuscript. FCC.

41. Thorek, Max, *A Surgeon's World.* Philadelphia: J.B. Lippincott Co., 1943, page 285.

42. Keith Pickering, a computer analyst proficient in navigational mathematics, pointed out that Cook's theory contains a "positive feedback loop" that virtually prevents its realization: "If Cook were trying this method and . . . drifted slightly westward from the magnetic meridian, the compass needle would then point him slightly farther westward; which would in turn cause an even more westward-deviating compass course; which would pull him farther west, in an ever-increasing cycle of westward deviation. . . .

"One way to illustrate a positive feedback loop is to gently bend a piece of cardboard to create a ridge, and try to roll a marble down the length of the ridge. Once the marble falls off the ridge (even a little), the feedback effect keeps pulling it farther and farther off the ridge. . . .

"The problem is also complicated by the fact that the magnetic meridians are not straight, but curving (and often wiggly curves at that). This virtually guarantees that Cook, if he were using this method, would fall off the magnetic meridian never to return." (Letter to the author dated December 21, 1993.)

Since Cook was north of the Magnetic North Pole, without correction, his compass would give him no reference to true North, as it could point at 180° constantly without any reference to the 180° isogon.

Ensign Green's calculations in the vicinity of the predicted position of Crocker Land indicated that the variation of the compass there was 178° westerly in 1914. This is confirmed by the earliest fairly reliable magnetic chart of the area produced by the Royal Geographical Society in 1922. However, an examination of Cook's positions given in his narrative and published field notes shows that his claimed course wandered between the 93rd and the 97th meridians, though generally he claimed to have been on the 97th to the 85th degree of latitude and on the 95th from there to the Pole. The 1922 chart shows that in the area along Cook's claimed route the declination would have been more in the neighborhood of 160°. If we assume the 1922 data to have an approximate applicability to Cook's 1908 journey, he would have had to have gone farther west than Green—to approximately 105° west longitude—before picking up his 180° "magnetic meridian." But Cook never claimed to have crossed even the 102nd meridian along which he said Bradley Land lay.

That Cook's idea of following an isogon has some practical application is illustrated by Will Steger's 1986 journey to the Pole. His navigator, Paul Schurke, said he used the 70°W isogonic line (which he, too, termed "magnetic meridian") as a rough check in cloudy weather, but he used celestial observations to maintain his course whenever he could. Schurke found that the variation changed about ten degrees from land to the Pole along his route, but he already knew the approximate true declination over the route he was traversing. Cook did not, and he made no celestial observations to check it.

43. FAC, "Range of Vision from an Altitude," pencil manuscript. FCC.

44. NYT, December 26, 1909.

45. MAP, page 318.

46. FAC, "Dr. Cook's Own Story," *Hampton's Magazine,* January 1911, page 62.

47. HNPBD, pages 387–388.

48. Cook's original notebook was returned to him on January 30, 1911 under a power of attorney given to Walter Lonsdale. (Letter, Wilhelm von Rosen to the author, dated January 3, 1993.)

49. "The Wonderful Adventures of Dr. Cook," *Living Age,* July 6, 1912, page 36.

50. Gibbs, Philip, *The Pageant of the Years.* London: Wm. Heinemann, Ltd., 1946, page 85.

51. NYT, September 5, 1909.

52. NYT, September 9, 1909. The same issue mentions that Gibbs first saw this letter "in Freuchen's hands." In the NYH, September 12, 1909, can be found Freuchen's admission.

53. Gibbs, Philip, *The Pageant of the Years.* London: Wm. Heinemann, Ltd., 1946, page 87.

54. Ibid., page 86.

55. NYT, October 15, 1909.

56. Letter, Frank D. La Lanne to FAC, dated October 1, 1909. FCC.

57. Duckworth, W.M., "Cook, the Man Who Hypnotized a Nation," London *Daily News,* no date, but c. May 1910 by content.

58. NYT, December 27, 1909. The complete, official list of recipients of the medal between the years 1890 and 1921 was published in *Geografisk Tidsskrift,* vol. 25 (1922): 161–162. (No gold medals have been given since 1921.) It does not list Cook's name. The medal, however, was never formally revoked. (Letter, Sofus Christiansen [secretary of the Royal Danish Geographical Society] to the author, dated February 18, 1993.) The whereabouts of Cook's medal are unknown; it is not on display with the rest at his burial place in Buffalo.

59. Philadelphia *Evening Bulletin,* October 1, 1909.

60. NYA, September 16, 1909, reported that a Captain Blandford had dined with Peary and showed him Cook's printed dispatch while he was still at Battle Harbour.

61. Thorek, Max, *A Surgeon's World.* Philadelphia: J.B. Lippincott Co., 1943, page 283.

62. Henson said in the *Boston American* for July 17, 1910: "For the crime of being present when the Pole was reached Commander Peary has ignored me ever since." In March of that year, while at the Grand Theatre in Syracuse to give one of his lectures, Henson said, "Commander Peary, for all the years I have known him, has been a selfish man, after his own glory and that of nobody else. Since he discovered the north pole I have had a chance to see that more plainly than ever before, and so have some others.

"I have had a little dealing with Peary since our return, but I can't say it was particularly satisfying to me. . . .

"Along about the 15th or 16th of October [1909] I was negotiating with William A. Brady for these lectures upon the polar trip, and then Peary, who had ignored my existence after our return, suddenly woke up to it." (NYT, March 11, 1910.)

Though Peary swore he was "through" with Henson over this incident, it is true that Peary later persuaded his publisher, Frederick A. Stokes, to publish Henson's book and wrote an introduction to it. But a reading of his correspondence with Stokes leaves the feeling that this was done only to gain editorial control over Henson's manuscript. In any case, this seems to be the last favor Peary ever did Henson, and his last formal dealing with his "man-servant" of 25 years. Considering all this, S. Allen Counter's telling his readers that Henson was Peary's "most loyal and trusted companion" and that "the two men were more like brothers than friends" appears to be uninformed revisionism. (*National Geographic,* September 1988, pages 428–429.)

Peary had earlier said of this same man with whom he never shared any part of his questionable glory, apparently, quite literally, "I can't do without him," and Donald MacMillan described Henson as "indispensable" to Peary. Nevertheless, the geographical establishment did not even invite Henson to the admiral's funeral or to the dedication of the monument over his grave identifying Peary as the "Discoverer of North Pole."

As a result of Counter's efforts, Henson has now been reinterred in Arlington National Cemetery next to the admiral; his epitaph reads: "Co-discoverer of the North Pole." Matt Henson's book, which originally sold only a handful of copies in 1912, in its reprinted versions is now far more common in the libraries of the United States than *The North Pole.* This is a justice that, surely, "the only white man to have ever reached the Pole" could never have imagined.

In fairness to Peary, it should be mentioned that Cook made a parallel statement, ignoring his two Eskimo companions: "That I, one white man, might alone succeed in this quest gave me an impetus only single-handed effort and the prospect of single-handed success can give." (MAP, page 72.)

63. Goodsell, John W., *On Polar Trails.* Austin, Texas: Eakin Press, 1983, page 137.

64. A photo of the inscription placed on the monument appeared in the *National Geographic Magazine,* October 1954, page 517.

65. NYT, November 29, 1909.

A note on dirty diaries

On the subject of explorers' notebooks, Anthony Fiala remarked, "I don't believe any one could come up with a substitute for those old blubber-stained, snow marked notebooks familiar to every arctic explorer. This is where the weak part of an attempt to deceive will be found." (*Fighting the Polar Ice,* page 155.) Nansen related that his notebooks were so soiled with grease that he could hardly read them and displayed one page photographically to emphasize his point. "If you only took hold of a piece of paper your fingers left a dark-brown, greasy mark," he said, "and if a corner of your clothes brushed across it, a dark streak appeared. Our journals of this period look dreadful. They are 'black books' in the literal sense of the term." (*Farthest North,* vol. 2, page 436.) And of Peary's own notebook of 1906, now disappeared, Bob Bartlett said, "He wrote a paragraph in his little greasy diary that I think is classic." (*The Log of Bob Bartlett,* page 163.)

Erich von Drygalski, who was asked to give his opinion as part of the case filed against Peary by his German publisher, said as to the merits of *The North Pole*'s contents as proof of Peary's having actually reached the Pole: "I have first to remark that unimpeachable proof of the reaching of the pole cannot be adduced either positively or negatively in a book, but only by original diaries, for the latter obtain a definite aspect from the locality at which they are kept . . . so that one can recognize with certainty from their appearance, whether they were kept in polar conditions, i.e. are genuine or not, and consequently also whether they contain conclusive evidence." (Statement by Drygalski on Peary's *The North Pole,* dated January 25, 1913. PFC.)

66. Peary, who was right-handed, was in the draftsman's habit of holding his pen between his index finger and his middle finger. Wearing mittens would therefore have made writing with his normal grip impossible, yet the diary is in his characteristic hand, slanted left, and is, in fact, far neater than many of his ordinary letters, presumably written at his leisure in comfortable surroundings.

67. "Facts bearing on the point raised in regard to the cleanness of Peary's Note-book." PFC. Arthur T. Anthony, a document examiner with the Division of Forensic Sciences, Georgia Bureau of Investigation, made a limited examination of the diary in May 1989. He concluded that the diary could not have been written under the conditions described by Peary and was "not a chronicling of events that were happening when the journal was written." (*Journal of Forensic Sciences,* vol. 36 [1991]: 1614–1624.)

68. In relation to Peary's two blank pages at the Pole, in 1935 Stefansson had an interview with Louis Bernacchi, who had been to the Antarctic with

Borchgrevink and also with Scott's first expedition. He had never seen Peary's diary. During the interview Bernacchi remarked, "There is only one way in which Peary could have faked [his observations] effectively and that is for him to have had the idea and decide that he would leave, say, two blank pages in his notebook to be filled in later. That is the way I would go about it if I were going to make a fake report. These blank pages would be all dirty and greasy like the rest of the notebook. . . .

". . . Then after reaching camp I would fill in the data. But it would have to be very carefully done and I would have to be very cautious. It is not possible to do the whole thing after you return in some other book. Expedition notebooks bear the stamp of a long journey that cannot be faked – seal oil grease, smudged pencil marks, and other dirt." (Typed transcript of conversation with Bernacchi, dated March 8, 1935. CSC.)

The most interesting thing Arthur Anthony (see note 67 above) noted was that the two loose sheets inserted in the diary, one containing Peary's famous entry on his arrival at the Pole, were consecutive pages out of a single signature because the halves of the single watermark on the two sheets matched perfectly, yet they were placed in two different signatures in the bound diary, leading Anthony to conclude that they were not original entries but were placed there after the fact.

What Peary originally sent to the National Geographic Society might account for the loose-leaf sheet proclaiming his arrival at the Pole. Everything he first sent that was "original" was on loose sheets. This way he could avoid sending the diary itself. But when the society called for additional evidence, he had to show his entire original diary. Since he had first shown these loose sheets and, subsequently, the diary to the National Geographic Society, the loose sheets had to be included when his diary was later submitted to the congressional subcommittee. None of the loose sheets were torn from the sequential places they should have been written in his diary, however, but came from another position in the diary or from another notebook. Peary had several others with him identical to the North Pole Diary.

69. If they were genuine, there could be no reason to suppress these two photos. Why then did Peary never reveal he even had them?

One of the pictures may hold the answer. It shows the sun above a relatively flat polar pack. Since it is shot into the sun, the aperture is stopped down and so the surface of the pack is very underexposed. In *The North Pole*, Peary displayed four photographs on a single page opposite page 299 and labeled them "The Four Directions from the Pole." Each of these photographs is cropped and shows only a narrow swath of sky above the horizon. Nevertheless, there is enough sky shown to expect to see in one of them the sun above the horizon at exactly the same height as in the picture just described.

The one labeled "Looking Towards Cape Chelyuskin" is very similar, having been taken into the sun with the aperture stopped down to prevent overexposure. However, no sun is visible, since the entire sky has been airbrushed out and is devoid of any of the original details. This is the only one of the four in the book that has been retouched.

The 1989 Navigation Foundation's report, which purports to confirm Peary's journey to the North Pole, unwittingly adds further evidence against Peary by reproducing these photographs in a different form. As printed in the report, the pictures show less of the width of the horizon than in Peary's book, but the portion of the sky visible above the horizon is much wider, and its original details are visible in all four photos—*except* for the same horizontal swath above the horizon in the "Chelyuskin" picture. As in Peary's book, this portion of the photo has been airbrushed out but the rest of the sky is intact. That the sun was visible in the unretouched version is indicated by the shadows on the pack, which suggest it should appear near the left-hand margin of the picture.

Why has the sun been removed from the sky in this photograph? Peary may not have wanted its altitude compared with his stated time and position—or with his other two hidden photographs showing the sun at the "Pole."

Peary was clearly desperate to get hold of Matt Henson's pictures, perhaps fearing that shadows visible in them would prove they were not taken anywhere near the Pole, and after he did get them, except for a few shadowless exceptions, they were never seen again.

70. One such apparent instance is the Navigation Foundation's assertion that Louis Wolf's diary mentions Crocker Land long before Peary made reference to it in public, in an attempt to show that it was not an after-the-fact fantasy aimed at parting George Crocker, the wealthy New York capitalist, from more of his money. However, the author read through Dr. Wolf's diary, twice, for all the dates after the date of Peary's alleged discovery of Crocker Land without finding any mention of it by Wolf.

Although Peary's diary for the alleged discovery date, June 24, 1906, states, "No land visible," Peary's 1906 diary does mention "Crocker Land." Like his 1909 diary, the 1906 diary also has many mercenary comments about the rewards of finding the North Pole. Among them is a suggestion to himself, "Name the land West of the 12 mile tumulus (?) channel 'Crocker Land?'" Obviously, this is not the Crocker Land Peary eventually described lying far to the northwest. But could this be a reference to Meighen Island? Peary's writings and map show that he was significantly disoriented as to direction at this time. See also note 109 below.

71. HNPBD, pages 359–360.

72. HNPBD, page 354. Many examples of travesties of natural and physical laws can be found in Peary's *The North Pole*. He reports, for instance, on page 305, a "howling gale" with "ice . . . raftering all about us and beneath our very feet," then on the next page tells his readers, "Luckily there was no lateral movement of the ice." In a more candid time, Peary described to a New York reporter the typical condition of the polar pack ice as being "piled in ridges 25–75 feet high, and crossing them is as hard as it would be to get . . .

from the East [River] to the North River if all the buildings were thrown down." (NYT, November 18, 1906.)

Dr. Harrison J. Hunt of the Crocker Land Expedition described the particulars of such a journey: "If the trail lies across piled-up floe ice, progress is agonizingly slow. The sledge is shoved and hauled over one pressure ridge, only to plunge down the other side and tip over or bury its nose in the next one—dogs, traces, and sledge in a mess." (*North to the Horizon,* Camden, Maine: Down East Books, 1980, page 26.) Yet in 1909 these conditions had vanished, allowing Peary to reach the Pole from where he left his last fully literate witness and return to land at a speed never attained before or equaled since.

73. Though Peary's observations have been generally accepted, Bartlett's do contain significant errors. In a letter to Peary dated October 25, 1909, which accompanied Bartlett's original notebook (not located in the PFC), the captain said he had taken only single-limb sights of the sun at culmination, since that was what he was used to doing at sea. Bartlett made a number of mistakes, associated with applying his corrections for parallax, refraction and semi-diameter. As a result, his last sight for Peary was off by four miles, placing him 137 miles from the Pole when they parted on April 1, 1909, rather than 133. One of Henson's accounts states that this observation was taken by Bartlett five to six miles north of their April 1 camp on Bartlett's attempt to reach the 88th parallel. If this is so, that would place his point of separation from Peary that much farther south. It appears that Bartlett had been turned down for a Master's certificate because he was deficient in navigational skills. MacMillan alluded to this in his book, *Four Years in the White North,* on page 21.

On page 348 of *The Noose of Laurels,* Wally Herbert states unequivocally, "Without a knowledge of one's position and a regularly up-dated check on the variation of the compass, it is impossible to reach the North Pole." No one has yet presented a convincing explanation of how Peary knew his position at any time after he left land.

For a discussion of the extreme difficulties of the navigational feat Peary and Cook claimed to have accomplished see Hinks, Arthur R., "Notes on Determination of Position near the Poles," *Geographical Journal,* vol. 35 (1910): 299–312.

74. In 1986 Will Steger gained the means to make a dogsledge journey to the Pole, in part by persuading the National Geographic Society to back him on the premise that if he reached the Pole unresupplied, it would help Peary's case. In his book, *North to the Pole,* Steger claimed to have done so; actually he did not. Two of his party had to be airlifted out, but when they went, the food they would have consumed was left on the expedition's sledges. However, when Steger reached the Pole on May 1, 1986, he had few rations, having abandoned most of them to lighten his load, and could not have possibly returned to his starting point on what remained. Peary and Cook both claimed to have carried everything they needed *round-trip.* Steger was airlifted

out, and so his journey bears no comparison to these two explorers' claimed feat.

Discussions of Peary's sledge speeds with their comparisons of straight-line distances versus actual miles covered including detours, conversions of statute miles to nautical miles or vice versa, comparisons of "miles per day" to "miles per march," and a number of other vagaries have presented limitless opportunity for understandable honest confusion as well as intentional dishonest obfuscation; in nearly every such discussion, for or against, can be found errors introduced by one or the other.

Steger said that his speed during the final few days on the journey supported Peary's contention that he could travel at the incredible speeds he claimed after he left his last fully-literate witness. However, Steger's dog teams traveled at a fast clip because the sledges were nearly empty, a luxury not available to Cook or Peary. And in his book Steger compared his *total miles per day* for this period, including detours, with Peary's claimed *straight-line distance*, without detours. A table on page 327 of Steger's book acknowledges this and reveals that his best day was 32 miles made good. His average was less than nine miles of progress north per day for the whole trip, and these mileages are given in statute miles, which are 15 percent shorter than the nautical miles Peary always used to express his traveling distances. Even at this pace, Paul Schurke, Steger's navigator, said, "We were exhausted every day." When the two claims are directly equated, Steger covered the distance from 87°50' north latitude to the Pole at a rate of 18.13 statute miles per day, as opposed to Peary's 30.95.

It took Steger 55 days to reach the Pole. Peary claimed the *round-trip* in 53 days; Cook claimed 88 days, round-trip.

So Steger's journey did not actually help bolster Peary's claim. But Steger's experiences did throw some additional light on the real-life difficulties of an actual unresupplied journey to the Pole by dogsledge, including the observation that 20 percent of his time was spent in helping his sledges over ridges or chopping ice to make a passage for them. Also, Steger was of the opinion that a short, medium-framed man with a low metabolic rate was best suited to arctic conditions—a description that fits Cook better by far than Peary. Cook had the second-lowest pulse rate of anyone on the North Greenland Expedition (Verhoeff's was lowest); Peary had the highest.

After his polar expedition that appeared to support Peary's claim, Steger received another grant from the National Geographic Society for his proposed crossing of Antarctica, which he subsequently accomplished.

For a detailed discussion of the techniques of travel over pack ice and real-life survival on drift ice, as well as the perilous ice phenomena encountered, see Nelson, Richard K., *Hunters of the Northern Ice*. Chicago: University of Chicago Press, 1969.

The first and as yet only expedition verified to have ever reached the North Pole and returned unresupplied was that of Richard Weber and

Mikhail Malakhov, who as part of a three-man team had come close to doing it in 1992. They left Ward Hunt Island on February 14, 1995, man-hauling 300-pound sledges, arrived at the Pole on May 12 and retraced their route, making landfall on June 16, accomplishing the round-trip, including some backhauling, in 123 days—35 days more than Cook claimed; 70 more than Peary. However, Cook's journey took him over a route of 1,040 miles. Malakhov and Weber's was 100 miles shorter—940 (not including backhauling); Peary's route was only 826. Unlike 1909, this incredible physical feat, perhaps the greatest in the history of exploration, received hardly any notice in the popular press.

75. From the author's notes of comments made at the symposium, "All Angles: Peary and the North Pole," presented at the 117th Annual Meeting of the United States Naval Institute, Annapolis, April 19, 1991. Handwritten notes in Peary's hand were found in the PFC in which he stated that he estimated his distance traveled was 25 percent more than his progress northward, up to and including the twentieth day out.

76. NYT, November 29, 1909.

77. Green, Fitzhugh, "Arctic Duty with the Crocker Land Expedition," *United States Naval Institute Proceedings,* vol. 43, no. 10 (October 1917): 2223.

78. Letter, Thomas F. Hall to FAC, dated August 17, 1916. FCC. Note also that Cook's scathing telegram of March 4, 1911, to President Taft about the Peary Bill was sent from Omaha, Hall's place of residence.

In the contents list of Cook's memoirs, which he wrote at Leavenworth, chapter 11 is entitled "The Murder of Prof. Ross Marvin." However, this chapter was missing from the manuscript. Cook told William Shea that he was thinking of removing it, since it did not seem to fit in with the rest. Did Dr. Cook send it to Captain Hall for incorporation into his monograph on the murder of Ross Marvin, which appeared in Henry Lewin's book, *The Great North Pole Fraud?* And if so, did Hall use it as the basis for his article? The chance for comparison came when the missing chapter turned up in the CSC. Chapter 11, entitled "The Suppressed Murder of Ross Marvin with its International Complications," is 3,500 words; Captain Hall's monograph is about twice that and has little in common with it in content or structure.

79. Balch, Edwin Swift, "Polar Controversies. II. Cook's Claims," *Independent,* November 28, 1925, page 608; quotes Wordie from "The Undiscovered North," *Discovery,* vol. 2 (1921):88–91.

80. MAP, page 246. Some Cook proponents have recently suggested that Cook saw one of the ice islands that are currently circulating in the Arctic Basin. This is unlikely because these ice islands are by no means permanent features. T-1, for instance, the largest ice island ever observed, which was first sighted in 1947, grounded in McClintock Channel in 1963 and had broken up completely by 1975. However, new ice islands are still being calved from Ellesmere Island's glacial fringe.

81. One is the photograph Wordie mentions, labeled as such in Cook's book, and the other, which appears at the top of the page opposite 237 of MAP, was identified as "the new land" in the October 1, 1909, issue of the NYH, where the picture was first published. Both show what appears to be coastline with distinct differences in elevation over its terrain, something not characteristic of an ice island.

Along with the Cook papers given to the Library of Congress came a mass of photographic prints. Many of these were made on Cook's polar expedition, distinguishable by their 3½-by-5½-inch size, unique among his photographs. Among them is an uncropped copy of the picture of Bradley Land published opposite page 236 in MAP. At the extreme left margin of the uncropped photo can be seen a bright spot well above the horizon, which appears to be the sun behind some haze. This is confirmed by a careful examination of the shadows of the sledges and dogs, which extend in the opposite direction. Since Cook claimed Bradley Land lay along the 102nd meridian in the west, the position of the sun indicates the picture was taken in the evening. But Cook says in his printed field notes: "March 30: Land, 9 A.M., cleared; land was seen; westerly clouds settled over it." This implies the sighting was in the morning when the sun would be in the east, not over Bradley Land to the west, though the text of the book is not clear on this point. However, his *Herald* article of October 1, 1909, states, "Awaking in time for observations on the morning of the 30th, the weather was found beautifully clear. The fog, which had persistently screened the west had vanished and land was discovered at some distance west. . . ." There is room in the text, however, to infer that the land may still have been visible in the evening, but the height of the sun in the uncropped picture certainly appears to be far too high above the horizon for that late in the day on March 30 or 31 at the latitude at which Cook placed Bradley Land.

82. FAC, "A Walk to the North and South Poles," *Canadian Magazine*, September 1900, page 422.

83. Apparently, Cook's belief in Crocker Land was ambivalent. In the letter he wrote to Captain Bernier in May 1909, which embodies the first report of his polar journey, he states that "Crocker Land was sighted and a new land to the north of it extending to the eighty-fifth. Beyond no land was seen." Yet in his letter to Rudolph Franke in March 1908, he says, "We have seen nothing of Crocker Land, and I am taking a straight course for the Pole." In his *Herald* series he reconciles these two statements by saying he noticed a belt of disturbed ice and "for a while I believed this to be an indication of Crocker land." On September 22, 1909, he told Dillon Wallace that Crocker Land did not exist, and that Peary probably had seen a mirage. In his 1911 book, he says he "prefers" to believe it exists even though the Eskimos said Peary never saw it. By 1914 we find him again telling Dillon Wallace that MacMillan was wasting his time looking for Crocker Land, as he knew, definitely, it did not exist. Still later, in the 1930s, he told William Shea that he

still believed Crocker Land might exist; then, when Shea expressed surprise at this statement, he backed away from it. (Bernier's letter appears in Helgesen, Henry T., "Dr. Cook and the North Pole," Extension of Remarks, *Appendix to the Congressional Record*, 64th Congress, 2nd session, September 4, 1916, p. 54; Wallace's letter to Edmund Platt, dated May 4, 1916, is quoted on the same page; FAC to William Shea, dated June 25 and 30, 1931. FCC.)

A comparison of the *Herald*'s publication with the version of the Bernier letter printed in the *Congressional Record* reveals highly significant differences showing that the *Herald* was just as willing to toy with the truth to protect its interests as was the *New York Times.*

In the original letter, for instance, Cook says he arrived at Annoatok on April 5, 1909. In the *Herald* it is printed as April 15, the date given in the logbook kept by Peary's cabin boy, Pritchard, and this was about eight days ahead of the true date. In Cook's notebook 1 (see note 99 below) the last entry is April 5, but other notes are added, giving the day of arrival as April 15.

84. Skeptics logically assumed that Bradley Land was a fantasy long before this was confirmed, since in his book Cook reported that on his return he crossed the 85th parallel at the 100th meridian. This placed him on May 24, 1908, just 10.5 miles from Bradley Land's reported position, yet he didn't see it, though he said the Eskimos saw it when he was asleep.

If it were really at this position, they pointed out, he might have visited it expecting to replenish his sledges, and could even have wintered there in an extremity. Yet he plunged on southward with dwindling supplies.

85. NTP, page 131. Those who have argued that Cook could not have based his description on these passages, since he hadn't the time to read Peary's book, which came out not long before Cook left the United States in 1907, are mistaken. Rudolph Franke, in a letter to Congressman Helgesen in 1916, specifically said that *Nearest the Pole* was one of the books in the arctic library at Annoatok, so it is possible that Cook may have relied on these descriptions as a basis for his Glacial Island. (Helgesen, Henry, T., "Dr. Cook and the North Pole." *Appendix to the Congressional Record*, 64th Congress, 2nd session, September 4, 1916, page 59.)

Some ice islands carry substantial debris from their point of origin. ARLIS II (Arctic Research Laboratory Ice Station), which was occupied by the U.S. Navy during the International Quiet Sun Year in 1965, had a hill 41 feet high made of boulders. But even these could never be confused with the solid land shown at the margin of Cook's uncropped lantern slide of his "Glacial Island."

86. Nansen, Fridtjof, "On North Polar Problems," *Geographical Journal*, vol. 30, no. 5 (November 1907): 469–487; vol. 30, no. 6 (December 1907): 585–601.

87. Perhaps this last was unnecessary. Recent aerial surveys indicate that the "Big Lead" is not a constant feature of the pack, as Peary and Cook assumed—and perhaps never was—though Cook may have actually encountered a southwest shear zone now known to exist along his claimed route.

88. FAC, "A Comparative View of the Arctic and the Antarctic," in *Report of the Eighth International Geographic Conference, Held in the United States,* 1904. Washington, D.C.: GPO, 1905, page 705; Spencer, J.W., "On the Physiographic Improbability of Land at the North Pole," *American Journal of Science,* May 1905, pages 333–340.

89. In *Peary at the North Pole; Fact or Fiction?* and in several articles previous to its publication, Dennis Rawlins stated that in 1908 the compass needle at the Pole would have pointed 30 degrees to the right of the North Magnetic Pole, and he used this as evidence against Cook's claim, since Cook said it pointed directly down the 97th meridian. Rawlins extrapolated this figure working backward from a chart of magnetic variation for the epoch 1965.0. According to correspondence to the author from Norman Peddie of the Global Seismology and Geomagnetism Branch of the U.S. Geological Survey, such an extrapolation is not possible since secular variation is not a constant and not susceptible to extrapolation from current data. The author asked Rawlins about this in October 1993, and though he did not admit that his method was invalid, he said that his figure was "only approximate." This seems supported by the Royal Geographical Society's chart of magnetic variation for epoch 1922. The placement of the 180° isogon seems to fall within ten degrees of Rawlins's estimate.

Peary never publicly mentioned any observations for magnetic variation, but a letter in the Peary papers written in 1912 indicates that Peary's compass pointed 90 degrees west of north during his journey to the Pole. This is apparently the only mention he ever made of magnetic data at any time during his polar attempt. (Letter, REP to Roth J. Rosenthal, dated April 2, 1912. PFC.)

90. Arthur, James, "Strange Scientific Anomalies at the North Pole," *Scientific American,* October 16, 1909, page 279.

91. Translated from Quervain, Alfred de, *Durch Grönlands eiswüste; reise der Deutsch-schweizerischen Grönlandexpedition 1909 auf das inlandeis.* Strassburg: J. Singer, 1911, page 180.

92. On page 144 of his original polar diary, Cook mentions "the spiral ascent of the sun," which de Quervain said Cook was not aware of on the return trip to Denmark in 1909, just as it appears in his published field notes. This contradiction is not easily explained, since it seems unlikely that the field notes as a whole could have been written after Cook's return to Greenland. But it might be explained as an addition. The entry for April 21 is split into two "paragraphs" on page 144. The second half of the entry might have been inserted. There are as many as eight blank lines between other consecutive entries in the field notes written in Cook's original diary—the same as there would be here if the paragraph containing reference to the "spiral ascent" were taken out. After this paragraph there is just one space before the entry for April 22 begins. It must be said, though, that there is no visible evidence that would indicate that it has been added. And in the copy of the field notes

(notebook 1) there is a continuous series of entries, including this one, with no intervening spaces. If Cook really copied this at Cape Sparbo, even this copy would predate de Quervain's report of Cook's ignorance of the phenomenon. However, the notes could just as easily have been copied over after his conversation with de Quervain.

As to other field data, in notebook 1's (see note 99 below) condensation of Cook's original narrative of his journey across Ellesmere Land, he twice notes "Compass Var" and once "Azimuths for our compass" but writes no figures. These notations are nowhere to be found in the original diary of the journey.

93. *Scottish Geographical Magazine,* vol. 30 (1914): 60.

94. RWP, "The Brilliant Coloring of the North," typescript. RPA.

95. Certainly, Cook wrote the first thought on this. On page 79 of Cook's original diary this sentence makes its first appearance under the date of March 2, 1908. But at that point he was more than 600 miles from his goal, surrounded by game and still accompanied by all his remaining Eskimo comrades. This does not necessarily mean that this passage was written on this date, however. The fact that it starts on the bottom of page 78 and runs over onto the unlined upper portion of 79 suggests that it was written in after the bulk of the material on page 79.

96. Letter, FAC to William Shea, dated March 18, 1931. FCC.

97. In a letter Cook wrote at Oomanui to John R. Bradley on December 6, 1907, he says the sun set on October 20. If this is so that would make the date February 25.

98. In a letter, REP to S.A. Mitchell, dated November 24, 1909. PFC. Mitchell was a professor in the Department of Astronomy at Columbia University. Peary was using him, in addition to Hastings, to check Cook's statements on astronomical matters in hope of finding flaws to use against him. Peary wrote of the notations in Billy Pritchard's Annoatok log, which was eight days ahead of the actual date when Peary got back: "Pritchard's statement in regard to seeing the sun for the first time on the 10th of March by his log (2d of March by the correct date) is undoubtedly entirely accurate. The high land back of Annoatok (Annoatok itself having a northern exposure) would readily prevent the sun from being actually seen at Annoatok for several days after it appeared." PFC.

99. Descriptions of the notebooks under discussion are as follows:

Notebook 1. Original field notes, February 19, 1908, to September 4, 1909. A small medical memorandum book, 2⅝ by 4¾ inches. The contents are almost exactly like "copy of the field notes" displayed in MAP pages 569–577, except there are also entries both before and after those printed in the book. After June 18, 1908, the entries are scattered and seem to be written after the fact.

Notebook 2. September 1, 1908, to April 30, 1909; same description and dimensions. This contains a record of events of the stay at Cape Sparbo, apparently as they happened. There is a partial typed copy of this notebook in Baldwin's papers—mostly the weather information has been extracted—but this copy is reasonably complete after the winter begins in October.

Notebook 3. Another tiny book, the same as those above. It apparently once contained sketches for Cook's projected polar book, of which only two pages and a table of contents survive, along with a list of flowery phrases, apparently for use in the book, some of which actually appear in *My Attainment of the Pole.* Most of the body of the book is now blank, having been erased. This note was attached to it: "Found in green book rest of pages empty. Destroyed because of working conditions. HCV 12/28/50."

Notebook 4. May 25, 1907, to June 13, 1909. Leather-bound book, 4¾ by 6¾ inches with "Record" printed in gold diagonally on the cover. There are entries for May 25–27, 1907, the last having been erased. The main body, however, begins March 20, 1908. There are 72 consecutively numbered pages. Some pages may be missing at the end, as the binding is broken, though it is impossible to tell for sure. This notebook would be a good candidate for the one Ralph Shainwald said was mutilated, presumably by E.B. Baldwin. It is in every way like Cook's Mount McKinley Diary, which contains 176 pages. However, Shainwald reported only 60 pages missing, and he said they were clipped out. This one, if it had 176 pages originally, is missing at least 104 pages, and several whole signatures have been removed. The other notebooks seem to be intact. This may be the one Cook showed the reporters at the Waldorf-Astoria in September 1909. At that time it was said to have 173 pages.

Including AWD and the "Hunting Diary," there are therefore six separate books kept by Cook on the Bradley Arctic Expedition of 1907–1909 at the Library of Congress, none larger than 8¼ inches in any dimension. But what of the "ten-inch-square" notebook Captain Loose said Cook read latitudes to him from? Did Loose simply misjudge the size?

In Walter Lonsdale's article in the June 1910 *Travel Magazine,* there is a picture on page 425 captioned "The note books on which the famous Copenhagen report was based." Leaning against a typewriter on a desk, are three notebooks. The one in the foreground is closed and lying on its side. Anyone familiar with these notebooks will recognize it as one of the small medical memorandum books, such as notebook 1 above. This notebook can be easily measured and compared in size with those behind it, which are standing upright with their pages open, though since they are leaning away from the camera, they are foreshortened and cannot be measured directly. The first of these with the pages open is larger than the one in front of it, so it must be one the size of notebook 4. The one behind it is still larger, and compared with the height of the typewriter, this could be the one that Captain Loose described. Perhaps it contained the rough draft of Cook's *Herald* series, since the Copenhagen submission was substantially like that account. If so, no such book has yet come to light.

100. Letter, William Adams to REP, dated June 17, 1909. PFC.

101. The two versions of the Bernier letter are found in the NYH, October 6, 1909, and the *Appendix to the Congressional Record*, September 4, 1909, page 54. That the text reproduced in the *Congressional Record* is authentic is borne out by the fact that Cook kept a handwritten copy of the letter. FCC. It is identical to this version, not to the one printed in the *Herald*.

102. Another example of "a story in the making" is illustrated by comparing a draft of the telegram sent from Lerwick with the actual text as transmitted. A carbon copy of this seven-page draft, written in Cook's hand and dated "Upernavik, June 18, 1909," was given to the Royal Danish Library by Governor Kraul. A copy was obtained after a personal inquiry by the author brought it to light.

In almost all respects the draft is like the telegram but for two passages. The first has to do with the return journey. Cook eventually said that he did not see Bradley Land as he returned southward from the Pole but that his Eskimos did while he was sleeping. However, the draft says, "On May 24 the sky cleared long enough to give us a peep of the new lands and a set of observations. We had reached the 84 parallel near the 97 meridian. The ice was much broken and drifted eastward leaving many open spaces of water." The words "a peep of the new lands and" were left out of the telegram, which simply says, "to give us a set of observations."

The other major deviation from the published telegram has to do with the number of dogs. Cook said little about his dogs other than that he started with 26 and came back with ten. Nowhere in his published writings does he state at what point he killed his dogs or exactly how many he had at any other point in the journey. But in this draft he says of April 14 above latitude 88°21': "Other dogs had been sacrificed for the good of the greatest number but there remained six pulls of well tried wolf force for each sled," meaning he had twelve dogs on April 14. Since he claimed to have returned with ten, that would mean only two died in the next two months before they reached land on June 15. This sentence, too, was stricken from the finished dispatch.

Among Cook's early published statements, his interview with W.T. Stead published in the NYA, September 15, 1909, varies in a number of significant details from his eventually published narrative.

103. Chapter 12 of HCP is entitled "Polar Packs – Making and Breaking." Its text begins: "My note books are packed with data bearing upon the making and breaking of the polar pack." The very first page of N. I has an essay entitled "The Making and Breaking of the Polar Pack." Though the content of the essay is not the same as the memoir chapter, such a coincidence suggests that Cook may have still had this now-missing notebook as late as the 1930s. There are 154 original prenumbered pages. The four occupied by the renum-

bered pages 155–158 make 158. Notes in the index list four more that had something already written on them—160, 169, 170, 177 (which might have been the flyleaf)—plus their reverses 159 and 178 make six, for a total of ten additional pages. So 164 pages are accounted for, leaving 12 pages missing (or 14 if we do not count the flyleaf). The implication is that these pages were not blank but may have held the actual events of the "missing week."

The diary in question, which was originally in the Royal Astronomical Library, was moved to the Rigsarkivet after an inquiry by the author uncovered it. All remarks on this diary are a result of an examination of a photocopy purchased from the Rigsarkivet. Not all of the copy provided to the author was entirely legible.

104. MAP, pages 75–76.

105. HNPBD, page 363.

106. HNPBD, page 344.

107. HNPBD, page 350.

108. See the series Lindsay, D.G., *Sea Ice Atlas of Canada*. Ottawa: Energy, Mines and Resources of Canada, 1961–1968; 1969–1974; 1975–1978, published in 1974, 1977 and 1981. Other studies confirm these data. When the Arctic Petroleum Operators Association was preparing data on ice movement in the Queen Elizabeth Archipelago, they didn't even bother to map the area between Axel Heiberg Island and the Ringnes Islands for June, since "it was found that June movements in the area of interest were nonexistent." (Lindsay, D.G., *Arctic Islands Sea Ice Movements Analysis from Ice Reconnaissance and Satellite Imagery Data*. A.P.O.A. Project #92, Ottawa: January 1976.) This report details the ice conditions in the areas where Cook claimed to have been adrift to the south:

> Sverdrup Channel: The ice cover in this area rarely breaks up. Typically a few cracks appear at the peak [September] of the break-up season.
>
> Peary Channel: The ice cover in this channel seldom breaks up. If break-up does occur it usually takes place after all other channels in the archipelago have broken up.
>
> Hassel Sound: Only the southern most part of this channel breaks up with any regularity during the summer season.

Cook said he drifted through Hassel Sound in June 1908, at the very beginning of summer. The Eskimos' story as published by the Peary Arctic Club says that they gathered duck eggs at Cape Vera. This supports a far more southerly position for Cook at his stated return date, since these birds' eggs can be found there between June 15 and July 15. Cape Vera is on Jones Sound, beyond the zone of immovable ice.

109. When Stefansson wanted to use some of Cook's material from MAP in his discussion of the discovery of Meighen Island in his book, *Unsolved Mysteries of the Arctic*, Cook revealed his ambivalence about whether he had

actually seen it. At first he gave permission through his lawyer for Stefansson to use the quotes he wanted, asking him only to correct one inaccuracy of direction in the text, then, a month later, he threatened to sue Stefansson because he did not want it to be said that he had not seen Meighen Island. The chapter on Meighen Island was then dropped from Stefansson's book but later was privately published and distributed to libraries by Stefansson. See the correspondence between Stefansson and Stanley Boriss, Anthony Fiala and Ted Leitzell, October to December, 1938. SPD.

A note on the "mystery" of Meighen Island

No physical evidence that Cook ever visited Meighen Island has ever been found. Some tin-plate containers found there in the 1960s were analyzed and proved to be of a manufacture after 1910, thus eliminating them as relics of such a visit. (Sebisty, J., et. al., *Examination of Metal Relics found on Meighen Island, N.W.T.* Ottawa: Mines Branch Investigation Report IR 64–67.)

Meighen Island mysteriously appeared on the map drawn for Peary by Cook's Eskimo companions in 1909, though it was not officially discovered until 1916. It then was used by Stefansson to "prove" that Cook did not even attempt a trip to the Pole, but had camped instead on this undiscovered island (see note 70 above).

Fitzhugh Green recovered the message from another Peary cairn either at Cape Thomas Hubbard or within one day's travel down the west coast of Axel Heiberg Island. (It is impossible to tell where it was from Green's muddled text.) Its text does not clear up Peary's movements after arriving at the cape. It is dated "June 30, 1906," whereas the other cairn message found at the cape itself was dated June 28. The message reads in part: "The 27th and 28th fine clear days giving good view of the northern horizon from the summit of the Cape. The 29th and 30th southwesterly gales with rain and snow. . . . Expect to start back tonight." It makes no mention of any travel to the southwest, but Green's text implies that the cairn was on the west shore. (See Green, Fitzhugh, "Arctic Duty with the Crocker Land Expedition," *United States Naval Proceedings*, vol. 43, no. 10 [October 1917]: 2224; vol. 43, no. 11 [November 1917]: 2457–2459.)

Might Peary have looked to the west and caught sight of Meighen Island "12 miles" across the Sverdrup channel, as he notes in his diary? The island actually lies about 25 miles to the closest point of Axel Heiberg Island, but Peary may have estimated it as closer. As Cook found with antarctic icebergs, distance in the polar regions is extremely difficult to estimate.

On page 523 of Stefansson's book, *The Friendly Arctic*, he says that on June 22, 1916, from a 200-foot elevation, "We could see Heiberg Island northward to the vicinity of Cape Thomas Hubbard." It appears from this passage that it may have been possible to have seen Meighen Island from the position of Peary's second cairn, whether on the cape or not. Keith C. Arnold, who spent some time on the island, confirms that the north end of Axel

Heiberg Island is visible from Meighen Island, but being about 100 miles away, it requires abnormal refraction to raise it above the horizon. ("Who Discovered Meighen Island?" in *Polarboken,* 1963–64, published by the Norwegian Polar Club.)

110. NYH, September 19, 1909.

111. HNPBD, pages 313–314. The Eskimos told Dr. Hunt of the Crocker Land Expedition that Cook still had four cartridges when he returned to Annoatok.

112. NYH, September 6, 1909.

113. Cape Hardy was the original name applied to the cape that Sverdrup renamed Cape Sparbo. It consists of twin headlands, 900 feet high, projecting into Jones Sound, attached to the main body of Devon Island by a thin neck of land. Cook's winter igloo is on a small projection on the east side of Cape Hardy; just south of the cape lies a lowland with many ponds before Devon Island rises to rocky highlands. About 1940, the cape Cook occupied reverted to its original name and the other headland was given the name Cape Sparbo.

114. Wordie, J.M., "An Expedition to North West Greenland and The Canadian Arctic in 1937," *Geographical Journal,* vol. 92, no. 5 (November 1938): 401. It is impossible to tell which of these artifacts belonged to Dr. Cook, because the *Beothic* visited the igloo in 1910 and so did Captain Adams in the *Morning* the same year. Both parties mounted a musk ox hunt before departing. In his original polar diary, Cook describes in detail the building of his house over the remains of an older dwelling, just as described by Wordie.

115. NYT, October 6, 1909.

116. There is considerable variance in the reports of the relations between Cook and Murphy at Annoatok. Murphy reported that he treated Cook amicably, lent him his own pants and even shaved Cook. Murphy said Cook's last words to him were "Murphy, as long as I live I will never forget you for your kindness to me." (NYA, October 7, 1909.) This account seems doubtful considering the several reports of animosity between Cook and Murphy. But Cook himself is reported to have said, "It isn't true that Murphy didn't treat me well when I returned, after reaching the Pole, to my base of supplies at Etah. It was I, I am afraid, who did not treat Murphy well. When I found him in my house, in charge of my supplies, I put him out." (NYA, September 22, 1909.)

According to the September 15, 1909, diary entry of Donald B. MacMillan preserved at Bowdoin College, Bo'sun Murphy said that Cook was more concerned about his monetary loss than anything else: "[Cook] told Bo'sun he had no right to use his stores, was like taking money out of his pocket. Quite a lot of his stores were still left which he gave to the Esquimaux on leaving. Was never denied stores but given all he needed and provisioned for sledge trip. Remarked that he had gone beyond Peary's record. Had a watch with one hand on it. Said he would not take $20,000 for flag. Gave this to Whitney, also sledge." The allegation that Cook cheated his Eskimos of their promised payment is, therefore, unjust. Cook's own letter gave the contents of his house to Etukishuk, Ahwelah and Koolootingwah but left them in the charge of Whitney. As shown by MacMillan's diary entry, he was well aware of this. If they did not get what was promised to them, it was Whitney's fault, not Cook's.

117. NYH, September 29, 1909.

118. Letter, T. Everett Harré to Edwin C. Hill, of WABC Radio, dated May 8, 1940.

119. NYW, September 18, 1910.

120. NYH, September 20, 1909.

121. NYA, September 22, 1909.

122. NYA, September 27, 1909; NYA, September 29, 1909. Cook confirmed this in his original polar diary by writing that he had left only material dated June 1–September 1, 1908, and the observations of his return journey with Whitney.

123. A copy of this 14-page handwritten record of the second Konsistorium's deliberations was obtained from the archives of the University of Copenhagen by the author.

124. Freuchen, Peter, *I Sailed with Rasmussen.* New York: Julian Messner, Inc., 1958, page 36.

125. Egan, Maurice Francis, "Dr. Cook in Copenhagen," *Century Magazine,* September 1910, page 763.

126. FAC, "Dr. Cook's Own Story," *Hampton's Magazine,* February 1911, page 166. Though Cook said, "It is ridiculous to say I have no knowledge of the Eskimo tongue. I lived three and one-half years among them and speak their language fluently," he showed little facility with languages. Several sources indicate his German was barely understandable; French, despite his confinement on the *Belgica,* remained a mystery to him. It is doubtful that Cook could master, even in three and a half years, a language that the missionary in Greenland, whom he interviewed in 1893, told him he had been unable to learn in more than 17 years of total immersion.

L.C. Bement recorded that when some Eskimos first came aboard the *Erik* in 1901, Cook "oiled up his Huskie" but that it took him an hour to find out the location of their village. (Bement, Louis C., Diary, July 27, 1901. Possession of Silas H. Ayer, III).

127. LK, "The Faked 'Confession' or How a Magazine Made History!" unpublished article, dated February 4, 1916, page 44. FCC.

128. NYT, September 3, 1911.

129. Letters, Ernest C. and Etta Rost to LK, the first dated June 7, 1914; the "message" letter is dated June 21, 1914. Both quotes are in Etta's postscripts to Ernest's letters. FCC.

130. Letter, LK to Ralph von Ahlefeldt, dated May 8, 1940. CSC. High, Fred, "Muck Raking and Muck Rakers," *Platform,* vol. iv, no. 12, May 1914, unpaged. High says the quote is taken from an interview given April 16,

1914, by Lilian Kiel. Kiel also told the Education Committee that Peary had little to do with the writing of his *Hampton's* articles and had "no data" of his own about his polar journey, later going so far as to say some of the material used in "Peary's Own Story" was directly lifted from Dr. Cook's *Herald* series. (LK, private recording made on April 7, 1953. CSC.) She strongly implied that Elsa Barker made up the story of Peary's journey based on only the sketchiest of details.

Elsa Barker said this was ridiculous, as Kiel knew that Peary came to the offices of *Hampton's* nearly every month and gave hours of dictation to a court stenographer to provide background material for the articles. (Barker, Elsa, "Facts Relative to the Writing of the Peary North Pole Articles for *Hampton's Magazine*." Statement dated 1936. PFC.) That Kiel was indeed aware of this is shown in her long article on the "faked confession," in which she described meeting Peary in the elevator coming from *Hampton's* offices. Kiel seemed to think that her story was worth a lot of money and even wrote to President Wilson about it in 1917.

131. MAP, New York: Polar Publishing Company, 1911, page x; MAP, New York: Mitchell Kennerley, 1913, page x.

132. All quotes of the reviewer of MAP are from "The Wonderful Adventures of Dr. Cook," *Living Age,* July 6, 1912, pages 28–36.

133. Letter, T. Everett Harré to Edwin C. Hill, May 8, 1940. FCC.

134. T. Everett Harré, *Behold the Woman.* Philadelphia: J.B. Lippincott Co., 1916, pages 158–159.

135. FAC, Miscellaneous notes for *The New Era.* FCC.

136. MAP, page 566.

137. NYH, September 9, 1909.

138. VS, "Cook and Peary," unpublished article, page 3, undated, but content dates it to after 1934. SCD.

139. In his 1901 diary, Clarence Wyckoff gave a hint as to how Bridgman accumulated so much wealth. He said Bridgman admitted to being a "noteshaver," that is, someone who practiced usury. Apparently, this was not Bridgman's only method. Among the Peary papers was a letter threatening to expose Bridgman for bilking two newlyweds out of their savings in a scam involving the sale of a piano. The writer said this happened when Bridgman was still working for the publisher Frank Leslie, so it would have been sometime in the late 1880s. (Letter, W. Brookman Pfister to HLB, dated July 24, 1912. PFC.)

140. Peter Freuchen said of MacMillan, "When one knows MacMillan one is surprised by nothing." According to his surgeon, Dr. Hunt, MacMillan had emulated Peary in many other ways. Hunt alleged that MacMillan set up a lucrative trade in fox furs, had an Eskimo wife and was in the exploration game solely for his own glory. He also didn't get along with his surgeon.

141. Bartlett, Robert A., *The Log of Bob Bartlett.* G.P. Putnam's Sons, 1928, page 201.

142. *Saturday Evening Post,* April 16, 1910, pages 17–19, 46.

143. Green, Fitzhugh, "The Crocker Land Expedition," *Natural History,* vol. 28 (1928): 475.

144. The murder of Pewahto took place when the Eskimo drove his sled ahead of Green, who was on foot, leading him to think the man intended to abandon him; Pewahto was probably only trying to get the white man to hurry. (Jean Malaurie mentions a similar incident in his classic book on the Polar Eskimos, *The Last Kings of Thule.*) Green later gloated ghoulishly over the killing: "He that had loomed hostile and deceit between me and safety lay now crumpled and inert in the unheeding snow.

"For once fate was balked. . . . I had baffled misfortune. The feeling sent red gladness to my anaemic humor. . . .

"The present was perfect, ecstatic. To prolong the moment was my impulse. I laughed, not fiendishly, but because I was glad." (*United States Naval Institute Proceedings,* vol. 43, no. 11 [November 1917]: 2456.) Coincidentally, Pewahto was Peary's Eskimo wife's real husband.

145. Grosvenor, Gilbert H., *The National Geographic Society and Its Magazine.* Washington, D.C.: National Geographic Society, 1957, page 51.

146. There are many suspicious things about Byrd's flight: Byrd dropped no flags at the Pole, though he carried hundreds of tiny ones for just that purpose (if Byrd had dropped them, Amundsen would certainly have seen them when he passed over the Pole in the *Norge*); contemporaneous meteorological records do not match Byrd's reports, especially of a convenient tailwind that whisked his lumbering plane back from the Pole, like Peary, in record time; though he didn't drop flags, Byrd did drop and damage his sextant immediately upon leaving the "Pole" and so could make no observations on the return flight; he took no solar altitude data.

On a flight from Detroit to Labrador in August 1928, Floyd Bennett, Byrd's pilot on the 1926 flight, took ill and died. In the spring of 1927, however, according to Bernt Balchen, Bennett's copilot and Byrd's pilot in Antarctica in 1929, Bennett had confided to him that the North Pole flight, for which both he and Byrd had been awarded the Congressional Medal of Honor and a gold medal from the National Geographic Society, was a fake. Byrd's claim to have flown over the South Pole in 1929, a flight on which Byrd was the navigator responsible for certifying the feat, and on which some have alleged the polar hero was stone drunk, also rests entirely on the favorable endorsement of the National Geographic Society, in a report dated January 9, 1931. Apparently all the copies of this report have disappeared except the one in the Byrd papers, box 1002, file 2, housed at Ohio State University. For more details on Byrd's career and his relationship to the National Geographic Society, see Rodgers, Eugene, *Beyond the Barrier* (Annapolis: Naval Institute Press, 1990), which cites this material.

The diary kept by Byrd on his North Pole flight was discovered among his papers in 1996. It seems to indicate that Byrd turned back about 150 miles short of the Pole when oil started to leak from one of the engines. Balchen had said that Floyd Bennett had told him the malfunction occurred early in the flight and that they had made no real attempt to reach the Pole, but had merely cruised back and forth, out of sight, long enough to simulate such a flight.

147. "More News from the Pole," *Nation,* December 16, 1909, page 591.

148. "More News from the Pole," *Nation,* December 16, 1909, pages 591–592.

149. Rochester *Post-Express,* quoted in the NYT, December 11, 1909.

150. NYH, October 5, 1909.

151. NYH, September 12, 1909. Yet today, none of those "foolish telegrams" exist. Though Peary kept every insult, Cook's papers contain not a single challenge to his claims. Though the newspapers tell us that Cook found more than 1,000 messages waiting for him at the Waldorf-Astoria upon his arrival in New York, and his lawyer wrote to him after his return to America in 1911 saying that his mail had piled up to such an extent that he had to store it in a secure place out of town (Letter, H. Wellington Wack to FAC, dated January 14, 1911. FCC.), relatively little of that correspondence remains today. But what does remain is entirely in praise of Dr. Cook's character or accomplishments.

152. Letter, August W. Loose to HLB, dated February 15, 1910. PFC.

153. There were some attempts by Clark Brown and others to show that the signature to the affidavit printed in the NYT was a forgery. Lightfoot had employed Loose as a watchman and had a number of checks signed by him, and it was said that analysis by handwriting experts showed the signatures on the checks did not match the one in the affidavit. Also, it was pointed out that Loose left the country just as Cook arrived from exile, preventing any confrontation between the two.

154. *The Fourth Estate,* quoted in the NYT, January 18, 1910.

Notes for Chapter 30: To Dream and Not to Count the Cost

1. Quoted in the NYT, December 12, 1909.

2. NYT, November 28, 1909.

3. NYT, December 21, 1909.

4. This letter is included in an undated typescript of an article by Thomas C. Stowell, whose content indicates it was published in an Albany newspaper c. 1913, probably the *Albany Knickerbocker.* CSC. The article says: "This written note, which Mr. Brown cherishes as the first communication of a growing friendship. . . ."

5. NYT, September 24, 1910.

6. OOJ, page 167.

7. Letter, FAC to "Dr. Carr," dated December 26, 1910. CSC. Cook forwarded a copy of this letter to Clark Brown, writing at the top, "I send it to you because it is the keynote of the policy that I will follow." CSC.

8. FAC, "Enmity vs. Indifference," *The New Era,* undated clipping. FCC.

9. OOJ, page 163.

10. HCP, preface, titled "Back to Inscription," page 1.

11. Letter, REP to HLB, dated June 29, 1915. PFC.

12. FAC, "The Prince of Liars." *American Weekly,* August 9, 1925.

13. Crockett, Albert Stevens, *When James Gordon Bennett Was Caliph of Bagdad.* Funk & Wagnalls Co., 1926, page 11.

14. FAC, miscellaneous notes. CSC.

15. A case in point can be found in Howard Abramson's biography of Cook, *Hero in Disgrace.* On pages 203–204, he quotes the letter of September 16, 1924, from Judge Wilson to Attorney General Stone (see chapter 24, note 15 above). Not only does Abramson fail to make clear to the reader the issue Judge Wilson is addressing—that is, Killits's objections to the Fifth Circuit Court of Appeals ruling, in July 1924, concerning whether Cook was a pauper or not, and not the substance of his appeal—but he even rearranges the sequence of Judge Wilson's paragraphs to imply something the judge did not say. Abramson concludes, "One is left to wonder how different Cook's fate might have been had Wilson followed through or had the defense been able to obtain copies of Wilson's correspondence." Anyone who obtains such copies will find that Abramson ends his quotation of Judge Wilson just before this unequivocal statement: "There is absolutely no question in the mind of anyone about the guilt of Dr Cook." Reading the whole letter in sequence, one must wonder about Abramson's "wonder," since Wilson was concerned not with any miscarriage of justice in Cook's conviction but only with his excessive sentence. In fact, Judge Wilson said that he was "anxious to see this case affirmed" and was worried that Killits's interference might overturn Cook's conviction.

As an author on the art of biography once wrote: "The moment that you invent or let your imagination roam, or the moment that you select detail improperly, you no longer have biography; you have fiction."

A file containing 1,550 items related to the mail fraud prosecutions in Texas, many of which deal with the PPA trial, was released from the Justice Department in 1986. These records are now in the Judicial Records (RG 60) at the National Archives II in College Park, Maryland. A Freedom of Information Act request by the author for documentation on Cook to the Justice Department went through numerous offices including the FBI's without turning up any other information.

16. Letter, Sheldon Cook-Dorough (historian of the Frederick A. Cook Society) to the author, dated July 13, 1992.

17. HCP, chapter 1, page 4. FCC.

18. Killits, John M., "Dr. Cook's Oil Scheme," written for William H. Hobbs, c. 1935. SPD. Also, letter, John M. Killits to William H. Hobbs, dated February 14, 1935. SCD.

19. One hearsay story related to the author during his research was that the 1923 divorce was an arrangement between Cook and his wife to save

personal assets. Curiously, Mrs. Cook's lawyers were Callaway and Wade—the very same firm that represented Dr. Cook at his trial—but though the Cooks seemed to have no animosity toward each other only a few months after their divorce, there seems little evidence for such an arrangement other than that some assets were transferred to her, including parcels of land, as late as August 1923. Marie worked as the manager of the Unity Cafeteria in Fort Worth at least until 1924 and was nearly destitute thereafter. She showed no evidence of any of the immense wealth Judge Killits suspected Dr. Cook had hidden. In December 1943 Marie Cook was found dead in her modest apartment in the Milner Hotel at Chestnut and 33rd Streets in Philadelphia. Her estate amounted to $1,013.69—not much more than enough to have her ashes interred next to her former husband's in Buffalo. Her granddaughter told the author, however, that she always kept a number of diamonds, sewn into her corset, which someone removed sometime after her death. This story is not confirmable.

    20. HCP, chapter 14, pages 17–18. FCC.

    21. FAC, "Capitalizing Calamity," *The New Era,* March 1929, page 8.

    22. FAC, "Somewhere within the Universe of Self," *The New Era,* December 1928, pages 14–15.

    23. Dunn, Robert, *Horizon Fever.* New York: Albert & Charles Boni, 1932, pages 140–141.

    24. FAC, "Dr. Cook's Own Story," *Hampton's Magazine,* January 1911, page 52.

    25. NYH, October 5, 1909.

    26. NYS, September 5, 1909.

    27. NYA, September 5, 1909.

    28. NYT, December 25, 1909.

    29. New York *Evening Telegram,* September 16, 1909.

    30. NYW, September 21, 1909.

    31. NYH, September 9, 1909.

    32. NYA, September 17, 1909.

    33. NYG, quoted in the NYT, December 10, 1909.

    34. Cook himself indulged in such associations in his memoirs. Though he later crossed them out of his draft, he had expanded Peary's metaphor of nailing the Stars and Stripes to the Pole by saying, "It sounds like the hammer of a crucifixion" and referred to "spiking of a polar cross." "The man nailed to this cross," he continued, "was Dr. Cook." (HCP, chapter 11, "The Suppressed Murder of Ross Marvin with Its International Complications," page 1. CSC.)

    35. HNPBD, page 475. Chimborazo, a high peak revered as a god in Ecuador, has an elevation of 20,498 feet.

    36. "Stealer of Trash and Honor," *Outlook,* December 5, 1923, page 575.

    37. "Psychology of the Cook Fake," *Independent,* December 30, 1909, pages 1513–1514.

38. Hayes, J. Gordon, *The Conquest of the North Pole.* New York: Macmillan Co., 1934, page 46.

39. Letter, Ben L. Reitman to FAC, dated December 18, 1934. FCC.

40. Philadelphia *Public Ledger,* quoted in the NYT, December 24, 1909.

41. FAC, miscellaneous notes. FCC.

42. Letter, Fred High to Henshaw Ward, dated April 16, 1935. HWA.

43. HCP, chapter 18, page 22. FCC.

44. FAC, "Parasites," pencil manuscript. FCC.

45. New York *Telegram and Evening Mail,* March 30, 1925.

46. "Stealer of Trash and Honor," *Outlook,* December 5, 1923, page 575.

47. OOJ, page 240.

48. Letter, T. Everett Harré to AF, dated June 15, 1937. FCC. Harré also related this story to others.

49. Letter, Marie Cook to FAC, dated May 11, 1931. FCC.

50. NYT, December 24, 1909.

51. Unattributed newspaper clipping, undated. CSC.

52. OOJ, pages 282–283.

53. OOJ, page 257.

54. OOJ, page 258.

55. Ibid.

56. OOJ, pages 258–259.

57. OOJ, page 283.

58. OOJ, page 306.

59. OOJ, page 255.

60. OOJ, page 257.

61. OOJ, page 254.

62. OOJ, page 306.

63. OOJ, page 252.

64. OOJ, pages 170–171.

65. OOJ, page 172.

66. OOJ, page 259.

67. NYH, September 20, 1909.

68. Letter, Ralph Shainwald to Miles Poindexter, dated December 31, 1913; photostat. CSC.

69. Letter, JDP to HLB, dated October 15, 1902. Collection of the Explorers Club, New York.

70. NYH, September 2, 1909.

71. Letter, Ivar Fosheim to AF, dated March 3, 1937. CSC.

72. In an article Peary wrote in 1905, an illustration shows the "Farthest North" reached by various explorers up to that time. Farthest down is the notation "Cook—1331 miles." (REP, "What I Expect to Find at the North Pole," *Ladies Home Journal,* July 22, 1905, page 5.) Could this have been meant to minimize Dr. Cook's accomplishments? If not, why 1,331 miles,

when he had been within 700 miles of the Pole on the 1892 trek across the Greenland ice cap with Peary himself? Peary may have meant Captain James Cook; he was more accurate if he did. Captain Cook reached latitude 70°44'—1,184 miles from the Pole—in the summer of 1778.

73. *Tacoma Daily Ledger,* September 2, 1909. Peary even may have named a geographical feature on Ellesmere Island after Dr. Cook during his 1898–1902 Expedition. The Canadian Geographical Names Data Base (CGNDB) lists Cook Peninsula (69°27'N, 76°50'W) which extends into Princess Marie Bay as probably named for Frederick A. Cook. Peary spent considerable time at Cape Sabine, just below it, so this is possible, but by no means certain.

74. NYA, September 9, 1909.

75. Letter, Isaiah Bowman to Edwin Swift Balch, dated March 25, 1915. BCV.

76. MAP, page 3.

77. Noyce, Wilfrid, *The Springs of Adventure.* Cleveland: World Publishing Co., 1958, pages 229–230. Permission of John Murray (Publishers) Ltd.

78. FAC, "Some Physical Effects of Arctic Cold, Darkness, and Light," *Medical Record of New York,* vol. 51 (June 12, 1897): 835.

79. FAC, "Dr. Cook's Own Story," *Hampton's Magazine,* January 1911, page 52.

80. Noyce, Wilfrid, *The Springs of Adventure.* Cleveland: World Publishing Co., 1958, page 123. Permission of John Murray (Publishers) Ltd.

81. FAC, "Memoirs of Polar Adventure," unfinished pencil manuscript notes. FCC.

82. OOJ, pages 307–308.

83. Letter, FAC to Ruth Cook, undated, but c. 1928 by content. CSC.

84. Noyce, Wilfrid, *The Springs of Adventure.* Cleveland: World Publishing Co., 1958, page 227. Permission of John Murray (Publishers) Ltd.

85. Letter, REP to Robert T. Collier, dated January 14, 1904. PFC.

86. FAC, "A Walk to the North and South Poles," *Canadian Magazine,* September 1900, page 419.

87. NYH, October 8, 1909. The article also tells of the way doctors in New York charged their patients on a sliding scale, depending on ability to pay.

88. Stanton, Theodore, "Dr. Cook at Copenhagen," *Independent,* October 7, 1909, page 819.

89. FAC, "Dr. Cook's Own Story," *Hampton's Magazine,* March 1911, pages 298–300. Perhaps in the sale of his newspaper rights to the *New York Herald* he had no choice. There are suggestions that he may have had a pre-arrangement with the newspaper to publish the results of his expedition. This is possibly hinted at in a letter from E.G. Wyckoff, dated September 24, 1909: "I mentioned that you had no pre-arrangement with the Herald — feeling that if the <u>Herald</u> <u>itself</u> were to publish the information – as it was to your advantage – you would not object." And there is this curious thing: opposite

page 12 in MAP there is a picture of Rudolph Franke in the box house at An-noatok. Behind him hangs a large sheet of paper on which only the words "NEW YORK HERALD" are printed over and over down its entire length. As we have seen, the *Herald* was willing to enter into a secret deal with Peary; did it have one with Cook as well?

It is an interesting coincidence that on August 29, 1909, just three days before Cook reached Lerwick, the *Herald* ran a feature story entitled "Have America's Explorers Discovered the North Pole?" in which it outlined Cook's and Peary's chances.

In Peary's case it has often been repeated that he made a mere $4,000 out of his exclusive rights deal with the *New York Times* while Cook made $25,000 for his. Actually, under the terms of his agreement, through royalties, Peary earned about $10,000 from this arrangement. When the far larger number of words that Cook supplied the *New York Herald* is taken into account (25,000 to 7,300), Peary was actually paid more per word.

90. FAC, "A Walk to the North and South Poles," *Canadian Magazine,* September 1900, page 419.

91. Letter of Robert A. Franks, mentioned in a letter, John A. Brashear to Colby M. Chester, dated December 30, 1909. PFC.

92. HCP, chapter 14, page 22.

93. His brother William even asserted that he never relinquished his share of Cook Brothers Milk and Cream Company but was a "silent partner," using the money for his expeditions. (NYA, September 4, 1909.)

94. Unattributed newspaper clipping, 1936. CSC.

95. Brannon, W.T., *"Yellow Kid" Weil.* Chicago: Ziff-Davis Publishing Co., 1948, pages 293–297.

96. Of his subject, W.T. Brannon had this to say in the introduction to his book: "Far from finding the Kid a man of superficialities, I discovered that he has many real accomplishments. One of these is his uncanny knowledge of human nature. In this respect, he may be far ahead of some of our more celebrated psychologists. He can size up a man and accurately forecast his reactions to almost any given set of circumstances." Recall that in his memoirs Cook said, "I could figure out reactions to all issues coming or going. At any rate I thought I could, which in the end amounted to the same thing."

97. OOJ, page 164.

98. FAC, "Peeps into the Beyond," pencil manuscript notes; both quotes. FCC.

99. OOJ, pages 127–128.

100. NYT, October 22, 1909.

101. Dunn, Robert, *The Shameless Diary of an Explorer.* New York: Outing Publishing Co., 1907, pages 7–10.

102. OOJ, page 244.

103. FAC, "Somewhere within the Universe of Self," *The New Era,* December 1928, page 15.

104. HCP, labeled "Incorporate into Chapter 2, etc.," page 1. FCC.

105. HCP, labeled "Incorporate into Chapter 2, etc.," pages 2–3. FCC.

106. FAC, "Somewhere within the Universe of Self," *The New Era*, December 1928, page 15.

107. HCP, labeled "Incorporate into Chapter 2, etc.," page 1. FCC.

108. OOJ, page 119.

Notes for Postscript: An Impertinence

1. Riesenberg, Felix, *Living Again.* Garden City, N.Y.: Doubleday, Doran & Co., 1937, pages 194–195.

2. FAC, notebook 4, pages 1–11. FCC.

3. HNPBD, pages 466–467.

4. MacMillan, Donald B., *Four Years in the White North.* New York: Harper & Bros., 1918, page 88.

Sources of or permissions to use previously unpublished or copyrighted pictorial material in this book are as follows:

Pages 59, 160, 220, 223, 295, 303, 442: Courtesy of Silas H. Ayer III.

Pages 51, 430, 543: National Archives.

Pages 217, 345, 346, 347, 914: Library of Congress.

Pages 239, 297, 585, 738, 753, 822, 827, 832, 834, 981: Permission of the Frederick A. Cook Society.

Page 247: Illustration by Mignon F. Linck. Permission of the American Alpine Club.

Page 828: Courtesy of Michael Hjelmeland.

Page 833: Permission of Dartmouth College and McGregor Robinson.

Page 908: From the *Geographical Journal,* vol. 92, no. 5, page 402. Permission of the Royal Geographical Society, London.

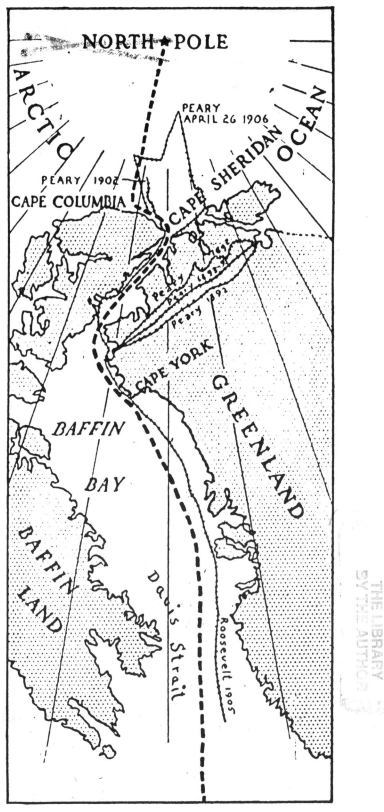

NORTH ★ POLE

PEARY
APRIL 26 1906

PEARY 1902

CAPE COLUMBIA

CAPE SHERIDAN

ARCTIC OCEAN

Peary 1892

Peary 1892

CAPE YORK

GREENLAND

BAFFIN

BAY

Davis Strait

BAFFIN

LAND

Roosevelt 1905